THE

LAW OF SCOTLAND

THE
LAW OF SCOTLAND

BY

The Late W.M. GLOAG, K.C., LL.D.

AND

The Late R. CANDLISH HENDERSON, Q.C., LL.D.

TENTH EDITION

EDITED BY

The Late W.A. WILSON, M.A., LL.B.
Lord President Reid Professor of Law, University of Edinburgh.

AND

ANGELO FORTE, M.A., LL.B.
Professor of Commercial Law, University of Aberdeen.

ASSISTANT EDITORS

The Rt. Hon. The LORD RODGER OF EARLSFERRY,
Q.C., F.B.A., D.C.L., LL.D., M.A., LL.B., D. Phil.
Lord Advocate

ANN PATON, Q.C., M.A., LL.B.

LAURA DUNLOP, LL.B.

Advocates

AND

PARKER HOOD, LL.B., LL.M.
Lecturer in Law, University of Edinburgh.

ANDREW R.W. YOUNG LL.B.
Advocate

W. GREEN/Sweet & Maxwell
Edinburgh
1995

First published   1927
Second edition   1933
Third edition   1939
Fourth edition   1946
Fifth edition   1952
Sixth edition   1956
Seventh edition   1968
Eighth edition   1980
Ninth edition   1987
Tenth edition   1995

Reprinted 1998

ISBN 0 41401068 X (Hardback)
ISBN 0 41401129 5 (Paperback)

Typeset by P.B. Computer Typesetting, Pickering, North Yorkshire
Printed in Great Britain by The Bath Press, Bath.

This Edition is Dedicated to

Bill Wilson

July 28, 1928—March 14, 1994

FOREWORD

by
The Right Hon. the Lord Hope of Craighead, P.C., LL.D.

When Gloag & Henderson's *Introduction to the Law of Scotland* was first published in 1927 it was listed in the catalogue of W. Green & Son Ltd as a student's textbook. The authors made it clear in their preface to the first edition that it was in order to meet the requirements of students that the book had been prepared. It was explained that no attempt had been made at such fullness of citation as might be expected by the practitioner. Simplicity and accuracy of treatment was to be its hallmark.

But Gloag & Henderson has always been much more than a book only for students. Despite the modest claims which the authors made for it, the work was from the outset plainly one of the highest quality. The breadth of its subject matter, its accuracy and its clarity soon earned for it a unique place as a textbook for the use of practitioners. I recall seeing the current edition in a prominent position on the Bench in the First Division Court Room when I first began to appear there as an Advocate. It sat there as a companion volume to the Parliament House Book, and it was by then pre-eminent among the books which were to be found on any practitioners's book shelf. Very few of the other textbooks listed in Green's 1927 catalogue are still in the publisher's current catalogue.

The characteristics of breadth, accuracy and clarity made the book particularly well suited for subsequent updating and re-editing. The earlier editions did not, as it happened, see much change in the text from the original. But from the sixth edition onwards, as the work of law reform at last gathered pace and the volume of case law and statutory provision grew also, the preparation of a new edition began to demand more and more of its editors. Each successive team of editors brought an enthusiasm and freshness to their editions which made the preparation of each edition far more than a mere exercise in updating.

That the current editors have responded to this challenge has been demonstrated very clearly in the tenth edition which is now being published. In keeping with the tradition set by their predecessors they have taken the opportunity of improving upon the text in its treatment of significant parts of the subject matter. This is plain to see in many passages throughout this edition, but more especially in its treatment of the law of unjustified enrichment and of reparation. The distinguished team who are responsible for this edition are worthy successors to the authors who placed such a valuable book before the public so long ago. The high quality of this edition will ensure that Gloag & Henderson will now serve as an important work of reference well into the next century.

July 1995   Hope of Craighead

PREFACE TO TENTH EDITION

Editorship of the tenth edition of this work was a source of genuine pleasure to Bill Wilson. Sadly, he did not live to see its publication and his death deprived this editor and the assistant editors of a valued colleague and friend. It is only fitting that this edition should be dedicated to his memory. As with the last edition, legislative changes have affected many of the topics included in it. The major difference, however, between this and earlier editions has been the redistribution and reworking of topics such as reparation, trusts and incorporeal moveable property into discrete chapters. It was also felt that the time was right to excise the chapter on criminal law from the compass of this work. The editors would also like to express their thanks to the staff at W. Green for their patience and assistance.

We have endeavoured to state the law as at March 31, 1995, though it has been possible in some instances to take account of later developments and changes, including the Requirements of Writing (Scotland) Act 1995. Readers' attention is also drawn to the Public Offers of Securities Regulations 1995 (S.I. 1995 No. 1537) which came into force too late to be incorporated in the text. These Regulations should be noted in connection with the text of paragraphs 51.17 and 51.18 of this work. In essence, the Public Offers of Securities Regulations 1995 amend Part IV of the Financial Services Act 1986 (Official Listing of Securities) by requiring a prospectus to be published (in lieu of listing particulars) where 'securities are to be offered to the public in the United Kingdom for the first time' before being admitted to the Official List. Both form and content of the prospectus will be given in the Stock Exchange *Yellow Book*. Part III of the Companies Act 1985 is repealed and replaced by a new prospectus regime applicable to public offers, for the first time, of unlisted securities. Exemptions from restrictions on advertising investments are added to and amended by the Financial Services Act 1986 (Investment Advertisements) (Exemptions) Order 1995 (S.I. 1995 No. 1266) and the Financial Services Act 1986 (Investment Advertisements) (Exemptions) (No. 2) Order 1995 (S.I. 1995 No. 1536).

May 1995   ADMF

PREFACE TO FIRST EDITION

SINCE its publication in 1754 Erskine's *Principles*, as revised and brought up to date by various editors, has held a leading place as a textbook in the classes of Scots Law in the Universities. The latest edition, issued in 1911 under the editorship of Sir John Rankine, is now out of print: and accordingly, in order to meet the requirements of students, it became necessary to consider the preparation either of another edition or of an entirely new book.

On the whole it appeared to us that it would be unwise to attempt a new edition. In the later editions Erskine's original work had been extensively altered by the inclusion of new material rendered necessary by the development of the law: and the addition of this new material in a book within the compass of a student's textbook was possible only at the cost of such compression as to make it extremely difficult for readers at the outset of their legal studies. As the present book is less comprehensive in its scope, we have been enabled to treat more fully the subjects embraced.

We have confined our work to those branches of the law which are usually dealt with in classes of Scots and of Mercantile Law. Conveyancing, Evidence and Procedure, Private International and Administrative Law are, therefore, only incidentally referred to.

It is hoped that few of the leading decisions have been omitted, but no attempt has been made at such fullness of citation as the practitioner, as distinguished from the student, might except.

We have to acknowledge the valuable assistance in the preparation of the work given by Mr. N. M. L. Walker and Mr. T. B. Simpson, Advocates.

W.M.G.
R.C.H.

October, 1927

CONTENTS

Page

TABLE OF CASES

TABLE OF STATUTES

PART I—INTRODUCTORY

CHAPTER 1

STATUTE AND COMMON LAW

1.1 Enacted Law.—The law of Scotland consists partly of enacted law, which has the authority of some body having legislative powers, and partly of common law, which is recognised by the courts as binding on some ground other than express enactment. Enacted law may include a Royal Proclamation or order; an Act of Parliament; a provision of a European Community treaty;[1] a regulation, directive or decision of the European Community Council or Commission; an Act of Sederunt; an Act of Adjournal; a by-law or regulation issued either by a department of state or by some local authority or body having statutory powers.

1.2 Legislative Authority of the Crown.—The legislative authority of the Crown, acting either through the Privy Council, or by some official, civil, naval or military, is a subject on which there is no direct authority in Scotland. Decisions of the House of Lords in English appeals cannot be taken as universally binding in questions of constitutional law in Scotland,[1a] but the following rules, enunciated in a leading English decision,[2] seem to be consistent with the Scottish approach: (1) in the absence of any national emergency,[3] the Crown has no legislative authority, and therefore a Royal Proclamation infers no obligation; (2) the Crown, in virtue of the royal prerogative, has legislative powers in cases of national emergency, *e.g.* invasion, and may delegate that power to a particular officer; (3) the validity of an order issued under the royal prerogative depends on the gravity of the emergency, and therefore, as no emergency can demand the seizure or the destruction as a precautionary measure of private property without payment of compensation, the person whose property is seized or commandeered may demand compensation as a right and not merely as an act of grace;[4]

---

[1] See also the inter-governmental provisions in the Treaty on European Union (*i.e.* Maastricht Treaty), titles V and VI; *R.* v. *Secretary of State for Foreign and Commonwealth Affairs, ex p. Rees-Mogg* [1994] Q.B. 552.

[1a] *Glasgow Corporation* v. *Central Land Board*, 1956 S.C. (H.L.) 1; see also *MacCormick* v. *Lord Advocate*, 1953 S.C. 396, *per* Lord President Cooper at p. 411.

[2] *Att.-Gen.* v. *De Keyser Hotel Co.* [1920] A.C. 508.

[3] See Emergency Powers Act 1920 (10 & 11 Geo. V, c. 55), as amended by Emergency Powers Act 1964.

[4] See *Burmah Oil Co. (Burmah Trading) Ltd.* v. *Lord Advocate*, 1964 S.C. (H.L.) 117; note also War Damage Act 1965 (c. 18).

1

(4) if a particular act (*e.g.* seizure of private property) is done which might be lawfully done either under the royal prerogative or under the provisions of a statute, it will be presumed that it was done under the statutory power and, therefore, under the statutory conditions.

1.3   Acts of Parliament.—A statute may be either a public general statute or a local or personal Act. There is a general presumption, in the absence of any express provision on the point, that a public general statute applies generally to Great Britain and Northern Ireland. This presumption may be rebutted, and the statute held not to be applicable to Scotland, either on the ground that it is expressed as an amendment of a statute in which Scotland was expressly excluded;[5] or, with less force, that it is expressed in technical terms of English law without an interpretation clause giving the equivalents in the law of Scotland.[6] A provision that the statute shall not apply to Ireland is a strong indication that it does apply to Scotland.[7] Historically, a division may be noted between statutes passed by the Scots Parliament prior to the Union in 1707 (usually termed Scots Acts) and statutes passed subsequently. Statutes of the English Parliament prior to 1707 are of no authority in Scotland, unless, as in the case of the Treason Act 1351, they have been applied to Scotland by a later Act.[8] The date at which a statute comes into force is generally stated; if not, it comes into force on the day when it receives the Royal Assent.[9]

1.4   Private Legislation Procedure Acts.—Local and personal, also called Private, Acts are statutes conferring powers on some local authority, body or company, or regulating the rights or status of some private individual. By the Private Legislation Procedure (Scotland) Act 1936,[10] where any public authority or persons desire a Private Act, they may apply to the Secretary of State for Scotland for a provisional order. If, after advertisement, no opposition is offered, the provisional order, after certain procedure detailed in the Act, will be issued; if objections are lodged, a local inquiry is held by commissioners. If their report is favourable, the provisional order is issued. A provisional order has no legislative force and it has to be confirmed by a Confirmation Act.[11] Provisions, for which reference must be made to the Act, are made excluding procedure by provisional order in projects which do not relate exclusively to Scotland or raise questions of public policy of novelty and importance.[12] A private Act cannot be impugned on the ground that Parliament in passing it was misled by fraud.[13]

---

[5] *Levy* v. *Jackson* (1903) 5 F. 646.
[6] *Scottish Drug Depot* v. *Fraser* (1905) 7 F. 1170.
[7] *Scottish Drug Depot, supra.*
[8] See Treason Act 1708.
[9] Interpretation Act 1978 (c. 30), s. 4.
[10] 26 Geo. V. & 1 Edw. VIII, c. 52.
[11] ss. 8, 9.
[12] s. 2.
[13] *British Railways Board* v. *Pickin* [1974] A.C. 765.

1.5 European Community Acts.—The European Communities Act 1972,[14] section 2 (1), provides that 'All such rights, powers, liabilities, obligations and restrictions from time to time created or arising by or under the Treaties, and all such remedies and procedures from time to time provided for by or under the Treaties, as in accordance with the Treaties are without further enactment to be given legal effect or used in the United Kingdom shall be recognised and available in law, and be enforced, allowed and followed accordingly.' 'The Treaties' are those specified in Part I of Schedule 1 to the Act, those specified in section 1 (2) of the Act and others specified in Orders in Council. The first effect of this enactment is that the provisions of the treaties, *e.g.* Articles 85 and 86 of the Treaty of Rome relating to competition,[15] and Article 119 relating to equal pay,[16] are part of the law of the United Kingdom. Secondly, directly applicable rules of Community law 'must be fully and uniformly applied in all the member states' and 'by their entry into force render automatically inapplicable any conflicting provision . . . of current national law.'[17] A British court may even have to give interim relief by suspending the operation of a United Kingdom statute.[18] A regulation made by the Council of Ministers or the European Commission has general application, is binding in its entirety and is directly applicable in all Member States of the European Union.[19] A directive is binding as to the result to be achieved upon each Member State to which it is addressed, but the choice of form and methods is left to the national authorities. However, in certain circumstances, a directive may be relied on by an individual against a Member State,[20] but not against another individual.[21] There are numerous decisions as to what entities are to be treated as 'the State' for this purpose.[22] A decision is binding

---

[14] c. 68.

[15] *Belgische Radio & T.V.* v. *S.A.B.A.M.* [1974] E.C.R. 313; *Garden Cottage Foods Ltd.* v. *Milk Marketing Board* [1984] A.C. 130.

[16] See *Garland* v. *British Rail Engineering Ltd.* [1983] 2 A.C. 751; *R.* v. *Secretary of State for Employment, ex p. Equal Opportunities Commission* [1995] 1 A.C. 1.

[17] *Amministrazione delle Finanze dello Stato* v. *Simmenthal SpA* [1978] E.C.R. 629.

[18] *Factortame Ltd. and Others* v. *Secretary of State for Transport* [1990] 2 A.C. 85; *R.* v. *Secretary of State for Transport, ex p. Factortame Ltd. and Others, (No. 2)* [1991] 1 A.C. 603; *R.* v. *Secretary of State for Transport, ex p. Factortame Ltd. (No. 3)* [1992] 1 Q.B. 680; *R.* v. *Secretary of State for Employment, ex p. Equal Opportunities Commission, supra.*

[19] Treaty of Rome, Art. 189; depending on its terms, a regulation may impose obligations on Member States and not on any individual: *Gibson* v. *Lord Advocate*, 1975 S.C. 136 at p. 143.

[20] *SpA S.A.C.E.* v. *Italian Ministry of Finance* [1970] E.C.R. 1213; *Van Duyn* v. *Home Office* [1974] E.C.R. 1337; *Becker* v. *Finanzamt Münster-Innenstadt* [1982] E.C.R. 53; *Foster* v. *British Gas plc* [1991] 1 Q.B. 405 (E.C.J.); [1991] 2 A.C. 306; *Kincardine and Deeside District Council* v. *Forestry Commissioners*, 1992 S.L.T. 1180, *per* Lord Coulsfield at p. 1186.

[21] *Marshall* v. *Southampton and South West Hampshire Area Health Authority (Teaching)* [1986] Q.B. 401.

[22] *Foster* v. *British Gas plc* [1991] 1 Q.B. 405 (E.C.J.); [1991] 2 A.C. 306; *Johnston* v. *Chief Constable of the Royal Ulster Constabulary* [1987] Q.B. 129; *Doughty* v. *Rolls Royce plc* [1992] 1 C.M.L.R. 1045; *Fratelli Costanzo SpA* v. *Comune di Milano* [1989] E.C.R. 1839.

in its entirety upon those to whom it is addressed; again, it may be invoked to affect legal relations between the addressee and a third party.[23] The Court of Justice of the Communities may review the legality of a regulation, directive or decision and declare it void; proceedings must be instituted within two months of the publication of the measure, or of its notification to the plaintiff or, in the absence thereof, of the day on which it came to his knowledge.[24]

1.6 Statutory Instruments.—There is a great deal of legislation, often referred to as 'subordinate' or 'secondary' legislation, by other authorities under powers conferred by Parliament, such as Orders in Council, orders by Ministers, rules of procedure made by courts, and by-laws by local authorities and other corporations.[25] Where an Act gives a power to Her Majesty in Council, exercisable by Order in Council, or to a Minister, exercisable by 'statutory instrument,' any document by which the power is exercised is a 'statutory instrument.'[26] Thus, Orders in Council made under the royal prerogative[27] and some subordinate legislation made by Ministers[28] are not statutory instruments. An order or regulation made by a Minister is liable to be attacked as *ultra vires*.[29]

1.7 Acts of Sederunt and Acts of Adjournal.—Acts of Sederunt are rules passed by the Court of Session, under powers originally conferred at its foundation.[30] In the seventeenth and eighteenth centuries, the court took a wide view of its powers and promulgated Acts of Sederunt amounting to general legislation, *e.g.* ordaining parties to a strike to resume work.[31] In modern times Acts of Sederunt relate exclusively to

[23] *Franz Grad* v. *Finanzamt Traunstein* [1970] E.C.R. 825.
[24] Art. 173.
[25] See *Macmillan* v. *McConnell*, 1917 J.C. 43; *Herkes* v. *Dickie*, 1958 J.C. 51.
[26] Statutory Instruments Act 1946 (9 & 10 Geo. VI, c. 36); see Mitchell, *Constitutional Law*, pp. 273 *et seq.*
[27] *e.g.* Territorial Waters Order in Council 1964 (*Post Office* v. *Estuary Radio Ltd.* [1968] 2 Q.B. 740: but see Territorial Sea Act 1987, s. 1(4)); see also *R.* v. *Secretary of State for Foreign and Commonwealth Affairs, ex p. Rees-Mogg* [1994] Q.B. 552 at p. 567.
[28] *e.g.* Breath Analysis Devices (Approval) (Scotland) Order 1983 (see *Annan* v. *Mitchell*, 1984 S.C.C.R. 32; *R.* v. *Clarke* [1969] 2 Q.B. 91).
[29] *Alexander & Sons* v. *Minister of Transport*, 1936 S.L.T. 553; *Islay Estates* v. *Agricultural Executive Committee for South Argyll*, 1942 S.L.T. 174; *Forster* v. *Polmaise Patent Fuel Co.*, 1947 J.C. 56; *City of Edinburgh District Council* v. *Secretary of State for Scotland*, 1985 S.C. 261; *Air 2000 Ltd.* v. *Secretary of State for Transport*, 1990 S.L.T. 335. See also *F. Hoffman-La Roche & Co. A.G.* v. *Secretary of State for Trade and Industry* [1975] A.C. 295, and, as to orders under the Royal prerogative, *Council of Civil Service Unions* v. *Minister for the Civil Service* [1985] A.C. 374. And see *R.* v. *Secretary of State for the Home Department, ex p. Fire Brigades Union* [1995] 2 W.L.R. 464 concerning the use of incorrect procedures regarding the non-introduction of an Act and the attempted introduction of a statutory scheme.
[30] College of Justice Act 1532 (c. 2). The Law Reform (Misc. Provs.) (Scotland) Act 1966, s. 10 provided that Acts of Sederunt and Acts of Adjournal made after that Act under enabling statutes enacted after the commencement of the Statutory Instruments Act 1946 are to be statutory instruments unless the enabling statute provides to the contrary.
[31] A.S. 1725. See Alexander, *Acts of Sederunt*.

procedure, and are usually passed in virtue of a specific authority in some particular statute. In such cases the repeal of the statute impliedly repeals the Acts of Sederunt which have been passed under it.[32] If the provisions of the statute admit of two interpretations, that consistent with the Act of Sederunt must be adopted.[33] In 1913 the existing Acts of Sederunt relating to procedure were collected, with amendments, in the Codifying Act of Sederunt, but in 1934 this, so far as regards procedure in the Court of Session, was in turn superseded by new Rules of Court made consequently upon the passing of the Administration of Justice (Scotland) Act 1933. In 1965 an Act of Sederunt[34] approved new consolidated rules, repealed the provisions of any statute or Act of Sederunt inconsistent with them,[35] and empowered the court to relieve any party from the consequences of failure to comply with the rules due to mistake, oversight or other cause, not being wilful non-observance.[36] An Act of Adjournal is an Act passed by the High Court of Justiciary for regulating procedure in that court and in inferior criminal courts. In 1988 the existing Acts of Adjournal were consolidated.[37]

1.8 Orders and By-laws.—If a by-law passed by a local authority or by a company has legislative force it must derive that force from a statute by which power to make by-laws is conferred. So a by-law issued by a company registered under the Companies Acts may be binding on the shareholders; if so, it is binding on principles of contract and because they have agreed to be bound by it, whereas a company founded on statute may have power to issue by-laws which have legislative force, and are binding on the general public as well as on the shareholders. The exact degree of legislative force possessed by an order or by-law depends on the terms of the statute by which the power to issue it was conferred. If it is there enacted that the by-law, when passed, is to be read as part of the statute it is still open to the objection that it is inconsistent with a section of the statute, or that the official empowered has gone completely beyond his province; any objections less weighty are excluded.[38] If there is a mere power to make by-laws for some particular object, these, when made, are valid only if they are *intra vires*, *i.e.*, if they relate to the object referred to;[39] if they are

[32] *Inglis's Trs.* v. *Macpherson*, 1910 S.C. 46.

[33] *Tonner* v. *Baird & Co.*, 1927 S.C. 870; *Carron Co.* v. *Hislop*, 1931 S.C. (H.L.) 75.

[34] S.I. 1965 No. 321 (replacing S.I. 1948 No. 1691).

[35] See *Graham* v. *Paterson & Co.*, 1938 S.C. 119.

[36] *Dalgety's Trs.* v. *Drummond*, 1938 S.C. 709.

[37] Act of Adjournal (Consolidation) 1988 (S.I. 1988 No. 110) (amended by Act of Adjournal (Consolidation Amendment) (Misc.) 1994 (S.I. 1994 No. 1769)).

[38] *The King* v. *Minister of Health* [1931] A.C. 494, explaining *Institute of Patent Agents* v. *Lockwood* (1894) 21 R. (H.L.) 61. And see *McEwen's Trs.* v. *Church of Scotland General Trs.*, 1940 S.L.T. 357, as to validity of a 'scheme' made under an Act of Parliament; *Cheyne* v. *Architects' Registration Council*, 1943 S.C. 468.

[39] *Shepherd* v. *Howman*, 1918 J.C. 78; *McAlister* v. *Forth Pilotage Authority*, 1944 S.L.T. 109.

reasonable;[40] and if they are not repugnant to the general law of the country.[41] There is, however, a strong presumption in favour of the validity of a by-law passed by a local authority, especially if it has been confirmed, in accordance with the provisions of the statute, by some public official, such as the Secretary of State for Scotland or the sheriff.[42] In such a case the function of the confirming authority is to determine the expediency of the by-law and not merely to consider its legality.[43] A by-law falls if the statute authorising it is repealed.[44]

1.9 **Repeal of Statutes: Desuetude.**—A statute may be repealed by a later Act, either expressly, or by the enactment of provisions inconsistent with it.[45] Repeal is not to be presumed if, consistently with the later statute, it is possible to give any reasonable meaning to the earlier.[46] The repeal of a repealing statute does not revive the statute repealed.[47] Statute Law Revision Acts, providing for the express repeal of statutes or sections impliedly repealed, have been passed at various dates. A statute may also be impliedly repealed by falling into desuetude, with the result that if appealed to, the courts will decline to give effect to it. This rule, probably, is not applicable except to Scots Acts; at least there is no case where a statute passed since 1707 has been held to have fallen into desuetude, and no analogous rule is recognised in England.[48] Mere age is not a sufficient ground for holding an Act to be in desuetude; it requires in addition the consideration that there is no recent case reported in which the Act has been given effect to, that it has for a long period been disregarded in practice, or that its provisions are out of accord with modern conditions.[49] A large number of Scots Acts were repealed by the Statute Law Revision (Scotland) Act 1906, and there is a presumption, not conclusive, that Acts not included in the Schedule thereto are still in observance.[50] The Statute Law Revision (Scotland) Act 1964[51] repealed about 145 other Acts which were obsolete, spent or unnecessary, or had been superseded, and deleted obsolete matter from many others; it also provided short titles for the remaining Acts, which may be used without prejudice to any other mode of citation.[52]

[40] *Saunders* v. *South-Eastern Ry.* (1880) 5 Q.B.D. 456; *De Prato* v. *Magistrates of Partick*, 1907 S.C. (H.L.) 5.
[41] *Dunsmore* v. *Lindsay* (1903) 6 F. (J.) 14.
[42] *Aldred* v. *Miller*, 1925 J.C. 21; *Baird* v. *Glasgow Corporation*, 1935 S.C. (H.L.) 21. See Local Government (Scotland) Act 1973 (c. 65), ss. 201–204.
[43] *Glasgow Corporation* v. *Glasgow Churches Council*, 1944 S.C. 97.
[44] *Watson* v. *Winch* [1916] 1 K.B. 688.
[45] See, for example, *Angus County Council* v. *Magistrates of Montrose*, 1933 S.C. 505.
[46] *Lang* v. *Munro* (1892) 19 R. (J.) 53.
[47] Interpretation Act 1978 (c. 30), s. 15.
[48] See opinion of Lord Deas, *Bute* v. *More* (1870) 9 M. 180.
[49] *McAra* v. *Magistrates of Edinburgh*, 1913 S.C. 1059; *Brown* v. *Magistrates of Edinburgh*, 1931 S.L.T. 456. See also *Britton* v. *R.W. Johnstone*, 1992 S.C.L.R. 947.
[50] *Brown* v. *Magistrates of Edinburgh*, *supra*.
[51] c. 80.
[52] s. 2 and Sched. 2. Further repeals were made by the Statute Law Repeals Act 1973 (c. 39), Sched. 1, Pt. XIII and the Statute Law (Repeals) Act 1993 (c. 50).

1.10 Interpretation of Statutes: Scots Acts.—The general rules applicable to the interpretation of statutes are not applicable to Scots Acts. These, expressed in nearly all cases briefly and without detailed provisions, have been interpreted in a very liberal spirit, sometimes in terms which cannot be reconciled with the words of the Act. In their construction, it is a recognised rule that, whatever the literal meaning of the statutory words, they are to be read as interpreted by decisions pronounced shortly after the Act was passed.[53]

1.11 Interpretation: General Principles.—The object of interpretation is to find the intention of Parliament from the words it has chosen to enact: 'We are seeking not what Parliament meant but the true meaning of what they said.'[54] In modern statutes[55] the most general rule is that if the meaning of the statute is plain and unambiguous it must receive effect. Arguments as to resulting inconvenience or injustice or anomaly[56] are irrelevant. If injustice would result from a statute, it is the province of the legislature, not the court, to amend it.[57] The rule probably yields to cases where a literal interpretation would result in positive absurdity.[58] 'Nothing short of impossibility should allow a judge to declare a statute unworkable.'[59] Any ambiguity will admit of the construction of the statute in a sense which will not render it nugatory, or result in obvious injustice or inconvenience, although it may not be the most obvious meaning of the words used.[60] Legislation which is intended to implement a European Community obligation should be given a purposive construction so that it is in conformity with the obligation.[61] Legislation which was not intended to implement a Community obligation, including legislation which was passed before the

---

[53] *Fergusson* v. *Skirving* (1852) 1 Macq. 232; *Heriot's Trust* v. *Paton's Trs.*, 1912 S.C. 1123, per Lord President Dunedin at p. 1135.

[54] *Black-Clawson International Ltd.* v. *Papierwerke Waldhof-Aschaffenburg A.G.* [1975] A.C. 591, per Lord Reid at p. 613.

[55] See Maxwell, *Interpretation of Statutes*; Craies, *Statute Law*.

[56] *Stock* v. *Frank Jones (Tipton) Ltd.* [1978] 1 W.L.R. 231; *Anderson* v. *Gibb*, 1993 S.L.T. 726, *per* Lord Penrose at p. 728, approving this statement in the 9th ed. hereof.

[57] *Lord Advocate* v. *Earl of Moray's Trs.* (1905) 7 F. (H.L.) 116; *Lawrie* v. *Banknock Colliery Co.*, 1912 S.C. (H.L.) 20, *per* Lord Shaw; *Feeney* v. *Miller*, 1925 J.C. 65. Also, the courts are extremely reluctant to imply words into a statute, and will only do so if it is necessary to give the provision "sense and meaning in its context", see *Bradley* v. *Motherwell District Council*, 1994 S.L.T. 739, pp. 741–742, applying *Tinkham* v. *Perry* [1951] 1 T.L.R. 91, p. 92.

[58] *Cal. Ry.* v. *N.B. Ry.* (1881) 8 R. (H.L.) 23, Lord Blackburn, p. 30.

[59] *Per* Lord Dunedin, *Murray* v. *Inland Revenue*, 1918 S.C. (H.L.) 111, at p. 124. In *Dumfries and Maxwelltown Co-operative Society* v. *Williamson*, 1950 J.C. 76, a statutory provision was found unworkable.

[60] *Inland Revenue* v. *Luke*, 1963 S.C. (H.L.) 65; *Paterson* v. *Ardrossan Harbour Co.*, 1926 S.C. 442. See also *Friel* v. *Initial Contract Services Ltd.*, 1994 S.L.T. 1216, *per* Lord McCluskey at p. 1221H–I that any ambiguity in a penal statute should be construed in favour of the liberty of the subject.

[61] *Pickstone* v. *Freemans plc* [1989] A.C. 66; *Litster* v. *Forth Dry Dock & Engineering Co. Ltd.*, 1989 S.C. 96; *Von Colson and Kamann* v. *Land Nordrhein-Westfalen* [1984] E.C.R. 1891; *N.U.P.E.* v. *Secretary of State for Employment*, 1993 G.W.D. 14–942.

Community obligation was adopted, must be construed, as far as possible, so that it complies with the obligation.[62]

1.12 Interpretation Sections.—Many statutes contain an interpretation section, giving the meaning to be assigned to expressions used in the Act. If the meaning of the word is defined, that meaning, though it may exclude the ordinary meaning, must be taken, unless the context plainly shows that this was not intended. 'If defined expressions are used in a context which the definition will not fit, then the words may be interpreted according to their ordinary meaning.'[63] Modern statutes frequently contain provisions that something is to be 'deemed' to be something else. If it is declared that a particular word shall 'include' something, the result is to enlarge the scope of the word, but not to exclude its ordinary meaning;[64] sometimes, however, 'includes' is equivalent to 'means and includes' and it then gives an exhaustive definition.[65] A general statute, the Interpretation Act 1978,[66] gives the meaning of a number of expressions in common use, such as 'person,' 'month,' 'Rules of Court,' 'writing.' The statutory meaning is to apply 'unless the contrary intention appears.' So it was held that although the word 'person' is defined as including male and female, yet in a statute relating to the admission of law agents its meaning might be restricted, on the ground of inveterate usage, to male persons.[67]

1.13 Meaning in Context.—If a word is not defined in the Act, it should be given the natural and ordinary meaning it had at the time the Act was passed.[68] Reference may be made to a dictionary[69] and especially to a judicial dictionary.[70] It is not permissible to lead evidence as to the meaning of an ordinary English word[71] but when a word is used in the technical sense it bears in a trade or industry, evidence of persons skilled in the trade or industry is competent.[72] It is important that the

---

[62] *Marleasing SA* v. *La Comercial Internacional de Alimentación SA* [1991] E.C.R. 4135. Cf. *Duke* v. *Reliance Systems Ltd.* [1988] A.C. 618; *Finnegan* v. *Clowney Youth Training Programme Ltd.* [1990] 2 A.C. 407; *Webb* v. *EMO Air Cargo (U.K.) Ltd.* [1992] 1 C.M.L.R. 793; *Kincardine and Deeside District Council* v. *Forestry Commissioners*, 1992 S.L.T. 1180.
[63] *Strathern* v. *Padden*, 1926 J.C. 9, *per* Lord Justice-General Clyde.
[64] *Ex p. Ferguson* (1871) L.R. 6 Q.B. 280.
[65] *Dilworth* v. *Stamps Commissioners* [1899] A.C. 99; *Inland Revenue* v. *Joiner* [1975] 1 W.L.R. 1701.
[66] c. 30 (consolidating the Interpretation Act 1889 and other enactments).
[67] *Hall* v. *Incorporated Society* (1901) 3 F. 1059. See also *Colquhoun* v. *Magistrates of Dumbarton*, 1907 S.C. (J.) 57.
[68] *Peart* v. *Stewart* [1983] 2 A.C. 109; *Sharpe* v. *Wakefield* (1888) 22 Q.B.D. 239; *Scottish Cinema* v. *Ritchie*, 1929 S.C. 350. Cf. *Dyson Holdings Ltd.* v. *Fox* [1976] Q.B. 503. A word may apply to something which did not exist at the time the Act was passed: *Leadbetter* v. *Hutchison*, 1934 J.C. 70; *Barker* v. *Wilson* [1980] 1 W.L.R. 884.
[69] *Baldwin & Francis* v. *Patents Appeal Tribunal* [1959] R.P.C. 221, *per* Lord Reid at p. 231; *Inland Revenue* v. *Russell*, 1955 S.L.T. 255.
[70] *Haigh* v. *Charles W. Ireland Ltd.*, 1974 S.C. (H.L.) 1.
[71] *Marquess Camden* v. *I.R.C.* [1914] 1 K.B. 641.
[72] *L. & N.E.Ry.* v. *Berriman* [1946] A.C. 278; *Unwin* v. *Hanson* [1891] 2 Q.B. 115.

word should be read in its context: 'Few words in the English language have a natural or ordinary meaning in the sense that they must be so read that their meaning is entirely independent of their context.'[73] Where a word is included in a list of words of greater precision in which some common characteristic can be discerned, the word should be given a meaning which shares the common characteristic—this is the principle *noscitur a sociis*.[74]

1.14   The Wider Context.—The word must also be considered in the context of the whole Act: 'A statute must, like any other continuous document, be read as a whole—*optimus statuti interpres statutum ipsum*'[75]—the best interpreter of a statute is the statute itself. The purpose and effect of other sections of the Act must be examined.[76] The title,[77] and the preamble[78] (usually omitted in recent statutes) may be referred to as determining the scope of the statute, though neither can override an express provision. It seems that it is permissible to refer to marginal notes, but they must not be given equal weight with the words of the Act.[79] Where a statute is divided into parts by specific headings, the heading limits the application of the sections which follow.[80] If a statute contains contradictory provisions the later sections override the earlier, but nothing in a schedule can overcome a provision in an enacting clause.[81] Other statutes *in pari materia* should be examined[82] and regard should be had to the social and political situation when the Act was passed[83] and the state of the law at that time.[84] The mischief which the

---

[73] *Re Bidie* [1949] Ch. 121, *per* Lord Greene M.R.

[74] *Ong Ah Chuan* v. *Public Prosecutor* [1981] A.C. 648; *Griffith* v. *Scottish Gas Board*, 1963 S.L.T. 286; *cf. Customs and Excise Commissioners* v. *Viva Gas Appliances Ltd.* [1983] 1 W.L.R. 1445.

[75] *Magistrates of Buckie* v. *Dowager Countess of Seafield's Trs.*, 1928 S.C. 525, *per* Lord President Clyde at p. 529. See also *Att.-Gen.* v. *Prince Ernest Augustus of Hanover* [1957] A.C. 436, *per* Viscount Simonds at p. 461, *per* Lord Normand at p. 465; *McArthur* v. *Strathclyde Regional Council*, 1994 S.C.L.R. 752.

[76] *Jennings* v. *Kelly* [1940] A.C. 206, *per* Viscount Maugham at p. 218.

[77] *Ayr* v. *St. Andrew's Ambulance Association*, 1918 S.C. 158; *Magistrates of Buckie* v. *Dowager Countess of Seafield's Trs.*, 1928 S.C. 525; *R.* v. *Secretary of State for Foreign and Commonwealth Affairs, ex p. Rees-Mogg* [1994] Q.B. 552, *per* Lloyd L.J. at p. 565F–G.

[78] *Att.-Gen.* v. *Prince Ernest Augustus of Hanover, supra*.

[79] *R.* v. *Schildkamp* [1971] A.C. 1, Lord Reid at p. 10; *Maxwell* (12th ed.), p. 49; *Craies* (7th ed.), p. 195; *Alexander* v. *Mackenzie*, 1947 J.C. 155, 166. *Cf. Nelson* v. *McPhee* (1889) 17 R. (J.) 1; *Magistrates of Buckie, supra*, opinion of Lord President Clyde.

[80] *Nelson, supra*; *Inglis* v. *Robertson & Baxter* (1898) 25 R. (H.L.) 70; *Magistrates of Buckie, supra*. *Cf. R.* v. *Schildkamp, supra*.

[81] *Jacobs* v. *Hart* (1900) 2 F. (J.) 33; *Kerr* v. *H.M. Advocate*, 1986 J.C. 41.

[82] *R.* v. *Loxdale* (1758) 1 Burr. 445. *Cf. Fane* v. *Murray*, 1995 G.W.D. 1–1—concerning the use of similar or equivalent English statutes as an aid to interpretation of Scottish Statutes.

[83] *Inland Revenue* v. *Hinchy* [1960] A.C. 748, *per* Viscount Kilmuir L.C. at p. 763; *Ealing L.B.C.* v. *Race Relations Board* [1972] A.C. 342; *Henretty* v. *Hart* (1885) 13 R. (J.) 9.

[84] *Rookes* v. *Barnard* [1964] A.C. 1129.

Act was intended to remedy should also be considered;[85] the court should ascertain the social ends the Act was intended to achieve and the practical means by which it was expected to achieve them: 'Meticulous linguistic analysis of words and phrases used in different contexts in particular sections of the Act should be subordinate to this purposive approach.'[86] The report of a Royal Commission or departmental committee on which the statute followed can be examined to ascertain the mischief aimed at and the state of the law as it was then understood to be, but it is not permissible to take into account the recommendations made in the report or any comments made on a draft Bill annexed to the report.[87] It seems that White Papers can be used in the same way.[88]

1.15 Extrinsic Sources.—Once an ambiguity has been established it becomes permissible to have regard to a wider range of materials. Recourse can be had to the legislative history of the subject[89] but not to the course of the Parliamentary proceedings relating to the particular statute.[90] At one time reference to Parliamentary debates was strictly prohibited[91] but now Hansard can be examined where the legislation is ambiguous or obscure or the literal meaning leads to absurdity and the material clearly discloses the mischief aimed at or the legislative intention; statements other than those of a Minister or promoter of the Bill are unlikely to meet these criteria.[92] In certain circumstances, *travaux préparatoires* have been used to construe an international convention which has been

[85] *Heydon's Case* (1584) 3 Co. Rep. 7a; *Black-Clawson International Ltd.* v. *Papierwerke Waldhof-Aschaffenburg A.G.* [1975] A.C. 591, *per* Lord Reid at p. 614.
[86] *R.* v. *National Insurance Commissioner, ex p. Hudson* [1972] A.C. 944, *per* Lord Diplock at p. 1005. See also *Kammins Ballrooms Co. Ltd.* v. *Zenith Investments (Torquay) Ltd.* [1971] A.C. 850; *Fothergill* v. *Monarch Airlines Ltd.* [1981] A.C. 251; *R.* v. *Cuthbertson* [1981] A.C. 470.
[87] *Black-Clawson* v. *Papierwerke Waldhof-Aschaffenburg A.G.* [1975] A.C. 591; *McIntyre* v. *Armitage Shanks Ltd.*, 1980 S.C.(H.L.) 46, *per* Lord Hailsham L.C. at p. 57. See, however, the *dicta* of Lord Browne-Wilkinson in *Pepper* v. *Hart* [1993] A.C. 593 at p. 635. As to the use of Scottish Law Commission Reports, see, *Barratt Scotland Ltd.* v. *Keith*, 1994 S.L.T. 1343; and *Archer Car Sales (Airdrie) Ltd.* v. *Gregory's Trustee*, 1993 S.L.T. 223 which say they should not be used where there is no ambiguity; *cf. McWilliams* v. *Lord Advocate,* 1992 S.L.T. 1045 at p. 1046J; and *Rehman* v. *Ahmad*, 1993 S.L.T. 741 at p. 745F.
[88] *Duke* v. *Reliance Systems Ltd.* [1988] A.C. 618, *per* Lord Templeman at p. 631; *Att.-Gen.'s Reference (No. 1 of 1988)* [1989] A.C. 971, *per* Lord Lowry at p. 992.
[89] *Lilley* v. *Public Trustee* [1981] A.C. 839 at p. 846; *cf. Grant* v. *D.P.P.* [1982] A.C. 190 at p. 201.
[90] *Cramas Properties Ltd.* v. *Connaught Fur Trimmings Ltd.* [1965] 1 W.L.R. 892, *per* Lord Reid at p. 899. Similarly, it is not permissible to look at subsequent amending legislation to aid interpretation, see *A.I.B. Finance Ltd.* v. *Bank of Scotland*, 1995 S.L.T. 2.
[91] *Davis* v. *Johnson* [1979] A.C. 264.
[92] *Pepper* v. *Hart* [1993] A.C. 593; *R.* v. *Warwickshire C.C., ex p. Johnson* [1993] A.C. 583; *Stubbings* v. *Webb* [1993] 2 W.L.R. 120; *Chief Adjudication Officer* v. *Foster* [1993] 2 W.L.R. 292; *Short's Tr.* v. *Keeper of the Registers of Scotland*, 1994 S.L.T. 65; *R.* v. *Secretary of State for Foreign and Commonwealth Affairs, ex p. Rees-Mogg* [1994] Q.B. 552; *Buchanan* v. *Secretary of State for Trade and Industry*, 1995 G.W.D. 11–600.

given the force of law in the United Kingdom.[93] Earlier[94] and later[95] statutes can be examined. An ambiguity in a consolidation statute justifies resort to the consolidated statutes.[96] Where the language of a statute has received judicial interpretation, and Parliament again uses the same language in a subsequent statute dealing with the same subject matter, there is a presumption that Parliament intended that the language so used by it in the subsequent statute should be given the meaning which meantime has been judicially attributed to it.[97] It seems that in some circumstances subordinate legislation made under powers contained in the statute can be used to construe the statute.[98] Where the statute has apparently been passed to implement the obligations of the United Kingdom under an international convention, there is a presumption that Parliament did not intend to act in breach of specific treaty obligations and where there is ambiguity a meaning should be attached to the legislation consonant with the obligations assumed under the convention.[99] If the convention is not referred to in the body of the statute it can be looked at only if the statute is ambiguous and there is cogent evidence that the enactment was intended to give effect to the particular convention.[1] If the Act gives effect to the convention as set forth in English in a schedule, it is permissible to resolve doubt or ambiguity by examining a text of the convention in another language which is stated to be the authentic text,[2] or to be an equally authentic text.[3] It has been held in the Outer House that the European Convention on Human Rights cannot be used as an aid to construction but a different view has been taken by the House of Lords in English decisions.[4]

1.16 Presumptions.—When the sole question is the construction of the statutory words, there is a general presumption that a statute is not

[93] *Fothergill* v. *Monarch Airlines Ltd., supra; Gatoil International Inc.* v. *Arkwright-Boston Manufacturers Mutual Insurance Co.,* 1985 S.C. (H.L.) 1.
[94] *Earl of Lonsdale* v. *Att.-Gen.* [1982] 1 W.L.R. 887.
[95] *Kirkness* v. *John Hudson & Co. Ltd.* [1955] A.C. 696.
[96] *Farrell* v. *Alexander* [1977] A.C. 59; *cf. Johnson* v. *Moreton* [1980] A.C. 37.
[97] *Barras* v. *Aberdeen Trawling Co.,* 1933 S.C. (H.L.) 21; *cf. Haigh* v. *Charles W. Ireland Ltd.,* 1974 S.C. (H.L.) 1; *Kelly* v. *MacKinnon,* 1982 S.C.C.R. 205.
[98] *British Amusements Catering Trades Association* v. *Westminster Council* [1989] A.C. 147; *Hanlon* v. *Law Society* [1981] A.C. 124. *Cf. Jackson* v. *Hall* [1980] A.C. 854.
[99] *Post Office* v. *Estuary Radio* [1968] 2 Q.B. 740.
[1] *Ellerman Lines* v. *Murray* [1931] A.C. 126, where, in the absence of ambiguity in the section under construction, the House of Lords refused to refer to the draft convention mentioned in the preamble and set forth in a schedule to the Act; *Salomon* v. *Commissioners of Customs and Excise* [1967] 2 Q.B. 116.
[2] *Fothergill* v. *Monarch Airlines* [1981] A.C. 251. In *Corocraft* v. *Pan American Airways* [1969] 1 Q.B. 616, the Court of Appeal proceeded on the ambiguous French text rather than the unambiguous English version.
[3] *James Buchanan & Co.* v. *Babco Forwarding and Shipping (U.K.)* [1978] A.C. 141.
[4] *Kaur* v. *Lord Advocate,* 1980 S.C. 319. See *Re M. and H. (Minors)* [1990] 1 A.C. 686, *per* Lord Brandon at p. 721; *R.* v. *Home Secretary, ex p. Brind* [1991] A.C. 696, *per* Lord Bridge at p. 747.

retrospective,[5] unless it expressly bears to be declaratory of the meaning of a prior Act, when the meaning so declared will apply to all pending questions, though not to cases already decided. A partial exception is that statutes introducing new forms of procedure apply to cases already in court.[6] And it may be a necessary inference from the language of the Act, even though there is no express enactment, that it was intended to be retrospective.[7] There is a presumption that a palpable injustice, such as enabling a party to profit by his own wrong or breach of contract, was not intended.[8] It has been laid down that 'an intention to take away the property of a subject without giving him a legal right to compensation for the loss of it is not to be attributed to the legislature unless that intention is expressed in unequivocal terms.'[9] If, however, the intention to take away property be clear, any claim to compensation must be founded on the terms of the statute.[10] Subordinate rules of construction are that the exclusion of the jurisdiction of the Court of Session is not to be presumed;[11] that where alternative constructions are equally open, that alternative is to be chosen which will be consistent with the smooth working of the system which the statute purports to be regulating;[12] and that the Crown (including departments of state) is not bound by a statute unless mentioned expressly[13] or by necessary implication.[14]

1.17 Ample and Restrictive Interpretation.—The theory that certain statutes should receive a beneficial, or ample, and others a restrictive interpretation,[15] is in modern law discredited, and it is held that the duty of the court is to interpret a statute according to its terms, without

---

[5] *Gardner* v. *Lucas* (1878) 5 R. (H.L.) 105; *Henshall* v. *Porter* [1923] 2 K.B. 193; and see also *L'Office Cherifien des Phosphates* v. *Yamashita-Shinnihon Steamship Co. Ltd.* [1994] 1 A.C. 486, *per* Lord Mustill at pp. 524–525 who noted the strong dispositive against retrospectivity, but expressed reservations about general presumptions and said the basis of the rule is unfairness.

[6] *Ballinten* v. *Connor* (1852) 14 D. 927. *Cf. Yew Bon Tew* v. *Kenderaan Bas Mara* [1983] 1 A.C. 553; and *L'Office Cherifien des Phosphates* v. *Yamashita-Shinnihon Steamship Co. Ltd.*, *supra*, at p. 523.

[7] *Wilson* v. *Wilson*, 1939 S.C. 102; *R.* v. *Governor of Pentonville Prison, ex p. Azam* [1974] A.C. 18; *L'Office Cherifien des Phosphates* v. *Yamashita-Shinnihon Steamship Co. Ltd. supra.*

[8] *Malins* v. *Freeman* (1838) 4 Bing. N.C. 395.

[9] *Per* Lord Atkinson, *Central Board* v. *Cannon Brewery Co.* [1919] A.C. 744, 752. See *Marshall* v. *Blackpool Corporation* (1932) 49 T.L.R. 148.

[10] *Hammersmith Ry.* v. *Brand* (1869) L.R. 4 H.L. 171; *Cal. Ry.* v. *Walker's Trs.* (1882) 9 R. (H.L.) 19; *Scott-Plummer* v. *Board of Agriculture*, 1916 S.C. (H.L.) 94, *per* Lords Haldane and Parmoor.

[11] *Dunbar* v. *Scottish County Investment Co.*, 1920 S.C. 210, *per* Lord Salvesen.

[12] *Shannon Realties Ltd.* v. *Ville de St. Michel* [1924] A.C. 185, *per* Lord Shaw at p. 192; *Hynd's Tr.* v. *Hynd's Trs.*, 1955 S.C. (H.L.) 1 *per* Viscount Kilmuir L.C. at p. 10.

[13] *Lord Advocate* v. *Dumbarton D.C.*, 1990 S.C. (H.L.) 1 (in which *dicta* of Lord Dunedin in *Magistrates of Edinburgh* v. *Lord Advocate*, 1912 S.C. 1085 were disapproved).

[14] *Province of Bombay* v. *Municipal Corporation of Bombay* [1947] A.C. 58.

[15] Erskine, I, i, 53.

any bias. There are still, however, certain cases in which a statute is read, *in dubio*, in a restrictive sense, *i.e.* in the narrowest sense which the words will bear. This applies to statutes extending the criminal law.[15a] Offences are not to be created by implication, unless the implication is so plain as to be equivalent to express enactment.[16] In construing revenue statutes, while considerations of hardship or apparent injustice are irrelevant if the meaning of the statute is clear,[17] it is a recognised rule that no one is to be subjected to taxation unless his case comes within the letter of the law,[18] and that no one can claim exemption from a general tax unless his case is expressly provided for.[19] A Private Act of Parliament, obtained by a public body or company, is to be read as a contract between them and the public, expressed in terms which they have chosen and, therefore, subject to the rule of construction *verba interpretanda sunt contra proferentes*, so that no privilege or right is conferred unless the words founded on as conferring it are unambiguous.[20]

1.18 *Ejusdem Generis* **Rule.**—When a list of things to which the statute is to apply is given followed by words of wide general import, the normal rule of construction, known as the rule of construction *ejusdem generis* (literally 'of the same kind'), is that the general words apply only to things of the same kind as those in the preceding list. So where betting was prohibited 'in any house, office, room or other place' it was held, construing the term 'other place' as a place of the same kind as a house, office or room, that the Act did not apply to a racecourse.[21] This rule of construction is a presumption only and may yield to the argument that the statutory provision was intended to be general, and that the list was given merely as an illustration.[22] It does not apply unless the things mentioned have some common and dominant feature. Where it was provided that a landlord, on certain specified conditions, might resume possession of the subjects let for 'building, feuing, planting or other purposes,' it was held that as building, feuing and planting could not be

---

[15a] See *Friel* v. *Initial Contract Services Ltd.*, 1994 S.L.T. 1216, *per* Lord McCluskey at p. 1221H–I, that any ambiguity should be construed in favour of the subject's liberty.

[16] *Barty* v. *Hill*, 1907 S.C. (J.) 36; *Remington* v. *Larchin* [1921] 3 K.B. 404.

[17] *Duncan* v. *Inland Revenue*, 1923 S.C. 388.

[18] *Coltness Iron Co.* v. *Black* (1881) 8 R. (H.L.) 67, *per* Lord Blackburn at p. 72; *Tennant* v. *Smith* (1892) 19 R. (H.L.) 1; *Scottish Milk Marketing Board* v. *Ferrier*, 1936 S.C. (H.L.) 39.

[19] *Gillanders* v. *Campbell* (1884) 12 R. 309.

[20] *Countess of Rothes* v. *Kirkcaldy Water Works* (1882) 9 R. (H.L.) 108; *Milligan* v. *Ayr Harbour Trustees*, 1915 S.C. 937; *North British Ry.*, v. *Birrell's Trs.*, 1918 S.C. (H.L.) 33 at p. 52; *Holburnhead Salmon Fishing Co.* v. *Scrabster Harbour Trs.*, 1982 S.C. 65.

[21] *Henretty* v. *Hart* (1885) 13 R. (J.) 9; *cf. Dawson* v. *Wright*, 1924 J.C. 121; *Murray* v. *Keith* (1894) 22 R. (J.) 16; *Chernack* v. *Mill*, 1938 J.C. 39; English cases are collected in Maxwell (12th ed.), pp. 297 *et seq.*, and Craies (7th ed.), pp. 178 *et seq.*

[22] *Symington* v. *Symington's Quarries* (1905) 8 F. 121; *Baird* v. *Lees*, 1924 S.C. 83. See *Quazi* v. *Quazi* [1980] A.C. 744, *per* Lord Scarman at p. 823; *Cormack* v. *Crown Estate Commissioners*, 1985 S.L.T. 426.

ascribed to any one genus there was no ground for limiting the generality of the words 'or other purposes.'[23]

1.19 Permissive Words.—When the words of a statute are permissive, where, for instance, it is provided that a party 'may' perform a certain act, or that 'it shall be lawful' for him to perform it, the general construction is, in accordance with the maxim *cuilibet licet renunciare juri pro se introducto* (anyone can renounce a right conceived in his own favour), that an option is conferred, and no obligation imposed.[24] But if such words are employed in a statute dealing with a matter in which the general public have an interest, permissive words may be read as imperative. So where a statute authorised road trustees to make and keep highways 20 feet in width it was held that an obligation to keep highways of that width was inferred.[25] Where a discretionary power is conferred on a court or on a public body, the statute, however absolute its terms may be, is to be construed subject to the implied limitation that the power is to be exercised in a judicial spirit, and under the conditions observed in judicial proceedings.[26]

1.20 *Casus Omissus*.—Circumstances may arise which show that a particular case has been overlooked by the framers of a statute. It is not within the power of the court, as interpreter, to read into the statute words which are not there.[27] But in non-contentious procedure an application to the Court of Session under the *nobile officium*, or equitable power, may get over the difficulty caused by a *casus improvisus* (an unforeseen case) in a statute. Thus the court has power to dispense with a statutory formality in a case where, owing to circumstances overlooked in the statute, its observance has been found to be impossible.[28] Though there was no statutory provision for the resuscitation of a company more than two years after its dissolution it was held to be within the power of the court,[29] and where there was no statutory power to recall a sequestration the court declared it at an end.[30] The limits of the power of the Court of Session in virtue of its *nobile officium* have not been determined, but if a statutory right is given to certain specified persons

---

[23] *Crichton Stuart* v. *Ogilvie*, 1914 S.C. 888; see also *Clark's Tr.*, *Noter*, 1993 S.L.T. 667; and *Secretary of State for Social Security* v. *McSherry*, 1995 S.L.T. 371.

[24] *Julius* v. *Bishop of Oxford* (1880) 5 App. Cas. 214; *Fleming & Ferguson* v. *Burgh of Paisley*, 1948 S.C. 547.

[25] *Gray* v. *St Andrew's District Committee*, 1911 S.C. 266. See Maxwell, *Interpretation of Statutes* (12th ed.), p. 234; Craies (7th ed.), p. 284.

[26] *Macbeth* v. *Ashley* (1874) 1 R. (H.L.) 14; *Goodall* v. *Bilsland*, 1909 S.C. 1152; *Sharp* v. *Wakefield* [1891] A.C. 173.

[27] *The Queen* v. *Ellis* (1844) 6 Q.B. 501, but see *McDermott* v. *Owners of S.S. Tintoretto* [1911] A.C. 35. See also *Piggins & Rix Ltd.* v. *Montrose Port Authority*, 1995 S.L.T. 418, where a plea of *casus omissus* failed.

[28] *Roberts* (1901) 3 F. 779; *Train & McIntyre*, 1923 S.C. 291. In *Murray* v. *Comptroller-General of Patents*, 1932 S.C. 726, an Outer House judge took similar action.

[29] *Forth Shipbreaking Co.*, 1924 S.C. 489.

[30] *Craig & Co.*, 1946 S.C. 19.

it cannot, even in a case where there is no opposition, be extended to others.[31]

1.21 Sources of Common Law.—Rules of law which are not referable to any legislative enactment constitute the common law. It is spoken of by Lord Stair as 'our ancient and immemorial customs,' in which he includes the law of succession,[32] and the law, in so far as not affected by statute, of feudal conveyancing.[33] The origin of these customs is not in every case ascertainable; but it is clear that the common law of Scotland is in considerable measure derived from the civil law; to a lesser extent, but in important particulars, from the canon law. Though there was probably no period at which the civil law was accounted part of the law of Scotland, yet that law, as explained and in some respects amended by the Dutch and French commentators of the sixteenth and seventeenth centuries, is the basis of the Scots law of contract and of property, apart from feudal conveyancing.[34] Before the Reformation much of the judicial business of Scotland was carried on in the ecclesiastical courts, with an ultimate appeal to the Papal Court at Rome, and the canon law as the law there administered. By the Act 1567, cap. 31, the authority of the canon law was expressly repudiated, but its influence remained, especially in the law relating to marriage and the domestic relations.[35] For more than a century the chief external factor, apart from legislation, in the development of the law of Scotland has been the law of England.

1.22 Custom as Forming Law.—Custom may still be recognised as a source of law, whether in the form of usage of trade[36] or of local custom affecting rights of property[37] or of usage sanctioning some particular method of government in a burgh[38] or determining the jurisdiction of a particular court.[39] Usage amounting to a rule of law is distinguishable from the more common case where it is appealed to as importing an unexpressed term into a contract. There, as its recognition is based on implied agreement, knowledge or notice of the usage must be brought home to the party against whom it is pleaded;[40] whereas if the usage has

---

[31] *Crichton Stuart's Tutrix*, 1921 S.C. 840. See opinions in *Gibson's Trs., Petrs.*, 1933 S.C. 190.

[32] As to the origin of the law of succession in moveables, see *Sommervill* v. *Murray's Creditors* (1744) Mor. 3902.

[33] Stair, I, i, 16.

[34] See, as to contrast with English law, *Cantiere San Rocco* v. *Clyde Shipbuilding Co.*, 1923 S.C. (H.L.) 105; *Sinclair* v. *Brougham* [1914] A.C. 398, opinion of Lord Dunedin.

[35] *Collins* v. *Collins* (1884) 11 R. (H.L.) 19; *Purves's Trs.* v. *Purves* (1895) 22 R. 513.

[36] *Bechuanaland Exploration Co.* v. *London Trading Bank* [1898] 2 Q.B. 658; *Clydesdale Bank Nominees* v. *Snodgrass*, 1939 S.C. 805 (Stock Exchange); *Wilkie* v. *Scottish Aviation*, 1956 S.C. 198.

[37] *Learmonth* v. *Sinclair's Trs.* (1878) 5 R. 548.

[38] *Gardner* v. *Magistrates of Kilrenny* (1828) 6 S. 693; *Magistrates of Dunbar* v. *Duchess of Roxburghe* (1835) 1 Shaw and McL. 134, at p. 195; Erskine, I, i, 20.

[39] *Neilson* v. *Vallance* (1828) 7 S. 182; *Duncan* v. *Lodijensky* (1904) 6 F. 408.

[40] See para. 6.18, *infra*.

acquired the force of law it falls under the general rule that everyone is
supposed to know the law, and knowledge or notice is immaterial.[41] It is
not possible to formulate exact rules as to the cases where a custom will
be recognised as part of the common law. It need not be universal
throughout Scotland; a special form of land tenure, prevailing in one
locality only, has been recognised.[42] It cannot prevail against the express
terms of a statute,[43] though it may be of material importance when the
plea is taken that a statute is in desuetude.[44] A usage of trade that the
transfer of a document of title to goods gives a real right to the goods
has been uniformly held to be a misunderstanding of a general principle
of law, to which no effect could be given.[45] The court refused to
sanction, on the plea of customary law, a local usage, under which a
certain class of creditors, without resort to legal process, satisfied their
debts by seizing the property of their debtors.[46] And a usage must be
reasonably fair. So it was held that a custom, proved to exist in
Shetland, by which landlords claimed a third of the proceeds of whales
killed on shore, had not the force of law, in respect that it amounted to
an exaction for which no return was given.[47]

1.23 Authorities.—The question whether a particular rule is recognised as
part of the common law must be determined, except in the case where
appeal is made to a custom or usage hitherto unrecognised, by
consideration of the authorities. The authorities may be statements by
legal writers, or reports of decided cases. A writer on law is not in any
proper sense an authority during his lifetime, unless he is raised to the
Bench. After his death his works acquire an authority, varying in degree
according to the reputation he may have attained. The works of certain
authors, usually referred to as the institutional writers, are in Scotland
treated with exceptional respect. Of these, the chief ones, in questions
of general law, are: Lord Stair, Lord Bankton, Erskine and Bell; in the
special sphere of criminal law: Hume[48] and Alison.

The authority of decisions as establishing a rule of law is a relatively
modern development. Erskine lays it down that a decision, even of the
House of Lords, is not binding when the same question is raised
between different parties, though he admits that a series of decisions

---

[41] *Learmonth* v. *Sinclair's Trs.* (1878) 5 R. 548.
[42] Kindly Tenants of Lochmaben. See Rankine, *Leases* (3rd ed.), p. 153; *Marquis of
Queensberry* v. *Wright* (1838) 16 S. 439; *Royal Four Towns Fishing Association* v.
Dumfries Assessor, 1956 S.C. 379. Not all local law is customary, however; the relics of
udal law, esp. udal tenure in Shetland, are attributable to the ancient connection with
Norway; see *Lord Advocate* v. *Univ. of Aberdeen,* 1963 S.C. 533.
[43] See *Walker Trs.* v. *Lord Advocate,* 1912 S.C. (H.L.) 12.
[44] *Supra,* para. 1.9.
[45] *Anderson* v. *McCall* (1866) 4 M. 765; *Dobell* v. *Neilson* (1904) 7 F. 281.
[46] *Brodie* v. *Watson* (1714) Mor. 14757.
[47] *Bruce* v. *Smith* (1890) 17 R. 1000.
[48] Hume's *Lectures,* published posthumously and not prepared for publication by him,
are not regarded as books of institutional authority: *Fortington* v. *Lord Kinnaird,* 1942
S.C. 239.

should be respected.[49] And there is modern sanction for the statement that a case is an authority only for what it actually decides, not for a proposition which may seem to follow logically from it.[50] In practice, however, more deference is paid to authority than these statements would suggest. A case two centuries old has been held binding in the Outer House.[51] The authority of a case depends upon the jurisdiction of the court by which it was pronounced. The decision of a sheriff principal is not binding outside his sheriffdom; the decision of the Court of Session is not binding on the House of Lords, though a decision which has ruled practice for a number of years will not readily be overturned merely because it is thought to be unfounded.[52] The decision of a single judge in the High Court of Justiciary is binding on a sheriff, it seems,[53] and it has been suggested that, by analogy, an Outer House decision binds a sheriff.[54] The decision of the House of Lords in a Scots appeal is binding on all courts in Scotland, and on the House itself, in so far as Scots law is concerned.[55] The House may, however, depart from a previous decision when it appears right to do so.[56] The power is exercised sparingly and according to stated principles but the fact that a case cannot be brought within the formulae used in other cases is not fatal to exercise of the power.[57] There must normally have been some change of circumstances.[58] This discretion to depart should only be exercised in rare cases in questions relating to the construction of statutes[59] and in matters of commercial law where there is a special need for certainty, consistency and continuity.[60] The power has been exercised in relation to a comparatively recent decision.[61] A decision of the House of Lords in an English appeal not turning on the interpretation of a statute applicable to both countries is not binding in Scotland, though if it proceeded on grounds of general jurisprudence

---

[49] Erskine I, i, 17. And see *Sugden* v. *H.M. Advocate*, 1934 J.C. at p. 127, where Lord Murray doubts whether the modern rule of *stare decisis* binds the High Court of Justiciary.

[50] *Quinn* v. *Leathem* [1901] A.C. 495, opinion of Lord Chancellor Halsbury.

[51] *American Express Europe Ltd.* v. *Royal Bank of Scotland plc (No. 2)*, 1989 S.L.T. 650.

[52] *Kirkpatrick's Trs.* v. *Kirkpatrick* (1874) 1 R. (H.L.) 37, qualified in *Nicol's Trustees* v. *Sutherland*, 1951 S.C. (H.L.) 21.

[53] *Jessop* v. *Stevenson*, 1988 J.C. 17.

[54] *Cromarty Leasing Ltd.* v. *Turnbull*, 1988 S.L.T. (Sh.Ct.) 62; *Chalmers* v. *Trs. of the Harbours of Peterhead*, 1991 S.L.T. 98, at p. 101. *Cf. Farrell* v. *Farrell*, 1990 S.C.L.R. 717; Maher, 1988 S.L.T. (News) 209.

[55] *London Street Tramways Co.* v. *London C.C.* [1898] A.C. 375. The House of Lords in an English appeal may apply Scots law, if that is the proper law, even though the Scots law has not been proved in the court below: *Elliot* v. *Joicey*, 1935 S.C. (H.L.) 57.

[56] Practice Statement (Judicial Precedent) [1966] 1 W.L.R. 1234. See, for example, *Dick* v. *Burgh of Falkirk*, 1976 S.C. (H.L.) 1.

[57] *Vestey* v. *I.R.C.* [1980] A.C. 1148.

[58] *Miliangos* v. *George Frank (Textiles) Ltd.* [1976] A.C. 443; *Fitzleet Estates Ltd.* v. *Cherry* [1977] 1 W.L.R. 1345; *Hesperides Hotels Ltd.* v. *Muftizade* [1979] A.C. 508.

[59] *R.* v. *National Insurance Commissioner, ex p. Hudson* [1972] A.C. 944.

[60] *Paal Wilson & Co. A/S* v. *Partenreederei Hannah Blumenthal* [1983] 1 A.C. 854.

[61] *R.* v. *Shivpuri* [1987] A.C. 1 (overruling *Anderton* v. *Ryan* [1985] A.C. 560); *Khera* v. *Secretary of State for the Home Department* [1984] A.C. 74.

and not on any specialty of English law, it ought to be treated with great respect.[62] An opinion by a judge on a point not necessary to the judgment (*obiter dictum*) has an authority varying with the reputation of the judge and the standing of the court. A decision clearly in point may be challenged on the ground that it is inconsistent with prior authorities which were not brought to the notice of the court;[63] that it proceeded upon views of morality, political economy, or religious observance which are no longer held in esteem;[64] that it had as its basis some theory of physical fact which modern science has shown to be baseless;[65] or that a statutory alteration of the law has altered the basis on which the previous decision rested.[66]

1.24 **Res Judicata.**—The plea of *res judicata* means that the question raised has been decided already in an action between the same parties,[67] or between parties in the same interest. It is a preliminary plea, which, if sustained, excludes all consideration of the merits of the case. Where the question raised is one of law, and a prior decision of the House of Lords is in point, the distinction between a plea of *res judicata* and the argument that the question is settled by authority is one of form rather than of substance. If, however, the prior authority is a decision, or series of decisions, in the Court of Session, then, although either the Lord Ordinary or the Division may consider that the question is closed in their courts, it remains open, if the parties to the action are not the same, on an appeal to the House of Lords, whereas, when the parties are the same, and the plea of *res judicata* is taken, the only question open in any court is whether the prior case decided the same point which the subsequent case proposes to raise.[68]

Apart from averments of *res noviter*[69] (new matter) a decision in favour of the pursuer, if *in foro*,[70] is *res judicata* in all cases. A defender is bound to set forth all his defences at once, and an attempt after decree has passed against him to reopen the question on new grounds is

---

[62] *Orr Ewing's Trs.* v. *Orr Ewing* (1885) 13 R. (H.L.) 1, *per* Lord Chancellor Selborne at p. 3; but see *Glasgow Corporation* v. *Central Land Board*, 1956 S.C. (H.L.) 1. See *Dalgleish* v. *Glasgow Corporation*, 1976 S.C. 32, *per* Lord Justice-Clerk Wheatley at pp. 51–53.

[63] *Mitchell* v. *Mackersy* (1905) 8 F. 198.

[64] *Bowman* v. *Secular Society* [1917] A.C. 406; *Commerzbank Aktiengesellschaft* v. *Large*, 1977 S.C. 375.
concludendi.[75]

[65] *Welldon* v. *Butterley Coal Co.* [1920] 1 Ch. 130.

[66] *Beith's Trs.* v. *Beith*, 1950 S.C. 66; *Douglas-Hamilton* v. *Duke & Duchess of Hamilton's Trs.*, 1961 S.C. 205, *per* Lord President Clyde at p. 217. The course of subsequent development of the common law is not such a ground: *Weir* v. *J.M. Hodge & Son*, 1990 S.L.T. 266.

[67] *Ryan* v. *McBurnie*, 1940 S.C. 173.

[68] *Duke of Atholl* v. *Glover Incorporation* (1899) 1 F. 658.

[69] See para. 1.25 *infra*.

[70] *Mackintosh* v. *Smith* (1865) 3 M. (H.L.) 6; see also *Esso Petroleum Co.* v. *Law*, 1956 S.C. 33; *Paterson* v. *Paterson*, 1958 S.C. 141.

met by the plea of competent and omitted.[71] A decree in favour of a defender, if one of dismissal on the ground of irrelevancy or incompetency, is not *res judicata*.[72] A decree of absolvitor, though *res judicata* as to any grounds of action which were in question, leaves open an action based on different *media concludendi*,[73] however, an opinion of high authority suggests that this rule is confined to actions of reduction;[74] for the purpose of the plea of *res judicata*, common law negligence and breach of statutory duty are not different *media concludendi*[75]

It is probably the law that a decree in the sheriff court, if allowed to become final, is *res judicata* in a subsequent action raised in the Court of Session.[76] A conviction or acquittal in a criminal court may be *res judicata* to bar an action or claim in a civil court, but only where the parties are the same, the ground of action the same and the remedy sought the same,[77] circumstances which can but seldom occur. Neither *res judicata* nor any analogous plea will preclude an appeal against an entry in the valuation roll.[78] No decree can found a plea of *res judicata* if the court, in pronouncing it, exceeded its jurisdiction;[79] if it is *ultra petita*, *i.e.* beyond the conclusions of the summons; or if it is founded on an error in calculation.[80]

In order to found a plea of *res judicata* the question in the later case must be the same as that in the earlier.[81] So a decision by a court which had authority to determine the parties who in right of hereditary offices were entitled to perform services at a coronation was held not to be *res judicata* when the question of the right to an office was raised in an action of declarator, in respect that it merely determined the right to serve at the coronation immediately in question, and not the right to the office.[82] And the parties in the two actions must be the same or must represent the same interest. A decision as to a right of property is *res judicata* in a question between the heirs or singular successors of the

---

[71] Erskine, IV, iii, 3; *Murray* v. *Seath*, 1939 S.L.T. 348.

[72] *Wallace* v. *Braid* (1900) 2 F. 754; *Cunningham* v. *Skinner* (1902) 4 F. 1124.

[73] *Phosphate Sewage Co.* v. *Molleson* (1879) 6 R. (H.L.) 113; *Edinburgh Water Trustees* v. *Clippens Oil Co.* (1899) 1 F. 899; *Weissenbruch* v. *Weissenbruch & Anr.*, 1965 S.L.T. 139; see also *Gibson & Simpson* v. *Pearson*, 1992 S.L.T. 894; *Zuiderent* v. *Schuerman*, 1992 G.W.D. 37–2213; and *Margrie Holdings Ltd.* v. *City of Edinburgh District Council*, 1994 S.L.T. 971 at p. 974G–J.

[74] *Glasgow and S.-W. Ry.* v. *Boyd & Forrest*, 1918 S.C. (H.L.) 14, opinion of Lord Shaw.

[75] *Matuszczyk* v. *N.C.B.*, 1955 S.C. 418.

[76] *Duke of Sutherland* v. *Reed* (1890) 18 R. 252; *Hynds* v. *Hynds*, 1966 S.C. 201. See, however, *Anderson* v. *Wilson*, 1972 S.C. 147 (apportionment between joint wrongdoers).

[77] *Young* v. *Mitchell* (1874) 1 R. 1011; *Wilson* v. *Murphy*, 1936 S.L.T. 564.

[78] *Lamond* v. *Assessor for Dumfriesshire* (1900) 2 F. 610; *Assessor for Angus* v. *Anderson Grice Co. Ltd.*, 1968 S.L.T. 345.

[79] *Pollock* v. *Thomson* (1858) 21 D. 173.

[80] Erskine III, iii, 3.

[81] *Murray* v. *Seath*, 1939 S.L.T. 348; *Malcolm Muir Ltd.* v. *Jamieson*, 1947 S.C. 314; *Crudens* v. *Tayside Health Board*, 1979 S.C. 142.

[82] *Earl of Lauderdale* v. *Wedderburn*, 1908 S.C. 1237, revd. (on other grounds) 1910 S.C. (H.L.) 35. See also *Burton* v. *Chapel Coal Co.*, 1909 S.C. 430.

original parties.[83] An action by a beneficiary founded on an alleged breach of trust by the trustees is *res judicata* in an action by any other beneficiary.[84] A declarator of right of way, which has been tried and decided in an action by a party suing merely as a member of the public, is conclusive in an action raised by any other member of the public.[85] But there is no such community between the various owners of salmon fishings in a river as to render a decision as to the legality of a particular method of fishing *res judicata* in an action brought against a different owner.[86]

1.25   **Res Noviter.**—The plea of *res noviter veniens ad notitiam*, as a replication to the plea of *res judicata*, or as a ground for the reduction of a decree, imports that new evidence is tendered of which the party was not aware at the former trial and which he could not have discovered by the exercise of reasonable diligence.[87] Nothing can be *res noviter* that was within the power of the party to discover with ordinary care.[88] It would appear that it is not enough to aver that witnesses, who might have given evidence at the previous trial, have been discovered.[89] An averment that a material document, supposed to have been lost, has been discovered is a relevant averment of *res noviter* if no negligence in the matter can be imputed to the party.[90] It is not enough to aver that a material witness gave evidence contrary to the truth, on the theory that it is the province of the court to decide on the credibility of the witnesses.[91] But proof of subornation of perjury, or any other preconcerted fraud on the court, will suffice for the reduction of a decree,[92] provided that proceedings have been taken within a reasonable time after the facts have come to the pursuer's knowledge.[93]

Further Reading

Bankton, *Institute* (1753), I, 1.
Bennion, *Statutory Interpretation* (2nd ed., 1992).
Craies on *Statute Law* (7th ed., 1971).
Erskine, *Institute* (1773, edited by Nicolson, 1871), I, 1.
Maxwell, *Interpretation of Statutes* (12th ed., 1969).
Mitchell, *Constitutional Law* (2nd ed., 1968).
Stair, *Institutions* (1681, edited by More, 1832), I, 1.
Stair Memorial Encyclopaedia, Vol. 22, paras. 35–393.
Sources and Literature of Scots Law (Stair Society, 1936).

[83] Erskine, IV, iii, 3.
[84] *Allen* v. *McCombie's Trs.*, 1909 S.C. 710.
[85] *Macfie* v. *Scottish Rights of Way Society* (1884) 11 R. 1094.
[86] *Duke of Atholl* v. *Glover Incorporation* (1899) 1 F. 658.
[87] *McCarroll* v. *McKinstery*, 1924 S.C. 396, revd. 1926 S.C. (H.L.) 1.
[88] *Per* Lord President McNeill in *Campbell* v. *Campbell* (1865) 3 M. 501, adopted in *McCarroll* v. *McKinstery, supra.*
[89] *Miller* v. *Mac Fisheries*, 1922 S.C. 157.
[90] *McCarroll* v. *McKinstery, supra.*
[91] *Mackintosh's Trs.* v. *Stewart's Trs.* (1906) 8 F. 467; but see *Maltman* v. *Tarmac Civil Engineering Ltd.*, 1967 S.L.T. 141.
[92] *Shedden* v. *Patrick* (1854) 1 Macq. 535; *Mackintosh's Trs. supra*; *Maltman, supra.*
[93] *Lockyer* v. *Ferryman* (1877) 4 R. (H.L.) 32 (delay of 30 years).

CHAPTER 2

COURTS AND JURISDICTION: ARBITRATION

2.1 House of Lords.—The ultimate appeal, in a civil case originating in Scotland, is to the House of Lords, which has inherited the jurisdiction exercised by the Scots Parliament prior to the Union in 1707. Until 1876 there was no definite distinction between the House of Lords as a legislative and as a judicial body. By the Appellate Jurisdiction Act 1876,[1] provision was made for the appointment of judicial officers, known as Lords of Appeal, and no appeal can be heard unless three of these are present.[2] The Act leaves untouched the right of any Peer of Parliament to sit and vote in any appeal but even before the Act was passed it had been recognised that lay peers should not sit and if they do their votes are not counted.[3] The House of Lords has no original jurisdiction. There is no appeal to it from the High Court of Justiciary.[4] Any final judgment of the Court of Session is subject to appeal, except in cases where appeal is excluded by statute,[5] or where the question is one of expenses only.[6] If the Court of Session, on an appeal from the sheriff court, has made findings-in-fact, appeal to the House of Lords is restricted to questions of law.[7] An interlocutory judgment (*i.e.* one which does not dispose of the whole cause) may be appealed if the judges were not unanimous, or, in any case, with the leave of the court.[8] An appeal lies from a judgment of the Court of Session in the exercise of its criminal jurisdiction.[9] By the Standing Orders of the House of Lords no appeal can be received unless it is lodged within three months of the last interlocutor appealed from.

[1] As amended by Appellate Jurisdiction Acts 1913–1947.

[2] s. 5. The Lords of Appeal, from whose number the quorum is constituted, include the Lord Chancellor and peers who have held high judicial office as well as Lords of Appeal in Ordinary appointed under the Act.

[3] Mitchell, p. 259.

[4] Criminal Procedure (Scotland) Act 1975, s. 281; *Mackintosh* v. *Lord Advocate* (1876) 3 R. (H.L.) 34.

[5] *e.g.* Agricultural Holdings (Scotland) Act 1991, Sched. 7, para. 21.

[6] *Caledonian Ry.* v. *Barrie* (1903) 5 F. (H.L.) 10.

[7] Court of Session Act 1988, s. 32(5); *Bogota* v. *Alconda*, 1924 S.C. (H.L.) 66; *Crerar* v. *Bank of Scotland*, 1922 S.C. (H.L.) 137; *Sutherland* v. *Glasgow Corporation*, 1951 S.C. (H.L.) 1; *Marshall* v. *William Sharp & Sons Ltd.*, 1991 S.L.T. 114; *Laing* v. *Scottish Grain Distillers Ltd.*, 1992 S.C.(H.L.) 64.

[8] Court of Session Act 1988, s. 40(1); *Ross* v. *Ross*, 1927 S.C. (H.L.) 4; *Adelphi Hotel (Glasgow)* v. *Walker & Eglinton Hotels (Scotland)*, 1960 S.C. 182 (interlocutor granting interim interdict). An appeal now lies, without leave, from an interlocutor granting a motion for a new trial (1988 Act, s. 40(2)).

[9] *Carse* v. *Lord Advocate* (1784) 3 Paton 1.

2.2 Privy Council.—In the seventeenth century the Scots Privy Council exercised a supreme jurisdiction in all questions relating to the public peace. It was abolished by 6 Anne, c. 40, and its functions transferred to the Privy Council of Great Britain, which has no jurisdiction of this character. The Privy Council, through its Judicial Committee, exercises a supreme jurisdiction in appeals from courts in certain Commonwealth countries but has no judicial functions in Scotland, except under particular statutes.[10]

2.3 Court of Session.—The Court of Session was established in 1532, superseding the jurisdiction of the Lords Auditors, a committee of Parliament, and courts known as the Session and the Daily Council, of which little is known.[11] As originally constituted it consisted of 14 ordinary judges, with a President. The King had power to nominate Extraordinary Lords, who might sit and vote, but this power was abolished by 10 Geo. I, c. 19. Until 1808 all the judges sat together in the Inner House as an appellate court, sending one of their body by rotation to hear cases as a judge of first instance, known as a Lord Ordinary, in the Outer House. In 1808 and in 1825 the court was reorganised.[12] It was divided into the First Division, presided over by the Lord President; the Second Division, presided over by the Lord Justice-Clerk, these two divisions constituting the Inner House; and the permanent Lords Ordinary. Since 1830 four judges have sat in each Division,[13] and the remainder as Lords Ordinary in the Outer House. The maximum number of judges who may be appointed is now 27,[14] and the retirement age is 75.[15] The Court of Session, as now existing, is a combination of two courts—the Inner House, with a jurisdiction mainly appellate, and the Outer House, a court of first instance. For detailed information as to the jurisdiction of the Court of Session, works devoted to procedure must be consulted.[16] Speaking generally, the Inner House sits as a court of appeal from the judgments of the Lords Ordinary or of any inferior civil court,[17] except in cases where the value, exclusive of interest and expenses, does not exceed £1,500[18] or where the inferior court is by statute declared to be final[19]: in the Outer

[10] *e.g.* Medical Act 1983, s. 12; *McAllister* v. *General Medical Council* [1993] A.C. 388.
[11] See *Acta Dominorum Auditorum* (1496–1501) and Neilson's Introduction, and (1501–1554) Hannay's Introduction.
[12] 48 Geo. III, c. 151; 6 Geo. IV, c.120.
[13] In practice, it is now unusual for more than three judges to sit in a Division.
[14] Court of Session Act 1988, s. 1(1) as amended by Maximum Number of Judges (Scotland) Order 1993 (S.I. 1993 No. 3154).
[15] Judicial Pensions Act 1959, s. 2. The retirement age is 70 for future appointments: Judicial Pensions and Retirement Act 1993, s. 26.
[16] See Mackay, *Manual*; Maclaren, *Court of Session Practice*; Maxwell, *The Practice of the Court of Session*.
[17] Erskine, I, iii, 20; *Jeffray* v. *Angus*, 1909 S.C. 400.
[18] Sheriff Courts (Scotland) Act 1907, s. 7. But see para. 2.6, n. 82. As to what is meant by 'value,' see *Brady* v. *Napier*, 1944 S.C. 18.
[19] *Adair* v. *Colville*, 1926 S.C. (H.L.) 51; *Arcari* v. *Dumbartonshire County Council*, 1948 S.C. 62; *Neill's Tr.* v. *Macfarlane's Trs.*, 1952 S.C. 356.

House actions may be brought originally, with the exception of cases where the value, exclusive of interest and expenses, does not exceed £1,500[20] and excluding certain cases where special statutory procedure is enjoined.[21] The criminal jurisdiction of the Court of Session, which at one time included cases of forgery, is in modern times confined to the imposition of penalties for breach of interdict or other contempt of court. The High Court of Admiralty (1681–1830), the Court of Exchequer (1707–1854)[22] and the Jury Court (1815–1830) are now merged in the Court of Session.

In addition to its ordinary functions the Court of Session has a general power to review, by suspension or reduction, the judgments of inferior courts or persons vested with judicial or administrative authority, on the ground that they have exceeded the jurisdiction committed to them, have contravened the principles of natural justice, or have been guilty of error in procedure so fundamental as to make their decision a nullity.[23] 'Wherever any inferior tribunal or any administrative body has exceeded the powers conferred upon it by statute to the prejudice of the subject, the jurisdiction of the Court to set aside such excess of power as incompetent and illegal is not open to dispute.'[24] A mere error of law if *intra vires* does not entitle the court to intervene with the decision of a body exercising a statutory jurisdiction.[25] In considering whether a tribunal has contravened the principles of natural justice, the question before the court is not whether the tribunal has arrived at a fair result, but whether it has dealt fairly and equally with the parties before it in arriving at that result.[26] Before recourse is had to the Court of Session it must be shown that any remedy provided by the statute by which the tribunal or administrative jurisdiction is founded is inapplicable.[27] The effect of statutory provisions that the decision of a particular body shall be final is not free from doubt. It is conceived that a statute may confer finality on the proceedings of an inferior court or of a statutory body in terms so wide as to exclude any interference by the Court of Session,[28]

[20] Sheriff Courts (Scotland) Act 1971, s. 31 as amended by S.I. 1976 No. 900 and S.I. 1988 No. 1993.
[21] Questions involving important patrimonial interests in Church matters may be outside the purview of the Court of Session: see *Ballantyne* v. *Presbytery of Wigtown*, 1936 S.C. 625.
[22] See *I.R.* v. *Barrs*, 1961 S.C. (H.L.) 22.
[23] See Mitchell, *Constitutional Law*, pp. 249 *et seq.*; *McDonald* v. *Lanarkshire Fire Brigade Joint Committee*, 1959 S.C. 141; *Lord Advocate* v. *Johnston*, 1983 S.L.T. 290.
[24] *Per* Lord Kinnear, *Moss's Empires* v. *Assessor for Glasgow*, 1917 S.C. (H.L.) 1, at p. 6. See *Cheyne* v. *Architects' Registration Council*, 1943 S.C. 468.
[25] *Watt* v. *Lord Advocate*, 1979 S.C. 120.
[26] *Barrs* v. *British Wool Marketing Board*, 1957 S.C. 72, *per* Lord President Clyde at p. 82.
[27] *Crawford* v. *Lennox* (1852) 14 D. 1029; *Lang* v. *Presbytery of Irvine* (1846) 2 M. 823; *British Railways Board* v. *Glasgow Corporation*, 1976 S.C. 224 (application to the court incompetent where statutory appeal procedure had not been exhausted and question raised could have been decided by statutory appeal).
[28] See *Adair* v. *Colville*, 1926 S.C. (H.L.) 51.

but in most cases finality clauses are read as applicable exclusively to procedure which is *intra vires* and regular and do not affect jurisdiction in cases of what have been termed constitutional nullities.[29] Applications to the supervisory jurisdiction of the court are now made by means of an application for judicial review and on such an application the court may make such order in relation to the decision in question as it thinks fit being an order which could be made in any action or petition and including an order for reduction, suspension, declarator, interdict, implement, restitution and payment.[30]

2.4 High Court of Justiciary.—The High Court of Justiciary, as a supreme criminal court, was established by the Courts Act 1672 (c. 16).[31] As now constituted, it consists of the Lord President, under the title of Lord Justice-General, the Lord Justice-Clerk and the other judges of the Court of Session.[32] Its permanent session is in Edinburgh, but provision is made for sittings elsewhere in Scotland.[33] The High Court of Justiciary has a universal jurisdiction as a court of first instance in all cases of crime, except where, in the case of minor offences, its original jurisdiction is excluded by statute. It possesses a paramount and overriding authority which has been described as similar to the *nobile officium* of the Court of Session.[34] When sitting in Edinburgh the court has at common law jurisdiction to review the decisions of inferior criminal courts where the proceedings have been initiated by complaint and not by indictment.[35] This jurisdiction has been extended by statute[36] but a power which previously existed to bring proceedings on indictment in the sheriff court under review by bill of suspension has been

---

[29] *Manson* v. *Smith* (1871) 9 M. 492 (Small Debt Court); *Walsh* v. *Magistrates of Pollokshaws*, 1907 S.C. (H.L.) 1, and *Goodall* v. *Bilsland*, 1909 S.C. 1152 (Licensing Court); *Moss's Empires* v. *Assessor for Glasgow*, 1917 S.C. (H.L.) 1 (Valuation Court).

[30] Rule of Court 58; *West* v. *Secretary of State for Scotland*, 1992 S.C. 385.

[31] History in Hume on *Crimes*, ii, 1.

[32] Criminal Procedure (Scotland) Act 1975, s. 113(1).

[33] *Ibid.*, s. 112.

[34] *Milne* v. *McNicol*, 1944 J.C. 151; *Wan Ping Nam* v. *Minister of Justice of German Federal Republic*, 1972 J.C. 43.

[35] Proceedings initiated by complaint are triable summarily by a sheriff or district court justice sitting alone. Proceedings on indictment (solemn procedure) are, on a plea of not guilty, tried by a jury. The common law methods of review, preserved by s. 455(1) of the 1975 Act, are advocation, suspension and suspension and liberation. Advocation is appropriate to review of a decision, disposing of the case or part of it, made in the preliminary stages of prosecution. It is not competent where a preliminary objection to competency or relevancy has been repelled (*Aldred* v. *Strathern*, 1929 J.C. 93) and so is normally of service only to the prosecutor. Suspension or suspension and liberation is appropriate where an illegal warrant, conviction or judgment is impugned. The grounds extend to lack of jurisdiction or title to prosecute, irrelevancy or incompetency of the complaint and oppression on the part of the judge including oppressive sentence (*Ferguson* v. *Brown*, 1942 S.C. 113) but not to the merits of a conviction (*Dunn* v. *Mitchell*, 1911 S.C. (J.) 46; *cf. Paterson* v. *Macpherson*, 1924 J.C. 38).

[36] 1975 Act, s. 442, which enables *inter alia* a limited review of the merits of a conviction by way of stated case.

abolished.[37] There is an appeal to the High Court sitting as a court of appeal by a person convicted on indictment against conviction or sentence or both and any alleged miscarriage of justice may be brought under review by such appeal.[38] Where a person tried on indictment is acquitted of a charge, the Lord Advocate may refer a point of law which has arisen in relation to that charge to the High Court for their opinion[39] but the opinion does not affect the acquittal.[40] The High Court has in respect of its *nobile officium* the power of interfering in extraordinary circumstances, for instance where no other procedure is available for review.[41] Three judges of the High Court constitute the court of appeal.[42] There is no appeal to the House of Lords.[43]

2.5 European Community Courts.—The Court of Justice of the European Communities[44] consists of 13 judges who are assisted by six advocates-general. One judge is elected President. The court may sit in chambers of three or five judges.[45] No dissenting opinions are given. The court has jurisdiction in the following: (1) actions brought by the Commission or a Member State against another Member State in respect of a failure to fulfil an obligation under the Treaty of Rome[46]; (2) actions to review the legality of acts adopted jointly by the European Parliament and the Council, of acts of the Council of Ministers, the Commission and of the European Central Bank other than recommendations and opinions[47]; (3) actions brought by the Member States or the other institutions against the European Parliament, Council or the Commission for failure to act when required to do so in terms of the Treaty[48]; (4) references by municipal courts and tribunals for preliminary rulings concerning the interpretation of the Treaty, the validity and interpretation of acts of the institutions of the Community (including the European Central Bank) and the interpretation of the statutes of bodies established by an act of the Council, where those statutes so provide[49]; (5) actions to enforce the

---

[37] 1975 Act, s. 230, re-enacting Criminal Appeal (Scotland) Act 1926, s. 13; see *George Outram & Co. Ltd.* v. *Lees*, 1992 S.L.T. 32.

[38] 1975 Act, s. 228.

[39] 1975 Act, s. 263 A (1).

[40] 1975 Act, s. 263 A (5). See *Lord Advocate's Reference No. 1 of 1983*, 1984 J.C. 52. The Lord Advocate may now appeal against sentence: 1975 Act, s. 228A, inserted by the Prisoners and Criminal Proceedings (Scotland) Act 1993, s. 42.

[41] *Wylie* v. *H.M. Advocate*, 1966 S.L.T. 149; *Rae, Petr.*, 1982 S.L.T. 233.

[42] 1975 Act, s. 245(1).

[43] *Mackintosh* v. *Lord Advocate* (1876) 3 R. (H.L.) 34; 1975 Act, s. 281.

[44] Treaty of Rome, Art. 164. Protocol on the Statute of the Court of Justice of the EEC signed in Brussels on April 17, 1957. Rules of Procedure [1991] O.J. L176/7.

[45] Art. 165.

[46] Arts. 169 and 170.

[47] Art. 173.

[48] Art. 175.

[49] Art. 177. European Communities Act 1972, s. 3; Rule of Court 65; Sheriff Court Rule 134. See *Mehlich* v. *Mackenzie*, 1984 S.L.T. 449; *Hamilton* v. *Whitelock* [1987] 3 C.M.L.R. 190; *Walkingshaw* v. *Marshall*, 1992 S.L.T. 1167; *Brown* v. *Secretary of State*, 1989 S.L.T. 402; *Wither* v. *Cowie*, 1994 S.L.T. 363.

contractual or non-contractual liability of the Community[50]; (6) disputes between the Community and its servants[51]; (7) disputes relating to the European Investment Bank and national central banks[52]; (8) matters submitted to arbitration under a contract concluded by or on behalf of the Community[53]; (9) disputes between Member States submitted under an agreement between the parties[54]; (10) matters arising under certain provisions of the European Coal and Steel Treaty and the Euratom Treaty.[54a] In addition the court has jurisdiction to interpret the Jurisdiction and Judgments Convention.[55] The court may be called upon to give an opinion as to whether an agreement between the Community and one or more states or an international organisation is compatible with the Treaty.[56]

The European Court of First Instance consists of 12 judges. It may sit in chambers of three or five judges.[57] The jurisdiction of the Court of First Instance has been extended and covers all staff cases and direct actions brought by national or legal persons under the EC, ECSC and Euratom Treaties.[58] There is an appeal on a point of law to the Court of Justice of the Communities.[59]

2.6 Sheriff Court.—The sheriff, as a ministerial and judicial officer, appears in the records of the law of Scotland from the twelfth century. By the eighteenth century the office had in most cases become hereditary. Hereditary jurisdictions were abolished by the Heritable Jurisdictions (Scotland) Act 1747,[60] under which, though sheriffs could be appointed by the Crown for a period not exceeding one year,[60] their duties were to be performed by a new officer, the sheriff-depute, who had to be an advocate of at least three years' standing, and was to hold office *ad vitam aut culpam*.[61] Sheriffs-substitute were appointed by the sheriffs-depute until 1877[62] but had been definitely recognised as judicial officers paid by the Crown in 1787. The use of the title 'sheriff' was authorised for the sheriff-depute by the Sheriff Courts (Scotland) Act 1825[63] and in

[50] Art. 178.
[51] Art. 179.
[52] Art. 180.
[53] Art. 181.
[54] Art. 182.
[54a] ECSC Treaty, Art. 95; Euratom Treaty, Arts. 12 and 103.
[55] See para. 2.13.
[56] Art. 228.
[57] Council Decision of October 24, 1988 [1988] O.J. L319/1; Rules of Procedure [1991] O.J. L136/1. Council Decision, Art. 2.
[58] For original jurisdiction see EC Treaty, Art. 168a(1); ECSC Treaty, Art. 32d(1); Euratom Treaty, Art. 140a(1). Jurisdiction has been extended by Council Decisions 93/350 and 94/149.
[59] Council Decision of October 24, 1988, Art. 51.
[60] *Ibid.*, s. 5.
[61] *Ibid.*, s. 29.
[62] Sheriff Courts (Scotland) Act 1877, s. 4.
[63] See also Circuit Courts (Scotland) Act 1828.

1971 he was, in accordance with what had become common usage, designated 'sheriff principal'.[64] At the same time the title of 'sheriff-substitute', for long a misnomer, was replaced by sheriff.[64] No one may be appointed to the office of sheriff principal or sheriff unless he is an advocate or solicitor of at least 10 years' standing.[65] The word 'sheriff' includes sheriff principal unless otherwise provided or the context is repugnant to the construction.[66] All resident sheriffs within a sheriffdom have jurisdiction throughout the sheriffdom.[67] Sheriffs principal and sheriffs are required to retire at the age of 72.[68]

The civil jurisdiction of the sheriff court, as extended by the Sheriff Court Acts of 1876, 1907 and 1913, extends to nearly all actions. The leading exceptions are certain actions involving status (*e.g.* declarator of marriage), reductions and petitions for judicial review, petitions for the winding up of a company if the paid-up capital exceeds £120,000,[69] suspension of charges upon decrees of the Court of Session[70] and actions of proving the tenor of a lost document.[71] Actions of divorce and for declarator of legitimacy, legitimation or illegitimacy, formerly competent only in the Court of Session, may now be brought in the sheriff court as also may actions for declarator of parentage or non-parentage and for declarator of death.[72] The sheriff's jurisdiction over actions of debt or damages is without pecuniary limit. In cases which are competent in the sheriff court and where the value, exclusive of interest and expenses, does not exceed £1,500 the jurisdiction of the sheriff is privative, *i.e.* such cases cannot be brought originally in the Court of Session.[73]

'Summary cause' procedure is applicable to all actions for payment of money not exceeding £1,500, exclusive of interest and expenses, to multiplepoindings, furthcomings and sequestrations for rent where the subject matter does not exceed £1,500 in value and to actions *ad factum praestandum* and actions for the recovery of heritable or moveable property unless there is an alternative or additional crave for payment of a sum exceeding £1,500.[74] If required to do so on joint motion of the parties, the sheriff is to direct that an ordinary cause be treated as a

---

[64] Sheriff Courts (Scotland) Act 1971, s. 4(1).

[65] *Ibid.*, s. 5(1).

[66] Interpretation Act 1978, Sched. 1.

[67] Sheriff Courts (Scotland) Act 1971, s. 7; *Spence* v. *Davie*, 1993 S.L.T. 217.

[68] The retirement age is 70 for future appointments: Judicial Pensions and Retirement Act 1993, s. 26.

[69] Insolvency Act 1986, s. 120.

[70] Sheriff Courts (Scotland) Act 1907, s. 5(5) as amended by the Law Reform (Misc. Provs.) (Scotland) Act 1980, s. 15.

[71] *Dunbar* v. *Scottish County Investment Co.*, 1920 1 S.L.T. 136.

[72] Divorce Jurisdiction, Court Fees and Legal Aid (Scotland) Act 1983, s. 1, amending Sheriff Courts (Scotland) Act 1907, s. 5; Law Reform (Parent and Child) (Scotland) Act 1986, s. 7; Presumption of Death (Scotland) Act 1977, Sched. 1.

[73] 1907 Act, s. 7, as amended by 1971 Act, ss. 31, 35 and 41 and S.I. 1988 No. 1993.

[74] 1971 Act, ss. 35(1) and 41 and S.I. 1976 No. 900, 1981 No. 842 and 1988 No. 1993.

summary cause or a summary cause as an ordinary cause and he may make the latter direction on the motion of any party if he is of the opinion that the importance or difficulty of the cause makes it appropriate to do so.[75] A 'small claim' is a form of process used for summary cause proceedings where the value does not exceed £750.[76] Small claims are exempt from rules relating to admissibility or corroboration of evidence. Expenses are awarded only where the value of the claim exceeds £200 and they may not exceed £75.[77] The sheriff also has jurisdiction to deal in a summary manner with a wide range of common law and statutory applications to which the 'summary application' procedure applies.[78] This procedure is entirely distinct from and unconnected with the 'summary cause'.

The judgment of a sheriff in his ordinary court may be appealed to the sheriff principal unless such appeal is excluded by statute. If the cause is not a summary cause or application the appeal may be either to the sheriff principal, from whom an appeal lies to the Court of Session, or directly to the Inner House of the Court of Session.[79] To render an appeal to the Court of Session competent, the judgment of the sheriff principal[80] or sheriff must either be final, or be an interlocutor granting interim decree for payment of money other than a decree for expenses, or sisting an action, or refusing a reponing note. In other cases the leave of the sheriff principal or sheriff, as the case may be, to appeal is required.[81] In summary causes appeal is competent only against a final judgment and only on a point of law.[81a] The appeal from the sheriff is to the sheriff principal from whose judgment there may be an appeal to the Court of Session only if he certifies the cause as suitable.[82] There is no appeal to the Court of Session in a small claim.[83] In a summary application at common law appeal to the sheriff principal and, subject to the value rule, to the Court of Session is competent but in statutory summary applications review is often restricted or excluded by the statute under which the application is brought.[84] In the case of

---

[75] 1971 Act, s. 37(1) and (2), as amended by the Law Reform (Misc. Provs.) (Scotland) Act 1980, s. 16(a); *Butler* v. *Thom*, 1982 S.L.T. (Sh. Ct.) 57.

[76] Law Reform (Misc. Prov.) (Scotland) Act 1985, s. 18, amending ss. 35–38 of 1971 Act; Small Claims Order 1988 (S.I. 1988 No. 1999).

[77] Small Claims Order 1988, art. 4 (but see 1971 Act, s. 36B(3)).

[78] 1907 Act, ss. 3(p), 50; Sheriff Court Summary Application Rules 1993 (S.I. 1993 No. 3240); Macphail, *Sheriff Court Practice*, Chap. 26.

[79] *Ibid.*, ss. 27 and 28.

[80] Appeal to the Court of Session will, however, be subject to the value rule (see *supra*, para. 2.3 and n. 18).

[81] Sheriff Courts (Scotland) Act 1907, s. 28 as amended by Sheriff Courts Act 1913.

[81a] 1971 Act, s. 38; an incompetent interlocutor may be the subject of an appeal even though the interlocutor is not a final judgment; *City of Glasgow District Council* v. *McAleer*, 1992 S.L.T.(Sh.Ct.) 41.

[82] 1971 Act, s. 38.

[83] 1971 Act, s. 38 as amended (see n. 76, *supra*).

[84] See Macphail, *Sheriff Court Practice*, pp. 884–892.

any ordinary cause the sheriff may, on the motion of any of the parties to the cause, remit the cause to the Court of Session if he is of the opinion that the importance or difficulty of the cause makes it appropriate to do so.[85]

In criminal matters the sheriff principal or sheriff is a competent judge in all crimes except treason, murder, attempt to murder, and rape. The sheriff court and the High Court have between them an inherent universal jurisdiction which can only be restricted or excluded by the express provision or clear implication of a statute.[86] In respect that a sheriff cannot inflict a penalty exceeding three[87] years' imprisonment it is mainly a question of the gravity of the alleged offence whether criminal proceedings should be taken in the sheriff court or in the High Court of Justiciary.

2.7   District Courts.—By the District Courts (Scotland) Act 1975 the Justice of the Peace Courts, Burgh Courts and Police Courts (which had until then exercised a petty criminal, and, in the case of the justices of the peace, a very limited civil, jurisdiction) were abolished and replaced by district courts.[88] There is a district court for each local authority district or islands area, except Orkney,[89] and its jurisdiction and powers are exercisable by one or more lay justices or by a stipendiary magistrate, where appointed, who must be an advocate or solicitor of at least five years' standing.[90] The jurisdiction and powers are those possessed by the former courts[91] and are restricted to the trial of offences summarily. But section 285 of the Criminal Procedure (Scotland) Act 1975[92] gives a list of offences, covering most common law offences of other than a minor character, which are excluded from the competence of the district court. And it is a general principle that statutory offences cannot be tried by courts such as the district court, unless jurisdiction is conferred upon them by statute, either expressly or by implication.[93] The maximum sentence which can be imposed is 60 days' imprisonment and a fine not exceeding £2,500.[94] These restrictions, however, only apply to

[85] 1971 Act, s. 37(1)(*b*), as amended by the Law Reform (Misc. Prov.) (Scotland) Act 1980, s. 16(*a*). *Mullan* v. *Anderson*, 1993 S.L.T. 835. For actions of divorce, custody or adoption, *cf.* s. 37(2A).
[86] See *Blythswood Taxis* v. *Adair*, 1944 J.C. 135, at p. 140; *Wilson* v. *Hill*, 1943 J.C. 124.
[87] Criminal Procedure (Scotland) Act 1975, s.2(2).
[88] District Courts (Scotland) Act 1975, s. 1.
[89] *Ibid.*, ss. 1, 1A and 26(1); Disestablishment of District Court (Orkney) Order 1986 (S.I. 1986 No. 1836).
[90] *Ibid.*, ss. 2(2) and 5(2).
[91] *Ibid.*, s. 3(1). The civil jurisdiction of the former justice of the peace courts and quarter sessions is, however, excluded.
[92] 1975 Act, as amended by Criminal Justice (Scotland) Act 1980, s. 7 and Sched. 8 and Criminal Justice Act 1982, Sched. 7.
[93] *Macpherson* v. *Boyd*, 1907 S.C. (J.) 42.
[94] Criminal Procedure (Scotland) Act 1975, s. 284 and s. 289E as amended by Criminal Justice Act 1991, s. 17.

the court when it is composed of lay justices. A stipendiary magistrate has the summary criminal jurisdiction and powers of a sheriff.[95]

2.8   Other Courts.[96]—*The Court of the Lord Lyon:* The Lord Lyon King of Arms has jurisdiction, subject to appeal to the Court of Session and the House of Lords, in questions of heraldry, and the right to bear arms.[97] He has no jurisdiction to determine rights of precedence,[98] nor to decide a disputed question of chiefship or chieftainship.[99]

The Scottish Land Court: This court was set up in 1911 with judicial functions under the statutes which relate to agricultural land and small holdings and crofts.[1] It consists of a legally qualified chairman, who has the status of a judge of the Court of Session, and a panel of lay members who are experienced in agriculture; one of the members must be a Gaelic speaker.[2]

The Lands Valuation Appeal Court: This court sits to dispose of appeals on rating questions from local valuation appeal committees and the Lands Tribunal for Scotland. It consists of three judges of the Court of Session (although there is provision for one judge to sit in certain circumstances).[3] Appeals come before it on questions of law by way of a stated case, which is final on the facts stated in it.[4] No appeal lies from the decisions of this court either to the Court of Session or the House of Lords.

The Restrictive Practices Court: A special United Kingdom court was established by the Restrictive Trade Practices Act 1956, to examine restrictive agreements and prohibit those found to be contrary to the public interest.[5] Its jurisdiction was widened by the Resale Prices Act 1964, to include the determination of whether particular classes of goods should be exempted from the provisions of that Act. Jurisdiction and powers are now governed by the Restrictive Trade Practices Act 1976 and Resale Prices Act 1976 and composition and procedure by the Restrictive Practices Court Act 1976. The court consists of five judges,

---

[95] District Courts (Scotland) Act 1975, s. 3(2). The reconciliation of this subsection with s. 285 of the Criminal Procedure (Scotland) Act 1975 is not, however, free from difficulty.
[96] See Walker, *Scottish Legal System* (6th ed.), pp. 278 *et seq.*
[97] *Hunter* v. *Weston* (1882) 9 R. 492; *Mackenzie* v. *Mackenzie*, 1920 S.C. 764, affd. 1922 S.C. (H.L.) 39.
[98] *Royal College of Surgeons* v. *Royal College of Physicians*, 1911 S.C. 1054.
[99] *Maclean of Ardgour* v. *Maclean*, 1938 S.L.T. 49; and see 1941 S.C. 613.
[1] See para. 33.27, *infra.*
[2] Scottish Land Court Act 1993, s. 1.
[3] See Armour, *Valuation for Rating* (5th ed.), pp. 122 *et seq.*; Valuation of Lands (Scotland) Amendment Act 1879, as amended by the Rating and Valuation (Amendment) (Scotland) Act 1984, s. 13.
[4] Valuation of Lands (Scotland) Amendment Act 1879, s. 7.
[5] See para. 10.14, *infra.*

one being a judge of the Court of Session nominated by the Lord President, and not more than 10 other, lay, members. The quorum is three, consisting of a presiding judge and at least two other members, and the court may sit as a single court or in two or more divisions. In Scotland an appeal on any question of law lies to the Court of Session.

The Employment Appeal Tribunal: set up under the Employment Protection Act 1975 has in all matters incidental to its jurisdiction the like powers, rights, privileges and authority as the Court of Session.[6] It consists of a judge of the Court of Session and judges of the High Court in England nominated for the purpose and of appointed members with special knowledge or experience of industrial relations as representatives of either employers or workers. Appeals are heard by a judge with two or four appointed members from industrial tribunals on questions of law and from the Certification Officer under Trade Union legislation. A further appeal lies on a question of law to the Court of Session and House of Lords.

Church Courts: Kirk Sessions, Presbyteries, and the General Assembly of the Church of Scotland are established courts of the realm.[7] They now, however, have only a domestic jurisdiction over members of the Church on matters affecting Church discipline, membership, doctrine and ritual.

2.9   European Court of Human Rights.—The European Court of Human Rights is set up under the European Convention on Human Rights 1953. The number of judges is equal to the number of Member States of the Council of Europe.[8] References to the court are made either by the European Commission on Human Rights to which complaints of violation of human rights are made and which must attempt to bring about a friendly settlement or, in some circumstances, by a Member State.[9] The court may afford a just satisfaction to an aggrieved party against a Member State.[10]

2.10   Children's Hearings.[11]—Children's hearings were created by the Social Work (Scotland) Act 1968. They have no power to determine disputed questions of law or fact but are entrusted with the determination of

---

[6] s. 87. See now Employment Protection (Consolidation) Act 1978, ss. 135, 136 and Sched. 11. See also para 2.11, *infra*.

[7] *Wight* v. *Presbytery of Dunkeld* (1870) 8 M. 921.

[8] Art. 38.

[9] Art. 43.

[10] Art. 50.

[11] See Social Work (Scotland) Act 1968, Pts. III and IV, ss. 30 to 68; *Kennedy* v. *B.*, 1973 S.L.T. 39; *H.* v. *McGregor*, 1973 S.L.T. 110; *B.* v. *Sinclair*, 1973 S.L.T. (Sh.Ct.) 47; *B.* v. *Kennedy*, 1974 S.L.T. 168; *H.* v. *Mearns*, 1974 S.L.T. 184; *K.* v. *Finlayson*, 1974 S.L.T. (Sh.Ct.) 51; *McGregor* v. *T.*, 1975 S.L.T. 76.

whether children referred to them are in need of compulsory measures of care and the application of such care by means of supervision requirements. Such conditions may be imposed in a supervision requirement as the hearing thinks fit, including a residential condition, and the child may be required to reside in a school or other institution registered with the local authority or Secretary of State for the purposes of the Act. The hearings also have certain advisory functions in relation to children and young persons brought before courts. A child may be in need of compulsory measures of care if any of the grounds mentioned in section 32 of the Act are satisfied. These grounds include the commission of an offence by the child, as well as those which formerly fell within the care and protection jurisdiction of juvenile courts, and the hearings have, accordingly, very largely replaced the functions of the courts so far as the measures to be adopted in the case of juvenile offenders are concerned. The decision on whether to refer a child to a hearing is taken by an officer known as the reporter. The hearing consists of a chairman and two members selected from the children's panel which must be formed under the Act for every local authority area. If the grounds on which the child is referred are disputed or are not understood by the child, the hearing, unless it discharges the referral, must direct the reporter to apply to the sheriff for a finding on whether the grounds are established.[12] An appeal lies to the sheriff at the instance of the child or its parents against any decision of a children's hearing and from the sheriff's decision on such an appeal, or on a finding as to whether the grounds of referral are established, an appeal lies at the instance of the child, its parents or the reporter to the Court of Session by way of stated case on a point of law.[13] In one case, the parents successfully petitioned the *nobile officium* for a rehearing of the grounds of referral.[13a]

2.11   Tribunals.[14]—Numerous tribunals have been set up under statutory authority for the determination of particular disputes. For the most part, these are concerned with the exercise of ministerial powers or the administration of statutory or governmental schemes in a judicial or quasi-judicial manner and as such fall outwith the scope of this book. Some, however, of which the most notable are industrial tribunals, have a function which is indistinguishable from that of courts in resolving, within the area of their competence, legal disputes between citizens.

Industrial tribunals were set up under the Industrial Training Act 1964 but now have an extensive jurisdiction, far exceeding that originally

[12] As to the standard of proof, corroboration and hearsay, see *Harris* v. *F.*, 1991 S.L.T. 242.
[13] See *Sloan* v. *B.*, 1991 S.L.T. 530.
[13a] *L, Petrs. (No. 1)*, 1993 S.L.T. 1310.
[14] Tribunals and Inquiries Act 1992; Walker, *Scottish Legal System* (6th ed.), pp. 282–299. Hepple & O'Higgins, *Employment Law* (3rd ed., 1979), Chaps. 4 and 22.

envisaged, under *inter alia* the Equal Pay Act 1970, the Sex Discrimination Act 1975, and the Employment Protection (Consolidation) Act 1978. They consist of a legally qualified chairman who must be an advocate or solicitor of at least seven years' standing and two lay members, one of whom is chosen from a panel of persons nominated after consultation with organisations representative of employers and the other after similar consultation with organisations representative of employed persons. An appeal lies from decisions of the tribunal to the Employment Appeal Tribunal.

The Lands Tribunal for Scotland consists partly of legally qualified persons (one of whom is President) and partly of persons with experience in the valuation of land. Its functions include the assessment of compensation for compulsory purchase of land and the variation and discharge of obligations affecting land.[15]

The working of virtually all tribunals is kept under review by the Council on Tribunals which has advisory and consultative functions in relation to them.

2.12   Jurisdiction over Persons.—Jurisdiction, in relation to the persons over whom it is exercised, has been defined as 'a power conferred on a judge or magistrate to determine debateable questions according to law, and to carry his sentences into execution.'[16] It is not, however, an absolute rule that the Scottish courts will refuse to pronounce a decree which cannot be carried into execution;[17] and in many cases they exercise their jurisdiction where their decree can be enforced only by proceedings in the courts of some other country.[18] The maxim *actor sequitur forum rei* (a pursuer follows the forum of the defender) imports that no actions can be entertained unless the court has jurisdiction over the defender, but there may be jurisdiction without power to enforce the decree. It is competent to sue the Crown for damages in respect of the negligence of its servants.[19] There are now substantial exceptions to the former rule that no Scottish court has jurisdiction to entertain a case against a foreign sovereign state, unless its immunity is departed from.[20] The immunity of ambassadors and other members of a diplomatic mission[21]

---

[15] Lands Tribunal Act 1949; Land Compensation (Scotland) Act 1963, Pt. II; Conveyancing and Feudal Reform (Scotland) Act 1970, Pt. I; The Lands Tribunal for Scotland Rules 1971 (S.I. 1971 No. 218).

[16] Erskine, I, ii, 2. See Anton, *Private International Law* (2nd ed.), Chap. 5.

[17] *Sons of Temperance Friendly Society*, 1926 S.C. 418.

[18] *e.g.* when jurisdiction is founded on arrestments to found jurisdiction, *infra*, para. 2.21.

[19] Crown Proceedings Act 1947, s. 2.

[20] State Immunity Act 1978; *Govt. of the Republic of Spain* v. *National Bank of Scotland*, 1939 S.C. 413; *Grangemouth and Forth Towing Co.* v. *Netherlands E.I. Govt.*, 1942 S.L.T. 228; *Forth Tugs Ltd.* v. *Wilmington Trust Company*, 1985 S.C. 317.

[21] Diplomatic Privileges Act 1964, which gave effect to the Vienna Convention on Diplomatic Privileges, 1961. Note that members of the administrative and technical staff are liable civilly, and members of the service staff are liable both criminally and civilly, for acts performed outside the course of their duties.

includes the chief representatives of Commonwealth countries and their staffs, and now extends to chief representatives of states or provinces of a country within the Commonwealth, to certain consular officers and persons in the service of Commonwealth governments or the government of the Republic of Ireland performing duties of a consular nature, and to other persons on whom it may be conferred by Order in Council.[22] It may also be conferred by Order in Council on certain international organisations and persons connected with them.[23] Under the Visiting Forces Act 1952, restrictions are placed on the power of United Kingdom courts to try members of visiting forces, as defined.

2.13 Jurisdiction under the Civil Jurisdiction and Judgments Act 1982.—Questions of whether a court has jurisdiction and against whom that jurisdiction extends depend on the nature of the action. In most classes of civil proceedings those questions are now governed by the Civil Jurisdiction and Judgments Act 1982.[24] The Act is not, however, exhaustive and several matters which fall outwith its scope, *e.g.* actions concerning status, are important and are noted below. The Act gives effect to the European Convention on Jurisdiction and Enforcement of Judgments in Civil and Commercial Matters 1968 and, going beyond what the Convention requires, makes provision for allocation of jurisdiction among the several parts of the United Kingdom and also for a new, although not entirely comprehensive, Scottish code of civil jurisdiction. It embodies in its application to Scotland a tripartite scheme of rules for determining jurisdiction (1) where the defender is domiciled in a Contracting State other than the United Kingdom or where, under the Convention, the courts of a Contracting State other than the United Kingdom have exclusive jurisdiction regardless of domicile;[25] (2) where the defender is domiciled in a part of the United Kingdom other than Scotland or where the courts of a part of the United Kingdom other than Scotland have exclusive jurisdiction regardless of domicile,[26] and (3) in other cases in which a person is sued in civil proceedings 'in the Court of Session or the Sheriff Court.'[27] The

---

[22] Consular Relations Act 1968 as amended by Diplomatic and Other Privileges Act 1971. *Cf.* Diplomatic Immunities (Conferences with Commonwealth Countries and Republic of Ireland) Act 1961. Reference must be made to the statutes for details of the extent of immunity, the conferral and withdrawal of which are, in some cases, subject to resolution by Order in Council.

[23] International Organisations Acts 1968 and 1981.

[24] For a full discussion see Anton & Beaumont, *Civil Jurisdiction in Scotland.* The Civil Jurisdiction and Judgments Act 1982 (Amendment) Order 1989 (S.I. 1989 No. 1346) amends the 1982 Act to give effect to the Greek Accession Convention. The Civil Jurisdiction and Judgments Act 1982 (Amendment) Order 1990 (S.I. 1990 No. 2591) gives effect to the Spanish and Portuguese Accession Convention, which amended the 1968 Convention in several respects.

[25] s. 2 and Sched.1, title II.

[26] s. 16 and Sched. 4.

[27] s. 20 and Sched. 8.

rules in the first category may conveniently be called 'the Convention rules,' those in the second category 'the United Kingdom rules' and those in the last category 'the Scottish rules.' In the event of conflict the Scottish rules yield to the United Kingdom rules and the Convention rules prevail over both.[28] Reference to a Contracting State is to the members of the European Community and this may include territories outwith Europe for which the member state is responsible.[29] The parts of the United Kingdom other than Scotland are (a) England and Wales, and (b) Northern Ireland.[30]

The Civil Jurisdiction and Judgments Act 1991 amends the 1982 Act to give effect to the Lugano Convention of 1988[31] which extends the 1968 Convention to the Member States of the European Free Trade Association.[32] The Spanish and Portuguese Accession Convention amends the 1968 Convention on certain points on which the Lugano Convention differed from the 1968 Convention[33] but some of the amendments differ slightly from the Lugano Convention.[34] The Court of Justice of the European Communities has jurisdiction to make preliminary rulings on questions of interpretation of the 1968 Convention referred by municipal courts[35] but there is no similar provision for the Lugano Convention. The courts of each Contracting State have 'to pay due account' to the principles laid down by decisions of courts of other states on the Convention. By declarations annexed to the Lugano Convention the Community Member States declare that they consider as appropriate that the Court of Justice of the European Communities when interpreting the Brussels Convention 'pay due account' to the rulings in the case-law of the Lugano Convention and the members of the European Free Trade Association declare that their courts should 'pay due account' to the rulings contained in the case-law of the Court of Justice of the European Communities and municipal courts in respect of the provisions of the Brussels Convention substantially reproduced in the Lugano Convention.[36]

2.14 The Scope of the 1982 Act.—The Convention and United Kingdom rules are specifically stated to apply only to civil and commercial

---

[28] ss. 16(4) and 20(1). It is important to note that while S.I. 1990 No. 2591 amends the text of the 1968 Convention in Sched. 1 to the 1982 Act to make several important changes, corresponding changes are not made in the 'United Kingdom rules' and 'the Scottish rules.'

[29] s. 1(3) as amended; Anton & Beaumont, paras. 3.42–3.46.

[30] s. 50.

[31] The Lugano Convention is sometimes known as the 'Parallel Convention.'

[32] Austria, Finland, Iceland, Norway, Sweden and Switzerland.

[33] There are changes to the text of Arts. 5, 6, 16, 17, 21, 31, 50, 52, 54, 54A, 57, 58, 60 and 64.

[34] Arts. 5, 16, 17.

[35] Protocol signed at Luxembourg, June 3, 1971 (1982 Act, Sched. 2); 1991 Act, s. 3.

[36] Lugano Convention, Protocol 2, Art. 1.

matters.[37] Not only criminal, but also revenue, customs and administrative cases are excluded. In addition, the Convention rules do not apply where the matter in issue concerns:[38]

(1) Status or legal capacity in natural persons.
(2) Rights in property arising out of a matrimonial relationship.
(3) Wills and succession.
(4) Bankruptcy.
(5) Winding up of insolvent companies or other legal persons, judicial arrangements, compositions and analogous proceedings.
(6) Social security.
(7) Arbitration.

The United Kingdom rules have the same list of exclusions as the Convention rules with the following additions:[39]

(1) Proceedings for the winding up of a company under the Insolvency Act 1986 (whether or not the company be insolvent) or proceedings relating to a company as respects which jurisdiction is conferred on the court having winding-up jurisdiction under the Act.
(2) Proceedings concerned with the registration or validity of patents, trademarks, designs or other similar rights required to be deposited or registered.
(3) Proceedings under s. 6 of the Protection of Trading Interests Act 1980.
(4) Proceedings on appeal from or for review of decisions of tribunals.
(5) Proceedings for or relating to maintenance and similar payments to local and other public authorities.
(6) Proceedings brought in pursuance of any statutory provision or rule of law which implements a Convention relating to specific matters overriding the general rules of the 1968 Convention.
(7) Proceedings in an Admiralty cause where the jurisdiction of the court is based on arrestment *in rem* or *ad fundandam jurisdictionem* of a ship, cargo or freight.
(8) Proceedings for the rectification of the Register of Aircraft Mortgages kept by the Civil Aviation Authority.
(9) Proceedings in pursuance of an order under s. 23 of the Oil and Gas (Enterprise) Act 1982.
(10) Proceedings arising out of the acts or omissions of a designated agency or other body under s. 188 of the Financial Services Act 1986.

[37] Sched. 1, Art. 1; s. 16(1).
[38] Sched. 1, Art. 1.
[39] ss. 16(1) and 17(1) and Sched. 5.

(11)   Proceedings under any enactment which confers jurisdiction on a Scottish court in respect of a specific subject matter on specific grounds.[40]

The scope of the Scottish rules is defined in terms different from the Convention and United Kingdom rules although the broad effect is similar. It embraces civil proceedings[41] and although commercial cases are not specifically mentioned, as they are in the Convention and the United Kingdom rules, they can be taken to be included. Criminal cases are thereby excluded but there is no exclusion of administrative, customs or revenue matters or of matrimonial property, wills and succession, social security or arbitration.[42] Otherwise the list of specific exceptions excludes from the Scottish rules all the matters which are excluded from the Convention and the United Kingdom rules and it is made clear that separation proceedings concern status and so are excluded from the scope of the Scottish rules as also are actions regulating the custody of children. Actions of affiliation and aliment, on the other hand, are within the scope of the rules.[43] The following further matters fall outwith the scope of the Scottish rules:

(1)   Guardianship of children and the management of the affairs of any incapax.
(2)   Commissary matters.
(3)   Remedies which are not in substance actions for decree against any person.
(4)   Jurisdiction conferred by any enactment in respect of a specific subject matter on specific grounds.[44]

2.15   Domicile under the 1982 Act.—The key jurisdictional concept of the 1982 Act is domicile. Domicile is not to be understood here in the sense in which it is encountered in international private law rules of status and succession ('the domicile of succession') but in a sense akin to what has been called the domicile of citation. A person is domiciled for the purposes of the Act in the United Kingdom or in a part of the United Kingdom or in a state other than a Contracting State if, and only if, he is resident in the United Kingdom or in a part of the United Kingdom or in a state other than a Contracting State, as the case may be, and the nature and circumstances of his residence indicate that he has a substantial connection therewith.[45] He is domiciled in a particular place in the United Kingdom if, and only if, he is domiciled in the part of the

[40] s. 17(1).
[41] s. 20(1).
[42] *Lord Advocate* v. *West End Construction*, 1990 S.C.L.R. 777 (Sh.Ct.).
[43] s. 21 and Sched. 9.
[44] s. 21(1)(*a*).
[45] s. 41(1), (2), (3) and (7).

United Kingdom in which that place is situated and is resident in that place.[46] Three months' residence in the United Kingdom or part of it gives rise to a presumption of substantial connection.[47] If a person is not by those rules domiciled in the United Kingdom and a question arises of whether he is domiciled in a Contracting State, the court is to apply the law of that state in order to determine whether he is domiciled there.[48]

The seat of a corporation or association is treated as its domicile.[49] It may have a seat in more than one place. If (a) a company or an association was incorporated or formed under the law of any part of the United Kingdom and has its registered office or some other official address in the United Kingdom, or (b) its central management and control is exercised in the United Kingdom, it will have a seat in any part of or place in the United Kingdom in which (i) it has its registered office or some other official address or (ii) its central management and control is exercised or (iii) it has a place of business.[50] A company or association has its seat in a state other than the United Kingdom if and only if it was incorporated or formed under the law of that state and has its registered office or some other official address in that state or its central management and control is exercised there,[51] but it is not to be regarded as having its seat in a Contracting State if it would not be so regarded by the courts of that state.[52] These rules for ascertaining the domicile of a company or association are subject to some modification in cases in which the court has an exclusive jurisdiction in relation to the company or association and also in certain other cases affecting company or association affairs.[53]

2.16 Grounds of Jurisdiction: The Scottish Rules of the 1982 Act.—The Scottish rules provide a code of jurisdiction where they are not in conflict with the Convention rules or the United Kingdom rules. In determining whether a Scottish court has jurisdiction, it is necessary to have recourse to the Convention and the United Kingdom rules only to ascertain whether there is such a conflict. The central principle of the Scottish rules is that persons, whether legal or natural, are to be sued in the courts for the place where they are domiciled.[54] That principle reflects corresponding provisions of the Convention rules and the United Kingdom rules and is not in conflict with them. Unless the special rules relating to exclusive jurisdiction regardless of domicile apply, any person

[46] s. 41(4).
[47] s. 41(6).
[48] Sched. 1, Art. 52.
[49] s. 42(1).
[50] s. 42(3), (4) and (5).
[51] s. 42(6).
[52] s. 42(7).
[53] s. 43.
[54] Sched. 8, para. 1.

domiciled in Scotland may therefore be sued in the Scottish courts and, subject to any rules regulating the jurisdiction of the Court of Session or the sheriff court on the basis of subject matter or value of the cause, any such person may be sued either in the Court of Session or the sheriff court. The sheriff court in which jurisdiction vests is that for the particular place within Scotland in which the defender is domiciled. Domicile, although the principal, is not, however, the only, ground of jurisdiction. In a variety of types of proceedings and circumstances there is under the Scottish rules concurrent jurisdiction in courts other than those of the defender's domicile.[55] Some of those grounds coincide or are compatible with the Convention rules and others are not. There appears to be no case of conflict with the United Kingdom rules. Where there is coincidence or compatibility and no rule of exclusive jurisdiction is transgressed, the Scottish courts will have jurisdiction even if the defender is domiciled in a Contracting State other than the United Kingdom. Where the rules of concurrent jurisdiction apply, there is jurisdiction in the Court of Session and also in the sheriff court for the place in question unless the Court of Session is expressly indicated as alone having jurisdiction. The following Scottish rules of concurrent jurisdiction coincide or are compatible with the Convention rules:[56]

(1) Where the person sued has no fixed residence, there is jurisdiction in the court within whose jurisdiction he is personally cited. This ground of jurisdiction does not coincide with any of the Convention or United Kingdom rules but is compatible with them as a person who has no fixed residence cannot be domiciled in another Contracting State or another part of the United Kingdom except in the case, probably rare, in which the law of a Contracting State so provides.

(2) In matters relating to a contract[57] there is jurisdiction in the courts for the place of performance of the obligation (the Convention, but not the Scottish rules, has been amended to provide that in an individual contract of employment the place of performance is where the employee habitually carries out his work; if the employee does not habitually carry out his work in any one country, the employer may also be sued in the courts for the place where the business which engaged the employee was or is situated).[58]

---

[55] Sched. 8, para. 2.

[56] Sched. 8, para. 2; cf. Sched. 1, Art. 5; Sched. 8, para. 5; cf. Sched. 1, Arts. 17 and 18.

[57] 'Matters relating to a contract' is an independent concept which is to be given a 'Community meaning': Peters v. ZNAV [1983] E.C.R. 987. On the other hand, 'the place of performance of the obligation' is to be determined by the law governing the obligation under the conflict rules of the court before which the matter is brought: Tessili v. Dunlop [1976] E.C.R. 1473. See Engdiv Ltd. v. G. Percy Trentham Ltd., 1990 S.C. 53.

[58] It is immaterial that the creditor has more than one place of business if he can insist on performance at one of them: Bank of Scotland v. Seitz, 1990 S.L.T. 584.

(3) In matters relating to delict or quasi-delict[59] there is jurisdiction in the courts for the place where the harmful event occurred.[60]

(4) A court seised of criminal proceedings has jurisdiction as regards a civil claim for damages or restitution which is based on an act giving rise to the criminal proceedings to the extent that that court has jurisdiction to entertain civil proceedings. It seems that the jurisdiction to entertain civil proceedings is here referable to the court's own rules.

(5) A court has jurisdiction in matters relating to maintenance if it is the court for the place where the maintenance creditor is domiciled or habitually resident or if the maintenance claim is ancillary to proceedings before it concerning the status of a person and it has jurisdiction to entertain those proceedings. An action for affiliation and aliment is to be treated as a matter relating to maintenance which is not ancillary to proceedings concerning status.

(6) As regards a dispute arising out of the operation of a branch, agency or other establishment, there is jurisdiction in the courts for the place in which the branch, agency or other establishment is situated.

(7) Where a person is sued in his capacity as settlor, trustee or beneficiary of a trust domiciled in Scotland, and created by the operation of statute, or by a written instrument, or created orally and evidenced in writing, there is jurisdiction in the Court of Session or the appropriate sheriff court within the meaning of section 24A of the Trusts (Scotland) Act 1921.

(8) In proceedings concerning an arbitration which is conducted in Scotland or in which the procedure is governed by Scots law, there is jurisdiction in the Court of Session. This ground of jurisdiction is compatible with the Convention rules because arbitration is expressly excluded from the scope of those rules.

(9) In proceedings which have as their object the decision of an organ of a company or other legal person or of an association of natural or legal persons, there is jurisdiction in the courts for the place where that company, legal person or association has its seat.

(10) Where the person sued is one of a number of defenders, there is jurisdiction in the courts for the place where any one of them is domiciled.

---

[59] 'Delict or quasi-delict' must be given an independent meaning: *Kalfelis* v. *Schröder, Münchmeyer, Hengst & Co.* [1988] E.C.R. 5565. A statutory claim against insurers is not a matter relating to delict or quasi-delict: *Davenport* v. *Corinthian Motor Policies at Lloyds*, 1991 S.C. 372.

[60] This covers both the place where the damage occurred and the place of the event giving rise to it: *Bier* v. *Mines de Potasse d'Alsace* [1976] E.C.R. 1735.

(11)   Where a person is sued as a third party in an action on a warranty or guarantee or in any other third party proceedings, there is jurisdiction in the courts seised of the original proceedings unless these were instituted solely with the object of removing him from the jurisdiction of the court which would be competent in his case.

(12)   On a counterclaim arising from the same contract or facts on which the original claim was based, there is jurisdiction in the court in which the original claim is pending.

(13)   Where the defender has prorogated the jurisdiction of the court.

The Convention and the Scottish rules have been amended to provide that in matters relating to contract, if the action may be combined with an action against the same defendant in matters relating to rights *in rem* in immoveable property, a person may be sued in the court of the place in which the property is situated.

Where a ground of jurisdiction is incompatible with the Convention rules, there is no jurisdiction in the Scottish courts where a defender is domiciled in another Contracting State or where the Convention rules otherwise indicate a jurisdiction outside Scotland. Certain of the Scottish rules fall into that category. Subject to exclusion on that ground, the Scottish courts have jurisdiction in the following further circumstances:[61]

(1)   Where the person sued is not domiciled in the United Kingdom, there is jurisdiction in the courts for any place where (a) any moveable property belonging to him has been arrested, or (b) any immoveable property in which he has any beneficial interest is situated.

(2)   In proceedings which have been brought to assert, declare or determine proprietary or possessory rights or rights of security in or over moveable property or to obtain authority to dispose of moveable property, there is jurisdiction in the courts for the place where the property is situated.

(3)   In proceedings for interdict, there is jurisdiction in the courts for the place where it is alleged that the wrong is likely to be committed.

(4)   In proceedings concerning a debt secured over immoveable property, there is jurisdiction in the courts for the place where the property is situated.

(5)   In proceedings principally concerned with the registration in the United Kingdom or the validity in the United Kingdom of patents, trademarks, designs or other similar rights required to be deposited or registered, there is jurisdiction in the Court of Session.

[61] Sched. 8, para. 2.

Special provisions of the Scottish rules, which reflect corresponding provisions of the Convention rules and the United Kingdom rules, apply to jurisdiction over consumer contracts.[62] The available grounds of jurisdiction are thereby widened in actions at the instance of consumers. The Convention rules, but not the United Kingdom or Scottish rules, also make special provision widening the grounds of jurisdiction when the action is against an insurer and restricting them when the action is at his instance.[63] The circumstances in which there may be a conflict between the Convention rules and the Scottish rules are thereby modified.

2.17 Exclusive Jurisdiction under the Scottish Rules of the 1982 Act.—The Scottish rules provide that in certain classes of proceedings a court shall have exclusive jurisdiction regardless of domicile or any other jurisdictional rule.[64] The classes of exclusive jurisdiction are as follows:[65]

(1) In proceedings which have as their object rights *in rem* in, or tenancies of, immoveable property, there is exclusive jurisdiction in the courts for the place where the property is situated. The Convention and the Scottish rules have been amended to provide that where the tenancy is for temporary private use for a maximum period of six consecutive months, the courts of the defendant's domicile shall also have jurisdiction, if the landlord and tenant are natural persons domiciled in the same country.

(2) In proceedings which have as their object the validity of the constitution, the nullity or the dissolution of companies or other legal persons or associations of natural or legal persons, there is exclusive jurisdiction in the courts for the place where the company, legal person or association has its seat.

(3) In proceedings which have as their object the validity of entries in public registers, there is exclusive jurisdiction in the courts for the place where the register is kept.

(4) In proceedings concerned with the enforcement of judgments, there is exclusive jurisdiction in the courts for the place where the judgment has been or is to be enforced.

(5) Where parties have prorogated the jurisdiction of a particular court, there is exclusive jurisdiction in that court.

The above rules are all compatible with the Convention rules and the United Kingdom rules. The Convention rules of exclusive jurisdiction are wider in two respects than the Scottish rules: (1) entries in registers of patents, trademarks, designs, etc., are not excluded from the exclusive jurisdiction given by the Convention to the courts of the

---

[62] Sched. 8, para. 3.
[63] Sched. 1, Arts. 7–12A.
[64] Sched. 8, para. 4.
[65] Sched. 1, Art. 16.

Contracting State in which a public register is kept and (2) the concurrent jurisdiction which the Scottish rules give in proceedings which have as their object a decision of an organ of a company, etc., is under the Convention rules an exclusive jurisdiction vested in the courts of the Contracting State in which the company, legal person or association has its seat. Neither of those features can, however, give rise to conflict with the Scottish rules. Where the Scottish rules of exclusive jurisdiction apply, they operate not only to vest jurisdiction in the Scottish courts but also to exclude the jurisdiction of a Scottish court wherever the rules indicate a court in another part of the United Kingdom or in another country whether or not a Contracting State.[66]

2.18 **Actions involving Status.**—Proceedings concerning status, being excluded from the scope of the Civil Jurisdiction and Judgments Act 1982, are subject to distinct jurisdictional rules. In actions of divorce and of separation and in declarators of marriage, of nullity of marriage and of freedom and putting to silence the Court of Session has jurisdiction if either of the parties to the marriage is domiciled in Scotland at the date when the action is begun or has been habitually resident in Scotland throughout the preceding year.[67] In declarators of marriage and of nullity of marriage it has, in addition, jurisdiction if either of the parties to the marriage is dead and was at death domiciled in Scotland or throughout the year preceding death was habitually resident there.[68] In declarators of parentage, non-parentage, legitimacy, legitimation or illegitimacy the Court of Session has jurisdiction if the child was born in Scotland or if (a) the alleged or presumed parent, or (b) the child, was domiciled in Scotland when the action was raised or was habitually resident in Scotland for not less than one year immediately preceding that date.[69] If the parent or child is dead the jurisdictional requirements apply to the date of death. In declarators of death there is jurisdiction if the missing person was domiciled in Scotland on the date on which he was last known to be alive or had been habitually resident there throughout the preceding year or if, in an action at the instance of his spouse, the spouse is at the date of raising the action domiciled in Scotland or has been habitually resident there throughout the preceding year.[70] The Court of Session has jurisdiction to entertain an action for reduction of any decree granted by a Scottish court.[71]

In an action for custody of children the Court of Session has jurisdiction where (1) the child is habitually resident in Scotland or (2) is present in Scotland and is not habitually resident in any part of the

---

[66] Sched. 8, para. 4(3).
[67] Domicile and Matrimonial Proceedings Act 1973, s. 7(1), (2) and (3) (*a*) and (*b*).
[68] *Ibid.*, s. 7(3)(*c*).
[69] Law Reform (Parent and Child) (Scotland) Act 1986, s. 7(2).
[70] Presumption of Death (Scotland) Act 1977, s. 1(3).
[71] Law Reform (Misc. Provs.) (Scotland) Act 1980, s. 20.

United Kingdom[72] unless, in either case, matrimonial proceedings are continuing in a court in any part of the United Kingdom in respect of the marriage of the parents of the child.[73] Where it has jurisdiction in an action of divorce, separation, declarator of marriage or declarator of nullity it has jurisdiction in questions relating to the custody of children.[74] It may also assume jurisdiction where the child is present in Scotland and the court considers that, for the protection of the child, it is necessary to make such an order immediately.[75]

In actions of divorce or separation the sheriff court has jurisdiction if the requirements of domicile and habitual residence in Scotland are satisfied and either party to the marriage was resident in the sheriffdom for 40 days preceding the raising of the action or was so resident for a period of at least 40 days ending within 40 days of the raising of the action and has, when the action is raised, no known residence in Scotland.[76] In actions of declarator of parentage, non-parentage, legitimacy, legitimation or illegitimacy there is jurisdiction if the child was born in the sheriffdom or if one of the grounds for Court of Session jurisdiction is satisfied and the parent or child was habitually resident in the sheriffdom at the date the action was raised or at the date of his death.[77] There is jurisdiction in declarators of death if any of the grounds for vesting jurisdiction in the Court of Session is satisfied and, in addition, the pursuer has been resident in the sheriffdom for a period of not less than 40 days ending with the date of raising the action.[78] In custody cases the sheriff has a jurisdiction on similar principles to those applying to the Court of Session.[79]

In actions concerning status, references to jurisdiction based on domicile are to the domicile of succession and not to domicile of citation or domicile in the sense of the Civil Jurisdiction and Judgments Act 1982.

2.19 Actions not involving Status and outwith the 1982 Act: the Court of Session.—In proceedings outwith the scope of the Civil Jurisdiction and Judgments Act 1982, other than those concerning status, neither domicile in the sense of that Act nor domicile of succession is, as a general rule, relevant to jurisdiction. In such cases the rules of jurisdiction which before the 1982 Act were generally applicable to personal actions remain in force.

[72] Family Law Act 1986, ss. 9, 10.
[73] *Ibid.*, s. 11.
[74] See *Battaglia* v. *Battaglia*, 1967 S.L.T. 49; 1973 Act, s. 10 and Sched. 2, Pt. I, para. 4; Family Law Act 1986, s. 13.
[75] Family Law Act 1986, s. 12.
[76] Domicile and Matrimonial Proceedings Act 1973, s. 8, as amended by Divorce Jurisdiction, Court Fees and Legal Aid (Scotland) Act 1983, Sched. 1, para. 18.
[77] Law Reform (Parent and Child) (Scotland) Act 1986, s. 7(3).
[78] Presumption of Death (Scotland) Act 1977, s. 1(4).
[79] Family Law Act 1986, ss. 8–13.

The two main grounds on which the Court of Session has been wont to assert jurisdiction, and may still proceed where the 1982 Act does not apply, and no question of status is in issue, are—(1) that defender is resident is Scotland or (2) that he is the owner of heritable property in Scotland. Residence is a ground of jurisdiction over all persons ordinarily resident in Scotland, or persons who have been resident for 40 days.[80] And residence means actual and not constructive residence.[81] In the case of a partnership or company the equivalent to residence is having a place of business[82] in Scotland, not merely having an agent there, if that agent has no power to bind his principal.[83] Jurisdiction is established over a friendly society if its rules are registered in Scotland or if it is incorporated and has a registered office in Scotland.[84] Ownership of, or a leasehold interest in, heritable property in Scotland will subject the owner to the jurisdiction of the Court of Session although the action may have no relation to that property.[85] Jurisdiction may also be founded by arrestment, by reconvention and by prorogation.[86]

2.20 Actions not involving Status and outwith the 1982 Act: the Sheriff Court.—The jurisdiction of the sheriff court is largely statutory. The principal rules, other than those already noticed for actions concerning status,[87] are contained in section 6 of the Sheriff Courts (Scotland) Act 1907 as amended by the Sheriff Courts (Scotland) Act 1913 and later legislation. These rules now receive effect subject to the Civil Jurisdiction and Judgments Act 1982[88] and are in part superseded by that Act. The following rules remain in force for cases to which the 1982 Act does not apply. A sheriff has jurisdiction, in actions competent in the sheriff court—(a) Where the defender (or where there are several defenders over each of whom a sheriff court has jurisdiction in terms of the Act, where one of them) resides[89] within the jurisdiction, or, having resided there for at least 40 days, has ceased to reside there for less than 40 days, and has no known residence in Scotland. (b) Where the

---

[80] Erskine, I, ii, 16; *Joel* v. *Gill* (1859) 21 D. 929; *Martin* v. *Szyska*, 1943 S.C. 203. The jurisdiction afforded by 40 days' residence ceases immediately on the defender's ceasing to reside in Scotland: see Maclaren, *Court of Session Practice*, p. 36; *Carter* v. *Allison*, 1967 S.L.T. 17.

[81] *Findlay* v. *Donachie*, 1944 S.C. 306; *Carter* v. *Allison*, *supra*.

[82] See *O'Brien* v. *Davies & Son*, 1961 S.L.T. 85.

[83] *Laidlaw Provident, etc., Insurance Co.* (1890) 17 R. 544.

[84] *Sons of Temperance Friendly Society*, 1926 S.C. 418; Friendly Societies Act 1992.

[85] *Ferrie* v. *Woodward* (1831) 9 S. 854; *Fraser* v. *Fraser & Hibbert* (1870) 8 M. 400; *Smith* v. *Stuart* (1894) 22 R. 130; *Thorburn* v. *Dempster* (1900) 2 F. 583; *Forth Tugs Ltd.* v. *Wilmington Trust Company*, 1985 S.C. 317.

[86] paras. 2.21, 2.22, and 2.23, *infra*.

[87] para. 2.18, *supra*.

[88] s. 20(3).

[89] There must be actual residence: *Findlay* v. *Donachie*, 1944 S.C. 306; *McCord* v. *McCord*, 1946 S.C. 198. The material date for determining the question of jurisdiction is the date of citation; *McNeill* v. *McNeill*, 1960 S.C. 30.

defender carries on business, and has a place of business, within the jurisdiction, and is cited either personally or at such place of business.[90] (c) Where the defender is a person not otherwise subject to the jurisdiction of the courts of Scotland and a ship or vessel of which he is owner or part owner or master, or goods, debts, money or other moveable property belonging to him have been arrested within the jurisdiction.[91] (d) Where the defender is the owner or part owner or tenant or joint tenant whether individually or as a trustee, of heritable property within the jurisdiction, and the action relates to such property or to his interest therein ... (g) Where in an action of furthcoming or multiplepoinding the fund or subject *in medio* is situated within the jurisdiction; or the arrestee or holder of the fund is subject to the jurisdiction of the court. (h) Where the party sued is the pursuer in any action pending within the jurisdiction against the party suing.[92] ... (j) Where the defender prorogates the jurisdiction of the court.[93]

2.21 **Arrestments to Found Jurisdiction.**—The mere possession of moveable property in Scotland does not afford jurisdiction.[94] But, under the process known as arrestment to found jurisdiction, if moveable property belonging to the defender (*e.g.* a ship) or a debt due to him in Scotland, is arrested, under a warrant from the Court of Session or from the sheriff court, he is subjected to the jurisdiction of the courts in Scotland in the action in respect of which the arrestments are used.[95] This applies only to actions with conclusions for payment of money or delivery of an article, not to actions affecting status, nor to a bare declarator or reduction.[96] Nor is it a process which will found jurisdiction in a petition for sequestration.[97] An arrestment to found jurisdiction has no effect except to found jurisdiction in the particular case; it does not give any nexus over the subject arrested, nor does it interpel the arrestee from paying the debt.[98] But the subject arrested must be one which could be arrested in execution.[99] This ground of jurisdiction is preserved by the Scottish rules of the 1982 Act but is not available against a defender who is domiciled in the United Kingdom; and it is incompatible with the

[90] *Bruce* v. *British Motor Trading Co.*, 1924 S.C. 908; *Hay's Trs.* v. *London and N.W. Ry.*, 1909 S.C. 707.
[91] See *infra*, para. 2.21.
[92] As to reconvention, of which this is an extension, see *infra*, para. 2.22. As to the limits of this statutory provision see *Kitson* v. *Kitson*, 1945 S.C. 434.
[93] See *infra*, para. 2.23.
[94] See paras. 2.19 and 2.20, *supra*.
[95] See form of warrants in Maclaren, *Court of Session Practice*, Chap. II. A right to expenses may be arrested to found jurisdiction: *Agnew* v. *Norwest Construction Co.*, 1935 S.C. 771.
[96] *Morley* v. *Jackson* (1888) 16 R. 78; *Williams* v. *Royal College* (1897) 5 S.L.T. 208.
[97] *Croil, Petr.* (1863) 1 M. 509.
[98] *Leggat Bros.* v. *Gray*, 1908 S.C. 67; *Fraser-Johnston Engineering Co.* v. *Jeffs*, 1920 S.C. 222.
[99] *Leggat Bros. supra*; as to arrestability, see para. 53.9, *infra*.

Convention rules and so is not available against a defender who is domiciled in a Contracting State.[1] In the sheriff court jurisdiction may be founded on arrestment only where the defender is not otherwise subject to the jurisdiction of the Scottish courts.[2]

2.22   Reconvention.—Where a party raises an action in the Court of Session he thereby submits himself to its jurisdiction in any counter action relating to the same dispute, as, for instance, in the case of cross actions arising from a collision between two ships.[3] He does not subject himself to the jurisdiction in an action relating to a separate question.[4] Reconvention will apply even although the action by the foreigner may not be the first in date.[5] It is not pleadable after the *actio conventionis* has been finally decided, though it may technically still be in court.[6] In order that jurisdiction may be founded on reconvention the foreigner must have sought the Scottish courts voluntarily. Where an English-woman, not otherwise subject to the jurisdiction, brought a suspension of a threatened charge on a bill it was held that she had not subjected herself to the jurisdiction of the Court of Session in an action for payment of the amount due on the bill, in respect that her proceedings were not voluntary but taken in self-defence.[7] The principle of reconvention is preserved by the 1982 Act to the extent that on a counterclaim arising from the same contract or facts on which the original claim was based, there is jurisdiction in the court in which the original claim is pending.[8]

2.23   Prorogation.—Jurisdiction may arise from prorogation. If a person submits himself to a court, either by express prior agreement,[9] or by appearing in answer to a citation without taking the plea of no jurisdiction before the record is closed,[10] he cannot afterwards take the objection that the court in question has no jurisdiction over him. Prorogation will not obviate the objection of want of jurisdiction in an action of divorce.[11] In any case prorogation only meets the objection that the court has no jurisdiction over the particular defender, not the

---

[1] See para. 2.16, *supra.*

[2] See para. 2.20, *supra.*

[3] *Morrison & Milne* v. *Massa* (1866) 5 M. 130. Even a sovereign state by invoking the Scottish court exposes itself to any lawful defence: see *Government of the Republic of Spain* v. *National Bank of Scotland*, 1939 S.C. 413, and cases there cited.

[4] *Thompson* v. *Whitehead* (1862) 24 D. 331. But see *Clydedock Engineering Ltd.* v. *Cliveden Compania Naviera SA* (O.H.) 1987 S.C.L.R. 540.

[5] *Morrison & Milne* v. *Massa* (1866) 5 M. 130.

[6] *Hurst, Nelson & Co.* v. *Whatley*, 1912 S.C. 1041.

[7] *Davis* v. *Cadman* (1897) 24 R. 297; see also *Macaulay* v. *Hussain*, 1967 S.L.T. 311.

[8] See para. 2.16, *supra.*

[9] *Elderslie S.S. Co.* v. *Burrell* (1895) 22 R. 389; *Lawrence* v. *Taylor*, 1934 S.L.T. 76 (prorogation by agreement to arbitrate in Scotland).

[10] *Fraser-Johnston Engineering Co.* v. *Jeffs*, 1920 S.C. 222.

[11] Fraser, *Husband and Wife*, ii, 1294; but see *A.B.* v. *C.D.*, 1957 S.C. 415 (cross actions of nullity and declarator of marriage).

objection that the case is one which the court, at common law or by statute, has no power to entertain. 'No parties can convey to a Court jurisdiction which does not belong to it.'[12] It has been held in the Outer House that the court might decline to accept jurisdiction, founded on a clause of prorogation, in an undefended case where neither the parties nor the matter in dispute had any connection with Scotland.[13] Any provision in a contract for the sale of an article whereby any party prorogates the jurisdiction of a particular sheriff court is void.[14] The same result is achieved in the case of consumer credit agreements,[15] including hire purchase agreements,[16] and consumer hire agreements[17] by the Consumer Credit Act 1974 which provides that no court other than the sheriff court where the debtor or hirer resides or carries on business shall have jurisdiction to enforce at the instance of the creditor or owner such an agreement or any security relating to it or to enforce against the debtor or hirer or his relative any linked transactions.[18] The principle of prorogation is preserved by the 1982 Act.

2.24   *Forum Non Conveniens*.—Either the Court of Session or the sheriff court may decline to exercise jurisdiction in a particular case on the plea of *forum non conveniens*, or, as it is stated in the earlier cases, *forum non competens*. The proper English equivalent of either term is, it has been laid down, 'appropriate.'[19] For the success of the plea it is necessary to show that some other court, in a civilised country, has concurrent jurisdiction.[20] The plea is one which will be most easily sustained in cases where foreign executors are sued in a Scottish court on the ground that as individuals they are subject to the jurisdiction,[21] but is open in any case. No rule has been laid down as to the grounds on which a court should hold that it is not the appropriate one to try a case where it has jurisdiction except in the very general form that the court has 'to consider how best the ends of justice in the case in question and on the facts before it, so far as they can be measured in advance, can be respectively ascertained and served.'[22] Elements of weight, but not necessarily conclusive, are that the question raised is one of foreign law, that the proof must be by foreign witnesses, that

---

[12] *Per* Lord Brougham, *Forest* v. *Harvey* (1845) 4 Bell's App. 197.

[13] *Styring* v. *Borough of Oporovec*, 1931 S.L.T. 493.

[14] Law Reform (Misc. Prov.) (Scotland) Act 1940, s. 4; *cf. English* v. *Donnelly*, 1958 S.C. 494.

[15] Consumer Credit Act 1974, s. 8(2).

[16] *Ibid.*, ss. 8(2) and 9(3).

[17] *Ibid.*, s. 15.

[18] *Ibid.*, ss. 141(3) and 141(3A).

[19] *Per* Lord Dunedin, *Société du Gaz* v. *Armateurs Français*, 1926 S.C. (H.L.) 13.

[20] *Clements* v. *Macaulay* (1866) 4 M. 583.

[21] See *Orr Ewing's Trs.* v. *Orr Ewing* (1885) 13 R. (H.L.) 1; *Robinson* v. *Robinson's Trs.*, 1929 S.C. 360; *Argyllshire Weavers Ltd.* v. *A. Macaulay (Tweeds) Ltd.*, 1962 S.C. 388. In *Dalziel* v. *Coulthurst's Exrs.*, 1934 S.C. 564, an action against executors, the stronger plea of 'no jurisdiction' prevailed.

[22] *Per* Lord Sumner, *Société du Gaz* v. *Armateurs Français*, 1926 S.C. (H.L.) at p. 22.

neither party is résident in Scotland, or that litiscontestation occurred earlier in this country.[23] It is irrelevant to consider on what grounds the jurisdiction of the Scottish court arises.[24] Where both the parties to the action were carrying on business in France, the question involved a claim for damages for unseaworthiness of a French ship, and all the witnesses were resident either in France or in England, the plea of *forum non conveniens* was sustained in reference to the sheriff court of Dumbarton, where, with jurisdiction established by arrestments, the action had been brought.[25] Under the Civil Jurisdiction and Judgments Act 1982 a defender is to be sued in the courts of his domicile unless one of the rules of exclusive jurisdiction or of concurrent jurisdiction can be invoked. Exclusive jurisdiction by definition precludes any question of choice of forum and under the rules of concurrent jurisdiction a right of choice appears to be given to the pursuer. There is therefore little, if any, scope for a plea of *forum non conveniens* in cases falling under the Act.

2.25 **Declinature.**—In any particular case the exercise of jurisdiction may be excluded by the declinature of the judge. This may be either on the ground of relationship to one of the parties, or of interest in the matters in the case. The Scots Acts[26] dealing with relationship have now been repealed[27] and the matter is dealt with administratively. Where the objection is that of interest in the cause any pecuniary interest will disqualify, such as that of holding shares in a company which is a party to the action,[28] with an exception, resting on Act of Sederunt, of the case where the judge is a shareholder (not a director) of a chartered bank in Scotland,[29] and by statute, where the judge is a partner in a life or fire insurance company, or the holder of shares in any company merely as a trustee.[30] Where the interest is not pecuniary it must be shown to be substantial, especially in cases where declinature would result in public inconvenience.[31] In practice, declinature, in cases where the interest is not really substantial, is elided by consent of parties; but if no such consent is given, or if the grounds of objection are not discovered until after decree, the decree will be reducible.[32]

---

[23] *Sim* v. *Robinow* (1892) 19 R. 665; *Société du Gaz, supra*; *Woodbury* v. *Sutherland's Trs.*, 1938 S.C. 689; *Argyllshire Weavers Ltd.*, *supra. Cf. Crédit Chimique* v. *James Scott Engineering Group*, 1979 S.C. 406, 1982 S.L.T. 131; *Mitchell* v. *Mitchell*, 1992 S.C. 372.
[24] Per Lord Shaw, *Société du Gaz* v. *Armateurs Français*, 1926 S.C. (H.L.) at p. 18.
[25] *Société du Gaz* v. *Armateurs Français*, 1925 S.C. 332, affd. 1926 S.C. (H.L.) 13.
[26] Declinature Act 1594 (c. 22); Declinature Act 1681 (c. 13).
[27] Court of Session Act 1988, s. 52(2), Sched. 2. The repeal of the 1681 Act is only so far as regarding the Court of Session.
[28] *Sellar* v. *Highland Ry.*, 1919 S.C. (H.L.) 19.
[29] A.S., Feb. 1, 1820.
[30] Court of Session Act 1868, s. 103.
[31] *Wildridge* v. *Anderson* (1897) 25 R. (J.) 27. See also *Rae* v. *Hamilton* (1904) 6 F. (J.) 42.
[32] *Ommanney* v. *Smith* (1851) 13 D. 678; *Sellar* v. *Highland Ry.*, 1919 S.C. (H.L.) 19.

2.26 Arbitration.—The jurisdiction of the courts may be excluded if the parties to any dispute agree to refer the matter to arbitration. Such an agreement is known as a reference or submission. It need not take the form of a probative deed, though it is doubtful whether a merely verbal submission is binding.[33] The effect is to give either party the right to object to an appeal by the other to the ordinary tribunals. Should such an appeal be made the court will decline to consider the case on the merits, and will sist the action to await the result of the arbitration.[34] The obligation to refer to arbitration is subject to prescription.[35] The Arbitration Act 1950 deals with arbitration between the subjects of different states which are parties to the agreements set out in the Act. The Arbitration Act 1975 provides for the enforcement of foreign arbitral awards. The UNCITRAL Model Law on International Commercial Arbitration has been given effect in Scotland.[36]

2.27 Agreements to Refer.—Prior to the Arbitration (Scotland) Act 1894, the general rule was that an agreement to refer to arbiters who were not named, for instance, to refer to the holder of some particular office, was not binding. By the Act it is provided that an agreement to refer shall not be invalid by reason of the reference being to a party not named, or to a person to be named by another person, or to a person merely described as the holder for the time being of any office or appointment. On failure to agree in the nomination of an arbiter, where the agreement is to refer to one, or on failure of a party to nominate an arbiter, where the agreement is to refer to two, the court, on the application of any party to the reference, may make the appointment.[37] An agreement to refer in the manner customary in a particular trade is valid, and proof will be allowed as to what that manner is.[38] In certain cases a particular form of arbitration is prescribed by statute[39]; where no statute is applicable there is no general rule, but the practice is to refer to a single arbiter, or to two arbiters and an oversman. Where the reference is to two arbiters, and there is no provision to the contrary, they have power to appoint an oversman, and, if they fail to agree in nomination, an oversman may be appointed by the court on the application of any party to the reference.[40] A mere agreement to refer to arbitration, without any indication of the method, will not justify an application to the court to appoint an arbiter, and it would seem doubtful by what procedure, if at all, it can be enforced.[41]

[33] *Otto* v. *Weir* (1871) 9 M. 660.
[34] *Hamlyn* v. *Talisker Distillery* (1894) 21 R. (H.L.) 21, opinion of Lord Watson.
[35] *Douglas Milne Ltd.* v. *Borders R.C.*, 1990 S.L.T. 558.
[36] Law Reform (Misc. Prov.) (Scotland) Act 1990, s. 66, Sched. 7.
[37] *Ibid.*, ss. 1–3.
[38] *Douglas* v. *Stiven* (1900) 2 F. 575; *United Creameries* v. *Boyd*, 1912 S.C. 617.
[39] *e.g.* Agricultural Holdings (Scotland) Act, 1991.
[40] Arbitration (Scotland) Act 1894, s. 4.
[41] *MacMillan* v. *Rowan & Co.* (1903) 5 F. 317.

2.28 Powers of Arbiter.—Some statutes provide for the determination of certain questions by arbitration and contain provisions as to the powers of the arbiters, and (in some cases) for an appeal to the courts on a question of law. In non-statutory arbitrations and those statutory arbitrations in which it is not competent, under the relevant statute, to appeal to a court or tribunal, or for a case to be stated for the court's or tribunal's opinions, provision is now made for a case to be stated for the opinion of the Court of Session on any question of law arising in the arbitration. The case may be stated by the arbiter at any stage on the application of a party[41a] and must be stated if the court on a party's application so directs.[42] It is, however, competent for parties by express agreement to exclude resort to the court.[43] Subject to these exceptions, the decision of the arbiter, or, where the arbiters differ, of the oversman, is final both as to fact and law.[44] An arbiter has implied power to award expenses,[45] but not, without express provision, to find either party liable in damages.[46] He has an implied power to award interest from the date of a final decree but no implied power to award interest from an earlier date.[47] He has no inherent power to enforce his decision; but it is usual to insert a clause of consent to registration for preservation and execution of the award, and diligence may proceed upon an extract from the register. Otherwise an action for decree conform is necessary. If no date is fixed the powers of the arbiter lapse after a year and a day from the date of the submission, unless the parties agree to prorogate the time, or express power to prorogate is conferred.[48]

2.29 Scope of Reference.—The scope of the reference depends upon the terms used.[49] In arbitration clauses in a contract the reference may be

---

[41a] The arbiter has discretion to postpone consideration of an application for a stated case until the facts have been ascertained: *Edmund Nuttall Ltd.* v. *Amec Projects Ltd.*, 1993 S.L.T. 255.

[42] Administration of Justice (Scotland) Act 1972, s. 3. An application after the final award is too late: *Fairlie Yacht Slip* v. *Lumsden*, 1977 S.L.T. (Notes) 41. The opinion of the Court of Session is not a judgment against which there can be an appeal to the House of Lords: *John G. McGregor (Contractors) Ltd.* v. *Grampian Regional Council*, 1991 S.C.(H.L.) 1. On the use of the procedure, see Davidson, 1989 S.L.T. (News) 89.

[43] See *Clydebank D.C.* v. *Clink*, 1977 S.C. 147; *Whatlings (Foundations) Ltd.* v. *Shanks & McEwan (Contractors) Ltd.*, 1989 S.L.T. 857. As to judicial review, see *Shanks & McEwan (Contractors) Ltd.* v. *Mifflin Construction Ltd.*, 1993 S.L.T. 1124.

[44] English law differs in this respect. See speeches of Lords Finlay and Dunedin in *Sanderson* v. *Armour*, 1922 S.C. (H.L.) 117.

[45] *Ferrier* v. *Alison* (1845) 4 Bell's App. 161. But parties must be heard on the question: *Islay Estates* v. *McCormick*, 1937 S.N. 28.

[46] *Mackay* v. *Leven Commissioners* (1893) 20 R. 1093.

[47] *John G. McGregor (Contractors) Ltd.* v. *Grampian Regional Council*, 1991 S.L.T. 136.

[48] Erskine, IV, iii, 29; *Lang* v. *Brown* (1855) 2 Macq. 93; *Graham* v. *Mill* (1904) 6 F. 886.

[49] *Beattie* v. *Macgregor* (1883) 10 R. 1094; *Mackay* v. *Leven Commissioners, supra*; *North British Ry.* v. *Newburgh, etc., Ry.*, 1911 S.C. 710.

merely executorial or ancillary, confined to questions arising in the course of the execution of the contract, in which case it is not to be carried beyond the term for which the contract endures[50]; or it may be of a more general character, covering all questions between the parties which may arise out of the contract. An averment that the adverse party has repudiated his contract may exclude the jurisdiction of the arbiter if the agreement to refer is merely executorial; it is now settled that it has not that effect if the reference is a general one of all questions that may arise under the contract.[51]

2.30   **Reduction of Award.**—An arbiter must be impartial; an award may be reduced if it is proved that the arbiter had an interest in the case such as would warrant the declinature of a judge, and that interest was not known to the party impugning the award at the date of the agreement to refer.[52] So where one of the parties to an arbitration was a railway company it was held to be a ground for the reduction of the award that the arbiter was a shareholder.[53] On the other hand, interest known to both parties is not a ground of disqualification. It is a common practice, in building and engineering contracts, to insert a clause referring all disputes that may arise to the employer's architect or engineer; and an agreement under which one of the parties to a contract was made sole arbiter has been sustained.[54] A party may by his conduct be held to have waived his objection to an arbiter.[55] That an arbiter has had business contacts of a regular kind with one of the parties does not in itself amount to disqualification.[55] An appointment of an arbiter, under statute, by a government department has been held to be an administrative act, so that the choice may not be challenged.[56] If the arbiter proceeds *ultra fines compromissi* (beyond the limits of the submission) and makes a pronouncement on a point not submitted to him, the award as a whole is open to reduction, unless the *ultra vires* part is clearly severable.[57] An award may also be reduced on the ground that the arbiter has mistaken the point at issue, or that he has not exhausted the questions submitted to him, but not merely because he has not dealt with the question of expenses.[58] By the Act of Regulations

[50] *Pearson* v. *Oswald* (1859) 21 D. 419; *Bellshill & Mossend Co-operative Society* v. *Dalziel Co-operative Society*, 1960 S.C. (H.L.) 64.
[51] *Sanderson* v. *Armour*, 1922 S.C. (H.L.) 117; *Scott* v. *Del Sel*, 1923 S.C. (H.L.) 37; *Charles Mauritzen Ltd.* v. *Baltic Shipping Co.*, 1948 S.C. 646; *Heyman* v. *Darwins* [1942] A.C. 356.
[52] *Magistrates of Edinburgh* v. *Lownie* (1903) 5 F. 711 (supervening interest).
[53] *Sellar* v. *Highland Ry.*, 1919 S.C. (H.L.) 19.
[54] *Buchan* v. *Melville* (1902) 4 F. 620; *Crawford Bros.* v. *Commissioners of Northern Lighthouses*, 1925 S.C. (H.L.) 22; see also *Fleming's Trs.* v. *Henderson*, 1962 S.L.T. 401.
[55] *Johnson* v. *Lamb*, 1981 S.L.T. 300.
[56] *Ramsay* v. *McLaren*, 1936 S.L.T. 35.
[57] *Miller* v. *Oliver & Boyd* (1903) 6 F. 77; *McIntyre* v. *Forbes*, 1939 S.L.T. 62; *Dunlop* v. *Mundell*, 1943 S.L.T. 286. In *McCoard* v. *Glasgow Corporation*, 1935 S.L.T. 117, interdict against the arbiter and against the other party was given.
[58] *Pollich* v. *Heatley*, 1910 S.C. 469; *Donald* v. *Shiell's Exrx.*, 1937 S.C. 52.

1695,[59] it is provided that no award of an arbiter may be reduced except on the ground of corruption, bribery or falsehood. These words are to be taken in their ordinary meaning, and an error in law cannot be made a ground of reduction under the name of 'constructive corruption.'[60] A decision on relevancy, whether or not the court might regard it as unsound, cannot be challenged.[61] But a serious error in procedure, such as hearing one party and refusing to hear the other, may be a ground of reduction, as a violation of what has been termed the 'principle of eternal justice.'[62] An award signed but improbative in form may not be sued upon.[63]

2.31   Remuneration of Arbiter.—In the earlier theory of law arbitration was assumed to be a service performed gratuitously, and an arbiter, or oversman, had no claim to remuneration, though he might stipulate for it without incurring the charge of corruption, within the meaning of that word in the Act of Regulations 1695.[64] On the more recent authorities the appointment of an arbiter implies an obligation to pay him a reasonable remuneration, either in statutory arbitrations,[65] or in any case where the arbiter is a professional man.[66] Each party is liable for half the arbiter's fee.[67]

Further Reading

Anton & Beaumont, *Civil Jurisdiction in Scotland* (2nd ed. 1995).
McBryde and Dowie, *Petition Procedure in the Court of Session* (2nd ed., 1988).
Mackay, *Court of Session Practice* (1879).
Mackay, *Manual* (1893).
Maclaren, *Court of Session Practice* (1916).
Macphail, *Sheriff Court Practice* (1988).
Maxwell, *The Practice of the Court of Session* (1980).
Russell, *Arbitration* (20th ed., 1982).
Stair Memorial Encyclopaedia, Vol. 6, paras. 801–1160.

---

[59] Printed in Irons, *Arbitration*, p. 376.

[60] *Adams* v. *Great North of Scotland Ry.* (1890) 18 R. (H.L.) 1. There may be appeal on a point of law in virtue of some special statutory provision. See, *e.g. L.M. & S. Ry.* v. *Glasgow Corporation*, 1940 S.C. 363.

[61] *Brown* v. *Associated Fireclay Companies*, 1937 S.C. (H.L.) 42.

[62] *Sharpe* v. *Bickerdike* (1815) 3 Dow 102; *Holmes Oil Co.* v. *Pumpherston Oil Co.* (1891) 18 R. (H.L.) 52; *Black* v. *Williams & Co.*, 1923 S.C. 510; *Islay Estates* v. *McCormick*, 1937 S.N. 28; *Fountain Forestry Holdings Ltd.* v. *Sparkes*, 1989 S.L.T. 853.

[63] *McLaren* v. *Aikman*, 1939 S.C. 222.

[64] *Fraser* v. *Wright* (1838) 16 S. 1049; *Duff* v. *Pirie* (1893) 21 R. 80.

[65] *Murray* v. *N.B.R.* (1900) 2 F. 460.

[66] *Macintyre Bros.* v. *Smith*, 1913 S.C. 129.

[67] *Macintyre Bros.*, *supra*.

CHAPTER 3

GENERAL LAW OF OBLIGATIONS

3.1 Meaning of Obligation.—The law deals with obligations and rights. The one necessarily involves the other. There can be no obligation unless the State, or some person, or body of persons, as the creditor, has the right to performance. An obligation has been defined as 'a legal tie by which we may be necessitated or constrained to pay or perform something.'[1] To which it should be added that the obligation may be of a negative character, and the obligant may be constrained to forbear from some action or course of action.

3.2 Obligation and Duty.—The word 'obligation' is sometimes used very loosely, as applicable to all legal ties, including the general duty to respect the rights of others sanctioned by the law, such as the right to liberty, to security of person, reputation or property. But such so-called obligations, in which all mankind are creditors, are more properly termed duties, and it is desirable to confine the term obligation to those legal ties which can be enforced only by some specific creditor. For instance, to refrain from defamatory statements about others is a duty, to observe an agreement not to make a particular statement about an individual is an obligation, and the defence that the statement was true, and therefore not actionable, though sufficient to meet any action founded on a breach of the duty, would be irrelevant as a defence to an action founded on a breach of the obligation.[2]

3.3 Sources of Obligations.—Taking an obligation in the narrower sense of the word indicated, as a legal tie by which one is bound to a specific creditor, or definite body of creditors, it may arise either with or without the consent of the debtor or obligant. If it arises with his consent it is said to arise from agreement or contract; if without his consent, it may either (*a*) be imposed by some external power or (*b*) arise from some act or omission of the obligant.

3.4 Statute.—In the latter class (*a*) are all obligations imposed by the legislature. As a general rule a statute imposes duties, and enjoins abstention from acts which would infringe the rights which it creates or

---

[1] Stair, iii, 1.
[2] See *R.* v. *S.*, 1914 S.C. 193.

54

protects, but certain statutes impose obligations in which either the State, as in revenue statutes, or some particular person, as under the Rent Acts, is the creditor.

3.5 Decree of Court.—Obligations may be imposed by the decree of a competent court. But it is at least arguable that a decree does not impose an obligation, but merely recognises and asserts an obligation which was already incumbent on the defender, though disputed by him. Thus, when a defender is found liable, the date of his obligation is not the date of the decree, but that of the act or omission which has occasioned his liability.[3] But a decree for expenses in favour of a litigant is an instance of an obligation resting solely on the decree.

3.6 Common Law.—Obligations may be imposed or recognised at common law. Such obligations, *e.g.* the obligation to restore property which does not belong to the possessor, are variously spoken of as arising from quasi-contract, as arising *ex lege*, or as obediential obligations. The term 'obediential', as it is explained by Stair, means that such obligations are exigible in accordance with the will of God.[4]

3.7 Breach of Contract, or of Duty.—In the second class, (*b*) are obligations which result from the act or failure of the obligant, apart from any consent of his. That act or failure may be a breach of contract, from which arises an obligation to pay damages for the breach. It may also be a breach of duty. The duty not to interfere with the rights of others gives rise, when it is not observed, to an obligation to make reparation to the particular person whose rights are infringed. At least according to older usage, when the infringement is of the nature of a deliberate act, the obligation is said to arise from delict or wrong; when it results from the failure to exercise the degree of care required by the law in the particular circumstances, it arises from quasi-delict or negligence.

3.8 Trust.—The obligations which arise from trust may be said to arise from agreement, and trust is treated by Stair and Erskine as a combination of the contracts of deposit and mandate. But the obligations involved in a position of trust, or in certain fiduciary relationships, extend so far beyond what the party who accepted that position may have intended, and are so often owed to parties with whom he clearly has no direct contractual relation, that it is more in accordance with modern decisions to regard trust, or fiduciary relationship, as an independent source of obligation. Thus, on a question of procedure, it was held that the liability of trustees for the loss of the trust funds was not to be considered as arising from breach of contract or from quasi-delict, but

[3] *Miller* v. *McIntosh* (1884) 11 R. 729; as to interest on damages, see para. 13.29, *infra*.
[4] Stair, I, i, 19.

from failure in the obligations recognised by law as resulting from the fiduciary relationship.[5]

3.9 **Rights.**—A right is defined by Holland as, 'capacity, residing in one man, of controlling, with the assent and assistance of the State, the actions of others.'[6] The definition indicates the difference between a right, as recognised in law, and a right as recognised in some system of morality, or by social usage. As the law of Scotland does not enforce gaming contracts, the man who has won a bet has no right to payment; he may be able to control the action of the loser, but he has that power by virtue of the force of public opinion and not by the assent and assistance of the State. The word 'right' is often used in a wider and looser sense, as indicating a freedom of acting in a particular way, without interference from the law, but without involving any control over the actions of others. Thus, it is said that a man has a right to open a shop or to make a will. A right in this wider sense may be termed a liberty or a licence.

3.10 **Real and Personal Rights.**—Under Holland's definition, a right may be the counterpart either of an obligation or of a duty. Thus, the right to receive an article which another has agreed to transfer consists in the capacity of controlling, with the assent and assistance of the State, the actions of the party who has made the agreement; the right of property in the article, when transferred, consists in the capacity of controlling the actions of all other persons, in so far as they may be forced to abstain from actions which would interfere with the proprietor's right to the article in question. In the former case, when the right is the counterpart of an obligation, it is known as a personal right, or *jus in personam*, and it gives a capacity of controlling the actions of the party who has undertaken the obligation, and of him only. A personal right is known also as *jus ad rem*. In the latter case, when the right is the counterpart of a duty, it is known as a real right, or *jus in re*, and gives a capacity of controlling the actions of all mankind. The distinction is indicated in Stair's definition of a right: 'A right is a power, given by the law, of disposing of things, or exacting from persons that which they are due.'[7] In the instance given above, the real right (*jus in re*) was a right of property, but it may also be a subordinate right, such as the right of a lessee or pledgee. Each, as distinguished from the personal right involved in an agreement to let or pledge, gives the power of controlling the actions of all persons in so far as they would infringe the right of the lessee or pledgee. The distinction between real and personal right is well expressed by Erskine:[8] 'A real right, or *jus in re*, whether of property or

---

[5] *Allen* v. *McCombie's Trs.*, 1909 S.C. 710.
[6] Holland, *Jurisprudence*, Chap. VII.
[7] Stair, I, i, 22.
[8] Erskine, III, i, 2.

of an inferior kind—as servitude—entitles the party vested with it to possess the subject as his own; or, if it be possessed by another, to demand it from the possessor, in consequence of the right which he hath in the subject itself; whereas the creditor in a personal right or obligation has only a *jus ad rem*, or a right of action against the debtor or his representatives, by which they may be compelled to fulfil that obligation, but without any right in the subject which the debtor is obliged to transfer to him.' The very important distinction between real and personal rights, as illustrated in the law of sale, securities and bankruptcy, will be noticed in the chapters devoted to these subjects.

3.11 Personal Bar.—The capacity of controlling the rights of others, either in the exercise of a real right in property or as the creditor in an obligation, may in particular circumstances be limited or abrogated by the operation of a principle known, according to Scottish terminology, as personal bar, according to English as estoppel.[9] In many cases the assertion of a right might conflict with ordinary conceptions of justice, either owing to the method by which the right was acquired or owing to the conduct of the party vested with it, and the principle of personal bar underlies many of the established rules of law. Thus, the rule that obligations induced by fraud or misrepresentation cannot be enforced, or that the informality of an obligation may be cured by acts following on it, may be said to rest on the ground that the party against whom the rules are pleaded is personally barred from asserting a right which he would otherwise have possessed. And the interpretation of all voluntary obligations must proceed on the principle that if a man expressed himself in ordinary language he is barred from asserting that his words were not intended to bear their ordinary meaning.[10] Many of the applications of the principle of personal bar have in Scots law become known by more specialised terms, such as *rei interventus*, homologation,[10a] adoption, acquiescence, and in the pages of this treatise dealing with these subjects illustrations of the general principle will be found.[11] For the present it may be sufficient to cite a definition of one main branch of the doctrine—personal bar by representation—and to add some annotations on it: 'Where A has by his words or conduct justified B in believing that a certain state of facts exists, and B has acted upon

[9] On this subject, see Rankine, *Personal Bar*; Spencer Bower and Turner, *Estoppel By Representation* (3rd ed., 1977); Everett and Strode, *Estoppel* (3rd ed., 1923); *Greenwood v. Martins Bank* [1933] A.C. 51.
[10] See para. 5.3 *infra*.
[10a] The rules of law referred to as *rei interventus* and *homologation* have been replaced by ss. 1(3) and (4) of the Requirements of Writing (Scotland) Act 1995.
[11] See Index. The statement that a party 'cannot be heard to deny' a certain fact does not, it is conceived, indicate a plea of personal bar, but means that the party, either by his prior acts or by his pleadings, has conclusively admitted the truth of the fact in question, or that his denial would conflict with the equitable rule that when a man does an act which he has a right to do he is not allowed to maintain that the act was intentionally and in fact done wrongly. See opinion of Jessel M.R., *Re Hallett* (1880) 13 Ch.D. 696, at p. 727.

such a belief to his prejudice, A is not permitted to affirm against B that a different state of facts existed at the same time.'[12] (1) A mere statement of intention is not a representation of any fact except that the intention has for the moment been formed, and therefore a party is not personally barred from affirming that his expressed intention has been altered.[13] (2) A man who neglects to assert his rights does not, in general, represent to those affected by the corresponding duty or obligation that his rights have been discharged or given up. So failure to state a defence to a claim does not bar the assertion of that defence at any time prior to the closing of the record in an action to enforce the claim.[14] (3) In Lord Birkenhead's definition above, B must be either a person with whom A had actual relations, or a person whom A, as a reasonable man, is bound to regard as interested, not merely a member of the general public. A man has no general duty so to regulate his conduct that third parties may not be justified in believing, and acting on the belief, that a certain state of matters exists. 'Law does not recognise a duty in the air, so to speak, that is, a duty to undertake that no one shall suffer from one's carelessness.'[15] A leaves his watch on a seat in the park; it is stolen and sold by the thief to B. A's conduct may be said to have justified B in forming and acting on the belief that the thief was the owner of the watch, but as A had no relations with B and was not bound to consider the possible results of his carelessness to members of the general public, A is not barred from asserting the true state of facts and recovering his watch from B.[16] This has been illustrated by cases bearing on the result of signing obligatory documents in a form which has facilitated fraudulent alteration. Where a man accepted a bill of exchange in a way which rendered it easy to alter the amount, he was not liable for more than the original amount to an indorsee, because the indorsee was merely a member of the general public, to whom the acceptor owed no duty to be careful.[17] But where a cheque for £2 was drawn carelessly, fraudulently altered to £120, and paid by the bank, it was held that as a customer does owe a duty to the bank to take reasonable care in drawing cheques, the bank was entitled to take credit for the £120 which had been paid.[18] (4) The party who pleads personal bar must show that in reliance on the other's words or acts he has altered his position, and altered it to his disadvantage. So, where a frontager, called upon by a local authority to make up a street, pleaded in defence that the local authority was barred by acts which had

[12] *Per* Lord Chancellor Birkenhead, *Gatty* v. *Maclaine*, 1921 S.C. (H.L.) 1.
[13] *Infra*, para. 5.8.
[14] *Morrison* v. *Gray*, 1932 S.C. 712. As to the effect of delay, see Chap. 15, *infra*.
[15] *Per* Greer L.J., *Bottomley* v. *Bannister* [1932] 1 K.B. 458.
[16] *Mitchell* v. *Heys* (1894) 21 R. 600; *Morrisson* v. *Robertson*, 1908 S.C. 332; *Low* v. *Bouverie* [1891] 3 Ch. 82; *Farquharson* v. *King* [1902] A.C. 325; *Jones* v. *Waring & Gillow* [1926] A.C. 670.
[17] *Scholfield* v. *Lord Londesborough* [1896] A.C. 514.
[18] *London Joint Stock Bank* v. *Macmillan* [1918] A.C. 777.

led him to suppose that the demand would not be made, it was held that, as he had suffered no disadvantage by the delay in enforcing his obligation, the plea of personal bar was untenable.[19]

3.12 **Personal Bar by Notice.**—As a general rule a person who acquires property, or to whom an obligation embodied in a negotiable instrument is transferred, is entitled to assume that the ostensible facts are the true ones, and that his author has an actual, as well as an apparent, right to convey or transfer. He is not concerned with latent claims, which might be asserted in a question with that author. But if he knew, or, as a reasonable man, should have known, that the latent claims existed, he is barred from asserting a right resting merely on the ostensible or apparent facts. So while a purchaser of lands is in general entitled to rely on the title as it stands on the Register of Sasines, if he knows that the subjects have already been sold to a third party he will be personally barred from asserting, in a question with that third party, his author's ostensible capacity to sell.[20] It would appear, however, that the purchaser of heritable property is entitled to assume that the seller has a complete and sufficient title to the subjects, and is not bound to verify grounds for suspecting that the title is in fact limited.[21]

3.13 **Obligations, Pure, Future, Contingent.**—An obligation may be pure, future or contingent.[22] An obligation is pure when, as in the case of a debt instantly payable, fulfilment is due at once. The term 'liquid' as applied to a debt, imports that it is pure, and also that it is either admitted, or constituted in such a form, as by a bill, bond or decree, that diligence can at once proceed. An obligation is termed future (as opposed to contingent) when it will become exigible either on a fixed date, or on the occurrence of some event (*e.g.* the death of some person) which is certain to happen. The maxim *dies statim credit, sed non venit*, means that, in the case of a future debt, the debt exists but cannot be enforced until the day of payment arrives. An obligation is contingent when it is subject either to a suspensive or a resolutive condition. There is a suspensive condition, also termed a condition precedent, when the obligation will arise only on the occurrence of an event which may or may not happen, or at some some period (*e.g.* the

---

[19] *Mags. of Alloa* v. *Wilson*, 1913 S.C. 6; *Bruce* v. *British Motor Trading Corporation*, 1924 S.C. 908; see also *Greater Glasgow Health Board* v. *Baxter Clark & Paul*, 1992 S.L.T. 35, *per* Lord Clyde at p. 43; *Bank of Scotland* v. *Smedley*, 1994 G.W.D. 21–1307.

[20] *Petrie* v. *Forsyth* (1874) 2 R. 214; *Stodart* v. *Dalzell* (1876) 4 R. 236; *Rodger (Builders)* v. *Fawdry*, 1950 S.C. 483.

[21] *Mossend Theatre Co.* v. *Livingstone*, 1930 S.C. 90; see also *Campbell* v. *McCutcheon*, 1963 S.C. 505.

[22] See Stair, I, iii, 7; Erskine, III, i, 6; Thomson, "Suspensive and Resolutive Conditions in the Scots Law of Contract," in *Obligations in Context* (ed. A.J. Gamble, 1990), p. 126; *Costain Building & Civil Engineering Ltd.* v. *Scottish Rugby Union plc*, 1994 S.L.T. 573, *per* Lord President Hope at pp. 576–577.

attainment by the creditor of a certain age) which may never arrive. There is a resolutive condition in the exceptional case of an obligation which is at once exigible but which will cease to be exigible on the occurrence of an uncertain event. Thus, where interim execution was authorised of a decree for expenses while the question between the parties was under appeal to the House of Lords, it was held that the claim for expenses was a contingent debt, in respect that although immediately exigible it would cease to be exigible if the judgment of the Court of Session was reversed.[23] A resolutive condition is also exemplified by a provision, in a disposition of property, that, on the occurrence of an uncertain event, the property shall revert to the disponer, or, a provision not uncommon in entails, shall pass to some third party.

3.14 Conditions.—A condition is termed potestative when it may be purified by an act which one or other of the parties has the power to do; casual, when the condition depends upon chance, or the action of third parties; mixed, when the concurrence of a potestative and a casual event is required. It is a general rule in the construction of wills that if a legacy is given on a condition which is partly potestative, it is held to be purified if the legatee has done all that he could to purify it, though he has failed. Thus if a legacy is given to A on the condition of his marriage with B, it is due if he had asked B to marry him and been refused.[24] In spite of a dictum of Erskine, it is conceived that this rule (grounded on the presumed intention of the testator) has no application to contracts, and that a party who has undertaken a conditional liability is not liable unless the condition is actually purified.[25] A party who has undertaken a conditional obligation impliedly undertakes that he will do nothing to impede the occurrence of the event on which the condition would be purified. So where A was a creditor in a bond which was not exigible by him for eight years provided that he remained the director of a particular company it was held that he did not acquire the right to immediate payment by the voluntary resignation of his directorship.[26] And if the scheme of a contract imports that something shall be done which cannot be done unless both parties concur in doing it, the construction of the contract is that each agrees to do all that is necessary to be done on his part for the carrying out of that thing, though there may be no express words to that effect.[27] So when a machine was sold on the condition that it should satisfy a certain test, to be carried out on

---

[23] *Forbes* v. *Whyte* (1890) 18 R. 182; another example is *Hardy* v. *Sime*, 1938 S.L.T. 18.
[24] Erskine, III, iii, 8; founding on Roman law; *Simpson* v. *Roberts*, 1931 S.C. 259.
[25] See Gloag, *Contract* (2nd ed.), p. 279.
[26] *Pirie* v. *Pirie* (1873) 11 M. 941. See also *Dowling* v. *Methven*, 1921 S.C. 948; *Leith School Board* v. *Clerk-Rattray's Trs.*, 1918 S.C. 94. See Rodger, 1991 S.L.T. (News) 253.
[27] See speech of Lord Blackburn, *Mackay* v. *Dick & Stevenson* (1881) 8 R. (H.L.) 37; 6 App.Cas. 251.

the premises of the buyer, it was held that he had impliedly agreed to give facilities for the test.[28] An agreement to sell goods at a time to be mutually agreed upon is not defeated by the fact that one party refuses to agree; the court will fix a reasonable time.[29] When goods were sold at a time when, to the knowledge of both parties, the sale could not be carried out unless the seller obtained a permit, it was held that the seller, though he had not guaranteed that he would obtain a permit, had impliedly undertaken to do all that he could to obtain one.[30] But questions of this kind turn on the interpretation of each contract; there is no absolute rule that because a man has undertaken a liability conditional on the performance of an act which he has the power to perform he has come under any implied obligation to perform it. When a railway company undertook to purchase lands if they constructed a certain line, it was held that the construction of the line remained a matter within their option, and that they were not in breach of their contract when they failed to construct it during the period within which they had statutory powers.[31] If a party adds to his offer or accceptance a condition which is purely in his own interest, he is entitled to waive compliance with it and insist on implement of the contract; whether a condition is purely in the interest of one party is a question of interpretation of the contract.[32]

3.15   Obligations by Co-debtors.—When an obligation is undertaken by more than one person the liability of each obligant in a question with the creditor may be either *in solidum*, for the whole debt, or only *pro rata*, for his proportionate share. When the matter is regulated by contract there is no doubt that if the parties are taken bound jointly and severally, or as principals and full debtors, the liability of each is *in solidum*. An obligation undertaken jointly, or conjunctly, involves liability only *pro rata*.[33] Where there is no express provision there is a general presumption in favour of liability *pro rata*.[34] This holds in bonds, cautionary obligations,[35] and as to the liability of underwriters in marine insurance.[36] But the exceptions are numerous and important. All the parties to a bill or promissory note are liable *in solidum*. Each

[28] *Mackay, supra.*
[29] *Pearl Mill Co.* v. *Ivy Tannery Co.* [1919] 1 K.B. 78; *Henry* v. *Seggie*, 1922 S.L.T. 5.
[30] *Re Anglo-Russian Merchant Traders and Batt* [1917] 2 K.B. 679.
[31] *Philip* v. *Edinburgh, etc., Ry.* (1857) 2 Macq. 514; *Maconochie Welwood* v. *Midlothian County Council* (1894) 22 R. 56; *Paterson* v. *McEwan's Trs.* (1881) 8 R. 646.
[32] Gloag, *Contract* (2nd ed.), p. 42; *Dewar and Finlay* v. *Blackwood*, 1968 S.L.T. 196 (O.H.); *Ellis and Sons Second Amalgamated Properties* v. *Pringle*, 1974 S.C. 200 (O.H.); *Imry Property Holdings Ltd.* v. *Glasgow Y.M.C.A.*, 1979 S.L.T. 261; *Gilchrist* v. *Payton*, 1979 S.C. 380.
[33] *Coats* v. *Union Bank*, 1929 S.C. (H.L.) 114; see also *Moss* v. *Penman*, 1994 S.L.T. 19, *per* Lord President Hope at p. 21.
[34] Stair, I, xvii, 20; Bell, *Prin.*, §51.
[35] Bell, *Prin.*, §267.
[36] Marine Insurance Act 1906, s. 67(2).

partner is liable for the whole debts of the firm.[37] When an order is given for goods or work by several persons acting in concert, though not partners, each is liable for the whole account.[38] And when the obligation is not for payment of money, but to do a particular act (*ad factum praestandum*), *e.g.* to return an article hired, the obligation is joint and several, so that, if the obligation is not fulfilled, each is liable for the whole amount awarded as damages.[39]

3.16 Rights of Relief.[40]—When a contractual obligation is joint and several there is a general legal implication, without any express agreement to that effect, that if one debtor pays the whole debt, or more than his *pro rata* share, he has a right of relief against the others. This right may be fortified by an assignation of the debt from the creditor, but exists without it.[41] It was extended to the case where one of two cautioners for an insolvent contractor completed the contract work at his own expense. He was entitled to recover half of the expenses incurred from the other.[42] If the obligation is *pro rata*, and the whole debt is exacted, no one has paid more or less than his share, and there can be no right of relief. But if less than the sum in the obligation is found to be due, one who has paid more than his share has a right of relief against others bound *pro rata* with him.[43] Where a party who has paid the whole debt claims relief, either on the general implication of law or in virtue of an assignation from the creditor, he cannot claim against any one of his co-debtors more than that co-debtor's *pro rata* share, but in computing the number of co-debtors those who are insolvent are not counted.[44]

3.17 Signatures of all Obligants Necessary.—It is a rule largely founded on the existence of the right of relief that when an obligation bears *ex facie* to be by more than one obligant, each who signs it does so on the implied condition that all the others will sign, and incurs no liability unless the signatures of all are obtained. This is an established rule in cautionary obligation,[45] with a doubtful exception in the case of judicial bonds of caution.[46] So, where a party whose debt to a bank was

[37] Partnership Act 1890, s. 9.

[38] *Walker* v. *Brown* (1803) Mor.App. *Solidum et pro rata*, No. 1. As to the competency of suing one obligant without calling the other, see *Neilson* v. *Wilson* (1890) 17 R. 608.

[39] *Darlington* v. *Gray* (1836) 15 S. 197; *Rankine* v. *Logie Den Land Co.* (1902) 4 F. 1074.

[40] As to joint wrongdoers, see para. 34.10, *infra*.

[41] Stair, I, viii, 9; Erskine, III, iii, 74; see also *Moss* v. *Penman*, 1994 S.L.T. 19, *per* Lord President Hope at p. 21, approving, *inter alios*, Stair and Erskine.

[42] *Marshall* v. *Pennycock*, 1908 S.C. 276.

[43] *Dering* v. *Lord Winchelsea* (1787) 1 Cox 318; *Ellesmere Brewery Co.* v. *Cooper* [1896] 1 Q.B. 75; Bell, *Comm.*, i, 367.

[44] *Buchanan* v. *Main* (1900) 3 F. 215.

[45] *Paterson* v. *Bonar* (1844) 6 D. 987; *Ellesmere Brewery Co.* v. *Cooper* [1896] 1 Q.B. 75.

[46] *Simpson* v. *Fleming* (1860) 22 D. 679.

guaranteed forged the name of one of the guarantors, it was held that the bank could not enforce the guarantee against the others.[47] The rule applies to analogous cases. When three persons had agreed to accept a lease, and one refused to sign, the other two, who had already signed, were held entitled to resile.[48]

3.18 Assignation by Creditor.—Where one of several co-obligants, bound jointly and severally, pays the whole debt he has a right to receive from the creditor an assignation of the debt, and of any securities which any of the other co-obligants may have granted for it.[49] This is a right which arises only on full payment; not where an obligant is bankrupt and the creditor has ranked for the whole debt and received a dividend.[50] But the creditor may refuse to assign if the assignation would conflict with any legitimate interest of his own. This, when an assignation merely of the debt is demanded, can be the case in exceptional circumstances only;[51] if an assignation of securities also is demanded the creditor's interest may be that he holds a prior security over the same subjects for a separate debt. He is not entitled to refuse an assignation on the ground that he has made subsequent advances on the same security.[52]

3.19 Effect of Discharge of One Co-Obligant.—A creditor is not entitled to do anything which would prejudice the right of relief possessed by co-obligants who are jointly and severally bound to him. He does so if he discharges one obligant without the consent of the others. The result, if the co-obligants are co-cautioners, is, by statute, that the others are discharged;[53] if they are not cautioners, the other obligants are relieved only in so far as their rights of relief are prejudiced, and therefore they remain liable for their own share of the debt.[54] But a *pactum de non petendo*, by which a creditor, without discharging an obligant, undertakes not to sue him, does not prejudice the rights of relief of the other obligants, and therefore does not affect their liability.[55] And if there is an express reservation of the creditor's right against the other co-obligants a discharge will be read as a *pactum de non petendo*, which neither bars the right of relief nor affects the liability of the other obligants. Thus, where a creditor acceded to a trust deed granted by one of his debtors, and to a discharge following thereon, reserving his rights against the other debtor, it was held the latter remained liable for the

---

[47] *Scottish Provincial Assurance Co.* v. *Pringle* (1858) 20 D. 465.

[48] *York Buildings Co.* v. *Baillie* (1724) Mor. 8435; *Gordon's Exrs.* v. *Gordon* (1918) 55 S.L.R. 497.

[49] Bell, *Prin.*, §255.

[50] *Ewart* v. *Latta* (1865) 3 M. (H.L.) 36.

[51] See *Bruce* v. *Scottish Amicable*, 1907 S.C. 637.

[52] *Sligo* v. *Menzies* (1840) 2 D. 1478.

[53] Mercantile Law Amendment (Scotland) Act 1856, s. 9.

[54] *Smith* v. *Harding* (1877) 5 R. 147.

[55] *Muir* v. *Crawford* (1875) 2 R. (H.L.) 148.

debt, and that his right of relief against the debtor who had been discharged was not affected.[56] It is provided by the Bankruptcy (Scotland) Act 1985[57] that a creditor in a sequestration may assent to the discharge of the bankrupt, with or without a composition, without prejudicing his rights against the bankrupt's co-obligants.

3.20   Creditors giving up Securities.—It is probably the general law, though the authorities have all related to the effect on a cautionary obligation of the release of securities granted by the principal debtor, that if a creditor gives up a security granted by one co-debtor he thereby releases the others in so far as their rights of relief are prejudiced.[58]

Further Reading

Bell, *Principles* (10th ed., 1899), §§5–85.
Erskine, *Institute*, Book III.
Holland, *Jurisprudence* (13th ed., 1924).
Paton, *Jurisprudence* (4th ed., 1972).
Salmond, *Jurisprudence* (12th ed., 1966).
Smith, *Short Commentary* (1962), Chaps. 8, 9 and 26.
Stair, Book I.
Stair Memorial Encyclopaedia, Vol. 11, paras. 1073–1112.

[56] *Morton's Trs.* v. *Robertson's Judicial Factor* (1892) 20 R. 72.
[57] s. 60.
[58] *Marshall* v. *Pennycook*, 1908 S.C. 276; *Taylor* v. *New South Wales Bank* (1886) 11 App. Cas. 596.

PART II—CONTRACT

CHAPTER 4

CAPACITY TO CONTRACT

4.1 The capacity of certain persons to enter into contracts is limited. The contractual powers of persons under the age of 16 years, lunatics, aliens and corporate bodies are the points which have to be considered.

4.2 Young Persons.—The Age of Legal Capacity (Scotland) Act 1991[1] abolishes the division of children under the age of 18 years into pupils and minors and replaces the office of tutor or curator with that of the guardian.[2] The Act groups young people into two age bands, namely, the under-16s and those between the ages of 16 and 18 years,[3] and applies to 'transactions' (which is defined to include contracts and unilateral promises).[4] The *quadriennium utile* is abolished, though 'prejudicial transactions' may be challenged in certain circumstances.[5]

4.3 Persons under 16.—The general rule is that persons under the age of 16 have no contractual capacity[6] and a contract made by such persons is void.[7] The child's guardian has power to contract on his or her behalf.[8] Provided that its terms are reasonable, a person under the age of 16 has the capacity to make the sort of contract which children of his or her

---

[1] The Act came into force on September 25, 1991: s. 11(2). It does not apply to transactions prior to this date and reference to paras. 6.2–6.4 of the 9th edition of this work may still be made in such cases. For commentaries on the legislation see Nichols, 'Can They or Can't They? Children and the Age of Legal Capacity (Scotland) Act 1991,' 1991 S.L.T. (News) 395; Norrie, 'The Age of Legal Capacity (Scotland) Act 1991,' (1991) 36 J.L.S. 434.

[2] s. 5(1). But the courts retain the power to appoint a *curator ad litem* or *curator bonis*: s. 1(3)(*f*).

[3] A young person becomes 16 or 18 at midnight on the date of his birth and not at the time of his birth on that date: s. 6.

[4] s. 9.

[5] s. 3(1). Discussed in para. 4.4 below.

[6] s. 1(1)(*a*).

[7] s. 2(5). Where restitution cannot be made, recourse will have to be made to the law of unjust enrichment.

[8] s. 5(1).

age and circumstances commonly make.[9] The Act makes no provision for the reduction of a contract made by a guardian on behalf of a child. Thus the common law right to have a contract reduced for enorm lesion within four years of attaining the age of majority has been abrogated.[10]

4.4   Persons between 16 and 18.—Young persons in this age group have full contractual capacity.[11] But a contract may be set aside on the ground that it is a prejudicial transaction[12] if the challenge is made before the challenger's 21st birthday.[13] A challenge may also be made by an executor, trustee in bankruptcy, trustee under a trust deed for creditors, or curator bonis, provided this is done before the young person reaches (or would have reached) 21 years.[14] The other party to the transaction, if an adult, cannot challenge it on this ground. But neither the young person nor the adult is precluded from challenging the transaction on the grounds of error, misrepresentation, undue influence or facility and circumvention. Whether a transaction is prejudicial or not is judged by asking: (a) if an adult, exercising reasonable care and prudence, would have made it had he been in the young person's shoes at that time; and (b) whether or not the transaction actually caused substantial prejudice or is likely to do so.[15] Some contracts cannot be set aside on this ground, *e.g.* (a) where a young person is in business or in trade or a profession and the contract is connected with these activities;[16] (b) where a young person holds himself out as being of full age and this fraudulent misrepresentation induces a contract;[17] and (c) if, after attaining majority, the young person ratifies the contract in the

[9] s. 2(1). Section 3(2) and (3) of the Sale of Goods Act 1979 are repealed in relation to the sale of 'necessaries' to minors. In *Nash* v. *Inman* [1908] 2 K.B. 1, it was decided that in order to qualify as 'necessaries' the seller had to show that a young person truly needed the goods in question and not simply that they were 'suitable to [his] condition in life.' Under s. 2(1) of the 1991 Act it will only be necessary to show the latter.

[10] Though an action for breach of trust might be raised against the guardian: Trusts (Scotland) Act 1921, s. 2.

[11] s. 1(1)(b).

[12] s. 3(1). Both the Court of Session and sheriff court have jurisdiction to hear such a petition: s. 3(5).

[13] s. 3(1).

[14] s. 3(4). Note *Harkness* v. *Graham* (1833) 11 S. 760; *Bruce* v. *Hamilton* (1854) 17 D. 265.

[15] s. 3(2). Substantial prejudice is undefined but some guidance may be sought from cases concerning the meaning of 'enorm lesion.' In *Robertson* v. *S. Henderson & Sons Ltd.* (1905) 7 F. 776, Lord President Dunedin observed (at p. 785): 'Lesion ... must not be trifling, but must be enorm, which means that the consideration ... must be immoderately disproportionate to what might have been got.' Note also *Faulds* v. *British Steel Corporation*, 1977 S.L.T. (Notes) 18, *per* Lord Stott at p. 19.

[16] s. 3(3)(f). *McFeetridge* v. *Stewarts & Lloyds*, 1913 S.C. 773; *Hill* v. *City of Glasgow Bank* (1879) 7 R. 68. In *O'Donnell* v. *Brownside Coal Co.*, 1934 S.C. 534, the court inclined strongly against treating an industrial employee as someone engaged in a 'trade.'

[17] s. 3(3)(g). The subsection refers to fraudulent misrepresentation about age or some other 'material' fact. It is thought that this covers the situation where a young person seeks to convey the impression that he is over 18: *e.g.* stating that he has a wife and family or is a dentist or engineer.

knowledge that he has a right to challenge the transaction on the ground of prejudice.[18]

An adult intending to contract with someone between the ages of 16 and 18 may be able to prevent it from being challenged as a prejudicial transaction. A joint application to have the proposed transaction ratified by a sheriff can be made.[19] Such an application may be refused where it is considered that no reasonable adult would make this contract in the present circumstances.[20] The sheriff's decision is final.[21] A transaction which has been judicially ratified cannot, subsequently, be challenged by the young person.[22] Judicial ratification must be sought prior to concluding any contract and cannot be applied for retrospectively.[23]

4.5 Insanity.—An insane person has no power to contract and contracts into which he enters are void.[24] If necessaries are sold and delivered to him, he must pay a reasonable price for them.[25] Generally his contracts are void, even although the other party may not have known that he was dealing with a person of unsound mind.[26] But continuing contracts, into which a party has entered while he was sane, are not necessarily avoided by his supervening insanity. Thus partnership is not dissolved merely by the insanity of a partner, though that is a ground on which its dissolution may be decreed by the court.[27] A factory and commission or power of attorney does not fall by virtue of the supervening insanity of the granter.[28] Drunkenness is not a ground for the avoidance of a contract unless it reaches a stage where the party no longer knows what he is doing and can give no true consent. Alcoholic overindulgence short of intoxication might render a person facile and present an opportunity to have it reduced on the ground of facility and circumvention.[29] An obligation undertaken in a drunken condition is voidable, provided that the party takes steps to avoid as soon as he recovers his senses and knows what he has done.[30]

4.6 Aliens.—Under the Rome Convention, a contract made during a period of residence in Scotland cannot be set aside on the ground that one of the parties was an alien who lacked contractual capacity under his or her own legal system; unless it is proved that the other party knew of the

---

[18] s. 3(3)(h).
[19] s. 4(1); (3).
[20] s. 4(2); i.e. that it would cause him substantial prejudice.
[21] s. 4(3).
[22] s. 3(3)(j).
[23] But see s. 3(3)(h).
[24] Stair, I, x, 3; Erskine, III, i, 16; Gall v. Bird (1855) 17 D. 1027.
[25] Sale of Goods Act 1979, s. 3.
[26] Loudon v. Elder's Curator, 1923 S.L.T. 226.
[27] Partnership Act 1890, s. 35.
[28] Law Reform (Misc. Provs.) (Scotland) Act 1990, s. 71(1).
[29] Jackson v. Pollock (1900) 8 S.L.T. 267.
[30] Pollok v. Burns (1875) 2 R. 497.

incapacity or was negligently unaware thereof.[31] The contractual capacity of aliens who are party to contracts to which the Rome Convention does not apply is subject to the proper law of the contract.[32] The only natural persons qualified to own a British ship, other than a fishing vessel, are:[33] British citizens; British Dependent Territories citizens; British Overseas citizens; British subjects under the British Nationality Act 1981; British Nationals (Overseas) citizens,[34] and citizens of the Republic of Ireland. In addition, a British ship may be owned by a company incorporated in the U.K. and having its principal place of business here.[35] Ownership of fishing vessels registered in the U.K. by nationals of any E.C. Member States is now competent.[36]

During wartime, any contract with an alien enemy is illegal[37] and an offence unless a licence from the Crown has been obtained.[38] There is a distinction to be observed between war and armed hostilities:[39] it is only when a state of war exists that the capacity of an alien may be affected.[40] Status as an alien enemy is determined, not by nationality or allegiance, but by voluntary residence in either an enemy state or enemy occupied territory.[41] The degree of control exercised by occupying forces over the occupied territory is relevant to the status of residents there.[42] A British prisoner of war held in enemy territory is not an alien enemy.[43] A national of an enemy or enemy occupied state residing in Scotland does not lose the power to contract[44] nor his right to resort to the Scottish courts.[45]

4.7 Corporate Bodies.—Apart from a few exceptional cases, corporations in Scotland owe their origin to a royal charter, to letters patent, to an Act of Parliament or to the machinery provided by the Companies Acts. A

---

[31] E.E.C. Convention on the Law Applicable to Contractual Obligations 1980, Art. 11. The Convention is implemented by the Contracts (Applicable Law) Act 1990, s. 2.

[32] Anton, *Private International Law* (2nd. ed.), pp. 276–78. See Art. 1 of the Rome Convention for contracts excluded from its ambit.

[33] Merchant Shipping Act 1988, s. 3(1). At the time of writing, the position stated in the text is unaffected by the Merchant Shipping (Registration, etc) Act 1993 which repeals ss. 1–10 and s. 14 of the 1988 Act.

[34] Under the Hong Kong (British Nationality) Order 1988 (No. 948).

[35] Merchant Shipping Act 1988, s. 3(1)(f).

[36] s. 14 as amended by the Merchant Shipping Act 1988 (Amendment) Order 1989 (S.I. 1989 No. 2006), art. 3. Note also *R.* v. *Secretary of State for Transport, ex p. Factortame Ltd.* [1991] 3 All E.R. 769.

[37] Trading with the Enemy Act 1939, as amended by the Emergency Laws (Misc. Provs.) Act 1953, s. 2.

[38] The procedure for obtaining a licence is found in McNair and Watts, *The Legal Effects of War* (4th ed.), p. 108.

[39] *Blomart* v. *Roxburgh* (1664) Mor. 16091.

[40] Armed hostilities may, however, amount to frustration of contract.

[41] *Janson* v. *Driefontein Mines* [1902] A.C. 484; *Sovfracht (V/O)* v. *Gebr. Van Udens Scheepvaart en Agentuur Maatschappij* [1943] A.C. 203.

[42] *Sovfracht* v. *Van Udens, supra*; *Re Anglo-International Bank* [1943] 1 Ch. 233.

[43] *Vandyke* v. *Adams* [1942] Ch. 155.

[44] *Schulze Gow & Co.* v. *Bank of Scotland*, 1914 2 S.L.T. 455.

[45] *Schulze*, 1917 S.C. 400; *Weiss* v. *Weiss*, 1940 S.L.T. 447.

particular body may act both under charter and under powers conferred by statute. The limitations of the contractual powers of a corporation depend upon its origin. A body acting under royal charter has the power to enter into any contract which is not expressly forbidden by its charter.[46] Any restriction on its activities rests, not on any limitation of its contractual powers, but on the principle that certain applications of its funds may amount to a breach of trust. So where the town council of a royal burgh, acting under charter, and possessed of property known as the common good, maintained the legality of applying its funds to further the candidature of persons in other burghs professing particular views, it was held that such expenditure amounted to a breach of trust and was *ultra vires*. The contention that a chartered body might do anything which an individual might lawfully do was repelled.[47]

4.8 Law of *Ultra Vires*.—A corporate body created by statute, or exercising statutory powers, cannot enter into any contract, or dispose of its funds in any way which is not authorised by the statute or reasonably incidental to the powers conferred. Thus a body established for one purpose cannot lawfully engage in any enterprise substantially different, or beyond the geographical limits within which it is authorised to act.[48] The mere fact that all the persons interested in the corporate body have consented will not validate an act which is *ultra vires*. So when a tramway company, incorporated by a private Act of Parliament, contracted to pay a lump sum to parties who had incurred expenses in procuring the Act, it was decided that the validity of the contract must depend upon some authority given in the Act, and, as that was lacking, that it could not be enforced just because all the shareholders had consented.[49]

4.9 Companies.—The memorandum of association of a company incorporated under the Companies Act 1985 must state, *inter alia*, its objects.[50] As a consequence of the *ultra vires* doctrine, the objects clause became a long and detailed list of the things which a company had the capacity to do: often followed by a general provision that it could do anything which, in the opinion of the directors, might honestly be considered as being ancillary to the specific objects.[51] Alternatively, the memorandum might state that each of the activities specified is to be

---

[46] *Conn* v. *Corporation of Renfrew* (1906) 8 F. 905.

[47] *Kemp* v. *Corporation of Glasgow*, 1920 S.C. (H.L.) 73. *Cf. Glasgow Corporation* v. *Secretary of State for Scotland*, 1966 S.L.T. 183, regarding payment from a common good fund.

[48] *Nicol* v. *Dundee Harbour Trs.*, 1915 S.C. (H.L.) 7; *Grieve* v. *Edinburgh Water Trs.*, 1918 S.C. 700.

[49] *Mann* v. *Edinburgh Northern Tramways Co.* (1892) 20 R. (H.L.) 7.

[50] Companies Act 1985, s. 2(1)(*c*). The objects clause and ramifications of the *ultra vires* doctrine are more fully discussed later: see para. 25.9 *infra*.

[51] *Bell Houses Ltd.* v. *City Wall Properties Ltd.* [1966] 2 Q.B. 656.

regarded as an independent object.[52] It is now competent for the
memorandum to declare only one, broad, object, namely, that of
carrying on 'business as a general commercial company.'[53] In such a
case the company has capacity 'to carry on any trade or business
whatsoever' and power to do whatever is 'incidental or conducive' to its
stated object.[54] It is an unsettled question whether it is competent for a
company to adopt, in addition to a number of independent objects, a
general object in the form described in the legislation.[55] Section 35 of
the Companies Act 1985[56] virtually abolishes the *ultra vires* doctrine in
relation to corporate transactions other than those made by charitable
companies. In this last case, the doctrine applies except where the party
dealing with the charitable company is ignorant of the fact that it is a
charity, or that the transaction is both onerous and outwith the
company's capacity (or beyond the directors' powers).[57]

4.10   Methods of Contracting.—Corporate bodies necessarily act through their
officers, directors or managers. Particular statutes sometimes enjoin a
particular form of contracting:[58] if not, no special form is required in
order to make a contract binding on a corporate body. So a verbal
compromise of a claim for augmentation, made between the minister of
a parish and the members of the governing body of a university, was
sustained.[59]

4.11   Trade Unions.—A trade union[60] is not, and cannot be treated as if it
were, a corporate body but it is capable of making contracts and can sue
and be sued in its own name in proceedings founded on contract.[61] The
purposes of any trade union are not, by reason only that they are in
restraint of trade, unlawful so as to make any member of the union
liable to criminal proceedings for conspiracy or otherwise or so as to
make any agreement or trust void or voidable. A rule of a trade union
is not unlawful or unenforceable by reason only that it is in restraint of
trade.[62]

An employers' association[63] may be a corporate body or an
unincorporated association. If it is unincorporated it is nevertheless

[52] *Cotman* v. *Brougham* [1918] A.C. 514; *Re Introductions Ltd.* v. *National Provincial Bank Ltd.* [1970] Ch. 199.
[53] Companies Act 1985, s. 3A: added by Companies Act 1989, s. 110(1).
[54] *Ibid.*
[55] The problem arises because, whereas s. 2(1)(c) refers to 'objects,' s. 3A envisages only a single 'object'.
[56] As substituted by Companies Act 1989, s. 108(1).
[57] Companies Act 1989, s. 112(3).
[58] See, as to companies, Companies Act 1985, s. 36; *Panorama Developments (Guildford)* v. *Fidelis Furnishing Fabrics* [1971] 2 Q.B. 711.
[59] *Park* v. *University of Glasgow* (1675) Mor. 2535.
[60] Defined in Trade Union and Labour Relations (Consolidation) Act 1992, s. 1.
[61] s. 10.
[62] s. 11.
[63] Defined in s. 122.

capable of making contracts and can sue and be sued in its own name.[64] The purposes and rules of an unincorporated employers' association, and, in or as far as they relate to the regulation of relations between employers and workers or trade unions, the purposes and rules of an association which is a corporate body, are not unlawful so as to give rise to criminal proceedings against the members or to make any agreement void or voidable or any such rule unenforceable.[65]

Neither a trade union nor an unincorporated employers' association can apply its funds directly or indirectly in the furtherance of political objects unless the furtherance of these objects has been approved as an object by a resolution passed on a ballot of members and rules governing the expenditure are approved by the Certification Officer.[66]

4.12 Building Societies.—The purpose and powers of building societies are prescribed by the Building Societies Act 1986. The principal (but not necessarily the exclusive) purpose of a building society must be the raising of funds, from members, in order to lend to those members against heritable securities.[67] Statutory powers conferred on building societies include: (a) the power to acquire and hold premises for business purposes;[68] (b) the power to raise funds by borrowing (subject to a prescribed limit).[69] A loan exceeding the society's borrowing limit is not invalid,[70] although the Building Societies Commission can take steps to prevent future breach.[71] Deposits exceeding the permitted limit are not invalid[72] but, again, the Building Societies Commission may take appropriate measures to prevent repetition of the breach. Borrowing for something other than the purpose of the society is *ultra vires*.[73] The directors' annual report must contain a statement about any activities believed to be outwith the society's powers.[74]

---

[64] s. 127.

[65] s. 128.

[66] ss. 71–96. The political objects affected are specified in s. 72.

[67] Building Societies Act 1986, s. 5(1). To reinforce this, s. 20 prescribes that commercial assets must be 'class 1 assets': *i.e.*, secured loans to members.

[68] s. 6.

[69] s. 7; Building Societies (Limit on Non-Retail Funds and Deposits) Order 1987 (S.I. 1987 No. 2131).

[70] s. 7(1).

[71] s. 37(3), (5), (6).

[72] s. 8(6).

[73] *Cross* v. *Fisher* [1892] 1 Q.B. 467; *Sinclair* v. *Brougham* [1914] A.C. 398.

[74] s. 75(1)(*c*).

CHAPTER 5

FORMATION OF CONTRACT

5.1 Obligations from Consent: Gratuitous Promise.—The law recognises as a general principle that an obligation may arise from mere consent: that if a man undertakes to do or pay something, or to abstain from some course of action, he has incurred an obligation which may be enforced against him by some form of legal process. The undertaking may take the form of a promise, when the resulting obligation is commonly termed unilateral, or of the acceptance of an offer, when the result is a mutual contract. Differing in this respect from the law of England, Scots law holds that consent will infer an obligation although there may be no consideration. An obligation to give, or to do or abstain from doing something without asking for any return is, in so far as its enforceability by legal process is concerned, on a par with an obligation for which a return or consideration is demanded and promised.[1] The distinction in this respect between the laws of England and Scotland is most clearly brought out in the case of an offer to sell, with an undertaking to keep the offer open for a certain period. Assuming that nothing is paid for the engagement to keep the offer open, it is an undertaking without consideration, and consequently, in English law, is not binding unless made in a deed under seal.[2] In Scotland, where consideration is not necessary, it is a binding obligation, and the offeree, if he accept within the time specified, and his acceptance be rejected, will be entitled to damages.[3]

5.2 Gratuitous, Onerous.—While the law of Scotland has rejected consideration as an essential element in the constitution of a voluntary obligation, this does not mean that the question of consideration is in all cases irrelevant, and that a gratuitous promise and a mutual contract stand in all respects on the same footing. Where a promise is made, other than one made in the course of business, writing is required for its constitution.[4] While in the case of an onerous contract the obligations are binding although one of the obligants may have entered into the

---

[1] *Morton's Trs.* v. *Aged Christian Friend Society* (1899) 2 F. 82.

[2] *Dickinson* v. *Dodds* (1876) 2 Ch.D. 463.

[3] *Littlejohn* v. *Hadwen* (1882) 20 S.L.R. 5; approved by Lord Dunedin in *Paterson* v. *Highland Ry.*, 1927 S.C. (H.L.) 32, at p. 38.

[4] Requirements of Writing (Scotland) Act 1995, s. 1(2)(a)(ii). To be formally valid, subscription by the promisor will be sufficient: s. 2(1).

contract by reason of some error or mistake on his own part, the man who has given a gratuitous promise, and can show that he gave it under essential error, is entitled to resile, even though he does not aver or prove that his error was induced by misrepresentation.[5] A difference between onerous and gratuitous obligations is also recognised in the law of bankruptcy. Certain prior obligations of the bankrupt are reducible or unenforceable if they were entered into gratuitously, whereas onerous contracts in the same circumstances would be unaffected.[6]

5.3 Mutual Contracts, Agreements.—A contract involves, and is dependent on, agreement. *Consensus in idem* occurs when agreement has been reached upon all the essentials of the contract; what the essentials are may vary according to the particular contract under consideration.[7] Agreement means generally that the minds of the parties are at one with regard to the point at issue. In most disputed cases, however, the question is to discover the parties' apparent, rather than their real, intentions. In matters of contract a party is generally entitled to act on the assumption that the other means what he says. The question whether the parties have agreed is to be decided not by proof of what each party really intended, but by considering what conclusion a reasonable person would draw from their words or acts. It is clear that if A uses words which have an ordinary meaning, and has no reason to suppose that B will interpret them otherwise, A cannot be heard to say that he attached a different meaning to his words, or spoke with a mental reservation.[8] Even if the parties are really at cross purposes, if one uses language which to a reasonable hearer would convey the impression that he meant to agree, he will be bound, unless the difference between their mental attitudes is so fundamental as to

[5] *McCaig* v. *University of Glasgow* (1904) 6 F. 918; *Hunter and Another* v. *Bradford Property Trust*, 1970 S.L.T. 173. See para. 9.18, *infra*.

[6] See para. 54.19, *infra*.

[7] See *Dempster* v. *Motherwell Bridge & Engineering Co.*, 1964 S.C. 308, *per* Lord President Clyde at p. 329, Lord Guthrie at p. 332. It has been held that the period of a loan and the payment of interest are not essential terms of a loan contract because a loan can be repayable on demand and may be interest free: *Neilson* v. *Stewart*, 1991 S.L.T. 523 (H.L.). In contracts for the sale of heritable property, it now appears to be settled that agreement as to date of entry is not essential: *Secretary of State for Scotland* v. *Ravenstone Securities Ltd.*, 1976 S.C. 171; *Gordon D.C.* v. *Wimpey Homes Holdings Ltd.*, 1988 S.L.T. 481; *Sloans Dairies Ltd.* v. *Glasgow Corporation*, 1977 S.C. 223. An offer which does not provide the means for determining the price of heritable property lacks an element essential for the conclusion of a contract: *MacLeod's Exr.* v. *Barr's Trs.*, 1989 S.L.T. 392. The subjects are also regarded as an essential element of a contract for the sale of heritage: *Grant* v. *Gauld & Co.*, 1985 S.C. 251. In a contract for the supply of goods, a reasonable price may be implied: *British Coal Corporation* v. *S.S.E.B.*, 1991 S.L.T. 302. In *Avintair Ltd.* v. *Ryder Airline Services Ltd.*, 1994 S.L.T. 613, it was held that where services were rendered under an agreement, where neither a price nor a method of calculating price had been settled, there was an implied term that a reasonable price should be paid on the principle *quantum meruit*.

[8] *Duran* v. *Duran* (1904) 7 F. 87, a form of marriage, with a mental reservation by one party.

preclude any real consent.[9] 'Commercial contracts cannot be arranged by what people think in their inmost minds. Commercial contracts are made according to what people say.'[10] Agreement may also be inferred from the parties' conduct[11] and conduct following verbal negotiations may be construed as concluding a contract on the basis of the verbal terms.[12]

Agreement for all legal purposes may be reached when a party has undertaken some definite obligation, though he may not be aware of the interpretation which the law will put on his expressions or acts, or may think that the terms to which he has bound himself are other than they are ultimately determined to be. It is for the court, not for either party, to interpret a contract, and decide upon the conditions, express or implied. So when a party had agreed to sell an entailed estate 'subject to the ratification of the Court' it did not affect the validity of the contract that he had formed an erroneous impression of the process involved in ratification by the court.[13]

5.4 Agreements in the Law.—It is not every agreement of which the courts will take cognisance.[14] The agreement must be one concerned with legal relations. Social engagements cannot be enforced by legal process. There are cases, however, where the parties may have meant to incur obligations, but where the question between them is not one which lies within the province of the courts to decide. To justify judicial interference a patrimonial interest—some material gain or loss, or chance of material gain or loss—must be involved. Thus the question whether a member of a club, averring that he has been wrongfully expelled, can find a legal remedy, depends upon whether the club possesses property in which the members have an interest. If it has none no patrimonial interest of the member expelled has been affected, and the court will not take account of the loss of opportunities of social intercourse.[15] A like principle applies to the case of a member of a voluntary church, alleging wrongful expulsion, in contrast with the case of a minister of a similar body, who, if expelled, loses a position which gives him a chance of employment and income, and may therefore obtain legal redress.[16]

An agreement, even a commercial one, will not be binding if it appears that the parties did not intend that it should be legally

[9] See *Stuart* v. *Kennedy* (1885) 13 R. 221, and paras. 8.19 *et seq., infra.*
[10] *Muirhead and Turnbull* v. *Dickson* (1905) 7 F. 686, *per* Lord President Dunedin.
[11] *Morrison-Low* v. *Paterson*, 1985 S.L.T. 255, *per* Lord Fraser at p. 266, following Gloag, pp. 46–47.
[12] *Gordon Adams and Partners* v. *Ralph Jessop*, 1987 S.C.L.R. 735.
[13] *Stewart* v. *Kennedy* (1890) 17 R. (H.L.) 25. See also *Laing* v. *Provincial Homes Co.*, 1909 S.C. 812; *Stobo Ltd.* v. *Morrisons (Gowns) Ltd.*, 1949 S.C. 184.
[14] As to *pacta illicita* and *sponsiones ludicrae* see Chap. 10, *infra.*
[15] *Anderson* v. *Manson*, 1909 S.C. 838.
[16] *Skerret* v. *Oliver* (1896) 23 R. 468.

enforceable. This may appear from the surrounding circumstances[17] or from the terms of the agreement.[18] In *Kleinwort Benson Ltd.* v. *Malaysia Mining Corporation Bhd.*,[19] comfort letters were given to a bank by a parent company in respect of loans to its subsidiary. These were not held to have created a legally enforceable obligation. The letters simply stated that it was the defendants' 'policy' to ensure the financial stability of their subsidiary. This clause was contrasted with another which stated that the defendants 'confirmed' that they would not withdraw capital support for the subsidiary: this was viewed as creating an enforceable obligation. A 'collective agreement' is conclusively presumed not to have been intended by the parties to be a legally enforceable contract unless it is in writing and contains a provision, however expressed, that the parties intended that the agreement would be legally enforceable; an agreement which satisfies these requirements is conclusively presumed to have been intended to be legally enforceable.[20] A 'collective agreement' is an agreement made by a trade union and an employer or an employers' association and relating to terms and conditions of employment.[21]

In order to be binding as a contract an agreement must be definite, and the test of whether it is sufficiently definite is whether it would be possible to frame a decree of specific implement.[22]

5.5 Definitions of Contract.—No satisfactory or comprehensive definition of what constitutes a contract has yet been formulated. Sometimes contracts are defined in terms of promises.[23] The institutional writers view it as an obligation distinguishable from other kinds of obligations including promises.[24] A modern work on our law of contract stresses the consensual nature of the obligation, the requirement of patrimonial interest and an intention to be bound.[25]

5.6 Offer and Acceptance.—A contract may be considered as consisting of an offer by one party and an acceptance by the other.[26] The offer, or

---

[17] *Ford Motor Co.* v. *Amalgamated Union of Engineering and Foundry Workers* [1969] 2 Q.B. 303. In England there is a presumption that an agreement between husband and wife is not intended to create a legal relationship: *Gould* v. *Gould* [1970] 1 Q.B. 275. But there is no reason why spouses cannot conclude a binding contract with each other: *Raith* v. *Raith* (1923) 39 Sh.Ct.Rep. 133.
[18] *Rose and Frank Co.* v. *Crompton* [1925] A.C. 445; *Tannahill* v. *Glasgow Corporation*, 1935 S.C. (H.L.) 15.
[19] [1989] 1 All E.R. 785 (C.A.).
[20] Trade Union and Labour Relations (Consolidation) Act 1992, s. 179.
[21] *Ibid.*, s. 178.
[22] *McArthur* v. *Lawson* (1877) 4 R. 1134; *Murray's Trs.* v. *St. Margaret's Convent Trs.*, 1907 S.C. (H.L.) 8, and cases collected at p. 12 of Gloag on *Contract*.
[23] See *e.g.* Restatement, Second, Contracts, s. 1; Chitty, para. 1. Note also Atiyah, *Promises, Morals, and Law* (1981), *passim*.
[24] Stair, I, x, 3; Ersk., *Inst.*, III, 1, ii *et seq.*; Bell, *Prin.*, §5, *Comm.*, I, 312.
[25] McBryde, para. 1.10.
[26] There may be types of contract which do not fit easily into the normal analysis of a contract as being constituted by offer and acceptance: *Gibson* v. *Manchester City Council* [1979] 1 W.L.R. 294, *per* Lord Diplock at p. 297.

the acceptance, or both, may be in words, spoken or written, or may be inferred from the actions of the parties. So when newspapers are laid out on a bookstall and one is taken a contract of sale is completed, though nothing may have been said. The keeper of the bookstall, by laying out the newspapers, offers to sell them, the party who takes one accepts the offer and agrees to pay the price. In sealed competitive bidding, a 'referential bid,' *i.e.* '£100 in excess of any other offer,' was held, in the circumstances, not to be a valid offer.[27]

5.7   Offer and Intention.—It may often be difficult, alike in the construction of words and of conduct, to distinguish between a mere expression of readiness to do business in a particular line and an offer to enter into a contract. A man who indicates that he is willing to contract does not necessarily make an offer which can be turned into a contract by acceptance. He may only be indicating his readiness to receive and to consider offers. The question whether a party has merely indicated an intention or has made an offer must depend on the circumstances of each case; words or acts which, if used in one connection, would amount to an offer, may, if used in another, merely indicate a readiness to chaffer. So while if a trader quotes prices of the commodity in which he deals, either in response to a request or *ex proprio motu*, he will, in general, be held to have made an offer to sell:[28] the statement of the lowest price which would be accepted for a particular estate, made in response to an inquiry as to the owner's readiness to sell, was read merely as an indication that he was willing to consider an offer of that price.[29] A shopkeeper, by placing goods in his window, with or without prices annexed, only indicates his readiness to trade,[30] but a party who is under a duty to exercise his vocation, such as a carrier or innkeeper, makes a continuous offer, subject, no doubt, to implied conditions, but which will bind him to carry or entertain any applicant who complies with these conditions.[31] The display of goods for hire beside a notice stating the hire charge has been treated as an offer, as has a vending machine dispensing car-park tickets.[32]

5.8   Expression of Intention not Binding.—It may probably be stated without qualification that if it is decided, on the particular facts, that a

---

[27] *Harvela Investments Ltd.* v. *Royal Trust Co. of Canada (C.I.) Ltd.* [1986] 1 A.C. 207.
[28] *Philp* v. *Knoblauch*, 1907 S.C. 994; but see *Scancarriers A/S* v. *Aotearoa International Ltd.* [1985] 2 Lloyd's Rep. 419, P.C., where quotation of freight rates by a carrier was held not to constitute an offer.
[29] *Harvey* v. *Facey* [1893] A.C. 552.
[30] That at least is the law in England: *Pharmaceutical Society of Great Britain* v. *Boots Cash Chemists (Southern) Ltd.* [1953] 1 Q.B. 401; *Fisher* v. *Bell* [1961] 1 Q.B. 394. But these cases leave unanswered the question of what constitutes acceptance of the customer's offer to purchase.
[31] *Campbell* v. *Ker*, Feb. 24, 1810, F.C.; *Rothfield* v. *North British Ry.*, 1920 S.C. 805.
[32] *Chapelton* v. *Barry Urban District Council* [1940] 1 K.B. 532; *Thornton* v. *Shoe Lane Parking Ltd.* [1971] 2 Q.B. 163.

party has only indicated an intention, he has incurred no liability. Where railway companies intimated that a reduced rate would be charged for a certain period, it was held that they were not precluded from withdrawing the concession before the period had expired.[33] A company circular which 'proposes' the issue of new shares does not commit the company to do this.[34] The announcement that I intend to do something does not bind me not to change my mind, and anyone who acts or incurs expense on the assumption that I will carry out my intention does so at his own risk. So when negotiations for a loan were broken off before any definite offer had been made, it was held that the party who had proposed to lend had no claim for the expenses he had incurred in investigating the other's title to subjects which were contemplated as security, nor to interest on the money which he had kept in hand in order to make the proposed advance.[35] Certain earlier cases,[36] quoted as authorities for the proposition that if A indicates an intention to contract, and knows that B is incurring expense in expectation of a contract, A, if he changes his mind, must meet the expenses B has incurred, were distinguished or overruled. But it was observed that to indicate an intention to contract when no such intention had been formed, and thereby to lead another party to incur expense, would be an actionable wrong,[37] and the most recent case would seem to leave it open to doubt whether a claim based on *Walker* v. *Milne*,[38] if supported by averments of definite loss, and not merely of deprivation of problematical gain, is or is not maintainable.[39] Where someone benefits from work done by another before there is a contract, a claim based on recompense may be allowed: but what is done must benefit or enrich that party.[40] It may be that a party who invites the submission of tenders obliges himself to consider these.[41] The effect of a 'letter of intent' depends on its terms and on the communings between the parties.[42]

5.9 Parties to Whom Offer Made.—An offer may be made to a particular individual, to a specified class, or to the general public, as in the case of

---

[33] *Paterson* v. *Highland Ry.*, 1927 S.C. (H.L.) 32.

[34] *Mason* v. *Benhar Coal Co.*, (1882) 9 R. 883.

[35] *Gilchrist* v. *Whyte*, 1907 S.C. 984. See also *Maddison* v. *Alderson* (1883) 8 App.Cas. 467.

[36] *Walker* v. *Milne* (1823) 2 S. 379; *Dobie* v. *Lauder's Trs.* (1873) 11 M. 749; *Hamilton* v. *Lochrane* (1899) 1 F. 478.

[37] *Per* Lord Ardwall in *Gilchrist* v. *Whyte*, 1907 S.C. 984.

[38] *Supra.*

[39] *Gray* v. *Johnston's Exr.*, 1928 S.C. 659.

[40] *Gilchrist* v. *White*, 1907 S.C. 984; *Microwave Systems (Scotland) Ltd.* v. *Electro-Physiological Instruments Ltd.*, 1971 S.C. 140; *Site Preparations Ltd.* v. *Secretary of State for Scotland*, 1975 S.L.T. (Notes) 41.

[41] *Blackpool and Fylde Aero Club Ltd.* v. *Blackpool Borough Council* [1990] 3 All E.R. 25.

[42] *Uniroyal Ltd.* v. *Miller & Co. Ltd.*, 1985 S.L.T. 101; *British Steel Corporation* v. *Cleveland Bridge and Engineering Co. Ltd.* [1984] 1 All E.R. 504.

an offer of a reward for the recovery of lost property,[43] or of insurance in timetables or diaries.[44] In such cases it is not necessary that the party who claims fulfilment of the offer shall have given any express acceptance; acceptance is implied in doing the act called for, though it is probably necessary that the act shall have been done in the knowledge that the offer has been made. Where the proprietors of a preventive for influenza offered a payment to anyone who used it in accordance with their directions and yet caught the disease, it was held that they could not refuse payment on the ground that the claimant had not expressly indicated that he accepted the offer and proposed to try the preventive.[45]

5.10 Express Acceptance, when Necessary.—Apart from offers to the general public, it is a question of construction in each case whether express acceptance of an offer is necessary to complete a contract. The question to be solved is whether the offer calls for an act, or for a promise to undertake a reciprocal obligation. So an order for goods does not require express acceptance; it is accepted by sending the goods.[46] On the other hand, when the directors of a company sent a circular offering to cancel the allotment of shares it was held that this offer required express acceptance, and therefore, in the ensuing liquidation of the company, that those shareholders who had accepted the offer were free from liability, while those who had done nothing were liable as contributors.[47]

5.11 Acts Amounting to Acceptance.—When a party who has received an offer proceeds to act in a way which is justifiable only on the assumption that he has accepted it, his acts, if unequivocal,[48] infer acceptance. So, in sale, if the goods have been delivered and the buyer, having had a reasonable opportunity to inspect them, does any act in relation to them which is inconsistent with the ownership of the seller, he is deemed to have accepted them, and cannot afterwards reject them as disconform to contract.[49] Action of this kind may be treated as equivalent to acceptance even if in words the offer has been refused. A ship had been stranded, and the owner offered to abandon her to the underwriters as a constructive total loss. The underwriters refused to accept the notice of abandonment, but proceeded in attempts to salve the ship in a manner which caused further damage. It was held that their actions, in spite of their formal refusal, amounted to acceptance of

---

[43] *Petrie* v. *Earl of Airlie* (1834) 13 S. 68.
[44] *Hunter* v. *General Accident Co.*, 1909 S.C. (H.L.) 30.
[45] *Carlill* v. *Carbolic Smoke Ball Co.* [1893] 1 Q.B. 256.
[46] Bell, *Comm.*, i, 343.
[47] *Edinburgh Employers Assurance Co.* v. *Griffiths* (1892) 19 R. 550.
[48] See *Oastler* v. *Henderson* (1877) 2 Q.B.D. 575. For an implied rejection, see *Lawrence* v. *Knight*, 1972 S.C. 26.
[49] Sale of Goods Act 1979, s. 35; *Mechan* v. *Bow, McLachlan & Co.*, 1910 S.C. 758.

the notice of abandonment, or, on an alternative view, were such as to bar them from maintaining that they had not accepted.[50]

Parties may agree that an offer is to be regarded as accepted if it is not refused within a specified time. And in ordinary business matters if a party receives an order for the goods in which he deals and does not promptly intimate his refusal he will be deemed to have accepted the order and will be liable in damages if he does not fulfil it.[51] In other cases a man is not entitled to force a contract merely by intimating that he will regard his offer as accepted if it is not refused. Goods sent without an order, and without a previous course of dealing from which an order may be implied, may safely be rejected.[52] When A, writing to B in reference to a dispute, proposed a compromise, and added that he would assume that his proposal was accepted if he did not hear to the contrary within a certain number of days, it was held that B's failure to reply did not make the compromise binding on him.[53] Where an employee continued to work after receiving notice of the terms of employment and failed to sign a written acknowledgment thereof, it was held that he had accepted employment on those terms.[54]

5.12 Incorporation of Terms.—An offer may be made conditionally: the conditions (or, more accurately, terms or stipulations) may be incorporated by express reference in the contract documents to the rules of an association,[55] or to printed conditions a copy of which is obtainable from the offerer,[56] or to articles of association of a company,[57] or to a foreign statute.[58] If the offer is met by general acceptance, without any express reference to the conditions, in ordinary cases this will be read as an acceptance of the offer in the terms in which it was made; but if the conditions to which reference is made would effect a substantial modification of the rights of the parties, the offerer must take reasonable steps to bring them to the notice of the other party by supplying a copy of them or by other means.[59] Even if there is no express incorporation in the principal contract, terms set out

[50] *Robertson* v. *Royal Exchange Assurance Corporation*, 1925 S.C. 1.
[51] *Barry, Ostlere & Shepherd* v. *Edinburgh Cork Importing Co.*, 1909 S.C. 1113.
[52] *Jaffrey* v. *Boag* (1824) 3 S. 375; *Gilbert* v. *Dickson*, 1803 Hume 334. Note also the Unsolicited Goods and Services Act 1971, s. 1.
[53] *Jaffrey* v. *Boag, supra.*
[54] *SOS Bureau Ltd.* v. *Payne*, 1982 S.L.T. (Sh.Ct.) 33.
[55] *Stewart Brown & Co.* v. *Grime* (1897) 24 R. 414.
[56] *Smith* v. *U.M.B. Chrysler (Scotland) and South Wales Switchgear Co.*, 1978 S.C. (H.L.) 1.
[57] *Muirhead* v. *Forth and North Sea Steamboat Mutual Insurance Association* (1893) 21 R. (H.L.) 1.
[58] *Standard Oil Co. of New York* v. *Clan Line Steamers Ltd.*, 1924 S.C. (H.L.) 1.
[59] *McConnell & Reid* v. *Smith*, 1911 S.C. 635; *Grayston Plant Ltd.* v. *Plean Precast Ltd.*, 1976 S.C. 206; *Continental Tyre & Rubber Co. Ltd.* v. *Trunk Trailer Co. Ltd.*, 1985 S.C. 163; *Wm. Teacher & Sons Ltd.* v. *Bell Lines Ltd.*, 1991 S.L.T. 876; *Interfoto Picture Library Ltd.* v. *Stiletto Visual Programmes* [1988] 1 All E.R. 348 (an example of a non-exclusionary term).

elsewhere—a letter heading,[60] a placard,[61] a ticket—may be imported
into the contract if reasonable steps have been taken to bring them to
the notice of the other party. 'Ticket cases' are perhaps in a special
category.[62] Further, in certain well-known types of case, in particular
those relating to carriage and deposit, it is now settled that a reference
to conditions, legibly printed on the face of the ticket, is sufficient
notice of conditions. The person who buys a railway ticket or a
cloakroom ticket is doing a thing which is now recognised by the public
in general as entering into a contract which may contain special
conditions. This is a situation which is now regarded as notorious and
customary.[63] Where a ticket is issued by a carrier, and conditions,
limiting the carrier's liability for the safe carriage of the passenger or his
luggage, are printed on or issued with it, such conditions may, if
sufficient notice has been given to the ticket-holder, be taken as being
part of the contract, and so binding upon him and his representatives.[64]
The question whether they are imported into the contract depends
partly on the character of the ticket, partly on the knowledge of the
passenger who takes it. If the conditions are printed on the back of the
ticket, and no indication of their existence is given on the front, the
passenger, if he can satisfy the court that he was not aware that there
were any conditions, is not bound by them.[65] If he has actually read the
conditions he is clearly bound by them. If he knew that there were
conditions, but did not read them, he will be bound by them, provided
that they are reasonable and of such a character as might be expected
on a ticket of the particular class.[66] On the other hand, where the
conditions are not issued with the ticket or otherwise expressly made
part of the contract, they cannot be incorporated into it by knowledge
on the part of the passenger that conditions were usually imposed
without knowledge of what they were.[67] If the front of the ticket
referred to conditions printed on the back, but the passenger did not
notice the reference, and was in fact unaware that there were any
conditions, the question depends on the adequacy of the means adopted
to bring them to his notice. A reference to conditions on the back,
printed on the front of a steamer ticket, was held ineffectual when it

[60] *Oakbank Oil Co.* v. *Love & Stewart*, 1918 S.C. (H.L.) 54.

[61] *W. N. White & Co.* v. *Dougherty* (1891) 18 R. 972; *Wright* v. *Howard Baker & Co.*
(1893) 21 R. 25; *Lewis* v. *Laird Line*, 1925 S.L.T. 316. See also *Palmer* v. *Inverness
Hospitals Board*, 1963 S.C. 311 (circular).

[62] *McCutcheon* v. *David MacBrayne Ltd.*, 1964 S.C. (H.L.) 28, *per* Lord Guest at p. 38,
per Lord Pearce at p. 45.

[63] *Taylor* v. *Glasgow Corporation*, 1952 S.C. 440, Lord Justice-Clerk Thomson at
p. 444.

[64] *e.g. McKay* v. *Scottish Airways*, 1948 S.C. 254.

[65] *Henderson* v. *Stevenson* (1875) 2 R. (H.L.) 71; *McCafferty* v. *Western S.M.T. Co.*,
1962 S.L.T. (Sh.Ct.) 39.

[66] *Lyons* v. *Caledonian Ry.*, 1909 S.C. 1185. *Cf. L'Estrange* v. *Graucob* [1934] 2 K.B.
394.

[67] *McCutcheon* v. *David MacBrayne, supra.*

was printed in the smallest known type, and in such a way as to be easily overlooked by a passenger, even if he were exercising ordinary care.[68] But when a ticket for a transatlantic voyage was enclosed in an envelope, with a distinct reference thereon to conditions printed on the ticket, it was held that the passenger was bound by them, though his evidence was that he had not noticed the reference and was unaware that there were any conditions on the ticket.[69] The ordinary form of a railway ticket, in which reference is made on the front to conditions on the back, and the conditions there contain nothing but a further reference to the carrier's timetables and bills, has been approved as affording sufficient notice to the passenger.[70] These rules will not readily be extended beyond tickets issued in relation to contracts of carriage or deposit.[71]

Conditions cannot be incorporated into a contract if they are not brought to the notice of the other party before the contract is completed.[72] But if there has been a consistent course of dealing between the parties and in each of the previous transactions conditions have been sent, after the contract was completed, by one party to the other, who has raised no query or objection, it may be held that the conditions are incorporated in a subsequent contract if each party has led the other reasonably to believe that he intended that the rights and liabilities which would otherwise arise by implication of law from the nature of the contract should be modified in accordance with the conditions.[73] Where both parties are in the same trade and of equal bargaining power the conditions habitually imposed in contracts of the particular type may be held to be incorporated on the basis of the common understanding of the parties that the usual conditions would apply.[74]

Where the offer refers to one set of conditions and the acceptance refers to a different set, there is the so-called 'battle of forms.' The result depends on the content of the conditions: if the two sets are reconcilable, both may apply; if they conflict, the 'acceptance' may be treated as a counter-offer and, if it is accepted, the conditions referred to therein may prevail.[75] If the offer contains an overriding clause, providing that the conditions referred to therein will apply unless a

---

[68] *Williamson* v. *North of Scotland Navigation Co.*, 1916 S.C. 554.
[69] *Hood* v. *Anchor Line*, 1918 S.C. (H.L.) 143.
[70] *Gray* v. *L. and N.E. Ry.*, 1930 S.C. 989; *Penton* v. *Southern Ry.* [1931] 2 K.B. 103.
[71] *Taylor* v. *Glasgow Corporation, supra.*
[72] *McCutcheon* v. *David MacBrayne, supra; Olley* v. *Marlborough Court* [1949] 1 K.B. 532; *Thornton* v. *Shoe Lane Parking* [1971] 2 Q.B. 163.
[73] *Henry Kendall & Sons* v. *William Lillico & Sons* [1969] 2 A.C. 31; *Hollier* v. *Rambler Motors (A.M.C.)* [1972] 2 Q.B. 71; *Grayston Plant* v. *Plean Precast*, 1976 S.C. 206. See, as to the specification of prior dealings, *McCrone* v. *Boots Farm Sales Ltd.*, 1981 S.C. 68; *G.E.A. Airexchangers Ltd.* v. *James Howden & Co. Ltd.*, 1984 S.L.T. 264.
[74] *British Crane Hire Corporation* v. *Ipswich Plant Hire* [1975] 1 Q.B. 303.
[75] *Uniroyal Ltd.* v. *Miller & Co. Ltd.*, 1985 S.L.T. 101; *Butler Machine Tool Co. Ltd.* v. *Ex-Cell-O Corporation (England) Ltd.* [1979] 1 All E.R. 965.

variation is confirmed in writing by the offerer, the offerer's terms should prevail.[76]

5.13   Withdrawal of Offer.—As a general rule, an offer may be withdrawn at any time before acceptance. But a man may promise to enter into a contract if the party to whom he makes his offer chooses to accept, and does so if he states that his offer is open for a certain time.[77] And while in the ordinary case an application for shares in a company may be withdrawn before it is accepted by allotment, an application expressly stated to be irrevocable binds the applicant to take the shares if they are allotted to him.[78] An offer is impliedly withdrawn by the death of either party or by the offerer's bankruptcy or his insanity, even although the insanity has not been made public by any legal process, and the party who has accepted the offer was not aware of it.[79] A formal written offer to purchase (or sell) heritable property may be withdrawn verbally so long as this is communicated to the offeree before he or she has accepted the offer.[80]

5.14   Conclusion of Contract by Acceptance: Time.—An offer cannot be withdrawn after acceptance. Where parties are in instantaneous communication with each other (across the table, or on the telephone, or by means of telex) the contract is concluded when the offerer actually becomes aware of the acceptance.[81] The rule is that acceptance takes effect when it is made in the manner indicated by the offer. In offers made by post it will be assumed, in the absence of any provision to the contrary, that an acceptance by letter is indicated; if so, the acceptance takes effect, and the contract is complete and binding, when the letter of acceptance is posted.[82] A message of any kind withdrawing the offer is too late if it does not arrive until after the acceptance has been posted.[83] But this rule assumes that both parties are acting in matters of business in an ordinary business way; when an offer was withdrawn by telegram which would have reached the offeree in time had he been at his place of business, it was held that the offer was effectually withdrawn although the offeree, writing to accept from some other place, had posted his letter before he actually received the telegram.[84] If there is a time fixed for acceptance it is sufficient for the acceptor to

---

[76] *Roofcare Ltd.* v. *Gillies*, 1984 S.L.T. (Sh.Ct.) 8.

[77] *Supra*, para. 5.1. There is, however, a distinction between stipulating a period during which the offer cannot be withdrawn and stipulating a period within which the offer must be accepted: *Effold Properties Ltd.* v. *Sprot*, 1979 S.L.T. (Notes) 84.

[78] *Premier Briquette Co.* v. *Gray*, 1922 S.C. 329.

[79] *Thomson* v. *James* (1855) 18 D. 1, at p. 10.

[80] *McMillan* v. *Caldwell*, 1991 S.L.T. 325.

[81] *Brinkibon Ltd.* v. *Stahag Stahl und Stahlwaren G.m.b.H.* [1983] 2 A.C. 34; *Entores Ltd.* v. *Miles Far East Corp.* [1955] 2 Q.B. 327.

[82] *Thomson* v. *James, supra.*

[83] *Thomson* v. *James, supra*; *Henthorn* v. *Fraser* [1892] 2 Ch. 27.

[84] *Burnley* v. *Alford*, 1919 2 S.L.T. 123.

show that he posted his letter in time, although, by a delay in the post, it arrived too late.[85] It has been held in England that proof that an acceptance has been posted is sufficient to complete the contract even though the letter never arrives,[86] but this has been doubted in Scotland,[87] and the question must be considered to be open.

5.15 Withdrawal of Acceptance.—From the theory that a contract is completed when an acceptance is dispatched it might be inferred that an acceptance cannot be withdrawn. But in the only decision on the subject it was held that an acceptance was withdrawn effectually if the notice of withdrawal reached the offerer before, or together with, the letter of acceptance.[88] The decision has been regarded with reserve by English academic writers on the grounds that it could be regarded as relating to withdrawal of an offer rather than an acceptance, and that it involved an element of agency;[89] a different result has been reached in other jurisdictions.[90] It may, however, be observed that under two international conventions relating to the sale of goods revocation of acceptance is treated as being effective so long as this is communicated before or together with the acceptance.[91]

5.16 Reasonable Time.—Acceptance must be within the time fixed by the offer, if any; if none, within a reasonable time. The question of what is a reasonable time may be solved by proof of a custom in the particular trade,[92] or may be decided on the whole circumstances of the case. Business offers, to buy or sell commodities which fluctuate in value, are assumed to be open for acceptance only by return of post.[93] An acceptance too late is in effect a new offer, which the original offerer may ignore without incurring any liability.[94] If a man admits that he has not accepted an offer within the proper time, and alleges that in the course of negotiation the time was extended, it lies on him to prove a definite agreement to that effect.[95]

---

[85] *Jacobsen* v. *Underwood* (1894) 21 R. 654.

[86] *Household Fire Insurance Co.* v. *Grant* (1879) 4 Ex.D. 216. *Cf. Holwell Securities Ltd.* v. *Hughes* [1974] 1 W.L.R. 155.

[87] *Mason* v. *Benhar Coal Co.* (1882) 9 R. 883. Note also *Higgins & Sons* v. *Dunlop, Wilson & Co.* (1847) 9 D. 1407, *per* Lord Fullerton at p. 1414; (1848) 6 Bell 195.

[88] *Countess of Dunmore* v. *Alexander* (1830) 9 S. 190.

[89] Winfield (1939) 55 L.Q.R. 499, 512; Hudson (1966) 82 L.Q.R. 169; Treitel, *Law of Contract* (8th ed., 1991), pp. 27–28, n. 77. See also Walker, *Contracts*, p. 133; McBryde, paras. 5–04 and 5–49.

[90] *Wenckheim* v. *Arndt* (N.Z.) 1 J.R. 73 (1873); *Morrison* v. *Thoelke*, 155 So. 2d. 889 (1963); *A to Z Bazaars (Pty.) Ltd.* v. *Minister of Agriculture*, 1974 (4) S.A. 392(C).

[91] Uniform Law on the Formation of Contracts for the International Sale of Goods (1964), art. 10: implemented in the U.K. by the Uniform Laws on International Sales Act 1967, s. 2 (1); United Nations Convention on Contracts for the International Sale of Goods (1980), art. 22; the U.K. has not yet ratified this Convention.

[92] *Murray* v. *Rennie* (1897) 24 R. 965.

[93] *Wylie & Lochhead* v. *McElroy* (1873) 1 R. 41, *per* Lord President Inglis.

[94] *Wylie & Lochhead* v. *McElroy, supra.*

[95] *Glasgow Steam Shipping Co.* v. *Watson* (1873) 1 R. 189.

5.17 Qualified Acceptance.—An acceptance must meet the offer.[96] If what
bears to be an acceptance proposes new conditions it is in effect a new
offer, which the other party may accept or not as he pleases. But if the
acceptance contains a meaningless condition, that condition will be
ignored and the contract, if otherwise good, held to be concluded.[97] A
request for more information or for clarification is not a rejection which
causes the offer to fall.[98] On the making of a qualified acceptance and
counter-offer, the original offer falls and, if the counter-offer is refused,
the party cannot fall back and accept the original offer.[99] Where an
exchange of missives reveals that there are two (counter-) offers in
existence, one by the purchaser the other by the seller, it is open to
either party to withdraw his offer and accept, without qualification, the
remaining offer.[1] A party who accepts an offer may be bound although
in his acceptance he may propose conditions as to the method in which
the contract may be carried into effect.[2] This question has arisen chiefly
in cases where an offer, made verbally or by letter, is met by an
acceptance 'subject to contract,' 'subject to formal contract,' or other
equivalent terms. Is this merely a condition as to the method in which
the contract which has been completed may be carried out, or does it
postpone the mutual agreement until the formal contract has been
drawn up and signed? In *Erskine* v. *Glendinning*,[3] an offer to let was
accepted with the qualification 'subject to lease drawn out in due form.'
It was held that a contract was completed by this acceptance, and that
the party who had accepted could not withdraw. But where an
imperfectly authenticated acceptance contained the words 'subject to
contract' it was held, distinguishing *Erskine* v. *Glendinning*, that the
obligation was suspended.[4] Where parties to an action agree to a
settlement, though with a provision that its terms are to be embodied in
a joint minute, the agreement is completely binding.[5]

5.18 *Locus Poenitentiae.*—While the engagement is still incomplete, *e.g.*
while the offer remains unaccepted, or the writing, where this is

[96] *Mathieson Gee (Ayrshire) Ltd.* v. *Quigley*, 1952 S.C. (H.L.) 38.

[97] *Nicolene Ltd.* v. *Simmonds* [1953] 1 Q.B. 543. But if terms are so interrelated that
the removal of one would affect the others, it will not be treated as *pro non scripto*:
MacLeod's Exr. v. *Barr's Trs.*, *supra*.

[98] *Stevenson* v. *McLean* (1880) 5 Q.B.D. 346; *Gibson* v. *Manchester City Council* [1979]
1 All E.R. 972.

[99] *Wolf and Wolf* v. *Forfar Potato Co.*, 1984 S.L.T. 100; *Rutterford Ltd.* v. *Allied
Breweries Ltd.*, 1990 S.L.T. 249. This case also rejected the argument that the terms of an
offer may be classified as being either essential or inessential, and that qualification or
variation of the latter should be treated as being a proposal for modification rather than as
a rejection.

[1] *Findlater* v. *Maan*, 1990 S.L.T. 465.

[2] See *Ingram-Johnson* v. *Century Insurance Co.*, 1909 S.C. 1032; *Thomson* v. *James*
(1855) 18 D. 1, at pp. 14 and 23.

[3] (1871) 9 M. 656.

[4] *Stobo Ltd.* v. *Morrisons (Gowns) Ltd.*, 1949 S.C. 184.

[5] *Dewar* v. *Ainslie* (1892) 20 R. 203; *Murphy* v. *Smith*, 1920 S.C. 104.

required by law or has been stipulated for,[6] has yet to be executed, parties have the right to withdraw from negotiations; this right is termed *locus poenitentiae*.[7] It may, in the case where an offer is met by a qualified acceptance, be lost if the party proposing to withdraw has allowed the other to act on the assumption that the contract is complete. Such actings are known as *rei interventus*.[8] The meaning of this term will be considered in dealing with verbal or informal agreements relating to heritage.[9] In cases where full agreement has never been reached but one or other of the parties has acted on the assumption that it has, it may be shown that they mistook each other's attitude so completely that the contract supposed to be accepted was a different one from that which was offered. In that event, in spite of any action that may have followed, the conclusion must be that since there was no agreement to any contract, matters must be restored as far as possible to their original position, and that neither party is under any obligation. This was the solution in a case where, owing to a misunderstanding, a tenant had made two offers for a farm, materially different in their conditions, and had entered into possession. It was held that there had been no agreement and that the tenant must remove.[10] In the more common case where substantial agreement has been reached, but minor details are still unsettled, it will be held that the offerer, if he knows that the other is proceeding to act in reliance on the contract, and does not interfere, has waived his objection to the terms proposed.[11] Where a person is barred by his actions from founding on the informality of contract, but it eventually proves that the other party cannot offer a valid title, he is entitled to repudiate.[12] A party may lose the right to resile by means of waiver. Waiver may be express or inferred but in either case, the party taking the plea must show that he has altered his position in reliance on the waiver.[13]

5.19   Implied Terms.—There are several types of implied term; a term may be implied in a contract because the law infers the term as an incident of contracts of a particular class;[14] a term may be implied by custom of

---

[6] *Infra*, para. 8.2; see *Stobo Ltd.*, *supra*, *per* Lord President Cooper at p. 192.

[7] Bell, *Prin.*, §25.

[8] Gloag, *Contract* (2nd ed.), pp. 46, 172.

[9] *Infra*, para. 8.4.

[10] *Buchanan* v. *Duke of Hamilton* (1878) 5 R. (H.L.) 69.

[11] *Colquhoun* v. *Wilson's Trs.* (1860) 22 D. 1035; *Roberts & Cooper* v. *Salvesen*, 1918 S.C. 794.

[12] *Kinnear* v. *Young*, 1936 S.L.T. 574.

[13] *Armia Ltd.* v. *Daejan Developments Ltd.*, 1979 S.C. (H.L.) 56; *Lousada & Co. Ltd.* v. *J. E. Lesser (Properties) Ltd.*, 1990 S.L.T. 823.

[14] Gloag, *Contract* (2nd ed.), p. 286; *Sterling Engineering Co.* v. *Patchett* [1955] A.C. 534 at p. 547, *per* Lord Reid; *Lister* v. *Romford Ice and Cold Storage Co.* [1957] A.C. 555, *per* Viscount Simonds at p. 579, Lord Tucker at p. 594; *Liverpool City Council* v. *Irwin* [1977] A.C. 239, *per* Lord Wilberforce at p. 253, Lord Cross at p. 257; *Prestwick Circuits Ltd.* v. *McAndrew*, 1990 S.L.T. 654.

trade;[15] a term may be implied by a previous course of dealing;[16] a term may be implied because in the circumstances of the particular contract it is necessary to give the contract business efficacy. As to the last of these cases—'The Court will only hold a term or condition to be implied in a written contract if its nature is such that it must necessarily be implied to give the contract business efficacy.'[17] A term may also be implied on the basis that 'every reasonable man ... would desire [it] for his own protection ... and that no reasonable man ... would refuse to accede to it.'[18] But implication of a term on the basis of presumed intention may be rebutted on the particular facts of a case. So, where goods hired under an agreement were bought at the hirers' request, were inspected only by them, and were not even delivered by the other party to the agreement, it was held that it was not an implied term of the hire agreement that the goods were hireworthy.[19] A term cannot be implied in a contract which contradicts its expressed terms.[20]

Further Reading

Bell, *Commentaries* (7th ed., 1870) I, 4 *et seq.*
Bell, Erskine, Stair as in Ch. 3.
Chitty, *Contracts* (26th ed., 1989).
Gloag, *Contract* (2nd ed., 1929).
McBryde, *The Law of Contract in Scotland* (1987).
Smith, *Short Commentary* (1962), Ch. 33.
Treitel, *Law of Contract* (8th ed., 1991).
Walker, *Law of Contracts* (2nd ed., 1985).

---

[15] *Infra*, para. 6.18.

[16] *Supra*, para. 5.12.

[17] *Per* Lord Jamieson, *McWhirter* v. *Longmuir*, 1948 S.C. 577, at p. 589. The well-known dictum of Bowen L.J. in *The Moorcock* (1889) 14 P.D. 64, at p. 68, has been criticised (Gloag, *Contract* (2nd ed.), p. 289). There is also the 'officious bystander' test: *Shirlaw* v. *Southern Foundries* [1939] 2 K.B. 206, *per* MacKinnon L.J. at p. 227; see also *Spring* v. *National Amalgamated Stevedores and Dockers Society* [1956] 1 W.L.R. 585; *Microwave Systems (Scotland)* v. *Electro-Physiological Instruments*, 1971 S.C. 140; *Prestwick Circuits Ltd.* v. *McAndrew, supra.*

[18] *Wm. Morton & Co.* v. *Muir Bros. & Co.*, 1907 S.C. 1211, *per* Lord McLaren at p. 1224.

[19] *G. M. Shepherd Ltd.* v. *North West Securities Ltd.*, 1991 S.L.T. 499.

[20] *Cummings* v. *Charles Connell & Co. (Shipbuilders)*, 1968 S.C. 305; *North American and Continental Sales Inc.* v. *Bepi (Electronics) Ltd.*, 1982 S.L.T. 47.

CHAPTER 6

RULES OF EVIDENCE IN RELATION TO CONTRACT

Though the law of evidence is beyond the scope of this work, this chapter will consider some of the rules affecting contracts. The law has been much altered since the previous edition by the reforms occasioned by the Requirements of Writing (Scotland) Act 1995 (subsequently referred to as 'the 1995 act').

6.1 **Proof *Prout de Jure.*—**When proof is allowed without qualification it is said to be proof *prout de jure*, proof by the evidence of witnesses (parole evidence) and by the production of any writings that may be available.

6.2 **Proof by Writ or Oath.—**Formerly, certain contracts which did not require to be constituted in writing nevertheless might only be proved by reference to the defender's writ or oath or by admission on record. Thus loans, obligations of relief and innominate and unusual contracts could only be proved by these restricted means. Proof by writ or oath has now been abolished[1] and, consequently, such contracts may be proved by any competent means.

6.3 **Self-proving Documents.—**When a document is subscribed by its granter or granters, signed by one witness and contains a statement of the latter's name and address then the authenticity of the granter's signature is presumed.[2]

6.4 **Attestation.—**The major change effected by the 1995 Act is the requirement that only one witness is needed to sign a document.[3] The witness must either see the granter subscribe or hear him acknowledge his signature.[4] If the witness does not see the granter subscribe his signature or signs it before the granter does, or if he does not sign *unico contextu* with the granter's acknowledgement of his signature, the presumption that the document was subscribed by the granter is displaced.[5] This presumption will also be displaced where what purports

---

[1] Requirements of Writing (Scotland) Act 1995, s. 11(1).
[2] *Ibid.*, s. 3(1).
[3] *Ibid.*, s. 3(1)(b).
[4] *Ibid.*, s. 3(7).
[5] *Ibid.*, s. 3(4)(d), (e).

to be the signature of the witness is not truly his signature, or where the witness is also the subscriber, or it can be established that at the time the witness signed he did not know the granter, or was under sixteen years of age, or was mentally incapable of acting as a witness.[6] The name and address of the witness, which need not be written by the witness himself, may be added at any time before the document is founded on in any legal proceedings or is registered for preservation in the Books of Council and Session or in the sheriff court books.[7]

6.5 Party Unable to Write.—A party who is blind or unable to write may subscribe by initial or mark if this is how he usually signs.[8] This will also be permitted where the granter intends that his initial or mark should be treated as being his signature.[9] Where the granter of a deed is blind or unable to write and does not choose to sign by initial or mark, the document may be subscribed on his behalf and with his authorisation by a practising solicitor,[10] an advocate, a justice of the peace or a sheriff clerk.[11] A notary public need only be used 'in relation to the execution of documents outwith Scotland'.[12] The person signing on behalf of the granter must only do so after reading out the document to be signed to the granter unless the latter expressly dispenses with the need to do so.[13] Subscription of a document in these circumstances must take place in the granter's presence.[14] Should such a document confer a right to either money or money's worth on the subscriber (or his spouse or children), that part of the document conferring the benefit will be invalid but the validity of the remainder of the document will not be affected. It is, therefore, no longer an objection on the validity of a document that it confers a benefit on the subscriber.[15]

6.6 Writs *in re Mercatoria*.—The 1995 Act declares that writs *in re mercatoria* no longer enjoy any privileged status.[16] Consequently, should the genuineness of a signature to such an instrument be challenged, this will have to be proved by the party founding on that signature.[17] A lease of business premises will require to be constituted in writing and, in order to be self-proving, it will require to be subscribed and attested.

---

[6] Requirements of Writing (Scotland) Act 1995, s. 3(4)(a)–(c).
[7] *Ibid.*, s. 3(3).
[8] *Ibid.*, s. 7(2)(c)(i).
[9] *Ibid.*, s. 7(2)(c)(ii).
[10] *i.e.*, who holds a practising certificate as defined in s. 4(c) of the Solicitors (Scotland) Act 1980.
[11] Requirements of Writing (Scotland) Act 1995, s. 9(6).
[12] *Ibid.*, s. 9(6).
[13] *Ibid.*, s. 9(1).
[14] *Ibid.*, s. 9(2).
[15] For the earlier law, see the 9th edition of this work, para 6.5.
[16] Requirements of Writing (Scotland) Act 1995, s. 11(3)(b)(ii).
[17] *McIntyre* v. *National Bank of Scotland*, 1910 S.C. 150 (This case concerned a bill of exchange).

Submissions to arbitration relating to moveables in mercantile matters no longer fall within the category of *obligationes literis* and need not be in writing.[18] Gratuitous cautionary obligations which are not undertaken in the course of a business must be constituted in writing and will need to be subscribed and attested in order to be self-proving. Such an obligation if onerous or undertaken in the course of a business need not be constituted in writing,[19] though it is unlikely that one would wish to do so.

6.7 Extrinsic Evidence in Written Contracts.—It is a general rule that where a contract has been entered into in writing it is incompetent to contradict or qualify its terms by parole evidence. Proof that the intention of the parties was not as it is expressed in the written contract is not excluded, but is limited to the writ, which must be subsequent to the contract, of the party proposing to maintain it,[20] or to an admission on a reference to his oath.[21] Thus where the subjects let were specified in a lease it was incompetent to prove, by the evidence of the landlord's factor, that additional subjects were intended to be included.[22] And when a party undertook, in unqualified terms, to deliver shares, it was held that parole evidence was not admissible to prove that he was acting merely as an agent, and that no personal liability was intended or expected.[23] Nor is it competent to prove by parole an agreement that the conditions which the law would imply should not hold in the particular case.[24]

These rules hold only in a question with a party who takes his stand on the written contract. An admission by a defender that the written contract does not accurately represent the agreement between the parties leaves it open to prove by parole what the real agreement was.[25] It is competent to establish by parole evidence a prior[26] or subsequent[27] oral agreement the subject-matter of which does not fall under the terms of the written contract although it may have some relation thereto. And when the question is not as to the meaning of the contract, but as to its validity, parole evidence is admissible. Thus there is no restriction as to

[18] On the new law with regard to this type of obligation, as effected by the 1995 Act, see para 8.2 below.
[19] Requirements of Writing (Scotland) Act 1995, s. 1(2)(a)(ii).
[20] *Stewart* v. *Clark* (1871) 9 M. 616.
[21] *Sinclair* v. *McBeath* (1869) 7 M. 934.
[22] *Gregson* v. *Alsop* (1897) 24 R. 1081.
[23] *Lindsay's* v. *Craig*, 1919 S.C. 139.
[24] *Johnston* v. *Edinburgh, etc., Union Canal Co.* (1835) 1 Sh. & M'L. 117; *Barclay* v. *Neilson* (1878) 5 R. 909.
[25] *Grant's Trs.* v. *Morison* (1875) 2 R. 377; *Cairns* v. *Davidson*, 1913 S.C. 1054: *McMenemy* v. *Forster's Trustee*, 1938 S.L.T. 555; but see *Pickard* v. *Pickard*, 1963 S.C. 604.
[26] *William Masson* v. *Scottish Brewers*, 1966 S.C. 9.
[27] *How Group Northern Ltd.* v. *Sun Ventilating Co. Ltd.*, 1979 S.L.T. 277.

the methods of proof of averments of fraud, misrepresentation, clerical error, or illegality.[28]

6.8 Bills of Exchange.—The general rule that parole evidence cannot be led to contradict the terms of a written contract has been impinged upon by statute in the case of bills of exchange. Section 100 of the Bills of Exchange Act 1882 provides: 'In any judicial proceedings in Scotland, any fact relating to a bill of exchange, bank cheque, or promissory note, which is relevant to any question of liability thereon, may be proved by parole evidence.' The generality of this enactment has been so far limited by decision that it has been held that parole evidence of payment is incompetent,[29] and that when the alleged liability is not rested exclusively on the bill, but on the bill as a method of carrying out a prior written contract, the section is not applicable.[30] So where a business carried on in leasehold premises was sold, and promissory notes given for the price, it was held that section 100 did not authorise parole evidence of the alleged verbal agreement that payment of the notes was not to be demanded until the lease had expired.[31] But it is competent to prove that the bill was granted for the accommodation of a particular party,[32] or that it had been agreed to renew it until the occurrence of a certain event.[33] The competency of proof that the holder had agreed that one of the parties to the bill should incur no liability is not settled.[34]

6.9 Proof of Additional Terms.—It is probably the law that it is incompetent to prove a term in a written contract which is not expressed, and which the law would not imply.[35] But there are cases which render it difficult to make any confident statement on the point.[36] It is competent to prove that an obligatory document has been delivered subject to the condition that it is not to be put in force until the occurrence of a certain event.[37]

6.10 Actions of Parties.—The cases as to the competency of interpreting a written contract by evidence of the actions of the parties under it result

---

[28] *Stewart's Trs.* v. *Hart* (1875) 3 R. 192; *Krupp* v. *Menzies*, 1907 S.C. 903; *Bell Bros.* v. *Aitken*, 1939 S.C. 577; *Anderson* v. *Lambie*, 1954 S.C. (H.L.) 43.

[29] *Robertson* v. *Thomson* (1900) 3 F. 5; *Nicol's Trs.* v. *Sutherland*, 1951 S.C. (H.L.) 21.

[30] *Stagg & Robson* v. *Stirling*, 1908 S.C. 675; *McAllister* v. *McGallagley*, 1911 S.C. 112.

[31] *Stagg & Robson* v. *Stirling, supra.*

[32] *Viani* v. *Gunn* (1904) 6 F. 989.

[33] *Dryburgh* v. *Roy* (1903) 5 F. 665. See also *Thompson* v. *Jolly Carters Inn*, 1972 S.C. 215.

[34] *National Bank of Australasia* v. *Turnbull* (1891) 18 R. 629.

[35] Dickson, *Evidence*, §1020. But as to collateral agreements, see Dickson, *Evidence*, §1033, and Walker and Walker, *Law of Evidence*, §262; *Perdikou* v. *Pattison*, 1958 S.L.T. 153.

[36] *Renison* v. *Bryce* (1898) 25 R. 521; *De Lassalle* v. *Guildford* [1901] 2 K.B. 215.

[37] *Abrahams* v. *Miller (Denny) Ltd.*, 1933 S.C. 171.

in the unsatisfactory rule that such evidence is competent, on the principle of *contemporanea expositio*, in contracts of ancient date,[38] not in contracts *de recenti*.[39] But where there were contradictory statements in the contract as to the acreage and boundaries of the subjects conveyed, it was held that evidence of acting upon it was competent, although the contract was of recent date.[40]

6.11 Patent and Latent Ambiguities.—It has been said that a patent ambiguity must be solved by a construction of its terms but in practice the distinction between patent and latent ambiguity seems to have been ignored and in a number of cases extrinsic evidence has been admitted to resolve a patent ambiguity.[41] A latent ambiguity in a contract may be resolved by extrinsic evidence. An ambiguity is latent when the meaning is only rendered doubtful by a knowledge of the surrounding circumstances, *e.g.* when property is conveyed by name, and it turns out that there are two properties to which that name would apply.[42]

6.12 Proof of Surrounding Circumstances.—Parole evidence is admissible to establish the state of knowledge of the parties at the time when their contract was made, in cases where, as in a sale for a particular purpose, the liabilities involved depend on that state of knowledge.[43] And there is a general and ill-defined principle that the court is entitled to know all the circumstances surrounding the parties at the time when the contract was made. 'What the court must do must be to place itself in thought in the same factual matrix as that in which the parties were.'[44] So where two ships were sold by separate bills of sale it was held competent to lead evidence, in the guise of surrounding circumstances, that it had been agreed that if the seller was unable to furnish one of the ships the purchaser was not bound to take the other.[45]

6.13 Usage of Trade.—The fact that a contract has been entered into in writing does not exclude proof of usage of trade, either to introduce an implied term into the contract, or to give to the words used a meaning which they would not ordinarily bear. Unless the contract is expressly made subject to the usage the latter cannot rule if it contradicts the actual provisions of the writing. Thus where a contractor accepted an offer for 'the whole of the steel' required for a bridge 'the estimated

---

[38] *North British Ry.* v. *Magistrates of Edinburgh*, 1920 S.C. 409.

[39] *Scott* v. *Howard* (1881) 8 R. (H.L.) 59, opinion of Lord Watson.

[40] *Watcham* v. *Att.-Gen. of East Africa* [1919] A.C. 533.

[41] See Walker and Walker, *Law of Evidence*, §269.

[42] *Raffles* v. *Wichelhaus* (1864) 2 H. & C. 906; *Houldsworth* v. *Gordon-Cumming*, 1909 S.C. 1198, revd. 1910 S.C. (H.L.) 49.

[43] *Jacobs* v. *Scott* (1899) 2 F. (H.L.) 70.

[44] *Reardon Smith Line* v. *Yngvar Hansen-Tangen* [1976] 1 W.L.R. 989, *per* Lord Wilberforce at p. 997.

[45] *Claddagh Steamship Co.* v. *Steven*, 1919 S.C. 184; 1919 S.C. (H.L.) 132.

quantity to be 30,000 tons, more or less,' it was held that the plain meaning of the words could not be qualified by proof of a usage in the steel trade that such an offer meant an offer to supply 30,000 tons only.[46] But there would seem no limit to the variation of meaning which may be given to any particular word. The word 'thousand' has been held to mean 'twelve hundred.'[47] If the contract expressly refers to a usage, as where in a charterparty the provisions for loading expressly refer to the custom of the port, it is immaterial that one or both parties may be unaware of what the actual custom is.[48] And where a man authorises another to deal for him on a particular exchange he must be deemed to have consented to his contract being interpreted in accordance with the usages of that exchange.[49] In other cases usage of trade will not affect a contract unless both parties were aware of it.[50] It has been held that while in a particular trade there may be a customary rate of wages which will be binding in the absence of express agreement, this will not prevail where as between parties there is a well-established practice of paying and receiving another rate.[51] A usage to be admissible must be reasonably fair,[52] and generally, though not necessarily universally, recognised in the trade,[53] It has been observed that a usage cannot be established by proof of a series of protests against it.[54]

6.14 Formal Deed Excludes Prior Writing.—In the cases referred to in the preceding pages the evidence tendered has been that of witnesses. But where a contract has been drawn up in a formal and probative form not only the evidence of witnesses, but evidence of all prior communings, whether verbal or in writing, is excluded, unless it is expressly incorporated or unless there has been an error in the deed.[55] The following explanation of the principle has been constantly cited: 'Where parties agree to embody, and do actually embody, their contract in a formal written deed, then in determining what the contract really was and really meant a Court must look to the formal deed and to that deed alone. This is only carrying out the will of the parties ... The very purpose of a formal contract is to put an end to the disputes which would inevitably arise if the matter were left upon verbal negotiations or upon mixed communings, partly consisting of letters and partly of

---

[46] *Tancred, Arrol & Co.* v. *Steel Co. of Scotland* (1887) 15 R. 215; affd. (1890) 17 R. (H.L.) 31; *Affréteurs Réunis* v. *Walford* [1919] A.C. 801; *Arthur Duthie & Co.* v. *Merson and Gerry*, 1947 S.C. 43, *Sworn Securities Ltd.* v. *Chilcott*, 1977 S.C. 53.

[47] *Smith* v. *Wilson* (1832) 3 B. & Ad. 728.

[48] *Strathlorne S.S. Co.* v. *Baird*, 1915 S.C. 956, revd. 1916 S.C. (H.L.) 134.

[49] *Forget* v. *Baxter* [1900] A.C. 467. See *Robinson* v. *Mollet* (1875) L.R. 7 H.L. 802.

[50] *Holman* v. *Peruvian Nitrate Co.* (1878) 5 R. 657.

[51] *Eunson* v. *Johnson & Grieg*, 1940 S.C. 49.

[52] *Bruce* v. *Smith* (1890) 17 R. 1000; *Devonald* v. *Rosser* [1906] 2 K.B. 728.

[53] *Hogarth* v. *Leith Cottonseed Oil Co.*, 1909 S.C. 955; *Dick* v. *Cochrane & Fleming*, 1935 S.L.T. 432.

[54] *Per* Lord Shaw, *Strathlorne S.S. Co.* v. *Baird*, 1916 S.C. (H.L.) 134.

[55] *Anderson* v. *Lambie*, 1954 S.C. (H.L.) 43. See para. 9.25, *infra.*

conversations.'[56] But parties may competently agree to waive the ordinary rule[57] and where the contract has been partly performed before the deed is executed, parole evidence may be competent to prove the terms on which parties were acting before execution.[58]

6.15 Conveyance as Superseding Prior Writs.—As a general rule, a disposition, even one which bears to be in execution of prior missives, supersedes the contract and becomes the sole measure of the rights and duties of the parties.[59] But where the missives contain a collateral obligation distinct from the obligation to convey the heritage, *e.g.* an undertaking to restore central heating to working order, this remains enforceable.[60] Where the missives, or a separate document, or the disposition provide for the continuance of some personal (non-collateral) obligation, that obligation remains enforceable.[61] Finally, where missives create obligations regarding moveable subjects, these remain enforceable since it is inappropriate to include these in the disposition.[62] Prior writings may also be referred to in a question as to the conditions on which a sale took place.[63] It may be proved that two conveyances, although executed without reference to each other, were really interdependent.[64] Where the terms of a written contract are ambiguous, it is probably legitimate to refer to writings of the parties (or their conduct) after the contract was concluded.[65]

6.16 Alteration of Written Contract.—Where parties have entered into a written contract a verbal agreement to alter its provisions is not binding, and, if no action has followed on it, either party may resile and insist on the performance of the contract in its original terms.[66] But if there has been an agreement to alter the terms of the contract, and one party, to the knowledge of and without objection from the other, has proceded to act upon the contract as altered, such action may amount to *rei*

---

[56] *Per* Lord Gifford, *Inglis* v. *Buttery* (1877) 5 R. 58, affd. (1878) 5 R. (H.L.) 87; *Norval* v. *Abbey* 1939 S.C. 724. As to reference to words deleted, see conflicting opinions in *Taylor* v. *John Lewis Ltd.*, 1927 S.C. 891.

[57] *Young* v. *McKellar*, 1909 S.C. 1340; *Fraser* v. *Cox*, 1938 S.C. 506.

[58] *Korner* v. *Shennan*, 1950 S.C. 285.

[59] *Lee* v. *Alexander* (1883) 10 R. (H.L.) 91. Note also, *Inglis* v. *Buttery & Co.* (1878) 5 R. (H.L.) 87; *Edinburgh United Breweries Ltd.* v. *Molleson* (1894) 21 R. (H.L.) 10; *Korner* v. *Shennan*, 1950 S.C. 285; *Winston* v. *Patrick*, 1980 S.C. 246; *Pena* v. *Ray*, 1987 S.L.T. 609; *Central Govan Housing Association Ltd.* v. *Maguire Cook & Co.*, 1988 S.L.T. 386; *Taylor* v. *McLeod*, 1990 S.L.T. 194; *Porch* v. *MacLeod*, 1992 S.L.T. 661.

[60] *Pena* v. *Ray*; *Central Govan Housing Association Ltd.* v. *Maguire Cook & Co.*; *Taylor* v. *MacLeod*; and *Winston* v. *Patrick, supra. Jamieson* v. *Welsh* (1900) 3 F. 176; *McKillop* v. *Mutual Securities Ltd.*, 1945 S.C. 166.

[61] *Winston* v. *Patrick*; *Taylor* v. *MacLeod*; and *Porch* v. *MacLeod, supra.*

[62] *Winston* v. *Patrick*; and *Jamieson* v. *Welsh, supra.*

[63] *Young* v. *McKellar*, 1909 S.C. 1340.

[64] *Claddagh Steamship Co.* v. *Steven*, 1919 S.C. (H.L.) 132.

[65] *Turner* v. *MacMillan-Douglas*, 1989 S.L.T. 293.

[66] See opinion of Lord President Inglis, *Kirkpatrick* v. *Allanshaw Coal Co.* (1880) 8 R. 327, at p. 332.

interventus and bar the right to resile.[67] Mere acquiescence in acts which, assuming that the original terms of the contract remained in force, would be a breach thereof, can at the highest merely bar a claim of damages for what is past, it can confer no sanction for the future.[68] To establish an alteration in the terms of the contract for the future there must either be a writing to that effect, an admission on reference to oath, or a verbal agreement on which action has followed.[69] And the action in question must be clearly inconsistent with the original terms of the contract. Thus where A, who was liable under a decree, averred that his creditor had agreed to accept payment by weekly instalments, and that certain instalments had been paid, it was held that as the acceptance of instalments was not inconsistent with the right to demand immediate payment of the balance, there were no relevant averments of *rei interventus*, and the alleged verbal agreement could not be admitted to proof.[70]

Further Reading

Dickson, *Evidence* (3rd ed., 1887).
Halliday, *Conveyancing Law and Practice in Scotland* (1985), Vol. I, Ch. 3.
Walker and Walker, *Law of Evidence* (1964).
Wilkinson, *The Scottish Law of Evidence* (1986).

---

[67] *Bargaddie Coal Co.* v. *Wark* (1856) 18 D. 772, revd. (1859) 3 Macq. 467; *Kirkpatrick* v. *Allanshaw Coal Co.*, *supra*.

[68] *Carron Co.* v. *Henderson's Trs.* (1896) 23 R. 1042.

[69] See *Earl of Ancaster* v. *Doig*, 1960 S.C. 203, *per* Lord Justice-Clerk Thomson, at p. 211.

[70] *Lavan* v. *Gavin Aird & Co.*, 1919 S.C. 345.

CHAPTER 7

AGREEMENTS VOID OR VOIDABLE

7.1 The statement that an obligation may result from mere consent is to be taken as a general rule, subject to important qualifications. There are many cases where real or apparent consent may have been given and yet no obligation may arise. This may result (1) from want of capacity in the party;[1] (2) from defect of form;[2] (3) from the nature of the means by which consent was obtained;[3] (4) from error precluding real consent;[4] or (5) from the illegality of the matter involved.[5]

7.2 Contracts Void, Voidable or Unenforceable.—These objections to the validity of consent may, according to the circumstances, render the obligation void, voidable or unenforceable. If an agreement, or apparent agreement, is void, it is to be treated, for all legal purposes, as a mere nullity. No one can enforce it, and, if it purports to convey property, no title to that property is given, even in a question with a third party, such as a sub-purchaser, who has no notice of the grounds of nullity. An agreement which is not void but merely voidable is valid until it is set aside by the party entitled to avoid it, with the result that if property has passed on a contract merely voidable, and has been transferred for value to a party who has no notice of any invalidity, that party's title is not affected by the reduction of the original contract.[6] An agreement is termed unenforceable when, owing to some statutory or other rule, it cannot be enforced by action, but is not so forbidden as to render it void, or to exclude the creation of incidental rights.

7.3 Conditions of Avoidance.—The fact that an obligation is voidable does not imply that in all circumstances it may be reduced. That is doubtless the general rule; in particular cases it may find exception on the grounds (a) that *restitutio in integrum* is impossible; (b) that the interests of third parties are involved; (c) that the validity of the obligation has been recognised by homologation, in the case of voidable contracts, or by adoption, in the case of a void contract or an apparent contract; (d) that there has been undue delay.

---

[1] Chap. 4.
[2] Chap. 8.
[3] Chap. 9.
[4] Paras. 9.13 to 9.25, *infra*.
[5] Chap. 10.
[6] See *Morrisson* v. *Robertson*, 1908 S.C. 332; *cf. MacLeod* v. *Kerr*, 1965 S.C. 253.

7.4 ***Restitio in Integrum.***—It is a general principle that where a party proposes to reduce a contract, he must be able to offer *restitutio in integrum*; in other words, must be able to restore the other party to the position in which he was before he entered into the contract. So if contractors have erected a building on a contract which proves to be voidable, the reduction of the contract is precluded, whatever remedies may in the particular case be available, on the ground that the original position of matters cannot be restored.[7] When an unincorporated company was incorporated under statute, it was held that, as the original shares had been so altered that they could no longer be restored, a reduction of the contract to take shares was impossible.[8] When a particular thing has been sold, and resold by the purchaser, he cannot reduce the sale because he cannot restore the thing. His title to reduce the sale is not improved by re-acquiring the thing from the sub-purchaser.[9] But when the sub-sale was also reducible on the same ground (a misrepresentation as to the condition of the thing), and was on that ground reduced by the sub-purchaser, it was held that a reduction of the original sale was competent.[10] *Restitutio in integrum* may be given in cases where the question depends on the possibility of restoring a particular thing, although that thing may in the meantime have diminished in value. So a contract to take shares may be reduced so long as the company is a going concern, though the shares may have become valueless.[11] The interest in a partnership could be restored though the business was openly insolvent.[12] If a particular thing has been transferred under the contract and has been accidentally destroyed, it would appear that the contract cannot be reduced.[13] But if it has perished owing to the fault of the party proposing to maintain the contract, as when a horse, warranted sound in work, ran away and was killed, that party cannot found upon his own wrong or breach of contract, and so cannot resist the reduction of the contract (involving repayment of the price) on the plea that *restitutio in integrum* cannot be offered.[14] And when a person by fraud has been able to purchase something, he may not in bar of restitution rely upon dealings with the thing purchased which his fraud has enabled him to carry out.[15]

---

[7] *Boyd & Forrest* v. *Glasgow and S.W. Ry.*, 1915 S.C. (H.L.) 20. See also *Hay* v. *Rafferty* (1899) 2 F. 302.

[8] *Western Bank* v. *Addie* (1867) 5 M. (H.L.) 80.

[9] *Edinburgh United Breweries* v. *Molleson* (1894) 21 R. (H.L.) 10.

[10] *Westville Shipping Co.* v. *Abram Shipping Co.*, 1922 S.C. 571; affd. 1923 S.C. (H.L.) 68.

[11] *Western Bank* v. *Addie* (1867) 5 M. (H.L.) 80, opinion of Lord Cranworth; *Armstrong* v. *Jackson* [1917] 2 K.B. 822.

[12] *Adam* v. *Newbigging* (1888) 13 App.Cas. 308.

[13] See opinion of Lord Atkinson, *Boyd & Forrest* v. *Glasgow and S.W. Ry.*, 1915 S.C. (H.L.) 20, 29.

[14] *Kinnear* v. *Brodie* (1901) 3 F. 540; *Rowland* v. *Divall* [1923] 2 K.B. 500.

[15] *Spence* v. *Crawford*, 1939 S.C. (H.L.) 52.

7.5 Interests of Third Parties.—The interests of third parties do not preclude the reduction of a contract in so far as that contract involves merely a personal obligation. So if a bond is granted under circumstances which render it voidable in a question with the original creditor, it remains voidable in a question with anyone to whom it may be assigned.[16] The obligation of an insurance company on a policy of insurance, if voidable on the ground of misrepresentation by the insured, may be reduced in a question with the assignee.[17] In cases of the assignation of a debt or other personal obligation (not embodied in a negotiable instrument) the maxim *assignatus utitur jure auctoris* (the assignee uses his author's right) applies, and the assignee may be met by any defence which was available against the cedent.[18] But if the result of the contract was not merely to create a personal obligation but to transfer a real right in some particular property—as where land is conveyed or goods are sold on a contract induced by misrepresentation—the original seller cannot reduce the contract so as to recover the property if it has been transferred to a third party either by sale or in security. The original sale carries a title to the property, and, though that title may be voidable, it is valid until reduced, and third parties may acquire indefeasible rights under it. This rule, recognised as a general principle in the earliest authorities,[19] may be stated in the language of the Sale of Goods Act 1979, section 23: when the seller of goods has a voidable title thereto, but his title has not been avoided at the time of the sale, the buyer acquires a good title to the goods, provided he buys them in good faith and without notice of the seller's defect in title.[20]

7.6 Interests of Creditors.—When third parties are interested in maintaining a contract, not as the holders of subordinate real rights, but merely as personal creditors of the original party, it is a general rule that their interests do not preclude the reduction of the contract. The distinction between the position of heritable creditors, who obtain a real right to the lands, and adjudgers, who were only personal creditors, was taken in an early and leading case.[21] And it is settled that a trustee in a sequestration cannot take advantage of the bankrupt's fraud, and therefore cannot maintain a right which the bankrupt has acquired by

---

[16] *Nisbet's Creditors* v. *Robertson* (1791) Mor. 9554; *McDonells* v. *Bell & Rannie* (1772) Mor. 4974.

[17] *Scottish Widows' Fund* v. *Buist* (1876) 3 R. 1078; *Graham Shipping Co.* v. *Merchants Marine Insurance* [1924] A.C. 294.

[18] See opinion of Lord President Inglis, *Scottish Widows' Fund* v. *Buist, supra.*

[19] Stair, IV, xl, 21.

[20] For illustrative cases, see *Bryce* v. *Ehrmann* (1905) 7 F. 5; *Morrisson* v. *Robertson*, 1908 S.C. 332 (contrast between void and voidable contract); *Price & Pierce* v. *Bank of Scotland*, 1910 S.C. 1095; affd. 1912 S.C. (H.L.) 19.

[21] *Thomson* v. *Douglas Heron & Co.* (1786) Mor. 10229; 3 Ross' Leading Cases, 132. See also opinion of Lord Watson, *Heritable Reversionary Co.* v. *Millar* (1892) 19 R. (H.L.) 43.

fraudulent means.[22] The chief exception to this rule is the case where shares are taken in reliance on misrepresentations in the prospectus. It is established law, proceeding largely on inferences derived from the terms of the Companies Acts, that the contract cannot be reduced after the company has gone into liquidation, on the ground that the real interest is then in the creditors, or, where all creditors are paid, in the other shareholders.[23] It has been observed that a partner, reducing the contract of partnership on the ground that he has been induced to enter into it by fraud, would remain liable to the creditors of the firm.[24]

7.7   **Homologation.**—Homologation is implied by any acts whereby a party, in the knowledge that a particular obligation is voidable, recognises its validity. 'The law of homologation proceeds on the principle of presumed consent by the party who does the acts to pass from grounds of challenge known to him, and *sciens et prudens* to adopt the challengeable deed as his own.'[25] Such acts as the payment or receipt of rent on a voidable lease,[26] payment of interest on a bond,[27] continuance of business with a banker on a system to which the customer might have objected,[28] amount to homologation and bar any subsequent challenge. Delivery of a deed lacking the required solemnities is not *per se* homologation.[29] As a rule, and in all cases of isolated acts, it is necessary to prove that the party alleged to have homologated was aware of all the material facts,[30] but in certain cases of long sustained relationship adequate means of knowledge have been held to be sufficient.[31] The effect of homologation is to validate the obligation from the date of its inception.

7.8   **Adoption.**—Adoption applies to cases where there is nothing but the semblance of an obligation. By recognising its validity the party may render himself liable on a new contract to be inferred from his acts. The

---

[22] *Colquhoun's Tr.* v. *Campbell's Trs.* (1902) 4 F. 739; *Gamage* v. *Charlesworth's Tr.*, 1910 S.C. 257.

[23] *Oakes* v. *Turquand* (1867) L.R. 2 H.L. 325; *Tennent* v. *City of Glasgow Bank* (1879) 6 R. (H.L.) 69; *Burgess' Case* (1880) 15 Ch.D. 507. Contrast the case where the contract to take shares is actually void, as where A, intending to apply for shares in one company, applied for shares in another: *Baillie's Case* [1898] 1 Ch. 110.

[24] Opinion of Lord Chancellor Cairns in *Tennent* v. *City of Glasgow Bank, supra.*

[25] *Gardner* v. *Gardner* (1830) 9 S. 138. Quoted and approved by Lord President Clyde, *Danish Dairy Co.* v. *Gillespie*, 1922 S.C. 656, 664. For a discussion of the limits of homologation, see *Westville Shipping Co.* v. *Abram Shipping Co.*, 1922 S.C. 571; affd. 1923 S.C. (H.L.) 68.

[26] *Rigg* v. *Durward* (1776) Mor. App. Fraud, No. 2; *Lord Advocate* v. *Wemyss* (1899) 2 F. (H.L.) 1.

[27] *McCalman* v. *McArthur* (1864) 2 M. 678.

[28] *Crerar* v. *Bank of Scotland*, 1921 S.C. 736; affd. 1922 S.C. (H.L.) 137.

[29] *Clark's Exr.* v. *Cameron*, 1982 S.L.T. 68.

[30] *Danish Dairy Co.* v. *Gillespie, supra.*

[31] *Lord Advocate* v. *Wemyss* (1899) 2 F. (H.L.) 1; *Crerar* v. *Bank of Scotland, supra.*

most important cases have related to forged bills. If a party whose signature is forged chooses to accept liability, he has adopted the bill, and he may act in such a way as to amount to adoption and consequent liability without any express recognition of his signature.[32] But this will not be easily inferred, and it is now established that mere silence, in face of an intimation that the bill is due, does not amount to adoption and infers no liability.[33] Where a person discovers that his signature has been forged to a document, it is his duty to inform the creditor at once, but the creditor can recover against him only if he can establish that he has been prejudiced by any delay in informing him.[34] If the objection to the contract be that the body which entered into it was acting *ultra vires*, no acts approving of it can cure the invalidity, or have any legal effect, unless in the meantime the contractual powers of the body have been enlarged.[35]

7.9 Delay.—In certain cases delay in taking action will preclude reduction of a contract.[36] This primarily depends on the nature of the defect which renders the contract voidable. Some grounds of avoidance are not maintainable unless they are taken advantage of within a specified or a reasonable time. Thus a contract entered into by a person between the ages of 16 and 18 may be reduced if it is a prejudicial transaction, but only if he takes action before attaining the age of 21.[37] The right to reject goods, and treat the contract as repudiated in the case where the goods are disconform to contract, must be exercised within a reasonable time.[38] The right to reduce a contract to take shares, on the ground of misrepresentation in the prospectus, must certainly be exercised within a reasonable time,[39] and probably must be followed by steps for the rectification of the register.[40] In other cases, for instance in the case of contracts voidable on the ground of fraud or misrepresentation, in a question between the original parties any delay, short of the negative prescription of five or 20 years, is not a bar to reduction.[41] But, if in consequence of unnecessary delay evidence has been lost, any point which it might have elucidated will be presumed in the defender's favour.[42] Where the interests of third parties are concerned, the law is

[32] *Greenwood* v. *Martins Bank* [1933] A.C. 51.
[33] *MacKenzie* v. *British Linen Co.* (1881) 8 R. (H.L.) 8; *British Linen Co.* v. *Cowan* (1906) 8 F. 704; *Muir's Exrs.* v. *Craig's Trs.*, 1913 S.C. 349.
[34] *Muir's Exrs.*, *supra*.
[35] *General Property Investment Co.* v. *Matheson's Trs.* (1888) 16 R. 282; and see Capacity to Contract, para. 6.8, *supra*.
[36] See also Extinction of Obligations, Chap. 14, *infra*.
[37] Capacity to Contract, para. 4.4, *supra*.
[38] Sale of Goods Act 1979, s. 11(5).
[39] *Aaron's Reefs* v. *Twiss* [1896] A.C. 273.
[40] *First National Re-Insurance Co.* v. *Greenfield* [1921] 2 K.B. 260.
[41] See *e.g. Robinson* v. *Robinson's Trs.*, 1934 S.L.T. 183.
[42] *Bain* v. *Assets Co.* (1905) 7 F. (H.L.) 104.

far from clear, but it would appear that unreasonable delay may preclude reduction.[43]

---

[43] See *Fraser* v. *Hankey* (1847) 9 D. 415; *Buckner* v. *Jopp's Trs.* (1887) 14 R. 1006. The numerous cases are collected and, so far as possible, reconciled in Rankine, *Personal Bar*, Chap. V.

CHAPTER 8

AGREEMENTS DEFECTIVE IN FORM: PROVINCE OF WRITING

8.1 Constitution in Writing.—The general rule is that writing is unnecessary for the constitution of a contractual obligation.[1] A contract may be entered into orally, or in writing, or it may be inferred from the conduct of the parties. And the fact that an obligation has been undertaken may be proved *prout de jure*.

8.2 Contracts Requiring to be Constituted in Writing.—Contracts or unilateral obligations for the creation, variation, or extinction of an interest in land require to be in writing in order to be validly constituted. Gratuitous unilateral obligations, though not ones under-taken in the course of business, and obligations creating, transferring, varying or extinguishing an interest in land, other than by the operation of a court decree, enactment or rule of law, also require to be constituted in writing.[2] 'Interest in land' is defined to mean 'any estate, interest or right in or over land, including any right to occupy or to use land or to restrict the occupation or use of land'.[3] However, a lease for less than one year or a right to occupy or use land for less than one year need not be constituted in writing.[4] Land does not include growing crops or moveable buildings or structures.[5] In order to be self-proving, such contracts or obligations will require to be subscribed by the granter and attested by one witness.[6] Missives for the sale and purchase of heritable property will need to be in writing since they represent a contract for the 'transfer of an interest in land'. They will not, however, require to be self-proving as they are not usually recorded or registered but they will need to be subscribed and witnessed: adoption as holograph will neither be necessary nor sufficient.

8.3 Personal Bar.—The Requirements of Writing (Scotland) Act 1995 retains the doctrine of *rei interventus* but in an altered form from the common law doctrine.[7] Where a contract is required by the Act to be

---

[1] Requirements of Writing (Scotland) Act 1995, s. 1(1).
[2] *Ibid.*, s. 1(2)(a)(i), (ii), and (b).
[3] *Ibid.*, s. 1(7).
[4] *Ibid.*, s. 1(7). Unless the tenancy or right is for recurring periods with a gap of more than a year between the start of the first period and the end of the last.
[5] *Ibid.*, s. 1(8).
[6] Discussed *supra*, paras 6.3 and 6.4.
[7] Though it replaces both *rei interventus* and homologation in relation to contracts and obligations specified in s. 1(2): see s. 1(5).

constituted in writing and this is not done, or is not done in the proper form, then, if one of the parties acts or refrains from acting in reliance on the contract with the knowledge and acquiescence of the other party, the latter is not entitled to resile from the contract and it will not be treated as being invalid,[8] provided that the first party's position has been affected to a material extent[9] and would be adversely affected to a material extent if withdrawal were permitted.[10] Similar provision is made in relation to the variation of contracts and obligations.[11] Where writing is absent or not in the proper form required by the Act there must still be evidence that the parties had reached *consensus in idem.*[12] It will not, however, be the case that proof of the existence of agreement between the parties will be restricted to the defender's writ or oath.[13]

8.4   Facts Amounting to Personal Bar.—The new form of *rei interventus* may consist in alterations in the property which is the subject of the contract,[14] in payment of the price or some substantial part of it,[15] or even, in the case of leases, in abstention, on the landlord's part, from efforts to obtain another tenant,[16] on the tenant's part, from efforts to obtain other accommodation[17]; this is, however, not an exhaustive list.[18]

8.5   Completion of Title.—Where an action on an improperly constituted agreement has been successful on proof of *rei interventus*, the defender may be ordained to execute a formal contract (sale or lease as the case may be) in accordance with the agreement established against him.[19] On his refusal a remit may be made to a conveyancer to draw up an appropriate instrument, and, on a continued refusal to sign, the Clerk of Court may be authorised to sign on the defender's behalf.[20]

8.6   Interests of Third Parties.—Before any proceedings have been taken to establish the validity of an informal sale followed by *rei interventus*, the

[8] Requirements of Writing (Scotland) Act 1995, s. 1(3).

[9] But not irretrievably so: see Bell, *Prin.*, § 26 which, in this respect, appears to be reflected in the legislation.

[10] Requirements of Writing (Scotland) Act 1995, s. 1(4).

[11] *Ibid.*, s. 1(6).

[12] *East Kilbride Development Corporation* v. *Pollock*, 1953 S.C. 370; *Colquhoun* v. *Wilson's Trs.* (1860) 22 D. 1035; *Wight* v. *Newton*, 1911 S.C. 762. Note also Gloag, *Contract* pp. 46–47, quoted with approval in *Morrison-Low* v. *Paterson*, 1985 S.C. (H.L.) 49.

[13] Requirements of Writing (Scotland) Act 1995, s. 11(1). *Errol* v. *Walker*, 1966 S.C. 93 is no longer good law.

[14] *Colquhoun* v. *Wilson's Trs.*, *supra.*

[15] *Foggo* v. *Hill* (1840) 2 D. 1322.

[16] *Sutherland* v. *Hay* (1845) 8 D. 283, *per* Lord Medwyn; *Kinnear* v. *Young*, 1936 S.L.T. 574.

[17] *Danish Dairy Co.* v. *Gillespie*, 1922 S.C. 656.

[18] See the broad terms of Bell's *Principles*, §26, note 9, *supra.*

[19] *Stodart* v. *Dalzell* (1876) 4 R. 236 (feu); *Wight* v. *Newton*, 1911 S.C. 762 (lease).

[20] *Whyte* v. *Whyte*, 1913 2 S.L.T. 85.

land in question may be resold to a third party. If he had no notice of the prior informal sale, his title is unchallengeable. If he had notice, he is bound to inquire and is not entitled to accept blindly the seller's statement that the prior negotiations had been broken off without reaching an agreement.[21] In the case of leases where the tenant has entered into possession any lease which could in any way be enforced against the landlord may be enforced against his singular successor.[22]

Further Reading

Halliday, *Conveyancing Law and Practice in Scotland* (1985), Vol. I.
MacPhail, *Evidence* (1987), Chaps. 14–15.
Rennie and Cusine, *The Requirements of Writing* (1995).
Walker and Walker, *Evidence* (1964), Chaps. IX–XI.

---

[21] *Petrie* v. *Forsyth* (1874) 2 R. 214; *Stodart* v. *Dalzell* (1876) 4 R. 236; *Rodger (Builders)* v. *Fawdry*, 1950 S.C. 483.
[22] *Wilson* v. *Mann* (1876) 3 R. 527.

CHAPTER 9

AGREEMENT IMPROPERLY OBTAINED

9.1 Means by which Consent Obtained.—A contract may be rendered void or voidable because the consent of one of the parties has been obtained by improper means, or given under error. Under this head may be considered the effect of (1) Fraud, (2) Misrepresentation, (3) Error, (4) Extortion, (5) Facility and Circumvention, and (6) Undue Influence.

I. FRAUD

9.2 Fraud.—Fraud is a machination or contrivance to deceive, by words or acts.[1] Unless the result of the fraud is to exclude any real consent, a contract induced by fraudulent practices is not void, but only voidable.[2] To induce a party to contract by fraud is a civil wrong, and therefore the party defrauded may not only reduce the contract but also recover damages for any loss he may have suffered. If, for reasons already explained,[3] the contract cannot be reduced, a claim for damages remains competent.[4] Where a contract has been induced by fraudulent misrepresentation, damages may be recovered even though the pursuer does not offer to rescind.[5]

It is impossible to enumerate the various words or acts which the law will regard as fraudulent, but some light may be thrown on the question from the negative side.

9.3 No Legal Fraud.—There is no such thing as legal, apart from moral, fraud. Conscious dishonesty must be proved. In the leading English case, *Derry* v. *Peek*,[6] the directors of an insolvent tramway company were sued for damages on the ground that the plaintiff had been

---

[1] Bell, *Prin.,* § 13. As to facility and circumvention as a separate ground for the reduction of a contract, see Gloag, *Contract* (2nd ed.), p. 484; *Mackay* v. *Campbell*, 1966 S.C. 237, affd. 1967 S.C. (H.L.) 53. As to facility and circumvention in relation to wills, see para. 44.2 *infra.*

[2] *Morrisson* v. *Robertson*, 1908 S.C. 332; *MacLeod* v. *Kerr*, 1965 S.C. 253, and see *infra*, para. 9.19.

[3] See para. 7.3, *supra.*

[4] *Boyd & Forrest* v. *Glasgow and S.W. Ry.*, 1912 S.C. (H.L.) 93.

[5] *Bryson & Co. Ltd.* v. *Bryson*, 1916 1 S.L.T. 361; *Smith* v. *Sim*, 1954 S.C. 357 (O.H.), an action founded on delict.

[6] (1889) 14 App. Cas. 337. See also *Boyd & Forrest* v. *Glasgow and S.W. Ry.*, 1912 S.C. (H.L.) 93; *Lees* v. *Tod* (1882) 9 R. 807.

induced to take shares by misrepresentation in the prospectus. The misrepresentation in question was that the company had obtained authority from the Board of Trade to work the tramway by steam power. This was proved to be untrue, but it was also proved that the directors honestly believed it to be true, having misapprehended the result of their negotiations with the Board of Trade. It was held, even on the assumption that the defendants had not taken reasonable care to verify their statement, that they were not liable in damages for fraud because there was no dishonesty.[7] In *Manners* v. *Whitehead*,[8] M had been induced to enter into a partnership with W by inaccurate statements contained in balance sheets of the business which W was carrying on. The business failed, and M sued for damages. He proved that the balance sheets were inaccurate; he did not succeed in proving fraud on the part of W. It was held that the action was not maintainable; a claim for damages in such circumstances, as the law then stood, had to rest on proof of conscious fraud. The general rule illustrated in these cases must be taken with the qualification that if a man does not know, or has forgotten, the truth on any particular question, he has no right to make any positive assertion on the subject, and therefore that fraud may be established although there may be no proof that the speaker was aware that his statement was untrue. It is enough that the real state of his mind was that he did not know whether it was true or not. And the absence of any reasonable grounds for belief may be evidence, to be taken with the other evidence in the case, that no positive belief existed.[9]

9.4   Disclosure.—Mere failure to disclose material facts does not amount to fraud; nor, except in certain special contracts, or where the parties stand to each other in some confidential relationship, is it a ground for the reduction of a contract. So a bank, when offered a guarantee for a customer's account, is not bound to inform the guarantor of the state of that account.[10] When A knew that B's mine contained a valuable seam

---

[7] In England and Scotland a negligent statement may now give rise to a claim for damages. See para. 9.9, *infra*.

[8] (1898) 1 F. 171. See para. 9.9, *infra*.

[9] See opinion of Lord President Inglis, *Lees* v. *Tod* (1882) 9 R. 807; of Lord Herschell in *Derry* v. *Peek* (1889) 14 App. Cas. 337.

[10] *Royal Bank* v. *Greenshields*, 1914 S.C. 259; *Mumford* v. *Bank of Scotland, Smith* v. *Bank of Scotland*, 1994 S.L.T. 1288. This stands in stark contrast to the position under English law with regard to the granting of a security by spouses or partners. In *Barclays Bank plc* v. *O'Brien* [1994] 1 A.C. 180, the House of Lords held that unless the creditor takes reasonable steps to ensure that a guarantor or surety signs a guarantee or mortgage willingly, free from pressure and in knowledge of the true facts, he is "fixed with notice of the surety's right to set aside the transaction". In order to escape being fixed with such constructive knowledge, the creditor should insist on a private meeting with the surety, without the other partner being present, and at that meeting the surety should be advised of the extent of his/her liability, warned of the risk being run and urged to take independent advice. This is now adopted as para. 14(1) of the second edition of *Good Banking* (the industry's code of practice). Note also: *CIBC Mortgages plc* v. *Pitt* [1994] 1 A.C. 180 and *Massey* v. *Midland Bank plc* [1995] 1 All E.R. 929.

of coal, and also knew that B was unaware of the fact, it was held that a lease obtained by A was unchallengeable.[11] A settlement of an action for £20 was sustained, although obtained by the defender in a private interview with the pursuer by concealing the fact that he had already made a tender of £50.[12] And it is probably established that the seller of goods is under no obligation to reveal latent defects.[13]

But this rule does not hold in insurance,[14] nor in guarantees for the fidelity of an official;[15] nor probably in negotiations for entering into partnership.[16] In these contracts (known as contracts *uberrimae fidei*) each party is bound to reveal all facts known to him which it would be material for the other to know. A similar duty of disclosure may arise from the fact that the parties stand to each other in some relationship. Thus concealment of material facts will serve to avoid a contract between parent and child,[17] trustee and beneficiary,[18] partners,[19] agent and principal.[20] A solicitor contracting with his client is under a particularly stringent obligation; he must not only reveal all material facts but show that the contract is one which he, if consulted in a case where he was not personally interested, would have advised the client to make.[21]

9.5   Half-Truths.—The general rule that concealment does not affect the validity of a contract applies only to a case of mere non-disclosure, when no representation has been made. It is fraudulent to tell a half-truth, that is, to make a statement true in itself, and withhold some explanation which would alter its whole bearing. A prospectus may satisfy the statutory conditions as to disclosure, and nevertheless, by the concealment of facts which would alter the impression conveyed by the facts disclosed, amount to fraud.[22] So if an agent for a bank makes any statement to a party who offers to guarantee an account he must reveal all the relevant facts.[23] Again, if a statement made is honestly but mistakenly believed, the party who makes it is bound to reveal the

---

[11] *Gillespie* v. *Russell* (1856) 18 D. 677; (1857) 19 D. 897; (1859) 3 Macq. 757.

[12] *Welsh* v. *Cousin* (1899) 2 F. 277.

[13] *Ward* v. *Hobbs* (1878) 4 App. Cas. 13; *Philip's Trs.* v. *Reid* (1884) 21 S.L.R. 698. As to possible exceptions in cases of sale see Chap. 16, *infra*.

[14] para 24.6, *infra*.

[15] *Bank of Scotland* v. *Morrison*, 1911 S.C. 593.

[16] See *Manners* v. *Whitehead* (1898) 1 F. 171; *Ferguson* v. *Mackay*, 1985 S.L.T. 94. There is no definite authority. A contract of employment is not *uberrimae fidei*: *Walker* v. *Greenock and District Combination Hospital Board*, 1951 S.C. 464.

[17] *Smith Cunninghame* v. *Anstruther's Trs.* (1872) 10 M. (H.L.) 39.

[18] *Dougan* v. *Macpherson* (1902) 4 F. (H.L.) 7.

[19] *Law* v. *Law* [1905] 1 Ch. 140. See also *Cassels* v. *Stewart* (1881) 8 R. (H.L.) 1.

[20] See *McPherson's Trs.* v. *Watt* (1877) 5 R. (H.L.) 9.

[21] *Aitken* v. *Campbell's Trs.*, 1909 S.C. 1217; *Gillespie* v. *Gardner*, 1909 S.C. 1053.

[22] *R.* v. *Lord Kylsant* [1932] 1 K.B. 442.

[23] *Falconer* v. *North of Scotland Bank* (1863) 1 M. 704; *Royal Bank* v. *Greenshields*, 1914 S.C. 259.

actual facts if they come to his knowledge. There is the same duty of disclosure if by a change of circumstances the original statement ceases to be true. So when A had honestly and truthfully stated that there was no risk that a machine, which B proposed to buy, would be requisitioned by the Government, it was held that A was bound to inform B of any change of attitude on the part of the Government officials.[24] The rule that mere failure to disclose is not fraudulent does not extend to the case of dealing with articles which *ex facie* pretend to be what they are not, such as forged stamps, faked antiques. A purchaser may reduce the contract to buy them, though the seller may have made no representation that the articles are genuine.[25] And it is fraudulent to exhibit unrepresentative specimens in an auction room, though the conditions of the sale may be that intending purchasers must satisfy themselves as to the condition of the goods in bulk.[26] Any devices to conceal defects in an article are clearly fraudulent.

9.6 Verba Jactantia.—The general rule that statements known to be untrue are fraudulent has certain qualifications. It is not to be applied too rigorously to advertisements, though the line which separates mere extravagant recommendation (*verba jactantia*) from fraudulent misstatements cannot be exactly drawn.[27] It has been decided by the Judicial Committee that when the manager of a company was bound by his duty to his employers not to disclose the fact that a particular report had been received, and knew that a refusal to make any statement would give the inquirer the information he wanted, he was not liable in damages for fraud though he gave an answer which was wilfully false.[28] But a good motive is no excuse for a fraudulent act.[29]

9.7 Attempts to Defraud.—Attempts to defraud cause no injury, and therefore afford no remedy. Where a seller adopted fraudulent devices to conceal the defects in a gun, and the buyer bought it without making any examination, it was held that, as he had not been deceived, he could not reduce the contract on the ground of fraud.[30] An action to reduce a contract to take shares failed where the shareholder was forced to admit that the particular statements in the prospectus which he could prove to be untrue had not affected his mind.[31] But it is no answer to

---

[24] *Shankland* v. *Robinson*, 1919 S.C. 715; revd. 1920 S.C. (H.L.) 103.

[25] *Patterson* v. *Landsberg* (1905) 7 F. 675, opinion of Lord Kyllachy; *Gibson* v. *National Cash Register Co.*, 1925 S.C. 500.

[26] *White* v. *Dougherty* (1891) 18 R. 972.

[27] Contrast *Bile Beans Co.* v. *Davidson* (1906) 8 F. 1181; and *Plotzker* v. *Lucas* (1907) 15 S.L.T. 186. Note also *Paul & Co.* v. *Glasgow Corporation* (1900) 3 F. 119.

[28] *Tackey* v. *McBain* [1912] A.C. 186.

[29] *Menzies* v. *Menzies* (1893) 20 R. (H.L.) 108, *per* Lord Ashbourne.

[30] *Horsfall* v. *Thomas* (1862) 1 H. & C. 90.

[31] *Smith* v. *Chadwick* (1884) 9 App. Cas. 187. *Cf. Ritchie* v. *Glass*, 1936 S.L.T. 591, a case of innocent misrepresentation.

an action based on fraud that the party defrauded could have discovered the true facts if he had taken the trouble to investigate.[32]

II. MISREPRESENTATION

9.8 Innocent Misrepresentation.—A statement honestly believed may nevertheless, if untrue, mislead the party to whom it is made, and induce him to contract under what is known as essential error.[33] This will render the contract voidable.[34] 'Error becomes essential whenever it is shown that but for it one of the parties would have declined to contract.'[35] This is probably a general rule though one case suggests that it is stated too broadly, and that there may be misrepresentations regarding collateral matters which, though in fact they induced the contract, are not sufficiently material, in the absence of fraud, to render it voidable.[36] On this theory such misrepresentations are spoken of as inducing, not essential error, but error *dans causam contractui*. But more recent authorities hold that a contract is voidable if it has been induced by any misrepresentation, giving more weight to the consideration that a man has no right to profit by a misrepresentation he has made, no matter how innocently, and would do so if he were allowed to retain the contract thereby induced.[37] If the misrepresentation in question relates to the credit of a third party it cannot be founded on as a ground for the reduction of the contract unless it is made in writing.[38]

9.9 Remedy for Negligent Misrepresentation.—The misrepresentation inducing a contract may be made either by some third party who does not stand in a contractual relationship with the party deceived or by one of the contracting parties. In the former case, a remedy in damages and based in delict lies against the third party.[39] But prior to the coming into force of the Law Reform (Miscellaneous Provisions) (Scotland) Act 1985, damages could not be claimed where the misrepresentor was the

---

[32] *Redgrave* v. *Hurd* (1881) 20 Ch.D. 1; *Gluckstein* v. *Barnes* [1900] A.C. 240; *Strover* v. *Harrington* [1988] 1 Ch. 390.

[33] For a comment on the use of this terminology see Smith, *Short Commentary*, pp. 809, 811.

[34] *Stewart* v. *Kennedy* (1890) 17 R. (H.L.) 25. As to the conditions for avoidance, see paras. 7.3 *et seq., supra.*

[35] *Per* Lord Watson, *Menzies* v. *Menzies* (1893) 20 R. (H.L.) 108, at p. 142.

[36] *Woods* v. *Tulloch* (1893) 20 R. 477; and see Erskine, III, i, 16; *Edgar* v. *Hector*, 1912 S.C. 348; and *Ritchie* v. *Glass*, 1936 S.L.T. 591.

[37] *Stewart* v. *Kennedy* (1890) 17 R. (H.L.) 25; *Mair* v. *Rio Grande Rubber Co.*, 1913 S.C. (H.L.) 74; *Westville Shipping Co.* v. *Abram S.S. Co.*, 1922 S.C. 571, opinion of Lord President Clyde (affd. 1923 S.C. (H.L.) 68).

[38] *Union Bank* v. *Taylor*, 1925 S.C. 835; *cf. Andrew Oliver & Son Ltd.* v. *Douglas*, 1981 S.C. 192, and see para. 20.5 *infra*.

[39] On the basis of *Hedley Byrne & Co.* v. *Heller & Partners* [1964] A.C. 465. The *Hedley Byrne* principle is endorsed in *Junior Books Ltd.* v. *The Veitchi Co. Ltd.*, 1982 S.L.T. 492; *Kenway Ltd.* v. *Orcantic Ltd.*, 1979 S.C. 422; and *Martins* v. *Bell-Ingram*, 1986 S.L.T. 575.

other party to the contract and the misrepresentation was negligent rather than fraudulent.[40] Such a claim is now competent under section 10(1) of the 1985 Act which states: 'A party to a contract who has been induced to enter into it by negligent misrepresentation made by or on behalf of another party to the contract shall not be disentitled, by reason only that the misrepresentation is not fraudulent, from recovering damages from the other party in respect of any loss or damage he has suffered as a result of the misrepresentation; and any rule of law that such damages cannot be recovered unless fraud is proved shall cease to have effect.' This provision merely alters the law as declared in *Manners* v. *Whitehead*[41] and permits the courts to award damages in respect of negligent misrepresentation as has been possible in England since at least 1967.[42] The pursuer will still have to show that (a) the misrepresentor owed him a duty of care, and (b) that the misrepresentation caused him to contract. It has been decided that under English law failure to take an opportunity to check up on a representation is no bar to a claim for damages provided that, in the circumstances, it was not reasonable to expect this.[43]

9.10 Representations and Contractual Terms.—It may often be difficult to determine whether a particular statement is to be regarded as a term of the contract, or merely as a representation. Thus the statement by a party selling an engine that it will develop a certain horse-power may be regarded as a representation to that effect, or as a guarantee of the engine's power.[44] If it is read as a representation, the only legal result (apart from allegations of fraud or negligence) of its untruth is to render the contract voidable, and then only if the statement was material, so that the purchaser would not have given the price he did had he known the true facts. If, on the other hand, the statement is read as a guarantee, the party who gives it is liable in damages for breach of contract if it is not fulfilled, and the terms of the contract may be such as to render it voidable even if the point guaranteed was not material. The latter question has been illustrated chiefly in cases relating to policies of insurance. These are commonly preceded by a proposal form, in which certain questions are answered by the insured. If it is expressly agreed that the validity of the policy is conditional on the truth of the answers in the proposal form, the policy will be avoided even if it may appear that the particular answer proved to be untrue related to a point which was not material.[45] In a case where there was no express

[40] *Manners* v. *Whitehead, supra.* Followed in *Foster* v. *Craigmillar Laundry Ltd.*, 1980 S.L.T. (Sh.Ct.) 100.
[41] See para 8.3, *supra.*
[42] See *Howard Marine and Dredging Co. Ltd.* v. *A. Ogden & Sons (Excavations) Ltd.* [1978] Q.B. 574 and other decisions on the Misrepresentation Act 1967.
[43] *Smith* v. *Eric S. Bush* [1990] 1 A.C. 831.
[44] *Robey* v. *Stein* (1900) 3 F. 278.
[45] *Standard Life Assurance Co.* v. *Weems* (1884) 11 R. (H.L.) 48.

provision that the validity of the policy should depend upon the accuracy of the answers in the proposal form, but it was provided in the policy that the proposal form should be the 'basis of the contract,' the House of Lords, by a narrow majority, held that the insured warranted the statements in the proposal form, and therefore that the policy was avoided by the inaccuracy of a statement therein, even though it was not material, and did not affect the amount of the premium charged.[46] Such a conclusion, however, will not be reached if there is any ambiguity in the terms of the policy.[47]

There are no *voces signatae* by which to distinguish between a representation and a contractual warranty. The latter is clearly excluded by an express provision that the statement in question is not guaranteed. And statements which do not relate to the *res* about which the parties are contracting, but to collateral matters which may affect motive, are merely representations. In the case of statements which do relate to the *res* it is always a question of intention whether they are to be regarded as representations or as contractual warranties.[48] It is merely an element in the question that one party had full means of information and the other had not.[49] The fact that the statement in question was made verbally in relation to a contract in writing does not necessarily preclude the conclusion that it was intended as a warranty. So a verbal assurance that the drains of a house were in good order, a point on which the lease was silent, was held to be a warranty, breach of which subjected the landlord to damages.[50]

9.11 Expressions of Opinion.—A statement may be construed neither as a representation nor as a warranty, but as an expression of the speaker's opinion or of his intentions for the future. While it is fraudulent to induce a contract by expressing an opinion or an intention which is not formed,[51] an honest statement of opinion, though unfounded, leaves the contract unaffected, and a person who states his intention does not represent that he will not change his mind.[52] While it must always be a question of construction whether a man has confined himself to stating his opinion, or has made a definite assertion, the former interpretation will generally be accepted in cases where in ordinary business the other party would make independent inquiries, *e.g.* a statement as to the

---

[46] *Dawsons Ltd.* v. *Bonnin*, 1922 S.C. (H.L.) 156; *McPhee* v. *Royal Insurance Co. Ltd.*, 1979 S.C. 304.

[47] *Provincial Insurance Co.* v. *Morgan* [1933] A.C. 240.

[48] *Hyslop* v. *Shirlaw* (1905) 7 F. 875, at p. 881.

[49] *Heilbutt* v. *Buckleton* [1913] A.C. 30.

[50] *De Lasalle* v. *Guildford* [1901] 2 K.B. 215. See also *Renison* v. *Bryce* (1898) 25 R. 521.

[51] *Edgington* v. *Fitzmaurice* (1885) 29 Ch.D. 459.

[52] para. 3.11, *supra*.

capacity of a farm to carry a certain head of stock.[53] A statement made in the course of business and in a context in which it is reasonable to rely on it without seeking independent advice may be treated as a misrepresentation.[54] Where an airline had a policy of overbooking flights and wrote to a customer 'confirming' a reservation, this was treated as a statement of fact and not of intention.[55] While a misrepresentation as to the legal effect of a contract will render it voidable,[56] it is probable that a statement as to a general principle of law would be regarded merely as an expression of opinion.[57]

9.12   Title to Sue on Misrepresentation.—A misrepresentation, innocent or fraudulent, affords no right of action except to the person or persons to whom, expressly or impliedly, it was addressed. Thus when A fraudulently induced B to accept a transfer of shares in a company it was held that the liquidator of the company had no title to reduce the contract, in order to place A on the list of contributories.[58] If the seller of an article, by fraudulent devices, obtains more than the proper price, a sub-purchaser, though he may be the actual loser, has no title to reduce the sale.[59] Anyone who acquires securities, whether from the company or on the market, has a right to compensation from those responsible for the listing particulars or prospectus, should he suffer loss as a consequence of any untrue or misleading statement therein or omission therefrom.[60] Misleading or false statements in other documents, such as rights circulars, may ground an action at common law.[61] If the speaker, as a reasonable man, must be aware that others than the party he addresses will act on his statement, he will be liable to them. So a banker, answering queries from another banker as to a customer's financial standing, must be aware that customers of the latter bank may be interested and will be liable to them if his statements are fraudulent.[62]

III.   ERROR

9.13   Error.—One who contracts under an erroneous belief which is due to his own misconception, is said to contract under error, or error in

[53] *Hamilton* v. *Duke of Montrose* (1906) 8 F. 1026.
[54] *Esso Petroleum Co.* v. *Mardon* [1976] Q.B. 801.
[55] *British Airways Board* v. *Taylor* [1976] 1 All E.R. 65 (H.L.); the statement being false, there was a successful prosecution under the Trade Descriptions Act 1968.
[56] *Stewart* v. *Kennedy* (1890) 17 R. (H.L.) 25.
[57] See *Brownlie* v. *Miller* (1880) 7 R. (H.L.) 66.
[58] *McLintock* v. *Campbell*, 1916 S.C. 966.
[59] *Edinburgh United Breweries Co.* v. *Molleson* (1894) 21 R. (H.L.) 10.
[60] Financial Services Act 1986, ss. 150(1), 166(1).
[61] *Peek* v. *Gurney* (1873) L.R. 6 H.L. 377; *Al Nakib Investments* v. *Longcroft* [1990] 1 W.L.R. 1390.
[62] *Robinson* v. *National Bank*, 1916 S.C. (H.L.) 154. See also *Fortune* v. *Young*, 1918 S.C. 1.

intention.[63] It is necessary to distinguish the various situations to which the word 'error' has been applied.

9.14 Error in Transmission.—Where an offer has been altered in a material respect in the course of transmission the offeree's acceptance does not result in the conclusion of a contract. So where an offer sent by telegram was misread by the telegraph clerk and was transmitted in a form materially different from its original terms, no contract resulted from the acceptance, because the circumstances precluded any real agreement.[64]

9.15 Mutual Error.—If the terms of an offer are intrinsically ambiguous and the offerer reasonably attaches one meaning to them there is no contract because there is no agreement. Where an order was given for stone coping at so much per 'foot,' a term equally applicable to a lineal and a superficial foot, it was held that the contract was not binding.[65] Where the parties were negotiating by telegram in code and the coded offer could reasonably be deciphered in a way different from that intended by the offerer and the offeree did read it in the alternative sense it was held that there was no binding contract.[66] Similarly, there may be no contract where the ambiguity arises from extrinsic circumstances. If parties are contracting about a particular thing, and use language which is equally applicable to some other thing, then, assuming that they differ as to the meaning of the terms which they employ, they have reached no agreement and concluded no contract. This may happen in the case of the sale of an estate by its name if there is a reasonable difference of opinion as to the extent of the lands covered by that name.[67] The result was the same in the sale of the cargo from 'the ship Peerless coming from Bombay' when there were two ships of that name coming from Bombay and the parties had different ships in mind.[68] If, in the course of negotiations, one party has indicated his interpretation of an ambiguous word and the other party has not contradicted him, the latter cannot subsequently advance an alternative meaning of the concluded contract.[69]

9.16 Error in Declaration.—Another class of case is where, by some slip on the part of the offerer, an offer reaches the offeree in a form which was not intended. In *Stuart's Trs.* v. *Hart*,[70] reduction of a disposition of heritable subjects was permitted where the seller thought that the

---

[63] The equivalent term in England is 'mistake.'
[64] *Verdin* v. *Robertson* (1871) 10 M. 35; *Henkel* v. *Pape* (1870) L.R. 6 Exch. 7.
[65] *Stuart* v. *Kennedy* (1885) 13 R. 221.
[66] *Falck* v. *Williams* [1900] A.C. 176.
[67] *Houldsworth* v. *Gordon Cumming*, 1910 S.C. (H.L.) 49.
[68] *Raffles* v. *Wichelhaus* (1864) 2 H. & C. 906.
[69] *Sutton & Co.* v. *Ciceri & Co.* (1890) 17 R. (H.L.) 40.
[70] *Steuart's Trs.* v. *Hart* (1875) 3 R. 192.

subjects were burdened with a *cumulo* feuduty of £9 15s but the buyer knew that this was only 3s and that the seller had made a mistake. Gloag doubted the correctness of this decision[71] and, more recently doubt has twice been cast upon it.[72] This notwithstanding, the most recent Outer House decision to consider the case follows it.[73] The matter will not be resolved until considered by a court of authority. If a party does not know that the offer which he receives is in a form which was not intended by the offeror and accepts this in good faith, the contract is binding.[74]

9.17 Error in Intention.—Cases where the agreement itself is entered into under error present more difficult problems. There is no doubt of the general rule that a party cannot reduce a contract on the ground that he has entered into it in error, if his contention is merely that he would not have contracted if he had known all the relevant facts. A plea to that effect has been judicially characterised as 'so utterly preposterous as to be undeserving of any attention.'[75] But the question is one of degree. Cases may arise where the error is so material as to preclude any real consent, and therefore to leave a contract, or apparent contract, without that basis of agreement on which all contractual obligation must rest. In such cases the apparent contract is not voidable on the ground of error but void because there never was a contract at all. While the interpretation of contractual obligation must accept, as a fundamental rule, that a party must be taken to mean what he says, and is barred from asserting that his words or acts did not represent his intention,[76] that rule may come in conflict with one equally fundamental, namely, that the contractual obligations of the parties must rest on their consent. The attempt of the law to reconcile the conflict may be approached by considering the various forms of error by which a contract, or apparent contract, may be affected.

9.18 Error Affecting Motive.—Certain forms of error clearly do not preclude consent, but only affect the motive of the party who gives it. Such cases are referred to in Bell's *Principles* as cases of *error concomitans*, as opposed to error in substantials. Under this head fall errors as to

[71] Gloag, *Contract* (2nd ed.), p. 438 points out: 'When a book is exposed for sale in a bookstall it is generally supposed that a collector may buy it at the price asked, though he knows that it is rare and valuable, and must know that the bookseller is unaware of its value, and yet in all essential points such a case is on all fours with *Steuart's Trs.* v. *Hart.*'

[72] *Brooker Simpson* v. *Duncan Logan (Builders)*, 1969 S.L.T. 304; *Spook Erection (Northern) Ltd.* v. *Kaye*, 1990 S.L.T. 676.

[73] *Angus* v. *Bryden*, 1992 S.L.T. 884. It is ventured that Gloag and the cases in note 72 express the better view. *Steuart's Trs.* v. *Hart* was decided before *Stewart* v. *Kennedy*, note 38, reshaped the meaning of 'essential' error.

[74] *Seaton Brick Co.* v. *Mitchell* (1900) 2 F. 550; *Steel's Tr.* v. *Bradley Homes (Scotland)*, 1972 S.C. 48; *cf. Sword* v. *Sinclair* (1771) Mor. 14241.

[75] Per Lord Fullerton, *Forth Marine Ins. Co.* v. *Burnes* (1848) 10 D. 689.

[76] para. 5.3, *supra*.

extraneous circumstances, which may lead a party mistakenly to suppose a contract advantageous. Such errors leave the contract unaffected and have no legal result, unless the error was induced by misrepresentation[77] or the obligation was gratuitous.[78] So the guarantor of a bank account may be able to say that he would not have given his guarantee had he known the true state of the account, yet, in the absence of any misrepresentation by the bank, he will be liable.[79] A case equally clear is an error as to the quality of the thing to which the contract relates; there is no doubt that when a man buys or hires a specific thing the contract is not affected by his error as to its value or suitability. Again, a contract is not rendered voidable by the fact that one of the parties mistook its legal result, or the obligations which it imposed; as already explained, these are matters for the court to determine.[80]

9.19 Error in Substantials.—Other forms of error arising as to material aspects of the contract are so fundamental as to exclude any agreement between the parties, and for this reason render the contract void *ab initio*.[81] 'Error in substantials, whether in fact or in law, invalidates consent, or rather excludes real consent, where reliance is placed on the thing mistaken.'[82] The question in such a case is not whether a contract is reducible on the ground of error, but whether there is any contract to enforce. Such error in substantials may arise in relation to (1) the nature of the contract itself, (2) the identity of the person with whom the contract is supposed to have been made, (3) the subject-matter of the contract, (4) in certain cases, the quality of the subject-matter, and (5) the price.[83] The question whether the error is such as to exclude consent is one of degree in each case. As has been stated, the normal effect of misrepresentation is to make the contract merely voidable, but where a misrepresentation induces an error in substantials the contract is void;[84] it is therefore appropriate to consider here such cases as well as those of uninduced error in substantials.

9.20 Error as to Contract.—The predominant and, it is submitted, the better view is that where one party avers uninduced unilateral error as to the nature of the obligation undertaken, then where there is a written,

---

[77] See para. 9.8, *supra*.

[78] para. 5.2, *supra*.

[79] *Royal Bank* v. *Greenshields*, 1914 S.C. 259. See also *Welsh* v. *Cousin* (1899) 2 F. 277; *Hogg* v. *Campbell* (1864) 2 M. 848.

[80] para. 5.3, *supra*; *Stewart* v. *Kennedy* (1890) 17 R. (H.L.) 25; see also *Manclark* v. *Thomson's Trs.*, 1958 S.C. 147.

[81] For a discussion of whether the contract might be rendered voidable rather than void, see Smith, *op. cit.*, pp. 810, 815; but note *MacLeod* v. *Kerr*, 1965 S.C. 253.

[82] Bell, *Prin.*, § 11 (10th ed.); Stair, I, x, 13; see opinion of Lord Watson in *Stewart* v. *Kennedy, supra*, at p. 28.

[83] Gloag, *Contract*, pp. 441–448.

[84] *Morrisson* v. *Robertson*, 1908 S.C. 332.

signed, onerous contract the courts will not look behind the written document to see what was in the mind of the party averring error.[85] Other than in cases involving gratuitous contracts,[86] it is unlikely that the courts will permit reduction of an onerous, written, contract on the basis of uninduced unilateral error.[87] It is otherwise where a party, intending to bind himself to one contract, is fraudulently induced to sign a document binding him to another, as where a party signed a guarantee, being told and believing that he was signing a policy of insurance. It was held that the contract was not merely voidable on the ground of fraud, but void on the ground of the want of real consent, and that no liability could be founded on the fact that, had he exercised reasonable care, the party would have discovered what he was signing.[88] But in order to sustain the plea of *non est factum*—that the party had no intention to bind himself—there must have been a definite mistake, so that the party thought he was entering into one contract while he was really entering into another. If obligatory documents are signed in reliance on an assurance that they are mere matters of form the party who signs them will be liable.[89] If a draft contract has been revised, and the party signs the extended copy without noticing that it has been fraudulently altered, he will be bound, in a question with anyone not involved in the fraud, unless the alteration is so material as to make it a different contract.[90]

9.21 **Error as to Identity.**—If a party believes that he was contracting with A, and in reality is contracting with B, he has given no consent and incurred no obligation, provided that, in the circumstances, the identity of the other party was material. So where A, pretending to be the son and agent of a well-known farmer, induced a dealer to sell him on credit and deliver two cows, and at once resold them, it was held that the dealer might recover them from the purchaser. He had not merely been induced to sell by A's fraud (which would only have rendered the sale voidable in a question with A); he had never intended to contract with A at all. The sale was not merely voidable, but void.[91] So again where a

---

[85] *Stewart* v. *Kennedy,* note 37 *supra; Hunter* v. *Bradford Property Trust Ltd.,* 1970 S.L.T. 173; *Steel* v. *Bradley Homes (Scotland) Ltd.,* 1972 S.C. 48; *The Royal Bank of Scotland* v. *Purvis,* 1990 S.L.T. 262; *Spook Erection (Northern) Ltd.* v. *Kaye, supra; McCallum* v. *Soudan,* 1989 S.L.T. 552.

[86] *Hunter* v. *Bradford Property Trust Ltd., supra.*

[87] *Cf. Ellis* v. *Lochgelly Iron Co.,* 1909 S.C. 1278.

[88] *Carlisle Banking Co.* v. *Bragg* [1911] 1 K.B. 489; *Foster* v. *Mackinnon* (1869) L.R. 4 C.P. 704; *Buchanan* v. *Duke of Hamilton* (1878) 5 R. (H.L.) 69.

[89] *Howatson* v. *Webb* [1908] 1 Ch. 1. And see opinion of Lord Sands in *Fletcher* v. *Lord Advocate,* 1923 S.C. 27.

[90] *Selkirk* v. *Ferguson,* 1908 S.C. 26; *Ellis* v. *Lochgelly Iron Co.,* 1909 S.C. 1278; *Hogg* v. *Campbell, supra.*

[91] *Morrison* v. *Robertson,* 1908 S.C. 332. This decision is discussed in *MacLeod* v. *Kerr,* 1965 S.C. 253; see also Smith (1967) 12 J.L.S.S. 206, 346. Error as to identity is not limited to the case where one person is mistaken for another: *Harrison* v. *Butters,* 1969 S.L.T. 183.

party obtained a consignment of goods by pretending in correspondence to be a well-known retail dealer, it was held that he obtained no title, and that the firm which had sent the goods could recover them from parties to whom they had been resold.[92] However, where both parties to the purported agreement were present at its making, the courts have tended to hold that the contract was intended to be made with the person who was present and not with the person whose identity he had falsely assumed.[93]

9.22 Error as to Subject-Matter.—Where certain barrels, some containing tow, others hemp, were put up for auction merely by their numbers, it was decided that a party who bid for a barrel of tow under the impression that it was a barrel of hemp had come under no obligation. His bid was read not as a bid for a particular barrel, but for a barrel of hemp; it was accepted as a bid for a barrel of tow.[94] But such cases are very exceptional; as a general rule if a party offers to sell goods of a particular description, and does so in words which, reasonably construed, have only one meaning, he is bound to fulfil his contract, though he may have mistakenly thought that the goods which he tenders were of the description which he has undertaken to supply.[95]

9.23 Error as to Price.—The mere fact that the contract does not settle the consideration to be paid does not raise a case of error. If no acts have followed it would generally be regarded as a case where negotiations had not reached the stage of contract;[96] if it has been carried into effect the court will fix a reasonable consideration.[97] In *Sword* v. *Sinclair*,[98] the seller's agent mistakenly offered to sell tea at 2s 8d per pound instead of 3s 8d per pound as his principal had instructed; it was held that the principal was not bound but no reason is given for the decision. In *Wilson* v. *Marquis of Breadalbane*,[99] although on the basis of what was said the parties appeared to have agreed on the price of stots, it was held in the Inner House that, as one believed that the price had been fixed and the other party thought that it was still to be fixed according to the quality of the cattle delivered, there was no *consensus in idem* and therefore no contract. Neither of these decisions can stand with

---

[92] *Cundy* v. *Lindsay* (1878) 3 App. Cas. 459.

[93] *MacLeod* v. *Kerr, supra*; *Phillips* v. *Brooks* [1919] 2 K.B. 243; *Lewis* v. *Averay* [1972] 1 Q.B. 198. *Ingram* v. *Little* [1961] 1 Q.B. 31, is the exception.

[94] *Scriven* v. *Hindley* [1913] 3 K.B. 564.

[95] Sale of Goods Act 1979, s. 13; *Wallis* v. *Pratt* [1911] A.C. 394.

[96] *Macarthur* v. *Lawson* (1877) 4 R. 1134; *Hillas* v. *Arcos* (1931) 36 Com. Cas. 353; *Foley* v. *Classique Coaches* [1934] 2 K.B. 1.

[97] Sale of Goods Act 1979; s. 8(2), 'Where the price is not determined ... the buyer must pay a reasonable price': *Glen* v. *Roy* (1882) 10 R. 239 (rent).

[98] (1771) Mor. 14241. In *Steel's Trs.* v. *Bradley Homes (Scotland Ltd.*, 1972 S.C. 48 at p. 55, Lord Dunpark suggested that *Sword* might have been a 'snatching at a bargain' case similar to *Steuart's Trs.* v. *Hart* (1875) 3 R. 192 (see para. 9.16, *supra*).

[99] (1859) 21 D. 957.

later authority. Where a contractor made an error in his private calculations and submitted a tender which was lower than it should have been he was held bound when the tender was accepted.[1] On the other hand where the contract is to be by schedule rates and the miscalculation is obvious on the face of the offer the parties will be taken to have contracted on the basis of the correctly calculated sum.[2]

9.24 **Shared Error.**[3]—Where both parties contract under the same mistaken belief there is common error and the contract is void.[4] In some cases, however, error need not be pleaded. Where, for example, specific goods have, unknown to the parties, perished at the time when a contract for their sale is made then the contract is void.[5] It may sometimes be difficult to distinguish the case where the continued existence of the thing was known to be doubtful, and each took the risk.[6] A mutual discharge of claims may be re-opened on proof of an error common to both, whether in fact or in law, which had induced the settlement.[7] And it would appear that even in the case where a thing sold has been examined by the purchaser, the contract may be void if it proceeded on the assumption, common to both, that the thing had some specific and essential quality which it did not in fact possess.[8] But—though the point may not be settled beyond question—it is conceived that a sale will stand though the article turns out to have a value which neither seller nor purchaser suspected, as in the case of the sale of a book afterwards discovered to be valuable as a rarity.[9] It has been held that a contract under which a director received compensation for loss of office could not be reduced on the ground that it was entered into when both parties were in ignorance of the fact that the director had been guilty of conduct which would have justified his dismissal.[10] When a contract is affected by common error neither party is entitled to insist on a contract such as would probably have been made if the true facts had been known.[11] Where both parties proceed on the basis of different mistaken beliefs, the error may be termed mutual. Mutual error produces

[1] *Seaton Brick Co.* v. *Mitchell* (1900) 2 F. 550. See also *Steel's Trs.* v. *Bradley Homes (Scotland) Ltd., supra.*
[2] *Jamieson* v. *McInnes* (1887) 15 R. 17; *Wilkie* v. *Hamilton Lodging House Co.* (1902) 4 F. 951.
[3] In earlier editions of this work, the heading of this section was 'Mutual Error.' In the last edition this was changed to 'Common Error.'
[4] *Grieve* v. *Wilson* (1828) 6 S. 454, affd. (1838) 6 W. & S. 543; *Hamilton* v. *Western Bank* (1861) 23 D. 1033.
[5] Sale of Goods Act 1979, s. 6. Note also *Couturier* v. *Hastie* (1865) 5 H.L.C. 673 and *Associated Japanese Bank* v. *Crédit du Nord S.A.* [1989] 1 W.L.R. 255.
[6] *Pender-Small* v. *Kinloch; Trs.,* 1917 S.C. 307.
[7] *Dickson* v. *Halbert* (1854) 16 D. 586; *Ross* v. *Mackenzie* (1842) 5 D. 151.
[8] *Edgar* v. *Hector,* 1912 S.C. 348. The report does not bring out clearly that both parties were in error as to the nature of the chairs in question.
[9] *Dawson* v. *Muir* (1851) 13 D. 843.
[10] *Bell* v. *Lever Bros.* [1932] A.C. 161.
[11] *Pender-Small* v. *Kinloch's Trs.,* 1917 S.C. 307.

dissensus. It may be simpler in many cases to rely on the rules relating to contract formation instead of pleading error.[12]

9.25 Error in Expression.—An error in expression occurs where parties, having reached an agreement in one form, further agree that the agreement should be recorded in another form, and the agreement is not accurately expressed in that second form. The most common case arises when, after a written contract is duly signed, it is discovered that owing to a mistake of an amanuensis it does not represent the agreement which the parties had made. Thus where a clerk was told to draw up an agreement between an hotel-keeper and his manager, and by an arithmetical mistake, which was not discovered until both parties had signed the agreement, gave the manager a larger share of the profits than had been agreed to, it was held that the mistake might be proved by witnesses and corrected.[13] Where the parties entered into missives for the sale of a farm and the subsequent disposition, owing to a mistake on the part of the solicitors concerned, conveyed, not only the farm, but also an adjacent coal-mine, it was held that the disposition could be reduced.[14] Accounts, docqueted as correct, may be challenged on the ground of arithmetical errors.[15] Where a document intended to express or give effect to an agreement fails to express accurately the common intention of the parties to the agreement at the date when it was made, the court now has a statutory power to rectify the document in any manner that it may specify in order to give effect to that intention.[16] In exercising this power the court may have regard to all relevant evidence, whether written or oral.[17] Any other document intended to express or give effect to an agreement which is defectively expressed by reason of the defect in the original document may also be rectified.[18] But where the parties' intentions differ as to the agreement reached, neither missives nor disposition may be rectified.[19] A rectified document shall have effect as if it had always been so rectified[20] and, where a document recorded in the Register of Sasines is rectified and the rectification order is likewise recorded, the document is to be treated as having been always recorded as rectified.[21] A rectification order is not to be made if the rectification would adversely affect to a material extent the interests of a person, other than a party to the agreement, who has acted or refrained from acting in reliance on the

[12] *Came* v. *City of Glasgow Friendly Society*, 1933 S.C. 69.
[13] *Krupp* v. *Menzies*, 1907 S.C. 903.
[14] *Anderson* v. *Lambie*, 1954 S.C. (H.L.) 43.
[15] *McLaren* v. *Liddell's Trs.* (1862) 24 D. 577.
[16] Law Reform (Misc. Prov.) (Scotland) Act 1985, s. 8.
[17] s. 8(2).
[18] s. 8(3).
[19] *Angus* v. *Bryden, supra.*
[20] s.8(4).
[21] s.8(5).

terms of the document or on the title sheet of an interest in land registered in the Land Register of Scotland, being an interest to which the document relates, with the result that his position has been affected to a material extent.[22]

IV. EXTORTION[23]

9.26   **Force or Fear.**[24]—It is probably the law that a contract induced by violence, or by threats sufficient to overcome the fortitude of a reasonable man, is void,[25] with an exception in the case of a bill of exchange, which is merely voidable, and may be enforced by a holder who can establish affirmatively that he gave value for the bill without notice of any objection.[26] Threats need not be of actual physical violence; an allegation by a workman of threatened loss of employment has been held relevant.[27] But threats of steps which the party may lawfully and warrantably take, such as proceedings in bankruptcy, or under the former law, imprisonment for debt, do not invalidate a payment or security thereby induced,[28] though they fall under the general rule of force and fear if used to extort consent to some independent contract.[29] And an obligation granted by a party who had been imprisoned under irregular diligence was reduced.[30] When a payment or promissory note is given in order to avoid a prosecution it is valid if it is given merely as repayment of what the giver has stolen.[31] The case of payment for the same purpose by a third party is more doubtful,[32] and it is probably settled that any payment or obligation extending beyond reimbursement of money stolen cannot be defended.[33] Threats of violence or injury to near relations have the same legal effect as threats to the party himself.[34] Threats by someone who is not a party to the contract may render the contract ineffectual in a question with a

[22] s.9.

[23] Since consent may be extorted in different ways, the generic term 'extortion' is thought preferable: see *Priestnell* v. *Hutchison* (1857) 19 D. 495, *per* Lord Deas at p. 499; *Hislop* v. *Dickson Motors (Forres)*, 1978 S.L.T. (Notes) 73. Note also Stair, I, ix, 8.

[24] Earlier editions of this work, have employed the heading 'Force and Fear' following Morison's *Dictionary*, *s.v. Vis et Metus*. Stair I, ix, 8 refers to force or fear indicating the possibility of separate pleas.

[25] Stair, I ix, 8; Erskine, III, i, 16. Cases in Morison, *s.v. Vis et Metus*.

[26] Bills of Exchange Act 1882, ss. 29, 30, 38.

[27] *Gow* v. *Henry* (1899) 2 F. 48. See *Pao On* v. *Lau Yiu Long* [1980] A.C. 614.

[28] *Ker* v. *Edgar* (1698) Mor. 16503; *Rudman* v. *Jay*, 1908 S.C. 552, opinion of Lord Ardwall; *Hunter* v. *Bradford Property Trust*, 1977 S.L.T. (Notes) 33; *Hislop* v. *Dickson Motors (Forres)*, 1978 S.L.T. (Notes) 73.

[29] *Nisbet* v. *Stewart* (1708) Mor. 16512.

[30] *McIntosh* v. *Chalmers* (1883) 11 R. 8.

[31] *Lamson Co.* v. *MacPhail*, 1914 S.C. 73.

[32] *Ferrier* v. *Mackenzie* (1899) 1 F. 597.

[33] *Canison* v. *Marshall* (1764) 6 Paton 759; *Kaufman* v. *Gerson* [1904] 1 K.B. 591; opinion of Lord Salvesen in *Lamson Co.* v. *MacPhail, supra*.

[34] Bell, *Prin.*, § 12.

party to the contract who is not responsible for, and not aware of, the threats.[35] Obligations granted by a married woman for her husband's debt may be reduced if they were obtained by threats used by the other party or by the husband; it is not sufficient that they were granted out of affection for him, and in order to save him from proceedings in bankruptcy.[36]

9.27 **Extortion.**—Except in the case of loans of money there is no authority at common law for holding it to be a relevant ground for the reduction of a contract that its terms are extortionate, even with the addition of averments that the defender had greatly the advantage of the pursuer in respect of education or business experience.[37] In the case of loans, until 1854, when they were finally repealed, the usury laws limited the rate of interest which might lawfully be charged. It has twice been held at common law that a loan by a moneylender might be challenged where the circumstances were exceptional and the borrower a person inexperienced in business.[38] The English law as to bargains with expectant heirs is not recognised in Scotland.[39] English law accepts that a contract may be avoided if entered into under 'economic duress': mere commercial pressure will not suffice.[40] It may be that extortion, a concept which encompasses not only force and fear but also 'pressure of a certain degree' could be applied to cover cases involving economic duress.[41]

V. FACILITY AND CIRCUMVENTION

9.28 **Facility and Circumvention.**—A contract (or disposition) may be avoided on the ground of facility and circumvention.[42] Three things must be proved: (a) facility; (b) lesion; and (c) circumvention.[43] These criteria need not be given equal weight: so where the facility is serious

---

[35] *Cassie* v. *Fleming* (1632) Mor. 10279; *Trustee Savings Bank* v. *Balloch*, 1983 S.L.T. 240; *cf. Stewart Brothers* v. *Keddie* (1889) 7 S.L.T. 92, *per* Lord Trayner at p. 93.

[36] *Priestnell* v. *Hutcheson* (1857) 19 D. 495.

[37] *Cal. Ry.* v. *N.B. Ry.* (1881) 8 R. (H.L.) 23, opinion of Lord Blackburn; *Wood* v. *N.B. Ry.* (1891) 18 R. (H.L.) 27; *Mathieson* v. *Hawthorne* (1899) 1 F. 468. The statutory provisions as to extortionate credit bargains are treated in para. 18.25, *infra*.

[38] *Young* v. *Gordon* (1896) 23 R. 419; *Gordon* v. *Stephens* (1902) 9 S.L.T. 397.

[39] *McKirdy* v. *Anstruther* (1839) 1 D. 855.

[40] *North Shipping Co. Ltd.* v. *Hyundai Construction Co. Ltd.* [1979] Q.B. 705; *Pao On* v. *Lau Yiu Long* [1980] A.C. 614; *Universe Tankships Inc. of Monrovia* v. *International Transport Worker's Federation* [1983] A.C. 366; *Alec Lobb (Garages) Ltd.* v. *Total Oil G.B. Ltd.* [1985] 1 All E.R. 303; *Atlas Express Ltd.* v. *Kafco (Importers & Distributors) Ltd.* [1989] Q.B. 833.

[41] *Hislop* v. *Dickson Motors (Forres)*, *supra*, *per* Lord Maxwell at p. 75. On the correct conceptual basis for the doctrine of economic duress in Scots law see Thompson, 1985 S.L.T. (News) 85 and, in response, McKendrick, 1985 S.L.T. (News) 277.

[42] *Gall* v. *Bird* (1855) 17 D. 1027.

[43] *Mackay* v. *Campbell*, 1967 S.C. (H.L.) 53; *Gibson's Exr.* v. *Anderson*, 1925 S.C. 774; *McGilivray* v. *Gilmartin*, 1986 S.L.T. 89; *Wheelans* v. *Wheelans*, 1986 S.L.T. 164.

and the lesion considerable, circumvention may be little more than a matter of inference.[44] 'Facility' means mental weakness (but not insanity) and may be attributable to age, grief, or illness. Alcoholic overindulgence which stops short of inebriation might render one facile. 'Lesion' simply means harm or loss. Circumvention is the most problematic aspect of the plea. In *Mackay* v. *Campbell*,[45] it was indicated that deceit or dishonesty had to be shown: which suggests that proof of fraud is necessary. That case may be contrasted with *Gibson's Executor* v. *Anderson*[46] in which the need to show fraud was rejected. It may be that the facts of the first case are special and that the general rule is that fraud need not be shown.[47]

VI. UNDUE INFLUENCE

9.29 So far as contracts are concerned,[48] undue influence involves neither fraud nor deceit nor coercion. It is the abuse or exploitation of the confidence or trust reposed by one party in another.[49] At one time, the relationships to which the doctrine might be applied were restricted but this is no longer the case.[50] The same facts may be capable of sustaining a plea of facility and circumvention as well as one of undue influence.[51] Undue influence renders a contract voidable.[52] There has been no case where a contract has been held to be voidable where the influence exercised was in genuine devotion to the interests of the person influenced and not in the interests of the other party to the agreement.[53]

Further Reading

Gloag, *Contract* (2nd ed., 1929).
McBryde, *The Law of Contract in Scotland* (1987) Chs. 9–12;
Smith, *Short Commentary* (1962), Ch. 37;
Walker, *Law of Contracts* (2nd ed., 1985), Chs. 14–15.

---

[44] *Mackay* v. *Campbell, supra.*
[45] *Supra*, note 37.
[46] *Ibid.* Note also *Anderson* v. *The Beacon Fellowship*, 1922 S.L.T. 111.
[47] McBryde, para. 11–23.
[48] It may be otherwise with wills. See *Weir* v. *Grace* (1899) 2 F. (H.L.) 80 and para. 43.2, *infra.*
[49] *Gray* v. *Binny* (1879) 7 R. 332; *Forbes* v. *Forbes' Trs.*, 1957 S.C. 325; *Honeyman's Exrs.* v. *Sharp*, 1978 S.C. 223.
[50] *Honeyman's Exrs.* v. *Sharp, supra* (an art dealer).
[51] *Honeyman's Exrs.* v. *Sharp*; *Anderson* v. *The Beacon Fellowship, supra.*
[52] *Logan's Trs.* v. *Wood* (1855) 12 R. 1094; *Gray* v. *Binny, supra.*
[53] *Forbes* v. *Forbes' Trs.*, 1957 S.C. 325; but see *Allan* v. *Allan*, 1961 S.C. 200.

CHAPTER 10

PACTA ILLICITA AND UNFAIR CONTRACT TERMS

10.1 Illegality.—An agreement may fail in obligatory effect because it is illegal, or because its object was the furtherance of some illegal purpose. The main grounds of illegality in contract may be divided into three classes—(a) When the object of the parties was to secure a result which is either criminal or generally recognised as immoral; (b) When the particular contract is forbidden by some positive rule, either of common law or statute; (c) When the particular method of contracting is prohibited. Instances of the various forms of illegality will appear in the sequel; for the present it may be enough to mention, in the first class, an agreement to secure the commission of a crime;[1] in the second, an unqualified agreement not to exercise a particular trade;[2] in the third, a sale where the subjects sold are estimated by other than weights and measures lawful for use for trade,[3] or a transaction requiring, yet lacking, a Government licence.[4]

10.2 Effects of Illegality.—To whichever class a particular contract may belong the contract is so far void that it cannot be directly enforced, nor can the party who refuses to carry it out be subjected in damages. It is the duty of the court to take notice of the illegality if it appears *ex facie* of the contract, although neither party may plead it.[5]

10.3 *Turpis Causa*.—Further results depend upon the nature of the illegality. To cases of the first class the maxims *in turpi causa melior est conditio defendentis* (in a claim arising out of an immoral consideration, the position of the defender is stronger) and *ex turpi causa non oritur actio* (no right of action arises from an immoral consideration) apply, with the result that even if the contract has been carried out the court will take no cognisance of the relations of the parties. The party who has happened to profit, though only by disregarding the terms to which he has agreed, may keep what he has secured; the party on whom a loss

---

[1] para. 10.11.
[2] para. 10.13.
[3] *Cuthbertson* v. *Lowes* (1870) 8 M. 1073.
[4] See *O'Toole* v. *Whiterock Quarry Co.*, 1937 S.L.T. 521.
[5] *Hamilton* v. *McLaughlan* (1908) 16 S.L.T. 341. See *North-Western Salt Co.* v. *Electrolytic Alkali Co.* [1914] A.C. 461; *Rawlings* v. *General Trading Co.* [1921] 1 K.B. 635.

has fallen cannot enforce an agreement to share it. In a question between a thief and a resetter the law cannot interfere. So when a director and the manager of a company entered into a contract, held to be a conspiracy to defraud the shareholders, by which a certain sum should be voted to the manager and he should pay a bonus to the director, the court declined to entertain an action for the bonus.[6] When a joint adventure, definitely illegal under an Order in Council, had resulted in a loss, the party on whom the loss had happened to light had no right to insist that the other should pay his share.[7]

To the general rule that the court will not interfere in a case involving *turpis causa* there are certain exceptions.

10.4 Parties not in *In Pari Delicto*.—While it is no objection that the defender is pleading and taking advantage of his own illegal act, there are certain cases where the parties, though both involved in illegality, are not regarded as equally blameworthy—are not *in pari delicto*. If so, the one less blameworthy may enforce rights incidentally arising under the contract. This rule is illustrated in our reports only in cases of collusive agreements in bankruptcy. While any secret payment by a bankrupt to an individual creditor is a *pactum illicitum*,[8] yet as the creditor who exacts and the bankrupt who may really be forced to accede are *in pari delicto* the trustee may recover what the bankrupt has paid, whereas the creditor cannot enforce an obligation to pay.[9]

10.5 Illegality in Interests of Special Class.—If it is held that the illegality of a contract is recognised or enacted for the benefit of a particular class, a member of that class may found upon it.[10] But this exception has very narrow limits; in general the illegality of a contract rests on the interests of the State, not of any particular class.[11]

10.6 Money Demanded Back Before Purpose Effected.—It has been decided in England that money paid in advance for an illegal purpose may be recovered if demanded before the illegal purpose has been carried out. So where money has been deposited with a stakeholder to await the result of an illegal bet it may be recovered at any time before it has actually been paid to the winner.[12] On this rule there is no decision in Scotland; and the limits of the English decisions are ill-defined. It is hardly conceivable that the man who has paid in advance for the

---

[6] *Laughland* v. *Millar* (1904) 6 F. 413; *Scott* v. *Brown* [1892] 2 Q.B. 724.
[7] *Stewart* v. *Gibson* (1840) 1 Robinson 260.
[8] *Farmers' Mart* v. *Milne*, 1914 S.C. (H.L.) 84; *Munro* v. *Rothfield*, 1920 S.C. (H.L.) 165.
[9] *Macfarlane* v. *Nicoll* (1864) 3 M. 237.
[10] *Phillips* v. *Blackhurst*, 1912 2 S.L.T. 254.
[11] *Mahmoud* v. *Ispahani* [1921] 2 K.B. 716.
[12] *Burge* v. *Ashley* [1900] 1 Q.B. 744; *Hermann* v. *Charlesworth* [1905] 2 K.B. 123.

commission of a theft could in any circumstances maintain an action for the recovery of his payment.[13]

10.7   Illegal Conditions Separable.—If a contract as a whole is lawful the mere fact that one clause involves an illegality does not necessarily taint the other provisions so as to affect their enforceability. The general test is whether the pursuer can maintain his case without founding on the illegal provision.[14] Thus while in a contract for the supply of goods a clause providing for the suspension of deliveries during war is contrary to public policy and illegal, the insertion of such a clause does not in any way affect the validity of the contract during peace.[15]

10.8   Contracts Merely Prohibited.—Contracts where the illegality does not consist in the object of the contract being to secure an illegal or immoral result, but merely in the fact that the particular contract, or method of contracting, is prohibited (*i.e.* cases falling within the second and third heads mentioned in para. 10.1) are at one with contracts involving *turpis causa* in respect that they cannot be enforced, but differ in respect that the court will not refuse to give effect to the rights of the parties when the contract has been carried into effect. So where there was a contract for the sale of potatoes calculated by a Scots measure, a method of contracting declared by statute to be 'void and null,' and the potatoes were actually delivered, it was held that, although the contract could not be enforced in defiance of the statute, still, as there was 'no turpitude in a man selling his potatoes by the Scots and not by the imperial acre,' the buyer was bound to pay the market price;[16] but this does not hold where the contract is actually prohibited and illegal.[17] While an insurance by a party who has no insurable interest is by statute 'null and void to all intents and purposes whatsoever,' yet if the insurance company has chosen to pay, the court will decide questions between competing claimants for the money.[18]

10.9   Rights of Third Parties.—As a general rule an illegal contract cannot be founded on even by third parties who have no notice of the illegality. Thus no one can acquire a title to stolen goods.[19] A bond for the price of goods which had been smuggled was held to be unenforceable even

---

[13] See *Berg* v. *Sadler & Moore* [1937] 2 K.B. 158; *Bigos* v. *Bousted* [1951] 1 All E.R. 92.

[14] See opinion of Lord Dunedin, *Farmers' Mart* v. *Milne*, 1914 S.C. (H.L.) 84. *Cf. Fegan* v. *Dept. of Health*, 1935 S.C. 823, where, however, the dissenting judgment of Lord Fleming seems correct.

[15] *Zinc Corporation* v. *Hirsch* [1916] 1 K.B. 541. See also *Kearney* v. *Whitehaven Colliery* [1893] 1 Q.B. 700.

[16] *Cuthbertson* v. *Lowes* (1870) 8 M. 1073.

[17] *Jamieson* v. *Watt's Tr.*, 1950 S.C. 265.

[18] *Hadden* v. *Bryden* (1899) 1 F. 710. The contrary has been decided in England, *Re London* v. *County Re–Insurance Co.* [1922] 2 Ch. 67.

[19] Bell, *Prin.*, § 527.

by a bona fide assignee.[20] There is statutory exception to this in the case of bills and notes granted for an illegal consideration.[21]

10.10 Statutory Illegality.—In endeavouring to indicate what contracts are illegal a distinction may be made between contracts rendered illegal by statute and contracts illegal at common law.[22] As a general rule, where a statute limits freedom of contract it does so either by declaring a particular contract or method of contracting to be void,[23] or by imposing a penalty on the persons who contract.[24] A contract declared by statute to be void can never be enforced, although, as has been explained, if the only objection is the statutory provision, the court will give effect to rights arising when the contract is performed.[25] If, without declaring a contract to be void, a statute imposes a penalty on the persons who enter into it, it is always a question of the construction of the particular statute whether or not avoidance of the contract is implied.[26] It is a strong argument against avoidance in cases where the method of contracting rather than the contract is penalised, that the penalty may be incurred by mere inadvertence.[27] Where the penalty is imposed for failure to stamp a contract the presumption is that the provision is merely for revenue purposes, and that the contract may be enforced.[28] Subject to these provisos, the general rule is that where a contract is subjected to a penalty its illegality and consequent avoidance is implied,[29] except in cases where the penalty is the deprivation of an office.[30] A defender who pleads statutory illegality, *e.g.* in defence of an action of payment for work carried out, must however relevantly aver and prove that the work was done unlawfully.[31]

10.11 Illegal at Common Law.—In contracts at common law there is a general, though not an exact, distinction between contracts objectionable on moral grounds and contracts contrary to public policy. In the former class are contracts for the commission of an act criminal at common law, involving a fraud on third parties,[32] or sexual immorality, with the exception of a provision made for a mistress after sexual

---

[20] *Nisbet's Creditors* v. *Robertson* (1791) Mor. 9554.
[21] Bills of Exchange Act 1882, ss. 30, 38.
[22] Gloag, *Contract*, p. 549.
[23] *e.g.* Unfair Contract Terms Act 1977, ss. 16, 19, 20, 21, 23. See also Sex Discrimination Act 1975, s. 77; Race Relations Act 1976, s. 72. As to exchange contracts, see *Mansouri* v. *Singh* [1986] 2 All E.R. 619.
[24] *e.g.* Mock Auctions Act 1961.
[25] *Cuthbertson* v. *Lowes* (1870) 8 M. 1073.
[26] *Whiteman* v. *Sadler* [1910] A.C. 514, *per* Lord Dunedin.
[27] *Whiteman* v. *Sadler, supra, per* Lord Mersey.
[28] *Learoyd* v. *Bracken* [1894] 1 Q.B. 114.
[29] *Jamieson* v. *Watt's Tr.*, 1950 S.C. 265.
[30] *Drysdale* v. *Nairne* (1835) 13 S. 348; *Aberdeen Ry.* v. *Blaikie* (1851) 14 D. 66, revd. on other grounds (1854) 1 Macq. 461.
[31] *Designers & Decorators (Scotland)* v. *Ellis*, 1957 S.C. (H.L.) 69.
[32] *Laughland* v. *Millar* (1904) 6 F. 413.

intercourse has ceased.[33] The rule extends beyond contracts where the direct consideration is the commission of a criminal, fraudulent or immoral act, and reaches cases where the contract is, to the knowledge of the parties, intended to further criminality or immorality. So where a brougham was hired to a prostitute 'as a part of her display, to attract men,' the hire could not be recovered.[34] A similar decision was given with regard to the rent of a house occupied, to the landlord's knowledge, by persons living in immoral relations.[35] The doctrine of public policy, as a ground for the avoidance of contracts, was at one time very loosely and widely applied in the English courts, reaching perhaps its culminating point in *Egerton* v. *Earl Brownlow*,[36] where it was held that a bequest to a peer, dependent on his obtaining a higher rank, involved a condition contrary to public policy, as tending to induce him to misuse his position as a legislator in order to obtain the higher rank. More recently, on the principle that it is a cardinal object of public policy that contracts should be observed, opinions have been expressed that the objection is open only where there is a direct precedent or plain analogy.[37] The mere fact that a direct precedent is forthcoming is not conclusive. It is open to the answer that instructed opinion may have altered on the point.[38]

10.12 **Illustrations of Public Policy.**—Among contracts which are illegal as contrary to public policy are included contracts interfering with the foreign policy of the State, such as a contract with an enemy State or with alien enemies.[39] On the same principle it is clear law in England that contracts involving the violation of the laws of a friendly State are unenforceable.[40] Contracts for smuggling;[41] for interfering with the free exercise of his duties by the holder of a public office[42] or member of a representative body;[43] for the employment of private influence to secure advantages from the Government;[44] for the evasion of legislative provisions limiting or regulating the sale of certain commodities;[45] for

[33] Bell, *Prin.*, § 37; *Webster* v. *Webster's Tr.* (1886) 14 R. 90.

[34] *Pearce* v. *Brooks* (1886) L.R. 1 Ex. 213.

[35] *Upfill* v. *Wright* [1911] 1 K.B. 506. But see *Heglibiston Establishments* v. *Heyman* (1977) 36 P. & C.R. 351.

[36] (1853) 4 H.L.C. 1.

[37] Per Lord Watson, *Nordenfelt* v. *Maxim Nordenfelt Gun Co.* [1894] A.C. 535; but see *McCaig's Trs.* v. *Kirk-Session of Lismore*, 1915 S.C. 426.

[38] *Bowman* v. *Secular Society* [1917] A.C. 406.

[39] para. 4.6, *supra.*

[40] *Ralli* v. *Compania Naviera* [1920] 2 K.B. 287; *Regazonni* v. *K.C. Sethia (1944] Ltd.* [1958] A.C. 301. On the other hand, income tax is payable on the fruits of such an adventure: see *Lindsay* v. *Inland Revenue*, 1933 S.C. 33.

[41] Bell, *Prin.*, § 42.

[42] *Henderson* v. *Mackay* (1832) 11 S. 225.

[43] *Hoggan* v. *Wardlaw* (1735) 1 Paton 148; *Amalgamated Ry. Servants* v. *Osborne* [1910] A.C. 87.

[44] *Stewart* v. *Earl of Galloway* (1752) Mor. 9465; *Montefiore* v. *Menday Motor Co.* [1918] 2 K.B. 241.

[45] *Trevalion* v. *Blanche*, 1919 S.C. 617; *Eisen* v. *McCabe*, 1920 S.C. (H.L.) 146.

suppression of information which might lead to a conviction of crime,[46] are all illegal as contrary to public policy. An agreement to indemnify a person against liability for defamation is not illegal unless the person knew that the matter published was defamatory and did not reasonably believe that he had a good defence.[47]

10.13   Restrictive Covenants.—As a general rule contracts which involve an undue interference with personal liberty are void as being oppressive. But this rule is qualified to the extent that it may be lawful, if certain conditions are satisfied, to secure freedom from competition by contracts, usually termed restrictive covenants, by which a party undertakes not to carry on a particular trade or profession. The test which is applied to decide whether restrictive agreements of this nature can be enforced is whether the agreement is reasonable as between the parties,[48] and is consistent with the interests of the public.[49] The court has to ascertain what were the legitimate interests of the party in whose favour the restriction was imposed which he was entitled to protect and then to see whether the restriction was more than adequate for that purpose.[50] The practical effects of the restriction, rather than its form, are to be examined.[51] In all cases it is probably necessary that there should be some limit, either in point of area or in point of time. Subject to this, where the seller of the goodwill of a business has agreed that in future he will not carry on a similar business in competition with the buyer of the goodwill, the only tenable objection to the restriction is that it is wider than is required in the interests of the business it is designed to protect. Thus while a world-wide restriction (limited as to time) was sustained in the case of a maker of cannon,[52] a restriction within the United Kingdom was held to be far too wide, and consequently unenforceable, in the case of the business of a local carrier.[53] Where the covenant is contained in a partnership agreement the fact that it is binding on each of the partners is a factor to be taken

---

[46] *Howard* v. *Odhams Press* [1938] 1 K.B. 1.

[47] Defamation Act 1952, s. 11.

[48] See *Nordenfelt* v. *Maxim Nordenfelt Gun Co.* [1894] A.C. 535; *Mason* v. *Provident Clothing Co.* [1913] A.C. 724; *Morris* v. *Saxelby* [1916] 1 A.C. 688; *Fitch* v. *Dewes* [1921] 2 A.C. 158; *Vancouver Malt and Sake Brewing Co.* v. *Vancouver Breweries Ltd.* [1934] A.C. 181. See also Gloag, *Contract*, pp. 569 *et seq.*

[49] *Vancouver Brewing Co.*, *supra*, *per* Lord Macmillan at p. 189; *George Walker & Co.* v. *Jann*, 1991 S.L.T. 771.

[50] *Bridge* v. *Deacons* [1984] 1 A.C. 705. *Cf. Dallas McMillan & Sinclair* v. *Simpson*, 1989 S.L.T. 454, where a 20-mile radius ban on a solicitor from acting for anyone, even persons who had never been clients of his old firm, was found to be unreasonable.

[51] *Stenhouse Australia* v. *Phillips* [1974] A.C. 391. The cases indicate clearly that the courts do not adopt a literal approach to the interpretation of restraints. Faced with two interpretations, one extreme (and probably absurd given the context), the other normal (*i.e.* easily referable to the facts) the latter interpretation will be chosen: *Scottish Farmers' Dairy Co.* v. *McGhee, infra; Bluebell Apparel Ltd.* v. *Dickinson, infra; Home Counties Dairies Ltd.* v. *Skilton* [1970] 1 W.L.R. 526.

[52] *Nordenfelt* v. *Maxim Nordenfelt Gun Co.* [1894] A.C. 535.

[53] *Dumbarton Steamboat Co.* v. *Macfarlane* (1899) 1 F. 993.

into account in determining whether it is reasonable between the parties.[54] Where a servant or apprentice has agreed that after leaving his present employer he will not take up employment with a competitor or set up business on his own account the limits of freedom of contract are much narrower. The result of the decisions in the House of Lords has been judicially summarised as follows: 'While a purchaser of the goodwill of a business may properly protect himself by covenant from the competition of his vendor, it is not permissible for an employer to protect himself merely from the competition of his former servant after his service has terminated. It is permissible for the employer by covenant to protect his trade or professional secrets, and to protect himself also against his clients being enticed away by his former assistant; in other words to protect his connection.'[55] So restrictions designed to protect business contacts, where an employee acquires influence over customers (including former and possibly even future customers) have been sustained.[56] A world-wide restriction for a period of two years has been upheld.[57] Restrictions on disclosure of a secret manufacturing process, confidential information regarding customer lists, or business pricing policy may be permitted.[58] When it was proved that the object of a restriction, imposed on a film actor, was not to protect a business but to obtain a hold upon the actor by rendering it difficult for him to obtain other employment, it was held that he was entitled to disregard it.[59]

The party who proposes to enforce a restrictive covenant must have an interest to enforce it, and cannot therefore do so if he has ceased to carry on, or has parted with, the business it was designed to protect.[60] He cannot enforce a restriction if he is himself in a material breach of contract, as where the servant restricted is unjustifiably dismissed.[61] A restriction imposed in a contract of service is not assignable.[62] If imposed on the seller of a business it may be assigned with that business, unless it appears that the restriction was undertaken solely in favour of the purchaser.[63] It is not settled whether a third party has a

[54] *Bridge* v. *Deacons, supra.* As to partnerships see *Trego* v. *Hunt* [1896] A.C. 7; *Whitehill* v. *Bradford* [1952] 1 Ch. 236; *Anthony* v. *Rennie*, 1981 S.L.T. (Notes) 11 (O.H.); *Kerr* v. *Morris* [1986] 3 All E.R. 217.
[55] *Per* Younger L.J., *Fitch* v. *Dewes* [1920] 2 Ch. at p. 185; [1921] 2 A.C. 158.
[56] *Scottish Farmers' Dairy Co.* v. *McGhee*, 1933 S.C. 148; *Stenhouse Australia* v. *Phillips* [1974] A.C. 391; *Rentokil* v. *Kramer.* 1986 S.L.T. 114. As to former customers, see *G.W. Plowman & Son Ltd.* v. *Ash* [1964] 2 All E.R. 10. As to future customers with whom contact was established prior to departure, see *Gledhow Autoparts* v. *Delaney* [1965] 3 All E.R. 288; *Rentokil* v. *Kramer, supra.*
[57] *Bluebell Apparel Ltd.* v. *Dickinson*, 1978 S.C. 16.
[58] *Commercial Plastics Ltd.* v. *Vincent* [1965] 1 Q.B. 623; *S.O.S. Bureau Ltd.* v. *Payne*, 1982 S.L.T. (Sh.Ct.) 33; *Faccenda Chicken Ltd.* v. *Fowler* [1987] Ch. 117. Restrictions on the disclosure of confidential information should indentify what is confidential: *Malden Timber Ltd.* v. *Leitch*, 1992 S.L.T. 757.
[59] *Hepworth Manufacturing Co.* v. *Ryott* [1920] 1 Ch. 1.
[60] *Berlitz Schools* v. *Duchene* (1903) 6 F. 181.
[61] *General Billposting Co.* v. *Atkinson* [1909] A.C. 118.
[62] *Berlitz Schools* v. *Duchene, supra.*
[63] *Rodger* v. *Herbertson*, 1909 S.C. 256.

title to maintain that a restrictive covenant is unenforceable.[64] If the restriction imposed is too wide it falls; the court will not enforce it within narrower limits.[65] But where there are two restrictions, one reasonable, the other oppressive, the contract may be regarded as separable, and the reasonable restriction enforced.[66] The effect of a term of a contract stating that the parties agree that a restraint is reasonable is unclear. It may be that such a term should be disregarded as an attempt to oust the jurisdiction of the courts.[67]

If a restraint is worded in a manner which prevents one party from setting up business on his own account, it will not apply to a rival company formed by that party and vice versa.[68]

10.14   Restraint of Trade.—Closely allied to the two kinds of restrictive covenant discussed above are those agreements which restrict a person's free exercise of his trade or business. Such agreements arise where manufacturers or merchants combine to regulate their trade relations, for instance by agreeing to restrict their output or to fix the selling price of a certain commodity.[69] While it was once the rule that contracts of this nature were contrary to public policy and, therefore, *pacta illicita*,[70] they are now regarded as a necessary part of commercial life. Such agreements are, at common law, legal and enforceable unless they involve a restriction on liberty greater than is necessary for the interest they are designed to protect, or their object is to raise wages or prices.[71] Again, the test in deciding whether any particular agreement is to be upheld, is the double standard of whether the agreement is reasonable as between the parties, and whether it is consistent with the public interest.[72] But in this case, where the parties themselves are regarded as

---

[64] *British Motor Trade Association* v. *Gray*, 1951 S.C. 586.

[65] *Dumbarton Steamboat Co.* v. *Macfarlane, supra.*

[66] *Mulvein* v. *Murray*, 1908 S.C. 528; *Attwood* v. *Lamont* [1920] 3 K.B. 571. *Mulvein* v. *Murray* may be contrasted with an Outer House decision, *Hinton & Higgs (U.K.) Ltd.* v. *Murphy*, 1989 S.L.T. 450. Here the contract provided that if the court considered the restrictions imposed to be unreasonable, but that they would be reasonable on deletion of some part or by reducing the period of the restraint, then the unreasonable part should be so deleted or amended. The Lord Ordinary described this as a contractual mechanism designed to operate on the occurrence of a particular event and declined to take the view that this was an attempt to have the contract rewritten by the court.

[67] *Hinton & Higgs (U.K.) Ltd.* v. *Murphy, supra, per* Lord Dervaird at p. 452.

[68] *WAC Ltd.* v. *Whillock*, 1990 S.L.T. 213; *Taylor* v. *Campbell*, 1926 S.L.T. 260.

[69] The categories of agreements in restraint of trade are not closed: see as to 'solus agreements,' *Petrofina (G.B.)* v. *Martin* [1966] Ch. 146, *per* Lord Denning M.R., at p. 169. See also *McIntyre* v. *Cleveland Petroleum Co.*, 1967 S.L.T. 95 (conditions contained in a back letter); *Esso Petroleum Co.* v. *Harper's Garage (Stourport)* [1968] A.C. 269; *A. Schroeder Music Publishing Co.* v. *Macaulay* [1974] 1 W.L.R. 1308 (exclusive services).

[70] *Barr* v. *Carr* (1766) Mor. 9564; *Corporation of Shoemakers* v. *Marshall* (1798) Mor. 9573; *Hilton* v. *Eckersley* (1855) 6 E. & B. 47; see dicta of Harman L.J., in *Petrofina (G.B.), supra*, at p. 175.

[71] *North-Western Salt Co.* v. *Electrolyte Alkali Co.* [1914] A.C. 461; *English Hop Growers* v. *Dering* [1928] 2 K.B. 174.

[72] *McEllistrim* v. *Ballymacelligott Co-operative Agricultural & Dairy Society* [1919] A.C. 548, *per* Lord Chancellor Birkenhead at p. 562.

being in an equal position of bargaining and the best judges of the fairness of the agreement, the court will not readily allow them to escape from their obligations by claiming that the agreement was unreasonable.[73] However, where a member of a co-operative union dedicated to a non-competitive system of trading was prohibited from trading in a certain area by a ruling of its union, it was held, on its resigning from the union, that the ruling ceased to be binding on it; it was unreasonable to suppose that on joining the union and agreeing to submit to its ruling, it intended to bind itself for all time, whether or not it continued to be a member.[74] The legality at common law of price-maintenance agreements, *i.e.* agreements by which an agent or retailer undertakes not to sell goods below list prices, seems to be established.[75]

The common law principles on this subject are now, however, relatively unimportant because of the far-reaching statutory provisions. The Restrictive Trade Practices Act 1976 provides for the registration of a wide range of restrictive trade agreements,[76] and for their judicial examination by a Restrictive Practices Court;[77] those agreements found to be contrary to the public interest are prohibited. The statutory presumption is that all such agreements are contrary to the public interest, unlike the common law where the onus of proving incompatibility with that interest lies on the party alleging it. The party seeking to justify the restrictive agreement must bring the restriction concerned within at least one of a list of circumstances, and also show that the agreement is not unreasonable having regard to those circumstances and any detriment which the agreement may cause to the public or third parties.[78] In addition, there is Article 85 of the Treaty of Rome which deals with restrictive agreements; agreements prohibited by the Article are automatically void. The Resale Prices Act 1976 prohibits individual resale price maintenance agreements,[79] except where such an agreement can be shown to be in the public interest. Where it can be shown to the satisfaction of the Restrictive Practices Court that without such an agreement in relation to a particular class of goods the public would suffer a detriment which would outweigh any detriment which would be caused by resale price maintenance, that court has power to make an order for the exemption of that class of goods.[80] The Act also

---

[73] *English Hop Growers, supra, per* Scrutton L.J. at p. 180.

[74] *Bellshill & Mossend Co-operative Society* v. *Dalziel Co-operative Society*, 1960 S.C. (H.L.) 64.

[75] *Dunlop Pneumatic Tyre Co.* v. *New Garage Co,* [1915] A.C. 79; *Palmolive Co.* v. *Freedman* [1928] 1 Ch. 264.

[76] s.1: Parts II, III. See also Restrictive Trade Practices Act 1977; *Sterling Financial Services Ltd.* v. *Johnston*, 1990 S.L.T. 111.

[77] Restrictive Practices Court Act 1976; Restrictive Trade Practices Act 1976, ss. 10, 19(1). See para. 2.8, *supra.*

[78] Restrictive Practices Act 1976, ss. 10, 19(1).

[79] Part II; the sanction afforded by the Act is a civil remedy, *e.g.* interdict or damages, for breach of statutory duty, rather than a criminal one.

[80] s. 14. See *Re Chocolate & Sugar Confectionery Reference* [1967] 1 W.L.R. 1175; *Re Footwear Reference (No. 2)* (1967) L.R. 6 R.P. 398; *Re Medicaments Reference (No. 2)* (1970) L.R. 7 R.P. 267.

contains a general prohibition of agreements or arrangements for the collective enforcement of conditions as to resale prices.[81]

10.15   Betting and Gaming.—Gaming contracts cannot be enforced. The ground of the refusal of action is not that they are illegal, but that they are *sponsiones ludicrae*, unworthy to occupy judicial time.[82] Accordingly, while the courts will not sustain an action for a bet, allow proof as to the result of a race,[83] or an action for recovery of money paid for losses, even on averments that the play was unfair,[84] yet if the result of a race or other contest be admitted the stakeholder must pay the winner,[85] and the court will entertain the question, who, according to the rules of the particular sport, is entitled to receive the prize.[86] A person employed to make bets, as he is not gambling but acting as an agent, may recover payments made on behalf of his principal.[87] The rights of parties under a joint adventure for gaming purposes may be judicially considered.[88] It has been held in the Outer House that money lent to pay gambling losses may be recovered.[89] The former English rule that an agreement to give time for payment or to refrain from making public the loser's default forms a new consideration on which direct action can be founded, is not law in Scotland,[90] and has now been abandoned in England.[91]

Certain forms of gaming are expressly made illegal by statute. Under the Betting, Gaming and Lotteries Act 1963, it is a criminal offence to use any premises, or to cause or knowingly permit any premises to be used, as a place for the purpose of betting,[92] or to loiter in or frequent a public place for that purpose;[93] contracts in connection with such a business are doubtless illegal. The Act legalises betting in certain closely regulated places, notably in licensed betting offices.[94] Under the Gaming Act 1968 most forms of gaming are closely regulated and certain conditions must be complied with; if gaming subject to the Act is

---

[81] Part I.

[82] *Wordsworth* v. *Pettigrew* (1799) M. 9524; *Knight* v. *Stott* (1892) 19 R. 959. The Betting, Gaming and Lotteries Act 1963 has not affected this principle: *Johnston* v. *T.W. Archibald*, 1966 S.L.T. (Sh.Ct.) 8.

[83] *O'Connell* v. *Russell* (1864) 3 Mor. 89; *Kelly* v. *Murphy*, 1940 S.C. 96 (football pool).

[84] *Paterson* v. *Macqueen* (1866) 4 M. 602.

[85] *Calder* v. *Stevens* (1871) 9 M. 1074. The promoter of a 'football pool' is not a stakeholder: *Wilson* v. *Murphy*, 1936 S.L.T. 564; *Kelly* v. *Murphy*, *supra*.

[86] *Graham* v. *Pollok* (1848) 10 D. 646, 11 D. 343.

[87] *Levy* v. *Jackson* (1903) 5 F. 1170.

[88] *Mollison* v. *Noltie* (1889) 16 R. 350; *Forsyth* v. *Czartowski*, 1961 S.L.T. (Sh.Ct.) 22.

[89] *Hopkins* v. *Baird*, 1920 2 S.L.T. 94. Not, on English authority, if the particular form of gaming is a criminal offence: *Moulis* v. *Owen* [1907] 1 K.B. 746. See, as to a cheque given in payment for chips in a gambling club, *Cumming* v. *Mackie*, 1973 S.C. 278.

[90] *Robertson* v. *Balfour*, 1938 S.C. 207.

[91] *Hill* v. *Wm. Hill (Park Lane) Ltd.* [1949] A.C. 350, a case which has no bearing on Scots law: Lord Normand, at p. 568.

[92] s. 1(1).

[93] s. 8.

[94] s. 9.

conducted otherwise than in accordance with these conditions, it is unlawful, the persons concerned will be committing an offence, and contracts in connection with that gaming will be unenforceable.[95] Under the Lotteries and Amusements Act 1976 all lotteries which do not constitute gaming are unlawful except as provided by the Act.[96] Those which are permitted under certain conditions are lotteries incidental to certain entertainments, 'private' lotteries and lotteries promoted by a society registered under the Act or promoted by a local authority.[97] The Act makes a saving for Art Unions,[98] but places restrictions on prize competitions conducted in or through newspapers.[99] A competition is a lottery although some skill is exercised, where the element of chance predominates.[1] Under the Financial Services Act 1986, section 63, betting on the movement of stocks and shares on a financial index, though clearly a form of wagering, is free from challenge.[2]

A bill, cheque or promissory note given for money lost at play is to be taken as given for an illegal consideration.[3] It cannot therefore be enforced, except by an indorsee who can prove that he has given value for it in good faith.[4] Where a bond is granted for money lost at cards it cannot be enforced against the granter even by a bona fide assignee, but the latter may recover what he has paid for it from the cedent, on the principle that everyone who assigns a debt gives implied warrandice *debitum subesse*.[5]

In the case of dealings on the stock exchange it has been held that if the forms of the exchange are observed, so that the one party is bound to deliver, the other to accept, stock, it is immaterial that the party never intended to take delivery but merely to pay or receive differences according to the rise and fall of the market. To bring the case within the category of gambling transactions, and therefore to preclude action on the contract, it must be proved that both parties regarded the sale-notes or other documents which passed between them as a mere form, not intended to have any legal effect. It is not enough that neither contemplated the actual transfer of the stock as a probable event.[6]

[95] *J.M. Allan (Merchandising) Ltd.* v. *Cloke* [1963] 2 Q.B. 340.
[96] s. 1; a lottery was not illegal at common law; *Clayton* v. *Clayton*, 1937 S.C. 619.
[97] ss. 3–6.
[98] s. 25(6); Art Unions Act 1846.
[99] s. 14.
[1] See *Strang* v. *Adair*, 1936 J.C. 56.
[2] *City Index Ltd.* v. *Leslie* [1991] 3 All E.R. 180.
[3] Gaming Act 1835, s. 1 (although there is doubt as to whether this applies to Scotland: *Cumming* v. *Mackie, supra*).
[4] Bills of Exchange Act 1882, s. 30.
[5] *Ferrier* v. *Graham's Trs.* (1828) 6 S. 818.
[6] *Shaw* v. *Cal. Ry.* (1890) 17 R. 466; *Universal Stock Exchange Co.* v. *Howat* (1891) 19 R. 128. For English authorities, which give more weight to the intention of the parties, see *Richards* v. *Starck* [1911] 1 K.B. 296, and *Woodward* v. *Wolfe* (1936) 53 T.L.R. 87 (speculation in cotton futures). See also Financial Services Act 1986, s. 63, Sched. 1, para. 33.

10.16   Unfair Terms.—The Unfair Contract Terms Act 1977 makes ineffectual
some types of contractual terms excluding or restricting liability for
breach of contract; in some cases the Act makes the term void; in other
cases, the term has no effect if it was not fair and reasonable to
incorporate it in the contract. It is not possible to evade the effect of the
Act by means of a secondary contract[7] or by a term applying, or
purporting to apply, a foreign law to the contract.[8] The following are
regarded as forms of exclusion or restriction:[9] (a) making the liability or
its enforcement subject to any restrictive or onerous conditions; (b)
excluding or restricting any right or remedy in respect of the liability, or
subjecting a person to any prejudice in consequence of his pursuing any
such right or remedy; (c) excluding or restricting any rule of evidence or
procedure; (d) excluding or restricting an obligation or duty implied by
law.[10] The Act has been extended to apply to non-contractual
disclaimers.[11] An agreement to submit any question to arbitration is not
an exclusion or restriction. The Act does not apply to international
contracts for the supply of goods.[12] The Act does not affect a
contractual provision which is authorised or required by the express
terms or necessary implication of an enactment or which, being made
with a view to compliance with an international agreement to which the
United Kingdom is a party, does not operate more restrictively than is
contemplated by the agreement.[13]

10.17   Contracts Affected.—The Act applies to any contract to the extent that
it—

   (a)   relates to the transfer of the ownership or possession of the
         goods from one person to another (with or without work
         having been done on them);
   (b)   constitutes a contract of service or apprenticeship;
   (c)   relates to services of whatever kind, including (without
         prejudice to the foregoing generality) carriage, deposit and
         pledge, care and custody, mandate, agency, loan and services
         relating to the use of land;
   (d)   relates to the liability of an occupier of land to persons
         entering upon or using that land;
   (e)   relates to a grant of any right or permission to enter upon or
         use land not amounting to an estate or interest in the land.[14]

---

[7] s. 23. See *Chapman* v. *Aberdeen Construction Group Ltd.*, 1991 G.W.D. 25–1446,
dealing with a term in a share option contract which purported to exclude rights under an
employment contract.

[8] s. 27(2).

[9] s. 25(3).

[10] s. 25(5).

[11] Law Reform (Miscellaneous Provisions) (Scotland) Act 1990, s. 68, amending Unfair
Contract Terms Act 1977, s.16(1). The amendment came into force on April 1, 1991: see
Law Reform (Miscellaneous Provisions) (Scotland) Act 1990 (Commencement No. 3)
Order 1991 (S.I. 1991 No. 330).

[12] s. 26.

[13] s. 29(1).

[14] s. 15(2).

Contracts of insurance and contracts relating to the formation, constitution or dissolution of any body corporate or unincorporated association or partnership are excepted.[15] It applies only to a limited extent to charter parties, and contracts of salvage or towage.[16] The Act does not affect the validity of any discharge or indemnity given by a person in consideration of the receipt by him of compensation in settlement of any claim which he had.[17]

10.18   Breach of Duty.—'Breach of Duty' is the breach of any obligation arising from the express or implied terms of a contract to take reasonable care or exercise reasonable skill in the performance of the contract or the breach of any common law duty to take reasonable care or exercise reasonable skill or the breach of the duty of reasonable care imposed by section 2(1) of the Occupiers' Liability (Scotland) Act 1960.[18] A term of a contract which purports to exclude or restrict liability for breach of duty arising in the course of any business or from the occupation of any premises used for business purposes of the occupier is void in any case where such exclusion or restriction is in respect of death or personal injury; in any other case the term has no effect if it was not fair and reasonable to incorporate the term in the contract.[19]

10.19   Unreasonable Exemptions.—The provision of the Act which has the widest effect applies to two types of terms in 'consumer contracts' and 'standard form contracts.' Terms in such contracts have no effect for the purpose of enabling a party to the contract—

(a)   who is in breach of a contractual obligation, to exclude or restrict any liability of his to the consumer or customer in respect of the breach;

(b)   in respect of a contractual obligation, to render no performance, or to render a performance substantially different from that which the consumer or customer reasonably expected from the contract;

if it was not fair and reasonable to incorporate the term in the contract.[20] Where a term in a holiday booking form reserved the right to change the mode of transport, and where a coach without a toilet was substituted for one with, as promised in a holiday brochure, it was

---

[15] s. 15(3)(*a*).
[16] s. 15(3)(*b*).
[17] s. 15(1).
[18] 2. 25(1).
[19] s. 16(1). The liability need not be that of a party to the contract; see *Melrose* v. *Davidson & Robertson*, 1992 S.L.T. 395.
[20] s. 17(1). It would seem that the expectation can be based on something other than the terms of the contract.

decided that the effect of this term would permit the tour operator to render performance substantially different from what a holidaymaker was reasonably entitled to expect.[21]

A 'consumer contract' is a contract (not being a contract of sale by auction or competitive tender) in which (a) one party to the contract deals, and the other party to the contract ('the consumer') does not deal or hold himself out as dealing, in the course of a business, and (b) in the case of contracts relating to the transfer of the ownership or possession of goods from one person to another, the goods are of a type ordinarily supplied for private use or consumption; the onus of proving that a contract is not to be regarded as a consumer contract lies on the party so contending.[22]

'Standard form contract' is not defined[23] but light is thrown on its meaning by the definition of customer as 'a party to a standard form contract who deals on the basis of written standard terms of business of the other party to the contract who himself deals in the course of a business.'[24] It includes any contract, whether wholly written or partly oral, which includes a set of fixed terms which the proponer applies, without material variation, to contracts of the kind in question.[25]

10.20   Unreasonable Imdemnity Clauses.—A term of a 'consumer contract' has no effect for the purpose of making the consumer indemnify another person (whether a party to the contract or not) in respect of 'liability' which that other person may incur as a result of breach of duty or breach of contract, if it was not fair and reasonable to incorporate the term in the contract.[26] 'Liability' means a liability arising in the course of any business or from the occupation of any premises used for business purposes of the occupier. The corresponding English section[27] makes it clear that the liability may be to the person dealing as consumer.

10.21   Guarantees of Consumer Goods.—A 'guarantee' is a document containing or purporting to contain some promise or assurance (however worded or presented) that defects will be made good by complete or partial replacement, or by repair, monetary compensation or otherwise. Section 19 affects a guarantee which relates to goods of a type ordinarily supplied for private use or consumption and which is *not* given by one

---

[21] *Elliot* v. *Sunshine Coast International Ltd.*, 1989 G.W.D. 28–1252.

[22] s. 25(1). A director's employment contract has been regarded as a consumer contract: *Chapman* v. *Aberdeen Construction Group Ltd.*, *supra*. Note also s. 15(2)(*b*).

[23] See *McCrone* v. *Boots Farm Sales Ltd.*, 1981 S.C. 68; *Border Harvesters Ltd.* v. *Edwards Engineering (Perth) Ltd.*, 1985 S.L.T. 128.

[24] s. 17(2).

[25] *McCrone* v. *Boots Farm Sales Ltd.*, *supra*. It may be that a term should not be regarded as fixed unless it has been employed more than once: see Cusine, 1981 S.L.T. (News) 241; *Border Harvesters Ltd.* v. *Edwards Engineering (Perth) Ltd.*, *supra*.

[26] s. 18.

[27] s. 4.

party to the other party to a contract under or in pursuance of which the ownership or possession of the goods to which the guarantee relates is transferred. A term of such a guarantee is void in so far as it purports to exclude or restrict liability for loss or damage (including death or personal injury) arising from the goods proving defective while in use otherwise than exclusively for the purposes of a business or in the possession of a person for such use and resulting from the breach of duty of a person concerned in the manufacture or distribution of the goods.

10.22 Supply Contracts.—The Act limits the exclusion or restriction of liability for breach of the terms as to title, description and quality or fitness implied by law in contracts of sale and hire-purchase.[28] It makes a similar provision in respect of the corresponding terms in other contracts relating to the transfer of ownership or possession of goods from one person to another (with or without work being done on them), *e.g.* contracts of hire or for work and materials.[29]

10.23 The 'Reasonableness' Test.—The onus of proving that it was fair and reasonable to incorporate a term in a contract lies on the party so contending.[30] In applying the 'reasonableness' test, regard is to be had only to the circumstances which were, or ought reasonably to have been, known to or in the contemplation of the parties to the contract at the time the contract was made.[31] Where a term in a contract purports to restrict liability to a specified sum of money, regard is to be had in particular to (a) the resources which the party seeking to rely on that term could expect to be available to him for the purpose of meeting the liability should it arise, and (b) how far it was open to that party to cover himself by insurance.[32] The 'guidelines' for application of the 'reasonableness' test provided in Schedule 2 to the Act[33] relate only to contracts of sale and hire purchase and other contracts for the supply of goods; but some of the 'guidelines' may be found to be of use in applying the 'reasonableness' test to other types of contract. A term is to be taken to have been fair and reasonable to incorporate if it is incorporated or approved by, or incorporated pursuant to a decision or

---

[28] s. 20. As to sale, see *Denholm Fishselling Ltd.* v. *Christopher Anderson Ltd.*, 1991 S.L.T. (Sh.Ct.) 24. See paras. 16.26 to 16.28, *infra*.

[29] s. 21. As to hire, see *G.M. Shepherd Ltd.* v. *North West Securities Ltd.*, 1991 S.L.T. 499.

[30] s. 24(4); see *Landcatch Ltd.* v. *Marine Harvest Ltd.*, 1985 S.L.T. 478 (a supply case); *George Mitchell (Chesterhall) Ltd.* v. *Finney Lock Seeds Ltd.* [1983] 2 A.C. 803 (decided under Sale of Goods Act 1979, s. 55); *Phillips Products Ltd.* v. *Hyland* [1987] 2 All E.R. 620; *Thompson* v. *Lohan* [1987] 1 W.L.R. 649; *Continental Tyre & Rubber Co. Ltd.* v. *Trunk Trailer Co. Ltd.*, 1987 S.L.T. 58. There is a requirement to aver that terms are reasonable or otherwise as the case may be, if one wishes to raise the issue: see *Landcatch Ltd.* v. *Marine Harvest Ltd.*, *supra* and *Wm. Teacher & Sons Ltd.* v. *Bell Lines Ltd.*, 1991 S.L.T. 876.

[31] s. 24.

[32] s. 24(3).

[33] See para. 16.32, *infra*.

ruling of, a 'competent authority' acting in the exercise of any statutory jurisdiction or function and is not a term in a contract to which the 'competent authority' is itself a party.[34] A 'competent authority' is any court, arbiter, government department or public authority.[35]

10.24 **Unfair Terms in Consumer Contracts.**—The E.C. Directive on Unfair Terms in Consumer Contracts[36] imposes controls over contract terms which are additional to those found in the Unfair Contract Terms Act 1977. Effect has been given to this in the United Kingdom by the Unfair Terms in Consumer Contracts Regulations 1994.[37] As the title indicates, the Directive and also the Regulations apply only to consumer contracts and a 'consumer' is a natural person who makes a contract 'for purposes which are outside his business'.[38] The contracts to which the Directive and Regulations apply are contracts for the sale of goods and contracts for the supply of goods and services. In both cases, the seller or supplier must be acting 'for purposes relating to his business'.[39] The Regulations apply only to contract terms which have not been 'individually negotiated' by the seller or supplier and the consumer:[40] thus standard form contracts are squarely within the ambit of the Regulations unless they are exempted.[41] Contracts to which the Regulations do not apply are: employment contracts; contracts relating to succession rights; contracts relating to rights under family law; and contracts relating to the incorporation and organisation of companies or partnerships.[42] The Regulations do not apply to contract terms which have been incorporated in order to comply either with United Kingdom legislation or delegated legislation, or with the provisions or principles of international conventions to which the E.C. or the Member States are party.[43] Also exempted are terms which define the 'main subject matter' of the contract and those which concern the adequacy of the price of remuneration as against the goods or services sold or supplied.[44] The onus of showing that a term was individually negotiated rests with the seller or supplier.[45] A contract term will be treated as unfair where, it causes a 'significant imbalance' between the rights and obligations of the contracting parties. Such a term is declared to be 'contrary to the

---

[34] s. 29(2).
[35] s. 29(3).
[36] Directive 93/13 1993 O.J. L95/29.
[37] S.I. 1994 No. 3159. The Regulations came into force on July 1, 1995.
[38] *Ibid.*, Reg. 2(1).
[39] *Ibid.*, Reg. 2(1).
[40] *Ibid.*, Reg. 3(1). Terms which have been drafted in advance of the conclusion of a contract and whose contents the consumer has been unable to influence are not to be regarded as having been individually negotiated: Reg. 3(3).
[41] If, looked at as a whole, a contract is a pre-formulated, standard form, agreement, the fact that one term has been individually negotiated does not prevent the Regulations being applied to the rest of the contract: S.I. 1994 No. 3159, Reg. 3(4).
[42] *Ibid.*, Reg. 3(1) and Sched. 1.
[43] *Ibid.*, Reg. 3(1) and Sched. 1.
[44] *Ibid.*, Reg. 3(2).
[45] *Ibid.*, Reg. 3(5).

requirement of good faith'.[46] In assessing good faith, regard may be had to the factors set out in Schedule 2 to the Regulations.[47] These are: (a) the strength of the parties' bargaining positions; (b) any inducement given to the consumer in order to secure his consent to the term in question; (c) whether the goods or services supplied were made or supplied to the consumer's special order; (d) the extent to which the seller or supplier has dealt fairly with the consumer. In assessing the fairness of the term, the nature of the goods or services supplied must be taken into account and fairness must be assessed taking into account all the circumstances at the time when the contract was concluded.[48] An indicative, but not exhaustive, list of terms which may be unfair is set out in Schedule 3.[49] The list includes the following terms: terms excluding or limiting a seller's or supplier's liability for death or personal injury caused by act or omission on their part; terms imposing a 'disproportionately' large sum by way of compensation; terms which permit a seller or supplier to vary, unilaterally, a contract's terms without having to specify a reason for doing so; terms which oblige the consumer to perform his part of the bargain but which does not impose a similar obligation on the seller or supplier. If a contract term is found to be unfair, it is unenforceable against the consumer but the contract itself remains valid so long as it can exist without the inclusion of the unfair term.[50] The Regulations also impose on sellers and suppliers a duty to word their contracts in 'plain, intelligible language' and, where there is doubt as to the meaning of the wording, it will be construed *contra proferentem*.[51] Opting out of the Regulations by means of a choice of law clause which declares the applicable law to be that of a non-member state is struck at where the contract has 'a close connection with the territory of a member state.'[52] In order to prevent the continued use of unfair contract terms in consumer contracts, the Director General of Fair Trading can act on any complaint made to him by seeking an interdict against its continued use.[53]

Further Reading

Gloag, *Contract* (2nd ed., 1929), Ch. xxxiii.
Heydon, *The Restraint of Trade Doctrine* (1971).
Trebilcock, *The Common Law of Restraint of Trade.*
Wilberforce, Campbell and Ellis, *Law of Restrictive Trade Practices and Monopolies* (2nd ed., 1966).
Yates and Hawkins, *Standard Business Contracts: Exclusions and Related Devices* (1986).

[46] S.I. 1994 No. 3159, Reg. 4(1). On the matter of good faith, see MacNeil, 'Good Faith and the Control of Contract Terms: The E.C. Directive on Unfair Terms in Consumer Contracts' (1995), J.R. 147.
[47] *Ibid.*, Reg. 4(3).
[48] *Ibid.*, Reg. 4(2).
[49] *Ibid.*, Reg. 4(4).
[50] *Ibid.*, Reg. 5.
[51] *Ibid.*, Reg. 6.
[52] *Ibid.*, Reg. 7.
[53] *Ibid.*, Reg. 8.

CHAPTER 11

TITLE TO SUE: ASSIGNABILITY

11.1 **Title to Sue.**—Scots law recognises the principle of privity of contract. In the ordinary case the only persons whose rights and liabilities are affected by a contract are the contracting parties. Strangers to the contract have no right to sue upon it and incur no liabilities under it. But this statement is subject to very wide exceptions. There are cases where others than the contracting parties have a right to sue and cases also where others may incur liabilities. One important case, contracts by agents, may be reserved for another chapter.[1] In the present we proceed to consider: (1) the possible rights and liabilities of third parties at the time when the contract was made; (2) the cases in which rights or liabilities may subsequently be transmitted or assigned.

11.2 **Contract Imposes no Liability on Third Parties.**—It is too clear to be illustrated by any express decision that a contract cannot impose any contractual liability on a third party. Contractual liability depends on consent, and the third party has given no consent. A and B, in contracting, cannot impose any liability on C, unless C has in some way authorised them to do so.

There is more complexity in the question whether a third party may acquire a title to sue.

11.3 **Laws of *Jus Tertii*.**—The primary rule is that the contracting parties alone have a title to enforce a contract, and that the mere fact that a third party may have an interest does not give him a title. An obligation imposed by a contract is *jus tertii* to third parties, and they have no right to enforce it.

This has been illustrated in various circumstances. A creditor has no title to sue his debtor's debtor. A, incurring a debt to B, is under no liability to B's creditor, unless the debt has been assigned.[2] And the mere fact that A has undertaken to B to pay B's creditors will not give them any direct right of action against him. Thus where a company took over a trader's business and agreed with him to pay all the outstanding debts, it was held that an individual creditor of the trader acquired no

---

[1] Chap. 22, *infra*.
[2] *Henderson* v. *Robb* (1889) 16 R. 341.

title to sue the company.[3] When a manufacturer attempted to recover charges made by a railway company on the ground that they exceeded the rates fixed in a contract between that railway and another, it was decided that as the contract was made between the two railways for their own purposes it conferred no rights upon anyone else.[4] Where it was the rule of a police force that no constable should sue any member of the staff without the consent of the chief constable it was held that the rule was *jus tertii* to a police surgeon, and that he could not plead it in bar of an action by a constable.[5] The fact that a particular enterprise by a firm is prohibited by the terms of the partnership deed, or, in the case of a company, is *ultra vires,* gives no right of interdict to a third party whose interests may be affected.[6] The tenants of a vassal under a feu have, in the absence of a *jus quaesitum tertio* in their favour, no title to sue the vassal's superior for the determination or enforcement of the rights and conditions contained in the vassal's grant from the superior.[7] In certain circumstances a third party's title, initially good, may lapse during the continuance of an action, with the result that he is no longer entitled to the remedy which he seeks.[8]

11.4 *Jus Quaesitum Tertio.*—The rule that the contracting parties alone have the right to enforce their contract suffers exception in cases where it is shown that their object or intention was to advance the interests of a third party. That may create a *jus quaesitum tertio*, which will give the third party, or *tertius*, a title to sue.[9] In order to make this possible the *tertius*, or a particular class of which he is a member, must be named or referred to in the contract. A contract intended to confer advantages on the general public would not confer a title on anyone who chose to sue upon it.[10]

11.5 Where Express Title given to *Tertius.*—Whether there is a *jus quaesitum tertio* or not is a question of the intention of the contracting parties, which means not only that the party creditor in the contract should have intended to confer a benefit on the *tertius*, but that the debtor should have intended to subject himself to liability to him. That intention may be shown by an express provision in the contract that liability to a *tertius* is undertaken.[11] So where money is lodged on deposit receipt, payable to a third party, that third party, though a stranger to the contract, may

[3] *Henderson* v. *Stubbs Ltd.* (1894) 22 R. 51.
[4] *Finnie* v. *Glasgow and S.W. Ry.* (1857) 3 Macq. 75.
[5] *A.* v. *B.*, 1907 S.C. 1154.
[6] *Nicol* v. *Dundee Harbour Trs.,* 1914 S.C. 374; 1915 S.C. (H.L.) 7.
[7] *Eagle Lodge* v. *Keir & Cawdor Estates*, 1964 S.C. 30.
[8] See *Donaghy* v. *Rollo*, 1964 S.C. 278.
[9] *Peddie* v. *Brown* (1857) 3 Macq. 65; *Finnie* v. *Glasgow and S.W. Ry., supra.*
[10] *Finnie* v. *Glasgow and S.W. Ry. supra, per* Lords Cranworth and Wensleydale.
[11] *Braid Hills Hotel Co.* v. *Manuel*, 1909 S.C. 120; *Nicholson* v. *Glasgow Blind Asylum,* 1911 S.C. 391, *per* Lord President Dunedin at p. 399; *Macdonald* v. *Douglas*, 1963 S.L.T. 191, *per* Lord Justice-Clerk Grant at p. 200.

demand payment from the bank.[12] And there would seem to be no rule of law which would deny effect to a provision in any contract whereby it is provided that a third party may sue upon it, even in cases where that third party has no personal interest involved.[13]

11.6 Where Sole Interest in *Tertius*.—Without any express provision a *jus quaesitum tertio* may be inferred in cases where the only party who has any substantial interest in the fulfilment of the contract is a *tertius*. Thus a promise to give a subscription to a charitable society may be enforced by the society, though not made to the society itself nor to anyone acting as agent for it.[14] Where the rules of a trade union provided benefits to the dependants of a member who had become insane it was held that a *jus quaesitum* was conferred.[15]

11.7 Where Contracting Party Retains Interest. Building Restrictions.
—Where one of the contracting parties has a substantial interest to enforce the contract, it is doubtful whether a *jus quaesitum tertio* can ever be inferred unless there is some indication, beyond the fact that the *tertius* has an interest, of an intention to confer a title to sue on him. His interest is only an incidental result of a contract between two parties for their own purposes, and is not enough to give him a title to sue.[16] Thus where a superior has imposed building restrictions on a number of co-feuars the mere fact that the same restrictions are imposed on all feuars, and that each feuar has an interest to enforce compliance with the restrictions, will not give one feuar a title to sue another. He is suing to enforce an obligation imposed in a contract to which he was not a party, and which one of the contracting parties, the superior, has an interest to enforce.[17] To give a title to sue there must, in the absence of any agreement between the feuars themselves, be either a reference to a common plan, or a stipulation in each feu contract that the same restrictions are to be imposed on all the others. Either of these provisions sufficiently indicates such a similarity of conditions and mutuality of interest between the co-feuars as to show the intention of each feuar to submit to enforcement of the restrictions at the instance of the others.[18] If, however, the superior reserves to himself the right to

[12] *Dickinson* v. *National Bank*, 1917 S.C. (H.L.) 50, *per* Lord Dunedin.
[13] See *Pagan & Osborne* v. *Haig*, 1910 S.C. 341.
[14] *Morton's Trs.* v. *Aged Christian Friend Society* (1899) 2 F. 82. See also *Lamont* v. *Burnett* (1901) 3 F. 797; *Cambuslang West Church* v. *Bryce* (1897) 25 R. 322.
[15] *Love* v. *Amalgamated Society of Printers*, 1912 S.C. 1078.
[16] *Finnie* v. *Glasgow and S.W. Ry.* (1857) 3 Macq. 75.
[17] *Hislop* v. *McRitchie's Trs.* (1881) 8 R. (H.L.) 95; the consent and concurrence of the superior will not confer a title: *Girls' School Co.* v. *Buchanan*, 1958 S.L.T. (Notes) 2. See opinion of Lord Dunedin, *Nicholson* v. *Glasgow Blind Asylum*, 1911 S.C. 391, at pp. 400–401.
[18] *Johnston* v. *Walker's Trs.* (1897) 24 R. 1061. The pursuer and defender must be subject to the same, or similar, restrictions; *Botanic Gardens Picture House* v. *Adamson*, 1924 S.C. 549.

waive the conditions or to sanction deviations from the plan, the mutuality of obligations between the co-feuars will be destroyed;[19] but where the title to sue is the subject of an express grant in the feu charter, the mere fact of such a reservation will not in itself be enough to negative the existence of a *jus quaesitum tertio*.[20] While the vassal, by consenting to be bound to his superior, prima facie concedes the superior's interest to enforce the conditions contained in the charter,[21] the onus is on the co-feuar, in order that he may enforce a condition as against another co-feuar, to show that he has a patrimonial interest, as well as a title, to do so.[22]

11.8   Actions of Damages.—There are several *obiter dicta* which indicate that although a third party may sue for non-performance of the contract he cannot sue for damages for defective performance thereof.[23] There are, however, cases which suggest that a claim for damages may be competent.[24] It has recently been opined that there is no reason in principle why a third party cannot sue for damages.[25] It is submitted that the better view is that damages for defective performance are competent.

11.9   *Jus Quaesitum*, when Irrevocable.—When A and B in contracting, make C the creditor in their contract, for instance in a bond or policy of insurance, it is clear that C has a title to sue, but it does not follow that he has a *jus quaesitum* in the money. In *Carmichael* v. *Carmichael's Executrix*[26] it was held that where, by contract between A and B, A was taken bound to pay to C, the mere terms of the contract were not enough to vest any irrevocable right in C. If there was nothing beyond the terms of the contract A and B were at liberty to alter their arrangement. On the other hand it was not absolutely necessary, in order to confer a *jus quaesitum* on C, that the document in which the

[19] *Turner* v. *Hamilton* (1890) 17 R. 494; *Red Court Hotel* v. *Burgh of Largs,* 1955 S.L.T. (Sh.Ct.) 2.

[20] *Lawrence* v. *Scott,* 1965 S.L.T. 390.

[21] *Earl of Zetland* v. *Hislop* (1882) 9 R. (H.L.) 40, *per* Lord Watson at p. 47; *Mactaggart* v. *Roemmele,* 1907 S.C. 1318, *per* Lord President Dunedin at p. 1323. For circumstances in which the superior's interest to enforce may be lost, see *Howard de Walden Estates* v. *Bowmaker,* 1965 S.C. 163, and cases cited therein.

[22] *Aberdeen Varieties* v. *James F. Donald (Aberdeen Cinemas),* 1940 S.C. (H.L.) 52; *Macdonald* v. *Douglas,* 1963 S.L.T. 191, *per* Lord Justice-Clerk Grant at p. 200.

[23] *Robertson* v. *Fleming* (1861) 4 Macq. 167; *Rae* v. *Meek* (1888) 15 R. 1033; (1889) 16 R. (H.L.) 1; *Tully* v. *Ingram* (1891) 19 R. 65; *Edgar* v. *Lamont,* 1914 S.C. 277. To like effect is Gloag, p. 239 and previous editions of this work.

[24] *Cullen* v. *James McMenamin Ltd.,* 1928 S.L.T. (Sh.Ct.) 2; *Blumer & Co.* v. *Scott & Sons* (1874) 1 R. 379. Note also Walker, *Principles of Scottish Private Law* (4th ed.), Vol. II, p. 127; S.L.C. Memorandum No. 38, *Stipulations in Favour of Third Parties* (1977), paras. 41–46; T.B. Smith, *Short Commentary,* pp. 782 *et seq.*

[25] *Scott Lithgow Ltd.* v. *G.E.C. Electrical Projects Ltd.,* 1992 S.L.T. 244.

[26] 1919 S.C. 636; revd. 1920 S.C. (H.L.) 195. See also *Drysdale's Trs.* v. *Drysdale,* 1922 S.C. 741.

contract was embodied should be delivered or formally intimated to him. It was a question of proof of the *animus donandi*, and of this the terms of the contract were important though not conclusive evidence. When the contract was expressed in C's favour, and he was made acquainted with the fact, the provision became irrevocable and he acquired a *jus quaesitum*.[27]

11.10   Title of Transferees of Property.—In cases where no one but the parties was originally interested in the contract third parties may acquire rights and liabilities as transferees of the subject or *res* to which the contract relates; as assignees of the contract; or as successors of the contracting parties. The law will be considered in this order.

11.11   Contracts Running with Lands: Superior and Vassal.—The cases where contractual rights and liabilities may be so attached to a particular subject that they pass with the ownership of that subject mainly relate to heritable property, and the law is commonly referred to as the law of contracts running with the lands. In contracts between superior and vassal it is the general rule that they run, not strictly with the lands, but with the successors of each party in the continuing contractual relationship as conditions of tenure. The obligations imposed, and the rights conferred, in a feu contract, are not read as imposed or conferred on the parties to the contract and their heirs, but on the parties and their successors as superior and vassal in the lands conveyed, and are binding on them[28] unless personal to the original parties.[29] Thus the obligation to pay feu-duty bound the feuar only so long as he retained that character; when he parted with the lands, and the title of the disponee was completed, he was no longer liable except for arrears, and the obligation to pay the feu-duty lay on the disponee.[30] The detailed law on this subject is beyond the scope of the present work.[31]

11.12   Disponer and Disponee.—When there is no continuing relationship, such as that of superior and vassal, it is less easy to infer that contracts will run with the lands. A disponer of lands may create a servitude over other lands which he retains, and the right and burden thus created will run with the ownership of the dominant and the servient tenements.[32] But, with the doubtful exception of a clause of warrandice,[33] any

[27] Gloag, *Contract* (2nd ed.), p. 230. See, however, *Allan's Trs.* v. *Lord Advocate*, 1971 S.C. (H.L.) 45, speech of Lord Reid at p. 54.

[28] *Hope* v. *Hope* (1864) 2 M. 670.

[29] *Duncan* v. *Church of Scotland General Trs.*, 1941 S.C. 145; *Jolly's Exrx.* v. *Viscount Stonehaven*, 1958 S.C. 635.

[30] Bell, *Prin.*, § 700. The feu-duty now has to be redeemed on transfer for valuable consideration.

[31] See Gloag, *Contract* (2nd ed.). p. 226.

[32] See, as to servitudes, Rankine, *Land-Ownership* (4th ed.).

[33] See *Christie* v. *Cameron* (1898) 25 R. 824.

personal obligation undertaken in a disposition of lands does not run with the lands so as to be enforceable by singular successors of the disponee, unless the right to enforce it is expressly assigned to them.[34] Nor will personal rights, which are valid against the disponer, be exercisable against his disponee, even if the disponee has prior knowledge of them.[35] An obligation undertaken by the disponee, if it is duly constituted a real burden in the disponee's title,[36] will form a preferable burden on the lands themselves and so be binding on singular successors in the lands, where an interest to enforce it can be shown.[37] But any positive obligations, to erect buildings on the lands in question,[38] are binding only on the disponee and his heirs, and cannot be directly enforced against a singular successor. If duly constituted as real burdens, obligations of this class will indirectly affect singular successors,[39] in so far as they form preferable burdens on the lands, but in order that a direct right of action, for the performance of an obligation *ad factum praestandum*, may run with the lands, the continuous relationship of superior and vassal is required.

11.13 Landlord and Tenant.—Contractual rights and liabilities may run with the relationship of landlord and tenant. This will be considered in a later chapter.[40]

11.14 Contracts do not Run with Moveables.—As a general rule contracts do not run with moveables. The purchaser of an article acquires no title to sue on contracts which the seller may have made in relation to that article, nor is he bound by them. So the rights under a charterparty do not pass to a purchaser of the ship.[41] When a firm of engineers had failed to carry out a contract to fit engines in a ship it was held that a purchaser of the ship had no title to sue them for damages. He was not the party with whom they had contracted, and the mere purchase of the ship conferred no title to sue on contracts relating to it.[42] Similarly, a

---

[34] *Maitland* v. *Horne* (1842) 1 Bell's App. 1; *Marquis of Breadalbane* v. *Sinclair* (1846) 5 Bell's App. 353; *Speirs* v. *Morgan* (1902) 4 F. 1069. This rule does not apply to a separate obligation expressed to be in favour of a party and his successors in a particular tenement: *Magistrates of Dunbar* v. *Mackersy*, 1931 S.C. 180.

[35] *Morier* v. *Brownlie & Watson* (1895) 23 R. 67; *Wallace* v. *Simmers*, 1960 S.C. 255.

[36] *Tailors of Aberdeen* v. *Coutts* (1840) 1 Rob. App. 296; Menzies, *Conveyancing*, pp. 577 *et seq.*; *Aberdeen Varieties* v. *James F. Donald (Aberdeen Cinemas)*, 1939 S.C. 788, affd 1940 S.C. (H.L.) 52.

[37] *Braid Hills Hotel Co.* v. *Manuel*, 1909 S.C. 120. Where the question arises between the original parties, it is for the disponee to show that the disponer's interest to enforce the restrictions has been lost: *S.C.W.S.* v. *Finnie*, 1937 S.C. 835; where the question arises between singular successors, however, the onus is on the dominant owner to show, as against the successor in the servient property, that he has an interest: *Aberdeen Varieties*, 1939 S.C. 788, *per* Lord Justice-Clerk Aitchison, at p. 798.

[38] *Marshall's Tr.* v. *McNeill* (1888) 15 R. 762.

[39] *Anderson* v. *Dickie*, 1915 S.C. (H.L.) 79.

[40] Chap. 41, *infra*.

[41] *Fratelli Sorrentino* v. *Buerger* [1915] 3 K.B. 367.

[42] *Blumer* v. *Scott* (1874) 1 R. 379; *Craig* v. *Blackater*, 1923 S.C. 472.

purchaser of moveables incurs no liabilities. If he is a sub-purchaser, he is not liable for the price to the original seller. At common law if goods were sold under a condition (usually termed a price-maintenance agreement) as to the price at which they might be resold, that condition was binding only on the party who had agreed to it; it did not run with the goods so as to be binding on anyone who acquired them.[43] Whether a sub-purchaser who has notice of the price-maintenance agreement is bound by it is an unsettled question.[44]

11.15 Exceptions in Shipping Law.—The general rule that contracts do not run with moveables finds some exceptions in shipping law. The right to freight runs with the ownership of the ship.[45] Under the Carriage of Goods by Sea Act 1992, the lawful holder of a bill of lading, a consignee named in a sea waybill, and any person entitled to delivery of goods in terms of a ship's delivery order 'shall ... have transferred to and vested in him all rights of suit under the contract of carriage as if he had been a party to that contract.'[46]

11.16 Title of Assignees.—When a contract is assigned the assignee acquires the right to sue and in some cases may be saddled with the liabilities arising under it. An assignee may sue in his own name, or may sist himself as pursuer in an action commenced by his cedent.[47] In cases where both the contracting parties consent to the assignation there is no difficulty, but it is a question of some complexity how far one party to a contract can assign without the consent of the other.

11.17 Assignability: Where Contract Executed.—It is an established rule that the benefit arising under a contract is assignable, in the absence of any express provision to the contrary.[48] Therefore if a contract is so far performed that nothing remains except to pay for what has been done, or to transfer a particular thing, the right to receive payment or the thing may be assigned. Such contracts are termed executed, as opposed

---

[43] See opinion of Lord Shaw, *National Phonograph Co.* v. *Menck* [1911] A.C. 336. In *British Motor Trade Association* v. *Gray*, 1951 S.C. 586, the petition contained such phrases as 'the vehicle concerned was subject to a covenant,' but this was not the ground of the judgment. Minimum re-sale price conditions are now, in general, void by virtue of the Resale Prices Act 1976, s. 9, but s. 26 of that Act does permit the enforcement of a lawful price-maintenance condition by the supplier against a person not a party to the sale who subsequently acquires the goods with notice of the condition as if that person had been a party to the sale.

[44] As to the common law, see *McGruther* v. *Pitcher* [1904] 2 Ch. 306; *Dunlop* v. *Selfridge* [1915] A.C. 847; *McCosh* v. *Crow* (1903) 5 F. 670; *Morton* v. *Muir*, 1907 S.C. 1211; *Lord Strathcona Co.* v. *Dominion Coal Co.* [1926] A.C. 108; *B.M.T.A.* v. *Salvadori* [1949] Ch. 556 (liability in tort).

[45] *Stewart* v. *Greenock Marine Insurance Co.* (1848) 1 Macq. 328.

[46] Carriage of Goods by Sea Act 1992, s. 2(1). This Act repeals *in toto* the Bills of Lading Act 1855.

[47] *Fraser* v. *Duguid* (1838) 16 S. 1130.

[48] *Aurdal* v. *Estrella*, 1916 S.C. 882; *Whiteley* v. *Hilt* [1918] 2 K.B. 808.

to executory or executorial contracts. So a debt is assignable, if there be not provision to the contrary.[49] Where there was an agreement for the sale of a ship it was held that the party who had agreed to sell could not object to an assignation of the right to receive, although in the particular circumstances he had a defence in a question with the purchaser which was not pleadable against the assignee.[50]

11.18   *Delectus Personae.*—Contracts where something more than mere payment or delivery of a particular thing remains to be done are as a general rule not assignable if it is a matter of reasonable inference that one party entered into the contract in reliance on the qualities possessed by the other. The contract is then said to involve *delectus personae*. The most obvious case is where a party agrees to do something which involves personal skill. It is clear, as has been judicially remarked,[51] that a contract with an artist to paint a portrait cannot either be assigned as a contract, or carried out by the agency of anyone else. And the principle covers all cases of personal service.[52] The more difficult cases arise when the performance involved, such as the supply of goods by a broker, could be given by any person in the same line of business, or where the work required must necessarily be done through the instrumentality of hired labour and not by the obligant personally.

It is not generally competent for a party to a contract, whatever its nature may be, to assign it so as to get rid of the liabilities he has undertaken. He may be entitled to tender performance by a third party, but will remain liable if that third party's performance be defective. So when a page was hired in a serial circular issued by a wine-merchant, it was held that the contract could not be assigned to a company which took over the business of the wine-merchant, and which was prepared to continue the issue of the circular. The company's position was not merely that they were entitled to tender performance, but to come in the place of the wine-merchant so as to relieve him of all liability.[53] The general rule that the debtor under a contract cannot delegate his liabilities finds an exception in the case of contracts which run with lands, where the element of property bulks more largely than the element of contract.[54] And if the contract is of a duration so great that it cannot be supposed that continued personal performance was contemplated, it may be held that both parties must have intended to make it completely assignable. This was the conclusion arrived at in the case of a contract whereby a quarrymaster undertook to supply a

---

[49] Stair, III, i, 3.

[50] *Aurdal* v. *Estrella, supra.*

[51] See opinion of Lord President Dunedin, *Cole* v. *Handasyde,* 1910 S.C. 68.

[52] *Hoey* v. *MacEwan & Auld* (1867) 5 M. 814; *Berlitz Schools* v. *Duchene* (1903) 6 F. 181.

[53] *Grierson, Oldham & Co.* v. *Forbes Maxwell & Co.* (1895) 22 R. 812.

[54] *Supra,* para 11.11.

company with all the chalk it might require. The contract was for 50 years, and it was held to be assignable to another company, although the assignee's requirements in chalk might be different from those of the cedent.[55]

11.19   Delegated Performance.—Though liability cannot be delegated a party may be entitled to assign his rights under the contract, or to tender performance by a third party. There is not necessarily *delectus personae* in all contracts, merely because the particular party has been chosen for the contract. If the contract is one which involves no special skill, and does not call for performance by the obligant personally, he may get it performed by a third party, and there would then seem to be no objection to his assigning to that third party the right to sue for the price of his work. The right to delegate performance has been sustained in the case of an upholsterer employed to beat and relay a carpet;[56] of a paviour who had contracted to lay and upkeep a street;[57] of a company which had undertaken to keep railway wagons in repair.[58] In none of these cases did it appear that the employer relied on any special skill in the party to whom he gave the order. This element was present in *Cole v. Handasyde*,[59] where a broker was employed to supply black grease, and selected because he was an expert in that commodity. But it was also provided that the grease might be rejected if it failed to pass a specified test, and it was held that this provision excluded *delectus personae*, and that the contract could be enforced by a party to whom it had been assigned, although he was not possessed of the broker's expert knowledge. There is a presumption against delegation though this may be rebutted by clearly expressed language which discloses an intention to delegate.[60]

11.20   Contracts Involving Mutual Obligations.—In all these cases the contract was reducible to an obligation to do a particular piece of work, or get it done, on the one side, and to pay for it on the other. If the contract is of a more complex character, involving further obligations on one party or other, it would seem that it is not assignable. So where, in a contract of a year's duration for the supply of eggs, the purchaser undertook not to buy eggs from any other dealer, it was held that this provision introduced the element of *delectus personae* and that the contract could not be enforced by a successor of the purchaser in business, to whom it had been assigned.[61] And when A ordered a particular machine from B,

---

[55] *Tolhurst* v. *Associated Portland Cement Co.* [1903] A.C. 414. See, however, *Magistrates of Arbroath* v. *Strachan's Trs.* (1842) 4 D. 538.
[56] *Stevenson* v. *Maule*, 1920 S.C. 335.
[57] *Asphaltic Limestone Co.* v. *Corporation of Glasgow*, 1907 S.C. 463.
[58] *British Waggon Co.* v. *Lea* (1880) 5 Q.B.D. 149.
[59] 1910 S.C. 68.
[60] *W.J. Harte Construction Ltd.* v. *Scottish Homes*, 1992 S.L.T. 948.
[61] *Kemp* v. *Baerselman* [1906] 2 K.B. 604.

undertaking to engage in a course of business which would involve ordering other machines, and B undertook to supply these machines at cost price, it was held that the contract, involving obligations on both sides other than supplying and paying for the initial machine, could not be enforced by a company to which B had assigned it.[62] *Delectus personae* may be involved in the fact that the party who orders goods or work is a creditor of the party to whom he gives the order, and would therefore be entitled to set off the price against his debt. The contract cannot then be assigned to a third party, so as to give him a right to fulfil the order and sue for the price.[63]

11.21 Title of Representatives.—On the death of one of the parties to a contract his representatives in succession may acquire a title to sue, and, in so far as they benefit in the succession, may incur liability. Debts pass to the executor of the creditor, and, in the absence of any provision to the contrary, may be recovered from the whole estate of the debtor.[64] In the case of uncompleted contracts the title of representatives to sue may depend on whether the contract involved *delectus personae*. Thus the death of either employer or employee dissolves the contract, and the relationship does not transmit to the representatives of either party.[65] But while, if it be clear that the personal qualities of an obligant are relied on, his death terminates the contract, there are cases where a contract may transmit to representatives though it would not be assignable *inter vivos*. Thus the interest of a tenant in a lease passes to his heir, although from the nature or the express terms of the lease it may not be assignable without the landlord's consent.[66] And probably all commercial or engineering contracts, unless it be clear that the personal attention of the obligant was promised, pass to and are enforceable against the personal representatives of the contracting parties.[67] Thus it was observed that, while a contract of service was ended by the death of the employer, a contract *operis faciendi*, such as a contract to build a house, would transmit to and be enforceable against the heir of the person who had ordered the work.[68]

11.22 Insolvency.—A permanent trustee in sequestration may have the right to enforce contracts in which the bankrupt was engaged. He is never bound to carry out the bankrupt's contracts, and a decree *ad factum praestandum* will not be pronounced against him. He may adopt any contract made by the bankrupt before sequestration where he considers

---

[62] *International Fibre Syndicate* v. *Dawson* (1900) 2 F. 636; affd. (1901) 3 F. (H.L.) 32.
[63] *Boulton* v. *Jones* (1857) 2 H. & N. 564.
[64] *Gardiner* v. *Stewart's Trs.,* 1908 S.C. 985.
[65] *Hoey* v. *MacEwan & Auld* (1867) 5 M. 814.
[66] Bell, *Prin.*, § 1219; Rankine, *Leases* (3rd ed.), p. 157.
[67] See the distinction between assignability and transmissibility drawn by Lord Lindley in *Tolhurst* v. *Associated Portland Cement Co.* [1903] A.C. 414.
[68] *Per* Lord President Inglis, *Hoey* v. *MacEwan & Auld, supra.*

that its adoption would be beneficial to the administration of the bankrupt estate, except where adoption is precluded by the express or implied terms of the contract.[69] If he refuses to adopt a contract the remedy of the other party is to lodge a claim for damages in the sequestration.[70] The authorities are not clear on the question how far the element of *delectus personae* in a contract precludes its adoption by a trustee in sequestration, or by the liquidator of a company. The trustee cannot adopt a contract when the personal services of the bankrupt are engaged.[71] It has been decided that a contract to publish a book did not pass to the trustee in the publisher's bankruptcy.[72] On the other hand the bankrupt's interest in a lease, though it may not be assignable, will pass to his trustee in sequestration, unless there is an express provision to the contrary.[73] The case of ordinary commercial contracts was considered in *Anderson* v. *Hamilton*.[74] The bankrupt had contracted to supply iron by instalments. The trustee intimated that he adopted the contract; the purchasers, that they regarded it as cancelled. The decision in the purchasers' favour was based on the ground that the trustee, assuming that he had a right to adopt the contract, had not intimated his decision to do so within a reasonable time, but from the opinions given, and from a later case,[75] there can be little doubt that a contract under which the bankrupt has undertaken to deliver goods, or to execute some building or engineering work, can be adopted by the trustee in his sequestration, even although its terms might be such as to preclude voluntary assignation by the bankrupt.[76]

The trustee must within 28 days of a written request from any party to a contract made by the bankrupt or within such longer period as the court may allow, adopt or refuse to adopt the contract; if he fails to reply in writing within the period allowed, he is deemed to have refused to adopt the contract.[77] Even where that procedure is not operated the trustee must intimate his intention to adopt the contract within a reasonable time or he will be taken to have abandoned it. In *Anderson* v. *Hamilton*[78] it was held that in a contract relating to goods which fluctuate in value each party was entitled to know at once whether the contract would be carried out, and that where the bankrupt failed on March 14, and the trustee did not intimate his decision to carry out the

[69] Bankruptcy (Scotland) Act 1985, s. 42(1).
[70] *Kirkland* v. *Cadell* (1838) 16 S. 860; *Asphaltic Limestone Co.* v. *Corporation of Glasgow,* 1907 S.C. 463.
[71] *Caldwell* v. *Hamilton*, 1919 S.C. (H.L.) 100, *per* Viscount Cave, at p. 104.
[72] *Gibson* v. *Carruthers* (1841) 8 M. & W. 321, opinion of Lord Abinger. See *Griffiths* v. *Tower Publishing Co.* [1897] 1 Ch. 21.
[73] Stair, II, ix, 26; Bell, *Prin.,* § 1216.
[74] (1875) 2 R. 355.
[75] *Asphaltic Limestone Co.* v. *Corporation of Glasgow, supra.*
[76] This is the law in England: see *Tolhurst* v. *Associated Portland Cement Co.* [1903] A.C. 414, opinion of Lord Lindley.
[77] Bankruptcy (Scotland) Act 1985, s. 42(2), (3).
[78] (1875) 2 R. 355.

contract until April 8, his intimation was too late, and the other party was entitled to hold the contract as cancelled.

A trustee in sequestration, if he decides to adopt a contract, cannot insist on fulfilment of the provisions in his favour unless he is prepared to implement the provisions incumbent on the bankrupt. So where A had undertaken to erect various buildings on land feued from B, and B had agreed to allocate the feu-duty on a building which was in course of erection, it was held that A's trustee in sequestration could not require fulfilment of the obligation to allocate the feu-duty unless he was prepared to adopt and implement the contract for the erection of the other buildings.[79] But if the bankrupt has two separate contracts with the same party, the trustee is entitled to adopt one and refuse to carry out the other.[80] If a trustee adopts a contract in which the bankrupt was engaged, or continues the bankrupt's business, he incurs personal liability.[81] In the case of a lease he renders himself personally liable for all the obligations incumbent on the tenant, including all arrears of rent.[82]

A liquidator is in the same position as a trustee in sequestration as to the adoption of contracts made by the company.[83] He must intimate his intention to adopt a contract within a reasonable time.[84] The court, on the application of any person who is entitled to the benefit or subject to the burden of a contract with the company, may make an order rescinding the contract in such terms as to payment by or to either party of damages for non-performance of the contract, or otherwise as the court thinks just.[85] Any damages payable under the order to such a person can be proved in the liquidation.

Where a receiver is appointed under a floating charge, a contract made by the company prior to his appointment continues in force (subject to its terms) but the receiver does not incur any personal liability on any such contract.[86] The receiver is personally liable on any contract entered into by him in the performance of his functions except in so far as the contract otherwise provides.[87] He is also personally liable on any contract of employment adopted by him in the carrying out of those functions but he is not to be taken to have adopted a contract of employment by reason of anything done or omitted to be done within 14 days after his appointment.[88] Where a receiver is

---

[79] *Mitchell's Tr.* v. *Galloway's Trs.* (1903) 5 F. 612.

[80] *Asphaltic Limestone Co.* v. *Corporation of Glasgow,* 1907 S.C. 463.

[81] *Mackessack* v. *Molleson* (1886) 13 R. 445; *Sturrock* v. *Robertson's Trs.,* 1913 S.C. 582.

[82] *Gibson* v. *Kirkland* (1833) 6 W. & S. 340; Rankine, *Leases* (3rd ed.), p. 698.

[83] *Asphaltic Limestone Concrete Co.* v. *Glasgow Corporation,* 1907 S.C. 463.

[84] *Crown Estate Commissioners* v. *Liqrs. of Highland Engineering Ltd.,* 1975 S.L.T. 58.

[85] Insolvency Act 1986, s. 186. There is a doubt as to whether this section is intended to apply to Scotland.

[86] *Ibid.,* s. 57(4).

[87] s. 57(2).

[88] s. 57(5).

personally liable on a contract he is entitled to be indemnified out of the property subject to the floating charge.[89] A contract made by a receiver continues in force even if his powers are suspended because of the appointment of a receiver under a prior floating charge.[90] The receiver is an agent of the company in relation to the property subject to the charge.[91]

An administrator appointed under Part II of the Insolvency Act 1986 is an agent of the company.[92] The appointment does not affect prior contracts made by the company (subject to their terms). He does not incur personal liability on contracts entered into, or contracts of employment adopted, by him but liabilities incurred under such contracts are a charge on the company's property in priority to any floating charge.[93] He is not to be taken to have adopted a contract of employment by reason of anything done or omitted to be done within 14 days after his appointment.[94]

---

[89] s. 57(3).
[90] s. 57(7).
[91] s. 57(1).
[92] s. 14(5).
[93] s. 19(5).
[94] s. 19(5).

CHAPTER 12

IMPOSSIBILITY OF PERFORMANCE

12.1   Contracts to Perform Impossibility.—It is generally supposed, though without any actual decision, that a contract to do something believed by all educated persons to be physically impossible would be void, even although both parties believed it to be possible.[1] But impossibility which is not obvious, but depends upon intricate calculations, as in the case of a contract to build a ship on a certain model and with a specified carrying capacity, leaves the contract unaffected.[2] The plea of commercial impossibility, that is, that the value of a ship when repaired would not cover the cost of repairs ordered, has been put forward, but unhesitatingly rejected.[3] Contracts to do something legally impossible, *i.e.* to do an act for which the law provides no facilities, as, for instance, to execute a valid entail after the Register of Tailzies was closed by the Entail Act, are void.[4]

12.2   Supervening Impossibility: Frustration.—A contract may be dissolved by a change of circumstances, or of the law, which either renders performance impossible or illegal, or so alters the conditions that performance, if given, would in substance be performance of a different contract from that to which the parties agreed. To such cases the term frustration of the adventure has been applied.[5] It is a general principle that the change in circumstances in question must have occurred from some cause independent of the volition of the contracting parties. So the statutory provision that on an agreement to sell specific goods the agreement is avoided if the goods perish before the risk passes to the buyer is qualified by the proviso that the goods shall have perished without any fault on the part of the seller or buyer.[6] And where a ship hired under a time charterparty was detained in a waterway when a war broke out, the contract was held to have been frustrated.[7]

---

[1] See Indian Contract Act 1872, s. 56. The illustration given is a contract to recover treasure by magic. See also Sale of Goods Act 1979, s. 6.

[2] *Gillespie* v. *Howden* (1885) 12 R. 800.

[3] *Hong-Kong, etc., Dock Co.* v. *Netherton Shipping Co.,* 1909 S.C. 34.

[4] *Caledonian Insurance Co.* v. *Matheson's Trs.* (1901) 3 F. 865; *George Packman & Sons* v. *Dunbar's Trs.,* 1977 S.L.T. 140.

[5] See paras. 12.14 and 12.15, *infra.*

[6] Sale of Goods Act 1979, s. 7. See *Mertens* v. *Home Freeholds Co.* [1921] 2 K.B. 526; and Gloag, *Contract* (2nd ed.), p. 344.

[7] *The Evia (No. 2)* [1983] 1 A.C. 736; *The Chrysalis* [1983] 1 Lloyd's Rep. 503.

12.3 **General Result of Impossibility.**—It is not an absolute rule that a contract is at an end because performance has become impossible. But the development of the law, starting with the principle that if an unqualified obligation has been undertaken its supervening impossibility may be a ground for excusing actual performance but is no answer to a claim for damages, has been in the direction of holding that obligations are rarely intended to be unqualified, but are undertaken under the implied condition that performance shall continue to be possible.[8] The result is that there are now few cases where impossibility is not an effectual plea. Still, it is probably the law that an agreement to sell a certain quantity of a particular commodity is not affected by the fact that the commodity has become unprocurable[9] where the contract does not stipulate the source from which the order is to be satisfied. It is an established rule in shipping law that if a certain number of days (lay-days) are provided in a charterparty for loading the ship, it is no answer to a claim for damages that owing to any circumstances, not expressly provided for and not due to the fault of the shipowner, it has proved to be impossible to load within the lay-days.[10] Even where there is no provision for lay-days the charterer is absolutely bound to have the cargo ready on receiving reasonable notice of the arrival of the ship, and is liable in damages for her detention even although his failure was due to conditions over which he had no control.[11]

12.4 **Contract with Time Limits.**—The strongest case for the enforcement of a contract according to its terms is where, as in the shipping cases above mentioned, there is an obligation to perform within a specified time, with a contractual provision for the consequences of failure. But even here it is not an absolute rule that impossibility of timely performance may not be a relevant defence. Thus when a joiner undertook to finish his work on a house by a given date, with a penalty in the event of the time being exceeded, and met a demand for the penalty by the plea that his delay was due to the fact that observance of the time limit was impossible owing to the failure of other tradesmen employed on the house, the opinions of the majority of the court were in favour of the validity of his plea.[12]

12.5 **Rei Interitus.**—The clearest case for the dissolution of a contract on the ground of impossibility is where an obligation is undertaken which cannot be performed unless some specific thing continues to exist and to

---

[8] See the history of the law traced by McCardie J., *Blackburn Bobbin Co.* v. *Allen* [1918] 1 K.B. 540; affd. [1918] 2 K.B. 467.

[9] *Blackburn Bobbin Co., supra. Re Badische Co.* [1921] 2 Ch. 331, does not contravert the view expressed in the text. One interpretation of this decision is that the contract was frustrated because both parties intended the subject-matter of the contract to come from Germany. Another is that the case concerns supervening illegality (*i.e.* the outbreak of the First World War) rather than supervening impossibility.

[10] *Hansa* v. *Alexander*, 1919 S.C. (H.L.) 122.

[11] *Ardan S.S. Co.* v. *Weir* (1905) 7 F. (H.L.) 126.

[12] *Duncanson* v. *Scottish County Investment Society*, 1915 S.C. 1106. The decision turned on a specialty.

be available for the contractual purposes. Then the accidental destruction of that thing (*rei interitus*) or, without actual destruction, some event which precludes the performance of the contract through its means, will put an end to the contract.[13] Thus if a specific thing sold has perished before the property has passed to the buyer;[14] if a subject has been accidentally destroyed,[15] or has been requisitioned by the Government,[16] or, in the case of a lease of salmon fishing, been so affected by the action of a Government department as to be incapable of possession as a fishing;[17] if a ship, though not actually lost, has been so injured as to become totally unfit for the purpose for which she was chartered;[18] if a music hall, hired for a particular day for the purpose of giving a concert, has been burned;[19] in all cases the contract is avoided or discharged, and no damages can be recovered from the party who has failed to fulfil his obligations. An analogous case is where a party has undertaken to perform some service, as, for example, to play at a concert, which is only possible if he remain in health. His illness amounts to *rei interitus*; he no longer exists as a concert-playing man; and the contract is dissolved.[20] It has been decided in Scotland that where the destruction or loss of a thing is due to the negligence of one of the contracting parties, this does not preclude a successful plea of frustration.[21] The position in England may be different and, in any event, is far less clearly stated.[22]

12.6 Building in Course of Erection.—When a building in course of construction is accidentally destroyed the question has been, not whether the contract is discharged (which would probably depend on the stage which the building had reached), but whether the builder has any claim for payment for his work or materials. In the cases in Scotland the question has been treated on the basis of property. As the property in the unfinished building has passed to the owner of the ground, on the principle of accession[23] the general maxim *res perit domino* applies, the loss falls on him and the builder has a claim for his work and materials.[24]

---

[13] Bell, *Prin.*, § 29.

[14] Sale of Goods Act 1979, s. 7; *Leitch v. Edinburgh Ice, etc., Co.* (1900) 2 F. 904.

[15] *Walker v. Bayne* (1815) 6 Paton 217; *Allan v. Robertson's Trs.* (1891) 18 R. 932; *Cantors Properties (Scotland) Ltd. v. Swears & Wells Ltd.*, 1978 S.C. 310.

[16] *Mackeson v. Boyd*, 1942 S.C. 56.

[17] *Tay Salmon Fisheries Co. v. Speedie*, 1929 S.C. 593.

[18] *London and Edinburgh Shipping Co. v. The Admiralty*, 1920 S.C. 309.

[19] *Taylor v. Caldwell* (1863) 3B. & S. 826.

[20] *Robinson v. Davidson* (1871) L.R. 6 Ex. 269.

[21] *London and Edinburgh Shipping Co. v. The Admiralty*, 1920 S.C. 309.

[22] In *The Super Servant Two* [1990] 1 Lloyd's Rep. 1, the Court of Appeal held that negligence did operate as a bar to frustration. This is contrary to *obiter dicta* in *Joseph Constantine S.S. Co. v. Imperial Smelting Corp. Ltd.* [1942] A.C. 154. Note also *The Hannah Blumenthal* [1983] 1 A.C. 854 and *Hare v. Murphy Bros. Ltd.* [1974] 2 All E.R. 940.

[23] See para. 37.6, *infra*.

[24] *McIntyre v. Clow* (1875) 2 R. 278; *Richardson v. Dumfriesshire Road Trs.* (1890) 17 R. 805.

12.7 Recovery of Payments in Advance.—When payment in advance has been made for a contract which is ultimately avoided on the ground of impossibility our law follows the *condictio causa data, causa non secuta* of the civil law, and holds that where money is paid in advance in consideration of some service to be rendered in future it may be recovered if that service is not rendered, even though, as in the case of impossibility, no breach of contract may be involved. Thus in a contract for the construction of ship's engines for an Austrian firm an instalment of the price was paid on signing the contract. Before the construction of the engines had begun war with Austria was declared. It was not in dispute that this put an end to the contract.[25] It was held on the conclusion of peace, that the Austrian firm might recover the deposit.[26]

12.8 Supervening Events Altering Value of Contract.—Some early cases on leases extended the principle of *rei interitus* to the case where the subjects let failed to produce the expected return. The lease was not avoided, but no rent was due for the period of sterility.[27] But the authority of these cases was called in question in *Gowans* v. *Christie*.[28] It was there held that a mineral lease was not avoided by the failure of the seam, and observed that in a lease for years the tenant expected to make his profit on a balance of good and bad years, and that there was no equity in refusing rent for a year which had proved unproductive. And generally, except in cases where the execution of the contract is interrupted and the plea of frustration of the adventure is available,[29] the fact that supervening events, or a change in the law, have made the contract more burdensome or less profitable is irrelevant.[30] Thus no rise or fall of prices or wages has so far been held to avoid a contract for the supply of goods or labour.[31] Inflation *per se* does not constitute frustration.[32] It is for the legislature, by emergency legislation, to provide for exceptional cases where a change in conditions would make the performance of certain contracts ruinous. There is a general statutory provision under which, when a new duty is imposed, or an existing duty increased or diminished, on any article which is the subject of a sale or an agreement to sell, an increase or diminution of the price, as the case may be, may be claimed by the seller or purchaser.[33] At common law it was held that the loss due to an alteration in duties must

[25] See para. 14.28, *infra*.
[26] *Cantiere San Rocco* v. *Clyde Shipbuilding Co.*, 1922 S.C. 723, revd. 1923 S.C. (H.L.) 105. The law of England has since been brought into line with Scots law: *Fibrosa Spólka Akcyjna* v. *Fairbairn & Co.* [1943] A.C. 32; Law Reform (Frustrated Contracts) Act 1943.
[27] *Foster* v. *Adamson* (1762) Mor. 10131.
[28] (1873) 11 M. (H.L.) 1.
[29] *Infra*, para. 12.15.
[30] *Holliday* v. *Scott* (1830) 8 S. 831.
[31] *Wilson* v. *Tennants* [1917] A.C. 495.
[32] *Wates Ltd.* v. *Greater London Council* (1983) 25 B.L.R. 1 (C.A.). Note also *British Movietonews Ltd.* v. *London and District Cinemas* [1952] A.C. 166 (currency depreciation) and *Multiservice Bookbinding Ltd.* v. *Marden* [1979] Ch. 84 (currency depreciation).
[33] Finance Act 1901, s. 10(1); scope enlarged by Finance Act 1902, s. 7. See also Value Added Tax Act 1983, s. 42.

fall where it might happen to light.[34] It may be regarded as an exception to the general rule that if a subject let is partially destroyed the tenant is entitled to an abatement of rent.[35]

12.9   Object of Contract Defeated.—Events, without rendering literal performance of the contract impossible, may disappoint the object for which one of the parties contracted. If this object was known to himself alone the contract is clearly unaffected; a seller is not concerned with the motives which induce the buyer to buy. Even if the object was known to both, its disappointment will not affect the contract unless the result be to render it completely nugatory. So an agreement for the sale of jute remained binding, although the export of jute was subsequently forbidden, since the contract did not provide that the sale was for export.[36] But there may be exceptional cases where the disappointment of the only purpose which could have induced it, even although no mention may have been made of that purpose in the contract itself, will avoid the contract. A series of cases, usually referred to as the Coronation cases, arose out of the postponement of a procession which had been fixed for the coronation of Edward VII. Rooms had been hired on the route of the procession, without any express mention of it, but on terms which clearly indicated the object for which they were rented. On the postponement of the procession it was held that the case could be treated as one where performance had been rendered impossible, and that the contracts were avoided.[37]

12.10   Violent Acts by Third Parties.—The effect of impossibility due to the violent or unwarrantable acts of third parties is not free from doubt, but it would appear that it is not a ground for the avoidance of a contract. Thus it has been held in England in cases which, though questioned, have not been overruled, that an obligation to load cargo at a particular port is not affected by the fact that civil disturbance or the unwarrantable acts of the port authorities have rendered it impossible.[38] In *Milligan* v. *Ayr Harbour Trustees* it was decided that the obligation of a harbour trust to provide facilities for unloading a ship was not excused by reasonable apprehensions that the result would be a strike, and in the opinion of Lord Guthrie, would not have been excused even if it had been certain that compliance would have brought the business of the harbour to a standstill.[39] Where a tenant's crops were carried off by rebel forces this was held to be no ground for a refusal to pay rent.[40]

---

[34] *Maclelland* v. *Adam* (1795) Mor. 14247.
[35] *Muir* v. *McIntyre* (1887) 14 R. 470; *Sharp* v. *Thomson*, 1930 S.C. 1092.
[36] *McMaster & Co.* v. *Cox McEuen & Co.*, 1920 S.C. 566, revd. 1921 S.C. (H.L.) 24.
[37] *Krell* v. *Henry* [1903] 2 K.B. 740; *Chandler* v. *Webster* [1904] 1 K.B. 493. Contrast *Herne Bay Steamboat Co.* v. *Hutton* [1903] 2 K.B. 683. It was further held in *Krell* and *Chandler* that the money paid in advance for the seats could not be recovered, but these decisions have been overruled on this point; see note 26.
[38] *Jacobs* v. *Credit Lyonnais* (1884) 12 Q.B.D. 589; *Ashmore* v. *Cox* [1899] 1 Q.B. 436. See opinions in *Matthey* v. *Curling* [1922] 2 A.C. 180.
[39] 1915 S.C. 937.
[40] *Strachan* v. *Christie* (1751) Mor. 10129.

12.11 Change in Law: Illegality.—If a change in the law renders performance illegal the contract is dissolved, on the theory that it is not to be presumed that a man bound himself to commit an illegal act. So, for example, a partnership is dissolved by the happening of any event which makes it unlawful for the business of the firm to be carried on, or for the members of the firm to carry it on in partnership.[41] The effect of a declaration of war as dissolving contracts with the enemy is considered later.[42] It is probably established that a contract which is to be performed in a foreign country is dissolved if a change in the law of that country renders performance illegal there.[43]

12.12 Change in Law: Impossibility.—If a change in the law renders performance impossible, the result is to dissolve the contract. Thus a contract for the export of goods is dissolved if their export is prohibited by statutory authority so long as the prohibition is absolute and applies to the whole time available for performance.[44] Where A contracted to leave a particular piece of ground unbuilt upon, and a railway company, under statutory powers, acquired the ground and built a station on it, it was held that A was not liable in damages.[45] But if, in similar circumstance, it is within the obligant's power to secure a clause which would safeguard his obligation, he is bound to do so.[46]

12.13 Impossibility: When Final.—A party is not entitled to cancel his contract on the ground that events are looming in the future which will probably render performance impossible, and, if he takes that course, will be liable in damages even although his apprehensions may be justified by the event.[47] The question how far it may be assumed that an existing bar to performance will remain permanent is in some respects doubtful. It is an established rule that no court can predict how long a war may last and, therefore, that contracts affected by war are dissolved at once.[48] Probably a statute which renders performance illegal or impossible may be regarded as conclusive. But this is not clear with regard to Orders in Council having statutory force, and in one case where the export of confectionery was prohibited by Order it was held that a party who had undertaken to export it was bound to wait to see whether the Order would remain in force, and was not justified in

---

[41] Partnership Act 1890, s. 34.

[42] para. 8, *infra*.

[43] *Ralli* v. *Compania Naviera* [1920] 2 K.B. 287; *Trinidad Shipping Co.* v. *Alston* [1920] A.C. 888.

[44] *Re Anglo-Russian Merchant Traders & Batt* [1917] 2 K.B. 679, distinguished in *Ross T. Smyth & Co. Ltd.* v. *W.N. Lindsay Ltd.* [1953] 1 W.L.R. 1280.

[45] *Baily* v. *De Crespigny* (1869) L.R. 4 Q.B. 180.

[46] *Leith School Board* v. *Rattray's Trs.*, 1918 S.C. 94.

[47] *Watts* v. *Mitsui* [1917] A.C. 227.

[48] *Horlock* v. *Beal* [1916] 1 A.C. 486; *Geipel* v. *Smith* (1872) L.R. 7 Q.B. 404.

rescinding the contract at once.[49] Where administrative measures taken by a foreign government rendered performance impossible it was held that the question whether the contract could be cancelled at once depended on whether there was or was not a reasonable probability that the measures in question would be altered in time to admit of the performance.[50]

12.14   Frustration of the Adventure.—The object of the principle known as frustration is to find some satisfactory way whereby the court may allocate between the parties to a contract the risk of supervening events. The general idea behind it has been judicially explained as follows.[51] 'When a lawful contract has been made and there is no default, a Court of law has no power to discharge either party from the performance of it unless either the rights of someone else or some Act of Parliament give the necessary jurisdiction. But a Court can and ought to examine the contract and the circumstances in which it was made, not of course to vary, but only to explain it, in order to see whether or not from the nature of it the parties must have made their bargain on the footing that a particular thing or state of things would continue to exist ... no Court has an absolving power, but it can infer from the nature of the contract and the surrounding circumstances that a condition which is not expressed was a foundation on which the parties contracted.' While the principle was, in the early stages of its history, developed particularly with regard to the interruption of business activities by delay, it admits of almost indefinite application, as diverse as are the possibilities of a contract being interrupted by a vital change of circumstances. The application of the general principle must depend on the circumstances of each case; and it is for the court to decide, looking to what has actually happened and its effect on the possibility of performing the contract, what is the true position between the parties.[52] Where there is frustration, a dissolution of the contract occurs automatically, independent of the choice or election of either party.[53] It is immaterial that the possibility of the frustrating event was within the contemplation of both parties; the only thing that is essential is that the parties should have made no provision for it in their contract.[54] Where a clause can be read as providing specifically for the event which occurred, the rule can have no application.[55]

---

[49] *Millar* v. *Taylor* [1916] 1 K.B. 402.

[50] *Embiricos* v. *Reid* [1914] 3 K.B. 45.

[51] By Lord Loreburn in *Tamplin Co.* v. *Anglo-Mexican Petroleum Co.* [1916] 2 A.C. 397, at p. 403, quoted by Lord Radcliffe in *Davis Contractors Ltd.* v. *Fareham U.D.C.* [1956] A.C. 696 at p. 727.

[52] *Per* Lord Wright in *James B. Fraser & Co.* v. *Denny Mott & Dickson*, 1944 S.C. (H.L.) 35 at pp. 42–43.

[53] *Hirji Mulji* v. *Cheong Yue S.S. Co.* [1926] A.C. 497 at p. 510.

[54] *Tamplin Co., supra; Ocean Tramp Tankers Corporation* v. *v/o Sovfracht (The Eugenia)* [1964] 2 Q.B. 226, *per* Lord Denning M.R. at p. 240.

[55] *Scott* v. *Del Sel*, 1922 S.C. 592, affd. 1923 S.C. (H.L.) 37; *The Evia (No. 2)* [1983] A.C. 736.

12.15 Theory or Principle of Frustration.—While the doctrine of frustration is itself now well established, the search for a theoretical basis for it has continued. Dicta in the House of Lords have over the years favoured a variety of theories, and, while the results have in most cases been consistent, it may be a matter of significance which theory is applied.[56] According to what may be called the 'implied term' theory, which has had wide support in past decisions of the House of Lords in English appeals, the principle upon which supervening impossibility was held to dissolve a contract was that it is an implied condition in the particular contract that performance is promised only if it remains possible and legal. The court, it was said, has no power to dissolve or vary a contract, but it has the power and duty to give effect to the intentions of the parties by interpreting the contract according to its conditions, implied as well as express.[57] The implied term theory was, however, not without its critics,[58] and seems now to have been rejected in favour of another which has had some currency in the past and seems more in line with the Scottish approach.[59] According to this view, which may be called the 'material change' theory, as contractual obligation rests on consent, there can be no obligation to perform in circumstances so altered that performance, if given, would in substance be the performance not of the original contract, but of a different contract, and one to which the parties have not consented. Lord Radcliffe in *Davis Contractors Ltd.* v. *Fareham U.D.C.*[60] has formulated the theory as follows: 'frustration occurs whenever the law recognises that without default of either party a contractual obligation has become incapable of being performed because the circumstances in which performance is called for would render it a thing radically different from that which was undertaken by the contract. *Non haec in foedera veni.* It was not this that I promised to do.' Lord Reid's opinion in the same case,[61] that frustration depends upon the true construction[62] of terms of the contract

---

[56] *Davis Contractors Ltd., supra, per* Lord Reid at p. 719, Lord Radcliffe at p. 728.

[57] See opinion of Earl Loreburn, *Tamplin Co.* v. *Anglo-Mexican Petroleum Co.* [1916] 2 A.C. 397, 405; of Lord Dundas, *Macmaster* v. *Cox, McEuen & Co.*, 1920 S.C. 566, revd. 1921 S.C. (H.L.) 24; of Lord Simon in *Joseph Constantine Steamship Line* v. *Imperial Smelting Corporation* [1942] A.C. 154 at p. 164; of Lord Simon and Lord Simonds in *British Movietonews* v. *London and District Cinemas* [1952] A.C. 166 at pp. 183, 187.

[58] See, *e.g.* Lord Wright in *James B. Fraser & Co., supra,* at p. 43; Lord Reid in *Davis Contractors Ltd., supra,* at p. 720.

[59] See opinion of Lord Dunedin, *Metropolitan Water Board* v. *Dick, Kerr & Co.* [1918] A.C. 119. The Scottish approach has been that the court in the exercise of its equitable jurisdiction does, upon a proper construction of the contract, what seems just in the circumstances: see Lord Cooper, 'Frustration of Contract in Scots Law' (1946) 28 J. Comp. Leg. 1 at p. 5.

[60] [1956] A.C. 696 at p. 729. See also *Tsakiroglou & Co. Ltd.* v. *Noblee Thorl GmbH* [1962] A.C. 93; *The Eugenia, supra, per* Lord Denning M.R. at pp. 238–40; *Pioneer Shipping Ltd.* v. *B.T.P. Tioxide Ltd.* [1982] A.C. 724 at p. 751.

[61] at p. 720.

[62] For an earlier statement of the 'true construction' approach, see Lord Simon in *British Movietonews, supra,* at p. 185; Lord Wright in *James B. Fraser & Co., supra,* at pp. 42–43.

and of the relevant surrounding circumstances when the contract was made, is really another way of saying the same thing. As he puts it, the question in each case is whether the contract which the parties did make is, on its true construction, wide enough to apply to the new situation; if not, it is at an end.

12.16 Illustrations.—The application of this rule will most easily be understood by examples. Where a servant is unable to attend to his duties through illness this does not form a breach of contract on his part, but if the time for which he is absent is in the circumstances material, it does bring the case within the law of frustration of the adventure, and the employer is entitled to cancel the contract.[63] In what is usually regarded as the leading case A undertook to send a ship to Cardiff to load a cargo for South America. His obligation was to arrive with all convenient speed, unless prevented by perils of the sea. By perils of the sea the ship was injured, with the result that her voyage to Cardiff took some five months more than the normal time. Though she had arrived in time according to the terms of the contract, it was held that the delay so altered the conditions as to entitle the charterer to declare it cancelled.[64] Where a house let furnished was requisitioned by the military authorities it was held that both landlord and tenant were liberated by 'constructive total destruction' of the premises.[65] And where a vessel which had been chartered to carry a cargo was so damaged by a violent explosion that she was unable to perform the charterparty, it was held that the voyage had been frustrated and that the owners were not liable in damages for non-performance.[66]

12.17 Limits of Principle of Frustration.—The principle does not apply to a change in economic conditions which may render the contract more onerous than had been contemplated; the fact that it had become more expensive or commercially less attractive for one party than he anticipated is not enough to bring about a frustration of the contract.[67] A policy of marine insurance is not affected by the declaration of war, however seriously that may affect the risk.[68] The principle of frustration of the adventure operates automatically for the good or ill of both

---

[63] *Manson* v. *Dowie* (1885) 12 R. 1103; *Poussard* v. *Spiers & Pond* (1876) 1 Q.B.D. 410; *Notcutt* v. *Universal Equipment Co. (London) Ltd.* [1986] 1 W.L.R. 641. There is no need for the employer (in a proper case) to give notice of termination: *Westwood* v. *Scottish Motor Traction Co.*, 1938 S.N. 8.

[64] *Jackson* v. *Union Marine Insurance Co.* (1874) L.R. 10 C.P. 125. See also *Nelson* v. *Dundee East Shipping Co.*, 1907 S.C. 927.

[65] *Mackeson* v. *Boyd*, 1942 S.C. 56; see also *Metropolitan Water Board* v. *Dick, Kerr & Co.* [1918] A.C. 119.

[66] *Joseph Constantine Steamship Line* v. *Imperial Smelting Corporation* [1942] A.C. 154.

[67] *Wilson* v. *Tennants* [1917] A.C. 495; *Davis Contractors Ltd.*, *supra*; *Tsakiroglou & Co.*, *supra*; *The Eugenia*, *supra*, *per* Lord Denning M.R. at p. 239.

[68] *Brown* v. *Maxwell* (1824) 2 Sh.App. 373.

parties, and the person who relies upon it lies under no obligation to disprove fault on his part in connection with the frustrating event.[69]

---

[69] *Joseph Constantine Steampship Line, supra.* As to the effect on a contract of employment of the employee being given a custodial sentence, see *F.C. Shepherd & Co. Ltd.* v. *Jerrom* [1986] 3 W.L.R. 801.

CHAPTER 13

BREACH OF CONTRACT

13.1 Right to Specific Implement.—When one party to a contract refuses, or fails, to fulfil his obligations the other may generally insist on specific implement. If the obligation in question is of a positive character, it may be enforced by a decree *ad factum praestandum*, and if of a negative, by interdict. A person who fails to obtemper a decree *ad factum praestandum* may be imprisoned until he does, but for not more than six months, and only if the court is satisfied that his refusal to comply with the decree is wilful.[1] Breach of interdict is punishable by fine or imprisonment. Subject to the discretion of the court to refuse decree when it would cause exceptional hardship,[2] the right to demand specific implement of a contract is, in Scots law, a general rule.[3] The following are the leading exceptions.

13.2 Cases where Specific Implement Refused.—(1) Where the obligation in question is the payment of money. As a rule the sole remedy of a creditor is to enforce payment by diligence; he is not entitled to a decree *ad factum praestandum*, which might result in the imprisonment of the debtor. Such a decree is by statute competent in the case of a contract to take up and pay for debentures of a company,[4] and may be granted in other cases where there is an order for consignation of money in court.[5]

(2) Where the contract if fulfilled would involve an intimate relationship, where forced compliance would be worse than none. So specific implement will not be granted of a contract of service,[6] or of a contract to enter into partnership.[7]

---

[1] Law Reform (Misc. Provs.) (Scotland) Act 1940, s. 1; *Nelson* v. *Nelson*, 1988 S.C.L.R. 663.

[2] *Grahame* v. *Magistrates of Kirkcaldy* (1882) 9 R. (H.L.) 91.

[3] *Stewart* v. *Kennedy* (1890) 17 R. (H.L.) 1; the English law is contrasted by Lord Watson, at p. 9. The court cannot, however, grant decree of specific implement against the Crown: Crown Proceedings Act 1947, s. 21(1).

[4] Companies Act 1985, s. 195.

[5] *Mackenzie* v. *Balerno Paper Mill Co.* (1883) 10 R. 1147.

[6] Trade Union and Labour Relations (Consolidation) Act 1992, s. 236; *Skerret* v. *Oliver* (1896) 23 R. 468, at p. 485. Cf. *Murray* v. *Dumbarton C.C.*, 1935 S.L.T. 239; interdict against transfer of a teacher, so as, in effect, to enforce compliance, refused. An industrial tribunal may make an order for reinstatement or re-engagement of an employee, failure to comply with which may result in an additional award of compensation: Employment Protection (Consolidation) Act 1978, ss. 69–71; see *infra*, para. 22.13.

[7] *Macarthur* v. *Lawson* (1877) 4 R. 1134, p. 1136; *Pert* v. *Bruce*, 1937 S.L.T. 475.

(3)   Where compliance with the decree would be impossible. As the only sanction of a decree *ad factum praestandum* is imprisonment it will not be pronounced where the defender cannot possibly comply with it, even if the impossibility may be due to his own fault.[8] Thus if a man undertakes something which he cannot lawfully do, *e.g.* to execute work on land to which he has no right of access, he may be liable in damages for failure, but specific implement is not an appropriate remedy.[9]

(4)   Where the court cannot enforce the decree. Where the defender is a foreigner, subject to the jurisdiction of the Scottish courts only on some exceptional ground, these courts, as they have no power to enforce a decree *ad factum praestandum* by his imprisonment, will not pronounce a decree which would be futile.[10] Nor will such a decree be pronounced in pursuance of an obligation which can be performed by a corporate body only as a whole, and not by its officials, and where there is no means of enforcement except by the imprisonment of all the individual members of the body.[11]

(5)   Where there is no *pretium affectionis*. In the case of generic sales, *i.e.* sales of a certain quantity of a commodity which can be procured in the open market, the purchaser's remedy is to supply himself at the seller's expense, and decree of specific implement against the seller is incompetent.[12] Where, how-ever, an alternative source of supply is unavailable, or not readily available, specific implement may be granted.[13]

13.3   **Remedies for Breach of Contract.**—Where specific enforcement of a contract is either incompetent, or not demanded, the party aggrieved by a breach is always entitled to damages, nominal or substantial where it causes him loss or, at least, inconvenience.[14] He may have other remedies. He may be entitled to exercise a right of retention, whereby, without ending the contract, he may withhold performance of the obligations incumbent on him until the obligations due to him are

---

[8] *Macarthur* v. *Lawson, supra, per* Lord President Inglis; *Rudman* v. *Jay*, 1908 S.C. 552.

[9] *Sinclair* v. *Caithness Flagstone Co.* (1898) 25 R. 703.

[10] Note, however, *Ford* v. *Bell Chandler*, 1977 S.L.T. (Sh. Ct.) 90, where it was held that a decree is competent against a party outwith the jurisdiction because an order for payment can be substituted for the warrant for imprisonment: Law Reform (Misc. Provs.) (Scotland) Act 1940, s. 1(2).

[11] *Gall* v. *Loyal Glenbogie Lodge* (1900) 2 F. 1187; contrast *Collins* v. *Barrowfield Oddfellows*, 1915 S.C. 190; *Ponder* v. *Ponder*, 1932 S.C. 233. See, as to the position of a receiver, *Macleod* v. *Alexander Sutherland*, 1977 S.L.T. (Notes) 44.

[12] *Union Electric Co.* v. *Holman*, 1913 S.C. 954.

[13] *Sky Petroleum Ltd.* v. *V.I.P. Petroleum Ltd.* [1974] 1 W.L.R. 576: *cf. Re London Wine Co. (Shippers)* [1986] P.C.C. 121. Note also *Howard E. Perry & Co.* v. *British Railways Board* [1980] 1 W.L.R. 1375 which seems to justify the view in *Sky Petroleum Ltd.*

[14] It is doubtful that nominal damages should be recoverable where loss or inconvenience are absent: *Aarons & Co.* v. *Fraser*, 1934 S.C. 137. Damages for inconvenience suffered were awarded in *Gunn* v. *National Coal Board*, 1982 S.L.T. 526.

tendered or performed. He may also have the right to break off all contractual relations, to rescind the contract, or, in the words of section 15B(1)(b) of the Sale of Goods Act 1979, to 'treat the contract as repudiated.'[14a] If one party shows by words or conduct that he does not intend to perform his obligations he is said to 'repudiate' the contract and the other party can accept the repudiation and rescind the contract. If one party fails to perform a material obligation under the contract, that is deemed repudiation and the other party can treat the contract as repudiated and rescind the contract.[15] Where a material breach is remediable, the party in breach should probably be given a second chance to put things right.[15a] Repudiation does not bring the contract to an end.[16] Firstly, the innocent party may choose to affirm his rights by raising an action for specific implement against the party in material breach.[17] Secondly, if he elects to rescind, this relieves him of his obligation to perform, further, his part of the bargain[18] but it does not absolve the party in breach from obligations already incurred under the contract.[18a] Thirdly, some contract terms, such as arbitration or exclusion or liquidate damages clauses, are worded so as to survive the breach of contract and govern its consequences.[19] A right to payment of interest for non-payment of the purchase price of heritable property will not be sustained if it is worded in a way which indicates that interest is due only where the contract is being performed.[19a] Postponing in the meantime the law of retention, we have to consider the circumstance which will justify a party in breaking off contractual relations on the ground that the other is in breach of the contract.

13.4 Rescission.—There is a source of confusion in that, in considering what justifies rescission, some authorities refer to 'material terms' and others

---

[14a] As added by s.5(1) of the Sale and Supply of Goods Act 1994.

[15] *Blyth* v. *Scottish Liberal Club*, 1982 S.C. 140, *per* Lord Dunpark at p. 149; *Lloyd's Bank plc* v. *Bamberger*, 1994 S.L.T. 424.

[15a] *Lindley Catering Investments* v. *Hibernian Football Club*, 1975 S.L.T. (Notes) 14. There is a trace of approval of this approach in *Millars of Falkirk Ltd.* v. *Turpie*, 1976 S.L.T. (Notes) 66.

[16] *Johannesburg Municipal Council* v. *Stewart*, 1909 S.C. 860, *per* Lord President Dunedin at p. 878: 'That does not mean that the contract is gone forever; on the contrary, the contract remains and is only the measure of liability for damages.' Note also, *Photo Production Ltd.* v. *Securicor Transport Ltd.* [1980] A.C. 827, *per* Lord Diplock at p. 844: 'when in the context of a breach of contract one speaks of "termination," what is meant is no more than that the innocent party, or in some cases, both parties, are excused for further performance.' Note also *Port Jackson Stevedoring Pty. Ltd.* v. *Salmond & Spraggon (Australia) Pty. Ltd.* [1980] 3 All E.R. 257; *G.L. Group plc* v. *Ash Gupta Advertising Ltd.*, 1987 S.C.L.R. 149.

[17] *Salaried Staff London Loan Co. Ltd.* v. *Swears and Wells Ltd.*, 1985 S.L.T. 326.

[18] *Heyman* v. *Darwins Ltd.* [1942] A.C. 356.

[18a] *Photo Production Ltd.* v. *Securicor Transport Ltd.*, supra; *Lloyd's Bank plc* v. *Bamberger*, supra.

[19] *Heyman* v. *Darwins Ltd.*, supra; *Alexander Stephen (Forth) Ltd.* v. *J.J. Riley (U.K.) Ltd.*, 1976 S.L.T. 269; *Sanderson & Son* v. *Armour & Co.*, 1922 S.C. (H.L.) 177; *Muir Construction Ltd.* v. *Hambly Ltd.*, 1990 S.L.T. 830.

[19a] *Lloyd's Bank plc* v. *Bamberger*, supra.

to 'material breach.' It seems that there are terms any breach of which is sufficient to justify rescission and others breach of which is not ground for rescission unless the consequences of the breach are sufficiently serious.

The following cases have to be considered: (1) The question whether any particular provision in a contract is a material term of the contract[20] is one which the parties may settle for themselves. If they choose to provide that the whole contract shall be dependent on the fulfilment of one provision or condition, then, no matter how trivial it may appear to be, the court will give effect to the expressed intention of the parties.[21] An implied intention will also be given effect.[22] (2) There may be an implication of law that breach of a certain term will justify rescission. Thus the Sale of Goods Act 1979 provides that breach of a term as to the quality of the goods or their fitness for a purpose in a consumer contract of sale shall be deemed to be a material breach.[23] (3) A declaration by one party that he refuses to perform his obligations under the contract entitles the other party to rescind.[24] Repudiation may be effected by conduct. 'If the defender has behaved in such a way that a reasonable person would properly conclude that he does not intend to perform the obligations he has undertaken, that is sufficient.'[25] An unjustified rescission may be treated as a repudiation which entitles the other party to rescind and recover damages.[26] An unjustified rescission need not be regarded as a repudiation where done in the honest belief that it is justified and on the clear understanding that should this belief be shown to be wrong, the contract will be performed according to its terms.[26a] (4) The breach itself may make further performance of the contract impossible, e.g. where the contract was to instal equipment in a factory and a defect in the equipment caused a fire which destroyed the factory[27] the contract is rescinded and the innocent party has no option as to accepting repudiation. (5) A total failure of performance is obviously material. (6) The terms of the contract may indicate that a stipulation is so material that breach of it per se justifies rescission. The term must be one which goes to the root and essence of the contract.

[20] The English term is 'condition precedent.' 'Precedent' refers to materiality, not to time.
[21] Standard Life Assurance Co. v. Weems (1884) 11 R. (H.L.) 48; Dawsons v. Bonnin, 1922 S.C. (H.L.) 156; Provincial Insurance Co. v. Morgan [1933] A.C. 240.
[22] Bunge Corp. v. Tradax Export S.A. [1981] 1 W.L.R. 711.
[23] Sale of Goods Act, 1979, s. 15B(2)(a); added by the Sale and Supply of Goods Act 1994, s. 5(1). But see para. 16.27, infra.
[24] Davie v. Stark (1876) 3 R. 1114; see para. 13.10, infra, as to anticipatory breach.
[25] Forslind v. Bechely-Crundall, 1922 S.C. (H.L.) 173, per Viscount Haldane at p. 179.
[26] Carswell v. Collard (1893) 20 R. (H.L.) 47; Forbes v. Campbell (1885) 12 R. 1065; Municipal Council of Johannesburg v. Stewart, 1909 S.C. 860, per Lord President Dunedin at p. 877.
[26a] Woodar Investment Development Ltd. v. Wimpey Construction U.K. Ltd. [1980] 1 All E.R. 57 (H.L.).
[27] Harbutt's 'Plasticine' Ltd. v. Wayne Tank and Pump Co. Ltd. [1970] 1 Q.B. 447.

Two cases may be narrated as illustrations. In *Wade* v. *Waldon*,[28] a comedian undertook to perform in a theatre on a date a year subsequent to the contract. It was stipulated that he should give a fortnight's notice, with bill matter, before the date of appearance. This stipulation he failed to comply with, and the manager of the theatre in consequence refused to fulfil his engagement. It was held that the comedian was entitled to damages, on the ground that, although he was in breach of contract in failing to send the notice, the breach was not sufficiently material to justify the manager in breaking off the whole contract. In *Graham* v. *United Turkey Red Co.*[29] an agent for the sale of goods undertook not to sell the same goods supplied by others. This condition he broke. It was accepted that it was a material condition, and that the breach precluded the agent from suing for the commission to which he was entitled under the contract. Any claim he might have must rest on the ground, apart from the contract, that his employers had taken benefit from his service. (7) There are cases where rescission is justified by the nature of the breach. While it is a term of a contract of service that the employee will obey orders, whether disobedience justifies rescission in a particular instance is a question of facts and circumstances.[30] The breach 'must fundamentally affect the fair carrying out of the bargain as a whole';[31] it must have 'the effect of depriving the other party of substantially the whole benefit which it was the intention of the parties that he should obtain from the contract'.[32]

13.5 Exclusion Clauses.—Apart from the provisions of the Unfair Contract Terms Act 1977 and those of the Unfair Terms in Consumer Contracts Regulations 1994,[33] it is open to the parties to a contract to provide by means of exclusion or exemption clauses that the failure by one of them in the performance of his obligations under the contract will not entitle the other to recover damages or to rescind the contract. It is now accepted that it is possible to frame a clause of this kind which will exclude liability for even a 'total' or 'fundamental' breach.[34] But such

---

[28] 1909 S.C. 571. The following passage in the opinion of Lord President Dunedin has been frequently referred to: 'It is familiar law, and quite well settled by decision, that in any contract which contains multifarious stipulations there are some which go so to the root of the contract that a breach of those stipulations entitles the party pleading the breach to declare that the contract is at an end. There are others which do not go to the root of the contract, but which are part of the contract, and which would give rise, if broken, to an action of damages.' To this general rule it would appear that the contract of sale of goods by description must be treated as an exception: para. 16.27, *infra*.

[29] 1922 S.C. 533.

[30] *Blyth* v. *Scottish Liberal Club*, 1982 S.C. 140.

[31] *Forslind* v. *Bechely-Crundall, supra, per* Lord Shaw at p. 190.

[32] *Photo Production Ltd.* v. *Securicor Transport Ltd., supra, per* Lord Diplock at p. 849.

[33] See paras. 10.16 *et seq, supra.*

[34] There is a problem of nomenclature. 'Fundamental term' may refer to a term breach of which justifies rescission: *Photo Production Ltd.* v. *Securicor Transport Ltd.* [1980] A.C. 827, per Lord Diplock at p. 849; or to a term breach of which, it was thought, could not be covered by an exclusion clause: *Smeaton Hanscomb & Co. Ltd.* v. *Sassoon I. Setty Son & Co.* [1953] 1 W.L.R. 1468, *per* Devlin J. at p. 1470. Similarly, 'fundamental breach' is used to refer to a breach which justifies rescission: *Suisse Atlantique Société d'Armament*

clauses are strictly construed, and it is a question of construction in each case whether the clause is so clearly and unambiguously expressed as to be effectual where there has been a fundamental breach of contract.[35] Clauses which merely limit liability must equally be strictly construed and read *contra proferentem* but they are to be judged by a less exacting standard.[36] In England it was at one time held that if, on a fundamental breach, the innocent party rescinded the contract, the other party could not then rely on a clause limiting liability because the contract, including the exclusion clause, had ceased to exist; and the result was the same where the fundamental breach itself brought the contract to an end.[37] Although it has been held that that is not the law of Scotland,[38] the Unfair Contract Terms Act 1977, section 22, provides 'for the avoidance of doubt' that where the Act requires that the incorporation of a term in a contract to which the Act applies must be fair and reasonable for that term to have effect—(a) if that requirement is satisfied, the term may be given effect to notwithstanding that the contract has been terminated in consequence of breach of that contract, (b) for the term to be given effect to, that requirement must be satisfied even where a party who is entitled to rescind the contract elects not to rescind it.

13.6   Building Contracts.—There is some difficulty in the law relating to building contracts, mainly due to the fact that a failure by a builder to observe the building conditions may not materially affect the value of the building and yet may not be remediable without inordinate expense. If the builder so far deviates from his contract as to produce a building substantially different from that ordered, the owner may reject it; if he prefers to keep it, he is not liable for the contract price, but only *quantum lucratus*, in so far as he is enriched by the building.[39] If the defects are of minor importance and admit of being remedied, the builder may recover the contract price under deduction of the sum necessary to bring the building into consonance with the plans.[40] If the deviation is irremediable without demolition, *e.g.* where the wrong kind of cement has been used, it was held in *Steel* v. *Young*,[41] that even if

Maritime S.A. v. *N.V. Rotterdamsche Kolen Centrale* [1967] 1 A.C. 361, *per* Lord Reid at p. 397; or to a breach which, it was thought, could not be covered by an exclusion clause: *Charterhouse Credit Co. Ltd.* v. *Tolly* [1963] 2 Q.B. 683, *per* Donovan L.J. at p. 704.

[35] *Pollock* v. *Macrae*, 1922 S.C. (H.L.) 192; *Mechans* v. *Highland Marine Charters*, 1964 S.C. 48. See, as to whether such a clause exempts a party from the consequences of his own negligence, *Canada Steamship Lines Ltd.* v. *The King* [1952] A.C. 192; *Smith* v. *U.M.B. Chrysler (Scotland) Ltd.*, 1978 S.C. (H.L.) 1; *Evans* v. *Glasgow District Council*, 1979 S.L.T. 270; *Verrico* v. *Geo. Hughes & Son*, 1980 S.C. 179; *Golden Sea Produce Ltd.* v. *Scottish Nuclear plc.*, 1992 S.L.T. 942.

[36] *Ailsa Craig Fishing Co. Ltd.* v. *Malvern Fishing Co. Ltd.*, 1982 S.C. (H.L.) 14.

[37] *Harbutt's 'Plasticine'* v. *Wayne Tank and Pump Co.* [1970] 1 Q.B. 447.

[38] *Alexander Stephen (Forth)* v. *J.J. Riley (U.K.)*, 1976 S.C. 151.

[39] *Ramsay* v. *Brand* (1898) 25 R. 1212.

[40] *Spiers* v. *Petersen*, 1924 S.C. 428.

[41] 1907 S.C. 360.

the difference in value was inappreciable the builder could not sue for the contract price, and that, if his action contained no conclusions for payment on the basis of *quantum lucratus*, it must be dismissed. But this decision has been doubted in *Forrest* v. *Scottish County Investment Co.*[42] From the opinions there given it would appear that if the contract had scheduled prices for each item (a measure and value, as distinguished from a lump-sum, contract) failure in one item would not preclude action for the amount due for the rest. The effect of an irremediable but immaterial failure in a lump-sum contract is doubtful;[43] in an English case opinions were given to the effect that the builder might sue for the contract price under deduction of any damage which the owner might have suffered.[44]

13.7   Materiality of Time of Performance.—The question whether time of performance is material, or, as it is sometime put, whether time is of the essence of the contract, depends upon the nature of the obligations undertaken. Time is clearly material, and failure will justify rescission, in contracts for the supply, or carriage, of goods which vary in price from day to day.[45] In other mercantile contracts, where the element of fluctuation in price is absent, performance on the actual day is not generally material, but any lengthened delay will justify rescission.[46] In contracts for the construction of a particular article delay is not generally sufficiently material to justify the rejection of the article when ultimately tendered.[47] Failure to tender a marketable title to heritage on the day fixed will not entitle a buyer to resile,[48] but will entitle him to intimate that he will resile if the title is not tendered at some definite date in the future.[49] It is clear that time of performance is not so material in a lease as to justify the tenant in throwing up the lease in the event of the landlord failing to execute improvements or repairs within the time stipulated.[50]

13.8   Degrees in Materiality.—There are degrees in materiality. A failure may not be sufficiently material to justify the rescission of the contract, yet may justify the party aggrieved in withholding performance of the obligations incumbent on him. This has been illustrated chiefly in the

---

[42] 1916 S.C. (H.L.) 28.

[43] See comments on *Forrest* v. *Scottish County Investment Co.* in *Graham* v. *United Turkey Red Co.*, 1922 S.C. 533.

[44] *Dakin* v. *Lee* [1916] 1 K.B. 566. See also *Eshelby* v. *Federated Bank* [1932] 1 K.B. 423.

[45] *Colvin* v. *Short* (1857) 19 D. 890; *Nelson* v. *Dundee East Coast Shipping Co.*, 1907 S.C. 927.

[46] *Carswell* v. *Collard* (1892) 19 R. 987; affd. (1893) 20 R. (H.L.) 47.

[47] *Macbride* v. *Hamilton* (1875) 2 R. 775.

[48] *Kelman* v. *Barr's Tr.* (1878) 5 R. 816.

[49] *Stickney* v. *Keeble* [1915] A.C. 386; see also *Rodger (Builders)* v. *Fawdry*, 1950 S.C. 483, *per* Lord Sorn (O.H.) at p. 492.

[50] *McKimmie's Trs.* v. *Armour* (1899) 2 F. 156.

case of leases. Failure by a landlord to place, or to uphold, the subject in the condition required by the contract may be so material as to justify the tenant in abandoning the subjects and claiming damages; or, where less material, may justify him in withholding payment of his rent; or may be in such a subordinate point that the tenant's only remedy is a claim for damages. The questions involved depend so much on the particular circumstance, and on the reasonableness, or otherwise, of the conduct of the parties, that it is not proposed to deal with the cases here.[51] Similar rules, equally insusceptible of precise definition, prevail in the case of a contract for the supply of goods by instalments.[52] It does not follow that because the loss caused by a breach is small, then the breach is trivial and not material.[53]

13.9 Unity of Contract.—There is a general presumption that a contract is to be regarded as a whole, that the stipulations on either side are the counterparts and consideration given for each other, and therefore that failure by one party will justify the other in breaking off contractual relations, or in withholding performance of the obligations incumbent on him, according to the degree of materiality of the breach in question.[54] And it is competent to prove that two contracts are so related to each other that their respective provisions are interdependent. Thus where a verbal contract for the sale of two ships was, for reasons of convenience, carried into effect by two separate bills of sale, it was held that there was really only one contract, and therefore that the seller, who was unable to supply one of the ships, could not insist on the purchaser taking the other.[55]

There is only a presumption that the provisions of a contract are dependent on each other. There is nothing to prevent two separate contracts, for instance a lease and an option to buy, being recorded in the same deed, and it is then a question of construction whether they are interdependent or not.[56] And even when there is clearly only one contract, some of its provisions may be independent covenants.

As illustrations of the general rule that the provisions of a contract are interdependent may be cited the decisions that where a restrictive covenant is imposed on an employee the employer cannot enforce it if he has wrongfully dismissed the employee and is therefore himself in breach of contract;[57] and that where a landlord undertook to take over

[51] See para. 41.10, *infra*; Rankine, *Leases* (3rd ed.), pp. 245, 326.
[52] para. 16.41, *infra*.
[53] *N.V. Devos Gebroeder* v. *Sunderland Sportwear Ltd.*, 1987 S.L.T. 331.
[54] Stair, I, x, 16; *Turnbull* v. *McLean & Co.* (1874) 1 R. 730; *Barclay* v. *Anderston Foundry Co.* (1856) 18 D. 1190; *Dingwall* v. *Burnett*, 1912 S.C. 1097; *Graham & Co.* v. *United Turkey Red Co. Ltd.*, *supra*; *Laurie* v. *British Steel Corp.*, 1988 S.L.T. 17.
[55] *Claddagh Steamship Co.* v. *Steven*, 1919 S.C. 184, 1919 S.C. (H.L.) 132.
[56] *Penman* v. *Mackay*, 1922 S.C. 385.
[57] *General Billposting Co.* v. *Atkinson* [1909] A.C. 118; *Measure Bros.* v. *Measure* [1910] 2 Ch. 248.

a sheep stock on a farm at the tenant's waygoing the tenant could not enforce the obligation when he was in breach of the material conditions of the lease.[58] Of the exceptional case where provisions are read as independent covenants the best illustration is *Pendreigh's Tr.* v. *Dewar.*[59] There a tenant undertook to lay out £200 on repairs, to be repaid on the expiry of the lease; it was held that, although the tenant was in breach of his contract under the lease, the right to repayment of the sum which he had expended was an independent stipulation, which was not affected by the fact that the other provisions of the lease had not been implemented.

13.10　Anticipatory Breach of Contract.—A definite refusal by one party to perform his obligations under a contract, even if made before the time for performance has arrived, may be treated by the other as an actual breach of contract which entitles him at once to the remedies which such a breach may entail.[60] He may accept the refusal as final; if he does so, any subsequent offer of performance comes too late.[61] He may decline to accept the refusal, and, when the time for performance arrives, sue for damages measured by the loss suffered at the date of failure, not at the date of the anticipatory refusal.[62] By adopting this attitude he puts it in the power of the other to reconsider his refusal, and also to take advantage of any intervening circumstance, such as a declaration of war, which, by rendering performance impossible or illegal, may offer a defence to a claim for damages.[63] In a case where he has the active duties under the contract, he has also the option, rather than accepting the refusal and claiming damages for breach of contract, of disregarding it so that the contract remains effectual. If he can carry out the contract without the co-operation, active or passive,[64] of the other party, he may proceed to do so and then claim for the full contract price.[65] It may be, however, that, if he has no legitimate interest to do so, he will not be allowed to saddle the other party with an additional burden which will involve no benefit to himself;[66] but it is for the other party to aver and

---

[58] *Marquis of Breadalbane* v. *Stewart* (1904) 6 F. (H.L.) 23.

[59] (1871) 9 M. 1037.

[60] *Hochester* v. *De La Tour* (1853) 2 E. & B. 678, as explained by Lords Haldane and Wrenbury in *Bradley* v. *Newsom* [1919] A.C. 16; *Monklands District Council* v. *Ravenstone Securities*, 1980 S.L.T. (Notes) 30.

[61] *Gilfillan* v. *Cadell & Grant* (1893) 21 R. 269.

[62] *Howie* v. *Anderson* (1848) 10 D. 355; *Millet* v. *Van Heek* [1921] 2 K.B. 369; *Tai Hing Cotton Mill* v. *Kamsing Knitting Factory* [1979] A.C. 91.

[63] *Avery* v. *Bowden* (1856) 6 E. & B. 953.

[64] *Hounslow L.B.C.* v. *Twickenham Garden Developments Ltd.* [1971] Ch. 233.

[65] *White & Carter (Councils)* v. *McGregor*, 1962 S.C. (H.L.) 1, overruling *Langford & Co.* v. *Dutch*, 1952 S.C. 15. See *Finelli* v. *Dee* (1968) 67 D.L.R. (2d) 393; *Decro-Wall International S.A.* v. *Practitioners in Marketing Ltd.* [1971] 1 W.L.R. 361; *Attica Sea Carriers Corpn.* v. *Ferrostaal Poseidon Bulk Reederei GmbH* [1976] 1 Lloyd's Rep. 250.

[66] *Per* Lord Reid in *White & Carter (Councils)*, supra, at p. 14; *Gator Shipping Corp.* v. *Trans-Asiatic Oil Ltd. S.A. and Occidental Shipping Establishment* [1978] 2 Lloyd's Rep. 357; *Clea Shipping Corp.* v. *Bulk Oil International Ltd.* [1983] 2 Lloyd's Rep. 645.

prove the absence of legitimate interest.[67] Mere indications of doubt as to ability to perform cannot safely be regarded as an anticipatory breach;[68] but where A had attempted to evade his obligations, and had persistently failed to give any definite answer to demands for performance, it was held that his whole attitude amounted to a refusal to perform, which entitled B to treat the contract as repudiated by him.[69] If performance is due on demand, or on the occurrence of an uncertain event, any act by which the obligant puts it out of his power to perform, as when A transfers to B the article which he has agreed to sell to C, on demand or on the occurrence of some event, amounts to a repudiation of the contract.[70] C in such a case has bargained not merely for ultimate performance, but for the expectation of performance in the meantime, and to deprive him of that expectation is a material breach of the contract.[71] If, on the other hand, the date for performance is fixed the obligant fulfils his contract if he is ready to perform when that date arrives, and it is doubtful whether any intervening act of his with regard to the subject to which the contract relates can be regarded as so irremediable as to amount to a refusal of ultimate performance.[72]

13.11 Retention.—In cases where a contract has been so far performed that its rescission would confer no advantage, and also in certain cases where the breach is not so material as to justify rescission, the party aggrieved by a breach of contract may find his remedy in withholding performance of the obligation incumbent on him. This right, when it takes the form of refusal to pay a debt, is always known as a right of retention; when it takes the form of a refusal to deliver a particular thing it is more commonly referred to as a lien. But in this connection the terms retention and lien are often used as synonymous.

13.12 Retention not a General Rule.—While on the principle of compensation debts which are liquid and payable may be set against each other and extinguished;[73] there is no general rule that a party who is debtor in a liquid debt has any right to refuse or delay payment in respect of any illiquid claim he may have against his creditor. His obligation is to pay the liquid debt at once; his only right is to receive payment when his illiquid claim is established. So a purchaser cannot refuse to pay for goods on the ground that he has a claim of damages for the defective

---

[67] *Salaried Staff London Loan Co. Ltd.* v. *Swears and Wells Ltd.*, 1985 S.L.T. 326.
[68] *Johnstone* v. *Milling* (1886) 16 Q.B.D. 460; *Thorneloe* v. *McDonald* (1892) 29 S.L.R. 409.
[69] *Forslind* v. *Bechely-Crundall*, 1922 S.C. (H.L.) 173.
[70] *Leith School Board* v. *Rattray's Trs.*, 1918 S.C. 94; *Synge* v. *Synge* [1894] 1 Q.B. 466.
[71] See opinion of Lord President Clyde, *Sanderson* v. *Armour*, 1921 S.C. 18, affd. 1922 S.C. (H.L.) 117.
[72] *Harvey* v. *Smith* (1904) 6 F. 511; *Smith* v. *Butler* [1900] 1 Q.B. 694.
[73] As to compensation, see para. 14.11, *infra*.

quality of goods previously supplied by the seller[74] or for the fraud by which he was induced to buy.[75] When a company had two contracts with the town council for the paving of streets, and, through its liquidator, executed one contract, it was held that the town council could not refuse to pay for the work done on the plea that they had a claim of damages in respect of the company's failure to carry out the other contract.[76] The provisions of rule 55 of the First Schedule to the Sheriff Courts (Scotland) Act 1907,[77] it has been held, made no alteration in the law.[78] But the general rule, that an action for a liquid debt cannot be met by a plea of retention based on an illiquid claim, must be stated with the qualification that it has been allowed in exceptional cases, either when the illiquid claim admitted of instant verification,[79] or where, in the opinion of the court, it would be inequitable to reject the plea.[80]

The more definite exceptions to the rule arise—(1) when both claims arise under the same contract; (2) when the creditor in the liquid claim is bankrupt.

13.13   **Retention where Debts Arise from the Same Contract.**—When two claims, one liquid, the other in the nature of a claim for damages, arise from the same contract the creditor in the claim for damages may withhold payment of his debt until the amount due to him as damages is established. On this principle is based the rule, in leases, that if the landlord fails, to any material extent, to execute repairs or improvements which he has agreed to make the tenant may withhold payment of his rent.[81] A carrier's demand for freight may be met by a claim for damages for injury done to the goods.[82] A purchaser of goods may retain the price, in respect of the seller's failure to deliver within a specified or within a reasonable time.[83] But if the price is payable by instalments the buyer is not entitled to retain earlier instalments in

---

[74] *Mackie* v. *Riddell* (1874) 2 R. 115.

[75] *Smart* v. *Wilkinson*, 1928 S.C. 383.

[76] *Asphaltic Limestone Co.* v. *Corporation of Glasgow*, 1907 S.C. 463.

[77] 'Where a defender pleads a counter claim it shall suffice that he state the same in his defences, and the sheriff may thereafter deal with it as if it had been stated in a substantive action, and may grant decree for it in whole or in part, or for the difference between it and the claim sued on.' The rule is now rule 54 (S.I. 1983 No. 747) and there are differences in wording, the sheriff being given power 'to regulate procedure as he thinks fit.' See also Rules of Court of Session (1965), II, 84.

[78] *Christie* v. *Birrell*, 1910 S.C. 986. But it is indisputable that this is not consistent with some of the reasoning in *Armour & Melvin* v. *Mitchell*, 1934 S.C. 94; see also *Croall & Croall* v. *Sharp*, 1954 S.L.T. (Sh. Ct.) 35.

[79] *Ross* v. *Ross* (1895) 22 R. 461.

[80] *Henderson* v. *Turnbull*, 1909 S.C. 510.

[81] *McDonald* v. *Kydd* (1901) 3 F. 923; *Earl of Galloway* v. *McConnell*, 1911 S.C. 846; *Haig* v. *Boswall-Preston*, 1915 S.C. 339. As to agreement not to withhold payment of rent, see *Skene* v. *Cameron*, 1942 S.C. 393.

[82] *Taylor* v. *Forbes* (1830) 9 S. 113. Cf. *Aries Tanker Corporation* v. *Total Transport* [1977] 1 W.L.R. 185.

[83] *British Motor Body Co.* v. *Shaw*, 1914 S.C. 922.

security for damages so long as the amount of the unpaid instalments exceeds the amount of his claim.[84] A bondholder in possession under a decree of mails and duties may be met by a plea of retention based on judgments in the tenants' favour in actions previously brought to enforce their rights under their leases.[85] The contract may exclude the right of retention expressly or by necessary implication.[86]

13.14 **Retention in Insolvency.**—In bankruptcy a party who is a debtor to the bankrupt and has an illiquid claim against him is entitled to withhold payment until the amount of his illiquid claim is ascertained, and then to compensate the one debt with the other, even although the two debts do not arise out of the same contract.[87] The principle applies in liquidation and it is not necessary to aver that the company is insolvent.[88]

13.15 **Lien: Special Lien.**—In contracts of employment, if the party employed has been placed in possession of an article or property belonging to his employer he has the right to retain until his claim for payment for his work is satisfied. This right, known as a special lien, is based on the principle that one party to a contract may withhold performance of his obligation to return the article until performance of the counter-obligation, namely, payment for the work, is made or tendered.[89] The substantial result is to create a right in security.[90]

13.16 **Provisions for Breach of Contract.**—The remedies for breach of contract considered in the preceding pages may in particular cases be supplemented by a provision for an irritancy or a penalty.

13.17 **Irritancies.**—An irritancy is a right to put an end to the contractual relation. When it is conditional on a breach of contract it is a general rule of construction that, no matter how it is expressed, it can be enforced only by the party aggrieved by the breach. It gives no right to the party in default. Thus a provision, in a contract between A and B, that the contract shall be void in the event of a specified breach by B, is read as rendering it voidable at A's option, not as giving B the opportunity of getting rid of his contract by committing a breach thereof.[91]

---

[84] *Dick & Stevenson* v. *Woodside Iron & Steel Co.* (1888) 16 R. 242.
[85] *Marshall's Trs.* v. *Banks*, 1934 S.C. 405.
[86] *Redpath Dorman Long Ltd.* v. *Cummins Engine Co. Ltd.*, 1981 S.C. 370.
[87] Bell, *Comm.*, II, 122.
[88] *Liquidators of Highland Engineering Ltd.* v. *Thomson*, 1972 S.C. 87; *G & A. (Hotels) Ltd.* v. *T.H.B. Marketing Services Ltd.*, 1983 S.L.T. 497.
[89] Bell, *Prin.*, §§ 1411, 1419; *Robertson* v. *Ross* (1887) 15 R. 67; *Paton's Trs.* v. *Finlayson*, 1923 S.C. 872.
[90] Rights in Security, Chap. 19, *infra*.
[91] *Bidoulac* v. *Sinclair's Tr.* (1889) 17 R. 144; *New Zealand Shipping Co.* v. *Société des Ateliers* [1919] A.C. 1.

13.18 Legal Irritancies.—Irritancies may be legal, imposed by law, or conventional, provided in the particular contract. The only legal irritancies known to the law relate to the non-payment of feu-duty or rent. Legal irritancies are purgeable, and an action to enforce them may be met by tender of payment at any time before decree is granted.[92]

13.19 Conventional Irritancies.—A conventional irritancy may be inserted in any contract, and is a matter which parties may arrange as they please. But what is in terms an irritancy may in substance amount to a penalty, and then cannot be enforced unless it can be regarded as a pre-estimate of damages.[93] So where in a contract of sale with a price payable by instalments a provision is made for the irritancy of the contract (involving forfeiture of all that has been paid) this is in substance a penalty and one which the law will not enforce.[94] A conventional irritancy cannot be purged; considerations of hardship are out of place in a question of enforcing an unambiguous provison in a contract.[95] But conventional provisions in feus, and probably in leases if they merely express the irritancy which the law would infer, may be purged[96] and a statutory modification has been made in relation to certain types of lease.[97] And the court has an equitable jurisdiction to allow an irritancy to be purged when its exercise could be shown to be oppressive, as where it was enforced without giving adequate notice that the debt was due.[98]

13.20 Irritancy as Precluding Damages.—The enforcement of an irritancy in a feu contract, by annulling the contract, not only precludes any claim for damages but bars any claim for arrears of feu-duties.[99] In leases, if the event for which the irritancy is provided is the bankruptcy of the tenant, its enforcement is a bar to any claim for damages.[1] But the charterer of a ship may take advantage of a cancelling clause in the charterparty, and also recover damages, if the non-arrival of the ship by the cancelling date is due to the fault of the shipowner.[2]

13.21 Penalty Clauses.—A provision in a contract for the incurring of a penalty in the event of a breach will not be enforced according to its

---

[92] Erskine, I, v, 27. See history of the law in *Duncanson* v. *Giffen* (1878) 15 S.L.R. 356.
[93] para. 13.21, *infra*.
[94] *Steedman* v. *Drinkle* [1916] 1 A.C. 275.
[95] *Lyon* v. *Irvine* (1874) 1 R. 512; *McDouall's Trs.* v. *MacLeod*, 1949 S.C. 593; *Anderson* v. *Valentine*, 1957 S.L.T. 57; *Dorchester Studios (Glasgow)* v. *Stone*, 1975 S.C. (H.L.) 56.
[96] *Duncanson* v. *Giffen* (1878) 15 S.L.R. 356; see *Anderson, supra.*
[97] See Law Reform (Misc. Provs.) (Scotland) Act 1985, ss. 4–7 and para. 41.25, *infra.*
[98] *Stewart* v. *Watson* (1864) 2 M. 1414; *McDouall's Trs., supra*; Precision Relays Ltd. v. *Beaton*, 1980 S.C. 220.
[99] *Magistrates of Edinburgh* v. *Horsburgh* (1834) 12 S. 593; *Malcolm* v. *Donald*, 1956 S.L.T. (Sh. Ct.) 101.
[1] *Buttercase and Geddie's Tr.* v. *Geddie* (1897) 24 R. 1128.
[2] *Nelson* v. *Dundee East Shipping Co.*, 1907 S.C. 927.

terms unless it admits of being construed as a pre-estimate of damages. 'If the penalty be truly a penalty—that is, a punishment—the Court will not allow that, because the law will not let people punish each other.'[3] Where, however, a contract term provides for payment of a penalty on the occurrence of an event other than breach of contract, it will be enforced;[4] unless it occurs in a consumer contract in which case it may be invalid under the Unfair Terms in Consumer Contracts Regulations 1994.[4a]

13.22 Penalty and Liquidate Damages.—The rule is general, and applies to a clause of irritancy if in substance it amounts to a penalty. It has been illustrated in cases where there is a provision for the payment of a specified sum in the event of a breach of the contract. This may be termed a penalty, or may be termed liquidate damages, but the result does not depend on the term used. It is regarded as a penalty unless it bears some intelligible relation to the loss which the breach will probably cause; as liquidate damages if it can be regarded as a fair, though not necessarily exact, pre-estimate of the amount of that loss. If the provision is sustained as liquidate damages, proof of the actual damage sustained is unnecessary,[5] and proof that damage has been sustained beyond the pre-estimate is inadmissible,[6] if regarded as a penalty, nothing can be recovered without proof of actual loss, and the amount fixed as a penalty is not a limit to the amount of damages that may be awarded.[7]

13.23 Penalties in Bonds and Leases.—There are two cases where clauses providing for a penalty or liquidate damages are inoperative. One is a clause in a bond, imposing a penalty on failure of punctual payment of interest. This is not enforceable according to its terms,[8] though there is no legal objection to the enforcement of a provision whereby, though interest at a lower rate than that fixed in the bond will be accepted, the full rate will be exacted on failure of punctual payment.[9] The other case is a provision in an agricultural lease for the payment of increased rent

---

[3] *Per* Lord Young, *Robertson* v. *Driver's Trs.* (1881) 8 R. 555. An interesting case on penalties, involving the Roman-Dutch law, is *Pearl Assurance Co.* v. *Union of South Africa* [1934] A.C. 570.

[4] *Bell Bros (H.P.) Ltd.* v. *Aitken*, 1939 S.C. 577; *Granor Finance Ltd.* v. *Liquidator of Eastore Ltd.*, 1974 S.L.T. 296; *E.F.T. Commercial Ltd.* v. *Security Change Ltd.*, 1993 S.L.T. 128. Note also *Highland Leasing Ltd.* v. *Lyburn*, 1987 S.L.T. 92.

[4a] para. 10.24 *supra*.

[5] *Clydebank Engineering Co.* v. *Castaneda* (1904) 7 F. (H.L.) 77.

[6] *Diestal* v. *Stevenson* [1906] 2 K.B. 345; *Cellulose Acetate Silk Co.* v. *Widnes Foundry* [1933] A.C. 20.

[7] *Dingwall* v. *Burnett*, 1912 S.C. 1097.

[8] *Nasmyth* v. *Samson* (1785) 3 Paton 9; Debts Securities (Scotland) Act 1856, s. 7 (not applicable to a standard security: Conveyancing and Feudal Reform (Scotland) Act 1970, s. 32, Sched. 8, para. 1).

[9] *Gatty* v. *Maclaine*, 1921 S.C. (H.L.) 1.

(usually termed 'pactional rent') or other liquidated damages for breach of the terms of the lease. By statute such a provision is unenforceable.[10]

13.24   **Liquidate Damages.**—Apart from these two special cases the tendency of modern decisions has been to sustain clauses providing for liquidate damages, unless the amount is plainly exorbitant, or where the same sum is fixed for any breach of a contract involving various obligations, some of trivial, and some of relatively great importance. Such a provision indicates that no real pre-estimate of damages was aimed at, only a punishment of the defaulter.[11] Thus where in a lease of an hotel various obligations were laid on each party it was held that a general clause providing for a payment of £50 by either in the event of any failure could not be regarded as a pre-estimate of damages, and, as a penalty, could not be enforced.[12] But it is not an objection that the same sum is fixed for a number of specified acts, if these acts are all of the same class, and if, from the nature of the case, the actual damage likely to result from each act is difficult or impossible to determine. So where agents for the sale of tyres agreed not to tamper with the tyre marks, to export without written consent, or to sell under list prices, a penalty of £5 per tyre was sustained.[13] In a leading case torpedo boats were ordered by the Spanish Government, with a penalty of £500 per week for late delivery. It was held that as it was impossible to prove the amount of loss which a nation might sustain owing to the want of torpedo boats any reasonable pre-estimate, whether termed a penalty or liquidate damages, would be sustained.[14] And it may perhaps be regarded as settled that in a contract for work to be done within a specified time, a penalty calculated at so much per day, week, or month will be sustained, unless plainly exorbitant.[15] In a hire-purchase case, where terms were agreed upon the basis of which the hirer had an option to return the hired article to the seller and he exercised that option, it was held that despite the use of the term 'liquidate damages' as applying to the sum to be paid, the case was truly neither one of penalty nor of liquidate damages.[16] On the other hand, where a hire-purchase contract was terminated by the owner on the ground that the hirer was in breach, it was found necessary to consider whether a clause requiring the hirer to pay in that event the same amount as he would

---

[10] Agricultural Holdings (Scotland) Act 1991, s. 48.

[11] See opinion of Lord Watson, *Lord Elphinstone* v. *Monkland Iron Co.* (1886) 13 R. (H.L.) 98. Such clauses, if exorbitant, are also struck at by the Unfair Terms in Consumer Contracts Regulations 1994 where they appear in a consumer contract: para. 10.24 *supra*.

[12] *Dingwall* v. *Burnett, supra*.

[13] *Dunlop Tyre Co.* v. *New Garage Co.* [1915] A.C. 79; followed, *Imperial Tobacco Co.* v. *Parslay* (1936) 52 T.L.R. 585.

[14] *Clydebank Engineering Co.* v. *Castaneda* (1904) 7 F. (H.L.) 77.

[15] *Cameron Head* v. *Cameron*, 1919 S.C. 627.

[16] *Bell Bros.* v. *Aitken*, 1939 S.C. 577. See also *Granor Finance* v. *Liquidator of Eastore*, 1974 S.L.T. 296.

have had to pay had he exercised his option to terminate was a penalty.[17]

13.25 Deposits on Sale.—In sale it is a common provision that the purchaser must deposit a portion of the price, to be forfeited if he fails to carry out his contract. This, though in substance a penalty, because it 'creates by the fear of its forfeiture a motive in the payer to perform the rest of the contract,'[18] is not so regarded, and the contract may be enforced according to its terms;[19] unless the sale is a consumer contract in which case such a term, if not individually negotiated, may be inavlid under the Unfair Terms in Consumer Contracts Regulations 1994.[19a]

13.26 Penalty Does Not Excuse Performance.—It is a general rule that where the consequences of a breach of contract are provided for by a penalty or by liquidate damages the provision is to be read as an addition to the remedies which the party aggrieved would otherwise possess, not as a licence to the other party to break his contract on payment of the penalty. So building restrictions, though fortified by a penalty, may be enforced by interdict,[20] and the same rule applies to the case where a party has agreed not to carry on a particular business.[21] Penalties are spoken of as 'by and attour performance.'

13.27 Damages.[22]—Where there is no conventional provision for the consequence of a breach of contract, or where that provision is found to be unenforceable, the party aggrieved is in almost all cases entitled to damages. The principal exception is where the breach consists in failure to pay money at the appointed date, when, though interest may be due, no general damages can be demanded.[23]

Damages are intended—and the rule holds in cases of wrongs as well as in cases of breach of contract[24]—as compensation to the injured party,[25] not as a punishment of the party in breach. It is, consequently, irrelevant to consider how far a party who has broken his contract has gained by doing so,[26] or the question whether he is rich or poor.[27]

---

[17] *Bridge* v. *Campbell Discount Co.* [1962] A.C. 600.
[18] *Zemhunt (Holdings) Ltd.* v. *Control Securities plc*, 1992 S.L.T. 150, *per* Lord Morison at p. 154K.
[19] *Commercial Bank* v. *Beal* (1890) 18 R. 80; *Roberts & Cooper* v. *Salvesen*, 1918 S.C. 794; *Zemhunt (Holdings) Ltd.* v. *Control Securities plc*, *supra*. In the last two cases a deposit was treated as a pledge or guarantee of performance.
[19a] Reg. 4(4) and Sched. 3, para. 1(d). For discussion of the regulations, see para. 10.24 *supra*.
[20] *Dalrymple* v. *Herdman* (1878) 5 R. 847.
[21] *Curtis* v. *Sandison* (1831) 10 S. 72.
[22] See Walker, *Law of Civil Remedies in Scotland* (1974) Part VIII.
[23] Erskine, III, iii, 86; Bell, *Prin.*, § 32.
[24] *Black* v. *N.B. Ry.*, 1908 S.C. 444.
[25] *Watson Laidlaw & Co.* v. *Pott, Cassels, & Williamson*, 1914 S.C. (H.L.) 18.
[26] *Teacher* v. *Calder* (1899) 1 F. (H.L.) 39.
[27] *Black* v. *N.B. Ry.*, *supra*.

Neither point affects the loss which the pursuer has sustained, and for which he is to be compensated. It was a general rule in cases of breach of contract that the law will consider material loss or inconvenience only, not injury to feelings arising from the breach or the circumstances in which it was made,[28] but in cases where one party was contracting on a non-commercial basis sums have been awarded in respect of mental distress, disappointment and frustration.[29] It is now established that, in accordance with the principle that compensation to the injured party should be limited to the true loss which he has suffered, consideration of his income tax liability is a necessary element in the calculation of the amount to be awarded as damages.[30]

Where injury is inflicted, whether by breach of contract or by a wrongful or negligent act, the damages that may be claimed are limited by the principle that the party who is aggrieved is bound to take all reasonable means to minimise his loss.[31] So a servant who has been wrongfully dismissed must endeavour to find other employment;[32] a buyer, if the seller has failed to supply the goods, must take measures to supply himself, if there is an available market in which the goods in question can be obtained.[33] Whether such efforts to minimise the loss have in fact been taken or not, the damages awarded will not exceed the loss which their adoption would not have prevented. Similarly, if reasonable care in the inspection of a defective article would have averted some item of loss, that loss will not be included in the damage recoverable from the party who supplied the article.[34] It has been laid down that 'a contracting party is not entitled to proceed so as to cause unnecessary loss to the other party without any resulting benefit to himself.'[35] Where, however, the pursuer can show that he has taken all reasonable means to minimise the loss, he has done enough; the defender cannot successfully avert a claim for damages by proof that some extraordinary or exceptional measures might have been adopted.[36]

13.28 **Measure of Damages.**—The formula as to the measure of damages in the case of breach of contract is often referred to as the rule of *Hadley*

---

[28] *Addis* v. *Gramophone Co.* [1909] A.C. 488.

[29] *Jarvis* v. *Swans Tours* [1973] 1 Q.B. 233; *Jackson* v. *Horizon Holidays* [1975] 1 W.L.R. 1468; *Diesen* v. *Samson*, 1971 S.L.T. (Sh. Ct.) 49.

[30] *McDaid* v. *Clyde Navigation Trs.*, 1946 S.C. 462; *British Transport Commission* v. *Gourley* [1956] A.C. 185. See also *Spencer* v. *Macmillan's Trs.*, 1958 S.C. 300; *Stewart* v. *Glentaggart*, 1963 S.L.T. 119.

[31] *The Admiralty* v. *Aberdeen Steam Trawling Co.*, 1910 S.C. 553.

[32] *Ross* v. *Macfarlane* (1894) 21 R. 396.

[33] *Warin & Craven* v. *Forrester* (1876) 4 R. 190; affd. 4 R. (H.L.) 75; Sale of Goods Act 1979, s. 50. It has been held in England that a disappointed buyer may even have to accept some offer by way of compromise made by the seller: see *Houndsditch Warehouse Co.* v. *Waltex* [1944] 1 K.B. 579.

[34] *Carter* v. *Campbell* (1885) 12 R. 1075; *Wilson* v. *Carmichael* (1894) 21 R. 732.

[35] *Dunford & Elliot* v. *Macleod* (1902) 4 F. 912, *per* Lord McLaren.

[36] *Gunter & Co.* v. *Lauritzen* (1894) 31 S.L.R. 359; *Clippens Oil Co.* v. *Edinburgh Water Trustees*, 1907 S.C. (H.L.) 9.

v. *Baxendale*,[37] but that case merely restated a principle which had long been recognised in Scotland.[38] The formula or rule is expressed in *Hadley* v. *Baxendale* in the following terms: 'Where two parties have made a contract which one of them has broken, the damages which the other party ought to receive in respect of such breach of contract should be such as may fairly and reasonably be considered either arising naturally, i.e., according to the usual course of things, from such breach of contract itself, or such as may reasonably be supposed to have been in the contemplation of both parties at the time they made the contract as the probable result of the breach of it.' The former alternative points to the general rule of what are known as ordinary damages: everyone, as a reasonable person, is taken to know the ordinary course of things and consequently what loss is liable to result from a breach of contract in that ordinary course.[39] The latter shows that to this knowledge, which a party in breach is assumed to possess whether he actually possesses it or not, there may have to be added in a particular case any knowledge which he does actually possess, through, *e.g.* prior notice or special experience, of special circumstances which would be liable, in the event of a breach, to cause more loss.[40] The measure, in short, depends upon the knowledge, actual or imputed, of the party in breach: 'a party who breaks his contract is liable for those consequences which a reasonable man, possessing the knowledge which the party had at the time of contracting, would have anticipated.[41] The breach itself does not have to have been foreseeable.[42]

In computing ordinary damages, an allowance for the inconvenience and dislocation of business involved in the breach of any mercantile contract is permissible, even where no actual pecuniary loss can be established.[43] There may also be included the expenses directly incurred by the party whose contract has been broken, if such expenses would have been incurred by a reasonable man;[44] the cost of litigation with third parties, if traceable to the breach of contract and if reasonably incurred;[45] the loss of a sub-contract, in cases of failure to supply or carry goods, if that sub-contract contained no exceptional conditions.[46]

---

[37] (1854) 9 Ex. 341; Bell, *Prin.*, §33; *A/B Karlshamns Oljefabriker* v. *Monarch S.S. Co.*, 1949 S.C. (H.L.) 1; *Victoria Laundry (Windsor)* v. *Newman Industries* [1949] 2 K.B. 528.

[38] Brown, *Sale*, p. 214 (published in 1821).

[39] See, *e.g. Waddington* v. *Buchan Poultry Products*, 1963 S.L.T. 168.

[40] *Den of Ogil Co.* v. *Cal. Ry.* (1902) 5 F. 99; *Victoria Laundry (Windsor), supra*, in which see opinion of Asquith L.J. at p. 539.

[41] Gloag, *Contract*, 2nd ed., p. 697; *Koufos* v. *C. Czarnikow* [1969] 1 A.C. 350; *Caledonian Property Group Ltd.* v. *Queensferry Property Group Ltd.*, 1992 S.L.T. 738; *Balfour Beatty Construction (Scotland) Ltd.* v. *Scottish Power plc*, 1994 S.L.T. 807 (H.L.).

[42] *H. Parsons (Livestock)* v. *Uttley Ingham & Co.* [1978] Q.B. 791.

[43] *Webster* v. *Cramond Iron Co.* (1875) 2 R. 752.

[44] *Le Blanche* v. *London & N.W. Ry.* (1876) 1 C.P.D. 286.

[45] *Munro* v. *Bennett*, 1911 S.C. 337; *Buchanan & Carswell* v. *Eugene*, 1936 S.C. 160.

[46] *Ströms Bruks A/B* v. *Hutchison* (1905) 7 F. (H.L.) 131. Contrast *Horne* v. *Midland Ry.* (1872) L.R. 8 C.P. 131.

In many cases a person who supplies an article impliedly warrants that it is fit for ordinary use, and any injury which may result from the fact that it is unsuitable or inadequate will form part of the damages.[47] Damages for injury resulting from some exceptional use of the article, on the other hand, will be due only where the party supplying it had notice that such a use of it was contemplated.[48] Among the items of loss which would not fall under ordinary damages, but might be recovered, as consequential damages, in cases where the party in breach had notice of the actual facts, are the loss incurred where goods are supplied or conveyed too late for a particular market;[49] or the loss involved by delay in the provision or carriage of an article from the want of which some larger enterprise is brought to a standstill.[50] In the latter case, e.g. where some necessary part of a mill or of a ship is delayed in transit, it is possibly the law that mere notice of the facts is not enough to render the carrier liable for the exceptional loss which his delay may cause; there must be something such as the payment of a special rate, indicating that he took the risk.[51]

13.29   **Interest.**—As already noticed, mere failure to pay at the appointed time does not give rise to any claim for damages for the loss which may have resulted. It may, however, render the party in delay liable for interest. This may be expressly provided, with or without a period of credit. Interest may also, but only in a limited class of cases, be due *ex lege*. It has been stated to be due when the pursuer 'is deprived of an interest-bearing security or a profit-producing chattel . . . or . . . by virtue of a principal sum having been wrongfully withheld and not paid on the day when it ought to be paid.'[52] It is due when possession is taken on the sale of land, even if the price is not settled or the title not complete.[53] It is due, after maturity, on a bill of exchange or promissory note.[54] It is also due on money lent,[55] unless the circumstances of the case were exceptional.[56] In the case of an I.O.U., interest, unless stipulated for, is due only from the date of citation.[57] It may be recovered by a solicitor on his outlays, but not on his professional charges.[58] It is due on money

---

[47] *Dickie* v. *Amicable Property Investment Co.*, 1911 S.C. 1079.

[48] *Cory* v. *Thames Ironworks, etc., Co.* (1868) L.R. 2 Q.B. 181.

[49] *Macdonald* v. *Highland Ry.* (1873) 11 M. 614; *Anderson* v. *N.B. Ry.* (1875) 2 R. 443.

[50] *Hadley* v. *Baxendale* (1854) 9 Ex. 341; *Den of Ogil Co.* v. *Cal. Ry.* (1902) 5 F. 99; *Hydraulic Engineering Co.* v. *McHaffie* (1878) 4 Q.B.D. 670.`

[51] See *British Columbia Saw Mills Co.* v. *Nettleship* (1868) L.R. 2 C.P. 499.

[52] *Kolbin & Sons* v. *Kinnear & Co.*, 1931 S.C. (H.L.) 128, *per* Lord Atkin at p. 137.

[53] *Greenock Harbour Trustees* v. *Glasgow and S.W. Ry.*, 1909 S.C. 1438, affd. 1909 S.C. (H.L.) 49; *Prestwick Cinema Co.* v. *Gardiner*, 1951 S.C. 98.

[54] Bills of Exchange Act 1882, s. 57.

[55] *Cunningham* v. *Boswell* (1868) 6 M. 890.

[56] *Forbes* v. *Forbes* (1869) 8 M. 85; *Smellie's Exrx.* v. *Smellie*, 1933 S.C. 725.

[57] *Winestone* v. *Wolifson*, 1954 S.C. 77.

[58] *Blair's Trs.* v. *Payne* (1884) 12 R. 104. *Cf. Drummond* v. *Law Society of Scotland*, 1980 S.C. 175 (counsel's fees).

paid under protest which ultimately turns out not to have been legally exigible.[59] It is not due on arrears of rent or feu-duties.[60] The general rule with regard to tradesmen's and professional accounts is that no interest is due unless there has been a judicial demand for payment, or an intimation that interest will be charged on the account if not paid on a specified date.[61] No interest is due on sums payable as demurrage.[62] Interest has been allowed on a salvage award.[63]

Where interest is due under the contract, the decree should award interest at the contract rate until payment.[64] Where legal action is taken, and the debt arises directly from contract, interest will be due from the date of citation.[65] Where the action concludes for damages, either for breach of contract or on some other ground, the general rule is that no interest is due until the damages are awarded, and the decree has become enforceable.[66] The court has, however, a discretion, to award interest on damages for the whole or any part of the period between the date when the right of action arose and the date of the decree.[67]

Further Reading

McBryde, *The Law of Contract in Scotland* (1987), Chs. 14 and 20.
Walker, *The Law of Civil Remedies in Scotland* (1974).

---

[59] *Haddon's Exrx.* v. *Scottish Milk Marketing Board*, 1938 S.C. 168.
[60] *Marquis of Tweeddale's Trs.* v. *Earl of Haddington* (1880) 7 R. 620; Rankine, *Leases* (3rd ed.), p. 460.
[61] *Somervell's Tr.* v. *Edinburgh Life Assurance Co.*, 1911 S.C. 1069.
[62] *Pollich* v. *Heatley*, 1910 S.C. 469, *per* Lord President Dunedin at p. 478.
[63] *The 'Ben Gairn,'* 1979 S.C. 98.
[64] *Bank of Scotland* v. *Davis*, 1982 S.L.T. 20.
[65] Erskine, III, iii, 10.
[66] *Roger* v. *Cochrane*, 1910 S.C. 1; *McCormack* v. *N.C.B.*, 1957 S.C. 277.
[67] Interest on Damages (Scotland) Act 1958, s. 1, as substituted by the Interest on Damages (Scotland) Act 1971, s. 1. See *Macrae* v. *Reed & Mallik*, 1961 S.C. 68; *R. & J. Dempster* v. *Motherwell Bridge & Engineering Co.*, 1964 S.C. 308; *Fraser* v. *Morton Wilson (2)*, 1966 S.L.T. 22; *James Buchanan & Co.* v. *Stewart Cameron (Drymen)*, 1973 S.L.T. (Notes) 78.

CHAPTER 14

EXTINCTION OF OBLIGATIONS

An obligation may be extinguished by a discharge by the creditor; by performance or payment; by compensation; by novation; by confusion; or by lapse of time. The result of impossibility of performance has already been considered.[1]

14.1 Acceptilation and Discharge.—Acceptilation is the technical term applicable when the creditor discharges his right without payment or performance. There are no longer restrictions as to the method of proof of the acceptilation.[2] The terms of an agreement and the circumstances in which it was made may give rise to an implication of a mutual surrender of rights.[3]

It is always a question of construction as to what debts are covered by a discharge. If the discharge was in general terms, without reference to any particular debt, or class of debts, the normal construction is that the debtor is freed from any claim of which the creditor was then aware, *e.g.* from a debt in which the debtor was merely cautioner.[4] If a list of debts is given, followed by general words of discharge, no debts of a different kind from those enumerated are included.[5] If it turns out that there existed a debt of which the creditor, at the time of granting the discharge, was not aware, a general discharge may be reducible on the ground that, so far as relates to the debt in question, it was gratuitous, and granted under error.[6] Fitted accounts, *i.e.* accounts rendered by one party and docqueted as correct by the other,[7] do not preclude proof that some item or items have been omitted or entered incorrectly, but they lay the onus of proof on the party who challenges their accuracy.[8] The

---

[1] *Supra*, Chap. 12.

[2] See Requirements of Writing (Scotland) Act 1995, s. 11. For a statement of the previous law, see Walkers, *Evidence* §125. There is still the possibility of 'waiver' by actings: *Armia Ltd.* v. *Daejan Developments Ltd.*, 1979 S.C. (H.L.) 56; *Lausada & Co. Ltd.* v. *J.E. Lesser (Properties) Ltd.*, 1990 S.L.T. 823; *British Coal Corporation* v. *South of Scotland Electricity Board (No. 2)*, 1993 S.L.T. 38; *Atlas Assurance Co. Ltd.* v. *Dollar Land Holdings plc*, 1993 S.L.T. 892.

[3] *Evenoon Ltd.* v. *Jackel & Co. Ltd.*, 1982 S.L.T. 83.

[4] *British Linen Co.* v. *Esplin* (1849) 11 D. 1104.

[5] *Greenock Banking Co.* v. *Smith* (1844) 6 D. 1340; *McAdam* v. *Scott* (1913) 50 S.L.R. 264.

[6] *Dickson* v. *Halbert* (1854) 16 D. 586; *Purdon* v. *Rowat's Tr.* (1856) 19 D. 206.

[7] *Fell* v. *Rattray* (1869) 41 Sc. Jurist 236.

[8] *Laing* v. *Laing* (1862) 24 D. 1362; *Struthers* v. *Smith*, 1913 S.C. 1116.

rule applies to entries made by a banker in his customer's pass-book; proof that the banker never received the money is competent.[9] Fitted accounts, or even a formal discharge, do not preclude a subsequent demand by a client for the taxation of his solicitor's account.[10]

14.2 Performance.—The question whether any obligation has been performed is one of fact in each case. Proof may be *prout de jure*.[11] The onus of proof is on the party alleging performance.[12]

14.3 Proof of Payment.—Proof of payment was at common law restricted in certain cases to writ or oath. This has now disappeared as a result of the Requirements of Writing (Scotland) Act 1995.[13]

14.4 Presumption of Payment.—In certain cases, there is a legal presumption of payment. Counsel's fees are presumed to be paid. It is conceived that no action is competent against the client, but counsel may recover from the agent fees which the latter has actually received.[14] The onus of proof that a hotel bill has not been paid after the guest has left lies on the hotel-keeper.[15]

14.5 Apocha Trium Annorum (Discharges for Three Years).—The production of receipts for three consecutive instalments of any termly payment, such as rent, feu-duty, interest, salaries or wages, raises a presumption that all prior instalments have been paid.[16] It is open to the creditor to prove, and by parole evidence, that payment has not in fact been made.[17] The presumption is not raised, and the onus of proof therefore remains with the debtor, if there is only one receipt, though for several instalments.[18] Nor do receipts for three instalments raise any presumption that a bill, granted for prior arrears, has been paid.[19]

14.6 Document of Debt in Debtor's Hands.—The maxim *chirographum apud debitorem repertum praesumitur solutum* imports that the fact that a document of debt is in the possession of the debtor raises a presumption that the debt has been paid. Parole evidence is admissible to prove the

---

[9] *Couper's Trs.* v. *National Bank* (1889) 16 R. 412.
[10] *Macfarlane* v. *Macfarlane's Trs.* (1897) 24 R. 574.
[11] See Requirements of Writing (Scotland) Act 1995.
[12] See *Svendborg* v. *Love & Stewart*, 1916 S.C. (H.L.) 187; *Carruthers* v. *Macgregor*, 1927 S.C. 816.
[13] s. 11.
[14] *Batchelor* v. *Pattison & Mackersy* (1876) 3 R. 914.
[15] *Barnet* v. *Colvil* (1840) 2 D. 337.
[16] *Erskine*, III, iv, 10; Bell, *Prin.*, § 567; Walkers, *Evidence*, § 64.
[17] *Cameron* v. *Panton's Trs.* (1891) 18 R. 728; *Stenhouse* v. *Stenhouse's Trs.* (1899) 6 S.L.T. 368.
[18] Dickson, *Evidence*, § 177.
[19] *Patrick* v. *Watt* (1859) 21 D. 637.

contrary.[20] It is competent to prove by parole that a receipt which is in the hands of the debtor was given without payment.[21]

14.7 Ascription of Payments.—Where a party owing more than one debt makes payments without ascribing them to any particular debt it is open to the creditor to ascribe them so as to diminish or extinguish any debt he pleases.[22] He cannot, however, thereby preclude the challenge of the validity of any debt.[23] Where there is a continuous account, such as that between banker and customer, the rule, usually termed the rule in *Clayton's Case*,[24] is that the earliest credit item wipes out out the earliest debit item. This principle, immaterial in questions solely between the debtor and creditor, is of importance where there are parties subsidiarily liable. Thus, where a cautioner is liable for a fixed period, and after that period the account is allowed to go on without any settlement, any payments subsequently made by the principal debtor, being applied, on the rule in *Clayton's Case*, to wipe out the earliest debit items, will extinguish *pro tanto* the debt for which the cautioner is liable, even though payments are made to the principal debtor which preserve the debit balance against him.[25] The rule is not applicable to a tradesman's account,[26] nor, probably, to any account except that of banker and customer, or other parties whose relationship is substantially the same.[27] Nor can the rule be applied where two separate accounts are kept with a bank.[28] Moreover, the rule does not apply where the parties' dealings reveal that it was not intended to do so.[29] Provision for the appropriation of payments in respect of two or more regulated agreements with the same person is made by the Consumer Credit Act 1974.[30]

14.8 Mode of Payment: Legal Tender.—A creditor, in the absence of any agreement to the contrary, is entitled to insist on payment in legal tender. Gold coins complying with any minimum weight specification are legal tender for payment of any amount.[31] Cupro-nickel or silver coins of denominations of more than 10 pence are legal tender for

---

[20] Bell, *Prin.*, § 566; Walkers, *Evidence*, § 66.
[21] *Henry* v. *Miller* (1844) 11 R. 713.
[22] Bell, *Prin.*, § 563. A mere uncommunicated intention of the debtor will not suffice: *Leeson* v. *Leeson* [1936] 2 K.B. 156.
[23] *Dougall* v. *Lornie* (1899) 1 F. 1187.
[24] *Devaynes* v. *Noble (Clayton's Case)* (1816) 1 Merivale 529, 572.
[25] *Royal Bank* v. *Christie* (1841) 2 Robinson 118; *Cuthill* v. *Strachan* (1894) 21 R. 549; *Deeley* v. *Lloyds Bank* [1912] A.C. 756.
[26] *Dougall* v. *Lornie* (1899) 1 F. 1187.
[27] *Cory Bros.* v. *Owners of the Mecca* [1897] A.C. 286; *Hay* v. *Torbet*, 1908 S.C. 781; *Macdonald, Fraser & Co.* v. *Cairns' Exrs.*, 1932 S.C. 699.
[28] *Bradford Old Bank* v. *Sutcliffe* [1918] 2 K.B. 833.
[29] *Montgomery & Sons* v. *Gallacher*, 1982 S.L.T. 138.
[30] s. 81.
[31] Coinage Act 1971, ss. 1, 2 (as substituted by the Currency Act 1983, s. 1(1), (3)); Royal Proclamation of April 20, 1983.

payments up to a maximum of £10; and if less than 10 pence up to a maximum of £5. Bronze coins are legal tender for payments no greater than 20 pence.[32] By Royal Proclamation other coins (*e.g.* the thirteenth Commonwealth Games £2 coin) may be declared legal tender.[33] Bank of England notes, approved by the Treasury, are legal tender in Scotland if less than £5:[34] but *any* such notes may be circulated in Scotland.[35] Bank notes issued by a Scottish bank are not legal tender.[36] Normally, a gold clause in a contract, the proper law of which is English, is interpreted as meaning that payment will be made in the sterling equivalent of the gold's value.[37] Decree for payment in a foreign currency may be granted in appropriate circumstances.[38] A cheque, if accepted, is conditional payment. The condition is resolutive, so that the debt is extinguished but revives if the cheque be dishonoured.[39] Payment by a credit card is not conditional upon it being paid by the credit card company.[40] If payment is made in any unusual or unbusinesslike way, any loss by theft or fraud will fall upon the debtor.[41]

14.9   Duty of Debtor to Tender Payment.—It is the duty of the debtor to tender payment, at the creditor's residence or place of business,[42] on the appointed date. Once the date of payment has arrived the creditor is within his rights in taking legal proceedings or using diligence without any formal demand. He must stop his proceedings or diligence on tender of payment in full and expenses, but is not bound to accept a tender of the debt without the expenses of the legal proceedings which he has taken.[43]

14.10   Bona Fide Payments.—Payment to a person honestly and reasonably believed to be the creditor is good, as, for instance, payment to the original creditor after he has assigned the debt but before intimation has been made. The rule holds even if payment is made before it is due.[44]

---

[32] Coinage Act 1971, ss. 2(1A) (as substituted by the Currency Act 1983, s. 1(3)(*a*)).

[33] Royal Proclamation of December 18, 1985.

[34] Currency and Bank Notes Act 1954, s. 1.

[35] *Ibid.*

[36] Smith, *Short Commentary*, p. 842.

[37] *Feist* v. *Société Intercommunale Belge* [1934] A.C. 161; *New Brunswick Ry. Co.* v. *British and French Trust Corp.* [1939] A.C. 1. *Cf. Treseder-Griffin* v. *Co-operative Insurance Soc.* [1956] 2 Q.B. 127.

[38] *Commerzbank Aktiengesellschaft* v. *Large*, 1977 S.C. 375.

[39] *Leggat Bros.* v. *Gray*, 1908 S.C. 67; *Bolt & Nut Co. (Tipton)* v. *Rowlands Nicholls & Co.* [1964] 2 Q.B. 10.

[40] *Re Charge Card Services Ltd.* [1987] Ch. 150; [1989] Ch. 497; *Customs and Excise Commrs.* v. *Diners Club Ltd.* [1989] 1 W.L.R. 1196.

[41] *Robb* v. *Gow* (1905) 8 F. 90; *Mitchell Henry* v. *Norwich, etc., Assurance Co.* [1918] 2 K.B. 67.

[42] *Bank of Scotland* v. *Seitz*, 1990 S.L.T. 584, *per* Lord President Hope at pp. 588–589, approving Gloag, p. 709. Note also *Arab Bank Ltd.* v. *Barclays Bank (Dominion, Colonial and Overseas)* [1954] A.C. 495, *per* Lord Reid at p. 531.

[43] *Pollock* v. *Goodwin's Trs.* (1898) 25 R. 1051.

[44] Bell, *Prin.*, § 561.

But a tenant who pre-pays his rent may have to pay again to a party to whom the subjects have been sold, though not to the trustee in the landlord's sequestration.[45] A banker granting a deposit receipt is bound to pay according to his contract, and incurs no liability if the payee (a trustee) should embezzle the money.[46] But where a deposit receipt was paid to a person who alleged he was the depositor's brother, and presented the deposit receipt and a letter of authority, it was held, on proof that he had stolen the documents, that the bank could not rely on the payment as a discharge.[47] Payment made to the creditor's agent is good if in fact he had authority to receive it, or if he was in a line of business such as to give ostensible authority.[48] A solicitor has ostensible authority to receive payment of a sum sued for,[49] or of the price of shares he has been employed to sell,[50] but not to receive payment of the principal sum in a bond.[51]

14.11 Compensation.—The right to compensate, or set off, one debt against another, with the result that each debt is *pro tanto* extinguished, is in Scotland referable to statute, namely, the Compensation Act 1592 (c. 143). The terms of the Act exclude compensation after decree, and it has accordingly been decided that if A allows a decree (*in foro* or in absence) to pass against him he must pay his debt and recover any counterclaim by separate proceedings.[52] This rule probably holds only while both parties are solvent,[53] and does not apply unless there was an opportunity of pleading compensation against a claim for a sum decerned for as expenses.[54]

14.12 Liquid Debts.[55]—Compensation is pleadable only between liquid debts, with an exception, largely in the discretion of the court, of cases where an illiquid debt may be rendered liquid without delay.[56] So there is no right to compensate a debt instantly payable by a future or contingent debt,[57] or by a claim of damages arising on a separate ground. The right of retention when debts arise out of the same contract, or where bankruptcy has supervened, has been already considered.[58]

[45] *Davidson* v. *Boyd* (1868) 7 M. 77.
[46] *Dickson* v. *National Bank*, 1917 S.C. (H.L.) 50.
[47] *Wood* v. *Clydesdale Bank*, 1914 S.C. 397.
[48] *International Sponge Importers* v. *Watt*, 1911 S.C. (H.L.) 57. *Cf. British Bata Shoe Co. Ltd.* v. *Double M. Shah Ltd.*, 1980 S.C. 311.
[49] *Smith* v. *North British Ry.* (1850) 12 D. 795.
[50] *Pearson* v. *Scott* (1878) 9 Ch.D. 198.
[51] *Richardson* v. *McGeoch's Trs.* (1898) 1 F. 145.
[52] *Cunninghame* v. *Wilson*, Jan. 17, 1809, F.C.
[53] Bell, *Comm.*, ii, 121.
[54] *Fowler* v. *Brown*, 1916 S.C. 597.
[55] See paras. 3.13–3.14, *supra*.
[56] See *Ross* v. *Ross* (1895) 22 R. 461.
[57] *Paul & Thain* v. *Royal Bank* (1869) 7 M. 361.
[58] para. 13.14, *supra*.

Compensation must be pleaded: cross debts are not extinguished *ipso facto*.[59] So a debt may prescribe although, during the years of prescription, compensation might have been pleaded against it.[60] But if compensation is ultimately sustained neither debt bears interest *ex lege* during the period of concourse.[61]

14.13 *Concursus Debiti et Crediti.*—To admit of compensation there must be *concursus debiti et crediti*. The parties must be debtor and creditor not only at the same time but in the same capacity. So an executor, when sued for his private debt, could not plead compensation in respect of a debt owed to him as executor.[62] A banker who has granted a deposit receipt payable to either of two persons cannot plead compensation in respect of a debt due by one of them,[63] and the same rule holds in all cases where there are joint creditors.[64] The death of a debtor does not raise a separation of interests so as to preclude a plea of compensation against his executor. So where A died in debt to his law agent, and the latter was employed to ingather the estate, it was held that he was entitled to satisfy his claim against the deceased out of the executry funds which he had ingathered.[65] There is no *concursus debiti et crediti* between a debt due to a principal and a debt due by his agent.[66] But if the agency was not disclosed and the party with whom the agent dealt was not aware of it, he may plead compensation on a debt due by the agent provided that the right to compensate had accrued before he was informed of the principal's interest in the matter.[67] In proceedings against a Government department, the Crown cannot, without leave of the court, avail itself of any set off or counterclaim if the subject-matter thereof does not relate to that department.[68]

14.14 **Compensation in Partnership.**—In partnership, a debtor to the firm cannot plead compensation due to him by an individual partner. A partner, sued for his private debt, cannot plead compensation on a debt due to the firm, unless the firm, while still solvent, is dissolved, when the partner becomes the creditor in a *pro rata* share of the debts to the

[59] Erskine, III, iv, 12; Bell, *Comm.*, ii, 124; *Cowan* v. *Gowans* (1878) 5 R. 581; *National Westminster Bank* v. *Halesowen Presswork* [1972] A.C. 785.
[60] *Carmichael* v. *Carmichael* (1719) Mor. 2677.
[61] Bell, *Comm.*, ii, 124.
[62] *Stuart* v. *Stuart* (1869) 7 M. 366.
[63] *Anderson* v. *North of Scotland Bank* (1901) 4 F. 49.
[64] *Burrell* v. *Burrell's Trs.*, 1916 S.C. 729.
[65] *Mitchell* v. *Mackersy* (1905) 8 F. 198, overruling *Gray's Trs.* v. *Royal Bank* (1895) 23 R. 199.
[66] *National Bank* v. *Dickie's Tr.* (1895) 22 R. 740; *Matthews* v. *Auld & Guild* (1874) 1 R. 1224.
[67] *Wester Moffat Colliery Co.* v. *Jeffrey*, 1911 S.C. 346; *Kaltenbach* v. *Lewis* (1885) 10 A.C. 617; *Greer* v. *Downs Supply Co.* [1927] 2 K.B. 28.
[68] Crown Proceedings Act 1947, s. 50; see *Atlantic Engine Co. (1920) Ltd.* v. *Lord Advocate*, 1955 S.L.T. 17; *Laing* v. *Lord Advocate*, 1973 S.L.T. (Notes) 81; *Smith* v. *Lord Advocate (No. 2)*, 1980 S.C. 227.

firm, and to that extent may plead compensation. A partner, suing for his private debt, may be met with a plea of compensation on a debt due by the firm. A firm may plead compensation on a debt due to an individual partner. The principle underlying these rules that a partner, so long as the firm remains undissolved, is not a creditor in debts due to the firm, whereas he is a debtor in debts due by the firm.[69]

14.15 Compensation in Insolvency.—The bankruptcy of one of the obligants so far enlarges the right of compensation that by the exercise of the right of retention compensation may be pleaded on illiquid debts due by the bankrupt.[70] In other respects, the bankruptcy of one party effects a separation of interests, which precludes *concursus debiti et crediti*. So the debtor to a bankrupt estate cannot plead compensation on debts which he has acquired after the bankruptcy,[71] nor on debts subsequently incurred to him by the bankrupt.[72] If, however, A is a contingent creditor of B, and the contingency is purified after B's bankruptcy, A has the right to plead compensation, as in the case where a bill, accepted by the bankrupt, was at the date of bankruptcy held by a bank, and was subsequently paid by the drawer.[73] There is no compensation between a debt due by the bankrupt and a debt subsequently incurred to the trustee. So when a liquidator adopted and carried out a contract in which the company was engaged it was held that his action for payment could not be met by a plea of compensation or retention in respect of separate claims against the company.[74] And where a landlord took over a waygoing crop from the trustee in the tenant's sequestration it was held that there was no *concursus debiti et crediti* between the price and a claim for arrears of rent. The one was a debt due by the bankrupt, the other a debt subsequently incurred to the trustee.[75] A debt due by a company can be set off against a claim by the receiver of the whole property and undertaking of the company for a debt due to the company.[76]

14.16 Specific Appropriation.—Compensation cannot be pleaded if the plea is in conflict with the express or implied terms of a contract between the

---

[69] See *Heggie* v. *Heggie* (1858) 21 D. 31; *Mitchell* v. *Canal Basin Co.* (1869) 7 M. 480.

[70] para. 13.14, *supra.*

[71] *Cauvin* v. *Robertson* (1783) Mor. 2581.

[72] *Meldrum's Trs.* v. *Clark* (1826) 5 S. 122.

[73] *Hannay's Tr.* v. *Armstrong Bros.* (1875) 2 R. 399; affd. (1877) 4 R. (H.L.) 43.

[74] *Asphaltic Limestone Co.* v. *Corporation of Glasgow*, 1907 S.C. 463. *Cf. Smith* v. *Lord Advocate*, 1978 S.C. 259, where both claims arose after liquidation.

[75] *Taylor's Tr.* v. *Paul* (1888) 15 R. 313; *Sutherland* v. *Urquhart* (1895) 23 R. 284.

[76] *McPhail* v. *Cunninghame D.C.*, 1985 S.L.T. 149; *cf. McPhail* v. *Lothian R.C.*, 1981 S.C. 119. In *Taylor* v. *Scottish and Universal Newspapers Ltd.*, 1981 S.C. 408, it was held that there need not be *concursus debiti et crediti* prior to the receiver's appointment, but this is not consistent with the reasoning of the Inner House in *Forth & Clyde Construction Co. Ltd.* v. *Trinity Timber & Plywood Co. Ltd.*, 1984 S.C. 1. Note also *Myles J. Callaghan Ltd.* v. *City of Glasgow D.C.*, 1987 S.C. 171 (an illiquid claim).

parties. So if money is placed in A's hands for a specific purpose, and that purpose cannot be effected, A cannot refuse to return the money on the ground that the depositor was otherwise indebited to him.[77]

14.17 **Novation.**—Where a new document of debt is accepted with the result of extinguishing all liability on the prior document, the case is said to be one of novation; when a new obligant is accepted, with the result of freeing the original debtor, the case is more strictly one of delegation. But the term novation is often used to cover both cases.[78] Either novation or delegation has the effect of releasing a cautioner for the original debt or for the original obligant.[79] But either requires the consent of the creditor and, although that consent may in certain circumstances be implied, there is a presumption against novation. A creditor who accepts a new voucher of his debt, or a new obligant, without any express discharge of the old, is presumed to have obtained an additional voucher or guarantor for his debt rather than to have surrendered the rights which he already held,[80] and it is only in exceptional cases, or on proof of a custom of trade,[81] that the original obligant, or a cautioner for him, can successfully maintain that he had been impliedly discharged.

The typical case of pure novation is the renewal of a bill of exchange. When a new bill is accepted, and the old one given up, the inference is that all liability on the old bill is extinguished,[82] though in one very special case it was held that the renewal of a promissory note given for a loan, at a time when the original note was on the verge of prescription, did not exclude a claim for interest on the loan during the currency of the original note, in spite of the fact that the note had been given up to the debtor.[83] If the original bill or note is retained by the creditor there would seem to be no case for novation. So where the original bill was renewed for one of a smaller amount, and the balance was not paid, it was held that there was no objection to an action for that balance against a party who had signed the original bill as a cautioner.[84]

14.18 **Delegation.**—The general presumption is also strongly against delegation. Where a creditor accepted a promissory note from his debtor's factor the liability of the debtor was in no way affected.[85] A statutory

---

[77] *Middlemas* v. *Gibson*, 1910 S.C. 577; *Reid* v. *Bell* (1884) 12 R. 178; *Mycroft, Petr.*, 1983 S.L.T. 342.

[78] Bell, *Prin.*, § 576.

[79] *Commercial Bank of Tasmania* v. *Jones* [1983] A.C. 313. The assignation of a debt, and consequent introduction of a new creditor, does not amount to novation, so as to liberate a cautioner: *Bradford Old Bank* v. *Sutcliffe* [1918] 2 K.B. 833.

[80] See opinion of Lord President Inglis, *McIntosh* v. *Ainslie* (1872) 10 M. 304.

[81] *North* v. *Basset* [1892] 1 Q.B. 333.

[82] *Stevenson* v. *Lord Duncan*, 1805 Hume 245.

[83] *Hope Johnstone* v. *Cornwall* (1895) 22 R. 314.

[84] *Hay & Kyd* v. *Powrie* (1886) 13 R. 777.

[85] *McIntosh* v. *Ainslie* (1872) 10 M. 304.

provision under which the personal obligation in a bond and disposition in security may transmit against a purchaser of the lands was construed as giving the creditor an additional obligant, not, without his express consent, as depriving him of the obligation of his original debtor.[86] Where a partner in a firm retires and the firm continues without the introduction of any new partners, the mere fact that the creditor in an outstanding debt continues to accept interest, or ultimately ranks in the bankruptcy of a firm, does not amount to delegation so as to discharge the liability of the retiring partner.[87] But in such a case delegation may be inferred from the fact that a party from whom the firm as originally constituted had ordered goods supplied them after the change, and in full knowledge of the facts, entered the new firm as his debtor in his books.[88] Where new partners are introduced the acceptance of the obligation of the firm as newly constituted, with some change in the form of the obligation (as where a bill, or deposit receipt, is renewed) will amount to delegation in a question with a partner who has retired.[89] It is laid down in England that where two companies amalgamate very clear evidence is required to prove that a creditor of one of the original companies has accepted the obligation of the amalgamation in substitution for that of his original debtors.[90]

14.19   Confusion.—When the same person is creditor and debtor in an obligation it may be extinguished *confusione*,[91] a doctrine which will not be extended to cases not covered by the prior authorities.[92] The obligation must be for the payment of money, and therefore a permanent right, such as that involved in a lease,[93] a superiority,[94] or a ground annual,[95] is not extinguishable *confusione*, though while the same person is debtor and creditor the annual prestations, such as rent or feu-duty, do not come into existence.

The merger of the interests of debtor and creditor may arise either by succession, when the debtor succeeds as heir to his creditor, or vice versa; or by contract, when the creditor in a bond acquires the subjects over which it is secured, under an arrangement by which the amount of the bond is deducted from the price, or where the owner of an estate

---

[86] *University of Glasgow* v. *Yuill's Tr.* (1882) 9 R. 643.

[87] *Morton's Trs.* v. *Robertson's Judicial Factor* (1892) 20 R. 72; *Smith* v. *Patrick* (1901) 3 F. (H.L.) 14; Partnership Act 1890, s. 17(3).

[88] *Pearston* v. *Wilson* (1856) 91 D. 197.

[89] *Buchanan* v. *Somerville* (1779) Mor. 3402; *Bilborough* v. *Holmes* (1876) 5 Ch.D. 255.

[90] *Re Family Endowment Society* (1870) L.R. 5 Ch. 118; Halsbury (4th ed.), Vol. 9, para. 584, p. 403.

[91] Stair, I, xviii, 9; Erskine, III, iv, 23. The English term is 'merger.'

[92] *Craig* v. *Mair's Trs.*, 1914 S.C. 893, *per* Lord President and Lord Johnston.

[93] *Lord Blantyre* v. *Dunn* (1858) 20 D. 1188.

[94] *Motherwell* v. *Manwell* (1903) 5 F. 619. As to the effect of consolidation, see *Earl of Zetland* v. *Glover Incorporation* (1870) 8 M. (H.L.) 144.

[95] *Craig* v. *Mair's Trs.*, 1914 S.C. 893.

acquires bonds which affect it. In such cases the confusion of interests is absolute and the debt is extinguished *ipso facto*, and, in the case of bonds, is not kept alive by the indication of intention involved in taking an assignation instead of a discharge. If for any reason it is desired that the bond shall still subsist it must be assigned to a trustee.[96]

14.20 Confusion Excluded by Separation of Interests.—Confusion does not operate where there is any separation of interests, but only where the full and absolute right of the creditor and the full and absolute right of the debtor merge in one person. Thus there is sufficient distinction between the position of a party deceased and his executor to preclude the extinction of a debt by *confusio* when a debtor confirms as executor to his creditor, or a creditor as executor to his debtor.[97] Bonds affecting an entailed estate are not extinguished when the creditor becomes heir in possession, because his right is a limited and not an absolute one.[98] The same rule holds when bonds are acquired by a fiar during the subsistence of a liferent.[99] Where a prior bondholder obtained, in security of a further advance, a disposition *ex facie* absolute of the subjects, it was held that the prior bond was not extinguished *confusione*[1]; and a similar decision was pronounced where, in course of the arrangements for the assignation of a prior bond, the right of creditor and debtor had temporarily been vested in the same party.[2] And no confusion takes place where a person only subsidiarily liable for the debt, such as a cautioner, acquires the right of the creditor. It may still be enforced against the principal debtor.[3]

14.21 Lapse of Time: End of Fixed Period.—The effect of lapse of time primarily depends upon whether the obligation or contract has been entered into for a definite period or not. When a contract is entered into for a definite period, as a general rule the lapse of that period extinguishes the obligation on either side. But this is subject, in contracts of lease, service and partnership, to the principle of tacit relocation, under which a new contract may be implied. There is no authority for extending the principle beyond these contracts.

14.22 Tacit Relocation: Leases.—A lease, if neither party gives due notice of his intention to end it at the expiry of its term, is continued by tacit relocation on the old terms, except in reference to duration. In that respect, if the lease was for less than a year, continuation for the same

[96] *Codrington* v. *Johnston's Trs.* (1824) 2 Sh.App. 118; *Balfour-Melville's Trs.* v. *Gowans* (1896) 4 S.L.T. 111.
[97] *Salaman* v. *Sinclair's Tr.*, 1916 S.C. 698.
[98] *Colville's Trs.* v. *Marindin*, 1908 S.C. 911.
[99] *Fraser* v. *Carruthers* (1875) 2 R. 595.
[1] *King* v. *Johnstone*, 1908 S.C. 684.
[2] *Whiteley* v. *Delaney* [1914] A.C. 132.
[3] Stair, I, xviii, 9.

period is inferred; if for more than a year, continuation for a year.[4] The period of notice depends on the nature of the subjects let.[5] The contract under tacit relocation is binding on both parties, whether the tenant continues in possession or not. Tacit relocation rests on implied contract, and is therefore excluded by an arrangement for a new lease, though not in probative form.[6] And where the landlord intimated an increase of rent, and the tenant, though refusing to pay it, did not give notice to end the lease, and in fact stayed on after the term, it was held that tacit relocation was inapplicable, and that the tenant must be taken to have assented to the landlord's terms.[7] But where a house and shop were let together, it was held that notice to quit the shop only was ineffectual, and did not exclude tacit relocation of the whole subjects.[8] The question whether, in case of joint tenancy, all the tenants must concur in giving notice in order to avoid a renewal by tacit relocation has been considered but not decided.[9] If a landlord, after giving notice to quit, takes no further steps, and allows the tenant to remain in possession, he may be held to have passed from his notice, and a new lease by tacit relocation may be inferred.[10] If a tenant, after giving notice, refuses to leave, he is in the position of an intruder without a title, and liable for violent profits, *i.e.* for the largest sum for which the subjects could be let.[11]

The inference of a new lease by tacit relocation has been held to be based on universal understanding, and is therefore probably not applicable to seasonal lets of grass parks, furnished houses, shootings or fishings. In these cases the obligations on either side terminate without notice.[12] And a party who occupies a house as part of his remuneration on a contract of service must remove when his contract comes to an end.[13]

14.23   Service.—In certain contracts of service the law of tacit relocation applies, and if neither party gives notice a reasonable time before the expiry of the term a new contract is inferred either for the original period, or, at the longest, for a year, on the same terms. 'The law of

---

[4] Stair, II, ix, 23; Rankine, *Leases* (3rd ed.), p. 598; Agricultural Holdings (Scotland) Act 1991, s. 3. See especially *Douglas* v. *Cassillis & Culzean Estates*, 1944 S.C. at p. 361, where Lord Justice-Clerk Cooper points out that, in tacit relocation, while the contract may be new, the lease is not; *Smith* v. *Grayton Estates*, 1960 S.C. 349, *per* Lord President Clyde at p. 354.
[5] See para. 41.24, *infra.*.
[6] *Buchanan* v. *Harris & Sheldon* (1900) 2 F. 935. For the modern law, see Requirements of Writing (Scotland) Act 1995.
[7] *McFarlane* v. *Mitchell* (1900) 2 F. 901.
[8] *Gates* v. *Blair*, 1923 S.C. 430.
[9] *Graham* v. *Stirling*, 1922 S.C. 90.
[10] *Taylor* v. *Earl of Moray* (1892) 19 R. 399.
[11] *Tod* v. *Fraser* (1889) 17 R. 226. See para. 40.12, *infra.*
[12] *Macharg* (1805) Mor. App. Removing, 4.
[13] *Dunbar's Trs.* v. *Bruce* (1900) 3 F. 137; *Sinclair* v. *Tod*, 1907 S.C. 1038; *Cairns* v. *Innes*, 1942 S.C. 164.

tacit relocation has reference only to specific classes of servants, agricultural, domestic, and the like.'[14] So it was held not to be applicable to a contract between dressmakers and the manager of their fur department.[15] It does not apply to contracts of service on exceptional terms, such as an arrangement, made during a strike, under which a workman, usually engaged and paid by the week, was guaranteed employment for a year.[16] Nor does it apply to part-time employments, nor, probably, to any employment for a period exceeding a year.[17]

14.24 Partnership.—In partnership for a fixed period no notice is required to terminate the contract at the expiry of the term.[18] But if the partnership business is continued a partnership at will is inferred, in which the rights and duties of the partners continue as they were, in so far as is consistent with a partnership at will.[19]

14.25 Delay in Enforcement.—In the case of obligations which have no definite period the effect of lapse of time depends upon whether the obligation in question was definitely constituted or whether it requires to be established by proof. In the former case the mere fact that the creditor in the obligation has not chosen to enforce it for any period short of the negative prescription[20] has no legal effect. 'I am not aware of anything short of prescription or express discharge which can cut off a liquid debt standing on a written contract. Delay in making a claim may be fatal if the claim depends on the ascertainment of facts, and the opposite party's case on the facts is prejudiced by the delay.'[21] So a bond has been held to be enforceable although no action had been taken upon it until one day before the expiry of the years of prescription.[22]

**14.26 *Mora.*—In the case of obligations which require to be constituted by proof the plea of *mora* and taciturnity may be put forward,[23] but delay *per se* is no bar to an action.[24] If the obligation is in origin contractual, *e.g.* a claim for damages for breach of contract, or a demand for

---

[14] *Per* Lord Justice-Clerk Moncrieff in *Lennox* v. *Allan* (1880) 8 R. 38, approved by Lord President Dunedin in *Stanley* v. *Hanway* (1911) 48 S.L.R. 757. But see *Stevenson* v. *N.B. Ry.* (1905) 7 F. 1106.
[15] *Stanley* v. *Hanway, supra.*
[16] *Lennox* v. *Allan, supra.*
[17] *Brenan* v. *Campbell's Trs.* (1898) 25 R. 423.
[18] *Wallace* v. *Wallace's Trs.* (1906) 8 F. 558; Partnership Act 1980, s. 27.
[19] Partnership Act 1890, s. 27. See *McGowan* v. *Henderson*, 1914 S.C. 839.
[20] As to prescription, see *infra* Chap. 15.
[21] *Per* Lord Stormonth-Darling, *Alexander's Trs.* v. *Muir* (1903) 5 F. 406.
[22] *Graham* v. *Veitch* (1823) 2 S. 594; *Cunninghame* v. *Boswell* (1868) 6 M. 890.
[23] See Rankine, *Personal Bar*, p. 117.
[24] See Maclaren, *Court of Session Practice*, p. 403; also *Halley* v. *Watt*, 1956 S.C. 370.

payment for work done without any definite agreement,[25] the law would appear to be, as in the case of the reduction of a contract, that mere lapse of time short of the prescriptive period does not extinguish the obligation, but increases the onus of proof which lies upon the party asserting the claim.[26] The same rule applies to belated claims on a trust or executry estate.[27] Excessive delay in intimating a claim for reparation or in instituting an action of reparation may appear from the pleadings to have affected the quantity or quality of the evidence available to such an extent as to render proof preferable to jury trial as the means of ascertaining the truth.[28] Unexplained delay may result in a pursuer being ordained to find caution for expenses.[29]

14.27 Acquiescence.—The plea of *mora*, taciturnity and acquiescence is a plea to the merits.[30] It applies to the case where the defender maintains that some act of his, involving an invasion of the pursuer's rights, unjustifiable and not easily remediable, was done with the knowledge of and without objection from the pursuer, and infers that the latter is barred from now insisting on the right invaded.[31] The vagueness of the plea makes it difficult to summarise the cases in which it is applicable.[32] It necessarily imports knowledge by the pursuer of the defender's act, and also power to intervene. So the plea of acquiescence cannot be sustained merely because the pursuer did not intervene while the defender was incurring expenditure on work which he was entitled to carry out, as, for example, alterations on a mill with a view to taking and using an increased quantity of water from a river, even although it may have been obvious that the work and expenditure would be useless unless followed by the aggression of which the pursuer complains.[33] Acquiescence is not a method by which the title to heritable property can be altered, and therefore if A builds on B's land the fact that B was aware of his proceedings and took no objection does not operate as a conveyance of the land to A.[34] But it may bar B's right to insist on the

[25] *Mackison* v. *Burgh of Dundee*, 1910 S.C. (H.L.) 27.
[26] *Bain* v. *Assets Co.* (1905) 7 F. (H.L.) 104; opinion of Lord President Dunedin in *Bishop* v. *Bryce*. 1910 S.C. 426; *McKenzie's Exrx.* v. *Morrison's Trs.*, 1930 S.C. 830. And see para. 7.9, *supra*.
[27] *Robson* v. *Bywater* (1870) 8 M. 757; *Miller's Exrx.* v. *Miller's Trs.*, 1922 S.C. 150.
[28] See cases cited in Walker on *Delict* (2nd ed.), p. 439, also *Conetta* v. *Central S.M.T. Co. Ltd.*, 1966 S.L.T. 302. As to limitation of actions, see para. 34.9, *infra*.
[29] *G.* v. *H.* (1899) 1 F. 701.
[30] See Maclaren, *cit. supra*.
[31] The distinction between failure to intervene while an act is in progress and failure to take timely objection after it has been done is drawn in *De Bussche* v. *Alt* (1877) 8 Ch.D. 286. As to 'waiver,' see *Armia Ltd.* v. *Daejan Developments Ltd.*, 1979 S.C. (H.L.) 56; *Cumming* v. *Quartzag Ltd.*, 1981 S.L.T. 205; *British Coal Corporation* v. *South of Scotland Electricity Board (No. 2)*, 1993 S.L.T. 38.
[32] See Rankine, *Personal Bar*, p. 54.
[33] *Earl of Kintore* v. *Pirie* (1903) 5 F. 818, affd. (on other grounds) (1905) 8 F. (H.L.) 16.
[34] *Nicol* v. *Hope* (1663) Mor. 5627; *Melville* v. *Douglas's Trs.* (1830) 8 S. 841.

removal of the building in a case where A acted in good faith and the invasion was due to a mistake as to the boundary between his own land and that of B.[35] And acquiescence in operations involving considerable expenditure may bar the right to object to such acts as the unjustifiable withdrawal of water from a river,[36] or the heightening of a building in contravention of a servitude *non altius tollendi*.[37] Where the same building restrictions are imposed in all feu contracts in a particular street or locality, and a number of the feuars have been allowed to disregard them without objection, with the result that the character of the locality has changed, the superior may be barred from enforcing the restrictions on the remaining feuars.[38] In such circumstances the superior is held to have lost his interest to enforce the restrictions.[39] Non-intervention by the superior does not necessarily bar action by a neighbouring feuar.[40] The bar raised by acquiescence is, except in special circumstances, personal to the person who acquiesced and his heirs, and will not bar a singular successor in the title.[41] Apart from cases of building restrictions, if the relations of the parties are regulated by a written contract the fact that one party has been allowed to disregard its terms, to the knowledge of and without objection from the other, though it may bar an action of damages for what has been done in the past, will not infer any licence for the future.[42] To amount to such a licence—in effect, to alter the terms of the contract—an agreement for such alteration, though it may be merely verbal, must be proved.[43] In a case where an employee had regularly accepted his salary and given unqualified receipts he was held to have acquiesced in payment of that salary, and he was not allowed to prove, in support of his contention that he was entitled to a higher salary, that he had frequently protested against the amounts paid.[44] A creditor may be held to have acceded to a private trust deed, and therefore to be barred from using independent diligence, if he takes no objection to proceedings following on it which are being done with his knowledge[45]; and a son, or the trustee in his

[35] *Duke of Buccleuch* v. *Magistrates of Edinburgh* (1865) 3 M. 528; *Wilson* v. *Pottinger*, 1908 S.C. 580.

[36] *Cowan* v. *Lord Kinnaird* (1865) 4 M. 236; *Bicket* v. *Morris* (1866) 4 M. (H.L.) 44, opinion of Lord Chelmsford.

[37] *Muirhead* v. *Glasgow Highland Society* (1864) 2 M. 420; *Grahame* v. *Magistrates of Kirkcaldy* (1882) 9 R. (H.L.) 91.

[38] *Campbell* v. *Clydesdale Bank* (1868) 6 M. 943.

[39] *Howard de Walden Estates* v. *Bowmaker*, 1965 S.C. 163; and see Gloag, *Contract* (2nd ed.), p. 252; para. 11.7, *supra*.

[40] *Mactaggart* v. *Roemmele*, 1907 S.C. 1318.

[41] *Brown* v. *Baty*, 1957 S.C. 351.

[42] *Carron Co.* v. *Henderson's Trs.* (1896) 23 R. 1042; see also *British Coal Corporation* v. *South of Scotland Electricity Board (No. 2)*, 1993 S.L.T. 38 at p. 40.

[43] *Bargaddie Coal Co.* v. *Wark* (1859) 3 Macq. 467; *Kirkpatrick* v. *Allanshaw Coal Co.* (1880) 8 R. 327.

[44] *Davies* v. *City of Glasgow Friendly Society*, 1935 S.C. 224; *Eunson* v. *Johnson & Grieg*, 1940 S.C. 49.

[45] *Marianski* v. *Wiseman* (1871) 9 M. 673.

sequestration, may be barred from claiming legitim by acquiescing in family arrangements for carrying out the provisions of his father's will.[46]

14.28 **Outbreak of War.**[47]—The general rule is that the outbreak of war between this country and another puts an end to all executory contracts which for their further performance require commercial intercourse between a British subject and an enemy alien.[48] The rule rests on the principle that it is contrary to public policy that a relationship should continue which may strengthen the enemy or facilitate communication with him. But the principle is not carried to its logical conclusion and there is no general rule that a state of war avoids all contracts between subjects and alien enemies.[49] A debt due to an alien enemy incurred before the declaration of war (including a debt arising from a contract which is itself abrogated) is not extinguished and at common law may be recovered after the war,[50] and property belonging to an enemy alien is not confiscated, though the existence of these rights may be an indirect source of strength to the enemy. But by statute enemy property, including debts, vests in the Custodian of Enemy Property and is dealt with by him on the restoration of peace.[51] In certain rare cases[52] such a contract has been held to have survived the outbreak of war, *e.g.* a lease,[53] a power of attorney[54] and a policy of life assurance.[55]

---

[46] *Bell's Tr.* v. *Bell's Tr.*, 1907 S.C. 872.

[47] See McNair and Watts, *Legal Effects of War* (4th ed., 1966).

[48] As to meaning of 'enemy alien' see para. 4.6, *supra*.

[49] See opinion of Lord Dunedin in *Ertel Bieber & Co.* v. *Rio Tinto Co. Ltd.* [1918] A.C. 260, at pp. 267–69.

[50] *Ertel Bieber & Co., supra*; *Schering Ltd.* v. *Stockholms Enskilda Bank Aktiebolag* [1946] A.C. 219, at p. 241; *Arab Bank* v. *Barclays's Bank* [1954] A.C. 495.

[51] Trading with the Enemy Act 1939, as amended by the Emergency Laws (Misc. Provs.) Act 1953 and the Foreign Compensation Act 1969, s.1.

[52] McNair and Watts, *op. cit.*, at p. 134.

[53] *Halsey* v. *Lowenfeld* [1916] 2 K.B. 707, a lease now being regarded as 'a concomitant of a right of property,' Lord Dunedin's phrase in *Ertel Bieber, supra*, at p. 269.

[54] *Tingley* v. *Müller* [1917] 2 Ch. 144, where the circumstances were very special.

[55] *Seligman* v. *Eagle Insurance Co.* [1917] 1 Ch. 519, a doubtful decision.

CHAPTER 15

PRESCRIPTION

15.1 Prescription and Limitation.—This chapter is concerned only with prescription, *i.e.* the establishment or definition of a right or title, or the extinction of a right or obligation, through lapse of time. The law relating to limitation, which does not affect the subsistence of rights or obligations but merely renders them unenforceable by court action after a certain time, is to be found in the chapter on Reparation.[1]

15.2 Common Law and the 1973 Act.—It is doubtful whether lapse of time can at common law fortify a right or extinguish an obligation. The effect of mere delay (*mora*) has already been considered.[2] It would appear that if a particular exaction has been submitted to for 40 years it becomes exigible at common law, though the creditor may be unable to explain the basis of his claim.[3] Most of the law relating to prescription is statutory. The Prescription and Limitation (Scotland) Act 1973[4] repeals much previous legislation and in Part I[5] enacts a comprehensive new scheme of prescription, consisting of the positive prescription, the long negative prescription, the quinquennial prescription, and a two-year prescription in the case of recovery between joint wrongdoers. The Consumer Protection Act 1987 inserted Part IIA[6] in the 1973 Act, creating a 10-year prescription in respect of rights and obligations arising out of damage caused by defective products.[7]

---

[1] para. 34.41, *infra*. Where a right or obligation is affected by limitation rather than by prescription, alternative methods of enforcement such as security or lien, remain open to the creditor. Furthermore, if payment has been made, the fact that the debt was affected by limitation does not afford ground for a *condictio indebiti*. Some rights and obligations may be subject to both prescription and limitation: for example rights and obligations arising from damage caused by defective products: see ss. 22A–22D of the Prescription and Limitation (Scotland) Act 1973 (as amended by Sched. 1 to the Consumer Protection Act 1987); and see para, 15.33, *infra*.

[2] para. 14.26, *supra*.

[3] *Kirk Session of South Leith* v. *Scott* (1832) 11 S. 75; *Mann* v. *Brodie* (1885) 12 R. (H.L.) 52, at p. 57.

[4] As amended by the Land Registration (Scotland) Act 1979, s. 10, the Law Reform (Misc. Provs.) (Scotland) Act 1980, the Prescription and Limitation (Scotland) Act 1984, the Bankruptcy (Scotland) Act 1985, the Law Reform (Misc. Provs.) (Scotland) Act 1985, the Prescription (Scotland) Act 1987, and the Consumer Protection Act 1987. All subsequent statutory references are to the 1973 Act as amended, unless otherwise indicated.

[5] ss. 1–16, Pt. I came into force on July 25, 1976: s. 25(2)(*b*).

[6] ss. 22A–22D.

[7] See para. 15.33, *infra*.

15.3 Choice of Law.[8]—Where the substantive law of a country other than Scotland falls to be applied by a Scottish court as the law governing an obligation,[9] the court is to apply any relevant rules of law of that country relating to the extinction of the obligation to the exclusion of any corresponding rule of Scots law.[10] The foreign law is not to be applied however where (a) it appears to the court that the application of the relevant foreign rule of law would be incompatible with the principles of public policy applied by the court;[11] or where (b) the application of the corresponding rule of Scots law had extinguished the obligation prior to the coming into force of the Prescription and Limitation (Scotland) Act 1984.[12]

15.4 Positive Prescription.—Positive prescription is the effect of continued possession in establishing and defining (a) title to interests in land, and (b) positive servitudes[13] and public rights of way. 'Land' includes heritable property of any description, including buildings and minerals.[14] An 'interest in land' is not defined, but it does not include a servitude.[15] The title to an interest in land is often, although not invariably, recorded in the General Register of Sasines,[16] or registered in the Land Register of Scotland.[17] The *dominium directum* of a superior, the *dominium utile* of a vassal, a liferent, a lease, and a heritable security are probably all interests in land.

15.5 Period.—(a) 10 years: Where possession of an interest in land is founded upon a recorded title or registered interest, the period of the positive prescription is 10 years.[18] If the foundation writ is a decree of

---

[8] 1973 Act, s. 23A inserted by Prescription and Limitation (Scotland) Act 1984, s. 4, implementing the recommendations of the Scottish Law Commission in their Report No. 74, *Prescription and Limitation of Actions: Report on Personal Injuries Actions and Private International Law Questions* (Nov. 1982). The Law Commission envisaged that any relevant foreign rule of prescription or limitation should be applied, irrespective of its classification as substantive or procedural: see paras. 1.3 and 1.4 of their Report.

[9] See generally Anton, *Private International Law* (2nd ed.); Cheshire & North, *Private International Law* (11th ed.); Dicey & Morris, *Conflict of Laws* (11th ed.).

[10] s. 23A.

[11] s. 23A(2).

[12] s. 23A(3), *i.e.* prior to September 26, 1984: see 1984 Act, s. 7(2). Note that s. 23A does not affect any proceedings commenced before September 26, 1984: 1984 Act, s. 5(2). The Law Commission comment that the state of the law prior to September 26, 1984 might have influenced the choice of forum, and it would therefore be inappropriate to apply s. 23A to proceedings already commenced.

[13] Negative servitudes can only be acquired by express grant: *Inglis* v. *Clark* (1901) 4 F. 288.

[14] s. 15(1).

[15] s. 15(1). Note that an 'interest in land' is defined in s. 28 of the Land Registration (Scotland) Act 1979 for the purposes of that Act.

[16] See, *e.g.* s. 1(2); s. 2.

[17] 1973 Act, s. 1, amended by the Land Registration (Scotland) Act 1979, s. 10.

[18] s. 1(1) of the 1973 Act; the Land Registration (Scotland) Act 1979, s. 10. The period of the positive prescription was originally 40 years: Prescription Act 1617 (c. 12). It was reduced (with the exception of servitudes, public rights of way and other public rights) to 20 years by the Conveyancing (Scotland) Act 1874, s. 34, as restated by the Conveyancing (Scotland) Act 1924, s. 16. It was further reduced (with the exception of servitudes, public

adjudication for debt, the prescriptive period does not begin to run until after the expiry of a 10-year period known as 'the legal.'[19]

(b) 20 years: In certain less common cases the period of the positive prescription is 20 years. Possession for 20 years is required in order to establish or define a title to an interest in foreshores and salmon fishings in any question with the Crown.[20] A period of 20 years is also necessary in certain special cases where the foundation writ does not require to be, and has not in fact been, recorded. Thus where prescriptive possession is founded upon an unrecorded lease or sub-lease or upon an unrecorded title to an interest in allodial lands,[21] or where prescriptive possession is relied upon in any other case where by virtue of pre-1973 law the foundation writ need not be recorded, a period of 20 years is required.[22] Finally, a period of 20 years is required where prescription is relied upon as establishing or fortifying a positive servitude[23] or public right of way.[24]

15.6 Requisites: Interests in Land.—If an interest in particular land has been possessed by any person[25] for a continuous period of 10 years openly, peaceably and without any judicial interruption, and if the possession was founded on and followed (i) the recording in the General Register of Sasines of a deed[26] which is sufficient in respect of its terms to constitute in favour of that person a title to that interest in the particular land[27] or (ii) registration of that interest in favour of that person in the

rights of way, other public rights; and foreshores and salmon fishings in any question with the Crown) to 10 years by the Conveyancing and Feudal Reform (Scotland) Act 1970, s. 8.

[19] s. 1(3). The debtor can redeem his land during the legal. He may also redeem his land after the expiry of the legal unless the adjudger obtains a decree of declarator of expiry of the legal without payment.

[20] s. 1(4). 10 years suffices where a claim is made against someone other than the Crown. Possession in relation to a foreshore was discussed in *Luss Estates Co.* v. *B.P. Oil Grangemouth Refinery Ltd.*, 1981 S.L.T. 97; affd. 1982 S.L.T. 457, 1987 S.L.T. 201; and briefly in *Hamilton* v. *McIntosh Donald Ltd.*, 1994 S.L.T. 793; and possession in relation to salmon fishings in *Fothringham* v. *Passmore*, 1984 S.C. (H.L.) 96. See too Rennie R., "Possession: Nine Tenths of the Law", 1994 S.L.T. (News) 261. Note the special provisions in the Land Registration (Scotland) Act 1979, s. 14, for notice to be given to the Crown where a person claims prescriptive possession of and title to the foreshore.

[21] Allodial lands are held of no superior: for example, the Crown's paramount superiority; and the Crown's own property: Erskine, II, iii, 8. Many allodial titles are unrecorded.

[22] ss. 2, 15(1). See for example, *Wallace* v. *University of St. Andrews* (1904) 6 F. 1093.

[23] s. 3(1), (2).

[24] s. 3(3); *Richardson* v. *Cromarty Petroleum Co. Ltd.*, 1982 S.L.T. 237; *Strathclyde (Hyndland) Housing Society Ltd.* v. *Cowie*, 1983 S.L.T. (Sh.Ct) 61; *Cumbernauld and Kilsyth D.C.* v. *Dollar Land (Cumbernauld) Ltd.*, 1993 S.C. (H.L.) 44.

[25] Or by any person and his successors: s. 1(1)(a).

[26] 'Deed' includes a judicial decree, and any instrument of sasine, notarial instrument or notice of title which narrates or declares that a person has a title to an interest in land: s. 5(1)—including, for example, a superiority title: *Love-Lee* v. *Cameron*, 1991 S.C.L.R. 61; 1990 G.W.D. 31–1814; or an *a non domino* disposition: *Hamilton* v. *McIntosh Donald Ltd.*, 1994 S.L.T. 793.

[27] Or in land of a description habile to include the particular land: s. 1(1)(b). See, *e.g.* *Lock* v. *Taylor & Anor.*, 1976 S.L.T. 238; *Suttie* v. *Baird*, 1992 S.L.T. 133.

Land Register of Scotland subject to an exclusion of indemnity under the Land Registration (Scotland) Act 1979, section 12(2),[28] the validity of the title so far as relating to the interest in land is rendered unchallengeable, except on the ground that the recorded deed is *ex facie* invalid or was forged or that registration proceeded upon a forged deed and the person in whose favour the registration was made was aware of the forgery at the time of registration.[29]

15.7 Recorded Deed or Registered Interest.—Where a deed forms the basis of prescription, the deed must be *ex facie* valid.[30] Intrinsic defects, such as the lack of the proper statutory solemnities of execution, are struck at, but not extrinsic defects such as fraud or duress.[31] Where a deed has been at any time *ex facie* invalid by reason of an informality of execution within the meaning of section 39 of the Conveyancing (Scotland) Act 1874 and the appropriate court has subsequently declared that it was subscribed by the granter or maker and the witnesses, the deed shall be deemed not to be *ex facie* invalid by reason of any such informality of execution.[32] The foundation deed must also be recorded in the General Register of Sasines or registered in the Land Register of Scotland,[33] except, as has been indicated, in certain special cases,[34] and in such cases possession for 20 years is required.[35]

It is no objection to the plea of prescription that the title proceeds from a party who had no title to the lands in question or no right to dispose of them.[36] This is indeed the very objection which it is the object of prescription to exclude: good titles stand in no need of prescription.[37] Nor is *bona fides* necessary: the plea of prescription may be taken by a party who has been in possession in the knowledge that his title was defective.[38]

---

[28] A title subject to exclusion of indemnity was thought to be the only case under a registration of title system which might require the benefit of the positive prescription in rendering a title unchallengeable; *cf.* dicta in *Short's Tr.* v. *Keeper of the Registers of Scotland*, 1994 S.L.T. 65.

[29] s. 1(1A) of the Prescription and Limitation (Scotland) Act 1973; see Land Registration (Scotland) Act 1979, s. 10.

[30] s. 1(1), (1A) of the 1973 Act, and the Land Registration (Scotland) Act 1979, s. 10. See, *e.g. Scammell* v. *Scottish Sports Council*, 1983 S.L.T. 462. The deed may be an *a non domino* disposition: *Hamilton* v. *McIntosh Donald Ltd.*, 1994 S.L.T. 793.

[31] *Cf.* Bell, *Prin.*, § 610; *Cooper Scott* v. *Gill Scott*, 1924 S.C. 309; *Abbey* v. *Atholl Properties*, 1936 S.N. 97; dicta in *Short's Tr.* v. *Keeper of the Registers of Scotland, supra.*

[32] s. 5(2).

[33] s. 1(1)(b); s. 15(1).

[34] Namely, the interest in land of the lessee under a lease or sub-lease; any interest in allodial land; any other interest in land the title to which could in terms of pre-1973 law be established without the necessity of recording the foundation writ: s. 2. *Cf.* para. 15.5, *supra.*

[35] s. 2(1) (*a*). If the deed has in fact been recorded, or an interest registered, 10 years' possession suffices: s. 2(3).

[36] Erskine, III, vii, 4; *Fraser* v. *Lord Lovat* (1898) 25 R. 603.

[37] *Cooper Scott* v. *Gill Scott*, 1924 S.C. 309 at pp. 315 and 326; *Hamilton* v. *McIntosh Donald Ltd., supra* (*a non domino* disposition); and see Rennie R., "Possession: Nine Tenths of the Law", 1994 S.L.T. (News) 261.

[38] *Duke of Buccleuch* v. *Cunynghame* (1826) 5 S. 57; contrary to Bell, *Prin.*, § 2004.

15.8 Possession.—Possession is a question of fact,[39] and may be actual or civil, through the actual possession of tenants. Possession must be continuous, and must be *nec vi nec clam, nec precario*, so that possession by force, by stealth, or by leave rather than as a matter of right will not suffice. Possession must be referable to the title,[40] and a person in possession under some subordinate right (*e.g.* a long lease) cannot, by obtaining an *ex facie* valid title from some party other than his landlord, and continuing to possess for the prescriptive period, maintain that his right is one of property.[41] Possession by an institute[42] under a deed which satisfies the statutory requirements, may be appealed to by any substitute[43] as excluding any extrinsic objection to the right which the deed confers upon him.[44] The requisite possession may fortify a title although the adverse right was a grant by the possessor himself, or his predecessor in title.[45]

15.9 Requisites: Servitudes and Public Rights of Way.—Unlike an interest in land, a positive servitude over land may be constituted or its existence proved by prescription without the necessity of a foundation deed, recorded or otherwise, or a registered interest. Mere possession of the servitude by any person also in possession[46] of the dominant tenement for a continuous period of 20 years openly, peaceably and without judicial interruption will render unchallengeable the existence of the servitude as so possessed.[47] Where a servitude is thus constituted, the extent of the possession affords the measure of the right acquired: *tantum praescriptum quantum possessum* (there is only prescription in so far as there has been possession).[48] However, if there be a deed[49] sufficient in respect of its terms, whether expressly or by implication, to constitute the servitude, the deed itself is the measure of the right[50] although where its terms are unclear they may be explained or interpreted by the prescriptive possession. The deed need not be recorded.[51] If the deed is followed by the requisite possession, the validity of the servitude as so constituted is unchallengeable except on the ground that the deed is *ex facie* invalid or was forged.[52]

---

[39] See, for example, *Bain* v. *Carrick,* 1983 S.L.T. 675; *Hamilton* v. *McIntosh Donald Ltd.,* 1994 S.L.T. 793.

[40] Possession in relation to a barony title was discussed in *Luss Estates Co.* v. *B.P. Oil Grangemouth Refinery Ltd.,* 1981 S.L.T. 97; affd. 1982 S.L.T. 457; 1987 S.L.T. 201.

[41] *Duke of Argyll* v. *Campbell,* 1912 S.C. 458.

[42] See para. 44.21, *infra.*

[43] *Ibid.*

[44] *Cooper Scott* v. *Gill Scott,* 1924 S.C. 309.

[45] *Wallace* v. *University of St. Andrews* (1904) 6 F. 1093.

[46] s. 3(4). The 1973 Act dispenses with the need for infeftment in the dominant tenement by the party claiming the servitude.

[47] s. 3(2).

[48] s. 3(2) and *cf. Kerr* v. *Brown,* 1939 S.C. 140.

[49] See note 26, *supra.*

[50] s. 3(1).

[51] s. 3(1)(*b*). *Cf.* Bell, *Prin.,* § 994; *Cowan* v. *Stewart* (1872) 10 M. 735.

[52] *Ibid.*

The existence of a public right of way becomes unchallengeable where it has been possessed[53] by the public for a continuous period of 20 years openly, peaceably, and without any judicial interruption.[54] Again the extent of the possession affords the measure of the right.

Servitudes and public rights of way are dealt with in greater detail in the chapter on Landownership.[55]

15.10 Computation of Period.—The Act provides certain rules for computation.[56] Where the prescriptive period commences at a time other than at the beginning of the day, the period is deemed to have commenced at the beginning of the next following day.[57] If the prescriptive period ends on a holiday (as defined[58]) the period is extended to include the next succeeding day which is not a holiday.[59] Any time during which any person against whom prescription is pled was under legal disability[60] is to be reckoned as if the person were free from that disability.[61] In general, regard is to be had to the principles formerly applicable in computing the prescriptive periods for the purposes of the Prescription Act 1617.[62]

Thus positive prescriptions will in most cases run from the midnight following upon the recording of the deed[63] or the registration of the

---

[53] As a matter of right: *Cumbernauld and Kilsyth D.C.* v. *Dollar Land (Cumbernauld) Ltd.*, 1993 S.L.T. 1318; *Lauder* v. *MacColl*, 1993 S.C.L.R. 753; *Renfrew D.C.* v. *Russell*, 1994 G.W.D. 34–2032.

[54] s. 3(3).

[55] Chap. 40, *infra*; see too *Richardson* v. *Cromarty Petroleum Co. Ltd.*, 1982 S.L.T. 237; *Strathclyde (Hyndland) Housing Society Ltd.* v. *Cowie*, 1983 S.L.T. (Sh.Ct) 61.

[56] s. 14.

[57] s. 14(1)(*c*).

[58] s. 14(2). 'Holiday' means a Saturday, a Sunday, and a Scottish bank holiday.

[59] s. 14(1)(*d*).

[60] Legal disability is defined in s. 15(1) as meaning legal disability by reason of nonage or unsoundness of mind. Section 1(2) of the Age of Legal Capacity (Scotland) Act 1991 (which came into force on September 25, 1991) provides that any reference to 'legal disability by reason of nonage' is to be construed as a reference to a person under the age of 16 years. The former categories of pupillarity and minority (see, *e.g. Fyfe* v. *Croudace Ltd.*, 1986 S.C. 80, 1986 S.L.T. 528; and Chap. 49 *infra*) are abolished. There are transitional provisions in s. 8 of the 1991 Act to avoid prejudice to persons who were aged between 16 and 18 immediately before the commencement of the 1991 Act.

[61] s. 14(1)(*b*) except in the circumstances in s. 6(4) (including that subsection as applied by s. 8A) which provides, *inter alia*, that 'any period during which the original creditor (while he is the creditor) was under legal disability shall not be reckoned as, or as part of, the prescriptive period.' As the Scottish Law Commission indicate in their Report No. 122, *Prescription and Limitation of Actions (Latent Damage and Other Related Issues)* (Oct. 1989) at para. 4.14: 'The reference to the "original creditor" indicates that the legal disability of an assignee of that creditor's rights would not postpone or suspend the prescriptive period.' It is not clear to what extent the 1973 Act affects the equitable common law plea of *non valens agere cum effectu* (not able to act effectually). There may be grounds other than nonage or unsoundness of mind which could form the basis of the plea: *cf. Campbell's Trs.* v. *Campbell's Trs.*, 1950 S.C. 48, *per* Lord President Cooper at p. 57. However it has been said that the plea should not be extended beyond the decided cases: *Pettigrew* v. *Harton*, 1956 S.C. 67 *per* Lord Justice-Clerk Thomson at p. 73.

[62] s. 14(1)(*c*).

[63] s. 1(1); s. 14(1)(*c*); and *cf. Simpson* v. *Marshall* (1900) 2 F. 447.

interest in land, or from the midnight following upon possession if possession is subsequent to recording or if recording is unnecessary. At common law, the appropriate period runs until the midnight on the same-numbered day in the same-numbered month.[64]

15.11 Effect.—The positive prescription excludes all inquiry into the previous titles and rights to the lands.[65] It may also define the extent of an interest in land, positive servitude or public right of way either where there is no foundation writ or where the extent of the right is not precisely set forth in the title.[66]

15.12 Interruption.—Only the interruption of possession or 'judicial' interruption will stop the running of the positive prescription.[67] Judicial interruption is defined[68] as the making in appropriate proceedings[69] by any person having a proper interest to do so of a claim[70] which challenges[71] the possession in question. The date of interruption is normally the date when the claim was made.[72] In arbitration proceedings where the nature of the claim has been stated in a preliminary notice the date of interruption is the date on which the preliminary notice is served by one party on the other requiring him to appoint an arbiter or to agree to the appointment of an arbiter or to submit the dispute to the arbiter previously designated.[73] Interruption

---

[64] Walker, *The Law of Prescription and Limitation of Actions in Scotland* (4th ed.), p. 97, citing *Cavers Parish Council* v. *Smailholm Parish Council*, 1909 S.C. 195.

[65] s. 1(1); and *cf. Fraser* v. *Lord Lovat* (1898) 25 R. 603.

[66] See, *e.g.* s. 3(3), (4), and long title to the Act. *Cf. Lord Advocate* v. *Cathcart* (1871) 9 M. 744; *Auld* v. *Hay* (1880) 7 R. 663, *per* Lord President Inglis at p. 681; dicta in *Hamilton* v. *McIntosh Donald Ltd.*, 1994 S.L.T. 793 at p. 797.

[67] s. 1(1); *British Railways Board* v. *Strathclyde R.C.*, 1981 S.C. 90; *George A. Hood & Co.* v. *Dumbarton D.C.*, 1983 S.L.T. 238; *G.A. Estates Ltd.* v. *Caviapen Trs. Ltd.*, 1993 S.L.T. 1051 (I.H.); 1993 S.L.T. 1045 (O.H.).

[68] s. 4.

[69] Appropriate proceedings are any proceedings in a court of competent jurisdiction and any arbitration proceedings provided that the arbitration award would be enforceable in Scotland: s. 4(2). No claim is made in an arbitration if no arbiter has been appointed at the material time; *Douglas Milne Ltd.* v. *Borders R.C.*, 1990 S.L.T. 558; *John O'Connor (Plant Hire)* v. *Kier Construction*, 1990 S.C.L.R. 761; *R. Peter & Co. Ltd.* v. *The Pancake Place Ltd.*, 1993 S.L.T. 322. The definition does not include proceedings initiated in the Court of Session by a summons which is not subsequently called: s. 4(2)(*a*). *Cf. Barclay* v. *Chief Constable Northern Constabulary*, 1986 S.L.T. 562, where held *obiter* that the *terminus a quo* is the citation of the defender, and that the calling of the summons may occur outwith the quinquennium provided that the summons is called within a year and a day of citation or within such lesser period as has been fixed by protestation under Rule of Court 80 (now Rule of Court 13.14).

[70] Which may be an initial writ grossly lacking in specification: *British Railways Board* v. *Strathclyde R.C.*, *supra*, or a writ ultimately requiring substantial amendment (see para. 15.28, *infra*) but probably not a writ giving rise to a fundamentally null action: *Shanks* v. *Central R.C.*, 1987 S.L.T. 410 (O.H.); 1988 S.L.T. 212 (Ex. Div.).

[71] See dicta in *Scammell* v. *Scottish Sports Council*, 1983 S.L.T. 462 at p. 467.

[72] s. 4(3)(*b*). The commencement of an action has been defined as the date of citation: *Miller* v. *N.C.B.*, 1960 S.C. 376, *per* Lord President at p. 383; *Barclay* v. *Chief Constable, Northern Constabulary*, cit. sup. (*cf.* authorities cited in Walker, *The Law of Prescription* (4th ed.) at p. 97).

[73] s. 4(3)(*a*) and (4); in relation to stating the nature of the claim, see *Douglas Milne Ltd.* v. *Borders R.C.*, 1990 S.L.T. 558. See also n. 26 to para. 15.20 *infra*.

may take place on the last day of the prescriptive period.[74] If a relevant claim is made, it is thought that the prescriptive period starts anew from the midnight following upon the date on which the interruption ends:[75] the point has been discussed in several cases.[76]

15.13 Negative Prescription: Long, Quinquennial, Ten Year and Two Year.—While lapse of time in the positive prescription has the effect of establishing or defining a right or title to heritable property, lapse of time in the negative prescription extinguishes rights and obligations relating to both heritable and moveable property. The creditor is deemed by his non-enforcement thereof to have abandoned his claim.[77]

Before the coming into force[78] of Part I of the Prescription and Limitation (Scotland) Act 1973 there were several negative prescriptions of differing periods which fell into two groups: (a) prescriptions which extinguished rights and obligations after certain periods of time;[79] and (b) prescriptions which did not extinguish rights and obligations but which merely affected the onus and method of proof.[80] Part I of and Schedule 5 to the 1973 Act as amended abolished these prescriptions and replaced them with two extinctive prescriptions, one of five years (the quinquennial) and one of 20 years (the long). The Prescription and Limitation (Scotland) Act 1984 introduced a third extinctive prescription of two years relating to joint wrongdoers.[81] The Consumer Protection Act 1987 introduced a fourth extinctive prescription of 10 years relating to product liability.[82] It is impossible to contract out of the statutory provisions relating to negative prescription.[83]

---

[74] *Simpson* v. *Marshall* (1900) 2 F. 447.

[75] Thus, for example, a fresh prescriptive period would begin to run from the midnight following upon the date of the final disposal of a relevant court action, including any appeal procedure.

[76] See *G.A. Estates Ltd.* v. *Caviapen Trs. Ltd.*, 1993 S.L.T. 1051 (I.H.); 1993 S.L.T. 1045 (O.H.) *obiter dicta* in *British Railways Board* v. *Strathclyde, supra* at pp. 99, 102, 104; *George A. Hood* v. *Dumbarton D.C.*, 1983 S.L.T. 238; *Hogg* v. *Prentice*, 1994 S.C.L.R. 426.

[77] *Macdonald* v. *North of Scotland Bank*, 1942 S.C. 369, *per* Lord Justice-Clerk Cooper at p. 373.

[78] See note 5, *supra*.

[79] The septennial prescription of cautionary obligations (Cautioners Act 1695 (c. 7)); the long negative prescription (Prescription Acts 1469 (c. 4); 1474 (c. 9); 1617 (c. 12)), although *quaere* whether the latter prescription was truly extinctive; see *Stirling's Trs.* v. *Legal and General Assurance Society*, 1957 S.L.T. 73; Anton, *Private International Law* (2nd ed.), p. 302.

[80] The triennial prescription (Prescription Act 1579 (c. 21)); the quinquennial prescription (Prescription Acts 1669 (c. 14) and 1685 (c. 14)); the sexennial prescription (Bills of Exchange (Scotland) Act 1772 (c. 72)); and the vicennial prescription of holograph writings (Prescription Act 1699 (c. 14)).

[81] See para. 15.32, *infra*. The two-year period relating to joint wrongdoers was previously a limitation, not a prescription: see 1973 Act, s. 20, repealed by the 1984 Act.

[82] See para. 15.33 *infra*.

[83] s. 13: commented on in *McPhail* v. *Cunninghame D.C.*, 1985 S.L.T. 149 at p. 153; *Ferguson* v. *McIntyre*, 1993 S.L.T. 1269.

15.14 Long Negative Prescription (20 Years).—If an obligation[84] becomes enforceable[85] and thereafter subsists for a continuous period of 20 years[86] without any relevant claim being made in relation to the obligation and without the subsistence of the obligation being relevantly acknowledged, then as from the expiration of that period the obligation is extinguished.[87] Similarly if a right[88] relating to property (heritable or moveable) becomes exercisable or enforceable and thereafter subsists for a continuous period of 20 years without being exercised or enforced, and without any relevant claim being made in relation to the right, then as from the expiration of that period the right is extinguished.[89]

15.15 To what Rights and Obligations Applicable.—The long negative prescription applies to all rights and obligations which have become enforceable including those obligations affected by the quinquennial prescription[90] but excluding obligations arising from damage caused by defective products;[91] those rights and obligations designated as imprescriptible[92] and any obligation to make reparation in respect of personal injuries within the meaning of Part II of the 1973 Act or in respect of the death of any person as a result of such injuries.[93] In pre-1973 law the long negative prescription has been held to apply to all

---

[84] Any reference to an obligation includes a reference to the right correlative thereto: s. 15(2).

[85] See 1973 Act, s. 11(4) for definition of 'enforceable' in the context of obligations to make reparation whether arising from any enactment, rule of law, or by reason of breach of contract or promise. See also paras. 15.17, 15.26 and 15.31 *infra*.

[86] The period of the long negative prescription was originally 40 years: Prescription Acts 1469 (c. 4); 1474 (c. 9); 1617 (c. 12). It was reduced (with the exception of servitudes, public rights of way and other public rights) to 20 years by the Conveyancing (Scotland) Act 1924, s. 17, as amended by the Conveyancing Amendment (Scotland) Act 1938, s. 4.

[87] s. 7(1).

[88] Any reference to a right includes a reference to the obligation (if any) correlative thereto: s. 15(2).

[89] s. 8. This section applies to any right relating to property (heritable or moveable) not being a right designated as imprescriptible (see para. 15.16, *infra*) nor a right falling within ss. 6 or 7 as being a right correlative to an obligation to which either of those sections applies: s. 8(2). It is thought that s. 8 was necessary, despite s. 7 and the provision for correlative rights in s. 15(2), for the reason that while every obligation must have a correlative right, the correlative of a right need not be an obligation. For example, a person may have a right to raise an action of reduction (*cf. Paul* v. *Reid*, 8 February 1814, F.C.; *Pettigrew* v. *Harton*, 1956 S.C. 67) but it would seem that no corresponding obligation (as distinct from, say, a liability to be disadvantaged) can arise unless and until decree of reduction is pronounced.

[90] s. 7(2). Because of the special rules applying to the quinquennial prescription (see para. 15.26, *infra*) it is possible that an enforceable obligation might subsist for 20 years without being extinguished by the quinquennial prescription. Hence the need for s. 7(2).

[91] s. 7(2) as amended by the Consumer Protection Act 1987; see para. 15.33, *infra*.

[92] See para. 15.16, *infra*.

[93] s. 7(2) of the 1973 Act as amended by s. 6(1) of and Sched. 1, para. 2 to the Prescription and Limitation (Scotland) Act 1984, implementing the recommendation of the Scottish Law Commission in their Report No. 74, *Prescription and Limitation of Actions: Report on Personal Injuries Actions and Private International Law Questions* (Nov. 1982). Section 7(2) as amended affects any obligation which had not been extinguished by the long negative prescription before the coming into force of the 1984 Act, *i.e.* before September 26, 1984: 1984 Act, s. 5(3).

ordinary debts;[94] reparation claims;[95] rights to land if merely personal;[96] the right to object to the use of property as a nuisance;[97] the right to reduce a contract on any extrinsic ground such as fraud;[98] the right to recover things which have been lost or lent;[99] the right of a bank customer to recover a sum placed on current account with the bank;[1] and a right of servitude.[2]

15.16   Imprescriptible Rights and Obligations: Schedule 3.—The rights and obligations specified in Schedule 3 can never prescribe.[3] These are, any real right of ownership in land;[4] the right in land of the lessee under a recorded lease; any right to recover property *extra commercium*; the obligation of a trustee[5] to account, make reparation in respect of any fraudulent breach of trust, or make trust property furthcoming;[6] any obligation of a *mala fide* recipient of trust property to make it furthcoming; any right to recover stolen property from the thief or anyone privy to the theft; any right to be served as heir to an ancestor or to take any steps necessary for making up or completing title to any interest in land;[7] and any right exercisable as a *res merae facultatis, i.e.* a right which the creditor may assert or not as he pleases, without losing the right by failure to assert it for the prescriptive period.[8]

[94] Bell, *Prin.*, § 608.

[95] *Cooke* v. *Falconer* (1850) 13 D. 157; but see paras. 15.29 *et seq., infra.*

[96] *Paterson* v. *Wilson* (1859) 21 D. 322; *Pettigrew* v. *Harton*, 1956 S.C. 67. Real rights of ownership in land are imprescriptible: Sched. 3, para. (*a*). See para. 15.16, *infra.*

[97] *Harvie* v. *Robertson* (1903) 5 F. 338.

[98] *Cubbison* v. *Hyslop* (1837) 16 S. 112, at p. 119.

[99] *Kirk Session of Aberscherder* v. *Kirk Session of Gemrie* (1633) Mor. 10972.

[1] *Macdonald* v. *North of Scotland Bank*, 1942 S.C. 369.

[2] Bell, *Prin.*, § 999; and see s. 3(5). See too para. 39.31, *infra.* Prior to the 1973 Act the period of the long negative prescription in relation to servitudes and public rights of way was 40 years. *Cf.* note 86, *supra.*

[3] ss. 7(2), 8(2).

[4] *Re* 'real right', see *Macdonald* v. *Scott*, 1981 S.C. 75; *Gibson* v. *Hunter Home Designs*, 1976 S.C. 23; *Sharp* v. *Thomson*, 1994 S.L.T. 1068.

[5] 'Trustee' is widely defined in s. 15(1) and includes not only executors, tutors, curators, and judicial factors, but anyone who could be said to be holding property in a fiduciary capacity for another. In *Sinclair* v. *Sinclair*, O.H. (Lord McCluskey) Sept. 24, 1985 (unreported), it was held that the duty of an executor-nominate to account for the executry estate is imprescriptible.

[6] *Hobday* v. *Kirkpatrick's Trs.*, 1985 S.L.T. 197: *sed quaere* whether Sched. 3, para. (*e*) (i)–(iii) was fully argued.

[7] See *e.g. Bain* v. *Bain*, 1994 G.W.D. 7–410. A contractual right to demand delivery of a disposition was held not to be an 'interest in land' within Sched. 3, para. (*h*): *Macdonald* v. *Scott*, 1981 S.C. 75. *Cf. Stewart's Exrs.* v. *Stewart*, 1993 S.L.T. 440, where it was held that an obligation to grant a disposition was not imprescriptible within the meaning of Sched. 3, para. (*h*). Note also *Porteous' Exrs.* v. *Ferguson*, 1995 G.W.D. 2–90, where the personal right of an uninfeft beneficiary was extinguished by the long negative prescription before the Act of 1973 came into effect.

[8] Rights exercisable as *res merae facultatis* include the right to exercise the ordinary uses of property: *Inglis* v. *Clark* (1901) 4 F. 288; a contractual right to open a door on to a common stair: *Gellatly* v. *Arrol* (1863) 1 M. 592; and the right of a superior to exact feuduties, although individual payments will be affected by the quinquennial prescription: see para 15.25, *infra*, and *cf. Duke of Buccleuch* v. *Officers of State* (1770) Mor. 10751. A right of servitude is not exercisable as a *res merae facultatis* and may therefore prescribe: see para. 15.15, *supra.*

Any right to challenge a deed on the ground that it is *ex facie* invalid or was forged is also imprescriptible.[9]

15.17 **Computation of Period.**—The rules set out in section 14 apply equally to the long negative as they do to the positive prescription.[10] Thus, the prescriptive period runs from the midnight after an obligation has become enforceable[11] (or a right exercisable or enforceable[12]). In the case of a debt, prescription runs from the midnight following upon the date when the debt became payable,[13] in the case of legitim and *jus relictae*, as a general rule, from the midnight following upon the date of death;[14] in the case of a positive servitude, from the midnight following upon the date of the last exercise of the servitude.

15.18 **Effect.**—The long negative prescription extinguishes rights and obligations which have not been enforced. When the prescriptive period expires, the right or obligation is gone. So, in the case of a debt, it is of no consequence that the debtor may admit that he never paid, and a reference to his oath is incompetent.[15]

15.19 **Interruption: Obligations: Section 7.**—To interrupt the running of the long negative prescription, a relevant claim in relation to the obligation must be made,[16] or the subsistence of the obligation must be relevantly acknowledged.[17] However in the case of an obligation arising from a bill of exchange or a promissory note, only a relevant claim will suffice to interrupt prescription.[18] If a relevant claim or a relevant acknowledgment is made, it is thought that the prescriptive period starts anew from the midnight following upon the date on which the interruption ends:[19] the point has been discussed in several cases.[20]

---

[9] s. 12(2).

[10] s. 14. See para. 15.10, *supra.*

[11] s. 7(1); s. 14(1)(*c*).

[12] s. 8(1); s. 14(1)(*c*).

[13] *Cf.* Erskine, III, vii, 36.

[14] *Cf. Sanderson* v. *Lockhart-Mure*, 1946 S.C. 298; *Campbell's Trs.* v. *Campbell's Trs.*, 1950 S.C. 48; but see *Mill's Trs.* v. *Mill's Exrs.*, 1965 S.C. 384.

[15] ss. 7 and 8. *Cf. Napier* v. *Campbell* (1703) Mor. 10656.

[16] s. 7(1); and see paras. 15.20 and 15.21, *infra.* The claim must be made against the debtor in the obligation: *Kirkcaldy D.C.* v. *Household Manufacturing Ltd.*, 1987 S.L.T. 617; but note *Bank of Scotland* v. *Laverock*, 1992 S.L.T. 73, where it was held that the claim may be made against the debtor's judicial factor or executor.

[17] *Ibid.*

[18] Proviso to s. 7(1).

[19] Thus, for example, a fresh prescriptive period would begin to run from the midnight following upon the date of the final disposal of a relevant court action, including any appeal procedure.

[20] See *G.A. Estates Ltd.* v. *Caviapen Trs. Ltd.*, 1993 S.L.T. 1051 (I.H.); 1993 S.L.T. 1045 (O.H.); *obiter dicta* in *British Railways Board* v. *Strathclyde R.C.*, 1981 S.C. 90; *George A. Hood* v. *Dumbarton D.C.*, 1983 S.L.T. 238; *Hogg* v. *Prentice*, 1994 S.C.L.R. 426; and *cf.* recommendations by the Scottish Law Commission in their Report No. 122 *(Prescription, Latent Damage)*, paras. 4.41 *et seq.*

15.20 Relevant Claim: Obligations.—A relevant claim in relation to section 7 is defined in section 9(1) as a claim made by or on behalf of the creditor for implement or part-implement of the obligation, being a claim made (a) in appropriate proceedings;[21] or (b) by the presentation of, or concurring in, a petition for sequestration or by the submission of a claim under the Bankruptcy (Scotland) Act 1985, section 22 or 48;[22] or (c) by a creditor to the trustee acting under a trust deed as defined in the Bankruptcy (Scotland) Act 1985,[23] section 5(2)(c); or (d) by the presentation of, or the concurring in, a petition for the winding up of a company or by the submission of a claim in a liquidation in accordance with rules made under section 411 of the Insolvency Act 1986.[24] Prior to the 1973 Act it was held that a summons, although not in proper form and therefore incompetent, could nevertheless interrupt prescription.[25]

Where a claim is made in an arbitration, and the nature of the claim has been stated in a preliminary notice, the date of interruption is the date on which the preliminary notice is served.[26] If diligence is executed against a debtor in an attempt to enforce an obligation, the diligence is deemed to be a relevant claim.[27]

15.21 Relevant Acknowledgment: Obligations.—Relevant acknowledgment is defined in section 10(1) as such performance by or on behalf of the

[21] See note 69, *supra.*

[22] s. 22 relates to the submission of claims by creditors to the interim trustee for the purposes of voting at the statutory meeting of creditors held within 28 days after the date of the award of sequestration; s. 48 relates to the submission of claims by creditors to the permanent trustee (with a view to obtaining a dividend or voting at any other meetings). The Prescription (Scotland) Act 1987 deals with the effect of the presentation of a petition for liquidation or submission of a claim in a liquidation.

[23] Subparas. (b) and (c) were inserted by the Bankruptcy (Scotland) Act 1985, Sched. 7, para. 11, brought into force on April 1, 1986 (s. 78(2) of the 1985 Act and S.I. 1985 No. 1924); and see s. 78(4) of the 1985 Act for transitional provisions. Note also ss. 8(5), 22(8), 48(7), 73(5) of and Sched. 5, para. 3 to the 1985 Act.

[24] Subpara. (d) was inserted by the Prescription (Scotland) Act 1987, effective as regards any claim (whenever submitted) in a liquidation in respect of which the winding up commenced on or after December 29, 1986: s. 1(3) of the 1987 Act; and see the sequence of the legislation in 1986 S.L.T. (News) 345.

[25] *Bank of Scotland* v. *Fergusson* (1898) 1 F. 96. See too *British Railways Board* v. *Strathclyde R.C.,* 1981 S.C. 90; *George A. Hood* v. *Dumbarton D.C.,* 1983 S.L.T. 238; but it has been observed that an action which is fundamentally null would not constitute an interruption of the prescriptive period: *Shanks* v. *Central R.C.,* 1987 S.L.T. 410 (O.H.); 1988 S.L.T. 212 (Ex. Div.); and an action of declarator has been held not to constitute a relevant claim in respect of an obligation to indemnify: *Wylie* v. *Avon Insurance Co. Ltd.,* 1988 S.C.L.R. 570.

[26] s. 9(3), (4); s. 4(4); *cf.* para. 15.12, *supra.* See *Douglas Milne Ltd.* v. *Borders R.C.,* 1990 S.L.T. 558 in relation to the necessity for stating the nature of the claim, and having an appointed arbiter at the material time. See also *John O'Connor (Plant Hire)* v. *Kier Construction,* 1990 S.C.L.R. 761; *R. Peter & Co. Ltd.* v. *The Pancake Place Ltd.,* 1993 S.L.T. 322. In another case where it was argued that there was no 'dispute' to be referred to arbitration in that the claim had prescribed, it was held that the issue of prescription was a further matter of dispute between the parties and should be decided by the arbiter: *Albyn Housing Society* v. *Taylor Woodrow Homes,* 1985 S.L.T. 309.

[27] s. 9(1); *Hogg* v. *Prentice,* 1994 S.C.L.R. 426.

debtor towards implement of the obligation as clearly indicates that the obligation still subsists,[28] or an unequivocal written admission by or on behalf of the debtor to the creditor or his agent clearly acknowledging that the obligation still subsists.[29] If the nature of the obligation requires the debtor to refrain from doing something or to permit or suffer something to be done or maintained, he will be regarded as acknowledging the obligation if he so refrains, permits or suffers.[30] If an obligation is relevantly acknowledged by the performance of, or on behalf of, one joint obligant, the running of prescription is interrupted as respects each joint obligant.[31] If, on the other hand, a written admission is made by or on behalf of one joint obligant, the running of prescription is only interrupted as respects that joint obligant.[32] Where an obligation affects a trust estate, it matters not whether one trustee acknowledges by performance or by written admission: the running of prescription is interrupted as respects the liability of the trust estate and any liability of each of the trustees.[33]

15.22 Interruption: Rights: Section 8.[34]—To interrupt the running of the long negative prescription, the right must be exercised or enforced, or a relevant claim in relation to the right must be made.[35]

15.23 Relevant Claim: Rights.—A relevant claim in relation to section 8 is a claim made in appropriate proceedings[36] by or on behalf of the creditor to establish the right or to contest any claim to a right inconsistent therewith.[37]

Where a claim is made in an arbitration, and the nature of the claim has been stated in a preliminary notice, the date of interruption is the date on which the preliminary notice is served.[38]

---

[28] For example, the payment of interest on a debt. *Cf. Kermack* v. *Kermack* (1874) 2 R. 156. However it has been held that the payment of interest under a principal bond does not interrupt the running of prescription against the obligation in a bond of corroboration: *Yuill's Trs.* v. *Maclachlan's Trs.*, 1939 S.C. (H.L.) 40. In *Gibson* v. *Carson*, 1980 S.C. 356, the fact that a landlord allowed a tenant to occupy a house for many years without payment of rent was held not to constitute a relevant acknowledgment by the landlord of an obligation on his part under an oral contract to grant a title to the tenant. In *Inverlochy Castle Ltd.* v. *Lochaber Power Co.*, 1987 S.L.T. 466, the supplying of electricity constituted performance.

[29] See, for example, *Fortunato's J.F.* v. *Fortunato*, 1981 S.L.T. 277 (resolution of trustees recorded in minute and communicated to creditor's agents); and cases cited in nn. 90 and 99 *infra*.

[30] s. 10(4).

[31] s. 10(2)(*a*).

[32] s. 10(2)(*b*).

[33] s. 10(3).

[34] For the ambit of s. 8, see s. 8(2) and n. 89, *supra*.

[35] s. 8(1).

[36] See n. 69, *supra*.

[37] s. 9(2) as amended by the 1984 Act, Sched. 1.

[38] s. 9(3), (4); s. 4(4); *cf.* para. 15.12, *supra*.

15.24 The Quinquennial Prescription (Five Years).—If after the 'appropriate date'[39] an obligation[40] to which section 6 applies subsists for a continuous period of five years without any relevant claim being made in relation to the obligation and without the subsistence of the obligation being relevantly acknowledged then as from the expiration of that period the obligation is extinguished.[41]

15.25 To what Obligations Applicable: Schedule 1.—Unlike the long negative prescription, the quinquennial prescription applies only to a limited but important group of obligations,[42] namely any obligation (a) to pay a sum of money due in respect of a particular period;[43] (b) based on redress of unjustified enrichment;[44] (c) arising from *negotiorum gestio*; (d) arising from liability to make reparation, other than reparation in respect of personal injuries or death;[45] (e) under a bill of exchange or promissory note,[46] (f) of accounting;[47] and (g) arising from, or by reason of any breach of, a contract or promise.[48]

Cautionary obligations are affected by the quinquennial prescription.[49] Prescription runs even where the cautionary obligation is constituted or

---

[39] See para. 15.26, *infra*.

[40] See s. 15(2) and n. 84, *supra*.

[41] s. 6(1). The five year period need not necessarily commence immediately after the appropriate date: *R. Peter & Co. Ltd.* v. *The Pancake Place Ltd.* 1993 S.L.T. 322. Note that s. 6 has been held to apply not only to private rights and obligations, but also to public law obligations: *Lord Advocate* v. *Butt*, 1992 S.C. 140.

[42] s. 6(2); Sched. 1, para. 1.

[43] *i.e.* interest, an annuity instalment, feuduty, ground annual, rent or other periodical payment in respect of the occupancy or use of land or a periodical payment under a land obligation: Sched. 1, para. 1 (*a*). It has been held that the quinquennial prescription does not apply to interest accruing on unpaid tax in terms of the Taxes Management Act 1970: *Lord Advocate* v. *Butt*, 1992 S.C. 140.

[44] Restitution, repetition, or recompense. For decisions on recompense, see *N.V. Devos Gebroeder* v. *Sunderland Sportswear Ltd.*, 1990 S.C. 291; *Alexander Hall & Son (Builders) Ltd.* v. *Strathclyde R.C.* 1989 G.W.D. 9–401.

[45] Sched. 1, para. 2 (*g*); and see paras. 15.29 *et seq., infra*. Certain obligations have been held not to arise from liability to make reparation within Sched. 1, para. 1 (*d*): see, for example, *Holt* v. *City of Dundee D.C.*, 1990 S.L.T. (Lands Tr.) 30 (a liability to pay statutory compensation under planning legislation); *Miller* v. *City of Glasgow D.C.*, 1988 S.C. 440 (a claim for reinstatement of premises altered as a result of a local authority refurbishment scheme).

[46] Cheques are therefore affected by the quinquennial prescription: Bills of Exchange Act 1882, s. 73. Bank notes are not: Sched. 1, para. 2(*b*) of the 1973 Act.

[47] Other than accounting for trust funds, which is imprescriptible: Sched. 3, para. (*e*). In *Lord Advocate* v. *Hepburn*, 1990 S.L.T. 530, and *Lord Advocate* v. *Butt*, 1992 S.C. 140, obligations in respect of unpaid tax and Class 4 contributions were held not to be obligations of accounting.

[48] See, for example, *Bank of Scotland* v. *Laverock*, 1992 S.L.T. 73 (sums outstanding in bank accounts); *Douglas Milne Ltd.* v. *Borders R.C.*, 1990 S.L.T. 558 (obligation in terms of clause 66 of I.C.E. Conditions of Contract to refer any difference or dispute to the contract engineer).

[49] 1973 Act, Sched. 1, paras. 2 (*c*) and 3. See *Royal Bank of Scotland* v. *Brown*, 1982 S.C. 89; *Smithy's Place Ltd.* v. *Blackadder & McMonagle*, 1991 S.L.T. 790; 1991 S.C.L.R. 512; *City of Glasgow D.C.* v. *Excess Insurance Co. Ltd.*, 1986 S.L.T. 585 (performance bond); *City of Glasgow D.C.* v. *Excess Insurance Co. Ltd. (No. 2)*, 1990 S.L.T. 225 (performance bond).

evidenced by a probative writ.[50] The 1973 Act provides[51] that where by virtue of a probative writ two or more persons are bound jointly and severally by an obligation to pay money to another party, the obligation shall, as respects the liability of each of the co-obligants, be regarded for the purposes of Schedule 1, paragraph 2(c) as if it were a cautionary obligation.[52]

The Act specifically provides[53] that the quinquennial prescription is not to apply to any obligation to recognise or obtemper a court decree, arbitration award, or an order of any tribunal or authority exercising jurisdiction under any enactment;[54] any obligation arising from the issue of a bank note; any obligation constituted or evidenced by a probative writ;[55] any obligation under a contract of partnership or of agency, not being an obligation remaining or becoming prestable on or after the termination of the relationship between the parties under the contract;[56] any obligation relating to land including an obligation to recognise a servitude;[57] any obligation to satisfy any claim to terce, courtesy, legitim, *jus relicti* or *jus relictae*, or to any prior right of a surviving spouse under sections 8 or 9 of the Succession (Scotland) Act 1964; any obligation to make reparation in respect of personal injuries[58] or in respect of the death of any person as a result of such injuries; any

---

[50] An exception to the general provision that obligations constituted or evidenced by probative writs are unaffected by the quinquennial prescription: Sched. 1, para. 2(c).

[51] Sched. 1, para. 2(3).

[52] Sched. 1, para. 3(1)—a paragraph which does not, however, affect the liability of a co-obligant where the creditor establishes that the co-obligant is truly a principal debtor, or that the original creditor was (at the time when the writ binding the co-obligant was delivered to the creditor) unaware that the co-obligant was not truly the principal debtor.

[53] Sched. 1, para. 2.

[54] 'Enactment' is defined in s. 15(1).

[55] The obligation must be 'constituted or evidenced by' the probative writ: *Hobday* v. *Kirkpatrick's Trs.*, 1985 S.L.T. 197; *Lord Advocate* v. *Shipbreaking Industries Ltd.*, 1991 S.L.T. 838. However, cautionary obligations and obligations to make periodical payments in terms of Sched. 1, para. 1(a), are affected by the quinquennial prescription whether or not incorporated in a probative writ: Sched. 1, para. 2 (c); see text, *supra*. 'Probative writ' is defined in Sched. 1, para. 4(b) as meaning a writ which is authenticated by attestation or in any such other manner as may be provided by an enactment (as defined by s. 15(1)) as having an effect equivalent to attestation. Holograph writs and writs adopted as holograph are therefore affected by quinquennial prescription, as they are not equivalent to attested writs by virtue of any enactment. Missives relating to heritage are usually adopted as holograph but are probably excluded from the quinquennial prescription as being obligations 'relating to land'; see *Barratt Scotland Ltd.* v. *Keith*, 1994 S.L.T. 1343 (missives); *Wright* v. *Frame*, 1992 G.W.D. 8–447 (missives); but see too *Lieberman* v. *G.W. Tait & Sons, S.S.C.*, 1987 S.L.T. 585 (letter of obligation).

[56] Discussed in *Sinclair* v. *Sinclair*, O.H. (Lord McCluskey), Sept. 24, 1985, unreported; see too *Coull* v. *Maclean*, 1991 G.W.D. 21–1249.

[57] But excluding those obligations to make periodical payments in terms of Sched. 1, para. 1 (a) to which the quinquennial prescription does apply. Missives may be an 'obligation relating to land': *Barratt Scotland Ltd.* v. *Keith*, 1994 S.L.T. 1343; *Wright* v. *Frame*, 1992 G.W.D. 8–447; but not a letter of obligation (*Lieberman* v. *G.W. Tait & Sons, S.S.C.*, 1987 S.L.T. 585) nor an obligation to make reparation for breach of an obligation to do something on land (*Lord Advocate* v. *Shipbreaking Industries Ltd.*, 1991 S.L.T. 838).

[58] 'Personal injuries' includes any disease and any impairment of a person's physical or mental condition: Sched. 1, para. 2 (g) and s. 22(1). See paras. 15.29 *et seq.*, *infra*.

obligation to make reparation or otherwise make good in respect of defamation within the meaning of section 18A of the 1973 Act;[59] any obligation arising from liability under section 2 of the Consumer Protection Act 1987, to make reparation for damage caused wholly or partly by a defect in a product;[60] and any obligation specified in Schedule 3 as imprescriptible.[61]

15.26 Computation of Period.—The rules set out in section 14 apply equally to the quinquennial prescription as they do to the positive and long negative prescriptions.[62] However, while the long negative prescription invariably commences when the obligation has become enforceable,[63] the quinquennial prescription begins to run after 'the appropriate date,' which is usually but not always the date when the obligation became enforceable.[64] Thus, for example, the prescription begins to run from the midnight of the date of a bill of exchange or cheque payable on demand;[65] or from the midnight after the expiry of the period of notice, where payment is due only after a certain period after demand.[66] An obligation to pay the price for heritage in terms of missives has been held to become enforceable only when a validly executed disposition was available for delivery.[67] Where a guarantee bound the guarantors to make payment of all sums due 'on demand,' the quinquennial prescription began to run on the date when the creditor wrote to each guarantor demanding payment of the balance still outstanding.[68] A principal debtor's obligation to repay the cautioner became enforceable on the date when payment was made to the creditor by the cautioner.[69] Where a performance bond became enforceable 'on default by the contractor,' the quinquennial prescription began to run on the date when a receiver was appointed to the contractor, that being a 'default' in terms of the building contract.[70] Where in terms of the parties' contract, liability to pay could only be ascertained from an architect's certificate, the quinquennial prescription began to run from the date of issue of the certificate and not from an earlier date when a receiver was

---

[59] Sched. 1, para. 2, as amended by the Law Reform (Misc. Provs.) (Scotland) Act 1985, s. 12(5).

[60] Sched. 1, para. 2, as amended by the Consumer Protection Act 1987, Sched. 1.

[61] See para. 15.16, *supra*.

[62] s. 14. See para. 15.10 *supra*.

[63] See para. 15.17, *supra*.

[64] s. 6(3). The five year period need not necessarily commence immediately after the appropriate date: *R. Peter & Co. Ltd.* v. *The Pancake Place Ltd.*, 1993 S.L.T. 322.

[65] *Cf. Stephenson* v. *Stephenson's Trs.* (1807) Mor. App. Bill No. 20.

[66] *Cf. Broddelius* v. *Grischotti* (1887) 14 R. 536.

[67] *Muir & Black* v. *Nee*, 1981 S.L.T. (Sh.Ct.) 68.

[68] *Royal Bank of Scotland* v. *Brown*, 1982 S.C. 89.

[69] *Smithy's Place Ltd.* v. *Blackadder & McMonagle*, 1991 S.L.T. 790; 1991 S.C.L.R. 512.

[70] *City of Glasgow D.C.* v. *Excess Insurance Co. Ltd.*, 1986 S.L.T. 585; contrast with *City of Glasgow D.C.* v. *Excess Insurance Co. Ltd. (No. 2)*, 1990 S.L.T. 225 (contractor's liability could only be determined by an architect's certificate, and the date of issue of that certificate was held to be the *terminus a quo*).

appointed to one of the parties.[71] Where cloth was supplied to manufacturers, an obligation to make recompense to the suppliers became enforceable when the manufacturers first became *lucrati* by making up and selling the cloth, and the quinquennial prescription began to run from that date.[72] In reparation actions, other than actions for personal injuries or death, the *terminus a quo* is the date on which there is a concurrence of *injuria* and *damnum*.[73]

'The appropriate date' is defined for certain special purposes in Schedule 2:

(a) Series of transactions: sale, hire or services rendered: where goods are supplied on sale[74] or hire, or where services are rendered, in the form of a series of transactions between the same parties charged on a continuing account, the appropriate date in respect of any obligation to pay for the goods or services is the date on which payment for the goods last supplied or the services last rendered became due.[75] Prescription cannot be elided by inserting a charge for keeping the account in question.[76] If an account has been definitely closed, the prescriptive period will begin to run on the appropriate date although trading between the parties may continue.[77] The death of the debtor is equivalent to the closing of the account.[78]

(b) Money lent to or deposited with the debtor:[79] the appropriate date is the date stipulated in the contract as the repayment date; or if no such date is stipulated, the date when a written demand for payment is first made.[80]

[71] *McPhail* v. *Cunninghame D.C.*, 1983 S.C. 246; 1985 S.L.T. 149.

[72] *N.V. Devos Gebroeder* v. *Sunderland Sportswear Ltd.*, 1990 S.C. 291; 1990 S.L.T. 473.

[73] As being 'the date when the loss, injury or damage occurred': s. 11(1) and see para. 15.31, *infra* and cases therein cited.

[74] Sale includes hire-purchase, credit-sale, or conditional sale: Sched. 2, para. 1(2)(*a*).

[75] Sched. 2, para. 1. See, for example, *H.G. Robertson* v. *Murray International Metals Ltd.*, 1988 S.L.T. 747; *R. Peter & Co. Ltd.* v. *The Pancake Place Ltd.*, 1993 S.L.T. 322. See also special provision for the termination of a series of transactions on the bankruptcy of a partnership or partner: para. 1(3).

[76] Sched. 2, para. 1(2)(*b*).

[77] *Cf. Christison* v. *Knowles* (1901) 3 F. 480.

[78] *Cf.* Bell, *Comm.*, i, 349.

[79] Note that 'debtor' does not include 'guarantor': *Royal Bank of Scotland Ltd.* v. *Brown*, 1982 S.C. 89.

[80] Sched. 2, para. 2. As to what may constitute a 'written demand for payment,' see *Bank of Scotland* v. *Laverock*, 1991 S.C. 117. The demand for payment may be made to the debtor's judicial factor or executor: *Bank of Scotland* v. *Laverock, cit. sup.* Note that in the context of banking the Scottish Law Commission recommended (in para. 74 of their Report No. 15 on *Reform of the Law Relating to Prescription and Limitation of Actions*) that the quinquennial prescription should run from the date when the creditor demands repayment, but that the long negative prescription should run (as before) from the date of deposit in accounts where the bank is debtor, and from the date of advance in accounts where the bank is creditor: *Macdonald* v. *North of Scotland Bank*, 1942 S.C. 369. This recommendation appears to have been implemented in the Act.

(c) Termination of partnership or agency: where an obligation arises under a contract of partnership or of agency, being an obligation remaining or becoming prestable on or after the termination of the relationship between the parties under the contract, the appropriate date is the date stipulated in the contract as the date on or before which performance of the obligation is due, and if no such date is stipulated, the date when the relationship terminated.[81]

(d) Payment or work by instalments: where there is an obligation to pay an instalment of a sum of money or to execute an instalment of work, the appropriate date is the date on which the last of the instalments is due to be paid or executed.[82]

In computing the five-year period, no account is to be taken of time during which the creditor was induced to refrain from making a relevant claim by reason of fraud on the part of the debtor or his agent, or error on the creditor's part induced by the debtor or his agent.[83] However once the creditor could with reasonable diligence[84] have discovered the fraud or error, any time elapsing thereafter is to be included in the prescriptive period.[85] Any period during which the original creditor (while he is the creditor) was under legal disability[86] is not to be reckoned as part of the prescriptive period.[87] The fact that any time is to be discounted on the ground of fraud, error or disability is not to be regarded as separating the periods before and after that time.[88]

15.27 Effect.—Unlike most of the former short prescriptions, which did not extinguish rights or obligations but merely affected the onus and method of proof, the quinquennial prescription extinguishes obligations (and

---

[81] Sched. 2, para. 3. See, for example, *Coull* v. *MacLean,* 1991 G.W.D. 21–1249 (*de facto* termination of partnership held relevant, rather than a date of dissolution deemed for accountancy purposes).

[82] Sched. 2, para. 4.

[83] s. 6(4)(*a*); *cf. Caledonian Railway* v. *Chisholm* (1886) 13 R. 773; *Inglis* v. *Smith,* 1916 S.C. 581; *Fisher & Donaldson* v. *Steven,* 1988 S.C.L.R. 337 (Sh.Ct.) (fraud); *Greater Glasgow Health Board* v. *Baxter Clark & Paul,* 1990 S.C. 237 (error); *Safdar* v. *Devlin,* 1994 G.W.D. 17–1085 (error).

[84] *Cf. Peco Arts* v. *Hazlitt* [1983] 1 W.L.R. 1315; *Greater Glasgow Health Board* v. *Baxter Clark & Paul,* 1990 S.C. 237; *Southside Housing Association Ltd.* v. *Harvey Scott & Partners,* 1992 G.W.D. 27–1593. *Dumfries Labour and Social Club and Institute Ltd.* v. *Sutherland Dickie & Copland,* 1993 G.W.D. 21–1314; *Sinclair* v. *MacDougall Estates Ltd.,* 1994 S.L.T. 76; *Glasper* v. *Rodger,* 1995 G.W.D. 8–456.

[85] Proviso to s. 6(4).

[86] Legal disability is defined in s. 15(1) as meaning legal disability by reason of nonage or unsoundness of mind. Legal disability by reason of nonage is to be construed as a reference to a person under the age of 16 years: see Age of Legal Capacity (Scotland) Act 1991, and para. 15.10, note 60, *supra.*

[87] s. 6(4)(*b*); and see para. 15.10, n. 61 *supra.*

[88] s. 6(5). Thus a creditor who, for example, becomes temporarily insane two years after an obligation has become enforceable will have a further three years after regaining his sanity within which to claim.

rights correlative thereto) which have not been enforced. When the prescriptive period expires, the obligation ceases to exist.

15.28 **Interruption.**—To interrupt the running of the quinquennial prescription, a relevant claim in relation to the obligation must be made,[89] or the subsistence of the obligation must be relevantly acknowledged.[90] However, in the case of an obligation arising from a bill of exchange or a promissory note, only a relevant claim will suffice to interrupt prescription.[91]

A relevant claim may be constituted by a writ with unspecific averments,[92] ultimately requiring substantial amendment after the expiry of the quinquennium.[93] But it has been held that no relevant claim was made where a writ required amendment outwith the quinquennium in order to substitute a new and distinct obligation in place of the original obligation, such as recompense for payment,[94] or contract for delict,[95] or a contract other than that originally founded upon;[96] nor where

[89] s. 6(1); s. 9; and see para. 15.20, *supra*. The execution of diligence may constitute a relevant claim: s. 9(1); *Hogg v. Prentice*, 1994 S.C.L.R. 426. The claim must be made against the debtor in the obligation: *Kirkcaldy D.C. v. Household Manufacturing Ltd.*, 1987 S.L.T. 617; but note *Bank of Scotland v. Laverock*, 1991 S.C. 117 (claim may be made against debtor's judicial factor or executor). Where the interruption sought to be relied upon is a claim made in an arbitration, there must be an arbitration in existence at the material time: *Douglas Milne Ltd. v. Borders R.C.*, 1990 S.L.T. 558; *cf. John O'Connor (Plant Hire) v. Kier Construction*, 1990 S.C.L.R. 761 (preliminary notice referring dispute to arbitration, but no subsequent claim in arbitration proceedings); *R. Peter & Co. Ltd. v. The Pancake Place Ltd.*, 1993 S.L.T. 322 (no concluded agreement to arbitrate).

[90] s. 6(1); s. 10; and para. 15.21, *supra*. See, for example, *Fortunato's J.F. v. Fortunato*, 1981 S.L.T. 277; *Greater Glasgow Health Board v. Baxter Clark & Paul*, 1990 S.C. 237; *Lieberman v. G.W. Tait & Sons, S.S.C.*, 1987 S.C. 213; *Barratt Scotland Ltd. v. Keith*, 1994 S.L.T. 1343; *Steel v. Dundaff Ltd.*, 1995 G.W.D. 8–457 (I.H.).

[91] Proviso to s. 6(1).

[92] *British Railways Board v. Strathclyde R.C.*, 1981 S.C. 90; *George A. Hood v. Dumbarton D.C.*, 1983 S.L.T. 238; *Kinnaird v. Donaldson*, 1992 S.C.L.R. 694 (whole writ, including crave or conclusions, condescendence and pleas-in-law, to be taken into account). However, it has been observed that a fundamentally null action would not constitute an interruption of the prescriptive period: *Shanks v. Central R.C.*, 1987 S.L.T. 410; 1988 S.L.T. 212, and an action of declarator has been held not to constitute a relevant claim in respect of an obligation to indemnify: *Wylie v. Avon Insurance Co. Ltd.*, 1988 S.C.L.R. 570.

[93] *Macleod v. Sinclair*, 1981 S.L.T. (Notes) 38; *Kinnaird v. Donaldson*, 1992 S.C.L.R. 694; *Mackinnon v. Avonside Homes Ltd.*, 1993 S.C.L.R. 976; *Safdar v. Devlin*, 1994 G.W.D. 17–1085. In assessing whether an amendment has been made within the quinquennium, the *punctum temporis* is the date when the minute of amendment was allowed to be received: *Boyle v. Glasgow Corporation*, 1975 S.C. 238; *Stewart v. Highlands & Islands Development Board*, 1991 S.L.T. 787. The lodging of the minute of amendment itself may amount to the making of a relevant claim, even though amendment was not allowed at the time: *Kinnaird v. Donaldson, supra*.

[94] *N.V. Devos Gebroeder v. Sunderland Sportswear Ltd.*, 1990 S.C. 291, distinguished in *Ductform Ventilation (Fife) Ltd v. Andrews-Weatherfoil Ltd.*, 1995 S.L.T. 88, where a claim, initially for payment under a contract, was amended outwith the quinquennium to a claim for damages for breach of that contract.

[95] *Middleton v. Douglass*, 1991 S.L.T. 726.

[96] *Lawrence v. J.D. McIntosh & Hamilton*, 1981 S.L.T. (Sh.Ct.) 73; *Wright v. Invergordon Distilleries Ltd.*, 1993 G.W.D. 22–1393.

amendment was required to add a conclusion for specific implement in a writ seeking declarator.[97]

If a relevant claim is made, the prescriptive period cannot run during the currency of the proceedings.[98] Similarly the prescriptive period cannot run during the currency of a relevant acknowledgment.[99] It is thought that the prescriptive period starts anew from the midnight following upon the date on which the interruption ends: the point has been discussed in several cases.[1]

15.29 Reparation.[2]—For the purposes of prescription the 1973 Act in effect divides reparation into two categories: (a) reparation in respect of personal injuries or death;[3] and (b) reparation in respect of any other loss, injury or damage, arising from, for example, negligent actings in relation to property, or breach of contract or promise. Rights and obligations arising from damage caused by defective products are the subject of special rules and are dealt with separately.[4]

15.30 Personal Injuries or Death.—An obligation to make reparation in respect of personal injuries or death cannot be extinguished by the quinquennial prescription,[5] nor by the long negative prescription.[6]

15.31 Other Loss, Injury or Damage.—Any other obligation to make reparation is extinguished by the quinquennial prescription.[7] Thus the

---

[97] *Wylie* v. *Avon Insurance Co. Ltd.*, 1988 S.C.L.R. 570.

[98] *G.A. Estates Ltd.* v. *Caviapen Trs. Ltd.*, 1993 S.L.T. 1051 (I.H.); 1993 S.L.T. 1045 (O.H.); *British Railways Board* v. *Strathclyde R.C. supra*; *George A. Hood & Co.* v. *Dumbarton D.C.*, 1983 S.L.T. 238. Thus an action may constitute an interruption even although the action is subsequently abandoned. But where a relevant claim was constituted by the service and registration of letters of inhibition on the dependence of an action (which was not itself proceeded with until over five years later) the interruption was held to have begun and ended on the day of registration: *Hogg* v. *Prentice*, 1994 S.C.L.R. 426.

[99] *Barratt Scotland Ltd.* v. *Keith*, 1994 S.L.T. 1343 (pursuer's unequivocal admission on record effective to prevent the running of the prescriptive period until minute of abandonment); *cf.* dicta at p. 1059G of *G.A. Estates Ltd.* v. *Caviapen Trs. Ltd.*, 1993 S.L.T. 1051. Note that in order to defeat a plea of prescription, the relevant acknowledgment must have been made within the five years preceding the raising of the action: *R. Peter & Co. Ltd.* v. *The Pancake Place Ltd.*, 1993 S.L.T. 322.

[1] See *G.A. Estates Ltd.* v. *Caviapen Trs. Ltd.*, *supra*; *British Railways Board* v. *Strathclyde R.C.*, *supra*. Thus, for example, a fresh prescriptive period would begin to run from the midnight following upon the date of the final disposal of a relevant court action, including any appeal procedure.

[2] Reparation is not defined in the Act, but appears to have been used in its widest sense, namely, the making good of any civil wrong usually by an award of damages. See, *e.g.* the terms of s. 11; *Miller* v. *Glasgow D.C.*, 1988 S.C. 440. Note that special prescriptive rules apply to reparation arising from product liability: see para. 15.33, *infra*.

[3] 'Personal injuries' includes any disease or any impairment of a person's physical or mental condition: s. 22(1); and see *Fleming* v. *Strathclyde R.C.*, 1992 S.L.T. 161.

[4] See Pt. IIA (ss. 22A–22D) of the 1973 Act, inserted by the Consumer Protection Act 1987: and para. 15.33 *infra*.

[5] Sched. 1, para. 2(g). However limitation may prevent enforcement by court action after three years: see para. 34.41, *infra*. For an interesting discussion involving both limitation (s. 17) and prescription (s. 6), see *Grindall* v. *John Mitchell (Grangemouth) Ltd.*, 1986 S.C. 121; 1987 S.L.T. 137, where an injured bankrupt and his trustee pursued claims for solatium and patrimonial loss respectively.

[6] The 1973 Act, s. 7(2) as amended by the 1984 Act, Sched. 1.

[7] s. 6(2); Sched. 1, para. 1(d).

quinquennial prescription applies to a variety of claims, including claims for breach of contract, property damage, and professional negligence resulting in loss or damage other than personal injuries or death.[8] In computing the prescriptive period, the obligation is regarded as having become enforceable on the date when the loss, injury or damage occurred;[9] or in the case of loss, injury or damage arising as a result of a continuing act, neglect or default, on the date when the latter ceased;[10] or where the creditor is unaware of any damage, on the date when the creditor first became aware or could with reasonable diligence[11] have become aware that the loss, injury or damage had occurred.[12] Latent defects in buildings and

[8] See e.g. Curran v. Docherty, 1994 G.W.D. 39–2321. In Hobday v. Kirkpatrick's Trs., 1985 S.L.T. 197, beneficiaries under a trust disposition and settlement raised an action of count reckoning and payment against the trustees seeking restoration to the trust estate of the value of trust property wrongly parted with: the obligation resting on the trustees was held not to be one arising from liability to make 'reparation' within para. 1(d) of Sched. 1.

[9] s. 11(1); See Dunlop v. McGowans, 1980 S.C. (H.L.) 73 (concurrence of injuria and damnum: here, the date on which the proprietor was deprived of the opportunity of obtaining vacant possession of subjects as a result of the defender's failure to serve a notice timeously); Highland Engineering Ltd. v. Anderson, 1979 S.L.T. 122 (in an action of negligence against an accountant and the partners of his firm, it was held that the quinquennial prescription in relation to partnership debts or obligations ran from the date on which the debt or obligation was constituted against the partnership by decree); George Porteous (Arts) Ltd. v. Dollar Rae, 1979 S.L.T. (Sh.Ct.) 51 (date on which local authority served demolition enforcement notice on proprietor following upon defenders' failure to obtain planning permission); Riddick v. Shaughnessy Quigley & McColl, 1981 S.L.T. (Notes) 89 (date on which pursuer was put out of premises); British Railways Board v. Strathclyde R.C., 1981 S.C. 90 (date on which tunnel collapsed); Renfrew Golf Club v. Ravenstone Securities Ltd., 1984 S.C. 22; 1984 S.L.T. 170 (where held that an underlying defect in a newly constructed golf course may not necessarily constitute damnum until some damage such as waterlogged greens occurred); East Hook Purchasing Corp. Ltd. v. Ben Nevis Distillery (Fort William) Ltd., 1985 S.L.T. 442 (date on which the depositary of whisky parted with possession of any quantity of the goods); Scott Lithgow Ltd. v. Secretary of State for Defence, 1989 S.C. (H.L.) 9 (date of discovery of defective submarine cables, being date when Secretary of State's contractual obligation to indemnify contractor arose); Beard v. Beveridge, Herd & Sandilands, W.S., 1990 S.L.T. 609 (date of execution of lease containing defective rent review clause); Roulston v. Boyds, 1990 G.W.D. 12–633 (date of recording of challenged standard security); Fergus v. MacLennan, 1991 S.L.T. 321 (date by which, as a result of positive prescription acting in favour of another, a beneficiary irretrievably lost her right to heritable property bequeathed to her but not conveyed to her despite her instructions to solicitors); Sinclair v. MacDougall Estates Ltd., 1994 S.L.T. 76 (date when certain major building defects and damage were evident or discovered). See too Gloag, Contract (2nd ed.), pp. 738–739. 'The computation of the prescriptive period starts from the day when it first became possible for the creditor to take action to enforce his claim.'

[10] s. 11(1). Fergus v. MacLennan, 1991 S.L.T. 321.

[11] Cf. Peco Arts v. Hazlitt [1983] 1 W.L.R. 1315; Greater Glasgow Health Board v. Baxter Clark & Paul, 1990 S.C. 237; 1992 S.L.T. 35; Southside Housing Association Ltd. v. Harvey Scott & Partners, 1992 G.W.D. 27–1593; Dumfries Labour and Social Club and Institute Ltd. v. Sutherland Dickie & Copland, 1993 G.W.D. 21–1314; Sinclair v. MacDougall Estates Ltd., 1994 S.L.T. 76; Glasper v. Rodger, 1995 G.W.D. 8–456.

[12] s. 11(3), i.e. loss, injury or damage giving rise to an obligation to make reparation: Dunfermline D.C. v. Blyth & Blyth Assocs., 1985 S.L.T. 345; Curran v. Docherty, 1994 G.W.D. 39–2321. In Greater Glasgow Health Board v. Baxter Clark & Paul, 1990 S.C. 237; 1992 S.L.T. 35, it was held that the pursuers' ignorance as to the identity of the person upon whom the obligation to make reparation lay did not defer the start of the prescriptive period: but see recommendations of the Scottish Law Commission in their Report No. 122 (Prescription, Latent Damage), paras. 2.37 et seq.

other construction works have given rise to difficult questions of prescription.[13]

15.32 Two-Year Prescription: Contribution between Wrongdoers.—Where two or more persons are found jointly and severally liable[14] in delict the court can apportion the damages between or amongst them.[15] A joint defender who pays more than his fair share of damages has then a right of relief against another joint defender and can recover the appropriate sum apportioned to that defender.[16] However, a pursuer may have elected to sue one or some but not all of a number of joint wrongdoers. The court cannot order a person who has not been called as a defender to pay damages.[17] Nevertheless there is a right of relief or contribution in terms of section 3(2) of the Law Reform (Miscellaneous Provisions) (Scotland) Act 1940 which provides that one joint wrongdoer who has paid damages or expenses in satisfaction of a decree against him is entitled to recover a proportion from any other person who, if he had been sued, might also have been held liable.

Section 8A[18] of the Prescription and Limitation (Scotland) Act 1973 provides that if the obligation to make a contribution by virtue of section 3(2) above has subsisted for a continuous period of two years after the date on which the right to recover the contribution became enforceable by the creditor in the obligation without any relevant claim[19] having been made in relation to the obligation, and without the subsistence of the obligation having been relevantly acknowledged,[20] then as from the expiration of that period the obligation is extinguished.[21] In computing the two-year period, no account is to be taken of time during which the creditor was induced to refrain from making a relevant claim by reason of fraud on the part of the debtor or

[13] Scottish Law Commission Report No. 122, *Prescription and Limitation of Actions (Latent Damage and Other Related Issues)* (Oct. 1989); H. McQueen, "Latent Defects, Collateral Warranties and Time Bar," 1991 S.L.T. (News) 77, 91, 99; *Sinclair* v. *MacDougall Estates Ltd.*, 1994 S.L.T. 76.

[14] As to 'found liable,' see *Comex Houlder Diving Ltd.* v. *Colne Fishing Co. Ltd.*, 1987 S.C. (H.L.) 85.

[15] s. 1(1) of the Law Reform (Misc. Provs.) (Scotland) Act 1940.

[16] Thus, where a settlement has been reached between the pursuer and one joint defender, the court will be reluctant to assoilzie that defender pending the establishment of any right of relief against him in the course of action: *Magee & Co. (Belfast) Ltd.* v. *Bracewell Harrison & Coton*, 1981 S.L.T. 107.

[17] See, for example, *Findlay* v. *N.C.B.*, 1965 S.L.T. 328. The Scottish Law Commission in their Report No. 74 comment that damages cannot be awarded against a person not called as a defender even although called as a third party.

[18] Inserted by the Prescription and Limitation (Scotland) Act 1984, s. 1.

[19] See s. 9 of the 1973 Act as amended and paras. 15.20 and 15.23, *supra*.

[20] See s. 10 of the 1973 Act as amended and para. 15.21, *supra*.

[21] Thus, the former two-year limitation under s. 10 of the Limitation Act 1963 and s. 20 of the 1973 Act is made an extinctive prescription, implementing the recommendations of the Scottish Law Commission in their Report No. 74. Section 20 is repealed by Sched. 1 of the 1984 Act.

his agent, or error on the creditor's part induced by the debtor or his agent.[22] Once the creditor could with reasonable diligence[23] have discovered the fraud or error, any time elapsing thereafter is included in the prescriptive period.[24] Any period during which the original creditor (while he is the creditor) is under legal disability[25] is not to be included in the computation. The fact that any time is to be discounted on the ground of fraud, error or disability is not to be regarded as separating the periods before and after the time.[26]

15.33 Product Liability.—Section 2 of the Consumer Protection Act 1987[27] imposed strict liability upon producers, importers and others in relation to damage caused by defective products.[28] The 1987 Act also amended the Prescription and Limitation (Scotland) Act 1973 by introducing a 10-year prescription of obligations arising from defective products,[29] and a three-year limitation of actions.[30]

15.34 Ten-Year Prescription: Defective Products.—In terms of section 22A of the 1973 Act, an obligation to make reparation for damage caused wholly or partly by a defect in a product is extinguished if a period of 10 years has expired from the relevant time,[31] unless a relevant claim[32] was made within that period and has not been finally disposed of.[33] No

---

[22] s. 8A(2); s. 6(4); s. 14(1)(b), as amended by the 1984 Act.

[23] Cf. *Peco Arts* v. *Hazlitt* [1983] 1 W.L.R. 1315; *Greater Glasgow Health Board* v. *Baxter Clark & Paul*, 1990 S.C. 237; 1992 S.L.T. 35; *Dumfries Labour and Social Club and Institute Ltd.* v. *Sutherland Dickie & Copland*, 1993 G.W.D. 21–1314; *Sinclair* v. *MacDougall Estates Ltd.*, 1994 S.L.T. 76; *Glasper* v. *Rodger*, 1995 G.W.D. 8–456.

[24] s. 8A(2); proviso to s. 6(4).

[25] See para. 15.10, nn. 60 and 61, *supra*.

[26] s. 6(5).

[27] c. 43. Section 2 came into force on March 1, 1988 (S.I. 1987 No. 1680).

[28] See Chap. xx, *infra*.

[29] See Sched. 1 to the 1987 Act, which also came into force on March 1, 1988 (S.I. 1987 No. 1680) and inserted Pt. IIA (ss. 22A–22D) in the 1973 Act.

[30] Limitation is outwith the scope of this chapter. For further details, see ss. 22B and 22C of the 1973 Act.

[31] s. 4(2) of the 1987 Act: the time when the product was supplied (or last supplied) to the consumer.

[32] 'Relevant claim' is defined in s. 22A(3) as meaning a claim made by or on behalf of the creditor for implement or part implement of the obligation, being a claim made—(a) in appropriate proceedings within the meaning of s. 4(2) of the 1973 Act (see para. 15.12, *supra*, n. 69); or (b) by the presentation of, or the concurring in, a petition for sequestration or by the submission of a claim under s. 22 or 48 of the Bankruptcy (Scotland) Act 1985; or (c) by the presentation of, or the concurring in, a petition for the winding up of a company or by the submission of a claim in a liquidation in accordance with the rules made under s. 411 of the Insolvency Act 1986. Where a relevant claim is made in an arbitration, and the nature of the claim has been stated in a preliminary notice (within the meaning of s. 4(4) of the 1973 Act), the date of service of the notice is deemed to be the date of the making of the claim: s. 22A(4); and *cf. Douglas Milne Ltd.* v. *Borders R.C.*, 1990 S.L.T. 558; and see generally para. 15.20, n. 26.

[33] If a relevant claim has been made but has not been finally disposed of, the obligation is extinguished when the claim is finally disposed of: s. 22A(2). For the definition of 'finally disposed of,' see s. 22A(3).

product liability obligation can come into existence after the expiration of the 10-year period.[34]

15.35 Transitional.—Part I of the Act did not come into force until July 25, 1976, *i.e.* three years after the passing of the Act on July 25, 1973.[35] The purpose of the three-year delay was to enable people to readjust to the new prescriptive periods, and to avoid penalising anyone by the unexpectedly early extinction of a right or obligation.[36] The fact that the Act is to some extent retroactive[37] also made the three-year delay necessary. Thus, if an obligation subject to the quinquennial prescription had become enforceable more than five years before the commencement of Part I, the obligation could not be extinguished before July 25, 1976.[38]

Where the subsistence of an obligation was by virtue of a former prescription provable only by writ or oath as at July 25, 1976, its subsistence was thereafter provable *prout de jure*.[39]

Rights and obligations affected by specific statutory limitations created before the passing of the 1973 Act are not to be extinguished by the new negative prescriptions until the end of the relevant statutory limitation period.[40]

Any proceedings brought before July 25, 1976 are not affected by the Act.[41]

15.36 The Crown.—The Act binds the Crown.[42] Prescription may therefore be pleaded against the Crown.[43]

---

[34] s. 22A(1) of the 1973 Act.

[35] s. 25(2)(*b*).

[36] For example, some rights and obligations formerly extinguishable only by the long negative prescription became extinguishable after five years: see *Dunlop* v. *McGowans*, 1980 S.C.(H.L.) 73.

[37] In terms of s. 14(1)(*a*) time occurring before the commencement of Pt. I is reckonable towards the prescriptive period in like manner as time occurring thereafter, so long as any time reckoned in terms of s. 14(1)(*a*) is less than the prescriptive period. A right which has been wholly extinguished by the long negative prescription prior to the coming into force of the Act of 1973 cannot be revived by the Act: *Porteous' Exrs.* v. *Ferguson*, 1995 G.W.D. 2–90 (personal right to land of uninfeft beneficiary).

[38] *Dunlop* v. *McGowans, supra.* Such an obligation might not be extinguished until after July 25, 1976 if (say) a period of legal disability were to delay the expiry of the prescriptive period. For the transitional provisions relating to legal disability by reason of nonage, see s. 8 of the Age of Legal Capacity (Scotland) Act 1991, and para. 15.10, n. 60, *supra.*

[39] s. 16(3).

[40] s. 12. If at the end of the limitation period any claim to establish the right or enforce the obligation has not been finally disposed of, the right or obligation is deemed to be extinguished on the date when the claim is so disposed of. S. 12 was commented on in *Riddick* v. *Shaughnessy Quigley & McColl*, 1981 S.L.T. (Notes) 89.

[41] s. 25(3).

[42] s. 24.

[43] Cf. *Lord Advocate* v. *Graham* (1844) 7 D. 183. See para. 15.5, *supra.*

Further Reading

Gordon, *Scottish Land Law* (1989).
Millar, *Prescription* (1893).
Napier, *Prescription* (1854).
Stair Memorial Encyclopaedia, Vol. 16.
Walker, *The Law of Prescription and Limitation of Actions* (4th ed., 1990).

PART III—PARTICULAR CONTRACTS

CHAPTER 16

SALE OF GOODS

16.1 Sale of Goods Act.—The law of sale of goods was first comprehensively regulated by the Sale of Goods Act 1893. That statute, in its main provisions applicable both to Scotland and England, was with regard to the law of England in substance a codification of the pre-existing law; in regard to the law of Scotland it made changes which may be called revolutionary. It was amended in important respects by the Supply of Goods (Implied Terms) Act 1973 and the Consumer Credit Act 1974. The law is now consolidated in the Sale of Goods Act 1979[1] which has been amended by the Sale and Supply of Goods Act 1994 (hereinafter referred to as 'the 1994 Act').[1a]

16.2 Meaning of 'Goods'.—Goods are defined as including, in Scotland, 'all corporeal moveables except money.' The term 'includes emblements, industrial growing crops and things attached to or forming part of the land which are agreed to be severed before sale or under the contract of sale.'[2] The provisions of the Act have been held applicable to the sale of ships,[3] standing trees,[4] and growing crops,[5] but not to a mineral lease.[6]

16.3 Sale as Contract and as Transfer of Property.—The effect of the alterations in the common law of Scotland introduced by the 1893 Act may be apprehended by considering that the law of sale has two main aspects.[7] It deals with sale as a contract, and indicates the contractual

---

[1] The Act applies to contracts made on or after January 1, 1894 but Sched. 1 modifies some sections as they apply to contracts made before various dates. For the background, see Rodger (1992) 108 L.Q.R. 570. The Act applies without modification to contracts made on or after May 19, 1985 (S.I. 1983 No. 1572).

[1a] The 1994 Act came into force on January 3, 1995 and applies to contracts of sale made on or after that date, s. 8(3). The 1994 Act was based on the joint report by the English and Scottish Law Commissions: *The Sale and Supply of Goods* (Law. Com. No. 160, Scot Law. Com. No. 104, Cm. 137).

[2] Sale of Goods Act 1979, s. 61(1).

[3] *Behnke* v. *Bede Shipping Co.* [1927] 1 K.B. 649.

[4] *Morison* v. *Lockhart*, 1912 S.C. 1017; *Munro* v. *Liquidator of Balnagown Estates Co.*, 1949 S.C. 49. See note 36, *infra*.

[5] *Kennedy's Tr.* v. *Hamilton* (1897) 25 R. 252; *Paton's Trs.* v. *Finlayson*, 1923 S.C. 872; *Allan* v. *Millar*, 1932 S.C. 620.

[6] *Morgan* v. *Russell* [1909] 1 K.B. 357.

[7] See also paras. 16.9 and 16.11, *infra* and para. 3.10, *supra*.

obligations on either side which will be implied in the absence of any express provision. In this aspect the alterations due to the Act are of minor importance, and may be indicated in summarising the statutory provisions. But it also deals with sale as a method of transferring the property (*jus in re*) of the thing sold, and in this aspect the law has been altered so fundamentally that it is desirable to insert a statement of the common law and of the modifications introduced by prior legislation.

16.4 Transfer of Goods Sold: Common Law.—By the common law of Scotland a contract to sell goods has no effect on the property of the goods in question. The property, and the real right, *jus in re*, remained with the seller (whether the price had been paid or not) until the goods were delivered to the buyer. Until delivery a purchaser had no right higher than that of a creditor in a personal obligation to deliver the goods. Sale was an example of the general rule, expressed in the maxim *traditionibus, non nudis pactis, dominia rerum transferuntur* (rights of property are transferred by delivery and not by mere agreements), that a contract for the transfer of a thing merely created a *jus in personam*, or personal claim against the transferor. It did not carry the real right in the thing. This was a rule of law, independent of the volition of the parties. It was, it is true, open to the parties, by selling under a suspensive condition, to reserve to the seller the property in the thing even after it had been delivered;[8] it was not within their power to transfer the property before delivery.[9] But the risk of accidental destruction or damage passed to the buyer before delivery: in the sale of specific goods, when the contract was concluded: in the sale of unascertained goods, when the seller appropriated particular goods to the contract for delivery to the buyer.[10]

16.5 Results of Rules of Common Law.—The most important practical results of the general rule that property in the goods sold could not pass until they were delivered were the following: (a) in the event of the sequestration of the seller before delivery the buyer, though he might have paid the price, could not obtain the article sold. It was still the property of the seller, and passed, with the rest of his property, to the trustee in his sequestration. The buyer had merely a claim for damages for the non-fulfilment of the contract, his right being to rank for a dividend on that claim with the other personal creditors of the seller.[11] (b) The seller, being still undivested owner, could, in a question with the purchaser or in his bankruptcy, retain the thing sold in security of

[8] *Macartney* v. *Macredies's Creditors* (1799) Mor.App. Sale No. 1; *Murdoch* v. *Greig* (1889) 16 R. 396.

[9] As to the common law, see Bell, *Comm.*, i, 181, and para. 3.10, *supra*.

[10] See the discussion of the common law in *Widenmeyer* v. *Burn Stewart & Co.*, 1967 S.C. 85.

[11] *Mathison* v. *Alison* (1854) 17 D. 274.

any debt which which might be due to him by the purchaser.[12] (c) The seller had a similar right in a question with a sub-purchaser. He was still the owner of the goods, the sub-purchaser had merely a personal right to delivery, and that personal right was postponed to the seller's right to retain his position as owner, and therefore to withhold delivery of the goods, until he had received payment, not only of the price,[13] but of any general balance which might be due to him by the original purchaser.[14]

16.6 Mercantile Law Amendment Act.—The general principle that the property in goods sold did not pass until delivery ruled until the Sale of Goods Act 1893 came into operation (1894), but certain of its practical results were affected by the Mercantile Law Amendment (Scotland) Act 1856, sections 1 to 5. As these sections were repealed by the Schedule to the Sale of Goods Act 1893, it is unnecessary to deal with their provisions in detail. Their general result was to entitle the purchaser of specific goods in a deliverable state to delivery in a question with the trustee in the sequestration of the seller,[15] and to abolish the right of an undivested seller to retain goods, in a question with a sub-purchaser, for any general balance due by the original purchaser.[16]

16.7 General Effect of Sale of Goods Act.—The provisions of the Sale of Goods Act with regard to the passing of the property in goods sold are detailed later,[17] but it may be stated generally that the 1893 Act introduced the English law on the subject, under which the passing of the property does not depend upon the delivery of the goods but on the force of the contract. The property passes at the time when the parties intend it to pass, whether the goods are delivered or not.

16.8 Sale of Goods Act: Construction and Scope.—With these preliminary explanations we pass to the consideration of the Act. It was laid down with reference to the 1893 Act as a general canon of construction that the fair meaning of the words used in the Act had to be taken, although that meaning might be inconsistent with the result of prior decisions, and although there might be no apparent reason for supposing that a change in the law was intended.[18] The Sale of Goods Act 1979, like the 1893 Act, does not deal with such questions as the effects of error, misrepresentation or fraud, which fall to be decided according to the general law of contract. Section 62(2) provides that the rules of the

---

[12] *Wyper* v. *Harveys* (1861) 23 D. 606.
[13] *McEwan* v. *Smith* (1849) 6 Bell's App. 340.
[14] *Melrose* v. *Hastie* (1851) 13 D. 880.
[15] *McMeekin* v. *Ross* (1876) 4 R. 154.
[16] See as to the result of the Mercantile Law Amendment Act, *Wyper* v. *Harveys* (1861) 23 D. 606; *Distillers' Co.* v. *Russell's Tr.* (1889) 16 R. 479.
[17] Paras. 16.14 *et seq., infra*.
[18] *Bristol Tramway Co.* v. *Fiat Motors* [1910] 2 K.B. 831.

common law, including the law merchant, save in so far as they are inconsistent with the express provisions of the Act, shall continue to apply to the contract of sale of goods. In the following pages the figures in square brackets refer to the sections of the Act as amended by the 1994 Act, which should in all cases be read.

16.9 Definition of Contract of Sale.—The contract of sale is defined [2] as a contract by which the seller transfers or agrees to transfer[19] the property in goods for a money consideration, called the price. Capacity to buy and sell is regulated by the general law as to capacity to contract, but where necessaries are sold and delivered to a person who, by reason of mental incapacity or drunkenness, is incompetent to contract, he must pay a reasonable price for them [3]. The contract may be entered into verbally, and proved by parole evidence. So a verbal sale of a ship is binding.[20] Such subjects as growing crops or standing trees, though included in the definition of 'goods,' are heritable, and probably a contract for their sale would require to be in writing.[21]

16.10 Sale and Other Contracts.—The definition serves to distinguish sale from such contracts as pledge, where there is no agreement to transfer the property in goods; donation, where there is no price; and barter, where the consideration is not in money.[22] And where in a contract for building a ship, it was provided that the ship, as she was constructed, and all materials intended for her, should become the property of the purchasers, it was decided that there was only a contract for the sale of a complete ship, and that the provision as to the unfinished ship and the materials was not a sale but an attempt to create a right in security, which required delivery in order to make it effectual.[23]

16.11 Sale and Agreement to Sell.—The Act draws a distinction between a sale and an agreement to sell. It depends on the transfer of the property in the goods. When the property is transferred under the contract it is a sale; where the transfer of the property is to take place at a future time or subject to some condition thereafter to be fulfilled, it is an agreement to sell. An agreement to sell becomes a sale when the time elapses or the conditions are fulfilled subject to which the property in the goods is to be transferred [2 (6)].[24] A 'sale,' under the Act, is both a contract and a transference of the property in goods; an 'agreement to sell' is merely a contract.

---

[19] These are the alternatives referred to in paras. 16.3, *supra* and 16.11, *infra*.
[20] *McConnachie* v. *Geddes*, 1918 S.C. 391.
[21] *Morison* v. *Lockhart*, 1912 S.C. 1017.
[22] For a modern case on barter, see *Widenmeyer* v. *Burn Stewart & Co.*, 1967 S.C. 85; see also para. 16.52 *infra*.
[23] *Reid* v. *Macbeth & Gray* (1904) 6 F. (H.L.) 25.
[24] *A.K. Stoddart* v. *Scott*, 1971 J.C. 18.

16.12 **Sale and Security.**—By section 62(4) it is provided that 'the provisions of this Act about contracts of sale do not apply to a transaction in the form of a contract of sale which is intended to operate by way of mortgage, pledge, charge, or other security.' In the case of such transactions the common law as to passing of the property in goods is still applicable, and, therefore, the property in the goods which are nominally sold does not pass without delivery. The mere contract does not confer on the nominal purchaser any real right in the goods, and he has no claim to them which he can vindicate in the bankruptcy of the nominal seller. So where £40 was advanced to a dealer in bicycles, and he granted a promissory note for that amount, and also a document in the form of a receipt for certain bicycles sold to the lender, it was decided that the sale of the bicycles was a transaction intended to operate by way of security; that the provisions of the Sale of Goods Act did not apply; and that the nominal purchaser had no real right in the bicycles until they were delivered.[25] The transaction was not really a sale, but an attempt to give a security in a method which the law of Scotland does not recognise. But it may be stipulated, without bringing the transaction within the purview of section 62(4), that the seller shall have a right to repurchase the goods at the same price,[26] or that the purchaser, if he make any profit by a resale of the goods, shall be bound to account for that profit to the seller.[27] And probably if the legal relations of buyer and seller are created the transaction is to be regarded as a sale to which the Act will apply, although it may be proved that the object of the parties in entering into the transaction was to give security for money borrowed. It is inconsistent with the legal relationship of buyer and seller that the nominal seller should be bound by some obligation (*e.g.* a promissory note) to repay the price; it is not inconsistent with that relationship that the seller should have an option to repay, and a right, on repayment, to recover the goods.[28]

16.13 **Price.**—The Act provides [8] that the price of goods sold may be fixed by the contract, left to be fixed in some manner agreed to, or determined by the course of dealing between the parties. If not so determined, the buyer must pay a reasonable price.[29] If it is agreed that the price shall be fixed by a third party, and that third party cannot or does not act, an agreement to sell is avoided, but if any part of the

[25] *Jones & Co.'s Tr.* v. *Allan* (1901) 4 F. 374; see also *Robertson* v. *Hall's Tr.* (1896) 24 R. 120; *Hepburn* v. *Law*, 1914 S.C. 918; *Scottish Transit Trust* v. *Scottish Land Cultivators*, 1955 S.C. 254; *G. & C. Finance Corporation* v. *Brown*, 1961 S.L.T. 408; *Ladbroke Leasing (South West) Ltd.* v. *Reekie Plant Ltd.*, 1983 S.L.T. 155. As to an 'all sums' retention of title clause, see para. 16.16.

[26] *Gavin's Tr.* v. *Fraser*, 1920 S.C. 674; *Newbigging* v. *Morton*, 1930 S.C. 273.

[27] *McBain* v. *Wallace* (1881) 8 R. (H.L.) 106.

[28] *Gavin's Tr.* v. *Fraser*, 1920 S.C. 674; see opinion of Lord President Clyde; *Newbigging* v. *Morton, supra.*

[29] *Glynwed Distribution Ltd.* v. *S. Koronka & Co.*, 1977 S.C. 1.

goods has been delivered to and appropriated by the buyer he must pay a reasonable price therefor. If the third party is prevented from fixing the price by the fault of the buyer or seller, the party in fault is liable in damages [9]. It is no objection to the validity of a contract of sale that the buyer is left to fix his own price.[30]

16.14   Transfer of Property: Unascertained Goods.—In dealing with sale as a method of transferring the property in goods it must be noted that the contract may either relate to particular and existing things, identified at the time the contract is made, and referred to in the Act as specific or ascertained goods (*venditio rei specificae*); or to future goods, goods to be manufactured or obtained by the seller after the contract is made; or to generic goods, so much of some particular commodity (*venditio generis*); or to an unsevered portion of some particular quantity of goods.[31] In the last three cases the goods are unascertained, and the property does not pass to the purchaser until they are ascertained [16]. They are ascertained when goods of that description and in a deliverable state[32] are unconditionally appropriated to the contract either by the seller with the consent of the buyer or by the buyer with the consent of the seller [18, Rule 5(1)].[33] Notification of such appropriation is not essential if the necessary consent can be implied from the terms of the contract.[34] If the seller delivers the goods to a carrier for transmission to the buyer, and does not reserve the right of disposal, he is deemed to have unconditionally appropriated them to the contract [18, Rule 5(2)].

16.15   Specific Goods: General Rules.—The general rule as to the transfer of the property in specific goods is given in section 17: '(1) Where there is a contract for the sale of specific or ascertained goods the property in them is transferred to the buyer at such time as the parties to the contract intend it to be transferred. (2) For the purpose of ascertaining the intention of the parties regard shall be had to the terms of the contract, the conduct of the parties, and the circumstances of the case.' In contrast with the common law, which demanded delivery in order to pass the property, this section places it in the power of the parties to the contract to decide when the property is to pass. It depends on their intention. In some cases that intention may be clear, either from the express terms of the contract or from the circumstances of the case. But in many cases the buyer and seller do not consider the question of the property in the goods, and have really no intention in the matter. It is a question which rises into importance if the creditors of the seller, or his

---

[30] *Lavaggi* v. *Pirie* (1872) 10 M. 312.
[31] See *Hayman* v. *McLintock*, 1907 S.C. 936.
[32] *Philip Head & Sons* v. *Showfronts* (1970) 113 Sol.J. 978.
[33] The appropriation may be by a third party; *Wardar's (Import & Export) Co.* v. *W. Norwood & Sons* [1968] 2 Q.B. 663.
[34] See *Widenmeyer* v. *Burn Stewart & Co. Ltd.*, 1967 S.C. 85, *per* Lord President Clyde at p. 101.

trustee in sequestration, assert a right to the goods, or if the goods are accidentally injured or destroyed, Where no actual intention can be ascertained the presumed intention is to be gathered from rules given in section 18. It must be remembered that these rules are not applicable if there is proof of intention to the contrary.[35]

Rule 1.—'Where there is an unconditional contract for the sale of specific goods[36] in a deliverable state the property in the goods passes to the buyer when the contract is made, and it is immaterial whether the time of payment or the time of delivery, or both, be postponed.' It may be presumed that in this, the general rule for the ordinary case of sale of specific articles, the term 'unconditional' means without any condition relating to the passing of the property, and that the property in an article which is sold in a deliverable state will pass at once to the purchaser, although the contract may involve conditions as to the quality of the article. Goods are in a deliverable state when they are in such a state that the buyer would, under the contract, be bound to take delivery of them [61 (5)].

Rule 2.—'Where there is a contract for the sale of specific goods and the seller is bound to do something to the goods for the purpose of putting them into a deliverable state, the property does not pass until the thing is done and the buyer has notice that it has been done.'[37] From the opinions in an English case it would appear that the rule does not apply, and that the passing of the property is not postponed, merely because the seller has undertaken to pack the goods, or because, as in the case of a billiard-table, the article sold must be taken to pieces before it can be removed. But where the article sold was at the date of the contract affixed to a building the property did not pass until it was severed.[38] And there may be a narrow distinction between putting goods into a deliverable state and initiating the process of delivery. When growing potatoes were sold, and the seller undertook to lift and put them in pits at maturity, and to cart them to the station, it was decided that the potatoes had reached a deliverable state, and that the property passed to the purchaser, when they were put into pits; the subsequent obligation of the seller, to cart the potatoes to the station, relating not to deliverable state but to actual delivery.[39]

Rule 3.—'Where there is a contract for the sale of specific goods in a deliverable state but the seller is bound to weigh, measure, test, or do some other act or thing with reference to the goods for the purpose of

---

[35] As examples see *Re Anchor Line* [1937] 1 Ch. 1; *Lacis* v. *Cashmarts* [1969] 2 Q.B. 400; *Aluminium Industrie Vaassen B.V.* v. *Romalpa Aluminium* [1976] 1 W.L.R. 676.

[36] Specific goods are 'goods identified and agreed on at the time a contract of sale is made' [61]. Standing trees sold for felling and removal cannot become the property of the buyer until they are severed from the ground; *Morison* v. *Lockhart*, 1912 S.C. 1017; *Munro* v. *Liquidator of Balnagown Estates Co.*, 1949 S.C. 49.

[37] *e.g. Lombard North Central Ltd.* v. *Lord Advocate*, 1983 S.L.T. 361.

[38] *Underwood* v. *Burgh Castle Syndicate* [1922] 1 K.B. 343.

[39] *Cockburn's Tr.* v. *Bowe*, 1910 2 S.L.T. 17. See also *Woodburn* v. *Motherwell*, 1917 S.C. 533; *Paton's Trs.* v. *Finlayson*, 1923 S.C. 872.

ascertaining the price, the property does not pass until the act or thing is
done, and the buyer has notice that it has been done.' This rule is
applicable only where the seller has undertaken to weigh, measure or
test the goods, not to the case where there is no agreement on the
point, though the price cannot as a matter of fact be ascertained until
such operation has been performed. So in the sale of 'my crop of hay'
the property was held to pass at once, though the sale was at so much
per ton, and the price consequently could not be ascertained until the
hay was weighed.[40] Similarly, when it was agreed that the goods should
be weighed at the station and the result accepted by both parties as
determining the price, it was held that Rule 3 was inapplicable because
there was no obligation on the seller to weigh the goods.[41]

(Rule 4, relating to the contract of sale and return, will be considered
subsequently, para. 16.49.)

16.16 **Reservation of Title.**—In recent years there has been much litigation as
to the effect of clauses providing that property will not pass to the buyer
until the price has been paid.[42] Such clauses may attempt to give the
seller, if the goods have been re-sold, rights against the sub-purchaser or
over the proceeds in the hands of the buyer; they may also purport to
give the seller rights over products which have been manufactured from
the goods by the buyer. It is clear that a simple provision that property
in the goods sold will not pass until the price has been paid will be given
effect and, in the event of the sequestration or liquidation of the buyer,
the seller can recover the goods.[43] He is not obliged to account to the
buyer for any part of the value of the goods but a partial payment may
be repayable.[44] However, where an administration order is made in
relation to the buyer under Part II of the Insolvency Act 1986, the rights
of a seller under a conditional sale agreement may be constrained. It has
now been established that a reservation of title until the price and all
other sums due to the seller or to members of its combine have been
paid is effectual; it is not an attempt to create a security in the form of a
sale.[45] It is not possible in a reservation of title clause to create an
effectual trust over proceeds to be received by the buyer at some future
time.[46] It is thought that a clause giving the seller rights over products

[40] *Kennedy's Tr.* v. *Hamilton* (1897) 25 R. 252.
[41] *Woodburn* v. *Motherwell*, 1917 S.C. 533.
[42] Such clauses are often called 'Romalpa clauses': see *Aluminium Industrie Vaassen
B.V.* v. *Romalpa Aluminium, supra.* In statutory usage an instalment sale subject to such
a clause is a 'conditional sale': Hire Purchase Act 1964, s. 29(1); Consumer Credit Act
1974, s. 189(1).
[43] *Archivent Sales & Development Ltd.* v. *Strathclyde Regionàl Council*, 1985 S.L.T. 154;
Zahnrad Fabrik Passau GmbH v. *Terex Ltd.*, 1985 S.C. 364.
[44] *per* Lord Keith, *Armour* v. *Thyssen Edelstahlwerke A.G.*, 1990 S.L.T. 891 at p. 895.
For a discussion of the various problems which can arise, see *Clough Mill* v. *Martin* [1985]
1 W.L.R. 111 and McCormack [1991] 12 L.S. 195.
[45] *Armour* v. *Thyssen Edelstahlwerke A.G.*, supra.
[46] *Clark Taylor & Co. Ltd. and Quality Site Development (Edinburgh) Ltd.*, 1981 S.C.
111. *Cf. Tay Valley Joinery Ltd.* v. *C.F. Financial Services Ltd.*, 1987 S.L.T. 207, and see
Reid, "Trusts and Floating Charges," 1987 S.L.T. (News) 113.

manufactured from the goods and other materials which were never the seller's property would be ineffectual as an attempt to create a security without possession.[47]

16.17   Risk: Generic Sales.—The question of risk, *i.e.* the question on whom the loss is to fall if goods sold are accidentally injured or destroyed, is, in general, raised only in the case of the sale of specific articles. If a man agrees to supply a certain quantity of a particular commodity there is nothing under the contract at risk. *Genus nunquam perit*, the particular commodity does not cease to exist, although the seller's whole stock may be accidentally destroyed. In all ordinary cases he remains liable under his contract.[48] Even if the particular commodity has ceased to exist, or has become unprocurable, the contract is not affected, if the buyer has no notice of the seller's sources of supply. So where A agreed to supply a certain quantity of Finnish birch, he was held liable in damages for failure to fulfil his contract, in spite of the fact that owing to war conditions it had become impossible to procure that particular commodity.[49] But where the subject of sale was a particular chemical, and both parties were aware that it was to be imported from Germany, and therefore during the war could not be obtained without trading with the enemy, it was held that the contract was avoided.[50]

16.18   Risk: Specific Goods.—Where the contract relates to specific goods, or to goods which have been unconditionally appropriated to the contract by one party with the consent of the other, the result of their accidental destruction depends upon the date of that occurrence. If, without the knowledge of the seller, they have perished at the date when the contract was made, the contract is void [6]. This has been held to apply to a case of partial destruction by theft.[51] Unless otherwise agreed, they are at the seller's risk until the property has passed to the buyer, thereafter at the buyer's risk whether they have been delivered or not [20].[52] If they are accidentally destroyed before the risk has passed to

---

[47] See *Re Bond Worth Ltd.* [1980] Ch. 228; *Borden (U.K.) Ltd.* v. *Scottish Timber Products Ltd.* [1981] Ch. 25; *Re Peachdart Ltd.* [1984] Ch. 131. These cases were largely concerned with whether a charge had been created which required registration pursuant to Companies Act 1948, s. 95 (now Companies Act 1985, ss. 395–396), a question which was also discussed in *Clough Mill* v. *Martin* [1985] 1 W.L.R. 111. In Scotland, a fixed security over corporeal moveables other than ships or aircraft did not require to be registered but the position is being altered by the Companies Act 1989, s. 93, amending s. 396 of the 1985 Act. Other English cases are: *Hendy Lennox (Industrial Engines) Ltd.* v. *Grahame Puttick Ltd.* [1984] 2 All E.R. 152; *Re Andrabell Ltd.* [1984] 3 All E.R. 407 (proceeds in buyer's hands); *Pfeiffer GmbH* v. *Arbuthnot Factors Ltd.* [1988] 1 W.L.R. 150; *Tatung (U.K.) Ltd.* v. *Galex Telesure Ltd.* (1989) 5 B.C.C. 325; *Re Weldtech Equipment Ltd.* [1991] B.C.L.C. 393 (rights against sub-purchaser).
[48] *Anderson and Crompton* v. *Walls* (1870) 9 M. 122.
[49] *Blackburn Bobbin Co.* v. *Allen* [1918] 2 K.B. 467.
[50] *Re Badische Co.* [1921] 2 Ch. 331.
[51] *Barrow Lane & Ballard* v. *Phillips* [1929] 1 K.B. 574.
[52] *Cf.* the common law rule that risk passed when the contract was completed, not when property in the goods passed: see *Widenmeyer* v. *Burn Stewart & Co. Ltd.*, 1967 S.C. 85.

the buyer the contract is avoided, and neither party is under any liability [7]. Otherwise the maxim *res perit domino* (a thing perishes to the disadvantage of its owner) applies, and if the risk has passed to the buyer he must pay the price.[53] It is, however, open to the parties to agree that the risk shall not pass with the property, and such agreement may be express or implied. If the seller has undertaken to deliver the goods the general rule is that both property and risk pass to the buyer when they are delivered to a carrier, and, by the transfer of the bill of lading or otherwise, they are placed at the buyer's disposal [18, Rule 5(2); 32] but if the contract is read as an obligation to deliver the goods at a particular place the risk is with the seller until they arrive there.[54] It is possible that the risk may be divided; the risk of total destruction being on one party, the risk of deterioration on the other. So where herrings were sold, and, owing to delay on the voyage, arrived in a state unfit for consumption, it was held that the buyer might reject them, even on the assumption that the property in the herrings, and with it the risk of their accidental destruction, had passed to him.[55]

16.19 **Risk: Where One Party is at Fault.**—In the case of specific goods the risk may be affected by the fact that one or other party was at fault. If the destruction of the goods is due to the fault of one or other party, he will be liable in damages. If delivery be delayed through the fault of buyer or seller, the risk is on the party at fault as regards any loss which might not have occurred but for that fault [20]. If goods are sent to the buyer by a route involving sea transit in circumstances where it is usual to insure, and the seller fails to give such notice to the buyer as may enable him to insure, the goods are at the seller's risk during the sea transit [32 (3)].

16.20 **Title of Buyer.**—As a general rule the purchaser of goods obtains no better title to them than the seller possessed.[56] So if the seller be a thief, or a person who has no right to be in possession of the goods or to dispose of them, the purchaser obtains no title in a question with the true owner. It is immaterial, in Scots law, that the sale may have taken place in a public market or market overt.[57] The general rule is qualified by the proviso to section 21(1)[58] and by other statutory provisions which give effect to the ostensible authority to dispose of goods which is

---

[53] *Woodburn* v. *Andrew Motherwell*, 1917 S.C. 533; *Wardar's (Import & Export) Co.* v. *W. Norwood & Sons* [1968] 2 Q.B. 663.

[54] *Henckell Du Buisson* v. *Swan* (1889) 17 R. 252.

[55] *Pommer* v. *Mowat* (1906) 14 S.L.T. 373. In such cases the buyer takes the risk of deterioration necessarily incident to the transit (s. 33). See also *Sterns* v. *Vickers* [1923] 1 K.B. 78.

[56] s. 21. As to the distinction between void and voidable agreements, see para. 7.2, *supra.*

[57] *Todd* v. *Armour* (1882) 9 R. 901.

[58] *Central Newbury Car Auctions* v. *Unity Finance* [1957] 1 Q.B. 371.

involved in possession of the goods or of the documents of title to them. The proviso to section 21(1) that the owner may be precluded by his conduct from denying the seller's authority to sell does not apply where there has been only an agreement to sell.[59]

16.21 Sales by Ostensible Owner.—By the Factors Act 1889 (extended to Scotland by the Factors (Scotland) Act 1890), section 2, it is provided: 'Where a mercantile agent is, with the consent of the owner, in possession of goods or of the documents of title to goods, any sale, pledge, or other disposition of the goods, made by him when acting in the ordinary course of business of a mercantile agent, shall, subject to the provisions of this Act, be as valid as if he were expressly authorised by the owner of the goods to make the same; provided that the person taking under the disposition acts in good faith, and has not at the time of the disposition notice that the person making the disposition has not authority to make the same.' By the Sale of Goods Act 1979 [24, 25] (re-enacting sections 8 and 9 of the Factors Act) similar provisions are made for the case of an unauthorised disposition of goods to a party who takes in good faith either (a) by a person who has sold goods but continues in possession of the goods or of the documents of title to them; or (b) by a person who has bought or agreed to buy goods and has obtained, with the consent of the seller, possession of the goods or of the documents of title to them. Section 24 provides: 'Where a person having sold goods continues or is in possession of the goods, or of the documents of title to the goods, the delivery or transfer by that person, or by a mercantile agent acting for him, of the goods or documents of title under any sale, pledge, or other disposition thereof, to any person receiving the same in good faith and without notice of the previous sale, has the same effect as if the person making the delivery or transfer were expressly authorised by the owner of the goods to make the same.' The test is continuity of possession regardless of any alteration of the legal title under which the possession is held.[60] 'The owner of the goods' must be read as 'the original buyer of the goods,' so that if the seller (X) having stolen the goods from W, sold them to Y and then, while still in possession of them, delivered them under a sale to Z, that delivery would not be treated as if it had been expressly authorised by W.[61]

Section 25(1) provides: 'Where a person having bought or agreed to buy goods obtains, with the consent of the seller, possession of the goods or the documents of title to the goods, the delivery or transfer by that person, or by a mercantile agent acting for him, of the goods or documents of title, under any sale, pledge, or other disposition thereof, to any person receiving the same in good faith and without notice of any

---

[59] *Shaw* v. *Commissioner of Police* [1987] 1 W.L.R. 1332.
[60] *Pacific Motor Auctions Pty.* v. *Motor Credits (Hire Finance)* [1965] A.C. 867; *Worcester Works Finance* v. *Cooden* [1972] 1 Q.B. 210.
[61] *National Employers' Mutual General Insurance Association Ltd.* v. *Jones* [1990] A.C. 24.

lien or other right of the original seller in respect of the goods, has the same effect as if the person making the delivery or transfer were a mercantile agent in possession of the goods or documents of title with the consent of the owner.' If the seller in fact consents it is immaterial that his consent has been obtained by fraud.[62] There must be a voluntary transfer of actual or constructive possession.[63] Delivery by the seller to the sub-purchaser satisfies the requirement of the section.[64] The buyer must be acting in the way in which a mercantile agent would normally be expected to act.[65] Once again the words 'the owner' in the last phrase of the subsection cause difficulty and must be read as 'the owner who entrusted them to him'; if a thief sells the goods to X who then sells them to Y, who takes in good faith, Y does not get a good title against the person from whom the goods were stolen. For purposes of section 9 of the Factors Act and section 25(1) of the Sale of Goods Act a buyer under a conditional sale agreement (as defined in the Consumer Credit Act 1974) is to be taken not to be a person who has bought or agreed to buy goods.[66] A private purchaser of a motor vehicle which is the subject of a prior conditional sale agreement may, however, acquire a good title to it if he purchases in good faith and without notice of the prior agreement.[67]

16.22 Meaning of Good Faith.—A person who takes goods or documents of title in the circumstances covered by these statutory provisions takes in good faith if he in fact takes honestly, whether he takes negligently or not [61(3)]. But absence of inquiry, or an inadequate price, may be evidence of want of good faith.[68] Where bills of lading were taken by A in the ordinary course of business, in the knowledge that the person from whom he took them (B) was in financial difficulties and had not paid for the goods, but without any notice that B had obtained the bills of lading fraudulently, it was held that A's title was unchallengeable.[69]

16.23 Mere Possession Confers no Power to Dispose of Goods.—There may be exceptional cases in which a party who is in possession of goods or of documents to title, but who is neither a mercantile agent, nor a seller left in possession, nor a buyer entrusted with possession, is able to confer a good title by a fraudulent sale of the goods, on the ground that

[62] *Du Jardin* v. *Beadman Bros. Ltd.* [1952] 2 Q.B. 712.

[63] *Ladbroke Leasing (South West) Ltd.* v. *Reekie Plant Ltd.*, 1983 S.L.T. 155.

[64] *Four Point Garage Ltd.* v. *Carter* [1985] 3 All E.R. 12.

[65] *Newtons of Wembley* v. *Williams* [1965] 1 Q.B. 560; *Archivent Sales and Development Ltd.* v. *Strathclyde Regional Council*, 1985 S.L.T. 154.

[66] Factors Act 1889, s. 9 (as amended by Consumer Credit Act 1974, Sched. 4, para. 2); 1979 Act, s. 25(2).

[67] Hire Purchase Act 1964, ss. 27–29, as substituted by Consumer Credit Act 1974, Sched. 4, para. 22. See para. 16.51 *infra*.

[68] See *Jones* v. *Gordon* (1877) 2 App. Cas. 616; *Hayman* v. *American Cotton Oil Co.* (1907) 45 S.L.R. 207; 15 S.L.T. 606.

[69] *Price & Pierce* v. *Bank of Scotland*, 1910 S.C. 1095; 1912 S.C. (H.L.) 19.

the party who allowed him to be in possession is personally barred from disputing his authority to sell.[70] But there is no general rule that mere possession of goods, as for instance by a hirer,[71] or a carrier or forwarding agent,[72] gives the possessor any ostensible right to dispose of them, or is any ground for a plea of personal bar put forward by a party who had bought the goods from the person in possession, and whose right is challenged by their true owner.[73]

16.24 **Warranties.**—Warranties by a seller of goods may be express, imposed by statute, implied, or annexed by custom of trade. The question whether a particular statement is to be read as a warranty, or merely as a representation, has been already considered.[74] An example of a warranty imposed by statute is the Agriculture Act 1970, section 72, by which, in a sale of any material for use as a feeding stuff for animals, there is implied a warranty by the seller that the material is suitable to be used as such. The term has effect notwithstanding any contract or notice to the contrary.

16.25 **Implied Terms.**—The terms implied in sale are dealt with by sections 12 to 15. An express term does not negative an implied term unless inconsistent with it.[75] The Act formerly provided for implied warranties and conditions which reflected a well established distinction in English law.[76] The 1994 Act removed this distinction in favour of the single concept of an implied term. Implied terms are of three classes: terms as to title, as to description, and as to quality.

16.26 **Implied Terms of Title.**—There are (a) an implied term on the part of the seller that, in the case of a sale, he has the right to sell the goods, and that, in the case of an agreement to sell, he will have a right to sell the goods at the time when the property is to pass; and (b) an implied term that the goods are free, and will remain free until the time when the property is to pass, from any charge or encumbrance not disclosed or known to the buyer before the contract is made and that the buyer will enjoy quiet possession of the goods except in so far as it may be disturbed by the owner or other person entitled to the benefit of any charge or encumbrance so disclosed or known [12(1) and (2)]. These provisions do not apply in the case in which there appears from the

---

[70] See *London Joint Stock Bank* v. *Simmons* [1892] A.C. 201, opinion of Lord Herschell; *Commonwealth Trust* v. *Akotey* [1926] A.C. 72, on which see opinion of Lord Sumner in *Jones* v. *Waring & Gillow* [1926] A.C. 670.
[71] *Mitchell* v. *Heys* (1894) 21 R. 600; *Lamonby* v. *Foulds*, 1928 S.C. 89; *George Hopkinson Ltd.* v. *Napier & Son*, 1953 S.C. 139 (diligence).
[72] *Martinez y Gomez* v. *Alison* (1890) 17 R. 332.
[73] *Mitchell* v. *Heys, supra*; *Farquharson* v. *King* [1902] A.C. 325.
[74] para. 8.10, *supra*.
[75] s. 55(2); *Douglas* v. *Milne* (1895) 23 R. 163.
[76] See, as to conditions and warranties in English law, s. 11; opinion of Fletcher Moulton L.J. in *Wallis* v. *Pratt* [1910] 2 K.B. 1003; *Baldry* v. *Marshall* [1925] 1 K.B. 260.

contract or is to be inferred from the circumstances of the contract an intention that the seller should transfer only such title as he or a third person may have; in such a case there is—(a) an implied term that all charges or encumbrances known to the seller and not known to the buyer have been disclosed to the buyer before the contract is made; and (b) an implied term that neither—(i) the seller, nor (ii) in a case where the parties to the contract intend that the seller should transfer only such title as a third person may have, that person, nor (iii) anyone claiming through or under the seller or that third person otherwise than under a charge or encumbrance disclosed or known to the buyer before the contract is made, will disturb the buyer's quiet possession of the goods [12(3), (4) and (5)]. Any term of a contract which purports to exclude or restrict liability for breach of the obligations arising from any of these implied undertakings as to title or to exclude or restrict the undertakings themselves is void.[77] With regard to these provisions it may be noted that if the buyer knows that the seller has only a limited right he cannot insist on an implied term of an absolute one.[78] It has been held that a seller did not fulfil the warranty of his right to sell when he supplied goods with a label which constituted an infringement of a third party's trade mark, and which the buyer could not deal with without risk of a law suit.[79] The implied term of 'quiet possession' does not import a warranty against unfounded claims by third parties, and therefore the buyer cannot recover from the seller the expenses he has incurred in resisting these.[80]

16.27   Implied Terms of Description.—'Where there is a contract for the sale of goods by description, there is an implied term that the goods will correspond with the description' [13]. A sale of goods is not prevented from being a sale by description by reason only that, being exposed for sale or hire, the goods are selected by the buyer [13(3)]. The word 'description,' which is not defined in the Act, may be synonymous with 'kind.'[81] Thus it has been observed: 'If a man offer to buy peas of another, and he sends him beans, he does not perform his contract, but that is not a warranty, there is no warranty that he should sell him peas; the contract is to sell peas, and if he sends him anything else in their

[77] Unfair Contract Terms Act 1977, ss. 20(1)(a), 25 (5).
[78] *Leith Heritages Co.* v. *Edinburgh Glass Co.* (1876) 3 R. 789.
[79] *Niblett* v. *Confectioners' Materials* [1921] 3 K.B. 387. See also *Microbeads A.G.* v. *Vinhurst Road Markings* [1975] 1 W.L.R. 218.
[80] *Stephen* v. *Lord Advocate* (1878) 6 R. 282; *Dougall* v. *Magistrates of Dunfermline*, 1908 S.C. 151.
[81] *Rutherford & Son* v. *Miln & Co.*, 1941 S.C. 125, at p. 135. In *Christopher Hill Ltd.* v. *Ashington Piggeries Ltd.* [1972] A.C. 441, it was said that description went to the identification of the goods. 'One must look to the contract as a whole to identify the kind of goods that the seller was agreeing to sell and the buyer to buy': *Berger & Co. Inc.* v. *Gill & Duffus S.A.* [1984] A.C. 382, speech of Lord Diplock at p. 394. See also *Harlingdon and Leinster Enterprises Ltd.* v. *Christopher Hull Fine Art Ltd.* [1991] 1 Q.B. 564.

stead, it is a non-performance of it.'[82] In this meaning of the word 'description,' there is no difficulty in holding that the party who orders goods of a particular description, and gets either different goods or a consignment, in part of the goods ordered, and in part of goods of a different description, is entitled to reject them.[83] But the word 'description' may refer to any statement as to the origin or history of the goods[84] as, for instance, that they form part of a particular stock,[85] that they have been shipped in a particular month,[86] that they have been carried,[87] or packed,[88] in a specified way. In such cases failure to answer the description may make no difference to the value of the goods. If the seller is in breach of the implied term that the goods will correspond with the description, the buyer can claim damages[89] and he may also be entitled to reject the goods if the breach is material[90] or if the contract of sale is a consumer contract made on or after January 3, 1995.[91]

16.28 Implied Terms as to Quality.—At common law the rule was expressed in the statement that a fair price demanded a fair article, and therefore it was held that, in the absence of any provision to the contrary, the seller undertook to supply goods of reasonably good quality.[92] The English law on the subject, generally referred to by the phrase *caveat emptor* (let the buyer beware), was applied to Scotland by section 5 of the Mercantile Law Amendment Act Scotland 1856, but that section is now repealed. Prior to amendment by the 1994 Act, the Act provided that in certain circumstances there could be an implied condition that the goods were of merchantable quality.[93] This implied condition is still relevant for contracts made prior to January 3, 1995 and consideration of the authorities on this concept has been retained in the text.[94] For contracts made on or after January 3, 1995, there may be an implied term that the goods will be of satisfactory quality.[95] Section 14 (as amended) provides as follows:

'(1) Except as provided by this section and section 15 below and subject to any other enactment, there is no implied term about the

---

[82] *Per* Lord Abinger, *Chanter* v. *Hopkins* (1838) 4 M. & W. 399.

[83] *Jaffé* v. *Ritchie* (1860) 23 D. 242; *Carter* v. *Campbell* (1885) 12 R. 1075; *Rutherford & Son* v. *Miln*, 1941 S.C. 125; see also *Christopher Hill* v. *Ashington Piggeries, supra,* and the opinions in *McCallum* v. *Mason,* 1956 S.C. 50, as to the effects of mixed ingredients.

[84] *Varley* v. *Whipp* [1900] 1 Q.B. 513.

[85] *Thomson Bros.* v. *Thomson* (1885) 13 R. 88.

[86] *Bowes* v. *Shand* (1877) 2 App.Cas. 455.

[87] *Meyer* v. *Travaru* (1930) 46 T.L.R. 553; contrast *Meyer* v. *Kivisto* (1929) 142 L.T. 480.

[88] *Moore* v. *Landauer* [1921] 2 K.B. 519.

[89] s. 15B(1)(a); see *infra,* para. 16.36.

[90] s. 15B(1)(b); see also s. 11(5) of the Act which was repealed by Sched. 3 to the 1994 Act.

[91] s. 15B(2); as to the meaning of a consumer contract, see para. 16.32, *infra.*

[92] *Whealler* v. *Methuen* (1843) 5 D. 402.

[93] See s. 14(2) of the Act prior to amendment.

[94] *Infra* para. 16.29.

[95] *Infra* para. 16.29.

quality or fitness for any particular purpose of goods supplied under a contract of sale.

(2) Where the seller sells goods in the course of a business, there is an implied term that the goods supplied under the contract are of satisfactory quality.

(2A) For the purposes of this Act, goods are of satisfactory quality if they meet the standard that a reasonable person would regard as satisfactory, taking account of any description of the goods, the price (if relevant) and all the other relevant circumstances.

(2B) For the purposes of this Act, the quality of goods includes their state and condition and the following (among others) are in appropriate cases aspects of the quality of goods—

(a) fitness for all the purposes for which goods of the kind in question are commonly supplied,
(b) appearance and finish,
(c) freedom from minor defects,
(d) safety, and
(e) durability.

(2C) The term implied by subsection (2) above does not extend to any matter making the quality of goods unsatisfactory—

(a) which is specifically drawn to the buyer's attention before the contract is made,
(b) where the buyer examines the goods before the contract is made, which that examination ought to reveal, or
(c) in the case of a contract for sale by sample, which would have been apparent on a reasonable examination of the sample.

(3) Where the seller sells goods in the course of a business and the buyer, expressly or by implication, makes known—

(a) to the seller, or
(b) where the purchase price or part of it is payable by instalments and the goods were previously sold by a credit-broker to the seller, to that credit-broker,

any particular purpose for which the goods are being bought, there is an implied term that the goods supplied under the contract are reasonably fit for that purpose, whether or not that is a purpose for which such goods are commonly supplied, except where the circumstances show that the buyer does not rely, or that it is unreasonable for him to rely, on the skill or judgment of the seller or credit-broker.

(4) An implied term or warranty about quality or fitness for a particular purpose may be annexed to a contract of sale by usage.'

A 'business' includes a profession and the activities of any government department (including a Northern Ireland department) or local or public authority [61(1)]. The provisions apply to a sale by a person who in the

course of a business is acting as agent for another as they apply to a sale
by a principal in the course of a business, except where the other is not
selling in the course of a business and either the buyer knows that fact
or reasonable steps are taken to bring it to the notice of the buyer
before the contract is made.[96] A displenishing sale of a farm and the
stock and plenishing thereof is a sale in the course of a business.[97] The
term that the goods will be of satisfactory quality will not be implied
into the contract if the seller specifically draws to the buyer's attention
any matter which makes the quality of the goods unsatisfactory or if the
buyer examines the goods prior to the contract and ought to have
discovered the matter.[98]

A 'credit-broker' is a person acting in the course of a business of
credit brokerage carried on by him, that is a business of effecting
introductions of individuals desiring to obtain credit—

   (i)   to persons carrying on any business so far as it relates to the
         provision of credit, or
   (ii) to other persons enagaged in credit brokerage.[99]

16.29 **Merchantable Quality and Satisfactory Quality.**—The phrase 'merchantable quality' is still relevant for contracts made prior to January 3, 1995.
Goods of any kind are of merchantable quality if they are as fit for the
purpose or purposes for which goods of that kind are commonly bought
as it is reasonable to expect having regard to any description applied to
them, the price (if relevant) and all other relevant circumstances.[1] It has
been held that the implied condition is not applicable where goods are
supplied which do not correspond with the description given, *e.g.*
sodium chlorate weedkiller instead of magnesium sulphate fertiliser.[2]
The implied condition relates to the physical quality of the goods
themselves and not to external circumstances affecting their
saleability—for example, in the case of a sale of cows, the existence of a
government order prohibiting movement of the cows.[3] The fact that the
defect is repairable or does not destroy the 'workable character' of the

---

[96] s.14(5). The provisions will apply even where the principal is undisclosed and is not
selling in the course of a business, but employs an agent who is so selling. In these
circumstances the buyer can elect to sue either the principal or the agent: *Boyter* v.
Thomson, 1994 S.L.T. 1315.

[97] *Buchanan-Jardine* v. *Hamilink*, 1983 S.L.T. 149.

[98] s. 14(2C) which largely follows the wording formerly found in s. 14(2)(a) and (b); see
also *Turnock* v. *Fortune*, 1989 S.L.T. (Sh.Ct.) 32.

[99] s. 61(1), added to s. 14(3) of the 1893 Act by Consumer Credit Act 1974, Sched. 4,
para. 3.

[1] See s. 14(6) of the Act prior to amendment by the 1994 Act; the definition was
inserted in the 1893 Act by the Supply of Goods (Implied Terms) Act 1973, s.7(2). In
England it has been said that in most cases it should now be unnecessary to have recourse
to the pre-1973 case law on the meaning of 'merchantable quality': *Rogers* v. *Parish
(Scarborough) Ltd.* [1987] Q.B. 933, *per* Mustill L.J. p. 942, Woolf L.J. at p. 947. *Cf. M/S
Aswan Engineering Establishment Co.* v. *Lupdine Ltd.* [1987] 1 W.L.R. 1.

[2] *McCallum* v. *Mason*, 1956 S.C. 50.

[3] *Buchanan-Jardine* v. *Hamilink, supra.*

goods does not mean that the goods are not unmerchantable. For example, in the case of a car, consideration must be given to the purchaser's purpose in driving it with the degree of comfort, ease of handling, reliability and pride in its appearance appropriate for the market at which the vehicle was aimed.[4] The identity of the artist is not a matter affecting the merchantable quality of a painting.[5] For contracts made on or after January 3, 1995, the relevant concept is satisfactory quality. Goods of any kind are of satisfactory quality if they meet the standard that a reasonable person would regard as satisfactory, taking account of any description of the goods, the price and all other relevant circumstances, [14(2A)]. The quality of goods includes their state and condition; fitness for all the purposes for which goods of that kind are commonly supplied; appearance and finish; freedom from minor defects; safety; and durability. The list detailing the different aspects of quality is not intended to be exhaustive [14(2B)].

16.30 **Fitness for Particular Purpose.**—The general application of the implied stipulation that the goods must be fit for a particular purpose may be illustrated by a case where hay was sold as 'good, sound, timothy hay.' The buyer's purpose, resale in a particular market, the conditions of which were known to the seller, was disclosed. The hay, though not of bad quality, did not satisfy the market conditions. It was held that the buyer was entitled to reject the hay, and recover damages, in respect that the seller had impliedly warranted that it was fit for the particular purpose for which, to his knowledge, the buyer required it. It was also decided that the circumstances involving the implied stipulation could be proved by parole evidence although the contract was in writing.[6] There is a strong body of authority to the effect that in the case of articles which are commonly used for one purpose only, e.g. milk,[7] articles of food,[8] a hot-water bottle,[9] coals,[10] the buyer's purpose is sufficiently made known to the seller merely by asking for the article, without any express statement as to the object for which he requires it. The stipulation can be implied in the sale of secondhand goods.[11]

---

[4] *Rogers* v. *Parish (Scarborough) Ltd.*, *supra*. See also *Bernstein* v. *Pamson Motors (Golders Green) Ltd.* [1987] 2 All E.R. 220; *M/S Aswan Engineering Establishment Co.* v. *Lupdine Ltd.*, *supra*; *Shine* v. *General Guarantee Corp. Ltd.* [1988] 1 All E.R. 911; *Business Applications Specialists Ltd.* v. *Nationwide Credit Corporation Ltd.* [1988] CCLR 135.

[5] *Harlingdon and Leinster Enterprises Ltd.* v. *Christopher Hull Fine Art Ltd.* [1991] 1 Q.B. 564.

[6] *Jacobs* v. *Scott* (1899) 2 F. (H.L.) 70. See also *Manchester Liners* v. *Rea* [1922] 2 A.C. 74; *Buchanan & Carswell* v. *Eugene*, 1936 S.C. 160; *Slater* v. *Finning Ltd.*, 1995 G.W.D. 2–105.

[7] *Frost* v. *Aylesbury Dairy Co.* [1905] 1 K.B. 608.

[8] *Wallis* v. *Russell* [1902] 2 Ir. R. 585, 'two nice fresh crabs for tea.'

[9] *Priest* v. *Last* [1903] 2 K.B. 148.

[10] *Duke* v. *Jackson*, 1921 S.C. 362.

[11] *Bartlett* v. *Sidney Marcus* [1965] 1 W.L.R. 1013; *Crowther* v. *Shannon Motor Co.* [1975] 1 W.L.R. 30.

16.31   Sale by Sample.—In the case of a sale by sample there is an implied term (a) that the bulk will correspond with the sample in quality; (b) that the goods will be free from any defect which makes their quality unsatisfactory and which would not be apparent on reasonable examination of the sample [14(2C)(c) and 15].[12] If the sale is also by description the bulk must correspond not only with the sample but with the description [13(2)]. A sale is a sale by sample when there is a term in the contract, express or implied, to that effect [15]. So where the conditions of a sale by auction provided that intending purchasers must satisfy themselves of the condition of the goods in bulk, it was held that the sale was not by sample, in spite of the fact that a sample was open to inspection in the auction room.[13]

16.32   Exclusion of Implied Terms.—A right, duty or obligation arising by implication under a contract of sale may be negatived or varied by express agreement, or by the course of dealing between the parties or by usage if the usage is such as to bind both parties to the contract,[14] but the extent to which this can be done effectually in respect of the implied terms discussed in the five preceding paragraphs is severely limited by the provisions of the Unfair Contract Terms Act 1977.[15]

Any term of a contract which purports to exclude or restrict[16] liability for breach of any obligation arising from the seller's implied undertakings as to description, quality, fitness for purpose or conformity with samples or to exclude or restrict the obligation itself,[17] is, in the case of a consumer contract, void against the consumer; in the case of other contracts, such a term has no effect if it was not fair and reasonable to incorporate the term in the contract.[18]

A consumer contract of sale is a contract of sale (not being a contract of sale by auction or competitive tender) in which one party to the contract deals, and the other party to the contract (the consumer) does not deal, or hold himself out as dealing, in the course of a business,[19] and the goods are of a type ordinarily supplied for private use or consumption.[20] The onus of proving that a contract is not to be regarded as a consumer contract lies on the party so contending.

---

[12] *Drummond* v. *Van Ingen* (1887) 12 App. Cas. 284; *F.E. Hookway Co.* v. *Alfred Isaacs & Son* [1954] 1 Lloyd's Rep. 491, *per* Devlin J., at p. 511; *Godley* v. *Perry* [1960] 1 W.L.R. 9.

[13] *White* v. *Dougherty* (1891) 18 R. 972.

[14] s. 55(1). Such terms are strictly construed: *Wallis* v. *Pratt* [1911] A.C. 394; *Baldry* v. *Marshall* [1925] 1 K.B. 260.

[15] See para. 9.16, *supra*. As to exclusion of the implied term of title, see para. 16.26, *supra*.

[16] Unfair Contract Terms Act 1977, s. 25(3). The references to sections in the succeeding part of this section are to sections of that Act.

[17] s. 25(5).

[18] s. 20(2); see *George Mitchell (Chesterhall) Ltd.* v. *Finney Lock Seeds Ltd.* [1983] 2 A.C. 803; *R. & B. Customs Brokers Co. Ltd.* v. *United Dominions Trust Ltd.* [1988] 1 W.L.R. 321.

[19] See *R. & B. Customs Brokers Co. Ltd.* v. *United Dominions Trust Ltd.*, *supra*.

[20] s. 25(1).

In determining whether it was fair and reasonable to incorporate a term in a contract which is not a consumer contract, regard is to be had only to the circumstances which were, or ought reasonably to have been, known to or in the contemplation of the parties to the contract at the time the contract was made.[21] Regard is to be had in particular to:[22]

(a) the strength of the bargaining positions of the parties relative to each other, taking into account (among other things) alternative means by which the consumer's requirements could have been met:[23]

(b) whether the customer received an inducement to agree to the term, or in accepting it had an opportunity of entering into a similar contract with other persons, but without having to accept a similar term;

(c) whether the customer knew or ought reasonably to have known of the existence and extent of the term (having regard, among other things, to any custom of the trade and any previous course of dealing between the parties);[23a]

(d) where the term excludes or restricts any relevant liability if some condition is not complied with, whether it was reasonable at the time of the contract to expect that compliance with that condition would be practicable;[23b]

(e) whether the goods were manufactured, processed or adapted to the special order of the customer.

Where the term purports to restrict liability to a specified sum of money regard should be had to—(a) the resources which the party seeking to rely on that term could expect to be available to him for the purpose of meeting the liability should it arise; (b) how far it was open to that party to cover himself by insurance.[24] The onus of proving that it was fair and reasonable to incorporate a term lies on the party so contending[25] and he must aver upon which of the above matters (a) to (e) he relies.[26]

16.33 Rules as to Delivery.—It is the obligation of the seller to deliver the goods, of the buyer to accept and pay for them, in accordance with the terms of the contract [27]. Unless otherwise agreed, delivery and payment of the price are concurrent conditions, so that the seller is not bound to deliver the goods unless the price is paid or tendered, while the buyer is not bound to pay the price unless the goods are delivered

---

[21] s. 24(1).
[22] s. 24(2); Sched. 2. See *Rasbora* v. *J.C.L. Marine* [1977] 1 Lloyd's Rep. 645.
[23] See *Denholm Fishselling Ltd.* v. *Anderson*, 1991 S.L.T. (Sh.Ct.) 24.
[23a] See *Knight Machinery (Holdings) Ltd.* v. *Rennie*, 1995 S.L.T. 166.
[23b] See *Knight Machinery (Holdings) Ltd.* v. *Rennie, supra.*
[24] s. 24(3).
[25] s. 24(4).
[26] *Landcatch Ltd.* v. *Marine Harvest Ltd.*, 1985 S.L.T. 478.

[28]. The case of a sale on credit is an obvious example of an agreement to the contrary. But in the absence of any express provision on the subject, inference from a previous course of dealing between the parties, or proof of custom of trade, a sale is presumably for cash, and the seller, if he chooses to stand on his strict rights, may refuse delivery unless the price is tendered.[27] Even where the sale is on credit, or a term is fixed for delivery before the term of payment, the seller is not bound to deliver the goods if the buyer is insolvent. He may retain them in the exercise of his right of lien, or, if they have been dispatched and are in course of transit, recover them by the exercise of his right of stoppage in transit.[28]

The time for delivery may be fixed; if not, the law will infer a time reasonable in the whole circumstances of the case [29 (3)]. Late delivery will give the buyer the right to retain the price in security of his claim for damages.[29] Whether it will entitle him to rescind the contract, and refuse to accept the goods, depends upon whether, in the particular case, the delay amounts to a material failure on the part of the seller.[30]

Whether the seller is to send the goods to the purchaser, or the purchaser to send for them, depends upon the agreement, express or implied, in each case. If the seller is to send them by carrier he must make a reasonable contract of carriage.[31] In the absence of any agreement to the contrary the expense of putting the goods in a deliverable state falls on the seller [29 (6)]. *Prima facie* the place of delivery is the seller's place of business, if he has one; if not, his residence. But if the contract is for specific goods, which, to the knowledge of the parties when the contract is made, are in some other place, then that place is the place of delivery [29(2)].

16.34 Remedies of Buyer: Failure to Deliver.—The remedies of the buyer depend on the nature of the seller's failure. If he fails to supply the goods, he is liable in damages. Where there is an available market for the goods,[32] the measure of damages is *prima facie* to be ascertained by the difference between the contract price and the market price at the time when they ought to have been delivered; if no time was fixed, then at the time of refusal to deliver [51]. The buyer may also demand specific implement of the contract [52], but this remedy is available only when the sale is of some specific article, and the buyer can show a *pretium affectionis*, some reason for preferring the thing he contracted for to other things of the same kind; it is not competent when the sale is

---

[27] *Hall* v. *Scott* (1860) 22 D. 413.
[28] *Infra*, paras. 16.45, 16.46.
[29] *British Motor Body Co.* v. *Shaw*, 1914 S.C. 922. See para. 13.13, *supra*.
[30] *Infra*, para. 16.36.
[31] *Young* v. *Hobson* (1949) 65 T.L.R. 365.
[32] *Marshall & Co.* v. *Nicoll & Son*, 1919 S.C. 244; affd. 1919 S.C. (H.L.) 129, on meaning of 'available market.' See also *Thompson* v. *Robinson* [1955] Ch. 177; *Charter* v. *Sullivan* [1957] 2 Q.B. 117.

merely of a certain quantity of some particular commodity.[33] If the seller delivers less than he contracted to sell, the buyer may reject the goods if the shortfall is material, but if he accepts them must pay for them at the contract rate. If the seller delivers goods in excess of what he contracted to sell and the excess is material, the buyer may accept the amount he contracted for and reject the rest, or he may reject the whole. If he accepts the whole of the goods delivered, he must pay for them at the contract rate [30]. If the seller delivers the goods contracted for mixed with goods of a different description, the buyer may accept the goods which are in accordance with the contract, and reject the rest, or he may reject the whole [35A]. For contracts made prior to January 3, 1995, the buyer only enjoys a right of partial rejection if some of the goods do not conform to the description.[34] There is no right of partial rejection if some of the goods, though of the same description, are of inferior quality.[35] For contracts made after January 3, 1995, the right of partial rejection applies when there has been a breach on the part of the seller which affects some or all of the goods. The right of partial rejection of the goods will not apply if a contrary intention appears in, or is to be implied from, the contract [35A].

16.35 Defective Quality: Common Law.—The law as to the remedies of the buyer where the goods delivered are not of the quality demanded by the contract, is a subject on which the 1893 Act made an important alteration in the law of Scotland. At common law the sole remedy of a buyer, if the goods tendered were disconform to contract, was to reject them, and, on doing so, to recover damages for breach of contract. If, however, he chose to accept the goods—and in certain cases the exigencies of his business might make acceptance unavoidable—then (except in the case of latent defects) he was held to have condoned their defects, and could not recover damages for their defective quality. The *actio quanti minoris*, which involves the right to retain goods and claim from the seller the difference between their value and the value they would have possessed had they fulfilled the contractual conditions, was not recognised by the law of Scotland.[36]

16.36 Remedies Provided by Act.—The remedies available to a buyer have been significantly altered by the 1994 Act. For contracts made prior to January 3, 1995, the buyer's remedies depend on section 11, which, it may be noted, has separate provisions for England and Scotland. 'In Scotland, failure by the seller to perform any material part of a contract of sale is a breach of contract, which entitles the buyer either within a reasonable time after delivery to reject the goods and treat the contract

---

[33] *Union Electric Co.* v. *Holman*, 1913 S.C. 954, 958.

[34] s. 30(4), repealed by 1994 Act, s. 3(3) and Sched. 3.

[35] *Aitken, Campbell & Co.* v. *Boullen*, 1908 S.C. 490.

[36] *McCormick* v. *Rittmeyer* (1869) 7 M. 854, opinion of Lord President Inglis.

as repudiated,[37] or to retain the goods and treat the failure to perform such material part as a breach which may give rise to a claim for compensation or damages'.[38] Under this provision, as interpreted by decisions, the buyer has alternative remedies, in the case where the seller's failure is material, *i.e.* (a) he may reject the goods, treat the contract as repudiated by the seller, and claim damages; (b) he may keep the goods and claim damages for their defective state, in substance the *actio quanti minoris* of the civil law.[39] For contracts made on or after January 3, 1995, the relevant provision of the Act is section 15B. If the seller is in breach of any term of the contract, the buyer can claim damages. In addition, if the breach is material, the buyer can reject any goods delivered and treat the contract as repudiated. If the contract of sale is a consumer contract[39a], a breach by the seller of any of the terms relating to quality, fitness for purpose, description or conformity with samples, is deemed to be a material breach of contract.[39b]

16.37   **Rejection Excluded by Acceptance.**—The right to reject is excluded if the buyer has accepted the goods,[40] even though after acceptance the goods reveal latent defects.[41] If he has not previously examined them, he is not deemed to have accepted them unless and until he has had a reasonable opportunity of examining them for the purpose of ascertaining whether they are in conformity with the contract and, in the case of a contract for sale by sample, of comparing the bulk with the sample [35(2)]. He is deemed to have accepted them when he intimates to the seller that he has accepted them[42] or when the goods have been delivered to him and he does any act in relation to them which is inconsistent with the ownership of the seller or when, after the lapse of a reasonable time he retains the goods without intimating to the seller that he has rejected them [35(2) and (4)]. Thus, where it was a

---

[37] As to the construction of clauses whereby the buyer undertakes not to reject goods tendered, with provision for arbitration as to their defects, see *Leary* v. *Briggs* (1904) 6 F. 857; *Munro* v. *Meyer* [1930] 2 K.B. 312.

[38] See ss. 11(5), 53 and 58 of the Act, and *George Cohen, Sons & Co.* v. *Jamieson & Peterson*, 1963 S.C. 289.

[39] It is conceived that there is nothing in the Act to affect the common law distinction between the laws of England and Scotland, to the effect that, according to Scots law, any material failure in the quality of the goods will entitle the buyer to reject them, whilst according to English law, rejection is incompetent for a failure in quality not amounting to a difference in kind, unless there is an express provision for it. See opinion of Lord Chelmsford in *Cousten, Thomson & Co.* v. *Chapman* (1872) 10 M. (H.L.) 74, at p. 81; referred to, as applicable to the existing law, by Lord Dunedin, *Pollock* v. *McCrae*, 1922 S.C. (H.L.) 192, at pp. 202–03.

[39a] ss. 15B(2) and 61(1); for the definition of consumer contract see para. 16.32 *supra*.

[39b] *cf. Millars of Falkirk* v. *Turpie* 1976 S.L.T. (Notes) 66.

[40] *Mechan* v. *Bow, McLachlan & Co.*, 1910 S.C. 758; *Woodburn* v. *Motherwell*, 1917 S.C. 533; *Hardy* v. *Hillerns* [1923] 2 K.B. 490 (resale); Gloag, *Contract* (2nd ed.), at p. 611.

[41] *Morrison & Mason* v. *Clarkson Bros.* (1898) 25 R. 427; *Mechans* v. *Highland Marine Charters*, 1964 S.C. 48.

[42] s. 35(1)(a); see also *Mechans* v. *Highland Marine Charters, supra* (unqualified acceptance).

condition of a contract for the supply of a boiler for a tank which was being built for the Navy that it should have passed Admiralty tests, it was held that the buyer, by fitting the boiler in the tank, had done an act inconsistent with the ownership of the seller, and could not reject it on the ground that the tests had not been passed.[43] But the fact that the property of a thing in course of construction may have passed to the buyer does not preclude his ultimate rejection of it. So where there was a contract to build a yacht, with provisions under which the property passed to the buyer as the various instalments of the price were paid, it was held that the buyer was still entitled to reject when, on completion, the yacht proved disconform to contract.[44] It has been held that it is not necessarily too late to reject after the lapse of two years when the goods had been stored and the defect was discovered only when they were taken out.[45] For contracts made on or after January 3, 1995, the Act provides that the buyer under a consumer contract cannot lose his right to have a reasonable opportunity of examining the goods by agreement, waiver or otherwise [35(3)]. In addition, the buyer is not deemed to have accepted the goods merely by asking for, or agreeing to, repair of the goods[46] or by delivering the goods to another under a sub-sale or other disposition [35(6)]. If the buyer accepts any goods included in a commercial unit, he is deemed to have accepted all the goods making up the unit [35(7)].

Conditions of Rejection.—Rejection is inconsistent with any further use of the goods. So it is established that if the buyer merely intimates rejection and, on the seller refusing to take the goods back, continues to use them, he cannot insist on his right to reject.[47] In one case it was decided that in these circumstances the buyer, having by his notice of rejection elected one of two alternative remedies, was bound by the election, and could not fall back on the alternative of keeping the goods and claiming damages for their defective condition.[48] But this decision has been authoritatively disapproved.[49] Where the buyer has lost or foregone his right of rejection and is confined to a claim for damages, a clause which purports to exclude liability may not be operative if there has been a fundamental breach of contract on the part of the seller.[50] But it has been emphasised that the applicability of such an exceptions clause in that situation depends upon the true construction of the particular contract.[51] Continued use after intimation of rejection will

---

[43] *Mechan* v. *Bow, McLachlan & Co., supra.* See also *Morrison & Mason* v. *Clarkson Bros., supra.*

[44] *Nelson* v. *Chalmers*, 1913 S.C. 441.

[45] *Burrell* v. *Harding's Exrs.*, 1931 S.L.T. 76 (a decision on relevancy).

[46] See *Munro & Co.* v. *Bennet & Son*, 1911 S.C. 337.

[47] *Electric Construction Co.* v. *Hurry & Young* (1897) 24 R. 312; *Croom & Arthur* v. *Stewart* (1905) 7 F. 563.

[48] *Electric Construction Co.* v. *Hurry & Young, supra.*

[49] *Pollock* v. *McCrae*, 1922 S.C. (H.L.) 192.

[50] *Pollock* v. *McCrae, supra.*

[51] *Suisse Atlantique* v. *N.V. Rotterdamsche* [1967] 1 A.C. 361; and see para. 13.5, *supra.*

still, it is conceived, bar rejection, but will not bar a claim for damages on the principle of the *actio quanti minoris*.

16.38 Duty When Goods Rejected.—When the buyer rejects the goods he has no right to retain them in security of his claim of damages.[52] In the absence of any express provision, he is not bound to return them to the seller [36]. But where a horse was rejected as unsound, and the seller refused to take it back, opinions were expressed that it was the duty of the buyer either to have it placed in neutral custody or to obtain judicial authority for its resale.[53] If the goods rejected are perishable the buyer is entitled, and probably bound, to resell them at once.[54]

16.39 Examination of Goods.—In a question of rejection, the buyer is bound to examine the goods within a reasonable time. What is a reasonable time is a question of the circumstances of each particular case.[55] But two general points are established. (a) When, as in the case of machinery, the defect is apparently remediable, and the seller, on being appealed to, attempts to remedy the defect, no lapse of time or continued use of the article while his attempts are still in progress will bar ultimate rejection by the buyer.[56] (b) Where goods are ordered for export, the buyer, unless he can prove that the circumstances rendered it impossible, should examine the goods before forwarding them, and failure to do so may preclude rejection on the ground of any defect which a prompt examination would have revealed, on the principle that a seller is entitled to have an opportunity to remedy the goods.[57]

16.40 Failure in Minor Respects.—The Act formerly contained no provision for the case of failure by the seller in some respect which was not material. The rule at common law is that the buyer is not then entitled to reject the goods, but may recover damages for the defect.[58] The Act, as amended by the 1994 Act, provides that a breach of any term of the contract which is not material entitles the buyer to claim damages [15B(1)(a)]. What is a material failure is a question of the circumstances of each case, and of degree. Any serious defect in quality is undoubtedly material. But at least in cases of machinery the buyer is not within his rights in instant rejection on the ground of some remediable defect.[59] Failure in respect of time of delivery is as a rule material in the case of mercantile contracts for the supply of goods where time is

[52] *Lupton* v. *Schulze* (1900) 2 F. 1118.
[53] *Malcolm* v. *Cross* (1898) 25 R. 1089.
[54] *Pommer* v. *Mowat* (1906) 14 S.L.T. 373.
[55] See *Hyslop* v. *Shirlaw* (1905) 7 F. 875.
[56] s. 35(6); and see *Munro & Co.* v. *Bennet & Son*, 1911 S.C. 337; *Aird & Coghill* v. *Pullan* (1904) 7 F. 258.
[57] *Pini* v. *Smith* (1895) 22 R. 699; *Magistrates of Glasgow* v. *Ireland* (1895) 22 R. 818; *Dick* v. *Cochrane & Fleming*, 1935 S.L.T. 432.
[58] *Webster* v. *Cramond Iron Co.* (1875) 2 R. 752; *Bradley* v. *Dollar* (1886) 13 R. 893.
[59] *Morrison & Mason* v. *Clarkson* (1898) 25 R. 427.

usually of the essence of the contract,[60] but not in the case of a contract for the supply of an article to be built or manufactured by the seller.[61] In consumer contracts made on or after January 3, 1995, the breach of any term relating to quality, fitness of purpose, description or conformity with samples, will be deemed to be a material breach [15B(2)].

16.41 Instalment Contracts.—Contracts for the supply of goods by instalments, with provisions for intermediate payments, have raised the question whether the delivery of defective goods, or failure of delivery, in respect of one instalment, and, conversely, whether delay in payment of one instalment of the price, will justify the party aggrieved in rescinding the contract as repudiated by the other. By section 31 it is stated that it is a question of the circumstances of each case. That question, it would appear, is whether the conduct of the party in default is such as to justify the other in inferring that he does not intend to fulfil his contract, or is unable to do so. That inference may more easily be drawn in the case of a party's failure in the early instalments. The law has been judicially stated as follows: 'If on one occasion the seller should tender goods inferior to contract quality, the purchaser would not in ordinary circumstances be justified in rescinding the whole contract, though he would be entitled to return the particular lot of goods which were objectionable. But if a seller systematically send goods which are not conformable to contract, and the contract is for successive deliveries, I do not doubt that, where such conduct is persisted in, so as to make it evident that the seller does not intend to fulfil his contract, the purchaser may rescind the contract and refuse to take further deliveries.'[62] Only in exceptional circumstances would delay in payment justify the seller in rescinding the contract.[63]

16.42 Rights of Seller: Refusal of Acceptance.—Questions as to the rights of the seller arise where the buyer wrongfully refuses to accept the goods, or when he fails to pay the price. In the case of refusal to accept and pay for the goods the seller may maintain an action of damages for non-acceptance, the measure of damages being, if there is an available market for the goods,[64] the difference between the contract price and the market price ruling at the date when the goods ought to have been

[60] *Shaw, Macfarlane & Co.* v. *Waddell* (1900) 2 F. 1070.
[61] *Macbride* v. *Hamilton* (1875) 2 R. 775.
[62] *Govan Rope Co.* v. *Weir* (1897) 24 R. 368; *per* Lord McLaren. See *Dunford & Elliot* v. *Macleod & Co.* (1902) 4 F. 912; *Mersey Steel Co.* v. *Naylor Benzon & Co.* (1884) 9 App. Cas. 434; *Maple Flock Co.* v. *Universal Furniture Products* [1934] 1 K.B. 148; *Regent OHG Aisenstadt und Barig* v. *Francesco of Jermyn Street Ltd.* [1981] 3 All E.R. 327.
[63] s. 10(1); *Barclay* v. *Anderston Foundry Co.* (1856) 18 D. 1190; *Linn* v. *Shields* (1863) 2 M. 88.
[64] *Thompson* v. *Robinson* [1955] Ch. 177 (where there was no available market); *Charter* v. *Sullivan* [1957] 2 Q.B. 117. *Cf. Lazenby Garages* v. *Wright* [1976] 1 W.L.R. 459.

accepted [50]. He is also entitled to a reasonable charge for the care and custody of the goods [37]. Refusal by the buyer, either to accept the goods or to pay the price, would seem to amount to a repudiation of the contract by him, which would justify the seller in an immediate resale, preferably under a warrant from the sheriff.[65]

16.43 Failure in Payment.—Where the buyer fails to pay the price we have to consider (a) the seller's right of action; and (b) his rights over the goods.

If the property in the goods has passed to the buyer, *i.e.* if the contract was a sale, as contrasted with an agreement to sell, the seller may maintain an action for the price [49 (1)]. He may also do so if the price was payable on a day certain,[66] irrespective of delivery, although the property in the goods has not passed, and the goods have not been appropriated to the contract [49 (2)]. In other cases his action is for damages for non-acceptance [50]. Mere failure to pay the price does not entitle the seller to rescind the contract and demand redelivery of the goods after the property has passed to the buyer.[67] But if the contract was induced by fraud, the seller may reduce it and recover the goods in a question either with the buyer himself or with the trustee in his sequestration, and it is sufficient proof of fraud if it be established that the buyer bought the goods without any intention to pay for them.[68]

16.44 Rights of Unpaid Seller over Goods.—The rights of a seller over the goods are dealt with in Part V of the Act, under the heading 'Rights of Unpaid Seller against the Goods.'[69] A seller is deemed to be unpaid (a) when the whole of the price has not been paid or tendered; (b) when a bill of exchange or other negotiable instrument has been received as conditional payment, and the condition on which it was received has not been fulfilled by reason of the dishonour of the instrument or otherwise [38].[70] The unpaid seller may have one or more of the following rights: lien; stoppage in transit; resale.

16.45 Lien.—Lien is the right of the seller while still in possession of the goods (whether the property has passed or not) to retain them until payment or tender of the price, in the following cases: (a) where the goods have been sold without any stipulation as to credit; (b) where the goods have been sold on credit but the period of credit has expired; (c) where the buyer becomes insolvent [41]. A buyer is deemed to be insolvent if he either has ceased to pay his debts in the ordinary course

[65] Bell, *Prin.*, § 128.
[66] On meaning of 'a day certain,' see *Henderson & Keay Ltd.* v. *A.M. Carmichael Ltd.*, 1956 S.L.T. (Notes) 58.
[67] *Muirhead & Turnbull* v. *Dickson* (1905) 7 F. 686.
[68] *Gamage* v. *Charlesworth's Tr.*, 1910 S.C. 257.
[69] See Gow, pp. 186 *et seq.*
[70] *McDowall & Neilson's Tr.* v. *Snowball Co.* (1904) 7 F. 35.

of business or cannot pay his debts as they become due [61 (4)]. A right of lien is lost (a) when the seller delivers the goods to a carrier for the purpose of transmission to the buyer without reserving the right of disposal; (b) when the buyer or his agent lawfully obtains possession of the goods[71]; (c) by waiver [43]. A right of lien is not affected by the fact that the buyer may have resold or pledged[72] the goods to a third party [47]. But in a case before the 1893 Act it was held that where A had sold to B on a month's credit and B resold to C, who intimated the subsale to A within the month, A had waived his right of lien in a question with C and must deliver to him, although B was bankrupt and could not pay A.[73] And if the buyer had obtained a document of title to the goods, and that document had been transferred to a person who took it in good faith,[74] and for valuable consideration, then if that transfer was by way of sale the original seller's right of lien is defeated, while if it was by way of pledge, the right of lien can only be exercised subject to the rights of the pledgee [47]. Delivery of part of the goods does not preclude the exercise of lien over the remainder [42].

16.46 Stoppage in Transit.—Stoppage in transit, formerly known as stoppage *in transitu*, is a principle which was introduced into the law of Scotland by the decision of the House of Lords in *Jaffrey* v. *Allan, Stewart & Co.*,[75] in place of a doctrine, which was then disapproved, that if a buyer took delivery of goods within three days of stopping payment (*intra triduum*) he was presumed to have taken them fraudulently, and the seller could recover them in a question with the trustee in his sequestration.

The right of stoppage in transit, as now regulated by the Act, is the right of an unpaid seller, in the case where the property has passed to the buyer, and the goods are in course of transit to him, to resume possession, and to retain the goods until payment or tender of the price [44]. Where the property has not passed to the buyer the unpaid seller has a right of withholding delivery similar to and co-extensive with the right of stoppage in transit [39 (2)]. The right of stoppage can be exercised only when the buyer becomes insolvent.[76] If the seller stops the goods and is unable to prove that the buyer is insolvent he is liable in damages.

Stoppage in transit may be effected either by taking actual possession of the goods, or by giving notice to the carrier requiring him to re-deliver the goods to the seller, at the latter's expense [46]. Notice may

---

[71] But where a seller retakes possession from the buyer, he does not necessarily regain his right of lien: *London Scottish Transport* v. *Tyres (Scotland) Ltd.*, 1957 S.L.T. (Sh.Ct.) 48; *Hostess Mobile Catering* v. *Archibald Scott Ltd.*, 1981 S.C. 185.

[72] Since *ex hypothesi* the seller is still in possession and pledge requires delivery (para. 19.10, *infra*), the circumstances in which the buyer can pledge must be exceptional.

[73] *Fleming* v. *Smith* (1881) 8 R. 548.

[74] As to the meaning of 'good faith,' see *supra*, para. 16.22.

[75] (1790) 3 Paton 191.

[76] As to the meaning of 'insolvency,' see *supra*, para. 16.45.

be given either to the actual custodier, or to his principal, *e.g.* to the shipping company. In the latter case it must be given in time to allow of communication with the actual custodier [46 (3)]. Where the contract of carriage has been made by the buyer, the seller, by giving notice to stop, incurs personal liability for the freight.[77] If the carrier disregards the notice, and delivers the goods to the buyer, the stoppage is defeated, and the goods fall to be treated as part of the assets in the buyer's sequestration, but the carrier is liable in damages to the seller.[78]

Stoppage in transit is competent only while the goods are in transit. The Act deals with the duration of the transit in seven rules [45]. These should be referred to, but it may be convenient to state the general law. The transit may end either at the actual place of delivery or when the buyer or his agent obtains possession at some intermediate place. Actual delivery is not necessary to end the transit, if the carrier acknowledges to the buyer that he holds the goods for him after their arrival at the place of destination. So where goods were sent by rail to a particular station, and the consignee there signed a receipt for them but did not take them away, it was held that the transit had ended, and that a subsequent notice to stop came too late.[79] There is no room for stoppage in transit if the buyer sends for the goods. If he charters a ship the goods are in his custody, and cannot therefore be stopped, as soon as they are put on board.[80] But the duration of the transit is not affected by the fact that the contract of carriage with the shipowner is made by the buyer, if the ship is not chartered by him in such a way as to make the captain of the ship his servant.[81]

If part of the goods is delivered to the buyer, the remainder may be stopped, unless the part delivery has been made in such circumstances as to show an agreement to give up possession of the whole [45 (7)]. When two lifeboats arrived by rail at Sunderland station, and one of them was delivered to a carter who had general instructions to take all goods arriving for the consignee, and the other would have been delivered to the carter if he had had room for it, it was held that the circumstances did not show an agreement by the railway company to give up possession of the second boat, and that it might still be stopped in transit.[82] Rules, similar to those applicable to lien,[83] apply where a document of title has been transferred to a third party either as a sub-purchaser or as a pledgee.

16.47 Resale.—The unpaid seller, if in possession of the goods, either under lien or after he has stopped them in transit, is entitled to resell them

[77] *Booth Co.* v. *Cargo Fleet Iron Co.* [1916] 2 K.B. 570.
[78] *Mechan* v. *N.-E. Ry.,* 1911 S.C. 1348.
[79] *Muir* v. *Rankin* (1905) 13 S.L.T. 60.
[80] *Rosevear China Clay Co.* (1879) 11 Ch.D. 560.
[81] *Booth Co.* v. *Cargo Fleet Iron Co.* [1916] 2 K.B. 570.
[82] *Mechan* v. *N.-E. Ry.,* 1911 S.C. 1348.
[83] s. 47, and see *supra*, para. 16.45.

either if they are perishable or if he has given notice to the buyer of his intention to resell, and the buyer does not within a reasonable time pay or tender the price. The contract of sale is not rescinded by the exercise of a right of lien or of stoppage in transit [48(1)] but, if the seller then resells, the contract is rescinded, whether the resale is of the whole of the goods or part of them, and the property in them reverts to the seller who may then recover from the original buyer damages for non-acceptance [48 (3)].[84] If the seller expressly reserves the right of resale in case the buyer should make default, and, on the buyer making default, resells, the original contract of sale is rescinded, without prejudice to any claim the seller may have for damages [48 (4)]. In all cases of resale the buyer obtains a good title to the goods as against the original buyer [48 (2)].

16.48 **Auction Sales.**—The law of sale by auction is regulated by section 57. *Prima facie* each lot is to be regarded as a separate contract of sale. So it was held that where wine was sold in lots the purchaser was entitled to reject lots which were defective and to keep the rest.[85]

A sale by auction is complete when the auctioneer announces its completion by the fall of the hammer. Until such announcement is made any bidder may retract his bid [57 (2)]. The common law, which will still rule in sales to which the Act does not apply, *e.g.* sales of heritage, was not settled, but probably was that a bid could not be retracted, unless it were refused, or a higher bid made.[86] It has been held to follow from the statutory provision that as each bidder may retract his bid the exposer has a corresponding right to withdraw the article even after the bidding has commenced.[87]

A reserve price is lawful [57 (3)] but, unless the right of the seller to bid is expressly reserved, it is unlawful and may be treated as fraudulent for him to bid or to employ anyone else, commonly spoken of as a white-bonnet, to bid for him [57 (4), (5)]. Should it transpire that fraudulent bids of this kind have been made, the highest bona fide bidder is entitled to the article at the last bid he made before the fraudulent bidding commenced.[88] If, however, the objection to the sale is merely that a person has made bids who was not entitled to do so, and there is no proof of fraud, the bidder to whom the article is ultimately adjudged must pay the full price he has offered.[89] But if the party disqualified proves to be the highest bidder the sale is open to reduction by other bidders or by anyone who can show an interest in obtaining the highest possible price.[90] It is a general rule that a party

[84] *R.V. Ward* v. *Bignall* [1967] 1 Q.B. 534.
[85] *Couston, Thomson & Co.* v. *Chapman* (1872) 10 M. (H.L.) 74.
[86] *Cree* v. *Durie*, 1st December, 1810, F.C.
[87] *Fenwick* v. *Macdonald, Fraser & Co.* (1904) 6 F. 850.
[88] *Faulds* v. *Corbet* (1859) 21 D. 587.
[89] *Wishart* v. *Howatson* (1897) 5 S.L.T. 84.
[90] *Shiell* v. *Guthrie's Trs.* (1874) 1 R. 1083.

directly interested in the sale is not entitled to bid. So a beneficiary may not bid in a sale by a trustee,[91] and one of several part-owners is equally disqualified.[92] It is doubtful whether the creditor in a bond and disposition in security, exposing the subjects for sale under the powers in his bond, is entitled to bid; in any event the disqualification does not apply where there are several creditors, and bids are made by one.[93]

It has twice been held in Scotland that when an intending bidder bribed others not to compete with him his conduct amounted to fraud on the exposer, which entitled the latter to reduce the sale and recover the expenses of it from the party implicated.[94] It was decided in England that such an agreement was not a *pactum illicitum*, and that its conditions could be enforced by the parties to it *inter se*.[95] However, by the Auctions (Bidding Agreements) Act 1927, if any dealer[96] agrees to give, or gives, or offers to give, any gift or consideration to any other person as a reward for abstaining, or for having abstained, from bidding at a sale by auction, he and any person who agrees to accept, or accepts, or attempts to obtain, any such gift commits a criminal offence. Where goods are purchased at an auction by a person who has entered into an agreement with another or others that the other or others (or some of them) will abstain from bidding for the goods (not being an agreement to purchase the goods bona fide on joint account) and he or the other party, or one of the other parties, to the agreement is a dealer, the seller may avoid the contract under which the goods were purchased. If restitution of the goods is not made, the parties to the bidding agreement are jointly and severally liable to make good to the seller the loss (if any) he sustained by reason of the operation of the agreement.[97] It is also an offence to permit or conduct an auction where (a) any person bidding has an article in a lot sold to him for less than his highest bid for that lot; or (b) part of the price at which it was sold is repaid or credited to him; or (c) the right to bid for any lot is restricted to persons who have bought or agreed to buy one or more articles; or (d) any articles are given away or offered as gifts.[98]

An auctioneer is entitled to give notice that he will not receive bids from particular parties, or from parties representing a particular interest, and his refusal of their bids does not constitute an actionable wrong.[99]

16.49   Sale or Return: Sale on Approval.—The contract of sale or return is usually entered into when goods are supplied by a wholesaler to a retail

[91] *Shiell, supra.*
[92] *Morrice* v. *Craig* (1902) 39 S.L.R. 609.
[93] *Wright* v. *Buchanan,* 1917 S.C. 73. As to a sale by a permanent trustee in a sequestration, see Bankruptcy (Scotland) Act 1985, s. 39(8).
[94] *Murray* v. *McWhan* (1783) Mor. 9567; *Aitchison* (1783) Mor. 9567.
[95] *Rawlings* v. *General Trading Co.* [1921] 1 K.B. 635.
[96] Defined as 'a person who in the normal course of his business attends sales by auction for the purpose of purchasing goods with a view to reselling them.'
[97] Auctions (Bidding Agreements) Act 1969, s. 3.
[98] Mock Auctions Act 1961. See *Allen* v. *Simmons* [1978] 1 W.L.R. 879.
[99] *Scottish Co-operative Society* v. *Glasgow Fleshers* (1898) 35 S.L.R. 645.

dealer on the condition, variously expressed, that the latter may sell
them to his customers, but has the option to return them. A sale on
approval implies that possession of an article is given, with an
unqualified option to buy it or to return it within a specified period.
When a horse was sold with a warranty, and delivered on a week's trial,
it was held that the contract was not a sale on approval. The buyer's
option to return the horse within the week was not unqualified: he could
do so only if it failed to fulfil the warranty.[1]

In the question of the passing of the property in the goods the
contracts of sale or return and sale on approval are dealt with in the
same subsection of the Act [18, Rule 4]: 'When goods are delivered to
the buyer on approval or on sale or return or other similar terms the
property in the goods passes to the buyer:—(a) when he signifies his
approval or acceptance to the seller or does any other act adopting the
transaction; (b) if he does not signify his approval or acceptance to the
seller but retains the goods without giving notice of rejection, then, if a
time has been fixed for the return of the goods, on the expiration of
that time, and, if no time has been fixed, on the expiration of a
reasonable time.'[2] In certain cases the retail dealer, having obtained
goods on sale or return, has pawned them, and the question of the title
of the pawnbroker in a question with the wholesale dealer has been
raised. If the contract merely provides that the retail dealer may sell the
goods or may return them it is probably established that by pawning
them (although fraudulently) he does an act adopting the transaction,
the property passes to him, and the pawnbroker obtains a good title.[3]
The wholesale dealer may seek to protect himself by stipulating that,
before disposing of any article, the retail dealer must have it invoiced by
him. In *Bryce* v. *Erhmann*[4] opinions were expressed that in spite of such
a clause a pawnbroker would obtain a good title but, in view of a
contrary English decision,[5] the law cannot be regarded as settled. Goods
on sale or return do not pass to the trustee in the sequestration of the
retail dealer,[6] nor, it is conceived, could they be attached by his
creditors by poinding. But as *invecta et illata* they are possibly covered
by the landlord's hypothec, and could be attached by him by
sequestration.[7]

16.50 **Sale: f.o.b.; c.i.f.**—In sale f.o.b. (free on board) or, in inland carriage,
f.o.r. (free on rail) the seller undertakes to ship the goods at the port of
shipment, or to load them at the station named, the expense of the
carriage, and of insurance, falling upon the buyer, on whom the risk

---

[1] *Cranston* v. *Mallow*, 1912 S.C. 112.
[2] See *Poole* v. *Smith's Car Sales* [1962] 1 W.L.R. 744.
[3] *Bryce* v. *Ehrmann* (1904) 7 F. 5; *Kirkham* v. *Attenborough* [1897] 1 Q.B. 201.
[4] *Kirkham* v. *Attenborough, supra.*
[5] *Weiner* v. *Gill* [1906] 2 K.B. 574.
[6] *Macdonald* v. *Westren* (1888) 15 R. 988.
[7] See para. 33.13, *infra.*

falls. The property in the goods may not pass to the buyer on shipment if the seller has reserved a right of disposal by taking the bill of lading with the goods deliverable to the seller or his agent.[8] Any charge necessarily payable before the goods are put on board, such as an export duty newly imposed, falls upon the seller.[9]

A sale c.i.f. (cost, insurance, freight) imports that the price includes the freight of the goods to their destination, and their insurance during transit. If, as is usual, the arrangement with the shipowner is that the freight is to be paid by the buyer or consignee on delivery of the goods, the amount is deducted from the invoice price. The obligation of the seller, in a contract c.i.f., is to ship the goods and transmit to the buyer the shipping documents, these being an invoice, a bill of lading and a policy of insurance. When these are sent to the buyer the property and risk pass to him[10] unless a contrary intention appears from the conduct of the parties and the circumstances of the case.[11] On tender of the shipping documents the buyer is bound to pay the price, and is not entitled to withhold payment until the goods arrive and he has had an opportunity of examining them.[12] Refusal to pay on presentation of the documents is a fundamental breach of contract.[13] But payment of the price does not imply acceptance of the goods, and if they arrive and are disconform to contract, the buyer may still reject them, and recover the price or damages.[14] If the goods are lost in transit the buyer cannot recover the price; his remedy lies in the policy of insurance.[15] When timber in New Brunswick was sold 'c.i.f. Glasgow' it was decided, in a question of stoppage *in transitu*, that it was in course of transit until it reached Glasgow, in spite of the fact that in the contract it was stated to be 'deliverable' at a New Brunswick port.[16]

A development of the c.i.f. contract is that the buyer agrees to open in favour of the seller a confirmed banker's credit on which the seller may draw on presentation of the shipping documents, possibly with other documents.[17] The buyer is bound to keep the credit open during the whole period allowed for shipping.[18]

---

[8] 1979 Act, s. 19; *Mitsui & Co. Ltd.* v. *Flota Mercante Grancolombiana S.A.* [1988] 1 W.L.R. 1145, C.A.

[9] *Bowhill Coal Co.* v. *Tobias* (1902) 5 F. 262.

[10] *Delaurier* v. *Wyllie* (1889) 17 R. 167.

[11] *The Albazero* [1977] A.C. 774.

[12] *Horst* v. *Biddel* [1912] A.C. 18.

[13] *Berger & Co. Inc.* v. *Gill & Duffus S.A.* [1984] A.C. 382.

[14] *Pommer* v. *Mowat* (1906) 14 S.L.T. 373; *Harrower, Welsh & Co.* v. *McWilliam*, 1928 S.C. 326; *Kwei Tek Chao* v. *British Traders and Shippers Ltd.* [1954] 2 Q.B. 459.

[15] *Delaurier* v. *Wyllie* (1889) 17 R. 167; *Manbre Saccharine Co.* v. *Corn Products Co.* [1919] 1 K.B. 198.

[16] *McDowall & Neilson's Tr.* v. *Snowball Co.* (1904) 7 F. 35.

[17] *Pavia & Co., S.P.A.* v. *Thurmann-Neilsen* [1952] 2 Q.B. 84; *Trans Trust S.P.R.L.* v. *Danubian Trading Co.* [1952] 2 Q.B. 297; *United City Merchants (Investments) Ltd.* v. *Royal Bank of Canada* [1983] 1 A.C. 168, *per* Lord Diplock at pp. 182–188. As to incorporation of the Uniform Customs and Practice for Documentary Credits, see *Forestal Mimosa Ltd.* v. *Oriental Credit Ltd.* [1986] 1 W.L.R. 631.

[18] *Ibid.*

16.51 **Hire-Purchase.**—The term 'hire-purchase' is commonly used to describe a variety of different types of agreement. Strictly, however, a contract of hire-purchase is one under which articles are taken on hire and the hirer is granted the option to purchase them on his fulfilling certain conditions of the contract.[19] This type of contract is to be contrasted with a contract of sale under which the buyer and seller are under binding obligations to each other respectively to buy and to sell.[20] Accordingly, if the terms of the hire-purchase agreement in any way bind the hirer to purchase the article hired, the contract is one of sale, not of hire-purchase.[21] This distinction is of importance in considering whether a hirer has conferred a good title upon an innocent third party to whom he has purported to sell the article hired. If the contract is only one of hire-purchase, the third party does not obtain a good title.[22] If on the other hand, it is one of sale, the hirer is a person who has bought or agreed to buy goods and is in possession of them with the consent of the owner; and under the provisions of section 25(1) of the Sale of Goods Act[23] he has the power to give a good title to the third party.[24] But where the contract is truly one of hire-purchase, the hirer has the right to acquire the article by completing the payments and this right he may assign to a third party. If he sells the article, at least if there is no proof that in doing so he acted fraudulently, it will be assumed that he transferred all the right he possessed, and the purchaser from him, though he will not get a complete title to the article, will be entitled to retain it and complete his right by payment of the remaining instalments of the hire-purchase, provided that there is no term in the agreement forbidding assignation.[25] Articles on hire-purchase do not pass to the trustee in the hirer's sequestration,[26] but presumably he has the power to adopt the contract and acquire them by completing the payments. They fall under the landlord's hypothec.[27]

Part III of the Hire-Purchase Act 1964[28] provides that where the hirer of a motor vehicle under a hire-purchase agreement or the buyer of such a vehicle under a conditional sale agreement disposes of the vehicle to a

[19] Compare, however, the definition of 'hire-purchase agreement' in the Consumer Credit Act 1974, s. 189.

[20] *Murdoch* v. *Greig* (1889) 16 R. 396, especially *per* Lord President Inglis at p. 400, and *per* Lord Shand at p. 402.

[21] The court will examine the substance of each agreement carefully to see whether it is one of hire-purchase or sale, whatever its terms: *Murdoch* v. *Greig, supra*; *Scottish Transit Trust* v. *Scottish Land Cultivators*, 1955 S.C. 254.

[22] *Helby* v. *Matthews* [1895] A.C. 471. Motor vehicles are now a statutory exception where sold to a private purchaser by the hirer: Hire Purchase Act 1964, Pt. III; see *infra*.

[23] See *supra*, para. 16.21.

[24] *Lee* v. *Butler* [1893] 2 Q.B. 318. But see para. 16.21, *supra* as to conditional sales which are subject to the Consumer Credit Act 1974.

[25] *Whiteley* v. *Hilt* [1918] 2 K.B. 808.

[26] Stewart, *Diligence*, pp. 341–43.

[27] *Rudman* v. *Jay*, 1908 S.C. 552.

[28] As substituted by Consumer Credit Act 1974, Sched. 4, para. 22.

private purchaser[29] who purchases in good faith and without notice[30] of the said agreement, the disposition has effect as if the title of the owner or seller to the vehicle had been vested in the hirer or buyer, immediately before the disposition.[31]

The Supply of Goods (Implied Terms) Act 1973 (as amended by the Consumer Credit Act 1974, Sched. 4, para. 35), sections 8 to 11, imposes implied stipulations as to the title, description, quality and fitness of goods let on hire-purchase, corresponding to those implied in the sale of goods. Section 20 of the Unfair Contract Terms Act 1977 applies to these terms.[32]

16.52 Contracts for the Transfer of Goods.—The Supply of Goods and Services Act 1982[33] provides for comparable terms to be implied into contracts for the transfer of goods. A contract is a contract for the transfer of goods if one person transfers or agrees to transfer to another the property in the goods.[34] It is irrelevant whether services are also provided under the contract. Nor is the nature of the consideration important. Contracts for the sale of goods, hire purchase agreements, contracts involving the exchange of trading stamps, gratuitous contracts and security contracts are excluded. The Act will principally apply to contracts involving barter, trading-in and the use of tokens or coupons in exchange for goods. Implied terms relating to title, description, quality or fitness and conformity of samples[35] may apply in a similar manner to the Sale of Goods legislation. Similar remedies are also applicable.[36]

Further Reading

Atiyah, *Sale of Goods* (8th ed., 1990).
Benjamin's *Sale of Goods* (3rd ed., 1987).
Brown, *Sale of Goods* (2nd ed., 1911).
Chalmers, *Sale of Goods Act 1979* (18th ed., 1981).
Goode, *Commercial Law* (1982), Pts. 2 and 4.
J.J. Gow, *Mercantile and Industrial Law of Scotland* (1964).

---

[29] To be contrasted with a 'trade or finance purchaser': s. 27(3). A person who carries on a part-time business of buying and selling motor-vehicles is a 'trade or finance purchaser' even in relation to a vehicle he acquires for his own private use: *Stevenson* v. *Beverley Bentinck* [1976] 1 W.L.R. 483.

[30] Notice of a prior hire-purchase agreement which has been paid off does not affect the private purchaser's title: *Barker* v. *Bell* [1971] 1 W.L.R. 983.

[31] It is doubtful whether, in Scotland, the person who let the vehicle on hire has any remedy against a trade purchaser, who, having acquired the vehicle in good faith from the hirer, resells it to a private purchaser, who thus may acquire a good title: *North-West Securities* v. *Barrhead Coachworks*, 1976 S.C. 68. *Cf. Finance* v. *Langtry Investment Co.*, 1973 S.L.T. (Sh.Ct.) 11, where the doctrine of *specificatio* was applied. For the English position, see *Moorgate Mercantile Co.* v. *Twitchings* [1977] A.C. 890.

[32] See para. 16.32, *supra.*

[33] Part 1A, introduced by the 1994 Act, s. 6 and Sched. 1.

[34] 1982 Act, s. 11A.

[35] 1982 Act, ss. 11B, 11C, 11D and 11E.

[36] 1982 Act, s. 11F.

CHAPTER 17

CONSUMER PROTECTION

The Unfair Contract Terms Act 1977 has already been discussed. In this chapter some miscellaneous statutory provisions are collected. No attempt is made to deal with the Food Safety Act 1990 or the Weights and Measures Acts.

17.1 Unsolicited Goods and Services.—A person who receives unsolicited goods may, as between himself and the sender, treat them as if they were an unconditional gift to him and any right of the sender to the goods is extinguished if the following conditions are satisfied: (i) the goods were sent to the recipient with a view to his acquiring them; (ii) the recipient has no reasonable cause to believe that they were sent with a view to their being acquired for the purposes of a trade or business and has neither agreed to acquire nor agreed to return them; (iii) the sender has not taken possession of the goods and the recipient did not unreasonably refuse to permit the sender to do so in the period of six months beginning with the day of receipt; (iv) not less than 30 days before the expiration of the six months the recipient gave written notice to the sender of the location of the goods and of the fact that they are unsolicited and the sender has not within the 30 days following the notice taken or tried to take possession of the goods.[1] It is an offence to demand payment or to assert a right to payment or to attempt to enforce payment for goods which are known to be unsolicited.[2] A person is not liable to make payment for inclusion of an entry relating to him in a directory unless an order or note satisfying specified requirements has been signed by him.[3] It is an offence to send or cause to be sent to another person, in the knowledge that it is unsolicited, a book, magazine or leaflet which describes or illustrates human sexual techniques or advertising material for such a publication.[4] An invoice or similar document stating the amount of any payment is regarded as asserting a right to payment unless it complies with the Unsolicited Goods and Services (Invoices, etc.) Regulations 1975.[5]

---

[1] Unsolicited Goods and Services Act 1971, s. 1.
[2] s. 2; *Readers Digest Association* v. *Pirie*, 1973 J.C. 42.
[3] An attempt to recover payment is again an offence.
[4] s. 4; *Director of Public Prosecutions* v. *Beate Uhse (U.K.)* [1974] Q.B. 158.
[5] S.I. 1975 No. 732; ss. 3A, 6 (2), as added by Unsolicited Goods and Services (Amendment) Act 1975.

17.2 Trade Descriptions Act 1968.—The Act makes it an offence to misdescribe goods or services or to give false indications as to the price of goods. A contract for the supply of any goods is not void or unenforceable by reason only of a contravention of the Act.[6]

It is an offence for a person in the course of a trade or business[7] to apply a false trade description to any goods or to supply or offer to supply any goods to which a false trade description is applied at the time of supply or has been so applied in the course of negotiations leading to such supply.[8] A person exposing goods for supply or having goods in his possession for supply is deemed to offer to supply them. The offence of applying a false trade description may be committed by a buyer if he is acting in the course of a trade or business[9] but the offence is not committed by a description given incidentally in the course of performance of the service of advising in regard to some matter affecting the goods.[10] A statement made after the sale or supply cannot give rise to an offence.[11]

A trade description is an indication, direct or indirect, and by whatever means given, of the quantity, composition,[12] fitness for purpose or other specified characteristics of the goods.[13] The mileage recorded on the mileometer of a car may be a trade description. [14] 'Extra value' on the wrapper of a bar of chocolate is not a trade description.[15]

17.3 False Description.—A false trade description is a trade description which is false to a material degree.[16] A trade description which, though not false, is misleading, *i.e.* likely to be taken for such an indication of the specified matters as would be false to a material degree, is deemed to be a false trade description.[17] Anything which, though not a trade description, is likely to be taken for an indication of any of the specified matters, and, as such an indication, would be false to a material degree, is deemed to be a false trade description.[18] An indication which appears

---

[6] 1968 Act, s. 35.
[7] See *Havering London Borough Council* v. *Stevenson* [1970] 1 W.L.R. 1375. *Cf. Davies* v. *Sumner* [1984] 1 W.L.R. 1301; *Blakemore* v. *Bellamy* [1983] R.T.R. 303.
[8] s. 1 (1); *Norman* v. *Bennett* [1974] 1 W.L.R. 1229.
[9] *Fletcher* v. *Budgen* [1974] 1 W.L.R. 1056.
[10] *Wycombe Marsh Garages* v. *Fowler* [1972] 1 W.L.R. 1156.
[11] *Hall* v. *Wickens Motors (Gloucester)* [1972] 1 W.L.R. 1418. *Cf. Fletcher* v. *Sledmore* [1973] R.T.R. 371.
[12] See *British Gas Corporation* v. *Lubbock* [1974] 1 W.L.R. 37.
[13] s. 2(1).
[14] *McNab* v. *Alexanders of Greenock*, 1971 S.L.T. 121; *Tarleton Engineering Co.* v. *Nattrass* [1973] 1 W.L.R. 1261.
[15] *Cadbury* v. *Halliday* [1975] 1 W.L.R. 649. *Cf. Robertson* v. *Dicicco* [1972] R.T.R. 431 ('beautiful car').
[16] s. 3(1).
[17] s. 3(2); *R.* v. *Inner London Justices, ex p. Wandsworth L.B.C.* [1983] R.T.R. 425 ('one owner').
[18] s. 3(3).

to be a false trade description may be shown not to be by a disclaimer which is as bold, precise and compelling as the indication itself, and which is effectively brought to the notice of any person to whom the goods may be supplied.[19]

17.4 Applying Description.—A person applies a trade description to goods if he:

'(*a*) affixes or annexes it to or in any manner marks it on or incorporates it with—

    (i) the goods themselves, or

    (ii) anything in, on or with which the goods are supplied; or

(*b*) places the goods in, on or with anything which the trade description has been affixed or annexed to, marked on or incorporated with, or places any such thing with the goods; or

(*c*) uses the trade description in any manner likely to be taken as referring to the goods'[20] [4(1)].

An oral statement may amount to the use of a trade description.[21] Where goods are supplied in pursuance of a request in which a trade description is used and the circumstances are such as to make it reasonable to infer that the goods are supplied as goods corresponding to that description, the supplier is deemed to have applied that description to the goods.[22] Where a trade description is used in relation to any class of goods in an advertisement, it is taken as referring to all goods of the class, whether or not in existence at the time the advertisement is published.[23] Repairs carried out in such a way as to conceal a defect in the goods may result in a false trade description but it is not 'applied' by someone who did not carry out the repairs and who was unaware of the defect.[24]

17.5 Services.—It is an offence for a person in the course of a trade or business to make a statement which he knows to be false or recklessly to make a statement which is false as to the provision, nature, time of provision, or evaluation of any services,[25] accommodation or facilities[26]

---

[19] *Norman* v. *Bennett, supra*; *R.* v. *Hammertons Cars* [1976] 1 W.L.R. 1243. See also *Doble* v. *David Greig* [1972] 1 W.L.R. 703; *Zawadski* v. *Sleigh* [1975] R.T.R. 113.

[20] See *Rees* v. *Munday* [1974] 1 W.L.R. 1284.

[21] s. 4(2).

[22] s. 4(3).

[23] s. 5.

[24] *Cottee* v. *Douglas Seaton (Used Cars) Ltd.* [1972] 1 W.L.R. 1408. See also *Donnelly* v. *Rowlands* [1970] 1 W.L.R. 1600.

[25] A statement as to the qualifications of the person providing services is a statement as to the provision of the services; *R.* v. *Breeze* [1973] 1 W.L.R. 994.

[26] 'Facilities' is to be construed *ejusdem generis* with 'services' and 'accommodation' and does not cover a closing down sale: *Westminster City Council* v. *Ray Allan Manshops Ltd.* [1982] 1 W.L.R. 383.

provided in the course of any trade or business[27] or as to the location or
amenities of any accommodation so provided.[28] Anything likely to be
taken for such a statement as would be false is deemed to be a false
statement;[29] 'false' means false to a material degree.[30] There is an
offence if the person had no knowledge of the falsity of the statement at
the time of its publication but knew of the falsity when it was read by a
customer.[31] Where services involve the application of any treatment or
process or the carrying out of any repair, statements as to the effect
thereof are covered by the section.[32] A statement made regardless of
whether it is true or false is deemed to be made recklessly, whether or
not the person making it had reasons for believing that it might be
false.[33] The statement need not be one inducing entry to the contract
and can be one made after the contract is concluded.[34] A promise,
forecast or warranty cannot be a false statement[35] but a statement of
present intention can be false and such a statement may be implied in a
promise or forecast.[36] Where the false statement is in a brochure, as
many offences are committed as there are readers.[37]

17.6 **Defences.**—In any proceedings under the Act it is a defence that the
commission of the offence was due to a mistake or to reliance on
information supplied or to the act or default of another person, an
accident or some other cause beyond the control of the person charged
and that he took all reasonable precautions and exercised all due
diligence to avoid the commission of such an offence by himself or any
person under his control.[38] The mistake must be that of the person
charged.[39] The act or default relied on may be that of a manager or
servant; but where the accused is a body corporate the other person
cannot be a director, manager, secretary or similar officer.[40] It is a
defence to a charge of supplying or offering to supply goods to which a
false trade description is applied that the person charged did not know,
and could not with reasonable diligence have ascertained, that the goods

---

[27] The statement may be about services to be proved by someone other than the person
making the statement: *Banbury* v. *Hounslow London Borough Council* [1978] R.T.R. 1.

[28] s. 14(1).

[29] s. 14(2)(*a*); *R.* v. *Clarksons Holidays* (1972) 57 Cr. App. R. 38.

[30] s. 14(4).

[31] *Wings Ltd.* v. *Ellis* [1985] 1 A.C. 272.

[32] s. 14(3).

[33] s. 14(2)(*b*). See *M.F.I. Warehouses* v. *Nattrass* [1973] 1 W.L.R. 307.

[34] *Breed* v. *Cluett* [1970] 2 Q.B. 459.

[35] *Beckett* v. *Cohen* [1972] 1 W.L.R. 1593.

[36] *British Airways Board* v. *Taylor* [1976] 1 W.L.R. 13; *R.* v. *Sunair Holidays* [1973] 1
W.L.R. 1105.

[37] *R.* v. *Thomson Holidays* [1974] Q.B. 592; appvd. *Wings Ltd.* v. *Ellis, supra.*

[38] s. 24(1); *Aitchison* v. *Reith and Anderson (Dingwall and Tain) Ltd.*, 1974 J.C. 12;
Costello v. *Lowe*, 1986 J.C. 231; *London Borough of Ealing Trading Standards Dept.* v.
Taylor [1995] Crim.L.R. 166.

[39] *Birkenhead and District Co-operative Society* v. *Roberts* [1970] 1 W.L.R. 1497.

[40] *Tesco Supermarkets* v. *Nattrass* [1972] A.C. 153.

did not conform to the description or that the description had been applied to the goods.[41]

17.7 Orders.—There are powers to make orders assigning definite meanings to expressions used in relation to goods, services, accommodation or facilities and an expression thus defined is deemed to have the assigned meaning for purposes of the Act when used in a trade description or in a statement about services, accommodation or facilities.[42] Orders may be made requiring that goods should be marked with or accompanied by information or instructions relating to the goods; contravention of such an order is an offence.[43] Orders may also be made requiring specified information to be included in advertisements relating to goods.[44] For purposes of the Act, goods are deemed to have been manufactured or produced in the country in which they last underwent a treatment or process resulting in a substantial change; orders may be made specifying what treatment or process is to be regarded as resulting in a substantial change and specifying what is to be regarded as the country of origin where different parts of goods are manufactured or produced in different countries.[45]

17.8 Price Indications.—It is an offence for a person to give, in the course of any business of his, to consumers an indication which is misleading as to the price at which any goods, services, accommodation or facilities are available.[46] It is also an offence to fail to take reasonable steps to prevent consumers from relying upon an indication of price which has become misleading.[47] An indication is misleading as to a price if what is conveyed by, or what consumers might reasonably be expected to infer from, the indication includes any of the following: (a) that the price is less than in fact it is; (b) that the applicability of the price does not depend on facts or circumstances on which its applicability does in fact depend; (c) that the price covers matters in respect of which an additional charge is in fact made; (d) that a person who in fact has no

---

[41] s. 24(3). See *Barker* v. *Hargreaves* [1981] R.T.R. 197; *Rotherham M.B.C.* v. *Raysun (U.K.) Ltd.* [1989] C.C.L.R. 1; *Hurley* v. *Martinez & Co. Ltd.* [1991] C.C.L.R. 1.

[42] ss. 7, 15.

[43] s. 8; Trade Descriptions (Country of Origin) (Cutlery) Order 1981 (S.I. 1981 No. 122). The Eggs (Marketing Standards) Regulations 1985 (S.I. 1985 No. 1271) and similar orders have been made under the European Communities Act 1972, s. 2.

[44] s. 9.

[45] s. 36; *e.g.* Trade Descriptions (Sealskin Goods) (Information) Order 1980 (S.I. 1980 No. 1150).

[46] Consumer Protection Act 1987, s. 20(1); see *R.* v. *Warwickshire County Council, ex p. Johnson* [1993] A.C. 583; *Toys 'R' Us* v. *Gloucestershire County Council, The Times,* February 14, 1995 in which it was held that no offence was committed when there was a discrepancy between the price displayed on an item in a shop and the price on the bar code and the shop charged the lower price. Section 22 applies the provision to services and facilities, and s. 23 applies it to accommodation. For defence, see s. 24. See also The Prices Indications (Resale of Tickets) Regulations 1994 (S.I. 1994 No. 3248), relating to reselling tickets for entertainment events.

[47] s. 20(2).

such expectation—(i) expects the price to be increased or reduced (whether or not at a particular time or by a particular amount); or (ii) expects the price, or the price as increased or reduced, to be maintained (whether or not for a particular period); or (e) that the facts or circumstances by reference to which the consumers might reasonably be expected to judge the validity of a comparison with another price or value made or implied by the indication are not what in fact they are.[48] A code of practice giving guidance as to desirable practices in the giving of price indications has been approved by the Secretary of State;[49] contraventions of, and compliance with, the code may be relied upon in criminal proceedings.[50] Where a trader charges different prices for different methods of payment he must give specified information as to this.[51]

17.9 Price Marking.—Orders may require that the price or charge is indicated on or in relation to goods which a person indicates are or may be for sale by retail and for services which a person indicates may be provided except those provided only for purposes of businesses carried on by other persons.[52] Where goods are subject to value added tax, the order may make provision as to the indication to be given of the tax included in, or payable in addition to, the price. Thus, in the case of petrol, a price including taxes and duties must be marked on the pump.[53] Orders may also be made requiring retailers to display information with respect to the range of prices at which certain goods are commonly sold by retail in the United Kingdom, or in a particular part thereof, at a particular date or during a particular period.[54]

17.10 Property Misdescriptions.—It is an offence to make a false or misleading statement about a prescribed matter in the course of an estate agency business or a property development business, other than in providing conveyancing services.[55] There is a due diligence defence.[56] The prescribed matters include the location, physical characteristics, history and price of the subjects.[57]

17.11 Fair Trading Act 1973.—The Director General of Fair Trading has a general duty to keep under review the carrying on of commercial

---

[48] s. 20(1).
[49] Code of Practice for Traders on Price Indications, annexed to S.I. 1988 No. 2078.
[50] s. 25(2).
[51] s. 26; Price Indications (Method of Payment) Regulations 1991 (S.I. 1991 No. 199).
[52] Prices Act 1974, s. 4 (as amended by Price Commission Act 1977), Price Marking Order 1991 (S.I. 1991 No. 1382 as amended by S.I. 1991 No. 1690) implementing Council Directive 79/581/EEC; see also *Allen* v. *Redbridge L.B.C.* [1994] 1 W.L.R. 139.
[53] Price Marking (Petrol) Order 1980 (S.I. 1980 No. 1121).
[54] 1974 Act, s. 5.
[55] Property Misdescriptions Act 1991, s. 1.
[56] s. 2.
[57] Property Misdescriptions (Specified Matters) Order 1992 (S.I. 1992 No. 2834).

activities which relate to goods or services supplied to consumers.[58] Under Part II of the Act the Director can initiate a procedure by which 'consumer trade practices'[59] can be regulated by an order made by the Secretary of State for Trade and Industry, a contravention of the order being a criminal offence. Several orders have been made. A person must not, in the course of a business, in a notice, advertisement, or document furnished to a consumer include a statement purporting to apply to consumer transactions a term which would be void by virtue of sections 6 or 20 of the Unfair Contract Terms Act 1977 or section 4 (1) (c) of the Trading Stamps Act 1964.[60]

A seller in the course of a business must not supply to a consumer pursuant to a consumer transaction a statement about the rights which the consumer has against him if the goods are defective unless in close proximity to the statement there is another conspicuous statement to the effect that the first mentioned statement does nct affect the rights of the consumer under the Sale of Goods Act 1979 (as amended), the Supply of Goods (Implied Terms) Act 1973 and the Trading Stamps Act 1964.[61] Similarly, a manufacturer or distributor must not furnish a guarantee, unless it includes a conspicuous statement that the statement of obligations accepted by him in relation to the goods does not affect the consumer's rights against the retailer under these statutes.[62] A mail order advertisement or catalogue must contain in legible characters the true name or registered business name of the person carrying on the mail order business and the address at which that business is managed.[63]

A person who is seeking to sell goods that are being sold in the course of a business must not publish an advertisement which indicates that the goods are for sale and which is likely to induce consumers to buy the goods unless it is reasonably clear from the contents of the advertisement, its format or size, the place or manner of its publication or otherwise that the goods are to be sold in the course of a business; this does not apply to sales by auction or competitive tender or to sales of horticultural and farm produce produced by the seller.[64]

17.12 Unfair Conduct.—If it appears to the Director General that a person in the course of carrying on a business has persisted in a course of conduct which is detrimental to the interests of, and unfair to, consumers, he may attempt to obtain from the person a satisfactory written assurance

---

[58] Fair Trading Act 1973, s. 1.

[59] As defined in s. 13.

[60] Consumer Transactions (Restrictions on Statements) Orders 1976 (S.I. 1976 No. 1813), as amended by Consumer Transactions (Restrictions on Statements) (Amendment) Order 1978 (S.I. 1978 No. 127), art. 3; *Hughes* v. *Hall* [1981] R.T.R. 430. Note, s. 4 of the Trading Stamps Act 1964 was amended by the Sale and Supply of Goods Act 1994, Sched. 2.

[61] art. 4.

[62] art. 5.

[63] Mail Order Transactions (Information) Order 1976 (S.I. 1976 No. 1812).

[64] Business Advertisements (Disclosure) Order 1977 (S.I. 1977 No. 1918).

that he will refrain from continuing that course of conduct and from carrying on any similar course of conduct in the course of that business.[65] A course of conduct is unfair if it consists of criminal offences, or breaches of contract or breaches of duties enforceable by civil proceedings.[66] If the person fails to give an assurance, or fails to observe an assurance he has given, the Director General may bring proceedings against him before the Restrictive Practices Court (or, in certain circumstances, the sheriff court[67]) which may, if no appropriate undertaking is given, make an order directing the person to refrain from continuing that, or a similar, course of conduct.[68] Where the person is a body corporate an order may be made against an officer of it, or a person controlling it, directing him to refrain from consenting to or conniving at the course of conduct in question or from carrying on any similar course of conduct in the course of any business carried on by him or from the carrying on of any such course of conduct by any other body corporate of which he is an officer or which he controls.[69]

17.13 Pyramid Selling.—Part XI of the Fair Trading Act empowers the Secretary of State to make regulations as to the practice known as 'pyramid selling.'[70]

17.14 Safety.—The Consumer Protection Act 1987, Part II, contains measures designed to prevent the supply of goods which are not safe. In what follows, 'supply' includes offering or agreeing to supply and exposing or possessing for supply. There is now a general offence of supplying unsafe goods; it is an offence to supply consumer goods which are not reasonably safe having regard to all the circumstances, including the way in which the goods are presented for marketing, any instruction or warnings given, any published safety standards and the existence of means by which it would have been reasonable for the goods to have been made safer.[71] Consumer goods are goods which are ordinarily intended for private use or consumption, not being growing crops, water, food, feeding stuff, fertiliser, gas, aircraft, motor vehicles, drugs, medicinal products or tobacco.[72] It is a defence for a retailer to show that he neither knew nor had reasonable grounds for believing that the goods were unsafe.[73] Regulations may be made to secure the safety of goods, and contravention of the regulations gives rise to criminal and

---

[65] s. 34(1) of the Fair Trading Act 1973.
[66] s. 34(2).
[67] s. 41. See Gamble, 1977 S.L.T. (News) 113; *Director General of Fair Trading* v. *Boswell*, 1978 S.L.T. (Sh. Ct.) 9.
[68] s. 37.
[69] ss. 38, 39.
[70] See Pyramid Selling Schemes Regulations 1989 (S.I. 1989 No. 2195, amended by S.I. 1990 No. 150).
[71] Consumer Protection Act 1987, s. 10(1), (2).
[72] s. 10(7).
[73] s. 10(4).

civil liability.[74] The Secretary of State may serve on a person a 'prohibition notice' prohibiting the person from supplying specified kinds of goods;[75] similarly, a 'notice to warn' may require a person to publish at his own expense a warning about goods he has supplied;[76] contravention of either type of notice is an offence.[77] An enforcement authority, if it has reasonable grounds for suspecting that a safety provision has been contravened, can serve a 'suspension notice' prohibiting the person concerned from supplying the relevant goods for a period of not more than six months without the consent of the authority;[78] contravention of a notice is an offence;[79] compensation is payable if there has in fact been no contravention of a safety provision and there has been no neglect or default on the part of the supplier.[80] The sheriff may order forfeiture for destruction of goods in relation to which there has been a contravention of a safety provision.[81] There is a defence of due diligence to the various offences.[82] Consumer safety measures may also be made under the European Communities Act 1972 to implement Community obligations.[83]

17.15   Trading Stamps.—An exchange of goods for stamps is not a sale. A 'trading stamp' is 'a stamp which is, or is intended to be, delivered to any person on or in connection with either (i) the purchase of any goods, or (ii) ... the hiring of any goods under a hire-purchase agreement (other than the purchase of a newspaper or other periodical of which the stamp forms part or in which it is contained), and is, or is intended to be, redeemable (whether singly or together with other such stamps) by that or some other person.'[84] Only a company or an industrial and provident society can carry on business as the promoter of a trading stamp scheme.[85] A stamp must bear on its face in clear and

---

[74] ss. 11(1), 12(1), 41; *e.g.* The General Product Safety Regulations 1994 (S.I. 1994 No. 2328); *R.* v. *Secretary of State for Health, ex p. United States Tobacco International Inc.* [1992] 1 Q.B. 353.

[75] s. 13(1)(*a*).

[76] s. 13(1)(*b*).

[77] s. 13(4).

[78] s. 14(1), (2); see *R.* v. *Birmingham City Council, ex p. Ferrero Ltd.* [1993] 1 All E.R. 530, that there is no duty to consult when issuing such a notice.

[79] s. 14(6)

[80] s. 14(7).

[81] s. 17.

[82] s. 39; *P. & M. Supplies (Essex) Ltd.* v. *Devon C.C.* [1991] C.C.L.R. 71; *Tesco Stores Ltd.* v. *Donnelly*, 1994 G.W.D. 27–1609; *Balding* v. *Lew Ways Ltd., The Times*, March 9, 1995, that showing compliance with a British Standard was insufficient; there had to be compliance with the regulations.

[83] *e.g.* Child Resistant Packaging and Tactile Danger Warnings (Safety) Regulations 1992 (S.I. 1992 No. 2006), implementing Council Directive 88/379/EEC and Commission Directives 90/35/EEC and 91/410/EEC; The General Product Safety Regulations 1994 (S.I. 1994 No. 2328).

[84] Trading Stamps Act 1964, s. 10.

[85] s. 1(1). (Consumer Credit Act 1974, Sched. 4, para. 26).

legible characters a value expressed in or by reference to current coin of the realm and the name of the promoter of the scheme.[86] If the holder of stamps having an aggregate value of not less than 25p so requests, the promoter must redeem them by paying over their aggregate cash value.[87] In the redemption of stamps there are implied stipulations as to the promoter's title to the goods, quiet possession, and satisfactory quality similar to those contained in sections 12 and 14 of the Sale of Goods Act 1979 (as amended);[88] it is not possible to exclude these implied stipulations.[89] A shop in which a trading stamp scheme is operated must display a notice stating the cash value of stamps issued under the scheme and giving such particulars as will enable customers readily to ascertain the number of trading stamps, if any, to which they are entitled on any purchase.[90] If a catalogue has been published for the scheme, it must contain a statement of the name of the promoter and the address of its registered office and a copy must be kept in the shop.[91] Any stamp book must contain the promoter's name and the address of its registered office.[92] It is an offence for the promoter to advertise in terms which convey the cash value of stamps by means of a statement which associates the worth of any trading stamps with what the holder pays or may pay to obtain them or in terms which are misleading or deceptive.[93]

Further Reading

Cunningham, *The Fair Trading Act 1973* (1974).
Harvey, *The Law of Consumer Protection and Fair Trading* (3rd ed., 1987).
O'Keefe, *The Law Relating to Trade Descriptions* (1990).

[86] s. 2.
[87] s. 3.
[88] s. 4 (as substituted by Supply of Goods (Implied Terms) Act 1973, s. 16, and amended by Sale and Supply of Goods Act 1994, Sched. 2, para. 2).
[89] s. 4(1).
[90] s. 7.
[91] ss. 5, 7(1)(*b*).
[92] s. 5(1).
[93] s. 6.

CHAPTER 18

CONSUMER CREDIT TRANSACTIONS

18.1   Scope of the Legislation.—The Consumer Credit Act 1974[1] establishes a system of licensing of persons concerned with the provision of credit and regulates consumer credit transactions of all kinds. It replaced the Pawnbrokers Acts, the Moneylenders Acts and the Hire-Purchase (Scotland) Act 1965. The mode of operation of ancillary credit business[2] and, in particular, of credit reference agencies,[3] is controlled.

The Director General of Fair Trading ('the Director') has the duty of generally superintending the working and enforcement of the Act, of administering the licensing system set up by the Act and of exercising various adjudicatory functions under the Act.[4]

18.2   Licensing.—A licence is required to carry on a consumer credit or consumer hire business or an ancillary credit business.[5] A regulated agreement (other than a non-commercial agreement) made when the trader or credit-broker was unlicensed is enforceable against the debtor only where the Director has made an order applying to the agreement.[6] A person is not to be treated as carrying on a particular type of business merely because occasionally he enters into transactions belonging to a business of that type.[7] A local authority and a body corporate

---

[1] The provisions of the Act are not fully implemented. It is not proposed to make regulations under ss. 53, 54, 55, 64(3), 112, 156 and 179: H.C. Deb., Vol. 28 (1982), col. 103.

[2] Pt. X.

[3] ss. 157–160; Consumer (Credit Reference Agency) Regulations 1977 (S.I. 1977 No. 329); Consumer Credit (Conduct of Business) (Credit References) Regulations 1977 (S.I. 1977 No. 330).

[4] s. 1.

[5] ss. 21, 147. Ancillary credit business is credit brokerage, debt-adjusting, debt-counselling, debt-collecting or the operation of a credit reference agency (s. 145). An advocate acting in that capacity and a solicitor engaging in business done in or for the purposes of proceedings before a court or an arbiter are not engaged in ancillary credit business (s. 146). As to credit brokerage, see *Hicks* v. *Walker* [1984] C.C.L.R. 19; *Brookes* v. *Retail Credit Cards Ltd.* [1986] F.L.R. 86.

[6] ss. 40, 149. See s. 148 as to the agreement between the customer and the unlicensed person carrying on an ancillary credit business. Sections 40, 148 and 149 are qualified where a party to an agreement is a credit institution authorised in another Member State of the EC: Banking Co-ordination (Second Council Directive) Regulations 1992 (S.I. 1992 No. 3218), reg. 61. An offer of loan by a person in business which is a private offer or a 'one-off', does not amount to a business activity and so no licence is required under s. 40, see *Hare* v. *Schurek* [1993] C.C.L.R. 47.

[7] s. 189(2); *R.* v. *Marshall* [1989] C.C.L.R. 47; *Hare* v. *Schurek, supra.*

empowered by a public general Act naming it to carry on a business do not need a licence.[8]

A 'standard licence' is issued to a person, a partnership or an unincorporated body of persons. A standard licence is granted to a person who satisfies the Director that he is a fit person to engage in activities covered by the licence and that the name under which he applies is not misleading or otherwise undesirable.[9] A 'group licence' covers such persons and such activities as are described in the licence and may be issued only where it appears to the Director that the public interest is better served by doing so than by obliging the persons concerned to apply separately for standard licences.[10] The Director has powers to vary, suspend or revoke a licence.[11] Decisions on these matters are subject to appeal to the Secretary of State[12] and from him on a question of law to the Court of Session.[13]

18.3 Definitions.—A 'personal credit agreement' is 'an agreement between an individual ("the debtor") and any other person ("the creditor") by which the creditor provides the debtor with credit of any amount.'[14] An 'individual' includes a partnership or other unincorporated body of persons not consisting entirely of bodies corporate.[15] 'Credit' includes a cash loan and any other form of financial accommodation.[16] An item entering into the total charge for credit is not treated as credit even though time is allowed for its payment.[17] A hire-purchase agreement is regarded as a provision of a fixed-sum credit to finance the transaction of an amount equal to the total price of the goods less the aggregate of

[8] s. 21.

[9] s. 25. A standard licence is valid for five years: Consumer Credit (Period of Standard Licence) Regulations 1975 (S.I. No. 2124, as amended by S.I. 1991 No. 817). On the death, sequestration or incapacity of the licensee the business may be carried on under the licence by some other person: s. 37; Consumer Credit (Termination of Licences) Regulations 1976 (S.I. 1976 No. 1002) (as amended by S.I. 1981 No. 614). See, as to refusal of a licence, *North Wales Motor Auctions Ltd.* v. *Secretary of State for Trade* [1981] C.C.L.R. 1.

[10] s. 22. A group licence issued to the Law Society of Scotland covers all solicitors holding practising certificates in respect of consumer credit, credit brokerage, debt-adjusting, and debt-counselling and debt-collecting in activities arising in the course of practice as a solicitor: Office of Fair Trading, General Notice No. 1038. A group licence has been issued to cover persons appointed to be a liquidator, receiver, executor, judicial factor, trustee in sequestration, curator bonis, or trustee under a deed of arrangement or trust deed: Office of Fair Trading, General Notice No. 1005.

[11] ss. 29–34.

[12] s. 41; Consumer Credit Licensing (Representations) Order 1976 (S.I. 1976 No. 191); Consumer Credit Licensing (Appeals) Regulations 1976 (S.I. 1976 No. 837).

[13] Tribunals and Inquiries Act 1992, s. 11(7). See Rule of Court 293A.

[14] s. 8(1).

[15] s. 189(1).

[16] s. 9(1).

[17] s. 9(4). Items included in the total charge for credit are specified in the Consumer Credit (Total Charge for Credit) Regulations 1980 (S.I. 1980 No. 51, as amended by S.I. 1985 No. 1192 and S.I. 1989 No. 596).

the deposit (if any) and the total charge for credit.[18] A hire-purchase agreement is an agreement, other than a conditional sale agreement, under which goods are hired in return for periodical payments and the property will pass to the hirer if the terms of the agreement are complied with and the hirer exercises an option to purchase, or any party to the agreement does another specified act or another specified event occurs.[19]

A 'consumer credit agreement' is a personal credit agreement by which the creditor provides the debtor with credit not exceeding £15,000.[20] A consumer credit agreement is a 'regulated agreement' if it is not an 'exempt agreement'.[21]

There is, however, another class of 'regulated agreement'—a consumer hire agreement is a regulated agreement if it is not an exempt agreement.[22] A 'consumer hire agreement' is an agreement for the hiring of goods to an individual, which is not a hire-purchase agreement, which is capable of subsisting for more than three months and which does not require the hirer to make payments exceeding £15,000.[23]

A 'running-account credit' is a facility under a personal credit agreement whereby the debtor can receive cash, goods and services to a value such that, taking repayments by the debtor into account, the credit limit is not exceeded, the credit limit being in any period the maximum debit balance permissible in the period, disregarding any term of the agreement which allows the maximum to be exceeded merely temporarily.[24] For purposes of the £15,000 limit in the definition of a consumer credit agreement, the running-account credit is taken not to exceed £15,000 if the credit limit does not exceed £15,000; but even if there is no credit limit or there is a limit exceeding £15,000, the credit may be taken not to exceed £15,000 if the debtor cannot draw more than £15,000 at one time *or* if the credit charge increases or the agreement otherwise becomes more onerous when the debit balance rises above a given amount not exceeding £15,000 *or* if 'at the time the agreement is made it is probable, having regard to the terms of the agreement and any other relevant considerations, that the debit balance will not at any time rise above' £15,000.[25] A 'fixed-sum credit' is any facility other than a running-account credit under a personal credit

[18] s. 9(3).
[19] s. 189(1).
[20] s. 8(2)(j). Consumer Credit (Increase of Monetary Limits) Order 1983 (S.I. 1983 No. 1878).
[21] s. 8(3).
[22] s. 15(2). For definition of "regulated agreement" see s. 189(1).
[23] s. 15(1); Consumer Credit (Increase of Monetary Limits) Order 1983 (S.I. 1983 No. 1878); *Apollo Leasing Ltd.* v. *Scott*, 1984 S.L.T. (Sh. Ct.) 90; *Lloyds Bowmaker Leasing Ltd.* v. *MacDonald*, [1993] C.C.L.R. 63.
[24] s. 10(1), (2). A bank overdraft is a running-account credit (Sched. 2, Exs. 18, 23).
[25] s. 10(3). If the agreement contains a term signifying that in the opinion of the parties the last of these conditions is not satisfied it should be taken not to be satisfied unless the contrary is proved (s. 171(1)).

agreement whereby the debtor is enabled to receive credit in one amount or by instalments.[26]

18.4 Exempt Agreements.—The following are 'exempt agreements':

(1) certain debtor-creditor-supplier and debtor-creditor agreements[27] secured over land where the creditor is a local authority, a building society, a bank or a body specified in an order made by the Secretary of State;[28]

(2) debtor-creditor-supplier agreements for a fixed-sum credit where the number of payments to be made by the debtor does not exceed four and those payments are to be made within a period not exceeding 12 months with the exception of: (a) agreements financing the purchase of land; (b) conditional sale agreements and hire-purchase agreements; and (c) agreements secured by a pledge (other than a pledge of documents of title or bearer bonds);[29]

(3) debtor-creditor-supplier agreements for running-account credit providing for payments by the debtor in relation to specified periods and requiring that the number of payments to be made in repayment of the whole amount of the credit provided in each such period shall not exceed one (there are the same exceptions as in (2));[30]

(4) debtor-creditor-supplier agreements financing the purchase of land where the number of payments to be made by the debtor does not exceed four;[31]

(5) certain debtor-creditor-supplier agreements for fixed-sum credit financing insurance premiums;[32]

(6) debtor-creditor agreements (other than those in which repayments may vary according to a formula and, with certain exceptions, those in which there is provision for an increase in the total charge for credit) where the total charge for credit does not exceed a prescribed rate;[33]

---

[26] s. 10(1)(b); e.g. a loan granted in instalments or a hire-purchase agreement (Sched. 2, Exs. 9, 10).

[27] These terms are defined in para. 18.7, infra. There is a circularity in the definitions: regulated agreements are consumer credit agreements which are not exempt agreements; exempt agreements include debtor-creditor-supplier and debtor-creditor agreements which are defined as including some regulated agreements.

[28] s. 16(1); Consumer Credit (Exempt Agreements) Order 1989 (S.I. 1989 No. 869, as amended by S.I. 1989 Nos. 1841 and 2337; S.I. 1991 Nos. 1393, 1949 and 2844; S.I. 1993 No. 346; and S.I. 1994 No. 2420), art. 2.

[29] art. 3(1)(a)(i).

[30] art. 3(1)(a)(ii).

[31] art. 3(1)(b).

[32] art. 3(1)(c), (d).

[33] art. 4(1)(a). The prescribed rate is the higher of (i) the sum of one per cent. and the highest of any base rates published by the clearing banks, being the latest rates in operation on the date 28 days before the agreement was made; and (ii) 13 per cent.

(7) debtor-creditor-supplier agreements for fixed-sum credit financing life insurance premiums connected with an exempt land mortgage agreement when the only charge for credit is interest at a rate not exceeding the rate payable under the land mortgage agreement and not exceeding the prescribed rate (with the exception of those under which repayments may vary according to a formula);[34]

(8) debtor-creditor agreements where the only charge for credit is interest which cannot at any time exceed the higher of the sum of one per cent. plus the highest bank base rate 28 days before that time and 13 per cent. (with the exception of those under which repayment may vary according to a formula);[35]

(9) agreements made in connection with trade in goods or services between the U.K. and other countries or within a country or between countries outside the U.K., being agreements under which credit is provided to the debtor in the course of a business carried on by him;[36]

(10) consumer hire agreements for meters or metering equipment owned by electricity, gas or water suppliers;[37]

(11) consumer credit agreements where the creditor is a housing authority and the agreement is secured on a dwelling.[38]

18.5 Restricted-Use Agreements.—A 'restricted-use agreement' is a regulated consumer credit agreement of one of three types: (a) financing a transaction between the debtor and the creditor; (b) financing a transaction between the debtor and someone other than the creditor (the 'supplier') whose identity need not be known when the agreement is made; (c) refinancing any existing indebtedness to the creditor or another person.[39] It is important to note that an agreement is not a restricted-use one if credit is in fact provided in such a way as to leave the debtor free to use it as he chooses, even though certain uses would contravene that or any other agreement.[40] An 'unrestricted-use agreement' is a regulated consumer credit agreement which is not a restricted-use one.[41]

18.6 Creditor-Supplier 'Arrangements.'—A consumer credit agreement is made under pre-existing arrangements between a creditor and a supplier if it is entered into in accordance with, or in furtherance of,

[34] art. 4(1)(*b*); the rate is that defined in note 33.
[35] art. 4(1)(*c*).
[36] art. 5(*a*). As to a further exemption where the creditor is listed and the debtor is connected with the U.S. forces see art. 5(*b*).
[37] art. 6.
[38] s. 16(6A).
[39] s. 11(1).
[40] s. 11(3).
[41] s. 11(2).

arrangements previously made between the creditor or his associate and the supplier or his associate.[42] 'Associates' are, broadly, relatives, partners and controlled bodies corporate.[43] A consumer credit agreement is entered into in contemplation of future arrangements if it is entered into in the expectation that arrangements will subsequently be made between the creditor or his associate and the supplier or his associate for the supply of cash, goods or services to be financed by the agreement.[44] If the creditor is an associate of the supplier's, the agreement is treated as entered into under pre-existing arrangements unless the contrary is proved.[45] Arrangements are disregarded if they are merely arrangements for the making, in specified circumstances, of payments to the supplier by the creditor and the creditor holds himself out as willing to make, in such circumstances, payments of the kind to suppliers generally.[46] Arrangements are also disregarded if they are for the electronic transfer of funds from a current account at a bank.[47]

18.7 Debtor-Creditor-Supplier Agreements.—A 'debtor-creditor-supplier agreement' is a regulated consumer credit agreement being:

   (a)   one financing a transaction between the debtor and the creditor, or

   (b)   one financing a transaction between the debtor and the supplier with 'arrangements,' pre-existing or contemplated, or

   (c)   an unrestricted-use agreement with pre-existing 'arrangements' and knowledge on the part of the creditor that the credit is to be used to finance a transaction between the debtor and the supplier.[48]

A 'debtor-creditor agreement' is a regulated consumer credit agreement being:

   (a)   one financing a transaction between the debtor and the supplier without 'arrangements,' or

   (b)   one refinancing any existing indebtedness to the creditor or another person, or

   (c)   an unrestricted-use agreement without 'arrangements' and without knowledge on the part of the creditor that the credit is to be used to finance a transaction between the debtor and the supplier.[49]

18.8 Other Definitions.—A 'multiple agreement' is an agreement part of which falls within one category of agreement and part in another or an

---

[42] s. 187(1).
[43] s. 184.
[44] s. 187(2).
[45] s. 187(5).
[46] s. 187(3).
[47] s. 187(3A), inserted by Banking Act 1987, s. 89.
[48] s. 12; *e.g.* a bank credit-card agreement so far as it relates to goods: Sched. 2, Ex. 16.
[49] s. 13; *e.g.* an agreement for a bank overdraft: Sched. 2, Ex. 18.

agreement which, or part of which, falls within two or more categories of agreement mentioned in the Act.[50] A part of a multiple agreement is to be treated as a separate agreement.[51] A transaction, other than one for the provision of security, is a 'linked transaction' in relation to an actual or prospective regulated agreement (the 'principal agreement') if it is entered into by the debtor or his relative in compliance with a term of the principal agreement, or if it is financed by a principal debtor-creditor-supplier agreement, or if the other party to the transaction is a person of a specified class and the transaction is suggested by a person of a specified class and it is entered into to induce the creditor to enter into the principal agreement, or for another purpose related to the principal agreement, or, where the principal agreement is a restricted-use credit agreement, for a purpose related to a transaction financed, or to be financed, by the principal agreement; the specified classes of persons are: the creditor, his associate, a person who knows that the principal agreement has been made or who contemplated that it might be made and a person who, in the negotiation of the transaction, is represented by a credit-broker who is also a negotiator in antecedent negotiations for the principal agreement.[52] A linked transaction entered into before the principal agreement has no effect until that agreement is made.[53]

A 'small agreement' is: (a) a regulated consumer credit agreement for credit not exceeding £50 other than a hire-purchase or conditional sale agreement or (b) a regulated consumer hire agreement which does not require the hirer to make payments exceeding £50, being, in either case, an agreement which is unsecured or secured only by a guarantee or indemnity.[54]

A 'non-commercial agreement' is a consumer credit or hire agreement not made by the creditor or owner in the course of a business carried on by him.[55]

18.9 Regulated Agreements.—The provisions of the Act which affect regulated agreements generally are summarised in this section;[56]

[50] s. 18(1).
[51] s. 18(2).
[52] s. 19. The 'negotiator' is defined by s. 56(1).
[53] s. 19(3). For exceptions see Consumer Credit (Linked Transactions) (Exemptions) Regulations 1983 (S.I. 1983 No. 1560).
[54] s. 17(1); Consumer Credit (Increase of Monetary Limits) Order 1983 (S.I. 1983 No. 1878). There are provisions to prevent evasion by the splitting of an agreement into several small agreements: s. 17(3), (4).
[55] s. 189(1). The following do not apply to a non-commercial agreement: ss. 55, 57–73; 75; 77–80; 82; 83; 103; 107–110; 112; 114–123.
[56] References to the 'debtor' include references to the hirer. There are important exceptions to some of the following provisions. Pt. V (ss. 55–74), dealing with entry into agreements, does not, except for s. 56, apply to non-commercial agreements or to certain current account overdraft agreements or to certain debtor-creditor agreements to finance certain payments arising on death: s. 74(1); Consumer Credit (Payments Arising on Death) Regulations 1983 (S.I. 1983 No. 1554); and does not, except for s. 56, apply to a small debtor-creditor-supplier agreement for restricted-use credit: s. 74(2). There are exceptions to the exception where a term of the agreement is expressed in writing s. 74(4).
—continued on p. 274

thereafter provisions affecting special kinds of regulated agreement will be noticed. In the antecedent negotiations, the negotiator is deemed to be the creditor's agent and he cannot validly be made the debtor's agent.[57] Regulated agreements must be in the prescribed form and have the prescribed content.[58] The document must be readily legible, must be signed by the debtor and the creditor and must embody all the terms of the agreement other than implied terms.[59] The debtor must be given a copy of the executed agreement and, if the agreement does not become executed when he signs it, a copy of the unexecuted agreement.[60] An agreement which does not conform to the foregoing requirements is 'improperly-executed' and is enforceable only on the order of the court.[61] An agreement may be cancelled by the debtor within a specified period if the antecedent negotiations included oral representation made by the negotiator in the presence of the debtor unless the agreement is secured on land or is for the purchase of land or the debtor signed the agreement at the premises of the creditor or the negotiator or any party to a linked transaction.[62] Any linked transaction is also cancelled.[63] Notice of his cancellation rights must be given to the debtor.[64] There are provisions for the recovery of sums paid by the debtor,[65] the return of goods and the repayment of any credit extended on cancellation;[66] these provisions also operate, so far as applicable, where the debtor has withdrawn from a prospective regulated agreement.[67]

—continued from p. 273

The seeking of business is governed by ss. 43–54; Consumer Credit (Advertisements) Regulations 1989 (S.I. 1989 No. 1125); Consumer Credit (Quotations) Regulations 1989 (S.I. 1989 No. 1126). See *Jenkins* v. *Lombard North Central plc* [1984] 1 W.L.R. 307; *R.* v. *Secretary of State for Trade and Industry, ex p. First National Bank plc* [1990] C.C.L.R. 105; *Metsoja* v. *H. Norman Pitt & Co. Ltd.* [1990] C.C.L.R. 12; *Ford Credit plc* v. *Normand*, 1994 S.L.T. 318; *Clydesdale Group plc* v. *Normand*, 1994 S.L.T. 1302. Discrimination in providing credit facilities is unlawful: Sex Discrimination Act 1975, s. 29(2)(c); Race Relations Act 1976, s. 20(2)(c).

[57] s. 56.

[58] s. 60; Consumer Credit (Agreements) Regulations 1983 (S.I. 1983 No. 1553, as amended by S.I. 1984 No. 1600, S.I. 1985 No. 666 and S.I. 1988 No. 2047). See, as to information about variation of the interest rate by the creditor, *Lombard Tricity Finance Ltd.* v. *Paton* [1989] C.C.L.R. 21.

[59] s. 61.

[60] ss. 62, 63.

[61] s. 65.

[62] ss. 67–69. A statement of fact or opinion or a future undertaking capable of inducing a debtor to enter into a credit agreement amounts to a 'representation' entitling the debtor, who signs the credit agreement at his premises, to be told of his right to cancellation under s. 67, see *Moorgate Services Ltd.* v. *Kabir, The Times*, April 25, 1995.

[63] s. 69(1)(i). For exceptions see Consumer Credit (Linked Transactions) (Exemptions) Regulations 1983 (S.I. 1983 No. 1560).

[64] s. 64; Consumer Credit (Cancellation Notices and Copies of Documents) Regulations 1983 (1983 No. 1557) (as amended by S.I. 1984 No. 1108 and S.I. 1985 No. 666); Consumer Credit (Notice of Cancellation Rights) (Exemptions) Regulations 1983 (S.I. 1983 No. 1558). It is not proposed to make regulations under s. 64(3).

[65] s. 70.

[66] ss. 71–72; Consumer Credit (Repayment of Credit on Cancellation) Regulations 1983 (S.I. 1983 No. 1559).

[67] s. 57.

Restrictions are placed on the creditor's liberty to do any of the following acts whether he is acting under the terms of the agreement or by reason of a breach of the agreement by the debtor:

    (i)   demanding earlier payment of any sum;

   (ii)   recovering possession of any goods or land;

  (iii)   treating any right of the debtor (other than a right to draw credit) as terminated, restricted or deferred;

  (iv)   terminating the agreement;

   (v)   enforcing any security.

In general, he cannot do any of these acts without giving notice to the debtor[68] and the debtor, on receipt of the notice, can apply to the court for relief. The creditor cannot enforce a term of an agreement by doing any of (i), (ii) or (iii) during the specified period of duration of the agreement without giving not less than seven days' notice to the debtor, unless the right to enforce arises from the debtor's breach of the agreement.[69] Similarly, the creditor cannot terminate the agreement for reasons other than the debtor's breach during the specified period of duration of the agreement without giving not less than seven days' notice to the debtor.[70]

If, under a power contained in the agreement, the creditor varies the agreement, the variation does not take effect before notice of it is given to the debtor in the prescribed manner.[71] The creditor is obliged to give the debtor, on request and payment of a fee, information as to the state of the debt[72] and the debtor is under a similar duty to inform the creditor as to the whereabouts of any goods to which the agreement relates and which are required by the agreement to be kept in the debtor's possession or control.[73] There are rules as to the appropriation of payments where there are two or more agreements.[74]

A credit-broker, a supplier or a negotiator is deemed to be the creditor's agent for the purpose of receiving any notice rescinding the agreement.[75]

It is an offence for a trader to fail to give a customer who serves an appropriate notice on him a counter-notice stating either that the

[68] Consumer Credit (Enforcement, Default and Termination Notices) Regulations 1983 (S.I. 1983 No. 1561, as amended by S.I. 1984 No. 1109).

[69] s. 76. A right of enforcement arising by reason of breach of the agreement is not affected: s. 76(6); nor is the creditor's right to restrict or defer the drawing on any credit: s. 76(4).

[70] s. 98. See note 68, *supra*.

[71] s. 82; Consumer Credit (Notice of Variation of Agreements) Regulations 1977 (S.I. 1977 No. 328, as amended by S.I. 1979 Nos. 661 and 667).

[72] ss. 77–79; Consumer Credit (Prescribed Periods for Giving Information) Regulations 1983 (S.I. 1983 No. 1569); Consumer Credit (Running-Account Credit Information) Regulations 1983 (S.I. 1983 No. 1570).

[73] s. 80.

[74] s. 81.

[75] s. 102.

customer's indebtedness is discharged or his grounds for alleging that the indebtedness is not discharged.[76]

18.10 Debtor's Death.—On the debtor's death, the creditor in an agreement which has a specified period of duration which has not ended cannot do any of the acts (i) to (v) specified in para. 18.9 if at the death the agreement is fully secured.[77] If the agreement is only partly secured or is unsecured, he can do them only on an order of the court which will be made only if the creditor proves that he has been unable to satisfy himself that the debtor's present and future obligations under the agreement are likely to be discharged.[78]

18.11 Default.—Where there is a breach of the agreement by the debtor the creditor cannot by reason of the breach do any of the acts (i) to (v) specified in para. 18.9 unless he has served on the debtor a default notice in the prescribed form.[79] This notice must specify, *inter alia*, what action is required to remedy the breach, or, if the breach is not capable of remedy, the compensation required to be paid therefor;[80] and if the action is taken or the compensation paid within a period of not less than seven days specified in the notice, the breach shall be treated as not having occurred.[81] Summary diligence cannot be used to enforce payment of a debt due under a regulated agreement or under any security related thereto.[82]

18.12 Time Orders.—There are three ways in which the agreement can come before the court: (a) when the creditor applies for an enforcement order; (b) on an application by the debtor, after service of a default notice, a notice of termination, or a notice of intention to do the acts (i), (ii) or (iii) specified in para. 18.9, *supra*, under the agreement; and (c) when the creditor brings an action to enforce the agreement or a security, or to recover possession of any goods or land.

In any of these circumstances the court may make a 'time order' providing for payment by instalments of any sum due under the agreement or for the remedying of any breach other than non-payment of money by the debtor within a specified time.[83] A time order cannot be made if a time to pay direction or order[84] has previously been made

---

[76] s. 103.

[77] s. 86. The creditor may, however, restrict or defer the drawing on any credit: s. 86(4); and the section does not affect the operation of an agreement that sums will be paid out of the proceeds of a policy of assurance on the debtor's life: s. 86(5).

[78] s. 128.

[79] s. 87. See note 68, *supra*.

[80] s. 88.

[81] s. 89.

[82] s. 93A, inserted by Debtors (Scotland) Act 1987, Sched. 6, para. 16.

[83] s. 129; *Murie McDougall Ltd.* v. *Sinclair*, 1994 S.L.T. 74 (Sh.Ct.); *Southern and District Finance plc* v. *Barnes, The Times*, April 19, 1995.

[84] See para. 18.9.

in relation to the debt.[85] Payment by instalments can be ordered only where it appears just to do so and in considering what is just the creditor's position, as well as the debtor's, must be taken into account.[86] In any order made in relation to an agreement the court may make the operation of a term conditional on the doing of certain acts by any party or may suspend the operation of any term.[87] The court may also include in the order such provision as it considers just for amending the agreement or security in consequence of a term of the order.[88] On the application of the creditor or owner, the court may make such order as it thinks just for the protection of his property or of property subject to a security pending the determination of the proceedings.[89]

18.13 Enforcement Orders.—Where an application is made for an enforcement order, there are some situations in which the court cannot make the order, *e.g.* where the agreement was a cancellable one and the debtor was not given a notice of his right to cancel.[90] In other situations, *e.g.* in the case of some improperly executed agreements, the court is to dismiss the application if it considers it just to do so having regard to the prejudice caused to any person by the contravention in question and the degree of culpability for it and having regard also to the court's powers, already mentioned, to make conditional or suspended orders or to vary the terms of the agreement.[91] In an enforcement order the court may reduce or discharge any sum payable by the debtor or by a surety to compensate him for any loss suffered as a result of the contravention.[92] Where the agreement is not in the correct form but the debtor did sign a document containing all the prescribed terms, the order may direct that the agreement is to have effect as if it did not include a term omitted from that document.[93]

18.14 Securities.—Documents embodying regulated agreements have to embody any security[94] provided in relation to the agreement by the debtor.[95] If the person by whom a security is provided (the 'surety') is not the debtor, the security must be expressed in writing, the document

---

[85] s.129(3), inserted by Debtors (Scotland) Act 1987, Sched. 6, para. 17.
[86] *First National Bank plc* v. *Syed* [1991] C.C.L.R. 37, C.A.
[87] s. 135.
[88] s. 136.
[89] s. 131.
[90] s. 127(4).
[91] s. 127(1).
[92] s. 127(2).
[93] s. 127(5).
[94] A 'security' means a mortgage (including a heritable security), charge, pledge, bond, debenture, indemnity, guarantee, bill, note or other right provided by the debtor or at his request to secure the carrying out of his obligations: s. 189. Note, however, that a document 'embodies' a provision if the provision is set out either in the document itself or in another document referred to in it: s. 189(4).
[95] s. 105(9); Consumer Credit (Agreements) Regulations 1983 (S.I. 1983 No. 1553), reg. 2(8).

containing all the terms of the security other than implied terms must be signed by or on behalf of the surety and a copy of the document and the principal agreement given to him.[96] If these requirements are not satisfied, the security is enforceable against the surety only on an order of the court and if an application for such an order is dismissed (except on technical grounds) the security is treated as never having effect, property lodged with the creditor for purposes of the security must be returned, any entry relating to the security in any register must be cancelled and any amount received by the creditor on realisation of the security must be repaid to the surety.[97] There is a partial exemption for heritable securities.[98] The creditor is obliged to give the surety on request a copy of the principal agreement and of the security instrument and information about the present state of the debtor's indebtedness.[99]

A copy of any default notice served on the debtor must be served on the surety.[1] A security cannot be enforced so as to benefit the creditor to an extent greater than would be the case if there were no security and the obligations of the debtor were carried out to the extent (if any) to which they would be enforced under the Act.[2] Accordingly, if a regulated agreement is enforceable only on a court order, or on an order of the Director, the security is enforceable only where an order has been made[3] and, generally, if the agreement is cancelled or becomes unenforceable, the security becomes ineffective.[4]

18.15   Pledges.[5]—It is an offence to take an article 'in pawn' from a minor.[6] It is also an offence for the 'pawnee' to fail to give the 'pawnor' a copy of the agreement, notice of his cancellation rights and a pawn-receipt.[7] The pawn is redeemable during the 'redemption period', *i.e.* six months after it was taken or the period fixed for the duration of the credit, if longer, or such longer period as the parties may agree; the pawn remains redeemable after the expiry of the redemption period until it is realised or the property in it passes to the pawnee.[8] No special charges or higher

---

[96] s. 105. A guarantee or indemnity must be in the prescribed form: Consumer Credit (Guarantees and Indemnities) Regulations 1983 (S.I. 1983 No. 1556).

[97] s. 106.

[98] s. 177(5).

[99] ss. 107–110.

[1] s. 111.

[2] s. 113(1).

[3] s. 113(2).

[4] s. 113(3).

[5] The provisions as to pledges do not apply to pledges of documents of title or of bearer bonds or to non-commercial agreements: s. 114(3) as amended by Banking Act 1979, s. 38(2).

[6] s. 114(2).

[7] s. 115. The form of receipt is prescribed by the Consumer Credit (Agreements) Regulations 1983 (S.I. 1983 No. 1553), reg. 4, Scheds. 1 and 2, where it is combined with the document embodying the agreement and otherwise by the Consumer Credit (Pawn-Receipts) Regulations 1983 (S.I. 1983 No. 1566).

[8] s. 116.

charges for safe-keeping of the pawn can be made on redemption after the expiry of the redemption period.[9]

The pawnee must deliver the pawn on surrender of the receipt and payment of the amount owing unless he knows or suspects that the bearer of the receipt is not the owner of the pawn.[10] If the owner claiming the pawn does not have the receipt he may make a statutory declaration (or, where the loan is not over £25,[11] a written statement in prescribed form) which is treated as the receipt.[12] It is an offence to fail without reasonable cause to allow redemption of a pawn.[13] Where a pawn is an article which has been stolen or obtained by fraud the court which has convicted a person of the offence may order delivery of the pawn to the owner subject to such conditions as to payment of the debt as it thinks fit.[14]

If the credit does not exceed £25, and the pawn has not been redeemed at the end of a redemption period of six months, the property in the pawn passes to the pawnee. In other cases, the pawn becomes realisable if it has not been redeemed at the end of the redemption period.[15] The pawnor must be given notice of the pawnee's intention to sell and, after the sale, information as to the sale, its proceeds and expenses. If the net proceeds are not less than the debt, the debt is discharged and any surplus is payable to the pawnor; otherwise the debt is reduced *pro tanto*. On challenge, it is for the pawnee to prove that he used reasonable care to ensure that the true market value was obtained and that the expenses of sale were reasonable.[16]

18.16 Negotiable Instruments.—Except in the case of a non-commercial agreement, a negotiable instrument cannot be taken as a security for discharge of a sum due under a regulated agreement and a negotiable instrument other than a bank note or cheque cannot be taken from a debtor or surety in discharge of a sum payable.[17] The person who takes the negotiable instrument is not a holder in due course and is not entitled to enforce it.[18] A cheque taken in discharge cannot be negotiated except to a banker[19] and negotiation to a non-banker is a

[9] s. 116(4).
[10] s. 117.
[11] Consumer Credit (Increase of Monetary Amounts) Order 1983 (S.I. 1983 No. 1571).
[12] s. 118; Consumer Credit (Loss of Pawn-Receipt) Regulations 1983 (S.I. 1983 No. 1567).
[13] s. 119.
[14] s. 122.
[15] s. 120.
[16] s. 121. Consumer Credit (Realisation of Pawn) Regulations 1983 (S.I. 1983 No. 1568); see also *Mathew* v. *T.M. Sutton Ltd., The Times*, June 22, 1994.
[17] s. 123; Consumer Credit (Negotiable Instruments) (Exemption) Order 1984 (S.I. 1984 No. 435).
[18] s. 125(1).
[19] s. 123(2).

defect in the negotiator's title.[20] Contravention of these provisions makes the agreement or security enforceable on order of the court only.[21] The rights of a holder in due course of a negotiable instrument are not affected but where the debtor or surety becomes liable to a holder in due course as a result of a contravention of these provisions the creditor must indemnify him.[22]

18.17 Consumer Credit Agreements.—The debtor under a regulated consumer credit agreement is not liable to the creditor for any loss arising from use of the credit facility by another person not acting, or to be treated as acting, as the debtor's agent.[23] The debtor is entitled to discharge his indebtedness under the agreement at any time by notice to the creditor and payment of all amounts due to the creditor; the debtor may be entitled to a rebate for early payment.[24]

There is a restriction on the rate of interest which can be charged on sums which the debtor, in breach of the agreement, has not paid.[25]

18.18 Agreements about Goods.—The creditor under a regulated hire-purchase, conditional sale or consumer hire agreement cannot enter premises to take possession of the goods except under an order of the court.[26] Contravention is actionable as a breach of statutory duty. Where, after the making of a time order in relation to such an agreement, the debtor is in possession of the goods, he shall be treated as the custodier of the goods notwithstanding that the agreement has been terminated.[27]

18.19 Hire-Purchase and Conditional Sale Agreements.[28]—If the debtor is in breach of a hire-purchase or conditional sale agreement relating to

[20] s. 125(2).
[21] s. 124.
[22] s. 125(3), (4).
[23] s. 83. This does not apply to any loss arising from misuse of an instrument to which the Cheques Act 1957, s. 4, applies.
[24] ss. 94–95; Consumer Credit (Rebate on Early Settlement) Regulations 1983 (S.I. 1983 No. 1562, as amended by S.I. 1989 No. 596). See *Forward Trust Ltd.* v. *Whymark* [1990] C.C.L.R. 1.
[25] s. 93.
[26] s. 92. It seems that in Scotland an owner is never entitled to retake goods at his own hand from a person who possesses them under a contract: Gow, *Law of Hire-Purchase* (2nd ed., 1968), p. 210. Section 134 dealing with 'adverse possession' purports to apply to Scotland but is incomprehensible.
[27] s. 130(4).
[28] A conditional sale agreement is an agreement for the sale of goods or land under which the purchase price or part of it is payable by instalments and the property in the goods or land is to remain in the seller (notwithstanding that the buyer is to be in possession of the goods or land) until such conditions as to the payment of instalments or otherwise as may be specified in the agreement are fulfilled: s. 189. The buyer under such an agreement which is a consumer credit agreement is deemed for purposes of s. 25(1) of the Sale of Goods Act 1979 not to be a person who has bought or agreed to buy goods: Sale of Goods Act 1979, s. 25(2). See para. 16.21, *supra.*

goods but has paid one-third or more of the total price, the goods, even although they are the creditor's property, are 'protected goods' and the creditor cannot recover possession of them without a court order.[29] If he does recover them without an order, the agreement is terminated and the debtor is released from all liability and can recover all that he has paid under the agreement.[30]

The debtor is entitled to terminate the agreement by giving notice at any time before the final payment.[31] He must, however, pay the creditor the amount (if any) by which one-half of the total price exceeds the aggregate of the sums paid and the sums due immediately before termination unless (a) the agreement provides for a small payment or does not provide for any payment, or (b) the court makes an order for payment of a lesser sum which it is satisfied is equal to the loss sustained by the creditor in consequence of the termination of the agreement.[32] In addition, the debtor must recompense the creditor if he has contravened an obligation to take reasonable care of the goods.

Goods comprised in a hire-purchase or conditional sale agreement which have not become vested in the debtor are not subject to the landlord's hypothec in the period between service of a default notice and the date on which the notice expires or is earlier complied with, or, if the agreement is enforceable on an order of the court only, in the period between the commencement and the termination of the creditor's action.[33]

A time order in relation to a hire-purchase or conditional sale agreement may deal with sums which, although not payable at the time the order is made, would if the agreement continued in force become payable under it subsequently.[34]

In an application for an enforcement order or a time order in relation to a hire-purchase or conditional sale agreement or in an action brought by the creditor to recover the goods, the court may make a 'return order' or a 'transfer order.'[35] A 'return order' is an order for return of the goods to the creditor; a 'transfer order' is an order for transfer to the debtor of the creditor's title to such of the goods as the court thinks just and the return to the creditor of the remainder of the goods. A transfer order can be made only where the amount of the total price which has been paid exceeds the part of the total price referable to the transferred goods by at least one-third of the unpaid balance of the total price. Notwithstanding the making of a return order or a transfer order, the debtor may, before the goods enter the creditor's possession, on

[29] s. 90.
[30] s. 91.
[31] s. 99.
[32] s. 100.
[33] s. 104.
[34] s. 130(2).
[35] s. 133.

payment of the balance of the total price and on fulfilment of any other necessary conditions, 'claim' the goods ordered to be returned.[36] When, under that provision, or under a time order, the total price is paid and any other necessary conditions are fulfilled, the creditor's title to the goods vests in the debtor. If goods are not returned under a return order or transfer order the court may revoke so much of the order as relates to those goods and order the debtor to pay the unpaid portion of so much of the total price as is referable to those goods.

18.20 Conditional Sale Agreements Relating to Land.—When the debtor is in breach of a conditional sale agreement relating to land, the creditor can recover possession of the land on an order of the court only.[37] A conditional sale agreement relating to land cannot be terminated after the title has passed to the debtor.[38]

18.21 'Land Mortgages.'—A 'land mortgage' is any security charged on land, 'land' being defined to include heritable subjects of whatever description.[39]

Before sending to the debtor for signature an unexecuted agreement where the prospective regulated agreement is to be secured on land, the creditor must give the debtor a copy of the unexecuted agreement containing a notice indicating the debtor's right to withdraw from the prospective agreement and how and when the right is exercisable.[40] This does not apply to a restricted-use credit agreement to finance the purchase of the land or to an agreement for a bridging loan in connection with the purchase of the 'mortgaged land' or other land.

A land mortgage is not properly executed unless in addition to the requirements applying to regulated agreements generally (a) the copy agreement and notice of the withdrawal right are sent to the debtor, (b) the unexecuted agreement is sent by post to the debtor for his signature not less than seven days after the copy was given to him, (c) in the period between the giving of that copy and the expiry of seven days after the sending of the unexecuted agreement for his signature (or its return signed if earlier) the creditor refrained from approaching the debtor, in person, by telephone or letter or otherwise, except in response to a specific request made by the debtor, (d) no notice of withdrawal by the debtor was received by the creditor before the sending of the unexecuted agreement.[41]

---

[36] The words ' ... may ... claim ... ' are presumably used to mean 'is entitled to retain.'

[37] s. 92(2). See also Tenants' Rights, Etc. (Scotland) Act 1980, s. 74.

[38] s. 99(3).

[39] s. 189.

[40] s. 58; Consumer Credit (Cancellation Notices and Copies of Documents) Regulations 1983 (S.I. 1983 No. 1557), reg. 4 (as amended by S.I. 1984 No. 1108, S.I. 1985 No. 666, S.I. 1988 No. 2047 and S.I. 1989 No. 591).

[41] s. 61.

A land mortgage securing a regulated agreement is enforceable (so far as provided in relation to the agreement) on order of the court only.[42] Nothing in the Act is to affect the rights of a creditor in a heritable security, other than one carrying on the business of debt-collecting, who became the creditor for value and without notice of any defect in title arising by virtue of the other provisions of the Act or who derived title from such a creditor.[43]

18.22 Consumer Hire Agreements.—The hirer is entitled to terminate a regulated consumer hire agreement by giving to the person entitled to receive the sums payable thereunder notice which is not to expire earlier than 18 months after the making of the agreement.[44] A minimum period of notice is prescribed according to the intervals at which payment is made. This power to terminate is not available where the hire payments exceed £900 in any year or where the goods are hired for purposes of a business carried on by the hirer.

If the owner recovers possession of the goods otherwise than by action, the court, on the hirer's application, may, if it appears just to do so, having regard to the extent of the hirer's enjoyment of the goods, order that any sums already paid by the hirer shall be repaid and that the hirer's obligation to pay any sums owed to the owner shall cease.[45] Similar provisions may be made by the court in an order for delivery of the goods to the owner.

18.23 Connected Lender Liability.—A substantial liability is imposed upon the creditor in a debtor-creditor-supplier agreement in which there are 'arrangements' between the creditor and the supplier.[46] If the debtor has, in relation to a transaction financed by such an agreement, any claim against the supplier in respect of a misrepresentation or breach of contract, he has a like claim against the creditor who is jointly and severally liable with the supplier but has a right to be indemnified by the supplier. The provision does not apply to a non-commercial agreement nor where the claim relates to any single item to which the supplier has attached a cash price not exceeding £100 or more than £30,000.

18.24 Credit-Token Agreements.—A credit-token is 'a card, check, voucher, coupon, stamp, form, booklet or other document or thing' given to an individual by a person carrying on a consumer credit business who undertakes that he will supply, or reimburse a third party who supplies

[42] s. 126.
[43] s. 177.
[44] s. 101.
[45] s. 132; *Automotive Financial Services Ltd.* v. *Henderson*, 1992 S.L.T. (Sh. Ct.) 63.
[46] s. 75. See A.S. (Consumer Credit Act 1974) 1985 (S.I. 1985 No. 705). See also *United Dominions Trust* v. *Taylor*, 1980 S.L.T. (Sh. Ct.) 28. *Cf. Porter* v. *General Guarantee Corporation Ltd.* [1982] R.T.R. 384.

cash, goods and services on credit on production of the token. A credit-token agreement is a regulated agreement for the provision of credit in connection with the use of a credit-token.[47]

It is an offence to give a person a credit-token if he has not asked for it.[48] In the case of credit-token agreements, there are relaxations of the requirements to send the debtor a copy of the executed agreement and to send a notice of cancellation rights.[49] The debtor is not liable under a credit-token agreement for use made of the token by any person, unless the use constituted an acceptance of it by him or he had previously accepted it by signing it or a receipt for it on first using it.[50] The debtor may be liable to the extent of £50 (or the credit limit if lower) for loss to the creditor caused by use of the token when it is outwith the possession of the debtor or of a person authorised by him to use it, the use being before the creditor has been given notice that the token is lost or stolen or for another reason liable to misuse.[51] The debtor may be liable to any extent for loss to the creditor from use (before similar notice) of the token by a person who got possession of it with the debtor's consent.[52] When, in connection with a credit-token agreement (other than a small agreement) a token (other than the first) is given to the debtor, the creditor must give him a copy of the executed agreement and of any other document referred to in it; if he fails to do this he cannot enforce the agreement and, if the default continues for one month, he commits an offence.[53]

The onus is on the creditor to prove that the token was lawfully supplied to the debtor and accepted by him. If the debtor alleges that any use of the token was not authorised by him, it is for the creditor to prove either that the use was so authorised, or that the use occurred before the creditor was given notice of the loss or theft of the token.[54]

18.25   Extortionate Credit Bargains.—A 'credit agreement' is an agreement between an individual and any other person by which that person provides credit of any amount. A 'credit bargain' is the credit agreement if no other transactions are to be taken into account in computing the total charge for credit; otherwise it means the credit agreement and those other transactions taken together.[55] The court is given power, if it finds a credit bargain extortionate, to reopen the credit agreement so as

---

[47] s. 14. Examples of credit-tokens are a bank credit-card (Sched. 2, Ex. 3) and a trading check (Ex. 14); *Elliott* v. *Director General of Fair Trading* [1980] 1 W.L.R. 977. As to credit card transactions, see *Richardson* v. *Worrall* [1985] S.T.C. 693; *Re Charge Card Services Ltd.* [1989] Ch. 497.

[48] s. 51.

[49] ss. 63(4), 64(2).

[50] s. 66.

[51] s. 84; Consumer Credit (Credit-Token Agreements) Regulations 1983 (S.I. 1983 No. 1555).

[52] s. 84(2).

[53] s. 85.

[54] s. 171(4).

[55] s. 137. As to the transactions to be taken into account, see para. 18.3, *supra*, n. 17.

to do justice between the parties. It is important to notice that this provision is not restricted to consumer credit agreements and is thus not subject to a financial limit.

A credit bargain is extortionate if it requires the debtor or a relative of his to make payments (whether unconditionally, or on certain contingencies) which are grossly exorbitant or if it otherwise grossly contravenes ordinary principles of fair dealing. In considering the question of extortion, regard shall be had to such evidence as is adduced concerning: interest rates prevailing when the bargain was made; the debtor's age, experience, business capacity and state of health; the degree to which, at the time of making the bargain, he was under financial pressure, and the nature of that pressure; the degree of risk accepted by the creditor, having regard to the value of any security provided; the creditor's relationship to the debtor; whether or not a colourable cash price was quoted for any goods or services included in the credit bargain; in relation to a linked transaction, how far the transaction was reasonably required for the protection of the debtor or creditor or was in the interest of the debtor; any other relevant considerations.[56]

If the debtor or surety alleges that the bargain is extortionate it is for the creditor to prove the contrary.[57]

The credit agreement may be reopened on an application for that purpose made by the debtor or surety or in any proceedings to enforce the agreement or a security or any linked transaction or in other proceedings in any court where the amount paid or payable under the agreement is relevant.[58] In reopening the agreement the court may, to relieve the debtor or surety from payment of any sum in excess of that fairly due and reasonable, direct an accounting to be made, set aside obligations, require the creditor to make repayments, direct the return of property to the surety or alter the terms of the credit agreement or of any security instrument.[59] These orders may be made notwithstanding that the effect is to place a burden on the creditor in respect of an advantage unfairly enjoyed by another person who is a party to a linked transaction.[60]

Further Reading

Bennion, *Consumer Credit Control* (1977) (Updated Service).
Goode, *Consumer Credit Law* (1989).
Guest and Lloyd, *Encyclopaedia of Consumer Credit Law* (1975) (Updated Service).
Stair Memorial Encyclopaedia, Vol. 5, paras. 801–965.

[56] s. 138. See *Ketley Ltd.* v. *Scott* [1981] I.C.R. 241; *Wills* v. *Wood* [1984] C.C.L.R. 7; *Davies* v. *Directloans Ltd.* [1986] 1 W.L.R. 823; *Woodstead Finance Ltd.* v. *Petrou* [1986] C.C.L.R. 107; *Coldunell Ltd.* v. *Gallon* [1986] Q.B. 1184.
[57] s. 171(7).
[58] s. 139(1).
[59] s. 139(2).
[60] s. 139(3).

CHAPTER 19

RIGHTS IN SECURITY

19.1 Nature of Right in Security.—The term 'right in security' may be read as denoting any right which a creditor may possess for the recovery of his debt in the event of the bankruptcy of his debtor, distinct from, and in addition to, the right which he possesses in common with all other creditors of claiming a ranking in the sequestration. It may be the corroborative obligation of some party other than the bankrupt.[1] Alternatively, the right may be a nexus over some particular property, acquired either by express contract, by implication of law, or by the use of diligence, but in all such cases the debtor retains an ultimate right over the subject-matter in question so that the creditor must account to the debtor for any surplus.[2] Taking 'right in security' in this meaning it is clear that it does not include such documents as a promissory note granted by the debtor, which is evidence of the debt but no security for it.[3] And a mere undertaking by the debtor to set aside some particular fund in order to meet the debt, unless it can be treated as a completed assignation of that fund, leaves the party who has received it to rank as an ordinary creditor, and is not a right in security.[4]

19.2 Sequestration as a Test of Security.—Sequestration (or, in the case of a company, liquidation) is the ultimate test by which it may be determined whether a security has been created, in contrast with an attempt or obligation to give one. The holder of a security can, in some way or other, and to a greater or lesser extent, satisfy his debt from the subjects impledged or hypothecated, whereas an undertaking or attempt to give a security, while it may have reached the stage at which it would found an action against the debtor while solvent, leaves the creditor in the same position as the other creditors who have relied on the personal credit of the debtor. And the theory that an obligation to transfer some specific thing in security made the obligant a trustee, with the corollary that the creditor might vindicate that thing, in the capacity of beneficiary, in the debtor's bankruptcy, was finally rejected in *Bank of Scotland* v. *Hutchison, Main & Co.*[5] There a company had undertaken

---

[1] See Chap. 20.
[2] *Armour* v. *Thyssen Edelstahlwerke A.G.*, 1990 S.L.T. 891 at p. 895, *per* Lord Keith of Kinkel.
[3] *Bow* v. *Spankie*, 1 June 1811, F.C. See *George Shaw* v. *Duffy*, 1943 S.C. 350.
[4] *Graham* v. *Raeburn & Verel* (1895) 23 R. 84; *Brown* v. *Port Seton Harbour Commissioners* (1898) 1 F. 373.
[5] 1914 S.C. (H.L.) 1.

to procure a certain debenture and assign it to a bank in security of a debt. The company went into liquidation after they had procured the debenture but before they had executed an assignation. It was held that the company did not hold the debenture in trust for the bank and accordingly that the bank had no security over it, but ranked as ordinary creditors.

19.3 **Necessity of Delivery.**—It is a general principle in the law of Scotland that a security, in the sense indicated in the preceding paragraphs, cannot be created by mere contract. The security holder must have a real right in the subject, and this involves some form of delivery, actual, symbolical or constructive. Nor will the law infer any right in security over property in favour of anyone who is not in possession thereof. To this general rule there are certain exceptions, known as hypothecs, where a security may be created by mere contract, or may be implied by law without possession.[6]

In addition, a statute may provide that a particular body shall have the power to create a security over its assets by some method which does not involve any form of delivery, or which is not in accordance with the general rules of Scottish conveyancing.[7] The validity of the security must be determined by considering whether it complies with the statutory conditions, and not by asking whether, if no statute were applicable, it would have been effectual at common law.[8] But such cases are exceptional; the general trend of the law is against any latent charges on property without any overt change in its possession.[9] There is nothing in the law of Scotland analogous to the English bill of sale in the case of corporeal moveables such as furniture.

19.4 **Securities Founded on Possession.**—In securities founded on possession a general distinction may be drawn between rights due to express contract between the parties and rights implied by law in particular circumstances. The latter class includes rights of retention and lien.

19.5 **Forms of Constituting Security.**—At common law the constitution of a security by express contract may take one or other of two general forms. It may be effected by transferring possession of the subject to the creditor expressly in security. Pledge of moveables and the pre-1970 bond and disposition in security may be taken as types. Alternatively, property in the security subject may be transferred to the creditor subject to an obligation to reconvey on repayment of the debt. The pre-1970 *ex facie* absolute disposition with back bond and, according to the

---

[6] See below, paras. 19.31–19.38.

[7] See especially floating charges under Pt. XVIII of the Companies Act 1985 (para. 19.39 below) and standard securities under the Conveyancing and Feudal Reform (Scotland) Act 1970 (para. 19.9 below).

[8] *Lord Advocate* v. *Earl of Moray's Trs.* (1905) 7 F. (H.L.) 116.

[9] Stair, I, xiii, 14; Bell, *Prin.*, § 1385.

authorities,[10] the transfer of documents of title to moveables with the intention to give a security are examples.

19.6 Power to Realise.—At common law, where a subject is transferred expressly in security, the creditor has no implied power of sale. His right is limited by his title and to realise the security subject, he must either have an express power of sale,[11] or obtain that power by application to the court.[12] This remains the position with pledges of documents of title, bearer bonds and with non-commerical pledges.[13] Where the Consumer Credit Act 1974 applies,[14] on the expiry of the redemption period, the pledgee may sell the pledge.[15] If, on the other hand, the creditor has an absolute title, qualified by a separate obligation to reconvey, he is invested with a power of sale which he can exercise without notice to the debtor.[16] Should he sell in violation of an agreement not to do so, or by some method involving disregard of the debtor's interests, he may be liable in damages, but the title of the purchaser is not affected.[17]

19.7 Scope of Security.—At common law the form in which the security is given may also affect its scope. If *ex facie* an express security, or pledge, it covers only the debt for which it was granted, and gives the holder no preferential right in the sequestration of the debtor for any debts subsequently contracted.[18] If the title of the creditor is in form absolute, his security, unless limited by some express contract,[19] involves a right of retention, which will cover any debt incurred in the future.[20] This right may be limited by notice that the reversion is no longer in the hands of the party who granted the security. Thus if he is sequestrated the creditor cannot retain his security for advances made after the date of the sequestration.[21] And notice that the reversionary right, or right to demand a reconveyance, has been assigned to a third party, will preclude any further advances on the faith of the security. Thus property was conveyed by A to the National Bank by an *ex facie*

---

[10] *Hamilton* v. *Western Bank* (1856) 19 D. 152; *Hayman* v. *McLintock*, 1907 S.C. 936. But see Bell, *Comm.*, ii, 21, n. 1 (Lord McLaren) and *North Western Bank* v. *Poynter* (1894) 22 R. (H.L.) 1. The language of s. 114(3) of the Consumer Credit Act 1974 also suggests that bills of lading can be pledged in the normal way.

[11] Such a power of sale was incorporated into all bonds and dispositions in security by s. 118 and Sched. FF, Form 1 of the Titles to Land Consolidation (Scotland) Act 1868.

[12] Bell, *Prin.*, § 207.

[13] Consumer Credit Act 1974, s. 114(3) as amended.

[14] Consumer Credit Act 1974, s. 74.

[15] s. 120(1)(*b*).

[16] *Baillie* v. *Drew* (1884) 12 R. 199; *Aberdeen Trades Council* v. *Shipconstructors, etc. Association*, 1949 S.C. (H.L.) 45.

[17] *Duncan* v. *Mitchell* (1893) 21 R. 37; *Davidson* v. *Scott*, 1915 S.C. 924; *Aberdeen Trades Council*, *supra*.

[18] *National Bank* v. *Forbes* (1858) 21 D. 79; *Colquhoun's Tr.* v. *Diack* (1901) 4 F. 358.

[19] *Anderson's Tr.* v. *Somerville* (1899) 36 S.L.R. 833.

[20] *Hamilton* v. *Western Bank* (1856) 19 D. 152; *National Bank* v. *Union Bank* (1886) 14 R. (H.L.) 1.

[21] *Callum* v. *Goldie* (1885) 12 R. 1137.

absolute conveyance. In a back letter it was provided that the property was to be held in security of a present advance and of all advances to be made in future. Subsequently, A assigned his reversionary right to the Union Bank, and the assignation was duly intimated to the National Bank. On A's bankruptcy it was held that the National Bank could not claim any preference over the subjects for any advances after they had been made aware, by intimation from the Union Bank, that the right to demand a reconveyance was no longer vested in their debtor.[22] Similarly, there is no preference for interest falling due after intimation.[23] The permanent trustee in the sequestration of a security holder who holds upon an *ex facie* absolute title, if called upon to fulfil the obligation to reconvey, is bound to do so.[24]

19.8   Subjects of Security.—While these distinctions made by the common law remain, since the introduction of the standard security the law with regard to securities arising by express contract turns chiefly on the nature of the subject over which the security is given.

19.9   Security over Heritable Property.—Until 1970, heritable securities were created by means of a bond and disposition in security, a cash credit bond and disposition in security or an *ex facie* absolute disposition with back bond or letter. While such securities may continue to affect subjects, the only means,[25] apart from a floating charge,[26] of creating[26a] a security over heritable subjects is now the standard security introduced by the Conveyancing and Feudal Reform (Scotland) Act 1970. Where a debtor grants a standard security in one or other of the two prescribed forms and it is recorded,[27] it operates to vest the interest over which it is granted in the creditor as security for performance of the contract to which it relates.[28] All standard securities are regulated by the standard conditions contained in Schedule 3 to the Act except in so far as they may be and have been varied.[29] The standard security gives security for a debt contracted after recording of the deed and no specific sum of money need be stated as the sum secured by the deed.[30] Where the

---

[22] *National Bank* v. *Union Bank* (1886) 14 R. (H.L.) 1. See also *Deeley* v. *Lloyds Bank* [1912] A.C. 756.

[23] *Campbell's J.F.* v. *National Bank*, 1944 S.C. 495.

[24] *Heritable Reversionary Co.* v. *Millar* (1892) 19 R. (H.L.) 43; *Forbes's Trs.* v. *Macleod* (1898) 25 R. 1012.

[25] s. 9(3) and (4).

[26] See para. 19.39.

[26a] *A.I.B. Finance Ltd.* v. *Bank of Scotland*, 1995 S.L.T. 2, dealing with the ranking of a standard security and floating charge.

[27] s. 9(2) and Sched. 2. Registrable under s. 2(3)(i) of the Land Registration (Scotland) Act 1979. *Cf. Sanderson's Trs.* v. *Ambion Scotland Ltd.*, 1994 S.L.T. 645 at p. 648H. For effects of recording as giving notice see *Trade Development Bank* v. *Warriner & Mason (Scotland) Ltd.*, 1980 S.C. 74 and *Trade Development Bank* v. *David W. Haig (Bellshill) Ltd.*, 1983 S.L.T. 510.

[28] s. 11(1).

[29] s. 11(2) and (3) (as amended by the Redemption of Standard Securities (Scotland) Act 1971, s. 1) and Sched. 3.

[30] s. 9(6).

creditor receives notice of the creation of a subsequent duly recorded security over the subjects or of a subsequent duly recorded assignation or conveyance in security, his preference is restricted to security for present advances and any future advances which he is required to make under his contract together with interest, reasonable expenses and outlays.[31] But the creditor and debtor may regulate the preference enjoyed by creditors in such manner as they think fit.[32] The debtor may redeem the standard security on giving two months' notice.[33] If a debtor fails to comply with a calling-up notice[34] requiring him to discharge the debt, the creditor may exercise his rights under the security,[35] including a right to take possession of and to sell the subjects.[36] In other cases of default, the creditor may apply for a warrant to exercise these rights.[36a] If the creditor is unable to sell the subjects or part of them, he may apply for a decree of foreclosure[37] giving him right to them or the unsold part of them.[38] A creditor in possession is liable to maintain the subjects, but not to pay a sum due by the debtor for repairs carried out before the creditor took possession.[39] The detailed rules with regard to heritable securities are not within the scope of this work.[40]

19.10 Security over Moveables.—The ordinary method by which corporeal moveables are used as a security is by the contract of pledge. Pledge requires the delivery of the article, and it is a well-established rule that an agreement to pledge, not followed by actual delivery, confers no preference in bankruptcy, and is in no sense a right in security.[41] The maxim, *traditionibus, non nudis pactis, dominia rerum transferuntur* (the ownership of things is transferred by delivery, not by bare agreement) applies. This has led to many attempts to create some form of security over subjects, such as furniture or stock-in-trade, which it would be inconvenient to deliver in pledge. How far the general rule that a security cannot be created over corporeal moveables without delivery can be evaded by a contract in the form of a sale has been already considered.[42] Attempts to evade it by placing a label on the goods,[43] by

---

[31] s. 13(1). For the position of the creditor's assignee, see *Sanderson's Trs., supra.*
[32] s. 13(3)(*b*); Sched. 2, note 5.
[33] s. 18; *G. Dunlop & Son's J.F.* v. *Armstrong*, 1994 S.L.T. 199.
[34] s. 19.
[35] s. 20(1).
[36] s. 20(2) with Standard Conditions 9 and 10; *Skipton Building Society* v. *Wain*, 1985 S.L.T. 96.
[36a] s. 24(1); *Halifax Building Society* v. *Gupta*, 1994 S.L.T. 339.
[37] s. 28(1).
[38] s. 28(5).
[39] *David Watson Property Management* v. *Woolwich Equitable Bldg. Soc.*, 1992 S.C. (H.L.) 21.
[40] Cf. *Stair Encyclopaedia*, Vol. 20, paras. 108–270.
[41] *Moore* v. *Gledden* (1869) 7 M. 1016.
[42] para. 16.12, *supra*. A power to create securities without delivery, in special statutory cases, in favour of a bank, is provided by the Agricultural Credits (Scotland) Act 1929, ss. 5–8.
[43] *Orr's Tr.* v. *Tullis* (1870) 8 M. 936.

a fictitious lease,[44] or by an imitation of the process, appropriate only in the case of heritage, of giving sasine,[45] or by purporting to create a trust,[46] have failed. But where there is a genuine sale, even though the purpose is to create a security, effect will be given to the transaction. So if, for instance, the object of a proposed loan is to enable the borrower to acquire some furniture, what is in effect a security for the loan may be obtained if the lender purchases the furniture, and places it in the possession of the borrower on a contract of hire. In the event of the borrower's bankruptcy his trustee cannot assert a right to the furniture preferable to that of the lender to remove it.[47] It is probably the law that if subjects are so situated that any form of delivery is impossible, as in the case of pipes sunk in the ground,[48] of subjects already in the lender's possession[49] or (it may be suggested) of goods in course of transit without any document of title, an assignation in writing would be effectual in the event of the borrower's bankruptcy.

19.11 Forms of Delivery.—Delivery does not in every case involve the physical transfer of the article. It may be actual, symbolical, or constructive. Actual delivery takes place when goods are physically transferred from one party to another. Also if the goods are in any confined space, and the complete command of that space is transferred, the goods are delivered. So where barrels in the yard of a company were enclosed by a fence, and the key of its gate was given to a party who had advanced money on the security of the barrels it was held that the security was completed by delivery.[50] The question whether goods can be held as delivered if they are set aside in the premises of the party who transfers them is not settled.[51]

19.12 Symbolical Delivery.—The main instance of symbolical delivery arises in the case where goods are shipped and a bill of lading is taken for them. The bill of lading is recognised as a symbol of the goods, and its transfer, in pursuance either of a sale or of a pledge of the goods to which it refers, should have the same legal effect as the physical delivery of the goods themselves,[52] but, as was seen above,[53] it has been held that transfer of a bill of lading in security vests the creditor with a right

---

[44] *Heritable Securities Investment Association* v. *Wingate's Tr.* (1880) 7 R. 1094.

[45] *Stiven* v. *Cowan* (1878) 15 S.L.R. 422.

[46] *Emerald Stainless Steel* v. *South Side Distribution*, 1982 S.C. 61. This aspect of the Lord Ordinary's reasoning was not referred to by the House of Lords when the case was overruled in *Armour* v. *Thyssen Edelstahlwerke A.G.*, 1990 S.L.T. 891.

[47] *Duncanson* v. *Jefferis' Tr.* (1881) 8 R. 563; *Union Bank* v. *Mackenzie* (1865) 3 M. 765. See also Goudy, *Bankruptcy*, p. 520.

[48] *Darling* v. *Wilson's Tr.* (1887) 15 R. 180.

[49] *Blundell Leigh* v. *Attenborough* [1921] 3 K.B. 235.

[50] *West Lothian Oil Co.* v. *Mair* (1892) 20 R. 64; contrast *Pattison's Tr.* v. *Liston* (1893) 20 R. 806.

[51] *Gibson* v. *Forbes* (1833) 11 S. 916; *Boak* v. *Megget* (1844) 6 D. 662.

[52] Bell, *Prin.*, § 417.

[53] para. 19.5, *supra.*

of property. It has been suggested, though not decided, that transfer of
the bill of lading has this effect even where the goods are not
ascertained, *e.g.* in the case where several bills of lading are taken for a
parcel of goods, and there are no means of identifying the *ipsa corpora*
to which each bill relates.[54] But, at least so far as sale is concerned, this
dictum seems inconsistent with the provisions of section 16 of the Sale
of Goods Act.[55]

Apart from the case of bills of lading, attempts to evade the necessity
of actual delivery by some symbolical form have not usually proved
successful, either in the case of sales before the Sale of Goods Act 1893,
or in the case of securities. A sale of standing trees was followed by
cutting and removing a few of them, with a written minute declaring
that the purchaser had thereby 'entered into his bargain.' It was held
that the trees were not delivered, and passed to the trustee in the
seller's sequestration.[56] When it was attempted to complete a right in
security over the moveable machinery in a mill by stopping the mill and
going through a form of taking sasine both of the mill and of the
machinery, it was decided that delivery of the machinery had not been
effected, and therefore that no effectual right in security had been
created.[57]

19.13 Constructive Delivery.—Constructive, as distinguished from symbolical,
delivery is the term applied when goods are in a store, and their
delivery is attempted either by a delivery order addressed to the
storekeeper, or by the indorsation of the storekeeper's warrant. This is
effectual to transfer a real right in the goods, *i.e.* is equivalent to actual
delivery, under the following conditions: (1) Intimation of the transfer
must be made to the keeper of the store. A delivery order, or
storekeeper's warrant, is not regarded as a symbol of the goods in the
sense that a bill of lading is. While the mere transfer of the bill of lading
carries the real right in the goods without any intimation to the captain
of the ship in which they are situated, the issue or transfer of a delivery
order or warrant leaves the right of the transferee merely personal (*jus
ad rem*) until it is completed by intimation to the custodier of the
goods.[58] The theory of the law is that the storekeeper, on intimation of
the transfer being made to him, ceases to hold the goods as custodier
for the transferor, and holds them subsequently as custodier for the
transferee. The latter has acquired civil possession and hence a *jus in re*,
through the actual possession of the custodier holding for him, and that
civil possession is not acquired until intimation is made.[59] (2) Intimation
must be made to the actual custodier, the keeper of the store in which

[54] *Hayman* v. *McLintock*, 1907 S.C. 936, 952 (Lord McLaren).
[55] Benjamin, *Sale of Goods* (4th ed., 1992), § 18–133.
[56] *Paul* v. *Cuthbertson* (1840) 2 D. 1286.
[57] *Stiven* v. *Cowan* (1878) 15 S.L.R. 422.
[58] *Widenmeyer* v. *Burn Stewart & Co.*, 1967 S.C. 85.
[59] *Inglis* v. *Robertson & Baxter* (1898) 25 R. (H.L.) 70.

the goods are. It is not sufficient to intimate to a party, for instance, an excise officer in a bonded store, who may have the control of the goods, but is not the keeper of the store.[60] A custom of trade to regard such intimation as sufficient is a misunderstanding of the law, to which no effect can be given.[61] (3) The custodier must be an independent third party, not the servant of the owner of the goods. The law does not recognise constructive delivery by the medium of orders addressed by the owner of goods to the keeper of his own store, and it is immaterial that the store may be used also for keeping goods belonging to third parties.[62] (4) The goods must be ascertained, so that in some way those referred to and transferred by the delivery order may be distinguished from the general mass of goods kept by the transferor in the particular store. So where there were a number of bags of flour in a store, with no marks whereby one bag could be distinguished from another, it was held that a delivery order for a certain number of bags, though intimated to the storekeeper and entered by him in the store books, did not effect constructive delivery, because there were no means of determining which bags were transferred and which were not.[63] In such a case, however, if the goods are subsequently ascertained, by being physically separated from the general mass, they are constructively delivered as at the date when they are so ascertained.[64]

19.14 Securities over Ships.[65]—The Merchant Shipping Act 1995 makes provision for the registration, discharge and transfer of mortgages over a British ship or shares thereof.[66] It may be the law that a bill of sale or other conveyance in writing, even although it was not registered, would form a security effectual in the bankruptcy of the owner, provided that it was followed by actual possession or by possession inferred from the receipt of the earnings of the ship.[67] If an instrument in the appropriate form creating a mortgage, *i.e.* a security over a ship or shares, is produced to the registrar, the registrar is directed to enter it in the register.[68] Preference depends on the order in which the mortgages appear in the register[69] but, as noted below, a mortgagee's right may be

---

[60] *Rhind's Tr.* v. *Robertson & Baxter* (1891) 18 R. 623. See also *Dobell* v. *Neilson* (1904) 7 F. 281.

[61] *Dobell* v. *Neilson, supra.*

[62] *Anderson* v. *McCall* (1866) 4 M. 765; *Pochin* v. *Robinow* (1869) 7 M. 622, *per* Lord President Inglis at pp. 628–29.

[63] *Hayman* v. *McLintock*, 1907 S.C. 936; contrast *Price & Pierce* v. *Bank of Scotland*, 1910 S.C. 1095; 1912 S.C. (H.L.) 19.

[64] *Black* v. *Incorporation of Bakers* (1867) 6 M. 136; *Pochin* v. *Robinow, supra.*

[65] For aircraft see the Mortgaging of Aircraft Order 1972 as amended by the Mortgaging of Aircraft (Amendment) Order 1981; Shawcross & Beaumont, *Air Law*, Vol. 1, paras. V, 54 *et seq.*

[66] s. 16 and Sched. 1.

[67] *Watson* v. *Duncan* (1879) 6 R. 1247.

[68] 1995 Act, Sched. 1, para. 7(2) and (3).

[69] Sched. 1, para. 8(1), subject to the registrar being given a priority notice (para. 8(2)); *Lombard North Central* v. *Lord Advocate*, 1983 S.L.T. 361.

defeated by the holder of a bond of bottomry or of a maritime lien.[70] It may also be affected by a lien acquired by a shipwright for repairs instructed by the mortgagor.[71]

19.15 Powers of Mortgagee of Ship.—A mortgagee has a statutory power of sale if the mortgage money or any part of it is due.[72] He is entitled to interdict any act of the owner which may imperil his security, *e.g.* a voyage uninsured.[73] Though the Act has no express provision on the subject, it has long been established that the statutory power of sale implies the right to take possession of the ship.[74] A mortgagee, if he enters into possession, not otherwise, is liable for furnishings supplied to the ship on the order of the master.[75]

19.16 Securities over Incorporeal Property.—A debt of any kind, for instance, a policy of insurance, may be transferred in security by a written assignation, followed by intimation to the debtor.[76] The law of Scotland does not recognise any security (known in England as an equitable mortgage) by the mere deposit of title deeds,[77] and therefore the mere transfer of the voucher of a debt (unless it is a negotiable instrument[78]) or a mere assignation not followed by intimation to the debtor,[79] creates no effectual security. So no preferential right is created by the transfer of a policy of insurance without intimation to the insurance company.[80] The same principles were applied to an assignation of the uncalled capital of a company, which was held to be ineffectual as a security unless it was completed by intimation to each shareholder.[81]

19.17 Shares in Company.—Shares in a company may be used as a security by transferring them to the creditor, subject to an obligation by him to retransfer, but such a transfer will be effective to create a security only if it is registered.[82] Under the prior law, it was held that it was no objection to the creditor's title that the transfer was registered within 60 days[83] of the debtor's sequestration[84] or even after the date of sequestration,[85] but under the 1985 Act a preference is created on the

---

[70] paras. 19.33 and 19.38, *infra.*
[71] *Tyne Dock Engineering Co.* v. *Royal Bank of Scotland,* 1974 S.L.T. 57.
[72] Sched. 1, para. 9; *Banque Indo Suez* v. *Maritime Co. Overseas Inc.,* 1984 S.C. 120.
[73] *Laming* v. *Seater* (1889) 16 R. 828.
[74] Bell, *Prin.,* § 1382A.
[75] *Havilland, Routh & Co.* v. *Thomson* (1864) 3 M. 313.
[76] As to assignation and intimation, see paras. 38.1 to 38.6, *infra.*
[77] *Christie* v. *Ruxton* (1862) 24 D. 1182.
[78] See para. 38.9, *infra.*
[79] *Gallemos Ltd. (in receivership)* v. *Barratt Falkirk Ltd.,* 1990 S.L.T. 98.
[80] *Strachan* v. *McDougle* (1835) 13 S. 954; *Wylie's Exrx.* v. *McJannet* (1901) 4 F. 195.
[81] *Liquidators of Union Club* v. *Edinburgh Life Assurance Co.* (1906) 8 F. 1143.
[82] Bankruptcy Act 1985, s. 36(3).
[83] The period under the 1985 Act is now six months before the date of sequestration.
[84] *Guild* v. *Young* (1884) 22 S.L.R. 520.
[85] *Morrison* v. *Harrison* (1876) 3 R. 406.

day it becomes completely effectual.[86] Moreover, before registration, the transfer is liable to be defeated by arrestments used by some other creditor, or by a fraudulent transfer by the debtor.[87] It is a practice, more common in England than in Scotland,[88] to deposit the share certificate with blank transfers, *i.e.* transfers executed by the transferor, but without the name of the transferee. The advantage is that it enables the creditor to transfer his right without any further procedure. The validity of a security by means of blank transfers is established in England; in Scotland it may be doubtful, and has not been decided, whether they are open to challenge under the Blank Bonds and Trusts Act 1696,[89] which declares that instruments delivered blank in the name of the creditor shall be void.[90]

19.18 Obligations of Security Holder.[91]—The obligation of a party who holds any property in security is to exercise reasonable care. Thus when a company offered new shares to its shareholders on advantageous terms it was decided that a party who was registered as owner of certain shares but really held them in security was bound either to take the new shares or to intimate the offer to the debtor, for whom he held.[92] But a creditor is not liable for the accidental loss or destruction of the subject he holds in security, nor is his right to recover his debt affected,[93] unless tender of payment has been made and the return of the security subjects wrongfully refused.[94] If, however, the creditor is unable to return the security, from some cause attributable to his own fault, he cannot demand payment of the debt.[95] As a general rule where a security, such as a pledge, is constituted by delivery, the creditor cannot restore the possession of the subjects pledged to the debtor without abandoning his right in security;[96] but it has been held, in the case of a bill of lading, and on grounds which are applicable generally, that a creditor, desirous of realising his security, might employ the debtor as his agent to effect a sale, and on that footing restore the subjects to the debtor's possession, without losing his preferable right to the proceeds of the sale.[97] On payment of the debt it is the duty of the creditor to restore the exact subject given in security, and hence it was held that a bank, to which

[86] 1985 Act, s. 36(3).
[87] *Rainford* v. *Keith* [1905] 1 Ch. 296.
[88] See *Crerar* v. *Bank of Scotland,* 1921 S.C. 736, affd. 1922 S.C. (H.L.) 137.
[89] c. 25.
[90] *Colonial Bank* v. *Cady* (1890) 15 App.Cas. 267; see *Shaw* v. *Caledonian Ry.* (1890) 17 R. 466, at p. 478.
[91] As to the regulation of pledge by the Consumer Credit Act 1974, see para. 18.15, *supra.*
[92] *Waddell* v. *Hutton,* 1911 S.C. 575.
[93] *Syred* v. *Carruthers* (1858) E.B. & E. 469.
[94] *Fraser* v. *Smith* (1899) 1 F. 487.
[95] *Ellis & Co.'s Tr.* v. *Dixon-Johnston* [1925] A.C. 489.
[96] *Hunter* v. *Slack* (1860) 22 D. 1166.
[97] *North-Western Bank* v. *Poynter* (1894) 22 R. (H.L.) 1. See also *Moore* v. *Gledden* (1869) 7 M. 1016 and *Wolifson* v. *Harrison,* 1977 S.C. 384.

shares had been transferred in security, was not justified in tendering in return equivalent shares of the same company unless in virtue of an agreement under which this method of dealing was sanctioned by the debtor.[98] Except by agreement, the creditor is not entitled to use the security subjects.[99]

In realising his security the creditor must proceed exactly in the terms, express, or in the case of heritable securities statutory, of his power of sale, and failure in this respect may entitle a purchaser to resile,[1] or afford ground for a reduction of the sale at the instance of the debtor.[2] He must also have regard to the interests of the debtor, and of postponed bondholders.[3] A sale without such regard may be interdicted, or may lead to a claim of damages but not, it is conceived, to a reduction of a sale to a bona fide purchaser.[4] A creditor proposing to realise his security is bound to assign the debt, and the security held for it, to anyone who tenders payment, and can show a reasonable interest,[5] though he may refuse an assignation of the security if he can show that his own interests would be prejudiced thereby,[6] or that he would be exposed to any liability.[7] A creditor, in selling the subject of his security, is not entitled to purchase,[8] except under the provisions, applicable to heritable securities only, of section 8 of the Heritable Securities (Scotland) Act 1894 or section 28 of the Conveyancing and Feudal Reform (Scotland) Act 1970. But a creditor may purchase at a sale by the trustee in the debtor's sequestration,[9] by another bondholder,[10] or by one of several creditors in the bond.[11]

19.19 Lien.—A lien is a right to retain property until some debt or other obligation is satisfied. If constituted by express contract it is a pledge under another name, and it is only liens implied by law which need be considered here.

'Lien' and 'right of retention' are sometimes used as synonymous terms, but, more strictly, a lien is a right founded on mere possession, retention a right founded on property. A lien is a right to remain in possession of a subject held on a limited title; a right of retention is the

[98] *Crerar* v. *Bank of Scotland*, 1921 S.C. 736, affd. 1922 S.C. (H.L.) 137. See also *McKirdy* v. *Webster's Trs.* (1895) 22 R. 340.

[99] *Wolifson, supra.*

[1] *Ferguson* v. *Rodger* (1895) 22 R. 643.

[2] *Stewart* v. *Brown* (1882) 10 R. 192.

[3] Bell, *Comm.,* ii, 271. This does not apply to a sale by a receiver: *Forth and Clyde Construction* v. *Trinity Timber and Plywood Co. Ltd.,* 1984 S.C. 1.

[4] *Beveridge* v. *Wilson* (1829) 7 S. 279; *Kerr* v. *McArthur's Trs.* (1848) 11 D. 301.

[5] *Adair's Tr.* v. *Rankin* (1895) 22 R. 975.

[6] *Smith* v. *Gentle* (1844) 6 D. 1164.

[7] *Bruce* v. *Scottish Amicable Insurance Co.,* 1907 S.C. 637.

[8] *Stirling's Trs.* (1865) 3 M. 851.

[9] *Cf.* Bankruptcy (Scotland) Act 1985, s. 39(8) with Bankruptcy (Scotland) Act 1913, s. 116.

[10] *Begbie* v. *Boyd* (1837) 16 S. 232.

[11] *Wright* v. *Buchanan,* 1917 S.C. 73.

right of a party, whose title is one of ownership subject to an obligation to convey, to refuse to implement his obligation until some counter-obligation due by the party entitled to demand conveyance has been fulfilled. The effect and limits of a right of retention have been considered in dealing with securities constituted by an *ex facie* absolute conveyance qualified by a backbond.[12] In what follows lien is taken in its more restricted sense as a right founded on possession of property belonging to another.

19.20 Special and General Liens.—Liens are classed as special and general. A special lien is a right implied by law to retain an article until some specific debt is paid. A general lien is a right to retain until some balance, arising on a contract of employment, is discharged. The law of Scotland does not recognise as a corollary from mere possession, as distinguished from ownership, any right in the possessor to continue in possession until all debts due to him by the owner are paid.[13] A lien is in all cases a limited right, and its extent depends either on the contract under which possession was obtained, or on usage of trade. The chief instances are in sale and in contracts for services. The lien of an unpaid seller has been already considered.[14]

19.21 Special Lien: In Contracts for Services.—In contracts for services it is a general rule, based, according to the Scottish authorities, on principles of mutual contract,[14a] that if the party employed has been placed in possession of an article belonging to his employer he has a right to retain it until he is paid for his work under that contract. The mutual obligations of the parties are on the one hand to pay for the work done; on the other to return the article, and the party employed is not bound to fulfil his obligation until the obligation due to him, and arising out of the same contract, is fulfilled. On this footing the assertion of a special lien does not require proof of custom of trade; it is an implied condition in all contracts for services.[15] So it is immaterial that no work has actually been done on the article over which the lien is claimed, and an accountant, who had been placed in possession of business books in order to collect debts, was held to be entitled to a lien over the books, and the defence that he had done no work on the books themselves was rejected.[16] But to found a special lien the party employed must be placed in possession of the article; a servant, who has merely the custody, and not the possession, of his master's property, has no lien.[17]

---

[12] para. 19.7, *supra*; and as to retention of debts, para. 13.11 *supra*.

[13] *Harper* v. *Faulds* (1791) Bell's 8vo Cases, 440; 2 Ross. L.C. 708; 27 Jan. 1791, F.C.; *Anderson's Tr.* v. *Fleming* (1871) 9 M. 718.

[14] para. 16.45, *supra*.

[14a] *National Homecare Ltd.* v. *Belling & Co. Ltd.*, 1994 S.L.T. 50.

[15] Bell, *Comm.*, ii, 92; *Miller* v. *Hutcheson* (1881) 8 R. 489; *Robertson* v. *Ross* (1887) 15 R. 67.

[16] *Meikle & Wilson* v. *Pollard* (1880) 8 R. 69. *National Homecare Ltd.*, *supra*.

[17] *Barnton Hotel Co.* v. *Cook* (1899) 1 F. 1190; contrast *Findlay* v. *Waddell*, 1910 S.C. 670.

Where a hire purchase contract forbids the creation of any lien by the hirer, a repairer who carries out repairs on the article on behalf of the hirer does not acquire a lien.[18]

19.22   General Lien.—A general lien is recognised by the custom of certain professions and trades. Its range depends on the usage of the particular trade, and varies from a right covering all debts arising from prior employment, as in the case of a solicitor,[19] to a right covering merely the balance due on the working of a particular year, as in the case of a bleacher.[20] In a case not covered by decision the question whether a general lien existed is to be determined on the evidence of parties engaged in the trade that their dealings were on the footing of a lien. The fact that a general lien is recognised in a particular trade in England is evidence, though not necessarily conclusive evidence, that it is also recognised in that trade in Scotland.[21]

Among cases of general lien particular notice may be taken of the lien of (a) a factor, (b) a banker, (c) a solicitior and (d) an innkeeper.

19.23   (a) Lien of Factor.—A factor or mercantile agent has a general lien over all goods, bills, money or documents belonging to his employer which have come into his possession in the course of his employment.[22] It covers all advances made to the principal, the factor's salary or commission, and any liabilities incurred on the principal's behalf.[23] It will not cover, in the principal's bankruptcy, debts due to the factor, but arising on some separate account.[24] A mercantile agent is defined, for the purposes of the Factors Act 1889, as a mercantile agent 'having in the customary course of his business as such agent authority either to sell goods, or to consign goods for the purpose of sale, or to buy goods, or to raise money on the security of goods.'[25] In questions of lien the term is used somewhat more widely, and the factor's or mercantile agent's lien has been held to belong to an auctioneer,[26] and to a stockbroker.[27]

19.24   (b) Lien of Banker.—A banker has a general lien over all bills, notes and negotiable securities. It covers any balance due by the customer.[28] There is no case in Scotland extending the lien to any instrument not

---

[18] *Lamonby* v. *Foulds Ltd.*, 1928 S.C. 89. See Gow, *Law of Hire-Purchase in Scotland* (2nd ed., 1968), p. 164; Wilson, *Debt* (2nd ed.), p. 95.

[19] para. 19.25, *infra.*

[20] *Anderson's Tr.* v. *Fleming* (1871) 9 M. 718.

[21] *Strong* v. *Philips* (1878) 5 R. 770 (packer).

[22] Bell, *Prin.*, § 1445.

[23] *Sibbald* v. *Gibson* (1852) 15 D. 217; *Glendinning* v. *Hope*, 1911 S.C. (H.L.) 73.

[24] *Miller* v. *McNair* (1852) 14 D. 955.

[25] s.1(1).

[26] *Miller* v. *Hutcheson* (1881) 8 R. 489.

[27] *Glendinning* v. *Hope*, 1911 S.C. (H.L.) 73.

[28] Bell, *Prin.*, § 1451.

negotiable, for instance, to share certificates. In order that negotiable securities may be subject to the lien they must have been lodged with the banker in his capacity as monetary agent, not merely for safe keeping. Thus when exchequer bills were sent to a bank in a locked box, of which the bank had no key, it was held that there was no lien over them, although the bills were periodically taken from the box and given to the banker in order that he might collect the interest.[29] But the terms of a receipt given by the bank and indicating that the documents were held for safe keeping does not necessarily exclude a lien, in a case where there is proof that the bank, relying on lien, had made advances to the customer.[30] Where negotiable securities are lodged with a banker by a stockbroker, the banker, in the absence of notice to the contrary, may be entitled to assume that they are the stockbroker's own property, and claim a lien over them, in the stockbroker's bankruptcy, in a question with the clients to whom they really belong. But where the banker has notice, either express, or from his knowledge of the usual course of business, that the securities are the property of the stockbroker's clients, there is a difference between a right founded on express pledge and one founded on the lien implied by law. Where securities are expressly pledged for a specific advance the banker is entitled to assume that the stockbroker has the authority of his clients so to pledge them, and may therefore, on the stockbroker's failure, retain them to meet the amount advanced. But a claim to retain them to meet the general balance due by the stockbroker, founded on lien and not on any specific pledge, is in a different position, because the banker has no right to assume that the stockbroker has any authority to subject his client's securities to a lien for his own general balance.[31] It would appear that a banker's right in the exercise of lien is merely to retain the securities, not to realise them.[32]

19.25   (c) **Lien of Solicitor.**—A solicitor has a general lien over all papers placed in his hands by his client. It extends over title deeds of any description, and miscellaneous documents, such as the client's will.[33] It does not entitle the solicitor to obstruct the course of justice by refusing to produce papers entrusted to him for the purposes of an action,[34] but it does entitle him to refuse production of papers required for a professional negligence case against him.[35] Nor can it be exercised over the register of shareholders of a company, which, because of the statutory right of the public to consult it,[36] cannot be subjected to any

---

[29] *Brandao* v. *Barnett* (1846) 12 Cl. & F. 787.

[30] *Robertson's Tr.* v. *Royal Bank* (1890) 18 R. 12.

[31] *National Bank* v. *Dickie's Tr.* (1895) 22 R. 740.

[32] *Robertson's Tr.* v. *Royal Bank* (1890) 18 R. 12.

[33] *Paul* v. *Meikle* (1868) 7 M. 235. See also *McIntosh* v. *Chalmers* (1883) 11 R. 8.

[34] *Callman* v. *Bell* (1793) Mor. 6255.

[35] *Yau* v. *Ogilvie & Co.*, 1985 S.L.T. 91.

[36] Companies Act 1985, ss. 211, as amended by s. 23 and para. 3 of Sched. 10 to the Companies Act 1989, and 219 as amended by s. 143 of the 1989 Act.

form of security.[37] It covers the solicitor's business accounts, and advances usually made in the ordinary course of business, such as to counsel or witnesses.[38] It does not cover cash advances to the client,[39] nor, it would appear, the account of an Edinburgh solicitor in Court of Session proceedings, if paid by the country solicitor;[40] nor the account of an English solicitor, unless a Scottish solicitor has paid it, or is liable for it.[41] The solicitor's lien, so far as it is a general lien, rests on professional usage, and is not enjoyed by persons similarly employed who are not solicitors. Thus an accountant has a lien over papers entrusted to him only for his charge for work done in connection with those papers, not a general lien for his whole professional account,[42] and the scope of the lien of the factor or land agent on an estate has been held to depend upon whether he is a qualified solicitor.[43]

19.26 Solicitor's Lien in Questions with Third Parties.—The lien of a solicitor may be exercised against the client, and also, in certain cases, against parties deriving right from him. Thus the solicitor of a seller may retain title deeds against the purchaser, the solicitor of a borrower against the lender on heritable security. In neither case can he exercise this right if he acts for both parties (*i.e.* for seller and purchaser, or for borrower and lender) unless he has intimated to the purchaser or lender that he holds the title deeds and proposes to claim a lien over them.[44] In any event a solicitor cannot acquire a lien, in a question with a heritable creditor, after the date of recording or registering the security.[45] Where the lien is exercised, the solicitor's right cannot be evaded by raising an action, obtaining a diligence for the recovery of documents, and calling on the solicitor to produce the title deeds as a haver.[46]

19.27 Solicitor's Lien in Sequestration.—A permanent trustee in sequestration,[47] or the liquidator of a company,[48] is entitled to insist on the production of all papers relating to the estate under his charge. The solicitor, who must give them up, does so under implied reservation of his lien: express reservation is unnecessary.[49] The result is not to give

[37] *Garpel Haematite Co.* v. *Andrew* (1866) 4 M. 617.
[38] *Richardson* v. *Merry* (1863) 1 M. 940, at p. 946.
[39] *Christie* v. *Ruxton* (1862) 24 D. 1182; *Wylie's Exrx.* v. *McJannet* (1901) 4 F. 195.
[40] *Largue* v. *Urquhart* (1883) 10 R. 1229.
[41] *Liquidator of Grand Empire Theatre* v. *Snodgrass*, 1932 S.C. (H.L.) 73.
[42] *Findlay* v. *Waddell*, 1910 S.C. 670; *Morrison* v. *Fulwell's Tr.* (1901) 9 S.L.T. 34.
[43] *Macrae* v. *Leith*, 1913 S.C. 901.
[44] *Gray* v. *Graham* (1855) 2 Macq. 435; *Drummond* v. *Muirhead & Guthrie Smith* (1900) 2 F. 585.
[45] Conveyancing (Scotland) Act 1924, s. 27; Land Registration (Scotland) Act 1979, s. 29(2).
[46] *Dalrymple* v. *Earl of Selkirk* (1751) 2 Elchies 198.
[47] Bankruptcy Act 1985, s. 38(4); *Garden, Haig Scott & Wallace* v. *Stevenson's Tr.*, 1962 S.C. 51.
[48] Insolvency Act 1986, s. 144; *Train & McIntyre* v. *Forbes*, 1925 S.L.T. 286 (accountants), applying *Renny & Webster* v. *Myles* (1847) 9 D. 619.
[49] *Adam & Winchester* v. *White's Tr.* (1884) 11 R. 863, *per* Lord President Inglis at p. 865; *Garden, Haig Scott & Wallace* v. *Stevenson's Tr.*, *supra*.

him any claim against the trustee or liquidator,[50] but to entitle him to be ranked for his account as a preferred creditor.[51] It is not decided how he ranks in competition with other preferred creditors, but he is postponed to the expenses of the liquidation or sequestration.[52]

The solicitor's lien does not give him the right to dispose of the papers, only to retain them.[53] Accordingly, his lien is worthless in a case where there is nothing in the bankrupt's estate over which he can be given a preference. In that case he ranks as an ordinary creditor.[54]

19.28   **(d) Lien of Innkeeper.**—An innkeeper has a lien over his guest's luggage for the amount of his bill.[55] He cannot detain the guest or the clothes he is wearing.[56] The lien covers articles not of the nature of ordinary luggage, such as a solicitor's letter book.[57] It does not cover articles not brought as luggage, but hired by the guest during his stay at the inn,[58] or articles, not luggage, handed to the innkeeper as security for the bill,[59] or delivered by a third party for the use of guests.[60] By statute it also does not cover 'any vehicle or any property left therein, or any horse or other live animal or its harness or other equipment.'[61] It may be exercised even if the articles brought as luggage do not belong to the guest, and the innkeeper is aware of the fact.[62] Under the Innkeepers Act 1878,[63] an innkeeper is entitled, after advertisement, to sell by auction goods brought to or left in his inn, provided that a debt for board and lodging, or for the keep of any horse, shall have been six weeks outstanding. He must account to the guest for any surplus.

19.29   **Limit of Rights under Liens.**—It has been laid down that lien is a right over which the court may exercise an equitable control, and therefore, that in particular circumstances a ship might be released from a lien for repairs on terms to be fixed by the court.[64] And no lien founded on possession can be asserted if it would conflict with the express or implied terms of the contract under which possession was obtained. Thus if a bill is sent to a banker for discount, and he refuses to discount

[50] *Adam & Winchester* v. *White's Tr., supra*; *Lochee Sawmills Co.* v. *Stevenson*, 1908 S.C. 559.
[51] *Skinner* v. *Henderson* (1865) 3 M. 867.
[52] *Miln's J.F.* v. *Spence's Trs.*, 1927 S.L.T. 425.
[53] *Ferguson* v. *Grant* (1856) 18 D. 536, at p. 538.
[54] *Garden, Haig Scott & Wallace* v. *Stevenson's Tr., supra*.
[55] Bell, *Prin.*, § 1428. This lien can be regarded as a special lien: see Gloag & Irvine, p. 397.
[56] *Sunbolf* v. *Alford* (1838) 3 M. & W. 248.
[57] *Snead* v. *Watkins* (1856) 1 C.B. (N.S.) 267.
[58] *Broadwood* v. *Granara* (1854) 10 Ex. 417.
[59] *Marsh* v. *Commissioner of Police* (1943) 60 T.L.R. 96.
[60] *Bermans and Nathans Ltd.* v. *Weibye*, 1983 S.C. 67.
[61] Hotel Proprietors Act 1956, s. 2(2).
[62] *Bermans and Nathans Ltd. supra.*
[63] s.1.
[64] *Garscadden* v. *Ardrossan Dry Dock Co.*, 1910 S.C. 178.

it, he cannot retain it under lien.[65] Where money was deposited with a
solicitor in order to effect a composition with the depositor's creditors,
and this proved impracticable, it was held that the solicitor could not
retain the money to meet a general balance on his business account in a
question with the trustee in the depositor's sequestration.[66] And it is a
general principle that when a security is constituted by express pledge it
cannot be extended, on the plea of lien, to cover other debts or a
general balance.[67] The primary purpose of a lien is to constitute a
security for payment of charges incurred in connection with the object
over which the lien exists.[68] But this is a right of limited value unless,
where the debtor proves recalcitrant, the object in question can be sold.

19.30 Extinction of Lien.—As a lien is founded on possession it is lost if
possession is relinquished,[69] with a probable exception, as in the case of
a pledge, where an article is restored to its owner on a contract whereby
he is constituted the agent of the holder of the lien for the purpose of
selling the article.[70] Some of the articles held under lien may be restored
without affecting the lien over the rest.[71] Where a bill is taken for the
debt, and subsequently dishonoured, the presumption is that the bill has
been taken as an additional security, and the lien is not affected, unless
the currency of the bill is unusually long, when the lien will be held to
have been relinquished unless it was expressly reserved.[72]

19.31 Hypothecs.—As was explained above,[73] even at common law certain
securities are recognised even though delivery of the subject-matter is
not made to the creditor. Hypothec is the general term used to denote a
security without possession. Hypothecs are either conventional, *i.e.*
created by express contract, or legal, implied by law in particular
circumstances.

19.32 Conventional Hypothecs.—The only conventional hypothecs which are
recognised in the law of Scotland are bonds of bottomry and of
respondentia.

19.33 Bottomry and Respondentia.—These, now nearly obsolete, are bonds
covering, in the case of bottomry, a ship, in the case of *respondentia*, a

---

[65] *Borthwick* v. *Bremner* (1833) 12 S. 121.
[66] *Middlemas* v. *Gibson*, 1910 S.C. 577.
[67] para. 19.7, *supra*.
[68] But in the case of a depositary to whom goods have been handed over for repairs,
etc., the depositary cannot exercise his lien over the goods to secure payment of garaging
or other storage costs unless that is a matter of separate agreement with the depositor:
Stephen v. *Swayne* (1861) 24 D. 158; *Carntyne Motors* v. *Curran*, 1958 S.L.T. (Sh.Ct.) 6.
[69] *Miller* v. *McNair* (1852) 14 D. 955, 959 *per* L.J.-C. Hope; Bell, *Comm.* ii, 89. For a
possible qualification see *Hostess Mobile Catering* v. *Archibald Scott Ltd.*, 1981 S.C. 185.
[70] para. 19.18, *supra*.
[71] *Gray* v. *Graham* (1855) 2 Macq. 435.
[72] *Palmer* v. *Lee* (1880) 7 R. 651; approving Bell, *Comm.*, ii, 109.
[73] See para. 19.3, *supra*.

cargo, granted by the owner or master of a ship, and constituting a floating charge without possession or any entry on the ship's register. Bottomry bonds by the owner are now unknown. The master of a ship has an implied power to grant a bond of bottomry when the ship is in a foreign port, unable to proceed on its voyage without an advance of money, and when no money is procurable on the personal credit of the owner.[74] Before granting a bottomry bond in these circumstances the master must communicate with the owner, if in the circumstances such communication is practicable; if not, he may grant the bond on his own authority.[75] The lender on bottomry has no claim unless he can show that the condition as to communication with the owner was fulfilled; that the circumstances justified the bond; and that the ship has arrived at her port of destination. As the bond depends on the safe arrival of the ship, in a competition between two bottomry bonds the one last in date, as presumably the means by which the ship ultimately arrived, is preferable.[76] While there is no established form of bottomry bond, it must indicate the risk, the voyage and the event on which it will become exigible. If it fails in these particulars it is not a bond of bottomry, and is not in any way binding on the owner.[77] Assuming the validity of the bond the lender may arrest the ship and insist on a judicial sale.[78] He is preferable to any ordinary creditor or to a mortgagee, although not to the seamen or master holding a maritime lien.[79]

A bond of *respondentia* covers the cargo. Communication with the cargo owner, if possible, is essential. If communication is not possible, it may be granted by the master, if there is no other means of raising money necessary for the prosecution of the voyage.[80] The bond is effectual if the cargo arrive at the port of destination, though the ship may not.[81] Where the cargo is attached and sold under a bond of *respondentia* the shipowner is liable to the cargo owner for its value.[82]

19.34 Legal Hypothecs.—The recognised legal hypothecs are those of a landlord, of a superior, of a solicitor, and certain maritime hypothecs.

19.35 Hypothec of Landlord: Superior.—The hypothec of a landlord is considered in the chapter on Leases.[83] A superior has a hypothec analogous to that of a landlord, which he may exercise by sequestration for the recovery of his feu-duty, although this will rarely arise in practice nowadays. Like the hypothec of a landlord it covers the *invecta et illata*

---

[74] Bell, *Prin.*, § 452.
[75] *Kleinwort, Cohen & Co.* v. *Cassa Marittima* (1877) L.R. 2 App.Cas. 156.
[76] Bell, *Prin.*, § 456.
[77] *Miller* v. *Potter, Wilson & Co.* (1875) 3 R. 105; *The Elwell* [1921] P. 351.
[78] *Lucovich, Petr.* (1885) 12 R. 1090.
[79] *The Daring* (1868) L.R. 2 Adm. 260.
[80] *Dymond* v. *Scott* (1877) 5 R. 196.
[81] Bell, *Comm.* i, 584.
[82] *Anderston Foundry Co.* v. *Law* (1869) 7 M. 836.
[83] paras. 41.12 to 41.16, *infra.*

and is not affected by the mercantile sequestration of the debtor or the liquidation of a company.[84] As it is not mentioned in the Hypothec Abolition Act 1880,[85] it probably exists in rural as well as in urban subjects.

19.36 **Hypothec of Solicitor.**—A solicitor who has defrayed the costs of an action has at common law a right in the nature of a hypothec over any expenses to which his client may be found entitled. This he may make effectual by moving for decree in his own name as agent-disburser. He thereby acquires a right preferable to that of any creditor of the client, and may obtain decree even after the client is sequestrated.[86] The party liable in expenses cannot oppose decree in the solicitor's name merely on the ground that he has a claim against the client on which he could plead compensation. But if cross awards of expenses are made in the course of an action, or in two actions arising out of the same matter (*ex eodem negotio*), the right of compensation thereon arising is preferable to the solicitor's claim under hypothec. So when A made an unsuccessful claim for damages against his employer, and was found liable in expenses, and was subsequently found entitled to expenses in proceedings under the Workmen's Compensation Act in connection with the same matter, decree in the name of A's solicitor was refused on the ground that the employer was entitled to set off the expenses to which he had been found entitled against those in which he had been found liable.[87] This does not hold if the decree in the first action has been extracted before the second action comes into court,[88] and is an exception to the solicitor's right which will not be extended.[89]

Should the solicitor allow decree to be pronounced in favour of his client he still has a right in security over the expenses, and by intimating his claim to the other party, will acquire a right preferable to that of the trustee in the client's sequestration.[90] But his claim will be excluded if the sum due for expenses is arrested,[91] or transferred by a duly intimated assignation.[92] And the party liable in the expenses may plead compensation on any debt due by the client.[93]

In certain cases a solicitor is entitled to be sisted as a party to the action in order to make his hypothec over expenses effectual. This may

[84] *Anderson's Trs.* v. *Donaldson*, 1908 S.C. 38.
[85] Erskine, II, vi, 63.
[86] *Hunter* v. *Pearson* (1835) 13 S. 495.
[87] *Lochgelly Iron Co.* v. *Sinclair*, 1907 S.C. 442; *Fine* v. *Edinburgh Life Assurance Co.*, 1909 S.C. 636; *Byrne* v. *Baird*, 1929 S.C. 624.
[88] *Baird* v. *Campbell*, 1928 S.C. 487.
[89] *Jack* v. *Laing*, 1929 S.C. 426.
[90] *McTavish* v. *Peddie* (1828) 6 S. 593.
[91] *Stephen* v. *Smith* (1830) 8 S. 847.
[92] *Fleeming* v. *Love* (1839) 1 D. 1097, *per* Lord Mackenzie.
[93] *Fleeming* v. *Love, supra.*

protect him where the client, without his consent, has settled or abandoned the action. This right is recognised in three cases: (1) where decree for expenses has been actually pronounced; (2) where an interlocutor has been pronounced of which decree for expenses is the legitimate sequel; (3) where the action has been settled in the knowledge that the client was insolvent and with the object of defeating the solicitor's right.[94]

19.37   **Solicitor's Charge over Subject of Action.**—At common law a solicitor's hypothec was confined to expenses; he had no preferable right over property which might be recovered in the action. By section 62(1) of the Solicitors (Scotland) Act 1980, the court in any action may declare the solicitor entitled in respect of the taxed expenses of or in reference to the action or proceeding to 'a charge upon, and a right to payment out of, any property (of whatsoever nature, tenure or kind it may be) which has been recovered or preserved[95] on behalf of the client by the solicitor in the action or proceeding.' The effect of such a declaration, it is provided, is that acts or deeds granted by the client after it, except acts or deeds in favour of a bona fide purchaser or lender, shall be absolutely void as against the solicitor's charge or right. A declaration is precluded by the sequestration of the client[96] but not by a prior arrestment.[97] A declaration in favour of the country solicitor, in Court of Session proceedings, is competent.[98] The court has a general discretion to grant or refuse a declaration,[99] but any charge will be restricted to the sum left after deduction of the other party's claim for expenses.[1]

19.38   **Maritime Hypothecs or Liens.**—Maritime hypothecs, more commonly termed maritime liens, give certain creditors a right in security over a ship, without possession, and with the power of enforcing the right by a judicial sale.[2] Such creditors are preferable to any mortgagee.[3] On this subject it has been laid down that the laws of England and of Scotland are the same.[4] Seamen have a maritime lien for wages, of which they cannot deprive themselves by contract;[5] the master, for his wages and

---

[94] *Ammon* v. *Tod*, 1912 S.C. 306; *Peek* v. *Peek*, 1926 S.C. 565.

[95] *Foxon* v. *Gascoigne* (1874) L.R. 9 Ch. App. 654 at p. 657, *per* Jessel M.R.; *cf. Hanlon* v. *Law Society* [1981] A.C. 124.

[96] *Tait* v. *Wallace* (1894) 2 S.L.T. 252; but see *Philip* v. *Wilson*, 1911 S.C. 1203 (liquidation).

[97] *Automobile Syndicate* v. *Cal. Ry.*, 1909 1 S.L.T. 499.

[98] *Bannatyne, Petr.*, 1907 S.C. 705.

[99] *Carruthers' Tr.* v. *Finlay & Watson* (1897) 24 R. 363.

[1] *O'Keefe* v. *Grieve's Trs.*, 1917 1 S.L.T. 305.

[2] For arrestment in this connection see *Mill* v. *Fildes*, 1982 S.L.T. 147.

[3] *Harmer* v. *Bell* (1851) 7 Moore P.C. 267; *Bankers Trust Ltd.* v. *Todd Shipyards* [1981] A.C. 221.

[4] *Currie* v. *McKnight* (1896) 24 R. (H.L.) 1.

[5] Merchant Shipping Act 1995, s. 39.

disbursements;[6] a salvor, for any sum found due for salvage.[7] There is a maritime lien for repairs executed or necessaries supplied in a foreign port; no such right, unless the ship is actually detained, for similar services in a home port.[8] There is a maritime lien for damages for a collision, provided that the ship was physically the agent of the injury; not, therefore, where the captain and crew of one ship had, without any actual collision, caused injury to another.[9] A party who pays seamen's wages is entitled, without written assignation, to the preference accorded to seamen, unless it is proved that he made the payment in reliance on the personal credit of the owner, when he is only an ordinary creditor, and postponed to a mortgagee.[10] In the same case it was decided that questions of maritime liens depend on the law of the place where the action is raised (*lex fori*).[11]

19.39   Floating Charges.—In modern law the most important security without possession is the floating charge, a creation of statute. Security may be given to the creditor of an incorporated company or society registered under the Industrial and Provident Societies Acts 1965 and 1967, by creating in favour of the creditor a floating charge over the company's heritable and moveable property.[12] The floating charge crystallises or attaches only upon the commencement of the winding up of the company[13] or upon the appointment of a receiver by the creditor;[14] but where a receiver is appointed on any subsequent winding up the charge attaches to property acquired by the company after the receiver was appointed.[15] Until crystallisation it 'floats' over the property in the sense that it is not attached to any specific item. When the charge crystallises, the holder is in the same position as the holder of an equivalent fixed security over the property.[16] When the charge has been registered with the registrar of companies a valid security is conferred without the transference of possession, the giving of intimation, or, in the case of heritage, registration in the Register of Sasines or recording in the Land

---

[6] 1995 Act, s. 40.

[7] *Harmer* v. *Bell, supra.*

[8] *Clydesdale Bank* v. *Walker & Bain*, 1926 S.C. 72.

[9] *Currie* v. *McKnight, supra.*

[10] *Clark* v. *Bowring*, 1908 S.C. 1168; doubted in *Clydesdale Bank* v. *Walker & Bain, supra.*

[11] See also *Bankers Trust Ltd., supra.*

[12] Companies Act 1985, Pt. XVIII; Industrial and Provident Societies Act 1967, s. 3(1) as substituted by the Companies Consolidation (Consequential Provisions) Act 1985, s. 26.

[13] 1985 Act, s. 463(1), as amended by the Insolvency Act 1985, Sched. 6, para. 18 and the Insolvency Act 1986, Scheds. 12 and 13, Pt. I.

[14] Insolvency Act 1986, s. 53(7).

[15] *Ross* v. *Taylor*, 1985 S.C. 156.

[16] 1985 Act, s. 463(2); Insolvency Act 1986, ss. 53(7) and 54(6); *Forth and Clyde Construction Ltd.* v. *Trinity Timber and Plywood Co. Ltd.*, 1984 S.C. 1; *Myles J. Callaghan Ltd.* v. *City of Glasgow D.C.*, 1988 S.L.T. 227.

Register.[17] A fuller discussion of floating charges will be found below in the chapter on Company Law.[18]

19.40 Certain other general principles relating to securities over both moveable and heritable property can be discerned in the cases.

19.41 **Equitable Restrictions on Contracts with Debtors.**—Freedom of contract, in cases between debtor and creditor, is in some respects limited on equitable grounds. Thus a creditor cannot enforce a provision for a penalty in the event of failure in punctual payment,[19] though he may secure the same result by a provision under which, if the interest is punctually paid, a lower rate is to be accepted than that stipulated in the bond.[20] The rule 'once a mortgage, always a mortgage' means that if a conveyance was in origin a security, although it may be expressed as an *ex facie* absolute transfer, a provision that the right of redemption shall expire after a certain period will not receive effect. A declarator that the right to redeem has expired is necessary, and may at any time be met by an offer of payment.[21] So where a party, borrowing money from an insurance company on the security of a contingent interest, took out a policy on his life, and assigned it and his contingent interest to the company, with a provision that if the contingent interest should lapse by his predecease the policy should become the property of the company, it was held, on his predecease, that the company must pay the policy to his executors, under deduction of the amount of the debt, on the ground that the policy was originally transferred in security and that a contract that the subject of a security should become the property of the creditor on the occurrence of a certain event was one to which the law would not give effect.[22] It is competent to provide that a creditor shall have the right to exact immediate payment, but that the right of redemption shall be postponed.[23] But the period of redemption cannot be so postponed as to preclude the return of any subject given in security on payment being made; it must not therefore, where the subject of the security is of a wasting character (*e.g.* a lease), be fixed at a period when that subject would have ceased to exist.[24] It is somewhat doubtful how far a creditor can enforce agreements for advantages other than the payment of his debt and interest. In Scotland an agreement that a borrower should not

[17] 1985 Act, s. 462(5). For the ranking of a floating charge and a standard security see *A.I.B. Finance Ltd.* v. *Bank of Scotland*, 1995 S.L.T. 2.

[18] para. 51.28.

[19] *Nasmyth* v. *Samson* (1785) 3 Paton 9.

[20] *Gatty* v. *Maclaine*, 1921 S.C. (H.L.) 1.

[21] *Smith* v. *Smith* (1879) 6 R. 794. As to the power of the creditor to acquire the subjects, see para. 19.18, *supra*.

[22] *Marquis of Northampton* v. *Salt* [1892] A.C. 1.

[23] *Ashburton* v. *Escombe* (1892) 20 R. 187.

[24] *Fairclough* v. *Swan Brewery Co.* [1912] A.C. 565.

start a rival business was sustained.[25] In England a bargain for some collateral advantage, if it is not unconscionable[26] and does not amount to an obstacle, or clog, on the borrower's right of redemption, is an admissible contract, and may be enforced, according to its terms, even after the loan has been repaid.[27]

19.42 Catholic and Secondary Securities.—When A has a prior bond or other security over two subjects belonging to the debtor, and B has a postponed bond over one of these subjects, A is termed the catholic and B the secondary creditor. If in these circumstances A chooses to realise the subjects over which B's security extends, and thereby obtains payment of his debt, he is bound to assign to B his security over the other subject.[28] And if both subjects are realised, and the debtor is bankrupt, it will be assumed that the catholic creditor exhausted first the subject over which the secondary bond did not extend, and therefore that the secondary creditor has a preferable right to the balance of the sum realised from both subjects, in a question with the general creditors of the debtor represented by the trustee in his sequestration.[29] But the secondary creditor has no direct control over the acts of the catholic creditor, and cannot object to a discharge of the bond over the subjects not covered by his own security.[30] And the catholic creditor may disregard the interests of the secondary creditor in pursuance of any legitimate interest of his own. So if he holds a bond for another debt over the subjects not covered by the secondary creditor's bond, he is entitled, in realising, to exhaust first the subjects covered by the secondary bond, so as to leave the largest possible surplus to meet his own postponed bond.[31]

If there are secondary bonds on each estate the burden of the catholic bond is, in a question between the secondary bondholders, to be apportioned rateably, according to the value of each estate, and irrespective of the question as to which secondary bond was prior in date.[32] The same principles apply in analogous cases. So, when a catholic bond covered two estates, and one of them was burdened with a secondary bond and the other sold, it was held that the burden of the

---

[25] *Stewart* v. *Stewart* (1899) 1 F. 1158.

[26] *Barrett* v. *Hartley* (1866) L.R. 2 Eq. 789 at p. 795, *per* Sir J. Stuart, V-C. and *James* v. *Kerr* (1889) 40 Ch.D. 449 at pp. 459–460 *per* Kay J.

[27] *Kreglinger* v. *New Patagonia Syndicate* [1914] A.C. 25. See Megarry and Wade, *The Law of Real Property* (5th ed., 1984), pp. 969–971.

[28] Bell, *Comm,* ii, 417.

[29] *Littlejohn* v. *Black* (1855) 18 D. 207; *Nicol's Tr.* v. *Hill* (1889) 16 R. 416.

[30] *Morton (Liddell's Curator)* (1871) 10 M. 292.

[31] *Preston* v. *Erskine* (1715) Mor. 3376. It was held in *Forth & Clyde Construction Co. Ltd.* v. *Trinity Timber & Plywood Co. Ltd.,* 1984 S.C. 1 at p. 11, *per* Lord President, that any equitable constraints imposed by the common law of catholic and secondary securities do not apply to receivers.

[32] *Ferrier* v. *Cowan* (1896) 23 R. 703.

catholic bond was, on the debtor's bankruptcy, to be apportioned rateably between the secondary creditor on the one estate and the purchaser of the other.[33]

Further Reading

Gloag and Irvine, *Rights in Security* (1897; reprinted 1987).
Gow, *Mercantile and Industrial Law of Scotland* (1964), Ch. 4.
Gretton, 'Pledge, Bills of Lading, Trusts and Property Law,' 1990 J.R. 23.
Rodger, 'Pledge of Bills of Lading,' 1971 J.R. 193.
Stair Memorial Encyclopaedia, Vol. 20 (1992), Rights in Security.
Wilson, *The Scottish Law of Debt* (2nd ed., 1991), Chs. 7–9.

[33] *Earl of Moray* v. *Mansfield* (1836) 14 S. 886.

CHAPTER 20

CAUTIONARY OBLIGATIONS

20.1 Nature of the Contract.—A cautionary obligation is defined by Bell as 'an accessory obligation or engagement, as surety for another, that the principal obligant shall pay the debt or perform the act for which he has engaged, otherwise the cautioner shall pay the debt or fulfil the obligation.'[1] The obligation may be for the payment of a debt already incurred; for debts to be incurred, or furnishings to be supplied, in the future; for the faithful performance of an office or contract of service; for the due execution of any contract;[2] or for the performance of some particular act. The person undertaking the obligation is called indifferently cautioner, guarantor, or surety; the party to whose debt or acts the obligation applies is known as the principal debtor; the party entitled to exact performance is the creditor.

20.2 Cautionry as an Accessory Obligation.—As an accessory obligation, cautionry requires the existence of a principal debt. If the apparent principal debt be unenforceable, as granted by a party with no power to contract, or in its nature a *pactum illicitum* (an unlawful agreement), the cautioner is not liable.[3] A guarantee, however, for some debt or other obligation to be contracted in the future is binding.[4] And there is some, though doubtful, authority to the effect that if the principal debtor, though a person (*e.g.* a person under the age of 16) unable to contract, has actually entered into a morally binding engagement, the obligation of the cautioner is enforceable.[5] If the party interposing as cautioner was aware that the principal obligation was invalid, as where directors guaranteed an undertaking of the company which they knew to be *ultra vires*, the doctrine of personal bar may be invoked so as to preclude the defence of invalidity.[6]

---

[1] *Prin.*, § 245. Cautionary obligations may be affected by the Consumer Credit Act 1974; see Consumer Credit, Chap. 18, *supra*.

[2] *Moschi* v. *Lep Air Services* [1973] A.C. 331, *per* Lord Kilbrandon; *Glasgow D.C.* v. *Excess Insurance*, 1986 S.L.T. 585 (performance bond), but see *Attock Cement Co.* v. *Romanian Bank for Foreign Trade* [1989] 1 W.L.R. 1147.

[3] The cautioner may be liable if the illegality is merely technical, *e.g.* the inability of a company to purchase its own shares, and the parties contracted on the assumption of legality; *Garrard* v. *James* [1925] 1 Ch. 616.

[4] *Fortune* v. *Young*, 1918 S.C. 1.

[5] See Bell, *Prin.*, § 251.

[6] *Yorkshire Railway Waggon Co.* v. *McClure* (1881) 19 Ch.D. 478; *Stevenson* v. *Adair* (1872) 10 M. 919.

20.3 Constitution of Cautionary Obligation.—A cautionary obligation may arise from an offer, addressed to a particular creditor, and offering to guarantee a particular debt or the conduct of a third party. It is then a question of construction, on which no definite rule can be given, whether an express acceptance is required, or whether the cautioner's liability is clinched when credit is given to the third party whose actings or dealings he has offered to guarantee.[7] A cautionary obligation may also arise from an undertaking to guarantee the debt or dealings of another, given to the party who is to be guaranteed, and not addressed to any particular creditor. In that case anyone who has given credit on the faith of the guarantee is entitled to enforce it, unless from its terms it appears that it was limited to some particular class of prospective creditors.[8]

20.4 Writing.—By the Mercantile Law Amendment Act Scotland 1856, it was provided (in general, though not exact, accordance with English statutory rules) that all guarantees, securities or cautionary obligations made or granted by any person for any other person should be in writing, and should be subscribed by the person undertaking the obligation, or by some person duly authorised by him, otherwise the same should have no effect.[9] A written undertaking to give a guarantee when required satisfied the conditions imposed by the Act.[10] It was not decided whether the writing by which a cautionary obligation was undertaken must be a probative writ.[11] But such writing did not need to be probative if the obligation was *in re mercatoria*,[12] or if in reliance on it advances had been made to the debtor, or there had been other actings amounting to *rei interventus*.[13] A signature in the firm name was sufficient to bind the partner who so signed.[14] That provision continues to apply to transactions entered into before August 1, 1995.[14a] Thereafter such obligations will require to be constituted in writing if they are gratuitous unilateral obligations which have not been undertaken in the course of business.[14b] If on the other hand a cautionary obligation, for example, is not gratuitous or is to be regarded

---

[7] See *Wallace* v. *Gibson* (1895) 22 R. (H.L.) 56.

[8] *Fortune* v. *Young*, 1918 S.C. 1.

[9] s. 6.

[10] *Wallace* v. *Gibson* (1895) 22 R. (H.L.) 56; *Scottish Metropolitan Property* v. *Christie*, 1987 S.L.T. (Sh. Ct.) 18.

[11] See the divergent judicial opinions in *Snaddon* v. *London, Edinburgh and Glasgow Assurance Co.* (1902) 5 F. 182; *Hylander's Exr.* v. *H. & K. Modes*, 1957 S.L.T. (Sh. Ct.) 69 at p. 71.

[12] *Johnston* v. *Grant* (1844) 6 D. 875; *B.O.C.M. Silcock Ltd.* v. *Hunter*, 1976 S.L.T. 217.

[13] *National Bank* v. *Campbell* (1892) 19 R. 885.

[14] *Fortune* v. *Young*, 1918 S.C. 1.

[14a] Requirements of Writing (Scotland) Act 1995, s. 14(2) and Sched. 5 repeals s. 6 of the 1856 Act, but by s. 14(3) the repeal does not affect transactions before that date.

[14b] Requirements of Writing (Scotland) Act 1995, s. 1(2)(ii). For the significance of actings where the obligation has not been constituted in writing see s. 1(3) and (4).

as one aspect of a bilateral transaction or has been undertaken in the course of business, then writing is not required.

20.5 Representations as to Credit.—Section 6 of the Mercantile Law Amendment Act also required writing in the case of 'representations and assurances as to the character, conduct, credit, ability,[15] trade or dealings of any person, made or granted to the effect or for the purpose of enabling such person to obtain credit, money, goods or postponement of payment of debt, or of any other obligation demandable from him.' Despite its general terms the section was held in the Outer House to apply to fraudulent representations and assurances only.[16] Where it applied, a verbal statement could not be founded on as a defence to an action on an obligation which had been induced by it.[17] The need for such representations and assurances to be in writing ceased on the commencement of the Requirements of Writing (Scotland) Act 1995.[17a]

20.6 Representations and Guarantees.—It is a question of construction whether a particular writing amounts to a guarantee or is merely a representation as to the character or credit of another.[18] If the former construction be adopted, the writer is liable directly on his contractual obligation; if the latter, no contractual obligation has been undertaken, but the statement may be a ground for the reduction of a contract or obligation induced by it and the writer may be liable *ex delicto* if his statement was fraudulent or negligent.[19] An honest, though mistaken, opinion as to the credit of another infers no liability even if made negligently,[20] unless the relations of the writer and the person he addresses are of such a fiduciary or other special character as to involve a duty to take reasonable care, as for example, where their relationship is that of solicitor and client[21] or where the person making the representation knows or ought to know that it will be relied upon[22] or assumes responsibility for the accuracy of what he says.[22a] In such a case it has been held in England that as the ground of action is failure in the duty involved in the relationship, action may lie although the representation was verbal.[23]

---

[15] Construed as meaning 'ability to pay,' *Irving* v. *Burns*, 1915 S.C. 260.

[16] *Andrew Oliver & Son Ltd.* v. *Douglas*, 1981 S.C. 192, not following *Union Bank* v. *Taylor*, 1925 S.C. 835; *Clydesdale Bank* v. *Paton* (1896) 23 R. (H.L.) 22.

[17] *Union Bank* v. *Taylor, supra; Muir* v. *Burnside*, 1935 S.N. 13.

[17a] The Act came into force on August 1, 1995. For representations made before that date, *cf.* s. 14(3)(a).

[18] *Park* v. *Gould* (1851) 13 D. 1049; *Fortune* v. *Young*, 1918 S.C. 1.

[19] *Union Bank* v. *Taylor, supra.*

[20] *Robinson* v. *National Bank*, 1916 S.C. (H.L.) 154.

[21] *Nocton* v. *Lord Ashburton* [1914] A.C. 923; *Banbury* v. *Bank of Montreal* [1918] A.C. 626.

[22] *Hedley Byrne & Co.* v. *Heller* [1964] A.C. 465; *Parks* v. *Gould* (1851) 13 D. 1049.

[22a] *Hedley Byrne & Co.* v. *Heller, supra; Spring* v. *Guardian Assurance plc* [1994] 3 W.L.R. 354; *White* v. *Jones* [1995] 2 W.L.R. 187.

[23] *Andrew Oliver & Son Ltd.* v. *Douglas*, 1981 S.C. 192; *Banbury* v. *Bank of Montreal, supra; Hedley Byrne & Co.* v. *Heller, supra.* See, however, previous para.

20.7 Cautionary or Independent Obligation.—There are many cases where it is difficult to say whether an independent or a cautionary obligation has been undertaken. If A orders goods to be supplied to B, and undertakes to be responsible for payment, this may, according to the circumstances, be an independent obligation by A, and provable by parole evidence, or a cautionary obligation for a debt primarily undertaken by B, and, if so, invalid if not constituted in writing.[24]

It has been decided in England that agency *del credere*, when the agent guarantees the solvency of the party with whom he deals on his principal's behalf, is not to be regarded, in a question as to the necessity of writing, as a contract of guarantee.[25] And a guarantee against loss from a contract, which does not involve any obligation of performance by any principal debtor, *e.g.* an obligation to take over shares if they do not reach a certain price, is not a cautionary obligation.[26] Contracts which do involve performance by a principal debtor, but are framed as policies of insurance, may really be cautionary obligations. So far as any rule can be stated in such cases, the incidents of the contract depend on the law of insurance if the guarantee is obtained by the creditor, on the law of cautionary obligations if it is obtained by the debtor.[27] It has been held in the Outer House that a performance bond is a cautionary obligation for the purposes of prescription,[28] but the Court of Appeal in England has held that a performance bond is not a guarantee for purposes of determining its proper law.[29]

20.8 Cautionry, Proper and Improper.—In form, a cautionary obligation may be proper or improper: proper, when the fact that the parties are principal debtor and cautioner appears in the instrument by which they are bound; improper, where, *ex facie* of the instrument, they appear as co-obligants, though *inter se* they are principal and cautioner.

20.9 Benefit of Discussion.—In proper cautionry the cautioner had at common law, unless otherwise agreed, the benefit of discussion (*beneficium ordinis*). That is to say, he was entitled to insist that before he was called upon, diligence should be used against the principal debtor. No such right was implied in the case of improper cautionry. The implied benefit of discussion was abolished by section 8 of the Mercantile Law Amendment Act Scotland 1856, and, since that Act, requires express stipulation. Without it there may be direct action against the cautioner, and it is not necessary to establish the failure of

---

[24] *Stevenson's Tr.* v. *Campbell* (1895) 23 R. 711.
[25] *Sutton* v. *Grey* [1894] 1 Q.B. 285.
[26] *Milne* v. *Kidd* (1869) 8 M. 250.
[27] *Laird* v. *Securities Insurance Co.* (1895) 22 R. 452; *Seaton* v. *Burnand* [1899] 1 Q.B. 782, revd. on other grounds [1900] A.C. 135; *Re Law Guarantee Society* [1914] 2 Ch. 617.
[28] *Glasgow D.C.* v. *Excess Insurance*, 1986 S.L.T. 585.
[29] *Attock Cement Co.* v. *Romanian Bank for Foreign Trade* [1989] 1 W.L.R. 1147.

the principal debtor before suing the cautioner and using diligence against him on the dependence of the action.[30]

20.10   **Benefit of Division.**—The right of division (*beneficium divisionis*) also depends on the distinction between proper and improper cautionry. In proper cautionry where more than one cautioner is expressly bound as such for an obligation in its nature divisible, such as a debt, none can be sued for more than his *pro rata* share, unless the others are insolvent.[31] In improper cautionry, when all the obligants are bound jointly and severally and *ex facie* as full debtors, anyone may be sued for the whole debt.[32]

20.11   **Obligations by More than One Cautioner.**—Where a cautionary obligation is to be undertaken by more than one cautioner it is as a general rule the duty of the creditor to secure that all become bound. Each cautioner who signs does so on the implied condition that the others are to be bound with him, and is not liable if this condition is not fulfilled. This rule holds even although the form of the obligation is joint and several, provided that the creditor was aware that some of the obligants were really cautioners. So where an insurance company agreed to lend money to A on condition that four other persons should become jointly and severally liable with him in a bond, and three of the four signed and A forged the signature of the fourth, it was held that the bond could not be enforced against any of the cautioners.[33] The general rule finds exception in judicial cautionry, where a bond is lodged in obedience to the orders of the court. No duty is then cast on the creditor to see that the signatures of all the obligants are obtained, and therefore an obligant who signed was held liable although the signature of the other obligant was forged.[34]

20.12   **Effect of Fraud: Concealment.**—On general principles of contract a cautionary obligation is not binding if obtained by fraud or misrepresentation on the part of the creditor. But the debtor, whose obligation is guaranteed, is not the creditor's agent, and fraud or misrepresentation by him will not liberate the cautioner.[35] In cautionary obligations for a debt there is no obligation on the creditor to disclose all the material facts. So a bank, accepting a guarantee for a customer's account, is not bound to inform the guarantor that the account is overdrawn, and may

[30] *Johannesburg Municipal Council* v. *Stewart*, 1909 S.C. (H.L.) 53; *Scottish Metropolitan Property* v. *Christie*, 1987 S.L.T. (Sh. Ct.) 18.
[31] Bell, *Prin.*, § 267.
[32] *Richmond* v. *Grahame* (1847) 9 D. 633.
[33] *Scottish Provincial Assurance Co.* v. *Pringle* (1858) 20 D. 465. See also *Ellesmere Brewery Co.* v. *Cooper* [1896] 1 Q.B. 75.
[34] *Simpson* v. *Fleming* (1860) 22 D. 679.
[35] *Young* v. *Clydesdale Bank* (1889) 17 R. 231. See also *Sutherland* v. *Low* (1901) 3 F. 972.

enforce the guarantee, although the guarantor may have been induced to intervene by fraudulent statements made by the customer.[36] A different rule applies in the case of guarantees for the fidelity of a servant or official, when the employer is bound to disclose all prior irregularities or other facts calculated to influence the mind of the guarantor.[37] The ground of the distinction between the two classes of cautionry is that in the latter class, fidelity guarantees, the contract is in substance one of insurance, and falls within the rule that in insurance all material facts must be disclosed.[38]

20.13   Extent of Cautioner's Liability.—The obligation undertaken by a cautioner may or may not be limited to a certain amount. It is a general rule that his undertaking is to be construed in the narrowest sense which the words will reasonably bear.[39] If there is no limitation in amount, the cautioner is liable for all loss resulting from the failure in fulfilment of the obligation guaranteed, *e.g.* for interest, or for expenses reasonably incurred in attempting to enforce the debt against the principal debtor.[40] As cautionry is an accessory obligation, the cautioner's liability can never exceed that of the principal debtor. So where the creditor advanced the sum of £300 and the cautionary obligation took the form of a blank promissory note, which was later filled in for £2000 by the principal debtor's agent, it was held that in the cautioner's sequestration the creditor could not rank for a greater amount than he had advanced to the principal debtor in order to draw his actual advance of £300 as a dividend.[41]

Where a cautionary obligation contains no limit of time, but does contain a limit of the amount for which the cautioner undertakes liability, it is a question of construction whether it is to be read as a continuing guarantee, such as a cash credit with a bank, or as a guarantee which is ended when the limit of liability is reached. In the former case the cautioner is liable for the balance due when his obligation is ultimately enforced; in the latter, any payments made by the principal debtor, after the maximum of liability has been reached, go to diminish the amount for which the cautioner is responsible, and he is not liable for advances subsequently made.[42] Where the guarantor undertakes to make payment 'on demand' his obligation is not enforceable until the creditor makes a demand.[43] Where the obligation

---

[36] *Royal Bank* v. *Greenshields*, 1914 S.C. 259; *Mumford* v. *Bank of Scotland*, 1994 S.L.T. 1288, but see *McCabe* v. *Shipton Building Society*, 1994 S.L.T. 1272, per the Lord Justice-Clerk at p. 1277 A—B.
[37] *French* v. *Cameron* (1893) 20 R. 966; *Bank of Scotland* v. *Morrison*, 1911 S.C. 593.
[38] *Wallace's Factor* v. *McKissock* (1898) 25 R. 642, *per* Lord McLaren at p. 653.
[39] *Harmer* v. *Gibb*, 1911 S.C. 1341; *Veitch* v. *National Bank*, 1907 S.C. 554.
[40] *Struthers* v. *Dykes* (1847) 9 D. 1437; *Moschi* v. *Lep Air Services* [1973] A.C. 331.
[41] *Jackson* v. *McIver* (1875) 2 R. 882.
[42] *Scott* v. *Mitchell* (1866) 4 M. 551.
[43] *Royal Bank of Scotland* v. *Brown*, 1982 S.C. 89.

is not incurred for any definite period, the cautioner may safeguard himself for any liability in the future by giving notice to the creditor that his guarantee is withdrawn. And a cautioner is entitled, on giving reasonable notice, to call upon the principal debtor to relieve him of all liabilities which he may have incurred. The principal debtor will be ordained to procure and deliver to the cautioner a discharge from the creditor.[44]

20.14 **Relief.**—A cautioner, on payment of the debt,[45] is entitled to recover what he has paid from the principal debtor. In the case where all are *ex facie* co-obligants, parole evidence as to their real relationship is competent, because the written instrument by which the debt is constituted is intended to regulate the contract between the creditor and the obligants, not the rights of the obligants *inter se*.[46] It is also a general rule, which will yield only to an express contract to the contrary, that where more than one cautioner is engaged, anyone who has paid more than his share may claim relief from the others. On this principle, where A and B were cautioners for a contractor, and A, on the contractor's failure, carried out the contract at his own expense, he was held entitled to recover half his outlay from B.[47] In determining the amount of relief, those cautioners who are insolvent are not counted, *e.g.* if A, B and C are cautioners, and C is insolvent, A, who has paid the whole debt, is entitled to recover half of what he has paid from B.[48] Where each cautioner is liable for a specified sum, and the whole debt is exacted, no one has paid more than his share, and there can be no claim of relief. But if less than the whole debt is due, anyone who has paid more than his proportionate share may claim relief if the cautioners are bound in the same instrument; if, in separate contracts, each cautioner engages for a specific sum, there is no right of relief.[49]

20.15 **Right to Assignation of Debt.**—On payment a cautioner is entitled to demand from the creditor an assignation of the debt, any security held for it, and any diligence done upon it, so as to enable him to enforce his right of relief against the principal debtor, or against co-cautioners.[50] Subject to the prohibition of double ranking, the cautioner as assignee of the creditor may rank in the principal debtor's sequestration.[51] It has been decided that no such right exists except upon full payment, so that where a cautioner was bankrupt, and a dividend was paid on the debt,

---

[44] *Doig* v. *Lawrie* (1903) 5 F. 295.
[45] *Smithy's Place Ltd.* v. *Blackadder & McMonagle*, 1991 S.L.T. 790.
[46] *Hamilton* v. *Freeth* (1889) 16 R. 1022; *Crosbie* v. *Brown* (1900) 3 F. 83.
[47] *Marshall* v. *Pennycook*, 1908 S.C. 276.
[48] *Buchanan* v. *Main* (1900) 3 F. 215.
[49] *Morgan* v. *Smart* (1872) 10 M. 610.
[50] Bell, *Prin.*, § 255; *Sligo* v. *Menzies* (1840) 2 D. 1478.
[51] Bankruptcy (Scotland) Act 1985, s. 60(3). See para. 20.17, *infra*.

his trustee could not demand an assignation.[52] In exceptional cases the creditor may refuse an assignation of the debt on the ground that to grant it would conflict with some legitimate interest of his own.[53] Where the demand is for the assignation of securities held for the debt, it cannot be refused on the ground that the creditor proposes to retain the securities to meet some other debt subsequently incurred.[54] It is a general principle that an assignation from the creditor, though it may afford a convenient means of enforcing a right of relief, does not in any way enlarge that right.[55] And it has been laid down that a cautioner, with or without an assignation, can enforce only securities over the estate of the debtor, not securities granted by third parties.[56]

20.16 Right to Share in Securities.—A cautioner is entitled to share in the benefit of any securities which any of his co-cautioners may have obtained over the estate of the principal debtor.[57] The rule applies, although the cautioner claiming the right to share had already engaged without any security.[58] But it yields to any express agreement to the contrary. And if one cautioner engages under a contract with the principal debtor whereby he obtains a security of which he is to have the whole benefit, the fact that the other cautioners have agreed to this may be proved by parole evidence.[59] The theory underlying the rule is that the estate of the principal debtor is to be regarded as a fund in which all the cautioners have an equal right to share, and therefore it was held that it did not extend to the case where one cautioner had obtained a security from a third party.[60]

20.17 Ranking in Bankruptcy.—On the bankruptcy of the principal debtor, if the creditor ranks for the debt, receives a dividend, and obtains payment of the balance from the cautioner, the latter is not entitled to a ranking for what he has paid, because to allow it would conflict with the principle that no debt can be ranked twice on a sequestrated estate.[61] Where the cautioner is liable for the whole debt, it is open to him to pay it, obtain an assignation and rank in place of the creditor. To this the creditor has no legitimate interest to object. If the cautioner's liability is limited to a fixed sum, and the principal debt exceeds this, the bond may be read as a guarantee of part of the debt. If so, the cautioner is entitled, on payment of the amount he has guaranteed, to

[52] *Ewart* v. *Latta* (1865) 3 M. (H.L.) 36.
[53] *Graham* v. *Gordon* (1842) 4 D. 903.
[54] *Fleming* v. *Burgess* (1867) 5 M. 856.
[55] *Thow's Tr.* v. *Young*, 1910 S.C. 588.
[56] *Thow's Tr., supra*, at p. 596, *per* Lord President Dunedin.
[57] Bell, *Comm.*, i, 367.
[58] *Steel* v. *Dixon* (1881) 17 Ch.D. 825.
[59] *Hamilton* v. *Freeth* (1889) 16 R. 1022.
[60] *Scott* v. *Young*, 1909 1 S.L.T. 47.
[61] *Anderson* v. *Mackinnon* (1876) 3 R. 608; *Mackinnon* v. *Monkhouse* (1881) 9 R. 393.

rank in place of the creditor for that amount, or, if the creditor ranks, the cautioner's liability is limited to the balance of the guaranteed amount remaining after payment of the dividend.[62] On the other hand, if the bond is read as a guarantee of the whole debt, with a limit of the amount for which the cautioner is liable, the general construction of the obligation is that the creditor is entitled to rank for his whole debt to and recover from the cautioner any balance remaining, in so far as that balance does not exceed the limit for which the cautioner has engaged.[63] But if, before the sequestration of the principal debtor, the cautioner has paid any part of the debt, the creditor is bound to deduct what has been paid and rank for no more than the balance, whether the cautioner makes a claim for a ranking or not.[64]

20.18 Discharge of Cautionary Obligations.—In addition to the methods applicable in general to the discharge of obligations the following require notice: (1) prescription; (2) extinction of the principal obligation; (3) death of principal debtor, cautioner or creditor; (4) discharge of co-cautioner; (5) giving time to principal debtor; (6) release of securities; (7) alteration of the contract; (8) change in a partnership.

20.19 Prescription.—By section 6 of the Prescription and Limitation (Scotland) Act 1973, the prescriptive period applicable to cautionary obligations is five years.[65] Thus, if a cautionary obligation, being an obligation arising from a contract, has subsisted for a continuous period of five years from the time when it became enforceable without any relevant claims having been made in relation to it and without the subsistence of the obligation having been relevantly acknowledged in terms of the Act, it will be extinguished.[66] Where the debtor fails to perform an obligation, the cautioner is immediately liable[67] and the prescriptive period will start to run, but where the cautioner's obligation is to pay 'on demand,' the period does not begin until a demand is made.[68]

20.20 Extinction of Principal Obligation.—As cautionry is an accessory obligation, the absolute discharge of the principal debtor implies the discharge of the cautioner. There is a statutory exception to this in the

[62] *Veitch* v. *National Bank*, 1907 S.C. 554.
[63] *Harvie's Trs.* v. *Bank of Scotland* (1885) 12 R. 1141.
[64] *Mackinnon's Tr.* v. *Bank of Scotland*, 1915 S.C. 411.
[65] Sched. 5. See Chap. 15, *supra*.
[66] s. 6(1)–(3), and Sched. 1, paras. 1 (*g*) and 2 (*c*); *Royal Bank of Scotland* v. *Brown*, 1982 S.C. 89. Sched. 2, para. 2 does not apply to cautionary obligations. A cautionary obligation may also be affected by the long negative prescription of 20 years: see para. 15.15, *supra*.
[67] *Moschi* v. *Lep Air Services* [1973] A.C. 331, *per* Lord Kilbrandon; *Glasgow D.C.* v. *Excess Insurance*, 1986 S.L.T. 585, as read with *Glasgow D.C.* v. *Excess Insurance (No. 2)*, 1990 S.L.T. 225.
[68] *Royal Bank of Scotland* v. *Brown, supra*.

case of the discharge of the bankrupt in sequestration.[69] And a distinction is recognised between a discharge, which extinguishes the principal debt and also frees the cautioner, and a *pactum de non petendo*, whereby the creditor gives up his right to sue the principal debtor but reserves his claim against the cautioner. In the latter case the cautioner is not discharged, and, on payment, may demand an assignation of the debt and sue the principal debtor thereon.[70] Apart from a discharge the cautioner may be liberated by the extinction of the principal debt by other methods, as where it is allowed to prescribe.[71] Novation of the principal debt, in the case where the principal debt is discharged and a new one substituted, will liberate the cautioner.[72] The assignation of the debt, merely substituting a new creditor, has no such effect.[73] The fact that at some period in the history of the transaction compensation might have been pleaded in respect of a debt due by the creditor to the principal debtor does not extinguish the debt and therefore does not liberate the cautioner, but the latter is entitled, on a claim being made against him, to insist on any ground of compensation then available to the principal debtor.[74] The debt for which the cautioner is liable, and consequently his own liability, may be extinguished by the application of the rule that where indefinite payments are made, the earliest credit item goes to wipe out the earliest debit item.[75] This may happen if, when the cautioner's obligation for a continuous account, such as a cash credit with a bank, is in any way withdrawn or terminated, the account is continued with the principal debtor without any definite break. Then, though there may be a continuous adverse balance against the debtor, any payments made by him, if ascribed to meet the earliest debt in the account, will in time extinguish the balance due when the cautionary obligation was withdrawn, and, by thus extinguishing the principal debt, will liberate the cautioner.[76]

20.21 Death of One of the Parties.—The death of a cautioner has no effect on his existing liability, which may be enforced against his representatives. And if the cautionary obligation is of the nature of a continuing guarantee—as in the case of a cash credit with a bank—the representatives of a deceased cautioner will remain liable for debts

---

[69] Bankruptcy (Scotland) Act 1985, s. 60(1). This does not cover private trust deeds for creditors.

[70] *Muir* v. *Crawford* (1875) 2 R. (H.L.) 148.

[71] Erskine, III, iii, 66.

[72] *Commercial Bank of Tasmania* v. *Jones* [1893] A.C. 313. See also *Hay & Kyd* v. *Powrie* (1886) 13 R. 777.

[73] *Bradford Old Bank* v. *Sutcliffe* [1918] 2 K.B. 833.

[74] *Bechervaise* v. *Lewis* (1872) L.R. 7 C.P. 372.

[75] *Devaynes* v. *Noble (Clayton's Case)* (1816) 1 Merivale 529, 572. For the application of the rule, see *Hay & Co.* v. *Torbet*, 1908 S.C. 781 and para. 14.7, *supra*.

[76] *Royal Bank* v. *Christie* (1841) 2 Rob. 118; *Cuthill* v. *Strachan* (1894) 21 R. 549.

subsequently incurred, unless they intimate that the guarantee is withdrawn. It is immaterial that the cautioner's representatives were not aware of the obligation, and no duty is cast upon the creditor to intimate to them.[77] The death of the principal debtor will, as a general rule, exclude the liability of the cautioner for any debt not then due.[78] But where caution for expenses was the statutory condition of an appeal from the sheriff court, it was held that the cautioner was liable for expenses incurred after the death of the appellant, when his representatives were sisted as parties and carried on the appeal.[79] The death of the creditor does not affect the liability of a cautioner for an existing debt. In guarantees for the fidelity of an employee the death of the employer terminates the guarantee, even although the party employed is kept on by his representatives.[80]

20.22 Discharge of Co-Cautioners.—Where there are several cautioners, the discharge of one without the consent of the others has, by statute, the effect of liberating them.[81] The section by which this rule is established expressly excepts the case of a cautioner's consent to the discharge of a co-cautioner who has become bankrupt.[82] It has been held in England that where the cautioner is released in such a way that the creditor expressly reserves his rights against a co-cautioner, the co-cautioner is not liberated.[83] And, by a decision in Scotland, the section applies only where the cautioners are bound jointly and severally for the whole debt, not to the case where each has engaged for a specific sum.[84]

20.23 Giving Time.—It is a general, and in some respects very technical, rule that a cautioner is liberated if the creditor has given time to the principal debtor.[85] By giving time is not meant failure to press the principal debtor for payment or to rank in his bankruptcy. For such failure the cautioner has his remedy by paying the debt, obtaining an assignation of it and exercising the rights of the creditor.[86] By giving time is meant any act by which the creditor deprives himself of the right to sue for immediate payment, and thus alters the contract for which the

---

[77] *British Linen Co.* v. *Monteith* (1858) 20 D. 557.

[78] *Woodfield Finance Trust (Glasgow)* v. *Morgan*, 1958 S.L.T. (Sh. Ct.) 14.

[79] *Wilson* v. *Ewing* (1836) 14 S. 262.

[80] *Stewart* v. *Scot* (1834) 7 W. & S. 211.

[81] Mercantile Law Amendment Act Scotland 1856, s. 9; *Royal Bank of Scotland* v. *Welsh*, 1985 S.L.T. 439.

[82] It has been suggested (probably wrongly) that the Act used 'cautioner' when 'creditor' was intended: Gloag and Irvine, *Rights in Security*, p. 912; Bell, *Prin.*, § 261A, n.(a). The scheme of the Bankruptcy (Scotland) Act 1985 means that the point may no longer be of great practical importance.

[83] *Thompson* v. *Lack* (1846) 3 C.B. 540.

[84] *Morgan* v. *Smart* (1872) 10 M. 610.

[85] Bell, *Prin.*, § 262.

[86] *Hay & Kyd* v. *Powrie* (1886) 13 R. 777, *per* Lord Rutherfurd Clark; *Hamilton's Exr.* v. *Bank of Scotland*, 1913 S.C. 743, where the effect of a clause entitling the creditor to give time is considered.

cautioner undertook liability. This may be by an express agreement not to sue, or by taking a bill payable at some future date,[87] or by an arrangement for payment by instalments.[88] By such agreements the cautioner is, or may be, prejudiced since, as he can only stand in the place of the creditor, he loses the power to enforce immediate payment from the debtor. On this footing it is an established rule that he is liberated, and it is immaterial that he is unable to show that he has suffered any actual prejudice,[89] or that, before time was given, he had repudiated his liability on other grounds.[90] If the cautionary obligation is for a debt already incurred, the giving of time for any period, however short, precludes recourse against the cautioner; if the obligation is to guarantee payment of furnishings to be supplied in the future, the creditor is not held to have given time by allowing any ordinary period of credit, or taking a bill for the price. But the cautioner may have a valid defence if he can prove that the amount of credit given, or the currency of the bill, was unreasonably long; it is not sufficient to prove that the credit given was more than was usual in the particular trade.[91]

The rule that a cautioner is liberated if time be given to the principal debtor does not apply if in the contract by which time is given the rights of the cautioner against the principal debtor are expressly reserved. The cautioner may then, by paying the debt and obtaining an assignation, enforce immediate payment and therefore, as he has suffered no injury, his liability is unaffected.[92] And if the creditor has obtained decree against the cautioner, the fact that he has subsequently given time to the principal debtor does not affect the cautioner's liability.[93]

20.24 Giving up Securities.—As a cautioner has the right, on payment of the debt, to an assignation of any security over the debtor's estate which the creditor may hold for it,[94] his position is prejudiced if, without his consent, any security is given up; and therefore the release of securities, if a voluntary act on the part of the creditor, will operate as a release to the cautioner.[95] Unless there is an express agreement that the creditor shall avail himself of a particular security before calling on the cautioner (when the release of that security operates as an absolute discharge),[96] the cautioner is released only in so far as he is prejudiced, *i.e.* to the extent of the value of the security which has been given up.[97] The same

[87] *Johnstone* v. *Duthie* (1892) 19 R. 624; *Goldfarb* v. *Bartlett* [1920] 1 K.B. 639.
[88] *Wilson* v. *Lloyd* (1873) L.R. 16 Eq. 60.
[89] *Johnstone* v. *Duthie, supra*; *Polak* v. *Everett* (1876) 1 Q.B.D. 669.
[90] *Johnstone* v. *Duthie, supra.*
[91] *Calder* v. *Cruikshank's Tr.* (1889) 17 R. 74.
[92] *Crawford* v. *Muir* (1875) 2 R. (H.L.) 148.
[93] *Aikman* v. *Fisher* (1835) 14 S. 56.
[94] *Supra*, para. 20.15.
[95] *Sligo* v. *Menzies* (1840) 2 D. 1478.
[96] *Drummond* v. *Rannie* (1836) 14 S. 437.
[97] *Wright's Trs.* v. *Hamilton* (1835) 13 S. 380.

rules apply to the case where the creditor, without giving up a security, fails to take the steps necessary to make it effectual, as where the holder of a bond and disposition in security failed to complete his title, with the result that the trustee in the debtor's sequestration acquired a preferable right to the subjects.[98] It may be the law that a cautioner is released to the extent that he is prejudiced by the creditor's failure to take due care in realising the security.[99]

20.25   Alteration of the Contract.—A cautioner is discharged if his position is adversely affected by an alteration of the contract between the creditor and the principal debtor without the consent of the cautioner.[1] Thus where the creditors in a composition contract took a trust deed from the debtor, it was held that they had liberated the cautioner.[2] The mere fact that the creditor failed to disclose to the cautioner that he had grounds for suspecting forgery by the principal debtor was held to be no ground on which the cautioner could dispute his liability, though it was observed that the creditor, in the case of a cash credit bond, would not be justified in making further advances without disclosing to the cautioner any circumstances materially affecting the honesty of the debtor.[3] Where, however, a guarantee was limited to a certain sum irrespective of the sum due by the principal debtor and advances were made beyond the limit, it was held that the cautioner was not adversely affected and was not released.[4]

In the case of fidelity guarantees, if in the original contract certain checks on the behaviour of the party guaranteed are provided for, the cautioner is discharged if they are not observed, and it is no defence to the creditor to prove that the checks would have been useless or that equivalent methods of supervision were instituted.[5] In the absence of any provision there is no implied obligation on the part of the creditor to exercise any special precautions, and therefore the cautioner will not escape liability by proof that more careful supervision would have precluded the failure in respect of which he is sued.[6] There is probably an exception to this in the case of a guarantee for the acts of a bank official, when the cautioner is entitled to rely on the checks, such as periodical audits, which are usual in banking business.[7] A change in the duties to be performed by the party guaranteed will release the

---

[98] *Fleming* v. *Thomson* (1826) 2 W. & S. 277.

[99] *Lord Advocate* v. *Maritime Fruit Carriers Co.*, 1983 S.L.T. 357.

[1] See Bell, *Prin.*, § 259; *N.G. Napier* v. *Crosbie*, 1964 S.C. 129.

[2] *Allan, Allan & Milne* v. *Pattison* (1893) 21 R. 195.

[3] *Bank of Scotland* v. *Morrison*, 1911 S.C. 593.

[4] *Bank of Scotland* v. *MacLeod*, 1986 S.C. 165; *Huewind Ltd.* v. *Clydesdale Bank*, 1995 S.L.T. 392.

[5] *Haworth* v. *Sickness, etc. Assurance Co.* (1891) 18 R. 563; *Clydebank Water Trs.* v. *Fidelity Co.*, 1916 S.C. (H.L.) 69.

[6] *Mayor of Kingston* v. *Harding* [1892] 2 Q.B. 494; *Mactaggart* v. *Watson* (1835) 1 S. & McL. 553.

[7] *Falconer* v. *Lothian* (1843) 5 D. 866, at p. 870.

cautioner if the terms of that party's appointment were made known to
him at the time when he undertook the cautionary obligation, even
when the change had no bearing on the loss for which the cautioner is
sued.[8] This has been held even where the change in duties was due not
to the act of the creditor but to the provisions of a statute.[9] The
cautioner has engaged for a party performing particular duties, and he is
not, without his consent, to be rendered liable for a party performing
duties of a different kind. If, however, the particular nature of the
duties to be performed was not known to the cautioner, and he gave a
general guarantee, he will remain liable unless he can prove that the
alteration in the contract of employment was material.[10] It has been
held that if an employer discovers an act of dishonesty on the part of an
official whose acts have been guaranteed, he is bound to give immediate
notice to the cautioner, and failure to do so will justify the cautioner in
repudiating his obligation even if he can offer no proof that the notice
which was withheld would have been of any advantage to him.[11]

20.26   Change in a Firm.—It is provided by section 18 of the Partnership Act
1890, re-enacting section 7 of the Mercantile Law Amendment Act
Scotland 1856, and in substance reproducing the common law,[12] that a
continuing guarantee or cautionary obligation given either to a firm or
to a third person in respect of the transactions of a firm is, in the
absence of agreement to the contrary, revoked as to future transactions
by any change in the constitution of the firm to which, or of the firm in
respect of the transactions of which, the guarantee or obligation was
given. The change in the firm may be effected either by the admission
of a new partner,[13] or by the retirement of an existing partner,[14] or,
without any change in the persons composing the firm, by its
registration as a company under the Companies Acts.[15]

Further Reading

Bell, *Principles* (10th ed., 1899), Ch. 8.
Gloag and Irvine, *Rights in Security* (1897; reprinted 1987), Chs. 19–25.
Gow, *Mercantile and Industrial Law of Scotland* (1964), Ch. 5.
Wilson, *The Scottish Law of Debt* (2nd ed., 1991), Ch. 10.

[8] *Bonar* v. *Macdonald* (1850) 7 Bell's App. 379; affirming, (1847) 9 D. 1537.
[9] *Pybus* v. *Gibb* (1856) 6 E. & B. 902.
[10] *Nicolson* v. *Burt* (1882) 10 R. 121.
[11] *Snaddon* v. *London, Edinburgh, etc. Assurance Co.* (1902) 5 F. 182.
[12] *Royal Bank* v. *Christie* (1841) 2 Rob. 118.
[13] *Spiers* v. *Houston's Exrs.* (1829) 3 W. & S. 392.
[14] *Royal Bank* v. *Christie, supra.*
[15] *Hay & Co.* v. *Torbet*, 1908 S.C. 781.

CHAPTER 21

EMPLOYMENT

21.1 Legislation.—Much of the law of employment is now statutory, the principal statute being the Employment Protection (Consolidation) Act 1978 (hereafter referred to as 'the 1978 Act') but it was extensively amended by the Employment Acts of 1980, 1982, 1988, 1989, 1990 and 1991 which are similarly referred to by the year in which they were passed. The 1978 Act has also been amended by the Trade Union Reform and Employment Rights Act 1993 (hereafter referred to as 'the 1993 Act'). The law relating to labour relations has been consolidated in the Trade Union and Labour Relations (Consolidation) Act 1992 ('the 1992 Act').

21.2 Definition of Employment.—Previous editions of this book, which discussed employment in terms of the relationship of master and servant,[1] offered the following definition of a servant: 'A servant is one who is employed to render personal service to his employer otherwise than in pursuit of an independent calling, and who in such service remains entirely under the control or direction of the other, who is called the master.'[2] The stress on control, as the distinguishing feature of the contract of employment, represents the classical view, and close control, where it exists, is still a sure indication that the person subject to control is an employee. In modern sophisticated classes of employment the control exercised by an employer may, however, often not extend to the manner in which the work is to be done[3] and may be so remote as to be scarcely distinguishable from that appropriate to other contractual relationships.[4] Accordingly it was suggested that the true test of employment is whether the work is done as an integral part

---

[1] The terminology had advantages in avoiding the ambiguities which sometimes attach to the use of 'employment.' It had, however, become increasingly archaic, was apt to cause confusion by perpetuating obsolete views of the relationship between employer and employee and, except for secondary purposes of definition, had been abandoned in the language of statute. In accordance with the statutory example, employer, employee and employment are the terms used in this edition unless the context renders the earlier terminology more appropriate.

[2] See, *e.g.* 6th ed., p. 233.

[3] *e.g.* a surgeon (*Macdonald* v. *Glasgow Western Hospitals Board,* 1954 S.C. 453), a trapeze artiste (*Whittaker* v. *Ministry of Pensions and National Insurance* [1967] 1 Q.B. 156), a professional footballer (*Walker* v. *Crystal Palace Football Club* [1910] 1 K.B. 87). See also *Morren* v. *Swinton and Pendlebury Council* [1965] 1 W.L.R. 576, *per* Lord Parker C.J. at pp. 581–82.

[4] *e.g.* agency and a contract to perform services (see *infra*, para. 21.4).

of the business or organisation in question,[5] and a multiple or mixed test
has also been suggested.[6] More recent authority favours the test: 'Is the
person who has engaged himself to perform these services performing
them as a person in business on his own account?'[7] There is no
exhaustive list of factors to be considered in answering that question but
relevant matters include, in addition to control, whether the person
provides his own equipment, whether he hires his own helpers, what
degree of financial risk he takes and whether he has the opportunity of
profiting from sound management in the performance of his task.

There is in Scotland no rule against a gratuitous obligation to work as
an employee. In an onerous contract the advantage accruing to the
person employed need not take the form of wages; it may consist in an
opportunity of earning, *e.g.* by tips, or by instruction in a trade or
profession. A person who attends in the hope of employment, even
although, if no employment be available, he may receive payment for
his attendance, is not an employee.[8] Often, however, the method of
remuneration is crucial to the distinction between a contract of
employment and a joint adventure.[9] The question whether a partner can
be an employee of his own firm has been raised but not settled.[10] It has
been decided that a partner does not by his negligence render the firm
liable to another partner who has been injured as a result of that
negligence.[11]

21.3 Employment and Agency.—The distinction between employment and
agency may be merely verbal, and the same person may act as an
employee and as an agent. The term 'agent' is, however, more properly
applicable to the case where the duties of the person employed are to
bring his employer into contractual relations with third parties.[12]

21.4 Contract to Perform Services.—A contract of employment may require
to be distinguished from a contract to perform services, either in the
case where the party who renders the services (*e.g.* a solicitor) has a
separate and independent occupation, or in the case, such as that of a
surgeon at a hospital, where, though there may be no separate
occupation, and the power to appoint and dismiss may be vested in a
particular body, yet that body has no right of interference or direction

[5] *Macdonald* v. *Glasgow Western Hospitals Board, supra, per* Lord President Cooper at
p. 478; *Bank voor Handel en Scheepvaart* v. *Slatford* [1953] 1 Q.B. 248, *per* Denning L.J.
at p. 295.
[6] *Ready Mixed Concrete (South East)* v. *Ministry of Pensions and National Insurance*
[1968] 2 Q.B. 497, *per* McKenna J. at p. 512.
[7] *Per* Cooke J., *Market Investigations Ltd.* v. *Minister of Social Security* [1969] 2 Q.B.
173, at p. 184, *appd.* in *Lee Ting Sang* v. *Chung-Keung* [1990] 2 A.C. 374. See also
O'Kelly v. *Trusthouse Forte plc* [1984] Q.B. 90.
[8] *Conlon* v. *Glasgow Corporation* (1899) 1 F. 869.
[9] See *Parker* v. *Walker*, 1961 S.L.T. 252.
[10] See *Fife County Council* v. *Minister of National Insurance*, 1947 S.C. 629 at p. 636.
[11] *Mair* v. *Wood*, 1948 S.C. 83; *Blackwood* v. *Robertson*, 1984 S.L.T. (Sh.Ct.) 68.
[12] Ch. 22, *infra.*

as to the way in which the work is to be done. In the former case, the contract will normally be for the performance of services[13] and clear contrary indications will be necessary for the constitution of a contract of employment. In the latter case, authorities in which it was held that a person so employed was not an employee, either in a question as to the employer's liability for his negligence,[14] or in the construction of statutes dealing with the incidents of service,[15] must now be regarded as obsolete.[16] Thus it has been held that a hospital board is liable for the negligence of resident medical staff,[17] and similar principles will apply in analogous cases with possible exceptions for visiting consultants and for certain classes of work done for charitable bodies.[18] If it is impossible to regard a person as being in business on his own account the inference that he is an employee may follow.[19] If the employer has an obligation to provide work, that is also indicative of a contract of employment.[20]

21.5 Constitution of Contract.—A contract of employment for more than a year requires to be constituted by writing which is attested by, or holograph of, both parties or by informal writing upon which *rei interventus* has followed.[21] If for less, it may be entered into orally, or implied from the relationship of the parties. But in nearly every contract of employment the employer must now within 2 months after the beginning of an employee's period of employment give the employee a written statement identifying the parties, specifying the date when the employment began, and giving certain statutory particulars of the terms of employment.[22] Where services are rendered without any express agreement, there is a general presumption (except in cases of near relatives) in favour of an implied contract of service and consequent right to payment.[23] The presumption is displaced by proof of a professional custom to render similar services gratuitously.[24] A belated claim, or one made by executors when no claim has been made by the

---

[13] See, *e.g. Renfrewshire and Port Glasgow Joint Committee* v. *Minister of National Insurance*, 1946 S.C. 83.

[14] *Foote* v. *Greenock Hospital*, 1912 S.C. 69; *Lavelle* v. *Glasgow Royal Infirmary*, 1932 S.C. 245; *Reidford* v. *Magistrates of Aberdeen*, 1933 S.C. 276.

[15] *Scottish Insurance Commissioners* v. *Edinburgh Infirmary*, 1913 S.C. 751.

[16] *Macdonald* v. *Glasgow Western Hospitals Board, supra*; *cf. Stagecraft Ltd.* v. *Minister of Pensions and National Insurance*, 1952 S.C. 288.

[17] *Macdonald, supra*; *cf. Kilboy* v. *South Eastern Fire Area Joint Committee*, 1952 S.C. 280.

[18] *Macdonald, supra, per* Lord President Cooper at p. 478.

[19] *Young and Woods* v. *West* [1980] I.R.L.R. 201.

[20] *Nethermere (St Neots)* v. *Gardiner* [1984] I.C.R. 612; [1984] I.R.L.R. 240.

[21] para. 8.9, *supra*; *Cook* v. *Grubb*, 1963 S.C. 1.

[22] 1978 Act, s. 1, as amended by 1993 Act, s. 23 and Sched. 4. Merchant seamen (s. 144) and employees who work wholly or mainly outside Great Britain (s. 141) are excluded. It has been held that the corresponding Northern Ireland legislation cannot give rise to a claim for damages for breach of statutory duty: *Scally* v. *Southern Health and Social Services Board* [1992] 1 A.C. 294.

[23] *Thomson* v. *Thomson's Tr.* (1889) 16 R. 333.

[24] *Corbin* v. *Stewart* (1911) 28 T.L.R. 99 (doctor attending widow of deceased colleague).

deceased, is regarded unfavourably.[25] Where the parties are nearly related, there is probably a presumption in favour of the pursuer in the case of a claim by a son who has assisted his father in his work or business;[26] in favour of the defender, in the case of a daughter or niece who claims payment for domestic services or for nursing.[27]

21.6 Obligations of Employee.—The varieties of types of employment preclude any but a very general statement of the obligations of an employee. He is bound to obey orders;[28] not to absent himself without leave during working hours; to refrain from such misconduct or immorality as may be incompatible with the reasonable performance of the particular service;[29] to do nothing to injure the employer's interests. Refusal to obey orders may be justified if the demand, not excused by an emergency, is to do work other than that which the employee engaged for;[30] if it is illegal;[31] or if compliance would expose the employee to some danger not contemplated at the time of engagement. So the crew of a ship were held to be justified in refusing to continue a voyage when the emergence of war had rendered that ship liable to seizure as carrying contraband.[32] It has been held that an ordinary contract of employment does not involve any fiduciary relationship, and therefore that an employee is not bound to reveal the fact that he has been guilty of a breach of contract,[33] but an employee in a managerial position may have a duty to report the misconduct of subordinates even if that involves disclosure of his own breach.[34] An employee, if he does not hold himself out as belonging to any particular trade or profession, does enough if he performs his duties with reasonable care.[35] One engaged as a member of some trade or profession *spondet peritiam artis* (promises skill in the art), and is liable in damages if he fails to exhibit the degree of skill reasonably to be expected from an ordinary member of his craft.[36]

21.7 Remedies of Employer.—Where an employer is held vicariously liable for the fault or negligence of his employee, he is entitled to claim an

---

[25] *Mackersy's Exrs.* v. *St Giles Managing Board* (1904) 12 S.L.T. 391; see *Mackison* v. *Burgh of Dundee,* 1910 S.C. (H.L.) 27.
[26] *Thomson* v. *Thomson's Tr., supra*; *Miller* v. *Miller* (1898) 25 R. 995; *Urquhart* v. *Urquhart's Tr.* (1905) 8 F. 42.
[27] *Russell* v. *McClymont* (1906) 8 F. 821.
[28] *Blyth* v. *Scottish Liberal Club,* 1983 S.L.T. 260.
[29] See Fraser, *Master and Servant,* p. 84. And see, as to fiduciary position of an employee or agent, para. 22.6, *infra.*
[30] *Thomson* v. *Douglas* (1807) Hume 392; *Moffat* v. *Boothby* (1884) 11 R. 501.
[31] *Morrish* v. *Henleys (Folkestone) Ltd.* [1973] 2 All E.R. 137. As to the illegality of Sunday labour, see *Middleton* v. *Trough,* 1908 S.C. (J.) 32; *Smith* v. *Beardmore,* 1922 S.C. 131.
[32] *Lang* v. *St Enoch Shipping Co.,* 1908 S.C. 103.
[33] *Bell* v. *Lever Bros.* [1932] A.C. 161.
[34] *Sybron Corp.* v. *Rochem Ltd.* [1984] Ch. 112.
[35] See *Gunn* v. *Ramsay* (1801) Hume 384; *Lister* v. *Romford Ice & Cold Storage Co.* [1957] A.C. 555; *Janata Bank* v. *Ahmed* [1981] I.C.R. 791.
[36] In the case of a doctor, see, *e.g. Hunter* v. *Hanley,* 1955 S.C. 200.

indemnity from the employee for the damages and expenses he has had to pay.[37] The remedy of an employer for an employee's breach of contract is dismissal, and a claim for damages. It has been said that where an employee is justifiably dismissed, no wages are due for the part of the term which he has served[38] but it is thought that that would now be accepted only in respect of any period affected by the breach leading to dismissal. If employees refuse to carry out the normal duties of their employment, the employer can suspend them and withhold pay for the period of suspension.[39] A decree *ad factum praestandum*, ordaining the employee to remain at his work, will not be pronounced.[40] A court cannot grant an order for specific implement or interdict which has the effect of compelling an employee to do any work or attend at any place for the doing of any work.[41] To harbour an employee, *i.e.* to give him employment in the knowledge that he is in desertion, is an actionable wrong to his employer.[42] It is also a wrong to induce him to break his contract.[43] The common law rule that workmen deserting their employment could be imprisoned would not be followed in a modern case,[44] and it is thought that a similar rule affecting apprentices[45] is also now obsolete.[46] An employee commits a criminal offence if he wilfully and maliciously breaks a contract of service in the knowledge that by the breach, whether done alone or in combination, serious injury to life or property will be entailed.[47] Seamen are subject to special civil and criminal liabilities in relation to their employment.[48]

21.8 Obligations of Employer.[49]—The obligations of an employer, like those of an employee, can be indicated only in general terms. He is bound to pay wages if, expressly or impliedly, wages are due. Suspension without pay is, unless it can be justified in terms of the contract, a breach of contract for which damages may be recovered.[50] Where remuneration is

[37] *Lister* v. *Romford Ice & Cold Storage Co.* [1957] A.C. 555.
[38] Fraser, *Master and Servant*, pp. 113, 119.
[39] *Laurie* v. *British Steel Corporation*, 1988 S.L.T. 17, *appvd. Miles* v. *Wakefield M.D.C.* [1987] A.C. 539.
[40] Fraser, *Master and Servant*, p. 37; *Rose Street Foundry Co.* v. *Lewis*, 1917 S.C. 341, *per* Lord Salvesen at p. 351.
[41] 1992 Act, s. 236.
[42] *Rose Street Foundry Co.* v. *Lewis*, 1917 S.C. 341.
[43] *Lumley* v. *Gye* (1853) 2 E. & B. 216; *Couper* v. *Macfarlane* (1879) 6 R. 683. See para. 31.8, *infra*.
[44] See Umpherston, *Master and Servant*, p. 134.
[45] *McDermott* v. *Ramsay* (1876) 4 R. 217.
[46] The statutory provisions for imprisonment of certain deserting apprentices laid down in the Employers and Workmen Act 1875 (ss. 6 and 12) have been repealed (Family Law Reform Act 1969, ss. 11(*b*) and 28(4)(*e*); Statute Law Repeals Act 1973, Sched. 1, Pt. XIII).
[47] Trade Union and Labour Relations (Consolidation) Act 1992, s. 240.
[48] Merchant Shipping Act 1970, ss. 27–41 as amended by the Merchant Shipping Act 1988, s. 32.
[49] See also paras. 21.37 to 21.42, *infra*.
[50] *McArdle* v. *Scotbeef Ltd.*, 1974 S.L.T. (Notes) 78; *cf. Bird* v. *British Celanese Ltd.* [1945] K.B. 336.

to be by piecework, and the engagement is for a fixed period, work must be provided.[51] In domestic service the employer is bound not only to pay wages but to supply board and lodging, and to exhibit a reasonable amount of care for the servants' welfare. So, though he is probably not bound to supply medical attendance, it was held that an employer in the case of illness, was bound to intimate to the panel doctor, and was liable in damages where, without doing so, he sent the servant home in a state when it was dangerous for her to travel.[52] It is settled that an employer is not bound to give an employee a character[53] or to answer inquiries, and doubtful whether a custom of trade can lay upon him the obligation to give a certificate of the fact of employment.[54] Seamen, on discharge, have a statutory right to such a certificate.[55] In giving a character an employer enjoys a qualified privilege, and averments of malice are necessary to the relevancy of an action of damages against him for defamation.[56] A character reference unduly laudatory may render him liable to a party who engages the employee in reliance on it and suffers loss.[57] There may be an implied obligation on the employer to take reasonable steps to publicise a term of the contract negotiated with a representative body which confers on the employee a valuable right contingent upon the employee's acting in a certain manner.[58]

21.9 Wages Act 1986.—Payment of wages in certain employments was formerly regulated by the Truck Acts of 1831, 1887, 1896 and 1940, as amended by the Payment of Wages Act 1960.[59] The object of the legislation was to ensure that manual workers were paid in cash and not in goods. The Truck Acts were repealed and in their place the Wages Act 1986 provided a new scheme for the protection of workers in relation to the payment of wages. A worker, for the purposes of the Act, is any individual who has entered into or works under (a) a contract of service, (b) a contract of apprenticeship, or (c) any other contract whereby he undertakes to do or perform personally any work or services for another party to the contract whose status by virtue of the contract is not that of a client or customer of any profession or

---

[51] *Devonald* v. *Rosser* [1906] 2 K.B. 728. See, as to agency, *infra*, Chap. 22.

[52] *McKeating* v. *Frame*, 1921 S.C. 382.

[53] *Fell* v. *Lord Ashburton*, December 12, 1809, F.C.; Fraser, *Master and Servant*, p. 127.

[54] *Grant* v. *Ramage & Ferguson* (1897) 25 R. 35; *Royce* v. *Greig*, 1909 2 S.L.T. 298.

[55] Merchant Shipping (Crew Agreements etc.) Regulations 1972 (S.I. 1972 No. 918). para. 26 (4)

[56] Bell, *Prin.*, § 188, para. 33.12, *infra*. On the question of negligence, see *Spring* v. *Guardian Assurance* [1994] 3 All E.R. 129.

[57] *Anderson* v. *Wishart* (1818) 1 Murray 429.

[58] *Scally* v. *Southern Health and Social Services Board* [1992] 1 A.C. 294.

[59] 1 & 2 William IV; 50 & 51 Vict.; 59 & 60 Vict; 3 & 4 Geo. VI; 8 & 9 Eliz. II. The amount of remuneration was in some cases controlled by Wages Councils but Wages Councils have been abolished with effect from October 1, 1993.

business undertaking carried on by the individual.[60] An employer is prohibited from making any deduction from the wages of any worker employed by him or receiving any payment from such a worker unless (a) the deduction or payment is authorised by statute[61] or by a relevant provision of the worker's contract, or (b) the worker has previously signified his agreement in writing.[62] Payments in lieu of notice which are damages for breach of contract are not 'wages' under the Act.[63] A relevant provision is a written term of the contract of which the employer has given the worker a copy prior to making the deduction or receiving the payment, or a term, which may be oral or implied, whose existence and effect have been notified to the worker.[64] Neither a relevant provision varying the contract nor the worker's agreement can operate so as to authorise any deduction or payment on account of any conduct of the worker or any event occurring before the variation took effect or the agreement was signified.[65] The prohibitions of the Act do not, however, apply to (a) reimbursement in respect of overpayment of wages or expenses, (b) deductions or payments in consequence of disciplinary proceedings held by virtue of any statutory provision, (c) any deduction in pursuance of a statutory requirement imposed on the employer to deduct and pay over, in accordance with a relevant determination of a public authority, amounts determined by that authority to be due to it from the worker, (d) any deduction in pursuance of arrangements established with the worker's written agreement under which the employer is to deduct and pay over to a third person, in accordance with a notification from that person, amounts notified as being due to him from the worker, (e) any deduction or payment on account of the worker's having taken part in a strike or other industrial action, or (f) any deduction made with the worker's prior written agreement or any payment received by the employer, where the purpose is the satisfaction of the order of a court or tribunal requiring payment by the worker to the employer.[66] Special provisions govern deductions made and payments received on account of cash shortages or stock deficiencies in retail employment.[67] A worker affected by a contravention of the statutory prohibitions may present a complaint to an industrial tribunal[68] which, if it finds the complaint to be well founded, must make a declaration to that effect and order the employer to pay or repay any amount unlawfully deducted or received.[69]

---

[60] s. 8(1) and (2).
[61] *e.g.* under an earnings arrestment: *Slater* v. *Grampian R.C.,* 1991 S.L.T. (Sh.Ct.) 72.
[62] s. 1(1) and (2).
[63] *Delaney* v. *Staples* [1992] 1 A.C. 687.
[64] s. 1(3).
[65] s. 1(4).
[66] s. 1(5).
[67] ss. 2, 3 and 4.
[68] s. 5(1).
[69] s. 5(4).

21.10 Wages: Other Statutory Provisions.—Statute now provides for guarantee payments to be made in respect of any whole day in which an employee, who has been continuously employed for at least one month, is not provided with work because of diminution in the requirements of the employer's business or other occurrence affecting its normal working.[70] The payment is not available in event of a strike, lock-out or other industrial action involving employees of the employer or an associated employer or of unreasonable refusal by the employee of suitable alternative work[71] or of failure to comply with reasonable requirements imposed with a view to ensuring the availability of the employee's services. Payments are at the guaranteed hourly rate, subject to a maximum of £14.10 per day, and cannot exceed five days in any period of three months.[72]

An employee who has been continuously employed for a least one month (or for more than three months in the case of employment under a contract which is for a fixed term of three months or less or which has been made in contemplation of the performance of a specific task not expected to last for more than three months) is entitled to a week's pay during each week up to 26 weeks during which he is suspended because of a requirement imposed by statute or a recommendation made under a Code of Practice authorised by the Health and Safety at Work Act 1974.[73] Employees who are incapable of work because of illness or injury, who unreasonably refuse alternative work or who do not make themselves available for work, are excepted.[74]

Unpaid wages up to a total of £800 owed by a bankrupt employer and accruing during the four months preceding bankruptcy constitute a preferential debt.[75] In addition, certain amounts owed by an insolvent employer may be recovered from the National Insurance Fund.[76] Payments in respect of arrears of pay are limited to eight weeks' pay and £205 in respect of any one week.[77] Every employee is now entitled to an itemised pay statement on each occasion that payment of wages or salary is made.[78]

---

[70] 1978 Act, s. 12(1).

[71] s. 13(3) and (4).

[72] ss. 14, 15; Employment Protection (Variation of Limits) Order 1992 (S.I. 1992 No. 312).

[73] ss. 19(1) and 20(1) as amended by the 1982 Act, s. 20 and Sched. 2, para. 2.

[74] s. 20(4).

[75] Insolvency Act 1986, s. 386, Sched. 6, para. 9; Insolvency Proceedings (Monetary Limits) Order 1986 (S.I. 1986 No. 1996), art. 4; Bankruptcy (Scotland) Act 1985, s. 51, Sched. 3, para. 5(1); Bankruptcy (Scotland) Regulations 1985 (S.I. 1985 No. 1925) (as amended by Bankruptcy (Scotland) Amendment Regulations 1986 (S.I. 1986 No. 1914)), reg. 14.

[76] s. 122.

[77] 1978 Act, s. 122(3)(a) and (5) as amended by the 1982 Act, Sched. 3, para. 4 (2) and Employment Protection (Variation of Limits) Order 1992 (S.I. 1992 No. 312). Other maxima apply to other debts.

[78] s. 8; see also Employment Protection (Part-time Employees) Regulations 1995 (S.I. 1995 No. 31) and 1978 Act, s. 146(4).

21.11 Sick Pay.—The employer is liable to pay statutory sick pay to the employee for the first 28 weeks of incapacity.[79] The amount paid is recoverable by small employers from the Department of Social Security.[80] Sick pay is not payable for the first three days of a period of incapacity.[81] Payment is at a prescribed weekly rate related to normal weekly earnings.[82]

21.12 Maternity Pay.—An employee who has been continuously employed for at least 26 weeks is entitled to statutory maternity pay from the employer for a period not exceeding 18 weeks during which she is absent from work because of pregnancy or confinement.[83] The first week of payment is normally the eleventh week before the expected week of confinement.[84] If the woman has been employed for a period of at least two years the payment is at the higher rate equivalent to nine-tenths of her normal weekly earnings for the first six weeks; otherwise, it is at a lower prescribed rate.[85] The employer may recover the payments from the Department of Social Security.[86] An employee is also entitled to maternity leave and may be entitled to return to work after confinement.[86a]

21.13 Pensions.—A term of a contract of employment that the employee must be a member of an occupational pension scheme is void.[87] Occupational pension schemes must give equal treatment to men and women.[88] The provisions of the pension scheme are overridden by this requirement[89] and the Occupational Pensions Board, on application by the trustees of the scheme, may modify a scheme to bring about equal treatment.[90] The trustees are required to give certain information to members.[91] Where employment is terminated before the normal pension age and certain conditions are satisfied, the pension must be preserved for payment at the normal age[92] and is also subject to revaluation.[93] An occupational scheme must also permit the transfer and buying-out of benefits. Certain criteria must be satisfied if the scheme is to benefit from tax privileges.[94]

---

[79] Social Security Contributions and Benefits Act 1992, ss. 151, 155.
[80] s. 158 as amended by the Statutory Sick Pay Act 1994, s. 1.
[81] s. 155.
[82] s. 157 as amended by the Social Security (Incapacity for Work) Act 1994, s. 6.
[83] Social Security Contributions and Benefits Act 1992, s. 164.
[84] s. 165.
[85] s. 166.
[86] s. 167.
[86a] See para. 21.15, *infra*.
[87] Pension Schemes Act 1993, s. 160.
[88] Social Security Act 1989, s. 23, Sched. 5.
[89] *Ibid.*, para. 3(1).
[90] *Ibid.*, para. 4(1).
[91] Pension Schemes Act 1993, ss. 113 and 114.
[92] *Ibid.*, ss. 69–82.
[93] *Ibid.*, ss. 83–86.
[94] Income and Corporation Taxes Act 1988, ss. 590–612 (as amended).

Other criteria have to be satisfied if the employer is to be allowed to 'contract-out' of the state pension scheme.[95] The value of pension rights may have to be considered in relation to damages for breach of the employment contract,[96] compensation for unfair dismissal,[97] damages in respect of personal injury[98] or death[99] and financial provision on divorce.[1]

21.14 Time Off.—An employer has a statutory obligation to permit an employee in any of the following categories to take time off during working hours for certain purposes:

(1) An official of an independent trade union recognised by the employer—if the time off is taken for the purpose of enabling him to carry out his official duties concerned with negotiations with the employer related to or connected with conditions of employment in relation to which the trade union is recognised by the employer and any other duties of such official concerned with the performance of any functions related to conditions of employment that the employer has agreed may be performed by the trade union, or to undergo approved training in aspects of industrial relations relevant to the carrying out of these duties.[2] 'Industrial relations' are confined to relations between employer and employees but within that context are not to be narrowly construed;[3]

(2) A member of an independent trade union recognised by the employer in relation to employees of the same description as the member seeking time off—if the time off is taken for the purpose of taking part in activities of that trade union or in other trade union activities in relation to which the employee is acting as a representative of his trade union, excluding activities consisting of industrial action;[4]

(3) A Justice of the Peace or a member of a local authority, statutory tribunal or certain other public bodies—if the time off is taken for the purpose of performing his public duties;[5]

(4) An employee who is given notice of dismissal by reason of redundancy and has been continuously employed for at least

---

[95] Pension Schemes Act 1993, Chaps. I and II.
[96] *Paterson* v. *South West Scotland Electricity Board*, 1950 S.C. 582.
[97] *Manpower Ltd.* v. *Hearne* [1983] I.C.R. 567.
[98] *Mitchell* v. *Glenrothes Development Corporation*, 1991 S.L.T. 284.
[99] *Davidson* v. *Upper Clyde Shipbuilders Ltd.*, 1990 S.L.T. 329.
[1] Family Law (Scotland) Act 1985, s. 10(5); *Little* v. *Little*, 1990 S.L.T. 785.
[2] 1992 Act, s. 168.
[3] *Sood* v. *G.E.C. Elliott Process Automation* [1979] I.R.L.R. 416; *Vine* v. *D.R.G. (U.K.)* [1978] I.R.L.R. 475; *Young* v. *Carr Fasteners Co.* [1979] I.R.L.R. 420; *Beal* v. *Beecham Group* [1982] 1 W.L.R. 1005.
[4] 1992 Act, s. 170.
[5] 1978 Act, s. 29(1), (2) and (3).

two years—if the time off is taken in order to look for new employment or make arrangements for training for future employment;[6] and

(5) An employee who is pregnant—if the time off is taken to enable her to attend for the purpose of receiving ante-natal care in accordance with an appointment made on the advice of a registered general practitioner, midwife or health visitor.[7]

The amount of time off which an employer is bound to permit to an employee in any of the above categories other than a pregnant employee and the conditions to which it may be subject are such as may be reasonable in all the circumstances.[8] The right of a pregnant employee is not to be unreasonably refused time off to enable her to keep the appointment.[9] In determining what is reasonable in the case of a trade union official or member, regard is to be had to any relevant provision of a code of practice[10] and, in the case of time off for public duties, to how much time is required for the performance of the duties, to how much time the employee has already been permitted, and to the circumstances of the employer's business and the effect of the employee's absence on its running.[11] Time off in the case of trade union officials, redundant employees and pregnant employees is to be paid, but there is no such requirement in the other categories.[12]

A complaint may be made to an industrial tribunal in the event of the employer's failure to permit time off as required by the Act.[13] On such a complaint by a trade union official or redundant employee or pregnant employee the tribunal may order the employer to pay to the employee the amount due to him or her,[14] and in all cases, except those of the redundant employee or pregnant employee, may award compensation having regard both to the employer's default and to any loss sustained by the employee.[15]

21.15   Maternity.—An employee who is absent from work on account of pregnancy or confinement has, subject to certain qualifications, and in addition to her entitlement to statutory maternity pay,[16] a right to return to work.[17] The qualifications are that: (1) she has continued to be

---

[6] 1978 Act, s. 31(1) and (2).

[7] 1978 Act, s. 31A as inserted by 1980 Act, s. 13.

[8] 1992 Act, ss. 168(3), 170(3); 1978 Act, ss. 29(4)' and 31(1). The words 'in all the circumstances' do not occur in s. 31(1).

[9] 1978 Act, s. 31A(1).

[10] 1992 Act, ss. 168(3), 170(3).

[11] 1978 Act, s. 29(4); see *Borders Regional Council* v. *Moule* [1993] I.R.L.R. 199.

[12] 1992 Act, s. 169; 1978 Act, ss. 31(3) to (5) and 31A(4) and (5).

[13] 1992 Act, ss. 168(4), 169(5), 170(4); 1978 Act, ss. 29(6), 31(6) and 31A(6).

[14] 1992 Act, s. 172(3); 1978 Act, ss. 31(8) and 31A(8).

[15] 1978 Act, s. 30(2).

[16] Maternity pay under the 1978 Act has been replaced by statutory maternity pay under Social Security Contributions and Benefits Act 1992, Pt. XII. See para. 21.12.

[17] ss. 33(1) and 39, (as introduced by 1993 Act, Pt. II).

employed until immediately before the beginning of the eleventh week before the expected week of confinement; (2) at that time she has been continuously employed for at least two years; and (3) she has informed her employer at least 21 days before her absence begins or, if that is not reasonably practicable, as soon as reasonably practicable, that she will be absent from work because of pregnancy or confinement and that she intends to return to work.[18] In order to avail herself of this right she must give the required information to her employer in writing and supply for his inspection a medical certificate stating her expected date of confinement.[19] The right is exigible at any time before the end of 29 weeks from the beginning of the week of confinement,[20] and is a right to be reinstated in the job in which she was employed under her original contract of employment, and on terms and conditions no less favourable than if she had not been absent.[21] Failure by the employer to permit return constitutes dismissal with effect from the notified day of return, and the dismissal is deemed to be for the reason for which she was not permitted to return.[22] Unless there is a supervening reason unconnected with her pregnancy which justifies dismissal, the remedies for unfair dismissal will ensue.[23] Dismissal of a woman who is employed under a contract of indefinite duration on the grounds of her pregnancy is direct sex discrimination under the European Equal Treatment directive.[24] All female employees, regardless of length of service or number of hours worked, are entitled to maternity leave of 14 weeks or until the baby is born during which period the employee is entitled to the benefit of the terms and conditions of her contract of employment other than any entitlement to remuneration.[24a]

21.16 Racial Discrimination.—A dismissal wholly, or mainly, on the ground of the employee's racial identity will almost always be unfair. The Race Relations Act 1976 provides, however, additional protection for employees against racial discrimination,[25] and extends that protection to workers supplied under contracts for the provision of services.[26] There is discrimination for the purposes of the Act if, on racial grounds, A treats B less favourably than he treats, or would treat, other persons, or if he applies to B a requirement or condition which (1) is such that the proportion of the persons of B's racial group who can comply with it is

[18] ss. 36, 37, 39 and 40.
[19] s. 37.
[20] s. 39(1).
[21] s. 39(2).
[22] s. 56
[23] See para. 21.28 *infra*. Redundancy (on which see s. 41) may be a supervening reason.
[24] *Webb* v. *Emo Air Cargo (UK) Ltd.* [1994] I.R.L.R. 482, applying art. 5(1) of directive 76/207.
[24a] ss. 33–38A, (as introduced by the 1993 Act).
[25] Pts. I and II.
[26] s. 7.

considerably smaller than the proportion of persons not of that group who can so comply, (2) he cannot show to be justifiable on other than racial grounds, and (3) is to B's detriment because he cannot comply with it.[27] To segregate a person from others on racial grounds is to treat him less favourably,[28] and the definition of racial grounds and racial group covers considerations of colour, nationality or ethnic or national origins as well as race.[29] If there is discrimination on the grounds of race it is immaterial that those grounds were not personal to the victim. So, an employee dismissed for refusal to obey a discriminatory order comes under the protection of the Act although the discrimination was not directed against him.[30] 'Ethnic' is a wider term than 'race' and connotes membership of a distinct community with, *inter alia*, a long shared history of which it is conscious and the memory of which it keeps alive as distinguishing it from other groups and with a distinct cultural tradition, social customs and manners.[31] Victimisation in connection with proceedings brought or steps taken under the Act, or in connection with allegations of contraventions of the Act, is treated as discrimination.[32]

It is unlawful to discriminate on racial grounds against an employee in the terms of employment afforded to him, or the access afforded to opportunities for promotion, transfer or training, or, with certain exceptions, to any other benefits, facilities or services, or by dismissing him or subjecting him to any other detriment; and it is unlawful to discriminate against a prospective employee in the arrangements made for the purpose of determining who should be offered employment, or in the terms offered, or by refusing or deliberately omitting to offer employment.[33] The provisions relating to the making of arrangements for offering employment, to refusal or deliberate omission to offer employment, and to access afforded to opportunities for promotion, transfer or training, are excluded where membership of a particular racial group is a genuine occupational qualification.[34] It is such a qualification where it is required for reasons of authenticity in a dramatic performance or other entertainment, or in work as an artist's or photographic model, or in the provision of food or drink to the

---

[27] s. 1(1).

[28] s. 1(2).

[29] s. 3(1).

[30] *Zarczynska* v. *Levy* [1979] I.C.R. 184; *Showboat Entertainment Centre* v. *Owens* [1984] I.R.L.R. 7. *Cf. Race Relations Board* v. *Applin* [1973] 1 Q.B. 815.

[31] *Mandla* v. *Dowell Lee* [1983] 2 A.C. 548. Among additional features relevant to whether a community is ethnic in character are common geographical or ancestral origins, common language, a common literature, a common religion distinct from the religion of neighbouring peoples, and the community's position as a minority or as an oppressed or dominant group within a larger community. *Cf. Crown Suppliers (Property Services Agency)* v. *Dawkins* [1991] I.C.R. 583.

[32] s. 2; see *Kirby* v. *Manpower Services Commission* [1980] I.R.L.R. 229.

[33] s. 4(1); *N.W. Thames Regional Health Authority* v. *Noone* [1988] I.C.R. 813, C.A.; *Dhatt* v. *McDonalds Hamburgers Ltd.* [1991] I.C.R. 238, C.A.

[34] s. 5(1).

public in a particular setting, or where personal services promoting the welfare of the group can most effectively be provided by a member of that group.[35] There are also exceptions for employment outside Great Britain;[36] for employment for the purpose of providing training and skills intended to be exercised outside Great Britain;[37] for seamen recruited abroad;[38] for the provision of education or training for persons not ordinarily resident in Great Britain;[39] for provision by any person of access to facilities for training to members of a particular racial group or encouraging such members to take advantage of opportunities for work where the group is under-represented among persons doing the work in question;[40] for discrimination, on the basis of nationality, place of birth or length of residence, in relation to selection to represent a country, place or area, or to eligibility for competition in any sport or game;[41] and for acts done under statutory authority[42] or for the purpose of safeguarding national security.[43]

Employers are liable not only for their own discriminatory acts but also (except for the purposes of criminal liability) for such acts done in the course of their employment by their employees, even if done without the employer's knowledge or approval, unless the employer can prove that he took such steps as were reasonably practicable to prevent the employee from doing the act in question, or from doing acts of that description in the course of his employment.[44] A person aggrieved by racial discrimination in respect of employment may complain to an industrial tribunal, which, if it finds the complaint well founded, may grant such of the following remedies as it considers just and equitable:

(1) an order declaring the rights of the complainant and the respondent;

(2) an order for compensation for any damages sustained by the complainant, including injury to feelings[45] (but an order for compensation cannot be made if the discrimination consists in the application to the complainant of a requirement or a condition applied equally to persons not of the same racial group, but with discriminatory results, and the respondent proves that the requirement or condition was not applied with the intention of treating the claimant unfavourably on racial grounds). There is no longer a statutory limit on the level of

---

[35] s. 5(2); *Tottenham Green Under Fives' Centre* v. *Marshall (No. 2)* [1991] I.C.R. 320.
[36] ss. 4(1) and (2) and 8.
[37] s. 6.
[38] s. 9.
[39] s. 36.
[40] ss. 37 and 38. Section 37 does not apply to discrimination rendered unlawful by s. 4(1) or (2): s. 37(3) substituted by 1989 Act, s. 7(3).
[41] s. 39.
[42] s. 41; *Hampson* v. *Department of Education and Science* [1991] 1 A.C. 171.
[43] s. 42.
[44] s. 32.
[45] *Sharifi* v. *Strathclyde R.C.* [1992] I.R.L.R. 259.

compensation which can be awarded and the tribunal can also award interest on the compensation payment;[45a] and

(3) a recommendation that the respondent take, within a specified period, action appearing to the tribunal to be practicable for the purpose of obviating or reducing the adverse effect on the complainant of any act of discrimination. (If the respondent fails, without reasonable justification, to comply with a recommendation of the tribunal, the tribunal may, if it thinks it just and equitable to do so, increase the amount of compensation which the respondent was required to pay or, if an order for compensation has not been made, may make such an order.)[46]

In addition to the remedies available to the individual, compliance with the Act, in relation to employment as well as other matters, may be secured at the instance of the Commission for Racial Equality by means of non-discrimination notices and consequent procedure.[47]

21.17   Equal Pay.—Under the Equal Pay Act 1970 an equality clause is, unless already expressed, deemed to be included in every contract under which anyone is employed at an establishment in Great Britain.[48] The Act extends to employment 'under a contract of service or of apprenticeship, or a contract personally to execute any work or labour'[49] and so embraces contracts for the provision of services. The effect of an equality clause is that for men and women employed on like work, or employed on work rated as equivalent, the terms and conditions of employment for one sex are not less favourable in any relevant respect than the terms and conditions applicable to the other sex.[50] By like work is meant work of the same or a broadly similar nature in which any differences between the things done are not of practical importance in relation to terms and conditions of employment.[51] Differences in duties and responsibilities, if sufficiently significant, may be of practical importance[52] but in many cases they may appropriately be compensated, as may differences in hours and shifts, by the payment of a premium and so do not justify a difference in basic pay.[53] An equality clause does not preclude the payment of such a premium for additional or different work actually done. By work rated as equivalent is meant a job which has been given an equal value to another job in terms of the demand made on a worker or which would have been given an equal value but

---

[45a] Race Relations (Remedies) Act 1994, ss. 1 and 2.
[46] ss. 54 and 56.
[47] ss. 58 to 66.
[48] As amended by the Sex Discrimination Act 1975, s. 8 and Sched. 1, Equal Pay (Amendment) Regulations 1983 (S.I. 1983 No. 1794).
[49] s. 1(6).
[50] s. 1(2).
[51] s. 1(4).
[52] *Noble* v. *David Gold and Son (Holdings)* [1980] I.R.L.R. 252.
[53] *Electrolux* v. *Hutchinson* [1977] I.C.R. 252.

for the evaluation being made on a system setting different values for men and women.[54] Although an evaluation has not been made by the employer, an employee may claim that his or her work is of equal value to the work of comparable persons of the opposite sex and, on such a claim, an industrial tribunal may order an evaluation to be made by an independent expert.[55] In cases both of like work and of equal value an equality clause shall not operate if the employer proves that a variation between a man's contract and a woman's is genuinely due to a material difference other than sex.[56] Differences of this kind may, and usually will, be differences which are not inherent in the work itself because differences pertaining to the work will already have been taken into account in an assessment of like work or equal value. Market forces cannot be a relevant factor, because the Act is designed to counteract such forces and factors extrinsic to the personal equation between the employees are to be disregarded, but a variation may be justified on the need to recruit, irrespective of sex, employees of a particular class.[57]

21.18 Equal Pay: Remedies.—Any claim in respect of the contravention of a contractual term arising out of the operation of an equality clause may be presented to an industrial tribunal or, where it appears to the Secretary of State that an employer may have contravened such a term but that it is not reasonable to expect the employees to take steps to have the question determined, the question may be referred to an industrial tribunal by him.[58] In either case, the tribunal may determine the claim, including any question of arrears of remuneration or damages in respect of the contravention, and where there is a dispute about the effect of an equality clause it may, on the application of an employer, make an order declaring the rights of parties.[59] A remedy for failure to comply with an equality clause may also be pursued as a breach of contract through the courts, subject, however, to the court's power where it considers that the claim can more conveniently be disposed of by an industrial tribunal to direct that the claim be struck out and, if it thinks fit, referred to an industrial tribunal.[60]

21.19 Equal Pay: Exceptions.—No claim in respect of the operation of an equality clause may be referred to an industrial tribunal, otherwise than on a reference directed or made by a court, unless the employee, in

[54] s. 1(5).
[55] ss. 1(2)(c) and 2A as amended by Equal Pay (Amendment) Regulations 1983. See also *Neil* v. *Ford Motor Co.* [1984] I.R.L.R. 339; *Hayward* v. *Cammell Laird Shipbuilders* [1988] A.C. 894.
[56] s. 1(3). *Leverton* v. *Clwyd C.C.* [1989] A.C. 706.
[57] *Clay Cross (Quarry Services)* v. *Fletcher* [1978] 1 W.L.R. 1429; *Rainey* v. *Greater Glasgow Health Board*, 1987 S.C. (H.L.) 1; see also *Enderby* v. *Frenchay Health Authority* [1993] I.R.L.R. 591.
[58] s. 2(1) and (2).
[59] s. 2(1A).
[60] s. 2(3).

respect of whom the claim is made, has been in the relevant employment within the six months preceding the date of the reference and no payments may be awarded in any proceedings, whether before a court or tribunal, by way of arrears of remuneration or damages, in respect of a time earlier than two years before the date on which the proceedings were instituted.[61] The Act also contains provisions for securing equality of treatment in agricultural wages orders.[62] The equal treatment requirement is excluded in so far as the terms and conditions of a woman's employment are affected by the law regulating the employment of women and in so far as any special treatment is accorded to women in connection with pregnancy or the birth of a child.[63] There is, moreover, no requirement of equal treatment as regards terms and conditions related to retirement or death, or to any provision made in connection therewith, other than a provision affording access to opportunities for promotion, transfer or training or providing for dismissal or demotion.[64] But equal access must be afforded to occupational pensions schemes[65] and any provision in contravention of Article 119 of the Treaty of Rome (which requires equal pay for equal work) cannot receive effect.[66] Article 119 can be founded on in British courts as having direct effect.[67]

21.20 **Sex Discrimination.**—The Sex Discrimination Act 1975 contains provisions on discrimination on the ground of sex or, in relation to employment, on the ground of marital status, corresponding *mutatis mutandis* to those already noticed as laid down by the Race Relations Act 1976 for discrimination on the ground of race.[68] The following special features should, however, be noted. A genuine occupational qualification means, in terms of the Sex Discrimination Act, (a) that the job calls for a person of one sex rather than the other for reasons of physiology (excluding physical strength or stamina), or, in dramatic performances or other entertainment, for reasons of authenticity, so that the essential nature of the job would be materially different if carried out by a person of the other sex, or (b) that the job needs to be held by a person of one sex rather than the other to preserve decency or privacy or, where the job is likely to involve working or living in a private home, because objection might reasonably be taken to allowing to a

[61] s. 2(4) and (5). Interest may be awarded on an award of arrears of remuneration or damages, see Sex Discrimination and Equal Pay (Remedies) Regulations 1993 (S.I. 1993 No. 2798).
[62] s. 5.
[63] s. 6(1).
[64] s. 6(1A) and (2) as amended by Sex Discrimination Act 1986, s. 2(4) and the Social Security Act 1989, Sched. 5, para. 13.
[65] *Ibid.*
[66] *Worringham and Humphreys* v. *Lloyds Bank (No. 2)* [1982] 1 W.L.R. 841.
[67] *Barber* v. *Guardian Royal Exchange Assurance Group* [1990] E.C.R. 1889 [1991] 1 Q.B. 344; *Coloroll Pension Trs Ltd.* v. *Russell* [1994] I.R.L.R. 586.
[68] See, as to sexual harassment, *Strathclyde R.C.* v. *Porcelli*, 1986 S.C. 137.

person of the other sex the degree of physical or social contact with an inmate of the home or the knowledge of intimate details of his life which is likely on account of the nature or circumstances of the job or the home, or (c) that it is impracticable for the employee to live elsewhere than in premises provided by the employer which are normally lived in by, and equipped with accommodation for, persons of one sex and it is not reasonable to expect the employer either to equip these premises with accommodation for the other sex or to provide other premises, or (d) that the premises within which the work is to be done are part of a hospital, prison or other establishment for persons requiring special care, supervision or attention and these persons are all of one sex and it is reasonable, having regard to the essential character of the establishment, that the job should not be held by a person of the other sex, or (e) that the holder of the job provides individuals with personal services, promoting their welfare or education or the like, and these services can most effectively be provided by a person of one sex rather than the other, or (f) that the job needs to be held by a person of one sex rather than the other because it is likely to involve the performance of duties outside the United Kingdom in a country whose laws or customs are such that the duties could not effectively be performed by a person of the other sex, or (g) that the job is one of two to be held by a married couple.[69]

21.21 Sex Discrimination: Exclusions.—Discrimination in employment outside Great Britain,[70] or in acts done under statutory authority,[71] or for the purpose of safeguarding national security,[72] is excluded, as it is under the Race Relations Act, and the provisions for discriminatory training are similar. In other respects the exclusionary provisions are, however, different. Subject to exceptions similar to those under the Equal Pay Act, the Act does not apply to discriminatory provisions in respect of retirement or death.[73] Regulations under sections 26 and 27 of the Police (Scotland) Act 1967 may discriminate in requirements relating to height, uniform or equipment or allowances in lieu thereof, in according special treatment to women in connection with pregnancy or child-birth, and in pensions of special constables or police cadets;[74] and discrimination as to requirements relating to height is also lawful in the recruitment and employment of prison officers.[75] Employment for the purposes of an organised religion is excluded where the employment is limited to one sex so as to comply with the doctrines of the religion or

[69] s. 7 as amended by Sex Discrimination Act 1986, s. 1(2).
[70] ss. 6(1) and 10.
[71] ss. 51, 51A inserted by Employment Act 1989, s. 3(3). See also 1989 Act, ss. 1, 4.
[72] s. 52; Sex Discrimination (Amendment) Order 1988 (S.I. 1988 No. 249).
[73] s. 6(4) as amended by Sex Discrimination Act 1986, s. 2(1) and Social Security Act 1989, Sched. 5, para. 14.
[74] s. 17.
[75] s. 18.

avoid offending the religious susceptibilities of a significant number of its followers, but not otherwise.[76] As provisions for conferring benefits on persons of one sex only are lawful if contained in a charitable instrument,[77] discrimination between one sex and the other in a purely charitable provision for any class of employees is lawful. In employment, as in other contexts, discrimination in respect of insurance is lawful if it is reasonable, having regard to actuarial or similar data,[78] and discrimination in respect of admission to communal accommodation, or in the provision of benefits, facilities or services which cannot properly and effectively be provided except for those using communal accommodation, is lawful, provided the accommodation is managed in a way which comes, in the given exigencies of the situation, as near as may be to fair and equitable treatment of men and women.[79] Midwifery is not now the subject of an exclusion.[80]

In questions of sex discrimination, the Equal Opportunities Commission plays a role similar to that played by the Commission for Racial Equality in matters of racial discrimination.[81] Article 119 of the Treaty of Rome can be founded on in British courts.[82] EC directives also have direct effect where the employer is the state or a body which has been made responsible by law for providing a public service under the control of the state and has special powers for that purpose.[83] There is no longer a statutory limit on the level of compensation available in cases of sex discrimination.[83a]

21.22   Duration of Contract: Notice at Common Law.—Most contracts of employment are now subject to a statutory minimum period of notice,[84] but there are some to which the common law still applies,[85] and the common law rules as to duration are not affected by statute. The duration of a contract of employment, when not expressly fixed,[86] may depend on various considerations. In certain cases there is an

---

[76] s. 19.

[77] s. 43; Sex Discrimination Act 1975 (Amendment of Section 43) Order 1977 (S.I. 1977 No. 528).

[78] s. 45.

[79] s. 46.

[80] s. 20; Sex Discrimination Act 1975 (Amendment of Section 20) Order 1983 (S.I. 1983 No. 1202).

[81] ss. 53 to 61, 67 to 76. See para. 21.16, *supra.*

[82] *Barber* v. *Guardian Royal Exchange Assurance Group* [1990] E.C.R. 1889; [1991] 1 Q.B. 344.

[83] *Foster* v. *British Gas plc* (Case 188/89) [1990] E.C.R. 3313: *Johnston* v. *Chief Constable of the Royal Ulster Constabulary* [1987] Q.B. 129; *Marshall* v. *Southampton and S.W. Hampshire Area Health Authority* [1986] Q.B. 401; *cf. Doughty* v. *Rolls Royce plc* [1992] I.C.R. 538.

[83a] Sex Discrimination and Equal Pay (Remedies) Regulations 1993 (S.I. 1993 No. 2798), which were introduced as a result of the decision of the European Court of Justice in *Marshall* v. *Southampton and S.W. Hampshire Area Health Authority* [1993] I.R.L.R. 445.

[84] Employment Protection (Consolidation) Act 1978, s. 49. See para. 21.23, *infra.*

[85] *Ibid.*, ss. 141(1) and 144(1).

[86] But see *ibid.*

established rule. Thus domestic servants, when their employment was common, were presumably engaged for a term ending at Whitsunday or Martinmas, out-door servants for a year.[87] An inference may be drawn from the terms of payment, an annual salary affording a presumption of an engagement for a year.[88] A tenure *ad vitam aut culpam* (for life or until fault) is not to be inferred except in established cases, such as those of judges, sheriffs, ministers of the established church, or professors in a university, who hold a *munus publicum*, an office involving duties to the public.[89] In most such *munera publica* tenure *ad vitam aut culpam* is now qualified by a requirement to retire on reaching a prescribed age. Where none of the considerations indicative of duration is applicable, the general presumption at common law is that the employment is terminable at the pleasure of either party, with or without notice. Notice, or payment of the amount that would have been earned during the period of notice, is usually necessary in engagements which take up the whole time of the party employed, *e.g.* that of a schoolmaster,[90] not in part-time employments, such as that of a solicitor,[91] or in commercial agency.[92] The term of notice required is that deemed reasonable in the particular case, of which the practice of other employers is evidence.[93] Even where the period of endurance is fixed, notice as a rule is necessary to bring the contractual relationship to an end.[94] In the case of domestic and agricultural servants, 40 days' notice before the term is the established rule;[95] in other cases notice must be for a reasonable time. If a servant is hired for the year or half-year ending at Whitsunday or Martinmas, he must remove on May 28 or November 28 in the absence of special agreement,[96] and 40 days' notice before these dates is sufficient.[97] Where no notice is given the contract will be, in certain cases, renewed by tacit relocation;[98] where the principle is inapplicable, the employer's failure to give notice will entitle the servant to a payment in lieu thereof.[99] Servants of the Crown, civil or military, though they may be appointed for a fixed period, remain, as

[87] Bell, *Prin.*, § 174; *Groom* v. *Clark* (1859) 21 D. 831; *Cameron* v. *Fletcher* (1872) 10 M. 301.
[88] *Campbell* v. *Fyfe* (1851) 13 D. 1041; *Dowling* v. *Henderson* (1890) 17 R. 921; *Stevenson* v. *North British Ry.* (1905) 7 F. 1106; but see *Robson* v. *Overend* (1878) 6 R. 213.
[89] *Hastie* v. *McMurtrie* (1889) 16 R. 715.
[90] *Morrison* v. *Abernethy School Board* (1876) 3 R. 945.
[91] *Cormack* v. *Keith & Murray* (1893) 20 R. 977; *Brenan* v. *Campbell's Trs.* (1898) 25 R. 423.
[92] *London, etc. Shipping Co.* v. *Ferguson* (1850) 13 D. 51; *Stewart* v. *Rendall* (1899) 1 F. 1002.
[93] *Forsyth* v. *Heathery Knowe Coal Co.* (1880) 7 R. 887.
[94] *Morrison* v. *Abernethy School Board* (1876) 3 R. 945, opinion of Lord Deas; Bell, *Prin.*, § 187.
[95] *Cameron* v. *Scott* (1870) 9 M. 233.
[96] Removal Terms (Scotland) Amendment Act 1890, ss. 2 and 3.
[97] *Stewart* v. *Robertson*, 1937 S.C. 701.
[98] As to tacit relocation, see para. 15.23, *supra*.
[99] *Lennox* v. *Allan* (1880) 8 R. 38.

a general rule, subject to dismissal at any time and without notice.[1] Special rules apply to the holders of judicial office: a judge can be removed only by Act of Parliament; a sheriff principal or sheriff by an order made by the Secretary of State for Scotland if the Lord President of the Court of Session and the Lord Justice-Clerk after a joint investigation report that he is unfit for office on the ground of inability, neglect of duty or misbehaviour.[2]

21.23 Statutory Notice.—Part IV of the Employment Protection (Consolidation) Act 1978[3] provides a statutory code relating to the minimum periods of notice which must be given by employers and employees when contracts of employment affected by the Act are terminated.[4] The Act defines an employee as an individual who has entered into or works under a contract of employment whether the contract be expressed or implied, oral or in writing, and whether it be a contract of service or of apprenticeship.[5] With the exception of certain specified contracts[6] the Act applies to all contracts of employment in which the employee has been continuously employed for at least one month. Where an employer terminates the employment of those who have been continuously employed (a) for one month or more but less than two years, he must give not less than one week's notice; (b) for two years or more but less than twelve years, he must give not less than one week's notice for each year of continuous employment; (c) for twelve years or more, he must give not less than 12 weeks' notice.[7] On the other hand, if an employee who has been continuously employed for at least one month wishes to terminate his contract of employment, he must give at least one week's notice.[8] These periods of notice are the minimum prescribed by statute.

[1] *Dunn* v. *The Queen* [1896] 1 Q.B. 116; *Mulvenna* v. *Admiralty*, 1926 S.C. 842 (doubtful in view of *Cameron* v. *Lord Advocate*, 1952 S.C. 165). But see *Riordan* v. *War Office* [1961] 1 W.L.R. 210; [1959] 1 W.L.R. 1046. Civil servants, but not members of the naval, military or air forces of the Crown, are however, in general protected against unfair dismissal (1978 Act, s. 138).

[2] Sheriff Courts (Scotland) Act 1971, s. 12. The removal can be effected only by statutory instrument which is subject to annulment by a resolution of either House of Parliament. For an example see Sheriff (Removal from Office) Order 1992 (S.I. 1992 No. 1677).

[3] ss. 49 to 53 as amended by the 1982 Act, s. 20 and Sched. 2, paras. 3 and 4.

[4] Similar provisions were first enacted in the Contracts of Employment Act 1963, which was repealed and replaced by the Contracts of Employment Act 1972, also now repealed.

[5] *Ibid.*, s. 153(1).

[6] See ss. 141(1), and 144(1). Members of the Armed Forces and civil servants are also excluded (ss. 138(1) and 138A). See also s. 49(4) and (4A). Under s. 49(4) a contract of employment for a fixed term of one month or less shall have effect as if it were for an indefinite period if the employee has been employed for three months or more and under s. 49(4A) a contract made in contemplation of the performance of a specific task which is not expected to last for more than three months does not for this purpose come within the ambit of the Act unless the employee has been continuously employed for a period of more than three months.

[7] s. 49(1).

[8] s. 49(2). See *Walmsley* v. *C. & R. Ferguson Ltd.*, 1989 S.L.T. 258,

They cannot be reduced by conventional provisions, but either party can agree to waive his right to notice, or to accept payment in lieu of notice.[9] The Act preserves the contractual or common law right of an employee to receive longer notice than the statutory minimum,[10] and retains the common law right of either party to treat the contract as terminable without notice by reason of such conduct as would have justified such termination before the Act.[11] The liability of an employer to an employee during a period of notice is set out in Schedule 3 to the Act.

21.24 Termination of Contract.—The termination of a contract of employment depends upon the general rules applicable to other contracts,[12] and only a few special cases require to be considered.

21.25 Dismissal: Common Law.—It is an established rule at common law that an employer is entitled to dismiss an employee at any time on paying wages, and, in certain employments, board wages, for the remainder of the term, and that such dismissal does not involve a breach of contract.[13] There is no analogous rule in favour of the employee.[14] A right of appeal against dismissal may, however, be incorporated in a contract of employment in terms which constitute an appellate committee as a quasi-judicial tribunal. In that event any material departure in the appeal procedure from the principles of natural justice may nullify the dismissal.[15]

21.26 Remedies: Common Law.—At common law the remedy of an employee, in the event of a material breach of contract on the employer's part, or unjustifiable dismissal, is an action of damages. In certain cases it may be possible to reduce the employer's resolution to dismiss.[16] He has no right to insist on remaining in a post from which he has been dismissed, even although the dismissal was not justified.[17] In special circumstances, however, the court may, where damages would not afford an adequate remedy, restrain the implementation of an invalid notice of dismissal.[18] The measure of damages in the case of

[9] ss. 49(3) and 140(1).

[10] s. 49(1) and (3).

[11] s. 49(5).

[12] *e.g.* it may be repudiated by fundamental breach on the part of either party (*cf. Donovan* v. *Invicta Airways* [1970] 1 Lloyd's Rep. 486; *Pepper* v. *Webb* [1969] 1 W.L.R. 514; *Carvill* v. *Irish Industrial Bank* [1968] I.R. 325).

[13] *Graham* v. *Thomson* (1822) 1 S. 309; *Mollison* v. *Baillie* (1885) 22 S.L.R. 595.

[14] *Wallace* v. *Wishart* (1800) Hume 383.

[15] *Palmer* v. *Inverness Hospitals Board of Management*, 1963 S.C. 311; *Dietmann* v. *Brent L.B.C.* [1988] I.C.R. 842.

[16] *Palmer* v. *Inverness Hospitals Board of Management*, 1963 S.C. 311; see para. 21.25, *infra.*

[17] *First Edinburgh Building Society* v. *Munro* (1884) 21 S.L.R. 291; *Chappell* v. *Times Newspapers* [1975] 1 W.L.R. 482.

[18] *Hill* v. *C.A. Parsons & Co.* [1972] 1 Ch. 305.

unjustifiable dismissal is normally the amount which the employee would have earned had the contract been duly fulfilled, not to be increased by proof that the dismissal had caused third parties to form unfavourable opinions of his character.[19] But certain parties, *e.g.* an actor to whom publicity is of value, may recover damages for the loss of opportunity for gain through enhanced reputation arising from wrongful dismissal[20] and although damages are not recoverable for hurt feelings as such, they may be awarded in respect of mental stress where that is within the contemplation of the parties as a likely consequence of the employer's breach.[21] Moreover an apprenticeship agreement is regarded as being of a special character and in the event of its wrongful termination by the employer damages may be awarded not only for loss of earnings during the remainder of the apprenticeship but for loss of training and loss of future prospects.[22] Where dismissal was justified, an action of damages by the employee is not rendered relevant by averments that the motives of the employer were malicious.[23] A dismissed employee is bound to minimise the loss by endeavouring to obtain other employment, and his claim for damages will be subject to deduction of what he has actually earned or with reasonable effort would have been able to earn.[24] The question whether a breach of contract will enable the employee to leave, and claim damages, depends generally, as in other contracts, on the materiality of the breach in question.[25] But a domestic servant, if ill-treated, must leave, and by staying on will be held to have abandoned any claim for damages.[26] Following his dismissal, an employee can bring an action seeking damages for breach of contract in either the civil courts or before an industrial tribunal.[26a]

21.27　Dismissal: Statutory Definition.—The employer's common law right to dismiss has been modified by statute. Under legislation originating in the Industrial Relations Act 1971 and now embodied in the Employment Protection (Consolidation) Act 1978 an employee, who has been continuously employed for a period of not less than two years,[26b] has a

---

[19] *Addis* v. *Gramophone Co.* [1909] A.C. 488; *Cull* v. *Oilfield Inspection Services Group plc*, 1990 S.L.T. 205.

[20] *Clayton & Waller* v. *Oliver* [1930] A.C. 209.

[21] *Cox* v. *Philips Industries* [1976] 1 W.L.R. 638.

[22] *Dunk* v. *Geo. Waller & Son* [1970] 2 Q.B. 163.

[23] *Brown* v. *Magistrates of Edinburgh*, 1907 S.C. 256.

[24] *Ross* v. *Macfarlane* (1894) 21 R. 396.

[25] para. 13.4, *supra*.

[26] *Fraser* v. *Laing* (1878) 5 R. 596.

[26a] Industrial Tribunals Extension of Jurisdiction (Scotland) Order 1994 (S.I. 1994 No. 1624), although there is a £25,000 limit on the amount of compensation which can be awarded by a tribunal under this jurisdiction.

[26b] s. 64. The qualifying period has been equalised between full-time and part-time employees by the Employment Protection (Part-time Employees) Regulations 1995 (S.I. 1995 No. 31), following the decision of the House of Lords in *R.* v. *Sec. of State for Employment ex p. Equal Opportunities Commission* [1994] I.R.L.R. 176.

right not to be unfairly dismissed.[27] There is a dismissal for the purposes of the Act:

(1) if the contract is terminated by the employer with or without notice,

(2) where a fixed term contract expires without renewal, and

(3) where the employee terminates the contract[28] with or without notice in circumstances such that he is entitled to terminate it without notice by reason of the employer's conduct.[29]

There is dismissal in the last of these senses only if the employer's conduct is a significant breach going to the root of the contract or shows that he no longer intends to be bound by one of its essential terms.[30] There is no dismissal and so no infringement of the employee's rights where a contract of employment is frustrated, as may happen after a long period of absence through illness.[31] Unless, however, certain qualifying provisions apply, there is a dismissal if an employee who has a right to return to work after an absence because of pregnancy is not permitted to return.[32]

21.28 **Dismissal: Unfairness.**—A dismissal is to be regarded as unfair if it was by reason of trade union membership or activities or, with certain exceptions, by reason of non-membership of a trade union[32a] or of pregnancy.[33] A dismissal by reason of redundancy is to be regarded as unfair if selection was by reason of trade union membership or activity or, again with certain exceptions, was by reason of non-membership of a trade union or was, without special reasons to justify it, in contravention of a customary arrangement or agreed procedure.[34] As from August 30 1993, a dismissal is also to be regarded as unfair if the employee was

[27] s. 54.

[28] *Greater Glasgow Health Board* v. *Mackay*, 1989 S.L.T. 729.

[29] s. 55.

[30] *Western Excavating (E.C.C.)* v. *Sharp* [1978] Q.B. 761; *Prestwick Circuits Ltd.* v. *McAndrew*, 1990 S.L.T. 654. As to the effect of rules made by the employer for the conduct of employees in the place of work within the scope of the contract, see *Dryden* v. *Greater Glasgow Health Board* [1992] I.R.L.R. 469.

[31] *Jones* v. *Wagon Repairs* (1968) 3 I.T.R. 168; *Pritchard* v. *Dinorwic Slate Quarries* (1971) 6 I.T.R. 102; *Marshall* v. *Harland & Wolff (No. 2)* (1972) 7 I.T.R. 150; *Egg Stores (Stamford)* v. *Leibovici* [1976] I.R.L.R. 376; *cf. Watts, Watts & Co.* v. *Steeley* (1968) 3 I.T.R. 363; *Farmer* v. *Willow Dye Works* (1972) 7 I.T.R. 226; *Hebden* v. *Forsey & Son* (1973) 8 I.T.R. 656.

[32] s. 56. For the provisions qualifying the circumstances in which there will be such a dismissal see s. 56A as inserted by the 1980 Act, s. 12 and further amended by 1993 Act, Sched. 8, para. 13.

[32a] 1992 Act, s. 152.

[33] s. 60 (as substituted the 1993 Act, s. 24(1)); *Brown* v. *Stockton-on-Tees B.C.* [1989] A.C. 20; *Shoner* v. *B. & R. Residential Lettings Ltd.* [1992] I.R.L.R. 317; *Webb* v. *Emo Air Cargo (U.K.) Ltd.* [1994] I.R.L.R. 482; *cf. Brown* v. *Rentokil Ltd.*, 1995 G.W.D. 6–334.

[34] 1992 Act, s.153.

dismissed for raising issues of health and safety at work[34a] or if the
employee was dismissed after attempting to assert his statutory rights.[34b]

Unless one of the special rules discussed above applies, the fairness or
unfairness of a dismissal depends on whether:

(1) the reason for dismissal related to the employee's capability,
     qualifications or conduct or was that the employee was
     redundant or that his continued employment would involve
     contravention of a statutory obligation or restriction or was
     some other substantial reason of a kind such as to justify
     dismissal, and

(2) having regard to the reason shown, the employer acted
     reasonably or unreasonably in the circumstances in treating
     that reason as a sufficient reason for dismissal.[35]

If on engaging an employee an employer informs him in writing that his
employment will be terminated on the resumption of work by an
employee absent because of pregnancy or of suspension on medical
grounds in accordance with a statutory requirement or recommendation,
dismissal of that employee on the return of the employee whom he was
replacing is to be regarded as having been for a substantial reason of a
kind such as to justify dismissal.[36] That is, however, without prejudice
to the question of the reasonableness of the dismissal.

21.29 Dismissal: Reasonableness.—It is for the employer to show the reason
for dismissal (or, if there was more than one, the principal reason[37]) and
that it falls within the ambit of those for which the Act provides. There
is no such onus on him in relation to the reasonableness or
unreasonableness of his actings.[38] That question is to be decided in
accordance with equity and the substantial merits of the case and among
the circumstances to be taken into account are the size and
administrative resources of the employer's undertaking.[39] Subject to
that, the employer's actings are to be considered in the light of the
adequacy of the procedures which he followed and the facts which were
known, or might, on a reasonable investigation, have been known to
him at the time the decision to dismiss was taken.[40] Accordingly, if an
employer acted unreasonably at that time the dismissal will be regarded
as unfair even if facts subsequently emerge on which it could have been
justified. On the other hand if an employer follows fair procedures and,

---

[34a] s. 57A, (as introduced by the 1993 Act).
[34b] s. 60A, (as introduced by the 1993 Act). The particular statutory rights are rights
conferred under the 1978 Act, the Wages Act 1986, the Sunday Trading Act 1994 and the
1992 Act, ss. 68, 86, 146 and 168–170.
[35] s. 57 as amended by 1980 Act, s. 6.
[36] s. 61; as amended by the 1993 Act, Sched. 8, para. 15.
[37] See *Smith* v. *City of Glasgow D.C.,* 1987 S.L.T. 605.
[38] *Post Office (Counters) Ltd.* v. *Heavey* [1990] I.C.R. 1.
[39] s. 57; *P.* v. *Nottinghamshire C.C.* [1992] I.R.L.R. 362 (C.A.).
[40] *Earl* v. *Slater & Wheeler (Airlyne) Ltd.* (1973) 8 I.T.R. 33; *A.J. Dunning & Sons
(Shopfitters) Ltd.* v. *Jacomb* (1973) 8 I.T.R. 453; *St. Anne's Board Mill Co.* v. *Brien*
(1973) 8 I.T.R. 453; *Merseyside & North Wales Electricity Board* v. *Taylor* (1975) 10

in appropriate cases, makes such investigations as may reasonably be required in the circumstances, it is immaterial that on facts which subsequently emerge he can be shown to have been mistaken. A failure to follow fair procedures will normally render a dismissal unfair.[40a] The test is what a reasonable employer would have done, not what a tribunal thinks appropriate, and so if a decision to dismiss is within a band of decisions which an employer might take without forfeiting the title of reasonableness, the dismissal will not be unfair.[41] Where a dismissal takes place in the course of a lock-out, strike, or other industrial action, proceedings for unfair dismissal cannot be entertained unless it is shown that there has been discrimination between the dismissed employee and other relevant employees.[42] If, however, the employee was taking part in unofficial industrial action at the time of his dismissal, he cannot complain of unfair dismissal.[43]

21.30 **Employee's Remedies.**—Where an employee is unfairly dismissed an industrial tribunal may, if the employee wishes it to do so, make an order for his reinstatement or re-engagement.[44] If reinstated, he is to be treated in all respects as if he had not been dismissed;[45] if the order is for re-engagement, its effect is that he is to be engaged in employment comparable to that from which he was dismissed, or other suitable employment, on terms specified in the order.[46] In exercising its discretion, the tribunal must first consider reinstatement, and take into account the dismissed employee's wishes, the practicability of reinstatement or re-engagement, and the justice of making an order where the employee caused or contributed to his dismissal.[47] If the employee does not wish reinstatement or re-engagement, or if the tribunal does not make an order, or in the event of non-compliance by the employer with the order, the employee is entitled to an award of compensation consisting of a basic award calculated on the same basis as a redundancy payment, and a compensatory award of such an amount as is just and equitable having regard to the loss sustained in consequence of dismissal, in so far as that is attributable to the employer's action.[48] The loss so sustained is to be taken to include any expense reasonably

---

I.T.R. 52; *W. Devis & Sons* v. *Atkins* [1977] A.C. 931; *British Home Stores* v. *Burchell* [1978] I.R.L.R. 379; *A. Links & Co.* v. *Rose*, 1993 S.L.T. 209.

[40a] *Polkey* v. *A.E. Dayton Services Ltd.* [1987] I.R.L.R. 503.

[41] *Grundy (Teddington)* v. *Willis* [1976] I.C.R. 323; *British Leyland (U.K.)* v. *Swift* [1981] I.R.L.R. 91; *Iceland Frozen Foods Ltd.* v. *Jones* [1982] I.R.L.R. 439; *Dooley* v. *Leyland Vehicles Ltd.*, 1986 S.C. 272.

[42] 1992 Act, s. 238.

[43] 1992 Act, s. 237. There are two exceptions to this provision, namely if the reason for dismissal, or selection for redundancy, was on the basis that the employee had raised issues of health and safety (s. 57A) or was pregnant (s. 60).

[44] 1978 Act, ss. 68(1) and 69.

[45] s. 69(2).

[46] s. 69(4).

[47] s. 69(5) and (6). In relation to re-engagement the employee's contribution to his dismissal is a factor which bears on what the terms of any re-engagement order should be, as well as on whether such an order should be made.

[48] ss. 68(2), 71(1), 73 and 74.

incurred in consequence of dismissal and any benefit which the employee might reasonably be expected to have had but for dismissal.[49] Where there has been non-compliance by the employer with an order for reinstatement or re-engagement the employee is entitled to an additional compensatory award of from 13 to 26 weeks' pay or, in cases of unlawful racial or sex discrimination, from 26 to 52 weeks' pay, unless the employer satisfies the tribunal that it was not practicable for him to comply with the order.[50] Those provisions for an additional compensatory award do not apply to dismissals which are held to be unfair because they were made by reason of membership or non-membership of a trade union or participation in its activities, but in such cases a special award of 104 weeks' pay or £13,400, whichever is the greater, is to be made (subject to a maximum of £26,800) and the minimum basic award is £2,700.[51] The basic award, any special award and the compensatory award may be reduced in respect of the employee's contribution to his dismissal,[52] and the basic and special awards may be reduced in respect of unreasonable refusal of an offer of reinstatement.[53] A dismissed employee has a duty to mitigate his loss and failure to do so, including cases in which the employer has unreasonably prevented an order for reinstatement or re-engagement from being complied with, is to be taken into account in calculating his loss for the purposes of a compensatory award.[54]

21.31   Trade Union Membership.—It is unlawful to refuse a person employment because he is, or is not, a member of a trade union or because he is unwilling to take steps to become, or cease to be, or to remain or not to become, a member of a trade union or to make payments or suffer deductions in the event of his not being a member of a trade union. The sanction is that an industrial tribunal may award compensation and may recommend that the person refusing employment take action to obviate or reduce the adverse effect arising from the refusal.[55] Dismissal on the ground of trade union membership or activities, or on the ground of membership of an independent trade union or non-membership of any trade union, is unfair in the statutory sense and gives rise to the remedies noticed in the previous paragraph.[56] An employee is, however, also entitled to be protected against action by his employer, short of dismissal, taken for the purpose of (1) preventing or deterring him from being, or seeking to become a member of an independent trade union,

[49] s. 74(2). The compensatory award is subject to a limit of £11,000 (s. 75 as amended by Unfair Dismissal (Increase of Compensation Limit) Order 1993 (S.I. 1993 No. 134)).
[50] s. 71(2) and (3), as amended by the 1993 Act, Sched. 5, para. 6.
[51] 1992 Act, ss. 152–158.
[52] 1978 Act, ss. 73(7B), 74(6), 1992 Act, s. 158(4); *Nairne* v. *Highland and Islands Fire Brigade,* 1989 S.L.T. 754.
[53] ss. 73(7A) and 75A(5); 1992 Act, s. 158(5).
[54] 1978 Act, ss. 74(4) and 71(5); *cf.* for special award, 1992 Act, s. 158.
[55] 1992 Act, ss. 137–143.
[56] 1992 Act, s. 152.

or from taking part in its activities at any appropriate time, or (2) penalising him on these grounds or (3) compelling him to become a member of a trade union.[57] In the event of infringement of any of these rights, a complaint may be made to an industrial tribunal which, if it finds the complaint well founded, may make a declaration to that effect and award such compensation as it considers just and equitable, having regard to the infringement of the complainant's right and any loss sustained by him (including expenses reasonably incurred, and loss of any benefit which he might reasonably be expected to have had but for his employer's actions).[58]

21.32 Redundancy.—Part VI of the Employment Protection (Consolidation) Act 1978, which substantially re-enacts provisions of the Redundancy Payments Act 1965,[59] imposes upon employers the obligation to make a 'redundancy payment' to any employee who, after continuous employment for two years,[60] is (a) dismissed by reason of redundancy, or (b) laid off or kept on short time for specified periods, provided that in the latter event he gives written notice of his claim.[61] An employee is dismissed by reason of 'redundancy' if his dismissal is due wholly or mainly to the cessation of the employer's business, or to the cessation or diminution of demands for particular work.[62]

21.33 Death of Either Party.—The death of either employer or employee terminates the contract. An engagement to serve a firm is dissolved by the death of a partner,[63] but not by a mere change in the constitution of the firm.[64]

21.34 Illness or Imprisonment of Employee.—Absence from illness or accident is not a breach of contract on the employee's part. But where the accident was due to the employee's own fault it was held that the employer was justified in dismissal, and that no further wages were due.[65] And prolonged absence from illness, though no fault may be attributed to the employee, may justify the employer in treating the contract as frustrated, and therefore at an end.[66] Where an employee is sentenced to a term of imprisonment which makes it impossible for him to perform his part of the contract, his employment is automatically terminated at the date of the sentence.[67]

---

[57] 1992 Act, s. 146.
[58] 1992 Act, ss. 147–150.
[59] s. 1.
[60] s. 81.
[61] *Ibid.*, s. 88.
[62] *Ibid.*
[63] Bell, *Prin.*, § 179.
[64] *Hoey* v. *McEwen & Auld* (1867) 5 M. 814.
[65] *McEwan* v. *Malcolm* (1867) 5 S.L.R. 62.
[66] *Manson* v. *Downie* (1885) 12 R. 1103; *Poussard* v. *Spiers & Pond* (1876) 1 Q.B.D. 410; *Westwood* v. *S.M.T. Co.*, 1938 S.N. 8.
[67] *Hare* v. *Murphy Bros.* [1974] 3 All E.R. 940; *F.C. Shepherd & Co. Ltd.* v. *Jerrom* [1985] I.R.L.R. 275.

21.35 Insolvency of Employer.—The sequestration or liquidation of an employer amounts to a breach of contract on his part. The employee is entitled to leave, and to claim the amount which he would have earned as wages. But his claim is for damages, not for wages, and is therefore not entitled to the preferential ranking accorded to wages.[68]

21.36 Apprenticeship.—A contract of apprenticeship differs from other contracts of employment in respect that it must in all cases be entered into in writing, usually known as an indenture.[69] An informal writing may be validated by part performance,[70] but a merely verbal agreement is not in any case binding.[71] There must be an obligation, express or implied, on the employer to teach his profession or trade; without it the contract is merely one of service.[72] In apprenticeship the employer is bound to instruct the apprentice in his business, either personally or through the agency of his other employees.[73] Where an apprentice baker was able to prove that instruction in part of his trade had not been given, and that in consequence he earned lower wages, he was found entitled to damages.[74] An apprentice cannot be assigned to another employer without his own consent.[75] On the death of the employer during the term of the apprenticeship the apprentice may recover a portion of the premium paid,[76] but no such repayment is due on the death of the apprentice.[77] The competency of imprisonment of a deserting apprentice has already been mentioned.[78]

21.37 Injury to Employee.—Although the relationship between an employer and his employee is regulated by contract, the liability of an employer to make reparation to an employee injured in the course of his employment is regarded as delictual.[79] The employer is vicariously liable where the negligence of one employee causes injury to another, the doctrine of common employment having been abolished.[80] The employer has a personal duty to take reasonable care for the safety of his employees.[81] Thirdly, he may be liable to an employee in respect of injury caused by breach of statutory duty.[82]

---

[68] *Day* v. *Tait* (1900) 8 S.L.T. 40.
[69] *Grant* v. *Ramage & Ferguson* (1897) 25 R. 35.
[70] *Neil* v. *Vashon* (1807) Hume 20.
[71] *Murray* v. *McGilchrist* (1863) 4 Irv. 461.
[72] *Royce* v. *Greig*, 1909 2 S.L.T. 298.
[73] *Gardner* v. *Smith* (1775) Mor. 593.
[74] *Lyle* v. *Service* (1863) 2 M. 115.
[75] *Edinburgh Glasshouse Co.* v. *Shaw* (1789) Mor. 597.
[76] *Cutler* v. *Littleton* (1711) Mor. 583.
[77] *Shephard* v. *Innes* (1760) Mor. 589.
[78] *Supra*, para. 21.7.
[79] *MacKinnon* v. *Iberia Shipping Co.*, 1955 S.C. 20.
[80] By the Law Reform (Personal Injuries) Act 1948, s. 1(1). See *Lindsay* v. *Connell*, 1951 S.C. 281.
[81] See para. 21.38.
[82] See para. 21.42.

21.38   Employer's Personal Duty.—An employer at common law owes a duty to his employee to take reasonable care for his safety throughout the course of his employment. He has no duty to protect an employee from risks necessarily attaching to the job and against which no reasonable precautions can be taken, but he has a general duty not to expose an employee to unnecessary risks and that duty may, in some circumstances, involve withdrawing an employee from positions of danger created by a third party. But, where the third party is independent of the employer, that will be so only if the danger is very likely to occur.[83] The employer's duty may extend, where the employer has relevant and special knowledge, to advice calculated to minimise the consequences of injury sustained by an employee in the course of his employment, even if the injury was not attributable to the employer's fault. Thus, where an employer becomes aware of past circumstances connected with the employment which make it desirable for present employees to have a medical examination, he has a duty to advise them of that.[84] And there may be a duty to advise a prospective employee of risks inherent in the job which are, or ought to be, known to the employer and which are not common knowledge if such risks would be likely to affect the decision of a sensible level-headed person contemplating such employment.[85]

Whether or not an employer is in breach of duty depends upon the facts and circumstances of each case.[86] This duty is personal to the employer, and while he may delegate performance of the duty to a third party, he cannot escape liability in the event of negligent performance by that party.[87] However, the employer is not in the position of an insurer of the safety of his employee. Thus under a rule of the common law now abrogated by statute an employer was held not to be liable for an injury to an employee arising from a latent defect in a tool obtained from a reputable supplier.[88] The tendency of the courts to classify the nature of the employer's personal duty to exercise reasonable care for the safety of his employees into three categories of provision of competent staff, adequate plant and machinery, and a proper system of

[83] *Longworth* v. *Coppas International (U.K.),* 1985 S.L.T. 111.
[84] *Wright* v. *Dunlop Rubber Co.* (1971) 11 K.I.R. 311; *cf. Stokes* v. *Guest, Keen & Nettlefold (Bolts and Nuts)* [1968] 1 W.L.R. 1776.
[85] *White* v. *Holbrook Precision Castings* [1985] I.R.L.R. 215.
[86] See Chap. 32 (negligence); para. 34.17 (contributory negligence); paras. 34.1 and 34.2 (exclusions of liability and *volenti non fit injuria*). As to the general nature of the employer's duty, see *English* v. *Wilsons and Clyde Coal Co.,* 1937 S.C. (H.L.) 46; *Paris* v. *Stepney Borough Council* [1951] A.C. 367; *Qualcast (Wolverhampton) Ltd.* v. *Haynes* [1959] A.C. 743; *Cavanagh* v. *Ulster Weaving Co.* [1960] A.C. 145, *per* Lord Keith at pp. 164–166; and see *Smith* v. *Austin Lifts* [1959] 1 W.L.R. 100 (H.L.), where employee working on the premises of a third party.
[87] *English* v. *Wilsons and Clyde Coal Co., supra, per* Lord Thankerton at p. 57; *per* Lord Wright at p. 64; *Donnelly* v. *Ronald Wilson (Plant Hire),* 1986 S.L.T. 90.
[88] *Davie* v. *New Merton Board Mills* [1959] A.C. 604.

work,[89] serves to illustrate the scope of the duty, but the categories are neither conclusive nor exhaustive.[90]

21.39 Competent Staff.—The vicarious liability of an employer for the negligence of a fellow employee has largely overridden this aspect of the personal duty of the employer. However, the employer remains personally liable when it is shown that he has failed to exercise reasonable care to select competent staff for the task in question, as where a skilled employee lacks the necessary experience to meet a situation which the employer ought to have foreseen,[91] or where an employer fails to discharge an employee who has shown himself through his habitual conduct to be a source of danger to his fellow employees.[92]

21.40 Plant and Machinery.—The employer is bound to exercise reasonable care in the provision and maintenance of adequate plant and materials for the job. Liability arises when the employer has not provided any plant,[93] or where the plant supplied is insufficient,[94] defective[95] or dangerous.[96] The extent of the duty is only to exercise reasonable care, and there is no liability for injury caused by a latent defect which reasonable inspection would not have revealed.[97] That formulation of the duty must now, however, be read subject to the statutory gloss that liability attaches to the employer where an employee suffers personal injury in the course of his employment in consequence of a defect in 'equipment' provided by his employer and the defect is attributable wholly or partly to the fault of a third party such as a manufacturer or supplier.[98] An employer may therefore be liable for a defect which is latent to him if it is attributable to the fault of someone else. 'Equipment' is to be interpreted broadly and ranges from soap[99] to a ship of 91,000 tons gross.[1]

21.41 Proper System.—The employer is bound to take reasonable care to institute and maintain a safe and proper system of work.[2] It is his duty to give such general safety instructions as a reasonably careful employer

---

[89] *English* v. *Wilsons and Clyde Coal Co., supra.*
[90] See n. 86, *supra.* Other examples are safe place of work and safe means of access.
[91] *Black* v. *Fife Coal Co.,* 1912 S.C. (H.L.) 33.
[92] *Hudson* v. *Ridge Manufacturing Co.* [1957] 2 Q.B. 348.
[93] *Williams* v. *Birmingham Battery & Metal Co.* [1899] 2 Q.B. 338; *Lovell* v. *Blundells & Crompton & Co.* [1944] 1 K.B. 502.
[94] *Machray* v. *Stewarts & Lloyds* [1965] 1 W.L.R. 602.
[95] *Henderson* v. *Carron Co.* (1889) 16 R. 633.
[96] *Robertson* v. *Thomas's* (1907) 15 S.L.T. 32 (vicious horse).
[97] *Gavin* v. *Rogers* (1889) 17 R. 206; *Milne* v. *Townsend* (1892) 19 R. 830; *McMillan* v. *B.P. Refinery (Grangemouth),* 1961 S.L.T. (Notes) 79.
[98] Employer's Liability (Defective Equipment) Act 1969, s. 1; *Yuille* v. *Daks Simpson,* 1984 S.L.T. 115; *Ralston* v. *Greater Glasgow Health Board,* 1987 S.L.T. 386.
[99] *Ralston* v. *Greater Glasgow Health Board, supra.*
[1] *Coltman* v. *Bibby Tankers Ltd.* [1988] A.C. 276.
[2] *English* v. *Wilsons and Clyde Coal Co.,* 1937 S.C. (H.L.) 46.

who has considered the problem presented by the work would give to his employees.[3] Each case, therefore, turns on its own facts and circumstances,[4] and even where facts closely correspond to a previous decision, no necessary inference as to the decision of the instant case arises.[5] Evidence of trade practice is not conclusive[6] but may be an indication of what reasonable care requires. If it is evident that a practice is dangerous, and a precaution which would avoid the risk could reasonably be adopted, it is no defence that accidents rarely occurred or that the practice was widespread.[7] Physical disability of the employee may render the performance of the duty by the employer more onerous, since the employer owes the duty to each of his employees as individuals.[8] The decided cases merely serve as illustrations of this aspect of the personal duty of the employer.[9]

21.42 **Statutory Provisions.**—Many industries are closely regulated by statute.[10] In most cases the observance of the statutory regulations is protected by the sanction of a fine, but civil liability is inferred if the person injured by their non-observance was one whose interests the regulation was designed to protect.[11] The harm which the pursuer sustains must be harm of a type which the statute envisages,[12] although it is not generally essential that the harm must be sustained in a particular manner.[13] As with liability at common law the pursuer must establish on a balance of probabilities that a breach of the statutory provisions caused him injury.[14] It depends upon the facts in each case whether the breach leads to a legitimate inference that the injury resulted from it.[15] Thus an employer will escape liability if he can show that, even if he had provided the safety equipment enjoined by the

[3] *General Cleaning Contractors* v. *Christmas* [1953] A.C. 180, *per* Lord Oaksey at p. 189.

[4] *Grace* v. *Alexander Stephen & Son*, 1952 S.C. 61.

[5] *Qualcast* v. *Haynes* [1959] A.C. 743.

[6] *Morris* v. *West Hartlepool Steam Navigation Co.* [1956] A.C. 552; *Cavanagh* v. *Ulster Weaving Co.* [1960] A.C. 145, applying *Morton* v. *Dixon*, 1909 S.C. 807, *per* Lord Dunedin at p. 809; *Brown* v. *Rolls Royce*, 1960 S.C. (H.L.) 22; *Riddick* v. *Weir Housing Corporation*, 1970 S.L.T. (Notes) 71; *Macdonald* v. *Scottish Stamping & Engineering Co.*, 1972 S.L.T. (Notes) 73.

[7] *Brown* v. *John Mills & Co. (Llanidloes)* (1970) 8 K.I.R. 702.

[8] *Paris* v. *Stepney Borough Council* [1951] A.C. 367.

[9] See Walker on *Delict* (2nd ed.), pp. 561–572; Munkman, *Employer's Liability* (10th ed.), pp. 129 *et seq.*

[10] See in general Factories Act 1961 and regulations made thereunder; Mines and Quarries Act 1954; Agriculture (Safety, Health and Welfare Provisions) Act 1956; Offices, Shops and Railway Premises Act 1963; Health and Safety at Work etc. Act 1974; Redgrave, *Health and Safety* (1993); see also relevant regulations implementing EC Directives.

[11] *Groves* v. *Lord Wimborne* [1898] 2 Q.B. 402; *Bett* v. *Dalmeny Oil Co.* (1905) 7 F. 787; *Macmillan* v. *Lochgelly Iron, etc. Co.*, 1933 S.C. (H.L.) 64; see also *Marshall & Son* v. *Russian Oil Products*, 1938 S.C. 773, and para. 34.3, *infra*.

[12] *Gorris* v. *Scott* (1874) L.R. 9 Ex. 125.

[13] *Grant* v. *N.C.B.*, 1956 S.C. (H.L.) 48.

[14] *Wardlaw* v. *Bonnington Castings*, 1956 S.C. (H.L.) 26.

[15] *Gardiner* v. *Motherwell Machinery and Scrap Co.*, 1961 S.C. (H.L.) 1.

statute, the injured workman would not have used it.[16] If the statutory duties are laid upon the employer, they involve liability for injury caused by failure to observe them, though the immediate cause of failure may have been the fault of a fellow employee or sub-contractor.[17] And it will not be easy for a defender to prove that statutory regulations supersede the common law duty of care.[18] If an absolute duty is placed upon an employer, his only defences in case of failure are such statutory defences as may be provided,[19] but this does not include defences provided against a criminal charge.[20] If they are laid upon a particular official, the employer is not necessarily liable for his negligence, but the onus of proof that the official was competent is laid upon him.[21] In a case based on failure to fence machinery in compliance with the Factories Act 1937 it was held that the duty related to the plant used in manufacturing and not to the machine being manufactured.[22] Contributory negligence may lead to apportionment of damages,[23] but the degree of care required of a man in a factory or mine may be lower than that required of an ordinary man not exposed to the noise, strains and risks of a factory or mine.[24] An employer who is in breach of statutory duty may avoid liability altogether if it is established that the conduct of the employee was the sole cause of the breach.[25]

Further Reading

Craig and Miller, *Employment Law in Scotland* (1991).
Encyclopaedia of Labour Relations Law (continuously revised).
Fraser, *Master and Servant* (3rd ed., 1882).
Harvey, *Industrial Relations and Employment Law* (continuously revised).
Hepple and O'Higgins, *Employment Law*.
Miller, *Industrial Law in Scotland* (1970).
Munkman, *Employer's Liability at Common Law* (10th ed., 1985).
Redgrave, Fife & Machin, *Health and Safety* (2nd ed., 1993).
Umpherston, *Master and Servant* (1904).

[16] *Qualcast* v. *Haynes* [1959] A.C. 743; *McWilliams* v. *Sir William Arrol & Co.*, 1962 S.C. (H.L.) 70; *McKinlay* v. *British Steel Corporation*, 1988 S.L.T. 810; and see n. 25, *infra*.

[17] *Bett* v. *Dalmeny Oil Co.*, *supra*; *Rodger* v. *Fife Coal Co.*, 1923 S.C. 108; *Alford* v. *National Coal Board*, 1952 S.C. (H.L.) 17; and see para. 34.33, *infra*, n. 19.

[18] *Matuszczyk* v. *National Coal Board*, 1953 S.C. 8; *Bux* v. *Slough Metals* [1973] 1 W.L.R. 1358.

[19] *Bain* v. *Fife Coal Co.*, 1935 S.C. 681; *Reilly* v. *Beardmore & Co.*, 1947 S.C. 275; *Millar* v. *Galashiels Gas Co.*, 1949 S.C. (H.L.) 31; *Taylor* v. *National Coal Board*, 1953 S.C. 349.

[20] *Riddell* v. *Reid*, 1942 S.C. (H.L.) 51.

[21] *Black* v. *Fife Coal Co.*, 1912 S.C. (H.L.) 33; *Connell* v. *Nimmo*, 1924 S.C. (H.L.) 84.

[22] *Parvin* v. *Morton Machine Co.*, 1952 S.C. (H.L.) 9.

[23] See para. 34.4, *infra*.

[24] *Caswell* v. *Powell Duffryn Associated Collieries Ltd.* [1940] A.C. 152; *Hunter* v. *Glenfield & Kennedy*, 1947 S.C. 536; *Barnes* v. *Southhook Potteries*, 1946 S.L.T. 295; *John Summers & Sons Ltd.* v. *Frost* [1955] A.C. 740.

[25] See *Ross* v. *Associated Portland Cement Manufacturers* [1964] 1 W.L.R. 768 and cases cited therein, where employee disobeyed instructions; also *Crowe* v. *James Scott & Sons*, 1965 S.L.T. 54, and *Horne* v. *Lec Refrigeration* [1965] 2 All E.R. 898; *cf. Quinn* v. *J.W. Green (Painters)* [1966] 1 Q.B. 509.

22.1 **Meaning of Agency.**—Agency has been defined as 'the fiduciary relationship which exists between two persons, one of whom expressly or impliedly consents that the other should act on his behalf, and the other of whom similarly consents so to act or so acts.' An agent has been defined as 'a person having express or implied authority to act on behalf of another party, who is called the principal.'[1] The express or implied power which the agent has to bring the principal into contractual relations with third parties is known as his 'authority.' So agency includes that branch of the law of employer and employed where the employment consists in bringing the employer into contractual relations with third parties. There are many cases where the principles of the law of agency apply but where the terms agent and principal are not commonly used: directors are the agents of the company; a receiver is the agent of the company, though he recovers debts for behoof of the floating-charge holder;[2] a partner, in dealing with partnership affairs, is the agent of the firm and of the other partners.[3] Moreover, aspects of the activities of certain agents have been subject to statutory regulation, *e.g.* directors by the Companies Acts, estate agents by the Estate Agents Act 1979, solicitors by the Solicitors (Scotland) Act 1980 and commercial agents by the Commercial Agents (Council Directive) Regulations 1993.[3a]

22.2 **Mandate.**—If the contract is gratuitous it is usually termed mandate instead of agency, and the terms mandant and mandatory are used instead of principal and agent.[4] If a mandate is given to do something in the mandatory's own interest it is known as a procuratory *in rem suam* (or, in English law, as an authority coupled with an interest), and differs from other mandates in being irrevocable without the mandatory's consent.[5] So it was held that a cheque, when granted for value, was a

---

[1] Bowstead, *Agency*, p. 1.

[2] Insolvency Act 1986, s. 57 (1); *Forth & Clyde Construction Co.* v. *Trinity Timber & Plywood Co.*, 1984 S.C. 1 at p. 11, *per* Lord President Emslie.

[3] Partnership Act 1890, s. 5; para. 50.12, *infra*.

[3a] S.I. 1993 No. 3053 implementing Council Directive 86/653/EEC. The definition of a commercial agent in reg. 2(1) would cover a wider spectrum than would be covered by the ordinary Scots law concept of an agent.

[4] *Stair Encyclopaedia*, Vol. 1, para. 665.

[5] Bell, *Prin.*, § 228.

mandate to the payee to draw the money in his own interest and therefore, when presented at the bank, constituted a completed assignation of any funds standing at the drawer's credit.[6] And if an application for shares in a company is given to one who has an interest in the shares being allotted the applicant is not entitled to withdraw his application.[7]

22.3 Constitution of the Contract.—The authority of an agent or mandatory may arise from express contract, which may be entered into orally;[8] may be inferred from the prior conduct of the parties; or may be assumed because an emergency has made action in the character of an agent reasonable or even necessary. The last case—termed in England agency of necessity[9]—arises when A is in possession of B's goods and some action by A with regard to the goods is necessary but communication with B is impossible. Thus a carrier, or seller, of perishable goods, when, owing to circumstances not due to his fault, delivery is delayed or rendered impossible, may assume authority to dispose of the goods, and his act will be binding on their owner.[10] The rule seems indistinguishable from the principle of *negotiorum gestio*.[11] The relationship of agency cannot be created after the death of the putative principal.[11a]

22.4 Ratification.—Where one party acts for another without any prior authority—express, inferred, or arising from necessity—the relationship of agent and principal may be constituted if the act of the ostensible agent is ratified or homologated by the party for whom he professed to act. Ratification need not be in express words: it may be inferred from conduct.[12] All the material facts must be known, unless the words or conduct of the party ratifying can be construed as a ratification of whatever the agent may have done.[13] To admit of the ratification of a contract made without authority so as to make the ratifier a party to the contract as a principal, the agent must have contracted ostensibly as agent; if he contracted ostensibly as principal, though in the expectation that his contract would be ratified by another, that other cannot ratify so as to acquire the right to sue or subject himself to liability to be

---

[6] *British Linen Co.* v. *Carruthers* (1883) 10 R. 923. See now Bills of Exchange Act 1882, s. 75A, inserted by the Law Reform (Misc. Provs.) (Scotland) Act 1985, s. 11.

[7] *Premier Briquette Co.* v. *Gray*, 1922 S.C. 329; *Carmichael's Case* [1896] 2 Ch. 643.

[8] Requirements of Writing (Scotland) Act 1995, s. 1. A commercial agent and the principal are entitled to a written document setting out the terms of the relationship: Commercial Agents (Council Directive) Regulations 1993, reg. 13.

[9] *Sims* v. *Midland Ry.* [1913] 1 K.B. 103; *Prager* v. *Blatspiel* [1924] 1 K.B. 566.

[10] *China Pacific S.A.* v. *Food Corporation of India* [1982] A.C. 939; *Forth Tugs Ltd.* v. *Wilmington Trust Co.*, O.H., Dec. 28, 1984, unreported (opinion of Lord Wylie); affd. 1985 S.C. 317.

[11] See para. 22.31, *infra*. But in England it is limited in its application. See Birks, *An Introduction to the Law of Restitution* (1989), pp. 199–202.

[11a] *Lord Advocate* v. *Chung*, 1995 S.L.T. 65 at p. 68.

[12] *Ballantine* v. *Stevenson* (1881) 8 R. 959; *Barnetson* v. *Petersen* (1902) 5 F. 86.

[13] *Fitzmaurice* v. *Bayley* (1856) 6 E. & B. 868.

sued.[14] Where ratification takes effect, it relates back to the time when the agent purported to contract. So where an agent purports to make a contract without authority and the other party seeks to withdraw, subsequent ratification by the principal makes the withdrawal ineffective.[15] And to make ratification possible the principal must have been in existence at the time when the agent acted, and therefore a company cannot ratify contracts made ostensibly on its behalf before it came into existence.[16] If the acts of the agent could not competently have been performed by the principal, the principal cannot ratify these acts.[17] Where the validity of an act depends on its being done within a certain time or before a certain event, and it is done timeously but without authority, subsequent ratification will not make the act valid.[18] It is an anomalous exception to this that in marine insurance a principal may ratify a contract of insurance made on his behalf and without his authority, even after he is aware of a loss.[19] And when ratification has to be inferred from conduct without any express statement, it has been held that that inference cannot be drawn unless the party ratifying had a choice in the matter. So where an agent had ordered repairs on a ship without authority, the shipowner did not ratify his act, and thereby incur liability to pay for the repairs, merely because he received and used the ship.[20]

22.5 Principal and Agent *Inter Se*.—In many respects the rights and liabilities of principal and agent, in questions solely *inter se* and where no third party is affected, are the same as those of master and servant.[21] The following paragraphs examine those rights and liabilities.[21a]

22.6 Fiduciary Character of Agency.—Agency is generally, but not invariably, a contract involving a fiduciary relationship. It depends on the facts and circumstances. Where there is a fiduciary relationship, it must be examined to determine the duties imposed by it.[22] The authorities

---

[14] *Keighley, Maxted & Co.* v. *Durant* [1901] A.C. 240.

[15] *Bolton Partners* v. *Lambert* (1889) 41 Ch.D. 295; *Bedford Insurance Co.* v. *Instituto de Resseguros* [1985] Q.B. 966; *Presentaciones Musicales* v. *Secunda* [1994] 2 W.L.R. 660.

[16] *Tinnevelly Sugar Refining Co.* v. *Mirrlees* (1894) 21 R. 1009; *Kelner* v. *Baxter* (1886) L.R. 2 C.P. 174; *Cumming* v. *Quartzag Ltd.*, 1980 S.C. 276. For the liability of the purported agent, see para. 22.30, *infra*.

[17] *Boston Deep Sea Fishing Co.* v. *Farnham* [1957] 1 W.L.R. 1051.

[18] *Goodall* v. *Bilsland*, 1909 S.C. 1152; *Ward & Co.* v. *Samyang Navigation Co. Ltd.*, 1975 S.C. (H.L.) 26; *Presentaciones Musicales, supra.*

[19] Marine Insurance Act 1906, s. 86. This does not hold in fire insurance: *Grove* v. *Mathews* [1910] 2 K.B. 401.

[20] *Forman* v. *The Liddesdale* [1900] A.C. 190. In Scots law the shipowner might be liable, on the principle of recompense, in so far as he was *lucratus*; see paras. 29.12–29.15, *infra* and para. 22.24 *infra*.

[21] Chap. 20.

[21a] The rights and obligations applying in respect of commercial agents are laid down in the Commercial Agents (Council Directive) Regulations 1993, Part II.

[22] *Sao Paulo Alpargatas S.A.* v. *Standard Chartered Bank*, 1985 S.L.T. 433, applying dicta of Lord Upjohn in *Boardman* v. *Phipps* [1967] 2 A.C. 46 at p. 127.

establish, however, than an agent is bound to account to his principal for any incidental advantage which, without the knowledge of the principal, or due to an error by the principal,[23] he has obtained from his position as agent. So a director must account to the company for any benefit which he has received from a promoter, even although it cannot be shown that the company has suffered any loss.[24] Where an agent employed to sell a ship but unable to find a buyer on the cash terms the principal demanded, purchased it himself, having received an offer of a higher price although on less advantageous cash terms which he did not disclose to the principal, it was held that he must account to the principal for the profit he made on the transaction.[25] The rule so far rests on principles of trust that the agent's liability is measured by the gain he has made, and not by the loss, if any, which the principal has sustained;[26] but it has been held in England, in the case of a secret commission, that the legal position of the principal was that of a creditor, and not that of a beneficiary. So in the bankruptcy of the agent the principal could rank only as a creditor, not as a beneficiary for whom the agent held money in trust.[27] There is no implied condition of contract between agent and principal, at least where the contract is constituted in writing, that the agent shall not without the permission of his principal act, even in an outside matter, in such a way as to bring his interests into conflict with those of his principal.[28]

22.7 Secret Commissions.—An agent employed to introduce business is not entitled, without the knowledge and consent of his principal, to take any commission from the party with whom he deals. The principal's consent may be presumed if the principal gave no payment, and if the agent's work was of a character not generally done gratuitously.[29] But a custom of trade, not known to the principal, is no defence for a secret commission.[30] Where an agent is proved to have received a secret commission certain civil consequences ensue.[31] (1) The principal may dismiss the agent from his employment, and, as a creditor, recover the amount of the commission from him.[32] (2) He may also, whether he has settled with the agent or not, recover damages from the party who gave

---

[23] *Trans Barwil Agencies (U.K.) Ltd.* v. *John S. Braid & Co.*, 1988 S.C. 222 and *Trans Barwil Agencies Ltd.* v. *John S. Braid & Co. (No. 2)*, 1990 S.L.T. 182 (liability for interest).

[24] *Henderson* v. *Huntingdon Copper Co.* (1877) 5 R. (H.L.) 1; *Boston Deep Fishing Co.* v. *Ansell* (1888) 39 Ch.D. 339; *Jubilee Cotton Mills* v. *Lewis* [1924] A.C. 958.

[25] *De Bussche* v. *Alt* (1878) 8 Ch.D. 286. See also *Graham* v. *Paton*, 1917 S.C. 203.

[26] *Ronaldson* v. *Drummond & Reid* (1881) 8 R. 956.

[27] *Lister* v. *Stubbs* (1890) 45 Ch.D. 1.

[28] *Lothian* v. *Jenolite*, 1969 S.C. 111.

[29] *Great Western Insurance Co.* v. *Cunliffe* (1874) L.R. 9 Ch. 525.

[30] *Ronaldson* v. *Drummond & Reid* (1881) 8 R. 956.

[31] For the criminal law consequences, see the Prevention of Corruption Act 1906 (c. 34) and the Prevention of Corruption Act 1916 (c. 64).

[32] *Ronaldson, supra*; in *Powell & Thomas* v. *Jones* [1905] 1 K.B. 11, this was held to apply even to sub-agents.

the secret commission, on the ground that such an act amounts to a civil wrong.[33] (3) The agent forfeits all claim to a commission (which the principal, if he has already paid it, may recover) for the particular transaction in question,[34] but not the right to his commission on other transactions in which he acted honestly.[35] (4) The principal, on discovering that his agent has been bribed, may rescind or refuse to carry out the contract,[36] and if, in the case of sale, he has made a deposit, he may recover it.[37] As the agent and the party who offers a secret commission are engaged in an illegal transaction, the agent, whether the promise of the bribe has influenced his conduct or not, cannot recover it by action.[38]

22.8 **Sale or Purchase between Agent and Principal.**—An agent, employed to buy, is not entitled, without the principal's knowledge, to supply his own goods. A custom of a particular trade, not known to the principal, will afford no justification.[39] Thus if an agent, employed by several persons to buy goods or shares, purchases a sufficient quantity to meet all his orders, and allocates to each principal the amount he has ordered at an average price, he is selling his own property instead of buying for his principal, and the latter is not bound by the contract.[40]

It is not necessarily illegal for an agent to purchase property belonging to his principal, even without disclosing the fact that he is the purchaser.[41] But such a transaction cannot stand if the agent was employed to sell the property in question; and a law agent must disclose to his client that he is the purchaser.[42]

22.9 **Delegation.**—It is a question depending on the nature of the employment in each particular case whether an agent has any implied power to delegate his work. The maxim *delegatus non potest delegare* (a person to whom a matter has been delegated cannot himself delegate it) is only a general presumption.[43] If the circumstances are such that delegation was permissible, the sub-agent and the principal may be brought into contractual relations, both in respect of the liability of the principal to pay for the services rendered, and in the application of the

---

[33] *Mayor of Salford* v. *Lever* [1891] 1 Q.B. 168; *Mahesan* v. *Malaysia Housing Society* [1979] A.C. 374.

[34] *Andrews* v. *Ramsay* [1903] 2 K.B. 635.

[35] *Graham* v. *United Turkey Red Co.*, 1922 S.C. 533.

[36] *Armagas Ltd.* v. *Mundogas S.A.* [1986] A.C. 717; *Logicrose Ltd.* v. *Southend United F.C.* [1988] 1 W.L.R. 1256.

[37] *Shipway* v. *Broadwood* [1899] 1 Q.B. 369; *Alexander* v. *Webber* [1922] 1 K.B. 642.

[38] *Harrington* v. *Victoria Graving Dock Co.* (1878) 3 Q.B.D. 549.

[39] *Robinson* v. *Mollett* (1874) L.R. 7 H.L. 802.

[40] *Maffett* v. *Stewart* (1887) 14 R. 506.

[41] See Gloag, *Contract*, pp. 522–23.

[42] *McPherson's Trs.* v. *Watt* (1877) 5 R. (H.L.) 9.

[43] *Robertson* v. *Beatson*, 1908 S.C. 921; *Black* v. *Cornelius* (1879) 6 R. 581; *Knox & Robb* v. *Scottish Garden Suburb Co.*, 1913 S.C. 872.

rule that no one in the position of an agent can obtain any secret advantage or commission.[44] Where, however, no privity exists between the principal and sub-agent, failure on the part of the sub-agent to carry out his duties in the proper way will infer the liability of the original agent.[45]

22.10 Relief.—An agent is entitled to be relieved by the principal of all liabilities which he may incur in the due performance of his contract as agent. Thus if, acting in accordance with his instructions, the agent so contracts as to render himself liable on the contract, the principal is bound to relieve him of his liability.[46] Where an agent was employed to make a report and a third party brought an unsuccessful action for damages for statements in the report which reflected on him, it was held that the principal was liable to the agent in the expenses—which the unsuccessful plaintiff was unable to pay—incurred in defending the action.[47]

22.11 Remuneration of Agent.—It is generally a question depending on circumstances whether an agent, in the absence of any express provision on the point, is entitled to remuneration. Where the services rendered are of the nature of supplying an introduction, or introducing business, and the party who has rendered the service is a broker or commission agent, he will be entitled to payment, in cases where a private individual would have been assumed to have acted gratuitously,[48] if his claim can be shown to be sanctioned by a custom of trade.[49] Though the actual business done may not be directly due to the broker, he may be entitled to commission if he was the means of bringing the parties into relations with each other;[50] not where the parties were already acquainted and the broker's claim is founded on a suggestion which was declined.[51] The general principle that a mercantile agent is entitled to remuneration in some form may be excluded by proof of a custom in a particular trade known to both parties that agents rely exclusively on the proceeds of the sale of goods placed in their hands.[52] In the absence of agreement a commercial agent is entitled to such remuneration as is customarily given to commercial agents selling such goods in the relevant place and,

---

[44] *De Bussche* v. *Alt* (1878) 8 Ch.D. 286.

[45] *Mackersy* v. *Ramsay, Bonar & Co.* (1843) 2 Bell's App. 30.

[46] *Robinson* v. *Middleton* (1859) 21 D. 1089. See Lord McLaren's note to Bell, *Comm.*, i, 534.

[47] *Famatina Development Corporation* [1914] 2 Ch. 271; distinguished in *Tomlinson* v. *Liquidators of Scottish Amalgamated Silks*, 1935 S.C. (H.L.) 1.

[48] See *White* v. *Munro* (1876) 3 R. 1011 at p. 1028, *per* L.J.-C. Moncreiff (dissenting).

[49] *Walker, Donald & Co.* v. *Birrell* (1883) 11 R. 369; *Kennedy* v. *Glass* (1890) 17 R. 1085; *Dawson* v. *Fisher* (1900) 2 F. 941; *Howard* v. *Manx Line Co.* [1923] 1 K.B. 110.

[50] *Walker, Donald & Co.*, *supra*; *Walker, Fraser & Steele* v. *Fraser's Trs.*, 1910 S.C. 222.

[51] *Van Laun* v. *Neilson* (1904) 6 F. 644.

[52] *Dinesmann* v. *Mair*, 1912 1 S.L.T. 217.

if there is no customary practice, to reasonable remuneration.[52a] If the agent is to receive commission on completion of the contract, and he finds a customer willing to complete, he is entitled to damages if his principal refuses to complete.[53]

22.12 **Obligation to Furnish Agent with Work.**—Some difficult questions are raised when an agent is appointed for a definite period, and his remuneration is to be by commission. Does the appointment imply an obligation on the part of the principal to continue his business in order that the agent may have an opportunity of earning a commission? If the agency has been in any way paid for, as where the agent subscribes for shares in a company by which he is engaged, there is a strong though not conclusive presumption that an obligation not to discontinue business voluntarily is implied.[54] If no payment has been made for the agency the general rule of construction is that the agent takes his chance of getting employment, and cannot complain if his employer discontinues or transfers his business.[55] If, however, the contract contains an obligation to employ the agent,[56] or to execute any orders which he may be able to obtain,[57] an obligation not to discontinue the business voluntarily may be implied. An appointment as sole selling agent does not preclude a sale by the principal himself, unless the terms of the contract amount to sale and not agency.[58]

22.13 **Lien.**—In security of his wages or commission, or of any debt incurred by the principal in the course of the agent's employment, a commercial agent has a general lien over any property of the principal which has been placed in his hands.[59] It has been laid down that 'every agent who is required to undertake liabilities or make payments for his principal, and who in the course of his employment comes into possession of property belonging to his principal over which he has power of control and disposal, is entitled, in the first place, to be indemnified for the moneys he has expended or the loss he has incurred, and, in the second

---

[52a] Commercial Agents (Council Directive) Regulations 1993, reg. 6(1). See further regs. 7 to 12. Regulations 17 and 18 provide for compensation or indemnification on termination.

[53] *Dudley Bros.* v. *Barnet*, 1937 S.C. 632. The House of Lords in *Luxor (Eastbourne)* v. *Cooper* [1941] A.C. 108 seems to have taken another view, but the Scottish decision seems preferable. See *Alpha Trading* v. *Dunnshaw-Patten* [1981] Q.B. 290 for a discussion of *Luxor*.

[54] *Galbraith* v. *Arethusa Shipping Co.* (1896) 23 R. 1011; *Ogden* v. *Nelson* [1905] A.C. 109.

[55] *Patmore* v. *Cannon* (1892) 19 R. 1004; *State of California Co.* v. *Moore* (1895) 22 R. 562; *Rhodes* v. *Forwood* (1876) 1 App.Cas. 256; *French* v. *Leeston Shipping Co.* [1922] 1 A.C. 451; Gloag, *Contract*, p. 294. Cf. *North American & Continental Sales Inc.* v. *Bepi (Electronics) Ltd.*, 1982 S.L.T. 47 and *Alpha Trading* v. *Dunnshaw-Patten* [1981] Q.B. 290.

[56] *Turner* v. *Goldsmith* [1891] 1 Q.B. 544.

[57] *Reigate* v. *Union Manufacturing Co.* [1918] 1 K.B. 592.

[58] *Bentall* v. *Vicary* [1931] 1 K.B. 253; *Lamb* v. *Goring Brick Co.* [1932] 1 K.B. 710.

[59] Bell, *Prin.*, § 1445; and see, as to lien, para. 19.22, *supra*.

place, to retain such properties as come into his hands in his character of agent.'[60] Proof that a general lien is recognised in the particular branch of agency is not required.[61] But the factor on an estate has no general lien, unless he happens to be a solicitor,[62] and it is doubtful whether an accountant could assert anything more than a special lien on the plea that the particular work on which his claim was based was of the nature of agency.[63]

22.14 Termination of the Contract.—In most respects the rules applicable to the termination of the contract of agency are the same as in other contracts of employment,[64] though, where they apply, the Commercial Agents (Council) Directive Regulations 1993 make provision for various matters including minimum periods of notice and compensation or indemnification for the agent.[64a]

22.15 Relations with Third Parties.—It is now necessary to examine the relationships which arise when an agent enters a legal relationship with a third party.

22.16 *Del Credere* Agency.—In the normal case an agent in entering into a contract on behalf of his principal does not guarantee that the party with whom he contracts will fulfil his contract. If, by arrangement with his principal, he does so guarantee, he is said to act *del credere*.[65] An agent *del credere* is substantially a cautioner, though the former rule that cautionary obligations must be entered into in writing did not apply.[66] He is not, if he discloses the name of his principal, a party to the contract, and cannot be sued by the other party to it. Where goods are supplied for resale, it may often be a narrow question whether the contract is one of *del credere* agency or of sale and return.[67]

22.17 Contracts with Third Parties.—When an agent, in pursuance of his authority,[67a] enters into a contract with a third party, the question as to the rights and liabilities thence arising depends materially on the method by which the agent has contracted. He may contract (1) as agent for a particular principal; (2) as an agent, but without disclosing for whom he is acting; (3) ostensibly as a principal, without disclosing the fact of agency.

---

[60] *Glendinning* v. *Hope*, 1911 S.C. (H.L.) 73, *per* Lord Kinnear at p. 78.

[61] *Glendinning, supra* (stockbroker).

[62] *Macrae* v. *Leith* 1913 S.C. 901. As to the lien of a solicitor, see para. 19.25, *supra*.

[63] See *Findlay* v. *Waddell*, 1910 S.C. 670.

[64] para. 21.25, *supra*. Death terminates the relationship: *Lord Advocate* v. *Chung*, 1995 S.L.T. 65 at p. 68.

[64a] Part IV and in particular regs. 15, 17 and 18. Regulation 14 provides for the situation where a fixed term contract continues to be performed after the expiry of the period.

[65] Bell, *Prin.*, § 286.

[66] *Sutton* v. *Grey* [1894] 1 Q.B. 285. *Cf.* para. 20.4 *supra*.

[67] *Michelin Tyre Co.* v. *Macfarlane*, 1917 2 S.L.T. 205 (H.L.).

[67a] An agent may not always be acting in that capacity. *Cf. McCabe* v. *Skipton Building Society*, 1994 S.L.T. 1272.

22.18 **(1) Contracts where Identity of Principal Disclosed.**—In the first case, where the agent names his principal, the general rule is that the principal alone is the contracting party, and that the agent is under no liability and has no title to sue on the contract.[68] The other party to the contract cannot, in respect of a debt arising out of it, plead compensation on a debt due to him by the agent—a rule which holds even if the name of the principal has not been disclosed,[69] but yields to proof of a custom of trade known to all the parties.[70] Payment to the agent is valid if the agent had authority to receive it, or if the nature of the agency was such as to involve ostensible authority to receive payment. Putting the picture broadly, it would appear that if an agent is in possession of goods the buyer may assume that he has authority to receive payment of the price; if he is merely a broker or traveller employed to take orders, without possession of the goods, a payment to the agent, if misapplied by him, leaves the buyer liable to the principal.[71] Where, however, the agent is more than a mere instrument and has an interest in the transaction, the general rule does not apply. So an auctioneer acting for a disclosed principal may himself sue a bidder for the price of goods sold.[72]

22.19 **Liability of Agent.**—While the general rule is that an agent who is acting within his authority and who names his principal incurs no liability, there are exceptional cases in which that rule does not hold.

If the contract is in writing, and the obligations under it are *ex facie* undertaken by the agent, he incurs personal liability even although the other party may have known that he was dealing with an agent, and may have known who the principal was.[73] So where a chartered accountant undertook to send a transfer of shares for signature it was held that it was incompetent to prove by parole evidence that he was merely an agent, and that this was known to the party with whom he dealt.[74] And where heritage was sold on behalf of a named client by a firm of solicitors who gave a letter of obligation to the purchaser's solicitors, undertaking to produce certain writs relating to the heritage within a specified period, the seller's solicitors were held personally liable when they failed to produce the writs.[75] Any qualification of the liability which the agent has apparently undertaken must appear from the terms of the writing.[76] Apart from cases of bills of exchange or

[68] See Bell, *Comm.*, i, 540, Lord McLaren's note. See, as illustration, *McIvor* v. *Roy*, 1970 S.L.T. (Sh.Ct.) 58.
[69] *Matthews* v. *Auld & Guild* (1874) 1 R. 1224.
[70] *Sweeting* v. *Pearce* (1861) 9 C.B. (N.S.) 534.
[71] *International Sponge Importers* v. *Watt*, 1911 S.C. (H.L.) 57.
[72] *MacKenzie* v. *Cormack*, 1950 S.C. 183.
[73] *Stewart* v. *Shannessy* (1900) 2 F. 1288; *Lindsay* v. *Craig*, 1919 S.C. 139; *Johnston* v. *Little*, 1960 S.L.T. 129; *Muirhead* v. *Gribben*, 1983 S.L.T. (Sh.Ct.) 102.
[74] *Lindsay* v. *Craig, supra.*
[75] *Johnston* v. *Little, supra.*
[76] See *Armour* v. *Duff*, 1912 S.C. 120.

promissory notes,[77] a signature 'as agent' or 'on behalf of' a principal, named or unnamed, will be sufficient to negative personal liability.[78]

With the exception of the case where an agent acts on behalf of a British Government department,[79] or a foreign Government[80] (where, though there may be no action against the principal, the agent is not personally liable) an agent incurs personal liability if the principal from whom he has received his authority, and on whose behalf he ostensibly contracts, is an unincorporated body which cannot be sued, such as a congregation,[81] or a club.[82]

22.20   Agent for Foreign Principal.—If an agent names as his principal a person not subject to the jurisdiction of the British courts he may be held to have incurred personal liability. In every case it is a question of fact for the court to determine what is the intention of the parties to the particular contract. But there is a presumption of fact that the agent himself intends to be bound by the contract, which is stronger in the case where the agent buys for a foreign principal—especially if the payment is stipulated to be immediate, or the credit given is short—and correspondingly weaker where the agent is selling goods to be supplied by a foreign house.[83]

22.21   (2) Contracts as Agent but Identity of Principal Undisclosed.—The legal results of a contract entered into as agent, but without disclosing the name of the principal, are a matter on which there is little authority in Scotland.[84] It may often be settled by a custom in a particular market or exchange that brokers deal with others as principals. Where there is no such custom in question, it will depend on the circumstances whether the third party, who knows that he is dealing with an agent, is looking only to the credit of the agent, or is looking to the credit of the unnamed principal.[85] But it is settled that, where an agent signs a written contract buying or selling specific articles, he is personally liable.[86] On the other hand, an auctioneer who gives a warranty does

---

[77] See para. 23.8, *infra.*

[78] *Universal Steam Navigation Co.* v. *McKelvie* [1923] A.C. 492; *Stone & Rolfe* v. *Kimber Coal Co.*, 1926 S.C. (H.L.) 45; *McLean* v. *Stuart*, 1970 S.L.T. (Notes) 77; *Digby Brown & Co.* v. *Lyall*, 1995 G.W.D. 11–596.

[79] *Dunn* v. *Macdonald* [1897] 1 Q.B. 555, discussed in Bowstead, *Agency*, p. 463.

[80] *Twycross* v. *Dreyfus* (1877) 5 Ch.D. 605.

[81] *McMeekin* v. *Easton* (1889) 16 R. 363.

[82] *Thomson* v. *Victoria Eighty Club* (1905) 43 S.L.R. 628.

[83] *Millar* v. *Mitchell* (1860) 22 D. 833 (opinion of majority of Whole Court); see also *Bennett* v. *Inveresk Paper Co.* (1891) 18 R. 975; and *Girvin Roper & Co.* v. *Monteith* (1895) 23 R. 129 (both cases in which the foreign principal was undisclosed); *cf. Miller, Gibb & Co.* v. *Smith & Tyrer* [1917] 2 K.B. 141; *Teheran-Europe Co.* v. *S.T. Belton (Tractors)* [1968] 2 Q.B. 545.

[84] Gloag, *Contract*, p. 138; Bowstead, *Agency*, p. 316.

[85] *N. & J. Vlassopulos Ltd.* v. *Ney Shipping Ltd.* [1977] 1 Lloyd's Rep. 478; *P. & M. Sinclair* v. *Bamber Gray Partnership*, 1987 S.L.T. 674.

[86] *H. O. Brandt & Co.* v. *H. N. Morris & Co.* [1917] 2 K.B. 784; *Hichens, Harrison Woolston & Co.* v. *Jackson & Sons* [1943] A.C. 266.

not bind himself personally if he discloses the name of the exposer, and was authorised by him;[87] he incurs personal liability if the name of the exposer is not given.[88] In the case of goods in the auction room he impliedly undertakes to deliver them, but not that the purchaser will obtain a good title.[89]

22.22 **(3) Contracts Ostensibly as Principal.**—Where an agent contracts ostensibly as principal the result generally is that both principal and agent are liable on the contract, and are entitled to sue upon it.[90] But it has been suggested that for the principal to be entitled to sue, the contract must be assignable.[91] It is no answer to an action or counterclaim by the agent for damages for breach of the contract that he personally has suffered no loss; he may sue on behalf of his principal.[92] Similarly, if the principal discloses himself and sues on the agent's contract he is subject to all the pleas which could have been maintained against the agent.[93] The other party to the contract may plead compensation based on a debt due by the agent, if that debt was incurred before he had notice of the existence of the principal.[94] And, on discovering the identity of the principal, he may sue him, and is not adequately met by the defence that the principal has already made payment to the agent.[95]

22.23 **Election between Agent and Principal.**—The liability of principal or agent, in the case where an agent has contracted ostensibly as principal, is alternative, and not joint and several.[96] The other party to the contract must at some time elect whether he will hold the principal or the agent as his debtor, and his election when once made is final.[96] Election implies knowledge of the right to elect, and therefore nothing done before the existence of the principal is discovered can amount to election of the agent as debtor. It does not necessarily amount to election that the agent has been debited,[97] or even that an action for payment has been raised against him,[98] after the principal has been disclosed. But a decree against either party, even although it be a

[87] *Fenwick* v. *Macdonald, Fraser & Co.* (1904) 6 F. 850.
[88] *Ferrier* v. *Dods* (1865) 3 M. 561.
[89] *Benton* v. *Campbell, Parker & Co.* [1925] 2 K.B. 410.
[90] Bell, *Comm.*, i, 540, Lord McLaren's note; *Siu Yin Kwan* v. *Eastern Insurance Co. Ltd.* [1994] 2 A.C. 199.
[91] Gloag, *Contract*, pp. 128–129. See discussion in *Siu Yin Kwan, supra*, at pp. 209 *et seq.*
[92] *Craig* v. *Blackater*, 1923 S.C. 472; *James Laidlaw & Sons* v. *Griffin*, 1968 S.L.T. 278.
[93] *Bennett* v. *Inveresk Paper Co.* (1891) 18 R. 975.
[94] *Wester Moffat Colliery Co.* v. *Jeffrey*, 1911 S.C. 346; *Greer* v. *Downs Supply Co.* [1927] 2 K.B. 28.
[95] *Irvine* v. *Watson* (1880) 5 Q.B.D. 414.
[96] *David Logan & Sons Ltd.* v. *Schuldt* (1903) 10 S.L.T. 598; *British Bata Shoe Co.* v. *D. M. Shah Ltd.*, 1980 S.C. 311.
[97] *Stevenson* v. *Campbell* (1836) 14 S. 562.
[98] *Meier* v. *Küchenmeister* (1881) 8 R. 642; *Clarkson Booker* v. *Andjel* [1964] 2 Q.B. 775.

decree in absence and nothing may be recoverable under it, amounts to election and precludes a claim against the other.[99] The same rule holds in the case of a ranking in the bankruptcy of either principal or agent,[1] unless perhaps the claim against the other is expressly reserved.[2] But it will probably not amount to election if only a claim in bankruptcy has been lodged.[3] Apart from any definite claim, a party's conduct under a contract may amount to election,[4] a question largely circumstantial. Where a horse was sold at auction, under circumstances which made both the auctioneer and the owner responsible for a warranty which had been given, it was held that the return of the horse to the owner was a conclusive election to treat him as the party responsible, and precluded a claim against the auctioneer for repetition of the price.[5]

22.24   Agent Acting without Authority.—If an agent enters into a contract without the authority of a principal the latter is generally not bound, whether the contract is expressly made on his behalf or not.[6] The principal may become a party to the contract by ratifying the agent's unauthorised act.[7] Indeed if A, wholly unconnected with B, professes to contract on B's behalf, ratification of A's act is the only ground on which B can be held to be liable under the contract. Even if the agent's act was wholly without authority, actual or ostensible, the principal might nevertheless be liable to the third party on the principle of recompense, *i.e.* to the extent of the principal's enrichment.[8]

22.25   Ostensible Authority.—A principal may also incur liability under a contract if the agent's act in entering the contract was within his ostensible, though not within his actual, authority. Liability on the ground of ostensible authority cannot arise unless there was some prior contractual relationship between the agent and the party sued as principal, or in circumstances where it can be established that the principal held the agent out as possessing authority or made a representation as to his authority.[8a] If A so behaves or allows B so to behave that the reasonable inference is that A has authorised B to act for him, and hence that B has any necessary actual authority, A may

---

[99] *Craig* v. *Blackater*, 1923 S.C. 472; *Morel* v. *Earl of Westmoreland* [1904] A.C. 11; *Moore* v. *Flanagan* [1920] 1 K.B. 919.

[1] *Scarf* v. *Jardine* (1882) 7 App.Cas. 345; *David Logan & Son Ltd.* v. *Schuldt, supra*; *British Bata Shoe Co.* v. *D. M. Shah Ltd., supra*. Contrast a case of joint and several liability, *Morton's Trs.* v. *Robertson's Judicial Factor* (1892) 20 R. 72.

[2] *Black* v. *Girdwood* (1885) 13 R. 243.

[3] See opinions in *Black* v. *Girdwood, supra*.

[4] *Ferrier* v. *Dods* (1865) 3 M. 561; *Lamont, Nisbet & Co.* v. *Hamilton*, 1907 S.C. 628.

[5] *Ferrier* v. *Dods, supra*.

[6] As to the agent's liability, see para. 22.30, *infra*.

[7] para. 22.4, *supra*.

[8] *Commercial Bank of Scotland* v. *Biggar*, 1958 S.L.T. (Notes) 46. See also paras. 29.12 to 29.15, *infra*.

[8a] *First Energy (U.K.) Ltd.* v. *Hungarian International Bank* [1993] 2 Lloyd's Rep. 194; *Armagas Ltd.* v. *Mundogas S.A.* [1986] A.C. 717.

incur liability to anyone dealing with B, though in a question between A and B there may be no contract, or a contract of a different kind.[9] The basis of liability is personal bar.[10] Cases of ostensible authority to enter a particular transaction will rarely arise.[11] Occasionally an agent may have apparent authority to communicate approval to third parties in relation to a transaction even though he has no authority on his own to enter into the transaction.[11a]

The usual cases of ostensible authority arise—(1) where authority has been conferred, but has been withdrawn; (2) where limited authority has been given and has been exceeded.

22.26   Original Authority Withdrawn.—Where a party has authorised another to act as his agent and has withdrawn his authority he is bound to give notice of the fact of withdrawal, and if he fails to do so, he will be liable on contracts which the agent may make with parties who deal with him in the belief that the authority is still in force. Notice by advertisement is sufficient in a question with parties who had no prior dealings with the agent; with those who had, some specific notice is required.[12] The general rule is well established, and, in the case of a partner retiring from a firm, is statutory.[13] So where a gardener bought seeds over a four-month period and his employer paid for them, the employer was held liable for further large purchases by the gardener from the same supplier who had not been told that the gardener no longer had authority to buy from the supplier.[14]

22.27   Authority Exceeded.—In the case of an agent who has some authority, but has exceeded it, a distinction is recognised between general and special agents. The former are persons who are employed either, as in the case of a factory and commission, to transact all the business of the principal, or, in the case of the master of a ship or a solicitor, to transact all the business of some particular kind. The latter are persons who are authorised for some special occasion or act. In the former case third parties are entitled to assume in the absence of notice to the contrary, that the agent possesses the powers which are usually conferred in agency of the particular kind;[15] in the latter case there is no presumption of any authority beyond that which has been actually

---

[9] See *Hayman* v. *American Cotton Oil Co.* (1907) 45 S.L.R. 207; *British Bata Shoe Co. Ltd.* v. *D. M. Shah Ltd., supra; Armagas Ltd.* v. *Mundogas S.A., supra; Dornier GmbH* v. *Cannon*, 1991 S.C. 310.

[10] *Armagas Ltd., supra, per* Lord Keith of Kinkel at p. 777 (estoppel); para. 3.11, *supra*.

[11] *Armagas Ltd., supra.*

[11a] *First Energy (U.K.) Ltd., supra, per* Steyn L.J. at p. 203.

[12] Bell, *Prin.*, § 288; *North of Scotland Bank* v. *Behn Möller & Co.* (1881) 8 R. 423.

[13] Partnership Act 1890, s. 36. See para. 50.15, *infra*.

[14] *Dewar* v. *Nairne* (1804) Hume 340.

[15] In *United Bank of Kuwait* v. *Hammoud* [1988] 1 W.L.R. 1051, at p. 1063, Staughton L.J. points out that the usual scope varies with changes in practice.

given.[16] But it may often be difficult to determine to which class a particular case belongs. Where the third party knows that an agent has limited authority, ostensible general authority can never arise.[17] The law may be illustrated by reference to the ostensible authority of a solicitor, and of a mercantile agent.

22.28 **Ostensible Authority of Solicitor.**—A solicitor has ostensible authority to receive payment of a sum decerned for in an action which he has been employed to conduct,[18] or to receive payments for shares which he has been employed to sell.[19] He has no such authority to receive payment of the principal sum due under a bond,[20] or to discharge a bond, or place it in the custody of the debtor.[21] There is no ostensible authority to bind the client to any contract, *e.g.* a lease,[22] or a bank overdraft.[23] The solicitor of a trust has no authority to have a trustee or executor registered as a shareholder in a company.[24] Employed to purchase lands or to arrange a heritable security, a solicitor has implied authority to authorise a search of the records for incumbrances, and has been held liable to his client for failure to do so.[25] In the conduct of litigation[26] counsel have a very wide authority to bind their client to any step in process,[27] and the solicitor has an implied authority to follow counsel's directions.[28] Where counsel is not employed, a solicitor has ostensible authority to take any ordinary step in procedure, including marking an appeal to a higher court,[29] but not to grant delay in the execution of diligence,[30] nor to compromise an action.[31]

22.29 **Ostensible Authority in Commercial Agency: Factors Acts.**—In commercial agency there is a general distinction between a factor and a broker, the former being a party entrusted with the possession of goods or documents of title to goods, the latter being a mere intermediary, without possession.[32] The ostensible authority of a broker depends

---

[16] Bell, *Prin.*, § 219.

[17] *Russo-Chinese Bank* v. *Li Yau Sam* [1910] A.C. 174; *Armagas Ltd., supra.*

[18] *Smith* v. *North British Ry.* (1850) 12 D. 795.

[19] *Pearson* v. *Scott* (1878) 9 Ch.D. 198.

[20] *Peden* v. *Graham* (1907) 15 S.L.T. 143.

[21] *Bowie's Trs.* v. *Watson*, 1913 S.C. 326.

[22] *Danish Dairy Co.* v. *Gillespie*, 1922 S.C. 656; *Hopkinson* v. *Williams*, 1993 S.L.T. 907; *Stewart's Exrs.* v. *Stewart*, 1993 S.L.T. 440.

[23] *Commercial Bank of Scotland* v. *Biggar*, 1958 S.L.T. (Notes) 46.

[24] *Smith* v. *City of Glasgow Bank* (1879) 6 R. 1017.

[25] *Fearn* v. *Gordon & Craig* (1893) 20 R. 352.

[26] *Brodt* v. *King*, 1991 S.L.T. 272.

[27] *Batchelor* v. *Pattison & Mackersy* (1876) 3 R. 914; *Duncan* v. *Salmond* (1874) 1 R. 329; *Zannetos* v. *Glenford Investment Holdings Ltd.*, 1982 S.L.T. 453; *Waugh* v. *H. B. Clifford & Sons* [1982] Ch. 374—which makes a clearer distinction between ostensible and implied authority than is found in the Scottish authorities.

[28] *Batchelor, supra*; Begg, *Law Agents* (2nd ed.), p. 95.

[29] *Riverford Finance Ltd.* v. *Kelly*, 1991 S.L.T. 300, distinguishing *Goodall* v. *Bilsland*, 1909 S.C. 1152.

[30] *Cameron* v. *Mortimer* (1872) 10 M. 817.

[31] *Cormie* v. *Grigor* (1862) 24 D. 985; (1863) 1 M. 357.

[32] See Bell, *Comm.*, i, 505.

largely on the rules of the particular market or exchange in which he deals, though it would seem that no usage will justify a broker, employed to buy, in supplying commodities or shares belonging to himself.[33] The ostensible powers of a factor or mercantile agent are defined by the Factors Acts. By section 2 of the Factors Act 1889, extended to Scotland by the Factors (Scotland) Act 1890, a mercantile agent,[34] who is in possession of goods or of documents of title[35] with the consent of the owner, has ostensible authority to sell or pledge them, and any sale, pledge or other disposition made in the ordinary course of his business to anyone who takes in good faith and for value,[36] is as valid as if the mercantile agent had the express authority of his principal.[37] It has been held in England that in the case of a sale or pledge under these conditions the purchaser takes a statutory title, although there may be a custom in the particular trade that agents have no authority to sell or pledge.[38] A pledge of the documents of title to goods (*e.g.* a bill of lading, dock warrant or delivery order) is, if made by a mercantile agent, deemed to be a pledge of the goods, and, probably, gives an instant right which does not require completion by intimation to the custodier of the goods or any form of delivery.[39] In the case of property other than goods or documents of title an agent in possession of negotiable securities has ostensible authority to pledge them. So a bank, taking securities from a stockbroker, is entitled to assume, in the absence of information to the contrary, that he has the authority of his clients to pledge them, though not that he has any authority to subject them to a lien for his own debit balance.[40] In the exceptional case of *indicia* of title other than documents of title to goods or negotiable instruments, it has been held in England that mere possession gives no ostensible title to dispose of them, but that if an agent has actual authority to pledge them the pledge is good though the authority be exceeded.[41]

22.30 Liability of Agent Exceeding his Authority.—Where a party contracts ostensibly as agent but in excess of his actual or ostensible authority, and with the result that no principal is bound by the contract, he will as a rule incur personal liability, but the nature and extent of that liability will depend on the circumstances of the case. If the contract is made professedly on behalf of a non-existent principal, the party who makes

---

[33] *Robinson* v. *Mollett* (1875) L.R. 7 H.L. 802; *Maffett* v. *Stewart* (1887) 14 R. 506.

[34] Defined by s. 1 (1).

[35] Defined by s. 1 (4).

[36] Factors Act 1889, s. 5 and Factors (Scotland) Act 1890, s. 1 (2).

[37] This does not apply to a pledge in security of an antecedent debt of the mercantile agent: Factors Act 1889, s. 4.

[38] *Oppenheimer* v. *Attenborough* [1908] 1 K.B. 221.

[39] Factors Act 1889, s. 3; *Inglis* v. *Robertson & Baxter* (1898) 25 R. (H.L.) 70.

[40] *National Bank* v. *Dickie's Tr.* (1895) 22 R. 740; *London Joint Stock Bank* v. *Simmons* [1892] A.C. 201.

[41] *Fry* v. *Smellie* [1912] 3 K.B. 282 (share certificates with blank transfers).

the contract is liable to carry it out and is treated as a party to it. So where someone purports to contract or to undertake an obligation as agent for a company which has not yet been formed, subject to any agreement to the contrary he is personally liable on the contract or under the obligation.[42] The same rule holds where the nominal principal is a body unable to bind itself by contract, with the exception of the case of a contract on behalf of a government.[43] Where the principal, though in existence and able to give authority, has in fact not done so, the agent is not a party to the contract. If his conduct was fraudulent he will be liable in damages for fraud and where he owes a duty of care to the other party, he will be liable in damages for negligence.[44] If he honestly thought he had the principal's authority, as where an auctioneer, by mere mistake, sold a horse which was not for sale,[45] or solicitors believed that they were representing a trust when in fact there were no trustees,[46] the agent will incur liability on the theory that an agent impliedly warrants that he has the authority of the principal whom he names, and is liable in damages for breach of that warranty if it turns out that he has no authority.[47] The damages are measured by the loss the other party has sustained in not having the obligation of the principal. Thus where an agent sells, without authority, he is liable for the difference between the price paid and the actual value of the article.[48] But where a plumber had done work on the instructions of an agent who, as it turned out, had no authority, but the principal named was a company which was insolvent and had no assets, it was held that as the obligation of the company was valueless, the plumber had lost nothing by the want of it, and therefore could recover no damages from the agent for breach of his implied warranty.[49]

The rule as to the implied warranty given by an agent does not apply where the question of the agent's authority is one of law, and the other party has the means of judging for himself what that authority is. So directors of a company which had no power to borrow were not liable on debentures which they honestly but mistakenly issued, the question as to the power to borrow being one of law.[50] But they did incur liability where the debentures were in excess of a borrowing limit, the question whether that limit had been reached being one of fact.[51]

---

[42] *Phonogram Ltd.* v. *Lane* [1982] Q.B. 938; Companies Act 1985, s. 36C (1) and (2) inserted by s. 130 of the Companies Act 1989 (c. 40); *Vic Spence Assocs.* v. *Balchin*, 1990 S.L.T. 10.

[43] Para. 22.19, *supra*.

[44] Bowstead, *Agency*, pp. 458–459.

[45] *Anderson* v. *Croall* (1903) 6 F. 153.

[46] *Scott* v. *J. B. Livingston & Nicol*, 1990 S.L.T. 305.

[47] *Collen* v. *Wright* (1857) 8 E. & B. 647; *Firbank's Exrs.* v. *Humphreys* (1886) 18 Q.B.D. 54.

[48] *Anderson* v. *Croall, supra*. See also *Salvesen* v. *Rederi Nordstjernan* (1905) 7 F. (H.L.) 101.

[49] *Irving* v. *Burns*, 1915 S.C. 260.

[50] *Beattie* v. *Lord Ebury* (1874) L.R. 7 H.L. 102. See now, however, Companies Act 1985, s. 35.

[51] *Firbank's Exrs., supra*.

22.31 **Negotiorum Gestio.**—The law of agency deals with cases where one person acts on behalf of another by agreement. Where one person acts on another's behalf without his agreement, there is no contract between the parties, but in certain circumstances rights and obligations may arise which are dealt with under the heading of *negotiorum gestio*. A *negotiorum gestor* is a person who, without any regular authority, intervenes to manage the affairs of another who, temporarily or permanently, is unable to manage them himself, and in a situation where it is reasonable to assume that authority would have been given had the circumstances rendered it possible to apply for it.[52] The position is held by a salvor[53] and by one who acts on behalf of an absentee[54] or of a person who has become insane.[55] A *negotiorum gestor* is entitled to be reimbursed for any expenditure he has incurred in the proper course of administration, even although it has not proved beneficial,[56] and to be relieved of all liabilities. On the other hand a *gestor* is not entitled to recover any enrichment which may have accrued to the other party as a result of his intervention. The *gestor* must account for his intromissions, and is liable for any loss caused by his failure to exercise the care and diligence which a prudent man would have shown in relation to his own property.[57] A person reasonably and properly employed by a *negotiorum gestor*, as, for example, a solicitor, has a direct right of action for his account against the party whose affairs have been managed.[58]

Further Reading

Bowstead, *Agency* (15th ed., 1985).
Fridman, *The Law of Agency* (6th ed., 1990).
Leslie, 'Negotiorum Gestio in Scots Law: the Claim of the Privileged Gestor', 1983 J.R. 12.
MacQueen and Sellar, 'Unjust Enrichment in Scots Law', in Schrafe, *Unjust Enrichment* (1995), p. 289 at pp. 301 *et seq*.
Powell, *The Law of Agency* (2nd ed., 1961).
Stair Memorial Encyclopaedia, Vol. 1 (1987), Agency and Mandate.
Stewart, *The Law of Restitution in Scotland* (1992), Chap. 9.
Stoljar, *The Law of Agency* (1961).
Story, *Commentaries on the Law of Agency* (9th ed., 1882).
Whitty, 'Negotiorum Gestio', *Stair Memorial Encyclopaedia* (forthcoming).
Zimmermann, *The Law of Obligations* (1990), Chap. 14.

---

[52] Stair, I, viii, 3; Erskine, III, iii, 52–53; Pothier, *Traité du contrat de mandat* (appendice); Kames, *Equity* (3rd ed.), i, 179 *et seq*.; Bell, *Prin.*, § 540; Zimmermann, *The Law of Obligations*, Chap. 14 and pp. 875 *et seq*. For the analogous principle of agency of necessity, see para. 22.3, *supra*.

[53] See Chap. 30.

[54] *Bannatine's Trs.* v. *Cunninghame* (1872) 10 M. 319; see *S.M.T. Sales & Services Co.* v. *Motor & General Finance Co.*, 1954 S.L.T. (Sh. Ct.) 107.

[55] *Dunbar* v. *Wilson & Dunlop's Tr.* (1887) 15 R. 210.

[56] Stair, I, viii, 3.

[57] *Kolbin & Son* v. *United Shipping Co.*, 1931 S.C. (H.L.) 128, *per* Lord Atkin at p. 139.

[58] *Fernie* v. *Robertson* (1871) 9 M. 437; *Dunbar* v. *Wilson & Dunlop's Tr., supra*.

CHAPTER 23

BILLS OF EXCHANGE

23.1 THE law of bills of exchange, cheques and promissory notes was codified by the Bills of Exchange Act 1882.[1] In its main provisions the Act applies both to Scotland and England.

23.2 Origin and Use of Bills.[2]—In origin a bill of exchange was a method whereby a merchant in one country might pay a debt due in another without the actual transmission of money. If A in London owed money to B in Paris, and was himself the creditor of C in Paris, a bill of exchange was the means by which the debt owed by C could be used to meet the debt due to B. A, known as the drawer, gave an order to C (the drawee) to pay to B (the payee). If C was willing to accede to this order he indicated the fact by signing his name on the bill, and thereby became the acceptor and incurred a direct liability to the payee. It was at an early period established that a bill of exchange in this, its ordinary form, was negotiable; that is to say, B, in the case supposed, by signing his name on the back of the bill (known as indorsement), could transfer his right as payee either to the bearer of the bill or to some named party. And in the case of ordinary mercantile bills an indorsee, who paid for the bill and took it regularly and honestly, acquired, by law originally resting on the recognition of mercantile custom, an independent title, and was not affected by any imperfection or qualification of the title of the person from whom he took it. Such an indorsee is termed in the Act a holder in due course.[2a]

23.3 Normal Relations of Parties.—The ensuing sketch of the main provisions of the Bills of Exchange Act will be more easily understood if it is borne in mind that while the holder of a bill is entitled to demand payment from anyone whose name appears on it, drawer, acceptor or indorser, the relations of these parties *inter se* are regulated by the character in which they became parties to the bill. Before the bill is accepted, the principal debtor is the drawer, and any indorsers may

---

[1] In this chapter references to sections without specifying any Act are references to sections of the 1882 Act. For an account of the background to the codification see Appendix 3 to Byles, *Bills of Exchange* and Rodger (1992) 108 L.Q.R. 570.
[2] See also Holden, *History of Negotiable Instruments in English Law* (1955).
[2a] s. 29(1).

recover from him and are liable among themselves in the order in which their names appear on the bill. After acceptance, the acceptor becomes the principal debtor; the drawer, and after him any indorsers in their order, are subsidiarily liable. In many respects the position of a person who becomes a party to a bill is that of a cautioner for those who are already parties to it, but, if forced to pay, he is entitled to recover the whole, and not merely a contribution, from anyone who, in the order of liability on the bill, ranks before him.

These rules as to the order of liability on a bill hold only in the absence of proof to the contrary. It is competent to prove in any particular case that the true relationship of the parties is not that which would appear on the face of the bill. It may be proved that the principal debtor is not the acceptor, but the drawer, or an indorser. Such cases generally arise when a bill is used, not for its original purpose of transferring a debt, but as a means whereby money is borrowed by one party, and a guarantee for its payment is given by another. Bills of this character are known as accommodation bills.[3]

In what follows it is proposed to deal first with the course of a normal bill of exchange, afterwards with exceptional cases, and finally with the law applicable to cheques and promissory notes.

23.4 Definitions.—The following statutory definitions should be noted:

A bill of exchange is an unconditional order in writing, addressed by one person to another, signed by the person giving it, requiring the person to whom it is addressed to pay on demand or at a fixed or determinable future time a sum certain in money to or to the order of a specified person, or to bearer.[4]

'Holder' means the payee or indorsee of a bill who is in possession of it, or the bearer thereof.[5] This definition is extended to include a collecting bank which takes delivery from a customer of an unindorsed cheque.[6]

A holder in due course is a holder who has taken a bill, complete and regular on the face of it,[7] under the following conditions, namely (a) that he became the holder of it before it was overdue, and without notice that it had been previously dishonoured, if such was the fact; (b) that he took the bill in good faith[8] and for value, and that at the time

---

[3] See *Macdonald* v. *Whitfield* (1883) 8 App. Cas. 733, and para. 23.32, *infra*.

[4] s. 3. See Cheques Act 1957, s. 5. A building society withdrawal form is not a bill: *Weir* v. *National Westminster Bank*, 1994 S.L.T. 1251. As to the meaning of an 'unconditional' order, see *Guaranty Trust* v. *Hannay* [1918] 2 K.B. 623. The sum may be expressed, and judgment given, in foreign currency; ss. 57(2) and 72(4) of the 1882 Act have ceased to have effect: Administration of Justice Act 1977, s. 4.

[5] s. 2.

[6] Cheques Act 1957, s. 2; *Midland Bank* v. *Harris* [1963] 1 W.L.R. 1021.

[7] See *Macdonald* v. *Nash* [1924] A.C. 625; *Arab Bank* v. *Ross* [1952] 2 Q.B. 216. As to cheques, see *Westminster Bank* v. *Zang* [1966] A.C. 182.

[8] *B.C.C.I.* v. *Dawson* [1987] F.L.R. 342. *Cf.* s. 90.

the bill was negotiated to him he had no notice of any defect in the title of the person who negotiated it.[9]

In particular the title of a person who negotiates a bill is defective within the meaning of the Act when he obtained the bill, or the acceptance thereof, by fraud, duress, or force and fear, or other unlawful means, or for an illegal consideration, or when he negotiates it in breach of faith, or under such circumstances as amount to a fraud.[10]

A holder (whether for value or not), who derives his title to a bill through a holder in due course, and who is not himself a party to any fraud or illegality affecting it, has all the rights of that holder in due course as regards the acceptor and all parties to the bill prior to that holder.[11]

23.5 Stamp.—A bill of exchange does not now require to be stamped.[12] A bill is not invalid by reason only that it is not stamped in accordance with the law of the place of issue.[13]

23.6 Inland and Foreign Bills.—A bill may be an inland or a foreign bill. It is an inland bill if it is or on the face of it purports to be (a) both drawn and payable within the British Islands, or (b) drawn within the British Islands on some person resident therein.[14] Unless the contrary appears on the face of the bill the holder may treat it as an inland bill.[15] The chief difference[16] between inland and foreign bills is that the latter, and not the former, when dishonoured by non-acceptance or non-payment, must be protested in order to preserve recourse against the drawer and indorsers.[17]

23.7 Methods of Signing Bills.—A person may become a party to a bill either when he signs it or when it is signed for him by a person to whom he has given authority. The latter case is termed a signature by procuration. A bill may be signed by initials or by a mark, and will then form a ground of action on proof that this was the party's usual method

---

[9] s. 29(1). A person who takes a negotiable instrument in contravention of s. 123(1) or (3) of the Consumer Credit Act 1974 is not a holder in due course and cannot enforce the instrument: Consumer Credit Act 1974, s. 125(1); see para. 18.16, *supra.*

[10] s. 29(2). Where a person negotiates a cheque in contravention of s. 123(2) of the Consumer Credit Act 1974, his doing so constitutes a defect in his title: Consumer Credit Act 1974, s. 125(2); see para. 18.16, *supra.*

[11] s. 29(3). The payee of a cheque is not, under any circumstances, a holder in due course: *Jones* v. *Waring & Gillow* [1926] A.C. 670; applied in *Williams* v. *Williams*, 1980 S.L.T. (Sh. Ct.) 25. The drawer may become a holder in due course if the bill is renegotiated to him by a party who was a holder in due course: *Jade International Steel Stahl und Eisen G.m.b.H. & Co. KG* v. *Robert Nicholas (Steels)* [1978] Q.B. 917.

[12] Finance Act 1970, s. 32 and Sched. 7, para. 2(2).

[13] s. 72(1).

[14] s. 4(1).

[15] s. 4(2).

[16] But see also s. 72(2).

[17] s. 51.

of signature.[18] The Act provides (section 23) that where a person signs a bill in a trade or assumed name he is liable thereon as if he had signed in his own name, and that the signature of the name of a firm is equivalent to the signature by the person so signing of the names of all the persons liable as partners of that firm. A bill of exchange is deemed to have been made, accepted or indorsed on behalf of a company if made, accepted or indorsed in the name of, or by or on behalf or on account of, the company by any person acting under its authority.[19] A signature by procuration operates as notice that the party has but a limited authority to sign, and the principal is only bound by such signature if the agent in so signing was acting within the actual limits of his authority.[20] But if the agent has authority the principal will be liable though the agent has misused his authority for his own purposes.[21]

23.8   Signature as Agent.—Where a person signs a bill as drawer, indorser or acceptor and adds words to his signature, indicating that he signs for or on behalf of a principal, or in a representative capacity, he is not personally liable thereon; but the mere addition to his signature of words describing him as an agent, or as filling a representative character, does not exempt him from personal liability.[22] In determining whether a signature on a bill is that of the principal or that of the agent by whose hand it is written, the construction most favourable to the validity of the instrument must be adopted.[23] So if a bill is signed on behalf of an unincorporated body, such as a club or a congregation, which has no power to incur liability by bill, the persons who sign, although they may do so expressly on behalf of the body, incur personal liability.[24] But it is always open to any drawer or indorser to insert an express stipulation negativing or limiting his own liability to the holder.[25]

23.9   Form of Bill.[26]—A bill of exchange is usually expressed as an order by one person, known as the drawer, addressed to another, known as the drawee, requiring the drawee to pay a sum of money to the drawer himself, or to his order, or to a named payee, or to the bearer. But a man may draw a bill on himself; if so, any holder may, in his option, treat it as a bill or as a promissory note. The same rule applies where

---

[18] Bell, *Prin.*, § 323.

[19] Companies Act 1985, s. 37; *Bondina Ltd.* v. *Rollaway Shower Blinds* [1986] 1 W.L.R. 517. For the position where the company name is not legible on the bill see s. 349(4) of the Companies Act 1985; *Scottish & Newcastle Breweries Ltd.* v. *Blair*, 1967 S.L.T. 72.

[20] s. 25; *Midland Bank* v. *Reckitt* [1933] A.C. 1.

[21] *North of Scotland Banking Co.* v. *Behn* (1881) 8 R. 423; *Bryant Powis & Bryant Ltd.* v. *La Banque du Peuple* [1893] A.C. 170.

[22] s. 26(1). See illustrative cases collected in Chalmers and Guest, *Bills of Exchange*, pp. 220–222; *Brebner* v. *Henderson*, 1925 S.C. 643.

[23] s. 26(2).

[24] *McMeekin* v. *Easton* (1889) 16 R. 363.

[25] s. 16(1).

[26] For conflict of laws see s. 72.

the drawee is a fictitious person or a person who has no capacity to contract.[27] To form a bill of exchange the order must be solely for payment of money, and must be, on the face of it, unconditional.[28] It is not unconditional if it is an order to pay out of some particular fund, but it may indicate the fund from which the drawee is to be indemnified, or the account which is to be debited.[29] An instrument which is expressed as a conditional order may, if transferred to a third party, be used by him as proof of a debt, but it is not a bill of exchange.[30]

23.10 Liabilities of Drawer.—The drawer of a bill incurs a conditional liability to subsequent holders. He is liable if the drawee refuses to accept the bill, or fails to pay it, provided that the requisite proceedings for notice on dishonour are duly taken.[31] He may exclude this liability by appropriate terms, the usual phrase being 'without recourse.'[32] He is precluded from denying to a holder in due course the existence of the payee and his then capacity to indorse.[33]

23.11 Negotiation of Bill.—Unless otherwise expressed a bill is negotiable. If payable to bearer, it may be negotiated by mere delivery;[34] if payable to a particular payee, it may be negotiated by that party indorsing the bill, *i.e.* writing his name on the back of it, followed by delivery.[35] If a bill contains words prohibiting transfer, or indicating an intention that it should not be transferred, it is valid as between the parties to it, but is not negotiable.[36] Ambiguous expressions, such as the words 'against cheque' will not readily be construed as indicating that a bill should not be negotiable.[37]

23.12 Term of Payment.—A bill of exchange may be payable on demand, and is assumed to be so if no term of payment is mentioned.[38] A bill may be payable on, or at a fixed period after, the occurrence of an event which is certain to happen, though the date of the occurrence is uncertain, but a document payable on the occurrence of an event which may or may not happen is not in any event a bill of exchange.[39] Bills are usually made payable either after a certain period from the date at which they are drawn, or at a certain period after sight or presentation. The bill is

---

[27] s. 5(2). Cf. *Universal Import Export GmbH* v. *Bank of Scotland* 1995 G.W.D. 12–633.
[28] s. 3(1).
[29] s. 3(3).
[30] See *Lawson's Exrs.* v. *Watson*, 1907 S.C. 1353.
[31] s. 55(1)(*a*).
[32] s. 16(1).
[33] s. 55(1)(*b*).
[34] s. 31(2).
[35] s. 31(3).
[36] s. 8(1).
[37] *Glen* v. *Semple* (1901) 3 F. 1134.
[38] s. 10(1)(*b*).
[39] s. 11.

due and payable on the last day of the time of payment as fixed by the bill or, if that is a non-business day, on the succeeding business day; there are now no days of grace.[40] Non-business days are Saturdays, Sundays, Good Friday, Christmas Day, bank holidays, days appointed by Royal proclamation as public fast or thanksgiving days, and days declared by order to be non-business days.[41]

23.13 **Presentment for Acceptance.**—If a bill is payable at a certain period after sight or presentation, presentment for acceptance to the drawee is necessary in order to fix its maturity. In other cases presentment for acceptance is not necessary to render any party liable on the bill, unless it is expressly stated that it is required, or the bill is payable elsewhere than at the residence or place of business of the drawee.[42] The following rules as to presentment for acceptance are provided by section 41(1): It must be made by or on behalf of the holder to the drawee or his agent at a reasonable hour on a business day and before the bill is overdue; if there are two or more drawees, who are not partners, presentment must be made to all, unless one has authority to accept for the rest; if the drawee is dead, presentment may be made to his personal representative; if bankrupt, to him or to his trustee; if authorised by agreement or usage, presentment may be made through the post office. The usual time allowed for acceptance is 24 hours, excluding non-business days.[43] If after the lapse of that period the bill is not accepted it must be treated as dishonoured by non-acceptance. Presentment is excused and the bill may be treated as dishonoured by non-acceptance where the drawee is dead or bankrupt, a fictitious person, or a person not having power to contract by bill, where it cannot be effected by reasonable diligence, or where, though the presentment has been irregular, acceptance is refused on some other ground. But reason to believe that the bill will be dishonoured is not an excuse for failure to present it.[44] Where presentment for acceptance is necessary the holder of the bill is bound to present or negotiate it within a reasonable time, and his failure discharges the drawer and all prior indorsers.[45]

23.14 **Acceptance by Other than Drawee.**—No one but the drawee, or an agent authorised by him, can accept a bill, except in two cases. (1) Where the drawer or an indorser has inserted the name of a party (the referee) to whom the holder may resort in case of need, that is if the bill is dishonoured by non-acceptance (or non-payment), it is in the option of the holder to resort to a referee.[46] (2) Where a bill has been

---

[40] s. 14(1) as substituted by Banking and Financial Dealings Act 1971, s. 3(2).

[41] s. 92 as amended by Banking and Financial Dealings Act 1971, ss. 3(1), 4(4).

[42] s. 39.

[43] Thomson, *Bills of Exchange* (2nd ed., 1865 by Dove Wilson), p. 213; *Bank of Van Diemen's Land* v. *Bank of Victoria* (1871) L.R. 3 P.C. 526.

[44] s. 41(2) and (3).

[45] s. 40(1) and (2).

[46] s. 15.

protested for non-acceptance and is not overdue, any person, not already a party liable on it, may with the consent of the holder sign the bill in the capacity of an acceptor for honour.[47] In the absence of any statement to the contrary such a party is presumed to engage for the honour of the drawer.[48] He incurs liability to the holder and to all parties to the bill subsequent to the party for whose honour he has accepted.[49] Except in these cases any party who becomes a party to a bill, other than the drawer or acceptor, incurs the liabilities of an indorser to a holder in due course.[50]

23.15 **Acceptance by Drawee: Qualified Acceptance.**—An acceptance must be in writing on the bill. The mere signature of the drawee is sufficient.[51] The acceptance may be general or qualified. It is qualified if it is (a) conditional; (b) partial, for part only of the amount of the bill; (c) local, payable only at a particular place; (d) qualified as to time; (e) the acceptance of one or more drawees, but not of all.[52] It is in the option of the holder to take a qualified acceptance, or to treat the bill as dishonoured by non-acceptance.[53] If he takes it without the express or implied authority of the drawer or of a prior indorser, or their subsequent assent, their liability is discharged.[54] This rule does not apply to the case of a partial acceptance of which due notice has been given.[55]

23.16 **Liabilities of Acceptor.**—An acceptor engages that he will pay the bill according to the tenor of his acceptance.[56] He is precluded from denying to a holder in due course (a) the existence of the drawer, the genuineness of his signature, and his capacity and authority to draw the bill; (b) if the bill is payable to the drawer's order, the then capacity of the drawer to indorse but not the genuineness or validity of his indorsement; (c) if payable to the order of a third party, the existence of the payee and his then capacity to indorse, but not the genuineness or validity of his indorsement.[57]

23.17 **Indorsement.**[58]—The holder of a bill may at any stage transfer it by indorsement and delivery. Where there are several indorsers their liability *inter se* is, in the absence of proof to the contrary, regulated by

---

[47] s. 65(1).
[48] s. 65(4).
[49] s. 66(2).
[50] s. 56.
[51] s. 17(2)(*a*). For conflict of laws, *cf.* s. 72(1).
[52] s. 19(2).
[53] s. 44(1).
[54] s. 44(2).
[55] s. 44(2).
[56] s. 54(1).
[57] s. 54(2).
[58] For conflict of laws, *cf.* s. 72(1).

the order in which the indorsements appear on the bill since that is assumed to be the order in which they were made.[59] The indorser by indorsing a bill engages that it shall be accepted and paid according to its tenor, and that if it be dishonoured he will compensate the holder or a subsequent indorser who is compelled to pay it, provided that the requisite proceedings on dishonour are duly taken.[60] He is precluded from denying to a holder in due course the genuineness and regularity of the drawer's signature and of all previous indorsements;[61] and from denying to any subsequent indorsee, whether a holder in due course or not, that the bill was at the time of his indorsement a valid and subsisting bill, and that he had then a good title thereto.[62]

23.18 **Holder in Due Course.**—Every holder of a bill is prima facie deemed to be a holder in due course;[63] but if in an action on a bill it is admitted or proved that the acceptance, issue or subsequent negotiation of the bill is affected with fraud,[64] duress, force and fear, or illegality, the burden of proof is shifted, unless and until the holder proves that, subsequent to the alleged fraud or illegality, value has in good faith been given for the bill.[65]

23.19 **Rights of Holder.**—A holder in due course may sue on the bill in his own name. He holds the bill free from any defect of title of prior parties, as well as from mere personal defences available to prior parties among themselves, and may enforce payment against all parties liable on the bill.[66] Thus a holder who takes under the conditions which make him a holder in due course gets a valid title to the bill although the person from whom he took it may be a thief, or may have obtained the bill by fraud. But a party who has been fraudulently induced to sign a bill under the impression that it was a document of a different character is not liable even to a holder in due course.[67] Even if his title is defective, a holder in due course who negotiates the bill to a holder in due course gives him a good title.[68] A holder in due course with a defective title can give a valid discharge for a bill.[69]

A holder of a bill who is not a holder in due course, may sue on the bill in his own name,[70] but even although he has given value for the bill, he takes no higher right than that of the indorser, and is subject to all

---

[59] s. 32(5).
[60] s. 55(2)(a).
[61] s. 55(2)(b).
[62] s. 55(2).
[63] Cf. s. 29(1) and para. 23.4, supra.
[64] i.e. common-law fraud: Österreichische Länderbank v. S'Elite Ltd. [1981] 1 Q.B. 565.
[65] s. 30(2). For definition of holder in due course, see s. 29(1) and para. 23.4, supra.
[66] s. 38(1) and 2.
[67] Foster v. Mackinnon (1869) L.R. 4 C.P. 704; Lewis v. Clay (1897) 67 L.J.Q.B. 224. As to forgery see para. 23.34, infra.
[68] s. 38(3).
[69] s. 38(3).
[70] s. 38(1).

equities affecting him. Such is the case of a party who takes the bill when it is overdue or has been dishonoured;[71] or when it is not complete and regular on the face of it and with notice, or with good reason to suppose, that the title of the party from whom he takes is defective[72] or that it was delivered conditionally.[73]

23.20 Payee.—A bill may be drawn payable to a named payee; or to two or more payees jointly; to the holder of an office;[74] or to order[75] or to bearer.[76] It becomes payable to bearer if indorsed by the payee in blank, that is, without specifying a particular indorsee.[77] When a bill has been indorsed in blank any holder may convert the blank indorsement into a special indorsement by writing above the indorser's signature a direction to pay the bill to, or to the order of, himself or some other person.[78] When the payee is a fictitious or non-existing person the bill may be treated as payable to bearer.[79] In the construction of this rule it has been held that it includes the case where the payee is actually non-existent and also the case where the name of an existing party is inserted by the drawer without any intention that that party should receive the money or have any connection with the bill,[80] but not the case where the drawer intended the payee (an existing person) to receive the money, though he may have been induced to form that intention by fraud and the payee may be unaware that his name has been used.[81] These authorities show that if the bill may be treated as payable to bearer anyone who takes with the name of the payee indorsed upon it (though that indorsement be a forgery) may enforce it against prior parties, whereas, if the bill cannot be so treated, no one can acquire a valid title except on a genuine signature by the nominal payee.

23.21 Presentment for Payment.—A bill payable on demand must be presented for payment within a reasonable time after its issue, in a question as to the liability of the drawer, or within a reasonable time after indorsement, in a question as to the liability of the indorser.[82] But the drawer of a cheque is not discharged by delay in presentment except in so far as he has suffered damage thereby.[83] When a bill is payable at

---

[71] *Semple* v. *Kyle* (1902) 4 F. 421; *cf.* s. 29(1).
[72] *Jones* v. *Gordon* (1877) 2 App. Cas. 616.
[73] *Martini* v. *Steel & Craig* (1878) 6 R. 342.
[74] s. 7(2).
[75] s. 3(1) and s. 8(4).
[76] s. 3(1) and s. 7(3).
[77] s. 34(1).
[78] s. 34(4).
[79] s. 7(3).
[80] *Bank of England* v. *Vagliano* [1891] A.C. 107; *Clutton* v. *Attenborough* [1897] A.C. 90.
[81] *North and South Wales Bank* v. *Macbeth* [1908] A.C. 137.
[82] s. 45(2).
[83] s. 74(1).

a fixed date it must be presented for payment at that date, failing which the drawer and indorsers are discharged.[84] Failure in presentment does not, however, affect the liability of the acceptor.[85]

23.22 **Excuses for Delay in Presentment for Payment.**—Delay in presentment is excused where caused by circumstances beyond the control of the holder, and not attributable to any default, misconduct or negligence of his.[86] Presentment is dispensed with when it cannot be effected by the exercise of reasonable diligence, by waiver, express or implied, where the drawee is a fictitious party, but not merely because the holder has reason to believe that the bill if presented will be dishonoured.[87]

The rules as to the method of presentment for payment are similar to those applicable to presentment for acceptance.[88]

23.23 **Notice of Dishonour.**—Where a bill has been dishonoured either by non-acceptance or non-payment, notice of dishonour must be given to the drawer and each indorser, and any of these to whom notice is not given is discharged.[89] The notice must be given within a reasonable time, and as a general rule it is not given within a reasonable time unless, if the parties reside in the same place, it is dispatched in time to reach the party on the day after the bill was dishonoured, or unless, if the parties reside in different places, it is posted on that day.[90] It is sufficient if the holder can prove that he posted the notice in time though it may be delayed in transit, or may never arrive.[91] The notice is bad if it was received before the bill itself was dishonoured.[92] Notice may be oral or in writing, and no special form of notice is specified by the Act.[93] The return of the dishonoured bill to the drawer or to an indorser is sufficient notice.[94] For the specific rules as to giving notice reference must be made to the Act (section 49).

23.24 **Protest: When Necessary.**—Besides giving notice the holder of a bill which on the face of it bears to be a foreign bill must, in order to preserve recourse against the drawer or prior indorsers, protest it in the case of either non-acceptance or non-payment.[95] Protest is not necessary

---

[84] s. 45(1).
[85] s. 52(1); *McNeill* v. *Innes Chambers & Co.*, 1917 S.C. 540 (summary diligence).
[86] s. 46(1); *Bank of Scotland* v. *Lamont* (1889) 16 R. 769.
[87] s. 46(2). As to circumstances amounting to waiver, see *McTavish's Factor* v. *Michael's Trs.*, 1912 S.C. 425.
[88] s. 45(3)–(8) and see para. 23.13, *supra*. For the application of these rules to modern banking practice, see *Barclays Bank* v. *Bank of England* [1985] 1 All E.R. 385; Chalmers & Guest, *Bills of Exchange*, pp. 373 *et seq*.
[89] s. 48. See *Lombard Banking* v. *Central Garage and Engineering Co.* [1963] 1 Q.B. 220.
[90] s. 49, r.12.
[91] s. 49, r. 15; *Dunlop* v. *Higgins* (1848) 6 Bell's App. 195.
[92] *Eaglehill* v. *J. Needham* [1973] A.C. 992.
[93] s. 49, rr. 5 and 7.
[94] s. 49, r. 6.
[95] s. 51(2).

in the case of an inland bill merely to preserve recourse,[96] but is necessary if it is desired to enforce the bill by summary diligence.[97]

23.25　Form of Protest: Noting.—For the purpose of protest the bill must be noted by a notary public not later than the succeeding business day after it has been dishonoured.[98] Noting is effected by the notary public marking on the bill the date of dishonour, his initials and the letters 'N.P.'[99] The protest may be subsequently extended as of the date of the noting.[1] It must contain a copy of the bill, must be signed by the notary making it and must specify the person at whose request the bill is protested, the place and date of protest, the cause or reason for protesting, the demand made and the answer given, or the fact that the drawee or acceptor could not be found.[2] If the bill has been lost or destroyed, or is wrongly detained from the person entitled to hold it, protest may be made on a copy or written particular thereof.[3] In a question of recourse protest is dispensed with by any circumstances which would dispense with notice of dishonour.[4]

Where the services of a notary public cannot be obtained at the place where the bill was dishonoured, any householder or substantial resident of the place may, in the presence of two witnesses, give a certificate, signed by the witnesses, attesting the dishonour of the bill, and the certificate shall in all respects operate as if it were a formal protest of the bill.[5] It is doubtful whether a householder's certificate will form a warrant for summary diligence.[6]

23.26　Summary Diligence.—Summary diligence is the method by which payment of a bill or promissory note may be enforced without the necessity of an action to constitute the debt. It has been held in the Outer House that it is incompetent on a dishonoured cheque.[7] The Bills of Exchange Act provides (section 98) that nothing in the Act or in any repeal effected thereby shall extend or restrict or in any way alter or affect the law and practice in Scotland on the subject. The statutes in force are the Bills of Exchange Act 1681, the Inland Bills Act 1696, and the Bills of Exchange (Scotland) Act 1772, sections 42 and 43. Summary diligence is competent when a bill (or note) is dishonoured either by non-acceptance or non-payment. In the latter case it is competent

---

[96] s. 51(1).

[97] See para. 23.26, *infra*.

[98] Bills of Exchange (Time of Noting) Act 1917, s.1.

[99] *Encyclopaedia of Scottish Legal Styles*, Vol. 1, p. 415.

[1] s. 51(4).

[2] s. 51(7); *Encyclopaedia*, Vol. 1, pp. 416–420.

[3] s. 51(8).

[4] s. 51(9).

[5] s. 94. See *Sommerville* v. *Aaronson* (1898) 25 R. 524.

[6] *Sommerville* v. *Aaronson, supra,* at p. 525 *per* Lord Kyllachy (Ordinary); *McRobert* v. *Lindsay* (1898) 14 Sh. Ct. Rep. 89; (1898) 5 S.L.T. 317.

[7] *Glickman* v. *Linda*, 1950 S.C. 18.

against any party to the bill, including the acceptor; in the former against any actual party to the bill, but not against the drawee who has refused acceptance. For summary diligence a regular protest is required, and therefore while presentment for payment is not necessary to render the acceptor liable, it is necessary, and must be regularly made, in order to justify summary diligence against him.[8] But the practice under which a period of six months is allowed for presentment to the acceptor, without prejudice to summary diligence against him, has been sustained.[9] The protest of the bill or note must be registered not more than six months after dishonour (by non-acceptance or non-payment as the case may be) in the Books of Council and Session or the books of a sheriff court to whose jurisdiction the party is subject.[10] The process cannot be used against a party who is not subject to the jurisdiction of the Scottish courts, even although the bill may be payable in Scotland.[11] When registered, an extract may be obtained, which is a warrant for arrestment, or for a charge for payment to be followed by poinding or by a petition for sequestration. The induciae of the charge are six days.[12]

23.27 **When Summary Diligence Competent.**—Summary diligence is competent only for the amount of the bill or note, with interest. Damages or expenses must be recovered by action.[13] It is generally competent only when the liability of the party appears on the face of the bill without extrinsic proof,[14] and hence is not competent against a party who has signed the bill merely by initials,[15] or against an acceptor who has accepted conditionally,[16] or on a bill which has been cancelled by mistake.[17] But it was held competent against a firm carrying on business under a descriptive name, in the case where the bill was signed by all the partners.[18]

23.28 **Bill as Assignation.**[19]—The Act provides (section 53(2)): 'Subject to section 75A of this Act, in Scotland, where the drawee of a bill has in his hands funds available for the payment thereof, the bill operates as an assignment of the sum for which it is drawn in favour of the holder, from the time when the bill is presented to the drawee.' This rule applies, in the case of bills, where the bill has been presented for

[8] *Neill* v. *Dobson* (1902) 4 F. 625.
[9] *McNeill* v. *Innes Chambers & Co.*, 1917 S.C. 540.
[10] Bills of Exchange Act 1681.
[11] *Charteris* v. *Clydesdale Bank* (1882) 19 S.L.R. 602; *Davis* v. *Cadman* (1897) 24 R. 297.
[12] Bills of Exchange Act 1681; Graham Stewart, *Diligence*, p. 313.
[13] Erskine, III, ii, 36.
[14] *Summers* v. *Marianski* (1843) 6 D. 286.
[15] *Munro* v. *Munro* (1820) Hume 81.
[16] Thomson, *Bills of Exchange*, p. 223.
[17] *Dominion Bank* v. *Bank of Scotland* (1889) 16 R. 1081; affd. (1891) 18 R. (H.L.) 21.
[18] *Rosslund Cycle Co.* v. *McCreadie*, 1907 S.C. 1208.
[19] See Cusine, 1977 J.R. 98.

acceptance, and acceptance has been refused. The holder acquires a
completed right to any funds in the hands of the drawee which are
available to meet the bill, in a question either with the drawee himself,
or with other parties having competing assignations.[20] As the principle is
that presentment operates as intimation of the assignation of the debt
due by the drawee to the drawer, it is no objection that it may have
been irregular in form.[21] In the case of cheques, presentment for
payment, though payment may be refused on the ground of insufficient
funds to meet the cheque, operates as a completed assignation of any
balance there may be to the drawer's credit, and, in the event of the
drawer's bankruptcy, will give the holder a preferential right to that
balance.[22] But in order that presentment may operate as an assignation
of the balance standing at the credit of the drawer of a cheque there
must be a debt due by the bank to him. In *Kirkwood* v. *Clydesdale
Bank*,[23] A had several accounts with a bank, including a current
account, in which there was a balance standing to his credit. He drew a
cheque on this account. It was presented and payment was refused on
the ground that notice of A's death had been received. On the various
accounts A was in debt to the bank, though the debt was covered by
securities. In a question between the payee of the cheque and the bank
it was held that presentment did not operate as an assignation of the
balance due on the current account, because, although there was a
credit balance on that account, there was no debt due by the bank to A.

23.29 **Discharge of Bill.**—A bill is discharged by payment in due course, when
made by or behalf of the drawee or acceptor.[24] Payment in due course
means payment at or after the maturity of the bill to the holder thereof
in good faith and without notice that his title is defective.[25] In the case
of an accommodation bill payment in due course by the person
accommodated discharges the bill.[26] Payment by the drawer or by an
indorser does not discharge the bill; it remains available as a document
of debt against the acceptor or other antecedent party.[27] When the
acceptor of a bill is or becomes the holder of it at or after its maturity,
in his own right, the bill is discharged.[28] On the other hand, the mere
fact that a party liable in a bill is in possession of it raises a presumption
of payment, but does not necessarily discharge the bill.[29] So where a

[20] *Watt's Trs.* v. *Pinkney* (1853) 16 D. 279.
[21] *Ibid.*, opinion of Lord Ivory, at p. 287.
[22] *British Linen Co.* v. *Carruthers* (1883) 10 R. 923. For the position where payment has
been countermanded, see para. 23.40, *infra*.
[23] 1908 S.C. 20.
[24] s. 59(1); *Coats* v. *Union Bank*, 1929 S.C. (H.L.) 114. Proof of payment must be by
writ or oath: *Nicol's Trs.* v. *Sutherland*, 1951 S.C. (H.L.) 21.
[25] s. 59(1).
[26] s. 59(3).
[27] s. 59(2) stating also certain qualifications.
[28] s. 61; and see *Nash* v. *De Freville* [1900] 2 Q.B. 72.
[29] Erskine, III, iv, 5.

promissory note was given up, and a new one granted, it was held that the fact that the debtor was in possession of the original note did not infer abandonment of any claim for interest on it.[30] A bill may also be discharged by a renunciation at or after its maturity by the holder of his rights against the acceptor, or any other party to the bill.[31] The renunciation, unless the bill is given up to the party discharged, must be in writing, and is not effectual in a question with a holder in due course without notice.[32] A bill is discharged by its cancellation by the holder or his agent,[33] and the liability of any party on the bill is discharged by the intentional cancellation of his signature by the holder or his agent, this carrying with it the discharge of any indorser who would have had a right of recourse against the party whose signature is cancelled.[34] Cancellation which is unintentional, without the authority of the holder, or done under a mistake, is inoperative, but the onus of proof is laid upon the party founding on the cancelled bill.[35]

23.30 **Alteration of Bill.**—Where a bill or acceptance is materially altered without the assent of all parties liable on it, the bill is avoided, except as against a party who has himself made, authorised or assented to the alteration, and subsequent indorsers, unless the alteration is not apparent, and the bill is in the hands of a holder in due course who may enforce payment of the bill according to its original tenor.[36] It is immaterial that the party founding on the alteration as involving avoidance has suffered no prejudice.[37] The drawee of a bill of exchange owes no duty to those into whose hands the bill may come to exercise any care in accepting it, and therefore where a bill was accepted with a blank space which rendered it possible to alter the amount, and the amount was altered, it was held that the acceptor was not liable to a holder in due course for any more than the original sum in the bill.[38] But this rule does not apply in a case between banker and customer.[39]

23.31 **Inchoate Bills.**—The Act provides (section 20): 'Where a simple signature on a blank paper is delivered by the signer in order that it may be converted into a bill, it operates as a prima facie authority to fill it up as a complete bill for any amount using the signature for that of the drawer, or the acceptor, or an indorser; and in like manner, when a bill is wanting in any material particular, the person in possession of it has a prima facie authority to fill up the omission in any way he thinks fit.'

[30] *Hope Johnstone* v. *Cornwall* (1895) 22 R. 314.
[31] s. 62(1).
[32] s. 62(2).
[33] s. 63(1).
[34] s. 63(2).
[35] s. 63(3). See *Dominion Bank* v. *Anderson* (1888) 15 R. 408.
[36] s. 64(1); *Slingsby* v. *District Bank* [1932] 1 K.B. 544.
[37] *Koch* v. *Dicks* [1933] 1 K.B. 307.
[38] *Scholfield* v. *Lord Londesborough* [1896] A.C. 514.
[39] See para. 23.38, *infra*.

Once the bill has been filled up and transferred, complete and regular on the face of it, to a holder in due course, it may be enforced by him according to its tenor,[40] although it has not been filled up according to the authority given, as where a larger sum than that agreed upon was inserted,[41] or after material delay, as where a blank acceptance was kept and filled up after the giver had become bankrupt and obtained a discharge.[42] In a question between the original parties it must be filled up 'within a reasonable time, and strictly in accordance with the authority given.'[43] Thus the party receiving the blank acceptance, at least if, as is usual, it was given for his accommodation, cannot fill it up after the giver has been sequestrated.[44] The onus of proof that the bill has not been filled up in accordance with the authority given rests on the party who signed and delivered it.[45] In the absence of any contract to the contrary there is implied authority to fill in the name of a third party as drawer,[46] or, in the case of a bill payable to the drawer's order, to the drawer to insert his own name as payee.[47] Where an acceptance addressed to A was found after his death still uncompleted, it was doubted whether his executor had any right to complete it as a bill of exchange, but held that he might sue upon it as a document of debt, which laid on the party who signed the onus of proof that it was not delivered as an acknowledgment of debt, or that the debt had afterwards been paid.[48]

23.32 Accommodation Bills.—According to Scots law the fact that no consideration has been given for a bill, as where it was, for instance, a donation, is no objection to its enforcement, either by the drawer in a question with the acceptor, or by any holder.[49] Every party whose signature appears on a bill is prima facie deemed to have become a party thereto for value.[50] If, however, it is admitted or proved that the true relations of the parties are not as they appear on the face of the bill, and that one or more of the parties have received no value for the liability they have incurred, the bill may be regarded as an accommodation bill, and differs in certain of its incidents from a bill granted for value. The normal case of an accommodation bill is where, as between themselves, the drawer is the true debtor, and the acceptor a party who has interposed as cautioner for him. The Act provides (section 28): 'An accommodation party to a bill is a person who has

---

[40] s. 20(2).
[41] *Lloyds Bank* v. *Cooke* [1907] 1 K.B. 794.
[42] *McMeekin* v. *Russell* (1881) 8 R. 587.
[43] s. 20(2).
[44] *McKeekin* v. *Russell, supra.*
[45] *Anderson* v. *Somerville* (1898) 1 F. 90.
[46] *Russell* v. *Banknock Coal Co.* (1897) 24 R. 1009.
[47] *Macdonald* v. *Nash* [1924] A.C. 625.
[48] *Lawson's Exrs.* v. *Watson*, 1907 S.C. 1353.
[49] *Law* v. *Humphrey* (1876) 3 R. 1192.
[50] s. 30(1).

signed a bill as drawer, acceptor or indorser, without receiving value therefor, and for the purpose of lending his name to some other person.'[51] In a question with any holder who has given value for the bill, an accommodation party is liable, and it is immaterial whether the holder did or did not know that the bill was an accommodation bill.[52] 'Holder' in this case includes a transferee of the bill, who has taken it for value, but without indorsement.[53] But in questions between the original parties their rights are regulated by the true relations between them which may be proved by parole evidence.[54] So where several directors had indorsed a promissory note it was held, on proof that they had done so as guarantors for the company, that the general rule that a prior was liable to a later indorser was displaced, and that the director who had been compelled to pay could recover a proportionate share from each of the others.[55] The holder of an accommodation bill, when the acceptor is the person lending his name and the claim is made against the drawer as the person accommodated, is not barred by failure to present the bill for payment,[56] failure to give notice of dishonour,[57] or failure to protest the bill for non-acceptance or non-payment.[58]

23.33 **Accommodation Bills in Bankruptcy.**[59]—Where an accommodation bill is discounted and the parties are sequestrated the bank as holder may rank on each estate for the whole amount of the bill. As no debt can be ranked twice on the same estate, the trustee on the estate of the party who has lent his name cannot rank on the estate of the party accommodated for the dividend paid by the estate under his charge on the bill. Nor can he secure the same result by claiming a right of retention over property in his hands belonging to the estate of the party accommodated, in the case where that property was not expressly pledged, to meet the liability arising on the bill.[60] If it was so pledged, the rule in Scotland is that it may be applied to relieve the estate of the party who has lent his name for any dividend paid on the bill, and that any surplus is an asset in the estate of the party accommodated; the English rule is that property so pledged may be taken by the holder of the bill, who deducts its value from the sum due on the bill, and ranks on the estates of the parties to it only for the balance.[61]

---

[51] 'Value' is defined by s. 27.
[52] s. 28(2).
[53] *Hood* v. *Stewart* (1890) 17 R. 749.
[54] s. 100.
[55] *Macdonald* v. *Whitfield* (1883) 8 App. Cas. 733.
[56] s. 46(2)(*c*).
[57] s. 50(2)(*c*). The same applies to an indorser: s. 50(2)(*d*).
[58] s. 51(9).
[59] Goudy, *Bankruptcy* (4th ed.), pp. 571–576.
[60] *Anderson* v. *Mackinnon* (1876) 3 R. 608. See also *Mackinnon* v. *Monkhouse* (1881) 9 R. 393.
[61] *Royal Bank* v. *Saunders' Trs.* (1882) 9 R. (H.L.) 67.

23.34 Forged Bills.—As a general rule no liability is incurred by a person whose name is forged as a party to a bill, or used without his authority.[62] He cannot ratify but may adopt the bill, and will then be liable upon it.[63] Short of adoption he may be personally barred from disputing the validity of his signature if his conduct has caused loss to the holder.[64] But such cases are very exceptional; and mere failure to repudiate the bill at once will not infer liability.[65]

The Act provides (section 24): 'Subject to the provisions of this Act, where a signature on a bill is forged or placed thereon without the authority of the person whose signature it purports to be, the forged or unauthorised signature is wholly inoperative, and no right to retain the bill or to give a discharge therefor, or to enforce payment thereof against any party thereto can be acquired through or under that signature, unless the party against whom it is sought to retain or enforce payment of the bill is precluded from setting up the forgery or want of authority.' The provisions of the Act forming exceptions to this rule are (1) the safeguards for a banker who pays a cheque on a forged indorsement;[66] (2) the right to treat the bill as payable to bearer when the payee is a fictitious or non-existent person;[67] (3) the rule that, in a question with a holder in due course, the acceptor is precluded from denying the genuineness of the signature of the drawer;[68] and an indorser from denying both the genuineness of the signature of the drawer or of prior indorsers[69] and, in a question with his immediate or a subsequent indorsee, that the bill was at the time of his indorsement a valid and subsisting bill, and that he had then a good title thereto.[70] Thus the acceptor of a bill, who pays on a forged indorsement, cannot charge the drawer, and a bank which pays on behalf of the acceptor cannot charge its customer.[71] A person who has unwittingly paid on a bill vitiated by forgery or after a material and unauthorised alteration may recover from the holder, unless by delay he had prejudiced the holder's right of recourse against other parties to the bill.[72]

23.35 Prescription.—The rules relating to prescription in connection with bills of exchange and cheques have been considered above.[73]

---

[62] s. 24. *Cf. Strathmore Group Ltd.* v. *Crédit Lyonnais*, 1994 S.L.T. 1023.
[63] *Mackenzie* v. *British Linen Co.* (1881) 8 R. (H.L.) 8.
[64] *Mackenzie* v. *British Linen Co., supra*; *Greenwood* v. *Martins Bank* [1933] A.C. 51.
[65] *Mackenzie, supra*; *British Linen Co.* v. *Cowan* (1906) 8 F. 704.
[66] See now Cheques Act 1957, s. 1; para. 23.39, *infra*.
[67] s. 7(3); para. 23.20, *supra*.
[68] s. 54(2)(a).
[69] s. 55(2)(b).
[70] s. 55(2)(c).
[71] *Bank of England* v. *Vagliano* [1891] A.C. 107 at p. 131, *per* Lord Watson.
[72] *Imperial Bank of Canada* v. *Bank of Hamilton* [1903] A.C. 49.
[73] para. 15.25, *supra*.

23.36   Evidence.—The construction of section 100, which allows parole evidence of any facts relevant to any question of liability on a bill, has been already considered.[74]

23.37   Cheques.[75]—The statutory definition of a cheque is, 'A bill of exchange drawn on a banker payable on demand.'[76] It is enacted that except where otherwise provided in Part III of the Act the statutory provisions applicable to a bill of exchange payable on demand apply to a cheque. So the holder of a cheque, if in circumstances which satisfy the provisions of section 29,[77] has all the rights of the holder in due course of a bill of exchange.[78] The chief difference is that delay in presentment of a cheque does not give the drawer any remedy except in so far as he has suffered prejudice, which he can only do in the event of the bankruptcy of the banker.[79]

23.38   Contract between Banker and Customer.[80]—A banker undertakes to pay cheques drawn by his customer so long as he has funds in his hands and to take reasonable care in doing so.[81] He may determine the contract at any time by giving notice, but, provided that he has funds to meet them, must pay cheques drawn before the notice was received.[82] He is under no obligation to allow an overdraft, and no such obligation can be inferred for the future merely from the fact that the customer has been allowed to overdraw in the past.[83] Even where a banker holds a cash credit bond there is no obligation, in the absence of express agreement, to allow the customer to overdraw to the extent of the cash credit, though a refusal to honour a cheque without prior notice to the customer would probably be wrongful.[84] Where a customer keeps several accounts, *e.g.* a current and loan account, with a banker, the latter is not entitled, without notice, to mass the accounts together and to refuse to honour a cheque in respect of a debit balance thence arising.[85] But it has been held that where a customer had current accounts with two branches of a bank, the bank was entitled, without notice, to refuse to honour a cheque on the ground that, taking the two accounts together, the customer was overdrawn.[86] A bank is not bound

---

[74] para. 6.13, *supra.*
[75] Wilson, *Debt* (2nd ed.), Chap. 6; Chalmers & Guest, *Bills of Exchange*, Pt. III; *First Sport Ltd.* v. *Barclays Bank plc* [1993] 1 W.L.R. 1229.
[76] s. 73; see Chalmers and Guest, *Bills of Exchange*, pp. 599 *et seq.*
[77] para. 23.4, *supra.*
[78] *McLean* v. *Clydesdale Bank* (1883) 11 R. (H.L.) 1.
[79] s. 74(1).
[80] See Chalmers and Guest, *op. cit.*, pp. 614 *et seq.*
[81] *Selangor United Rubber Estates Ltd.* v. *Craddock (No. 3)* [1968] 1 W.L.R. 1555; *Lipkin Gorman* v. *Karpnale Ltd.* [1989] 1 W.L.R. 1340. The duty is contractual: *National Bank of Greece* v. *Pinios Co. No. 1* [1990] 1 A.C. 637 (Court of Appeal).
[82] *King* v. *British Linen Co.* (1899) 1 F. 928.
[83] *Ritchie* v. *Clydesdale Bank* (1886) 13 R. 866.
[84] *Johnston* v. *Commercial Bank* (1858) 20 D. 790.
[85] *Kirkwood* v. *Clydesdale Bank*, 1908 S.C. 20, at p. 25.
[86] *Garnett* v. *McKewan* (1872) L.R. 8 Ex. 10.

to pay at a branch other than that where the account is kept.[87] Dishonour of a cheque, without adequate grounds, is a breach of contract, and one for which the customer has been found entitled to damages; but damages will usually be nominal unless the customer is a trader, whose credit may be injured,[88] or can show that he has sustained actual loss.[89] Entries in a bank pass-book or counterfoil are prima facie evidence of the receipt of that amount of money against a bank which disputes their accuracy, and the onus of displacing the presumption of accuracy lies upon the bank.[90]

The customer's duties to his banker are strictly limited. He owes a duty to take reasonable care in drawing cheques and, if he draws them in a manner which facilitates alteration and the banker pays an altered cheque in good faith and without negligence, he may debit the customer with the full amount he has paid.[91] The customer is also under a duty to disclose forgeries when he becomes aware of them, and he will be barred from raising the matter at a later stage if he remains silent and allows the banker to pay.[92] It is a condition of the contract between the bank and its customer regulating the use of a cheque card that the customer who draws a cheque in conjunction with a card cannot countermand it. In addition the bank gives its customer authority, within specified limits, by using the card to bind the bank to pay the cheque, irrespective of the state of the customer's account.[93] A bank which issues travellers' cheques may be under a duty to refund the value of lost or stolen cheques.[94]

23.39 **Indorsement.**—The object of the Cheques Act 1957 was to restrict the circumstances in which indorsement of cheques is required. To that end it is provided that when a cheque drawn on a banker is paid by the banker in good faith and in the ordinary course of business, he is deemed to have paid the cheque in due course, although there is no indorsement or the indorsement of the name of the payee is irregular,[95] e.g. where the initials of the indorsement do not match those of the

---

[87] *Clare* v. *Dresdner Bank* [1915] 2 K.B. 576; *Richardson* v. *Richardson* [1927] P. 228.

[88] *King* v. *British Linen Co.* (1899) 1 F. 928.

[89] *Gibbons* v. *Westminster Bank* [1939] 2 K.B. 882. These rules relate to dealings with a customer's current account. They may not be applicable where the dealings are with the type of deposit account on which cheques cannot be drawn: *Gibb* v. *Lombank*, 1962 S.L.T. 288.

[90] *Couper's Trs.* v. *National Bank* (1889) 16 R. 412; *Docherty* v. *Royal Bank of Scotland*, 1963 S.L.T. (Notes) 43.

[91] *London Joint Stock Bank* v. *Macmillan* [1918] A.C. 777; *Slingsby* v. *District Bank* [1932] 1 K.B. 544; *Tai Hing Cotton Mill Ltd.* v. *Liu Chong Hing Bank* [1986] A.C. 80.

[92] *Greenwood* v. *Martins Bank* [1933] A.C. 51.

[93] *R.* v. *Charles* [1977] A.C. 177, *per* Lord Diplock at p. 182; *Re Charge Card Services* [1987] Ch. 150 at p. 166, *per* Millett J.; point left open by the Court of Appeal, [1989] Ch. 497); Chalmers & Guest, *Bills of Exchange*, pp. 621–22. On the position where a forged cheque is presented with a cheque card, see *First Sport Ltd.* v. *Barclays Bank plc, supra.*

[94] *El Awadi* v. *B.C.C.I.* [1990] 1 Q.B. 606; Chalmers & Guest, *Bills of Exchange*, pp. 606–9.

[95] Cheques Act 1957, s. 1.

payee. He may therefore charge his customer with the amount so paid, and incurs no liability by reason only of the absence of, or irregularity in, indorsement. Consequently the banker may in practice ignore indorsements. But the protection thus given to a banker does not apply where the cheque, before payment, has obviously been altered in a material particular,[96] nor where the cheque is crossed and the banker pays in disregard of the crossing.[97] In such circumstances the banker pays the cheque at his own risk. And the section applies only to the banker on whom the cheque is drawn, and does not protect any third party who may pay on a forged indorsement.[98]

To allow the collecting banker to sue on a cheque which has not been indorsed, it is provided that a banker who gives value for, or has a lien on, a cheque payable to order which the holder delivers to him for collection without indorsing it, has such (if any) rights as he would have had if, upon delivery, the holder had indorsed it in blank.[99] This is so even where the holder lodges the cheque for collection for an account other than his own.[1]

An unindorsed cheque which appears to have been paid by the banker on whom it is drawn is evidence of the receipt by the payee of the sum payable by the cheque.[2]

The practical effect is that the payee is not now required to indorse the cheque when he lodges it with his bank for collection. As a matter of banking practice,[3] an indorsee is required to indorse the cheque when he lodges it for collection. It is still, of course, necessary for the payee to indorse the cheque if he is negotiating it to a third party.

23.40   **Determination of Authority to Pay.**—The 1882 Act provides (section 75) that the duty and authority of a banker to pay a cheque drawn on him are determined by countermand of payment and notice of his customer's death. When payment is countermanded, the banker is treated as having no funds available for payment of the cheque.[4] On notice of the customer's death the cheque (if duly presented) will operate as an assignation in favour of the payee of any funds in the banker's hands available to meet the cheque, but in determining whether any funds are available, the balance on all the accounts kept by the customer must be considered.[5] Countermand of payment does not affect the liability of the drawer to any indorsee of the cheque who is in

---

[96] *Slingsby* v. *District Bank, supra.*
[97] *Smith* v. *Union Bank* (1875) 1 Q.B.D. 31.
[98] *Ogden* v. *Benas* (1874) 9 C.P. 513; but for statutory protection of collecting banker, see para. 23.43, *infra*, and 1957 Act, s. 4 and s. 3 of the Cheques Act 1992.
[99] 1957 Act, s. 2; see *Midland Bank* v. *Harris* [1963] 1 W.L.R. 1021.
[1] *Westminster Bank* v. *Zang* [1966] A.C. 182.
[2] 1957 Act, s. 3; see as to the effect of this, *Westminster Bank* v. *Zang, supra.*
[3] See the Memorandum of the Committee of London Clearing Bankers set out in Chalmers & Guest, *Bills of Exchange*, pp. 699 *et seq.*
[4] s. 75A inserted by s. 11 of the Law Reform (Misc. Provs.) (Scotland) Act 1985.
[5] *Kirkwood* v. *Clydesdale Bank*, 1908 S.C. 20; and see para. 23.28, *supra*.

the position of a holder in due course, for instance, to the bank to whom the payee may have paid the cheque.[6] The authority of a banker to pay a cheque is terminated by the vesting of the customer's estate in a permanent trustee in sequestration,[7] but if the banker proves that, when he paid the cheque in the ordinary course of business, he was unaware of the sequestration and had no reason to believe that the customer's estate had been sequestrated or was the subject of sequestration proceedings, the payment will be valid.[8] The banker's authority to pay is also determined by the liquidation of a customer company,[9] by the appointment of a *curator bonis* on a customer's estate,[10] or by arrestment.[11] A banker is under no obligation to inquire into the motives of the payee in taking payment.[12]

23.41 Crossed Cheques.—A cheque is crossed generally when it bears across its face two parallel lines, with or without the words '& Co.,' and with or without the words 'not negotiable.' It is crossed specially, and to the banker named, when it bears across its face the name of a banker, with or without the words 'not negotiable.'[13] A cheque may be crossed by the drawer, or by any holder. Where a cheque is crossed generally the holder may cross it specially, and may add the words 'not negotiable.' Where a cheque is crossed specially the banker to whom it is crossed may again cross it specially to another banker for collection. Where an uncrossed cheque, or a cheque crossed generally, is sent to a banker for collection, he may cross it specially to himself.[14] Except in these respects it is not lawful for any person to add to, or alter the crossing. The crossing is a material part of the cheque, and any unauthorised alteration avoids it.[15] But when the obliteration or alteration of the crossing is not apparent on the face of the cheque a banker who pays in good faith and without negligence may charge his customer with the amount so paid.[16]

23.42 Effect of Crossing.—The effect of a general crossing is that if the banker on whom it is drawn pays to anyone except a banker he is liable to the customer for any loss sustained owing to the cheque being so paid; of a special crossing, that the same liability is incurred by payment to anyone except the banker to whom the cheque is crossed, or his agent for

[6] *McLean* v. *Clydesdale Bank* (1883) 11 R. (H.L.) 1.
[7] Bankruptcy (Scotland) Act 1985, s. 32(8).
[8] *Ibid*, s. 32(9).
[9] Insolvency Act 1986, s. 127; *cf. Re Gray's Inn Construction Co. Ltd.* [1980] 1 W.L.R. 711 for validation.
[10] *Mitchell & Baxter* v. *Cheyne* (1891) 19 R. 324.
[11] Wallace and McNeil, *Banking Law* (10th ed., 1991), pp. 210–211.
[12] *Dickson* v. *National Bank*, 1917 S.C. (H.L.) 50.
[13] s. 76(2).
[14] s. 77(6).
[15] s. 78; see as to alteration of a material part, para. 23.30, *supra*.
[16] s. 79(2).

collection being a banker.[17] If it is paid in good faith and without negligence[18] in accordance with the crossing, the banker is placed in the same position and has the same rights as if payment had been made to the true owner of the cheque, *i.e.* the banker may debit his customer although the cheque has been stolen or paid on a forged indorsement.[19]

23.43 Protection of Collecting Bank.—Section 4 of the Cheques Act 1957 extended to a banker collecting on uncrossed cheques and other instruments the protection which was formerly provided by section 82 of the 1882 Act to a banker collecting upon a crossed cheque. Where in good faith and without negligence he receives payment for a customer of a cheque,[20] bank draft, customer's payment order or certain other instruments,[21] or, having credited a customer's account with the amount of such an instrument, receives payment thereof for himself, and the customer has no title or a defective title thereto, the banker will not incur any liability to the true owner by reason only of having received such payment.[22] To render a person a 'customer' within the meaning of the section he must have had some form of account with the bank before the cheque in question was presented; it is not enough that the bank had on previous occasions cashed cheques for him.[23] A banker is not to be treated as having been negligent[24] for this purpose by reason only of his failure to concern himself with the absence of or irregularity in indorsement of the instrument;[25] but the onus is on the banker to show that he acted in good faith and without negligence.[26]

23.44 Cheques Marked 'Not Negotiable.'—When a crossed cheque bears on it the words 'not negotiable' it does not mean that the cheque cannot be transferred but that the transferee gets no better title than his author had, and no better title can be obtained by an indorsee from him.[27] It is

---

[17] s. 79(2).

[18] But see s. 81A(2) inserted by s. 1 of the Cheques Act 1992.

[19] s. 80. The section does not apply to the case where a cheque has been materially altered (*Slingsby* v. *District Bank* [1932] 1 K.B. 544) but does apply to a cheque which is not transferable under s. 81A or otherwise: Cheques Act 1992, s. 2.

[20] Including a cheque which is not transferable under s. 81A or otherwise: Cheques Act 1992, s. 3.

[21] See 1957 Act, s. 4(2).

[22] 1957 Act, s. 4(1).

[23] *Great Western Ry.* v. *London and County Bank* [1901] A.C. 414; *Commissioners of Taxation* v. *English, Scottish and Australian Bank* [1920] A.C. 683; *Woods* v. *Martins Bank* [1959] 1 Q.B. 55.

[24] As to facts amounting to negligence, see *Underwood* v. *Bank of Liverpool* [1924] 1 K.B. 775; *Midland Bank* v. *Reckitt* [1933] A.C. 1; *Marfani & Co.* v. *Midland Bank* [1968] 1 W.L.R. 956; *Lumsden & Co.* v. *London Trustee Savings Bank* [1971] 1 Lloyd's Rep. 114. Negligence is not necessarily excluded by proof that an established banking practice has been followed: *Lloyds Bank* v. *Savory* [1932] 2 K.B. 122; affd. [1933] A.C. 201.

[25] s. 4(3). For contributory negligence, see Banking Act 1979, s. 47.

[26] *Lloyds Bank* v. *Savory* [1933] A.C. 201, *per* Lord Wright at p. 229; *Marfani & Co.* v. *Midland Bank, supra.*

[27] s. 81; *Ladup Ltd.* v. *Shaikh* [1983] Q.B. 225.

probably the law that no other words on a cheque can make it not negotiable.[28]

23.45 Non-Transferable Cheques.—Where a cheque is crossed 'account payee' or 'a/c payee,' whether or not with the word 'only,' the cheque is not transferable, and is only valid as between the parties to it.[29]

23.46 Certified Cheques.—When a bank certifies a cheque it undertakes that the customer has funds to meet it, and therefore will be liable on his failure.[30] Where, after certification, the cheque was fraudulently altered in amount, and, as altered, was paid to the holder by the certifying bank, it was held that the bank was entitled to recover from the holder.[31]

23.47 Promissory Notes.[32]—Promissory notes are dealt with by sections 83 to 89 of the Act. The statutory definition is (section 83(1)): 'A promissory note is an unconditional promise in writing made by one person to another signed by the maker, engaging to pay, on demand, or at a fixed or determinable future time, a sum certain in money to, or to the order of, a specified person or to bearer.' It is inchoate and incomplete until delivered to the payee or bearer.[33] The section provides that an instrument payable to maker's order is not a note within the section until it has been indorsed by the maker,[34] and that a note is not invalid merely because it contains a pledge of collateral security with a power to dispose thereof.[35] An instrument may be a promissory note though the words 'agree to pay,' and not 'promise to pay,' are used,[36] but not if it reserves an option to pay at an earlier date than the fixed date and so creates an uncertainty or contingency as to the time of payment.[37] A document which contained, in addition to a promise to pay, further and separate contractual stipulations was held not to be a promissory note.[38] In questions of stamp law it has been held that documents expressed as an obligation to pay a debt of unspecified amount,[39] or as a written obligation of indebtedness,[40] or as a mere receipt,[41] or as a promise to

---

[28] *Glen* v. *Semple* (1901) 3 F. 1134 (against cheque); *Importers Co.* v. *Westminster Bank* [1927] 2 K.B. 297.
[29] s. 81A(1), inserted by s. 1 of the Cheques Act 1992.
[30] *Gaden* v. *Newfoundland Bank* [1899] A.C. 281.
[31] *Imperial Bank of Canada* v. *Bank of Hamilton* [1903] A.C. 49.
[32] See Gow, *Mercantile Law*, pp. 455–56; Wilson, *Debt* (2nd ed.), pp. 75–77.
[33] s. 84.
[34] s. 83(2).
[35] s. 83(3).
[36] *Macfarlane* v. *Johnston* (1864) 2 M. 1210; *Vallance* v. *Forbes* (1879) 6 R. 1099; *McTaggart* v. *MacEachern's J.F.*, 1949 S.C. 503.
[37] *Williamson* v. *Rider* [1963] 1 Q.B. 89; *Claydon* v. *Bradley* [1987] 1 W.L.R. 521.
[38] *Dickie* v. *Singh*, 1974 S.L.T. 129.
[39] *Henderson* v. *Dawson* (1895) 22 R. 895.
[40] *Todd* v. *Wood* (1897) 24 R. 1104.
[41] *Welsh's Trs.* v. *Forbes* (1885) 12 R. 851.

pay a certain sum with interest at an unspecified rate,[42] were not promissory notes. A mere obligation to pay, not addressed to anyone, and not bearing to be payable to bearer, was held not to be a promissory note, and to be invalid as a 'blank bond' under the Blank Bonds and Trusts Act 1695.[43] It is no objection to the validity of a note that it contains provisions safeguarding the holder in the event of time being given to one or other of the joint makers.[44]

The provisions of the Act as to bills apply also to promissory notes.[45] In applying them the maker of a note corresponds with the acceptor of a bill, the first indorser with the drawer of an accepted bill payable to drawer's order.[46] The provisions relating to (a) presentment for acceptance, (b) acceptance, (c) acceptance supra protest, and (d) bills in a set do not apply to promissory notes.[47] A further difference is that where a foreign note is dishonoured protest is unnecessary.[48]

Presentment for payment is necessary in order to make an indorser liable,[49] but is not necessary in order to make the maker liable, unless it is in the body of it made payable at a particular place.[50] It must then be presented at that place, but not necessarily at the date of payment of the principal sum or of any instalment.[51] If a note payable on demand is not presented for payment within a reasonable time of indorsement the indorser is discharged.[52] But it is not deemed to be overdue, so as to affect a holder with defects of title of which he had no notice, because it appears that a reasonable time for presenting it for payment had elapsed.[53]

The maker of a note, by making and delivering it, engages that he will pay it according to its tenor, and is precluded from denying to a holder in due course the existence of the payee and his then capacity to indorse.[54]

Further Reading

Bell, *Commentaries* (7th ed.) i, 411.
Byles, *Bills of Exchange* (26th ed., 1988).
Chalmers and Guest, *Bills of Exchange* (14th ed., 1991).
Goode, *Commercial Law* (1982), Ch. 17.
Hamilton, *Bills of Exchange Act* (1904).
Holden, *History of Negotiable Instruments in English Law* (1955).
Wilson, *The Scottish Law of Debt* (2nd ed., 1991), Ch. 5.

[42] *Lamberton* v. *Aiken* (1899) 2 F. 189.
[43] c. 25. *Duncan's Trs.* v. *Shand* (1872) 10 M. 984.
[44] *Kirkwood* v. *Carroll* [1903] 1 K.B. 531.
[45] s. 89(1).
[46] s. 89(2).
[47] s. 89(3).
[48] s. 89(4).
[49] s. 87(2).
[50] s. 87(1).
[51] s. 87(1); *Gordon* v. *Kerr* (1898) 25 R. 570.
[52] s. 86(1).
[53] s. 86(3).
[54] s. 88; as to delivery, see s. 84.

CHAPTER 24

INSURANCE

24.1 Nature of Contract.—Insurance may be a contract to indemnify against possible loss or to make payment on the occurrence of a certain event.[1] The contract need not necessarily provide for payment of a sum of money so long as it confers a benefit equivalent to payment—*i.e.* money's worth.[2] The continued existence or safety of anything, or the occurrence or non-occurrence of any event, may be made the subject of a policy of insurance, and there has been no case where, apart from questions of insurable interest, a policy has been held void as in substance a bet or *sponsio ludicra*.[3] The main distinction between contracts classed under the general name of insurance is between those cases where the contract is one of indemnity, and the insured recovers and can only recover, the amount of his loss, except in the case of valued policy,[4] and those which are merely contracts to pay on a certain condition being fulfilled. In the former class are fire and marine and third party accident insurance, in the latter, whole-life and endowment insurance. Marine insurance law, which has many specialities, has been codified by the Marine Insurance Act 1906. Before dealing with particular forms it may be well to consider certain principles which are generally applicable.

24.2 Terminology.—The party effecting the insurance is termed the insured or the assured; the party insuring, the insurer, office or (in marine insurance) underwriter; the consideration is known as the premium.

24.3 Restrictions upon Insurance Companies.—The right to act as insurer, in various forms of insurance, including life, fire and accident, motor

---

[1] Insurance contracts are unaffected by the Unfair Contract Terms Act 1977: 1977 Act, s. 15(3)(*a*). There are, however, two codes of practice promulgated by the Association of British Insurers, the *Statement of Long-Term Insurance Practice* and the *Statement of General Insurance Practice* (1986), dealing respectively with life and indemnity cover. These *Statements* only apply to contracts made with an ABI member and then only when the insured acts in a private capacity. Effectively, therefore, the *Statements* apply to consumer contracts.

[2] *Department of Trade and Industry* v. *St. Christopher Motorists' Association* [1974] 1 W.L.R. 99. *Cf. Medical Defence Union Ltd.* v. *Department of Trade* [1980] Ch. 82.

[3] See *Carlill* v. *Carbolic Smoke Ball Co.* [1893] 1 Q.B. 256; *Re London County, etc., Re-insurance Co.* [1922] 2 Ch. 67. However, public policy may render a contract unenforceable: *Gray* v. *Barr* [1971] 2 Q.B. 554.

[4] See paras. 24.24, 24.38, *infra.*

vehicle, marine, aviation and transit, is limited by legislation. The Insurance Companies Act 1982[5] regulates the entry of new companies into the insurance business[6] and the conduct of insurance business generally.[7] The Act has been amended to provide for the harmonisation of insurance authorisation throughout the European Community.[7a] The fundamental requirement[8] is that a person must have authorisation from the Secretary of State for the Department of Trade in order to carry on an insurance business of one of the specified classes.[9] The Secretary of State may not issue an authorisation unless the applicant insurance company has submitted proposals as to the conduct of business, financial forecasts and such other information as may be required by regulations. He must withhold authorisation if it appears to him that any director, controller or manager of the insurance company is not a fit and proper person to hold that office.[10] Once in business, an insurance company to which the Act applies must, *inter alia*, produce annual accounts, obey rules as to advertising and the conduct of insurance agents,[11] and maintain a margin of solvency.[12] The powers of the Secretary of State under the 1982 Act are far-reaching. He may communicate with an insurance company concerning inaccuracies or deficiencies in its accounts.[13] He may object to the appointment of a director or chief executive in the company.[14] He may in certain circumstances[15] actively intervene by imposing requirements and restrictions on the company, or ordering that an actuarial investigation be carried out.[16] He may also in certain circumstances petition for the winding up of the company.[17]

The Financial Services Act 1986 does not apply to insurers carrying on only indemnity (*i.e.* general) business. It does apply to life assurance business containing an investment element such as annuity and capital redemption contracts. It does not apply to companies providing only whole-life cover: *i.e.* policies with no savings element.[18] A company

[5] As amended.
[6] 1982 Act, Pt. I.
[7] 1982 Act, Pts. II and III.
[7a] Insurance Companies (Third Insurance Directives) Regulations 1994 (S.I. 1994 No. 1696).
[8] A requirement introduced by the Companies Act 1967.
[9] 1982 Act, ss. 1–3. Exceptions include Lloyd's, friendly societies, trade unions or employers' associations making provisions for strike benefits, and bankers.
[10] 1982 Act, s. 7(3).
[11] 1982 Act, ss. 17, 72 *et seq.* Contraventions may result in penalties. See for example *R. v. Clegg* [1977] C.L.Y. 619.
[12] 1982 Act, s. 32.
[13] 1982 Act, s. 22(5).
[14] 1982 Act, s. 60.
[15] For example, where there is a risk that a company may be unable to meet its liabilities, or where it has furnished the Secretary of State with misleading information: 1982 Act, s. 37.
[16] 1982 Act, ss. 38–45. He may also demand that information be supplied, or that the company take such action as he thinks appropriate.
[17] For example, where a company is in breach of its duties under the 1982 Act, s. 54.
[18] Financial Services Act 1986, s. 1(1), Sched. 1, para. 10.

authorised to carry on investment business under the Insurance Companies Act 1982 is automatically an authorised person under the Financial Services Act 1986, not only with reference to investment insurance but to investment business generally: *e.g.* managing a pension fund.[19]

24.4 Formation of Contract: Writing.—The generally accepted (and better) view is that contracts of insurance are not *obligationes literis* and that oral contracts, subject to proof, are competent.[20] The principal exception to this is a contract of marine insurance which is 'inadmissible in evidence' unless in writing.[21] Policies of insurance are almost invariably written documents. An indemnity policy is, however, often preceded by a temporary contract of insurance which may or may not be in writing. A written contract for a specified, limited period, during which the applicant is insured while the company decides whether it will take the risk, is called a 'cover note.' This forms a binding contract and the company will be liable even although the risk is ultimately declined.[22] In the ordinary practice of marine insurance the policy is preceded by a document known as a slip, by which the underwriters indicate that they accept the risk and settle the amount which each will contribute on a loss. At one time the view taken was that a marine slip was not a contract.[23] This may no longer be the case.[24] Where a formal policy is not required a slip can be converted into a policy by affixing a suitably worded 'Slip Policy.' Contracts of insurance affected by the Insurance Companies Act 1982 may be void if the sum assured is unlimited in amount.[25]

24.5 Insurable Interest Generally.—Both at common law and by statute, such as the Life Assurance Act 1774 and the Marine Insurance Act 1906,

---

[19] 1986 Act, s. 22.

[20] Bell, *Comm.*, i, 653 concedes that insurance is not an *obligatio literis*. *Christie* v. *North British Insurance Co.* (1825) 3 S. 519 and *Parker & Co. (Sandbank) Ltd.* v. *Western Assurance Co.*, 1925 S.L.T. 131 suggest that writing is unnecessary: *cf. McElroy* v. *London Assurance Corp.* (1897) 24 R. 287. The Scottish Law Commission have suggested that insurance contracts 'should not be included in the list of contracts requiring writing for their constitution': Consultative Memorandum No. 66 — *Constitution and Proof of Voluntary Obligations and the Authentication of Writings* (1985), para. 4.7. Note also, *Murfitt* v. *Royal Insurance Co. Ltd.* (1922) 38 T.L.R. 334; *Stockton* v. *Mason* [1978] 2 Lloyd's Rep. 430.

[21] Marine Insurance Act 1906, s. 22.

[22] *Neil* v. *S.E. Lancashire Insurance Co.*, 1932 S.C. 35; *Cunningham* v. *Anglian Ins. Co.*, 1934 S.L.T. 273.

[23] *Clyde Marine Insurance Co.* v. *Renwick*, 1924 S.C. 113.

[24] *Bhugwandass* v. *Netherlands India Sea & Fire Insurance Co. of Batavia* (1888) 14 App. Cas. 83; Finance Act 1959, ss. 30(6), 37(5); Sched. 8, Pt. II. Note also *Home Marine Insurance Co.* v. *Smith* [1898] 2 Q.B. 351. Arnould, *Marine Insurance*, para. 48 concludes that a slip containing the 'statutory particulars' is a marine policy under the Marine Insurance Act 1906.

[25] 1982 Act, s. 36.

possession of an insurable interest is a prerequisite of a valid contract of insurance: a contract without such an interest is void.[26] The Life Assurance Act 1774 applies not only to life insurance but also to non-marine indemnity contracts other than ones relating to 'goods or merchandises.'[27] In England it has been held that the 1774 Act does not apply to real property.[28] Since the owner of heritable property manifestly has an insurable interest therein, the applicability or otherwise of the Act is not unduly problematic. If an insurer honours a claim under a policy, otherwise void for lack of interest, the court will entertain an action to decide who is entitled to the proceeds.[29] A tenant has an insurable interest in the subjects leased. If the lease stipulates that the tenant is obliged either to insure the subjects against damage or destruction or to rebuild them if destroyed, he has an interest in their full value. If his obligation is merely to maintain and repair premises let, he does not have an insurable interest in their full value.[30] A tenant does not have an insurable interest in a part of building not occupied by him under the lease.[31] Property owned by a company or partnership and held in its name does not confer an insurable interest on a shareholder or partner.[32] Creditors do not have an insurable interest in a debtor's property.[33] A carrier or custodier of goods, who will be liable for their loss or destruction, has an insurable interest.[34] If A, without B's authority, and with no insurable interest, insures B's property against fire, and the insurance company pay on a loss without objection, it would appear that B has no claim to the money.[35] The return of the premiums paid may be claimed if the insurance was induced by the fraudulent representations of the insurance agent,[36] but not merely because the insured was unaware of the law.[37] The question what amount to an insurable interest depends upon the particular form of insurance involved.

[26] Life Assurance Act 1774, s. 14; Marine Insurance Act 1906, s. 4(2)(*a*); Bell, *Prin.*, §§ 457, 520.
[27] s. 4.
[28] *Mark Rowlands Ltd.* v. *Berni Inns Ltd.* [1986] Q.B. 211; [1985] 3 All E.R. 473; *Siu Yin Kwan* v. *Eastern Insurance Co. Ltd.* [1994] 2 A.C. 199.
[29] *Hadden* v. *Bryden* (1899) 1 F. 710; *Carmichael* v. *Carmichael's Exrx.*, 1919 S.C. 636. The position under English law is less clear. *Gedge* v. *Royal Exchange Insurance Corp.* [1900] 2 Q.B. 214 indicates that an insurer cannot ignore an illegality and waive the requirement of interest; *cf. Attorney-General* v. *Murray* [1904] 1 K.B. 165.
[30] *Fehilly* v. *General Accident Fire and Life Assurance Corp.*, 1982 S.C. 163.
[31] *Aberdeen Harbour Board* v. *Heating Enterprises (Aberdeen) Ltd.*, 1990 S.L.T. 416.
[32] *Macaura* v. *Northern Assurance Co.* [1925] A.C. 619; *Arif* v. *Excess Insurance Group Ltd.*, 1987 S.L.T. 473.
[33] *Macaura* v. *Northern Assurance Co.*, supra.
[34] *Dalgleish* v. *John Buchanan & Co.* (1854) 16 D. 332.
[35] *Ferguson* v. *Aberdeen P.C.*, 1916 S.C. 715.
[36] *Hughes* v. *Liverpool Friendly Society* [1916] 2 K.B. 482.
[37] *Harse* v. *Pearl Life Co.* [1904] 1 K.B. 558; see also *London, etc., Re-insurance Co.* [1922] 2 Ch. 67; *Came* v. *City of Glasgow Friendly Society*, 1933 S.C. 69, a decision under the Industrial Assurance Act 1923, which provides expressly for repayment of premiums.

24.6 Duty of Disclosure.—All forms of insurance are *uberrimae fidei*, in which each party is bound to reveal all material facts known to him. Failure in this respect, *a fortiori* any misrepresentation in any material point, whether fraudulent or not, renders the policy voidable.[38] Though most cases have related to concealment by the insured, the same rules apply to the insurer.[39] At present, under English law, the materiality of an undisclosed fact in both life and indemnity insurance is defined by reference to the reaction of a reasonable insurer to the non-disclosure.[40] In Scotland it has been held that in life insurance, the test is that of the reasonable insured.[41] In indemnity contracts, it has recently been decided by a court of authority that the appropriate test is that of the reasonable insurer.[42] So, while the tests of materiality adopted by both jurisdictions coincide in relation to indemnity contracts,[43] they diverge in relation to life contracts. The reasonable insurer test is applied to marine contracts made in England or Scotland.[44] Circumstances may make any fact material, so though the name of the party having interest in a ship is not usually material, when the party having the main interest was a Greek, and ships belonging to Greeks were at the time uninsurable, it was held that concealment of his identity was sufficient to render a policy voidable.[45] Where the policy is preceded by a proposal form and one of the queries therein is left unanswered without objection, it will be assumed that the insurers accept the point as not material,[46] but the fact that the queries are all answered does not justify

---

[38] Bell, *Prin.*, §§ 474, 522; *Comm.*, i, 665; *Craig* v. *Imperial Union Accident Assurance Co.*, (1894) 1 S.L.T. 646; *Highlands Insurance Co.* v. *Continental Insurance Co.* [1987] 1 Lloyd's Rep. 109; *The Dora* [1989] 1 Lloyd's Rep. 69.

[39] The Marine Insurance Act 1906 stresses that a marine policy may be avoided if the utmost good faith 'be not observed by *either* party.' Note also *Life Association of Scotland* v. *Foster* (1873) 11 M. 351. For a recent example in which non-disclosure by the insurer was an issue, see *Banque Financière de la Cité S.A.* v. *Westgate Insurance Co. Ltd.* [1990] 2 All E.R. 947 (H.L.).

[40] *Lambert* v. *Cooperative Insurance Society* [1975] 2 Lloyd's Rep. 485; *Mutual Life Insurance Co. of New York* v. *Ontario Metal Products Co. Ltd.* [1925] A.C. 344; *Highlands Insurance Co.* v. *Continental Insurance Co.* [1987] 1 Lloyd's Rep. 109.

[41] *Life Association of Scotland* v. *Foster* (1873) 11 M. 351: referred to with approval by the Second Division in *Samuel Hooper* v. *Royal London General Insurance Co. Ltd.*, 1993 S.L.T. 679.

[42] *Samuel Hooper* v. *Royal London General Insurance Co. Ltd., supra.*

[43] As things stand at present, however, they may not be applying the same version of that test. In *Samuel Hooper* v. *Royal London General Insurance Co. Ltd., supra*, it was held, referring to the Marine Insurance Act 1906, s. 18(2), that a material fact is one which would have a decisive influence on a reasonable insurer: *i.e.* a fact which would either make him decline the risk or accept it on altered terms. In *Pan Atlantic Insurance Co. Ltd.* v. *Pine Top Insurance Co. Ltd.* [1994] 3 W.L.R. 677, the House of Lords held that a material circumstance was one which would have had an effect on the mind of a reasonable insurer although it did not require to have a decisive effect on the insurer's decision.

[44] Under both of the ABI *Statements of Practice* the test applied is a blend of the reasonable insured and the reasonable insurer tests. ABI members have agreed not to reject a claim for non-disclosure if the insured could not reasonably be expected to have disclosed a fact.

[45] *The Spathari*, 1925 S.C. (H.L.) 6.

[46] *Joel* v. *Law Union Co.* [1908] 2 K.B. 863.

the concealment of a material point regarding which there is no query.[47] In the case of certain policies, amongst which are fire and accident policies, where the insurers may decline to renew the policy at the expiry of the original period, each renewal is made on the understanding that the original representations remain true and that no new fact has emerged which ought to be disclosed.[48] The points on which disclosure is not required are, in marine insurance and probably also in other forms, the following.[49] (a) Any circumstance which diminishes the risk; (b) any circumstance which is known or presumed to be known to the insurer. The insurer is presumed to know matters of common notoriety or knowledge, and matters which an insurer in the ordinary course of his business, as such, ought to know;[50] (c) any circumstance as to which information is waived by the insurer;[51] (d) any circumstance which it is superfluous to disclose by reason of any express or implied warranty.[52]

24.7 **Disclosure in Questions with Agents.**—Where insurance is effected through an intermediary such as an insurance broker the law is unclear as to the effect of non-disclosure by the intermediary to the insurer of a material fact disclosed to him by the insured.[53] Where, on the facts, the intermediary can be viewed as the insurer's agent, failure to pass on such information will not entitle the insurer to avoid the contract for non-disclosure.[54] Where the converse obtains and the intermediary is the insured's agent, the insurer is entitled to avoid the contract but the intermediary may be liable in damages to the insured.[55] The principles to be applied in such cases are that what is known to the agent is deemed to be known to his principal[56] and that an agent to insure is assumed to know, and bound to disclose, every circumstance which in the ordinary course of business ought to be known by, or to have been communicated to, him, and every material circumstance which the insured is bound to disclose, unless it comes to his knowledge too late to be communicated to the agent.[57] Misrepresentation of facts not

---

[47] *Life Association* v. *Foster* (1873) 11 M. 351.

[48] *Law Accident Ins. Society* v. *Boyd.* 1942 S.C. 384; *Lambert* v. *Cooperative Insurance Society, supra.*

[49] Marine Insurance Act 1906, s. 18(3).

[50] See *London General Insurance Co.* v. *Guarantee, etc., Association* [1921] 1 K.B. 104.

[51] *Mann, Macneal & Steeves* v. *Capital, etc., Insurance Co.* [1921] 2 K.B. 300.

[52] See opinion of Lord President Dunedin, *Gunford Ship Co.* v. *Thames, etc., Insurance Co.,* 1910 S.C. 1072, revd. 1911 S.C. (H.L.) 84.

[53] *Life and Health Assurance Assoc. Ltd.* v. *Yule* (1904) 6 F. 437; *McMillan* v. *Accident Ins. Co. Ltd.,* 1907 S.C. 484; *National Farmers Mutual Insurance Soc. Ltd.* v. *Tully,* 1935 S.L.T. 574.

[54] *Cruikshank* v. *Northern Accident Insurance Co. Ltd.* (1895) 23 R. 147; *Stockton* v. *Mason* [1978] 2 Lloyd's Rep. 430; *Woolcott* v. *Excess Insurance Co. Ltd. (No. 2)* [1979] 2 Lloyd's Rep. 210.

[55] *McNealy* v. *Pennine Insurance Co. Ltd.* [1978] 2 Lloyd's Rep. 18; *Dunbar* v. *A. and B. Painters Ltd.* [1986] 2 Lloyd's Rep. 38; *Roberts* v. *Plaisted* [1989] 2 Lloyd's Rep. 341.

[56] *Stockton* v. *Mason, supra; Woolcott* v. *Excess Insurance Co. Ltd. (No. 2), supra.*

[57] Marine Insurance Act 1906, s. 19.

disclosed to the insured's agent may render him liable in damages to the insured should the insurer avoid the policy.[58] Non-disclosure or misrepresentation by an intermediary will not invalidate other policies on the same risk effected through other brokers.[59]

24.8 Warranties.—Where reduction of a policy is attempted on the ground of failure in disclosure, or of misrepresentation, the fact in question must be material to the risk. But certain facts may be warranted by the insured, either (in marine insurance) impliedly,[60] or expressly. If a particular fact or statement is warranted, the validity of the policy depends on the warranty being fulfilled, and it does not matter whether the fact or statement be material or not. Thus if the policy is preceded by a proposal form, and is issued expressly on the condition that the answers to the queries in the proposal form are true, any untruth, even on a minor point will vitiate the policy.[61] The same rule was applied where it was provided that the proposal form 'shall be the basis of the contract and be held as incorporated herein.' A misstatement as to the place where a motor car, which was the subject of the policy, was garaged, was held to render the policy voidable, though it was not material to the risk, and in spite of an express provision that only material misstatements should avoid the contract.[62] And in such cases where the accuracy of the answers in the proposal form is contractually the test of the validity of the policy, it is no answer to the company that the true facts were within the knowledge of their agent, or that the proposal form was actually filled up by him, and the inaccuracy due to his misunderstanding of the information furnished by the insured.[63] Nor will it necessarily save the policy that the statement was one (e.g. as to freedom from latent disease) of which the insured could have no actual knowledge; although, in doubtful cases, such statements will be read as assertions of opinion and not of fact.[64] Where the answers to the questions asked by a proposal form are declared to be true to the best of the insured's knowledge and belief, he must have a reasonable basis

[58] *Warren* v. *Henry Sutton & Co.* [1976] 2 Lloyd's Rep. 276.
[59] *Blackburn* v. *Haslam* (1888) 21 Q.B.D. 144. As to a broker's duties and liabilities generally, see the Insurance Brokers (Registration) Act 1977; *Claude R. Ogden & Co.* v. *Reliance Sprinkler Co.* [1975] 1 Lloyd's Rep. 52; *Warren* v. *Henry Sutton & Co.* [1976] 2 Lloyd's Rep. 276; *Beattie* v. *Furness Houlder Insurance,* 1976 S.L.T. (Notes) 60; *Cherry* v. *Allied Insurance Brokers* [1978] 1 Lloyd's Rep. 274.
[60] *Infra,* para. 24.31.
[61] *Standard Life Assurance Co.* v. *Weems* (1884) 11 R. (H.L.) 48; *Unipac (Scotland) Ltd.* v. *Aegon Insurance Co. (U.K.) Ltd.,* 1995 G.W.D. 9–513. The ABI *Statement of General Insurance Practice* exhorts insurers not to use a 'basis of the contract' clause as a means of creating past and present (though not future) warranties: they are enjoined to create only specific, express, warranties.
[62] *Dawsons* v. *Bonnin,* 1922 S.C. (H.L.) 156; *cf. Provincial Ins. Co.* v. *Morgan* [1932] 2 K.B. 70, affd. [1933] A.C. 240, where answers in the proposal form were held to be merely descriptive of the risk.
[63] *McMillan* v. *Accident Insurance Co.,* 1907 S.C. 484; *National Farmers, etc., Society* v. *Tully,* 1935 S.L.T. 574.
[64] *Standard Life Assurance Co.* v. *Weems, supra,* opinion of Lord Blackburn.

for believing his opinions to be correct. It has been held that an inaccurate guess, where the facts were readily ascertainable, will justify the insurer's refusal to meet a claim.[65]

24.9   Assignation.—A policy of insurance is assignable unless there is a provision to the contrary.[66] The transfer of the subject at risk does not amount to an assignation of the policy.[67] The assignation of a policy requires writing; the mere physical transfer of the policy does not give the transferee any right to sue the insurance company, and is not a completed gift in a question with the executors of the insured.[68] When the question is one of donation no special words are necessary to constitute an assignation; in doubtful cases the construction of the writing may be assisted by parole evidence of the circumstances under which it was prepared, executed and delivered.[69] Where the question is with the other creditors of the insured or with the trustee in his sequestration, a mere assignation, with or without the transfer of the policy, is not sufficient to give the assignee a real right in the policy or in its proceeds. The assignation must be followed by intimation to the insurance company.[70] Both at common law and by statute[71] an assignee of the policy may sue in his own name. But he is subject to any defence which the insurer could state in a question with the original insured.[72] Thus, in life insurance, the company may refuse payment to an assignee on the ground of misstatements by the insured in the proposal form. The brocard *assignatus utitur jure auctoris* applies.[73] In marine insurance, when a ship is lost by the fault of the owner, a claim by a mortgagee will fail if he is merely the assignee of the policy,[74] but may succeed if his interest, as well as that of the owner, was originally insured, and where therefore he has an independent and not merely a derivative right.[75]

24.10   Rights under Policy in Bankruptcy.—In the ordinary case, if the policy is not assigned, and is not made payable to any third party, any sum becoming due under it passes to the trustee in the sequestration of the insured. At common law, there was no exception to this rule in the case of insurance against liability arising from injury to third parties.[76] Under

[65] *McPhee* v. *Royal Insurance Co. Ltd.*, 1979 S.C. 304. The ABI *Statement of General Insurance Practice* suggests that proposal forms should declare that all answers are given on the basis that they are true to the best of the proposer's knowledge and belief.

[66] Bell, *Prin.*, § 516; Marine Insurance Act 1906, s. 50.

[67] *Rayner* v. *Preston* (1881) 18 Ch.D. 1 (fire); Marine Insurance Act 1906, s. 15.

[68] *Scottish Provident* v. *Cohen* (1888) 16 R. 112; *Brownlee* v. *Robb*, 1907 S.C. 1302; *United Kingdom Co.* v. *Dixon* (1838) 16 S. 1277.

[69] *Brownlee* v. *Robb*, *supra*; *Carmichael* v. *Carmichael's Exx.*, 1920 S.C. (H.L.) 195.

[70] *Strachan* v. *McDougle* (1835) 13 S. 954; *Wylie's Exx.* v. *McJannet* (1901) 4 F. 195.

[71] Policies of Insurance Act 1867, s. 1.

[72] See para. 24.10, *infra*, as to statutory assignations.

[73] *Scottish Equitable* v. *Buist* (1877) 4 R. 1076, affd. (1878) 5 R. (H.L.) 64.

[74] *Graham Shipping Co.* v. *Merchants' Marine Insurance Co.* [1924] A.C. 294.

[75] *Samuel* v. *Dumas* [1924] A.C. 431.

[76] *Hood's Trs.* v. *Southern Union Insurance Co.* [1928] 1 Ch. 793.

the Third Parties (Rights against Insurers) Act 1930,[77] where 'a person
is insured against liabilities to third parties which he may incur,' and is
bankrupt, or has made a composition with his creditors (or, in the case
of a company, in the event of a winding-up order, an administration
order, a receivership, a voluntary arrangement in terms of the
Insolvency Act 1986), his rights under the policy are transferred to, and
vest in, the party to whom the liability has been incurred, whether the
injury to him occurred before or after the bankruptcy. The party to
whom the claim under the policy is transferred takes no higher right in a
question with the insurance company, than the insured possessed.[78] It is
a prerequisite for a valid claim under the Act that liability of the insured
be established and quantified.[79] It has been decided in England that,
where the insolvent insured's liability is unascertained, the third party
should obtain the court's leave to sue the insured and so fix his
liability.[80] The insurer is not entitled to set off against the claim of a
judgment creditor the amount of premiums due from a judgment
debtor.[81] In cases involving compulsory employer's liability insurance,
the insurer cannot rely on terms of the policy requiring notification of
an accident to be made within a specific time, or making liability
contingent on taking reasonable precautions, against an employee.[82]

24.11 Protection for Policyholders.—Provision has been made for the
protection of policyholders whose insurance companies are unable to
meet their liabilities.[83] Only holders of United Kingdom policies[83a]
issued by authorised insurance companies or friendly societies are
protected.[84] Certain insurance companies incorporated under the laws of
member countries of the European Community are regarded as
authorised insurance companies.[84a] A body known as the Policyholders
Protection Board is empowered, subject to guidance from the Secretary
of State for Trade,[85] to indemnify or otherwise assist policyholders who
have been or may be prejudiced by an insurance company's inability to

---

[77] As amended by, *inter alia*, the Insolvency Act 1986 and the Bankruptcy (Scotland)
Act 1985.
[78] *Greenlees* v. *Port of Manchester Ins. Co.*, 1933 S.C. 383. But see para. 24.12, *infra*.
[79] *Post Office* v. *Norwich Union Fire Insurance Society* [1967] 2 Q.B. 363; *Bradley* v.
Eagle Star Insurance Co. Ltd. [1989] A.C. 957; *Firma C-Trade S.A.* v. *Newcastle
Protection and Indemnity Association* [1991] 2 A.C. 1.
[80] *Post Office* v. *Norwich Union Fire Insurance Society, supra.*
[81] *Murray* v. *Legal & General Assurance Society* [1970] 2 Q.B. 495.
[82] Employers' Liability (Compulsory Insurance) Act 1969, s. 1(3)(*a*) and the Employers'
Liability (Compulsory Insurance) General Regulations 1971 (S.I. 1971, No. 1117).
[83] Policyholders Protection Act 1975, as amended by the Insurance Companies Acts
1980, 1981, the 1982 consolidating Act, the Friendly Societies Act 1992, and by statutory
instruments.
[83a] For classification of a U.K. policy, see *Scher* v. *Policyholders Protection Board* [1994]
2 A.C. 57.
[84] 1975 Act, ss. 3, 4.
[84a] Insurance Companies (Third Insurance Directives) Regulations 1994 (S.I. 1994 No.
1696).
[85] 1975 Act, s. 2.

meet its liabilities, and also to impose levies on insurers in order to finance these protective measures.[86] In certain cases, a policyholder will be indemnified in full;[87] in other cases, only in part.[88] The Board has no duty to assist a policyholder who is insured with two or more companies, one of which is an authorised insurance company not in liquidation.[89] Protection may be given although no policy has been issued.[90]

24.12 Motor Vehicle Insurance.—By the Road Traffic Act 1988,[91] it is provided that it is unlawful for any person to use, or to cause or permit any other person to use,[92] a motor vehicle on a road unless there is in force in relation to the use of the vehicle by that person or that other person a policy of insurance covering third party risks which complies with the requirements of that Act.[93] This provision does not, however, render the owner of a motor vehicle personally liable in a case where he has permitted a third party, covered by his insurance, to drive it, and the third party's negligence has caused injury.[94] But the owner of a car who allows another person to use it, when there is no adequate policy in regard to third party risks, is liable for any loss caused by the fault of the driver which the driver cannot meet.[95]

An injured person who has obtained judgment against a wrongdoer, to whom a policy has been issued in accordance with the statutory requirements, may recover direct from the insurer such a sum as is payable under the policy.[96] This will not be the case, however, where the risk is not one covered by the policy.[97] The right of direct recovery avails even though the insurer is entitled to avoid the policy or has already done so.[98] Despite the presence of certain exceptions to liability in the policy, e.g. relating to the vehicle's condition or the number of occupants permitted, these are no defence to a claim by the third party.[99] These restrictions on the rights of insurers to avoid meeting

[86] 1975 Act, ss. 1, 5–16, 18 et seq., as amended by S.I. 1977 No. 1552. See for example *Policyholders Protection Board* v. *Official Receiver* [1976] 1 W.L.R. 447.
[87] For example, compulsory insurance under Pt. VI of the Road Traffic Act 1988; 1975 Act, ss. 6, 7.
[88] 1975 Act, ss. 8, 10 (as amended by S.I. 1977 No. 1552).
[89] 1975 Act, s. 9.
[90] 1975 Act, s. 23.
[91] As amended by the Road Traffic Act 1991.
[92] s. 143. See *Houston* v. *Buchanan*, 1940 S.C. (H.L.) 17; also *Kelly* v. *Cornhill Insurance Co.*, 1964 S.C. (H.L.) 46.
[93] s. 145 as amended by the Motor Vehicles (Compulsory Insurance) Regulations 1992 (S.I. 1992 No. 3036). Provided that the insurer is a member of the Motor Insurers' Bureau, it is no longer a requirement that the insurer be authorised to carry on motor insurance business within the U.K.: s. 145(5). Note also s. 148.
[94] *Lindsay* v. *Robertson*, 1933 S.C. 158. As to the liability of an employee under a contract of service, see *Lister* v. *Romford Ice & Cold Storage Co.* [1957] A.C. 555.
[95] *Houston* v. *Buchanan, supra*; *Fleming* v. *McGillivray*, 1946 S.C. 1.
[96] s. 151.
[97] *Robb* v. *McKechnie*, 1936 J.C. 25.
[98] s. 151(5).
[99] s. 148.

liability are, however, subject to several exceptions.[1] For example, under section 152(2), insurers may obtain a declaration that the policy may be avoided for non-disclosure or misrepresentation of a material fact. To be effective, this declaration must be obtained no later than three months after judgment has been obtained against the actual insured. In these proceedings, the claimants or the insured are entitled to be heard.[2] The third party's right, it should also be noted, was substantially underwritten by an agreement made in June 1946 between the Minister of Transport and the Motor Insurers' Bureau. The current agreements are the Motor Insurers' Bureau (Compensation of Victims of Uninsured Drivers) Agreement of December 21, 1988, and the Motor Insurers' Bureau (Compensation of Victims of Untraced Drivers) Agreements of November 22, 1972 and December 7, 1977.[3] Under each agreement the Bureau undertakes to satisfy any unsatisfied decree arising from any liability required by the Act[4] to be covered by a policy of insurance. It is a condition for recovery from the Bureau of whole or part of the damages and expenses awarded against an uninsured person that notice of the action is given to the Bureau within seven days of its commencement. Where the Motor Insurers' Bureau is involved, it may not be possible to obtain an interim award of damages.[5]

Where a car has been comprehensively insured, the insurers may be liable in damages if there has been undue delay in having the car repaired.[6]

FIRE INSURANCE

24.13 Nature of Contract.—Fire insurance is a contract of indemnity, in which the insured must prove the amount of his loss and can recover no more.[7] A policy under which the subjects insured are valued beforehand may nevertheless be valid, unless there appears to be fraudulent intent.[8] Unless the policy contains an average clause applicable where there has been under insurance,[9] the whole amount of the insurance may be recovered on a partial loss, provided that damage to that amount has

---

[1] s. 152.

[2] *Zurich, etc., Ins. Co.* v. *Livingston*, 1938 S.C. 582. For sequel, see *Zurich, etc., Ins. Co.* v. *Leven*, 1940 S.C. 406.

[3] Full texts of the agreements are to be found in an appendix to Ivamy, *Fire and Motor Insurance* (6th ed.); Digby Jess, *Butterworths Insurance Law Handbook* (3rd ed.), Pt. 5.

[4] See *Lees* v. *Motor Insurers' Bureau* [1952] 2 All E.R. 511.

[5] *Martin* v. *McKinsley*, 1980 S.L.T. (Notes) 15.

[6] *Davidson* v. *Guardian Royal Exchange Assurance*, 1979 S.C. 192 (40 weeks for repair).

[7] Bell, *Prin.*, § 511.

[8] Assessment of loss, *e.g.* the value of property destroyed or damaged, may not be easy: see *Carrick Furniture House Ltd.* v. *General Accident Fire & Life Assurance Corporation Ltd.*, 1977 S.C. 308 (market value or reinstatement value); Macgillivray, *Insurance*, para. 1880; Gow, *Mercantile Law*, p. 343. Overvaluation of the property may be evidence of fraud; *cf. Hercules Insurance* v. *Hunter* (1835) 14 S. 1137.

[9] *Buchanan* v. *Liverpool, London and Globe* (1884) 11 R. 1032.

been suffered. This contrasts with an average policy, usual in marine insurance, when the insured is entitled on a partial loss, to no more than a proportional part of the sum insured. The insured may be unable to recover this loss if he has failed to comply with specific conditions in the policy.[10]

24.14 Insurable Interest.—Fire insurance is one of the forms of insurance to which the Life Assurance Act 1774 applies and the insured must probably have an interest at the time when the insurance is effected and certainly at the time when the loss occurs. That interest may consist in the ownership of the subjects insured,[11] or in some subordinate right, such as that of a lessee or the holder of a security.[12] A mere expectancy, such as that of an heir, does not furnish an insurable interest.[13] A shareholder, even though he holds all the shares, has no insurable interest in the property of the company.[14] Neither has a creditor in the property of his debtor.[15] Where property which is insured is sold and the risk has passed to the purchaser before the price is paid the right under the policy does not pass to the purchaser unless the policy is assigned to him.[16] Should a fire then occur the seller has still an interest which will entitle him to recover from the insurance company, in respect that the buyer may fail to pay the price, but if the price is met, the company may recover when they have paid.[17] As an alternative to assignation of the seller's policy, the purchaser can effect his own insurance as soon as missives are concluded.[18]

24.15 Subrogation.—From the principle that fire insurance is a contract of indemnity, in which the insured is not entitled to recover more than he has lost, spring the rights of subrogation and of contribution. The right of subrogation arises when some third party is liable for the loss covered by the policy, either by contract, or because the loss arose from his wrongful or negligent act. The insurance company is not entitled to refuse payment of the sum due on the policy merely on the ground that

[10] *Laidlaw* v. *John M. Monteath & Co.*, 1979 S.L.T. 78 (failure to have fire-extinguishing appliances available at places where blow-torches were being used).

[11] *Arif* v. *Excess Insurance Group Ltd.*, 1987 S.L.T. 473.

[12] Bell, *Prin.*, § 509. *Fehilly* v. *General Accident Fire and Life Assurance Corp.*, 1983 S.L.T. 141.

[13] Bell, *Prin.*, § 461; *Lucena* v. *Craufurd* (1806) 2 Bos. & P. (N.R.) 325.

[14] *Macaura* v. *Northern Assurance Co.* [1925] A.C. 619; see too *Arif* v. *Excess Insurance Group Ltd.*, *supra*: no insurable interest where a hotel was a partnership asset but the policy was taken out in name of an individual.

[15] *Macaura, supra.*

[16] *Rayner* v. *Preston* (1881) 18 Ch.D. 1.

[17] *Castellain* v. *Preston* (1883) 11 Q.B.D. 380.

[18] Thus making provision for the situation which arose in *Sloan's Dairies Ltd.* v. *Glasgow Corporation*, 1976 S.L.T. 147, affd. 1977 S.C. 223 (subjects damaged by fire before disposition delivered). A further alternative is a provision in the missives that risk shall not pass to the purchaser until the price has been paid, the seller remaining responsible for adequate insurance until that date.

a third party is liable for the loss,[19] nor, conversely, is that third party entitled to plead the insurance as a defence.[20] But the company, on payment, and without any assignation, is subrogated to the rights of the insured, and may recover from any third party who would have been liable in a question with the insured.[21] Another aspect of the principle of subrogation is that if the insured, after payment on the policy, recovers anything from a third party who is liable for the loss, he must account to the insurance company for what he has recovered.[22] If the insured recovers more from the third party than he has received under the policy, subject to the wording of the policy, he is not obliged to account to the insurers for the excess.[23] The insured cannot, after a loss has occurred, defeat the insurer's right of subrogation by any gratuitous discharge of his claims against third parties. Should he do so he must give credit to the insurance company for the value of the claim which he has abandoned.[24] If the insured has waived liability to him by a third party, he has no rights to which his insurer can be subrogated.[25]

24.16 Contribution.—The right of contribution arises where property is insured in more than one office, and a fire causes loss less than the combined amount of the policies. Then prima facie the insured may recover from any one office the whole amount insured by it,[26] but there is usually a clause in the policy providing that each shall be liable to contribute rateably only.[27] Any company which has paid more than its rateable share of the total loss has, by implication of law and without any assignation from the insured, a right of contribution, *i.e.* a right to recover from the other companies their rateable shares.[28] To admit of the right of contribution the insurances must not only be over the same physical subject, but over the same interest in that subject. If parties having separate interests insure, there is no right of contribution. Thus where a wharfinger, who was liable for corn stored with him in the

---

[19] *Castellain* v. *Preston, supra*; Marine Insurance Act 1906, s. 14(3).

[20] *Port-Glasgow Sailcloth Co.* v. *Cal. Ry.* (1892) 19 R. 608.

[21] *Castellain* v. *Preston, supra*; *King* v. *Victoria Ins. Co.* [1896] A.C. 250. As to interest on damages, see *H. Cousins & Co.* v. *D. & S. Carriers* [1971] 2 Q.B. 230.

[22] *Darrell* v. *Tibbits* (1880) 5 Q.B.D. 560; *Castellain* v. *Preston, supra*. Also the insurer must have indemnified the insured; *cf. Scottish Union National Insurance Co.* v. *Davis* [1970] 1 Lloyd's Rep. 1 (motor vehicle).

[23] *L. Lucas Ltd.* v. *Export Credits Guarantee Department* [1974] 2 All E.R. 889; *Yorkshire Insurance Co.* v. *Nisbet Shipping Co.* [1962] 2 Q.B. 330.

[24] *West of England Fire Co.* v. *Isaacs* [1897] 1 Q.B. 226; *Phoenix Assurance Co.* v. *Spooner* [1905] 2 K.B. 753.

[25] *Mark Rowlands Ltd.* v. *Berni Inns Ltd.* [1985] 3 W.L.R. 964.

[26] *Glasgow Provident Society* v. *Westminster Fire Office* (1887) 14 R. 947, affd. (1888) 15 R. (H.L.) 89, *per* consulted judges, 14 R. 965; Marine Insurance Act 1906, s. 32.

[27] As to rateable proportion clauses, see *Commercial Union Assurance Co.* v. *Hayden* [1977] Q.B. 804. Where two insurance policies cover the same risk, and each contains a clause excluding liability in the event of the risk being covered by another policy, the general rule is that both companies are equally liable subject to any rateable proportion clause: *Steelclad Ltd.* v. *Iron Trades Mutual Insurance Co. Ltd.*, 1984 S.L.T. 304.

[28] *Sickness, etc., Association* v. *General Accident Co.* (1892) 19 R. 977.

event of fire, insured it, and the owners also insured, it was held that the company with which the wharfinger had insured had no right of contribution against the company with which the owners had insured.[29] The same principle was applied, and the right of contribution was negatived, where separate policies were effected covering the interest of prior and of postponed bondholders over a building which was destroyed by fire.[30] If, as is usual in such cases, the policies are taken out by the debtor to cover his own interest and that of the respective bondholders, there is the apparent objection to the recovery on both policies that the owner, by the extinction or reduction of the sum due on the bonds, will gain more than he has lost by the fire. But this is met by holding that the company, paying on its policy to the postponed bondholder, is entitled to an assignation of the bond.[31]

24.17 Reinstatement.—Fire policies invariably contain a provision entitling the company, at their option, to reinstate or replace the property which has been injured, instead of paying the amount of the loss.[32] It would appear that if the company indicate which course they propose to take, by entering into negotiations as to the amount of the damage, they have conclusively elected to pay and not to reinstate.[33]

24.18 Notice of Loss.—In fire, as also in accident insurance policies, there are generally provisions whereby the claim on the policy is made contingent on notice of a loss being given within a certain period. Such conditions are effectual, and failure to comply with them is not excused on the ground that it was due to circumstances beyond the insured's control.[34] But the company may be barred from taking the objection, as in a case where they had intimated rejection of the claim upon another and untenable ground.[35]

24.19 Indirect Loss.—In the absence of any special provision a fire policy covers only loss directly resulting from the destruction or injury of the subject insured, not indirect loss, such as injury to business or the loss of rent.[36]

LIFE INSURANCE

24.20 Nature of Contract.—Life insurance is a contingent contract, payment being made on the death of the insured, or in the case of an endowment

[29] *North British and Mercantile Co.* v. *London Liverpool and Globe* (1876) 5 Ch.D. 569.
[30] *Scottish Amicable, etc., Association* v. *Northern Assùrance Co.* (1883) 11 R. 287.
[31] *Glasgow Provident Society* v. *Westminster Fire Office, supra.*
[32] See, *e.g. Carrick Furniture House* v. *General Accident,* 1977 S.C. 308.
[33] *Scottish Amicable, etc., Association* v. *Northern Assurance Co. supra.*
[34] *Worsley* v. *Wood* (1796) 6 T.R. 710; *London Guarantee Co.* v. *Fearnley* (1880) 5 App.Cas. 911, Lord Blackburn.
[35] *Shiells* v. *Scottish Assurance Corporation* (1889) 16 R. 1014; *Donnison* v. *Employers Accident Co.* (1897) 24 R. 681.
[36] *Menzies* v. *North British Insurance Co.* (1847) 9 D. 694.

policy, on attaining an agreed age. Where a life policy is linked to an investment scheme the Financial Services Act 1986 may apply. The promotion and marketing of life insurance is governed partly by the 1986 Act, partly by the rules of Self Regulatory Organisations approved by the Securities and Investments Board, and partly by an ABI code of practice.[37] Neither the indemnity principle nor the doctrine of subrogation applies to life insurance. As a non-renewable contract, there is no continuing duty of disclosure after the contract is concluded.[38]

24.21 Insurable Interest.—Under the Life Assurance Act 1774, the party who takes out a policy of life insurance must have an insurable interest.[39] A man has always an interest in his own life. But if he merely takes the policy, and assigns it without paying any premium, it may be held void as an evasion of the Act.[40] In order to support a policy on the life of another the interest in the life must be of a pecuniary nature, not mere relationship. The pecuniary interest may be contractual, or may consist in a right to aliment. On the former ground a creditor has an interest, limited to the amount of his debt in the life of his debtor;[41] a cautioner, in the life of the principal debtor;[42] an employee, if engaged for a specific term, in the life of his employer;[43] an employer in the life of an agent through whose endeavour he obtains business.[44] On the latter ground, an obligation to aliment, husband and wife have an interest in each other's lives.[45] A child under the age of 25[46] probably has an insurable interest in its parents' lives. Parents do not have an insurable interest in their children's lives on this basis[47] but they may enjoy it on some other basis.[48] Where a person maintains a foster-child for reward, he is deemed to have no insurable interest in the child's life.[49] If there was an insurable interest at the time when the policy was taken, it may be kept up after the interest has lapsed,[50] and assigned to an assignee who has no interest.[51]

[37] See, generally, R.W. Hodgin, *Insurance Intermediaries: Law and Regulation* (1992).
[38] *Banque Financière de la Cité S.A.* v. *Westgate Insurance Co. Ltd.* [1990] 2 All E.R. 947.
[39] *Supra*, para. 24.5. Note also Bell, *Prin.*, § 520.
[40] *Macdonald* v. *National Association* (1906) 14 S.L.T. 173, 249.
[41] *Lindsay* v. *Barmcotte* (1851) 13 D. 718; *Simcock* v. *Imperial Insurance Co.* (1902) 10 S.L.T. 286.
[42] *Stevenson* v. *Cotton* (1846) 8 D. 872.
[43] *Hebdon* v. *West* (1863) 3 B. & S. 579.
[44] *Turnbull* v. *Scottish Provident* (1896) 34 S.L.R. 146; *Glenlight Shipping Ltd.* v. *Excess Insurance Company Ltd.*, 1981 S.C. 267 (dispute as to whether employee's death 'accidental').
[45] *Wight* v. *Brown* (1849) 11 D. 459.
[46] See the Family Law (Scotland) Act 1985, s. 1(1)(c), (5).
[47] 1985 Act, s. 1(1) does not include children in the list of those under an obligation of aliment.
[48] *e.g.* as a creditor or an employer.
[49] Foster Children (Scotland) Act 1984, s. 18.
[50] *Turnbull* v. *Scottish Provident* (1896) 34 S.L.R. 146.
[51] Bell, *Prin.*, § 520.

24.22 No Insurance until Premium Paid.—Proposals for life insurance are commonly accepted subject to the condition that there is no insurance until the premium is paid. The result of this condition is that the company may refuse to accept the premium, and to issue a policy, if there has been any intervening and material change, *e.g.* a change in the health of the applicant.[52]

MARINE INSURANCE

24.23 Generally.—The law of marine insurance,[53] which developed largely from recognition of the customs of those engaged in the trade,[53a] presents so many special features that only the leading points can be considered here. For other aspects of the law, in so far as not dealt with in the preceding pages, reference must be made to the Marine Insurance Act 1906, or to the leading textbook.[53b] The Act expressly bears to be a codifying statute, but in certain respects it has been held to alter the law.[54] By section 91 the rules of the common law, including the law merchant, save in so far as they are inconsistent with the express provisions of the Act, are preserved.

24.24 How Far Contract of Indemnity.—Marine insurance is described in the Act (section 1) as a contract of indemnity. But it is a recognised and common practice that the value of the subject matter insured may be agreed on beforehand and specified in the policy, and that in such a policy, known as a valued policy, the amount agreed upon is, in the absence of averments of fraud, conclusive as between the parties, except for the purpose of ascertaining whether there has been a constructive total loss.[55] Thus where the rules of a mutual insurance society provide that a certain proportion of the ship must remain uninsured, it is a proportion of the agreed-on, and not the actual, value, that has to be considered.[56]

24.25 Policy.—The contract must be embodied in a policy of insurance which may be issued at the time the contract is concluded or afterwards.[57] The policy must specify the name of the assured, or of his agent, and must

[52] *Canning* v. *Farquhar* (1886) 16 Q.B.D. 727; *Sickness, etc., Assurance* v. *General Accident* (1892) 19 R. 977.
[53] See Gow, *Mercantile Law*, p. 353.
[53a] *Moore* v. *Evans* [1918] A.C. 185.
[53b] *Templeman on Marine Insurance.*
[54] *Polurrian S.S. Co.* v. *Young* [1915] 1 K.B. 922.
[55] 1906 Act. s. 27. Policies generally provide that the agreed-on value is to be conclusive in a question of a constructive total loss: Arnould, *Marine Insurance*, §§ 395, 423 *et seq.* As to the business reasons for valued policies, see *Gunford Ship Co.* v. *Thames, etc., Insurance Co.*, 1911 S.C. (H.L.) 84.
[56] *Muirhead* v. *Forth, etc., Association* (1894) 21 R. (H.L.) 1.
[57] Act, s. 22. As to a 'slip', see *supra*, para. 24.4.

be signed by him or on his behalf.[58] The subject matter insured must be designated with reasonable certainty.[59] The policy need not be stamped.[60]

24.26 Subjects of Marine Adventure.—A policy of marine insurance must relate to a marine adventure: the risk must be 'consequent upon or incidental to the navigation of the sea.'[61] It may cover a ship in course of building, or being launched, or actually exposed to maritime perils. It may also cover goods so exposed, freight, profit, the security for any advance, loan or disbursements, or liability to third parties by reason of maritime perils.[62] But a time policy on specific goods is not a marine policy, or subject to the provisions of the Act, merely because the goods are sent to a destination involving sea transit.[63]

24.27 Floating Policy.—A floating policy is one effected by a merchant to cover goods which he intends to ship, usually specifying the particular kind of goods, the ports of loading and discharge, and a limit of time, but not the ship in which the goods are to be sent. It is expressed to be 'by ship or ships to be declared.'[64] The effect is that the policy vests at once, and the goods are covered as soon as they are shipped.[65] The insured is bound to declare each shipment (usually by indorsement on the policy) as soon as he is aware of it. He is bound to declare all shipments falling within the terms of the policy in their order, and therefore is not entitled to leave some shipments uninsured, or insured with third parties.[66] If he fails to declare any shipment the underwriter may treat it as declared, and if in this way the sum fixed in the policy is exhausted, may refuse to pay for a loss on a subsequent shipment.[67] If by inadvertence a shipment is not declared, it is the duty of the insured to rectify the omission, and he may do so even after a loss has occurred.[68] But where the policy provided for a declaration within a time limit it was held that the declaration was a condition precedent to any claim, and therefore that the insured could not recover for a loss on a shipment which had been declared too late.[69] As the underwriter in a

[58] Act, ss. 23(1), 24(1).
[59] *Ibid.*, s. 26(1); see Gow, pp. 356–57.
[60] The Finance Act 1970 abolished the requirement of stamping.
[61] *Continental Illinois National Bank and Trading Co. of Chicago* v. *Bathhurst* [1985] 1 Lloyd's Rep. 625.
[62] 1906 Act, ss. 2, 3. As to the possible twofold insurance in the case of goods, namely in respect of the goods themselves and of the adventure, *see Rickards* v. *Forestal Land, Timber and Ry.* [1942] A.C. 50.
[63] *Moore* v. *Evans* [1918] A.C. 185.
[64] 1906 Act, s. 29.
[65] Arnould, *Marine Insurance*, §§ 271 *et seq.*; *Stephens* v. *Australasian Insurance Co.* (1872) L.R. 8 C.P. 18 (customs of trade proved and accepted as law).
[66] 1906 Act, s. 29; *Stephens, supra.*
[67] *Dunlop Bros.* v. *Townend* [1919] 2 K.B. 127.
[68] 1906 Act, s. 29(3).
[69] *Union Insurance Society of Canton* v. *Wills* [1916] 1 A.C. 281.

floating policy has undertaken liability for any shipments made he cannot refuse payment on the ground of failure in disclosure or innocent misrepresentation regarding the character of the ship actually selected. So where, on a particular shipment, a declaration on a floating policy was made, and also a new and independent policy was taken out, it was held that the latter, but not the former, was rendered voidable by a material but not fraudulent misstatement as to the age of the ship.[70]

24.28   Insurable Interest.—The insured must have an insurable interest at the time of a loss under the policy; not necessarily at the time when the policy is effected.[71] He cannot acquire an interest after he is aware of a loss.[72] If, in the usual form, the subject matter is insured 'lost or not lost,' the insured may recover though he may not have acquired his interest until after the loss, unless at the time of effecting the contract the assured was aware of the loss, and the insurer was not.[73] The Act, reproducing earlier legislation, provides (section 4): '(1) Every contract of marine insurance by way of gaming or wagering is void. (2) A contract of marine insurance is deemed to be a gaming or wagering contract—(a) Where the assured has not an insurable interest as defined by this Act, and the contract is entered into with no expectation of acquiring such an interest; or (b) Where the policy is made "interest or no interest" or "without further proof of interest than the policy itself" or "without benefit of salvage to the insurer," or subject to any other like term; Provided that, where there is no possibility of salvage, a policy may be effected without benefit of salvage to the insurer.'[74] It has been held that where a policy is effected in such terms (usually known as p.p.i., policy proof of interest; or f.i.a., full interest admitted) it is void, even although the insured had in fact an insurable interest.[75] By the Marine Insurance (Gambling Policies) Act 1909, the issue of a marine policy without interest is a criminal offence on the part of the insurer, insured or broker. In spite of these statutory regulations, p.p.i. policies are still in common use and their existence is a material fact which the insured must disclose to subsequent underwriters.[76]

24.29   Nature of Interest.—Insurable interest is thus defined (section 5): 'Subject to the provisions of this Act, every person has an insurable interest who is interested in a marine adventure. In particular a person is interested in a marine adventure where he stands in any legal or equitable relation to the adventure or to any insurable property at risk therein, in consequence of which he may benefit by the safety or due

---

[70] *Ionides* v. *Pacific, etc., Co.* (1871) L.R. 6 Q.B. 674.
[71] 1906 Act, s. 6(1).
[72] *Ibid.*, s. 6(2).
[73] *Ibid.*, s. 6(1) and Sched. I, r. 1.
[74] See *Re London County Re-insurance Co.* [1922] 2 Ch. 67.
[75] *Cheshire* v. *Vaughan* [1920] 3 K.B. 240.
[76] *Gunford Ship Co.* v. *Thames, etc., Insurance Co.*, 1911 S.C. (H.L.) 84.

arrival of insurable property, or may be prejudiced by its loss, or by damage thereto, or by the detention thereof, or may incur liability in respect thereof.' The interest may be defeasible, contingent or partial. The insurer has an interest to reinsure. A mortgagor or lender on bottomry, to the extent of the amount due, the master and seamen in respect of wages, a party who has paid freight in advance have all insurable interests.[77] The owner of property has an insurable interest in respect of the full value thereof though some third party may have agreed, or be liable to indemify him in case of loss.[78]

24.30 Insurable Value.—Except in the case of a valued policy the insurable interest is limited to the insurable value of the subject matter at risk. Reference must be made to the Act for a definition of the insurable value of a ship, of freight and of goods.[79]

24.31 Warranties; Seaworthiness.—The rules with regard to disclosure of material facts, innocent misrepresentation, and express warranties are in their main aspects the same as those applicable to other forms of insurance.[80] They are set forth in the Act in sections 17 to 21 and 33 to 35. The principal implied warranty is that of seaworthiness. It is warranted, in the absence of any provision to the contrary, in a voyage policy, *i.e.* in a policy from one port to another, not in time policies, when the insurance is for a definite period of time. In the latter case if the ship is, with the privity of the insured, sent to sea in an unseaworthy state, the insurer is not liable for any loss attributable to unseaworthiness.[81] In voyage policies the warranty is that the ship is seaworthy at the commencement of the voyage; in voyages performed in different stages, during which the ship requires different kinds of or further preparation of equipment, the warranty is that at the commencement of each stage the ship is seaworthy in respect of such preparation of equipment for the purposes of that stage.[82] There is no implied warranty, in a policy on goods, that they are seaworthy, but in a voyage policy on goods there is an implied warranty that at the commencement of the voyage the ship is not only seaworthy as a ship but also that she is reasonably fit to carry the goods to the destination contemplated by the policy.[83]

---

[77] 1906 Act, ss. 7–14.

[78] *Ibid.*, s. 14(3).

[79] 1906 Act, s. 16; *Williams* v. *Atlantic Assurance Co.* [1933] 1 K.B. 81; *Berger and Light Diffusers* v. *Pollock* [1973] 2 Lloyd's Rep. 442.

[80] *Supra*, paras. 24.6 to 24.8.

[81] 1906 Act, s. 39; *Compania Maritima* v. *The Oceanus Mutual* [1977] Q.B. 49; *The Eurysthenes* [1976] C.L.Y. 2571; *Murray* v. *Scottish Boatowners Mutual Insurance Association*, 1986 S.L.T. 329; *Stephen* v. *Scottish Boatowners Mutual Insurance Association*, 1989 S.L.T. 283. As to the meaning of seaworthiness, see para 27.4, *infra*.

[82] 1906 Act, s. 39. So, in a voyage in stages, the ship must have sufficient fuel for each stage, not necessarily for the whole voyage: *Greenock Co.* v. *Maritime Insurance Co.* [1903] 2 K.B. 657.

[83] 1906 Act, s. 40. See *Elder, Dempster & Co.* v. *Paterson* [1924] A.C. 522.

24.32 Deviation.—An insurer may be discharged from liability by a change in the voyage, or by deviation. A change in the voyage occurs when the destination of the ship is voluntarily changed from the destination contemplated by the policy. In the absence of any provision to the contrary the insurer is discharged from the time when determination to change was manifested, although the loss may have occurred before the ship has actually left her course.[84] An insurer is also discharged from liability by deviation from the course contemplated by the policy. In general the rules as to deviation in questions of affreightment apply in questions of marine insurance,[85] but the provision, in the Carriage of Goods by Sea Act 1971, by which deviation in attempting to save property at sea, or any reasonable deviation, is excused,[86] is not applicable to policies of insurance. In the Marine Insurance Act the following excuses for deviation (also for delay) are enumerated: (a) when authorised by any special term in the policy; (b) where caused by circumstances beyond the control of the master and his employer; (c) where reasonably necessary in order to comply with an express or implied warranty; (d) where reasonably necessary for the safety of the ship or subject matter insured; (e) for the purpose of saving human life or aiding a ship in distress where human life may be in danger; (f) where reasonably necessary for the purpose of obtaining medical or surgical aid for any person on board the ship; (g) where caused by barratrous conduct of the master or crew, if barratry be one of the perils insured against.[87] There is often a clause in the policy authorising a change of voyage or deviation, at an increase of premium to be mutually agreed upon, provided that notice of the change be given.[88]

24.33 Perils Insured Against.—The sum due under a policy becomes payable when there has been a loss, total or partial, of the subject matter of the insurance, and that loss has been occasioned by one of the perils insured against. What these perils are may depend on the terms of the particular policy; the following are enumerated in the statutory form:[89] 'Touching the adventures and perils which we the assurers are contented to bear and do take upon us in this voyage: they are of the seas,[90] men of war, fire, enemies, pirates, rovers, thieves, jettisons, letters of mart and countermart, surprisals, takings at sea, arrests, restraints and detainments of all kings, princes, and people, of what nation, condition, or quality soever, barratry of the master and mariners, and of all other perils, losses and misfortunes, that have or shall come to the hurt,

[84] s. 45.
[85] *Infra.* para 27.19.
[86] 1971 Act, Sched., art. IV, r. 4.
[87] 1906 Act, s. 49.
[88] See *Maritime Assurance Co.* v. *Stearns* [1901] 2 K.B. 912, at p. 917.
[89] 1906 Act, Sched. I. In the rules given in the Schedule the meaning of the terms used in the policy is explained.
[90] *Stephen* v. *Scottish Boatowners Mutual Insurance Association, supra* ('peril of the sea').

detriment or damage of the said goods and merchandises, and ship etc.,
or any part thereof.' The general words with which this enumeration
ends include only perils similar in kind to the perils specifically
mentioned,[91] and 'perils' refers only to fortuitous accidents or casualties
of the seas, and does not include the ordinary action of the winds and
waves.[92]

24.34 *Causa Proxima.*—The general rule has been long recognised that in
considering whether a particular loss was due to one of the perils
insured against the maxim *causa proxima non remota spectatur* applies.
The rule is expressed in the Act as follows (section 55): 'Subject to the
provisions of this Act and unless the policy otherwise provides,[93] the
insurer is liable for any loss proximately caused by a peril insured
against, but, subject as aforesaid, he is not liable for any loss which is
not proximately caused by a peril insured against.' In recent cases it has
been explained that the term proximate cause does not necessarily mean
the cause latest in time.[94] In considering the question, not infrequently
raised, whether a stranding or collision has been caused by a warlike
operation or a marine risk, the House of Lords has reiterated the rule
that the proximate cause of the loss of a ship is not necessarily that
which operates last, but is the effective and predominant cause, selected
from among co-operating causes.[95] Thus where a ship was torpedoed,
and necessarily towed to a harbour where she was stranded and
wrecked, it was held that the war risk involved in the torpedo, and not
the subsequent stranding, was the cause of her loss. It was observed that
the term *causa proxima* might be rendered 'dominant cause' or 'cause
proximate in efficiency.'[96] A distinction is recognised between loss due
to a peril insured against and loss resulting from measures due to
apprehension of that peril. Thus where, in 1914, a German ship, not
actually pursued by Allied ships, put into a neutral port, with resultant
loss, it was held that the loss was not due to 'restraint of princes,' but to
measures adopted to avoid that restraint.[97] But restraint of princes was
held to apply where, on hearing of the declaration of war, and without
any actual compulsion, a British ship abandoned a voyage to a German
port.[98] Other questions have led to equally fine distinctions. Thus if a

[91] 1906 Act, Sched. I, r. 12.
[92] *Ibid.*, r. 7; *Samuel v. Dumas* [1924] A.C. 431; *Rhesa Shipping Co. v. Edmunds (The Popi M.)* [1985] 2 All E.R. 712 (H.L.).
[93] *Oei v. Foster* [1982] 2 Lloyd's Rep. 170; *The Miss Jay Jay* [1987] 1 Lloyd's Rep. 32.
[94] See, *e.g. Wayne Tank and Pump Co. v. Liability Assurance Corporation* [1974] Q.B. 49.
[95] *Yorkshire Dale S.S. Co. v. Minister of War Transport* [1942] A.C. 691.
[96] *Leyland Shipping Co. v. Norwich Union* [1918] A.C. 350. See also *Britain S.S. Co. v. The King* [1921] 1 A.C. 99; *Canada Rice Mills v. Union Marine & General Ins. Co.* [1941] A.C. 55; *Wayne Tank and Pump Co. v. Employers' Liability Assurance Corporation* [1974] Q.B. 57; *Soya G.m.b.H. v. White* [1983] 1 Lloyd's Rep. 122 (H.L.).
[97] *Becker, Gray & Co. v. London Assurance* [1918] A.C. 101.
[98] *British and Foreign Insurance Co. v. Sanday* [1916] 1 A.C. 650.

particular peril is encountered owing to negligent navigation, the peril in question, and not the preceding negligence, is the proximate cause of the loss,[99] whereas if the peril is incurred owing to an act deliberately wrongul, with the intent to wreck the ship, the wrongful act, and not the subsequent peril, is the proximate cause.[1] The distinction has been explained on the ground that in the former case, and not in the latter, there is the element of the fortuitous or unexpected in the mishap.[2] There can be more than one proximate cause of loss or damage.[3] If the policy covers loss or damage caused by one such cause and does not refer to the other, the insurer incurs liability.[4] But if one cause is covered and the other is specifically excluded the insurer does not incur liability.[5]

24.35 **Total and Partial Loss.**—A loss may be total or partial. A partial loss may in certain cases, and at the option of the insured, be treated as a constructive total loss. In the absence of any provision to the contrary an insurance against total loss includes a constructive, as well as an actual, total loss.[6] The Act provides that there is an actual total loss when the subject matter is destroyed, or so damaged as to cease to be a thing of the kind insured, or where the assured is irretrievably deprived thereof, or where a ship is missing, and after a reasonable time no news of her has been received.[7] Thus, for example, if goods insured arrive in an unmarketable state,[8] or if they are sold at an intermediate port on the ground that symptoms of decay show that they cannot be safely carried to their destination,[9] there is an actual total loss. Where a ship is sunk the question whether she is an actual total loss depends on the possibility of raising her.[10] Where a ship is abandoned by her crew and taken possession of by salvors, the loss is only partial, but if she is sold by a decree of a competent court at the instance of the salvors, there is an actual total loss.[11] There is no total loss of freight if, by the arrival of the cargo, it is earned, though it may never be paid, or though, owing to the abandonment of the ship to the underwriters, they, and not the insured, are entitled to payment.[12] But there is a total loss of freight where the cost of temporary repairs to a vessel would exceed the repaired value.[13] In the event of an actual total loss the insured is

---

[99] 1906 Act, s. 55(2); *Trinder, Anderson & Co.* v. *Thames, etc., Assurance Co.* [1898] 2 Q.B. 114.

[1] *Samuel* v. *Dumas* [1924] A.C. 431.

[2] *Trinder, Anderson & Co., supra.*

[3] *The Miss Jay Jay, supra.*

[4] *Ibid.*

[5] *Wayne Tank and Pump Co.* v. *Employers' Liability Assurance Corporation, supra.*

[6] 1906 Act, s. 56(3).

[7] *Ibid.*, ss. 57, 58.

[8] *Asfar* v. *Blundell* [1896] 1 Q.B. 123.

[9] *Roux* v. *Salvador* (1836) 2 Bing N.C. 266.

[10] *Blairmore Co.* v. *Macredie* (1898) 25 R. (H.L.) 57.

[11] *Cossman* v. *West* (1887) 13 App.Cas. 160.

[12] *Scottish Marine Ins. Co.* v. *Turner* (1853) 1 Macq. 334.

[13] *Kulukundis* v. *Norwich Union* [1937] 1 K.B. 1.

entitled to recover under the policy without giving notice of abandonment.[14]

24.36 Constructive Total Loss.—Where the loss is not an actual total loss, it may amount to a constructive total loss. In that event the insured may either treat the loss as a partial loss or abandon the subject matter insured to the insurer and treat the loss as if it were an actual total loss.[15] There is a constructive total loss where the subject matter insured is reasonably abandoned on account of an actual total loss appearing to be unavoidable, or because it could not be preserved from actual total loss without an expenditure which would exceed its value when the expenditure had been incurred.[16] In the case of loss of possession, *e.g.* by enemy capture, there is a constructive total loss if the cost of recovery would exceed the value when recovered, or if it is unlikely that the subject can be recovered.[17] Under this provision it is no longer, as it was before the Act, sufficient to prove that the recovery of a captured ship was uncertain; the proof must establish that it was unlikely.[18] Where a ship is damaged the Act provides that she is a constructive total loss if the cost of repairing her would exceed her value when repaired.[19] It is doubtful whether this provision, which leaves out of account the break-up value of the wreck, excludes the test established by the prior authorities, which was whether a prudent owner, if uninsured, would repair the ship or not.[20] In the case of damage to goods there is a constructive total loss when the cost of repairing the damage and forwarding the goods to their destination would exceed their value on arrival;[21] also if the voyage is frustrated, though the goods are not damaged, as where, on the declaration of war, it became illegal to proceed to the enemy port of destination and the goods were landed intact at a British port.[22]

24.37 Notice of Abandonment.—Where the insured proposes to claim as on a constructive total loss he must give notice of abandonment to the underwriter,[23] unless there is nothing to abandon, and no possibility of benefit to the underwriter,[24] as in the case of a policy on freight when the ship is wrecked,[25] or a policy on a ship which is captured by an

---

[14] 1906 Act, s. 57(2).

[15] *Ibid.*, s. 61.

[16] *Ibid.*, s. 60. The definition in the section is exhaustive: *Irvin* v. *Hine* [1950] 1 K.B. 555.

[17] *Ibid.*, s. 60(2).

[18] *Polurrian S.S. Co.* v. *Young* [1915] 1 K.B. 922; as to barratry, see *Marstrand Fishing Co.* v. *Beer* (1936) 53 T.L.R. 287.

[19] 1906 Act, s. 60(2).

[20] See *Macbeth* v. *Maritime Ass. Co.* [1908] A.C. 144.

[21] 1906 Act, s. 60(2).

[22] *British and Foreign, etc., Co.* v. *Sanday* [1916] 1 A.C. 650.

[23] 1906 Act, s. 62; *Watt's Tr.* v. *Scottish Boatowners Mutual Insurance Association,* 1968 S.L.T. (Sh.Ct.) 79.

[24] *Ibid.*, subs. (7).

[25] *Rankin* v. *Potter* (1872) L.R. 6 H.L. 83.

enemy.[26] Notice may be given verbally or in writing.[27] It must be given with reasonable diligence after the receipt of reliable information of the loss.[28] On receiving notice the underwriter may accept it, expressly or by implication.[29] His mere silence is not acceptance.[30] If, without express acceptance, he takes measures for the safety or recovery of a wreck, it is a question of circumstances whether he thereby indicates acceptance of the notice, or whether he is acting as a salvor of property which has been abandoned and become *res nullius*.[31] It would appear that notice of abandonment or acceptance of notice given under a material mistake of fact is a nullity.[32]

24.38 **Measure of Indemnity.**—On an actual or constructive total loss, in a valued policy, the sum fixed by the policy may be recovered; in an unvalued policy, the insurable value of the subject matter.[33] This is termed in the Act the measure of indemnity.[34]

24.39 **Subrogation.**—On payment as for a total loss, actual or constructive, the insurer is entitled, on the principle of subrogation, to exercise the rights of the insured in the subject matter of the policy.[35] He may recover the damages due from the third party from whose wrongful or negligent act the loss has resulted,[36] but where the insured himself recovers damages from the third party, the insurer may not recover from the insured a greater sum than he himself has already paid over to the insured.[37] If a ship has reached her port of destination, and earned freight, but has arrived so damaged as to be abandoned to the underwriters, they are entitled to the freight.[38] They are also entitled, where a ship has been abandoned as a constructive total loss, to a transfer which will enable them to be registered as her owners.[39] But the insurers, in virtue of their right of subrogation, stand in the same position as the insured, and may be met by any defence which would have been available against him. So where two ships belonging to the same owner came into collision, and the underwriters of the ship which was not in fault, and which was wrecked, paid the insurance, it was held that they had no

---

[26] *Roura, etc.* v. *Townend* [1919] 1 K.B. 189; *Nomikos* v. *Robertson* [1938] 2 K.B. 603.
[27] 1906 Act, s. 62.
[28] *Ibid.*, subs. (3). See *Fleming* v. *Smith* (1848) 6 Bell's App. 278; *Kaltenbach* v. *Mackenzie* (1878) 3 C.P.D. 467.
[29] *Watt's Tr.* v. *Scottish Boatowners Mutual Insurance Association, supra.*
[30] s. 62, subs. (5).
[31] *Shepherd* v. *Henderson* (1881) 9 R. (H.L.) 1; *Robertson* v. *Royal Exchange Corporation*, 1925 S.C. 1.
[32] *Norwich Union* v. *Price* [1934] A.C. 455.
[33] 1906 Act, s. 68.
[34] *Ibid.*, s. 67.
[35] *Ibid.* s. 79; see *Boag* v. *Standard Marine Insurance Co.* [1937] 2 K.B. 113.
[36] *North of England Assurance Co.* v. *Armstrong* (1870) L.R. 5 Q.B. 244.
[37] *Yorkshire Insurance Co.* v. *Nisbet Shipping Co.* [1962] 2 Q.B. 330.
[38] *Stewart* v. *Greenock Insurance Co.* (1848) 1 Macq. 328.
[39] *Whitworth* v. *Shepherd* (1884) 12 R. 204.

right to a ranking on the amount paid into court to meet claims against
the offending ship. They could make no claim which the insured could
not have made, and he could not have claimed against himself.[40] It has
been held that where a P. & I. club's rules contain a 'pay to be paid'
clause, a third party having a claim against a member of the club, who
has gone into liquidation, is bound by that rule.[40a] These clauses do not
contravene section 1(3) of the Third Parties (Rights Against Insurers)
Act 1930 since they attempt neither to avoid the contract of indemnity
nor alter the parties' rights thereunder.

24.40 Liabilities in Case of Abandonment.—Abandonment when accepted
divests the insured of the property in the subject matter, and also frees
him from any liabilities subsequently effeiring to it, such as the liability
to meet the expenses of local authorities having statutory powers to
remove wrecks.[41] It would seem to be a doubtful point whether the
insurer, if on abandonment he merely pays for a total loss and takes no
active steps to invest himself with the subject mater, comes under any
liability.[42]

24.41 Partial Loss: Particular Average.—Where damage occurs through a peril
insured against which is not of sufficient gravity to amount to a
constructive total loss, or which the insured does not choose to treat as
such, there is a partial loss. The partial loss may result from a sacrifice
which amounts to a general average act, and is then known as a general
average loss.[43] Where there is not a general average loss, a partial loss
is known as a particular average, or sometimes as an average, loss.[44]
Where, in a policy covering ship and cargo, certain kinds of goods are
'warranted free from average,' the insurer is not liable for a partial loss
of the goods in question, unless the contract be apportionable. The
contract may be apportionable either expressly, *e.g.* by the insertion of
such words as 'to pay average on each package as if separately insured,'
or impliedly, *e.g.* where the insurance is general, but on separate articles
wholly distinct in their nature.[45] In such cases the underwriter is liable
for a total loss of any separate package or article. Where goods are
warranted free from average under a certain percentage of their value,
he is not liable unless the damage exceeds that percentage.[46] Such
conditions are inserted in a clause, known as the memorandum,

---

[40] *Simpson* v. *Thomson* (1877) 5 R. (H.L.) 40. See also *Société du Gaz* v. *Armateurs Français*, 1925 S.C. 332.
[40a] *Firma C-Trade S.A.* v. *Newcastle Protection and Indemnity Association* [1991] 2 A.C. 1.
[41] *Barraclough* v. *Brown* [1897] A.C. 615.
[42] *Templeman*, Chap. 7.
[43] As to general average, see Chap. 30, *infra*.
[44] 1906 Act, s. 64.
[45] See generally *Templeman*, Chap. 8.
[46] 1906 Act, s. 76.

appended to the policy. In the statutory form of policy the words are 'free from average, unless general, or the ship be stranded.' Under a policy in these terms the insurer is liable if the ship be stranded, although the stranding may not be the cause of the injury to the goods.[47] To stranding is added, in some policies, sinking, burning and collision.[48]

24.42 Measure of Indemnity.—The amount which may be recovered as a partial loss, or the 'measure of indemnity,' is, in the case of injury to a ship which has been repaired, the reasonable cost of the repairs, 'less the customary deductions, but not exceeding the sum insured in respect of any one casualty.'[49] The principal customary deduction, recognised before the Act as a custom of trade, is a deduction of one-third of the cost of the repairs in respect of the advantage gained by the insured in having new material instead of old.[50] If the ship is partially repaired the insured is entitled to the cost of repairs, under like deduction, and also to the depreciation resulting from the unrepaired damage. When the ship has not been repaired, and has not been sold in her damaged state during the risk, the insured is entitled to the depreciation in value, provided that does not exceed the reasonable cost of repair.[51] If she is sold unrepaired, the measure of indemnity is the difference between her value, if undamaged, at the place of sale, and the actual price obtained.[52] When there is a partial loss of freight the measure of indemnity is such proportion of the sum fixed by the policy, in the case of a valued policy, or of the insurable value in the case of an unvalued policy, as the proportion of freight lost by the assured bears to the whole freight at the risk of the assured under the policy.[53] For the complicated rules with regard to the measure of indemnity in the case of a partial loss of good reference must be made to the Act, and to the exposition in *Templeman on Marine Insurance*.[54]

24.43 Successive Losses.—Unless the policy otherwise provides the insurer is liable for successive losses, even although the total amount of such losses may exceed the sum insured.[55] But when a partial loss has not been repaired and is followed by a total loss, whether from a peril insured against or not, the underwriter is not liable for the partial loss, and it is immaterial that under another policy by which the cause of the total loss is covered a deduction may be made for the loss in value caused by the partial loss.[56]

---

[47] *The Alsace Lorraine* [1893] P. 209.
[48] See *The Glenlivet* [1894] P. 48 (burning).
[49] s. 69(1).
[50] *Aitchison* v. *Lohre* (1879) 4 App.Cas. 755.
[51] ss. 69(2), (3); *Irvin* v. *Hine* [1950] 1 K.B. 555.
[52] *Pitman* v. *Universal Marine Insurance Co.* (1882) 9 Q.B.D. 192.
[53] s. 70.
[54] s. 71; *Templeman*, pp. 273 *et seq.*
[55] s. 77.
[56] *British and Foreign Insurance Co.* v. *Wilson Shipping Co.* [1921] 1 A.C. 188.

24.44 **Suing and Labouring Clause.**—In certain cases, under a clause in the policy known as the suing and labouring clause, a sum in excess of that fixed in the policy may be recovered. This clause, in its usual form, provides that in case of any loss or misfortune, it shall be lawful to the assured 'to sue, labour and travel for in and about the defence safeguard and recovery' of the ship or goods, and that the insurers will contribute to the charges thereof.[57] This clause is read as supplementary to the contract of insurance, and entitles the insured to recover from the underwriters any sums reasonably expended in endeavour to prevent or minimise a loss, provided that it was a loss insured against under the policy.[58] A claim of this nature may be made although the underwriters have paid for a total loss,[59] or, in the case of a partial loss, though the policy was free of particular average.[60] The clause does not cover anything paid for salvage, although services of a similar kind, if rendered under contract and not as salvage, fall within it.[61] Nor does it include general average losses and contribution.[62] The Act provides that 'it is the duty of the assured and his agent, in all cases, to take such measures as may be reasonable for the purpose of averting or minimising a loss.'[63] This has been interpreted as requiring the insured to act as any reasonable person would to safeguard his property and unusual expenditure may be recovered if it can be shown that a prudent insured would have incurred it.[64]

24.45 **Marine Insurance Policies and Arrestment of Ships.**—An action to enforce a contract of marine insurance has been held not to provide a proper basis for the arrestment of a ship in terms of section 47 of the Administration of Justice Act 1956.[65]

Further Reading

Birds, *Modern Insurance Law* (3rd ed., 1993).
Clarke, *The Law of Insurance Contracts* (1989) with Supplement (1991).
Ivamy, *Fire and Motor Insurance* (4th ed., 1984).
Ivamy, *Marine Insurance* (4th ed., 1985).
Ivamy, *Personal, Accident, Life and Other Insurance* (2nd ed., 1980).
Ivamy, *Principles of Insurance Law* (6th ed., 1993).
MacGillivray & Parkington, *Insurance* (8th ed., 1988).
Templeman on Marine Insurance (6th ed., 1986).

[57] *Templeman*, Chap. 12.
[58] 1906 Act, s. 78(3); *Kidston* v. *Empire Marine Insurance Co.* (1867) L.R. 2 C.P. 357; *Wilson's Bobbin Co.* v. *Green* [1917] 1 K.B. 860; *Nishina Trading Co.* v. *Chiyoda Fire and Marine Insurance Co.* [1969] 2 Q.B. 449.
[59] s. 78(1); *Aitchison* v. *Lohre* (1879) 4 App.Cas. 755.
[60] s. 78(1); *Kidston, supra.*
[61] *Aitchison* v. *Lohre, supra.*
[62] s. 78(2).
[63] s. 78(4).
[64] *Integrated Container Service Inc.* v. *British Traders Insurance Co.* [1984] 1 Lloyd's Rep. 154 (C.A.).
[65] *West of England Ship Owners* v. *Aifanourios Shipping S.A., The Aifanourios,* 1980 S.C. 346; *Gatoil International Inc.* v. *Arkwright-Boston Manufacturers Mutual Insurance Co.,* 1985 S.L.T. 68.

CHAPTER 25

HIRING, LOAN AND DEPOSIT

25.1 Forms of Location.—Location is a general term for contracts whereby the owner of an article places it in possession of another or a person hires out his services to another.[1] There may be distinguished—(1) *locatio conductio rei*, the letting for hire of a thing; (2) *locatio custodiae*, or deposit; (3) *locatio operis faciendi*, or contract to do work on an article;[2] and (4) *locatio conductio operarum*, the letting for hire of services. The letting for hire of services is dealt with in the chapters on Employment and on Agency; the contract of location, where the subject let is heritable property, in the chapter on Leases; the law as to hire-purchase in the chapter on Sale.

25.2 Hiring Terms.—Hiring is the location of moveable property. The party who takes the thing, and agrees to pay the hire, is the hirer (conductor); for the other party the most convenient term, in spite of its connection with heritable property, is lessor (locator). Hiring includes finance leasing, where the customer hires goods from a company which has bought them from the retailer.[3]

25.3 Obligations of Lessor.—The lessor undertakes to supply either a specific thing, or a thing of a particular kind, according to the terms of the contract. He is bound to take care that the article he supplies is of satisfactory quality and also, where the purpose of the hire is known, either expressly or by implication, that the article is reasonably fit for that purpose, and he is liable for failure in either respect.[4] But if the

---

[1] For the contracts considered in this and three succeeding chapters there is no general term established in Scots law. Bell (*Prin.*, § 84) describes them as 'contracts in the course and existence of which the property of one is necessarily entrusted to the care or custody of another.' The English term 'bailments' is sometimes met with in Scotland. For its meaning, see Beven, *Negligence* (4th ed.), p. 903. Added to the legal terminology must be commercial descriptions of arrangements such as 'finance leases', 'operating leases' and 'equipment leases'.

[2] Where a car is placed with a garage for repair, the contract comprises both *locatio operis faciendi* and *locatio custodiae*: *Verrico* v. *Hughes*, 1980 S.C. 179.

[3] Scottish Law Commission, Consultative Memorandum No. 58, *Sale and Supply of Goods* (1983), p. 133; *Stair Memorial Encyclopaedia*, Vol. 14 (Location), paras. 1005 *et seq.*

[4] Supply of Goods and Services Act 1982, s. 11J(2), (5) and (6): added by the Sale and Supply of Goods Act 1994, s. 6 and Sched. 1. Implied terms as to the right to transfer possession and where hire is by description or by sample are found in ss. 11H(1), 11I and 11K.

lessor can demonstrate that the hirer did not rely on his skill or judgment, or that it was unreasonable for the hirer to do so, the implied term as to fitness is displaced.[5] Should the thing cause injury to the hirer the lessor is clearly liable if he was aware of its dangerous character and failed to give warning.[6] A mere lender on gratuitous terms has no further duty, and is not liable merely because he has failed to examine the thing he lends.[7] Should the thing hired occasion some exceptional expense to the hirer—where, for instance, a horse falls lame, and has to be left at a livery stable—the lessor will be liable for the expense, provided that it was necessary and not due to any fault of the hirer, and that notice was given by the hirer to the lessor as soon as the circumstances permitted.[8] Where damage is caused by a defective product, the lessor may be liable.[9] The lessor may also be guilty of a criminal offence if he supplies[10] consumer goods which fail to comply with certain safety requirements.[11] Further, in terms of the Health and Safety at Work etc. Act 1974, the lessor has a duty to ensure, so far as is reasonably practicable, that an article supplied for use at work is safe and without risks to health.[12]

25.4 **Obligations of Hirer.**—The hirer is bound to pay the hire agreed upon or, in the absence of any express agreement, a reasonable hire. The accidental destruction of the thing terminates the contract, and with it the obligation to pay hire; an accidental injury gives the hirer the option of terminating the contract or claiming a proportionate reduction of the hire.[13]

25.5 **Degrees of Care.**—The hirer is bound to take reasonable care for the safety of the article hired. The care required is such as a diligent and prudent man takes of his own property. In estimating it the value of the article is obviously a relevant consideration. The civilian distinction between *culpa lata*, *culpa levis* and *culpa levissima*, though possibly still

---

[5] Supply of Goods and Services Act 1982, s. 11J(7).

[6] *Coughlin* v. *Gillison* [1899] 1 Q.B. 145. See *Clarke* v. *Army and Navy Stores* [1903] 1 K.B. 155.

[7] *Oliver* v. *Saddler*, 1929 S.C. (H.L.) 94, *per* Lord Atkin at p. 101.

[8] Bell, *Comm.*, i, 482; *Johnston* v. *Rankin* [1687] Mor. 10080.

[9] ss. 2(3) and 46 of the Consumer Protection Act 1987. Liability arises where the lessor fails to identify the manufacturer or trademark-owner or importer, despite being requested to do so: see s. 2 and Chap. 17, *supra*. Note that in finance leasing, the dealer or retailer rather than the finance company is liable: s. 46(2) of the 1987 Act. See also Health and Safety (Leasing Arrangements) Regulations 1992 (S.I. 1992 No. 1524).

[10] In the course of his business: s. 46(5) of the 1987 Act.

[11] ss.10 *et seq.* (Pt. II) of the 1987 Act. A contravention of the safety regulations can give rise to a civil action: s. 41. Note that in finance leasing the dealer or retailer rather than the finance company is liable: s. 46(2).

[12] s. 6(1) of the 1974 Act, as amended by s. 36 of and Sched. 3 to the Consumer Protection Act 1987.

[13] Bell, *Prin.*, § 141; *Muir* v. *McIntyre* (1887) 14 R. 470.

recognised in the law of Scotland,[14] is difficult to apply in any concrete case. If the distinction is still maintainable at all, the liability of a hirer, as the contract of hire is one beneficial to both parties, is for *culpa levis*:[15] liability for *culpa levissima* would be appropriate, in commodate, where the contract is beneficial only to the party in fault, and liability for *culpa lata* would be applicable in contracts like gratuitous mandate or deposit where the party alleged to be in fault is acting solely in the interests of the other. It has been suggested, though not decided, that a party who hires an article, or undertakes the care of it for reward, is liable for loss or injury due to the fault of his employee, even though acting outwith the scope of his employment, whereas no such liability would rest on a gratuitous depositary.[16]

25.6 Facts Indicating Fault.—Fault, or want of reasonable care, on the part of a hirer, may consist in overloading or overworking the article hired (as in the case of a horse[17]), or using it in some way involving an extra risk, which was not contemplated at the time of the contract.[18] Probably if the article is injured by use in the way contemplated by the contract, the onus of proof that he was not in fault lies on the hirer.[19] It may also consist in the want of reasonable precautions against loss or theft, a question necessarily of circumstances;[20] or in failure to take the proper steps after an injury or loss has occurred, as where an agister of cattle failed to give notice, either to the owner or the police, that the cattle had been stolen, and was held to be liable unless he could prove that the notice would have been useless.[21] It is cogent evidence of negligence that the hirer took less care of the article hired than he did of his own property.[22] It is no defence that he treated his own property with the same lack of care.[23]

25.7 Exclusion Clauses in Hire Contracts.—The Unfair Contract Terms Act 1977[24] applies to contracts of hire.[25] Thus contractual terms or a

---

[14] *Wernham v. McLean, Baird & Neilson,* 1925 S.C. 407. See, however, opinion of Lord Atkin, *Kolbin v. Kinnear,* 1931 S.C. (H.L.) 128, at p. 139. In *Giblin v. McMullen* (1868) L.R. 2 P.C. 317, Lord Chelmsford said: 'though degrees of care are not definable, they are with some approach to certainty distinguishable.'

[15] Bell, *Comm.,* i, 483.

[16] *Central Motors Co.* v. *Cessnock Garage Co.,* 1925 S.C. 796; *Coupé Co.* v. *Maddick* [1891] 2 Q.B. 413.

[17] *Pullars* v. *Walker* (1858) 20 D. 1238.

[18] *Seton* v. *Paterson* (1880) 8 R. 236; *Gardner* v. *McDonald* (1792) Hume 299,

[19] *Hinshaw* v. *Adam* (1870) 8 M. 933.

[20] See *Davidson* (1749) Mor. 10081; *McLean* v. *Warnock* (1883) 10 R. 1052; *Giblin* v. *McMullen* (1868) L.R. 2 P.C. 317.

[21] *Coldman* v. *Hill* [1919] 1 K.B. 443.

[22] *Campbell* v. *Kennedy* (1828) 6 S. 806.

[23] *Re United Service Co., Johnston's Claim* (1871) L.R. 6 Ch. 212; *Raes* v. *Meek* (1889) 16 R. (H.L.) 31, at p. 33 (trust).

[24] See *Pacta Illicita* and Unfair Contract Terms, Chap. 10, *supra.*

[25] ss. 15(2)(*a*) *et seq.* But rights, duties or liabilities arising under a contract for the hire of goods may be negatived or varied if not struck at by the 1977 Act: Supply of Goods and Services Act 1982, s. 11L(1).

provision of a notice[26] purporting to restrict or exclude liability for breach of duty may be void or unenforceable[27] as may terms purporting to exclude implied terms as to description, quality, fitness for purpose or title.[28]

25.8 Obligation to Restore Article: Unauthorised Disposal.—The hirer is bound to restore the article on the expiry of the time agreed upon, or, if no time was fixed, on demand. Failure in this respect involves liability for accidental loss.[29] Otherwise he is not liable for deterioration by ordinary wear and tear, nor for the accidental destruction of the article. But it would appear, from analogous cases, that the onus of proof of accidental loss lies on the hirer.[30] A hirer, or, it is conceived, a borrower or depositary, has no ostensible authority to dispose of the article, nor to subject it to a lien, and third parties acquire no right against its owner.[31]

25.9 Claim by Third Party.—Where an article hired is claimed by a third party the hirer should have recourse to an action of multiplepoinding. A refusal to return the article to the lessor, based merely on the ground of notice of an adverse claim, is a breach of contract unless the hirer can prove that the adverse claim was well founded.[32]

25.10 Regulated Consumer Hire Agreements.—Certain hire agreements (a) involving the supply of credit to an individual, (b) capable of subsisting for more than three months, and (c) not requiring the hirer to make payments exceeding £15,000, are regulated consumer hire agreements.[33] A person entering into such an agreement may require to be licensed.[34] The Act restricts advertising and canvassing in relation to such agreements, and regulates entry into, matters arising during, and the termination of, such agreements.[35] It is impossible to contract out of the Act.[36]

---

[26] As defined in s. 25, as amended by the Law Reform (Misc. Provs.) (Scotland) Act 1990, s. 68.
[27] s. 16, as amended by the Law Reform (Misc. Provs.) (Scotland) Act 1990, s. 68.
[28] s. 21; *G.M. Shepherd Ltd.* v. *North West Securities Ltd.*, 1991 S.L.T. 499; *Stair Memorial Encyclopaedia*, Vol. 14 (Location), paras. 1052, 1059.
[29] *Shaw* v. *Symmons* [1917] 1 K.B. 799.
[30] *Wilson* v. *Orr* (1879) 7 R. 266; *Copland* v. *Brogan*, 1916 S.C. 277. See also conflicting opinions in *Moes Moliere & Co.* v. *Leith, etc., Shipping Co.* (1867) 5 M. 988; *Mustard* v. *Paterson*, 1923 S.C. 142.
[31] *Murdoch* v. *Greig* (1889) 16 R. 396, and see, as to hire-purchase, para. 16.51, *supra*; *Mitchell* v. *Heyes* (1894) 21 R. 600; *Lamonby* v. *Foulds*, 1928 S.C. 89. See, however, *Albemarle Supply Co.* v. *Hind* [1928] 1 K.B. 307.
[32] *Ex p. Davies* (1881) 19 Ch.D. 86.
[33] Consumer Credit Act 1974, s. 15 as amended by S.I. 1983 No. 1878. See Chap. 18. The monetary limit is alterable by the Secretary of State: s. 181; see, *e.g.*, S.I. 1983 No. 1878, *cit. sup.*, increasing the limit from £5,000 to £15,000 with effect from May 20, 1985.
[34] s. 21.
[35] Pts. IV, V, VI and VII; *Automotive Financial Services* v. *Henderson*, 1992 S.L.T. (Sh. Ct.) 63.
[36] s. 173.

25.11 Loan.—Loan[37] is a contract under which the owner of a thing gives, for the temporary accommodation of another, the use or services derivable from it.[38] If the obligation is to return the particular thing the contract is known as commodate, or proper loan; if it is to return an equivalent amount, as in the case of money, or goods which are consumed by use, it is known as *mutuum*, or improper loan. In commodate the property in the thing does not pass to the borrower, and, on his bankruptcy, it may be recovered by the lender; in *mutuum* the property passes and the lender is merely a personal creditor.[39] In *mutuum* the borrower takes the risk of accidental destruction;[40] in commodate, while the standard of care required is a high one, proof of accidental loss, or accidental injury, the onus of proof being on the borrower, will excuse him. But the borrower is bound not to put the article to a use other than that (if any) indicated, and will be liable for any loss due to his failure in this respect.[41] Certain loans to individuals are governed by the Consumer Credit Act 1974.[42]

25.12 Deposit.—Similar rules apply to the contract of deposit, *locatio custodiae*.[43] The obligations of a depositary are to provide a secure place of custody, and to exercise due care to prevent damage or loss in connection with the property.[44] A contractual term or a provision of a notice[45] purporting to exclude or restrict liability for breach of duty may be void or unenforceable.[46] The fact that the contract was gratuitous,

[37] See Wilson, *Scottish Law of Debt* (2nd ed.), para. 4.1 *et seq.*; Gow, *Mercantile Law*, pp. 261 *et seq.*; *Stair Memorial Encyclopaedia*, Vol. 13 (Loan); as to proof of loan, see para. 6.2, *supra*.
[38] Bell, *Prin.*, § 194. It is unnecessary to specify the time and manner of restoration or repayment: *Neilson* v. *Stewart*, 1991 S.L.T. 523 (H.L.); 1990 S.L.T. 346 (I.H.).
[39] Bell, *Prin.*, § 1315. As to following trust money, see para. 46.14, *infra*.
[40] *Anderson & Crompton* v. *Walls* (1870) 9 M. 122, opinion of Lord Neaves.
[41] *Bain* v. *Strang* (1888) 16 R. 186.
[42] See Chap. 18. *Inter alia*, lenders require to be licensed. There are restrictions on advertising and canvassing. There are provisions for cooling-off periods and the supply of adequate information and documentation to the borrower. Extortionate loan agreements may be reopened by the court.
[43] See McBryde, *Contract*, paras. 6–54 *et seq*; *Stair Memorial Encyclopaedia*, Vol. 8 (Deposit). As to deposit in the context of a money deposit in the purchase of property, see *Zemhunt (Holdings) Ltd.* v. *Control Securities*, 1992 S.L.T. 151; and article, W.J. Stewart, "Restitution," 1992 S.L.T. (News) 47.
[44] Bell, *Prin.*, § 155, adopted in *Ballingall* v. *Dundee Ice, etc., Co.*, 1924 S.C. 238. See as to motor parking place, *Ashby* v. *Tolhurst* [1937] 2 K.B. 242; *Drynan* v. *Scottish Ice Rink Co.*, 1971 S.L.T. (Sh.Ct.) 59; garage, *Tognini Bros.* v. *Dick Bros.*, 1968 S.L.T. (Sh.Ct.) 87; *B.G. Transport Service* v. *Marston Motor Co.* [1970] 1 Ll. Rep. 371; *Verrico* v. *Hughes*, 1980 S.C. 179; bonded warehouse, *Brooks Wharf* v. *Goodman* [1937] 1 K.B. 534; restaurant, *Martin* v. *Alongi*, 1987 G.W.D. 20–758; friend for safe-keeping, *Fisher* v. *Donnelly*, 1990 G.W.D. 35–1984. Many of these cases must be read in the light of the Unfair Contract Terms Act 1977.
[45] As defined in s. 25 as amended by the Law Reform (Misc. Provs.) (Scotland) Act 1990, s. 68.
[46] Unfair Contract Terms Act 1977, ss. 15(2)(c) *et seq*. See Chap. 10. Alternatively the terms of any notice may be insufficient to exclude negligence or breach of duty on the part of the depositary: *Verrico* v. *Hughes*, *cit. sup.* Additionally, a term may be invalid under the Unfair Terms in Consumer Contracts Regulations 1994: para. 10.24 *supra*.

might, in narrow and doubtful cases, be of weight in determining whether sufficient care had been taken to exclude liability for the loss of the article.[47] So the degree of care required from bankers taking articles for safe custody has been held to depend on whether they make any charge.[48] But where a carrier undertook, gratuitously, to carry a parcel, and lost it, it was held that he was liable for its value unless he could explain the loss or prove that he had exercised reasonable care.[49] Where the deposit is for reward the standard of care, unless the depositary is an innkeeper or livery stable keeper, is that required from a hirer.[50] If a person undertakes to repair, or do other work on, an article for the owner (*locatio operis faciendi*) and has the article in his possession for that purpose, the contract normally includes an element of *locatio custodiae*, with the consequent obligations.[51]

25.13 **Innkeepers and Livery Stable Keepers.**—An innkeeper and a livery stable keeper may in certain cases incur a slightly higher degree of liability than other depositaries. They, like common carriers,[52] fall under the provisions of the Praetorian Edict.[53] Under the head of *stabularii* are included all livery stable keepers, whether attached to an inn or not,[54] but probably not the keeper of a motor garage.[55] In England, the exceptional liability of an innkeeper is held to depend on the custom of the realm and not on the Praetorian Edict.[56]

25.14 **Liability under Edict.**—An innkeeper or livery stable keeper is at common law liable for the loss of, or injury to, property brought to the inn or stable, unless he can prove that the loss or injury arose from the negligence of the owner[57] or is attributable to the Queen's enemies or to the act of God.[58] This latter term excludes liability for fire caused by pure accident, but the onus is on the depositary to prove the cause of the fire, or at least to exclude his own negligence.[59] Act of God has been defined generally as an accident due to natural causes, directly and

---

[47] Stair, I, xiii, 2; *Cogs* v. *Bernard* (1703) 1 Smith L.C. (13th ed.), p. 125; *Houghland* v. *R.R. Low (Luxury Coaches)* [1962] 1 Q.B. 694; *Walker* v. *Scottish & Newcastle Breweries*, 1970 S.L.T. (Sh.Ct.) 21; *Verrico* v. *Hughes, cit. sup.*

[48] *Giblin* v. *McMullen* (1868) L.R. 2 P.C. 317.

[49] *Copland* v. *Brogan*, 1916 S.C. 277.

[50] *Central Motors* v. *Cessnock Garage Co.*, 1925 S.C. 796; *Verrico* v. *Hughes, cit. sup.*

[51] *Sinclair* v. *Juner*, 1952 S.C. 35; *Macrae* v. *K. & I.*, 1962 S.L.T. (Notes) 90; *Forbes* v. *Aberdeen Motors*, 1965 S.L.T. 333; *Miller* v. *Howden*, 1968 S.L.T. (Sh.Ct.) 82; *Uprichard* v. *J. Dickson & Son Ltd.*, 1981 S.L.T. (Sh.Ct.) 5 (repair of gun: element of deposit).

[52] As to carrier, see Chap. 26, *infra*.

[53] Dig., IV, 9, 1. *Nautae, caupones, stabularii, quod cujusque salvum fore receperint, nisi restituant, in eos judicium dabo.*

[54] *Mustard* v. *Paterson*, 1923 S.C. 142.

[55] *Central Motors* v. *Cessnock Garage Co.*, 1925 S.C. 796; *Verrico* v. *Hughes; cit. sup.*

[56] *Calye's Case*, 1 Smith L.C. (13th ed.), p. 130.

[57] *Medawar* v. *Grand Hotel Co.* [1891] 2 Q.B. 11.

[58] Bell, *Prin*, § 237.

[59] *Sinclair* v. *Juner, cit. sup*; *Burns* v. *Royal Hotel (St. Andrews)*, 1958 S.C. 354.

exclusively, without human intervention, which could not have been prevented by any amount of foresight and pains and care reasonably to be expected.[60] As it is clear that a depositary for reward is in any event liable for loss due to the negligence of his servants, and is probably also liable for any loss or injury from unexplained causes, the practical difference between one who is, and one who is not, subject to the edict, would seem to be that the former alone is liable for loss by theft or by the wrongful act of third parties.[61]

25.15   Hotel Proprietors Act.—The liability of hotel proprietors is regulated by the Hotel Proprietors Act 1956, which repealed the Innkeepers' Liability Act 1863. An establishment, but only such an establishment, which is a hotel within the meaning of the Act,[62] is deemed to be an inn; and its proprietor, as an innkeeper, has the same duties, liabilities and rights which before the commencement of the Act attached to an innkeeper as such, in particular under the Edict. The proprietor's liability under the Edict extends to the making good to any guest of any damage to property brought to the hotel, as well as the loss of such property.[63] On the other hand he is not subject to the liability of an innkeeper under the Edict, whatever may be his liability under contract or for negligence, in respect of any loss of or damage to any vehicle or property left therein, or any horse or other live animal or its harness or equipment, nor does his lien extend to these articles.[64]

Without prejudice to any other ground of liability, the proprietor is only liable as an innkeeper to make good loss or damage to the property of a traveller for whom at the time of the loss or damage sleeping accommodation had been engaged, and where the loss or damage occurred during the period commencing with the midnight immediately preceding, and ending with the midnight immediately following, a period for which the traveller was a guest at the hotel and entitled to use such accommodation.[65] The proprietor may also limit his liability as an innkeeper to £50 for any one article or £100 in the aggregate, provided that at the time when the property in question was brought to the hotel a notice in statutory form[66] was conspicuously displayed in a place where it could conveniently be read by guests at or near the reception desk or, if none, at or near the main entrance. But this limit

---

[60] James L.J. in *Nugent* v. *Smith* (1876) 1 C.P.D. 423; adopted by Lord Hunter in *Mustard* v. *Paterson*, 1923 S.C. 142.

[61] *Mustard* v. *Paterson, supra*; *Macpherson* v. *Christie* (1841) 3 D. 930; *Whitehouse* v. *Pickett*, 1908 S.C. (H.L.) 31; *Winkworth* v. *Raven* [1931] 1 K.B. 652.

[62] 'Hotel' is defined (s. 1(3)) as 'an establishment held out by the proprietor as offering food, drink and, if required, sleeping accommodation, without special contract, to any traveller presenting himself who appears able and willing to pay a reasonable sum for the services and facilities provided and who is in a fit state to be received.'

[63] s. 1(2).

[64] s. 2(2).

[65] s. 2(1).

[66] See Schedule.

will not apply where (a) the property was stolen, lost or damaged through the default, neglect or wilful act of the proprietor or his employee,[67] (b) the property was deposited expressly for safe custody, or (c) if not so deposited, it had been offered for deposit and refused, or if not so offered, where the guest wishing to offer it for deposit was unable to do so through the default of the proprietor or his employee.[68] It has been held under the 1863 Act that in order to satisfy the condition that the property has been 'deposited expressly' the fact of the deposit must be definitely brought to the innkeeper's notice, and that where there is no such express deposit the onus of proof of fault or neglect on the part of the innkeeper lies on the guest.[69]

Further Reading

Bell, *Prin.*, pp. 133 *et seq.*
Gow, *Mercantile Law* (1964), Ch. 3.
Paton, *Bailment* (1952).
Stair Memorial Encyclopaedia, Vol. 8 (Deposit); Vol. 13 (Loan); Vol. 14 (Location).
Wilson, *Scottish Law of Debt* (2nd ed., 1991).

---

[67] *Kott & Kott* v. *Gordon Hotels* [1968] 2 Ll. Rep. 228.
[68] s. 2(3).
[69] *Whitehouse* v. *Pickett*, 1908 S.C. (H.L.) 31.

CHAPTER 26

CARRIAGE BY LAND

26.1 Common Carriers.—A carrier may or may not be a common carrier. A common carrier is one who undertakes for hire[1] to transport the goods of all who choose to employ him in the business which he professes to ply. He may be a common carrier though he limits the class of goods which he is willing to carry, or though he indicates that certain goods will be carried only on special conditions, but it is essential that he should profess to be willing to carry for all those who choose to employ him.[2] If he makes no such profession he is a private carrier. Until September 1, 1962 the railways, although nationalised by the Transport Act 1947, were common carriers. The Transport Act 1962 altered this and the Railways Board has freedom to impose such terms in its contracts of carriage as it wishes,[3] which results in its being a private carrier. The old law relating to the Standard Terms and Conditions[4] now no longer applies. Cabmen[5] and removal contractors[6] are private carriers. Bus companies and road hauliers are common carriers but in most cases their liability as such for loss or damage to goods is modified by contract.[7] The Post Office is not a common carrier.[8]

26.2 Obligation to Carry.—The distinction between common and private carriers is of importance in two respects—(1) in the obligation to accept employment; (2) in the degree of liability for loss or injury to goods. A private carrier may accept any offer of employment or refuse it. A common carrier makes a continuous offer to carry[9] provided, in the case of goods, that they are of the class he professes to carry, that they are not dangerous or insufficiently packed; that they arrive in time; that he

---

[1] See *Barr* v. *Caledonian Ry.* (1890) 18 R. 139.

[2] *Great Northern Ry.* v. *L.E.P.* [1922] 2 K.B. 742.

[3] s. 43(3).

[4] As settled by the Railway Rates Tribunal under the Railways Act 1921; see para. 26.12, *infra.*

[5] *Ord* v. *Gemmell* (1898) 1 F. 17.

[6] *Pearcey* v. *Player* (1883) 10 R. 564. As to wharfingers, see *Consolidated Tea Co.* v. *Oliver's Wharf* [1910] 2 K.B. 395.

[7] To the extent permitted by the Unfair Contract Terms Act 1977. See para. 26.8, *infra.*

[8] See *Harold Stephen & Co.* v. *Post Office* [1977] 1 W.L.R. 1172 at p. 1177; ss. 29 and 30 of the Post Office Act 1969, as amended by the British Telecommunications Act 1981, Scheds. 3 and 6, and the Telecommunications Act 1984, s. 99 and Sched. 7.

[9] See, *e.g., A. Siohn & Co. and Academy Garments (Wigan)* v. *R.H. Hagland & Son (Transport)* [1976] 2 Lloyd's Rep. 428.

has room in his conveyance; that his charges are paid or tendered; in the case of passengers also that they are in a reasonably fit state to be carried.[10] An unjustifiable refusal is a ground for an action for damages.[11] A common carrier is bound by a list of fares publicly advertised,[12] and in any case is not entitled to charge more than a reasonable fare.[13]

26.3   Strict Liability of Common Carrier.—The exceptional liability for the loss of goods which rests on a common carrier is in Scotland based on the Praetorian Edict; in England, on the custom of the realm.[14] The common carrier is in the position of an insurer, and is liable for loss of or damage to goods without affirmative proof of negligence. Proof that the goods were stolen is no defence.[15] For loss by accidental fire, which was an exception to the carrier's liability at common law,[16] a common carrier by land, though not by sea, is liable by statute.[17] It is a valid defence to the carrier that the goods have been lost by the fault of the sender, as where they are insufficiently addressed;[18] by act of God; by the Queen's enemies, including the case of a rebellion, not of a mere riot;[19] or by their inherent vice, as where a horse struggled through an opening left as a feeding window.[20] These defences are available only if the carrier has not deviated from the route agreed upon, or can show that the particular event would have happened even if he had not deviated.[21] In addition he must show that neither he nor his servants contributed to the casualty through their negligence.[22] In the absence of express agreement to the contrary, a carrier who issues a ticket or consignment note is responsible for the whole journey, though it is known that he carries only part of it.[23]

---

[10] Bell, *Prin.*, § 159; *Clarke* v. *West Ham Corporation* [1909] 2 K.B. 858. Note the analogous obligation of an innkeeper: *Rothfield* v. *N.B.R.*, 1920 S.C. 805.

[11] Bell, *Prin.*, § 159.

[12] *Campbell* v. *Ker*, Feb. 24, 1810, F.C.

[13] *Great Western Ry.* v. *Sutton* (1868) L.R. 4 H.L. 226, at p. 237.

[14] Dig., IV, 9, 1; Stair, I, xiii, 3; Bell, *Prin.*, § 235; and see *supra*, para. 25.13; and *Burns* v. *Royal Hotel (St. Andrews)*, 1958 S.C. 354. A private carrier is liable only for fault or negligence: Stair, I, xiii, 3; Bell, *Prin.*, § 235; *Copland* v. *Brogan*, 1916 S.C. 277 (gratuitous carriage).

[15] Bell, *Prin.*, § 238.

[16] See *supra*, para. 25.14 and *Burns* v. *Royal Hotel (St Andrews)*, *supra*, as to onus of proof.

[17] Mercantile Law Amendment (Scotland) Act 1856, s. 17. A private carrier is also liable under s. 17: *James Kemp (Leslie)* v. *Robertson*, 1967 S.L.T. 213; *Graham* v. *The Shore Porters Society*, 1979 S.L.T. 119; *Boomsma* v. *Clark & Rose*, 1983 S.L.T. (Sh.Ct.) 67. It may be possible to contract out of the statutory liability under s. 17: *Graham* v. *The Shore Porters Society*, *supra*; *Boomsma* v. *Clark & Rose*, *supra*.

[18] *Caledonian Ry.* v. *Hunter* (1858) 20 D. 1097.

[19] See *Curtis* v. *Matthews* [1919] 1 K.B. 425.

[20] *Ralston* v. *Caledonian Ry.* (1878) 5 R. 671.

[21] *Morrison* v. *Shaw Savill, etc., Co.* [1916] 2 K.B. 783.

[22] *Burns* v. *Royal Hotel (St. Andrews)*, *supra*.

[23] *Logan* v. *Highland Ry.* (1899) 2 F. 292. Referred to, *Aberdeen Grit Co.* v. *Ellerman's Wilson Line*, 1933 S.C. 9.

26.4 Passenger's Luggage.—A common carrier is liable for the loss of passenger's luggage.[24] The relevant rules were largely formulated in cases relating to luggage accompanying rail passengers. Although the Transport Act 1962 has removed the railways from the class of common carriers, these rules are probably still applicable to operators of public service vehicles.[25] There is liability for loss even if the luggage is inside the vehicle with the passenger unless the carrier can show that its loss was due to lack of reasonable care on the part of the passenger.[26]. The liability ends when the luggage is delivered at the end of the journey, though it may then be left with the carrier as a depositary or custodier,[27] in which case he is only liable for negligence.[28] A carrier is not bound to carry, as passenger's luggage, anything the passenger may choose to bring with him. The following general definition of passenger's luggage has been given: 'Whatever the passenger takes with him for his personal use or convenience, according to the habits or wants of the particular class to which he belongs, either with reference to the immediate necessities or to the ultimate purpose of the journey.'[29] The carrier is also entitled to refuse to carry, without additional charge, articles requiring special care in carriage, such as a bicycle, gun or fishing-rod, not so packed as to be readily carried without special precautions.[30] Where, without notice to the carrier, articles are taken which are not properly passenger's luggage he is not liable for their loss.[31]

26.5 Delay in Transit.—The obligation of a common carrier does not amount to insurance against loss or injury caused by delay in transit. It is an obligation to carry within a time reasonable in the circumstances. So where goods were damaged by delay due to a general strike of railwaymen,[32] or to a block on the line caused by an accident not due to the company's negligence,[33] it was held that there was no liability. The carrier, if aware of circumstances likely to cause delay, is bound to warn the passenger or sender of goods.[34] Should delay threaten damage to perishable goods the carrier, as an agent by necessity, is entitled to sell them, but before doing so is bound to communicate with the owner, if reasonably practicable.[35] An obligation to carry within a particular time

[24] *Parker* v. *L.M.S. Ry.*, 1930 S.C. 822; *Campbell* v. *Cal. Ry. Co.* (1852) 14 D. 806.
[25] See para. 26.15, *infra*.
[26] *Jenkyns* v. *Southampton Steam Packet Co.* [1919] 2 K.B. 135; *Vosper* v. *G.W. Ry.* [1928] 1 K.B. 340; *Parker* v. *L.M.S. Ry.*, 1930 S.C. 822.
[27] *Parker* v. *L.M.S. Ry.*, *supra.*
[28] *Lyons* v. *Caledonian Ry.*, 1909 S.C. 1185.
[29] *Jenkyns* v. *Southampton Steam Packet Co.*, *supra*; *Buckland* v. *The King* [1933] 1 K.B. 329.
[30] *Britten* v. *Great Northern Ry.* [1899] 1 Q.B. 243.
[31] *Macrow* v. *Great Western Ry.* (1871) L.R. 6 Q.B. 612.
[32] *Sims* v. *Midland Ry.* [1913] 1 K.B. 103.
[33] *Anderson* v. *N.B.R.* (1875) 2 R. 443.
[34] *McConnachie* v. *Great North of Scotland Ry.* (1875) 3 R. 79; *Jarvie* v. *Cal. Ry.* (1875) 2 R. 623.
[35] *Springer* v. *Great Western Ry.* [1921] 1 K.B. 257.

may be expressly undertaken, or may be inferred from advertisement, as where a railway advertises trains to meet a particular market.[36] Proof that a railway company regularly gave preference in transit to goods marked perishable was held to render them liable for injury on an occasion when they had failed to do so.[37]

26.6 Delay in Carriage of Passengers.—With regard to passengers the general obligation is merely to carry within a time reasonable in all the circumstances of the case. It has never been held that the publication of a time-table indicating times of departure and connections amounts to an undertaking that these times will be observed,[38] but it may amount to an undertaking that the trains indicated will be run.[39] It has been held that where a connection was missed owing to want of reasonable care on the part of the company the question whether the passenger could recover, as damages, the expense of a special train which he had ordered depended upon whether he would probably have done the same if he had had no recourse.[40] As has been seen the Railways Board will only incur liability arising from a breach of the terms of its private contract, but these rules still apply in substance to the liability of a common carrier who has not made special contractual arrangements with his customer.

26.7 Liability for Negligence.—Quite apart from the strict liability of common carriers, all carriers, whether common or private, are subject to the ordinary principles of the law of reparation.[41] Thus a carrier is liable for his own or his servants' negligence, whether it constitutes a breach of the implied conditions of the contract or a breach of the carrier's duty to take reasonable care for the safety of persons or property lawfully placed in his charge.[42] Negligence involves failure in a duty, and therefore in cases where the responsibility of a common carrier does not attach, there is no liability for injury by pure accident, by the criminal or wrongful acts of parties, such as fellow passengers, for whom the carrier is not responsible,[43] or from a breakdown in the carriage which could not have been prevented by a reasonable system of inspection.[44] If goods are delivered to a private carrier in good condition, and tendered by him in a damaged state, that is prima facie evidence of fault.[45] Similarly anything in the nature of a railway accident

[36] *Finlay* v. *N.B.R.* (1870) 8 M. 959.
[37] *Macdonald* v. *Highland Ry.* (1873) 11 M. 614.
[38] See Deas on *Railways* (2nd ed.), p. 724.
[39] *Denton* v. *Great Northern Ry.* (1856) 5 E. & B. 800.
[40] *Le Blanche* v. *L. and N.-W. Ry.* (1876) 1 C.P.D. 286.
[41] See Chap. 31 *et seq.*
[42] *Meux* v. *Great Eastern Ry.* [1895] 2 Q.B. 387; *Boomsma* v. *Clark & Rose*, 1983 S.L.T. (Sh.Ct.) 67.
[43] *East Indian Ry.* v. *Mukerjee* [1901] A.C. 396.
[44] *Readhead* v. *Midland Ry.* (1869) L.R. 4 Q.B. 379; *Reynolds* v. *Lanarkshire Tramways Co.* (1908) 16 S.L.T. 230.
[45] *Sutton & Co.* v. *Ciceri & Co.* (1890) 17 R. (H.L.) 40.

is prima facie evidence of negligence, and it rests with the Railways Board to prove that the accident was due to some cause, for example a latent and undiscoverable flaw, for which they were not responsible.[46] It would appear that the carrier's duty of care does not extend to persons who travel surreptitiously, or in violation of the carrier's regulations.[47] But his responsibility does extend to persons carried gratuitously.[48]

26.8 **Exclusion of or Limitation of Liability by Contract.**—The Carriers Act 1830 leaves it open to a common carrier to make special arrangements with individuals excluding or restricting liability for loss of or damage to goods, and private carriers were always free to contract to their own terms.[49] However the Unfair Contract Terms Act 1977 applies to all contracts of carriage.[50] A contractual term or a provision of a notice[51] purporting to exclude or restrict liability for breach of duty[52] arising in the course of the carrier's business or from the occupation of the carrier's business premises is void if it excludes or restricts liability in respect of death or personal injury, and may be unenforceable if it was not fair and reasonable to incorporate the term in the contract or to allow reliance on the provision of the notice[53] The fact that a passenger agreed to, or was aware of, the term or provision is not in itself sufficient evidence that he knowingly and voluntarily assumed the risk.[54] 'Breach of duty' does not extend to duties higher than the duty to use reasonable care and skill, and thus the Act does not cover any clause avoiding the strict liability of the common carrier.[55] But neither a private nor a common carrier may exclude liability for death or injury caused by their negligence.[56] A clause purporting to exclude or restrict liability for breach of contract or for unsatisfactory performance may be unenforceable if the contract of carriage is either a consumer contract[57] or a standard form contract.[58]

---

[46] *Ballard* v. *N.B.R.* , 1923 S.C. (H.L.) 43.

[47] *Thompson* v. *N.B.R.* (1882) 9 R. 1101; *Grand Trunk Ry.* v. *Barnett* [1911] A.C. 361.

[48] *Austin* v. *Great Western Ry.* (1867) L.R. 2 Q.B. 442.

[49] A clause seeking to exclude liability for negligence or breach of contract will be construed *contra proferentem*: *Graham* v. *The Shore Porters Society*, 1979 S.L.T. 119; *Boomsma* v. *Clark & Rose, supra.*

[50] 1977 Act, s. 15(2)(c); *Boomsma* v. *Clark & Rose*, 1983 S.L.T. (Sh.Ct.) 67.

[51] ss. 15 and 16 of the 1977 Act as amended by the Law Reform (Misc. Provs.) (Scotland) Act 1990, s. 68. 'Notice' includes an announcement whether or not in writing, and any other communication or pretended communication: s. 25(1) as amended by the 1990 Act.

[52] 'Breach of duty' is defined in s. 25(1).

[53] 1977 Act, s. 16(1) as amended; *Boomsma* v. *Clark & Rose, supra.* As to reasonableness, see para. 10.23, *supra.*

[54] 1977 Act, s. 16(3), as amended.

[55] See Rogers & Clarke, *The Unfair Contract Terms Act 1977.*

[56] 1977 Act, s. 16. See too the Public Passenger Vehicles Act 1981, s. 29, in relation to operators of public service vehicles.

[57] 'Consumer contract' is defined in s. 25(1).

[58] 1977 Act, ss. 15(2)(c), 17, 25(1). As to purported indemnity clauses in consumer contracts, see s.18. See generally Chap. 10, *supra.*

Any valid exclusion or restriction clause must be shown to have been incorporated in the contract.[59] It has been held that if a carrier deviates from the agreed route, he loses the benefit of any valid conditions in his favour, and is liable for damages however caused.[60] The right of the carrier to found on a valid limitation clause may be lost by actings which amount to repudiation of the contract.[61]

26.9 Statutory Limitation of Liability.—The Carriers Act 1830, section 1, provides that the liability of a common carrier by land for loss or injury to goods (including passengers' luggage[62]) is excluded, in the case of certain specified goods, unless their nature and value have been declared when they are placed in the carrier's hands, and an increased charge, if demanded, has been paid. Thirty-six classes of goods are specified, having the common characteristic of great value relative to their bulk, and including the precious metals, bank notes or securities, jewellery, pictures, furs and lace. Such goods must be declared if their value exceeds £10. If an increased charge is to be made it must be posted in the office or receiving-house of the carrier, but failure in this respect does not deprive the carrier of the statutory immunity.[63] The nature and value of the goods must be declared; it is not sufficient to make a general statement that they are valuable.[64] The Act does not protect the carrier from loss due to any theft, embezzlement or forgery of his servants, but the sender of the goods must prove circumstances, beyond the mere fact of opportunity, which render it more likely that the goods have been stolen by the carrier's servants than by some other thief.[65]

26.10 Ejection from Conveyance.—There is some authority for the view that any carrier has at common law the right to eject from his conveyance a passenger who refuses to pay the fare.[66] The Railways Board has express statutory power to arrest and detain any person who travels, or attempts to travel, without paying his fare, and with the intent to avoid payment;[67] and this has been held to justify summary expulsion of a

---

[59] See para. 5.12, *supra*; *cf. McCutcheon* v. *MacBrayne*, 1964 S.C. (H.L.) 28; *William Teacher & Sons Ltd.* v. *Bell Lines Ltd.*, 1991 S.L.T. 876. As to provisions of notices, see s. 16(1A) of the 1977 Act, as amended.
[60] *Lord Polwarth* v. *N.B.R.*, 1908 S.C. 1275; *L. and N.-W. Ry.* v. *Neilson* [1922] 2 A.C. 263; *Hain S.S. Co.* v. *Tate & Lyle* [1936] 2 All E.R. 597.
[61] *John Carter (Fine Worsteds)* v. *Hanson Haulage (Leeds) Ltd.* [1965] 2 Q.B. 495. Contrast with actings amounting to material breach entitling the other party to rescind: see 1977 Act, s. 22, and Chap. 10, *supra*.
[62] *Casswell* v. *Cheshire Lines Committee* [1907] 2 K.B. 499.
[63] *Rusk* v. *N.B.R.*, 1920 2 S.L.T. 139.
[64] *Rusk, supra.*
[65] Carriers Act 1830, s. 8, as amended by the Criminal Law Act 1967; *Campbell* v. *N.B.R.* (1875) 2 R. 433.
[66] *North-Eastern Ry.* v. *Mathews* (1866) 5 Irvine 237; but see opinions in *Harris* v. *N.B.R.* (1891) 18 R. 1009.
[67] Railway Clauses Act 1845, ss. 96, 97; *Gerber* v. *British Railways Board*, 1969 J.C. 7.

passenger who had a ticket which was not available on a particular day, though there was no averment that he had any intention to travel without paying his fare.[68] In England, it was held not to cover the case of a passenger who has lost his ticket, and refused to comply with a demand that he should pay the fare from the place from which the train started.[69] Any unnecessary violence in ejecting a passenger will found an action for damages.[70]

26.11 Lien of Carrier.—A carrier has at common law a special lien over goods for his charges for their carriage, but no lien for a general balance.[71] He is not entitled to detain a passenger, or any part of his clothing, for the fare.[72] A contract between a carrier and a trader whereby the former obtains a general lien is effectual in a question with the trustee in the sequestration of the trader.[73] A provision in a contract whereby goods were carried at owner's risk, under which the goods were subjected to a general lien for all charges due by the 'owners,' was held not to preclude the senders of the goods, as unpaid sellers, from exercising their right of stoppage *in transitu*, and thereby acquiring a right to delivery preferable to a claim by the railway company for a general balance due by the consignee.[74]

26.12 Carriage of Goods by Rail.—The railways are now under the general control of the Railways Board and have ceased to be common carriers.[75] Accordingly the Standard Terms and Conditions in force prior to 1962 have ceased to have any effect.[76] While the General Conditions of Carriage issued by the Railways Board bear some resemblance to the old standard conditions, these conditions are no more than the framework for each *ad hoc* contract made by the Board. The Board is not now an insurer of the goods it carries but can only be liable for negligence, subject to any valid condition in the contract in question limiting or excluding that liability.[77] Similarly the Carriers Act 1830 no longer applies to carriage of goods by rail.

26.13 Passengers.—Any person who holds himself out as willing to carry members of the public is a common carrier of passengers inasmuch as he is bound to carry persons willing to pay the fare unless there is some good reason for not doing so.[78] However, there is no edictal liability imposed for the safety of the passengers carried.[79]

---

[68] *Highland Ry.* v. *Menzies* (1878) 5 R. 887.
[69] *Butler* v. *Manchester, etc., Ry.* (1888) 21 Q.B.D. 207.
[70] *Maxwell* v. *Cal. Ry.* (1898) 25 R. 550.
[71] *Peebles* v. *Cal. Ry.* (1875) 2 R. 346.
[72] *Wolf* v. *Summers* (1811) 2 Camp 631.
[73] *Great Eastern Ry.* v. *Lord's Tr.* [1909] A.C. 109.
[74] *U.S. Steel Products Co.* v. *G.W. Ry.* [1916] 1 A.C. 189.
[75] See para. 26.1, *supra*.
[76] For a statement of the position prior to September 1, 1962, see Gow, *Mercantile and Industrial Law of Scotland*, pp. 480–481.
[77] See Transport Act 1962, s. 43(3) and para. 26.8, *supra*.
[78] *Clarke* v. *West Ham Corporation* [1909] 2 K.B. 858.
[79] As to liability for negligence, see para. 26.7, *supra*.

26.14 Road Haulage.—With certain exceptions[80] no haulier may use a goods
vehicle for the carriage of goods for hire or reward or in connection
with his trade or business without an operator's licence.[81] An operator's
licence may be standard or restricted, national or international.[82] All
hauliers are subject to the common law, as modified by the Carriers Act
1830,[83] and any conditions contained in licences. A road haulier may,
and usually does, limit his liability by special conditions.[84] The modern
practice is for road hauliers to limit their profession to that of private
carriers.

26.15 Public Service Vehicles.—Any motor vehicle is a public service vehicle
if it is adapted to carry more than eight passengers and is used for
carrying passengers for hire or reward, or is not so adapted but is used
for carrying passengers for hire or reward at separate fares in the course
of a business of carrying passengers.[85] Local services are governed by
sections 6 to 9 of the Transport Act 1985.[86] Prescribed particulars of the
service must be registered with the local traffic commissioner,[87] and
traffic regulation conditions may be imposed.[88] Each vehicle requires a
PSV operator's licence.[89]

The liabilities of the owner of a public service vehicle in respect of
injury to passengers or their luggage are those of common carriers,[90]
although in most cases his liability is modified or restricted by
contract.[91]

26.16 International Carriage.—International carriage by land has been the
subject of several international conventions.[92] The Unfair Contract
Terms Act 1977 does not strike at any restriction or exclusion clause

[80] See for example the Goods Vehicles (Operators' Licences, Qualifications and Fees)
Regulations 1984 (S.I. 1984 No. 176), as amended.
[81] Transport Act 1968, ss. 59–61, as amended, *Alderton* v. *Richard Burgon Associates
(Manpower)* [1974] R.T.R. 422.
[82] See the Goods Vehicles (Operators' Licences, Qualifications and Fees) Regulations
1984 (S.I. 1984 No. 176), as amended. See too, the International Road Haulage Permits
Act 1975.
[83] s. 6.
[84] para. 26.8, *supra*; *e.g.* the Conditions issued by the Road Haulage Association.
[85] Transport Act 1985, s. 137(2); Public Passenger Vehicles Act 1981, s. 1(1). *Re* 'hire
or reward' see 1981 Act, s. 1(5) and 1985 Act, s. 137(3).
[86] 'Local services' are defined in s. 2 of the 1985 Act. There is special provision for
London local services in Pt. II.
[87] 1985 Act, s.6.
[88] 1985 Act, s.7.
[89] 1985 Act, ss. 18–31; s. 137(2); 1981 Act, s. 82 and Pt. II.
[90] See paras. 26.4 and 26.7, *supra*.
[91] The courts are reluctant to hold that a carrier is a common carrier: see *Belfast
Ropeworks* v. *Bushell* [1918] 1 K.B. 210. In relation to modification or restriction by
contract, see para. 26.8, *supra*.
[92] See *infra*. The texts of the conventions are detailed, and should be referred to in any
particular case.

authorised by such conventions if the United Kingdom is a party thereto.[93]

26.17 **International Carriage by Road: Goods (CMR).**—The Carriage of Goods by Road Act 1965[94] applies to every contract for the carriage of goods by road[95] in vehicles[96] for reward, when the place of taking over of the goods and the place designated for delivery, as specified in the contract, are situated in two different countries, at least one being a contracting country.[97] The residence or nationality of the contracting parties is irrelevant.[97] With certain limited exceptions,[98] it is impossible to contract out of the statutory provisions.[99] Carriage should be effected under a consignment note, containing certain particulars. The note is prima facie evidence of the contract, and gives rise to certain presumptions.[1] The sender's rights and obligations are set out in detail, as are the carrier's.[2] The carrier is liable for loss of or damage to goods, and for delay in delivery.[3] However in certain circumstances,[4] his liability is excluded and, if not excluded, is limited.[5] However he cannot benefit from the Act's protection where he has been guilty of wilful

---

[93] 1977 Act, s. 29.

[94] The 1965 Act implements the Geneva Convention on the Contract for the International Carriage of Goods by Road 1956, the terms of which are set out in the Schedule to the Act. The Schedule has been amended by s. 4(2) of the Carriage by Air and Road Act 1979 (see S.I. 1980 No. 1966).

[95] As to carriage partly by road and partly by other modes of transport, see 1965 Act, Sched., art. 2; and see *Thermo Engineers* v. *Ferrymasters* [1981] 1 All E.R. 1142 (goods damaged while being loaded by stevedores).

[96] 'Vehicles' are defined in art. 1(2) of the Schedule.

[97] 1965 Act, Sched., art.1(1). See, *e.g.* the Carriage of Goods by Road (Parties to Convention) Order (S.I. 1967 No. 1683 as amended by S.I. 1980 No. 697). The Act does not apply to carriage performed under the terms of any international postal convention; to funeral consignments; or to furniture removals: *ibid.*, art. 1(4). The Act does apply to carriage by states and governmental institutions: art. 1(3). Note that for the purposes of the CMR convention, Jersey is not a different country from the U.K. : *Chloride Industrial Batteries* v. *F. & W. Freight* [1989] 1 W.L.R. 823 (C.A.).

[98] *Ibid.*, art. 40.

[99] 1965 Act, Sched., art. 41.

[1] *Ibid.*, arts. 4–9; *SGS-Ates Componenti Elettronici S.p.A.* v. *Grappo* [1977] R.T.R. 442.

[2] 1965 Act, Sched., arts. 7–16. The sender may *inter alia* stop the goods in transit, or change the consignee. The carrier may, *inter alia*, sell perishable goods.

[3] *Ibid.*, art. 17.

[4] *Ibid.*, arts. 17–18; for example, where the loss or damage was caused by the claimant's wrongful act; or by the claimant's instructions; or by inevitable accident; or by inherent vice. The following cases illustrate unsuccessful attempts by carriers to rely on arts. 17–18: *Ulster-Swift and Pig Marketing Board (Northen Ireland)* v. *Taunton Meat Haulage* [1975] 2 Lloyd's Rep. 502 (heating of carcasses not 'inherent vice'); *Michael Galley Footear* v. *Laboni* [1982] 2 All E.R. 200 (theft); *Centrocoop Export-Import S.A.* v. *Brit. European Transport* [1984] 2 Lloyd's Rep. 618 (freezing of meat not unavoidable circumstances); *W. Donald & Son (Wholesale Meat Contractors) Ltd.* v. *Continental Freeze Ltd.*, 1984 S.L.T. 182 (freezing of meat not decay); *Silber J.J.* v. *Islander Trucking* [1985] 2 Lloyd's Rep. 243 (robbery not unavoidable circumstances).

[5] *Ibid.*, arts. 23–26, as amended by the Carriage by Air and Road Act 1979, s. 4(2); *William Tatton & Co.* v. *Ferrymasters* [1974] 1 Lloyd's Rep. 203; *James Buchanan & Co.* v. *Babco Forwarding & Shipping (U.K.)* [1978] A.C. 141.

misconduct or default.[6] Where several carriers are liable, damages will be apportioned.[7] Any action under the 1965 Act must be raised within certain time limits.[8] Where a right of action is time-barred, it may not be exercised by way of set off.[9] A foreign litigant may be ordained to sist a mandatary.[10]

26.18   International Carriage by Road: Passengers and Luggage.—The Carriage of Passengers by Road Act 1974, when brought into force,[11] will regulate every contract for the carriage[12] of passengers[13] and their luggage in vehicles[14] by road[15] when the contract provides that the carriage shall take place in the territory of more than one state, and that either or both the place of departure or place of destination is situated in a contracting state's territory.[16] It will be impossible to contract out of the Act.[17]

26.19   International Carriage by Rail (COTIF).—One convention governs the international carriage by rail of goods, passengers and luggage.[18] There is provision for the establishment at Berne of a permanent organisation for international carriage by rail (OTIF).[19] Disputes arising from the convention may be referred to arbitration.[20]

[6] *Ibid.*, art. 29; *Texas Instruments* v. *Nason (Europe)* [1991] 1 Lloyd's Rep. 146.
[7] *Ibid.*, arts. 34–39; *Cummins Engine Co.* v. *Davis Freight Forwarding (Hull)* [1981] 1 W.L.R. 1363 C.A. But see art. 40. One carrier may seek contribution or indemnity from another carrier by way of third party proceedings: *cf.* English decision, *ITT Schaub-Lorenz* v. *Birkart Johann Internationale Spedition* [1988] 1 Lloyd's Rep. 487 (C.A.).
[8] *Ibid.*, art. 32; *Poclain S.A.* v. *S.C.A.C. S.A.* [1986] 1 Lloyd's Rep. 404 (C.A.); *Muller Batavier* v. *Laurent Transport Co.* [1977] R.T.R. 499; *I.C.I. plc* v. *M.A.T. Transport Ltd.* [1987] 1 Lloyd's Rep. 354; *Microfine Minerals & Chemicals Ltd.* v. *Transferry Shipping Co. Ltd.* [1991] 2 Lloyd's Rep. 630.
[9] *Ibid.*, art. 32.
[10] Notwithstanding the terms of art. 31(5): *General Trading Corp.* v. *James Mills (Montrose) Ltd.*, 1982 S.L.T. (Sh.Ct.) 30.
[11] The 1974 Act is to be brought into force on a date to be appointed: s. 14(5). It will implement the Convention on the Contract for the International Carriage of Passengers and Luggage by Road (Geneva, 1973) with amendments made by the Carriage by Air and Road Act 1979, s. 4(3). However the United Kingdom is not yet a contracting party to the Convention.
[12] The carrier must be acting in the course of a trade or business: 1974 Act, Sched., art.1(2). Taxis and hired cars with drivers are excluded.
[13] 'Passengers' and 'Vehicles' are defined in art. 1(2) of the Schedule to the 1974 Act.
[14] *Ibid.*
[15] As to carriage partly by road and partly by other modes of transport, see arts. 2, 3.
[16] 1974 Act, Sched., art. 1(1). Parties' residences and nationalities are irrelevant.
[17] *Ibid.*, art. 23.
[18] The Convention concerning International Carriage by Rail (Berne 1980) (or Convention relative aux Transports Internationaux Ferroviaires—COTIF) brought into force in the U.K. on May 1, 1985: ss. 1 and 11(3) of the International Transport Conventions Act 1983 and S.I. 1985 No. 612. The text of the Convention is to be found in Cmnd. 8535 (1982), as amended by Pt. I of the Protocols of Decisions adopted by the Revision Committee at Berne, first and second sessions (December 14–21, 1989, and May 28–31, 1990): see the International Transport Conventions Act 1983 (Amendment) Order 1992 (S.I. 1992 No. 237), and Command Papers Cm. 1690 and Cm. 1689.
[19] COTIF, arts. 1, 5–11.
[20] COTIF, arts. 12–16.

26.20 **International Carriage by Rail: Passengers and Luggage (COTIF Appendix A: CIV).**—The Uniform Rules[21] in COTIF Appendix A regulate (a) any carriage of passengers and luggage under international transport documents made out for a journey over the territories of at least two member states[22] and exclusively over listed lines or services;[23] and (b) persons accompanying consignments effected in accordance with the convention relating to carriage of goods by rail (CIM).[24] The rules regulate, *inter alia*, liability for death or personal injury; loss of or damage to luggage; and delay in delivery.[25] Claims may become time-barred, and rights of action may in certain circumstances be extinguished.[26]

The railway is liable for death or personal injury to a passenger caused by an accident arising out of the operation of the railway and happening while the passenger was in, entering or alighting from railway vehicles.[27] The railway is also liable for loss of or damage to hand luggage.[28] The railway is relieved of liability in certain circumstances,[29] and its liability in respect of certain heads of claim is limited[30] although the limits are doubled when the railway is guilty of gross negligence, and do not apply at all where the railway's misconduct caused the loss.[31] It is impossible to contract out of liability for personal injury or death.[32]

The railway is also liable for delay in delivery of, and loss[33] of or damage to, registered luggage, *i.e.* luggage, other than hand luggage, registered for carriage under a luggage registration voucher.[34] There are

---

[21] Replacing the Convention Internationale concernant le transport des voyageurs et des bagages par chemins de fer (CIV Berne 1970).

[22] The identity of member states may from time to time be certified by Order in Council: s. 2 of the 1983 Act.

[23] Listed lines and services: COTIF, App. A, arts. 3 and 10.

[24] COTIF, App. A, art. 1; and see para. 26.21, *infra*.

[25] In the absence of specific provisions in the rules, national law applies: COTIF, App. A, art. 8.

[26] COTIF, App. A, arts. 48–55. For example, art 53: right of action for death or personal injury extinguished (with certain exceptions) if 'notice of the accident' is not given within three months of becoming aware of the loss or damage; art. 54: acceptance of registered luggage may (with certain exceptions) extinguish a claim; art. 55(1): period of limitation for actions for damages for death or personal injury: three years from the day after the accident (or three years from the day after the death of the passenger, subject to a maximum of five years from the day after the accident); art. 55(2): period of limitation for other actions: one year (two years where wilful misconduct or fraud). A claim presented under art. 49 may suspend the running of the limitation period: art. 55(4).

[27] COTIF, App. A, art. 26.

[28] COTIF, App. A, art. 26 (provided that the railway was at fault: art. 47).

[29] COTIF, App. A, art. 26: for example, passenger's own fault; third party's behaviour; circumstances unconnected with the operation of the railway.

[30] For example, art. 30: damages for loss of earnings or loss of support limited to 70,000 units of account per passenger; art. 31: damages for hand luggage limited to 700 units of account per passenger.

[31] COTIF, App. A., art. 42.

[32] COTIF, App. A., art. 32.

[33] For presumption of loss on non-delivery within 14 days of a request for delivery, see COTIF, App. A, art. 37.

[34] COTIF, App. A, arts. 17–20; art. 35.

detailed provisions relating to the damages recoverable.[35] In certain circumstances, the railway may be relieved of liability,[36] or liability may be limited.[37]

26.21 International Carriage by Rail: Goods (COTIF Appendix B: CIM).—The Uniform Rules[38] in COTIF Appendix B regulate all consignments of goods for carriage under a through consignment note made out for a route over the territories of at least two Member States and exclusively over listed lines or services.[39] The rules regulate liability for loss of or damage to goods, and delay in transit.[40] Claims may become time-barred, and rights of action may in certain circumstances be extinguished.[41]

The railway is liable for loss[42] of or damage to the goods between the time of acceptance for carriage and the time of delivery, and for loss or damage resulting from the transit period being exceeded.[43] There are detailed provisions relating to the damages recoverable.[44] The railway is relieved of liability in certain circumstances,[45] and its liability in respect of certain heads of claim is limited,[46] although the limits are doubled where the railway's wilful misconduct caused the loss.[47]

Further Reading

Chitty, *Contracts* (26th ed., 1989), Vol. 2.
Clarke, *International Carriage of Goods by Road: CMR* (2nd ed., 1991).
Kahn Freund, *The Law of Inland Transport* (4th ed., 1965).
Stair Memorial Encyclopaedia, Vol. 3 (Carriage).

[35] COTIF, App. A, arts. 38–41.
[36] COTIF, App. A, art. 35(2): passenger's own fault: passenger's order; inherent vice, unavoidable circumstances or consequences. Art 35(3): 'special risks' such as inadequate packing; special nature of luggage; despatch of unacceptable articles.
[37] To a certain number of units of account per kilogramme or per item: COTIF, App. A, arts. 38–41.
[38] Replacing the Convention Internationale concernant le transport des marchandises par chemins de fer (CIM, Berne 1970).
[39] COTIF, App. B, arts. 1, 11–13, 18. And see notes 23 and 24, *supra*.
[40] In the absence of specific provisions in the rules, national law applies: COTIF, App. B, art. 10.
[41] COTIF, App. B, arts. 53–58. For example, art. 57; acceptance of goods may (with certain exceptions) extinguish a claim; art. 58: period of limitation for actions arising from contract—one year (two years in certain circumstances including wilful misconduct and fraud). The dates of commencement of the relevant periods are set out in art. 58(2). A claim presented under art. 53 may suspend the running of the limitation period: art. 58(3).
[42] For presumption of loss on non-delivery within 30 days after the expiry of the transit period, see COTIF, App. B, art. 39.
[43] COTIF, App. B, art. 36.
[44] COTIF, App. B, arts. 40–47.
[45] COTIF, App. B, art. 36(2): if the loss, etc. was caused by the fault or order of the 'person entitled'; inherent vice; unavoidable circumstances and consequences. Art. 36(3): 'special risks', including carriage by open wagon, poor packing, and breakable or perishable goods.
[46] For example, COTIF, App. B, art. 40(2): compensation for loss of goods limited to 17 units of account per kilogramme of gross mass short; art. 41: percentage allowance for goods subject to wastage; art 43(1): where transit period exceeded, compensation limit of three times carriage charges.
[47] COTIF, App. B, art. 44.

CHAPTER 27

CARRIAGE BY SEA

27.1 Constitution of the Contract.—A contract for the carriage of goods by sea, or affreightment, may be entered into verbally,[1] and its terms are then to be gathered from proof of the words or actions of the parties, from advertisements, or from their prior business relations.[2] More commonly the contract of affreightment is entered into in writing. Then the relationship of the parties may depend upon a charterparty; on the combined effect of a charterparty and a bill of lading; on a bill of lading alone; on a document known as a receipt;[3] on a sea waybill; or a ship's delivery order.[4] The edict *nautae, caupones, stabularii*, although applying to carriage by sea, has largely been superseded by legislation.[5]

27.2 Charterparty.—A charterparty is a contract whereby a ship, or some portion thereof, is hired either for a definite time (time charter) or for a particular voyage (voyage charter) in return for a payment known as freight. It may either take the form of the hire of the ship or merely of the accommodation in the ship. In the first form, usually termed a demise of the ship, the charterer takes for the time being the position of an owner, and the responsibility to third parties, *e.g.* in the case of a collision, rests solely with him.[6] The master of the ship, in signing a bill of lading, binds the charterer, and not the owner.[7] Where merely the accommodation in the ship is hired these responsibilities remain with the

---

[1] *Nordstjernan* v. *Salvesen* (1903) 6 F. 64, at p. 75; Bell, *Comm.*, i, 586.

[2] *Hill* v. *Scott* [1895] 2 Q.B. 371, 713.

[3] The receipt was introduced by the Carriage of Goods by Sea Act 1924. See now the Carriage of Goods by Sea Act 1971, Sched., art. VI; and para. 27.17, *infra*. The 1971 Act came into force on June 23, 1977 (S.I. 1977 No. 981) when it repealed the 1924 Act. However the unamended Hague Rules as set out in the 1924 Act may still have relevance: see 1977 Lloyd's M.C.L.Q. 512.

[4] See Carriage of Goods by Sea Act 1992 (c.50) which came into force on September 16, 1992, implementing the recommendations of the Law Commissions in their report *Rights of Suit in Respect of Carriage of Goods by Sea*, Scot. Law Com. Report No. 130 (1991). The 1992 Act repeals the Bills of Lading Act 1855. The 1992 Act is not retrospective.

[5] For example, the Merchant Shipping Act 1894, the Merchant Shipping Act 1970, the Carriage of Goods by Sea Act 1971, the Merchant Shipping Act 1979, the Merchant Shipping Act 1988, and the Carriage of Goods by Sea Act 1992. The Carriers Act 1830 does not apply to carriage by sea.

[6] *Clarke* v. *Scott* (1896) 23 R. 442; *The Briton* [1975] 1 Lloyd's Rep. 319; *Attica Sea Carriers Corporation* v. *Ferrostaal Poseidon Bulk Reederei G.m.b.H.* [1976] 1 Lloyd's Rep. 250.

[7] *Baumwoll Manufactur* v. *Furness* [1893] A.C. 8.

445

owner. Where not only the ship but its master and crew are hired, the contract will not be read as a demise of the ship merely because it is stated that the crew are to be in the service of the charterer, unless the power of appointment and dismissal is also vested in him.[8]

27.3   Normal Form of Charterparty.—A charterparty, a term derived from the ancient custom of executing the document in duplicate and cutting it across, is a contract usually entered into by a printed form, with or without additional clauses, typed or in manuscript. In its normal form, in voyage charters, it describes the ship, the voyage proposed, and contains an undertaking to deliver the cargo to the charterer or his assignee on payment of freight. Provisions as to time for loading or unloading are added, and responsibility for loss occasioned by certain specified causes excluded.[9]

27.4   Seaworthiness.—In a charterparty it is open to the contracting parties to exclude the liability of the shipowner for any cause of loss to the cargo.[9] But in the absence of any express stipulation to the contrary the law implies a warranty of seaworthiness, which is not excluded by any general exception of loss due to the negligence of the officers or crew, and is a guarantee that the ship is seaworthy, not merely that the owner has taken all reasonable steps to make her so.[10] Seaworthiness has been defined as 'that degree of fitness which an ordinary careful and prudent owner would require his vessel to have at the commencement of her voyage, having regard to all the probable circumstances of it.'[11] The warranty is that the ship is fit to encounter the normal dangers of the voyage and to carry the cargo contracted for, that her refrigerating machinery, for instance, is in good order.[12] It involves the provision of a qualified master and competent crew.[13] It is a warranty that the ship is ready to receive the cargo at the time of loading, *e.g.* that a cattle ship has been properly disinfected,[14] and is fit to sail at the time of sailing.

---

[8] *Manchester Trust* v. *Furness* [1895] 2 Q.B. 539. See also *Wills* v. *Burrell* (1894) 21 R. 527.

[9] But see para. 27.17, *infra*; Unfair Contract Terms Act 1977. A clause in a charterparty excluding liability for loss or damage arising out of 'errors of navigation' has been held in England not to provide exemption in respect of negligent navigation: *Seven Seas Transportation* v. *Pacifico Union Marina Corp.* [1983] 1 All E.R. 672; [1984] 2 All E.R. 140; *Industrie Chimiche Italia Centrale S.p.A.* v. *NEA Ninemia Shipping Co. S.A.* [1983] 1 All E.R. 686.

[10] *Steel & Craig* v. *State Line Co.* (1877) 4 R. (H.L.) 103; *A/B Karlshamns Oljefabriker* v. *Monarch S.S. Co.*, 1949 S.C. (H.L.) 1.

[11] Carver, *Carriage by Sea*, § 148, approved, *McFadden* v. *Blue Star Line* [1905] 1 K.B. 697.

[12] *Maori King* v. *Hughes* [1895] 2 Q.B. 550. As to the distinction between unfitness to receive the cargo, and bad stowage, see *Elder Dempster* v. *Paterson* [1924] A.C. 522. As to overloading the ship, see *Actis Co.* v. *Sanko S.S. Co.* [1982] 1 All E.R. 390.

[13] *Gunford Ship Co.* v. *Thomas, etc., Insurance Co.*, 1911 S.C. (H.L.) 84; *Standard Oil Co.* v. *Clan Line*, 1924 S.C. (H.L.) 1; *Hong Kong Fir Shipping Co.* v. *Kawasaki Kisen Kaisha* [1962] 2 Q.B. 26. As a result of these decisions there would not appear to be any disagreement between English and Scots law as to the effect of a breach of this warranty on the charterparty as a whole. Cf. *Universal Cargo Carriers Corp.* v. *Citari* [1957] 2 Q.B. 401 for a breach by the charterers.

[14] *Tattersall* v. *National S.S. Co.* (1884) 12 Q.B.D. 297.

But for defects occurring during the voyage, and not due to initial un-seaworthiness, the shipowner's obligation is only to execute and pay for repairs, not a warranty that repairs will not be necessary, and therefore he is not liable for delay due to a breakdown of machinery.[15] The question whether a temporary defect, *e.g.* a porthole left open or failure to case a pipe, is unseaworthiness, or a defect attributable to the negligence of the crew, depends upon whether, in the particular circumstances, it could be remedied during the voyage.[16] The onus of proving unseaworthiness primarily rests with the charterer who asserts it, but is displaced by proof that the ship broke down in the initial stage of her voyage.[17] The warranty of seaworthiness formerly applied in cases arising under bills of lading as well as under charterparties, but the law in this respect was altered by the Carriage of Goods by Sea Act 1924, section 2.

27.5 Lay-Days and Demurrage.—It is a common though not an invariable provision in charterparties that a certain number of days, known as lay-days, are allowed for loading and unloading, with a further provision for the payment of a fixed sum for a certain number of days after the lay-days have expired. The fixed sum is known as demurrage. Should the period of demurrage be exceeded damages for detention are due by the charterer, but where demurrage is not restricted to a certain fixed period of time any damages claimed by the shipowners for delay owing to the detention of the vessel in circumstances where the demurrage provisions apply must be restricted to the sum fixed by those provisions.[18] A provision for loading or unloading at a fixed rate per day is equivalent to a provision for lay-days, and has the same legal results.[19] Where the provision is for 'days' or 'running days' the period is calculated without considering whether the days are working days or not; the term 'working days' excludes Sundays and holidays at the port.[20] The obligation to load or unload the ship within the lay-days is an absolute one, and demurrage will be due although the delay is due to causes beyond the control of the charterer. His only relevant defences are either that the delay was occasioned by the fault of the shipowner, or that it was due to some cause excepted in the charterparty.[21] But

[15] *Giertsen* v. *Turnbull*, 1908 S.C. 1101.
[16] *Steel & Craig* v. *State Line Co.*, *supra*; *Gilroy* v. *Price* (1892) 20 R. (H.L.) 1.
[17] *Klein* v. *Lindsay*, 1911 S.C. (H.L.) 9.
[18] *Suisse Atlantique Société d'Armement Maritime S.A.* v. *N.V. Rotterdamsche Kolen Centrale* [1967] 1 A.C. 361, where the House of Lords regarded the demurrage clause as an agreed damages clause.
[19] *Hansa* v. *Alexander*, 1919 S.C. (H.L.) 122.
[20] *Holman* v. *Peruvian Nitrate Co.* (1878) 5 R. 657.
[21] *Hansa* v. *Alexander*, *supra*; *Reardon Smith Line* v. *Ministry of Agriculture, Food and Fisheries* [1963] A.C. 691, where the whole question is extensively reviewed; *Tramp Shipping Corp.* v. *Greenwich Marine Incorp.* [1975] 1 W.L.R. 1042; *Armada Lines* v. *Naviera Murueta S.A., The Elexalde* [1985] 2 Lloyd's Rep. 485 (strike). A contractual provision that time spent treating the ship's holds shall not count cannot be relied upon where such treatment takes place after the permitted lay-days: *Dias Compania Naviera S.A.* v. *Louis Dreyfus Corp.* [1978] 1 W.L.R. 261.

there can be no claim where the ship is totally destroyed.[22] It has been held in England that the charterer is in breach of contract if he fails to load within the lay-days,[23] disapproving the suggestion of Lord Trayner that days on demurrage are really lay-days which have to be paid for.[24] The lay-days do not begin to run until the ship has arrived, and is ready to load or discharge, as the case may be.[25] Where the charterparty contains no provisions for lay-days and demurrage the obligation of the charterer is merely to load within a time reasonable in the circumstances and in determining this any special causes of delay, such as a shortage of labour at the port, are to be taken into account.[26] He is, however, bound to have the cargo ready, and, in the absence of any express provisions in the charterparty, will be liable in damages for failure to do so, even although caused by circumstances beyond his control.[27]

27.6 Obligations of Shipowner.—The obligation of the shipowner is to have the ship ready to load at the time fixed by the charterparty, or, if no time be fixed, within a reasonable time, unless prevented by causes specified in the contract. If delay is caused by an excepted cause, as for example by the perils of the sea, the shipowner has not committed a breach of contract, yet the delay may be so great as to amount to frustration of the adventure, and to entitle the charterer to declare the contract at an end.[28] As this is a question of degree it is common to provide a clause, known as a cancelling clause, giving the charterer the option to declare the contract at an end if the ship is not ready to load by a certain date.[29] If the failure of the ship to arrive is due to the fault of the shipowner he is liable in damages.[30]

27.7 Dead Freight.—A charterer is usually taken bound to provide a full and complete cargo. Failure to do so, or in any case to provide the amount and kind[31] of cargo agreed upon, involves liability for dead freight, which is a payment in compensation for the stow-room left empty. If not fixed in amount by the charterparty it is, in the case where the whole cargo is loaded by one charterer, the difference between the freight

---

[22] *A/S Gulnes* v. *I.C.I.* [1938] 1 All E.R. 24.

[23] *Aktieselskabet Reidar* v. *Arcos* [1927] 1 K.B. 352.

[24] *Lilly* v. *Stevenson* (1895) 22 R. 278.

[25] For decisions as to when a ship has arrived, see Scrutton, *Charterparties* (19th ed.), pp. 138–145; *E.L. Oldendorff & Co. G.m.b.H.* v. *Tradax Export S.A.* [1974] A.C. 479; *Federal Commerce and Navigation Co. Ltd.* v. *Tradax Export S.A.* [1978] A.C. 1; *Micosta S.A.* v. *Shetland Islands Council*, 1986 S.L.T. 193; [1984] 2 Lloyd's Rep. 525.

[26] *Rickinson* v. *Scottish Co-operative Society*, 1918 S.C. 440.

[27] *Ardan S.S. Co.* v. *Weir* (1905) 7 F. (H.L.) 126.

[28] *Jackson* v. *Union Marine Insurance Co.* (1874) L.R. 10 C.P. 125.

[29] See, *e.g. The Mihalis Angelos* [1971] 1 Q.B. 164.

[30] *Nelson* v. *Dundee East Coast Shipping Co.*, 1907 S.C. 927; *Monroe* v. *Ryan* [1935] 2 K.B. 28.

[31] *Angfartygs A/B* v. *Price & Pierce* [1939] 3 All E.R. 672.

actually earned and the freight that would have been earned had the whole cargo been provided; in a general ship it has to be calculated under deduction of any expense saved to the shipowner, and of any sums he has received, or might have received, from carrying the goods of third parties.[32]

27.8 Cesser Clause.—A clause, known as the cesser clause, is commonly inserted in charterparties, whereby the charterer's liability under the contract ceases when the goods are put on board, and the shipowner's lien over the goods, which at common law only covers the freight, is extended to cover claims for dead freight and demurrage. This clause, unless expressed so as plainly to cover all grounds of liability, will not exempt the charterer from claims where his exemption would leave the shipowner without any remedy, as in the case of detention at the port of loading beyond the days allowed on demurrage.[33]

27.9 Freight *Pro Rata Itineris*.—As a general rule no freight is due unless and until the goods arrive at their destination. But if the voyage be interrupted by causes beyond the control of the shipowner, and the party entitled to the goods chooses to take delivery at some intermediate place, having the option to have the goods forwarded to their destination, he comes under an implied obligation to make a payment, estimated as a proportionate part of the freight and known as freight *pro rata itineris*.[34] To found a claim of this character there must be circumstances from which it may be inferred that the cargo owner dispenses with further carriage; the mere fact that he has accepted the goods at an intermediate port, when he had no option in the matter, is not enough to infer any liability.[35]

27.10 Advance Freight.—It is sometimes provided in a charterparty that the freight, or an instalment thereof, shall be paid in advance. The Scottish courts, disagreeing with the English rule, but agreeing with the commercial law of other countries, have held that if the voyage cannot be accomplished the amount paid as advance freight may be recovered.[36]

---

[32] *McLean & Hope* v. *Fleming* (1871) 9 M. (H.L.) 38; *Henderson* v. *Turnbull*, 1909 S.C. 510.

[33] *Gardiner* v. *Macfarlane* (1889) 16 R. 658; *Salvesen* v. *Guy* (1885) 13 R. 85; and see *Hill S.S. Co.* v. *Hugo Stinnes*, 1941 S.C. 324 (charterparty with cesser clause; charterer named as shipper in bill of lading); *Overseas Transportation Co.* v. *Mineralimportexport: The Sinoe* [1972] 1 Lloyd's Rep. 201.

[34] Bell, *Prin.*, § 425; *The Soblomsten* (1866) L.R. 1 Ad. & Ecc. 293.

[35] *The Iolo* [1916] P. 206.

[36] *Watson* v. *Shankland* (1871) 10 M. 142; affd. (1873) 11 M. (H.L.) 51. See also *Cantiere San Rocco* v. *Clyde Shipbuilding Co.*, 1923 S.C. (H.L.) 105.

27.11 Primage: Petty Average.—In addition to freight the usual form of a charterparty or bill of lading contains an obligation to pay primage and petty average, fixed as a certain percentage on the freight. Primage was originally a payment made to the master of the ship for his care of the goods.[37] Petty average, to be distinguished from particular and general average,[38] is a percentage on the freight in place of certain customary charges for towage and beaconage.[39]

27.12 Charterparty Followed by Bill of Lading.—A contract of charterparty may be, and usually is, followed by a bill of lading when the goods are put on board. If there is any discrepancy between the terms of the charterparty and the bill of lading, and the question raised is between shipowner and charterer, the charterparty is the ruling instrument and the bill of lading is regarded as a mere receipt.[40] Thus where the charterparty contained a provision exempting the shipowner from loss resulting from the negligence of master or crew, and no such provision appeared in the bill of lading, it was held that the shipowner was entitled to found on the negligence clause in a question with the charterer or with a party for whom he was acting as agent.[41] But this, which is the general rule, will yield to proof (which may be by parole evidence) that the parties intended to vary their contract by the bill of lading.[42] From the definition of 'contract of carriage' in the Carriage of Goods by Sea Act 1971,[43] it would appear that the rules relating to bills of lading and contracts thereunder which are provided by that Act do not apply to cases where the charterparty is the ruling contract but the charterparty may contain a clause paramount embodying these rules.[44] Where the bill of lading has been indorsed and the question is between the shipowner and the indorsee the contract is that contained in the bill of lading and not that contained in the charterparty.[45] And a mere reference to the charterparty, *e.g.* 'other conditions as per charter,' is construed as importing only conditions affecting the consignee at the port of discharge, not as introducing into the bill of lading an exemption from the consequences of negligence which is to be found in the

---

[37] See *Howitt* v. *Paul, Sword & Co.* (1877) 5 R. 321.

[38] See General Average, Chap. 30, *infra.*

[39] Bell, *Comm.*, i, 614.

[40] *President of India* v. *Metcalfe Shipping Co.* [1970] 1 Q.B. 289, a rule thought not to have been altered by the Carriage of Goods by Sea Act 1992: see Current Law Statutes Commentary by James Cooper at p. 50–55. Where the question (as to the operation of a cesser clause) was between the owner and the charterer, *qua* shipper, it was held that the bill of lading ruled: *Hill S.S. Co.* v. *Hugo Stinnes*, 1941 S.C. 324. A bill of lading may incorporate terms from a charterparty: *Skips A/S Nordheim* v. *Syrian Petroleum Co., The Varenna* [1984] Q.B. 599.

[41] *Delaurier* v. *Wyllie* (1889) 17 R. 167; *Rodocanachi* v. *Milburn* (1886) 18 Q.B.D. 67. The rule is questioned in Scrutton, *Charterparties* (19th ed.), pp. 60 *et seq.*

[42] *Davidson* v. *Bisset* (1878) 5 R. 706.

[43] See para. 27.15, *infra.*

[44] *Adamastos Shipping Co.* v. *Anglo-Saxon Petroleum Co.* [1959] A.C. 133.

[45] But see *President of India* v. *Metcalfe Shipping Co., supra.*

charterparty.[46] It lies on the charterer to see that bills of lading are not signed in terms inconsistent with the charterparty, and he will be liable to relieve the shipowner should the latter in consequence incur liability to an indorsee.[47]

27.13 **Bill of Lading.**—A bill of lading is the normal document under which goods are carried in a general ship. It is considered here in its aspects as a receipt for the goods and as a contract of carriage.[48]

27.14 **Bill of Lading as Receipt.**—In its ordinary form a bill of lading is signed by the master of a ship, acknowledges receipt of the goods, and contains an undertaking to deliver them to the shipper, or his assigns by indorsement. The Carriage of Goods by Sea Act 1971 provides that the carrier[49] must, on the demand of the shipper, furnish a bill of lading stating (a) the leading marks for identification of the goods; (b) either the number of packages, or the quantity, or weight, as furnished in writing by the shipper; (c) the apparent order and condition of the goods, with the proviso that there is no obligation to state any marks, number, quantity or weight which the master has reasonable ground for suspecting not to be accurate, or which he has no reasonable means of checking.[50] The shipper is deemed to have guaranteed the accuracy of the information furnished by him, and is bound to indemnify the carrier for any loss, damages or expenses resulting from its inaccuracy.[51] The bill of lading is prima facie evidence of the receipt by the carrier of the goods as therein described, but, if the bill is transferred to a third party acting in good faith, proof to the contrary is not admissible.[52] Section 4 of the Carriage of Goods by Sea Act 1992 further provides that a bill of lading[53] signed by the master of the vessel[54] is conclusive evidence in favour of the lawful holder[55] of the bill against the carrier that the goods have been shipped or received.[56]

[46] *Delaurier* v. *Wyllie, supra; cf. The Annefield* [1971] P. 168.

[47] *Kruger* v. *Moel Tryvan Co.* [1907] A.C. 272.

[48] Other aspects of bills of lading are dealt with in para. 19.12, *supra.*

[49] 'Carrier' is defined in art. I of the Schedule as including the owner or the charterer who enters into a contract of carriage with the shipper.

[50] 1971 Act, Sched., art. III, r. 3.

[51] *Ibid.*, art. III. See *Attorney-General of Ceylon* v. *Scindia Steam Navigation Co.* [1962] A.C. 60.

[52] art. III, r. 4.

[53] *i.e.* a transferable bill of lading (such as 'to X or order') and not a non-transferable or 'straight' bill of lading ('to X') nor a sea waybill, which is in effect a non-transferable bill of lading. While the 1992 Act applies to both 'shipped' and 'received for shipment' bills of lading, it does not apply to non-transferable bills of lading: see s. 1(2) and Scot. Law Com. Report No. 130, paras. 2.48, 2.50.

[54] Or by the carrier's agent: s. 4 of the 1992 Act.

[55] As defined in s. 5(2) of the 1992 Act. The holder must be in good faith.

[56] s. 4 of the Carriage of Goods by Sea Act 1992 (replacing s. 3 of the Bills of Lading Act 1855, which made the bill of lading conclusive evidence against the signatory of the bill rather than against the carrier: see 1992 *Current Law Statutes* Commentary by James Cooper).

27.15   **Bill of Lading as Contract.**—The incidents of a bill of lading as a
contract of carriage are now largely regulated by the provisions of the
Carriage of Goods by Sea Acts 1971 and 1992. The 1971 Act supplies
rules,[57] which are to have effect in relation to and in connection with
the carriage of goods by sea in ships where the port of shipment is a
port in the United Kingdom,[58] or where the goods[59] are carried between
ports in two different states and either the bill of lading is issued in a
contracting state, or the carriage is from a port in a contracting state, or
the bill of lading provides that the rules or legislation of any state giving
effect to them are to govern the contract.[60] A 'contract of carriage' is
defined as applying only 'to contracts of carriage covered by a bill of
lading or any similar document of title, in so far as such document
relates to the carriage of goods by sea, including any bill of lading or
any similar document as aforesaid issued under or pursuant to a
charterparty from the moment at which such bill of lading or similar
document of title regulates the relations between a carrier and a holder
of the same.'[61] In a contract of carriage, as thus defined, there is no
warranty that the ship is seaworthy, though the carrier is bound to
exercise due diligence (a) to make the ship seaworthy; (b) properly to
man, equip and supply the ship; (c) to make the holds, refrigerating and
cool chambers, and all other parts in which goods are carried fit and
safe.[62] When loss or damage has resulted from unseaworthiness the
burden of proving the exercise of due diligence lies on the carrier.[63] The
carrier does not discharge this obligation merely by showing that he
exercised reasonable care in the selection of an independent contractor
to render the ship seaworthy.[64]

The Carriage of Goods by Sea Act 1992 provides that the lawful
holder[65] of a bill of lading, whether or not he owns the property in the
goods, has vested in him all rights of suit under the contract of carriage
as if he had been a party to that contract.[66] A person who acquires the

---

[57] Known as the Hague-Visby Rules.
[58] As to live animals and deck cargo, see 1971 Act, s. 1(7); Sched., art. I(c).
[59] 1971 Act, s. 1(3).
[60] 1971 Act, s. 1(6)(a); Sched., art. X.
[61] Sched., art. I; *Harland & Wolff* v. *Burns and Laird Lines*, 1931 S.C. 722.
[62] Carriage of Goods by Sea Act 1971, s. 3, Sched., art. III; *cf. Riverstone Meat Co.
Pty.* v. *Lancashire Shipping Co.* [1961] A.C. 807.
[63] *Ibid.*, Sched., art. IV.
[64] *Riverstone Meat, supra.*
[65] Defined in s. 5(2).
[66] s. 2 of the 1992 Act, enacting one of the important changes brought about by this
Act, namely that ownership of the goods is no longer a necessary prerequisite to the
acquisition of the contractual rights of suit. A consignee of a sea waybill or a ship's
delivery order ('the person to whom delivery . . . is to be made') is similarly able to assert
contractual rights against the carrier and, in these particular cases, even without possession
of the relevant document: s. 2(1). Note also s. 2(3), which provides for the vesting of
contractual rights in sub-buyers with ship's delivery orders each relating to part of a larger
bulk. In the context of sea waybills and ship's delivery orders (but not bills of lading) the
original shipper and other intermediate holders retain their title to sue: s. 2(5).

bill of lading after delivery of the goods may sue on the bill provided he obtained it under arrangements made before the delivery.[67] A person with rights of suit may exercise them on behalf of another who has suffered the loss or damage.[68] The person who asserts the contractual rights against the carrier becomes subject to the liabilities under the contract.[69]

27.15A Electronic Data Interchange.—Section 1(5) and (6) of the Carriage of Goods by Sea Act 1992 permits regulations to be made so as to apply the provisions of the 1992 Act to paperless transactions conducted by means of a telecommunication system or any other information technology.[70]

27.16 Claims for Injury to Goods.—The 1971 Act makes provision as to the effect of the receipt and removal of the goods. Unless notice in writing of loss or damage is given by the person entitled to receive the goods at the port of discharge prior to their removal, or, if the damage be not apparent, within three days, their removal is prima facie evidence of their delivery in the state described in the bill of lading. Such notice need not be given if the state of the goods has been at the time of their receipt the subject of joint survey or inspection. In any event the carrier is discharged from all liability in respect of loss or damage unless suit is brought within one year after delivery of the goods or the date when the goods should have been delivered.[71] However the parties may agree to extend the period after the cause of action has arisen. An action for indemnity against a third person may be brought even after the expiry of the year, provided that the action is not time-barred by the *lex fori*.[72]

---

[67] s. 2(2) of the 1992 Act. Similarly a person who acquires the bill after the goods have been destroyed may sue on the bill, provided he obtained the bill under arrangements made before the destruction of the goods: s. 2(2). In each case, the bill of lading ceased to be a transferable document of title before coming into the hands of the holder. One purpose of s. 2(2) is to prevent the indorsement of exhausted bills of lading to those who have no interest in the goods but simply wish to buy a cause of action against the carrier: see Scot. Law Com. Report No. 130, paras. 2.43–2.44, and draft bill, p. 49; and *Current Law Statutes* Commentary by James Cooper.

[68] s. 2(4) of the 1992 Act.

[69] s. 3 of the 1992 Act; and see para. 27.22, *infra*.

[70] Including 'any computer or other technology, by means of which information or other matter may be recorded or communicated without being reduced to documentary form': s. 5(1). The Scottish Law Commission, in their Report No. 130 at p. 39, comment: 'E.D.I. may eventually render otiose the concept of negotiability. A single paper transfer will be replaced by a series of teletransmitted undertakings by the carrier to successive transferees, the communication of each undertaking giving constructive delivery to the person receiving the communication.'

[71] Carriage of Goods by Sea Act 1971, Sched., art. III, r. 6. See *Aries Tanker Corp.* v. *Total Transport* [1977] 1 W.L.R. 185.

[72] 1971 Act, Sched., art. III, r. 6 bis. The *lex fori* must allow at least three months from the date when the pursuer settled the claim or was served with process in the action against him.

27.17   Exemption from and Exclusion of Liability.—Where carriage is effected
under a bill of lading,[73] the Carriage of Goods by Sea Act 1971 provides
that neither the carrier[74] nor the ship shall be liable for injury resulting
from the undernoted causes,[75] nor in certain circumstances for loss of or
damage to goods which were dangerous.[76] Nor is the carrier liable for
loss of or damage to goods if the shipper knowingly misstated the nature
or value of the goods in the bill of lading.[77] Other exemptions from
liability under the 1971 Act have already been mentioned.[78] The
Merchant Shipping Act 1995, section 186[79] provides that a shipowner[80]
is not liable for any loss or damage caused by fire on board ship, or by
theft of gold, silver, watches, jewels, or precious stones, unless the
owner or shipper has, at the time of shipment, declared their nature and
value in the bill of lading or otherwise in writing.[81] Liability is not
excluded where it is proved that the loss resulted from personal act or
omission, committed with intent to cause such loss, or recklessly and
with knowledge that such loss would probably result.[82]

A clause in a bill of lading excluding liability in any manner other
than that permitted by the Carriage of Goods by Sea Act 1971 is void.[83]

---

[73] Or possibly a receipt: Carriage of Goods by Sea Act 1971, s. 1(6)(b).

[74] As to his servants or agents, see 1971 Act, Sched., art. IV bis.

[75] 1971 Act, Sched., art. IV, r. 2: '(a) Act, neglect or default of the master, mariner,
pilot or the servants of the carrier in the navigation or in the management of the ship. (b)
Fire, unless caused by the actual fault or privity of the carrier. (c) Perils, dangers and
accidents of the sea or other navigable waters. (d) Act of God. (e) Act of war. (f) Act of
public enemies. (g) Arrest or restraint of princes, rulers or people, or seizure under legal
process. (h) Quarantine restrictions. (i) Act or omission of the shipper or owner of the
goods, his agent or representative. (j) Strikes or lock-outs or stoppage or restraint of
labour from whatever cause, whether partial or general. (k) Riots and civil commotions.
(l) Saving or attempting to save life or property at sea. (m) Wastage in bulk or weight or
any other loss or damage arising from inherent defect, quality or vice of the goods. (n)
Insufficiency of packing. (o) Insufficiency or inadequacy of marks. (p) Latent defects not
discoverable by due diligence. (q) Any other cause arising without the actual fault or
privity of the carrier, or without the fault or neglect of the agents or servants of the
carrier, but the burden of proof shall be on the person claiming the benefit of this
exception to show that neither the actual fault or privity of the carrier nor the fault or
neglect of the agents or servants of the carrier contributed to the loss or damage.' The
term 'in the navigation or in the management of the ship' in (a) *supra* has been construed
in England as limited to navigation, as distinguished from care of the cargo. Thus it does
not cover defective stowage: *Gosse Millard* v. *Canadian Marine, etc., Co.* [1929] A.C. 223;
The Washington [1976] 2 Lloyd's Rep. 453; but see *Ismail* v. *Polish Ocean Lines* [1976]
Q.B. 893; nor failure in refrigerating machinery, *Foreman & Ellams* v. *Federal Steam
Navigation Co.* [1928] 2 K.B. 424. See *Albacora S.R.L.* v. *Westcott and Laurence Line*,
1966 S.C. (H.L.) 19 (note the doubt cast upon *Gosse Millard, supra*) and *Leesh River Tea
Co.* v. *British India S.N. Co.* [1967] 2 Q.B. 250.

[76] 1971 Act, Sched., art. IV, r. 6.

[77] *Ibid.*, r. 5 (h).

[78] paras. 27.15, 27.16, *supra*.

[79] s. 186 replaces s. 15 of the Merchant Shipping Act 1979.

[80] Or partowner, charterer, manager, operator of the ship: s. 186(1). Also any master,
member of the crew or servant: s. 186(2).

[81] s. 186(1) of the 1995 Act.

[82] s. 186(3), referring to the 1995 Act, Sched. 7, Pt. I, art. 4.

[83] 1971 Act, Sched., art. III, r. 8. However, the carrier may validly contract to
surrender his own rights and immunities under the 1971 Act: Sched., art. V.

Where carriage is effected under a receipt,[84] the parties may agree on any terms which are not contrary to public policy.[85] A clause in a charterparty, or a clause in a contract for the carriage of goods by ship, or a provision of a notice,[86] may be void if it excludes liability for death or personal injury, or may be unenforceable if one contracting party is a consumer and it was unfair and unreasonable to incorporate the clause in the contract or to allow reliance on the provision of a notice.[87] In a contract for the carriage by sea of passengers, a carrier cannot exclude liability for death or personal injury or loss of or damage to passengers' luggage occurring during the course of carriage and due to his own or his servants' or agents' fault or neglect.[88]

Non-contracting parties, such as stevedores, may benefit from a valid exclusion clause.[89]

27.18 Limitation of Liability.—Where a carrier is neither exempted nor excluded from liability, his liability may nevertheless be limited. The Carriage of Goods by Sea Act 1971[90] provides that, in the case of loss of, or damage to, goods carried under a bill of lading,[91] a carrier[92] shall not be liable beyond 666.67 units of account[93] per package or unit,[94] or two units of account per kilogramme of gross weight, whichever is the higher, unless the nature and value of the goods were declared by the shipper before shipment, and were inserted in the bill of lading.[95] A higher limit may be fixed by agreement.[96] Where a carrier and his

---

[84] A non-negotiable instrument, marked as such, used in cases where shipments are not of an ordinary commercial character made in the ordinary course of trade: 1971 Act, Sched., art. VI.

[85] *Ibid.*: subject, however, to the Unfair Contract Terms Act 1977.

[86] 'Notice' includes an announcement, whether or not in writing, and any other communication or pretended communication: s. 25 of the Unfair Contract Terms Act 1977, as amended by the Law Reform (Misc. Provs.) (Scotland) Act 1990, s. 68 and Sched. 9.

[87] Unfair Contract Terms Act 1977, ss. 15(3), 16, 25, as amended by the Law Reform (Misc. Provs.) (Scotland) Act 1990, s. 68 and Sched. 9.

[88] 1977 Act, s. 28: *cf.* art. 3 of the Athens Convention relating to the Carriage of Passengers and their Luggage by Sea, 1974.

[89] *New Zealand Shipping Company* v. *A.M. Satterthwaite & Co.; The Eurymedon* [1975] A.C. 154.

[90] As amended by the Merchant Shipping Acts, 1979 and 1981.

[91] Or possibly a receipt: 1971 Act, s. 1(6)(*b*).

[92] As to his servants or agents, see 1971 Act, Sched., art. IV bis.

[93] A unit of account is a special drawing right as defined by the International Monetary Fund. The amount is converted into sterling on the basis of the value of sterling on the date of decree or judgment: 1971 Act, Sched., art. IV, r. 5 (*d*) and ss. 2(5) and 3 of the Merchant Shipping Act 1981. The total amount recoverable is calculated by reference to the value of the goods at the place and time where in terms of the contract the goods were or should have been discharged: 1971 Act, Sched., art. IV, r. 5 (*b*) and (*c*).

[94] If the number of packages or units packed in a container, pallet or similar article is stated in the bill of lading, that number is deemed the number of packages or units for purposes of limitation; otherwise the article of transport is considered the package or unit: art. IV, r. 5 (*c*).

[95] 1971 Act, Sched., art. IV, r. 5 (*a*).

[96] *Ibid.*, r. 5 (*g*). But any restriction clause not permitted by the Act is void: art. III, r. 8.

servants or agents are sued, the aggregate amount recoverable cannot exceed the specified limits.[97] However, the carrier cannot benefit from the limitation provisions where it is proved that the loss or damage resulted from an act or omission of the carrier, done with intent to cause damage, or recklessly with knowledge that damage would probably result.[98] The Merchant Shipping Act 1995 enables a shipowner to limit his liability in respect of certain claims, including loss of life or personal injury and damage to property occurring on board or in direct connection with the operation of the ship.[99] There can be no limitation if it is proved that the loss resulted from personal act or omission, committed with the intent to cause such loss or recklessly and with knowledge that such loss would probably result.[1] Nor is there any limitation in respect of a claim by a person on board the ship or employed in connection with that ship under a United Kingdom contract of employment.[2] The limits of liability are calculated by units of account[3] related to the ship's tonnage.[4] Priority is given to claims for death and personal injury.[5] If legal proceedings are instituted, a shipowner may constitute a limitation fund with the court.[6]

27.19 Deviation.—At common law a contract of carriage by sea implied a warranty that the carrier would not deviate from the prescribed course, or, where no course was prescribed, from that usual and customary.[7] Deviation was excused in order to save life, not in order to save

[97] 1971 Act, Sched., art. IV bis, r. 3.
[98] 1971 Act, Sched., art. IV, r. 5 (e).
[99] s. 185 of the Merchant Shipping Act 1995 and Sched. 7, replacing s. 17 of the Merchant Shipping Act 1979. Sched. 7 gives effect to the London Convention on Limitation of Liability for Marine Claims 1976, brought into force with effect from December 1, 1986 (S.I. 1986 No. 1052). A list of claims subject to limitation is set out in art. 2(1). Claims in respect of oil pollution and nuclear damage are excluded: art. 3.
[1] art. 4. of Sched. 7. Contrast with the wording of s. 503 of the Merchant Shipping Act 1894 where limitation could be claimed where the loss, injury or damage occurred without the owner's 'actual fault or privity': *Dreyfus* v. *Tempus Shipping Co.* [1931] A.C. 726; *The Norman* [1960] 1 Lloyd's Rep. 1; *The Lady Gwendolen* [1965] P. 294; *Groen* v. *The England (Owners)* [1973] 1 Lloyd's Rep. 373; *The Devotion II*, 1979 S.C. 80; *The Garden City* [1982] 2 Lloyd's Rep. 382; *Richard Irvin* v. *Aberdeen Trawlers*, 1983 S.L.T. 26; *The Marion* [1984] A.C. 563 (H.L.).
[2] s. 185(4) of the 1995 Act; for example, a seaman, master, pilot, caterer, or servant of the shipowner: Sched. 7, Pt. I, art. 3 (e).
[3] Each unit being a special drawing right as defined by the International Monetary Fund: art. 8. See Sched. 7, Pt. II (conversion into sterling).
[4] Sched. 7, arts. 6 and 9. And see Sched. 7, Pt. II and the Merchant Shipping (Liability of Owner and Others) (Calculation of Tonnage) Order 1986 (S.I. 1986 No. 1040).
[5] art. 6(2) of Sched. 7. If the limitation fund constituted in respect of personal injury claims is insufficient, the personal injury claimants can rank rateably in respect of the unpaid balance upon the limitation fund constituted by reference to the property claims.
[6] art. 11 of Sched. 7. Note that in a decision under s. 503 of the 1894 Act, it was held that interest runs *ex lege* on the limitation fund: see *The Devotion II, supra*, where the defenders' tender (of the amount of the limitation fund and expenses) made no explicit reference to interest.
[7] Bell, *Prin.*, § 408; Scrutton, *Charterparties* (19th ed.), p. 259.

property.[8] It was also excused if necessary for the repair of ship or cargo,[9] or if due to the unseaworthiness of the ship,[10] or to credible information of some imminent danger on the proper course.[11] The result of deviation if not so justified, was to displace the contract, and, consequently, to render the shipowner liable for any injury to the cargo, though arising from a cause excepted in the charterparty, and although the loss occurred after the proper course has been resumed.[12] The shipowner could plead in defence, when the loss occurred from the act of God, of the Queen's enemies, or from the inherent vice of the goods carried, that the loss would have occurred even if no deviation had taken place.[13] The law is so far modified by the Carriage of Goods by Sea Act 1971,[14] that, in cases to which the rules under that Act apply, deviation in saving or attempting to save property at sea, or any reasonable deviation,[15] shall not be deemed an infringement of those rules or of the contract of carriage, and the carrier shall not be liable for any loss or damage resulting therefrom. In circumstances where the contract of carriage has been held to be displaced by the deviation of the ship, the question arises of the freight that may be claimed by the shipowner on completion of the voyage, when no damage has been caused to the cargo. A claim for freight on the principle of *quantum meruit* appears possible.[16]

27.20 Delivery of Goods.—At the conclusion of the voyage the carrier is bound to deliver the goods to the holder of the bill of lading. In the absence of any provision to the contrary the actual work of unloading falls to be done by the carrier or at his expense.[17] In any question as to injury to the goods they are to be regarded as delivered as soon as they pass over the ship's side and are received by porters employed by the consignee.[18] As bills of lading are commonly made out in sets of three, with a provision that on one being accomplished the others are to stand void, it is possible for the shipper fraudulently to indorse copies of the bill of lading to different indorsees, and thus to raise competing rights. The shipmaster, if he has no notice of any competing right, is entitled to deliver the goods to the first party presenting a bill of lading; if he has

---

[8] *Scaramanga* v. *Stamp* (1880) 5 C.P.D. 295.
[9] *Phelps* v. *Hill* [1891] 1 Q.B. 605.
[10] *Kish* v. *Taylor* [1912] A.C. 604.
[11] *The Teutonia* (1872) L.R. 4 C.P. 171.
[12] *Thorley* v. *Orchis Co.* [1907] 1 K.B. 660; *Hain S.S. Co.* v. *Tate & Lyle* (1936) 41 Com. Cas. 350. See *Lord Polwarth* v. *N.B.R.*, 1908 S.C. 1275 (land carriage).
[13] *Morrison* v. *Shaw Savill, etc., Co.* [1916] 2 K.B. 783.
[14] Sched., art. IV, r. 4.
[15] *Stag Line* v. *Foscolo Mango & Co.* [1932] A.C. 328; *Lyric Shipping Inc.* v. *Intermetals* [1990] 2 Lloyd's Rep. 117.
[16] See *Hain, supra.*
[17] *Ballantyne* v. *Paton*, 1912 S.C. 246.
[18] *Knight S.S. Co.* v. *Fleming Douglas & Co.* (1898) 25 R. 1070.

notice, he must select the true claimant at his peril, or refuse delivery.[19] Delivery in these circumstances does not affect the ownership of the goods.[20] Should a party alleging right to the goods be unable to produce the bill of lading, as in cases where it has been lost or has not reached the consignee at the time when the ship arrives, the master's duty is either to deliver the goods on receiving a guarantee or letter of indemnity against any possible liability,[21] or else to unload them and place them in a warehouse. Should he unreasonably refuse to take either course nothing can be recovered for the consequent detention of the ship.[22]

27.21 Warehousing.—If the goods are not claimed on arrival, or if the holder of the bill of lading fails to pay the freight, the shipmaster is at common law entitled, after waiting for a reasonable time, to warehouse the goods under reservation of his lien for freight.[23] This right is commonly expressly conferred in the bill of lading. Statutory provisions apply to the case of ships arriving from a foreign port.[24] In that case if the owner of the goods fails to make entry[25] thereof, or to take delivery at the time fixed in the charterparty, bill of lading or agreement, or, if no time has been fixed, within 72 hours (exclusive of Sundays and holidays) after the ship is reported, the shipowner may place the goods in a warehouse under lien for the freight. They may then be detained both for freight and for warehouse rent. Ninety days afterwards, in the event of no payment being made, the warehouse-keeper on the demand of the shipowner is bound to sell the goods by auction, after advertisement and notice to the owner of the goods, if his address be known. He has also discretionary power to sell perishable goods at any time. The proceeds, after payment of the warehouse rent and the shipowner's charges in respect of the goods, are to be paid to their owner.

27.22 Liability for Freight.—A charterer, or the shipper of goods under a bill of lading, is liable for the freight, unless his liability is excluded by a

[19] *Glyn Mills & Co.* v. *East & West India Dock Co.* (1882) 7 App. Cas. 591; delivery will not decide ownership: *Pirie* v. *Warden* (1871) 9 M. 523.
[20] *Barber* v. *Meyerstein* (1870) L.R. 4 H.L. 317; *Pirie* v. *Warden, supra*; and see Carriage of Goods by Sea Act 1992, s. 2.
[21] In modern transactions, frequent use is made of letters of indemnity in lieu of a bill of lading. Delivery is made by the carrier against a letter of indemnity given by the seller to cover the carrier against any loss caused by delivering against a document other than a bill of lading: see Payne & Ivamy, *Carriage of Goods by Sea* (13th ed., 1989), p. 4; Scot. Law Com. Report No. 130, p. 7, fn. 18.
[22] *Carlberg* v. *Wemyss Co.*, 1915 S.C. 616.
[23] Bell, *Comm.*, i, 605.
[24] Merchant Shipping Act 1894, ss. 492–501. See *Smailes* v. *Dessen* (1906) 12 Com. Cas. 117.
[25] *i.e.* the entry required by the customs laws to be made for the landing or discharge of goods from an importing ship (s. 492).

cesser clause. Should the full cargo, as stated in the bill of lading, not be forthcoming at the port of discharge, the shipowner is entitled to freight only for what he has actually carried, but if the full freight has been paid he may set off a claim for dead freight in an action for repetition of the balance.[26] Liability for freight has been extended by statute to any lawful holder of a bill of lading[27] who demands delivery of the goods from the carrier, or who takes delivery, or who makes a claim against the carrier.[28]

27.23 **Lien.**—At common law a shipowner has a lien over the goods for freight, unless this is excluded by the terms of the contract, as where the freight was payable at a certain time after delivery,[29] or bills given for it were still current at the time when delivery was demanded.[30] Apart from express contract there is no lien for dead freight or demurrage.[31] Nor is there any lien for a general balance due to the shipowner on another account.[32] Release of the cargo under reservation of the right of lien can give rise to difficulties.[33]

27.24 **Arrestment of Ship, Cargo.**—A ship may be arrested on the dependence of an action arising out of, *inter alia*, any agreement relating to the carriage of goods in the ship, whether by charterparty or otherwise.[34] At common law, cargo may be arrested on the dependence of such an action.[35] If a ship is to be sold under a warrant sale, the cargo owner may be directed to discharge the cargo.[36]

[26] *Henderson* v. *Turnbull*, 1909 S.C. 510; and note *Aries Tanker Corp.* v. *Total Transport* [1977] 1 All E.R. 398 (H.L.); *The Alfa Nord* [1977] 2 Lloyd's Rep. 434 (C.A.).

[27] As 'the person in whom rights are vested' by virtue of s. 2(1), which includes persons holding the bill as a security: see Scot. Law Com. Report No. 130, paras. 2.30 *et seq.* (and contrast with the previous law, *Sewell* v. *Burdick* (1884) 10 App. Cas. 74). For persons demanding delivery, etc., prior to receiving the bill of lading, see s. 3(1)(c). For provisions relating to sea waybills and ship's delivery orders, see ss. 1–3 of the 1992 Act.

[28] ss. 3 and 2(1) of the Carriage of Goods by Sea Act 1992. section 3 provides that upon demanding delivery, etc., the lawful holder becomes 'subject to the same liabilities under [the contract of carriage] as if he had been a party to that contract.' In such circumstances, the shipper also remains liable for the freight and other obligations as an original party to the contract of carriage: s. 3(3).

[29] *Foster* v. *Colby* (1858) 3 H. & N. 705.

[30] *Tamvaco* v. *Simpson* (1866) L.R. 1 C.P. 363.

[31] *McLean & Hope* v. *Fleming* (1871) 9 M. (H.L.) 38.

[32] *Stevenson* v. *Likly* (1824) 3 S. 291.

[33] *Georgia Pacific Corporation* v. *Evalend Shipping Co. S.A.*, 1988 S.L.T. 683.

[34] s. 47 of the Administration of Justice Act 1956, as amended by the Merchant Shipping (Salvage and Pollution) Act 1994: see *The Aifanourios*, 1980 S.C. 346; 1981 S.L.T. 233; *The Grey Dolphin*, 1982 S.C. 5; *Gatoil International Inc.* v. *Arkwright-Boston Manufacturers Mutual Insurance Co.*, 1984 S.L.T. 462; 1985 S.L.T. 68; *Clipper Shipping Co.* v. *San Vincente Partners*, 1989 S.L.T. 204 (arrestment in Scotland, although substantive court proceedings commenced in Denmark); *Nederlandse Scheepshypotheekbank N.V.* v. *Cam Standby Ltd.*, 1994 S.C.L.R. 956.

[35] *cf. Svenska Petroleum A.B.* v. *H.O.R. Ltd.*, 1982 S.L.T. 343.

[36] *Banque Indo Suez* v. *Maritime Co. Overseas Inc.*, 1985 S.L.T. 117.

27.25   **Cargoes of Oil.**—Ships carrying cargoes of oil in bulk are subject to special legislation.[37]

27.26   **Carriage by Sea: Passengers and Luggage.**—Liability for negligence during the carriage of passengers and luggage[38] by sea is regulated by the Merchant Shipping Act 1995.[39] The carrier is liable for the death of or injury to a passenger, and for loss of or damage to luggage, if caused by the fault or neglect of the carrier or his servants or agents.[40] His liability may be limited.[41] However he cannot benefit from limitation where there was intent to damage, or reckless behaviour.[42] There are detailed provisions relating to performing carriers,[43] valuables,[44] contributory fault,[45] time-limits in respect of giving notice to the carrier of damaged or lost luggage,[46] a two-year time-bar for reparation actions,[47] jurisdiction,[48] and nuclear damage.[49] It is impossible to contract out of the statutory provisions.[50] The 1995 Act applies only to liability for negligence. Other aspects of carriage by sea of passengers and their luggage, such as delay or deviation not arising from negligence, or the provision of reasonable accommodation, continue to be governed by the common law and the Unfair Contract Terms Act 1977.[51]

27.27   **Dangerous Vessels.**—A harbour master may direct a shipowner or master or other person in possession of a ship not to enter a harbour, or to remove a vessel therefrom, if the vessel presents a grave and imminent danger or risk.[52]

---

[37] See, *e.g.* the Merchant Shipping (Oil Pollution) Act 1971, as amended by the Merchant Shipping (Salvage and Pollution) Act 1994; Prevention of Oil Pollution Act 1971, as amended by the Merchant Shipping (Salvage and Pollution) Act 1994; Merchant Shipping Act 1974, as amended by the Merchant Shipping (Salvage and Pollution) Act 1994; and relevant subordinate legislation; *Davies* v. *Smith*, 1983 S.L.T. 644; *Esso Petroleum Co. Ltd.* v. *Hall Russell & Co. Ltd.*, 1988 S.L.T. 33, [1989] A.C. 643.

[38] Excluding live animals.

[39] ss. 183–184, and Sched. 6, implementing the Athens Convention 1974 and a Protocol of 1976, and operative as respects international carriage from December 1, 1986 (S.I. 1986 No. 1052) and as respects domestic carriage from April 30, 1987 (S.I. 1987 No. 635; S.I. 1989 No. 1881).

[40] art. 3(1) of the Convention (Sched. 6). In certain circumstances (shipwreck, collision, stranding, explosion or fire, or defect in the ship) fault on the part of the carrier is presumed, and the onus of proof lies with the carrier: art. 3(3). Similarly where luggage other than cabin luggage is lost or damaged, fault is presumed and the onus lies with the carrier: art. 3(3).

[41] arts. 7, 8, 9, 10, 12, 13, and Sched. 3, Pt. III (introducing units of account: S.I. 1989 No. 1881).

[42] art. 13.

[43] art. 4.

[44] art. 5.

[45] art. 6.

[46] art. 15.

[47] art. 16.

[48] art. 17, as amended by S.I. 1980 No. 1092, and S.I. 1987 No. 670.

[49] art. 20.

[50] art. 18.

[51] 1979 Current Law Statutes Commentary by D.R. Thomas, p. 39/14.

[52] Dangerous Vessels Act 1985, s. 1. The harbour master is himself subject to directions from the Secretary of State: s. 3.

27.28 **Safety at Sea.**—The Merchant Shipping Act 1995 makes provision for health and safety regulations on board ship.[53] Improvement notices and prohibition notices may be served upon persons contravening statutory regulations.[54] Deaths on board a United Kingdom registered ship must be the subject of an inquiry,[55] and accidents involving ships the subject of investigation.[56] The master and owner may be guilty of an offence if a ship is dangerously unsafe,[57] and the master or seamen may be guilty of an offence where they endanger the safety of their ship.[58] A shipowner must take all reasonable steps to ensure that the ship is operated in a safe manner.[59]

27.29 **Limitation in Marine Claims.**—Any action to enforce any claim or lien against a vessel or her owners in respect of any damage or loss to another vessel, her cargo or freight, or any property on board her, or damages for loss of life or personal injuries suffered by any person on board her, caused by the fault of the former vessel, must be commenced[60] within two years from the date when the damage or loss or injury was caused.[61] A court may extend the two-year period to such extent and on such conditions as it thinks fit.[62]

27.30 **Terrorism and Carriage by Sea.**—The Aviation and Maritime Security Act 1990[63] is concerned with protection against terrorism. Part II[64] gives effect to the Rome Convention 1988, and makes it an offence, *inter alia*, to hijack a ship; to damage a ship; to act violently on board ship so as

---

[53] ss. 85–108. Regulations are to be found in statutory instruments. For example, the Merchant Shipping (Means of Access) Regulations 1981 (S.I. 1981 No. 1729) as amended; the Merchant Shipping (Health and Safety: General Duties) Regulations 1984 (S.I. 1984 No. 408) as amended; the Merchant Shipping (Protective Clothing and Equipment) Regulations 1985 (S.I. 1985 No. 1664): see, for example, *Smith* v. *Brown*, 1988 S.L.T. 150 (relating to S.I. 1981 No. 1729); *Mearns* v. *Lothian R.C.*, 1991 S.L.T. 338 (relating to S.I. 1984 No. 408). As to limitation and exclusion of liability for personal injury, etc., see paras. 27.17 to 27.18, *supra*.

[54] ss. 261–262. Notices are served by Department of Trade inspectors: s. 256.

[55] s. 271.

[56] s. 267.

[57] s. 98. In certain circumstances, charterers and ship managers could be prosecuted.

[58] s. 58.

[59] s. 100. Failure in this duty is an offence: *Seaboard Offshore Ltd.* v. *Secretary of State for Transport* [1994] 1 W.L.R. 541. Demise charterers and ship managers may also be guilty in terms of s. 31.

[60] The commencement of an action has been defined as the date of citation: *Miller* v. *N.C.B.*, 1960 S.C. 376, Lord President at p. 383; *Barclay* v. *Chief Constable, Northern Constabulary*, 1986 S.L.T. 562.

[61] Maritime Conventions Act 1911, s. 8, as amended by the Merchant Shipping (Salvage and Pollution) Act 1994.

[62] s. 8: see *Brown* v. *Devanha Fishing Co.*, 1968 S.L.T. (Notes) 4; *Taft* v. *Clyde Marine Motoring Co. Ltd.*, 1990 S.L.T. 170.

[63] c.31; the majority of the provisions came into force on September 26, 1990.

[64] ss. 9–17.

to endanger safety; and to place devices such as bombs on board ship. The Secretary of State may give directions to harbour authorities, shipowners and charterers prohibiting a ship from going to sea, or persons or property from being taken on board.[65] Powers of inspection and search are also provided for.[65]

27.31 Hovercraft.—A hovercraft is a vehicle which is designed to be supported when in motion wholly or partly by air expelled from the vehicle to form a cushion of which the boundaries include the ground, water or other surface beneath the vehicle.[66] Many principles of maritime law have been made applicable to hovercraft.[67]

Further Reading

Carver, *Carriage by Sea* (13th ed., 1982).
British Shipping Laws Series.
Payne & Ivamy, *Carriage of Goods by Sea* (13th ed., 1989).
Scrutton, *Charterparties* (19th ed., 1984).
Stair Memorial Encyclopaedia, Vol. 21 (Shipping and Navigation).

[65] Pt. III (ss. 18–46).

[66] Hovercraft Act 1968, s. 4(1).

[67] See, *e.g.* the Hovercraft (Civil Liability) Order 1986 (S.I. 1986 No. 1305), applying, with modifications, principles of maritime law to carriage by hovercraft. The Hovercraft (Application of Enactments) Order 1972 (S.I. 1972 No. 971 as amended) also applies to hovercraft a number of enactments relating to ships. The Merchant Shipping Act 1995 including ss. 183–184 and Sched. 6 (international carriage by sea of passengers and luggage) and ss. 185–186 and Sched. 7 (exclusion and limitation of liability) applies to hovercraft: s. 310 of the 1995 Act. The liability of hovercraft owners for personal injury and loss of or damage to property may be limited: Hovercraft (Civil Liability) Order 1986 (S.I. 1986 No. 1305 as amended), operative on December 1, 1986.

CHAPTER 28

CARRIAGE BY AIR

28.1 General.—As will be seen in the chapter on Landownership, property in land extends *a coelo usque ad centrum*, so that in strictness the passage of aircraft over a man's land is a trespass. Since, however, the maintenance of such a rule would largely defeat travel by air, the owner's rights have been restricted by a statutory provision to the effect that no action shall lie in respect of trespass or nuisance by reason only of the flight of aircraft at a reasonable height above the ground, provided that the statutory requirements have been complied with.[1]

The law relating to the use of the air has developed rapidly.[2] While largely statutory, some common law principles apply. Thus the ordinary principles of reparation have been resorted to.[3] Similarly an air carrier might in some circumstances be held to be a common carrier, although as indicated below the possibility seems remote.[4] This chapter outlines some of the more important rules specifically relating to carriage by air.

28.2 The Aircraft and the Outsider.—The concession already noted as having been made by section 76(1) of the Civil Aviation Act 1982 is in respect of the bare fact of flight over another's property and that only at a reasonable height. But where material loss or damage is caused to any person or property on land or water by an aircraft,[5] the owner is liable without proof of fault except in the case of contributory negligence.[6] In certain circumstances the owner may have a right to be indemnified by a third party against a claim for loss or damage.[7] Where the aircraft has been bona fide let or hired out for a period exceeding 14 days, and no

---

[1] Civil Aviation Act 1982, s. 76(1), formerly s. 40(1) of the 1949 Act. See *Cubitt* v. *Gower* (1933) 47 Ll. L. Rep. 65; *Bernstein* v. *Skyviews & General* [1978] Q.B. 479; *Steel-Maitland* v. *British Airways Board*, 1981 S.L.T. 110.

[2] Shawcross and Beaumont, *Air Law* (4th ed.) provides a useful noter-up.

[3] See for example *Fosbroke-Hobbes* v. *Airwork* [1937] 1 All E.R. 108, where the doctrine of *res ipsa loquitur* was applied to the negligent handling of an aeroplane; Shawcross and Beaumont, *op. cit.*, Vol. 1, Pt. V, §§ 80 *et seq.*

[4] *Aslan* v. *Imperial Airways* (1933) 49 T.L.R. 415; Shawcross and Beaumont, *op. cit.*, Vol. 1, Pt. VIII, § 78; McNair, *Law of the Air* (3rd ed.), pp. 138–144.

[5] Or by a person in the aircraft, or an article, animal or person falling from the aircraft.

[6] Civil Aviation Act 1982, s. 76(2).

[7] s. 76(3).

pilot, commander or other operative is employed by the owner, the hirer is liable.[8] Dangerous flying is discouraged by heavy penalties.[9] A helicopter flight over a congested city area without written permission from the Civil Aviation Authority has been held to constitute an offence.[10] The potentialities of injury to others posed by aircraft are obviously great and the legislature has made provisions for lessening them. Thus, for example, an aircraft is bound to be registered, to bear the proper marks, to hold a certificate of 'airworthiness,' to have a certified and licensed crew, and to carry certain papers.[11] Similarly an air transport licence is required where an aircraft is used for the carriage for reward of passengers or cargo.[12] However the law imposes no statutory obligation upon the owner of aircraft to insure against third party risks.[13] Noise, vibration, and other pollution from aircraft is regulated by statute.[14]

The analogy of the law of sea-transport has been and will probably continue to be influential in the development of the law of the air. Examples are the law relating to wreck, the salvage of life or property, and in particular allowing to the owner of aircraft a reasonable reward for salvage services.[15]

The 1982 Act gives power to make regulations for the prevention of collisions at sea involving seaplanes on the surface of the water.[16] The general regulations applying to lights, signals and the rule of the air will be found in the schedule to the Rules of the Air Regulations 1991.[17]

28.3   Aircraft as Carrier.—At common law the liability of the carrier of goods depends on whether he is a common carrier or not.[18] If he is, he is liable for loss of or damage to the goods without proof of fault; if he is

---

[8] s. 76(4).

[9] s. 81; the Air Navigation Order 1989 (S.I. 1989 No. 2004) as amended, arts. 50 et seq., art. 99 and Sched. 12.

[10] Cameron v. Smith, 1982 S.L.T. 398.

[11] Air Navigation Order 1989 (S.I. 1989 No. 2004) as amended and Air Navigation (General) Regulations 1981 (S.I. 1981 No. 57), as amended, the latest amendment being S.I. 1989 No. 669.

[12] Civil Aviation Act 1982, ss. 64 et seq. See too Civil Aviation Authority Regulations 1991 (S.I. 1991 No. 1672); Corner v. Clayton [1976] 1 W.L.R. 800; Air Ecosse v. Civil Aviation Authority, 1987 S.L.T. 751.

[13] Compulsory third party insurance in relation to aircraft was the subject of two conventions at Rome, one in 1933 and one in 1952. The United Kingdom intended to give effect to the 1933 Convention but never did so, and the enabling legislation has been repealed (ss. 43–46 and 49(1) and Schedule 6 to Civil Aviation Act 1949 were repealed by the Companies Act 1967, s. 128; and ss. 42, 48, and 50, and Sched. 5 to the 1949 Act were repealed by the Civil Aviation Act 1968, s. 26).

[14] See, for example, s. 19 of the Civil Aviation Act 1968, ss. 5, 6, 81 and 82 of the Civil Aviation Act 1982.

[15] Civil Aviation Act 1982, s. 87.

[16] Ibid., s. 97.

[17] S.I. 1991 No. 2437, as amended; cf. Dickson v. Miln, 1969 J.C. 75.

[18] para. 26.3, supra.

not, fault must be proved. In either case he has no liability for injury to passengers except on proof of fault.[19] It has been held that there is no common law obligation to supply an 'airworthy' aircraft.[20] However the common law has been superseded in both international and non-international carriage by the provisions of the Warsaw Convention, as applied by the Carriage by Air Act 1961,[21] the Carriage by Air (Supplementary Provisions) Act 1962,[22] the Carriage by Air Acts (Application of Provisions) Order 1967,[23] and the Civil Aviation Act 1982.[24] Moreover each airline has detailed conditions of contract.[25] The result is that the likelihood of an airline or aircraft operator ever being regarded as a common carrier must be considered very remote.

28.4   International Carriage.—The Warsaw Convention[26] applies only to 'international carriage,' which is defined as 'any carriage in which according to the agreement between the parties the place of departure and the place of destination ... are situated either within the territories of two High Contracting Parties or within the territory of a single High Contracting Party, if there is an agreed stopping place within the territory of another state,[27] even if that state is not a High Contracting Party.'[28] Carriage between two points within the territory of a single High Contracting Party without an agreed stopping place in another state is not international carriage. The carrier must hand over the appropriate document, *i.e.* passenger ticket, luggage ticket or air consignment note, and if he fails to do so cannot rely on the provisions

[19] See para. 26.13, *supra. Chisholm* v. *British European Airways* [1963] 1 Lloyd's Rep. 626.

[20] *Aslan* v. *Imperial Airways* (1933) 49 T.L.R. 415. See para. 27.4, *supra.*

[21] As amended by, *inter alia*, the Prescription and Limitation (Scotland) Act 1973, Sched. 4, and the Carriage by Air and Road Act 1979.

[22] As amended by, *inter alia*, the Carriage by Air and Road Act 1979.

[23] S.I. 1967 No. 480, as amended, the latest amendment being S.I. 1981 No. 44.

[24] s. 85 and Sched. 11, relating to the body known as the Airworthiness Requirements Board. Air Navigation Orders regulate air navigation including air traffic control: s. 60 of the Civil Aviation Act 1982 as amended; and see *Stair Memorial Encyclopaedia*, Vol. 2 (Aviation), paras. 954 *et seq.*

[25] See for example the passenger ticket conditions and the air waybills conditions to be used by airlines who are members of the International Air Transport Association: Shawcross and Beaumont, *op cit.*, Vol. 1, Pt. VII, § 47.

[26] All references are to the 1961 Act and Sched. 1, setting out the amended Warsaw Convention. The 1967 Order sets out the unamended Warsaw Convention. The Carriage by Air and Road Act 1979, Sched. 1 contains the text of the Warsaw Convention as further amended following upon protocols signed at Montreal on September 25, 1975. However that schedule and s. 1 of the 1979 Act are not yet in force: see s. 7(2) of the 1979 Act and Commencement Order No. 1 (S.I. 1980 No. 1966). Note that the text of the Convention is given in both English and French, which can give rise to difficulties: *Rothmans Ltd.* v. *Saudi Airlines* [1981] Q.B. 368 (jurisdiction).

[27] art. 1; *Grein* v. *Imperial Airways Ltd.* [1937] 1 K.B. 50. The 1961 Act does not apply where the places of departure and destination and any agreed stopping places are all within the territory of a single foreign state: *Holmes* v. *Bangladesh Biman Corporation* [1989] A.C. 1112.

[28] For a list of the High Contracting Parties, see the Carriage by Air (Parties to Convention) Order 1988 (S.I. 1988 No. 243).

which exclude or limit his liability.[29] He is liable in damages for death of
or injury to a passenger by accident on board or in embarking or
disembarking,[30] for loss of or damage to registered luggage or goods
while in his charge on board or in an aerodrome,[31] and for any delay in
the carriage of passengers, luggage or goods.[32] But he avoids liability if
he proves that he and his agents[33] or employees have taken all
'necessary measures'[34] to avoid the damage or that it was impossible for
him or them to take such measures. This applies equally to passengers,
luggage and cargo.[35] If there was contributory negligence the court may,
according to its own law, exonerate him wholly or partly.[36] Unless by
special contract a higher sum is agreed, liability for injury to a passenger
is limited to 250,000 francs, for registered luggage and goods to 250
francs per kilogramme and for hand luggage to 5,000 francs per
passenger.[37] Any condition relieving the carrier of liability or fixing a
lower limit is null.[38] The carrier cannot rely on provisions excluding or
limiting his liability if the damage is caused by his own act or omission[39]
or that of any agent or employee acting within the scope of his
employment, done with intent to cause harm or recklessly and with
knowledge that damage would result.[40] The Unfair Contract Terms Act
1977, while applying to contracts of carriage by air,[41] does not affect
exclusion or limitation clauses authorised by an enactment such as the

[29] arts. 3–16; *Lisi* v. *Alitalia-Linee Aeree Italiane, S.P.A.* [1967] 1 Lloyd's Rep. 140;
Corocraft v. *Pan American Airways* [1969] 1 Q.B. 616; *Ludecke* v. *Canadian Pacific
Airlines* [1975] 2 Lloyd's Rep. 87; [1979] 2 Lloyd's Rep. 260; *Canadian Pacific Airlines* v.
Montreal Trust Co. [1975] 2 Lloyd's Rep. 90; but see *Collins* v. *British Airways Board*
[1982] Q.B. 734 (limitation allowed despite failure to complete baggage check details).
[30] art. 17; 1961 Act, s. 3; *Adatia* v. *Air Canada* [1992] P.I.Q.R. p. 238.
[31] art. 18; *Fothergill* v. *Monarch Airlines* [1978] Q.B. 108; [1980] Q.B. 23; [1981] A.C.
251; *Gatewhite Ltd.* v. *Iberia Lineas Aeras de Espana S.A.* [1990] 1 Q.B. 326.
[32] art. 19. See, *e.g. Panalpina International Transport Ltd.* v. *Densil Underwear Ltd.*
[1981] 1 Lloyd's Rep. 187.
[33] art. 20.
[34] This must mean 'proper' or 'reasonable.' If he took all necessary measures, there
would be no damage. See also *Rustenberg Platinum Mines* v. *Pan American World
Airways* [1979] 1 Lloyd's Rep. 19.
[35] art. 20.
[36] art. 21.
[37] art.22. These limits are to be replaced by limits of 16,600 special drawing rights, 17
special drawing rights, and 332 special drawing rights respectively in terms of s. 4(1) of the
Carriage by Air and Road Act 1979. However s. 4(1) is not yet in force: see s. 7(2) of the
1979 Act and Commencement Order No. 1 (S.I. 1980 No. 1966). Cases illustrating
limitation of liability include *Samuel Montagu & Co.* v. *Swiss Air Transport Co.* [1966] 2
Q.B. 306; *Bland* v. *British Airways Board* [1981] 1 Lloyd's Rep. 289; and *Datacard Corp.*
v. *Air Express International Corp.* [1983] 2 All E.R. 639; [1984] 1 W.L.R. 198. Note that
it has been held in England that the limits are comprehensive of everything except
expenses, and may not be exceeded by an award of interest upon damages: *Swiss Bank
Corp* v. *Brink's M.A.T. Ltd.* [1986] Q.B. 853 (contrast with the Scottish decision in
carriage by sea: *The Devotion II*, 1979 S.C. 80).
[38] art. 23.
[39] Replacing the phrase 'wilful misconduct' contained in the 1932 Act. See *Bastable* v.
N.B.R., 1912 S.C. 555.
[40] art. 25; *Goldman* v. *Thai Airways International Ltd.* [1983] 1 W.L.R. 1186; *S.S.
Pharmaceutical Co. Ltd.* v. *Quantas Airways Ltd.* [1989] 1 Lloyd's Rep. 319.
[41] 1977 Act, s. 15(2)(c).

Carriage by Air Act 1961.[42] Complaint of damage to luggage must be made within seven days of delivery, of damage to cargo within 14 and of delay within 21 of receipt by the carrier.[43] Any right to damages is lost if the action is not brought within two years.[44] Where carriage is performed by various successive carriers, each is subject to the Convention.[45] Where a carrier delegates performance of a contract to another[46] both are subject to the Convention, the former for the whole of the carriage contemplated in the agreement, the latter solely for the carriage which he performs.[47] The delegating carrier is vicariously liable for the acts and omissions of the actual carrier and of his employees and agents acting within the scope of their employment.[47]

28.5 Non-International Carriage.—The Warsaw Convention does not extend to carriage by air not falling within the definition of 'international carriage.'[48] However, the Convention has been applied with modifications[49] to 'non-international' carriage, by the Carriage by Air Acts (Application of Provisions) Order 1967.[50] Thus the two year time-bar applies.[51]

28.6 Safety of Aircraft.—Air Navigation Orders regulate the carriage of dangerous goods[52] and prohibit reckless or negligent behaviour likely to endanger aircraft, person or property.[53]

28.7 Protection for Air Passengers.—Air travel organisers (*i.e.* persons who make available or who hold themselves out as persons who may make available accommodation for the carriage of persons on aircraft) must be licensed.[54] An Air Travel Reserve Fund has been established to meet customers' losses when air travel organisers cannot meet their financial commitments.[55]

[42] 1977 Act, s. 29.
[43] art. 26; *Fothergill* v. *Monarch Airlines* [1978] Q.B. 108; [1980] Q.B. 23; [1981] A.C. 251.
[44] art. 29.
[45] art. 30.
[46] The 'actual carrier.'
[47] Carriage by Air (Supplementary Provisions) Act 1962, Sched.
[48] See para. 28.4, *supra.*
[49] For example arts. 3–16 (Chap. II) of the Convention do not apply to non-international carriage. Also liability for injury to a passenger is limited to 100,000 special drawing rights: art. 22.
[50] S.I. 1967 No. 480, as amended, the latest amendment being S.I. 1981 No. 440.
[51] See, *e.g. Hardy* v. *British Airways Board,* 1983 S.L.T. 45.
[52] The Air Navigation (Dangerous Goods) Regulations 1994 (S.I. 1994 No. 3187), and the Air Navigation Order 1989 (S.I. 1989 No. 2004) as amended, art. 47.
[53] The Air Navigation Order 1989 (S.I. 1989 No. 2004), as amended, art. 50 *et seq.*
[54] Civil Aviation Act 1982, s. 71; Civil Aviation (Air Travel Organisers' Licensing) Regulations 1972 (S.I. 1972 No. 223), as amended, the latest amendment being S.I. 1981 No. 314; *Jet Travel* v. *Slade Travel Agency* [1983] C.L.Y. 179; [1983] Com. L.R. 244; *Stair Memorial Encyclopaedia,* Vol. 2 (Aviation), paras. 1000 *et seq.*
[55] Air Travel Reserve Fund Act 1975, as amended by, *inter alia,* the Civil Aviation (Amendment) Act 1982.

28.8 The Civil Aviation Authority.—The Civil Aviation Authority[56] is responsible for the licensing of air transport.[57] It has other important functions, including the registration of aircraft, air safety, the control of air traffic, the certification of aircraft operators and the licensing of air crews.[57] The Authority's objectives are to provide a safe but economic air transport service, to promote the United Kingdom air industry, and to further the reasonable interests of users of air transport services.[58] The Secretary of State may in certain circumstances give the Authority directions[59] although the Authority is neither a servant nor agent of the Crown.[60] The Secretary of State is required in certain circumstances to obtain advice from the Authority.[61]

28.9 Contract Conditions.—As international carriage is regulated by the Warsaw Convention, little freedom of contract is conferred upon the airlines. Only when the statutory provisions are silent does the question of individual conditions arise, and even then the conditions may have been drafted to comply with standards, recommended practices, or standard conditions laid down by the International Civil Aviation Organisation or the International Air Transport Association.[62]

28.10 Prevention of Crime and Terrorism.—Legislation has been passed to combat crime and terrorism relating to aircraft.[63]

28.11 Air Accidents.—An accident involving aircraft may be the subject of an inspector's investigation,[64] a public inquiry,[65] or a fatal accident inquiry.[66]

---

[56] The Authority consists of six to 16 persons appointed by the Secretary of State for Transport: Civil Aviation Act 1982, s. 2 as amended by s. 72 of the Airports Act 1986; and the Transfer of Functions (Trade and Industry) Order 1983 (S.I. 1983 No. 1127).

[57] 1982 Act, s. 3; *R.* v. *Secretary of State for Transport, ex p. Pegasus Holdings (London) Ltd.* [1988] 1 W.L.R. 990 (Romanian-licensed pilots failing British C.A.A. examinations).

[58] 1982 Act, s. 6; *Laker Airways* v. *Department of Trade* [1977] Q.B. 643.

[59] 1982 Act, s. 6; but see *Laker Airways, supra.*

[60] 1982 Act, s. 2(4).

[61] For example, before issuing regulations relating to air traffic distribution: s. 31(4) of the Airports Act 1986: *Air 2000 Ltd.* v. *Secretary of State for Transport (No. 2)*, 1990 S.L.T. 335; see too 1989 S.L.T. 698 (title and interest to sue); *Stair Memorial Encyclopaedia*, Vol. 2 (Aviation), para. 921.

[62] See Shawcross and Beaumont, *op. cit.*, Vol. 1, Pt. VII, § 47 and Vol. 2, App. AB.

[63] Tokyo Convention Act 1967 as amended; Airports Authority Act, 1975, s. 12; Civil Aviation Act 1978 as amended; Civil Aviation Act 1982; Aviation Security Act 1982; Aviation and Maritime Security Act 1990.

[64] The Civil Aviation (Investigation of Air Accidents) Regulations 1989 (S.I. 1989 No. 2062); *Stair Memorial Encyclopaedia* Vol. 2 (Aviation), paras. 1011 *et seq.*

[65] S.I. 1989 No. 2062; *Stair Memorial Encyclopaedia*, paras. 1017 *et seq.*

[66] Fatal Accidents and Sudden Deaths Inquiry (Scotland) Act 1976, s. 1; article "FAIs — after Lockerbie," 1991 S.L.T. (News) 225.

28.12 Hovercraft.—A hovercraft is part aircraft, part ship.[67] Its hybrid nature is reflected in the relevant subordinate legislation.[68] The Unfair Contract Terms Act 1977 applies to hovercraft, to a limited extent.[69]

Further Reading

Blackshaw, *Aviation Law and Regulation* (1992).
McNair, *Law of the Air* (3rd ed., 1964).
Shawcross and Beaumont, *Air Law* (4th ed., 1977).
Stair Memorial Encyclopaedia, Vol. 2 (Aviation), Vol. 3 (Carriage).

---

[67] Hovercraft Act 1968 as amended; and see the Civil Aviation Act 1982, s. 100.
[68] Hovercraft (Civil Liability) Order 1986 (S.I. 1986 No. 1305); Hovercraft (General) Order 1972 (S.I. 1972 No. 674) as amended; Hovercraft (Application of Enactments) Order 1972 (S.I. 1972 No. 971) as amended, the latest amendment being S.I. 1990 No. 2594.
[69] ss. 15(3), (4).

PART IV—UNJUSTIFIED ENRICHMENT AND SALVAGE

CHAPTER 29

UNJUSTIFIED ENRICHMENT

29.1 The Concept.—A person may be said to be unjustifiably enriched at another's expense when he has become owner of the other's money or property or has used that property or otherwise benefited from his actings or expenditure in circumstances which the law regards as actionably unjust, and so as requiring the enrichment to be reversed.[1] The obligation does not depend on agreement but is obediential, arising by operation of law.[2] Although the underlying principles are the same in the various spheres,[3] as a general rule Scots law treats cases involving recovery of money under the heading of repetition, and those involving recovery of moveable property fall under the heading of restitution, while cases in which the defender has benefited unjustifiably from expenditure or actings of the pursuer or from the use of his property are dealt with under the heading of recompense.[3a]

29.2 Repetition.—The plea of repetition allows recovery of money which has been paid in circumstances where it would be unjust for the defender to keep the money. The cases are grouped under headings which reflect the Roman law origins of some of the principles involved and the

---

[1] See P. Birks, *An Introduction to the Law of Restitution* (revised ed., 1989), pp. 16 *et seq.*; P. Birks, *Restitution—The Future* (1992), Chap. 1. For *negotiorum gestio* see para. 22.31 *supra*.

[2] Stair, I, vii, 1; Erskine, III, i, 9 and 10.

[3] In *Royal Bank of Scotland* v. *Watt*, 1991 S.C. 48, there are remarks which suggest that enrichment or benefit to the defender may not be necessary in an action of repetition of money. But, as the judges recognised, a defender who becomes the creditor of a sum of money, for however short a period, is thereby prima facie enriched. The question then is whether in the circumstances of the case it would be equitable to make him repay the money. See, however, para. 29.9 below. 'The fact of the payment of money is itself *prima facie* proof of enrichment, but not conclusive proof. In assessing whether defendant has been enriched by the payment, account must be taken of any performance rendered by defendant which was juridically connected with his receipt of the money': *Govender* v. *Standard Bank of South Africa Ltd.*, 1984 (4) S.A. 392(C), at p. 404, *per* Rose-Innes J. On that decision see *First National Bank of Southern Africa Ltd.* v. *B. & H. Engineering*, 1993 (2) S.A. 41. See further S.L.C., *Recovery of Benefits*, Vol. 2, pp. 96 *et seq.*

[3a] *Cf. Morgan Guaranty Trust Co. of New York* v. *Lothian R.C.* 1995 S.L.T. 299 at p. 309J *per* Lord President Hope. For a historical analysis, see H.L. MacQueen and W.D.H. Seller, 'Unjust Enrichment in Scots Law,' *Unjust Enrichment*, E.J.H. Schrage (ed.), (1995), p. 289.

terminology used in some of the cases: the *condictio causa data causa non secuta*; the *condictio indebiti*; the *condictio ob turpem vel injustam causam* and the *condictio sine causa* (a term not much used in Scottish writings).[4] These terms are not straitjackets but merely serve to distinguish various situations in which repetition may be available, and it may be that some cases could be classified under more than one heading.

29.3 ***Condictio Causa Data Causa Non Secuta* (Claim for Something Given on a Basis which has Failed).[5]**—In these cases the pursuer seeks recovery of money paid in advance for an anticipated consideration which has not been received.[6] The defender must repay the amount by which he has been enriched.[7] Although the name used in Justinian's Digest is preserved, the doctrine has a rather different scope in Scots law[8] where it is possible to identify four main types of case.

(1) Performance of the contract is frustrated[9] and the defender is released from his obligation to supply the consideration. Thus in a contract for the construction of ship's engines for an Austrian firm, an instalment of the price was paid on signing the contract. Before the construction of the engines had been begun, war with Austria was declared and this put an end to the contract. It was held, on the conclusion of peace, that the Italian successors of the Austrian firm might recover the deposit.[10] Similarly where the price was put on deposit receipt pending settlement of the sale of subjects which were destroyed by fire before settlement, the purchaser was entitled to recover the price.[11] (2) The defender, in breach of contract, fails to supply the consideration and the pursuer terminates the contract. Here

---

[4] The *condictio furtiva* of Roman law has not been received into Scots law.

[5] On the translation see Birks (1983) 36 Current Legal Problems 141 at p. 156.

[6] D.12.4; Voet, *Commentarius ad Pandectas* (1698, 1704), 12.4; Stair, I, vii, 7; Erskine, III, i, 10; *Watson* v. *Shankland* (1871) 10 M. 142, *per* Lord President Inglis at p. 152; *Haggarty* v. *Scottish Transport and General Workers Union*, 1955 S.C. 109, *per* Lord Sorn at p. 114; *Connelly* v. *Simpson*, 1994 S.L.T. 1096. Along with this *condictio*, Stair, I, vii, 7 discusses the *condictio ob non causam* (or *ob causam finitam*) covering cases where the initial legal cause for the payment later ceases.

[7] *Ogilvy* v. *Hume* (1683) 2 Br. Supp. 34, approved by Lord Shaw of Dunfermline in *Cantiere San Rocco* v. *Clyde Shipbuilding Co.*, 1923 S.C. (H.L.) 105, at pp. 119–120; *Cutler* v. *Littleton* (1711) Mor. 583.

[8] For the difference and the development from Roman law, see R. Zimmermann, *The Law of Obligations* (1990), pp. 843–844; pp. 857–862; Buckland (1933) 46 Harv.L.R. 1281; Evans-Jones (1993) 109 L.Q.R. 663.

[9] For the case where the impossibility existed from the outset see para. 29.5, *infra*.

[10] *Cantiere San Rocco* v. *Clyde Shipbuilding Co.*, 1923 S.C. (H.L.) 105. Lord Shaw of Dunfermline (at p. 119) purports to explain the reference to D.12.4.5.4, Ulpian 2 *disputationum*, in Erskine, III, i, 10, but misunderstands the Digest text to which Erskine refers. See Buckland, *A Textbook of Roman Law* (3rd ed., 1963), pp. 545–546; (1933) 46 Harv.L.R. 1281, especially at p. 1284; Zimmermann, *Obligations*, pp. 858–859. Lord Shaw's reference (at p. 117) to Roby, *Roman Private Law*, Vol. 2, p. 78 should be read against this background. The passage still causes difficulties: *Connelly* v. *Simpson*, 1991 S.C.L.R. 295, at pp. 297–298.

[11] *Singh* v. *Cross Entertainments Ltd.*, 1990 S.L.T. 77.

the position is less clear. In the leading case[12] the pursuer agreed to pay for shares in a private company and paid in two stages. No shares were ever issued to him because, the pursuer not having wanted them until his divorce was over, the defender eventually put the company into liquidation. By a majority, the Extra Division refused to allow the pursuer to recover the price. Lord McCluskey based his decision on the broad ground that the *condictio* is not available, and the only remedy is damages, where a defender is in wilful breach of contract.[12a] Lord Sutherland, on the other hand, held that the payments were not recoverable because on a proper construction of the contract they constituted payments of the price then due and payable;[13] if they had been advances towards a price not due and payable until delivery of the shares, they would, in principle, have been recoverable.[14] (3) Where the pursuer, having paid a sum in advance, thereafter repudiates a contract before the defender performs his obligations, the pursuer can recover the advance, subject to any counterclaim by the defender for loss suffered due to the pursuer's breach of contract.[15] But if the sum is paid in advance as a deposit in security of the pursuer's performing the contract and he repudiates it, the pursuer cannot recover the deposit.[16] (4) Where the contract is subject to a suspensive condition which does not materialise, and as a result the defender comes under no obligation to supply the consideration, the pursuer can recover any prepayment.[17]

29.4   *Condictio Indebiti* (Claim for Recovery of a Payment which is not Due).—Money paid by the pursuer under the mistaken belief that it was due to be paid under a legal obligation to the recipient can be recovered in a personal action against the recipient,[18] unless the defender establishes factors which would make retention of the money equitable.[19] The pursuer's mistake may be as to the facts or as to the

---

[12] *Connelly* v. *Simpson*, 1994 S.L.T. 1096. Lord Brand dissented.

[12a] *Ibid.* at p. 1106C.

[13] 1994 S.L.T. 1096 at p. 1110. As in *Leitch* v. *Wilson* (1868) 7 M. 150.

[14] *Watson* v. *Shankland* (1871) 10 M. 142, esp. at pp. 152 *et seq.* The House of Lords deleted a passage related to certain aspects of the Lord President's remarks from the Court of Session interlocutor: (1873) 11 M. (H.L.) 51. Lord Sutherland (1994 S.L.T. 1110C) treats *Cantiere San Rocco* as ample authority for recovery of advances where the future event is not performed 'for whatever reason.' On Lord McCluskey's approach *Crofts* v. *Stewart's Trs.*, 1927 S.C. (H.L.) 65 may be regarded as a case of non-wilful breach.

[15] *Zemhunt (Holdings) Ltd.* v. *Control Securities*, 1992 S.L.T. 151, *per* Lord Morison at p. 155.

[16] *Roberts and Cooper Ltd.* v. *Christian Salvesen and Co. Ltd.*, 1918 S.C. 794; *Zemhunt (Holdings) Ltd.* v. *Control Securities*, *supra*.

[17] Voet 12.6.3. See *Brown* v. *Nielson* (1825) 4 S. 271. It is not clear whether this case should be classified under this heading or elsewhere.

[18] D.12.6; Voet 12.6; Stair, I, vii, 9; Erskine, III, iii, 54; Bell, *Prin.*, § 531; Hume, *Lectures*, iii, 172. See as to exceptions *Bell* v. *Thomson* (1867) 6 M. 64. For the scope of the *condictio indebiti* see *Govender* v. *Standard Bank of South Africa*, 1984 (4) S.A. 392, at pp. 396 *et seq.*, *per* Rose-Innes J. The theory of *promutuum* adopted by Stair, Erskine and Bell from Cujas (*Paratitla* on D.12.6 and *Observationes* 8.33) has not taken root in Scots law. See generally S.L.C., *Recovery of Benefits*, Vol. 2.

[19] *Morgan Guaranty Trust Co. of New York* v. *Lothian R.C.* 1995 S.L.T. 299, *per* Lord President Hope at p. 316F. Erskine, III, iii, 54; Gloag, *Contract* (2nd ed.), p. 61; *Bell* v.

law relating to the transaction.[19a] So the pursuer may have been mistaken as to facts which indicated that the sum was due, *e.g.* he paid a debt, being unaware that it had already been paid.[20] Thus where a feuar, on making use of a mutual gable, paid half the cost of erecting it, he was entitled to recover what he had paid on discovering that it had already been paid by his superior.[21] So also where as a result of common error a purchaser bought land with buildings and houses, but in fact most of the buildings were on a neighbouring feu, the contract of sale was reduced and the purchaser was entitled to recover the purchase price.[22] Likewise averments that, due to a representation by the contractors which the pursuer had been unable to check, the purchaser had overpaid a contractors' account were held relevant in a claim to recover the excess payment.[23] Similarly where a local authority entered into a currency exchange agreement with a merchant bank which both wrongly believed to be valid but which was in fact invalid because it was ultra vires the local authority, it was held that the merchant bank was entitled to recover the balance paid to the local authority, even though its belief that the sum was due had been based on an error of law.[23a] Earlier cases involving error of law require to be read in the light of this decision of a Court of Five Judges. Where, in any case the mistake was avoidable and the pursuer could have discovered the true facts, these factors will be relevant to any decision as to whether to grant the pursuer's claim on the grounds of equity.[24] Where, however, the pursuer waived any objection to payment, recovery will be denied.[25]

29.5 Excluded Cases.—Repetition is not allowed in the case of money paid as a compromise, even one offered due to a mistake in fact,[26] since the compromise itself forms a fresh obligation to pay.[27] The *condictio indebiti* has also been held not to lie in the case of money paid as a

Thomson, supra, especially *per* L.J.-C. Patton at p. 69, apparently citing Pothier, *Traité du Contract de Prêt de Consomption*, nn. 140–141; *Crédit Lyonnais* v. *George Stevenson & Co. Ltd.* (1901) 9 S.L.T. 93, *per* Lord Kyllachy at p. 95; *Haggarty* v. *Scottish Transport and General Workers Union*, 1955 S.C. 109; *Royal Bank of Scotland* v. *Watt*, 1991 S.C. 48. A proof will therefore usually be necessary to explore the equities: *Haggarty*. Interest is generally payable from the date of the erroneous payment either on the principle of restitution (*Gwydyr* v. *Lord Advocate* (1894) 2 S.L.T. 280) or on the analogy of loan interest (*Duncan, Galloway & Co.* v. *Duncan Falconer & Co.*, 1913 S.C. 265). But *cf. Sprot's Trs.* v. *Lord Advocate* (1903) 10 S.L.T. 452 (interest from date of payer's formal demand for repayment).
[19a] *Morgan Guaranty, supra*, overruling *Glasgow Corporation* v. *Lord Advocate*, 1959 S.C. 203 and *Taylor* v. *William's Trs.*, 1975 S.C. 146.
[20] Gloag, *Contract* (2nd ed.), pp. 60 *et seq.*
[21] *Robertson* v. *Scott* (1886) 13 R. 1127.
[22] *Hamilton* v. *Western Bank* (1861) 23 D. 1033; *supra*, para. [8.24].
[23] *Balfour* v. *Smith* (1877) 4 R. 454.
[23a] *Morgan Guaranty, supra*.
[24] *Morgan Guaranty, supra* at p. 316F *per* Lord President Hope; at p. 320I–J *per* Lord Clyde and at p. 322D–F *per* Lord Cullen.
[25] *Dalmellington Iron Co.* v. *Glasgow & S.W. Railway Co.* (1889) 16 R. 523.
[26] Erskine, III, iii, 54; Bell, *Prin.*, § 535.
[27] *Ibid.*

charity,[28] because there can have been no erroneous belief that the payment was legally due, but only as to the circumstances which made it expedient or desirable. Money paid under a decree cannot be recovered merely because facts have come to light which would have formed a complete defence to the action, *e.g.* a receipt for the debt for which decree has been granted.[29]

29.6 *Condictio Ob Turpem Vel Injustam Causam* **(Claim on Account of a Base or Unjust Consideration).**[30]—Money paid under an unwarranted threat by the recipient can be recovered. So where someone pays money to avert a crime such as a threatened assault on himself or a near relation, or to prevent someone giving false testimony,[31] it may be recovered, whether or not the threat is carried out.[32] Payments made under economic duress can be recovered,[33] even if the duress was lawful in the country where it was applied.[34] On the other hand, money paid merely because the creditor threatens to take legal proceedings cannot be recovered[35] and a mere protest will not justify recovery of money really paid to avoid the expense and inconvenience of a law suit.[36] But if a sum has been paid under protest to avoid some immediate inconvenience, such as seizure of goods for failure to pay market dues or threatened ejection from a conveyance, it may be recovered on its being established, in an action raised by a third party, that the demand in question was unwarrantable.[37]

29.7 *Condictio Sine Causa* **(Claim for Something Retained Without Legal Justification).**[38]—Although this heading is not generally used,[39] it covers a number of cases where Scots law recognises a right to repayment in situations which do not fit conveniently under any of the previous headings. They are cases where without legal justification the defender

---

[28] *Masters and Seamen of Dundee* v. *Cockerill* (1869) 8 M. 278; but see *Re Glubb* [1900] 1 Ch. 354 and para. 29.7, n. 45, *infra*.

[29] *Marriot* v. *Hampton* (1797) 7 T.R. 269; 2 Smith, L.C. 13th ed., 286.

[30] D.12.5; Voet 12.5; Stair, I, vii, 8; Bankton, I, viii, 22; Erskine, III, i, 10; Cowan, 'Repetition,' *Encyclopaedia of the Laws of Scotland*, Vol. 12 (1931), para. 1183; S.L.C., *Recovery of Benefits*, Vol. 2, pp. 201 *et seq.*

[31] Erskine, III, i, 10; Kames, *Principles of Equity* (5th ed.), p. 53.

[32] *Cf.* D.12.5.1.2, Paul 10 *ad Sabinum*; 12.5.5, Julian 3 *ad Urseium Ferocem*.

[33] *Universe Tankships Inc. of Monrovia* v. *I.T.F.* [1982] A.C. 366. For coercion affecting a bargain, *cf. Sutherland* v. *Montrose Fishing Co. Ltd.* (1921) 37 Sh.Ct. Rep. 239.

[34] *Dimskal Shipping Co. S.A.* v. *I.T.F.* [1992] 2 A.C. 152.

[35] para. 9.26.

[36] For payment without prejudice, see *British Railways Bòard* v. *Glasgow Corporation*, 1976 S.C. 224.

[37] *Maskell* v. *Horner* [1915] 3 K.B. 106; *Brocklebank* v. *The King* [1925] 1 K.B. 52.

[38] Sometimes referred to as the *condictio sine causa specialis*. See Zimmermann, *Obligations*, pp. 856 *et seq.* and pp. 871 *et seq. Cf.* Voet 12.7.1 and H. Grotius, *Inleiding tot de Hollandsche Rechts-geleertheyd* (1631) 3.30.18 (translated by R.W. Lee, *Introduction to the Jurisprudence of Holland* (corrected edition, 1953), Vol. 1, pp. 454–455).

[39] See, however, *Morgan Guaranty, supra*, at p. 309L *per* Lord President Hope and at p. 321F *per* Lord Cullen.

has been paid a sum of money to which the pursuer is entitled.[40] In particular, although some of these cases are sometimes regarded as examples of the *condictio indebiti*,[41] they do not really form part of that group since either they do not involve any payment by the pursuer or, where they do involve such a payment, there was no mistake on the part of the pursuer that in making the payment he was discharging a debt which was legally due by him to the defender.[42] So, if, for instance, A makes a gift of money to B, using C's money without his knowledge, it is thought that C is prima facie entitled to recover the money from B, even though he did not make the payment himself.[43] Where a stockbroker's clerk forged a cheque in favour of his employer and the cheque bore to be drawn on, and was ultimately paid by, the Clydesdale Bank, the bank was entitled to recover the sum from the stockbroker whose debt had been discharged by the clerk using the funds obtained from the bank.[44] In such circumstances the bank was entitled to recover, not because it could ever have thought that it was indebted to the stockbroker payee,[45] but because as a result of the clerk's forgery the bank believed that it was under a duty to its own customer to make the payment and the payee gave no valuable consideration.[46] But where the defender has given value for the payment and neither knew, nor ought to have inquired about, the source of the payment, the pursuer will not be entitled to recover his money which was wrongfully used to make the payment. So where a debtor to a bank by fraudulent misrepresentations induced the pursuer to purchase certain shares and used the price to pay

---

[40] In *Morgan Guaranty, supra*, the court left open the question whether a claim for repetition could have been based simply on the fact that payment had been made in respect of a contract which was subsequently held to be void.

[41] *e.g. Royal Bank of Scotland* v. *Watt*, 1991 S.C. 48. See further note 48 *infra*. See also W. Wallace & A. McNeil, *Banking Law* (10th ed., 1991), p. 137. Gloag, *Contract* (2nd ed.), p. 332, sees a resemblance to recompense.

[42] The opinion of Rose-Innes J. in *Govender* v. *Standard Bank of South Africa Ltd.*, 1984 (4) S.A. 392 (C) at pp. 396 *et seq.* contains an invaluable analysis. See further *First National Bank of S.A. Ltd.* v. *B. & H. Engineering*, 1993 (2) S.A. 41 (T) and *Commissioner of Customs & Excise* v. *Bank of Lisbon International*, 1994 (1) S.A. 205 (N). *Cf.* also *G.M. Scott (Willowbank Cooperage) Ltd.* v. *York Trailer Co. Ltd.*, 1969 S.L.T. 87; 1970 S.L.T. 15, *per* Lord President Clyde at 1969 S.L.T. 88. It may be that in *Masters and Seamen of Dundee* v. *Cockerill* (1869) 8 M. 278 the additional sum, which could not be recovered under the *condictio indebiti*, would have been held recoverable if this wider aspect of repetition had been considered. See the criticism of Birks, 1985 J.R. 227 at p. 240.

[43] *Cf.* Grotius, *Inleiding* 3.30.18.

[44] *Clydesdale Bank* v. *Paul* (1877) 4 R. 626. It makes no difference that the money is in cash or negotiable instruments: *M. & I. Instrument Engineers Ltd.* v. *Varsada*, 1991 S.L.T. 106.

[45] *Govender* v. *Standard Bank of South Africa, supra*. In *Royal Bank* v. *Watt, supra*, the alteration of the cheque by the rogue meant that the pursuers thought that they were under an obligation to their customers, Messrs W. & J. Burness, to honour their cheque by crediting the defender's account with the increased sum. But, as drawee bankers, they could not have believed that they were under a legal obligation to the defender who was simply the customer of another bank who had presented the cheque for payment. Hence, despite the terminology used, the head of repetition was not properly classified as the *condictio indebiti* See, however, S.L.C., *Recovery of Benefits*, Vol. 2, para. 2.10.

[46] *Clydesdale Bank, supra*, at p. 629 *per* Lord Shand.

off his debt to the bank, the pursuer was not entitled to recover the price from the bank which had given value by *pro tanto* discharging the fraudster's debt and releasing its security.[47] Similarly, where trustees instructed a broker to sell shares and he used the price to reduce his personal overdraft with a bank, the bank was not liable to repay the trustees since there was nothing unusual in brokers making such payments into their private accounts and the bank neither knew about, nor had any reason to inquire into, the fraudulent misapplication of the trustees' funds.[48] Recent authority indicates also that where a public body makes a demand for payment of taxes or other levies under an *ultra vires* enactment, prima facie an action of repetition may lie even though the pursuer did not labour under any mistake about this liability when he paid the sum demanded.[49] The same may apply where the demand was wrongful for some other reason such as a misconstruction of the relevant legislation or regulation.[50] In determining whether to grant repetition, it may be relevant to consider what the public body has done with the revenue raised[51] and whether the pursuer has passed on the payment in charges to customers.[52]

29.8 Defences.[53]—(1) In *condictio indebiti* cases where money which was not due has been paid in error[54] it is reclaimable unless it is inequitable in the circumstances that the defender should be obliged to pay back the sum of money[55] or the residue which the defender retains.[56] Often such

---

[47] *Gibbs* v. *British Linen Co.* (1875) 4 R. 630.

[48] *Thomson* v. *Clydesdale Bank* (1893) 20 R. (H.L.) 59; *Style Financial Services Ltd.* v. *Bank of Scotland*, 1995 G.W.D. 14–761; *Eagle Trust* v. *S.B.C. Securities* [1992] 4 All E.R. 488; *Cowan de Groot Properties Ltd.* v. *Eagle Trust* [1992] 4 All E.R. 700. *Thomson* is analysed in detail in *Westpac Banking* v. *Savin* [1985] 2 N.Z.L.R. 41, at pp. 61–63 and 70, *per* Sir Clifford Richmond. See Birks [1989] Lloyd's M.C.L.Q. 296.

[49] *Woolwich Building Society* v. *I.R.C.* [1993] A.C. 70; *British Oxygen Co. Ltd.* v. *South West Scotland Electricity Board*, 1959 S.C. (H.L.) 17; *British Railways Board* v. *Glasgow Corporation*, 1976 S.C. 224; *Amministrazione delle Finanze dello Stato* v. *SpA San Giorgio*, Case 199/82 [1983] E.C.R. 3595. For a survey of the position on repayment of unlawfully paid levies in European systems, see J. Schwarze, *European Administrative Law* (1992), pp. 1161 *et seq.*

[50] *Woolwich Building Society*, supra, *per* Lord Goff at p. 177 and *per* Lord Slynn at p. 205.

[51] *Bell* v. *Thomson* (1867) 6 M. 64; *National Bank of Scotland* v. *Lord Advocate* (1892) 30 S.L.R. 579. Cf. *Tower Hamlets London B.C.* v. *Chetnik Developments Ltd.* [1988] A.C. 858, at pp. 879 *et seq.*, *per* Lord Bridge and, p. 882, *per* Lord Goff.

[52] *Amministrazione delle Finanze dello Stato*, supra; but see *Air Canada* v. *British Columbia* (1989) 59 D.L.R. (4th) 161, at pp. 169–170, *per* Wilson J. (dissenting); *Woolwich Building Society*, supra, *per* Lord Goff at pp. 177–178. For discussion of some of the difficulties see B. Rudden & W. Bishop (1981) 6 European L. Rev. 243.

[53] For prescription, see Chap. 15. See generally S.L.C., *Recovery of Benefits*, Vol. 2, pp. 63 et seq.

[54] *Crédit Lyonnais* v. *George Stevenson & Co.* (1901) 9 S.L.T. 93.

[55] *Royal Bank of Scotland* v. *Watt*, 1991 S.C. 48, discussed in Gretton [1992] J.B.L. 108 and MacQueen [1992] J.B.L. 333; Stewart, *Restitution*, paras. 4.53 *et seq.* See generally Zimmermann, *Obligations*, pp. 895 *et seq.*

[56] Cf. *Lipkin Gorman* v. *Karpnale Ltd.* [1991] 2 A.C. 548, at p. 580, *per* Lord Goff (plaintiff's money paid by thief to innocent donee).

a defence will involve some kind of change of position on the part of the defender. So where the pursuer, wrongly believing himself to be the debtor, pays money to the defender who receives it in good faith and therefore surrenders his rights against the true debtor[57] or fails to sue him before his bankruptcy[58] or within the prescriptive period, repetition may be refused on equitable grounds. On the other hand if the recipient has spent the money on an asset[59] or has changed his position in bad faith or has acted wrongfully[60] or unreasonably[61] he will be obliged to repay. But an agent or intermediary, who receives payment in that capacity and pays it over to his principal in discharge of his obligation to the principal, is not liable in repetition, and the person seeking repetition must look to the principal.[62] Where on the other hand the nature of the alleged relationship with the principal should have put the defender on inquiry and the pursuers were not told of it, the defender was held liable in repetition even though most of the money had been paid to the alleged principal.[63] (2) There is a conflict of Outer House authority as to whether an equitable defence applies to payments made for a purpose which does not materialise.[64] (3) It has been said *obiter* that an innocent donee of a thief who gives the money to charity may have a defence.[65] (4) Similarly, it has been indicated that equitable considerations would not be allowed to defeat a claim for repetition of payments made under improper compulsion.[66] (5) Personal bar is a defence to a *condictio indebiti*[67] but, unlike the general equitable defence of change of position, it requires that the detrimental change in the defender's position flow from his reliance on an express or implied representation by the pursuer.[68] (6) There are conflicting authorities on whether the defence of bona fide consumption[69] applies to interest on a principal sum recoverable by a *condictio indebiti*[70] and on whether it

---

[57] Bell, *Prin.*, § 536; *Wallet* v. *Ramsay* (1904) 12 S.L.T. 111.

[58] *Ker* v. *Rutherford* (1684) Mor. 2928; *Duke of Argyle* v. *Lord Halcraig's Representatives* (1723) Mor. 2928; Kames, *Principles of Equity* (5th ed.), p. 200; Bell, *Prin.*, § 536.

[59] *Armour* v. *Glasgow Royal Infirmary*, 1909 S.C. 916.

[60] *Lipkin Gorman, supra*, at p. 580, *per* Lord Goff.

[61] *Royal Bank, supra* (treated by the court as a *condictio indebiti*).

[62] *Continental Caoutchouc Co.* v. *Kleinwort* (1904) 9 Com. Cas. 240; *Royal Bank, supra*; *A.N.Z. Banking Group* v. *Westpac Banking Corp.* (1988) 164 C.L.R. 662.

[63] *Royal Bank, supra*.

[64] *Grieve* v. *Morrison*, 1993 S.L.T. 852 (no such defence) which was not cited in the Outer House decision in *Connelly* v. *Simpson*, 1991 S.C.L.R. 295 where the defence was recognised. That decision was reversed in the Inner House (1994 S.L.T. 1096) but on another point.

[65] *Lipkin Gorman, supra*, at p. 579.

[66] *Unigate Foods Ltd.* v. *Scottish Milk Marketing Board*, 1975 S.C. (H.L.) 75, at p. 90, *per* Lord President Emslie.

[67] *Dixon* v. *Monkland Canal Co.* (1831) 5 W. & S. 447 (acquiescence).

[68] *Allied Times (Theatres) Ltd.* v. *Anderson*, 1958 S.L.T. (Sh.Ct.) 29.

[69] para. 40.12.

[70] For: Erskine, II, i, 26; *Ferguson* v. *Lord Advocate* (1906) 14 S.L.T. 52. Against: *Haldane* v. *Ogilvy* (1871) 10 M. 62.

applies to the principal sum itself rather than merely to interest on that sum.[71] (7) While *restitutio in integrum* is not a requirement of a *condictio indebiti*,[72] the pursuer may be required, as a condition of repetition, to restore benefits received from the defender[73] on the ground that 'they who ask equity must be prepared to give it.'[74]

29.9   Restitution.—In Scots law the term 'restitution' is used rather confusingly to describe two distinct remedies: (1) the claim of an owner to have something which remains his property restored to him (sometimes referred to as 'vindication'); (2) the claim of the pursuer that the defender has been unjustly enriched at his expense and should accordingly transfer ownership of some thing to the pursuer or compensate him for the defender's enjoyment of the thing.[75] The former claim is based on the pursuer's real right in the property, while the second is based on a personal right of the pursuer against the defender. Only the second kind of restitution falls to be considered in the present context.

29.10   *Condictio Indebiti.*—Just as a person who pays money in error may be entitled to recover it,[76] so also a person who delivers property to another in the erroneous belief that he is under an obligation to do so may be entitled to recover it.[77] Though there is little Scottish authority on the point,[78] the same general principles must apply since in each case the payment or transfer is made where it is not due.[79] So, for instance, just as a sum of money paid by an executor to a person not entitled to it can be recovered,[80] so also, it is thought, can a corporeal or incorporeal moveable which the executor has transferred to the wrong person. If the

[71] See *Hunter's Trs.* v. *Hunter* (1894) 21 R. 949, at p. 953, *per* Lord Young (defence applicable to principal). Contrast *Darling's Trs.* v. *Darling's Trs.*, 1909 S.C. 445, esp. at p. 451, *per* Lord President Dunedin; approved by Lord Skerrington (dissenting) in *Morrison* v. *School Board of St. Andrews*, 1918 S.C. 51, at p. 64. Opinions reserved in *Rowan's Trs.* v. *Rowan*, 1939 S.C. 30, at p. 39, *per* Lord President Normand and at p. 48, *per* Lord Moncrieff.
[72] *Cf. General Property Investment Co.* v. *Matheson's Trs.* (1888) 16 R. 282.
[73] *North British and Mercantile Insurance Co.* v. *Stewart* (1871) 9 M. 534.
[74] *Ibid.*, at p. 537, *per* Lord Ormidale.
[75] Birks, 1985 J.R. 227, at pp. 233 *et seq.*; Carey Miller, *Corporeal Moveables in Scots Law*, paras. 10.02 *et seq.*; S.L.C., *Recovery of Benefits*, Vol. 2, pp. 108 *et seq.*
[76] para. 29.4, *supra*.
[77] Stair, I, vii, 9; Bell, *Prin.*, § 531; Voet 12.6.1; *Morgan Guaranty, supra* at p. 310B *per* Lord President Hope; *Govender* v. *Standard Bank of South Africa*, 1984 (4) S.A. 392, at p. 396, *per* Rose-Innes J.
[78] *Cf.* however *Pride* v. *St. Anne's Bleaching Co.* (1838) 16 S. 1376 (on which Stewart, *Restitution*, para. 7.6); *Caledonian Ry.* v. *Harrison & Co.* (1879) 7 R. 151.
[79] Pothier, *Traité du Contrat de Prêt de Consomption*, nn. 140 *et seq.* and nn. 165 *et seq.*; Voet 12.6.1.
[80] *Armour* v. *Glasgow Royal Infirmary*, 1909 S.C. 916. *Anderson* v. *Lambie*, 1954 S.C. (H.L.) 43 may be based, though not explicitly, on a similar kind of principle applied to heritable property.

recipient of the property which has been transferred by mistake is in good faith, his obligation is to restore the property in the state in which it is at the time when the demand for restitution is made.[81]

29.11 **Other Cases.**—In the same way it is thought that the remedy of restitution would lie for property transferred or taken in circumstances covered by the *condictio causa data causa non secuta*,[82] the *condictio ob turpem vel injustam causam*[83] or the *condictio sine causa*.[84]

An obligation of restitution also arises where someone is enriched by the use of another's property.[85] Even though a bona fide possessor who has ceased to possess another's property is not liable in restitution for the value of the property,[86] he is liable for any profit which he has made[87] but not for any fruits which he has consumed in good faith.[88] This applies when the bona fide possessor parts with possession to another from whom the owner can recover his property.[89] But the view has been expressed that, where a bona fide possessor destroys another's property, he is liable to make restitution of its value.[90] Thus where oil merchants mixed the pursuers' oil with other substances to make lard which belonged to the merchants by virtue of the doctrine of specification, the merchants were liable to the pursuers for the value of the oil which had ceased to exist.[91] A person who in bad faith[92] parts with or puts an end to the possession of another's property is liable in the value of the property[93] and of any fruits consumed in bad faith.[94]

---

[81] Pothier, *Traité*, n. 166, but see Bell, *Prin.*, § 537.

[82] para. 29.3, *supra*. Stair, I, vii, 7; Erskine, III, i, 10; Bankton, I, viii, 21. *Cf. Savage* v. *McAllister* (1952) 68 Sh.Ct. Rep. 11; *Nicolson* v. *Schaw* (1711) Mor. 9166 and *Grieve* v. *Morrison*, 1993 S.L.T. 852.

[83] para. 29.6, *supra*. *Nisbet's Creditors' Tr.* v. *Robertson* (1791) Mor. 9554; Bell's Octavo Cases 349; *A* v. *B.*, 21 May 1816 F.C., not argued on this point in the House of Lords: *Duke of Hamilton* v. *Esten* (1820) 2 Bligh 196.

[84] para. 29.7, *supra*.

[85] It is possible that these cases should properly be classified under the heading of recompense in para. 29.19, *infra*. See further S.L.C., *Recovery of Benefits*, Vol. 2, pp. 108 *et seq.*

[86] Erskine, III, i, 10.

[87] Stair, I, vii, 11; Erskine, III, i, 10; Hume, *Lectures*, iii, 234, *Scot* v. *Low* (1704) Mor. 9123; *Faulds* v. *Townsend* (1861) 23 D. 437, at p. 439, *per* Lord Ordinary (Ardmillan) *obiter*. If the bona fide possessor has acted carelessly he may be liable for the whole value of the object: *Faulds, supra*; *Oliver & Boyd* v. *Marr Typefounding Co.* (1901) 9 S.L.T. 170.

[88] Stair, I, vii, 11; II, i, 23; Erskine, II, i, 25; Hume, *Lectures*, iii, 240 *et seq.*; *Houldsworth* v. *Brand's Trs.* (1876) 3 R. 304; Carey Miller, *Corporeal Moveables*, paras. 6.04 *et seq.*; Gordon, *Scottish Land Law*, paras. 14.48 *et seq.*

[89] *Faulds, supra*; *International Banking Corporation* v. *Ferguson, Shaw & Sons*, 1910 S.C. 182, *per* Lord Low at pp. 191–192.

[90] *International Banking Corporation, supra, per* Lord Low at p. 192. Lord Ardwall disagreed (at p. 193) and his view was adopted by Lord McDonald in *North-West Securities* v. *Barrhead Coachworks Ltd.*, 1976 S.C. 68.

[91] *International Banking Corporation, supra*.

[92] Serious fault may be treated as equivalent to fraud: *Faulds, supra*.

[93] Stair, I, vii, 13; *Faulds, supra*.

[94] Stair I, vii, 13; Erskine, II, i, 26; Hume, *Lectures*, iii, 240.

29.12   Recompense.[95]—While unjustified enrichment by the payment or taking of money is dealt with under repetition, and unjustified enrichment by the transfer or taking of property is dealt with under restitution, cases where the defender has been unjustifiably enriched by the pursuer's expenditure, services or other actings or by the defender's use of the pursuer's property are generally treated in Scots law under the heading of recompense.

The principle of recompense is defined in Bell's *Principles* in the following terms: 'Where one has gained by the lawful act of another, done without any intention of donation, he is bound to recompense or indemnify that other to the extent of the gain.'[96] This definition, though useful as indicating the general nature of the plea of recompense, is too widely expressed, since it would cover cases of incidental benefits arising without loss to the party who has conferred them.[97]

29.13   Elements.—It has been said that the limits of the plea of recompense are indicated by the maxim *nemo debet locupletari ex aliena jactura* (no-one should be enriched by another's loss).[98] Five elements must occur.[99] (1) The pursuer must have suffered loss.[1] The loss must consist in expenditure which has not met with the expected return or in work or service for which no payment has been received, but even where loss of this kind is incurred the pursuer may not have any remedy in recompense. So where a company supplied plans and did work in order to secure a contract with the defender, but no contract materialised, the company was not entitled to recompense for the plans which the defender retained.[2] Similarly where A performs work or service under a contract, 'his intention is to further his own interests by performance of his contract'[3] with the other party, B and, where no guarantor is involved, A will usually rely on the faith or credit of B.[4] Where B does

---

[95] Stewart, *Restitution*, Chap. 8. H.L. MacQueen and W.D.H. Sellar, 'Unjust Enrichment in Scots Law' in *A Comparative Legal History of the Law of Restitution*, E.J.H. Schrage (ed.) (1995), pp. 305 *et seq.*

[96] Bell, *Prin.*, § 538; Stair, I, viii, 6–7; Erskine, III, i, 11; Hume, *Lectures*, iii, 165. Aspects of the Scots law of recompense have their origins in the post-Justinianic *actio de in rem verso*. On which see Zimmermann, *Obligations*, pp. 878 *et seq.*; Stewart, *Restitution*, paras. 10.32 *et seq*; MacQueen and Seller in *Unjust Enrichment, supra*, pp. 300 *et seq.* (treating it as a distinct head). In fact the Scottish law of recompense seems to be composed of elements derived from a variety of sources.

[97] *Edinburgh Tramways Co.* v. *Courtenay*, 1909 S.C. 99; *Varney (Scotland) Ltd.* v. *Lanark Town Council*, 1974 S.C. 245.

[98] *Cf.* D.4.3.28, Gaius 4 *ad edictum provinciale*; 23.3.6.2, Pomponius 4 *ad Sabinum*; 50.17.206, Pomponius 9 *ex variis lectionibus*; *Edinburgh Tramways Co., supra*, at p. 105 where it is not altogether clear to which passage in Pothier Lord Dunedin refers.

[99] Given the diverse nature of the cases which fall within the plea, it may be wondered whether all five elements must occur in every case before recompense should be allowed.

[1] *Buchanan* v. *Stewart* (1874) 2 R. 78, at p. 87, *per* Lord Neaves; *Exchange Telegraph Co.* v. *Giulianotti*, 1959 S.C. 19. See also the cases cited under (4) *infra* on actings *in suo*.

[2] *Site Preparations* v. *Secretary of State for Scotland*, 1975 S.L.T. (Notes) 41.

[3] *Gouws* v. *Jester Pools (Pty.) Ltd.*, 1968 (3) S.A. 563 (T), at p. 571, *per* Jansen J.

[4] *Cf. Fernie* v. *Robertson* (1871) 9 M. 437.

not pay, A's loss is due to B's breach of contract[5] and, if C has the benefit of A's work, A cannot claim compensation from C.[6] While the underlying principles are not worked out fully in the judgments of the courts, it is clear that there is no doctrine in the law of Scotland that every person who has profited by work done under a contract is to be liable for that work.[7] So where a garage carried out repairs under a contract with an insurance company which went into liquidation, the owner of the car was not liable to pay the garage the amount by which he had benefited from the repairs.[8] Similarly in a case where the plaintiffs constructed a swimming pool on land which they believed belonged to the other contracting party and he subsequently disappeared without paying, it was held that the plaintiffs could not recover from the true owner of the land any sum representing its increase in value.[9] On the other hand when tradesmen did work on the house of an incapacitated old lady under a contract with her daughter whom they regarded as acting for the old lady, the tradesmen were entitled to recover in recompense from the old lady's estate since they had had in view the responsibility of both the old lady and her daughter.[10] (2) The pursuer must have had no intention to make a gift to the defender.[11] (3) The defender must have gained as a result of the pursuer's loss. A man is not *lucratus*, in a question of recompense, merely because a debtor has paid a debt which was owed to him.[12] Therefore in a bankruptcy a creditor has no preference on the ground that work which he has done under contract to the bankrupt has increased the value of the bankrupt's estate. The other creditors are not *lucrati* merely because the dividend on their debts is larger.[13] Again, a party is not *lucratus* by the acquisition of a thing for which he has paid, or which some party other than the pursuer in the action for recompense is bound to provide. Therefore where an accountant undertook to carry out the amalgamation of two companies for a contract price, it was held that those who employed him, and who had paid the contract price were under no liability to a law agent who, on the accountant's instructions, had drawn up a necessary agreement.[14] (4) The pursuer must not have carried out the operation for his own benefit (*in suo*).[15] If a man has expended

---

[5] See de Vos 1960 J.R. 142 and 226, at pp. 244 *et seq.*; *Gouws, supra*, at p. 574.

[6] *Cf.* Gloag, *Contract* (2nd ed.), p. 330.

[7] *Cran* v. *Dodson* (1893) 1 S.L.T. 354, *per* Lord Kyllachy.

[8] *Express Coach Finishers* v. *Caulfield*, 1968 S.L.T. (Sh.Ct.) 511; *Kirklands Garage (Kinross) Ltd.* v. *Clark*, 1967 S.L.T. (Sh.Ct.) 60.

[9] *Gouws* v. *Jester Pools, supra*.

[10] *Fernie* v. *Robertson, supra*, at p. 442, *per* Lord Benholme.

[11] Bell, *Prin.*, § 538.

[12] Kames, *Principles of Equity* (5th ed.), p. 99; Gloag, *Contract* (2nd ed.), p. 331; *Universal Import Export GmbH* v. *Bank of Scotland* 1995 G.W.D. 12–633 *per* Lord Caplan.

[13] *Burns* v. *McLellan's Creditors* (1735) Mor. 13402; *Mess* v. *Sime's Tr.* (1898) 1 F. (H.L.) 22.

[14] *Robertson* v. *Beatson, McLeod & Co..*, 1908 S.C. 921; *Thomson, Jackson, Gourlay & Taylor* v. *Lochhead* (1889) 16 R. 374, at p. 377, *per* L.J.-C. Macdonald.

[15] *Buchanan* v. *Stewart* (1874) 2 R. 78, *per* Lord Neaves at p. 82. See also the cases cited under (1) *supra* on the pursuer's loss.

money for a particular purpose, and that purpose has been attained, he cannot appeal to the principle of recompense in support of a claim for payment from a party who has incidentally gained by the expenditure in question. In the leading case, the defender had leased advertising rights on a company's tramcars and had agreed to supply boards on which to place his advertisements. In order to satisfy government regulations the company constructed new tramcars with boards in a roughly similar position. When the defender placed his advertisements on these boards, the company claimed a sum for the use of the boards on the ground that the lessee was saved the expense of erecting boards for himself. The claim was rejected: although the defender was a gainer by the company's expenditure, his gain was merely the incidental result of an expenditure which had secured its purpose.[16] And where a person holding property on a limited title, as in the case of a liferenter, expends money on improvements, it will generally be assumed that he did so with a view to his own advantage, and his representatives will have no claim against the fiar for the amount by which the improvements have enriched him.[17] Such a claim, however, may be established on proof that the liferenter acted on a reasonable expectation that his expenditure would be repaid.[18] And there is early authority for the statement that if a house is destroyed by fire, and rebuilt by a liferenter, his representatives have a claim against the fiar.[19] It would appear to be the law that a heritable creditor in possession and expending money on the subjects has a claim against the debtor in so far as the subjects are increased in value.[20] Any claim by a tenant for improvements must rest on express contract or statutory provision.[21] (5) Except in special circumstances, the pursuer must have no other legal remedy.[22] So where a local authority refused to comply with their statutory duty to construct sewers, and contractors constructed the sewers themselves, the contractors were not entitled to recover their costs since they could have brought proceedings to enforce the local authority's statutory duty.[23] Similarly where the person who was contractually bound to repair a road failed to do so and commissioners did the work themselves instead

---

[16] *Edinburgh Tramway Co.* v. *Courtenay*, 1909 S.C. 99. See also *Exchange Telegraph Co.* v. *Giulianotti*, 1959 S.C. 19; *Microwave Systems (Scotland)* v. *Electro-Physiological Instruments*, 1971 S.C. 140.

[17] *Wallace* v. *Braid* (1900) 2 F. 754, *per* Lord Trayner at p. 760; *Rankin* v. *Wither* (1886) 13 R. 903.

[18] *Morgan* v. *Morgan's Factor*, 1922 S.L.T. 247.

[19] *Halliday* v. *Garden* (1706) Mor. 13419.

[20] *Nelson* v. *Gardine* (1874) 1 R. 1093. See Gloag, *Contract* (2nd ed.), p. 326.

[21] *Thomson* v. *Fowler* (1859) 21 D. 453; *Walker* v. *McKnight* (1886) 13 R. 599.

[22] *Varney (Scotland) Ltd.* v. *Lanark Town Council*, 1974 S.C. 245; *Glasgow D.C.* v. *Morrison McChlery*, 1985 S.C. 52; *N.V. Devos Gebroeder* v. *Sunderland Sportswear Ltd.*, 1990 S.C. 291. But a pursuer may frame his pleadings with an alternative remedy in recompense if the principal claim fails: *Bennett* v. *Carse*, 1990 S.L.T. 454; *N.V. Devos Gebroeder*, *supra*.

[23] *Varney (Scotland) Ltd.*, *supra*.

of taking action to enforce their contract, it was held that they were not entitled to recover the cost of the work.[24] There is a conflict of views as to whether a mistake of fact is a requisite of the claim.[25] As the principle is an equitable one, the particular circumstances of each case must be considered.[26]

29.14 Application.—The principle of recompense is properly applicable either to cases where there is no contract between the parties, or to cases where work has been done under a contract in circumstances which preclude any direct contractual claim. It is not a plea which is open to someone who has done work under a contract and has the right to sue the other party for the contract price. So a contractor cannot claim recompense on the ground that the work he has done has enriched the employer to an amount greater than the price.[27] And a claim for payment for extra work done under a contract must, it is conceived, be founded on an express or implied agreement to pay, not on the principle of recompense.[28] When work has been done under a contract which makes no express provision for payment, a claim for payment, though sometimes referred to as a claim for recompense,[29] is more properly a claim under an implied contract for payment, measured, on the principle of *quantum meruit*, by the market value of the services rendered, and maintainable whether they have proved beneficial or not, in contrast to a claim *quantum lucratus*, measured and limited by the advantage which the services have produced to the recipient.[30] In such cases, however, assuming that the work has proved beneficial, a claim based either on recompense or on implied contract may be open.[31]

29.15 Relation to Implied Contract.—The typical cases for a plea of recompense as contrasted with a claim for payment under an implied contract would appear to be four. (1) Where a party has expended money on property in the bona fide but ill-founded belief that it is his own and is compelled to give it up to the true owner, he has a claim for his expenditure in so far as it has proved beneficial and the true owner consequently is enriched.[32] He has no such claim if his possession was

---

[24] *Northern Lighthouse Commissioners* v. *Edmonston* (1908) 16 S.L.T. 439.

[25] See *Rankin* v. *Wither* (1886) 13 R. 903; *Gray* v. *Johnston*, 1928 S.C. 659; *Varney (Scotland) Ltd., supra.*

[26] *Lawrence Building Co. Ltd.* v. *Lanark C.C.*, 1978 S.C. 30.

[27] *Boyd & Forrest* v. *G. and S.-W. Ry.*, 1915 S.C. (H.L.) 20, *per* Earl Loreburn at pp. 22–23.

[28] *Wilson* v. *Wallace* (1859) 21 D. 507; *Tharsis Co.* v. *McElroy* (1875) 5 R. (H.L.) 171.

[29] As in Bell, *Prin.*, § 539.

[30] See *Landless* v. *Wilson* (1880) 8 R. 289.

[31] *Anderson* v. *Anderson* (1869) 8 M. 157; *Mellor* v. *Beardmore*, 1927 S.C. 715.

[32] Erskine, III, i, 11; Gordon, *Scottish Land Law*, paras. 14–52 *et seq.*; *Magistrates of Selkirk* v. *Clapperton* (1830) 9 S. 9; *Newton* v. *Newton*, 1925 S.C. 715. A purchaser who pays for the improved subjects is not liable to the improver: *Beattie* v. *Lord Napier* (1831) 9 S. 639.

not bona fide.[33] (2) Where a party has done work or supplied goods[34] under a contract, but has so far departed from the contractual terms that a claim for the contract price is excluded. Thus, if a builder produces a building materially different from that ordered he may have no claim directly under his contract, but if the employer does not choose to reject the building he is at least liable *quantum lucratus*.[35] And where a commission agent had broken a term in his contract under which he was precluded from acting for rival traders, it was held that he could not recover commission for the period in which he was thus in breach of his contract but observed that he might have a claim for recompense on proof that his employers had benefited by the business he introduced.[36] (3) Where goods have been supplied or work done in circumstances where a direct contractual claim for the price must fail, either because the defender could plead his lack of contractual power[37] or because the contract is one which has been declared by statute to be void,[38] a claim for the value of the goods or work is generally relevant. (4) Where the defender uses the pursuer's property in the knowledge that the pursuer does not intend to give him the use gratuitously, the defender is liable to pay a reasonable sum for it.[39] So where the defender had possession of shootings under a lease which was held to be invalid, he was liable to pay a 'just and reasonable consideration,'[40] and where a person hired the pursuer's sacks from a railway company, but kept them beyond the hire period, he was liable to pay the pursuer's charges.[41] The principle applies to the use of incorporeal property also, so that where the pursuer's employers used an invention which he had patented, without agreeing any payments to him and after he had demanded a royalty, it was held that they were bound to pay him a reasonable sum by way of royalty.[42]

[33] *Barbour* v. *Halliday* (1840) 2 D. 1279; *Trade Development Bank* v. *Warriner & Mason (Scotland) Ltd.*, 1980 S.C. 74.

[34] *N.V. Devos Gebroeder* v. *Sunderland Sportswear*, 1990 S.C. 291.

[35] *Ramsay* v. *Brand* (1898) 25 R. 1212; (1898) 35 S.L.R. 927; *Forrest* v. *Scottish County Investment Co.*, 1916 S.C. (H.L.) 28. As to the conditions excluding the builder's claim for the contract price, see para. 13.6, *supra.*

[36] *Graham* v. *United Turkey Red Co.*, 1922 S.C. 533; *Abrahams* v. *Campbell*, 1911 S.C. 353.

[37] See Sale of Goods Act 1979, s. 3; *Sinclair* v. *Brougham* [1914] A.C. 398, *per* Lord Dunedin at pp. 434–435; *Stonehaven Magistrates* v. *Kincardineshire C.C.*, 1939 S.C. 760.

[38] *Cuthbertson* v. *Lowes* (1870) 8 M. 1073, distinguished in *Jamieson* v. *Watt's Tr.*, 1950 S.C. 265, where the contract was illegal. See also *Duncan* v. *Motherwell Bridge and Engineering Co.*, 1952 S.C. 131 and para. 10.8, *supra.*

[39] Gloag, *Contract* (2nd ed.), pp. 40 and 329–330; Wark, 'Recompense,' *Encyclopaedia of the Laws of Scotland*, Vol. 12 (1931), para. 728; K. Zweigert & H. Kotz, *An Introduction to Comparative Law* (2nd ed., 1987), pp. 236 *et seq.* See also para. 29.11, *supra.*

[40] *Earl of Fife* v. *Wilson* (1864) 3 M. 323. See also *H.M.V. Fields Properties Ltd.* v. *Skirt 'n' Slack Centre*, 1986 S.C. 114; *Shetland Islands Council* v. *B.P. Petroleum Development Ltd.*, 1990 S.L.T. 82.

[41] *Chisholm* v. *Alexander & Son* (1882) 19 S.L.R. 835.

[42] *Mellor* v. *William Beardmore*, 1927 S.C. 597, criticised by Gloag, *Contract* (2nd ed.), p. 291, n.11.

Further Reading

J. Beatson, *The Use and Misuse of Unjust Enrichment* (1991).

P. Birks, 'Restitution: A View of the Scots Law' (1985) 38 C.L.P. 57.

P. Birks, 'Six Questions in Search of a Subject — Unjust Enrichment in a Crisis of Identity,' 1985 J.R. 227.

P. Birks, 'Misdirected Funds: Restitution from the Recipient' [1989] Lloyd's M.C.L.Q. 296.

P. Birks, *An Introduction to the Law of Restitution* (revised ed., 1989).

P. Birks, *Restitution — The Future* (1992).

P. Birks & G. Macleod, 'The Implied Theory of Quasi-Contract: Civilian Opinion Current in the Century before Blackstone,' [1986] O.J.L.S. 46.

J. Blaikie, 'Unjust Enrichment in the Conflict of Laws,' 1984 J.R. 112.

W.W. Buckland, '*Casus* and Frustration in Roman and Common Law' (1933) 46 Harv.L.R. 1281.

A.S. Burrows (ed.), *Essays on the Law of Restitution* (1991).

A.S. Burrows, *The Law of Restitution* (1993).

Lord Goff of Chieveley & G. Jones, *The Law of Restitution* (4th ed., 1993).

A.M. Honoré, '*Condictio* and Payment,' 1958 *Acta Juridica* 135.

A.M. Honoré, 'Third Party Enrichment,' 1960 *Acta Juridica* 236.

R. Evans-Jones, 'Identifying the Enriched,' 1992 S.L.T. (News) 24.

R. Evans-Jones, 'Payments in Mistake of Law — Full Circle?' (1992) 37 J.L.S. 92.

R. Evans-Jones, 'Unjust Enrichment, Contract and the Third Reception of Roman Law in Scotland' (1993) 109 L.Q.R. 663.

J.G. Lotz, 'Enrichment,' in *The Law of South Africa* (ed. by W.A. Joubert), Vol. 9 (1978), p. 45.

D.R. Macdonald, 'Restitution and Property Law,' 1988 S.L.T. (News) 81.

D.R. Macdonald, 'Mistaken Payments in Scots Law,' 1989 J.R. 49.

H.L. MacQueen & W.D.H. Seller, 'Unjust Enrichment in Scots Law,' in E.J.H. Schrage (ed.), *Unjust Enrichment The Comparative Legal History of the Law of Restitution* (1995).

B. Nicholas, 'Unjustified Enrichment in the Civil Law and Louisiana Law' (1962) 36 Tulane L.R. 605 and 37 Tulane L.R. 49.

Scottish Law Commission, *Recovery of Benefits Conferred under Error of Law* (Discussion Paper No. 95, 1993).

T.B. Smith, *A Short Commentary on the Law of Scotland* (1962), pp. 623–632.

W.J. Stewart, *The Law of Restitution in Scotland* (1992).

S.J. Stoljar, *The Law of Quasi-Contract* (2nd ed., 1989).

W. de Vos, 'Liability Arising from Unjustified Enrichment in the Law of the Union of South Africa,' 1960 J.R. 125 and 226.

N.R. Whitty, 'Indirect Enrichment in Scots Law,' 1994 J.R. 200.

R. Zimmermann, *The Law of Obligations* (1990), Chap. 26.

For a useful analysis of the case law and literature, see P. Birks and R. Chambers, *The Restitution Research Resource 1994*, published as a Supplement to the Restitution Law Review and intended to be updated every two years.

CHAPTER 30

GENERAL AVERAGE. SALVAGE

30.1 Particular and General Average.—Average is the term used in shipping law for any loss or injury to ship or cargo during a voyage. Such a loss may be a particular or a general average loss. Under the head of particular average falls any loss which is not due to a voluntary act, as, for instance, injury to a ship by striking a rock, or cargo being washed overboard. It also includes losses which, though they are voluntarily incurred, do not satisfy the conditions of general average. In relation to marine insurance it is enacted that 'a particular average loss is a partial loss of the subject-matter insured, caused by a peril insured against, and which is not a general average loss.'[1] A particular average loss must be borne by the party whose property is injured.[2]

30.2 History of General Average.—The law of general average was recognised in civil law as derived from the maritime law of Rhodes, the *lex Rhodia de jactu*,[3] and has been adopted, though with differences in detail, in all mercantile countries. In Scotland the law of England on the subject has been recognised. As the result of international conferences, rules known as the York-Antwerp Rules, have been drawn up on the subject, and were last revised in 1974.[4] They have no statutory authority, but are commonly incorporated in bills of lading. They differ, in certain minor respects, from the common law, which holds where the Rules have not been expressly incorporated.

30.3 Nature of General Average Act.—The theory of general average is that when one of the three main interests at stake during a voyage, the ship, the cargo and the freight, is voluntarily sacrificed for the safety of all, the loss must be borne rateably by all interested. Such a voluntary sacrifice, known as a general average act, has been defined as follows: 'There is a general average act when, and only when, any extraordinary sacrifice or expenditure is intentionally and reasonably made or incurred

---

[1] Marine Insurance Act 1906, s. 64. See para. 27.41, *supra*.

[2] See Bell, *Prin.*, § 437; *Comm.*, i, 630.

[3] *Digest* 14.2.1, Paul 2 *sententiarum*: 'Lege Rhodia cavetur ut, si levandae navis gratia iactus mercium factus est, omnium contributione sarciatur quod pro omnibus datum est.' For relevant texts see Lowndes and Rudolf, *General Average*, App. 1; Buckland, *A Textbook of Roman Law* (3rd ed., 1963), p. 506. See also *Goulandris* v. *Goldman* [1958] 1 Q.B. 74 at p. 93.

[4] See Lowndes and Rudolf, *General Average*, section 3. For interpretation, see the Rule of Interpretation; Lowndes and Rudolf, *op cit.*, A 0.4—A 0.7.

for the common safety for the purpose of preserving from peril the property involved in a common maritime adventure.'[5]

30.4 Instances of General Average.—A general average act may cause loss to the cargo, to the ship, or to the freight. There is a general average loss to the cargo, when it is jettisoned for the safety of the ship; when, with the same object, it is landed at some place other than its destination;[6] or when, though the cargo may not be actually touched, its value is affected by measures, other than mere delay, taken for the common safety.[7] There is a general average loss to the ship when some portion, *e.g.* the mast or sails, is sacrificed, or where, without any actual sacrifice, the appurtenants of the ship are used in some abnormal way, with consequent injury, as where the engines were used to move a ship which had been stranded, and were damaged in the process.[8] Voluntary stranding to avoid a threatened wreck is probably general average at common law, and is recognised with a modification in Rule V of the York-Antwerp Rules.[9] Where a ship, to avoid being wrecked or stranded, entered a harbour, knowing that in entering she would probably strike the pier, it was held that both the injury to the ship and the damages fixed for injury to the pier were general average.[10] The freight is affected when cargo is sacrificed, and the freight for it consequently lost.[11] Mere delay, resulting in a loss of market for the cargo, or a partial loss of freight in a time charter, is not a general average loss.[12] A payment made under an indemnity in a towage contract may be a general average loss.[13]

30.5 Contribution.—Those who have to contribute to meet a general average loss are the owners of the ship, the various owners of the cargo, and the parties entitled to the freight. Although the aim of the York-Antwerp Rules is to keep matters of alleged fault separate from the average adjustment,[14] a party whose fault gave rise to the peril in question is not entitled to recover contribution in general average.[15] The owner of the property sacrificed contributes rateably according to its value.[16] There is

---

[5] York-Antwerp Rules, 1974, Rule A; Lowndes and Rudolf, *op. cit.*, p. 63. For a statutory definition, see Marine Insurance Act 1906, s. 66.

[6] *Royal Mail Steam Packet Co.* v. *English Bank* (1887) 19 Q.B.D. 362.

[7] *Anglo-Argentine Live Stock Co.* v. *Temperley Shipping Co.* [1899] 2 Q.B. 403.

[8] *The Bona* [1895] P. 125.

[9] See *The Seapool* [1934] P. 53.

[10] *Austin Friars Co.* v. *Spillers & Bakers* [1915] 1 K.B. 586.

[11] *Iredale* v. *China Traders' Insurance Co.* [1900] 2 Q.B. 515.

[12] *The Leitrim* [1902] P. 256.

[13] *Australian Coastal Shipping Commission* v. *Green* [1971] 1 Q.B. 456.

[14] York-Antwerp Rules, Rule D.

[15] *Goulandris* v. *Goldman, supra*; *Diestelkamp* v. *Baynes (Reading), The Aga* [1968] 1 Lloyd's Rep. 431; *E.B. Aaby's Rederi A/S* v. *Union of India, The Evje (No. 2)* [1976] 2 Lloyd's Rep. 714; *The Hellenic Glory* [1979] 1 Lloyd's Rep. 424; York-Antwerp Rules, 1974, Rule D.

[16] *Strang, Steel & Co.* v. *Scott* (1889) 14 App. Cas. 601.

no claim on passengers, their luggage or their effects carried without a bill of lading.[17] The owner of deck cargo, unless it is carried under a custom of trade or with the consent of the other cargo owners, has no claim if his property is jettisoned,[18] but is bound to contribute to another general average loss.[19] The party in right of the respective interest at the completion of the voyage, not the party in such right at the time when the sacrifice was made, is liable.[20]

30.6   Lien.—The owner of cargo which has been jettisoned has a lien over the rest of the cargo for a general average contribution. The captain is impliedly his agent in this respect, and is entitled to enforce the lien, and liable in damages if when called upon he refuses or fails to do so.[21]

30.7   Conditions of Right to Contribution.—The right to a general average contribution depends upon an act which has caused loss and which has been done for the safety of all. So a claim was rejected for damage caused by turning on steam into the hold under the mistaken impression that the ship was on fire.[22] It is a question in the circumstances of each case whether a general average act was done reasonably. Only those whose interests were actually in peril can be called upon to contribute. Thus where gold was landed to ensure its safety, and not for the purpose of lightening the ship, its owner, as his property was not in peril, was not liable to contribute in respect of cargo that was afterwards jettisoned.[23] The party to whose fault the peril is due, *e.g.* the shipowner, when the peril is due to the negligence of the captain, has no claim to a general average contribution,[24] with an exception in the case of fire.[25]

30.8   General Average Expenditure.—Certain expenditure by the shipowner, known as general average expenditure, may be the subject of contribution if it was incurred for the safety of all.[26] As a shipowner is bound under his contract to take measures for the safety of the ship he has no claim to an average contribution unless the circumstances were exceptional or abnormal.[27] So on the ground that risk from submarines

---

[17] Bell, *Comm.*, i, 636; York-Antwerp Rules, 1974, Rule XVII; Lowndes and Rudolf, *General Average*, paras. 17.58 *et seq.*

[18] *Strang, Steel & Co.* v. *Scott, supra.*

[19] Bell, *Comm.*, i, 636.

[20] *Ranking* v. *Tod* (1870) 8 M. 914.

[21] *Strang, Steel & Co.* v. *Scott, supra.*

[22] *Watson* v. *Firemen's Fund Insurance Co.* [1922] 2 K.B. 355.

[23] *Royal Mail Packet Co.* v. *English Bank* (1887) 19 Q.B.D. 362.

[24] *Strang, Steel & Co.* v. *Scott, supra; cf. Diestelkamp* v. *Baynes (Reading), The Aga, supra; E.B. Aaby's Rederi A/S* v. *Union of India, The Evje (No. 2), supra.*

[25] Merchant Shipping Act 1995, s. 186(1); *Dreyfus* v. *Tempus Shipping Co.* [1931] A.C. 726, decided on the construction of s. 502 of the Merchant Shipping Act 1894 (now repealed).

[26] York-Antwerp Rules, Rule A; *Australian Coastal Shipping Commission* v. *Green* [1971] 1 Q.B. 456.

[27] *Ocean Co.* v. *Anderson Tritton & Co.* (1883) 13 Q.B.D. 651; (1884) 10 App. Cas. 107.

was a normal incident during war and there was no proof that the ship had been in actual peril, the owner of a sailing ship was refused contribution for the expenses of a tug hired to speed up the voyage and so to lessen the risk.[28] When a ship is forced to put in to a port of refuge the expense of unloading the cargo with a view to repairs[29] is in all cases allowed as a general average charge; but the expense of reloading, though allowed by the York-Antwerp Rules,[30] is at common law admissible only if the reason why the port of refuge was necessary was a general average act, *e.g.* the deliberate sacrifice of some part of the ship's equipment as contrasted with accidentally springing a leak.[31]

30.9 General Average in Marine Insurance.[32]—In questions of insurance, an underwriter, in the absence of any provision to the contrary, is liable to the assured for any general average contribution which may be payable in respect of his interest covered by the policy.[33] He is liable for the whole amount if the interest in question is insured to its full contributory value; to a proportional amount if the insurance was only partial.[34] The assured may recover from the underwriters the proportion of any general average expenditure which falls upon him, and in the case of a general average sacrifice, the whole loss, without having enforced his right of contribution from the other parties liable to contribute.[35] Though all the interest in the ship, the cargo and the freight may be vested in one person, the insurer of any one of these interests is liable in a general average contribution in the same way as if they had been vested in different persons.[36]

SALVAGE

30.10 Nature of Salvage.—A claim for salvage does not rest on any contract but on an obligation implied by maritime law. At common law salvage was defined as 'a reward or recompense given to those by means of whose labour, intrepidity or perseverance a ship, or goods, have been saved from shipwreck, fire or capture'[37] but the law is now substantially to be found in the terms of the Merchant Shipping Act 1995[38] giving the force of law to the International Convention on Salvage 1989. Article 1

[28] *Société Nouvelle d' Armement* v. *Spillers & Bakers* [1917] 1 K.B. 865.
[29] The cost of temporary repairs qualifies as general average expenditure if they effect a saving in expense which would have been incurred and allowed in general average if such repairs had not been effected: *The Bijela* [1994] 1 W.L.R. 615.
[30] Rule X. (a); Lowndes and Rudolf, *General Average*, paras. 10.26–10.40.
[31] *Atwood* v. *Sellar* (1880) 5 Q.B.D. 286; *Svendson* v. *Wallace* (1885) 10 App. Cas. 404; Lowndes and Rudolf, *General Average*, paras. 10.02–10.20.
[32] Arnould, *Marine Insurance and Average*, Chap. 26.
[33] Marine Insurance Act 1906, s. 66(5).
[34] *Ibid.*, s. 73.
[35] *Ibid.*, s. 66(4).
[36] *Ibid.*, s. 66(7); *Montgomery* v. *Indemnity Insurance Co.* [1902] 1 K.B. 734.
[37] Bell, *Prin.*, § 443; *Comm.*, i, 638.
[38] The Convention is in Sched. 11, Part I.

of the Convention defines a salvage operation as 'any act or activity undertaken to assist a vessel or any other property in danger in navigable waters or in any other waters whatsoever', but in our law the Convention provisions do not apply if the salvage operation takes place in inland waters[39] of the United Kingdom and all the vessels involved are of inland navigation, or if the salvage operation takes place in inland waters of the United Kingdom and no vessel is involved.[40] So a person who saves the property of others on land has no claim,[41] nor, for example, has a person who saves another's lorry from an inland loch by using a crane operating from the bank. Salvage is applicable to the rescue of any ship[42] or craft or any structure capable of navigation,[43] but not to the rescue of fixed or floating platforms or mobile offshore drilling units when they are on location engaged in exploration, exploitation or production of sea-bed mineral resources.[44] Salvage is also applicable to the rescue of all kinds of property not permanently and intentionally attached to the shoreline, including cargo, stores, equipment, passengers' effects and freight at risk.[45] No remuneration is due from a person whose life has been saved[46] but if the person who saved the life took part in the services rendered on the occasion of the accident giving rise to salvage, then he is entitled to a fair share of the payment awarded to the salvor for salving the vessel or other property or for preventing or minimising damage to the environment.[47] To justify a claim for salvage, the subjects salved must have been in a position of danger, or at least believed by those in charge of them to be so.[48] Assistance to a ship which is disabled, but in no danger, is merely towage, a service which founds a claim for payment, but not for payment at salvage rates.[49] When a vessel is injured on going to the rescue of a ship run down by a third, she is not exposed to the plea that she assumed the risk. She goes in pursuance of a duty.[50]

30.11 Parties Entitled to Salvage.—The persons entitled to salvage are those who perform salvage operations[51] and so may include the owners of the

---

[39] Not including waters within the ebb and flow of the tide at ordinary spring tides or the waters of certain docks connected with such waters: Sched. 11 Part II, para. 2(2).

[40] Sched. 11, Part II, para. 2(1).

[41] cf. *Falcke* v. *Scottish Imperial Assurance Co.* (1886) 34 Ch. D. 234.

[42] For State-owned vessels see Art. 4.

[43] Art. 1(b).

[44] Art. 3.

[45] Art. 1(c).

[46] Art. 16.1.

[47] Art. 16.2. For environmental damage see para. 30.14 *infra*.

[48] *The Charlotte* (1848) 3 W. Rob. 68; *The Phantom* (1866) L.R. 1 A. & E. 58; Brice, *Maritime Law of Salvage* (2nd ed.), pp. 45 *et seq*.

[49] *Robinson* v. *Thoms* (1851) 13 D. 592; *Lawson* v. *Grangemouth Dockyard Co.* (1888) 15 R. 753; *The Kangaroo* [1918] P. 327; *The Troilus* [1951] A.C. 820; *Aberdeen Harbour Board* v. *Marz H.F.*, 1971 S.L.T. (Notes) 34; *The Texaco Southampton* [1983] 1 Lloyd's Rep. 94.

[50] *The Gusty* v. *The Daniel* [1940] P. 159.

[51] Art. 1(a).

ship or ships, which have rendered assistance, their masters and crew.[52] Since no payment is due unless the services rendered exceed what can be reasonably considered as due performance of any contract entered into before the danger arose,[53] the claimant must be a person who was not under any obligation to render the services prior to the emergency which rendered them necessary.[54] This excludes any claim by the master and crew of the ship salved; they are bound by their contract to do everything in their power for the safety of the ship.[55] Where the rules of a mutual assurance society provided that each assured should render assistance to every other, it was held that as such assistance was given under a contractual obligation, it afforded no ground for salvage.[56] An agent for the shipowner may recover salvage, but any bargain which he may make will be unfavourably regarded and such claims are rare.[57] Passengers, though not contractually bound, are under an obligation to assist in their own rescue and that of others, and a claim by them is not maintainable except in the case where, having an opportunity of leaving the ship, they voluntarily remained and assisted in saving her.[58] A ship which has been injured by a collision, though under a statutory obligation to render assistance to the other ship involved,[59] is, if not in fault, entitled to salvage,[60] and possibly even if she was in fault.[61] When salvage services are rendered by one of Her Majesty's ships, any claim by the officers and crew requires the consent of the Secretary of State for Defence.[62] It has been said that such a claim must be supported by proof of services of an exceptional kind,[63] but statute provides that the position of the Crown in relation to salvage claims by or against the Crown is the same as that of any other ship owner.[64] Where a public body, such as the Coast Guard, the police or the fire service provides

[52] See *Bennet* v. *Henderson* (1887) 24 S.L.R. 625; *The Golden Falcon* [1990] 2 Lloyd's Rep. 366. Agreements by which seamen give up their claim to salvage are, in general void: Merchant Shipping Act 1970, s. 16; *Nicholson* v. *Leith Salvage, etc., Co.*, 1923 S.C. 409.

[53] Art. 17.

[54] *cf. The Gregerso* [1973] Q.B. 274. However a salvage contract may be, and with professional salvors usually is, entered into after the emergency has arisen. Lloyd's has a standard form of salvage agreement. The Unfair Contract Terms Act 1977 applies to salvage contracts, to a limited extent: 1977 Act, s. 15(3)(b); see Chap. 10, *supra*. For a discussion of the circumstances in which a master may bind the cargo owners by such an agreement see *The Choko Star* [1990] 1 Lloyd's Rep. 516.

[55] Bell, *Prin.*, § 444. See *The Albionic* [1942] P. 81.

[56] *Clan Steamer Trawling Co.* v. *Aberdeen Trawling Co.*, 1908 S.C. 651.

[57] *The Crusader* [1907] P. 196; Brice, *Maritime Law of Salvage* (2nd ed.), p. 90.

[58] Kennedy, *Salvage*, para. 529; *Newman* v. *Walters* (1804) 3 B. & P. 612.

[59] Merchant Shipping Act 1995, s. 92(1).

[60] *Melanie (Owners)* v. *San Onofre (Owners)* [1925] A.C. 246.

[61] *The Kafiristan* [1925] A.C. 136.

[62] Merchant Shipping Act 1995, s. 230(3). If consent has not been given, the claim is dismissed: s. 230(5).

[63] *The Ulysses* (1888) 13 P.D. 205; *Swanney* v. *Citos*, 1925 S.L.T. 491; *The Valverda* [1938] A.C. 173.

[64] Crown Proceedings Act 1947, s. 8 as amended by Sched. 2, para. 3 of the 1994 Act.

assistance, they may do so in fulfilment of a statutory duty and if so on general principles no claim for salvage will be available, but if the public body merely has a power to provide the service or go beyond the requirements of any statutory duty, then, depending on the terms of any relevant legislation, a claim for salvage may be brought.[65] A salvor may require a licence if carrying out operations at or near a wreck of historical, archaeological or artistic importance.[66] A salvor may be directed by a harbour master not to enter a harbour, or to remove a vessel therefrom, if the vessel presents a danger or risk.[67]

30.12 Conditions of Salvage Claim.—Except in cases where an express bargain to pay for attempts to salve is proved[68] or the salvor has prevented or minimised damage to the environment,[69] success is a condition of a claim for salvage.[70] The efforts of a voluntary salvor, if unsuccessful, go unrewarded.[71] If nothing is saved, nothing is due.[72] If the ship is ultimately saved, those who were invited to assist her, though their efforts proved unsuccessful, have a claim.[73] Where a salvor removed the ship from a position of danger but left her in a position no more favourable, although the ship was ultimately saved, it was held that no salvage was due because the efforts to salve had met with no success.[74] Misconduct on the part of salvors, for instance fraud or other dishonest conduct such as looting, may deprive those implicated of the whole or part of the payment otherwise due.[75] A successful salvor may be liable for negligence on his part,[76] subject to the benefit of limitation of liability in terms of the Merchant Shipping Act 1995.[77]

30.13 Parties Liable.—The parties liable for salvage are all those who have a beneficial interest in the vessel and other property which is saved, generally the owners of the ship and cargo, and the persons entitled to

[65] See the discussion in Brice, *Maritime Law of Salvage* (2nd ed.), pp. 62 *et seq.*
[66] Protection of Wrecks Act 1973, s. 1.
[67] Dangerous Vessels Act 1985, s. 1: a grave and imminent danger to persons or property, or a grave and imminent risk that the vessel might founder and prejudice the use of the harbour. The harbour master is himself subject to directions from the Secretary of State: s. 3.
[68] *cf. The Valverda, supra,* holding that such a bargain is a true salvage agreement.
[69] Art. 14.
[70] Art. 12.1 and 12.2.
[71] *Steel & Bennie* v. *Hutchison,* 1909 2 S.L.T. 110.
[72] See Carver, *Carriage by Sea,* para. 1281.
[73] *Ross & Marshall* v. *Davaar (Owners)* (1907) 15 S.L.T. 29.
[74] *Melanie (Owners)* v. *San Onofre (Owners), supra.*
[75] Art. 18. *cf. The Clan Sutherland* [1918] P. 332.
[76] *The Tojo Maru* [1972] A.C. 242; *obiter dicta* in *The St. Blane* [1974] 1 Lloyd's Rep. 557. Such a claim might be made by way of a counter-claim.
[77] s. 185 and Sched. 7. Note that in terms of s. 185(4) there is no limitation of liability where loss of life or personal injury or loss of or damage to property has been sustained by a person who is on board the ship or employed in connection with that ship or with the salvage operations under a U.K. contract of employment.

the freight.[78] They may be sued personally[79] and are liable *pro rata* for the proportion which the value of their interest bears to the total value of all the property salved.[80] As a general rule, all those who are liable to contribute must be called as defenders, but where the peril of the ship was due to the fault of the shipowner, and he, had she been lost, would have been liable to the owners of the cargo, it was held that an action against him alone was competent; and opinions were expressed that in the case of a general ship, where the owners of the cargo are numerous, the action may be directed against the shipowner.[81] A claim for salvage may also be enforced by the retention of the property salved, if in the salvor's possession, or in that of the Receiver of Wreck for the district.[82] And the salvor has a maritime lien or hypothec, in virtue of which the ship may be arrested.[83] The salvor's lien, which cannot be enforced if he has been given satisfactory security for his claim,[84] takes priority over all other maritime liens.[85]

30.14 **Amount of Salvage Award.**—The amount payable as salvage may be settled by agreement between the parties. But such an agreement may be reduced or modified if it was entered into under undue influence or the influence of danger and its terms are inequitable, or if the payment due under the contract is in an excessive degree too large or too small for the services actually rendered.[86] Where there has been no agreement, and the amount has to be settled by the court, the reward should be fixed with a view to encouraging salvage operations.[87] The assessment by a court of first instance will hardly ever be disturbed.[88] The criteria to be taken into account in assessing or apportioning[89] a reward are: the salved value of the vessel and other property; the skill and efforts of the salvors in preventing or minimising damage to the environment; the measure of success obtained by the salvor; the nature and degree of the danger; the skill and efforts of the salvors in salving the vessel, other property and life; the time used and expenses and losses incurred by the salvors; the risk of liability and other risks run by the salvors or their equipment; the promptness of the services rendered;

---

[78] Art. 13.2. For freight, see Brice, *Maritime Law of Salvage* (2nd ed.), pp. 214 *et seq.*; para. 30.4, *supra*.

[79] *Duncan* v. *Dundee, etc. Shipping Co.* (1878) 5 R. 742.

[80] Art. 13.2. *cf. The M. Vatan* [1990] 1 Lloyd's Rep. 336.

[81] *Duncan, supra*.

[82] Merchant Shipping Act 1995, s. 226; *Walker, etc. Co.* v. *Mitre Co.*, 1913 1 S.L.T. 67.

[83] *Hatton* v. *Durban Hansen*, 1919 S.C. 154; *The Lyrma (No. 2)* [1978] 2 Lloyd's Rep. 30.

[84] Art. 20.2.

[85] *The Lyrma (No. 2), supra*.

[86] Art. 7. As previously indicated, the Unfair Contract Terms Act 1977 applies in a modified way to salvage contracts: s. 15(3)(b).

[87] Art. 13.1.

[88] But see *The Evaine* [1966] 2 Lloyd's Rep. 413. *cf.* Brice, *Maritime Law of Salvage* (2nd ed.), pp. 188–189.

[89] Art. 15.1.

the availability and use of vessels or other equipment intended for salvage operations and the state of readiness and efficiency of the salvor's equipment and the value thereof.[90] The salved value of the vessel and property is a controlling element since the reward, exclusive of interest and recoverable legal costs, cannot exceed that value[91] and in no modern case has the award of salvage exceeded half the value of the property saved, except in the case of a derelict, where there is no claim put forward by the owners.[92] In addition, if a vessel by itself or its cargo threatened damage to the environment, then a salvor is entitled to special compensation to cover his expenses even though the salvage operations failed.[93] If those operations actually prevented or minimised damage to the environment, the court may increase the special compensation up to a maximum of 30 per cent of the salvor's expenses and, if it deems it fair and just to do so and bearing in mind the criteria mentioned above, the court may increase it further up to a maximum of 100 per cent of the expenses.[94] The total special compensation is to be paid only if and to the extent that it is greater than the ordinary salvage reward, but the court is not obliged to maximise that reward before assessing special compensation.[95] In salvage actions the court has an equitable power to award interest.[96]

30.15   **Procedure.**—With the repeal of Section 547 of the Merchant Shipping Act 1894 the special rules on jurisdiction cease and the general provisions regulating the jurisdiction of the sheriff court and the Court of Session apply.[97] Proceedings must, however, be commenced within two years of the rendering of salvage services.[98] The period may only be extended by the potential defender making a declaration to the claimant during the two year period.[99]

Further Reading

Arnould, *Maritime Insurance and Average* (16th ed., 1981).
Brice, *Maritime Law of Salvage* (2nd ed., 1993).
Carver, *Carriage by Sea* (13th ed., 1982).
Kennedy, *Salvage* (5th ed., 1985).
Lowndes and Rudolf, *General Average* (11th ed., 1990).
Mackenzie, *Shipping and Navigation, Stair Memorial Encyclopaedia* Vol. 21 (1994), paras. 431 *et seq.* and paras. 700 *et seq.*

[90] Art. 13.1.
[91] Art. 13.3.
[92] See Kennedy, *Salvage*, paras. 1088 *et seq.*
[93] Art. 14.1 and 14.3. Such compensation may be lost or reduced if the salvor's negligence resulted in him failing to prevent or to minimise damage to the environment: Art. 14.5.
[94] Art. 14.2.
[95] Art. 14.4 and Sched. 1, para. 4.
[96] *The Ben Gairn*, 1979 S.C. 98; Art. 24.
[97] Section 547 was repealed by s. 8(4) and Sched. 5, Part II of the Merchant Shipping (Registration etc.) Act 1993, commenced with effect from May 1, 1994 by S.I. 1993 No. 3137.
[98] Art. 23.1.
[99] Art. 23.2.

PART V — DELICT

CHAPTER 31

REPARATION: GENERAL PRINCIPLES

31.1 **Terminology.**—Reparation is the term used in Scots law for making good, so far as possible in terms of money, loss (*damnum*) caused (*datum*) by a legal wrong (*injuria*), provided that the loss is not too remote from the wrong. The maxim applicable is *damnum injuria datum* and all three elements of the maxim must be present before liability to make reparation arises.[1] A legal wrong may be defined as an invasion of the legal rights of another without lawful justification or excuse. The wrong may be done by an act or omission. It is not necessary for the act to be conscious and deliberate. Accordingly, it is immaterial whether or not it constitutes a criminal offence; the law of reparation is concerned only with its civil consequences. The term 'delict' is now often used for those wrongs in which intention must be proved, all others being known as 'quasi-delicts,' but an alternative, and better, terminology is to apply 'delict' to all legal wrongs other than those of strict liability and to apply 'quasi-delict' to the latter.[2] 'Negligence' has numerous meanings. It may be used broadly in the sense of neglect of (*i.e.* failure to fulfil) a legal duty, whether that failure is intentional or unintentional.[3] It may also be used to denote unintentional wrongs only, as distinct from intentional wrongs. But nowadays it is most often used in the narrow sense of failure to exercise such care as is reasonable in all the circumstances to avoid damage to others and to their property.[4] *Culpa* or fault has been used as synonymous with negligence in all its meanings. There is a question as to whether *culpa* should not be restricted to denote only breach of the common law duty of taking reasonable care.[5] Discussion of this question is beyond the scope of this book but, as the English phrase 'strict liability' is to be found in recent textbooks on Scots law,[6]

---

[1] See paras. 32.10 and 32.11, *infra*; also discussion of terminology in *Miller* v. *City of Glasgow D.C.*, 1989 S.L.T. 44.

[2] See Smith, *Short Commentary*, p. 633.

[3] See *Bastable* v. *N.B. Ry.*, 1912 S.C. 555, *per* Lord President Dunedin at pp. 565–566; and *Hester* v. *Macdonald*, 1961 S.C. 370, *per* Lord Guthrie at p. 390.

[4] See Glegg, pp. 8–22; also paras. 32.1 and 32.8, *infra*.

[5] *Ibid.*; Smith, *op. cit.*, pp. 639–641, 663–672; Walker, *Delict*, pp. 46–49; *cf.* Lord Hunter in *Henderson* v. *John Stuart (Farms) Ltd.*, 1963 S.C. 245, at p. 248.

[6] Smith, *supra*; Walker, *supra*; *cf.* Glegg.

for the sake of uniformity liability to make reparation for invasion of legal rights which is neither intentional nor due to breach of a duty to exercise reasonable care is treated in this edition under the head of 'strict liability.'[7] The basis of liability in such cases is clear whether or not it is labelled as *culpa*.

31.2 Invasion of Rights: Classification.—It is not proposed to attempt any enumeration of actionable wrongs, but some indication may be given by considering rights or liberties which the policy of the state will protect. A man is clearly entitled to personal security, and therefore violence, or threats of violence, are actionable.[8] Personal liberty is also safeguarded, and therefore an invasion of it amounts to a wrong.[9] A man has a right to be safeguarded from unfounded aspersions on his character, and therefore slander amounts to a wrong.[10] Fraud may be categorised as an invasion of a right not to be deceived, or as an invasion of a right of property. In that latter category of wrong may also be included all aggressions on property, corporeal or incorporeal, either directly, or by acts which amount to a nuisance,[11] as well as irregular diligence, abuse of legal process,[12] or efforts at redress *brevi manu*,[13] where property which a party may be entitled to claim is taken by improper means. The extent to which a person has a right to protection of his general economic interests, as distinct from specific items of property, is, however, problematic. Such interests are protected against fraud but difficulties surround questions of remedy for other forms of intentional harm as for negligence. These questions are considered later.[14] Cases in which there is no liability for harming economic interests, whether intentionally or through lack of care, may be classified as instances of *damnum absque injuria*.

31.3 Breach of Statutory Provisions.—The fact that a particular act which is done wilfully and which causes injury is a criminal offence at common law may, it is conceived, be regarded as a sufficient indication that it also constitutes a civil wrong. With regard to acts penalised by statute, there is no inflexible rule. So although sexual intercourse with a girl under 16 is by statute a criminal offence, even if she consents, it was held that the statute had not altered the common law rule that it did not

---

[7] See Chap. 33 *infra*.

[8] See *Godwin* v. *Uzoigwe* [1992] T.L.R. 300 — assault and intimidation of a young girl working as a domestic help.

[9] For example, *Henderson* v. *Chief Constable, Fife Police,* 1988 S.L.T. 361 and *Walsh* v. *Secretary of State for Scotland*, 1990 S.L.T. 526. See also *Weldon* v. *Home Office* [1992] 1 A.C. 58 (lawfully convicted prisoner has no right of action regarding restraint within prison).

[10] Chap. 35, *infra*.

[11] As to nuisance, see para. 31.10, *infra*.

[12] paras. 35.25 to 35.27, *infra*.

[13] *Brash* v. *Munro* (1903) 5 F. 1102; and see *infra*, para. 34.5.

[14] See paras. 31.6 to 31.9 and 32.6, *infra*.

constitute an actionable wrong unless accomplished by fraud or circumvention.[15] When failure to observe some statutory regulation has caused injury to an individual, it is a question of the construction of the statute whether civil liability as well as criminal responsibility was intended.[16] The mere fact that a duty has been created by a statute does not entitle a person injured by the breach to claim damages therefor.[17] There must be a clear intention to confer a right to civil damages for breach of the statutory duty and a definite class of persons upon whom the right is conferred.[18] If the statute is aimed only at preventing a certain kind of injury, then civil liability results only if that kind of injury is caused by a breach.[19] So where sheep in course of transit were not penned in accordance with statutory regulations, and were washed overboard, it was held that the statute was irrelevant in the question of the carrier's liability in respect that the regulations were designed for the prevention of infection and not for the safety of the animals during transit.[20] But a statutory provision designed to prevent accidents will not be narrowly construed.[21] The question in each case is whether the legislature intended to impose public duties only[22] or, in addition, duties enforceable by any individuals injured by breach.[23] In determining this question the scope and purpose of the statute as a whole, as well as the state of the pre-existing law, must be considered.[24] Thus the purpose of section 143 of the Road Traffic Act 1988, in making it an offence to allow a car to be used without insurance against third party risks, being to provide third parties with better protection, involves a party in breach thereof in civil liability to injured third parties.[25]

Where the provisions of European Community Law are concerned, an individual who suffers loss through the failure of a Member State to implement a directive may be able to claim damages from the Member State.[26] The conditions which require to be satisfied are (1) that the particular directive is designed to result in the conferring of rights upon

[15] *Murray* v. *Fraser*, 1916 S.C. 623.

[16] *Atkinson* v. *Newcastle Water Works* (1877) 2 Ex.D. 441; *Cutler* v. *Wandsworth Stadium* [1949] A.C. 398; *Pullar* v. *Window Clean*, 1956 S.C. 13; *Weldon* v. *Home Office, supra;* see also Walker, *Delict*, pp. 307–314.

[17] *Atkinson* v. *Newcastle Water Works, supra, per* Lord Chancellor Cairns at p. 448. *Balmer* v. *Hayes*, 1950 S.C. 477; and see para. 32.5.

[18] *Pullar* v. *Window Clean, supra, per* Lord President Clyde at p. 22.

[19] *Grant* v. *N.C.B.*, 1956 S.C. (H.L.) 48, *per* Lord Reid at p. 57.

[20] *Gorris* v. *Scott* (1874) L.R. 9 Ex. 125.

[21] *Grant* v. *N.C.B., supra.*

[22] *West* v. *David Lawson*, 1949 S.C. 430 (Road Transport Lighting Act 1927, s. 1).

[23] *Byrne* v. *Tindal's Exrx.*, 1950 S.C. 216 (duty under Burgh Police (Scotland) Act 1892 to maintain lighting in common stair).

[24] *Cutler* v. *Wandsworth Stadium, supra, per* Lord Normand at p. 413; *Pullar* v. *Window Clean, supra, per* Lord President Clyde at p. 21; *Phillips* v. *Britannia Hygienic Laundry Co.* [1923] 2 K.B. 832; *Byrne* v. *Tindal's Exrx., supra.*

[25] *Monk* v. *Warbey* [1935] 1 K.B. 75; *Houston* v. *Buchanan*, 1940 S.C. (H.L.) 17; *cf. Balmer* v. *Hayes, supra.*

[26] *Francovich* v. *Italian Republic* [1992] I.R.L.R. 84.

individuals; (2) that the content of those rights may be determined by reference to the directive concerned; and (3) that there is a causal link between the breach by the Member State and the loss suffered.[27]

31.4 ***Damnum Absque Injuria.***—The invasion of a mere liberty, or advantage enjoyed on sufferance, is known as *damnum absque injuria* (loss without legal wrong) and infers no liability. So competition in trade, whatever injury it may inflict, is not *per se* a legal wrong, because a trader, though he may in fact have enjoyed it, has no legal right to a monopoly in his trade. But the law protects an injured trader (1) if the interference with his trade is carried out by unlawful means,[28] or (2) if the act causing the interference is done by a combination of persons and their predominant purpose is to injure the party with whom they interfere.[29] Competition does not, however, become a wrong giving rise to a right to reparation for delict merely on the ground that the newcomer may be acting in breach of his contract with a third party, or, in the case of a corporate body, *ultra vires*. So a shipowner, catering for excursion parties on a navigable river, had no title, merely as a shipowner, to interdict a statutory body which proposed to use a ship for the same purpose, although such use was prohibited by statute.[30] Parties interested in a river cannot claim damages for loss of water caused by a diversion of the underground springs, on the theory that the continuance of the springs is merely an advantage enjoyed on sufferance, not a right which can be vindicated by legal action.[31]

31.5 **Elements in Wrong: Intention and Motive.**—Intention to invade the rights of others is clearly immaterial in the case of an invasion resulting from negligence. In the domain of wilful wrongs, intention to deceive is the element which distinguishes fraud, involving a wrong and consequent liability in damages, from innocent misrepresentation, which may be a ground for the reduction of a contract, but which does not generally give rise to delictual liability.[32] But the English rule, founded on historical considerations peculiar to English law, that any invasion of a legal right, however innocent, amounts to a legal wrong, is no part of the law of Scotland.[33] Thus a party who, without negligence, has purchased and re-sold stolen goods is in England liable for their value in

---

[27] *Ibid.*

[28] *Infra*, para. 31.7.

[29] *Infra*, para. 31.6.

[30] *Nicol* v. *Dundee Harbour Trustees*, 1915 S.C. (H.L.) 7.

[31] *Chasemore* v. *Richards* (1859) 7 H.L.C. 349; *Mayor of Bradford* v. *Pickles* [1895] A.C. 587; *Stephens* v. *Anglian Water Authority* [1987] 1 W.L.R. 1381, though see paras. 31.5 and 40.13 regarding the differing attitudes of Scots and English law to acts intended to annoy a neighbour.

[32] para. 9.9 *supra*; and see para. 35.2, *infra*, where malicious intent is presumed.

[33] See *Leitch* v. *Leydon*, 1931 S.C. (H.L.) 1, *per* Lords Dunedin and Blanesburgh, as to the application to Scotland of the English law of conversion and trespass.

respect of a wrongful conversion;[34] in Scotland his liability depends upon the obligation of restitution, and not of reparation, and is limited to any profit he may have made on the re-sale.[35] And an unintentional trespass on land belonging to another, where there is no ground to suppose that the trespass will be repeated, will afford in Scots law no remedy, either by an action for nominal damages or by an application for interdict.[36]

Intention must be distinguished from motive or purpose, which is the actor's reason for doing the intentional act. 'The words "motive," "object," "purpose," are in application to practical matters difficult strictly to define or distinguish. Sometimes mere animus, such as spite or ill will, malevolence or a wanton desire to harm without any view to personal benefit is meant. But motive is often used as meaning purpose, something objective and external, as contrasted with a mere mental state.'[37] When the sole reason for an act is to harm someone, the motive is said to be malicious. But a man may have more than one reason for doing something and one purpose may predominate over others. His motive, object or purpose is in most cases irrelevant as will be seen from the following propositions which are illustrated in the next three paragraphs.

Proposition 1: If an intentional act is plainly lawful, the actor's motive for or purpose in doing it is irrelevant. There is liability to make reparation only if the act is unlawful.

Proposition 2: If an intentional act is plainly unlawful, motive or purpose is again irrelevant.[38] The act is not excused, for purposes of delictual liability, by the fact that the actor was not moved by desire to injure but acted in order to call attention to a defect in the law or in order to forward what he conceived to be the true interest of the party injured. So too, if A causes loss to B through interference with B's rights by unlawful means,[39] it is no defence that A's motive, object or purpose was to protect his own interest.

Proposition 3: Motive, although generally irrelevant, may exceptionally be relevant to whether an act is lawful or unlawful. The exceptions are noticed in Proposition 4. Otherwise, the considerations determining the lawfulness of an act are various but do not include motive.

Proposition 4: As the law stands there are only three clearly recognised exceptions to the general irrelevance of motive: (1) actings in concert with the predominant purpose of harming another;[40] (2)

---

[34] See Clerk and Lindsell, Chap. 22.

[35] *Scot* v. *Low* (1704) Mor. 9123.

[36] *Hay's Trs.* v. *Young* (1877) 4 R. 398.

[37] *Crofter Hand Woven Harris Tweed Co.* v. *Veitch*, 1942 S.C. (H.L.) 1, *per* Lord Wright at p. 29.

[38] But see para. 31.8, *infra*.

[39] See paras. 31.7 and 31.8, *infra*.

[40] *Crofter, etc., Co.* v. *Veitch, supra, per* Lord Simon L.C. at p. 10; and see para. 31.6, *infra*.

operations on land *in aemulationem vicini*;[41] and (3) inducement of breach of contract.[42]

The view that there is room in Scots law for a wider doctrine of abuse of rights has been canvassed[43] but remains unsettled.

31.6   Malice: Trade Competition.—It follows from the general irrelevance of motive that, where a party acts in the exercise of his own right, the fact that his motive in acting is a desire to injure another, usually stigmatised as malice, is generally insufficient to convert an otherwise lawful act into an actionable wrong. But interference with opportunities of trade or work is regarded as an exceptional case. If A, by inducements in themselves lawful, induces B not to deal with C, or not to employ C, A's motive, if he has a legitimate interest to act as he did, is irrelevant to whether his act is lawful or unlawful.[44] But if the same thing be done by a combination of persons acting in concert, the character of their act—as lawful or unlawful—will depend upon whether their predominant purpose or object was to advance their own material interest or to injure C.[45] The former and more usual result followed where a combination of shipowners, by offering rebates to those exporters who agreed to deal with them alone, injured the trade of a shipowner who was not in the combine, and were held not to have inflicted upon him any actionable wrong;[46] where a combination of butchers intimated that they would refuse to bid at auction sales of imported meat unless bids from co-operative stores were refused;[47] where an association of owners of newspapers cut off a newsagent's sources of supply;[48] and where trade union officials directed their members not to handle the goods of a company whose trade practices were supposed to be detrimental to the concerns for which the defenders' members worked.[49] In these cases it was decided that the members of the combination were acting legitimately in pursuance of their own business interests. In the exceptional case of *Quinn* v. *Leathem*,[50] on the other hand, the officials of a trade union, acting in concert, had intimated to one of L's customers that his men would be called upon to strike if he continued to deal with L, who had employed non-union labour. L in consequence suffered loss. In the circumstances

---

[41] For the sole purpose of annoying a neighbour. See para. 40.13, *infra*, and Smith, *Short Commentary*, on 'abuse of rights,' at pp. 662–663.

[42] See para. 31.8, *infra*.

[43] Smith, *Short Commentary*, *supra*.

[44] *Mackenzie* v. *Iron Trades Association*, 1910 S.C. 79; *Allen* v. *Flood* [1898] A.C. 1.

[45] *Sorrell* v. *Smith* [1925] A.C. 700.

[46] *Mogul S.S. Co.* v. *Macgregor* [1892] A.C. 25.

[47] *Scottish Co-operative Society* v. *Glasgow Fleshers* (1898) 35 S.L.R. 645.

[48] *Sorrell* v. *Smith, supra*.

[49] *Crofter Hand Woven Harris Tweed Co.* v. *Veitch*, 1942 S.C. (H.L.) 1; see *per* Lord Simon L.C. at p. 10. On p. 28 Lord Wright comments that the distinction between conduct by one man and conduct by two or more may be difficult to justify.

[50] [1901] A.C. 495, as explained in *Sorrell* v. *Smith, supra*; see also *Hewit* v. *Edinburgh & District Lathsplitters Assn.* (1906) 14 S.L.T. 489.

of the case the court arrived at the conclusion that the dominant purpose of the union officials was to injure L and held that they were liable in damages. The trade union officials would probably not be protected by the Trade Union and Labour Relations (Consolidation) Act 1992 since they were not pursuing a 'trade dispute' but rather a spite or grudge against L.[51]

31.7   Interference with Rights: Illegal Means.—Interference with trade or employment is actionable if the means employed are illegal.[52] It does not matter that the predominant purpose of the alleged wrongdoers is to further or protect their own legitimate interests.[53] The service of a strike notice of proper length is not illegal.[54] Nor is it illegal to offer advantage to B if he will refrain from dealing with C, or to influence B by intimating that the speaker, or others with whom he is acting, will refuse to work if C is employed.[55] But any violence or threats addressed to B in order to induce him to abstain from dealing with or employing C, with resulting loss to C, will amount to a wrong (intimidation) for which C can claim damages.[56] In this connection a mere intimation that a party proposes to do some lawful act (*e.g.* to abstain from working) is not to be construed as a threat merely because the speaker's attitude was menacing.[57] And to induce B by fraud to act in a way detrimental to C's business interests is a wrong to C. So where a manufacturer placed certain dealers on a stop list, and directed his agents not to supply them with goods, and one of these dealers obtained supplies by fraudulently concealing his identity, it was held that he was liable in damages even on the assumption that the agent who supplied him could not be regarded as in breach of contract.[58]

31.8   Inducing Breach of Contract.—Knowingly to induce a man to break a contract is in general a wrong for which the party whose contractual anticipations are disappointed may claim damages.[59] He may, on principles of contract, claim redress from the breaker of the contract; on principles of reparation, redress from the party who induced the breach.[60] The breach may be of implied conditions of the contract, as

---

[51] See para. 31.9, *infra.*
[52] But see para. 31.9, *infra.*
[53] *Lonrho plc* v. *Fayed* [1992] 1 A.C. 448, concerning the alleged use of unlawful means in a takeover battle.
[54] *Morgan* v. *Fry* [1968] 2 Q.B. 710.
[55] *Mogul S.S. Co.* v. *Macgregor, supra.*
[56] *Conway* v. *Wade* [1909] A.C. 506; *Rookes* v. *Barnard* [1964] A.C. 1129. See Walker, *Delict*, pp. 932–934; 1964 S.L.T. (News) 81.
[57] *Ware* v. *Motor Trades Manufacturing Co.* [1921] 3 K.B. 40; *Sorrell* v. *Smith* [1925] A.C. 700.
[58] *National Phonograph Co.* v. *Edison Bell & Co.* [1908] 1 Ch. 335.
[59] But see para. 31.9, *infra.*
[60] *Couper* v. *Macfarlane* (1879) 6 R. 683; *B.M.T.A.* v. *Gray,* 1951 S.C. 586; *Exchange Telegraph Co.* v. *Giulianotti,* 1959 S.C. 19. See also *D.C. Thomson* v. *Deakin* [1952] Ch. 646; *J.T. Stratford & Son* v. *Lindley* [1965] A.C. 269; Walker, *op. cit.*, pp. 919–924; and *Middlebrook Mushrooms Ltd.* v. *T.G.W.U.* [1993] I.R.L.R. 232.

where a clerk or workman is induced to betray his employer's secrets.[61] Where property has been transferred in breach of contract, however, it is not an actionable wrong for a third party, knowing of the breach, to accept transfer of the property from the party who induced the breach.[61a] In cases of inducing breach of contract motive may be a determining element. It is recognised throughout the cases that a party incurs no liability merely because the advantageous terms he offers in fact lead to a breach of contract, that is, of a contract of which he was not aware.[62] In the absence of actual awareness, mere recklessness is not enough.[63] Even where he is aware of the contract, his inducements to breach are not actionable if his conduct was justifiable as, for instance, where he was acting in pursuance of a social or professional duty.[64] So a doctor advising a patient to leave a service prejudicial to his health would incur no liability; and the same rule was applied where a society induced the owner of a theatre to break his contract with a touring company on the ground that the wages paid were in the nature of a public scandal.[65] Conduct can also be justified where the person inducing the breach of contract possesses rights in relation to one party to the contract which are equal or superior to the rights conferred by the contract.[66] A father who induces his minor son to break off an engagement to marry is presumed to have done so in the proper exercise of parental control and an action founded on that act will not be sustained without relevant averments of malice or other oblique motive.[67] In the absence of such a presumption in favour of the defender, however, a bare averment that the actings were unjustified will suffice.[67a]

It is an actionable wrong to employ a servant in the knowledge that he is in breach of an unexpired contract with another employer, although there may have been no inducement to break the contract.[68] But the first employer cannot recover damages from the second employer if it is established that in no circumstances would the servant have returned to his former employment.[69]

31.9 Trade Unions and Trade Disputes.—In the case of allegedly wrongful acts done by a trade union, or done by any person in contemplation or

---

[61] *Roxburgh* v. *Macarthur* (1841) 3 D. 556.

[61a] *Law Debenture Trust Corporation* v. *Ural Caspian Oil Corporation Ltd.* [1994] 3 W.L.R. 1221.

[62] *D.C. Thomson* v. *Deakin, supra; cf. J.T. Stratford & Son* v. *Lindley, supra.*

[63] *Rossleigh Ltd.* v. *Leader Cars Ltd.,* 1987 S.L.T. 355.

[64] *Glamorgan Coal Co.* v. *South Wales Federation* [1905] A.C. 239; *B.M.T.A.* v. *Gray, supra, per* Lord President Cooper at p. 600.

[65] *Brimelow* v. *Casson* [1924] 1 Ch. 302.

[66] *Edwin Hill & Partners* v. *First National Finance Corp. plc* [1989] 1 W.L.R. 225.

[67] *Findlay* v. *Blaylock,* 1937 S.C. 21.

[67a] *Akram* v. *Commission for Racial Equality & Ors.,* 1994 G.W.D. 22–1372.

[68] *Rose Street Foundry Co.* v. *Lewis,* 1917 S.C. 341.

[69] *Jones Bros. (Hunstanton) Ltd.* v. *Stevens* [1955] 1 Q.B. 275.

furtherance of a trade dispute, action may be limited by statute. The circumstances in which a trade union is accountable for allegedly wrongful acts are set out in the Trade Union and Labour Relations (Consolidation) Act 1992, as amended by the Trade Union Reform and Employment Rights Act 1993. There is under the 1992 Act no general immunity from proceedings in delict but, if a trade union is sued in respect of certain acts done in contemplation or furtherance of a trade dispute, the act is to be taken to have been done by the union only if it was authorised or endorsed by the union. Particular criteria must be satisfied before an act can be taken as authorised or endorsed by the union.[70] The 1992 Act also limits the amount of damages which may be awarded against a trade union in actions in delict other than actions in respect of personal injuries or for breach of duty in connection with the ownership, occupation, possession, control or use of property or for actions relating to product liability.[71]

An act done by a person in contemplation or furtherance of a trade dispute is not actionable on the ground only that it induces another person to break a contract, or interferes or induces another person to interfere with its performance, or that it consists in threatening such actions.[72] An agreement or combination to do such an act is not actionable if the act itself is not otherwise actionable.[73] There is authority for the view that even the use of unlawful means to interfere with business is protected.[74] To attract immunity, however, most such acts done by a trade union now require the support of a ballot in favour of such action, and compliance with certain notice requirements.[75] A trade dispute is a dispute between workers and their employer relating wholly or mainly to one of the matters specified in the Act.[76] Protection is removed where action is taken in an attempt to compel employers to employ only those who are members of a trade union, or of a particular trade union or unions.[77] Any union membership requirement in a contract for the supply of goods or services is void,[78] as is a requirement on a party to the contract to recognise one or more trade unions.[79] A refusal to deal with a supplier or prospective supplier of goods or services on grounds of union membership[80] or lack of union

[70] ss. 20 and 21.

[71] s. 22.

[72] s. 219(1).

[73] s. 219(2).

[74] *Shell U.K. Ltd.* v. *McGillivray*, 1991 S.L.T. 667, following *Plessey Co. plc* v. *Wilson*, 1983 S.L.T. 139, which was decided on the now repealed s. 13(2) of the 1974 Act; *cf.* 1991 S.L.T. (News) 367.

[75] 1992 Act, ss. 226–235.

[76] s. 244; see also *Conway* v. *Wade* [1909] A.C. 506; *J.T. Stratford & Son* v. *Lindley* [1965] A.C. 269; *Camden Exhibition & Display* v. *Lynott* [1966] 1 Q.B. 555 and *Square Grip Reinforcement Co.* v. *Macdonald*, 1966 S.L.T. 232; 1968 S.L.T. 65.

[77] ss. 222(1), (5).

[78] s. 144.

[79] s. 186.

[80] s. 145.

recognition[81] is prohibited. Acts designed to induce a person to breach these provisions relating to contracts for the supply of goods or services are therefore not protected,[82] nor are certain other acts designed to compel union recognition which interfere with the supply of goods or services whether under a contract or not.[83] Further, no protection is afforded where action is taken in protest at the dismissal of employees engaged in unofficial industrial action,[84] or where there has occurred 'secondary action' which does not amount to lawful picketing.[85] Lawful picketing is peaceful picketing by workers employed or last employed by the employer involved in the dispute, or by certain trade union officials.[86] Peaceful picketing is picketing amounting to the peaceful obtaining or communication of information, or to peaceful persuasion, which is taking place at or near a person's own place of work or, in the case of a union official, the place of work of a member whom he is accompanying and whom he represents.[87] Picketing can be at or near a place of work if it is at the nearest location to the place of work at which it can be carried out without trespassing.[88]

31.10   Nuisance.—'Nuisance' is the term commonly used to denote the infringement of a natural right of property. But the term is used by Bell in a wider sense: 'Whatever obstructs the public means of commerce and intercourse whether in highways or navigable rivers; whatever is noxious, or unsafe, or renders life uncomfortable to the public generally or to the neighbourhood; whatever is intolerably offensive to individuals in their dwelling-houses, or inconsistent with the comfort of life, whether by stench, by noise or by indecency is a nuisance.'[89] This definition includes what are in England called public nuisances which have nothing necessarily to do with the law of neighbourhood at all, but concern the public generally. Thus, the owner of a traction engine travelling on the highway has been held to commit a nuisance if he allows sparks to be emitted whereby the trees or houses of people living near the highway are injured.[90] Noise, vibration, and fumes from a launderette may amount to nuisance.[91] Piling operations causing soil movement, withdrawal of support and structural damage to neighbouring property may amount to nuisance.[92] The collapse of a sewer or

---

[81] s. 187.
[82] s. 222(3) (union membership) and s. 225(1) (union recognition).
[83] s. 225(2).
[84] s. 223.
[85] s. 224.
[86] s. 224(3).
[87] s. 220.
[88] *Rayware* v. *T.G.W.U.* [1989] 1 W.L.R. 675.
[89] *Prin.*, § 974: *Fleming* v. *Hislop* (1886) 13 R. (H.L.) 43.
[90] *Slater* v. *McLellan*, 1924 S.C. 854; see also *Ogston* v. *Aberdeen Tramways Co.* (1896) 24 R. (H.L.) 8.
[91] *MacNab* v. *McDevitt*, 1971 S.L.T. (Sh.Ct.) 41.
[92] *Lord Advocate* v. *The Reo Stakis Organisation Ltd.*, 1980 S.C. 203; 1981 S.C. 104; and *cf. Duncan's Hotel (Glasgow)* v. *J. & A. Ferguson*, 1974 S.C. 191.

culvert causing flooding may amount to nuisance.[93] The noise of erecting a steel scaffolding to provide seating at an annual military tattoo has been held to amount to nuisance.[94] Again, there are many statutory nuisances which do not depend on the law of neighbourhood.[95] But the most common instances of nuisance are those referred to in the latter part of Bell's definition, which consist in the disturbance of an owner of property in his use and enjoyment thereof. The owner has a right to the comfortable enjoyment of his property, and the law of nuisance is designed to protect this right. Interdict may be granted against nuisance and damages may be sought by one who has suffered loss as the result of nuisance. Liability in damages is based on culpa.[96] It is not, however, necessary for the pursuer in an action of damages for nuisance to aver and prove all that would be necessary to succeed in a case of negligence.[96a]

The proper approach to a case of alleged nuisance is rather from the standpoint of the victim of the loss or inconvenience than from the standpoint of the alleged offender.[97] Where the operations complained of interfere with the complainer's comfort and enjoyment the circumstances of the locality must be taken into account.[98] What is a nuisance in a residential neighbourhood would not necessarily be one in an industrial district. But an addition to the existing noises or smells in a district may be such as to give a cause of action.[99] If a nuisance exists it will not avail the wrongdoer to plead that it was in existence, and was known by the complainer to exist, when he purchased his property or came to the neighbourhood.[1] Nor is it any defence that other parties or even the complainer himself is contributing to the nuisance,[2] or that the

---

[93] *R.H.M. Bakeries (Scotland) Ltd.* v. *Strathclyde R.C.*, 1985 S.C. (H.L.) 17 (but note that the pursuers' case was held irrelevant because it excluded any reference to fault on the part of the defenders); *Plean Precast Ltd.* v. *N.C.B.*, 1986 S.L.T. 78.

[94] *Webster* v. *Lord Advocate*, 1985 S.C. 173.

[95] See, for example, the Control of Pollution Act 1974, s. 58(8) and *Hammersmith London B.C.* v. *Magnum Automated Forecourts Ltd.* [1978] 1 W.L.R. 50 (noise from 24-hour taxi care centre); *Tudhope* v. *Lee*, 1982 S.C.C.R. 409 (noise from a public house); *Strathclyde R.C.* v. *Tudhope*, 1983 S.L.T. 22 (noise from roadbreaking operations); the Countryside (Scotland) Act 1981, s. 11; the Litter Act 1983; the Public Health and Burgh Police Acts; *Tontine Hotel (Greenock)* v. *Greenock Corporation*, 1967 S.L.T. 180; *Rae* v. *Burgh of Musselburgh*, 1973 S.C. 291; *Clydebank D.C.* v. *Monaville Estates Ltd.*, 1982 S.L.T. (Sh.Ct.) 2.

[96] *R.H.M. Bakeries (Scotland) Ltd.*, *supra*.

[96a] *Kennedy* v. *Glenbelle Ltd.*, 1995 G.W.D. 7–398.

[97] *Watt* v. *Jamieson*, 1954 S.C. 56 at p. 57 *per* Lord President Cooper.

[98] But not so, according to English law, where actual injury to property is caused—*St. Helens Smelting Co.* v. *Tipping* (1865) 11 H.L.C. 642; *Shotts Iron Co.* v. *Inglis* (1882) 9 R. (H.L.) 78. It has been held in England that the victim of a continuing nuisance causing damage to his property is entitled to recover the cost of remedying such damage, including that which occurred prior to his acquiring an interest in the property: *Masters* v. *Brent London Borough Council* [1978] Q.B. 841.

[99] *St. Helens Smelting Co.* v. *Tipping*, *supra*; *Maguire* v. *Charles McNeil*, 1922 S.C. 174; *Polsue & Alfieri* v. *Rushmer* [1907] A.C. 121.

[1] *Fleming* v. *Hislop* (1886) 13 R. (H.L.) 43.

[2] *Duke of Buccleuch* v. *Cowan* (1866) 5 M. 214.

public or a large number of people benefit by that which causes the nuisance,[3] or that the defender was merely making a normal and familiar use of his own property.[4] But there is substantial authority to the effect that the owner or occupier of property from which a nuisance originates will be liable only if he had created or caused the nuisance, or if he had knowledge or the means of knowledge that actual nuisance was likely to be committed by other persons.[5] The right to object to a nuisance will be excluded if it has existed without challenge for the period of the long negative prescription[6] — 20 years;[7] but no shorter period will suffice, and even after the lapse of that period any increase in the extent of the nuisance may be challenged. Further, the objection may be met by showing consent on the part of the complainer, which may be either express agreement or acquiescence or such *rei interventus* as will create a personal bar.[7a] Moreover, what would otherwise be an actionable nuisance may be legalised by statute.[8] If a statute gives an absolute authority to do that which is complained of, irrespective of its consequences in creating a nuisance, no action to prevent it will lie; but it may, on the other hand, be that the statutory authority is provisional in the sense that it is given on the express or implied condition that what is authorised can be done without injury to the rights of others, and in this case the right to complain would not be cut off. Nor will statutory authority afford a defence if the nuisance is due to negligence in carrying out the operation authorised if without such negligence it would be unobjectionable.[9]

Further Reading

Clerk and Lindsell, *Torts* (16th ed., 1989).
Glegg, *Reparation* (4th ed., 1955).
Smith, *Short Commentary* (1962).
Stewart, *Delict* (2nd ed., 1993).
Thomson, *Delictual Liability* (1994).
Walker, *Delict* (2nd ed., 1981).
Winfield and Jolowicz, *Tort* (12th ed., 1989).

[3] *Shotts Iron Co.* v. *Inglis* (1882) 9 R. (H.L.) 78.

[4] *Watt* v. *Jamieson, supra.*

[5] See *Gourock Ropework Co.* v. *Greenock Corporation*, 1966 S.L.T. 125; *Noble's Trs.* v. *Economic Forestry (Scotland) Ltd.*, 1988 S.L.T. 662; *cf. Smith* v. *Scott* [1973] Ch. 314.

[6] Prescription and Limitation (Scotland) Act 1973, ss. 7 and 8; and *cf. Harvie* v. *Robertson* (1903) 5 F. 338.

[7] See Chap. 15, *supra.*

[7a] See discussion in *G.A. Estates Ltd.* v. *Caviapen Trs. Ltd. (No. 1)*, 1993 S.L.T. 1037.

[8] See, *e.g.* Civil Aviation Act 1982, ss. 76 and 77 and discussion in *Steel-Maitland* v. *British Airways Board*, 1981 S.L.T. 110.

[9] *Metropolitan Asylum District* v. *Hill* (1881) 6 App.Cas. 193; *Rapier* v. *London Tramways Co., supra*; *Manchester Corporation* v. *Farnworth* [1930] A.C. 171; see para. 34.6, *supra.*

CHAPTER 32

NEGLIGENCE

In this chapter, the term 'negligence' is used in what has already been described as its narrow sense, namely, failure to exercise such care as is reasonable in all the circumstances to avoid damage to others and to their property.[1] Liability for negligence depends upon proof of three things, namely, (1) that the defender owed to the pursuer the duty to take reasonable care for the safety of the pursuer's person or property; (2) that the defender was in breach of that duty; and (3) that the breach caused damage to the pursuer's person or property.[2]

32.1 Duty of Care: Development.—The best known formulation of the duty to take care is to be found in the case of *Donoghue* v. *Stevenson*.[3] In holding that the manufacturer of a bottle of ginger beer owed to the ultimate consumer a duty of care regarding the contents of the bottle, Lord Atkin stated:[4] 'You must take reasonable care to avoid acts or omissions which you can reasonably foresee would be likely to injure your neighbour. Who then in law is my neighbour? The answer seems to be — persons who are so closely and directly affected by my act that I ought reasonably to have them in contemplation as being so affected when I am directing my mind to the acts or omissions which are called in question.' As the law of negligence has evolved, however, it has become apparent that this formulation of the duty is not conclusive; while foreseeability of injury between the parties is necessary before a duty can arise, not every situation falling within Lord Atkin's definition of neighbourhood will give rise to liability when loss is sustained. There have been several attempts by the courts to formulate a test applicable to every situation. In *Home Office* v. *Dorset Yacht Company*,[5] a case where liability was held to attach to prison officers who had been negligent in their supervision of Borstal boys in their charge, allowing the boys to damage property nearby, Lord Reid expressed the view that the Atkin dictum ought to apply as a test of liability unless there were

---

[1] See para. 31.1, *supra*.
[2] Note that a defender is not necessarily liable for all the consequences of his negligence, those heads of loss which are 'too remote' from the negligence being excluded: see para. 32.11, *infra*.
[3] 1932 S.C. (H.L.) 31.
[4] At p. 44.
[5] [1970] A.C. 1004.

507

some justification for its exclusion. In *Anns* v. *London Borough of Merton*,[6] Lord Wilberforce formulated a two-stage test of liability: a prima facie duty of care arose if there was sufficient proximity or neighbourhood between the parties to lead to foreseeability by one party that his carelessness would injure the other, this prima facie duty then being negatived by particular considerations appropriate to individual situations. Between 1985 and 1990, in a succession of cases mainly dealing with economic loss rather than physical injury or damage to property, the House of Lords expressed reservations about the width of the test propounded by Lord Wilberforce. Finally in *Murphy* v. *Brentwood District Council*[7] the House of Lords departed from *Anns*.

In many cases where damages are sought for negligence, however, it is unnecessary to analyse whether or not the relationship between the parties is capable of giving rise to a duty of care. Particular relationships such as employer and employee or fellow road users are well recognised as giving rise to a duty of care, insofar as personal injury or damage to property is concerned. To establish a duty of care where the pursuer has sustained only economic loss has often posed greater difficulty.[7a] In a case in which damage to one party is a foreseeable result of carelessness by the other, but the relationship of the parties is not well established as giving rise to a duty of care in respect of the kind of loss sustained, the correct approach is now to determine whether there is an additional element in the relationship between the parties which justifies the imposition of the duty.[8] The nature of this additional element has been stated to be incapable of further definition,[9] but it has often been described as 'proximity.' It has also been stated that the courts can take into account whether it is just and reasonable that a duty of care should be held to exist;[10] whilst this requirement is expressed as a separate consideration, it has tended to be relied on by the courts as an additional factor demonstrating that the requisite degree of proximity is either present in or absent from a particular relationship. In three English House of Lords cases involving the provision of professional or quasi-professional services by the defendant, the test for the existence of a duty of care has been stated to be whether or not the defendant assumed responsibility to the plaintiff for the provision of such services,

[6] [1978] A.C. 728.

[7] [1991] 1 A.C. 398.

[7a] See para. 32.6, *infra*.

[8] *Caparo Industries plc* v. *Dickman* [1990] 2 A.C. 605. See also *Marc Rich & Co. A.G.* v. *Bishop Rock Marine Co. Ltd.* [1994] 1 W.L.R. 1071, where the Court of Appeal adopted this appraoch in a case based on damage to property. This incremental approach to the law of negligence has always been preferred in Australia, where *Anns* was not followed; see the oft-quoted dictum of Brennan J. in *Sutherland Shire Council* v. *Heyman* (1985) 60 A.L.R. 1, at pp. 43–44.

[9] *Caparo Industries plc, supra*.

[10] *Governors of the Peabody Donation Fund* v. *Sir Lindsay Parkinson & Co.* [1985] A.C. 210, *per* Lord Keith at pp. 240–241; *Caparo Industries, supra*, at p. 633.

on which the plaintiff relied.[10a] In the following paragraphs, the
requirement of foreseeability is first examined, and thereafter types of
claim giving rise to difficulty in deciding whether or not a duty of care
exists are discussed.

32.2 Duty of Care: Foreseeability.—The duty to take care is not owed to the
world at large, but to those to whom injury may reasonably and
probably be anticipated if the duty is not observed.[11] The duty may be
owed by a motorist to A, with whom he collides, but not to B who has
sustained nervous shock as a result of hearing the noise of the accident
from a point outwith the area of potential danger.[12] There may be
liability to parties who are injured in preventing or attempting to
prevent injury to other persons[13] or damage to property[14] imperilled by
the defender's acts. For example, a person who negligently starts a fire
can be liable to a fireman injured while fighting the fire.[15] There is,
however, no duty owed by an occupier of premises to firemen to
provide means of access and egress which will remain safe during the
fire, even if a duty to provide similar precautions might be owed to
employees.[16] Trespassers are within the class of persons to whom an
occupier of or operator on land owes the duty of care, if the presence of
the trespasser at the material time was reasonably foreseeable.[17] It has
been held in England that the duty is owed to a child *in utero* at the
time of an accident in respect of injuries attributable to that accident
which persist after birth.[18] If the presence of disabled people is
foreseeable, the defender may owe a duty to take care regarding
situations dangerous to them, even if no risk is posed to able-bodied
people.[19]

The test of 'reasonable foreseeability' of injury can thus be seen as
defining the class of persons to whom the duty of care is owed, but it
may also be used to determine whether or not the defender is liable in

---

[10a] The speech of Lord Goff in *Spring* v. *Guardian Assurance plc* [1994] 3 W.L.R. 354;
Henderson v. *Merrett Syndicates Ltd.* [1994] 3 W.L.R. 761; and *White* v. *Jones* [1995] 2
W.L.R. 187.

[11] *Bourhill* v. *Young*, 1942 S.C. (H.L.) 78, *per* Lord Macmillan at p. 88.

[12] *Bourhill* v. *Young, supra.*

[13] *Haynes* v. *Harwood* [1935] 1 K.B. 146; *Baker* v. *Hopkins* [1959] 1 W.L.R. 966;
Videan v. *B.T.C.* [1963] 2 Q.B. 650; see also *Carmarthenshire C.C.* v. *Lewis* [1955] A.C.
549.

[14] *Steel* v. *Glasgow Iron & Steel Co.*, 1944 S.C. 237. But note that the deceased had
responsibilites for the safety of his employer's property: see Lord Justice-Clerk Cooper at
p. 250.

[15] *Ogwo* v. *Taylor* [1988] A.C. 431.

[16] *Bermingham* v. *Sher Bros.*, 1980 S.C. (H.L.) 67.

[17] *McGlone* v. *B.R.B.*, 1966 S.L.T. 2 (H.L.), *per* Lord Reid at p. 9; and see para.
32.14, *infra*; Walker, p. 598, and *Videan* v. *B.T.C., supra*, where English trespass cases
are considered.

[18] *B.* v. *Islington Health Authority* [1992] 3 W.L.R. 637, following *Watt* v. *Rama* [1972]
V.R. 353. In *Cohen* v. *Shaw*, 1992 S.L.T. 1022, Lord Cullen declined to express a view on
whether or not the same approach as in *B.* v. *Islington* would be adopted in Scotland.

[19] *Haley* v. *London Electricity Board* [1965] A.C. 778.

damages for the consequences of his acts or omissions.[20] 'Legal liability
is limited to those consequences of our acts which a reasonable man of
ordinary intelligence and experience so acting would have in contemplation.'[21] To attract liability it is necessary that the kind of injury
sustained[22] and the manner in which it was sustained[23] should be
reasonably foreseeable but the precise chain of events leading up to the
particular accident need not be foreseeable.[24] Where negligence in the
manufacture of products is concerned, if it is not foreseeable that the
product will reach the consumer without intermediate examination or
testing, a manufacturer may not be liable for injury to a consumer.[25]
Negligence is not, therefore, synonymous with carelessness.[26] It involves
a failure to exercise the duty of care, and the existence of this duty
depends upon injury to the pursuer's person or property being a
reasonably foreseeable consequence of that failure.

32.3 Duty of Care: Nervous Shock.—Before damages can be awarded for
nervous shock, the pursuer must have sustained more than mere fright
or distress of mind; such an emotional reaction must have been followed
by some physical, mental or nervous injury.[27] If the pursuer is within
the area of potential danger (*i.e.* of reasonably foreseeable physical
injury) created by a careless act, the duty of care exists and the
defender will be liable to make reparation for nervous shock caused by
fear of bodily harm, although the pursuer may escape physical injury.[28]
It may also be sufficient that the pursuer reasonably thought he was in
physical danger or, although originally outwith the area of physical
danger, he later came within it as a rescuer.[28a] Whether there is liability
for nervous shock sustained by a person outwith the area of potential
physical danger as a result only of seeing or hearing an accident to a
third party or of becoming aware of its consequences, has given rise to
much difficulty. In *Bourhill* v. *Young*,[29] a motorcyclist negligently

[20] Note that this is a different question from that of the defender's liability for all the
consequences of his negligence: see para. 32.11, *infra*; and *McKillen* v. *Barclay Curle*,
1967 S.L.T. 41.
[21] See *Muir* v. *Glasgow Corporation*, 1943 S.C. (H.L.) 3, *per* Lord Macmillan at p. 10.
[22] *Hughes* v. *Lord Advocate*, 1963 S.C. (H.L.) 31; *Blaikie* v. *B.T.C.*, 1961 S.C. 44.
[23] *Hughes, supra*; *Malcolm* v. *Dickson*, 1951 S.C. 542; see also *Doughty* v. *Turner Mfg.
Co.* [1964] 1 Q.B. 518 and *Bell* v. *Scottish Special Housing Association*, 1987 S.L.T. 320.
[24] *Harvey* v. *Singer Mfg. Co.*, 1960 S.C. 155; and see *Carmarthenshire C.C.* v. *Lewis*
[1955] A.C. 549, *per* Lord Reid at p. 564.
[25] *Donoghue* v. *Stevenson*, 1932 S.C. (H.L.) 31, at p. 57; see, however, *Clay* v. *A.J.
Crump* [1964] 1 Q.B. 533 and para. 32.10 regarding cases where the subsequent negligence
of a third party has not broken the chain of causation leading from the original
wrongdoer.
[26] See *Donoghue* v. *Stevenson, supra, per* Lord Macmillan at p. 70.
[27] *Simpson* v. *I.C.I.*, 1983 S.L.T. 601.
[28] *Brown* v. *Glasgow Corporation*, 1922 S.C. 527; and see Walker, at p. 678; *cf. Page* v.
Smith [1995] 2 W.L.R. 644.
[28a] *McFarlane* v. *E.E. Caledonia Ltd.* [1994] 2 All E.R. 1.
[29] 1942 S.C. (H.L.) 78.

collided with a car and was killed. The pursuer, a fishwife unloading her creel from a tramway car nearby, did not see the collision but heard the noise. She suffered nervous shock, and a miscarriage which she alleged was caused by the nervous shock. It was held that the motorcyclist owed no duty to the pursuer, injury to a person in her position not being reasonably foreseeable. Where, however, the plaintiff was informed that her husband and three children had been involved in a road accident two hours earlier and taken to hospital where she saw her family and learned that her youngest daughter had been killed, it was held that she was entitled to recover damages for nervous shock.[30] It is necessary to show that the pursuer is within the class of persons to whom nervous shock was foreseeable, and that there is the required degree of proximity between the pursuer and the alleged wrongdoer.[31] The first limb of this test can be presumed to be satisfied where the relationship between the pursuer and the injured person is a close family one; the necessary degree of proximity may, however, be lacking where the pursuer has only learned of an accident by watching television.[32] Conversely, one who witnesses an accident to a fellow employee, in which he is not himself involved, is not within the class of persons who can recover damages for nervous shock.[32a] In deciding whether a duty exists in respect of nervous shock, time, space, distance, the relationship of the victims to the pursuer, the nature of the injuries and the means by which the shock is caused are all, therefore, relevant factors.[33] In limited circumstances, damages may also be recoverable for nervous shock sustained as a result of witnessing damage to one's property.[34]

32.4 Duty of Care: Actions of Third Parties.—A pursuer suffering loss or injury caused directly by the actions of a third party may seek damages from a defender on the basis that but for the alleged negligence of the defender, the third party would not have been able to cause the damage.[35] Typically, this occurs where the third party causing the damage is unidentified or has no assets with which to satisfy an award of damages. The third party may have acted negligently or deliberately and his actions may amount to a crime. In such cases, the courts are concerned to impose some limit or control mechanism to prevent liability attaching simply for omitting to prevent the infliction of harm,

[30] *McLoughlin* v. *O'Brian* [1983] 1 A.C. 410.
[31] *Alcock* v. *Chief Constable of South Yorkshire Police* [1992] 1 A.C. 310; *McFarlane, supra.*
[32] *Ibid.*
[32a] *Robertson* v. *Forth Road Bridge Joint Board*, 1995 G.W.D. 12–690.
[33] *McLoughlin* v. *O'Brian, supra*; see also *Bourhill* v. *Young, supra*; *Hambrook* v. *Stokes* [1925] 1 K.B. 141, where negligence admitted; *Boardman* v. *Sanderson* [1964] 1 W.L.R. 1317; *cf. Chadwick* v. *British Transport Commission* [1967] 2 All E.R. 945.
[34] *Attia* v. *British Gas plc* [1988] Q.B. 304.
[35] Note that this is different from cases where the defender is liable for the actions of a third party, even though he has not himself been negligent, because of a principle of law such as vicarious liability. See para. 33.5.

rather than for active conduct. The circumstances in which liability will attach to a defender for damage which is directly caused by a third party were reviewed by the House of Lords in *Maloco* v. *Littlewoods Organisation Ltd.*[36] There, vandals entered a disused cinema belonging to the defenders and started a fire which spread to a neighbouring café and church, belonging to the pursuers. It was held that the defenders were not liable to the pursuers. Lord Mackay saw the question as one of foreseeability, to be answered by examining from the standpoint of the defenders the level of likelihood of the conduct of the third party causing the damage. Lord Goff, however, considered that the case could not be resolved solely by assessing foreseeability but necessitated a consideration of the circumstances in which it would be appropriate to impose on a defender a duty to prevent the infliction of damage on others by a third party. Thus the duty could arise because of the relationship between the pursuer and defender, or between the defender and the third party,[37] or because the defender negligently causes or permits to be created a source of danger, or has knowledge or means of knowledge of previous similar incidents. It is therefore clear that liability will not be imposed simply because the defender has created the opportunity for a third party to act in a way which could have been anticipated[38] but, as in cases of economic loss, it is not possible to articulate any single principle to be used in determining those instances in which liability will result, each case turning on its own facts and circumstances.

32.5 Duty of Care: Public Bodies.—Although a pursuer has suffered injury, or loss of or damage to property, as a result of the actings of a public body exercising its powers or implementing its duties, he may be unable to recover damages because no common law duty of care was owed. A distinction has been recognised between the actings of a public body falling within the ambit of the exercise of discretion and actions in implementation of discretionary decisions. If the public body is acting within the ambit of its discretion it will not be liable in damages unless bad faith is present. Thus, where children have allegedly sustained injury as a result of an adverse reaction to vaccination it has been held that, in the absence of allegations of bad faith, no liability attaches to the Secretary of State, who has the responsibility of promoting the vaccination of children, for the content of information made available to the public about risks.[39] In the field of financial regulation, the courts have been similarly unwilling to recognise a duty of care. In *Yuen Kun*

[36] 1987 S.L.T. 425.
[37] As in *Home Office* v. *Dorset Yacht Company* [1970] A.C. 1004.
[38] See also *P. Perl (Exporters)* v. *Camden London Borough Council* [1984] Q.B. 342; *Topp* v. *London Country Bus (South West) Ltd.* [1993] 1 W.L.R. 976.
[39] *Bonthrone* v. *Secretary of State for Scotland*, 1987 S.L.T 34; *Ross* v. *Secretary of State for Scotland*, 1990 S.L.T. 13; see also *Johnstone* v. *Traffic Commissioner*, 1990 S.L.T. 409.

Yeu v. *Attorney General of Hong Kong*[40] it was held that the Commissioner of Deposit Taking Companies in Hong Kong did not owe a duty of care to individual depositors, who were thus unable to sue him for alleged failures to discover irregularities in the conduct of the affairs of a finance company which later collapsed. When exercising his discretion whether or not to register a company, the Commissioner had no special relationship either with the company or with potential depositors.[41] Once a public body moves into what is termed the operational area of its activities, a duty of care towards individuals may arise, although there can be difficulty in distinguishing discretionary and operational decisions.[42] In addition, such a distinction is only of use in identifying decisions which do not give rise to a duty of care; merely because a public body is within the operational area of its activities does not necessarily mean that a duty of care is owed to individuals.[43]

The question of the existence of such a duty will depend on a number of factors, including what is perceived to be the purpose for which the body is endowed with the powers concerned. Attempts have been made in a number of cases to argue that a local authority responsible for monitoring the construction of buildings owes a duty to the owner of the building to take reasonable care that the building is constructed properly. The House of Lords has held, however, that no such duty is owed; the statutory power of a local authority to control the construction of buildings is conferred for the purpose of protecting the safety of the public, not to safeguard the economic interests of the owner.[44] A further factor which is likely to militate against the imposition of a duty of care is the availability in public law of a means of challenging the decision complained of, such as judicial review or a statutory appeal procedure.[45]

Whether or not the police owe a duty of care in respect of their actions will also depend on the circumstances in individual cases. No specialty arises in situations which are well recognised as giving rise to a duty of care, for example individual police officers on the public road owe duties of care to other road users. A duty of care can also be owed by the police to a drunk[46] or suicidal[47] man in their custody. Where, however, police officers take action in the course of their duty and

---

[40] [1988] A.C. 175.

[41] See also *Davis* v. *Radcliffe* [1990] 1 W.L.R. 821; *cf. Lonrho plc* v. *Tebbit* [1992] 4 All E.R. 280; and *Deloitte Haskins & Sells* v. *National Mutual Life Nominees Ltd.* [1993] A.C. 774.

[42] *Rowling* v. *Takaro Properties Ltd.* [1988] A.C. 473.

[43] *Ibid.*

[44] *Governors of the Peabody Donation Fund* v. *Sir Lindsay Parkinson & Co.* [1985] A.C. 210, at p. 241. See the further discussion of cases concerning defective buildings in para. 32.6.

[45] See *Jones* v. *Department of Employment* [1989] Q.B. 1; *Johnstone* v. *Traffic Commissioner, supra.*

[46] *Wilson* v. *Chief Constable, Lothian and Borders Police*, 1989 S.L.T. 97.

[47] *Kirkham* v. *Chief Constable of Greater Manchester Police* [1990] 2 Q.B. 283.

injury is caused, they are protected from actions of damages unless their actings were malicious and without probable cause.[48] In the context of the investigation of crime, the House of Lords has held that the necessary degree of proximity is lacking between the police officers charged with the investigation of past crimes and the potential future victims of the criminal.[49] There is, thus, no duty of care capable of giving rise to liability for allegedly negligent failures in detection; in addition, to impose such a duty would be contrary to public policy.[50]

32.6   Duty of Care: Pure Economic Loss.—Where the loss sustained by a pursuer is purely economic, as distinct from injury to his person or damage to his property, it is generally more difficult to recover damages.[51] This is not so much because of the character of the loss in itself as because the scope of a duty of care may not be wide enough to include those whose loss is purely economic. There is, in general, no duty to take care to avoid causing financial loss to individuals who suffer such loss as a direct result of negligence which kills or injures other persons with whom they had some form of relationship by contract or otherwise. Thus, an employer cannot claim reparation for the loss caused to him by the death or injury of an employee through the fault of a third party, even if the employer has been injured in the same accident.[52] Nor, cases of death apart, is any duty owed to relatives in respect of the loss of the support or services of an injured person on which they relied.[53] Similarly, there is, in general, no duty owed to individuals who sustain financial loss when deprived of services through damage, negligently caused, to the property of another. Thus when, on the pursuers' averments, contractors negligently damaged an electricity supply cable belonging to the electricity board so that the supply of electricity to the pursuer's factory was cut off and loss of production with consequent financial loss ensued, the action was dismissed.[54] Similarly, where contractors were laying a pipe belonging to the Gas

---

[48] See *Ward* v. *Chief Constable, Strathclyde Police*, 1991 S.L.T. 292.

[49] *Hill* v. *Chief Constable of West Yorkshire* [1989] A.C. 53; see also *Clough* v. *Bussan* [1990] 1 All E.R. 431, and *Ancell* v. *McDermott* [1993] 4 All E.R. 355 (unsuccessful attempts to establish liability for alleged failure by the police to deal with hazards on the highway); also *Alexandrou* v. *Oxford* [1993] 4 All E.R. 328 (unsuccessful attempt to establish liability for alleged failure to respond to an emergency call).

[50] *Hill, supra.*

[51] *Caparo Industries, supra*, pp. 618–619; *Weir* v. *National Westminster Bank plc*, 1994 S.L.T. 1251.

[52] *Reavis* v. *Clan Line Steamers*, 1925 S.C. 725.

[53] *Robertson* v. *Turnbull*, 1982 S.C. (H.L.) 1. The injured person can now seek damages for inability to render services or for services which require to be rendered to him. See Administration of Justice Act 1982 and para. 34.11.

[54] *Dynamco* v. *Holland and Hannen and Cubitts (Scotland)*, 1972 S.L.T. 38; cf. *S.C.M. (United Kingdom)* v. *W.G. Whittall and Sons* [1971] 1 Q.B. 137; *Spartan Steel Alloys* v. *Martins and Co. (Contractors)* [1973] Q.B. 27. See also *East Lothian Angling Association* v. *Haddington Town Council*, 1980 S.L.T. 213; *Candlewood Navigation Corpn.* v. *Mitsui OSK Lines* [1986] A.C. 1; *Scott Lithgow* v. *G.E.C. Electrical Projects Ltd.*, 1992 S.L.T. 244.

Board and were responsible for any damage to the pipe during laying, they were unable to recover damages from a third party who damaged the pipe.[55] If, however, the pursuer can demonstrate that he has rights in connection with the property which, though falling short of ownership, amount to a possessory title, he may be able to recover damages.[56]

Where the owner of property discovers a defect in the property which is due to allegedly negligent construction, his claim for the cost of rectifying the defect or replacing the property, or for loss sustained on resale of the property, is a claim for pure economic loss. The House of Lords has held that damages are not recoverable for such loss. This exclusion has been applied to a claim by developers in respect of a failure by a local authority to prevent the developers from departing from approved plans, resulting in a defective building[57] and where plans which did not comply with building regulations were prepared by experts employed by the developers, approved by the local authority and utilised to the financial loss of the developers.[58] It has also been applied where defects in construction have emerged during the ownership of, or occupation by, a subsequent acquirer of the building who has attempted to claim damages from the builder[59] or from the local authority which passed the plans.[60] Dicta in some of the earlier cases suggested that damages were recoverable where the defect, when discovered, posed a risk to health or safety but it is now established that even such a risk does not make the economic loss recoverable.[61]

It has been suggested that claims which at first sight appear to be pure economic loss claims may in fact be cases in which the pursuer has suffered damage to other property which he owns. Thus, in a complex structure such as a building, a defect in one part may cause damage to another part of the structure.[62] The difficulties incurred in attempting to formulate and apply such a test have, however, now been acknowledged.[63] It has been stated that in Scots law there is no automatic

---

[55] *Nacap* v. *Moffat Plant*, 1987 S.L.T. 221.

[56] *North Scottish Helicopters Ltd.* v. *United Technologies Corp. Inc.*, 1988 S.L.T. 77, following dicta in *Leigh and Sillavan Ltd.* v. *Aliakmon Shipping Co. Ltd.* [1986] A.C. 785; the concept of a possessory title does not fit easily into the Scots law classification of rights as real or personal: see Chap. 3. See also *Mull Shellfish Ltd.* v. *Golden Sea Produce Ltd.*, 1992 S.L.T. 703.

[57] *Governors of the Peabody Donation Fund* v. *Sir Lindsay Parkinson & Co.* [1985] A.C. 210.

[58] *Investors in Industry Commercial Properties Ltd.* v. *South Bedfordshire D.C.* [1986] Q.B. 1034 (C.A.).

[59] *D. & F. Estates Ltd.* v. *Church Commissioners for England* [1989] 1 A.C. 177; *Department of the Environment* v. *Thomas Bates & Son Ltd.* [1990] 3 W.L.R. 457.

[60] *Murphy* v. *Brentwood D.C.* [1991] A.C. 398, overruling *Anns* v. *Merton London Borough Council* [1978] A.C. 728.

[61] *Murphy, supra.*

[62] *D. & F. Estates Ltd., supra,* per Lord Bridge at pp. 206–207; *McLeod* v. *Scottish Special Housing Association*, 1990 S.L.T. 749.

[63] *Murphy, supra,* per Lord Bridge at pp. 476–479.

exclusion of claims in delict for the diminution in value of property resulting from negligent work on that property.[64]

There are some cases where the pursuer has suffered pure economic loss but the relationship between the parties is of such a character that damages are recoverable. A category of case in which it has been recognised that pure economic loss may be recoverable is that of negligent misrepresentation, which is discussed in the next paragraph. In two English appeals, the House of Lords has held that the principles underlying recovery of loss in cases of negligent misrepresentation can be extended to other situations in which the defendant provides professional or quasi-professional services to the plaintiff. In both *Henderson* v. *Merrett Syndicates Ltd.*[65] and *White* v. *Jones*[65a] the House of Lords held that the relationship between the parties disclosed an assumption of responsibility by the defendant to the plaintiff and a concomitant reliance by the plaintiff on the quality of the services provided, leading to liability when the services fell below the requisite standard. The latter case concerned failures by solicitors in the preparation of a will, leading to loss to potential beneficiaries. In a nineteenth century Scottish appeal to the House of Lords, it was stated that there could be no liability in such a situation.[65b] This approach continues to be followed in Scotland[65c] although the dicta concerning a disappointed legatee were, strictly, obiter[65d] and have been superseded by other developments in the law.[65e]

The class of cases not involving negligent misrepresentation or any assumption of responsibility in which the relationship of the parties is sufficiently close for a duty of care to exist in respect of economic loss must be seen as very limited. It has included a relationship between the owner of property and a nominated subcontractor working on the property, in *Junior Books Ltd.* v. *The Veitchi Co. Ltd.*[66] In other similar cases, such factors as nomination by the pursuers of the defenders as subcontractors and whether or not the pursuers can be said to have relied on the defenders will be important.[67] In subsequent cases, it has been emphasised that the relationship in *Junior Books* which led to liability was particularly close,[68] the relationship being described by

[64] *Parkhead Housing Association Ltd.* v. *Phoenix Preservation Ltd.*, 1990 S.L.T. 812, at p. 816.

[65] [1994] 3 W.L.R. 761.

[65a] [1995] 2 W.L.R. 187.

[65b] *Robertson* v. *Fleming* (1861) 4 Macq. 167.

[65c] *Weir* v. *J.M. Hodge & Son*, 1990 SLT 266; *MacDougall* v. *MacDougall's Exrs*, 1994 S.L.T. 1178.

[65d] *White, supra, per* Lord Goff at p. 198.

[65e] *Ibid.*

[66] 1982 S.C. (H.L.) 244; see also *Parkhead Housing Association Ltd., supra.*

[67] *Scott Lithgow Ltd.* v. *G.E.C. Electrical Projects Ltd.*, 1992 S.L.T. 244.

[68] The relationship was described as 'unique' by Lord Bridge in *D. & F. Estates* at p. 202; *cf.* observations of Lord Clyde in *Scott Lithgow, supra* at p. 250 that the structure of relationships in *Junior Books* is relatively common in practice.

Lord Fraser in *Junior Books*[69] as 'only just short of a direct contractual relationship.' The significance in a delictual claim of a contractual relationship between the parties has not always been clear.[70] It has now been stated by the House of Lords in *Henderson* that the correct approach is to consider whether the plaintiff is precluded by his contract from suing in tort; if not, he may choose to sue in either.[71]

32.7 Duty of Care: Negligent Misrepresentation.—When the alleged negligence relates to statements, verbal or written, and not to deeds, it has long been recognised that a duty to take reasonable care that such statements are accurate may arise from special relationships in special circumstances.[72] In *Hedley Byrne & Co.* v. *Heller and Partners* the House of Lords considered the circumstances in which a party sustaining financial loss as a direct result of acting upon an incorrect statement, given by another with whom there was no contractual relationship, might sue for damages on the ground of negligence.[73] The 'special relationships' contemplated by the House of Lords were independent of contract and extended beyond fiduciary relationship. Lord Reid could see 'no logical stopping place short of all those relationships where it is plain that the party seeking information or advice was trusting the other to exercise such a degree of care as the circumstances required, where it was reasonable for him to do that, and where the other gave the information or advice when he knew or ought to have known that the inquirer was relying on him.'[74]

The principle established in *Hedley Byrne* was applied in a subsequent case where a local authority clerk failed to disclose to a third party the recording in a Land Register of a charge in favour of the plaintiffs, thus rendering the charge unenforceable against the third party, to the loss of the plaintiffs.[75] Where a surveyor is instructed by a lender to value property but knows that his report will be communicated to and probably relied upon by the borrower, the surveyor owes a duty of care to the borrower.[76] Similarly, surveyors instructed by a borrower can owe a duty of care to a lender.[77] A surveyor instructed by a potential purchaser, A, can owe a duty to another person, B, who joins A in the purchase of the property but whose existence as a potential purchaser is not known to the surveyor.[78] A solicitor acting for a client can owe a

---

[69] 1982 S.C. (H.L.) 244, at p. 265.
[70] Contrast e.g., *Middleton* v. *Douglass*, 1991 S.L.T. 726 and *Comex Houlder Diving Ltd.* v. *Colne Fishing Co. Ltd. (No. 2)*, 1992 S.L.T. 89.
[71] *Henderson, supra*, at p. 789.
[72] *Robinson* v. *National Bank of Scotland*, 1916 S.C. (H.L.) 154.
[73] [1964] A.C. 465. See *John Kenway* v. *Orcantic*, 1979 S.C. 422, acknowledging the existence of this principle in Scots law.
[74] *Ibid.*, at p. 486.
[75] *Ministry of Housing* v. *Sharp* [1970] 2 Q.B. 223.
[76] *Martin* v. *Bell-Ingram*, 1986 S.L.T. 575; *Smith* v. *Eric S. Bush* [1990] 1 A.C. 831.
[77] *U.C.B. Bank plc* v. *Dundas & Wilson, C.S.*, 1989 S.L.T. 243.
[78] *Smith* v. *Carter*, 1995 S.L.T. 295.

duty of care to a third party who is relying on advice or information given to him by the solicitor, provided the necessary degree of proximity is present.[79]

The circumstances in which liability will attach for the making of a negligent statement, written or verbal, were again reviewed by the House of Lords in *Caparo Industries plc* v. *James Dickman*.[80] In that case, the plaintiffs had begun to purchase shares in a company a few days before the annual accounts were published to shareholders. In reliance on those accounts, they purchased further shares and took over the company. They alleged that they had since discovered that the accounts presented a falsely optimistic picture of the company and that if they had known the true picture they would not have taken over the company at all, or at any rate not at the price paid. The House of Lords considered whether or not the auditor of the accounts could be held to have owed a duty of care to the plaintiffs, either as existing shareholders or as potential future investors. It was held that no such duty was owed. As in many such cases, the judges were reluctant to hold that such a duty existed in respect of representations which could potentially be relied upon by many different people in different situations and for many purposes.[81] Lord Bridge saw the limiting or control mechanism as being knowledge by the defendant that his statement would be communicated to the plaintiff, specifically in connection with a particular transaction, and that the plaintiff would be very likely to rely on it for the purpose of reaching a decision regarding that transaction.[82] The dissenting judgment of Lord Denning in *Candler* v. *Crane Christmas & Co.*,[83] a case overruled by the House of Lords in *Hedley Byrne*, was again approved by the House. The criteria set out in *Caparo* have since been applied by the Court of Appeal in England in other cases concerning failures by accountants in the preparation or auditing of accounts or other financial statements. In *James McNaughton Paper Group Ltd.* v. *Hicks Anderson & Co.*[84] it was held that no duty was owed because of the particular circumstances surrounding the preparation of the accounts and the unlikelihood of reliance; whereas in *Morgan Crucible Co. plc* v. *Hill Samuel & Co. Ltd.*[85] it was held that a duty could be owed not to mislead.[86] Auditors appointed to a local authority under statute owe a statutory duty and may also owe a common law duty of care to the local authority as the body whose

---

[79] *Midland Bank plc* v. *Cameron, Thom, Peterkin & Duncans*, 1988 S.L.T. 611.

[80] [1990] 2 A.C. 605.

[81] *Ibid.*, p. 621 where Lord Bridge of Harwich quotes the familiar caveat of Cardozo C.J. that there could ensue 'liability in an indeterminate amount for an indeterminate time to an indeterminate class'—*Ultramares Corporation* v. *Touche* (1931) 174 N.E. 441, at p. 444.

[82] *Ibid.*, at p. 621.

[83] [1951] 2 K.B. 164.

[84] [1991] 2 Q.B. 113.

[85] [1991] Ch. 295.

[86] See also *Galoo Ltd.* v. *Bright Grahame Murray* [1995] 1 All E.R. 16.

accounts are being audited.[87] Liability for negligent misrepresentation can also be established where an employer issues an inaccurate reference concerning a former employee to a potential employer of that employee, causing the loss of an opportunity of employment.[88] The duty may be excluded, in circumstances in which it would otherwise arise, by an express disclaimer of responsibility.[89] Negligent misstatements can now afford a ground of action as representations inducing a contract which has resulted in loss.[90] Formerly fraudulent misrepresentation had to be proved.[91]

32.8 Negligence: Standard of Care.—The standard of care applied to determine whether or not the defender was negligent is that of a reasonable man of ordinary intelligence and experience.[92] 'The reasonable man is presumed to be free both from over-apprehension and from over-confidence but there is a sense in which the standard of care of the reasonable man involves in its application a subjective element. It is still left to the judge to decide what in the circumstances of the particular case the reasonable man would have had in contemplation and what accordingly the party sought to be made liable ought to have foreseen.'[93] It is a question not only of what the reasonable man would have foreseen but also of the risks against which he would have taken precautions. The degree of care varies directly with the risk involved. Thus a higher degree of care is required in activities which are obviously highly dangerous.[94] At the other end of the scale the risk may be so small that a reasonable man would feel justified in disregarding it.[95] The appropriate degree of care is not determined by reference solely to the actual knowledge of the defender but also to the sources of knowledge open to him and to the actual knowledge of kindred persons.[96] Where the pursuer alleges that a system of work was unsafe, evidence that that system is standard practice in the industry is not conclusive in favour of the defenders.[97] The pursuer's own

[87] *West Wiltshire D.C.* v. *Garland* [1995] 2 W.L.R. 439.
[88] *Spring* v. *Guardian Assurance plc* [1994] 3 W.L.R. 354. See also *Johnstone* v. *Traffic Commissioner*, 1990 S.L.T. 409.
[89] *Hedley Byrne, supra*; *Commercial Financial Services Ltd.* v. *McBeth & Co.*, 1988 S.L.T. 528.
[90] See Law Reform (Misc. Provs.) (Scotland) Act 1985, s. 10.
[91] See para. 9.8, *supra*.
[92] *Muir* v. *Glasgow Corporation*, 1943 S.C. (H.L.) 3.
[93] *Ibid., per* Lord Macmillan at p. 10.
[94] *Dominion Natural Gas Co.* v. *Collins* [1909] A.C. 640, *per* Lord Dunedin at p. 646; *Read* v. *Lyons & Co.* [1947] A.C. 156, *per* Lord Macmillan at p. 171—'an exacting standard of care is incumbent on manufacturers of explosive shells.'
[95] See *Carmarthenshire C.C.* v. *Lewis* [1955] A.C. 549, *per* Lord Reid at p. 565; also *Overseas Tankship (U.K.)* v. *Miller Steamship Co.* [1967] 1 A.C. 617 (P.C.), at pp. 641–44 and *Bolton* v. *Stone* [1951] A.C. 850.
[96] See *Balfour* v. *Beardmore & Co.*, 1956 S.L.T. 205; *cf. Quinn* v. *Cameron & Roberton*, 1956 S.C. 224, *per* Lord President Clyde at p. 232 (reversed on another ground, 1957 S.C. (H.L.) 22); *Cramb* v. *Caledonian Ry.* (1892) 19 R. 1054; *Roe* v. *Minister of Health* [1954] 2 Q.B. 66.
[97] *Cavanagh* v. *Ulster Weaving Co.* [1960] A.C. 145.

knowledge and experience are also relevant to the question of what precautions were reasonable in the circumstances.[98] A greater degree of care is due to parties with abnormal susceptibilities or infirmities.[99] The magnitude of the risk must be weighed against the difficulty and expense of taking precautions and the importance of the particular operation.[1] An emergency may justify the taking of a risk which in other circumstances might be negligent.[2]

32.9 Standard of Care: Professional Negligence.—Where a person professes to have a particular skill, in carrying out the work with which he is thereby entrusted he must display the same standard of care as other members of the profession, whether or not he possesses the same qualifications.[3] The standard of care against which the actions of a professional are measured depends on the state of scientific and technical knowledge prevailing at the time.[4] A professional person will not be held to have been negligent in the exercise of his judgment unless he has followed a course which no ordinarily competent member of his profession would have adopted if acting with ordinary care.[5] A court faced with conflicting testimony of experts as to the course which should have been adopted is not entitled simply to prefer one body of opinion over another.[6] If, however, one of the competing bodies of evidence is found not to be credible and reliable, the opposing testimony may be preferred.[7] The standard of reasonably competent members of the profession covers the giving of advice as well as the carrying out of work; thus, a doctor in omitting to warn a patient of the risk inherent in a particular form of treatment will not be faulted if he has followed an accepted practice, albeit that other doctors might have alerted the patient to the risk.[8] In issuing advice, a professional should take into account the nature, experience and understanding of the client

[98] *Qualcast* v. *Haynes* [1959] A.C. 743, *per* Lord Radcliffe at p. 754; *Ross* v. *A.P.C.* [1964] 1 W.L.R. 768 (H.L.).
[99] *McKibbin* v. *Glasgow Corporation*, 1920 S.C. 590, and *Haley* v. *London Elec. Board* [1965] A.C. 778 (blind persons); *Paris* v. *Stepney B.C.* [1951] A.C. 367 (man known to have only one eye); as to children, see *Taylor* v. *Glasgow Corp.*, 1922 S.C. (H.L.) 1; *Miller* v. *S.S.E.B.*, 1958 S.C. (H.L.) 20; *Hughes* v. *L.A.*, 1963 S.C. (H.L.) 31; also para. 32.14, *infra*.
[1] *Morris* v. *West Hartlepool Steam Navig. Co.* [1956] A.C. 552, *per* Lord Reid at p. 574; *per* Lord Cohen at p. 579; *Daborn* v. *Bath Tramways Co.* [1946] 2 All E.R. 333, *per* Asquith L.J. at p. 336.
[2] See, *e.g.*, *Watt* v. *Hertfordshire C.C.* [1954] 1 W.L.R. 835; also *Latimer* v. *A.E.C. Ltd.* [1953] A.C. 643, where it was held that failure to close a factory to prevent employees slipping on a flooded floor was not negligent.
[3] *Dickson* v. *Hygienic Institute*, 1910 S.C. 352; *cf. Kirkcaldy D.C.* v. *Household Manufacturing Ltd.*, 1987 S.L.T. 617.
[4] *Roe* v. *Minister of Health* [1954] 2 Q.B. 66.
[5] *Hunter* v. *Hanley*, 1955 S.C. 200.
[6] *Maynard* v. *West Midlands R.H.A.* [1984] 1 W.L.R. 634; *Gordon* v. *Wilson*, 1992 S.L.T. 849.
[7] *Peach* v. *Iain G. Chalmers & Co.*, 1992 S.C.L.R. 423.
[8] *Sidaway* v. *Bethlem Royal Hospital Governors & Ors.* [1985] A.C. 871; *Moyes* v. *Lothian Health Board*, 1990 S.L.T. 444.

concerned.[9] An advocate is protected from suit, at least as far as his conduct of a litigation is concerned,[10] although this immunity may not extend to opinion work.[11] A solicitor is also protected when acting on the instructions of counsel.[12]

32.10 **Negligence: Causation.**—Once negligence is established, liability depends upon proof that it caused the damage in issue. Where the alleged negligence was failure to provide a workman with a safety belt, it was suggested that there were four steps of causation: (1) a duty to supply a safety belt; (2) a breach; (3) that, if there had been a safety belt, the workman would have used it; and (4) that, if the workman had been using a safety belt, he would not have been killed, and the failure to prove the third step rendered the first two steps inoperative.[13] The first two steps, however, are not truly links in the chain of causation, the tracing of which does not begin until the question is posed—'Did the proven breach of duty cause this event?'[14] The pursuer's claim will fail if it can be demonstrated as a matter of fact that the event would have occurred even if the breach of duty had not taken place.[15] Where a number of factors contribute to an event, any one which makes a material contribution thereto will be treated as a cause for the purpose of establishing liability.[16] If the defender's conduct materially increased the risk of harm occurring, it will be treated as having made a material contribution.[17] Where there are a number of possible causes of a disease or disability, only one of which is the negligence of the defender, the onus remains on the pursuer to show that the negligence made at least a material contribution.[18] In a medical negligence case where the evidence demonstrated that on the balance of probabilities the disability was not caused by the negligence, it was held by the House of Lords that there was no scope for an award of damages to compensate for the loss of a chance of a better medical result.[19]

Once it has been established that the defender's conduct was a cause of the harm suffered by the pursuer, it is necessary to decide whether or not it was a cause of sufficient importance to lead to liability. Such a

[9] *Stewart* v. *McLean, Baird & Neilson*, 1915 S.C. 13; *County Personnel (Employment Agency) Ltd.* v. *Alan R. Pulver & Co.* [1987] 1 All E.R. 289.
[10] *Batchelor* v. *Pattison and Mackersy* (1876) 3 R. 914; *Rondel* v. *Worsley* [1969] 1 A.C. 191.
[11] *Saif Ali* v. *Sydney Mitchell & Co.* [1980] A.C. 198.
[12] *Batchelor, supra.*
[13] *McWilliams* v. *Wm. Arrol & Co.*, 1962 S.C. (H.L.) 70, *per* Lord Chancellor Kilmuir at p. 77. See also for failure to wear safety glasses, *McKinlay* v. *British Steel Corporation*, 1988 S.L.T. 810.
[14] See para. 32.1, *supra.*
[15] *Kay's Tutor* v. *Ayrshire & Arran Health Board*, 1987 S.L.T. 577; see, however, para. 32.11 for consideration of the effect on recovery of damages of evidence that a particular loss would still have been suffered by the pursuer but after a lapse of time.
[16] *Wardlaw* v. *Bonnington Castings*, 1956 S.C. (H.L.) 26.
[17] *McGhee* v. *National Coal Board*, 1973 S.C. (H.L.) 37.
[18] *Wilsher* v. *Essex Area Health Authority* [1988] A.C. 1074.
[19] *Hotson* v. *East Berkshire Area Health Authority* [1987] A.C. 750.

cause has been variously described as the real or efficient cause, or as the *causa causans*. The assessment of causation is 'dealt with broadly, and upon common sense principles as a jury would probably deal with it.'[20] Two or more causes may combine concurrently to cause an accident, with each being regarded as a *causa causans*.[21] Difficulty may arise when a number of factors operate consecutively to produce a result. The mere fact that a subsequent act of negligence has been the immediate cause of the disaster does not exonerate the original wrongdoer if there is no sufficient separation of time, place and circumstances to justify the exclusion of the original negligence as an efficient cause.[22] This principle applies even if the final act of negligence is that of the pursuer himself[23] unless the final act is held to be the sole efficient cause of the accident.[24] But the chain of causation between the original negligent act and the ultimate consequences may be broken by 'a new cause which disturbs the sequence of events, something which can be described as either unreasonable or extraneous or extrinsic, outside the exigencies of the emergency.'[25] That new cause may be some act by the injured party himself or by a third party. If it is held to break the chain of causation, it is known as a *novus actus interveniens*; and, in determining whether or not such an act is sufficient to break the chain, the test of reasonable foreseeability may be applied.

The pursuer's own act will break the chain of causation if the effect of it is to render useless the precaution desiderated by him,[26] or if he has acted in wilful defiance of orders,[27] but probably not if he has merely been careless (which results in apportionment of blame), and certainly not if he has acted reasonably in the circumstances.[28] An error of judgment made by the pursuer when acting in an emergency created by the defender's negligence will not break the chain.[29] While the

[20] *The Volute* v. *Admiralty Commissioners* [1922] A.C. 129, *per* Lord Chancellor Birkenhead at p. 136.
[21] *Boy Andrew* v. *St. Rognvald*, 1947 S.C. (H.L.) 70.
[22] *The Volute, supra, per* Lord Chancellor Birkenhead at pp. 144–45; see also *Grant* v. *Sun Shipping Co.*, 1948 S.C. (H.L.) 73, *per* Lord du Parcq at p. 94; *Stapley* v. *Gypsum Mines* [1953] A.C. 663, *per* Lord Reid at pp. 681–82; and *Drew* v. *Western S.M.T.*, 1947 S.C. 222; *Rouse* v. *Squires* [1973] 1 Q.B. 889; *Wright* v. *Lodge* [1993] 4 All E.R. 299.
[23] Blame is then apportioned under the Law Reform (Contributory Negligence) Act 1945; and see *Ross* v. *A.P.C.* [1964] 1 W.L.R. 768 (H.L.).
[24] See cases of deliberate disobedience of instructions referred to by Lord Reid in *Ross* v. *A.P.C., supra*, at pp. 776–77; and para. 34.4, *infra.*
[25] *Per* Lord Wright in *The Oropesa* [1943] P. 32, at p. 39.
[26] *e.g.* by refusing to wear a safety belt: see *McWilliams* v. *Wm. Arrol & Co.*, 1962 S.C. (H.L.) 70.
[27] See *Stapley* v. *Gypsum Mines Ltd.* [1953] A.C. 663; *Ginty* v. *Belmont Building Supplies* [1959] 1 All E.R. 414; *Horne* v. *Lec Refrigeration* [1965] 2 All E.R. 898; also *Crowe* v. *James Scott & Sons*, 1965 S.L.T. 54.
[28] *Steel* v. *Glasgow Iron & Steel Co.*, 1944 S.C. 237, in particular, Lord Jamieson at p. 268; *cf. Malcolm* v. *Dickson*, 1951 S.C. 542; *Macdonald* v. *MacBrayne*, 1915 S.C. 716. See also *Emeh* v. *Kensington Area Health Authority* [1985] Q.B. 1012 (reasonable to refuse to have an abortion after a failed sterilisation operation).
[29] See *S.S. Baron Vernon* v. *S.S. Metagama*, 1928 S.C. (H.L.) 21, *per* Viscount Dunedin at pp. 26–27.

deliberate unwarranted intervention of a third party will break the chain if it is thought to be the proximate cause or not reasonably foreseeable,[30] an act which is reasonable in the circumstances will not. So a man who threw a lighted squib into a crowded market place was found liable in damages to the person injured when it exploded, notwithstanding the fact that it had only reached the injured party through the intervention of two other people who, acting in the interests of their own safety, had picked it up and thrown it onwards.[31] There is liability for all the natural and probable consequences of the negligent act;[32] and the fact that the last link in the chain is a wrongful[33] or negligent[34] or voluntary act[35] of a third party will not exclude liability if that act is a reasonably foreseeable consequence of the defender's original negligence. Negligent conduct is more likely to break the chain of causation than non-negligent conduct and positive acts are more likely to do so than inaction.[36]

32.11 Negligence: Remoteness of Damage.—'A wrongdoer is not held responsible for all the results which flow from his negligent act. Practical considerations dictate, and the law accepts, that there comes a point in the sequence of events when liability can no longer be enforced.'[37] Liability for injury to a person or damage to property through negligence extends to all the natural and direct consequences of that injury or damage.[37a] There must be an unbroken causal connection between the original damage and every item of loss claimed to flow therefrom.[38] 'The grand rule on the subject of damages is that none can be claimed except such as naturally and directly arise out of the wrong done, and such, therefore, as may reasonably be supposed to have been in the view of the wrongdoer.'[39] Although this statement was made

---

[30] See *Weld-Blundell* v. *Stephens* [1920] A.C. 956; *cf. Marshall* v. *Caledonian Ry.* (1899) 1 F. 1060. See para. 32.4 for discussion of the separate but allied question of whether a defender not otherwise negligent is liable where the actions of a third party were the direct cause of loss.

[31] *Scott* v. *Shepherd* (1773) 2 W. Bl. 892; see also *Clark* v. *Chambers* (1878) 3 Q.B.D. 327; *The Oropesa* [1943] P. 32; and *Haynes* v. *Harwood* [1935] 1 K.B. 146.

[32] *Scott's Trs.* v. *Moss* (1887) 17 R. 32; *Miller* v. *S.S.E.B.*, 1958 S.C. (H.L.) 20; *Steel* v. *Glasgow Iron & Steel Co.*, 1944 S.C. 237, *per* Lord Jamieson at p. 268.

[33] *Marshall* v. *Caled. Ry.*, supra.

[34] *Miller* v. *S.S.E.B.*, supra; *cf. S.S. Singleton Abbey* v. *S.S. Paludina* [1927] A.C. 16.

[35] See *Haynes* v. *Harwood* [1935] 1 K.B. 146 (where boys caused horses to bolt), *Baker* v. *Hopkins* [1959] 1 W.L.R. 966 and *Hosie* v. *Arbroath Football Club*, 1978 S.L.T. 122.

[36] *Knightley* v. *Johns* [1982] 1 W.L.R. 349.

[37] *Malcolm* v. *Dickson*, 1951 S.C. 542, *per* Lord Justice-Clerk Thomson at p. 547.

[37a] Liability having been established by the reasonable foreseeability of the kind of damage sustained and the manner in which it was sustained: see para. 32.2, *supra*. See also *Adm. Commrs.* v. *S.S. Susquehanna* [1926] A.C. 655, *per* Lord Dunedin at p. 661; approved in *Hutchison* v. *Davidson*, 1945 S.C. 395, by Lord Russell at p. 404, and by Lord Moncrieff at p. 410, and by Lords Mackay and Patrick in *Pomphrey* v. *Cuthbertson*, 1951 S.C. 147, at pp. 157 and 162.

[38] See *The Vitruvia*, 1925 S.C. (H.L.) 1; *The Cameronia* v. *The Hauk*, 1928 S.L.T. 71; and *Carslogie S.S. Co.* v. *Royal Norwegian Govt.* [1952] A.C. 292.

[39] *Allan* v. *Barclay* (1864) 2 M. 873, *per* Lord Kinloch at p. 874.

obiter by Lord Kinloch, it is an accurate statement of the rule in Scotland governing liability for both the immediate and subsequent consequences of negligence. It is, however, open to construction. 'Naturally' means 'according to the ordinary, usual or normal course of things' and this includes reasonable human conduct.[40] 'Directly' means 'without any break in the chain of causation.'[41] Everything which arises in the ordinary course of things from the negligence without the intervention of any extraneous act or factor is in law deemed to have been in the view of the wrongdoer.[42] Damages which flow directly and naturally (*i.e.* in the ordinary course of things) from the wrongful act cannot be regarded as too remote.[43] While the foreseeability test may be of assistance in certain cases in determining whether the loss claimed has arisen from the negligent act 'in the ordinary course of things' and is, therefore, a natural, ordinary or normal result as opposed to an unnatural, extraordinary and abnormal result,[44] our law does not permit that test to be pressed to the length of excluding liability for any item of loss which has arisen naturally and directly (in the sense beforementioned) from the negligence. For example, there is liability for all medical expenses reasonably incurred as a natural and direct consequence of physical injury and this liability extends to the expense of unnecessary treatment wrongly, but not negligently, prescribed by doctors.[45] The foreseeability test cannot be applied first and in isolation exclude liability for such expenses.[46]

32.12 'The personal injuries of the individual himself will be properly held (*i.e.* deemed) to have been in the contemplation of the wrongdoer.'[47] In other words, the negligent party 'must take his victim as he finds him' and is liable for all the natural and direct effects of the original injury

---

[40] See *S.S. Baron Vernon* v. *S.S. Metagama*, 1928 S.C. (H.L.) 21, *per* Lord Haldane at p. 25; *The Oropesa* [1943] P. 32, *per* Lord Wright at pp. 37–38, *Steel* v. *Glasgow Iron & Steel Co.*, 1944 S.C. 237, at pp. 248 and 268; and *McKew* v. *Holland & Hannen & Cubitts (Scotland) Ltd.*, 1970 S.C. (H.L.) 20 where the pursuer was held to have acted unreasonably.

[41] See para. 32.10, *supra.*

[42] Note: If 'naturally' is construed in the broader sense above mentioned instead of the narrow sense of 'in the ordinary course of nature,' the difficulties created in England by the *Polemis* case ([1921] 3 K.B. 560) do not arise in respect that liability for the fire damage in both the *Polemis* case and *The Wagon Mound* ([1961] A.C. 388) must be excluded as being an unnatural (*i.e.* extraordinary or abnormal) consequence and such, therefore, as cannot reasonably be supposed to have been in the view of the wrongdoer.

[43] See *Clyde Navigation Trs.* v. *Bowring S.S. Co.*, 1929 S.C. 715, *per* Lord Hunter at p. 723, quoting Lord Herschell.

[44] See *Steel* v. *Glasgow Iron & Steel Co.*, 1944 S.C. 237, *per* Lord Justice-Clerk Cooper at p. 248, and *per* Lord Jamieson at p. 268.

[45] *Rubens* v. *Walker*, 1946 S.C. 215. If the treatment had been negligently prescribed, that negligence might be held on the facts to be a *novus actus interveniens* excluding the defender's liability for such expenses but exposing the doctors to a claim against them.

[46] See also *H.M.S. London* [1914] P. 72, where a claim for loss of use of a vessel in dock for collision repairs was allowed to cover the period of a shipyard strike as natural and direct loss.

[47] *Allan* v. *Barclay* (1864) 2 M. 873, *per* Lord Kinloch at p. 874.

on the particular pursuer.[48] These include the consequences of inappropriate medical treatment if that was not negligent.[49] Where, following a negligently performed sterilisation operation, the plaintiff became pregnant and gave birth to a handicapped child, it was held that the additional cost of caring for the child was not too remote to sound in damages.[50] But death by suicide is neither a natural nor a direct result of a moderate eye injury.[51] Similar rules regarding remoteness of damage apply to patrimonial loss. Where a house is damaged with the result that it is left unoccupied, the person liable for that damage is not liable for further damage caused by squatters who enter the empty property.[52] Probable loss due to prospects of promotion being prejudiced is relevant, but the loss of hypothetical gain is too remote.[53] It has been held that an injured company director and principal shareholder could not claim for a share of the profits lost by the company due to his absence from business because the company itself had no right of action and his loss was, therefore, too remote.[54] Lastly, in assessing the measure of damages applicable to the loss of working plant through negligence, extraordinary or abnormal loss, sustained by the owners as a result of their inability through impecuniosity to purchase a replacement, may be too remote, the financial embarrassment of the owners being an extrinsic and unusual factor which was the effective cause of that loss.[55] It has, however, been held that it was reasonable for a plaintiff to defer incurring expenditure on repairs, even though the deferral led to an increase in the cost of such repairs.[56] Unless the particular circumstances of the pursuer were or ought to have been known to the defender, the cost of obtaining loans will not be recoverable, it not being inevitable that the infliction of financial loss will lead to the need to borrow money.[57]

Where the wrongful act of a third party is not a consequence of the defender's negligence and so operates that the physical effects of that negligence are brought to an end and replaced by other and more serious injuries, the extent of the defender's liability in damages is

---

[48] *McKillen* v. *Barclay Curle & Co.*, 1967 S.L.T. 41. This also appears to be the law of England: see *Smith* v. *Leech Brain & Co.* [1962] 2 Q.B. 405.

[49] *Cf. Robinson* v. *Post Office* [1974] 1 W.L.R. 1176, where although there was negligence in the medical treatment that negligence was not a cause of the condition which resulted from the treatment and so did not constitute *novus actus interveniens*.

[50] *Emeh* v. *Kensington Area Health Authority* [1985] Q.B. 1012.

[51] *Cowan* v. *N.C.B.*, 1958 S.L.T. (Notes) 19. It may, however, be possible to establish death by suicide as a natural and direct consequence of a severe head injury.

[52] *Lamb* v. *Camden London Borough Council* [1981] Q.B. 625.

[53] See *McCall* v. *Foulis*, 1966 S.L.T. 47, and cases cited therein.

[54] *Young* v. *Ormiston*, 1936 S.L.T. 79; *cf. Lee* v. *Sheard* [1956] 1 Q.B. 192, where the Court of Appeal held that the pursuer could recover his share of lost profits *because* the company could not.

[55] See *Liesbosch* v. *S.S. Edison* [1933] A.C. 449, in particular Lord Wright at pp. 460 and 465–466.

[56] *Dodd Properties (Kent) Ltd.* v. *Canterbury C.C.* [1980] 1 W.L.R. 433.

[57] *Margrie Holdings Ltd.* v. *City of Edinburgh D.C.*, 1994 S.L.T. 971.

unaffected. Thus where a plaintiff sustained leg injuries caused by the fault of the defendant and was subsequently shot in the same leg by criminals with the result that the leg had to be amputated, it was held that the defendant was liable not only for the consequences of his negligent act up to the time of amputation but also for the damages prospectively attributable to his act if the shooting had not taken place.[58] That decision is, however, difficult to reconcile with the principle that, in assessing the extent of the pursuer's loss attributable to the defender, all relevant factors are to be taken into account including those which limit the effect of the defender's act.[59] Where the supervening act or event is not wrongful it may have the effect of restricting the extent of the defender's liability. So, where, as a result of his employer's negligence an employee suffered a partially disabling injury and some three years later a totally disabling and unconnected condition supervened, it was held that the occurrence of that total disability could not be disregarded and the damages for which the employer was liable were reduced accordingly.[60]

32.13 **Proof of Negligence: *Res Ipsa Loquitur*.**—The burden of proving negligence generally rests upon the pursuer and it must be established on 'the balance of probabilities.'[61] Thus the decision may ultimately turn upon the question of whether or not the pursuer has discharged the burden of proving negligence.[62] In some cases the pursuer may establish a prima facie case of negligence which transfers to the defender a tactical burden of proving that he was not negligent.[63] The pursuer may be assisted in establishing a prima facie case by proving that the defender was convicted of an offence in connection with the circumstances of the accident.[64] In other cases the admitted or proved fact that an accident occurred may *per se* yield an inference of negligence which must be negatived by the defender.[65] It is to the latter type of case 'where the thing is shown to be under the management of the defendant or his servants, and the accident is such as in the ordinary case does not happen if those who have the management use proper care,'[66] that the maxim *res ipsa loquitur* ('the thing itself speaks')

[58] *Baker* v. *Willoughby* [1970] A.C. 467.
[59] See *Dalgleish* v. *Glasgow Corporation*, 1976 S.C. 32, where it was held *obiter* that the death of the child who was the subject of the award of damages before the case was heard in the Inner House should not be taken into account in the appeal.
[60] *Jobling* v. *Associated Dairies* [1982] A.C. 794.
[61] *Hendry* v. *Clan Line Steamers*, 1949 S.C. 320.
[62] *Ibid., per* Lord Justice-Clerk Thomson at p. 322; see also *Brown* v. *Rolls Royce Ltd.*, 1960 S.C. (H.L.) 22, *per* Lord Denning, as to the difference between the legal and provisional burden of proof.
[63] See, *e.g. Gunn* v. *McAdam*, 1949 S.C. 31.
[64] Law Reform (Misc. Provs.) (Scotland) Act 1968, s. 10.
[65] See, *e.g. Ballard* v. *N.B. Ry. Co.*, 1923 S.C. (H.L.) 43; *McQueen* v. *The Glasgow Garden Festival (1988) Ltd.*, 1995 S.L.T. 211.
[66] *Per* Erle C.J. in *Scott* v. *London, etc., Docks Co.* (1865) 3 H. & C. 596, adopted by the House of Lords in *Ballard* v. *N.B. Ry. Co., supra.*

applies. It is a presumption of law to which, therefore, if the conditions for its operation are satisfied, effect must be given.[67] In this as in other similar cases 'it is the policy of the law that intervenes to relax the logical stringency of proof and so invert the normal onus in order to avoid denial of justice to those whose rights depend on facts incapable of proof by them, and often exclusively within the knowledge and control of their opponent.'[68] Thus where shop owners were sued as a result of an accident due to spillage on the floor of the shop it was held that there was an onus on them to show that the accident did not occur through want of care on their part.[69] Once the onus is inverted, the defender can only exclude liability by proof that he was not negligent. It has been said, however, that it is essential to the application of *res ipsa loquitur* that the pursuer cannot reasonably be expected to know the exact cause of the accident and that, if he does, he must aver the cause and prove negligence. If the *res* does not *per se* exclude the possibility of the event having been caused by the pursuer or a third party for whom the defender is not responsible,[70] the pursuer, in order to establish a prima facie case, must adduce evidence which, if accepted, excludes interference by the pursuer and third parties.[71] If the pursuer fails to establish a prima facie case by his evidence, the legal burden of proving negligence remains on the pursuer throughout.[72]

If the cause of an accident is averred by the pursuer to have been a defect in the defender's plant, the onus of proving that the defect was patent (*i.e.* discoverable by reasonable inspection) and that the defender was at fault in failing to discover it is on the pursuer.[73] If the pursuer does not aver the exact nature of the defect and cannot reasonably be expected to do so, proof by the pursuer that the plant collapsed brings the maxim *res ipsa loquitur* into play so that the defender must exculpate himself.[74] If the defender pleads that the defect was latent and, therefore, not ascertainable by reasonable examination, the defender must prove that defence.[75] But the defender will not exculpate himself by proving only that the defect was latent if it is a reasonable

[67] *Henderson* v. *Henry E. Jenkins and Sons* [1970] A.C. 282.

[68] *Elliot* v. *Young's Bus Service*, 1945 S.C. 445, *per* Lord Justice-Clerk Cooper at p. 456; see also p. 454, where the Lord Justice-Clerk points out that it is 'unsafe to generalise upon the question of who must prove what without due regard to the precise legal relationship between the parties.'

[69] *Ward* v. *Tesco Stores* [1976] 1 W.L.R. 810.

[70] See *Macfarlane* v. *Thompson* (1884) 12 R. 232.

[71] *Inglis* v. *L.M.S. Ry. Co.*, 1941 S.C. 551; *cf. Easson* v. *L. & N.E.R.* [1944] K.B. 421; *Lloyds* v. *West Midlands Gas Board* [1971] 1 W.L.R. 749.

[72] *Connelly* v. *L.M.S. Ry. Co.*, 1940 S.C. 477; see also *Moore* v. *R. Fox & Sons* [1956] 1 Q.B. 596 (alternative ground).

[73] *Gavin* v. *Rogers* (1889) 17 R. 206; *Milne* v. *Townsend* (1892) 19 R. 830.

[74] *Macaulay* v. *Buist & Co.* (1846) 9 D. 245; *Fraser* v. *Fraser* (1882) 9 R. 896; *Walker* v. *Olsen* (1882) 9 R. 946.

[75] *Elliot* v. *Young's Bus Service*, 1945 S.C. 445, *per* Lord Justice-Clerk Cooper at p. 456; *Gibson* v. *Concrete*, 1954 S.L.T. (Notes) 7; see also *Moore* v. *R. Fox, supra, per* Evershed M.R. at pp. 611–612.

inference from the whole evidence that careless handling of the plant was an effective cause of the breakage.[76] If the exact cause of the accident is unknown to either party, proof or admission of the accident throws upon the defender the burden of proving that it happened without negligence on his part (*i.e.* that he had taken reasonable care in the circumstances of the case).[77] In the case of defective plant the defender may achieve this by proving that the plant was regularly and properly inspected and no defect found.[78]

Where the accident is of a kind which may occur without fault on the part of the person having control of the object causing the accident (*e.g.* a vehicle) *res ipsa non loquitur*. In such cases the pursuer must first establish a prima facie case of negligence by proving that the vehicle stopped or swerved suddenly for no apparent reason; thereafter, the defender can only exculpate himself by proving a reason for the driver's emergency action which negatives negligence on his part.[79] If, however, the pursuer avers that the sudden stop or swerve was made in order to avoid a collision with some person or thing on the roadway, the onus of proving negligence remains on the pursuer throughout.[80]

In Scotland, therefore, once the pursuer has established a prima facie case, or has led sufficient evidence to invoke the maxim *res ipsa loquitur*, the court will find for the pursuer unless the defender has cleared himself of negligence by 'full legal proof.'[81] But the pursuer is tied to his pleadings. Where the case established in evidence differs from that made out by the pursuer in his pleadings, he will not succeed on a case which is 'new, separate and distinct' but will be successful if the case made out in evidence is only a variation, modification or development of the case in his pleadings.[82]

32.14 Occupiers' Liability (Scotland) Act 1960.[83]—The effect of this Act is to abolish the categories of invitee, licensee and trespasser which were introduced to the law of Scotland in 1929 by the House of Lords' decision in *Dumbreck* v. *Addie & Sons*.[84] Section 2 of the Act provides:

[76] *Ballard* v. *N.B. Ry. Co.*, 1923 S.C. (H.L.) 43.

[77] *Elliot* v. *Young's Bus Service, supra; Marshall & Son* v. *Russian Oil Products*, 1938 S.C. 773, *per* Lord Justice-Clerk Aitchison at p. 791; *Devine* v. *Colvilles*, 1969 S.C. (H.L.) 67. See also *Woods* v. *Duncan (The Thetis)* [1946] A.C. 401.

[78] *Devine* v. *Colvilles, supra; Elliot* v. *Young's Bus Service, supra, per* Lord Justice-Clerk Cooper at pp. 454–455.

[79] *Mars* v. *Glasgow Corp.*, 1940 S.C. 202; *O'Hara* v. *Central S.M.T. Co.*, 1941 S.C. 363; *Doonan* v. *S.M.T.*, 1950 S.C. 136. See also *Roberts* v. *Matthew Logan*, 1966 S.L.T. 77; *Ludgate* v. *Lovett* [1969] 1 W.L.R. 1016.

[80] *Ballingall* v. *Glasgow Corp.*, 1948 S.C. 160; see also *McGregor* v. *Dundee Corp.*, 1962 S.C. 15, where the court inferred that a skid was caused by excessive speed.

[81] *O'Hara* v. *Central S.M.T., supra.*

[82] *Burns* v. *Dixon's Iron Works Ltd.*, 1961 S.C. 102; *McCusker* v. *Saveheat Cavity Wall Insulation Ltd.*, 1987 S.L.T. 24; *cf. Connelly* v. *L.M.S. Ry. Co.*, 1940 S.C. 477.

[83] See Walker, *Delict*, pp. 581–599. There is a similar, but not identical, Act for England: Occupiers' Liability Act 1957.

[84] 1929 S.C. (H.L.) 51; now disapproved even as a statement of the duty owed to a trespasser (*British Railways Board* v. *Herrington* [1972] A.C. 877).

'The care which an occupier of premises is required, by reason of his occupation or control of the premises, to show towards a person entering thereon in respect of dangers which are due to the state of the premises or to anything done or omitted to be done on them and for which the occupier is in law responsible shall, except in so far as he is entitled to and does extend, restrict, modify or exclude by agreement his obligations towards that person, be such care as in all the circumstances of the case is reasonable to see that that person will not suffer injury or damage by reason of any such danger.' 'Occupier of premises' is defined in section 1(1) as 'a person occupying or having control of land or other premises.' This includes 'any fixed or moveable structure, including any vessel, vehicle or aircraft' and the duty extends towards all persons and property on such premises.[85] The Act substantially restores the pre-1929 common law relating to the duties of occupiers of land[86] and the 'category' decisions between 1929 and 1959 are no longer relevant except on the question of 'control.'

The statutory concept of occupation or control is the same as the common law basis of liability, namely, possession and control.[87] The duty of care rests upon the person who has the right and means in the circumstances of taking effective steps to protect the visitor from the particular danger whether by removal, notice, fencing or forbidding entry to the premises.[88] Thus physical occupation *per se* will not impose the duty on a resident. The duty is owed by the occupier only if he is in control of the premises; if he is not, the obligation rests upon the party in control,[89] who may be the owner or tenant or a contractor conducting operations on the premises.[90]

The Act does not differentiate between public and private property, and the degree of care required from any occupier to any individual is deducible from and referable to the particular facts of the case.[91] Accordingly, there is no general rule as to the liability of an occupier for damage caused by the faulty work of an independent contractor

[85] 1960 Act, s. 1(3). See *A.M.F. International* v. *Magnet Bowling* [1968] 1 W.L.R. 1028.
[86] See *Shillinglaw* v. *Turner*, 1925 S.C. 807, *per* Lord President Clyde at p. 816; *per* Lord Sands at p. 820; and Walker, Vol. II, pp. 595–596.
[87] See *Laurie* v. *Mags of Aberdeen*, 1911 S.C. 1226; and *Laing* v. *Paull and Williamsons*, 1912 S.C. 196; *Kennedy* v. *Shotts Iron Co. Ltd.*, 1913 S.C. 1143; *McIlwaine* v. *Stewart's Trs.*, 1914 S.C. 934.
[88] *Murdoch* v. *A. & R. Scott*, 1956 S.C. 309; *Devlin* v. *Jeffray's Trs.* (1902) 5 F. 130, where owner had no right of entry.
[89] *Kennedy* v. *Shotts Iron Co.*, *supra*; *McPhail* v. *Lanarkshire C.C.*, 1951 S.C. 301; *Wheat* v. *Lacon & Co.* [1966] A.C. 552, where the House of Lords held that the owners were occupiers of premises although their manager resided there under a service agreement.
[90] See *Murdoch* v. *A. & R. Scott, supra*; also *Hartwell* v. *Grayson, etc., Docks* [1947] K.B. 901; *Telfer* v. *Glasgow Corpn.*, 1974 S.L.T. (Notes) 51.
[91] See *McKinley* v. *Darngarvil Coal Co.*, 1923 S.C. (H.L.) 34, *per* Lord Dunedin at p. 37; *cf. McMurray* v. *Glasgow School Board*, 1916 S.C. 9, where there was no averment that the occupiers knew that the gate was being used as a swing.

employed by him.[92] The dangers which section 2 of the Act requires the occupier to guard against are those which are (a) due to the state of the premises; (b) due to anything done on the premises; and (c) due to anything omitted to be done on the premises. 'The state of the premises' certainly covers all dangers due to structural defects[93] and poisonous shrubs,[94] and probably also to unfenced shafts or excavations,[95] although the latter may be alternatively classified as a danger due to omission (i.e. to fence). Machinery which is not in use, such as an unlocked turntable upon which children were known to play,[96] must also come under this head. 'Anything done on the premises' covers all dangers created by operations thereon[97] and is probably wide enough to cover keeping a vicious dog[98] and placing a savage horse in a field used by the public.[99] While the failure to fence or light holes and keep doors leading to cellars locked[1] may be classified under 'state' or 'omission,' some dangers created by operations carried on may be due to omissions, e.g. the failure of a railway company's employees to close carriage doors before a train started.[2]

While the standard of care required of the occupier is that of the reasonable, prudent man, the degree of care required is 'such care as in all the circumstances of the case is reasonable.' The antiquity of a building may be a circumstance to be taken into account.[3] The type of person likely to be present will also affect the range of care, which will vary from the maximum, in the case of a very young child on the premises for the first time by invitation of the occupier and known to him to be unaccompanied by an adult, to the minimum in the case of a trespasser whose presence is unknown to the occupier. 'The section applies both to trespassers and to persons entering property by invitation or licence express or implied. But that does not mean that the occupier must always show equal care for the safety of all such persons ... In deciding what degree of care is required, ... regard must be had both to the position of the occupier and to the position of the person entering his premises and it may often be reasonable to hold that an occupier must do more to protect a person whom he permits to be on

---

[92] See para. 33.9, last subpara.

[93] See Glegg, pp. 295–307.

[94] See *Taylor* v. *Glasgow Corp.*, 1922 S.C. (H.L.) 1.

[95] See Glegg, pp. 274–279, 281–282.

[96] *Cooke* v. *M.G.W. Ry. of Ireland* [1909] A.C. 229.

[97] e.g. *Messer* v. *Cranston* (1897) 25 R. 7 (defective stow); *Ross* v. *McCallum's Trs.*, 1922 S.C. 322 (petrol in water pail); *Excelsior Wire Rope Co.* v. *Callan* [1930] A.C. 404 and *Murdoch* v. *A. & R. Scott, supra* (moving machinery).

[98] *Smillies* v. *Boyd* (1886) 14 R. 150; *Hill* v. *Lovett*, 1992 S.L.T. 994.

[99] *Lowery* v. *Walker* [1911] A.C. 10.

[1] *Cairns* v. *Boyd* (1879) 6 R. 1004.

[2] *Tough* v. *N.B. Ry. Co.*, 1914 S.C. 291. For additional examples of dangers on land and premises, see cases cited in Glegg, pp. 60–72, and in Walker, *Delict*, p. 591.

[3] *Hogg* v. *Historic Building & Monuments Commission for England* [1989] C.L.Y. 2573.

his property than he need do to protect a person who enters the property without permission.'[4] An occupier may not be required to fence a quarry or other dangerous place which is so far from a public road that it is not reasonably foreseeable that members of the public will come near it,[5] but secure fencing will be necessary if injury to the particular victim is reasonably foreseeable through proximity of the danger to a public road[6] or otherwise.[7] While the pre-1929 law relating to trespassers was far from clear,[8] the Act now imposes upon an occupier the duty of taking such care as is reasonable in the circumstances to protect from reasonably foreseeable injury a trespasser whose presence is reasonably foreseeable. In the case of a boy injured while climbing an electric transformer, that duty was held to be discharged by the erection of a barrier which could only be overcome by a deliberate act intended to defeat its obvious function.[9] The age and capacity of persons entering premises are relevant considerations along with the likelihood of them being there. 'A measure of care appropriate to the inability or disability of those who are immature or feeble in mind or body is due from others who know of, or ought to anticipate, the presence of such persons within the scope and hazard of their own operations.'[10] The Act probably does not alter the law that the owner of a public park is not required to fence obvious dangers, such as a pond[11] or a river bank,[12] against which it is the duty of parents to protect their children; but parents are entitled to rely on such proprietors taking reasonable care to protect their children from injury from anything in the nature of a hidden danger or trap, whether natural or artificial.[13] And a very high degree of care is incumbent upon local authorities who provide children's playgrounds and thus invite parents to send their children there unaccompanied.[14]

[4] *McGlone* v. *B.R.B.*, 1966 S.L.T. 2 (H.L.), *per* Lord Reid at p. 9.

[5] *Prentices* v. *Assets Co.* (1890) 17 R. 484; *Holland* v. *Lanarkshire C.C.*, 1909 S.C. 1142, *per* Lord President Dunedin at p. 1149; *Melville* v. *Renfrewshire C.C.*, 1920 S.C. 61.

[6] *Black* v. *Cadell* (1804) Mor. 13905; *Gibson* v. *Glasgow Police Commrs.* (1893) 20 R. 466 (a public highway case, but the ratio is relevant to s. 2 of the Act).

[7] *Hislop* v. *Durham* (1842) 4 D. 1168; *McFeat* v. *Rankin's Trs.* (1879) 6 R. 1043; *British Railways Board* v. *Herrington* [1972] A.C. 877.

[8] See *McGlone* v. *B.R.B.*, *supra, per* Lord Reid at p. 9.

[9] *McGlone* v. *B.R.B.*, *supra.* 'The liability of an occupier cannot fairly be made to depend on the outcome of a conflict between his precautions to exclude entry and the ingenuity and agility of a youthful and determined trespasser': *per* Lord Guthrie at p. 8.

[10] *Per* Lord Sumner, *Taylor* v. *Glasgow Corp.*, 1922 S.C. (H.L.) 1, at p. 15; see also *Johnstone* v. *Mags. of Lochgelly*, 1913 S.C. 1078, *per* Lord Kinnear at p. 1089; *Cooke* v. *M.G.W. Ry. of Ireland* [1909] A.C. 229, *per* Lord Atkinson at p. 238: 'The duty ... must ... be measured by his [the occupier's] knowledge, actual or imputed, of the habits, capacities and propensities of those persons,' and *Southern Portland Cement* v. *Cooper* [1974] A.C. 623.

[11] *Hastie* v. *Mags. of Edinburgh*, 1907 S.C. 1102.

[12] *Stevenson* v. *Glasgow Corp.*, 1908 S.C. 1034.

[13] *Taylor* v. *Glasgow Corp.*, 1922 S.C. (H.L.) 1 (poisonous berries); and see Lord Shaw at pp. 10–12.

[14] *Plank* v. *Stirling Mags.*, 1956 S.C. 92. See Lord Justice-Clerk Thomson at pp. 105, 107; Lord Patrick at p. 115; and Lord Mackintosh at p. 118.

32.15 Exclusion of Occupier's Liability.—Section 2(1) of the Act permits an occupier, in so far as he is entitled to do so,[15] to extend, restrict, modify or exclude his obligations to any person by agreement, *i.e.* by contract, written or verbal.[16] The English Act[17] adds 'or otherwise' which seems to permit this to be done by the mere posting of a restricting or exempting notice,[18] whereas the Scottish Act does not. But the existence of such a notice in relation to a particular danger would be a relevant factor in determining whether or not the injured party had agreed to run the risk of injury through the occupier's lack of care, since the defence of *volenti non fit injuria* is expressly retained by the Act.[19] Where the premises are used for the business purposes of the occupier these rules on exclusion of liability have now to be read subject to the provisions of the Unfair Contract Terms Act 1977.[20]

32.16 Landlord's Liability.—Where premises are occupied or used by virtue of a tenancy or subtenancy under which the landlord is responsible for maintenance or repair of the premises, section 3 of the Act imposes on the landlord the same duty of care towards persons or property as section 2(1) imposes on the occupier, but only in respect of dangers arising from faulty maintenance or repair.[21] 'Tenancy' includes a statutory tenancy which does not in law amount to a tenancy[22] and includes also any contract conferring a right of occupation.[23] This section alters the law laid down in *Cameron* v. *Young*,[24] and anyone in the house, be he tenant, member of the tenant's family, lodger or visitor, now has a title to sue the landlord for injury caused through breach of his duty. Section 3 is silent as to the right of a landlord to vary his statutory liability by agreement. It seems that he retains the right, in appropriate circumstances, to plead *volenti non fit injuria*.[25] The Act applies to the Crown.[26] The Housing (Scotland) Act 1987[27] imposes obligations regarding maintenance on the landlords of let properties.[28]

---

[15] *e.g.* the operator of a public service vehicle is not entitled to do so: see Public Passenger Vehicles Act 1981, s. 29.

[16] *e.g.* by notice on ticket of such conditions: see para. 5.12, *supra* (ticket cases).

[17] 1957, s. 2(1).

[18] See *Ashdown* v. *Williams* [1957] 1 Q.B. 409, decided before the English Act was passed.

[19] s. 2(3). See para. 34.1, *infra*, and *McGlone* v. *B.R.B.*, *supra, per* Lord Pearce at p. 12.

[20] 1977, s. 16. See para. 34.1, *infra*.

[21] For illustrations of the extent of his liability, see Walker, Vol. II, pp. 603–607.

[22] *i.e.* under the Rent Acts: see Chap. 41, *infra*.

[23] *e.g.* under a service agreement.

[24] 1908 S.C. (H.L.) 7.

[25] See para. 41.9, *supra*.

[26] See s. 4.

[27] s. 113 and Sched. 10.

[28] See para. 41.7.

32.17 Public Roads and Streets.[29]—The Occupiers' Liability Act does not apply to public roads, streets or footpaths which at common law or by public or private Acts are the responsibility of public bodies. Public authorities responsible for the management and maintenance of public roads, streets and footpaths are bound to take reasonable care to maintain them in a condition safe for use by all members of the public.[30] They are liable to individuals injured by any type of danger of which they knew or ought to have known if regular inspections had been made.[31] A local authority is not liable, however, for a defect in a footpath of such a nature as to be obvious to a pedestrian exercising reasonable care for his own safety.[32] As the basis of liability is 'possession and control,' the owner of the solum of a footpath is not liable for defects therein unless he also has control of it;[33] but he may be jointly liable with the local authority for failure to fence off a dangerous subsidence.[34] And a local authority may assume by private Act a joint responsibility with the owner for the safety of a private footpath.[35] Works on roads and streets by the providers of public services are controlled by a code laid down in the New Roads and Street Works Act 1991. In England it was held that the previous Act[36] did not confer upon an individual the right to bring an action for breach of statutory duty[37] although decisions under previous statutes tended to suggest that there would be such liability.[38] In Scotland, when the Gas Board were sued under the previous Act, they did not challenge the allegations of breach of statutory duty and it was held that the Act did not diminish the responsibility of a local authority.[39]

Further Reading

Charlesworth & Percy, *Negligence* (8th ed. 1990).
Jackson & Powell, *Professional Negligence* (3rd ed. 1992).
Thomson, *Delictual Liability* (1994).
Walker, *The Law of Delict in Scotland* (2nd ed. 1981).

---

[29] See Glegg, pp. 104–05, 301–03; and Walker, *Delict*, pp. 599–608. As to liability for hazardous work, see 33.9, *infra*.

[30] Including blind persons; see *McKibbin* v. *Glasgow Corp.*, 1920 S.C. 590; *Haley* v. *L.E.B.* [1965] A.C. 778; and see para. 32.8, *supra*.

[31] The English distinction between liability for misfeasance and no liability for nonfeasance is not part of the law of Scotland.

[32] *McClafferty* v. *British Telecommunications plc.*, 1987 S.L.T. 327.

[33] *Laing* v. *Paull & Williamsons*, 1912 S.C. 196.

[34] *Laurie* v. *Mags. of Aberdeen*, 1911 S.C. 1226.

[35] *Rush* v. *Glasgow Corp.*, 1947 S.C. 580; *Kinnell* v. *Glasgow Corp.*, 1950 S.C. 573; *Black* v. *Glasgow Corp.*, 1958 S.C. 260.

[36] Public Utilities Street Works Act 1950.

[37] *Keating* v. *Elvan Reinforced Concrete* [1968] 2 All E.R. 139.

[38] See Charlesworth & Percy, para. 11–17, p. 851.

[39] *McNair* v. *Dunfermline Corporation*, 1953 S.C. 183.

CHAPTER 33

STRICT LIABILITY AND STATUTORY DUTY

It is not always necessary for an injured party to aver and prove that the defender was negligent in the sense of failing to exercise reasonable care. In certain cases, it is sufficient for the pursuer to prove that an act or omission occurred to cause him loss. Liability imposed without proof of negligence is termed absolute or strict liability. Strict liability for certain actions is imposed at common law or by statute. In other situations, the defender is vicariously liable for the negligence of another person, usually because of the nature of the relationship between the defender and that person. Examples of strict liability at common law are: (1) Edictal liability; (2) Unintentional slander; and (3) Liability for flooding damage caused by interference with the natural flow of water. The last mentioned example is considered in this chapter, as are particular areas of activity where liability is now regulated by statute, namely damage caused by animals or by defective products. Finally, vicarious liability is examined. Even where the pursuer is able to found on a rule of strict liability and does not require to show that the defender was negligent, he will still require to show that there has been a breach of duty and that the breach caused him loss which he is entitled to recover. Concepts already discussed in the context of negligence-based liability such as causation and remoteness of damage[1] will still therefore be relevant.

33.1 **Strict Liability: Interference with Natural Flow of Water.**—Anyone who erects a *novum opus* in a stream on his own property for the purpose of collecting water in a dam is liable for damage to adjacent property caused by flooding which would not have occurred if the stream had been left unaltered.[2] An unprecedented fall of rain is not a *damnum fatale* which exempts the proprietor from liability.[2a] The Lord Ordinary (Ardmillan) decided this case on the ground that the failure of the defender's dam raised a presumption of fault which he had not rebutted, but the Lord Justice-Clerk (Hope) at one point required the defender to 'secure' his works against danger.[3] This decision was approved by the

---

[1] See Chap. 32.
[2] *Kerr* v. *Earl of Orkney* (1857) 20 D. 298.
[2a] *Ibid.*
[3] *Ibid.*, at pp. 301 and 302.

House of Lords on the basis of strict liability in *Caledonian Railway Co.*
v. *Greenock Corporation.*[4] The reasoning behind the imposition of strict
liability has been stated to be that either the work could not be done
without causing damage to a neighbour, and therefore should not have
been done at all, or it was carried out negligently.[4a]

In the early editions of this book the learned authors and editors
treated as applicable to Scotland the general rule of *Rylands* v.
Fletcher,[5] namely, 'that a man who brings anything to land which, if it
escapes, is likely to cause injury, does so at his peril.' That view is,
however, controversial. It has been said that this 'extreme form of the
rule of absolute liability is simply a modern revival or survival of the
medieval principle of English common law that a man acts at his peril,'[6]
which has never been part of Scots law. While support for the
application of the broad *Rylands* v. *Fletcher* principle can be found in
the opinions delivered in *Chalmers* v. *Dixon*,[7] all the judges considered
the defenders to have been at fault in accumulating on their land a huge
bing of combustible materials, presumably on the ground that they knew
or ought to have known that they were liable to ignite and emit noxious
fumes to the harm of neighbouring properties and their crops. In *Miller*
v. *Robert Addie & Sons' Collieries*[8] Lord Justice-Clerk Aitchison
pointed out that 'in those cases in which the doctrine of *Rylands* v.
Fletcher has been held to apply, the obligation to take adequate
precautions has been of so onerous and imperative a kind that the mere
occurrence of damage and injury has of itself been sufficient to justify
an inference of negligence. In *Rylands* v. *Fletcher* negligence on the part
of the engineer who had constructed the reservoir was expressly found
to be established.' Accordingly, it has been argued that cases such as
Kerr v. *Earl of Orkney* and *Caledonian Railway Co.* v. *Greenock
Corporation* could now be decided on the ground that the facts raised an
almost irrebuttable presumption of negligence, flood damage being a
reasonably foreseeable consequence of the work done.[9] They were not,
however, so decided and should, rather than *Rylands* v. *Fletcher*, be
seen as the source of a Scottish doctrine of strict liability which extends

---

[4] 1917 S.C. (H.L.) 56.

[4a] *G.A. Estates Ltd.* v. *Caviapen Trs. Ltd. (No. 1)*, 1993 S.L.T. 1037 at p. 1041.

[5] (1866) L.R. 1 Ex. 265; (1868) L.R. 3 H.L. 330.

[6] *Per* Lord President Cooper in *McLaughlan* v. *Craig*, 1948 S.C. 599 at p. 610; see also
Bell, *Prin.*, § 970; the Reparation section in Green's *Encyclopaedia of the Law of
Scotland*, Vol. 12, contributed by the late Hector McKechnie, Q.C., especially at
pp. 488–496; Glegg, pp. 18–21; Smith, *Short Commentary*, pp. 642–647; and Walker, Vol.
II, pp. 973–985.

[7] (1876) 3 R. 461; see also *Gemmill's Trs.* v. *Cross* (1906) 14 S.L.T. 576; *Reynolds* v.
Lanarkshire Tramways Co. (1908) 16 S.L.T. 230; and *Western Silver Fox Ranch* v. *Ross &
Cromarty C.C.*, 1940 S.C. 601 (as to which, see criticism in Walker, *supra*, at
pp. 984–985).

[8] 1934 S.C. 150, at p. 155.

[9] See 7th ed. of this book where it is also suggested that *Rylands* v. *Fletcher* could have
been decided on the vicarious liability of the proprietor for the negligence of his agent.

at least to interference by a *novum opus* with the natural flow of water on land. There is, moreover, no principle which can readily justify the limitation of the doctrine to such cases. That someone who creates a risk should be strictly liable for its consequences is not a medieval peculiarity but is to be found, applied to circumstances of peculiar danger, in Roman law and in modern systems. A number of Scottish authorities support this extension.[10] In general, however, *culpa*, as the established basis of liability, has been applied to cases in which a thing or operation inherently dangerous causes damage to persons or property, as to other cases.[11] There is no liability for the detonation of dangerous articles, such as fireworks, without proof of fault.[11a] Where an operation not inherently dangerous caused damage by altering the quantity and quality of surface water draining on to a neighbour's land, it was held that it was necessary to show *culpa* before liability could result.[12] There is no liability for the escape of domestic gas[13] or water[14] without proof of negligence, but the greater the risk, the greater the degree of care required.[15]

33.2   Strict Liability: Statutory Liability.[16]—Breach of statutory provisions or regulations which prescribe the degree of care to be exercised in particular circumstances may reasonably be described as 'statutory negligence,'[17] notwithstanding the fact that the degree prescribed is higher than that required by the common law. But in some cases on grounds of policy there is imposed an absolute duty, which amounts to insurance and is not related to care.[18] In such cases, while a plea of contributory negligence may competently be taken, neither inevitable accident nor *volenti non fit injuria*[19] may be pled in defence. Most cases involving strict liability under statute arise in relation to industrial safety legislation. There is also strict liability for injury or property damage

---

[10] See n. 7, *supra*.

[11] *Mackintosh* v. *Mackintosh* (1864) 2 M. 1357 (escape of muir-burning fire to neighbour's lands); *Gray* v. *Caley Ry. Co.*, 1912 S.C. 339 (hot cinders from railway engine); *Gilmour* v. *Simpson*, 1958 S.C. 477 (fire caused by painter's blow-lamp).

[11a] *McQueen* v. *The Glasgow Garden Festival (1988) Ltd.*, 1995 S.L.T. 211.

[12] *Noble's Trs.* v. *Economic Forestry (Scotland) Ltd.*, 1988 S.L.T. 662.

[13] *McLaughlan* v. *Craig*, 1948 S.C. 599.

[14] *Moffat* v. *Park* (1877) 5 R. 13; *Miller* v. *Addie & Sons' Collieries*, 1934 S.C. 150; *R. Wylie Hill & Co.* v. *Glasgow Corp.*, 1951 S.L.T. (Notes) 3.

[15] *Muir* v. *Glasgow Corp.*, 1943 S.C. (H.L.) 3, *per* Lord Macmillan, at p. 10; *Gilmour* v. *Simpson*, *supra*, *per* Lord Wheatley at p. 479.

[16] Note that civil liability for the breach of a statutory provision does not automatically arise. The statute may provide expressly for liability to attach to breach of its provisions; otherwise it is a question of construction whether or not a right of action is conferred on an individual affected by the breach of a statutory provision. See para. 31.3, *supra*.

[17] *Per* Lord President Cooper in *Hamilton & Co.* v. *Anderson & Co.*, 1953 S.C. 129, at p. 137; and see Smith, *Short Commentary*, pp. 639–641.

[18] *e.g.* see Factories Act 1961, s. 22(1): 'Every hoist or lift shall be ... properly maintained,' *i.e.* in efficient working order (s. 176(1)); *Millar* v. *Galashiels Gas Co.*, 1949 S.C. (H.L.) 31. See also para. 33.9, *infra*.

[19] See *I.C.I.* v. *Shatwell* [1965] A.C. 656.

caused by nuclear installations[20] and for damage caused by the unauthorised deposit of waste on land.[21]

33.3 Liability for Animals.—Liability for animals is mainly regulated by the provisions of the Animals (Scotland) Act 1987. The Act provides that if an animal belongs to a species whose members generally are by virtue of their physical attributes or habits likely (unless controlled or restrained) to injure severely or kill persons or animals, or damage property to a material extent, the keeper of the animal is liable for any injury or damage caused by the animal and directly referable to such physical attributes or habits.[22] The keeper is any person who owns the animal or has possession of it at the time or who has actual care and control of a child under 16 who owns the animal or has possession of it.[23] Dogs and dangerous wild animals within the meaning of section 7(4) of the Dangerous Wild Animals Act 1976 are deemed to be likely to injure severely or kill by biting, savaging, attacking or harrying; and cattle, horses, asses, mules, hinnies, sheep, pigs, goats and deer are deemed to be likely to damage to a material extent land and the produce of land whether harvested or not.[24] There is no liability under the Act where the injury consists of disease transmitted by means which are unlikely to cause severe injury other than disease,[25] or where injury or damage is caused by the animal's mere presence on a road or in any other place[26] or is caused to persons or animals present on land without authority or entitlement.[27] In the last case, however, there is no exemption from liability if the animal causing the damage was kept for the purpose of protecting persons or property unless the keeping of it there and the use made of it was reasonable and, in the case of a guard dog, there was compliance with section 1 of the Guard Dogs Act 1975.[28] Defences of the pursuer's sole fault, of contributory negligence and of *volenti non fit injuria* are competent.[29] Liability for negligence is unaffected by the provisions of the Act. In situations not provided for, the rules of the common law are, therefore, relevant. At common law, it is the duty of the owner or custodier of all animals to take reasonable care to prevent them from injuring third parties or their property[30] and there will be

[20] Nuclear Installations Acts 1965 & 1969; see *Merlin & Anr.* v. *British Nuclear Fuels plc* [1990] Q.B. 557.
[21] Environmental Protection Act 1990, s. 73.
[22] s. 1(1).
[23] s. 5(1).
[24] s. 1(3).
[25] s. 1(4).
[26] s. 1(5).
[27] s. 2(1)(c).
[28] s. 2(2).
[29] ss. 1(6) and 2(1)(a) and (b).
[30] See *Henderson* v. *John Stuart (Farms)*, 1963 S.C. 245, where Lord Hunter reviews the authorities; Glegg, p. 357.

liability for accidents caused by negligently allowing animals to stray on to the highway, even sheep and cattle, if injury to a road user is a natural and probable consequence of their presence at the locus.[31]

33.4   Statutory Liability: Defective Products.—Part I of the Consumer Protection Act 1987 implements E.C. Directive 85/374, which imposes strict liability for defects in products.[32] The Act supplements, but does not replace, the common law.[33] The Act applies where any damage is caused wholly or partly by a defect in a product. Product is defined as any goods or electricity and includes a product comprised in another product.[34] Goods are widely defined, to include any natural or artificial substance, growing crops and things comprised in land, and any ship, aircraft or vehicle.[35] By section 2(2) of the Act, liability is imposed on the producer[36] of the product, on any person who, by putting his name or other mark on the product, has held himself out as the producer,[37] and on any person who has imported the product from outwith the member States into a member State. Liability may also be incurred by any person who has ever supplied the product if a person who has suffered damage caused by a product requests the supplier to identify one or more of the people referred to in section 2(2), the request is made within a reasonable time after the damage occurs and at a time when such identification is not reasonably practicable for the maker of the request, and the supplier fails either to comply with the request or to identify the person who supplied the product to him.[38] Those who supply game or agricultural produce are exempt from liability if their only supply of such produce is at a time when it has not undergone an industrial process.[39]

The test for whether or not a product is defective depends on the expectation of the consumer; a product is defective if it is not as safe as persons generally are entitled to expect.[40] Relevant to this test are such factors as the marketing of the product, its presentation, any instructions or warnings and the use which might be expected to be made of the

---

[31] *Gardiner* v. *Miller*, 1967 S.L.T. 29 (O.H.). Note Lord Thomson's reference to the probable difference of the law of England on this point. For illustrations of liability for damage done by animals on the basis of negligence, see Walker, *op. cit.*, pp. 621–623 and 634.

[32] The first draft Directive was published in 1974, and the Law Commission and the Scottish Law Commission reported jointly in 1977.

[33] s. 2(6).

[34] s. 1(2).

[35] s. 45.

[36] As defined by s. 1(2).

[37] This would include those companies who sell goods manufactured by others as their 'own brand,' although affixing a name or mark, for example as a sponsor or promoter, would not *per se* amount to 'holding out.' Even labelling narrating that the goods have been 'produced for' a seller might be sufficient to evade this provision.

[38] s. 2(3).

[39] s. 2(4).

[40] s. 3(1).

product.[41] Section 3(2)(c) also makes provision for account to be taken of the time when the product is supplied. A product is not rendered defective merely because the safety of a product subsequently supplied is greater.

A number of defences are set out in section 4 of the Act. Defects caused by compliance with any enactment or with any Community obligation do not incur liability.[42] The defender may also evade liability by showing that he did not at any time supply the product.[43] Any person who supplies a product outwith the course of business and either does not fall within section 2(2) at all, or does so only in relation to non-profit-making activities, is exempt from liability.[44] A defender may also establish that at the relevant time the defect did not exist in the product,[45] or that the state of scientific and technical knowledge at the relevant time was not such as to give rise to an expectation that a producer of such products would discover the defect.[46] It is also a defence to show that a defect was attributable to a subsequent product in which the product concerned was comprised.[47] In an appropriate case, a defender may plead that the pursuer was contributorily negligent.[48]

Death and personal injury fall within the definition of damage for which liability is imposed by the Act. Because the statute is designed to protect consumers, property damage may only be compensated if the property was of a type ordinarily intended for private use, occupation or consumption and was in fact so intended by the person suffering the damage.[49] Property damage for which the amount awarded would be £275 or less is not covered by the Act.[50]

33.5 Strict Liability: Vicarious Liability.[51]—A person may involve himself as a joint delinquent in a wrong which he did not personally commit by expressly authorising or subsequently ratifying the wrongful act, but his liability is then direct, not vicarious. In certain cases, however, the maxim *qui facit per alium facit per se*[52] is applied to produce vicarious liability for the act of another. It applies only to certain contractual

---

[41] ss. 3(2)(a) and (b).
[42] s. 4(1)(a).
[43] s. 4(1)(b).
[44] s. 4(1)(c). See para. 43 of Scot. Law Com. Report No. 45, pointing out the unreasonableness of imposing liability on a housewife who makes jam for a local church or a man who sells apples to a neighbour over a garden fence.
[45] s. 4(1)(d).
[46] s. 4(1)(e).
[47] s. 4(1)(f).
[48] s. 6(4).
[49] s. 5(3).
[50] s. 5(4).
[51] See Glegg, Chap. 17, pp. 409 *et seq.*; Walker, *Delict*, pp. 124–155.
[52] 'He who does something through the actions of another is treated as having done it himself.'

relationships, namely, those of partnership, principal and agent, employer and employee, and exceptionally to employer and independent contractor.[53] On principles of agency, vicarious liability for the negligence of the driver of a vehicle may attach to the owner of the vehicle if the driver was using it for the owner's purposes under delegation of a task or duty, but, where a car is owned by one spouse, vicarious liability for the negligent driving of the other spouse or someone driving on his behalf does not attach to the owner on the ground merely that the car is treated as a family car.[54] If the owner spouse is to be vicariously liable the car must have been used for his purposes under delegation of some task or duty. It is not sufficient that it was being used for the general purposes of the household.[55] A parent who, for the purpose of his child being conveyed as a passenger, lends his car to another may be liable for the driver's negligence if the proposal for use of the car originated from the parent but not if it originated from the child.[56] It has been suggested, *obiter*, that the vicarious liability of a principal for an agent may be less extensive than that of an employer for an employee in that 'it has never been laid down as a general proposition that all principals (as distinguished from employers) are liable for the negligence of their agents (as distinguished from servants) in the execution of their mandate.'[57] It is thought, however, that the only material distinction between the two is that the right of an employer at all times to direct his employee how his work is to be done[58] may extend the net of his vicarious liability wider than that of a principal for an agent, who is normally free of his principal's control as regards the manner in which he executes his mandate. In agency the test is whether the act causing the damage was within the scope of the agent's authority, express or implied; in contracts of service the same test is applied, although 'scope of authority' is usually termed 'scope of employment.' As the same principles apply to vicarious liability both in agency and *locatio operarum*, it is proposed to treat both under the general head of employer and employee. The law in cases of partnership will be considered later.[59]

33.6 Vicarious Liability: Employer and Employee.—It has long been established law that an employer is vicariously liable for the wrongful or negligent acts of his employee committed within the general scope of his employment.[60] Without attempting to lay down an exhaustive definition of the phrase, 'scope of employment' limits liability to those acts which

---

[53] See para. 33.9, *infra*.
[54] *Morgans* v. *Launchbury* [1973] A.C. 127; *Nottingham* v. *Aldridge* [1971] 2 Q.B. 739.
[55] *Norwood* v. *Nevan* [1981] R.T.R. 457.
[56] *Carberry* v. *Davies* [1968] 1 W.L.R. 1103.
[57] *Per* Lord President Cooper, in *Mair* v. *Wood*, 1948 S.C. 83 at p. 87.
[58] See para. 21.2, *supra*.
[59] Para. 50.13, *infra*.
[60] Bell, *Prin.*, § 547.

the employee is required or entitled to do under his contract of service and to acts incidental thereto[61]—in other words, to acts related to the employer's business which he can only perform through an agent.[62] Where the phrase 'course of employment' is used, it must be construed in this context in the same sense as 'scope of employment,' because the emphasis is upon the scope of the authority expressly or impliedly delegated to the servant or other agent by his employer. A principal is liable in damages to third parties 'for the frauds, deceits, concealments, misrepresentations, torts, negligences, and other malfeasances, or misfeasances, and omissions of duty, of his agent, in the course of his employment, although the principal did not authorise, or justify, or participate in, or indeed know of such misconduct, or even if he forbade the acts, or disapproved of them.'[63] 'But although the principal is thus liable for the torts and negligences of his agent, yet we are to understand the doctrine with its just limitations, that the tort or negligence occurs in the course of the agency, for the principal is not liable for the torts or negligences of his agent beyond the scope of his agency, unless he has expressly authorised them to be done, or he has subsequently adopted them for his own use and benefit.'[64] Whether the agent is acting within the scope of his authority,[65] or the employee acting within the scope of his employment, is largely a question of fact.[66] An employer who entrusts the general management of his business to an employee is liable for the fraud of his employee on a client, although the employer obtained no benefit from it.[67] Conversely, benefit to the employer from the fraud of his employee will not render the employer liable if the employee had no authority to perform honestly the act which he performed dishonestly.[68] Although the particular act which gives the cause of action may not be authorised, still if the act is done in the course of employment which is authorised, then the employer is liable for the act of the employee.[69] The general rule, which is often difficult to apply, is that an employer is liable for authorised acts done in an unauthorised way but not for acts of a kind altogether unauthorised.[70] Thus, a general mandate of management involves the employer in liability for all acts, including criminal acts, of

[61] See *Bell* v. *Blackwood Morton & Sons*, 1960 S.C. 11, *per* Lord Sorn at p. 26.
[62] See *Neville* v. *C. & A. Modes*, 1945 S.C. 175.
[63] Story on *Agency* (9th ed.), s. 452.
[64] *Ibid.*, s. 456, quoted by Viscount Haldane in *Percy* v. *Glasgow Corp.*, 1922 S.C. (H.L.) 144 at p. 151, as applicable to a master and servant relationship.
[65] See *Laing* v. *Provincial Homes Investment Co.*, 1909 S.C. 812.
[66] *Kirby* v. *N.C.B.*, 1958 S.C. 514, *per* Lord President Clyde at p. 532; *Bell* v. *Blackwood Morton & Sons*, 1960 S.C. 11.
[67] *Lloyd* v. *Grace, Smith & Co.* [1912] A.C. 716.
[68] *Sinclair Moorhead & Co.* v. *Wallace & Co.* (1880) 7 R. 874 (borrowing money); *Armagas Ltd.* v. *Mundogas S.A.* [1986] A.C. 717.
[69] *Per* Lord Lindley in *Citizen's Life Assurance Co.* v. *Brown* [1904] A.C. 423, at pp. 427–428; quoted by Lord Justice-Clerk Macdonald in *Mackenzie* v. *Cluny Hill Hydropathic*, 1908 S.C. 200 at p. 205.
[70] *Kirby* v. *N.C.B.*, *supra*.

his manager done in that capacity.[71] But in more restricted fields of employment, the employer is not liable for acts which the employee was not employed to do.[72] 'The criterion is whether the act which is unauthorised is so connected with acts which have been authorised that it may be regarded as a mode—although an improper mode—of doing the authorised act, as distinct from constituting an independent act for which the employer would not be liable.'[73] Examples of the former are as follows: smoking while working with inflammable materials;[74] use by employee of own uninsured motor car on employer's business;[75] garage attendant driving a car when instructed to move cars by hand;[76] blacksmith's apprentice without a driving licence voluntarily driving a car which was impeding his work;[77] and a substantial deviation from the direct route by a driver implementing his employer's contract to convey passengers from A to B.[78] An independent journey, undertaken for the employee's private purposes, is not within the scope of his employment.[79] But an act may fall within the scope of employment although prohibited.[80] The relevant connection of service between employer and employee commences, in the ordinary case, when the employee enters his employer's premises for the purpose of going to work[81] and

[71] *Lloyd* v. *Grace Smith & Co.*, *supra*; *Central Motors (Glasgow)* v. *Cessnock Garage, etc., Co.*, 1925 S.C. 796 (garage night watchman borrowing car); *Mackenzie* v. *Cluny Hill Hydropathic*, *supra*; *Dyer* v. *Munday* [1895] 1 Q.B. 742.

[72] *Martin* v. *Wards* (1887) 14 R. 814; *Beard* v. *London General Omnibus Co.* [1900] 2 Q.B. 530 (conductor driving bus); cf. *Ricketts* v. *Tilling* [1915] 1 K.B. 644 (where driver negligent in permitting conductor to drive); *O'Brien* v. *Arbib*, 1907 S.C. 975; and see Glegg, pp. 421–425.

[73] *Kirby* v. *N.C.B.*, 1958 S.C. 514, *per* Lord President Clyde at p. 533. Another test suggested is 'whether the activity was reasonably incidental to the performance of his duties': see Lord Pearce in *Williams* v. *A. & W. Hemphill*, 1966 S.C. (H.L.) 31 at p. 44.

[74] *Jefferson* v. *Derbyshire Farms Ltd.* [1921] 2 K.B. 281; *Century Insurance Co.* v. *N.I.R.T.B.* [1942] A.C. 509.

[75] *C.P.R. Co.* v. *Lockhart* [1942] A.C. 591.

[76] *L.C.C.* v. *Cattermoles (Garages) Ltd.* [1953] 1 W.L.R. 997.

[77] *Mulholland* v. *Reid & Leys*, 1958 S.C. 290.

[78] *Williams* v. *A. & W. Hemphill*, 1966 S.C. (H.L.) 31. 'It is a question of fact and degree in each case whether the deviation is sufficiently detached from the master's business to constitute a frolic of the servant unconnected with the enterprise for which he was employed': *per* Lord Pearce at p. 45. Cf. *Angus* v. *Glasgow Corporation*, 1977 S.L.T. 206 (deviating driver is outside the scope of his employment only when he departs altogether from his employer's business) and *R. J. McLeod (Contractors)* v. *South of Scotland Electricity Board*, 1982 S.L.T. 274 (employer vicariously liable where, despite unauthorised diversion, original purpose of driver's journey had not been completely superseded).

[79] See cases in Glegg, pp. 422–423; cf. *Central Motors* v. *Cessnock Garage Co.*, 1925 S.C. 796, where delegation to a servant of the care of customers' cars brought 'a frolic' of the servant within the scope of employment.

[80] *C.P.R. Co.* v. *Lockhart*, *supra*; *L.C.C.* v. *Cattermoles (Garages)*, *supra*; *Limpus* v. *London General Omnibus Co.* (1862) 1 H. & C. 526 (bus driver racing another bus driver). For examples of prohibited acts which the servant was not employed to do, see *Alford* v. *N.C.B.*, 1951 S.C. 248 (shot-firing); *Twine* v. *Bean's Express* (1946) 62 T.L.R. 458 (C.A.), and *Conway* v. *George Wimpey & Co.* [1951] 2 K.B. 266 (drivers giving prohibited lifts); see also *Roberts* v. *Matthew Logan* (O.H.), 1966 S.L.T. 77; *Rose* v. *Plenty* [1976] 1 W.L.R. 141.

[81] *Compton* v. *McClure* [1975] I.C.R. 378.

continues while the employee is leaving a factory by an inside stairway after finishing work;[82] but an employee who goes to an unauthorised place for the sole purpose of performing a prohibited act, namely smoking during a work break, has temporarily broken that connection.[83] Exceptionally, the connection may commence when the employee begins his journey to work, if he is sent by his employer to work temporarily at a different location. This is so even if he departs from home to travel to the different location, or is returning directly to his home after finishing the work.[84] It is not enough to create vicarious liability that the act is done for the benefit of or at the request of the employer if it is outwith the scope of employment and is not part of a delegated task or duty.[85] Firemen, and others, called out by their employer are, however, acting within the scope of their employment while travelling to work,[86] although it has been held that firemen travelling deliberately slowly to a fire as part of a programme of industrial action are acting outwith the scope of their employment.[87]

33.7 An employer is not liable for the act of an employee which the employer himself had no power to do,[88] but he is liable for the use of excessive force or wrongous detention by an employee to whom he has delegated, expressly or impliedly, the power to use force against persons or to detain them,[89] unless the employee was actuated by personal motives, such as hatred or spite.[90] Vicarious liability for defamation rests upon the same principles as other wrongs.[91] The only specialty arises when the employer is entitled to plead qualified privilege. In that event, express malice may be inferred from the reckless and extreme nature of charges made by the employee within the scope of his employment and the employer will be liable;[92] but the personal malice of the employee due to ill will and in no way connected with the employer's business excludes his liability.[93]

[82] *Bell* v. *Blackwood Morton & Sons Ltd.*, 1960 S.C. 11.

[83] *Kirby* v. *N.C.B.*, 1958 S.C. 514.

[84] *Thomson & Ors.* v. *British Steel Corporation*, 1977 S.L.T. 26; *Smith* v. *Stages* [1989] A.C. 928.

[85] *Nottingham* v. *Aldridge* [1971] 2 Q.B. 739.

[86] *Stitt* v. *Woolley* (1971) 115 S.J. 708. (The act of a passenger in grabbing hold of the steering wheel of the vehicle in which he is travelling is, however, in these circumstances, outwith the scope of his employment.)

[87] *General Engineering Services Ltd.* v. *Kingston & St. Andrews Corporation* [1989] 1 W.L.R. 69.

[88] *Poulton* v. *L. & S.W. Ry. Co.* (1867) L.R. 2 Q.B. 534 (wrongous detention).

[89] See cases in Glegg, pp. 426–429; *Percy* v. *Glasgow Corp.*, 1922 S.C. (H.L.) 144.

[90] See *Power* v. *Central S.M.T. Co.*, 1949 S.C. 376.

[91] See *Ellis* v. *National Free Labour Association* (1905) 7 F. 629; *Finburgh* v. *Moss Empires*, 1908 S.C. 928; *Neville* v. *C. & A. Modes*, 1945 S.C. 175; and *cf. Riddell* v. *Glasgow Corporation*, 1911 S.C. (H.L.) 35 (where the House of Lords held that the servant had no authority to make any statement on the point); *Eprile* v. *Cal. Ry.* (1898) 6 S.L.T. 65 (O.H.); and *Mandelston* v. *N.B. Ry. Co.*, 1917 S.C. 442.

[92] *Finburgh* v. *Moss Empires, supra*: see Lord Ardwall's opinion at p. 940.

[93] *Aitken* v. *Cal. Ry. Co.*, 1913 S.C. 66.

A distinction was formerly drawn between employees engaged to exercise professional skill and others, but this distinction is no longer valid and an employer is now vicariously liable for the negligence of full-time salaried employees in the exercise of their professions.[94] The existence of a contract of service is not, however, the factor which determines vicarious liability. There may be vicarious liability even in the case of a joint adventure if the person against whom vicarious liability is pleaded exercised superintendence and control of the work.[95] And A may have a contract of service with B and yet be acting as agent or servant *pro hac vice* of C. Thus if C borrows a car and appoints A to drive it on C's business, C will be liable for A's negligent driving jointly with A.[96] But difficulty may arise when the employee of A is lent or hired to B and the question is whether A or B is vicariously liable for the employee's act. There is on the injured party a heavy onus of proving that the employee was transferred *pro hac vice* to the service of B.[97] In the case of a negligent act, regard must be had to all the circumstances of the case to determine whether A or B had the right to control the way in which that act was done.[98] Where a ship is let out on hire with its master to a charterer, or a vehicle let out with a driver,[99] or plant with an operator, the owner remains vicariously liable for the negligent control of the operator unless he has divested himself of all possession and control of his property in favour of another. 'The reason is that he has delegated to the driver the task of driving his vehicle and he must be responsible for the way in which his delegate does his work.'[1] The case of the owner of a vehicle hiring the employee of another to drive the hirer's vehicle presents no difficulty because the real interest in the method of driving is in the owner and the car is being driven on his business.[2]

[94] *Macdonald* v. *Glasgow Western Hospitals*, 1954 S.C. 453 (resident physicians and surgeons); *Fox* v. *Glasgow South Western Hospitals*, 1955 S.L.T. 337 (nurse). A regional health board is not, however, liable for the negligence of a general practitioner within its area (*Bonthrone* v. *Secretary of State for Scotland*, 1987 S.L.T. 34).
[95] *Bruce* v. *Clapham*, 1982 S.L.T. 386.
[96] *Elliot* v. *Beattie*, 1926 S.L.T. 588 (O.H.); and see *Smith* v. *Moss* [1940] 1 K.B. 424 (son driving mother's car on mother's business); *cf. Hewitt* v. *Bonvin* [1940] 1 K.B. 188 (son driving father's car on son's business).
[97] *Malley* v. *L.M.S. Ry.*, 1944 S.C. 129, *per* Lord Justice-Clerk Cooper at pp. 136–138; *Mersey Docks & Harbour Board* v. *Coggins & Griffith Ltd.* [1947] A.C. 1, *per* Viscount Simon at p. 10; *McGregor* v. *J.S. Duthie & Sons*, 1966 S.L.T. 133 (where the onus was held to be discharged—but the driver was driving a vehicle belonging to the temporary employer on that employer's business at the material time); *Moir* v. *Wide Arc Services Ltd.*, 1987 S.L.T. 495.
[98] See *Malley* and *Mersey Docks, etc., supra.*
[99] See *Anderson* v. *Glasgow Tramways Co.* (1893) 21 R. 318.
[1] *John Young & Co. Ltd.* v. *O'Donnell*, 1958 S.L.T. (Notes) 46, *per* Lord Denning. Note that a term in such a hiring contract that the driver or operator is to be the servant of the hirer will not exclude the owner's liability for injury to a third party: see *Mersey Docks etc., supra*, at pp. 2 and 10. An indemnity clause provides the only effective protection.
[2] *Bowie* v. *Shenkin*, 1934 S.C. 459.

The position of authorised pilots is different; the general rule is that the employer of a duly authorised and licensed pilot is not vicariously responsible for damage caused by his negligence during pilotage, because when navigating the pilot is acting as an independent professional.[3] By statute the owners of the vessel are liable for such fault.[4] There may, however, be situations where a harbour authority which is actually the employer of an authorised pilot will be vicariously liable for his negligence.[5] Mere authorisation of a pilot does not, however, make a harbour authority vicariously liable for his negligence.[6] The Crown is vicariously liable for delicts committed by its servants or agents, including independent contractors,[7] and firemen are the servants of the statutory fire authorities set up under the Fire Services Act 1947.[8]

33.8 *Culpa Tenet Suos Auctores.*—The vicarious liability of an employer does not affect the employee's personal liability, as everyone is responsible for the consequences of his own wrongful or negligent acts.[9] It is no defence that he was acting in accordance with instructions from a party whom he was contractually bound to obey,[10] or even, as in the case of a soldier obeying an unjustifiable order to fire, one to whom his obedience was due by statute.[11] An independent contractor is personally liable for his own acts or omissions (and for acts of his servants within the scope of their employment), whether or not his employer is also liable to the injured party.[12]

33.9 **Liability of Employer of Independent Contractor.**—In *Stephen* v. *Thurso Police Commrs.*[13] Lord Justice-Clerk Inglis said: 'The law is well established. In the first place, a master is liable for the injurious act of his servant. In the second place, if the wrongdoer be a contractor who is subject to the control of his employer, the latter is responsible; and, in the third place, if the contractor be independent, and may do as he pleases as regards the execution of the work, he is to be viewed as the principal, and alone is liable.' There are no exceptions to the first two propositions. Although the contract in the first is a *locatio operarum* (a letting of his services by the servant) and in the second a *locatio operis*

---

[3] *Esso Petroleum Co. Ltd.* v. *Hall Russell & Co. Ltd.*, 1988 S.L.T. 874, at pp. 886–891.

[4] Pilotage Act 1987, s. 16; *Thom* v. *J. & P. Hutchison*, 1925 S.C. 386.

[5] *Ibid.*; s. 22 of the 1987 Act, by imposing a financial ceiling on the amount of damages payable, appears to contemplate such liability.

[6] *Ibid.*, s. 22(8).

[7] Crown Proceedings Act 1947, ss. 2 and 38(2). Note that s. 2(6) excludes, *inter alia*, police; vicarious liability was imposed on chief constables: Police (Scotland) Act 1967, s. 39.

[8] *Kilboy* v. *S.E. Fire Area Joint Committee*, 1952 S.C. 280.

[9] See para. 21.7.

[10] *Miller* v. *Renton* (1885) 13 R. 309.

[11] *Rogers* v. *Rajendro Dutt* (1860) 13 Moore P.C. 209.

[12] *Grieve* v. *Brown*, 1926 S.C. 787.

[13] (1876) 3 R. 535, at p. 540.

faciendi (a letting out of a job or piece of work to be done by a contractor), the maxims *qui facit per alium facit per se* and *respondeat superior* apply to both. If the employer of an independent contractor retains control of the work, he has the right to direct the contractor and his employees as to how the work is to be done, with the result that the contractor and his employees are deemed to be the employees *pro hac vice* of the employer.[14] The third proposition, above, lays down the general rule that the contractor alone is liable, and this is true provided that the employer is not personally at fault. Thus, when normal building operations were being carried out on private land, neither the owner nor the principal contractor was liable to a third party injured by colliding with a heap of lime left on the public street by servants of the plastering subcontractor.[15] But an employer may himself be negligent, *e.g.* by careless selection of an incompetent contractor, by ordering dangerous work,[16] or by failing to take steps to remove or guard an obstacle placed on the highway by the contractor's men if the employer knew or ought to have known it was there,[17] in which case he will be liable for damage caused by his own negligence, whether or not the contractor has been negligent. But, in addition to breach of this duty, certain other duties have been held to be personal to the employer so that, if they are not performed, he is liable, however careful he may have been in the selection of a competent contractor to perform them on his behalf. The exceptions now recognised to the general rule that an employer is not liable for damage caused by work done by an independent contractor are as follows.

(1) When the employer has no legal right to do the work ordered by him, he will be liable not only for the infringement of the rights of others caused by the work *per se* but also for any other injuries which third parties may suffer as a result of negligence of the contractor or his servants. For example, a gas company, which had no authority to make excavations in the street but employed a contractor for that purpose, was held liable for injury to a member of the public caused by a heap of stones negligently left on the roadway by the contractor's servants.[18] The same principle would apply to the case of an employer instructing or authorising a contractor to execute lawful work in an unlawful manner to the injury of neighbouring proprietors.[19]

---

[14] *Nisbett* v. *Dixon & Co.* (1852) 14 D. 973; *Stephen* v. *Thurso Police Commrs., supra; Gregory* v. *Hill* (1869) 8 M. 282; *Marshall* v. *William Sharp & Sons Ltd.*, 1991 S.L.T. 114, although this case may be an exception to the third proposition in *Stephen*, rather than an example of the second.

[15] *MacLean* v. *Russell* (1850) 12 D. 887; *Blake* v. *Woolf* [1898] 2 Q.B. 426 (owner not liable for overflow from cistern after repair by competent plumber).

[16] *Boyle* v. *Glasgow Corp.*, 1949 S.C. 254.

[17] See *Stephen* v. *Thurso Police Commrs., supra*, per Lord Justice-Clerk Inglis at p. 538, and *Burgess* v. *Gray* (1845) 1 C.B. 578.

[18] *Ellis* v. *Sheffield Gas Co.* (1853) 2 E. & B. 767.

[19] See *Cameron* v. *Fraser* (1881) 9 R. 26 and *Miller* v. *Renton* (1885) 13 R. 309, although no question of incidental negligence arose in these cases.

(2) Certain duties are personal to the obligant, so that he cannot escape liability for breach by delegating the performance to competent parties or by any other means. An employer's duty of care to his employee is non-delegable in the sense that he is personally liable for its performance. If therefore the duty is delegated by the employer and not properly performed, the employer remains liable to the employee.[20] Merely because a third party is involved in the provision of equipment[21] or the organisation of work for an employee[22] does not, however, make him an agent or delegate of the employer. Examples of statutory duties personal to the obligant are as follows: (a) absolute duties;[23] (b) duties laid on contractors and employers of workmen undertaking operations and works to which the various construction regulations apply;[24] (c) statutory provisions requiring or empowering some specific act to be done;[25] and (d) the obligation imposed by the Carriage of Goods by Sea Act 1971 on a shipowner in the work of repair of using 'due diligence' to make the ship seaworthy.[26]

(3) In certain cases, where damage is the natural and probable consequence of negligent execution of the work, the employer has the personal obligation of seeing that the work is carefully and properly done. These cases fall broadly into two classes. The first covers excavations and other hazardous work on public roads and streets;[27] the second relates to hazardous work on private property, such as building operations which expose adjacent property to risk of damage,[28] work involving the risk of fire spreading to adjacent property[29] or injuring

[20] *McDermid* v. *Nash Dredging* [1987] A.C. 907; see also para. 21.37.

[21] *Davie* v. *New Merton Board Mills* [1959] A.C. 604—note that the provision of equipment is now regulated by the Employers' Liability (Defective Equipment) Act 1969, which makes the employer liable for defective equipment even though the defect is attributable to the fault of a third party.

[22] *Marshall* v. *William Sharp & Sons Ltd.*, 1991 S.L.T. 114.

[23] See, *e.g.*, *Millar* v. *Galashiels Gas Co.*, 1949 S.C. (H.L.) 31: 'Every hoist ... shall be properly maintained,' etc.; and *Wolfson* v. *Forrester*, 1910 S.C. 675, *per* Lord President Dunedin at p. 680.

[24] See S.I.s 1961 No. 1580, reg. 3(1); 1966 No. 94, reg. 3(1); 1966 No. 95, reg. 4(1), but note reg. 4(2); see also *Mulready* v. *Bell* [1953] 2 Q.B. 117 (C.A.), and *Donaghey* v. *O'Brien* [1966] 1 W.L.R. 1170 (C.A.), at p. 1177.

[25] *Stephen* v. *Thurso Police Commrs.* (1876) 3 R. 535, 538 (cleansing streets); *Robinson* v. *Beaconsfield R.D.C.* [1911] 2 Ch. 188 (disposal of sewage); *Hole* v. *Sittingbourne Ry.* (1861) 6 H. & N. 448 (erection of bridge suitable for river traffic): referred to in *Hardaker* v. *Idle D.C.* [1896] 1 Q.B. 335, at pp. 340 and 345.

[26] *Riverstone Meat Co. Pty. Ltd.* v. *Lancashire Shipping Co. Ltd.* [1961] A.C. 807.

[27] *Gray* v. *Pullen* (1864) 5 B. & S. 970 (subsidence of pavement after construction of drain); *Hardaker* v. *Idle D.C.*, *supra* (gas main broken during construction of sewer); *Penny* v. *Wimbledon U.D.C.* [1899] 2 Q.B. 72 (heap of soil on road after dark); *Holliday* v. *Nat. Tel. Co.* [1899] 2 Q.B. 392 (risk of explosion during work on highway).

[28] *Bower* v. *Peate* (1876) 1 Q.B.D. 321 (excavation of foundations); *Dalton* v. *Angus* (1881) 6 App.Cas. 740 (interference with right of support); *Hughes* v. *Percival* (1883) 8 App.Cas. 443; and see *Cameron* v. *Fraser* (1881) 9 R. 26, *per* Lord Young at p. 29 (truly a nuisance case); *Borders Regional Council* v. *Roxburgh District Council*, 1989 S.L.T. 837; and *G.A. Estates Ltd.* v. *Caviapen Trs. Ltd. (No. 1)*, 1993 S.L.T. 1037.

[29] *Black* v. *Christchurch Finance Co.* [1894] A.C. 48; *Balfour* v. *Barty-King* [1956] 1 W.L.R. 779. *Emanuel (H. & N.)* v. *Greater London Council* [1971] 2 All E.R. 835.

persons present[30] or any work involving an obvious inherent risk of serious injury.[31] The case of *Tarry* v. *Ashton*[32] may be fitted under this head, where a lamp projecting over a public street was an obvious danger to the public if not secure. The owner was held liable to a passer-by, upon whom it fell, for the negligent execution of repair work by an independent contractor shortly before the accident. The perplexing case of *Cleghorn* v. *Taylor*,[33] where a chimney-can fell and damaged adjacent property shortly after its repair by a master slater, could also have been decided under this head, although it is not the stated *ratio decidendi*.

There is therefore no general rule that an employer is not liable for breach of his personal duties to an employee injured through the negligent work of an independent contractor employed by the employer, nor is there any general rule that an occupier of premises is not liable for damage to persons or property on the premises caused by such faulty work. The question of whether or not the employer has discharged his duty of taking reasonable care for the safety of his employee, or an occupier for the person who or whose property is injured on the premises, by selecting a skilled contractor of established reputation to carry out any work on plant or premises, including the inspection thereof, is a question of fact and degree in all the circumstances of the particular case and every decision on this subject should be treated as turning on its own facts.[34]

33.10   Landlord and Tenant.—While the mere relationship of landlord and tenant does not involve the landlord in vicarious liability analogous to that of a master, there are cases in which a landlord may be held liable for damage caused by his tenant's operations. This may come about because the lease expressly or impliedly authorises the tenant to commit a wrongful act, such as the working of minerals which the lessor has no right to work[35] or the use of a mill which necessarily involves the

---

[30] *Honeywill & Stein* v. *Larkin Bros.* [1934] 1 K.B. 191, in which the words 'absolute obligation' were used in lieu of 'strict liability': see *Pass of Ballater* [1942] P. 112, *per* Langton J. at pp. 115–116.

[31] *Stewart* v. *Adams*, 1920 S.C. 129 (contract for removal of poisonous paint scrapings on pasture land: employer liable for death of cow).

[32] (1876) 1 Q.B.D. 314.

[33] (1856) 18 D. 664. See comment of Lord Justice-Clerk Inglis in *Campbell* v. *Kennedy* (1864) 3 M. 121, at p. 126; and Rankine on *Land-Ownership* (4th ed.), p. 375. Note: it is unnecessary to classify it under the *actio de positis vel suspensis* of Roman law as Professor Walker does: *Delict*, Vol. I, p. 292.

[34] See opinions in *Davie* v. *New Merton Board Mills* [1959] A.C. 604; *Sumner* v. *Henderson & Sons* [1964] 1 Q.B. 450; [1963] 2 W.L.R. 330, where Phillimore J. purported to lay down a general rule and was reversed by the Court of Appeal, [1963] 1 W.L.R. 823. For property cases, see *MacDonald* v. *Reid's Trs.* (O.H.) 1947 S.C. 726, and cases cited therein; also *Green* v. *Fibreglass* [1958] 2 Q.B. 245, *per* Salmon J. at p. 253 (and note s. 2(4)(*b*) of the English Occupiers' Liability Act 1957, the terms of which are implied in s. 2(1) of the Occupiers' Liability (Scotland) Act 1960).

[35] *N.B. Ry. Co.* v. *Budhill Coal Co.*, 1910 S.C. (H.L.) 1.

pollution of a river.[36] Moreover, if damage is a reasonably foreseeable result of the tenant's occupation, the landlord will be liable for it.[37]

---

[36] *Robertson* v. *Stewart* (1872) 11 M. 189; *Cal. Ry.* v. *Baird* (1876) 3 R. 839 (sewage from workmen's houses).
[37] See opinion of Lord President Dunedin in *Fleming* v. *Gemmill*, 1908 S.C. 340, at p. 349.

CHAPTER 34

DEFENCES AND IMMUNITIES; RECOVERY OF DAMAGES

In some cases, the pursuer in an action of reparation is unable to recover damages because a complete defence is available to the defender. In other cases, no duty of care arises because of the context in which the harmful event occurred. The identity of the proposed defender may also be relevant to the question of whether or not damages can be recovered; certain individuals and bodies are immune from liability to make reparation. Finally, the question of what damages can be recovered may be affected by the identity of the pursuer. Title to sue in respect of personal injuries generally, but not invariably, rests with the victim. These matters are considered in this chapter.[1]

34.1 Exclusion of Liability; Contractual Terms; Notice.—Under the Unfair Contract Terms Act 1977, a term of a contract which purports to exclude or restrict liability for breach of duty arising in the course of any business, or from the occupation of any premises used for business purposes, is void where the exclusion or restriction is in respect of personal injury or death and in any other case is of no effect if it is not fair and reasonable[2] or if it is not fair and reasonable to allow reliance on the provision.[3] Where the Act does not apply, delictual liability may generally be excluded by a contractual term to that effect agreed between the wrongdoer and the person injured. Formerly, the Scottish provisions of the Act did not apply to non-contractual disclaimers but the Act was amended by section 68 of the Law Reform (Miscellaneous Provisions) (Scotland) Act 1990, to include attempts to exclude or restrict liability by notice.[4]

34.2 *Volenti Non Fit Injuria*.—The phrase *volenti non fit injuria* means that in certain circumstances a pursuer will be held to have accepted the risk of the injury which has befallen him, and on that ground to be precluded from claiming damages from the party who has caused the injury.[5] It is to be observed that *injuria* means, strictly, an unlawful act,

---

[1] Though see para. 31.9 *re* immunity of trade unions.
[2] 1977, s. 16(1).
[3] s. 16.
[4] The effect of the 1977 Act on disclaimers of liability in reports prepared by surveyors was considered by the House of Lords in *Smith* v. *Eric S. Bush* [1990] 1 A.C. 831.
[5] See Walker, *Delict*, pp. 346–353.

not an injury. Where a term of a contract is void or of no effect under the Unfair Contract Terms Act 1977, agreement to or knowledge of that term is not of itself sufficient evidence that a risk was knowingly and voluntarily assumed so as to found a plea of *volenti non fit injuria*.[6] 'The question raised by a plea of *volenti non fit injuria* is not whether the injured party consented to run the risk of being hurt, but whether the injured party consented to run that risk at his own expense so that he and not the party alleged to be negligent should bear the loss in the event of injury. In other words, the consent that is relevant is not consent to the risk of injury but consent to the lack of reasonable care that may produce that risk.'[7] The consent must be free and voluntary and so the plea may not be open to a defender in a question with an employee of a third party who incurred the risk in the course of his employment.[8] Where, however, the risk has been accepted, it is immaterial that it was done on a false premise.[9] The principle applies to injuries sustained in any lawful game or sport, provided the rules be observed. But where the rules are breached or risks otherwise incurred to which consent is not to be implied, a participant in sport owes a duty of care to other participants for neglect of which he will be liable.[10] The principle of assumption of risk has also been applied to spectators at games and sports who take the risk of physical damage caused to them by any act of a participant of adequate skill and competence, unless the participant's conduct is such as to evince a reckless disregard of the spectator's safety.[11] But the maxim is only required if harm has been caused by a wrongful act or omission; if there is no legal wrong, there is no need for this defence. The plea is excluded by statute where a passenger in a motor vehicle sues the driver on the ground of the latter's negligence.[12] It has been applied to a passenger agreeing to ride in a plane flown by a drunken pilot.[13]

In cases between employer and workman, when the ground of the action is an injury sustained through faulty organisation, the plea of *volenti non fit injuria* cannot be sustained merely by showing that the workman knew of the risk and continued to work in spite of it. The word in the maxim is *volenti*, not *scienti*.[14] Accordingly, the defence of *volenti* is rarely applicable in master and servant cases,[15] and, since the abolition of contributory negligence as a complete defence, there has

---

[6] 1977, s. 16(3).

[7] *McCaig* v. *Langan*, 1964 S.L.T. 121, *per* Lord Kilbrandon at p. 124; *cf. Bankhead* v. *McCarthy*, 1963 S.C. 263, *per* Lord Walker at p. 265; Smith, *Short Commentary*, p. 704.

[8] *Burnett* v. *British Waterways Board* [1973] 1 W.L.R. 700.

[9] *Bennett* v. *Tugwell* [1971] 2 Q.B. 267.

[10] *Condon* v. *Basi* [1985] 1 W.L.R. 866; *Lewis* v. *Buckpool Golf Club*, 1993 S.L.T. (Sh. Ct.) 43. See also the treatment of this topic in Stewart, *Skiing and the Law*.

[11] *Wooldridge* v. *Sumner* [1963] 2 Q.B. 43; *Hall* v. *Brooklands Auto Racing Co.* [1933] 1 K.B. 205.

[12] Road Traffic Act 1988, s. 149; *Winnik* v. *Dick*, 1984 S.L.T. 185.

[13] *Morris* v. *Murray* [1991] 2 Q.B. 6.

[14] *Smith* v. *Baker* [1891] A.C. 325; *Wallace* v. *Culter Paper Co.* (1892) 19 R. 915.

[15] But see *Keenan* v. *City Line*, 1953 S.L.T. 128.

been increasing reluctance to find *volenti* as a defence.[16] It has been held in England that *volenti* is not a defence to a breach of the employer's own statutory duty,[17] but it does afford a complete defence to the employer's vicarious liability for the acts of a fellow-servant when the pursuer invited or freely aided and abetted his fellow-servant's disobedience of an order.[18]

The maxim has been applied in cases between landlord and tenant. It has been held that the proper course for a tenant, on discovering that the subjects let are in a dangerous condition, is to give notice to the landlord and, if the defect is not remedied within a reasonable time, to abandon the lease.[19] If he stays on without giving notice, or if, having given notice, he remains in face of the danger for more than a reasonable time, he may be held to have taken the risk.[20] The authorities for that view are, however, before the coming into force of the Occupiers' Liability (Scotland) Act 1960, which puts a landlord's liability on a new basis and it is doubtful if they would now be followed.[21] In any event, the tenant's acquiescence cannot detract from the landlord's liability to other persons injured on the premises.[22] There may, however, be other circumstances on which a plea of *volenti non fit injuria* can be founded by a landlord, and the plea is open to an occupier of property who is sued for damages by a person injured thereon.[23] So, a person struck by a train while crossing a railway line is taken voluntarily to have accepted that risk.[24]

The plea of *volenti* will not avail a person whose fault creates a situation of peril which he ought reasonably to have foreseen would invite rescue by another person who voluntarily exposes himself to danger in attempting rescue.[25] And the right of a servant to interfere in circumstances of danger for the safeguarding of an employer's property is also recognised.[26]

34.3   Participation in Criminal Enterprise.—A pursuer's claim may be barred where the injury of which he complains was sustained in the course of a criminal enterprise in which he participated jointly with the defender. This rule has been applied when the pursuer was injured as a result of the defender's negligent driving of a car in which the pursuer was a

---

[16] *I.C.I.* v. *Shatwell* [1965] A.C. 656, *per* Lord Pearce at p. 686.
[17] *Wheeler* v. *New Merton Board Mills* [1933] 2 K.B. 669.
[18] *I.C.I.* v. *Shatwell, supra; Hugh* v. *National Coal Board,* 1972 S.C. 252.
[19] *Dickie* v. *Amicable Investment Co.,* 1911 S.C. 1079.
[20] *Smith* v. *Maryculter School Board* (1898) 1 F. 5; *Hardie* v. *Sneddon,* 1917 S.C. 1; *Mullen* v. *C.C. of Dunbartonshire,* 1933 S.C. 380.
[21] *Hughes' Tutrix* v. *Glasgow District Council,* 1982 S.L.T. (Sh.Ct.) 70.
[22] *Ibid.*
[23] See Occupiers' Liability (Scotland) Act 1960, s. 2(3); and para. 32.14, *supra.*
[24] *Titchener* v. *British Railways Board,* 1984 S.L.T. 192.
[25] *Haynes* v. *Harwood* [1935] 1 K.B. 146; *Baker* v. *Hopkins* [1959] 3 All E.R. 225 (C.A.); *Videan* v. *B.T.C.* [1963] 2 Q.B. 650, *per* Lord Denning M.R. at p. 669.
[26] *Steel* v. *Glasgow Iron & Steel Co.,* 1944 S.C. 237.

passenger and in the theft of which he had been involved along with the defender,[27] and where the pursuer knew that the defender was under age for driving and was driving without the consent of the owner of the car.[28] It may also apply where, to the pursuer's knowledge, the defender is guilty of breaches of the Road Traffic Act, such as driving while intoxicated.[29] The rule is not, however, an absolute one and its application will sometimes only be capable of ascertainment after proof of the particular facts of the case.[30] It has been held in England that damages cannot be awarded for loss of an opportunity where the exercise of that opportunity would have involved the commission of an illegal act.[31]

34.4   Contributory Negligence.—Although the fault of the pursuer is not now a complete defence, the fact that the pursuer was contributorily negligent can be invoked by the defender to justify a reduction in the damages which he is found liable to pay. 'The technical meaning of "contributory negligence" is negligence on the part of the pursuer which is itself jointly causative of the accident along with the negligence of the defender,'[32] but in ordinary usage it means fault on the part of a pursuer either wholly causing or materially contributing to his injury. In this context 'fault' connotes breach of a legal duty only in the sense that the law requires a man in his own interest to take reasonable care of himself.[33] The burden of proving that the pursuer's fault was at least one of the effective causes of his injury is on the defender.[34] Up to 1945,[35] if the pursuer was held to any extent to blame for his injury, his claim failed and he could recover nothing. To mitigate the harshness of this doctrine the courts developed the so-called 'last opportunity' rule,[36] under which he who had the last opportunity of avoiding the accident was held liable. The fault of the first party was regarded as a *causa sine qua non*; that of the second and later party was regarded as the *causa causans* of the accident. This 'was a fallacious test because the efficiency of the causes did not depend on their proximity in point of time.'[37]

[27] *Lindsay* v. *Poole*, 1984 S.L.T. 269; *Sloan* v. *Triplett*, 1985 S.L.T. 294.

[28] *Wilson* v. *Price*, 1989 S.L.T. 484.

[29] See dicta of Lord Hunter in *Winnik* v. *Dick*, 1984 S.L.T. 185, at p. 189; *Pitts* v. *Hunt* [1991] 1 Q.B. 24.

[30] As in *Weir* v. *Wyper*, 1992 S.L.T. 579—pursuer a passenger with someone she knew to be the unsupervised holder of a provisional licence.

[31] *Rance* v. *Mid Downs Health Authority* [1991] 1 Q.B. 587.

[32] *Robinson* v. *Hamilton (Motors)*, 1923 S.C. 838, *per* Lord President Clyde at p. 841.

[33] *Nance* v. *British Columbia Electric Ry. Co.* [1951] A.C. 601, *per* Viscount Simon at p. 611; *Davies* v. *Swan Motor Co.* [1949] 2 K.B. 291, *per* Bucknill L.J. at p. 308: *per* Denning L.J. at p. 324.

[34] See para. 32.10, *supra*.

[35] Law Reform (Contributory Negligence) Act 1945.

[36] *Davies* v. *Mann* (1842) 10 M. & W. 546; *Carse* v. *North British Steam Packet Co.* (1895) 22 R. 475; *British Columbia Electric Co.* v. *Loach* [1916] 1 A.C. 719; *Ward* v. *Revie*, 1944 S.C. 325, *per* Lord Moncrieff at p. 335.

[37] *Per* Denning L.J. in *Davies* v. *Swan Motor Co.* [1949] 2 K.B. 291, at p. 321; and see *Boy Andrew* v. *St. Rognvald*, 1947 S.C. (H.L.) 70; para. 32.10, *supra*.

The common law rule as to contributory negligence did not, however, apply to collisions between ships. By the Maritime Conventions Act 1911, it is provided that when, by the fault of two or more vessels, damage or loss is caused to one or more of these vessels, to their cargoes or freights, or to any property on board, the liability to make good the damage or loss shall be in proportion to the degree in which each vessel was in fault, with the proviso that if, having regard to all the circumstances of the case, it is not possible to establish different degrees of fault, the liability shall be apportioned equally.[38]

The principle of the Maritime Conventions Act 1911 was made generally applicable by the Law Reform (Contributory Negligence) Act 1945, which provides (section 1(1)) that 'where any person suffers damage as the result partly of his own fault and partly of the fault of any other person or persons, a claim in respect of that damage shall not be defeated by reason of the fault of the person suffering the damage, but the damages recoverable in respect thereof shall be reduced to such extent as the court thinks just and equitable having regard to the claimant's share in the responsibility for the damage.' This subsection is not to operate to defeat any defence arising under a contract (section 1(1)(a)). The judge or jury must determine the total damages recoverable by the claimant had he not been at fault (section 1(2) and (6)). The jury can also determine the extent to which these damages are to be reduced (section 1(6)) in the same way as the court under section 1(1). Where any person dies as the result partly of his own fault and partly of the fault of any other person, the damages or loss of society award recoverable by any dependant of the deceased may be reduced according to the share of the deceased in the responsibility for his death (section 1 (4)).[39]

Under the Act the court assesses the measure of contribution made by the pursuer to the end result and apportions liability accordingly.[40] Where more than one defender is found liable, the correct approach is to assess the pursuer's contribution as compared with the totality of the contribution made by the defenders. Thus, where the plaintiff and each of two defendants were all found to blame for an accident, contributory negligence was assessed at 50 per cent. before any question of contribution between the defendants *inter se* was dealt with.[41] Regard must be had both to the relative importance of the pursuer's act in causing the damage and also to his relative blameworthiness.[42] Consideration is not restricted to causation of the accident in a narrow

---

[38] See Marsden, *Collisions at Sea (British Shipping Laws* (1961), Vol. 4), § 27. As an example see *Boy Andrew* v. *St. Rognvald, supra.*

[39] See, *e.g., Kelly* v. *Glasgow Corporation*, 1951 S.C. (H.L.) 15.

[40] See *per* Denning L.J., in *Davies* v. *Swan Motor Co., supra*, at p. 322.

[41] *Fitzgerald* v. *Lane* [1989] A.C. 328.

[42] *Stapley* v. *Gypsum Mines* [1953] A.C. 663, *per* Lord Reid at p. 682; *Kilgour* v. *N.C.B.*, 1958 S.L.T. (Notes) 48.

sense, but extends to all the factors in respect of which fault can be imputed, contributing to the damage.[43]

The standard of care required of a pursuer is such care for his own safety as is reasonable in the circumstances. He will be guilty of contributory negligence if he ought reasonably to have foreseen that, if he did not act as a reasonable, prudent man, he might hurt himself, and he ought to take into account the possibility of others being careless.[44] What amounts to reasonable care depends upon the circumstances of each case.[45] Allowance must be made for inadvertence due to necessary haste, fatigue or familiarity,[46] and also for emergency action necessitated by the negligence of the defender.[47] In the case of children it is always a question of circumstances whether they are guilty of contributory negligence. Relevant factors are their age and whether or not they appreciated or should have appreciated the danger.[48] A child should only be found guilty of contributory negligence if he or she is of such an age as to be expected to take precautions for his or her own safety; even then the child is only to be found guilty if blame should be attached.[49] It is contributory negligence to fail to wear a seat-belt,[50] or to allow oneself to be driven in a car in the knowledge that the driver is so drunk[51] or tired[52] as to be unable to drive safely. A servant or employee may be held to be negligent although his claim is based upon breach of statutory duty on the part of his master or employer;[53] but his erroneous assumption that the duty has been performed may not amount to negligence.[54]

34.5 Self-Defence.—Self-defence, or defence of those whom one has a duty to protect, is an excuse for injury inflicted on the aggressor, unless the injury was unreasonably greater than the occasion warranted.[55] Even if it was, the attack or provocation may be proved in mitigation of

[43] *Davies* v. *Swan Motor Co., supra; Froom* v. *Butcher* [1976] Q.B. 286. The onus is, however, on the defender to show that the injuries sustained were, in part at least, caused by failure to adopt the precaution desired (*e.g.* wearing a seat-belt) (*Barker* v. *Murdoch*, 1977 S.L.T. 75).

[44] *Jones* v. *Livox Quarries* [1952] 2 Q.B. 608, *per* Denning L.J. at p. 615.

[45] See *Caswell* v. *Powell Duffryn Assoc. Collieries* [1940] A.C. 152, *per* Lord Wright at p. 176.

[46] *Ibid.*, at pp. 178–179; and see *John Summers & Sons* v. *Frost* [1955] A.C. 740.

[47] *Laird Line* v. *U.S. Shipping Board*, 1924 S.C. (H.L.) 37.

[48] *Fraser* v. *Edinburgh Tramways Co.* (1882) 10 R. 264; *Yachuk* v. *Oliver Blais & Co.* [1949] A.C. 386; see also *Hughes* v. *Lord Advocate*, 1961 S.C. 310, *per* Lord Wheatley at p. 323.

[49] *Gough* v. *Thorne* [1966] 1 W.L.R. 1387, *per* Lord Denning M.R. at p. 1390. But *cf.* *Barnes* v. *Flucker, Thomson* v. *Flucker*, 1985 S.L.T. 142.

[50] *Hill* v. *Chivers*, 1987 S.L.T. 323.

[51] *Ibid.; Winnik* v. *Dick*, 1984 S.L.T. 185.

[52] *Smith* v. *Stages* [1989] A.C. 928.

[53] *Caswell* v. *Powell Duffryn Assoc. Collieries, supra; Cakebread* v. *Hopping Bros. Ltd.* [1947] K.B. 641.

[54] *Grant* v. *Sun Shipping Co. Ltd.*, 1948 S.C. (H.L.) 73, *per* Lord du Parcq at p. 97.

[55] Glegg, *Reparation*, p. 131.

damages.[56] Because it is a matter which depends essentially on the circumstances of each case, limits of the right to defend property, or to resort to self-help, cannot be clearly defined. Probably a thief could not claim damages for injury inflicted in an attempt to recover the stolen property. And a mere squatter, or a person whose title to possess has expired, and who refuses to remove, may be removed by force, without any liability except on the ground that the measures taken involved more injury than was reasonably necessary.[57] But if a title to possess can be shown, even though that title may be voidable, measures of self-help are not justifiable, and will found an action for damages for any injury that may have resulted.[58] A carrier has a very wide discretion in the use of force to remove passengers who refuse to pay the fare or to submit to reasonable regulations.[59] A similar discretion is accorded to the managers of a place of entertainment or of a public meeting.[60] The limits of the right to use force against trespassers have never been definitely settled.[61]

34.6 Statutory Authority.—What would otherwise amount to a wrong may be excused if it is done under the authority of a statute. 'No action can be maintained for anything which is done under the authority of the legislature, though the act is one which, if unauthorised by the legislature, would be injurious and actionable.'[62] Any right to compensation must be founded on some provision in the statute in question.[63] But the defence of statutory authority is available only where the statutory operation is carried out without negligence, and negligence may consist either in carrying out work without reasonable care, or in neglecting precautions to avoid injury to third parties where such precautions are within the statutory powers.[64] It has been held that if work authorised by statute can be done in two ways, one injurious to a third party, the other innocuous, the body exercising the statutory powers is bound to choose the latter method, even though it be the more expensive.[65] In Private Acts the plea of statutory authority is often in substance elided by a clause providing that nothing in the Act shall

---

[56] *Falconer* v. *Cochran* (1837) 15 S. 891.

[57] *Macdonald* v. *Watson* (1883) 10 R. 1079; *Sinclair* v. *Tod*, 1907 S.C. 1038; *Hemmings* v. *Stoke Poges Golf Club* [1920] 1 K.B. 720.

[58] *Brash* v. *Munro* (1903) 5 F. 1102.

[59] *Highland Ry.* v. *Menzies* (1878) 5 R. 887; *Whittaker* v. *London* C.C. [1915] 2 K.B. 676.

[60] *Wallace* v. *Mooney* (1885) 12 R. 710; *Doyle* v. *Falconer* (1866) L.R. 1 P.C. 328.

[61] See *Wood* v. *N.B. Ry.* (1899) 2 F. 1.

[62] Per Lord Blackburn, *Cal. Ry.* v. *Walker's Trs.* (1882) 9 R. (H.L.) 19, 32.

[63] As to the construction of the phrase 'injuriously affected' in private Acts incorporating the Companies Clauses or Railway Clauses Acts, see *Cal. Ry.* v. *Walker's Trs., supra.*

[64] *Edinburgh Water Trs.* v. *Somerville* (1906) 8 F. (H.L.) 25; *Farnworth* v. *Manchester Corporation* [1930] A.C. 171.

[65] *West* v. *Bristol Tramways* [1908] 2 K.B. 14; see also *Metropolitan Asylums District Board* v. *Hill* (1881) 6 App.Cas. 193.

excuse those acting under it from liability for the commission of a nuisance.[66]

When the legislature authorises a particular thing to be done, it impliedly legalises all results which necessarily flow from its being done. So, as railway companies, as they then were, ran their trains under statutory powers, it was held that their duty was merely to use the best type of spark arrester, and that they were not liable for fires caused by sparks which the spark arrester failed to prevent.[67]

34.7   Proceedings Against the Crown.[68]—Before 1947 the Crown, in modern times at least,[69] was not vicariously liable for the wrongful acts of its servants or agents.[70] The effect of the Crown Proceedings Act 1947, however, is to render the Crown liable for wrongs committed by its servants or agents, provided that, apart from the provisions of the Act, the act or omission complained of would have rendered the servant or agent liable.[71] The Crown is also made liable in respect of any breach of those duties which a person owes to his servants and agents as their employer, and in respect of any breach of the duties attaching at common law to the ownership, occupation, possession or control of property.[72] Where the Crown is bound, whether expressly or by necessary implication, by a statutory duty which is binding also upon persons other than the Crown and its officers, it is liable for breach of such a duty in the same way as if it were a private person.[73] No proceedings, however, will lie against the Crown in respect of acts or omissions by judicial persons[74] or by public servants, such as policemen,[75] not directly or indirectly appointed by the Crown and paid out of the Consolidated Fund or certain other national sources.[76] It is not competent to pronounce interdict, or interim interdict, against the Crown.[76a] The Post Office is no longer regarded as an agent of the Crown or as enjoying Crown immunity.[77] The generality of the Crown's liability is further limited by section 11 of the Act, which specifically

---

[66] *Farnworth* v. *Manchester Corporation, supra.*

[67] *Port-Glasgow, etc., Sailcloth Co.* v. *Cal. Ry.* (1893) 20 R. (H.L.) 35. The rule was modified by statute (see Railway Fires Acts 1905 and 1923).

[68] See generally Mitchell, *Constitutional Law* (2nd ed.), pp. 304–312.

[69] At one stage it seems that an action of reparation against the Crown was competent; see Mitchell, p. 304.

[70] *Macgregor* v. *Lord Advocate*, 1921 S.C. 847.

[71] s. 2(1)(*a*). This proviso prevents the Crown from being sued where the defence of act of state would protect the individual; see n. 79, *infra.* 'Agent' is defined as including an independent contractor employed by the Crown (s.38).

[72] ss. 2(1)(*b*) and (*c*). The Occupiers' Liability (Scotland) Act 1960, s.4, binds the Crown.

[73] s. 2(2).

[74] s. 2(5), which has been held to cover sheriff clerks: *Wood* v. *Lord Advocate*, 1994 S.C.L.R. 1034.

[75] But see Police (Scotland) Act 1967, s. 39.

[76] s. 2(6).

[76a] s. 21(1); *McDonald* v. *Secretary of State for Scotland*, 1994 S.L.T. 692.

[77] Post Office Act 1969, s. 6(5).

preserves all powers and authorities of a prerogative nature or conferred on the Crown by any statute, particularly those connected with defence. Section 10, which formerly protected the Crown from suit at the instance of injured members of the armed forces, was repealed with effect from May 15, 1987.[78] An executive officer of the Crown may incur personal liability in respect of his own wrongful or negligent act.[79]

The sheriff court has jurisdiction in actions against the Crown, subject to the power of the Lord Advocate to have cases which are important remitted to the Court of Session.[80] In Scotland, actions against the Crown or any public department may be raised against the Lord Advocate, who before representing the Crown or the public department must have their authority to do so.[81]

34.8 Judicial Immunity.—Judges of the Court of Session, the High Court of Justiciary and probably the sheriff court[82] enjoy absolute immunity at common law from civil action for anything done by them in their judicial capacity.[83] At common law, judges of an inferior court, such as magistrates or justices of the peace, probably could be sued for damages in respect of acts done in excess of their jurisdiction apart altogether from malice,[84] but their position is now regulated by statute. Under the Criminal Procedure (Scotland) Act 1975[85] no judge, clerk of court or prosecutor in the public interest may be found liable in damages in respect of any proceedings taken, act done or judgment, decree or sentence pronounced under that Act unless (1) the person claiming damages was imprisoned in consequence thereof, (2) the proceeding complained of has been quashed, (3) malice and want of probable cause are specifically averred and proved and (4) the action is begun within two months of the proceeding complained of. Where a judge acts in an administrative capacity,[86] he will be liable only on averment and proof that he acted maliciously and without probable cause.[87]

The Lord Advocate is protected by absolute privilege in respect of matters in connection with criminal proceedings on indictment.[88] Since

---

[78] Crown Proceedings (Armed Forces) Act 1987; the subsection can, however, be revived if justified by national emergency.

[79] *Macgregor* v. *Lord Advocate*, 1921 S.C. 847; *Bainbridge* v. *Postmaster General* [1906] 1 K.B. 178. For the defence of act of state, see *Poll* v. *Lord Advocate* (1899) 1 F. 823; *Johnstone* v. *Pedlar* [1921] 2 A.C. 262; and Mitchell, *op. cit.*, at p. 180.

[80] s. 44.

[81] Crown Suits (Scotland) Act 1857.

[82] *Harvey* v. *Dyce* (1876) 4 R. 265; but see Mitchell, p. 262.

[83] *Haggart's Trs.* v. *Hope* (1824) 2 Shaw's App. 125; *McCreadie* v. *Thomson*, 1907 S.C. 1176, *per* Lord Justice-Clerk Macdonald at p. 1182.

[84] *McPhee* v. *Macfarlane's Exr.*, 1933 S.C. 163, *per* Lord President Clyde at p. 169.

[85] s. 456; *cf.* Summary Jurisdiction (Scotland) Acts 1908 and 1954, ss. 59 and 75 respectively.

[86] On the distinction between 'administrative' and 'judicial' acts, see Walker, *Delict*, pp. 105–106.

[87] *Beaton* v. *Ivory* (1887) 14 R. 1057; *McPherson* v. *McLennan* (1887) 14 R. 1063.

[88] *Henderson* v. *Robertson* (1853) 15 D. 292; *Hester* v. *Macdonald*, 1961 S.C. 370.

all prosecutions on indictment must have the authority of the Lord Advocate either in person or through his deputes,[89] that privilege extends to procurators fiscal and depute procurators fiscal acting on his authority and instructions.[90] In summary proceedings, procurators fiscal are protected by the Criminal Procedure (Scotland) Act 1975.

34.9 Prescription and Limitation.—Negative prescription is to be distinguished from limitation of actions. By negative prescription an obligation and its correlative right are extinguished. By limitation it is merely the right to sue that is cut off; substantive rights and obligations, although no longer directly enforceable, remain in force and may be pleaded by way of exception. Prescription is therefore substantive while limitation is procedural.[91]

The law as to limitation of actions[92] is now contained in the Prescription and Limitation (Scotland) Act 1973 which provides that no actions of damages, where the damages claimed consist of or include damages or solatium in respect of personal injuries, shall be brought unless commenced[93] within three years of the date when the injuries were sustained or, where there has been a continuing act or omission, within three years of the date on which the act or omission ceased, whichever is the later.[94] Where, however, the pursuer was not at that date aware that the injuries were sufficiently serious to justify his bringing an action of damages,[95] or that they were attributable to an act or omission or that the defender was a person to whose act or omission they were attributable, the three year period runs from the date on which he became aware, or on which, in the opinion of the court, it would have been reasonably practicable for him to become aware, of all those facts.[96] A three year limitation period applies on similar principles, but running from the date of death, to actions in which, following the death of any person from personal injuries, damages are claimed in respect of the injuries or death.[97] But no such action can be brought if the person who sustained the injuries allowed the limitation period applicable to an action by him to elapse without taking

---

[89] See Criminal Procedure (Scotland) Act 1975, s. 41.

[90] *Hester* v. *Macdonald, supra.*

[91] See Chap. 15.

[92] For the prior law, see Walker, *The Law of Prescription and Limitation of Actions in Scotland* (4th ed.), pp. 3–4.

[93] As to the meaning of 'commenced,' see *McGraddie* v. *Clark,* 1966 S.L.T. (Sh.Ct.) 36; see also *Miller* v. *N.C.B.,* 1960 S.C. 376, *per* Lord President Clyde at p. 382.

[94] ss. 17(1) and (2) as amended by the Prescription and Limitation (Scotland) Act 1984, s. 2.

[95] In *Mackie* v. *Currie,* 1991 S.L.T. 407, it was held that the triennium had begun to run at the time of an accident because the pursuer had been aware that he had suffered injuries which were not *de minimis* and would have justified the bringing of an action; *cf. Blake* v. *Lothian Health Board,* 1993 S.L.T. 1248.

[96] *Ibid.*

[97] s. 18.

proceedings.[98] If the pursuer is the person injured or, in an action following the death of the person injured, is a relative of that person, any time is to be disregarded, in computation of the limitation period, during which the pursuer was under legal disability by reason of nonage[99] or of unsoundness of mind.[1] It is not necessary for there to be a causal connection between the legal disability and the delay.[1a] It has been held that the limitation period does not apply where a pursuer seeks compensation for a wrong consisting of allowing his right of action against his employer or other person as a result of whose act he has suffered personal injury to lapse without having been exercised, as where a trade union official or a solicitor fails to raise the action within the statutory period; such an action is not one relating to damages for personal injuries.[2] Conversely, where the pursuer in an action concerning property damage makes averments of consequent distress and inconvenience, the three year limitation period applies to that aspect of the claim.[3] In any case where proceedings are barred by the expiry of the limitation period, the court may, nonetheless, allow the action to be brought if it seems to it equitable to do so.[4] The discretion thus given to the court is unfettered and is to be exercised according to the circumstances of the case. All the relevant equitable considerations are to be balanced and a decision reached on the basis of the side on which the balance of equity falls. The prejudice to which either party may be subject and the availability to the pursuer of an alternative remedy are relevant factors.[5] The fact that for part of the time since an accident the triennium has not been running because the pursuer has been under a legal disability should not however be viewed as creating unfairness to the defender.[5a]

The court will not in general allow a pursuer by amendment to change the basis of his case or cure a radical incompetence in his action,[6] to

---

[98] s. 18(4).

[99] i.e. 16—Age of Legal Capacity (Scotland) Act 1991, s.1(2); but see transitional provisions in s. 8.

[1] ss. 17(3) and 18(3).

[1a] *Paton* v. *Loffland Brothers North Sea Inc.*, 1994 S.L.T. 784; *cf. Bogan's C.B.* v. *Graham*, 1992 S.C.L.R. 920.

[2] *Robertson* v. *Bannigan*, 1965 S.C. 20; *McGahie* v. *Union of Shop Distributive & Allied Workers*, 1966 S.L.T. 74.

[3] *Fleming* v. *Strathclyde Regional Council*, 1992 S.L.T. 89.

[4] s.19 A was inserted by the Law Reform (Misc. Provs.) (Scotland) Act 1980, s.23(a).

[5] *Donald* v. *Rutherford*, 1984 S.L.T. 70; *Forsyth* v. *A.F. Stoddard and Co.*, 1985 S.L.T. 51; *Anderson* v. *City of Glasgow D.C.*, 1987 S.L.T. 279; *Elliot* v. *J. & C. Finney*, 1989 S.L.T. 605; *McLaren* v. *Harland & Wolff Ltd.*, 1991 S.L.T. 85.

[5a] *McCabe* v. *McLellan*, 1994 S.L.T. 346.

[6] See *Pompa's Trs.* v. *Edinburgh Mags.*, 1942 S.C. 119, *per* Lord Justice-Clerk Cooper at p. 125; *Dryburgh* v. *N.C.B.*, 1962 S.C. 485; *O'Hare* v. *Western Heritable Investment Co., Ltd.* 1965 S.L.T. 182. For cases in which amendments have been allowed on the view that they did not alter the basis of the pursuer's case see *Emslie* v. *Tognarelli's Exrs.*, 1969 S.L.T. 20, *Mazs* v. *The Dairy Supply Co.*, 1978 S.L.T. 208 and *Meek* v. *Milne*, 1985 S.L.T. 318.

substitute or call in another defender[7] or to amend his conclusion so as
to enable the court to grant decree against a third party,[8] if he seeks to
make such amendments outwith the period of the statutory limitation;
but an amendment may be allowed if it would be equitable to override
the time bar.[9]

34.10 Liability of Joint Wrongdoers *Inter Se*.—Joint wrongdoers, while each is
jointly and severally liable to the person wronged by them, are entitled
to relief *inter se* in such proportions as seem just to the court, whether
both have been sued in one action or not.[10] A decree of a Scottish
court,[11] or some equivalent instrument constituting the debt, is an
essential prerequisite to an action of relief by one wrongdoer against
another; an extrajudicial settlement by one wrongdoer acting on his own
which is not embodied in a decree[12] will not suffice for this purpose.[13]
Relief is available against any person who if sued to judgment might
also have been found liable.[14] The fact that such liability would have
arisen for breach of contract, rather than in delict, does not prevent
relief from being obtained.[15] Absolvitor or dismissal obtained as a result
of a settlement with the injured party[16] or as a result of successfully
founding on a plea of limitation[17] does not protect the person in whose
favour it is granted from claims for a contribution in relief at the
instance of others.

RECOVERY OF DAMAGES

34.11 Title to Sue.—The title to sue for damages in respect of a wrongful or
negligent act rests with the party injured. Insurance against the
particular injury is no objection to title.[18] If death has resulted from the
injury, certain near relatives have a title to sue, but third parties, who
may have suffered loss from the want of the injured person's services,
have no such title.[19] Where injury to the health of X resulted in loss to

---

[7] *Miller* v. *N.C.B.*, 1960 S.C. 376; *Maclean* v. *B.R.B.* 1966 S.L.T. 39 (an attempt to
include further pursuers); *Marshall* v. *Black,* 1981 S.L.T. 228; *Boslem* v. *Paterson*, 1982
S.L.T. 216; but see *Pompa's Trs.* v. *Edinburgh Mags., supra* and *Dailly* v. *Wilson*, 1990
S.L.T. 106.

[8] *Aitken* v. *Norrie*, 1967 S.L.T. 4; *Travers* v. *Neilson*, 1967 S.L.T. 64.

[9] *McCullough* v. *Norwest Socea*, 1981 S.L.T. 201; *Carson* v. *Howard Doris*, 1981 S.C.
278.; *Webb* v. *B.P. Petroleum Development Ltd.*, 1988 S.L.T. 775.

[10] Law Reform (Miscellaneous Provisions) (Scotland) Act 1940, s. 3; *Central S.M.T. Co.*
v. *Lanarkshire County Council*, 1949 S.C. 450.

[11] *Comex Houlder Diving Ltd.* v. *Colne Fishing Co. Ltd.*, 1987 S.L.T. 443.

[12] *Ibid.*

[13] *N.C.B.* v. *Thomson*, 1959 S.C. 353.

[14] See *Comex Houlder Diving Ltd.* v. *Colne Fishing Co. Ltd.*, *supra.*

[15] *Engdiv Ltd.* v. *G. Percy Trentham Ltd.*, 1990 S.L.T. 617.

[16] *Singer* v. *Gray Tool Co. (Europe)*, 1984 S.L.T. 149.

[17] *Dormer* v. *Melville Dundas & Whitson Ltd.* 1990 S.L.T. 186.

[18] *Port-Glasgow Sailcloth Co.* v. *Cal. Ry.* (1892) 19 R. 608.

[19] *Reavis* v. *Clan Line Steamers*, 1925 S.C. 725; *Gibson* v. *Glasgow Corporation*, 1963
S.L.T. (Notes) 16.

a limited company, of which X was the manager, secretary and principal shareholder, it was held that he could not recover in respect of loss of dividends.[20] And a relative cannot claim damages in respect of the loss of services previously rendered to him by a person who has been injured.[21] The injured person himself may, however, now include in his claim a reasonable sum by way of damages for his inability to render to a relative personal services which he might have been expected to render gratuitously and which, if rendered by a person other than a relative, would ordinarily be obtainable on payment.[22] He may also include in his claim a sum representing reasonable remuneration and repayment of reasonable expenses in respect of necessary services rendered by a relative to him in respect of his injuries.[23] The relative has no direct claim in respect of those matters but the injured person has an obligation to account to him. Necessary services may include management of the household and housekeeping.[24] A claim for necessary services rendered by the defender is unsustainable.[24a]

The law formerly refused an action of reparation by one spouse against another on the ground of the intimate relationship obtaining between them.[25] Since the Law Reform (Husband and Wife) Act 1962 however, each spouse has had the right to bring an action against the other in respect of a wrongful or negligent act or omission,[26] but the court has power to dismiss proceedings if it appears that no substantial benefit would accrue to either party from the continuation of the action.[27] An action of reparation has always been competent at the instance of a child against his parent,[28] and at the instance of a parent against his child.[29]

34.12   Title to Sue: Claims by Executors and Trustees in Sequestration.—If the injury causes patrimonial loss, the right to sue therefor passes, on the death of the injured party, to his executor; on his bankruptcy, to his trustee.[30] Should the injured party be an undischarged bankrupt at the

---

[20] *Young* v. *Ormiston*, 1936 S.L.T. 79; *cf. Lee* v. *Sheard* [1956] 1 Q.B. 192.

[21] *Robertson* v. *Turnbull*, 1982 S.L.T. 96.

[22] Administration of Justice Act 1982, s. 9.

[23] *Ibid.*, s. 8. In *Forsyth's C.B.* v. *Govan Shipbuilders Ltd.*, 1989 S.L.T. 91, it was held that the claim extended only to expenses prior to the proof; the right to claim damages for services to be rendered in the future was, however, expressly conferred by s. 69 of the Law Reform (Misc. Provs.) (Scotland) Act 1990.

[24] *Denheen* v. *British Railways Board*, 1986 S.L.T. 249.

[24a] *Hunt* v. *Severs* [1994] 2 A.C. 350 at p. 363; see acknowledgement of this view in *Kozikowska* v. *Kozikowski* 1995 G.W.D. 7–392.

[25] *Harper* v. *Harper*, 1929 S.C. 220; and see *Cameron* v. *Glasgow Corporation*, 1936 S.C. (H.L.) 26.

[26] s. 2(1). s. 2 applies to Scotland only.

[27] s. 2(2).

[28] *Young* v. *Rankin*, 1934 S.C. 499.

[29] *Wood* v. *Wood*, 1935 S.L.T. 431. Capacity to raise and defend proceedings is regulated by the Age of Legal Capacity (Scotland) Act 1991.

[30] *Muir's Tr.* v. *Braidwood*, 1958 S.C. 169, at p. 173; *Smith* v. *Duncan Stewart & Co. (No. 2)*, 1961 S.C. 91; *Russell* v. *B.R.B.*, 1965 S.L.T. 413.

time of his accident his claim for patrimonial loss will vest in his trustee in sequestration.[31] The right to sue may be assigned, but does not pass, without express assignation, with the transfer of a damaged thing.[32]

The position in relation to actions by an executor is now regulated by the Damages (Scotland) Act 1976. The rights to damages in respect of personal injuries sustained by a deceased person which transmit to his executor are the like rights as were vested in the deceased immediately before his death including the right to solatium, but damages by way of solatium or by way of compensation for patrimonial loss attributable to any period after the deceased's death are excluded.[33] The effect is that the executor's rights are restricted to recovery of solatium and patrimonial loss attributable to the period before death and compensation for services rendered by a relative to the deceased before his death.[34] He may enforce recovery of that loss by action whether or not the deceased had raised an action in his lifetime.[35] Any right which the deceased had to damages in respect of the death of another will transmit to his executor, but in assessing damages the court will have regard only to the period ending immediately before the relative's death.[36]

If an action of damages is raised by an injured party and he thereafter becomes bankrupt, his trustee in sequestration may sist himself as pursuer in lieu of the bankrupt and recover damages for solatium and patrimonial loss.[37] The trustee in sequestration cannot, however, initiate an action claiming solatium on behalf of the bankrupt, even if he has intimated a claim before sequestration.[38] If no action has been raised before sequestration, the title of the trustee is restricted to suing for patrimonial loss to the estate, unless the right to claim solatium has been assigned to him by the injured party.[39] If, however, a bankrupt raises an action of damages for personal injuries after sequestration, the trustee may be sisted as pursuer in the claim in respect of conclusions relating to both solatium and patrimonial loss.[40]

34.13 Claims by Relatives of Deceased Persons.—The right of a relative to damages for an injury resulting in death is regulated by the Damages (Scotland) Act 1976 which now governs the right of relatives of a deceased person to recover damages attributable to his death where that

[31] *Grindall v. John Mitchell Grangemouth Ltd.* 1987 S.L.T. 137.
[32] *Symington v. Campbell* (1894) 21 R. 434.
[33] 1976 Act, ss. 2(1)–(3), as substituted by the Damages (Scotland) Act 1993. See s. 6 of the 1993 Act for transitional provisions and specification of the deaths to which it relates.
[34] See ss. 7 and 8 of the Administration of Justice Act 1982.
[35] *Ibid.*, s. 2A, as inserted by the Damages (Scotland) Act 1993.
[36] *Ibid.*, s, 1A, as inserted by the Damages (Scotland) Act 1993, which also repealed s. 3 of the 1976 Act.
[37] *Thom v. Bridges* (1857) 19 D. 721.
[38] *Smith v. Duncan Stewart & Co (No. 1)*, 1960 S.C. 329; *Muir's Tr. v. Braidwood, supra.*
[39] *Traill v. Dalbeattie* (1904) 6 F. 798; *Cole-Hamilton v. Boyd*, 1963 S.C. (H.L.) 1; *cf. Muir's Tr. v. Braidwood, supra.*
[40] *Watson v. Thompson*, 1991 S.L.T. 683.

has been caused by the wrongful act of another.[41] The class of relatives who may sue has been enlarged and the principles regulating the award of damages redefined. A spouse, any person who immediately before the death of the deceased was living with the deceased as husband or wife, a parent or child[42] (including adopted and illegitimate children or their parents, as the case may be) and anyone accepted by the deceased as a child of his family may sue for damages for loss of support, and also for distress endured in contemplation of the suffering of the deceased before his death, grief caused by the death and loss of the society of the deceased.[43] The claim of a parent of a child who dies as a result of injuries sustained *in utero* is not excluded by the terms of section 1(1).[44] Any ascendant or descendant (other than a parent or child), a brother, sister, uncle, aunt, or any of their issue and, where the deceased had been divorced, an ex-spouse, may sue in respect of loss of support only.[45] Loss of support is to be measured by the extent to which the deceased, if he had not died, would have been likely to provide or contribute to support, and a legally enforceable alimentary obligation, although relevant to the question of likelihood, is not essential.[46] Funeral expenses, if incurred, may also be claimed[47] as may loss of personal services which had been rendered to the relative by the deceased.[48] In assessing loss of support, the court will take into account any part of a provisional award of damages relating to future patrimonial loss which was intended to compensate the deceased for a period beyond the date on which he died.[49] In assessing damages payable to a widow in respect of the death of her husband, whether for loss of support or loss of society, no account is taken of her remarriage or prospects of remarriage.[50] There are conflicting decisions on the relevance of a widow's cohabitation with another man after her husband's death.[51] A claim by the executor is not barred by the making of a claim by a relative nor is a relative's claim barred by a claim by the executor.[52] Action at the instance of the executor or relatives is, however, barred if liability has been excluded or discharged by the deceased during his lifetime.[53]

---

[41] 1976 Act, s.1.

[42] Which includes a posthumous child—*Cohen* v. *Shaw*, 1992 S.L.T. 1022.

[43] *Ibid.*, ss. 1(1), (3) and (4), and 10(2), and Sched. 1, para. 1 as amended by the Administration of Justice Act 1982, s. 14(4). Section 1(4) was amended by the Damages (Scotland) Act 1993, the transitional provisions of which are contained in s. 6.

[44] *Hamilton* v. *Fife Health Board*, 1993 S.L.T. 624.

[45] *Ibid.*, ss. 1(1) and (3) and Sched. 1, para. 2.

[46] *Ibid.*, ss. 1(3) and (6).

[47] *Ibid.*, s. 1(3).

[48] Administration of Justice Act 1982, s. 9(2).

[49] 1976 Act, s. 1(5A), as inserted by the Damages (Scotland) Act 1993.

[50] Law Reform (Misc. Provs.) Act 1971, s. 4.

[51] *Donnelly* v. *Glasgow Corp.*, 1949 S.L.T. 362; *cf. Morris* v. *Drysdale*, 1992 S.L.T. 186.

[52] Damages (Scotland) Act 1976, s. 4 as amended by the Administration of Justice Act 1982, s. 14(2)(a).

[53] *Ibid.*, ss. 1(2), 1A and 2A.

The right to redress for a wrongful or negligent act depends in part on the *lex loci delicti*, and therefore, in respect that English law does not recognise any claim for solatium, it was held, in an action by a father for damages for the death of his son in a railway accident which had occurred in England, that no damages on that ground could be given by the Court in Scotland in which the action was raised.[54] In an exceptional case, however, the *lex loci delicti* can be excluded to enable a party to rely on the *lex fori*, or vice versa.[55]

34.14   Damages and Title to Sue: Quantification of Damages.—As we have seen,[56] a wrongdoer is liable to make good all loss caused naturally and directly by his wrongful act. Damages are normally assessed on a once and for all basis but in personal injury cases where there is a risk that the injured person will develop a serious disease or suffer a serious deterioration in his condition, the court may award provisional damages.[57] Thus, the damages are assessed on the basis that the disease or deterioration will not occur but if it does, the injured person can return to court to claim further damages.[58] It is also possible in appropriate cases to obtain an award of interim damages.[59] A person who is injured through the breach of duty of another is entitled to claim solatium as pecuniary reparation for pain and suffering inflicted upon him.[60] Such a claim covers wounded feelings, physical injuries or nervous shock. The effects of injury which are thereby compensated are (1) pain and suffering, (2) loss of faculties and amenities, and (3) shortened life expectancy.[61]

Damages will also include wages lost by the injured party,[62] but not those of a spouse who voluntarily stops working to nurse the injured party:[63] pension rights lost by the injured party:[64] all medical expenses reasonably incurred[65] and other outlays: repair of a damaged article plus

---

[54] *Naftalin* v. *L.M.S. Ry.*, 1933 S.C. 259. Followed in *McElroy* v. *McAllister*, 1949 S.C. 110.

[55] *Chaplin* v. *Boys* [1971] A.C. 356; *Red Sea Insurance Co. Ltd.* v. *Bouygues S.A.* [1995] 1 A.C. 190.

[56] See para. 32.11, *supra.*

[57] Administration of Justice Act 1982, s. 12.

[58] See McEwan & Paton, Chap. 2.

[59] *Ibid.*, Chap. 1.

[60] See Bell, *Prin.*, § 2032; *Traynor's Exrx.*. v. *Bairds & Scottish Steel*, 1957 S.C. 311 (O.H.), *per* Lord Guthrie at p. 314.

[61] *Balfour* v. *Beardmore & Co.*, 1956 S.L.T. 205, at p. 215; and see *Dalgleish* v. *Glasgow Corp.*, 1976 S.C. 32.

[62] *Doonan* v. *S.M.T.*, 1950 S.C. 136.

[63] *Edgar* v. *P.M.G.*, 1965 S.L.T. 158; *Collins* v. *South of Scotland Electricity Board*, 1977 S.L.T. 93. But see now the provisions of the Administration of Justice Act 1982, discussed below, for remuneration of necessary services.

[64] See consideration of the quantification of such a loss in *Mitchell* v. *Glenrothes Development Corporation*, 1991 S.L.T. 284.

[65] *Rubens* v. *Walker*, 1946 S.C. 215; and see s. 2(4) of the Law Reform (Personal Injuries) Act 1948.

the cost of hiring a replacement pending repair[66] and, in the case of destruction, the market value of that article less its scrap value plus the cost of hire for a reasonable period pending the acquisition of a replacement.[66] If there is no market for the article destroyed, the actual cost of replacement may be allowed.[67] Future loss of income, and damages for the future cost of caring for an injured party, are normally calculated by computing an annual loss (the multiplicand) to which is applied a multiplier appropriate to the age of the party and other relevant circumstances. This produces a lump sum which, when invested, should provide an annual income equivalent to the loss. Multipliers are selected on a broad basis but it is permissible to have regard to actuarial tables as a cross reference.[68] Where the pursuer's expectation of life has, as a result of personal injuries to him, been reduced, that reduction is, for the purposes of assessing patrimonial loss, ignored; and the court may, for those purposes, have regard to any amount by way of benefits in money or money's worth, other than benefits from his own estate, which, in its opinion, he would have received in the period up to the date when he would have been expected to die if he had not sustained the injuries in question, less expenses which might reasonably have been incurred in that period.[69] The pursuer's right to damages by way of solatium for shortened expectation of life depends on whether or not he is aware that his expectation of life has been reduced.[70] Damages may also be awarded for the loss of a chance, although a distinction can be drawn between the loss of a chance which is itself a matter of legal right, such as a chance to bring an action or an appeal, and a chance of achieving some other benefit.[71] In the latter case, the chance of success may be too speculative to be taken into account.[72] In cases involving the failure of a sterilisation operation, and consequent pregnancy of the pursuer, damages awarded can include pain and suffering associated with pregnancy and birth, together with wage loss and the cost of rearing the child.[72a] When heritable property is totally destroyed, reinstatement value will only be allowed in exceptional cases.[73] Interest may be awarded from the date when the right of action arose, or when the

[66] *Pomphrey* v. *Cuthbertson*, 1951 S.C. 147.

[67] *Clyde Navigation Trs.* v. *Bowring S.S. Co*, 1929 S.C. 715.

[68] *O'Brien's Curator Bonis* v. *British Steel Corporation*, 1991 S.L.T. 477.

[69] Damages (Scotland) Act 1976, s. 9.

[70] *Ibid.*, s. 9A, as inserted by the Damages (Scotland) Act 1993.

[71] *Kyle* v. *P. & J. Stormonth Darling*, 1993 S.C.L.R. 18, following *Yeoman's Exrx.* v. *Ferries*, 1967 S.L.T. 332.

[72] *Neill* v. *Scottish Omnibuses Ltd.*, 1961 S.L.T. (Notes) 42.

[72a] *Allen* v. *Bloomsbury Health Authority* [1993] 1 All E.R. 651; *Allan* v. *Greater Glasgow Health Board* 1994, G.W.D. 6–348.

[73] *Hutchison* v. *Davidson*, 1945 S.C. 395; *Fraser* v. *Morton Wilson*, 1965 S.L.T. (Notes) 81 (O.H.). The Lord Ordinary also allowed interest from the date of citation: 1965 S.L.T. (Notes) 85.

damage suffered became capable of ascertainment.[74] Where damages are awarded for personal injuries, unless there are special circumstances in a particular case, the court must award interest on these damages.[75] It is competent to award damages in foreign currency.[75a]

In awarding damages the court should take into account the decline in the value of money,[76] and must deduct the appropriate income tax[77] and National Insurance contributions[78] and pension contributions[79] from a sum given for loss of earnings. Social security benefits must also be considered. Where damages are paid for an accident or injury occurring on or after January 1, 1989, or for a disease for which a benefit is first claimed on or after that date, the total of relevant benefits paid to the injured person in consequence of the injury or disease during the five years from the accident or from the first claim for benefit in respect of the disease must be deducted from the damages and repaid to the Department of Social Security in terms of the Social Security Administration Act 1992.[80] The responsibility for making the deduction and repayment is that of the payer of the damages. By section 81, certain compensation payments, such as payments below a certain amount[81] and damages awarded under the Damages (Scotland) Act 1976[82] are exempt. Unlike the previous law, deductions can be made from damages awarded as solatium, as well as from those awarded for patrimonial loss. Claims predating these rules, and small payments, will still be governed by the provisions of the Law Reform (Personal Injuries) Act 1948. There are also provisions governing deductions from damages in the Administration of Justice Act 1982. By section 10, any benefit payable from public funds and designed to secure a minimum level of subsistence is to be taken into account so far as payable in respect of any period before the award of damages but not if payable in respect of a later period. Any remuneration or earnings from employment, unemployment benefit and any benevolent payment made by the person responsible for the damages, where made directly and not through a trust or other fund, are to be taken into account so as to reduce damages but *not* any contractual pension or benefit, any pension

---

[74] Interest on Damages (Scotland) Act 1958, s. 1; see *Macrae v. Reed & Mallik*, 1961 S.C. 68; *Killah v. Aberdeen Milk Marketing Board*, 1961 S.L.T. 232 (O.H.); *R. & J. Dempster v. Motherwell Bridge, etc., Co.*, 1964 S.C. 308, *per* Lord President Clyde at pp. 333–334; *Boots the Chemist Ltd. v. G.A. Estates Ltd.*, 1993 S.L.T. 136.

[75] *Ibid.*, s. 1A, inserted by the Interest on Damages (Scotland) Act 1971; *Orr v. Metcalfe*, 1973 S.C. 57.

[75a] *Fullemann v. McInnes's Exrs.*, 1993 S.L.T. 259.

[76] *Kelly v. Glasgow Corporation*, 1951 S.C. (H.L.) 15.

[77] *British Transport Commission v. Gourley* [1956] A.C. 185; *Stewart v. Glentaggart*, 1963 S.C. 300; see also *Cockburn & Co. v. Scottish Motor Omnibus Co.*, 1964 S.L.T. (Notes) 7.

[78] *Gibney v. Eric Johnson Stubbs*, 1987 S.L.T. 132.

[79] *Dews v. N.C.B.* [1988] A.C. 1.

[80] ss. 81 and 82.

[81] s. 85, the amount being prescribed under Regulations—currently £2,500.

[82] s. 81(3).

or retirement benefit from public funds (other than those noticed above), any statutory redundancy payment, or its equivalent,[83] any payment made by an employer subject to an obligation of reimbursement in the event of an award of damages and any benevolent payment (other than that noticed above.)[84] Any saving which is attributable to the maintenance of the injured person at public expense in a hospital or other institution is to be set off against any income lost by him.[85] Proceeds of insurance policies are normally to be regarded as collateral and non-deductible but in some circumstances a discretionary payment made by an employer to an employee in respect of an accident may be deductible.[86] In an action in respect of a person's death no account is to be taken of any gain or advantage accruing by way of succession or settlement, or any insurance money, benefit under the Social Security Act 1975, any payment by a friendly society or trade union for the relief or maintenance of a member's dependants, or any pension or gratuity payable as a result of the deceased's death.[87] A widow's private means are not a relevant factor.[88]

Further Reading

McEwan & Paton, *Damages in Scotland* (2nd ed., 1989).
McGregor, *Damages* (15th ed., 1988).

---

[83] Which does not include severance pay received on redundancy: *Duncan* v. *Glacier Metal Co. Ltd.*, 1988 S.L.T. 479.

[84] Administration of Justice Act 1982, s. 10; McEwan & Paton, Chap. 5.

[85] *Ibid.*, s. 11.

[86] *Wilson* v. *National Coal Board*, 1978 S.L.T. 129.

[87] Damages (Scotland) Act 1976, s. 1(5).

[88] *Cruickshank* v. *Shiels*, 1953 S.C. (H.L.) 1.

CHAPTER 35

DEFAMATION: ABUSE OF LEGAL PROCESS

35.1 **Defamation.**—Defamation is a civil wrong, which grounds an action for damages, or an interdict against publication or repetition,[1] and in its widest sense covers all imputations which are injurious. The courts, however, have drawn a distinction between slander, which has been confined to injurious imputations against character, credit or reputation, and other types of verbal injury, *e.g.* (a) statements exposing a person to public hatred and contempt;[2] (b) slander of title; (c) slander of property;[3] and (d) slander of goods or business.[4] In this chapter the words 'defamation' and 'defamatory' are used in the narrow sense and are not related to those other aspects of verbal injury.

35.2 **Requisites of Defamation.**—Defamation consists of the communication of a false statement or idea, which is defamatory of the pursuer.[5] If the statement is untrue and defamatory, malice is irrelevant unless privilege is pleaded or there has, because of the defender's malice, been greater injury to the pursuer's reputation than would otherwise have occurred.[6] The statement may be oral, in writing, or, in exceptional cases, inferred from acts, as where the waxwork figure of the plaintiff was placed in the department of an exhibition devoted to the effigies of notorious criminals.[7] Technically, written defamation is known as libel, oral as slander,[8] but the distinction is not of importance in the law of Scotland.

35.3 **Statement must be Untrue: *Veritas*.[9]**—To be actionable the statement must be untrue, as is indicated in the maxim *veritas convicii excusat*[10] (the truth of an insult excuses). In the case of statements which are defamatory there is a presumption of their untruth, and the defender, if

---

[1] *British Legal Life Co.* v. *Pearl Ins. Co.* (1887) 14 R. 818.
[2] See para. 35.18, *infra.*
[3] See para. 35.19, *infra.*
[4] See Walker, pp. 906–907.
[5] See paras. 35.5 and 35.6, *infra.*
[6] *Stein* v. *Beaverbrook Newspapers,* 1968 S.C. 272; *cf.* para. 35.9, *infra.*
[7] *Monson* v. *Tussauds* [1894] 1 Q.B. 671; *Adamson* v. *Martin,* 1916 S.C. 319; *Tolley* v. *Fry* [1931] A.C. 333: and see Defamation Act 1952, s. 16(1). For limits of slander by acts, see *Drysdale* v. *Lord Rosebery,* 1909 S.C. 1121.
[8] A representation in words and pictures in a film is libel not slander: *Youssoupoff* v. *M.G.M.* (1934) 50 T.L.R. 581.
[9] See Walker, pp. 794–798; also para. 35.15, *infra.*
[10] *McKellar* v. *Duke of Sutherland* (1859) 21 D. 222.

569

he relies on *veritas*, must affirm the truth of his statement in his defences, and, where trial is by jury, table a definite counter-issue. Without such a counter-issue, evidence of the truthfulness of the statement is not admissible.[11] Where there are two separate charges, it is competent to take a counter-issue with regard to one of them.[12] By the Defamation Act 1952,[13] where a statement sued on contains two or more charges against a pursuer, a defence of *veritas* is not to fail by reason only that the truth of every charge is not proved, provided that the words not proved to be true do not materially injure the pursuer's reputation in view of the proven truth of the remaining charges. Where the alleged defamatory statement consists of a reference to a criminal conviction of the pursuer which by virtue of the Rehabilitation of Offenders Act 1974 is spent, the defence of *veritas* remains open unless malice is proved.[14]

35.4   Publication.—In Scotland it is not necessary that the statement be communicated to a third party. It is sufficent if it was made or sent to the injured party because damages are recoverable for injured feelings.[15] The dictation of a defamatory letter to a clerk is not publication and no action would lie if the letter was not despatched.[16]

35.5   What Amounts to Defamation.—Whether or not the words complained of are reasonably capable of bearing a defamatory meaning, either *per se* or by innuendo,[17] is a question of law for the court.[18] In determining this question the whole statement must be read.[19] Thus, the contents of a newspaper report, when read together with the heading, may negative the defamatory meaning of the heading alone.[20] If the court holds that the language may be construed in a defamatory sense, it is then a question for the jury to decide whether or not the proper construction in all the circumstances of the case is defamatory or innocent. Evidence may be led of the sense in which the words used were understood by those who read or heard them.[21]

Imputations against a man's moral character are defamatory.[22] Imputations of guilt of crime or of attempt to commit a crime or of

[11] *Craig* v. *Jex-Blake* (1871) 9 M. 973; *Browne* v. *Macfarlane* (1889) 16 R. 368.
[12] *O'Callaghan* v. *Thomson & Co.*, 1928 S.C. 532.
[13] s. 5; *Polly Peck (Holdings)* v. *Trelford* [1986] Q.B. 1000.
[14] Rehabilitation of Offenders Act 1974, s. 8(5); *Herbage* v. *Pressdram* [1984] 1 W.L.R. 1160.
[15] *Mackay* v. *McCankie* (1883) 10 R. 537; *Ramsay* v. *Maclay* (1890) 18 R. 130.
[16] See *Evans* v. *Stein* (1904) 7 F. 65.
[17] See para. 35.6, *infra.*
[18] *Russell* v. *Stubbs*, 1913 S.C. (H.L.) 14, *per* Lord Kinnear at p. 20; *Fraser* v. *Mirza*, 1993 S.C. (H.L.) 27.
[19] *Campbell* v. *Ritchie & Co.*, 1907 S.C. 1097.
[20] *Leon* v. *Edinburgh Evening News*, 1909 S.C. 1014.
[21] *Muirhead* v. *George Outram & Co.*, 1983 S.L.T. 201.
[22] *Brownlie* v. *Thomson* (1859) 21 D. 480, *per* Lord Justice-Clerk Inglis at p. 485. See Cooper, *op. cit.*, and Walker, pp. 771–780, for examples of defamatory imputations.

criminal intent are clearly defamatory, as also are allegations of dishonesty, immorality and drunkenness, if seriously made. Words which are prima facie defamatory may be held to have been used in their slang sense[23] or in the heat of a quarrel (in rixa)[24] as words of mere abuse, but not if a definite charge is made.[25] While the law affords no remedy for a reflection on manners, a definite charge of conduct usually regarded as dishonourable, either in general society,[26] or in a particular class to which the pursuer belongs,[27] is actionable. To say of a man that he is an informer may be actionable.[28]

Any imputation on solvency is actionable.[29] In the case of 'black lists,' i.e. lists of persons against whom decrees in absence have been pronounced, the publication of such a list, compiled from official sources, and accurate, cannot be made the subject of an action on the ground merely that it may be read as an imputation on the solvency of the parties whose names are included.[30] But it becomes actionable if prefaced by a caution against giving credit,[31] or if it is averred that the publication is generally read as inferring insolvency.[32] A party whose name is entered by mistake may claim damages. A prefatory statement, to the effect that the publication of a name does not import any inability to pay, will preclude an innuendo, by a party whose name has been inserted by mistake, that the insertion involves a charge of insolvency,[33] but not an innuendo that it involves a statement that he is a party to whom credit should not be given.[34]

False statements which disparage a man's professional or business capacity or fitness for his office or vocation may be defamatory,[35] but they must be distinguished from those which, while injurious, do not impugn his character or business reputation. The latter are not defamatory. While they are actionable under the general head of verbal injury, malice must be specifically averred and proved by the pursuer.[36] There is also a material distinction between private individuals and

[23] *Murdison* v. *Scottish Football Union* (1896) 23 R. 449; *Agnew* v. *British Legal Assce. Co.* (1906) 8 F. 422.
[24] *Watson* v. *Duncan* (1890) 17 R. 404.
[25] *Christie* v. *Robertson* (1899) 1 F. 1155, *per* Lord McLaren at p. 1157; and see Walker, pp. 792–793.
[26] *Menzies* v. *Goodlet* (1835) 13 S. 1136 (anonymous letter).
[27] *Griffen* v. *Divers*, 1922 S.C. 605; *Tolley* v. *Fry* [1931] A.C. 333; *Cuthbert* v. *Linklater*, 1936 S.L.T. 94; *Lloyd* v. *Hickley*, 1967 S.L.T. 225.
[28] *Winn* v. *Quillan* (1899) 37 S.L.R. 38. *Aliter* in England and Ireland: see *Byrne* v. *Dean* [1937] 1 K.B. 818; *Maure* v. *Pigott* (1869) I.R. 4 C.L. 54; *Berry* v. *Irish Times* [1973] I.R. 368.
[29] *A.B.* v. *C.D.* (1904) 7 F. 22; see cases in Walker, pp. 775–777.
[30] *Taylor* v. *Rutherford* (1888) 15 R. 608; *McLintock* v. *Stubbs* (1902) 5 F. 1.
[31] *Andrews* v. *Drummond* (1887) 14 R. 568.
[32] *Barr* v. *Musselburgh Merchants*, 1912 S.C. 174.
[33] *Russell* v. *Stubbs*, 1913 S.C. (H.L.) 14.
[34] *Mazure* v. *Stubbs*, 1919 S.C. (H.L.) 112.
[35] See cases cited in Walker, pp. 777–779, and Glegg on *Reparation*, p. 150; *Muirhead* v. *George Outram & Co., supra.*
[36] See para. 35.18, *infra.*

public figures, critics of the latter being allowed a wide latitude in the public interest.[37] It is, however, defamatory of the holder of a public office to make criticisms from which it can reasonably be inferred that he is dishonest or guilty of dishonourable behaviour or that his public conduct is combined with base and indirect motives.[38]

35.6 Innuendo.[39]—In some cases it may be necessary to explain technical, ironical or ambiguous language or to supply a stigma which may, but does not necessarily, lurk in the words used. This is done by setting forth on record and putting in issue an innuendo, *i.e.* the precise defamatory meaning which the pursuer attaches to the words.[40] The language itself may support the innuendo, but the pursuer may also aver facts extrinsic to the libel which tend to show that the language may reasonably be construed in the sense of the innuendo.[41] It is for the court to determine whether the innuendo is one which the words actually used may reasonably bear and for the jury to decide as matter of fact whether the language ought to be construed in the sense of the innuendo.[42] 'The innuendo must represent what is a reasonable, natural, or necessary inference from the words used, regard being had to the occasion and the circumstances of their publication.'[43] The words must be judged not in isolation but in the context of the publication as a whole.[43a] If the innuendo consists of a special meaning dependent on knowledge of specific facts, publication to persons aware of those facts at that time must be proved.[44] An innuendo is also used when the slander is in a foreign language and may be used to extract the substance of the charge from a series of letters or articles, and to gather together the expressions therein which are defamatory.[44a]

35.7 Defences.—The following defences are open in an action for defamation:

---

[37] See Glegg, pp. 183–184, and para. 33.15, *infra*.
[38] *Mutch* v. *Robertson*, 1981 S.L.T. 217; *cf. Fairbairn* v. *Scottish National Party*, 1979 S.C. 393.
[39] See Walker, pp. 765–771; Glegg, pp. 146–153.
[40] *Murdison* v. *S.F.U.* (1896) 23 R. 449, per Lord Kinnear at p. 463; *James* v. *Baird*, 1915 S.C. 23; *Fraser* v. *Mirza, supra*.
[41] *James* v. *Baird*, 1916 S.C. (H.L.) 158, *per* Lord Kinnear at p. 165; *Smith* v. *Walker*, 1912 S.C. 224; *Gordon* v. *Leng*, 1919 S.C. 415; *Gollan* v. *Thompson Wyles*, 1930 S.C. 599, *per* Lord President Clyde at pp. 603–604; *Lewis* v. *Daily Telegraph* [1964] A.C. 234 (turns in part on procedural rules which do not apply in Scotland).
[42] *Langlands* v. *Leng*, 1916 S.C. (H.L.) 102; *Ritchie & Co.* v. *Sexton* (1891) 18 R. (H.L.) 20, affirming (1890) 17 R. 680; *Slim* v. *Daily Telegraph* [1968] 2 Q.B. 157.
[43] *Per* Lord Shaw, *Russell* v. *Stubbs*, 1913 S.C. (H.L.) 14, at p. 24; *Lord Hamilton* v. *Glasgow Dairy Co.*, 1931 S.C. (H.L.) 67. See *Fullam* v. *Newcastle Chronicle and Journal* [1977] 1 W.L.R. 651, on requirements of pleading where innuendo would be drawn only by those with special knowledge.
[43a] *Chalmers* v. *Payne* (1835) 2 Cr. M. & R. 67; *Charleston* v. *News Group Newspapers* [1995] 2 W.L.R. 450.
[44] *Grappelli* v. *Derek Block (Holdings)* [1981] 1 W.L.R. 822; *cf. Hayward* v. *Thomson* [1982] Q.B. 47.
[44a] *Neilson* v. *Johnston* (1890) 17 R. 442.

(1) That the words founded on were not used by the defender.[45]
(2) That the statement did not refer to the pursuer and could not reasonably be construed as referrring to him.[46]
(3) That the words used were not reasonably capable of bearing the alleged defamatory meaning.[47]
(4) That the words used could not in all the circumstances bear the meaning ascribed to them.[47]
(5) That the slander was unintentional, coupled with an offer of amends.[48]
(6) That the pursuer expressly or impliedly assented to the statement being made.
(7) That the statement was true (*veritas*).[49]
(8) Absolute privilege.[50]
(9) Qualified privilege.[51]
(10) Fair retort.[52]
(11) Fair comment.[53]

35.8 Unintentional Slander.—The pursuer in an action of defamation does not require to prove that the defender intended to disparage him or that he even knew of his existence. His obligation is to satisfy the court, as a matter of relevancy, that the words used might reasonably be read as referring to him, and to satisfy the jury that they were in fact so read. In *Jones* v. *Hulton*[54] a newspaper article was defamatory of 'Artemus Jones,' the name given by the author to a fictitious character. A person of that name, who was unknown to the author of the article and to the editor of the paper, proved that the article had been read as referring to him and was found entitled to damages from the publishers. An action of damages lies for publication of a statement which is *ex facie* innocent but which is reasonably read in a sense defamatory of the pursuer by persons with knowledge of facts unknown to the defender. It is no defence that the author or publisher was unaware of these extrinsic factors.[55] So, in the case of a newspaper notice inserted by an unknown party, it has been held that malice may be inferred from the failure of the publishers to make sufficient inquiry into the genuineness of the notice and that the circumstances surrounding the publication of the notice are relevant only to quantum of damages.[56]

---

[45] The plea of *veritas* may be taken as an alternative defence.
[46] See para. 35.8, *infra*.
[47] See para. 35.5, *supra*.
[48] See para. 35.8, *infra*.
[49] See para. 35.3, *supra*. If the truth of the statement is evident from the pursuer's pleadings, the action is irrelevant: *Carson* v. *White*, 1919 2 S.L.T. 215.
[50] See paras. 35.9 and 35.10, *infra*.
[51] See paras. 35.9 and 35.11, *infra*.
[52] See para. 35.14, *infra*.
[53] See para. 35.15, *infra*.
[54] [1910] A.C. 20, followed in *Wragg* v. *Thomson*, 1909 2 S.L.T. 409.
[55] *Morrison* v. *Ritchie* (1902) 4 F. 645; *Cassidy* v. *Daily Mirror* [1929] 2 K.B. 331.
[56] *Morrison* v. *Ritchie, supra*; but note opinions of Lords Salvesen and Kinnear in *Wood* v. *Edinburgh Evening News*, 1910 S.C. 895. See Walker, pp. 783–784.

Nonetheless, if a slander is unintentional, the person claiming innocent publication[57] may offer 'amends' by way of published correction and apology and by notifying persons known to have received copies of the slanderous statement.[58] The offer must be accompanied by a signed declaration specifying the facts relied upon to demonstrate innocent publication.[59] If this offer is accepted and fulfilled, no proceedings for libel or slander can be taken or continued against the offeror.[60] Rejection of the offer enables the offeror to set up as a complete defence on the merits of an action the fact of innocent publication coupled with a timeous offer of amends.[61]

35.9   Privilege.[62]—In cases of defamation, privilege may be absolute or qualified. Where privilege is absolute no action can be based on defamatory words. Averments of malice are irrelevant. Where privilege is not absolute, but qualified, action is not excluded, but malice on the part of the defender must be averred and proved.[63]

35.10   Absolute Privilege.[64]—The following are the leading cases of absolute privilege: Any statement made in Parliament, in a petition to Parliament, in a report authorised by Parliament,[65] including reports broadcast by wireless telegraphy,[66] official reports to any department of State, or to a colonial government,[67] a memorandum by an acting ambassador to his home government;[68] any statement by a judge, of any court, while acting in his judicial capacity[69]; any statement by an advocate (*i.e.* by any person professionally addressing a court)[70] or by a witness whether made in court, on precognition,[71] or by way of some less formal interview.[71a] But the privilege of a litigant, in statements made on record, or in statements which he instructs his counsel or solicitor to make in court, is not absolute.[72] And submission to an agreed industrial conciliation procedure does not imply acceptance of absolute privilege for what is said in the course of the proceedings.[73]

[57] Defamation Act 1952, s. 4(5).
[58] s. 4(3).
[59] ss. 4(2) and 14 (c).
[60] ss. 4(1)(a) and (4) and 14 (d).
[61] s. 4(1)(b).
[62] See Glegg on *Reparation*, Chap. 9, pp. 160 *et seq.*
[63] *Langlands* v. *Leng*, 1916 S.C. (H.L.) 102, *per* Lord Shaw at p. 109.
[64] See Walker, pp. 798–805.
[65] *Dillon* v. *Balfour* (1887) 20 L.R.Ir. 600; Parliamentary Papers Act 1840; *Mangena* v. *Wright* [1909] 2 K.B. 958; *Dingle* v. *Associated Newspapers* [1964] A.C. 371; Erskine May. *Parliamentary Practice* (21st ed., 1989), pp. 86 *et seq.*
[66] Defamation Act 1952, s. 9(1).
[67] *Dawkins* v. *Lord Paulet* (1869) L.R. 5 Q.B. 94; *Isaacs* v. *Cook* [1925] K.B. 391.
[68] *Fayed* v. *Al-Tajir* [1988] Q.B. 712.
[69] *Primrose* v. *Waterston* (1902) 4 F. 783.
[70] *Williamson* v. *Umphray* (1890) 17 R. 905; *Rome* v. *Watson* (1898) 25 R. 733.
[71] *Watson* v. *McEwan* (1905) 7 F. (H.L.) 109.
[71a] *B.* v. *Burns*, 1994 S.L.T. 250.
[72] *Williamson* v. *Umphray, supra; M.* v. *H.*, 1908 S.C. 1130; and see para. 35.11, *infra.*
[73] *Tadd* v. *Eastwood and Daily Telegraph* [1985] I.C.R. 132.

Absolute privilege attaches, however, on the same principles as are applicable to judicial proceedings,[74] to statements made in the course of tribunal proceedings provided the tribunal is recognised by law and has similar attributes to those possessed by a court of justice.[75]

Absolute privilege extends to a fair report of what took place on any privileged occasion, such as the proceedings in Parliament, or in any court. The report need not be verbatim, and it is for the jury to decide whether any omission deprives it of the character of a fair report.[76] The privilege covers the publication of any decree, or official record.[77] While it is doubtful whether privilege covers a report of statements made in the closed record of an action, it is clear that it does not extend to statements before the record is closed.[78] The publication of such statements amounts to contempt of court, and may be visited by penalties.[79]

35.11 Qualified Privilege.[80]—Qualified privilege does not relate to persons or to the nature of statements but to occasions, and it is for the court to decide whether or not the occasion is privileged, although it may not be possible to do so until the relevant facts have been ascertained.[81] 'The proper meaning of a privileged communication is only this; that the occasion on which the communication was made rebuts the inference [of malice] prima facie arising from a statement prejudicial to the character of the plaintiff, and puts it upon him to prove that there was malice in fact—that the defendant was actuated by motives of personal spite or ill-will, independent of the occasion on which the communication was made.'[82] As misuse of the occasion is the essence of the matter,[82a] it may be sufficient to prove that the statement was actuated by malice even if the pursuer was not the object of that malice.[83] Absence of belief in the truth of a defamatory allegation actually or intended to be conveyed is usually conclusive evidence of an improper motive amounting to malice. So the privilege will be lost in respect of an untrue

[74] For arbitrations see *Neill* v. *Henderson* (1901) 3 F. 387; *Slack* v. *Barr*, 1918 1 S.L.T. 133.

[75] *Trapp* v. *Mackie*, 1979 S.C. (H.L.) 38.

[76] *Wright & Greig* v. *Outram* (1890) 17 R. 596; *Duncan* v. *Associated Newspapers*, 1929 S.C. 14; *Harper* v. *Provincial Newspapers*, 1937 S.L.T. 462; see Walker, pp. 884–885.

[77] *Buchan* v. *N.B. Ry.* (1894) 21 R. 379.

[78] *Macleod* v. *J.P. of Lewis* (1892) 20 R. 218.

[79] *Young* v. *Armour*, 1921 1 S.L.T. 211.

[80] See Walker, pp. 805–817.

[81] *Adam* v. *Ward* [1917] A.C. 309; *Mintner* v. *Priest* [1930] A.C. 558, *per* Viscount Dunedin at pp. 571–572.

[82] *Wright* v. *Woodgate* (1835) 2 C.M. & R. 573, *per* Parke B. at p. 577, quoted by Lord Hunter in *Cochrane* v. *Young*, 1922 S.C. 696, at pp. 701–702.

[82a] *Horrocks* v. *Lowe* [1975] A.C. 135 *per* Lord Diplock at pp. 149–150; *Fraser* v. *Mirza* 1993 S.C. (H.L.) 27 *per* Lord Keith of Kinkel at p. 33.

[83] Gatley, § 767; *Anderson* v. *Palombo*, 1984 S.L.T. 332 at p. 334 (see also n. 27, *infra*.) *Quaere*, however, if this view wholly consists with the explanation that the occasion, in the absence of proof of malice, rebuts the inference of malice (against the pursuer).

defamatory allegation, even though it is less serious than the one which the defendant intended to convey.[83a]

Qualified privilege exists where the statement is 'fairly made by a person in the discharge of some public or private duty, whether legal or moral, or in the conduct of his own affairs, in matters where his interest is concerned.'[84] As is added later in the same judgment, the communication must be to some person legitimately interested in the matter but the privilege is not lost merely because someone else happens to be present.[85] Publication in a specialist journal of matters of concern to the readership may fall within the necessary reciprocity of interest.[86]

A well-recognised instance for the invocation of privilege is criticism by an employer of his employee,[87] either to himself, in giving him a character, or in speaking to some party who has an interest to inquire, but not in repeating his criticism unnecessarily to third parties.[88] An employer is also privileged in speaking to his employees of the character of their associates.[89] Where a dismissed employee wrote to a television company complaining about his former employers and the television company communicated with the employers, their reply giving the reasons for his dismissal was held to be privileged.[90] Charitable intention has been held to afford privilege to a statement regarding the treatment of pauper patients by a doctor.[91] An elector has qualified privilege in speaking of a candidate in his own constituency,[92] not in another.[93] A Member of Parliament has a qualified privilege in passing on to the appropriate body a complaint received from a constituent about the conduct of a professional man.[94] A defamatory statement published by or for a candidate at a local or Parliamentary election is not privileged on the ground that it is material to a question at issue in the election.[95] The members of a public body or board are privileged in discussing any matter pertinent to the business.[96] The Public Bodies

---

[83a] *Fraser* v. *Mirza, supra* at p. 33 *per* Lord Keith of Kinkel.

[84] *Per* Parke B., in *Toogood* v. *Spyring* (1834) 1 C.M. & R. 181 at p. 193, adopted in *McIntosh* v. *Dun* [1908] A.C. 390; *A.B.* v. *X.Y.,* 1917 S.C. 15; *Hines* v. *Davidson*, 1935 S.C. 30, *per* Lord Anderson at p. 38.

[85] See *Watt* v. *Longsdon* [1930] 1 K.B. 130.

[86] *Star Gems* v. *Ford* [1980] C.L.Y. 1671.

[87] A comparable case is chairman and employee of a company; see *McGillivray* v. *Davidson*, 1934 S.L.T. 45.

[88] *Bryant* v. *Edgar*, 1909 S.C. 1080.

[89] *Hunt* v. *Great Northern Ry.* [1891] 2 Q.B. 189; *A.B.* v. *X.Y. supra;* but see *Milne* v. *Smith* (1892) 20 R. 95.

[90] *Sutherland* v. *British Telecommunications*, 1989 S.L.T. 531.

[91] *James* v. *Baird*, 1916 S.C. (H.L.) 158.

[92] *Bruce* v. *Leisk* (1892) 19 R. 482.

[93] *Anderson* v. *Hunter* (1891) 18 R. 467.

[94] *Beach* v. *Freesan* [1972] 1 Q.B. 14.

[95] Defamation Act 1952, s. 10; and see *Plummer* v. *Charman* [1962] 1 W.L.R. 1469; *Fairbairn* v. *Scottish National Party*, 1979 S.C. 393.

[96] *Shaw* v. *Morgan* (1888) 15 R. 865; *Griffen* v. *Divers*, 1922 S.C. 605; *Mutch* v. *Robertson*, 1981 S.L.T. 217.

(Admission to Meetings) Act 1960, section 1(5) confers qualified privilege on the agenda of any meeting required by the Act to be open to the public, a copy of which is supplied to a member of the public attending the meeting or supplied for the benefit of a newspaper. A trade protection society, established for profit, and issuing lists of persons to whom it is dangerous to give credit, has no privilege,[97] but privilege is allowed where similar lists are issued by a private body of traders, as the list may be regarded as the communication by one trader to another of facts in which he has a legitimate business interest.[98] And it would seem that an answer to a specific inquiry regarding the credit of a particular party is privileged.[99] A statement made by one litigant to another that the latter's manager had tampered with a juryman is privileged in an action for libel brought by the manager.[1]

No special privilege is enjoyed at common law by a newspaper[2] or broadcast, but the Defamation Act 1952[3] confers privilege in a number of cases. Thus the publication in a newspaper or in certain broadcasts[4] of a 'fair and accurate' report of the following matters is privileged unless proved to be made maliciously: public proceedings of a dominion legislature outside Great Britain: public proceedings of an international organisation or conference in which the United Kingdom participates: public proceedings of an international court; proceedings before a court with jurisdiction in H.M. dominions outside Britain or court-martial proceedings outside Britain; public proceedings at an inquiry instituted by a government in H.M. dominions outside Britain. Similarly privileged is a fair and accurate copy or extract from a public register kept in pursuance of an Act of Parliament and a notice or advertisement published by or on the authority of a United Kingdom court. Then section 7(2) confers privilege in the following cases, but subject to the defender publishing at the request of the pursuer a reasonable explanation or contradiction in the newspaper in which the original publication was made: a fair and accurate report of the findings or decisions in respect of members of, or in respect of persons controlled by, associations formed for various purposes such as the encouragement of art, science, religion or learning, the promoting or safeguarding of

---

[97] *Mackintosh* v. *Dun* [1908] A.C. 390.

[98] *Barr* v. *Musselburgh Merchants*, 1912 S.C. 174; *Keith* v. *Lauder* (1905) 8 F. 356.

[99] *Bayne & Thomson* v. *Stubbs* (1901) 3 F. 408.

[1] *Hines* v. *Davidson*, 1935 S.C. 30.

[2] *Wright & Greig* v. *Outram* (1890) 17 R. 596; *Langlands* v. *Leng*, 1916 S.C. (H.L.) 102, *per* Lord Shaw at p. 110. See also *Brims* v. *Reid* (1885) 12 R. 1016 and *McKerchar* v. *Cameron* (1892) 19 R. 383, in which pleas of privilege were repelled in relation to publication of anonymous letters. It is thought that 'privilege' was not an appropriate plea as the subject matter was of public interest. See *Merivale* v. *Carson* (1887) 20 Q.B.D. 275, *per* Lord Esher M.R. at p. 280. Qualified privilege attaches to reports relating to documents founded on in a court hearing although not read out: *Cunningham* v. *The Scotsman Publications Ltd.*, 1987 S.C. 107.

[3] s. 7 and Schedule, as amended by the Local Government (Access to Information) Act 1985 (c. 43), s. 3 and Sched. 2, para. 2.

[4] Broadcasting Act 1990 (c. 42), s. 116(3).

trade, business or profession, and the promoting of the interests of games, sports or pastimes played or viewed by the public. The privilege is extended also to fair and accurate reports of the proceedings of public meetings in the United Kingdom, the proceedings at meetings of local authorities, justices of the peace, commissions, tribunals, etc., appointed for the purposes of inquiry and other like purposes, the proceedings at the general meetings of companies incorporated by Royal Charter or under the Companies Act 1985, and to a notice issued for public information by a government department, officer of state, local authority or chief of police. Protection for reports of such notices applies, however, only where the notice has been formally issued and therefore is not automatically available to a report based merely on what an official has said even if in the course of his employment.[5] It should be observed that by section 9 the protection given to newspapers is substantially extended to cover statements made by broadcasting. The latitude thus given to newspapers is not to protect the publication of any matter whose publication is prohibited by law, or any matter which is not of public concern and the publication of which is not for the public benefit.[6]

The term 'judicial slander' includes oral statements made in court and written statements in pleadings. Both occasions are absolutely privileged *quoad* the advocate or solicitor,[7] but the litigant himself enjoys only a qualified privilege in relation to oral statements made in court by himself,[8] or by the pleader on his instructions,[9] and to statements inserted in his pleadings. If the latter are defamatory and not pertinent to the question at issue, the litigant is not entitled to plead privilege,[10] but, if the defamatory statements are relevant, the litigant is protected by a qualified privilege.[11] The party who sues upon them is not bound to aver want of probable cause, but is bound to aver malice and facts from which malice may reasonably be inferred.[12] It is not enough to aver that the statements were made without belief in their truth.[13] Statements by a party, verbal or written, in answer to a threat of legal action are also subject to qualified privilege.[14]

---

[5] *Blackshaw* v. *Lord* [1984] Q.B. 1.

[6] Defamation Act 1952, s. 7(3).

[7] See para. 35.10, *supra; Williamson* v. *Umphray* (1890) 17 R. 905; *Rome* v. *Watson* (1898) 25 R. 733.

[8] *Neill* v. *Henderson* (1901) 3 F. 387.

[9] *Williamson* v. *Umphray, supra;* see also *Bayne* v. *Macgregor* (1862) 24 D. 1126, where the solicitor was sued on the ground that he had maliciously instructed counsel to make the statement.

[10] *Mackellar* v. *Duke of Sutherland* (1859) 21 D. 222, where the averments were treated as pertinent, although irrelevant—see Lord Ordinary at p. 225, and *Scott* v. *Turnbull* (1884) 11 R. 1131, *per* Lord President Inglis at p. 1134. For an example of irrelevance and impertinence, see *Brodie* v. *Blair* (1834) 12 S. 941.

[11] *Scott* v. *Turnbull, supra.*

[12] *Ibid; M.* v. *H.,* 1908 S.C. 1130; *Webster* v. *Paterson,* 1910 S.C. 459; *Mitchell* v. *Smith,* 1919 S.C. 664.

[13] *Mitchell* v. *Smith, supra.*

[14] *Campbell* v. *Cochrane* (1905) 8 F. 205.

The question of whether communications passing between solicitor and client on a subject upon which the client has retained the solicitor are protected by absolute or qualified privilege has not been decided in Scotland.[15] While it is thought that qualified, not absolute, privilege applies to all statements made by solicitors to third parties in their clients' interests,[16] it may be impossible to decide as a matter of relevancy whether or not the particular statement has gone beyond what is necessary to protect the client's interest. In such a case the whole circumstances in which it was made must be ascertained before the judge can decide that the occasion is privileged and direct the jury to decide whether or not malice is proved.[17] If the statement made by the solicitor is expressed in terms which may reasonably be read as an expression of his own opinion and not that of his client, malice must be proved.[18] In the ordinary case an agent's liability for publishing defamatory matter on the instructions of his principal stands or falls with that of his principal,[19] but a solicitor who publishes defamatory matter which is prima facie in his client's interests, upon his client's instructions, is entitled to plead at least qualified privilege in his own right whether or not the occasion is privileged *quoad* his client.[20]

35.12 Averments of Malice.[21]—While it is recognised that there may be exceptional cases where a statement is so violent as to afford evidence that it could not have been fairly and honestly made,[22] in most cases of qualified privilege a mere general averment that the defender acted maliciously is not sufficent. Facts and circumstances from which malice may be inferred must be set forth, and it is for the court to decide whether they are relevantly stated.[23] Averments of a prior quarrel or ill-feeling are sufficient,[24] or, possibly, a definite averment that the

[15] The answer may differ according to circumstances, but it is thought that the English decision of *More* v. *Weaver* [1928] 2 K.B. 520 is consistent on its facts with public policy in respect that the communications seem to have been made in confidential circumstances in which it was not reasonably foreseeable that they would be disclosed by the solicitor to any third party; but see *Mintner* v. *Priest* [1930] A.C. 558, where opinions on this point were reserved.
[16] *Baker* v. *Carrick* [1894] 1 Q.B. 838; *cf.* opinions in *Crawford* v. *Adams* (1900) 2 F. 987.
[17] See opinions in *Adam* v. *Ward* [1917] A.C. 309 and *Wilson* v. *Purvis* (1890) 18 R. 72. *Ramsay* v. *Nairne* (1833) 11 S. 1033 should be treated as a case in which the judge left it to the jury to decide whether or not malice was proved.
[18] *Crawford* v. *Adams* (1900) 2 F. 987.
[19] Gatley, pp. 168–169. *Adam* v. *Ward, supra, per* Lord Finlay L.C. at p. 320.
[20] But see opinions of Lords Young, Trayner and Moncreiff in *Crawford* v. *Adams, supra,* which suggest that statements made by a solicitor to third parties in strict accordance with his client's instructions are absolutely privileged.
[21] See Glegg on *Reparation*, pp. 154–156; Walker, pp. 808–814.
[22] *Lyal* v. *Henderson*, 1916 S.C. (H.L.) 167.
[23] *Suzor* v. *McLachlan*, 1914 S.C. 306; *Rogers* v. *Orr*, 1939 S.C. 121. Malice depends on the defender's subjective state of mind. Malice may be established by the defender's malicious intentions in respect of an allegation which he intended to make but which on an objective construction his communication failed to convey: *Fraser* v. *Mirza*, 1993 S.C. (H.L.) 27. See para. 35.11 *supra*.
[24] *Dinnie* v. *Hengler*, 1910 S.C. 4.

defender, at the time when he spoke, knew that the charge was unfounded,[25] but in an extreme case malice may be inferred simply from the language of the defamatory statement.[26] It has been held that a history of making unfounded complaints about members of a particular class may give rise to an inference of malice in a further statement defamatory of a member of that class.[27] But it is not enough to say that the charge was made without due inquiry,[28] or, short of recklessness, that it was the result of unreasonable prejudice[29] or that the defender refused to listen to the pursuer's explanation of his conduct,[30] or refused to withdraw the charge after it had been held unfounded in an official inquiry.[31]

In a rare type of case it has been held competent to aver and prove malice on the part of the defender in order, not to defeat a plea of privilege, but to strengthen an inference that the defender was the author of a particular libel, namely, an anonymous letter.[32]

35.13 **No Probable Cause.**—Want of probable cause, as well as malice, must be averred and proved (1) where the statement complained of is made in reporting an alleged crime to the criminal authorities,[33] and (2) where it is made by a public officer in the discharge of his duty. Such statements receive the additional protection on the ground of public interest.[34] In an ordinary action of defamation the words 'without probable cause' have no place at all.[35]

35.14 **Fair Retort.**—The fact that a party has been slandered is no justification for a slander by him.[36] But in repelling a charge made publicly, as by publication in a newspaper, the party who has been attacked is entitled to the privilege of fair retort, to the extent that his repudiation of the charge is not actionable on the ground that it involves, or states, an imputation against the party by whom the charge was made.[37] 'If A should charge B with theft, a denial by B of the charge would not

---

[25] *Couper v. Lord Balfour*, 1913 S.C. 492; but see *Mitchell v. Smith*, 1919 S.C. 664; and *McGillivray v. Davidson*, 1934 S.L.T. 45.

[26] *Anderson v. Palombo*, 1986 S.L.T. 46.

[27] *Anderson v. Palombo*, 1986 S.L.T. 46; 1984 S.L.T. 332.

[28] *A.B. v. X.Y.*, 1917 S.C. 15; *Hayford v. Forrester-Paton*, 1927 S.C. 740.

[29] *Horrocks v. Lowe* [1975] A.C. 135 (privileged if there was honest and positive belief coupled with absence of abuse of privileged position).

[30] *A.B. v. X.Y.*, *supra*.

[31] *Couper v. Lord Balfour*, 1913 S.C. 492.

[32] *MacTaggart v. MacKillop*, 1938 S.C. 847; and see *Swan v. Bowie*, 1948 S.C. 46.

[33] *Infra*, para. 33.24.

[34] *Macdonald v. Martin*, 1935 S.C. 621; *Notman v. Commercial Bank of Scotland*, 1938 S.C. 522.

[35] *Webster v. Paterson & Sons*, 1910 S.C. 459, *per* Lord Dunedin at p. 468; *Notman v. Commercial Bank of Scotland*, *supra*.

[36] *Milne v. Walker* (1893) 21 R. 155.

[37] *Gray v. Society for Prevention of Cruelty to Animals* (1890) 17 R. 1185.

warrant an action of damages by A however vigorous or gross the language might be in which B's denial was couched. But if B should go on to charge A with theft, that would be actionable, and would not be protected or privileged to any extent on account of A's previous attack.'[38]

35.15   Fair Comment.[39]—Anyone is entitled to comment on matters of public interest, such as the policy and administration of a government department or local authority, the administration of justice, the conduct of the holder of any public office or aspirant thereto, literary or artistic productions, public exhibitions and entertainments, and indeed any published matter which invites comment from the general public. This liberty is the basis of the defence of 'fair comment,' which requires proof of the following: (1) that the facts stated are true; (2) that the comment on or criticism of those facts was such as could be honestly made; (3) on a matter of public interest. 'Fair comment' differs from the defence of qualified privilege in respect that the latter arises out of the special relationship of the pursuer and defender as individuals,[40] whereas the former is based upon the interests of the public and is the prerogative of all members of the public.[41] The distinction between 'fair comment' and *veritas* is that 'to succeed upon the plea of justification the defendant must prove not only that the facts were truly stated, but also that the innuendo is true ... Upon fair comment, however, if it be established that the facts stated are true, the defence of fair comment will succeed even if the imputation or innuendo be not justified as true, but be fair and *bona fide* comment upon a matter of public interest.'[42]

35.16   Fact and Comment.—A comment is a statement of opinion or inference drawn from facts.[43] It may be expressed in the form of a statement of fact[44] and it may often be difficult to distinguish between fact and comment.[45] The respective scope of the pleas of *veritas* and fair comment may be considered in the following circumstances: (1) If all the alleged defamatory matter is contained in statements of fact, the

[38] *Per* Lord Kincairney, Lord Ordinary, in *Milne* v. *Walker, supra*, at p. 157.

[39] See Walker, pp. 837–847, and *Burton* v. *Board* [1929] K.B. 301, *per* Sankey L.J. at p. 306.

[40] See para. 35.11, *supra.*

[41] See *Merivale* v. *Carson* (1887) 20 Q.B.D. 275, *per* Lord Esher at p. 280.

[42] *Peter Walker & Son* v. *Hodgson* [1909] 1 K.B. 239, at p. 253 *per* Buckley L.J., quoted by Lord Anderson in *Wheatley* v. *Anderson*, 1927 S.C. 133, at p. 147; see also *Broadway Approvals* v. *Odhams Press* [1965] 1 W.L.R. 805, *per* Sellers L.J. at p. 817.

[43] See *Cooper* v. *Lawson* (1838) 8 A. & E. 746, at p. 752, *per* Patterson J.: 'He has murdered his father, and therefore is a disgrace to human nature,' quoted by Lord Shaw of Dunfermline in *Sutherland* v. *Stopes* [1925] A.C. 47, at p. 83.

[44] *e.g.* 'he is a disgrace to human nature.'

[45] 'Comment ... is often to be recognized and distinguished from allegations of fact by the use of metaphor': *Grech* v. *Odhams Press* [1957] 3 All E.R. 556, at p. 558 *per* Donovan J., approved [1958] 2 Q.B. 275, at p. 282 (C.A.).

plea of fair comment is inept[46]; (2) If the only matter alleged to be defamatory arises from a statement which appears at the end of a factual narrative, it may be obvious that it is merely an expression of the writer's opinion based upon the facts stated.[47] In that event the plea of fair comment is appropriate and the plea of *veritas* unnecessary, although competent; (3) The imputation may stem from a statement of opinion only without any express statement of facts upon which the opinion is based.[48] If a sufficient substratum of fact may be implied by the public from that statement in its context, the plea of fair comment is competent and may be supported by averments of particular facts which, although not published, are alleged to be true, to have been known to the writer at the time of publication, and to have formed the basis of the comment.[49] If the court holds that a sufficient substratum of fact cannot reasonably be implied from the words published, they must be construed as an allegation of fact, thus excluding the defence of fair comment. But unpublished facts cannot be used for the purpose of turning what on the face of it is a statement of fact into a comment.[50] (4) Fact and comment may be so bound up together that it is difficult to distinguish the one from the other. In that situation both pleas may be taken and the jury has to decide into which category, fact or comment, the statements respectively fall, under direction from the judge as to the legal effect of their classification.[51] (5) It is for the court to decide as a matter of law whether the statements founded on by the defender as comment may reasonably be classified in their context as such.[52] (6) If comment is so much mixed up with fact that they cannot reasonably be separated, the whole publication may have to be treated as containing allegations of fact only. The plea of fair comment would then fall to be repelled.[53] (7) If the defender establishes the substantial truth of the imputation, whether arising from fact or comment or both, the plea of *veritas* will be sustained, thereby rendering redundant a plea of fair comment.[54]

---

[46] 'Fair comment is a defence to comment only and not to defamatory statements of fact': see *Broadway Approvals* v. *Odhams Press* [1964] 2 Q.B. 683, and [1965] 1 W.L.R. 805 (C.A.), at p. 818.

[47] See, *e.g. Gray* v. *S.P.C.A.* (1890) 17 R. 1185.

[48] *Kemsley* v. *Foot* [1952] A.C. 345— 'Lower than Kemsley.'

[49] *Ibid.*, see also *Wheatley* v. *Anderson*, 1927 S.C. 133, *per* Lord Justice-Clerk Alness at p. 143, and *per* Lord Anderson at p. 147; *cf.* Lord Hunter at pp. 145–146.

[50] *Telnikoff* v. *Matusevich* [1992] 2 A.C. 343.

[51] *Hunt* v. *Star Newspaper* [1908] 2 K.B. 309; *Aga Khan* v. *Times Publishing Co.* [1924] 1 K.B. 675, *per* Bankes L.J. at pp. 680–681; *Jones* v. *Skelton* [1963] 1 W.L.R. 1362 (P.C.), at pp. 1379–1380. In *Sutherland* v. *Stopes* [1925] A.C. 47, the 'rolled-up' plea was held to be a plea of fair comment only. See Gatley, pp. 437–438, and Walker, p. 840, n. 42, for form of plea. See also *London Artists* v. *Littler* [1969] 2 Q.B. 375, where it was held that the defence of fair comment could not apply to an allegation of a plot as that was an allegation of fact.

[52] *Aga Khan* v. *Times Publishing Co., supra; Jones* v. *Skelton, supra.*

[53] *Hunt* v. *Star Newspaper, supra, per* Fletcher Moulton L.J. at pp. 319–320; approved by Lord Anderson in *Wheatley* v. *Anderson*, 1927 S.C. 133, at p. 147.

[54] See *Sutherland* v. *Stopes, supra, per* Viscount Cave L.C. at p. 55; also Defamation Act 1952, s. 5.

35.17 Requisites of Fair Comment.—(1) As has already been pointed out,[55] the first requisite of a plea of fair comment is that the facts upon which the comment is based are proved or admitted to be true, and the defender may in his defences expand and elucidate facts which the libel clearly adumbrates.[56] It is no longer necessary to prove the truth of every such fact provided that sufficient is proved to enable the judge or jury to hold the comment to be fair.[57] Honest belief in the truth of such facts will not found the plea of fair comment but may mitigate damages.[58] Where the defence is based on unproven statements made on a privileged occasion, the defender must show that he has given a fair and accurate report of the occasion.[59]

(2) The second requisite is that the comment on or criticism of these facts must be such as could be honestly made. In cases where the comment follows logically from a preceding narrative of facts, which are proved or admitted to be true, it may be possible for the court to hold as matter of law that the criticism does not exceed the bounds of fair comment.[60] Normally it is for the jury to decide whether the comment was fairly and honestly made. There are two elements here. The first is that the comment must be warranted by true facts, stated or implied, in the sense that upon those facts a fair-minded man might reasonably hold that opinion.[61] This is an objective test and the jury are not entitled to substitute their own opinion for that of the defender.[62] Moreover, every latitude must be given to opinion and to prejudice.[63] The test for a theatrical review has been stated to be: 'Would any fair man, however prejudiced he may be, however exaggerated or obstinate his views, have said that which this criticism has said of the work which is criticised?'[64] The defender does not need to prove that the comment is an honest

---

[55] para. 35.15.

[56] *Wheatley* v. *Anderson*, 1927 S.C. 133, *per* Lord Justice-Clerk Alness at p. 143, and *per* Lord Anderson at pp. 147–148: 'The jury are entitled to know what was in a defender's mind at the time he made the comment.' See also Gatley, pp. 300–305, and cases cited therein.

[57] See Defamation Act 1952, s. 6. This section does not apply if any of the allegations of fact is defamatory: *Broadway Approvals* v. *Odhams Press* [1964] 2 Q.B. 683, and [1965] 1 W.L.R. 805 (C.A.), at p. 818.

[58] See Gatley, p. 294.

[59] *Brent Walker Group* v. *Time Out* [1991] 2 Q.B. 33.

[60] See *Gray* v. *S.P.C.A.* (1890) 17 R. 1185 (in which the plea of fair comment could have been taken), *per* Lord McLaren at p. 1200; *Dakhyl* v. *Labouchere* [1908] 2 K.B. 325n., *per* Lord Atkinson at p. 329; *McQuire* v. *Western Morning News Co.* [1903] 2 K.B. 100, *per* Collins M.R. at pp. 110–111.

[61] *Wheatley* v. *Anderson, supra; Peter Walker & Son Ltd.* v. *Hodgson* [1909] 1 K.B. 239, *per* Buckley L.J. at p. 253.

[62] *McQuire* v. *Western Morning News, supra, per* Collins M.R. at p. 109.

[63] *Merivale* v. *Carson* (1887) 20 Q.B.D. 275, *per* Lord Esher M.R. at p. 280. 'The basis of our public life is that the crank, the enthusiast, may say what he honestly thinks just as much as the reasonable man or woman who sits on a jury': *per* Diplock J. in *Silkin* v. *Beaverbrook Newspapers* [1958] 1 W.L.R. 743, at p. 747.

[64] *Merivale* v. *Carson, supra, per* Lord Esher M.R. at p. 281; and see *Crotty* v. *Macfarlane*, Outer House, January 27, 1891 (Lord Stormouth-Darling), referred to in Glegg at p. 178.

expression of his views.[65] But criticism cannot be used as a cloak for mere invective or for personal imputations not arising out of the subject matter.[66] Accordingly, if a personal attack on the character of a public man or the author of a published work or a public entertainer is mounted upon facts which, although true, do not warrant such an attack, the defence of fair comment will fail. The right of comment is exercisable in the public interest, not for the gratification of the writer's personal spite. The second element is that the defender will lose the defence of fair comment if the pursuer proves that the comment was in fact published maliciously[67] by the defender or was not his honest opinion. Where a newspaper publishes an anonymous letter and the editor refuses to disclose the identity of the author, it has been held, however, that the pursuer does not need to aver malice.[68]

(3) The third requisite of the defence of fair comment is that the comment must be upon a matter of public interest. This covers a wide field.[69] It is in the public interest that the conduct of public officials should be open to criticism,[70] but the right does not extend to criticism of their character or private conduct[71] unless their fitness for office is being questioned.

35.18   **Verbal Injury.**[72]—The courts have drawn a basic distinction between statements which are *per se* or by innuendo defamatory in the narrow sense of the word[73] and other false injurious statements. Whereas, in the case of the former, malice is irrelevant and once the defamatory statements are proved to have been made, they are presumed to be false, a pursuer who founds on statements of the latter must not only prove that they have been made by the defender but must also aver and prove that they were untrue and were made with deliberate intent to injure him or at least with such reckless disregard of injury as to yield the inference of such intent.[74] Certain statements which are not defamatory, in respect that they do not impugn the morality, solvency or business capacity of the person regarding whom they are made, may

---

[65] *Telnikoff* v. *Matusevich* [1992] 2 A.C. 343.

[66] *McQuire* v. *Western Morning News, supra, per* Collins M.R. at p. 109.

[67] *Cherneskey* v. *Armadale Publishers Ltd.* [1979] 1 S.C.R. 1067, at pp. 1098–1099, *per* Dickson J. (dissenting) (Canadian Supreme Court), approved by Lloyd L.J., *Telnikoff* v. *Matusevich* [1991] 1 Q.B. 102, at p. 119, affd. by the House of Lords, [1992] 2 A.C. 343; *Thomas* v. *Bradbury, Agnew & Co.* [1906] 2 K.B. 627; *Crotty* v. *Macfarlane, supra.*

[68] *Brims* v. *Reid* (1885) 12 R. 1016; *McKerchar* v. *Cameron* (1892) 19 R. 383.

[69] See Walker, pp. 846–850.

[70] *Langlands* v. *Leng*, 1916 S.C. (H.L.) 102, *per* Viscount Haldane at pp. 106–107.

[71] *Gray* v. *S.P.C.A.* (1890) 17 R. 1185, *per* Lord McLaren at p. 1200.

[72] See Walker, pp. 730–740, where he divides verbal injury into three categories, namely, defamation, *convicium* and malicious falsehood. For a different view of the nature of verbal injury and the characteristics which distinguish it from slander see T.B. Smith, *Short Commentary*, pp. 724–732.

[73] See para. 35.1 *supra.*

[74] *Paterson* v. *Welch* (1893) 20 R. 744, *per* Lord President Robertson at p. 749; *Lamond* v. *Daily Record*, 1923 S.L.T. 512; *Steele* v. *Scottish Daily Record*, 1970 S.L.T. 53. See comments in Walker, *supra*, pp. 732–734.

be actionable as 'verbal injury.' One case is where the pursuer maintains that a statement holds him up to public hatred and contempt, as by ascribing to him the expression of unpopular opinion.[75] Mere ridicule, where the element of public hatred is absent, is not actionable.[76] Where a pursuer takes an issue of public hatred and contempt, the onus of proving the untruth of the statement, *i.e.* of proving that he had not expressed the opinion ascribed to him, lies upon him. Provided that the words on which the action is based 'are calculated to cause pecuniary damage,' special damage need not be proved.[77]

35.19 Slander of Title: Property.[78]—Other forms of verbal injury are known as slander of title and slander of property, in which the pursuer must also aver and prove that the statements were untrue and were made maliciously. Slander of title is an assertion that the pursuer has no right to an article, or no right to dispose of it, as where a patentee said that the article the pursuer proposed to sell was an infringement of his patent.[79] Slander of property imports a statement reflecting on the pursuer's property. On this basis an issue was allowed on an allegation that a row of houses was built on an insecure foundation,[80] and that typhoid fever had broken out in a dairy.[81] But it does not amount to verbal injury for a dealer to state that his article is better than that of his rival, and to give reasons for his statement, even although his reasons involve disparagement of the rival commodity.[82]

35.20 Title to Sue.—Anyone who is defamed has a title to sue.[83] A defamatory statement about a deceased person does not afford any action to his representatives, unless, possibly, it can be read as amounting to a reflection on them.[84] When the injurious statement is made of a class of persons, it is a question of degree whether that class is sufficiently limited in numbers to make an imputation on the individual.[85] A member of an association cannot sue if the statements are comments upon the society and not upon individual action.[86] While

---

[75] *Paterson* v. *Welch, supra; Waddell* v. *Roxburgh* (1894) 21 R. 883; *Lamond* v. *Daily Record supra.*

[76] *McLaughlin* v. *Orr* (1894) 22 R. 38.

[77] Defamation Act 1952, s. 14 (*b*).

[78] See Walker, pp. 903–907, where additional categories of slander of goods and business are included.

[79] *Harpers* v. *Greenwood* (1896) 4 S.L.T. 116; *Philip* v. *Morton* (1816) Hume 865. There is a statutory remedy for such statements (Patents Act 1949, s. 65; Patents Act 1977, s. 70). See *Speedcranes Ltd.* v. *Thomson* 1972 S.C. 324.

[80] *Bruce* v. *Smith* (1898) 1 F. 327.

[81] *McLean* v. *Adam* (1888) 16 R. 175.

[82] *White* v. *Mellin* [1895] A.C. 154; *Hubbuck* v. *Wilkinson* [1899] 1 Q.B. 86.

[83] One spouse may sue the other but the court has power to dismiss such an action if it appears that no substantial benefit would accrue to either party: Law Reform (Husband and Wife) Act 1962, s. 2.

[84] *Broom* v. *Ritchie* (1904) 6 F. 942; and see Walker, pp. 750–752.

[85] *Campbell* v. *Ritchie*, 1907 S.C. 1097; *Browne* v. *Thomson*, 1912 S.C. 359; *Knupfer* v. *London Express Newspaper* [1944] A.C. 116; and see Walker, pp. 745–748.

[86] *Campbell* v. *Wilson*, 1934 S.L.T. 249.

a company or corporate body with a corporate reputation which is capable of being damaged by a defamatory statement can sue in libel to protect that reputation,[87] it would be contrary to the public interest for organs of central or local government to have the right to sue for defamation.[88] While a voluntary association may be able to sue for defamation,[89] in England it has been held that a tort can be committed only on a body with legal personality.[90] Two or more persons may sue together in one action in respect of one defamatory statement alleged to refer to one or other or all of them provided that each concludes separately for damages.[91]

35.21 Parties Liable.[92]—The person who originates,[93] and the person who repeats, a defamatory statement, are equally liable in damages. A common report may be proved in mitigation of damages, though not as a complete defence to the action.[94] A printer or publisher may be sued.[95] Persons, such as newsagents or librarians, who circulate a publication alleged to be defamatory, may escape liability by proving that they did not know that the publication contained a libel and that their ignorance was not due to negligence on their part.[96] The liability of an agent who publishes defamatory matter on the instructions of his principal follows that of his principal unless the agent is entitled to plead privilege in his own right.[97] The principles of vicarious liability for slander by an agent are the same as for employer and employee.[98] It is incompetent to conclude for damages jointly and severally against two or more defenders in respect of separate slanders without averments of conspiracy.[99]

35.22 Damages.[1]—A pursuer who proves that he has been defamed is *eo ipso* entitled to an award of damages, which may be nominal.[2] In addition he

---

[87] *Derbyshire C.C.* v. *Times Newspapers Ltd.* [1993] A.C. 534; *North of Scotland Bank* v. *Duncan* (1857) 19 D. 881; and see cases in Walker, p. 748.

[88] *Derbyshire C.C.*, *supra*.

[89] *Highland Dancing Board* v. *Alloa Publishing Co.*, 1971 S.L.T. (Sh.Ct.) 50.

[90] *Electrical, Electronic, Telecommunication and Plumbing Union* v. *Times Newspapers* [1980] Q.B. 585. But see Walker, p. 749.

[91] *Mitchell* v. *Grierson* (1894) 21 R. 367. Compare *Golden* v. *Jeffers*, 1936 S.L.T. 388 (truly a case of a conspiracy to slander) with *Turnbull* v. *Frame*, 1966 S.L.T. 24.

[92] As to the legality of an indemnity, see Defamation Act 1952, s. 11.

[93] For liability for unauthorised repetitions see *Slipper* v. *B.B.C.* [1991] 1 Q.B. 283.

[94] *Macculloch* v. *Litt* (1851) 13 D. 960.

[95] *A.B.* v. *Blackwood* (1902) 5 F. 25.

[96] *Emmens* v. *Pottle* (1885) 16 Q.B.D. 354; *Vizetelly* v. *Mudie* [1900] 2 Q.B. 170; and see *Morrison* v. *Ritchie* (1902) 4 F. 645, *per* Lord Moncreiff at p. 651.

[97] See Gatley, p. 373; *Adam* v. *Ward* [1917] A.C. 309, *per* Lord Finlay at p. 320; and n. 17, *supra*, re solicitors.

[98] See para. 33.5, *supra*; also Walker, p. 813.

[99] *Hook* v. *McCallum* (1905) 7 F. 528; *Turnbull* v. *Frame*, *supra*; *Golden* v. *Jeffers*, *supra*.

[1] See Walker, pp. 785–788; also Walker on *Damages*, Chap. 25.

[2] *Bradley* v. *Menley and James*, 1913 S.C. 923, *per* Lord Justice-Clerk Macdonald at p. 926.

may recover special damages on proof that he has suffered or is likely to suffer financial loss. Evidence of the circumstances of publication may aggravate the damages, *e.g.* proof of deliberate intention, recklessness or persistent repetition.[3] Ground for mitigation, on the other hand, has been found in the fact that there was provocation to make the statement, that there was probable cause for making it, that it was common talk and that the pursuer had a bad character.[4] By the Defamation Act 1952[5] it is competent to mitigate by proving that damages have been recovered or action has been brought in respect of publication of words similar to those on which the action is based, or that the pursuer has settled or agreed to settle in respect of such a publication. A tender in a defamation action must offer not only a sum of money but also a withdrawal and apology.[6]

35.23 **Expenses.**—Where a tender is lodged, and the damages ultimately awarded are less than the amount tendered, the tender has not its normal effect of entitling the defender to expenses after its date unless it is accompanied by a retraction and apology.[7] But it is sufficient to offer an apology without any admission that the statement complained of was made.[8] The Defamation Act 1952 makes provision for awards of expenses when an offer of amends is made.[9]

35.24 **Criminal Charge.**[10]—To give information to the police or criminal authorities, to institute a prosecution, or in the case of a party entitled to arrest, to arrest on suspicion of a crime, are acts which are not actionable merely on the ground that they were founded on a mistake but only on averments and proof of malice and want of probable cause.[11] Facts and circumstances from which malice may be inferred must be stated. 'A man has probable cause if, in giving information, he is acting in a way in which a reasonable man, swayed by no illegitimate motives, would act.'[12] A conviction on the charge made is fatal to the action, since it proves that probable cause existed;[13] an acquittal standing by itself is not enough to establish that there was no probable

---

[3] See Cooper, *Law of Defamation* (2nd ed.), p. 250; *Cunningham* v. *Duncan* (1889) 16 R. 383.

[4] Cooper, *op. cit.*, p. 254; *C.* v. *M.*, 1923 S.C. 1; *Bryson* v. *Inglis* (1844) 6 D. 363; *Hobbs* v. *Tinling* [1929] 2 K.B. 1.

[5] s. 12.

[6] See Walker, p. 787, for cases.

[7] *Faulks* v. *Park* (1854) 17 D. 247. See *Green's Encyclopaedia*, Vol. 5, para. 1171; *Encyclopaedia of Scottish Legal Styles*, Vol. 4, pp. 211–212.

[8] *Malcolm* v. *Moore* (1901) 4 F. 23.

[9] s. 4(4)(*b*).

[10] See Walker, pp. 870–876.

[11] *Hill* v. *Campbell* (1905) 8 F. 220; *Mills* v. *Kelvin & White*, 1913 S.C. 521; *Norman* v. *Commerical Bank of Scotland*, 1938 S.C. 522. And see para. 35.14, *supra*.

[12] *Mills* v. *Kelvin & White*, *supra*, per Lord President Dunedin at p. 528.

[13] *Hill* v. *Campbell*, *supra*.

cause.[14] A person making an arrest cannot, however, claim the protection of privilege where his actings have been unlawful. So, if an arrest is made without lawful warrant and in the absence of grounds on which such arrest may be justified, it is unnecessary for the person aggrieved to aver or prove malice.[15] The exercise of powers of search and its abuse are subject to similar principles.

Procurators fiscal and deputes acting on the authority of the Lord Advocate enjoy the same absolute privilege as the Lord Advocate in relation to prosecutions on indictment.[16] *Quoad* summary proceedings there is at common law no distinction in the law applicable in an action directed against a public or a private prosecutor.[17] By statute, however, actions against the former arising out of proceedings under provisions of the Criminal Procedure (Scotland) Act 1995[18] are subject to a statutory time limit,[19] and are competent only where the pursuer has suffered imprisonment, the proceedings have been quashed, and the pursuer avers that the actings were malicious and without reasonable cause.[20] Express provision is moreover made that it is a defence to such an action that the pursuer was guilty of the offence in question and had undergone no greater punishment than was assigned by law.[21] A letter, intimating the charge, and followed by a prosecution, is to be taken as part of the prosecution, and its actionability to be judged by the same standards.[22]

35.25 **Unfounded Litigation.**[23]—No damages can be claimed for bringing a civil action, even if it proves to be unfounded. It would seem a doubtful point whether averments that the action in question was brought maliciously would make a claim for damages relevant.[24] It is not wrong to take a decree irregularly, as where a decree in absence was obtained when the defender had not been properly cited, provided that no diligence has followed on the decree. If it has, averments and proof of malice will found a claim for damages.[25]

35.26 **Wrongful Diligence.**[26]—The use of diligence may found a claim for damages either because it has been carried out irregularly, or because it

---

[14] *Chalmers v. Barclay, Perkins & Co.*, 1912 S.C. 521.
[15] *Dahl v. Chief Constable of Central Scotland Police*, 1983 S.L.T. 420.
[16] *Hester v. Macdonald*, 1961 S.C. 370.
[17] *Chalmers, supra.*
[18] *Graham v. Strathern*, 1924 S.C. 699.
[19] Two months: s. 456(3).
[20] s. 170(1). *Graham, supra*; *Robertson v. Keith*, 1936 S.C. 29; *Hester v. Macdonald*, 1961 S.C. 370; *Bell v. McGlennan*, 1992 S.L.T. 237.
[21] s. 170(2).
[22] *Chalmers, supra.*
[23] See Walker, pp. 848–859.
[24] See *Hallam v. Gye* (1835) 14 S. 199.
[25] *McGregor v. McLaughlin* (1905) 8 F. 70.
[26] See Walker, at pp. 859–870; *Stair Encyclopaedia*, Vol. 8, para. 124 (Diligence); Graham Stewart, *Law of Diligence*, Chaps. 41 and 42.

was used on some untenable claim. Irregular diligence of any kind is a wrong which is in no way privileged. It may be irregular either because it proceeds on an insufficient warrant,[27] or because the statutory forms have not been observed. In either case the creditor who sets the diligence in motion is personally liable, though the actual fault or mistake may be on the part of the solicitor,[28] messenger-at-arms, or sheriff officer.[29] Probably the solicitor is only liable for his own act or omission,[30] not for a mistake on the part of the officials he employs.[31] A messenger-at-arms or sheriff officer is not liable unless he knew, or should have known, that the diligence was irregular.[32]

Where the ground for an action of damages is that diligence has been done on an unfounded or untenable claim, the law depends on the nature of the diligence. Certain forms of diligence, of which arrestment and poinding are examples, can be carried out on the appropriate warrant without any special application to the court. In these cases there is no liability for a mere mistake, as in the case where property is arrested or poinded for a debt which has in fact been paid. In order to found action there must be averments and proof of malice and want of probable cause.[33] Other forms of diligence, including landlord's sequestration[34] and certain statutory warrants for arrestment,[35] are granted, as is interim interdict,[36] only on an *ex parte* statement of facts which render them necessary. Such forms are granted at the risk of the person who applies (*periculo petentis*), and he is responsible for the truth of the statement he makes, and will be liable in damages if that statement proves to be untrue. No privilege is involved, and therefore there is no necessity for averments of malice or of want of probable cause.[37]

Further Reading

Carter-Ruck, *Libel and Slander* (4th ed., 1992).
Cooper, *The Law of Defamation* (2nd ed., 1906).
Duncan and Neill, *Defamation* (2nd ed., 1984).
Gatley, *Libel and Slander* (8th ed., 1981).
Glegg, *The Law of Reparation in Scotland* (4th ed., 1955), Chs. 8–11.
Walker, *The Law of Delict in Scotland* (2nd ed., 1981), Chs. 23 and 24, and pp. 902–907.

[27] *Wilson* v. *Mackie* (1875) 3 R. 18. See *McGregor* v. *McLaughlin*, *supra*, as to the distinction between taking a decree irregularly and using diligence upon it.
[28] *Smith* v. *Taylor* (1882) 10 R. 291; *Clarke* v. *Beattie*, 1909 S.C. 299, *per* Lord President Dunedin at pp. 303–304.
[29] *Le Conte* v. *Douglas* (1880) 8 R. 175.
[30] *McRobbie* v. *McLellan's Trs.* (1891) 18 R. 470.
[31] *Henderson* v. *Rollo* (1871) 10 M. 104; Graham Stewart, *Diligence*, p. 799.
[32] *Clarke* v. *Beattie*, 1909 S.C. 299.
[33] *Wolthekker* v. *Northern Agricultural Co.* (1862) 1 M. 211; *Grant* v. *Magistrates of Airdrie*, 1939 S.C. 738, 758.
[34] *Gray* v. *Weir* (1891) 19 R. 25; *Shearer* v. *Nicoll*, 1935 S.L.T. 313.
[35] *Gray* v. *Magistrates of Airdrie*, *supra*.
[36] *Kennedy* v. *Fort-William Commissioners* (1877) 5 R. 302; *Glasgow District Ry.* v. *Glasgow Coal Exchange* (1885) 12 R. 1287; *Clippens Oil Co.* v. *Edinburgh Water Trustees*, 1907 S.C. (H.L.) 9 (measure of damages).
[37] *Wolthekker*, *supra*; *Grant*, *supra*.

PART VI—PROPERTY

CHAPTER 36

PROPERTY: HERITABLE AND MOVEABLE

36.1 **Property or Ownership.**—In the Civil law property was analysed into three rights: *usus* (or right of use); *fructus* (or right of enjoying its fruits); and *abusus* (or right of using and disposing of it). Erskine speaks of property as 'the right of using and disposing of a thing as our own.'[1] It is seldom, if ever, that these rights are enjoyed without restriction. The owner of a house, for example, nowadays finds himself restrained in the exercise of his powers at various points, not only by the necessity for respecting the rights of others, but also by state and municipal regulations of the widest range and complexity.[2] Or it may be, as in the case of an heir of entail, that the conditions of his title disable him from exercising one or other of these rights. But despite such restrictions, the right in the subjects may nevertheless be such as is regarded in law as property. Erskine recognises this, for he qualifies the words quoted above by adding 'except in so far as we are restrained by law or paction.'

It is clear, therefore, that a person may have a right of property in a subject although he does not possess all the above powers to their full extent.[2a] One or more of the constituent rights which go to make up the aggregation which constitutes property in the fullest sense may be detached and enjoyed apart from the residue without necessarily reducing the sum of the remaining rights below the measure of what is recognised as property. It is not uncommon, for example, for the right of possession and enjoyment of the fruits to be severed from the other rights in the subject. B has a liferent of property inherited by A, or is tenant under a lease of part of A's estate. In each of these cases B has a limited right in the estate, but A's right would remain a right of property. Or, again, it may be that A holds lands in common with others. Here also his right is one of property, although his power over the land is necessarily limited by the rights of his co-owners.

---

[1] *Inst.*, II, ii, 1; see *Anstruther* v. *Anstruther* (1836) 14 S. 272, at p. 286.

[2] See, *e.g.* Town and Country Planning (Scotland) Act 1972, *passim*.

[2a] For example, the seller of heritable property who has granted a disposition which has not yet been recorded by the purchaser, retains the right of property although he is limited in the use which can be made of the subjects, see *Sharp* v. *Thomson*, 1994 S.L.T. 1068.

Property is the largest right which can be possessed in a subject. As the illustrations given above indicate, there may be more limited rights. The owner of a liferent or servitude over another's estate has a right in that estate; the liferent and servitude belong to the class of *jura in re aliena*, but they are not rights of property, nor would their owner be described as proprietor of the estate. 'Two different persons cannot have each of them the full property of the same thing at the same time,'[3] but these inferior rights may exist consistently with the right of property in another person. Subject to the existence of such rights the owner or owners of a subject have an exclusive right which enables them to prevent others from interfering with it.[4] The owner of land may interdict others from trespassing on it, and the owner of rights may prevent others from infringing these rights.

36.2 Classification of Property.—'Property,' in Erskine's definition, is used as meaning ownership. But the term is also employed with another significance. It is commonly used to denote the subjects of ownership: such things as are owned and have material value. The citizen has certain rights as regards his person, reputation and liberty, but these are not considered to be property as they have no patrimonial value. Nor can there be property in a person,[5] or in such things as the air, or the sea, or the water flowing in a stream, although the water may become property when it is appropriated.[6]

Property, when it is used as meaning the subjects of ownership, may be classified in various ways. Thus there is corporeal property, consisting of things such as a house, or book, or money; and incorporeal property, consisting of rights. Typical instances of incorporeal property are patent rights, copyright, goodwill, and a *jus crediti* or right to a debt by another. *Jura in re aliena* are always incorporeal. These rights may be of great value and will be included among the assets of the owner if he is sequestrated, and will pass on his death to his representatives or heirs. Another distinction is between fungibles and non-fungibles. Fungibles are such things as are estimated by weight, number or measure, and which can be replaced by equal quantities, *e.g.* money and grain. It is clearly a matter of indifference to a lender whether he receives repayment of his loan in the actual coin lent or others of like value. On the other hand, a horse or a picture is not fungible because 'their values differ in almost every individual.'[7] But of all the classifications, the most important is that which divides property according as it is heritable or moveable.

---

[3] Erskine, *Inst.*, II, i.

[4] 'Correctly speaking, property imports dominium—the entire and exclusive dominion over the thing spoken of—the proprietor being the dominus and having the sole disposal of it,'—Bell, *Comm.*, i, 177.

[5] *Reavis* v. *Clan Line Steamers*, 1925 S.C. 725.

[6] *Morris* v. *Bicket* (1864) 2 M. 1082, *per* Lord Neaves; affd. 4 M. (H.L.) 44.

[7] Erskine, *Inst.*, III, i, 18.

36.3   Heritable and Moveable Property.—The nomenclature here is not beyond criticism. 'Heritable' points to succession; 'moveable' refers to the nature of the subject. 'Anything is called moveable, which, by its nature and use, is capable of motion'; immoveables 'are called heritable, because they descend not to executors, to whom only moveables befall, but to heirs, and so the distinction cometh ordinarily of moveables and heritables,'[8] This distinction applies to both corporeal and incorporeal property. It is now of less significance than formerly, since by virtue of the Succession (Scotland) Act 1964 both heritable and moveable property fall to be administered by the executor; but it remains important in questions relating to testate succession and legal rights.[9]

36.4   Land and its Pertinents.—The typical instance of heritable (or immoveable) property is land with its pertinents. Stones and minerals, as constituents of the land, are heritable until they are removed from the land, when they become moveable.[10] Trees also, as *partes soli*, while unseparated from the ground are heritable;[11] cut timber, on the other hand, is moveable. The natural fruits of the land which do not require seed and cultivation are also, while unseparated, heritable. It is laid down in the institutional writers that industrial crops are considered to be moveable as they 'go with the property of the seed and labour as manufactures in which the productive powers of the soil are employed';[12] but it is explained in *Chalmers's Tr.* v. *Dick's Tr.*[13] that the true position is that the crop before separation is *pars soli*, and, therefore, heritable, but that the tenant who has sown it is allowed by the law to separate and remove it unless he has contracted not to do so.

36.5   Fixtures.—When a moveable thing is brought into connection with heritage, the question may arise in a variety of circumstances as to the effect of this connection upon the moveable. On this matter a mass of decisions (not always reconcilable) has accumulated, embodying the law

---

[8] Stair, II, i, 2. In English law the term corresponding to 'heritable' is 'real,' to 'moveable,' 'personal.' But the words 'real' and 'personal' are used in a different sense in Scots Law. A 'real' right is one which affects the subject itself; a 'personal' is one which is founded in obligation (Erskine, III, i, 2; IV, i, 10). A person having a right to lands has a 'real' right if he has completed his title by the appropriate legal procedure (*e.g.*, infeftment); his right is 'personal' if he has not done so. A burden on lands is said to be 'real' if it is so imposed that it attaches to the lands, whoever the owner of them may be. Similarly, a *vitium reale* or 'real' defect is one which affects the subject, into whosesoever hands it may come; thus, if goods be stolen, the theft is said to be a *vitium reale, i.e.* a defect in the title not only of the thief but of anyone who acquires them from the thief. See para. 3.10, *supra.*

[9] See para. 42.1 *infra*; para. 43.3, *infra.*

[10] *Bruce* v. *Erskine* (1707) Mor. 14092.

[11] *Paul* v. *Cuthbertson* (1840) 2 D. 1286; see also *Burns* v. *Fleming* (1880) 8 R. 226 (ornamental shrubs planted by a tenant). See para. 16.2, *supra.*

[12] Erskine, *Inst.*, II, ii, 4; Bell, *Prin.*, §1473; see also McLaren on *Wills and Succession*, i, 197.

[13] 1909 S.C. 761. Cf. *English Hop Growers* v. *Dering* [1928] 2 K.B. 174, *per* Scrutton and Sankey L.JJ.

of fixtures.[14] The word 'fixture' is used in more than one sense. It has been authoritatively defined as meaning anything annexed to heritable property, that is, fastened to or connected with it, and not in mere juxtaposition,[15] and it is in this sense that the term is used here. The annexation may be either to the soil directly or to something, such as a building, which itself has become annexed to the soil. In the case of a building the term 'fixture' signifies something which has been affixed as accessory to the house, and does not include things, such as windows, which were made part of the structure of the house when it was constructed.[16] In accordance with the maxim *Inaedificatum solo, solo cedit* all buildings and things annexed to the soil 'are accounted as parts of the ground.'[17] To this rule, as Lord Cairns points out in *Brand's Trs. v. Brand's Trs.*,[18] there is no exception. The owner of the moveable before it was annexed to the heritable loses on annexation his right of property in it; and, while it is annexed, it must, as part of the heritage, belong to the owner of the heritage. It has been held to be a legal impossibility, apart from statute, to sever property in land from property in pipes and drains traversing the land.[19] A second general rule is that what has once become part of the heritage cannot lawfully be severed and removed by a limited owner. But to this rule exceptions are allowed. In certain circumtances the limited owner has the right to sever and remove that which he has annexed to the heritage. Two questions, therefore, usually arise: First, has the thing been so affixed to the heritage as to become part of it? Secondly, assuming this to be so, can the thing, in a question with the owner of the heritage, be removed?

Whether an article has become a fixture is a question of fact to be decided in the circumstances of each case.[20] The following matters are to be taken into account but the list is not exhaustive:

(1) the degree of attachment to the solum, a factor which may be conclusive in some cases;

(2) whether the attachment is of a permanent or quasi-permanent character;

---

[14] See Rankine on *Land-ownership* (4th ed.), pp. 116 *et seq.*; Amos and Ferrard on *Fixtures* (3rd ed., 1883); Adkin and Bowen's *Law relating to Fixtures* (1923); Elwes v. Maw (1802) 2 Smith's Leading Cases (12th ed.), p. 188; Smith, *Short Commentary*, p. 500.

[15] *Brand's Trs.* v. *Brand's Trs.* (1876) 3 R. (H.L.) 16, *per* Lord Chelmsford at p. 23. The wording is also used as meaning removable fixed things, *Re de Falbe* [1901] 1 Ch. 523, *per* Rigby and Stirling L.JJ. at pp. 530 and 538; Amos and Ferrard, p. 2.

[16] *Boswell* v. *Crucible Steel Co.* [1925] 1 K.B. 119.

[17] Stair, II, i, 40.

[18] *Supra*. This was followed in *Millar* v. *Muirhead* (1894) 21 R. 658, and *Howie's Trs.* v. *McLay* (1902) 5 F. 214. There are observations in English cases inconsistent with it; see *Wake* v. *Hall* (1883) 8 App.Cas. 195, and *Re Hulse* [1905] 1 Ch. 406. In *Dowall* v. *Miln* (1874) 1 R. 1180, Lord Justice Clerk Moncreiff discusses the law of fixtures.

[19] *Crichton* v. *Turnbull*, 1946 S.C. 52.

[20] *Howie's Trs.* v. *McLay* (1902) 5 F. 214, *per* Lord President Kinross at p. 216; *Scottish Discount Co. Ltd.* v. *Blin*, 1986 S.L.T. 123, approving *Green's Encyclopaedia of the Laws of Scotland*, Vol. VII, paras. 362–363 by Professor Gloag.

(3)   whether the article can be removed from the soil or building without causing damage to the article itself and without causing damage to the soil or building;

(4)   whether the article is specially adapted to the building;

(5)   whether the building is specially adapted to the article;

(6)   whether the installation of the article in the building is a substantial, costly and time-consuming operation;

(7)   the intention of the party attaching the article determined objectively—not from extrinsic evidence—but from the nature of the article and the building and the manner of attachment.

Prima facie, an article which is unattached is not a fixture; there may, however, be circumstances in virtue of which, despite its non-attachment, an article is regarded as part of the heritage, but the onus lies on those who assert that this is so.[21] Thus, articles retained in position merely by their own weight may be so specially adpated to a building or to their surroundings as to become fixtures.[22] So also articles accessory to a principal, which is heritable, may be fixtures, although there is no physical connection between the principal and the accessory. Such things are known as constructive fixtures. Thus the keys of a house, the bell of a factory,[23] and the loose articles which are necessary for the use of fixed machinery, provided these articles are so constructed as to form part of the particular machine and are not equally capable of being applied in their existing state to other machines of the same kind, are notionally fixtures.[24]

On the other hand, the mere fact that there is some attachment to the heritage is not conclusive. Things so slightly attached as carpets nailed to the floor, or pictures hanging from a nail in the wall of a house, or a tent placed on the land, are not fixtures.

Questions as to fixtures may arise between parties standing to each other in various relationships and the right in the fixtures is affected by the nature of the relationships. In the cases which most commonly occur the conflicting interests are those of (1) (prior to the Succession (Scotland) Act 1964) the heir and executor as to fixtures added by their ancestor; (2) the seller and the buyer of heritage; (3) a heritable creditor maintaining that fixtures added by the debtor are included in the heritage covered by his security, and the general creditors of the debtor; (4) a liferenter of the heritage and his representatives, on the one hand,

---

[21] *Holland* v. *Hodgson* (1872) L.R. 7 C.P. 328, *per* Blackburn J. See *Assessor for Glasgow* v. *R.N.V.R. Club (Scotland)*, 1974 S.L.T. 291; *Assessor for Lothian Region* v. *Blue Circle Industries plc*, 1986 S.L.T. 537.

[22] *Niven* v. *Pitcairn* (1823) 2 S. 270; *D'Eyncourt* v. *Gregory* (1866) L.R. 3 Eq. 382 (unattached vases and statues forming part of architectual design); *Monti* v. *Barnes* [1901] 1 K.B. 205 (heavy dog-grates substituted for fixed grates). See also *Christie* v. *Smith's Exr.*, 1949 S.C. 572, a summerhouse remaining in position by weight alone: *Oman* v. *Ritchie*, 1941 S.L.T. (Sh.Ct.) 13.

[23] *Barr* v. *McIlwham* (1821) 1 S. 124.

[24] *Fisher* v. *Dixon* (1845) 4 Bell's App. 286; *Brand's Trs.* v. *Brand's Trs.*, *supra*.

and the owner of the fee on the other; and (5) a tenant and his landlord.

Where the rival claimants were the heir and the executor the rule which sinks the fixture in the heritage was applied with most rigour.[25] As both derived their title from the deceased owner of the heritage, there was no reason for favouring the latter at the expense of the former. The problem remains, although the executor now administers both the heritable and the moveable estate of the deceased, in deciding whether an item is heritable or moveable for the purposes of legal rights. Where the fixture has been annexed by one who was owner of the heritage, the question is not whether he has lost, for the benefit of another, the right to recover the property in the fixture, but whether, as his property, it would have passed in one or the other line of his succession. The question depends, therefore, on the character of the fixtures whether they are or are not part of the heritage.[26] In the case of a bequest of heritage the terms of the will may indicate the extent of the bequest; otherwise, the legatee is in the same position as the heir-at-law under the previous law of intestate succession.

In the case of the seller and purchaser of heritage, the terms of the contract may show what is included. If this is not so, although there may be room for allowing greater weight to the element of intention,[27] the rule appears to be the same as in that of heir and executor. The question is one of fact, namely, has the article been so permanently affixed as to become part of the heritage or, on the other hand, is it so attached that it can be removed without injury to itself and the heritage?[28] On the sale of a house it was held (after a remit to a reporter) that built-in gates, lustres, gas-brackets, and mirrors were removable by the seller.[29]

The same rule applies in a question between a heritable creditor and the general creditors, or a trustee in sequestration,[30] in valuation cases,[31] and in determining the appropriate diligence to be used with reference to fixtures.[32]

When the question arises between a landlord or fiar on the one hand, and the tenant or liferenter on the other, considerations of public policy have led to a more liberal admission of the right to remove the fixture. Both the liferenter and the tenant have no more than a temporary right

---

[25] *Elwes* v. *Maw* (1802) 2 Smith's Leading Cases (12th ed.), p. 188; *Norton* v. *Dashwood* [1896] 2 Ch. 497.

[26] *Brand's Trs.* v. *Brand's Trs.*, *supra*, *per* Lord Chelmsford.

[27] *Cochrane* v. *Stevenson* (1891) 18 R. 1208, *per* Lord Kyllachy.

[28] *Ibid.*, *per* Lord Kinnear; *Jamieson* v. *Welsh* (1900) 3 F. 176.

[29] *Nisbet* v. *Mitchell-Innes* (1880) 7 R. 575; see also *Cowans* v. *Assessor for Forfarshire*, 1910 S.C. 810. Electrical off-peak storage heaters were held to be heritable: *Assessor for Fife* v. *Hodgson*, 1966 S.C. 30.

[30] *Reynolds* v. *Ashby & Sons* [1904] A.C. 466; *Holland* v. *Hodgson*, *supra*; *Monti* v. *Barnes*, *supra*; and *Howie's Trs.* v. *McLay* (1902) 5 F. 214.

[31] *Weir* v. *Assessor for Glasgow*, 1924 S.C. 670, at p. 682; but see *Assessor for Fife* v. *Hodgson*, *supra*.

[32] Stewart on *Diligence*, p. 70.

in the heritage, and if a fixture cannot be removed the result is that the property in it is irrevocably transferred to the owner of the heritage. This being so, it is for the general advantage that the liferenter and the tenant should not be discouraged from making additions to the heritage by the operation of a rule of law which would make these for all time the property of the owner of the heritage.

It has long been settled, therefore, that a tenant may remove fixtures attached by him for the purposes of his trade;[33] and he may also remove such articles as he has annexed for ornament or for the better enjoyment of the article itself.[34] There is this limitation on that right, that the articles must be such as can be removed without material injury to the heritage and without being destroyed or losing their essential character or value.[35] But it will not prevent plant and machinery being removable that it is necessary for this purpose to take them to pieces, provided they can be fitted together in the same form in another place.[36]

In leases of agricultural subjects the common law was less favourable to the tenant;[37] but in holdings to which the Agricultural Holdings (Scotland) Act 1991[38] applies, the matter is now regulated by section 18 of that Act. Any engine, machinery, fencing or other fixture affixed by a tenant, and any building erected by him remain (under certain conditions specified in the section), the property of the tenant and removable by him up to six months from the expiry of the lease.

The case of the liferenter or his representatives has not been regarded as so strong as that of the tenant; but the tendency has been to place them in very much the same position as the tenant.[39] A liferenter may remove articles annexed for the purpose of trade or ornamentation under the same limitations as apply in the case of the tenant.

The right to remove a fixture as it exists under the above rules of the law may be modified by agreement. The person affixing the article may do so on the terms that he is to be entitled to remove it, although under the general law it might not be removable, and an agreement to this effect will be binding on the parties who have entered into it. In *Hobson* v. *Gorringe*[40] an engine was supplied on the hire-purchase system by the plaintiff to King, the owner of a saw-mill, on the terms that it was not to become his property until all instalments had been paid, and that on

---

[33] *Syme* v. *Harvey* (1861) 24 D. 201; *Marshall* v. *Tannoch Chemical Co.* (1886) 13 R. 1042.

[34] *Spyer* v. *Phillipson* [1931] 2 Ch. 183.

[35] Amos and Ferrard, pp. 71, 72.

[36] *Whitehead* v. *Bennett* (1852) 27 L.J.Ch. 474; *Pole-Carew* v. *Western Counties Manure Co.* [1920] 2 Ch. 97.

[37] Hunter on *Landlord and Tenant* (4th ed.), p. 312; Rankine on *Leases* (3rd ed.), p. 301.

[38] See para. 33.28, *supra*.

[39] *Re Hulse* [1905] 1 Ch. 406; *Fisher* v. *Dixon* (1845) 4 Bell's App. 286, *per* Lord Cottenham at p. 356.

[40] [1897] 1 Ch. 182, see also *Reynolds* v. *Ashby* [1904] A.C. 466, and *Ellis* v. *Glover & Hobson* [1908] 1 K.B. 388.

default in payment of any instalment it was to be removable by the plaintiff; and the engine was so attached to the heritage as to become part of it. King did not complete the required payments, and therefore never became owner of the engine in terms of the agreement with the plaintiff. He granted a mortgage over his property in favour of the defendant who was unaware of the terms of the agreement, and who on King's bankruptcy entered into possession of the premises. In a competition between the plaintiff and the defendant, it was held that the former could not remove the engine: it had become part of the heritage, and, as such, was included in the mortgage, and the right of removal reserved under the agreement was not enforceable as against a creditor who had in ignorance of it taken a security over the heritage. In *Scottish Discount Co. Ltd.* v. *Blin*,[41] however, it was said that when the matter is in fine balance the existence of a hire-purchase agreement may be of some relevance in deciding whether the installation was intended to be a permanent or quasi-permanent addition to the land.

36.6 Destination.—Even without actual annexation, corporeal moveables may, by destination, become part of the heritage in questions of succession, if the deceased has unequivocally manifested an intention to unite them to the heritage. Thus window-frames and building material collected on the ground for use in a building in the course of erection by a deceased person[42] and the funds required to complete it[43] have been held to be heritable *quoad* the succession to his estate.

In a question as to the succession to a tenant of a farm, the dung made on the farm was held to belong to the heir, as the tenant was under an obligation to apply it to the land, and it was to be presumed that his intention was to fulfil that obligation.[44]

36.7 Rights.—Passing from corporeal property to rights, the general rule is that these are heritable or moveable according to the nature of the subject matter. Rights connected with land (such as leases and servitudes) are heritable; a right of freshwater fishing is heritable;[45] a claim to money is, on the other hand, moveable. Thus, even claims for indemnification against the loss of, or injury to, heritable property are moveable.[46] Shares in companies[47] and the interest of a partner in a firm and its property, are moveable although the property may include

---

[41] 1985 S.C. 216.

[42] Erskine, *Inst.*, II, ii, 14; *Johnston* v. *Dobie* (1783) Mor. 5443; *Gordon*, v. *Gordon* (1806), Hume 188; *cf. Stewart* v. *Watson's Hospital* (1862) 24 D. 256.

[43] *Bank of Scotland* v. *White's Trs.* (1891) 28 S.L.R. 891; *Malloch* v. *McLean* (1867) 5 M. 335; see *Fairlie's Trs.* v. *Fairlie's Curator Bonis*, 1932 S.C. 216, *per* Lord President Clyde.

[44] *Reid's Exrs.* v. *Reid* (1890) 17 R. 519.

[45] Freshwater and Salmon Fisheries (Scotland) Act 1976, s. 4.

[46] *Heron* v. *Espie* (1856) 18 D. 917, at p. 951; *Caledonian Ry.* v. *Watt* (1875) 2 R. 917; *Kelvinside Estate Co.* v. *Donaldson's Trs.* (1879) 6 R. 995.

[47] Companies Act 1985, s. 182(1); *Hog* v. *Hog* (1791) Mor. 5479.

heritable subjects;[48] so are rights of patent and copyright.[49] It is a question of circumstances whether the goodwill of a business is so connected with the premises in which it is carried on as to be heritable; otherwise it is moveable.[50]

36.8 Feu-Duties and Rents.—These, as the produce of heritable subjects, are heritable. But in a question of succession the arrears are moveable, for the law 'suffers not chance to govern but supposes everything to be performed which ought to have been performed and will not put it in the power of a dilatory debtor to hurt the executor.' In other words, the arrears are treated as being in the pocket of the creditor.[51] The liability for arrears of feu-duty is primarily a burden on the moveable and not on the heritable estate of the deceased vassal.[52]

36.9 Heritable Securities.—From their connection with lands, sums secured over heritage were under the common law heritable as regards both the creditor's and debtor's succession. By section 117 of the Titles to Land Consolidation (Scotland) Act 1868,[53] such securities are made moveable as regards the general sucession of the creditor, but by express provision of the statute they remain heritable as to the fisc (*i.e.*, the Crown's right to the moveable estate of a person denounced rebel), and as regards the legal rights of spouses and issue (*i.e.* are not now subject to legal rights at all).[54] It is no longer possible to make a bond heritable for all purposes by taking a destination excluding executors.[55] The 1868 Act altered the law with reference only to the succession of the creditor; and such debts still remain heritable in a question between the debtor's heirs and representatives.[56] If a creditor in a heritable security in his will makes different dispositions of his heritable and moveable estate, without referring specifically to the security, it will fall under the disposition of the moveable estate.[57]

[48] Partnership Act 1890, s. 22; *Lord Advocate* v. *Macfarlane's Trs.* (1893) 31 S.L.R. 357; *Murray* v. *Murray* (1805) Mor., 'Heritable and Moveable,' App. No. 4; *Minto* v. *Kirkpatrick* (1833) 11 S. 632; see also *Irvine* v. *Irvine* (1851) 13 D. 1267.
[49] *Advocate-General* v. *Oswald* (1848) 10 D. 969; Patents Act 1977, s. 31(2); Copyright, Designs and Patents Act 1988, s. 90(1).
[50] *Muirhead's Trs.* v. *Muirhead* (1905) 7 F. 496; see para. 38.10, *infra*
[51] *Martin* v. *Agnew* (1755) Mor. 5457; 5 Brown's Sup. 830; *Logan's Trs.* v. *Logan* (1896) 23 R. 848; *Watson's Trs.* v. *Brown*, 1923 S.C. 228.
[52] *Johnston* v. *Cochran* (1829) 7 S. 226.
[53] As amended by Succession (Scotland) Act 1964, Sched. 3. For the definition of 'heritable security,' as used in the Act, see s. 3. It does not include 'securities by way of ground annual whether redeemable or irredeemable, or absolute dispositions qualified by back bonds or letters.' Securities by way of real burden are moveable *quoad* succession (Conveyancing (Scotland) Act 1874, s. 30, as amended by Succession (Scotland) Act 1964, Sched. 3). Section 117 of the 1868 Act applies to a standard security (Conveyancing and Feudal Reform (Scotland) Act 1970, s. 32).
[54] See para. 42.3, *infra*.
[55] See Meston, *Succession (Scotland) Act 1964* (4th ed., 1993), p. 59.
[56] *Bell's Trs.*, v. *Bell* (1884) 12 R. 85.
[57] *Hughes' Trs.* v. *Corsane* (1890) 18 R. 299.

36.10   Personal Bonds.—The veneration which the feudal system commanded in ancient times led to the inclusion under heritable property of rights which had no connection with heritable property. Rights were so treated for no better reason than that they had a certain degree of permanence, and, therefore, should be given to the heir in heritage. This is illustrated in the case of the rights noticed in this and the next paragraph. Under the common law 'contracts and obligations for sums of money' containing clauses for payment of interest were from the first heritable if the date of payment were uncertain or distant, and became in any case heritable after the first term at which the interest or capital was payable.[58]

But the Bonds Act 1661 (c. 32) (re-enacting an earlier statute[59]) altered this and made such contracts and obligations moveable. The statute contains a provision that if the bond contains an express obligation to infeft the creditor in security of the debt, or excludes the executors of the creditor, it is to remain heritable. The statute also expressly left such bonds heritable *quoad* fiscum, and the widow's *jus relictae*, but the latter exception was abolished by the Conveyancing (Scotland) Act 1924.[60]

36.11   Rights Having a Tract of Future Time.—'These are rights of such a nature that they cannot be at once paid or fulfilled by the debtor, but continue for a number of years, and carry a yearly profit to the creditor while they subsist, without relation to any capital sum or stock, e.g. a yearly annuity or pension for a certain number of years.'[61]

An annuity is heritable and, as such, a burden on the heritable succession of the person liable to pay it, although the termly payments as they become due are moveable.[62] So also where a liferent was assigned, it was held that this passed to the heir, and not the executor, of the assignee.[63] But where there is a capital sum or stock, its character will determine that of its fruits or income. Thus the income of a sum of money is always moveable.[64]

36.12   Conversion.—The character of property may be altered by conversion, actual or constructive. Thus the quality of the beneficial right in subjects held in trust depends on the nature of these according as they are heritable or moveable; but that quality may be constructively converted

---

[58] See *Heath* v. *Grant's Trs.*, 1913 S.C. 78, and cases there cited.

[59] 1641, c. 57.

[60] s. 22.

[61] Erskine, *Inst.*, II, ii, 6.

[62] *Hill* v. *Hill* (1872) 11 M. 247; *Reid* v. *McWalter* (1878) 5 R. 630; *Marquis of Breadalbane's Trs.* v. *Jamieson* (1873) 11 M. 912; *Countess de Serra Largo* v. *De Serra Largo's Trs.*, 1933 S.L.T. 391.

[63] *Allan* v. *Williamson*, 1741, Elchies' Heritable, No. 12; *Drummond* v. *Ewing*, 1752, Elchies' Heritable, No. 16.

[64] *Hill* v. *Hill, supra.*

from heritable into moveable, or vice versa, by the terms of the truster's directions or by what is found to be necessary in the course of the trust administration. So also rights in the succession may be affected by contracts entered into by the deceased for the purchase or sale of heritage, the completion of which by the necessary deed of conveyance has been interrupted by his death. These questions are considered elsewhere.[65]

Further Reading

Bells' *Principles*, §§ 1470–1505.
Dobie, *Manual of the Law of Liferent and Fee* (1941).
Erskines' *Institutes*, II.
Stair Memorial Encyclopedia, Vol. 18 (Property).

[65] See paras. 43.8, *infra* and 46.3, *supra*.

CHAPTER 37

MOVEABLE PROPERTY: CORPOREAL

37.1 Possession.—From the long controversy among jurists as to the nature of possession, various theories have emerged, an account of which may be found in works on general jurisprudence. In this place it is necessary to refer only to the views of the institutional writers in our law, and among these there is substantial agreement on this matter. According to Stair, possession is the holding or detaining of anything by ourselves or others for our use. 'To possession there must be an act of the body which is detention and holding; and an act of the mind which is the inclination or affection to make use of the thing detained.'[1] The material element, the detention, must depend to some extent on the nature of the thing possessed; since it is obviously impossible, for example, to require the same kind of acts in regard to heritage as in regard to moveables. 'By possession is meant possession of that character of which the thing is capable.'[2] The mental element, the act of the mind, is the intention to hold the thing for one's own benefit. This is presumed from the fact of detention unless the holding of the thing as his own would infer a crime on the part of the holder.[3] The person who holds or detains the thing is not required to prove that he does so with this intention; it rests on him who disputes it to establish its absence. The absence of the *animus possidendi* distinguishes custody from possession. A servant in charge of his master's property is not regarded as possessing it; he has the custody, but not the possession of it.[4] It is not necessary, however, that the subject should be held on a rightful title; a thief holding the goods stolen is possessor of these, as both elements of the definition are satisfied.

Possession is divided into natural and civil.[5] Natural possession is actual possession of the subject. Thus the owner of a moveable is in natural possession if he keeps it in his hands or repositories; the owner of land if he cultivates it; the owner of a house if he occupies it. Civil possession is possession through an intermediary or representative. Thus

---

[1] Stair, II, i, 17; see also Erskine, *Inst.*, II, i, 20; Bankton, i, 510. See Smith, *Short Commentary*, p. 461.

[2] *Young* v. *N.B. Ry.* (1887) 14 R. (H.L.) 53, *per* Lord Fitzgerald at p. 56.

[3] Erskine, *Inst.* II, i, 20.

[4] Stair, Erskine and Bankton, *supra; Barnton Hotel Co.* v. *Cook* (1899) 1 F. 1190. For observations as to the distinction between custody and possession, see *Sim* v. *Grant* (1862) 24 D. 1033.

[5] Erskine, *Inst.*, II, i, 22; Bell, *Prin.*, § 1312.

a person possesses things through his servants or agents or custodiers for his behoof; a landlord through his tenant;[6] trustees owning a house through a liferenter in possession.[7]

Possession is exclusive. Two persons cannot each have the full possession of the same subject at the same time. But there may be concurrent possession by two or more persons having different rights which are not antagonistic. Thus a subject may be possessed by several persons in common; a tenant possesses for his own interest and at the same time the landlord possesses through him; a pledgee possesses the thing pledged and the proprietor also possesses so far as necessary to support his right of property.[8]

37.2 Presumption of Ownership.—Seeing that 'there use not witnesses or writ to be adhibited in the commerce of moveables,' the possessor of a corporeal moveable is, in a question with a wrong-doer or a person asserting an adverse title, presumed to be its owner.[9] This presumption may be displaced by proof; but the possessor is entitled to stand upon his possession and require his adversary to establish his right of property.[10] The latter must show not only that he lost possession but that he did so in some way consistent with the retention of the ownership, as, for instance, that the goods were stolen from him or that they passed from him by 'some title not alienative of property as loan or the like.'[11] In certain circumstances however, the presumption, if it exists at all, is but slight; there is little ground for presuming ownership from possession in the case of one, such as a carrier, whose avocation requires the possession by him of goods entrusted to him by others.[12]

37.3 Reputed Ownership: Effect of Possession.—The object of the doctrine of reputed ownership was to afford protection to creditors who had been misled by the false credit acquired by their debtor owing to his having been permitted to possess as apparent owner property which belonged to another; and its effect was to preclude the true owner from asserting his right against these creditors.[13] Owing to changes in the law this doctrine is no longer of much importance.[14] The occasions on which the possession of, and the property in, goods may be separated are so frequent that creditors and others transacting with the possessor are not

---

[6] *Union Bank* v. *Mackenzie* (1865) 3 M. 765.

[7] *Mitchell's Trs.* v. *Gladstone* (1894) 21 R. 586.

[8] Erskine, *Inst.* II, i, 22–23.

[9] *Scot* v. *Elliot* (1672) Mor. 12727; Stair, II, i, 42; III, ii, 7; IV, xxx, 9; Erskine, II, i, 24; *Macdougall* v. *Whitelaw* (1840) 2 D. 500. See also *Glenwood Property Co.* v. *Phillips* [1904] A.C. 405, at p. 410.

[10] *Brownlee's Exr.* v. *Brownlee*, 1908 S.C. 232, *per* Lord President Dunedin at p. 239.

[11] *Russel* v. *Campbell* (1699) 4 Brown's Sup. 468; *Hariot* v. *Cuningham* (1791) Mor. 12405; *Prangnell-O'Neill* v. *Lady Skiffington*, 1984 S.L.T. 282.

[12] *Warrander & Sterling* v. *Alexander & Thomson* (1715) Mor. 10609. *Sed quaere* if a carrier has possession.

[13] See *Shearer* v. *Christie* (1842) 5 D. 132; Bell's *Comm.*, i, 269.

[14] *Robertsons* v. *McIntyre* (1882) 9 R. 772, *per* Lord Justice-Clerk Moncreiff.

warranted in assuming that he is the owner. Possession does not give the possessor even an apparent authority to dispose of the property; and the mere fact that the true owner has allowed another to be in possession of his property will not preclude him from asserting his right as against those who purport to have acquired the property or rights over it from the possessor.[15] Other circumstances must be present if the owner is to be personally barred from vindicating his property.[16] The possession by a liferenter will not entitle his creditors to carry away the goods to the prejudice of the fiar,[17] nor the creditors of a tenant to attach moveables held by him under a contract with his landlord, the true owner.[18]

37.4 Acquisition of Property: Occupation.—Property may be acquired either by an original title, as *e.g.* by occupation, or by a derivative title from the former owner. Occupation is the taking possession of a thing with the intention of becoming owner of it.[19] *Quod nullius est fit occupantis.* This mode of acquisition is not applicable to heritage, because under the feudal system the sovereign is the original proprietor of all the land within his dominions, nor to things which once have had an owner. Property in things which have never had an owner, such as wild animals, may be acquired in this way. Without specific appropriation a wild animal, although protected and preserved on private property, does not belong to anyone,[20] and it will become the property of him who takes or kills it, although he may be a trespasser or acting in contravention of the law. A poacher acquires the property in the animals which he takes unless these are forfeited by statute.[21] If such animals have once been appropriated and possession of them is retained by him who has thus become their owner, they are not capable of being acquired by another by occupation. But if the animal escapes and reverts to its original liberty 'the property is lost so soon as the owner ceaseth to pursue for possession,'[22] and it may again be acquired by this means. Domesticated animals, or such as have a homing instinct (pigeons, bees) or carry a mark indicating private property, are not acquired by one who seizes and detains them and thereby prevents their returning to their owner.[23]

37.5 Treasure-Trove; Lost Property; Wrecks.—Treasure discovered hidden in the ground, the ownership of which cannot be traced, belongs not to the

[15] *Lamonby* v. *Foulds*, 1928 S.C. 89; *Mitchell* v. *Heys & Sons* (1894) 21 R. 600; *Robertsons* v. *McIntyre* (1882) 9 R. 772. Cf. *Jones* v. *Waring & Gillow* [1926] A.C. 670, *per* Lord Sumner, and *Mercantile Bank of India* v. *Central Bank of India* [1938] A.C. 287.
[16] *Bryce* v. *Ehrmann* (1904) 7 F. 5. See para. 22.29, *supra,* for the Factors Act.
[17] *Scott* v. *Price* (1837) 15 S. 916, *per* Lord Mackenzie.
[18] *Hogarth* v. *Smart's Tr.* (1882) 9 R. 964.
[19] Stair, II, i, 33; Erskine, *Inst.,* II, i, 10; Bell, *Prin.,* §§ 1287–1294.
[20] *Wilson* v. *Dykes* (1872) 10 M. 444, *per* Lord Justice-Clerk Moncreiff.
[21] *Scott* v. *Everitt* (1853) 15 D. 288; see also *Leith* v. *Leith* (1862) 24 D. 1059, at pp. 1062 and 1077; *Livingstone* v. *Breadalbane* (1791) 3 Pat. App. 221.
[22] Stair, *supra.*
[23] Erskine, *Inst.,* II, i, 10; Bell's *Prin.,* § 1290. There are special rules applicable to whalefishing—see *Sutter* v. *Aberdeen Arctic Co.* (1862) 4 Macq. 355; Bell's *Prin.,* § 1289.

finder or to the owner of the ground, but to the Crown.[24] Erskine[25] and
Bell[26] state that goods lost, abandoned and ownerless (*bona vacantia*)
also fall to the Crown under the rule *Quod nullius est fit domini regis*.
The Civic Government Act (Scotland) 1982 provides that a person who
finds lost or abandoned property shall not by reason of finding it have
any right to claim ownership of it; there is a requirement to deliver
property to the police and provision for its subsequent disposal.[27] In
England it has been held that banknotes accidentally dropped in a shop
by an unknown person belonged not to the shopkeeper, but to the
finder;[28] articles embedded in the soil and discovered in the course of
operations were held to belong not to the discoverer, but to the owner
of the soil.[29] Strayed cattle, Erskine says, do not belong to the finder;
he must give public notice and, if within a year and a day the proprietor
does not claim his goods, they become escheat and fall to the Crown,
sheriff, or other person to whom a grant has been made of such
escheats. Under the Winter Herding Act 1686 (c. 11), the owner of
'horses, nolt, sheep, swine or goats' straying on another's lands was
made liable, in addition to his liability for any damage done, in a
penalty of half a merk for each beast, and the beasts might be detained
till this and the expenses of keeping them were paid but the Act is now
repealed.[30] Wrecks, which belonged to the Crown, but could be claimed
by the owner of the ship if a living thing were found on board,[31] are
now placed under the general superintendence of the Department of
Trade, which has power to appoint receivers, to whom any person
finding or taking possession of the wreck must give notice. Provision is
made for the disposal of the wreck whether claimed or unclaimed by the
owner.[32]

37.6   Accession.—In this way a person becomes owner of something of an
accessory nature by reason of his ownership of another, the principal,

---

[24] Stair, II, i, 5; Erskine, II, i, 12; *Gentle* v. *Smith*, 1 Bell's *Illustrations*, 184; *cf.*
Cleghorn & Bryce v. *Baird* (1696) Mor. 13522; *Sands* v. *Bell & Balfour*, May 22, 1810,
F.C.; *Lord Advocate* v. *University of Aberdeen*, 1963 S.C. 533.

[25] II, i, 12.

[26] *Prin.*, § 1291 (3); but *cf.* Stair, I, i, 3.

[27] ss. 67–79. 'If the finder at once, or within a short period, appropriate the article, theft
is committed': Macdonald's *Criminal Law* (5th ed.), p. 32; contra, Hume, i, 62, and
Alison, i, 360–1. See also *Lawson* v. *Heatly*, 1962 S.L.T. 53; Gordon, *Criminal Law* (2nd
ed., 1978), pp. 464 *et seq.* As to the finder's right to recover what he may have expended
on the goods, see the opinion of Scrutton L.J. in *Jebara* v. *Ottoman Bank* [1927] 2 K.B.
254.

[28] *Bridges* v. *Hawkesworth* (1851) 15 Jur. 1079; see Smith, *Short Commentary*, p. 464.

[29] *Elwes* v. *Brigg Gas Co.* (1886) 33 Ch.D. 562; *South Staffordshire Water Co.* v.
Sharman [1896] 2 Q.B. 44. See also *Att.-Gen.* v. *Trustees of British Museum* [1903] 2 Ch.
598, and Goodhart's *Essays in Jurisprudence*, p. 75.

[30] Animals (Scotland) Act 1987, s. 8(2), Schedule.

[31] Bell's *Prin.*, § 1292.

[32] Merchant Shipping Act 1995, ss. 231 *et seq.*; *Lord Advocate* v. *Hebden* (1868) 6 M.
489.

subject.[33] *Accessorium sequitur principale.* Thus, the proprietor of an animal becomes proprietor of its offspring;[34] and things affixed to heritable property become part of that property.[35] On this ground also the interest produced by a fund and not otherwise disposed of has been held to belong to the owner of the fund.[36] This method of acquiring property is illustrated in the case of heritable rights. The imperceptible addition made to one's ground, as by the retreat of the sea or the shifting of a river bed or by what is washed by a river from other grounds (*alluvio*), accrues to the owner of the ground receiving the addition. On the other hand, where there is *avulsio*, a sudden and sensible addition to land as contrasted with *alluvio*, there is no transference of property. An island formed in a river belongs to the owner of the *alveus* at that spot.[37]

37.7 **Specification.**—This is the making of a new subject by one person with materials belonging to another. Apart from the works of the institutional writers, there is little authority either on this matter or on the kindred modes of acquiring property dealt with in the next paragraph. In a passage[38] which was cited with approval in a modern case,[39] Bell (agreeing with Erskine) states the rules in these terms: 'If the materials, as a separate existence, be destroyed in bona fide, the property is with the workman; the owner of the materials having a personal claim for a like quantity and quality, or for the price of the materials; if still capable of restoration to their original shape, the property is held to be with the owner of the materials; a claim against him for work and indemnity in *quantum lucratus* being competent to the workman.' In the former case the operation has resulted in the creation of a new subject; but the equitable doctrine by which its ownership passes to the workman cannot be invoked if the materials or part of them were stolen by the workman from their rightful owner.[40]

37.8 **Confusion of Liquids and Commixtion of Solids.**—These 'raise a common property, if the commodities be of the same kind; and of such

---

[33] Erskine, II, i, 14–15. See *Zahnrad Fabrik Passau GmbH* v. *Terex Ltd.*, 1986 S.L.T. 84.

[34] *Lamb* v. *Grant* (1874) 11 S.L.R. 672.

[35] See para. 36.5, *supra.*

[36] *Gillespies* v. *Marshall* (1802) Mor., App. I, 'Accessorium' No. 2. *Cf. Stewart* v. *Stewart* (1669) Mor. 50. See McLaren on *Wills, i, 329.*

[37] *Erskine, supra*; Bell's *Prin.*, § 934; Rankine on *Land-Ownership* (4th ed.), p. 112; see also *Stirling* v. *Bartlett*, 1992 S.C. 523.

[38] Bell's *Prin.*, § 1298; see also Stair, II, i, 41; Erskine, II, i, 16. For the Civil Law, see *Inst.*, II, i, 25 *et seq.*; Girard, *Manuel de Droit Romain*, 3, 2, 3, 4; Buckland's *Text Book of Roman Law.*, (3rd ed.), p. 215. The doctrine does not apply to the situation in which a motor vehicle has been sold to a 'private purchaser' so as to give him a good title under the Hire-Purchase Act 1964: *North-West Securities* v. *Barrhead Coachworks*, 1976 S.L.T. 99; *cf. F.C. Finance* v. *Langtry Investment Co.*, 1973 S.L.T. (Sh.Ct.) 11.

[39] *International Banking Corporation* v. *Ferguson, Shaw & Sons*, 1910 S.C. 182. See also *Armour* v. *Thyssen Edelstahlwerke A.G.*, 1986 S.L.T. 452.

[40] *McDonald* v. *Provan*, 1960 S.L.T. 231.

property *pro indiviso* the shares are in proportion to quantity and value, where either the union is by common consent, or where, having been made by accident or without fault, the commodities are inseparable. The property is unchanged if the articles be capable of separation. If the union be of substances different, so as to create a *tertium quid* the property is (according to the rule in specification) with the owner of the materials, or with the manufacturer, according to the possibility or impossibility of restoring the original substances.'[41]

But, where two or more persons have agreed to contribute to the production of a new subject, either materials or skill and labour, or both, the subject will belong to them as common property in shares corresponding to the value of their respective contributions.[42]

37.9 **Voluntary Transference of Property.**—The law of Scotland requires for the voluntary transmission of property in corporeal moveables, both the intention or consent of the owner to the transmission and delivery of the subject in pursuance of that intention.[43] A contract to transmit the property is in itself ineffectual for that purpose; it creates nothing more than an obligation, on the one hand, to give, and a right, on the other, to receive, delivery. 'A mere assignation of corporeal moveables *retenta possessione* is nothing whatever but a personal obligation';[44] without delivery, the property or real right in the subject does not pass. *Traditionibus non nudis pactis transferuntur rerum dominia.* This rule applies to all forms of contract for the transference of moveables. Thus in the case of donation *inter vivos*[45] it must be established that there were both the *animus donandi* and delivery of the thing which is gifted and clear proof is required, as the presumption is against donation.[46] 'The donor must divest himself of, and invest the donee with, the subject of the gift.'[47] Although a person has come under obligation to give a thing to one party, if he delivers it to another, the latter becomes the proprietor of the thing.[48] An exception to the rule has, however, been made by statute in the case of the sale of goods.[49] The necessity for, and the effect of, tradition and the various modes of delivery, actual, symbolical and constructive,[50] have been considered in the earlier chapters dealing with the different classes of contracts. It has also

---

[41] This passage is taken from Bell's *Prin.*, § 1298 (2). *Cf.* Lord Moulton's speech in *Tyzack & Branfoot S.S. Co.* v. *Sandeman & Sons,* 1913 S.C. (H.L.) 84.

[42] *Wylie & Lochhead* v. *Mitchell* (1870) 8 M. 552.

[43] Erskine, *Inst.* II, ii, 18; Stair, III, ii, 5; Bell's *Comm.*, ii, 11.

[44] *Clark* v. *West Calder Oil Co.* (1882) 9 R. 1017, *per* Lord President Inglis.

[45] See para. 44.38, *infra.*

[46] *Brownlee's Exrx.* v. *Brownlee,* 1908 S.C. 232; *Milne* v. *Grant* (1884) 11 R. 887; *Thompson* v. *Dunlop* (1884) 11 R. 453; *Grant's Trs.* v. *McDonald,* 1939 S.C. 448. See *Newton* v. *Newton,* 1923 S.C. 15.

[47] *McNicol* v. *McDougall* (1889) 17 R. 25, *per* Lord Young.

[48] Erskine, III, iii, 90.

[49] Sale of Goods Act 1979; see paras. 16.7, 16.14 *et seq.*

[50] paras. 19.11–19.13, *supra.*

been seen that contracts regarding moveables do not run with these moveables.[51] In *Leitch & Co.* v. *Leydon*[52] it was held that the pursuers, manufacturers who issued their goods in receptacles (of which they retained the property), could not interdict the defender from helping a member of the public in lawful possession of one of these receptacles to put it to a use which, although not injurious to it, was objected to by the pursuers.

37.10 Property in Ships.—Ships are moveable property, but are subject to special rules which require separate notice.[53] Considerations of national policy led the English Parliament, in the seventeenth century, to legislate in regard to shipping, and this legislation was copied in Scotland after the Restoration. The regulation of shipping thus introduced has been continued in modern times. The leading statute now in force is the Merchant Shipping Act 1995.

37.11 Registration and Transfer of Ships.—The term 'ship' includes every description of vessel used in navigation not propelled by oars. The former registration of British ships in three registers is now replaced by a single register.[54] The new register must contain a separate part for the registration of fishing vessels and may be divided into other parts 'so as to distinguish between classes or descriptions of ships.'[55] A ship is a British ship if, *inter alia*, it is registered in the U.K. under the 1995 Act[56] and ships on bareboat charter to a person qualified to own British ships may also be entered in the register even though registered in another country.[57] Registration regulations will determine what persons are qualified to own British ships and the extent of the ownership qualification.[58] The registered owner of a ship or a share therein has a power of disposal thereof.[59] Transfer of a ship or a share therein is effected by a bill of sale unless this will result in the vessel ceasing to have a British connection.[60] The registration regulations will prescribe the form of the bill of sale and the information and evidence needed to accompany an application to the registrar,[61] as well as the manner in

---

[51] para. 10.14, *supra*.
[52] 1931 S.C. (H.L.) 1. See also *Wilson* v. *Shepherd*, 1913 S.C. 300.
[53] Temperley's *Merchant Shipping Acts* (7th ed.), 1976.
[54] Merchant Shipping Act 1995, ss. 8–23.   [55] s. 8(5).
[56] s. 1.
[57] s. 17. The registrar may, however, refuse registration where this would be inappropriate: s. 9(3).
[58] ss. 9(1), (2) and 10.
[59] s. 16, Sched. 1, para. 1(1).
[60] s. 16, Sched. 1, para. 2(1).
[61] s. 10(6), Sched. 1, para. 2(1); s. 10(2)(*b*). Section 10 should be consulted for the other prerequisites prior to registration which will be prescribed by the registration regulations.

which the bill of sale is to be registered.[62] While the provisions of the 1993 Act relate to the mode of transfer of the property in a ship or shares therein, a contract for the sale of these is valid though made without writing.[63]

Further Reading

Carey Miller, *Corporeal Moveables in Scots Law*.
Temperley, *Merchant Shipping Acts* (7th ed., 1976) (British Shipping Laws, Vol. II).

.

[62] s. 16, Sched. 1, para. 2(3).
[63] *McConnachie* v. *Geddes*, 1918 S.C. 391.

CHAPTER 38

MOVEABLE PROPERTY: INCORPOREAL

Within the category of incorporeal moveable property are included subjects so diverse as rights to debts (*nomina debitorum*) or obligations, claims *ex contractu* and *ex delicto*, rights to shares in companies, goodwill, patents, copyright and trade marks and names. Some of these are dealt with in other parts of this book. The main topic for consideration here is the mode and effect of the transference of incorporeal moveable property.

38.1   Assignations.—Corporeal moveables, as was shown in the preceding chapter, are transferred by delivery or possession. This is impossible in the case of incorporeal property; and, therefore, some deed by which it may be made clear that the right in the property has passed from the owner to another is required. The deed by which this is accomplished is known as an assignation. This term is applied to deeds conveying either such moveable rights or rights in heritage which are either incapable of infeftment or on which infeftment has not followed. If the subject is heritage, and the deed is granted by one who is infeft in that heritage, it is styled a disposition.[1] The grantor of an assignation is known as the cedent; the grantee as the assignee or (less commonly) cessionary. It is a general rule that unilateral deeds are not effective unless they are delivered.[2]

As a general rule anyone in right of a subject may at pleasure convey it to another. The exceptions to this are few. An alimentary provision and rights which are personal to the creditor from the *delectus personae* or choice made of him by the grantor of the right cannot be assigned.[3] Strictly speaking, a liferent is not assignable, but its profits may be assigned.[4] A conditional obligation, or *spes successionis*, may be assigned, and the assignation will become effectual if the condition is purified or the *spes* comes to be vested in the cedent.[5]

---

[1] Stair, III, i, 1 and 16; Erskine, *Inst.* II, vii, 2, and III, v, 1. Erskine's view that a particular moveable subject is transmitted by assignation and not by disposition is controverted by Ross (*Lects.*, i, 189) and Menzies (*Conveyancing*, p. 270).

[2] *Connell's Trs.* v. *Connell's Tr.*, 1955 S.L.T. 125.

[3] Erskine, *Inst.*, III, v, 2; see para. 10.18, *supra*.

[4] See para. 47.11, *infra*.

[5] *Bedwells & Yates* v. *Tods*, 2 Dec. 1819, F.C.; *Kirkland* v. *Kirkland's Tr.* (1886) 13 R. 798, at p. 805.

38.2 Form of Assignation.—In the earliest times it was considered that a creditor could not substitute another as creditor in his place without the consent of the debtor; and, consequently, a direct assignation of a debt was impossible. Hence the device was hit upon of making the assignee the mandatory of the cedent for the purpose of exacting and discharging the debt but without any obligation to account to the cedent. The older bonds were in the form of mandates, but in course of time deeds of direct conveyance came into use and have long been sanctioned. The Transmission of Moveable Property (Scotland) Act 1862, without prohibiting the use of the forms then in existence, provides short forms of assignation.

But no particular form need be adopted.[6] 'If anything is settled in the law of Scotland it is that no words directly importing conveyance are necessary to constitute an assignation but that any words giving authority or directions, which if fairly carried out will operate a transference, are sufficient to make an assignation.'[7] Thus a bill of exchange drawn by a beneficiary for whom trustees held funds on these trustees in favour of another was treated as constituting an assignation in his favour;[8] and a writing containing the words 'I hand over my life policy to my daughter,' was held to be a valid assignation of the grantor's right in the policy.[9]

38.3 Obligations of Cedent.—In assignations the law implies that the cedent confers on his assignee everything which is necessary to make the assignation effectual.[10] It is also implied that the cedent warrants that the debt is subsisting: that the bond, decree or other deed assigned is such as can never be reduced: and that the cedent has undoubted right to the debt.[11] But there is no implied warranty of the solvency of the debtor.[12]

38.4 Intimation.—As between the cedent (or his executor) and the assignee the execution and delivery of the assignation is sufficient to give the latter a valid right.[13] But for the purpose of giving the assignee a right effectual as against all parties, intimation of the assignation to the debtor or holder of the fund is necessary. By this means the assignation is brought to the knowledge of the debtor or holder so as to interpel him from paying the debt or making over the fund to the original

---

[6] In regard to special subjects there may be statutory provisions as to the mode of transfer.

[7] *Carter* v. *McIntosh* (1862) 24 D. 925, *per* Lord Justice-Clerk Inglis; see also *Gallemos Ltd.* v. *Barratt Falkirk Ltd.*, 1989 S.C. 239. See para. 23.28, *supra*.

[8] *Carter* v. *McIntosh, supra*.

[9] *Brownlee* v. *Robb*, 1907 S.C. 1302.

[10] *Miller* v. *Muirhead* (1894) 21 R. 658.

[11] *Barclay* v. *Liddel* (1671) Mor. 16591; *Reid* v. *Barclay* (1879) 6 R. 1007.

[12] *Ibid.*; Erskine, *Inst.*, II, iii, 25.

[13] *Thome* v. *Thome* (1683) 2 Brown's Sup. 49; Stair, III, i, 15.

creditor or to any other assignee; and if thereafter he chooses to do so, this will afford him no defence to the claim by the assignee who gave him intimation.[14] Further, it has long been settled that intimation is necessary to complete the assignee's right. 'The assignation itself is not a complete valid right till it be orderly intimated to the debtor.'[15] It is the point from which the passing of the right is dated and also the criterion by which the right of the assignee is determined in a question with other assignees or claimants to the fund or debt. If A, having assigned a debt due to him to B, subsequently assigns it to C, the assignation to C, although later in date, will if it is first intimated, carry the debt. So also an arrestment prior in date to the intimation, though subsequent to the assignation itself, will prevail over the assignation; but if it is later in date than the intimation, the assignation will be preferred.[16] Further, the intimation of the assignation of a debt will prevent the debtor X from pleading compensation against the assignee B, in respect of a debt due by the cedent A, which X has acquired after the date of the intimation; the right to the debt having passed from A with the intimation, there is no proper concourse of credit and debt between the same persons.[17] But if prior to the intimation the right to compensate was vested in the debtor X, then it will be available to him against the assignee B.[18] The intimation also has the effect of making it incompetent to prove any exception against the debt, whether of payment or otherwise, by the oath of the cedent unless the subject has been rendered litigious before intimation or the assignee admits on reference to his oath that the assignation is gratuitous or in trust for the cedent.[19]

38.5 Forms of Intimation.—The old, and still competent, form of regular intimation was that a procurator for the assignee delivered to the debtor in the presence of a notary and witnesses a copy of the assignation and took instruments in the notary's hands.[20] But by the Transmission of Moveable Property Act 1862 alternative forms are introduced. These are: (a) delivery by a notary of a certified copy of the assignation, or (b) transmission by the holder of the assignation or his agent of a certified copy by post, the first being vouched by the notary's certificate of intimation, the second by the debtor's written acknowledgment. The latter mode was valid at common law. Of a complex deed only a copy of

[14] See *McGill* v. *Laureston* (1558) Mor. 843; *McDowal* v. *Fullerton* (1714) Mor. 576, 840.
[15] Stair, III, i, 6; Erskine, *Inst.*, III, v, 3; Bell, *Comm.*, ii, 16; *Liquidator of Union Club* v. *Edinburgh Life Assurance Co.* (1906) 8 F. 1143, *per* Lord McLaren.
[16] Stair, III, i, 43 and 44; Erskine, *Inst.* III, vi, 19; *Liquidator of Union Club* v. *Edinburgh Life Assurance Co. supra.*
[17] See para. 14.13 *supra.*; *Macpherson's J.F.* v. *Mackay*, 1915 S.C. 1011; *Wallace* v. *Edgar* (1663) Mor. 837; *Chambers' J.F.* v. *Vertue* (1893) 20 R. 257.
[18] *Shiells* v. *Ferguson, Davidson & Co.* (1876) 4 R. 250.
[19] *Lang* v. *Hislop* (1854) 16 D. 908.
[20] For details see Bell's *Lectures on Conveyancing* (3rd ed.), i, 311.

the part containing the assignation need be sent. Where there are several obligants, as in the case of trustees, or joint debtors, intimation should be made to all unless some one or more of them take the whole management; for otherwise, while intimation to one would complete the assignation, it would not interpel the others from paying the cedent.[21] An absentee may be notified in the statutory modes, or at the edictal citation office. According to the common law, a corporation is notified through its treasurer; a bank, through the manager and the agent of the branch where the fund lies; and firm, through all its partners, or a manager, if such there be, formally appointed.[22] In the Companies Act 1985,[23] it is provided that documents may be served on a company by delivery at, or posting to, the company's registered office.

38.6   Equivalents of Intimation.—The law admits equivalents of intimation where the notice of the assignation given to the debtor is equally strong. Thus, diligence or a suit against the debtor founded on the assignation at the instance of the assignee, or a claim in a multiplepoinding to which the debtor is a party supplies the want of intimation, as these are judicial and public acts which bring the assignation to the eyes of the public and of the debtor.[24] The assignee's possession of the right by entering into enjoyment of the rents or interest is also equal to an intimation, for it imports not only notice to, but actual compliance by, the debtor.[25] An assignation of a lease, or of the rents and profits of land is perfected by intimation to the landlord and the assignee's possessing the ground or levying the rents. Assignations of heritable bonds, real burdens, registered leases and securities over these are completed by registration in the Register of Sasines or the Land Register;[26] but the registration of assignations of personal rights as bonds, contracts, etc., in the Books of Council and Session or of the sheriff courts does not suffice, as these are merely for preservation and diligence and not for publication.[27] Notice to the common debtor's factor in entire control of the estate, followed by entry thereof in his books,[28] and an assignee's attending and voting at the meeting of a company in virtue of the share assigned to him[29] have also been held sufficient proof of intimation.

[21] Erskine, *Inst.*, III, v, 5; *Jameson* v. *Sharp* (1887) 14 R. 643. See *Browne's Tr.* v. *Anderson* (1901) 4 F. 305.
[22] *Hill* v. *Lindsay* (1846) 8 D. 472; but see Partnership Act 1890, s. 16.
[23] s. 725 (extended to apply to European Economic Interest Groupings: S.I. 1989 No. 638).
[24] *Whyte* v. *Neish* (1622) Mor. 854; *Dougall* v. *Gordon* (1795) Mor. 851.
[25] Erskine, *Prin.*, III, v, 3.
[26] *Edmond* v. *Mags. of Aberdeen* (1858) 3 Macq. 116. It should be noted that, in the case of a 'long lease,' registration in the Land Register is the only means of obtaining a real right in an area in respect of which the Land Registration (Scotland) Act 1979, has come into operation; see para. 41.4, *infra*.
[27] *Tod's Trs.* v. *Wilson* (1869) 7 Mor. 1100; see *Cameron's Trs.* v. *Cameron*, 1907 S.C. 407.
[28] *Earl of Aberdeen* v. *Earl of March* (1730) 1 Pat. 44.
[29] *Hill* v. *Lindsay* (1847) 10 D. 78.

In a competition between an unintimated assignation and other claims, the defect in the assignee's title due to the absence of intimation will not be cured by the fact that the debtor was aware of the assignation.[30] But the following have been held to be equivalents of intimation: a written promise by the debtor, to pay the debt to the assignee;[31] payment by him of part of the capital, or the interest, of the debt;[32] the participation by him as a party[33] (not as a witness[34]) to the assignation.

If the assignation is granted to the debtor in the obligation, or to or by the person to whom intimation would in the ordinary course fall to be made, intimation is unnecessary. Thus, where the beneficiary under a trust was also the sole trustee, it was held that intimation of an assignation by him was not required, seeing that he intimated it to himself as trustee when he granted the deed.[35]

38.7   Effect of Assignation.—The effect of an assignation is to place the assignee in the shoes of the cedent. He may sue and do diligence to enforce the right which has been assigned to him. But that right is vested in him subject to all the contingencies which affected the author. *Assignatus utitur jure auctoris.*

No higher right can be conferred by the cedent than that which he himself possesses. *Nemo plus juris ad alium transferre potest quam ipse habet.*[36] Thus a person who has a temporary right, or one which is liable to be withdrawn or defeated, cannot give to his assignee a permanent or absolute right; if the right comes to an end or is withdrawn or defeated, the assignee's right falls.[37] In *Johnstone-Beattie* v. *Dalziel*[38] a sum was settled by a father in his daughter's marriage-contract in trust to pay a sum on his death to the husband. The husband assigned this sum in security to creditors. Subsequently he was divorced and thereby forfeited his right to the sum, and it was held that the right of his assignees was resolved by this forfeiture. So also, if trustees have a discretionary power to withdraw or reduce the interest of a beneficiary

---

[30] *Lord Rollo* v. *Laird of Niddrie* (1665) 1 Brown Sup. 510. It would seem (although the point is not altogether clear) that, according to the decisions, even where there is no such competition, the debtor's knowledge of the assignation will not render him liable to the assignee if he pay the debt to the cedent while no intimation has been given. See Stair, II, i, 24, and More's Note CCLXXXI; Bell, *Comm.*, ii, 18; *Dickson* v. *Trotter* (1776) Mor. 873; Hailes 675; *Faculty of Advocates* v. *Dickson* (1718) Mor. 866; *L. Westraw* v. *Williamson & Carmichael* (1626) Mor. 859; *Adamson* v. *McMitchell* (1624) Mor. 859; and *cf. Leith* v. *Garden* (1703) Mor. 865, and Erskine, *Inst.*, III, v, 5.

[31] *Home* v. *Murray* (1674) Mor. 863.

[32] *Livingston* v. *Lindsay* (1626) Mor. 860.

[33] *Turnbull* v. *Stewart* (1751) Mor. 868.

[34] *Murray* v. *Durham* (1622) Mor. 855.

[35] *Browne's Trs.* v. *Anderson* (1901) 4 F. 305; *Russell* v. *Breadalbane* (1831) 5 W. & S. 256.

[36] *Dig.*, 50, 17, 54.

[37] *Resoluto jure dantis, resolvitur jus accipientis.*

[38] (1868) 6 M. 333.

the exercise of that power will be effectual in a question with one to whom the beneficiary has assigned his interest.[39]

Moreover, the right passes to the assignee subject to all the pleas and exceptions pleadable by the debtor against the cedent. As against the assignee, the debtor may avail himself of every defence which would have been competent to him against the cedent; and it matters not that the assignee is a bona fide purchaser.[40] Thus, if a person who takes out an insurance on his life is guilty of misrepresentations which render the policy reducible in a question with him, this is pleadable by the insurance company against an onerous assignee of the insurer.[41] And if one party to a contract assigns it, the other may maintain against the assignee the claims arising out of the contract or in respect of its breach which would have been available against the cedent.[42] Thus, in *Arnott's Trs.* v. *Forbes*,[43] a vassal was held entitled to retain his feu-duty in respect of a breach of contract by his superior in a question with a heritable creditor to whom the superiority had been disponed in security.

This rule is without exception in the sphere in which it is applicable—the assignation of personal obligations. It does not apply to the transmission of heritable estate 'for there the disponee rests upon the faith of the records and so may disregard all rights granted by his author upon which an infeftment has not been taken before that which proceeded on his own disposition'; or to the sale of corporeal moveables, or to negotiable instruments, because 'a free course of commerce' must be secured.[44]

But a person may waive his rights under the law, and so the debtor in an obligation may undertake in express terms that the pleas and counterclaims between the original parties shall not be pleadable in a question with assignees.[45] This undertaking will receive effect; and, according to a series of cases in England concerned with such documents as debentures and letters of credit, even without express stipulation the same result will follow when it appears from the nature or terms of the contract that it must have been intended to be assignable free from and unaffected by such pleas and counterclaims.[46] Moreover, the debtor may by his behaviour towards the assignee be precluded from urging pleas

---

[39] *Chambers' Trs.* v. *Smiths* (1878) 5 R. (H.L.) 151; *Train* v. *Clapperton*, 1907 S.C. 517; affd. 1908 S.C. (H.L.) 26.

[40] Stair, I, x, 16; III, i, 20, and IV, xl, 21; Erskine, *Inst.*, III, v, 10; *McDonells* v. *Bell & Rennie* (1772) Mor. 4974.

[41] *Scottish Widows' Fund* v. *Buist* (1876) 3 R. 1078, 5 R. (H.L.) 64; *Shiells* v. *Ferguson, Davidson & Co.* (1876) 4 R. 250.

[42] Elchies' *Annotations*, 62; *Government of Newfoundland* v. *Newfoundland Ry.* (1887) 13 App.Cas. 199.

[43] (1881) 9 R. 89; see also *Duncan* v. *Brooks* (1894) 21 R. 760.

[44] Erskine, *Inst.*, III, v, 10; *Scottish Widows' Fund* v. *Buist, supra, per* Lord President Inglis; see para. 38.9, *infra*.

[45] See *Bovill* v. *Dixon* (1854) 16 D. 619, *per* Lord Rutherford, affd. 3 Macq. 1; *Re Goy & Co.* [1900] 2 Ch. 149.

[46] Pollock on *Contracts* (13th ed.), pp. 180 *et seq.*

which otherwise would have been open to him. Thus, if an insurance company, in the knowledge that there were clear objections to the validity of an insurance policy, continued to receive the premiums from an assignee of the policy, this might deprive them of the right to challenge the policy.[47]

38.8   **Latent Trusts and Claims.**—The general rule that an assignee takes subject to all the pleas which would have been available against the cedent must not be understood as meaning that he is necessarily exposed to all the latent claims to which the cedent is open. This is brought out in the case of *Redfearn* v. *Somervail*.[48] There, one who appeared to the world as owner of a share in a private company, but in reality had acquired it as trustee for a firm of which he was a partner, assigned it to a creditor in security of a private loan. The assignation was taken by the creditor in the honest belief that the cedent was the absolute owner of the share and it was duly intimated. A competition then ensued between the firm claiming the share as partnership property and the creditor as assignee, in which it was held that the latter's claim must prevail. The ground on which this decision proceeded was that the question was not between the debtor in the obligation, the company, and the assignee 'but between the assignee and a person setting up a collateral claim in the nature of that of a cestui que trust.'[49] Under the rule *assignatus utitur jure auctoris* the assignee was obnoxious to all the pleas which would have been available to the company against the cedent; but that rule had no application to the case of another party intervening to set up a right to the subjects as beneficiary under a latent trust.

The principle established in this decision is that if an assignation is onerous and is taken in good faith, the assignee takes the subject free from all latent trusts or equities affecting the cedent's right. It is otherwise if the assignee is aware of the equity, or does not take the assignation in the honest belief that the cedent is entitled lawfully to enter into the transaction; or, if the assignee, although taking in good faith, does not give any valuable consideration for the assignation. Gratuitous assignees are not protected. Nor does the principle of *Redfearn* v. *Somervail* apply to the case of a general body of creditors under a sequestration who take the rights of the bankrupt *tantum et tale* as they stand in his person.[50] Thus, where a bankrupt appeared on the Register of Sasines as owner of heritable property, but had executed an unregistered declaration that he held this property as trustee for a company, it was held that the property did not pass to the trustee in his

[47] *Scottish Equitable Life Assurance Society* v. *Buist* (1877) 4 R. 1076, *per* Lord President Inglis; *Bovill* v. *Dixon, supra.*
[48] 1813, 1 Dow 50; see also *Burns* v. *Laurie's Trs.* (1840) 2 D. 1348. Contrast *Scottish Widows' Fund* v. *Buist, supra.*
[49] The English term for a beneficiary under a trust.
[50] *Gordon* v. *Cheyne* (1824) 2 S. 675.

sequestration, for the trustee merely represented creditors who had no dealings with the bankrupt in relation to that property and who had given no value for the interest in it which he claimed. The trustee was not therefore in a position to found on the principle which protects onerous bona fide alienees.[51] Now, by statute, property held by the bankrupt in trust for any other person does not vest in the trustee in the sequestration.[52]

38.9 Negotiable Instruments.—Any person obtaining money in good faith and for valuable consideration is entitled to retain it notwithstanding that it has been lost or stolen from a former owner.[53] A different rule, as has been shown, prevails in regard to the assignation of rights and claims; the holder of the assignation is affected by infirmities in the title of his author. But there is a class of documents which the law, following mercantile usage, assimilates to money and treats as in effect part of the currency. The documents belonging to this class are known as negotiable instruments.[54]

A negotiable instrument is a document containing an obligation to pay money and possessing two distinguishing characteristics. The document must be such that (1) delivery of it will transfer to the transferee the right to the obligation contained in it, and (2) a bona fide holder for value will acquire a title valid against all the world notwithstanding any defect in the title of the transferor or prior holders.

Both of the above characteristics must be present, otherwise the document is not a negotiable instrument.[55] In the first place the document must be such that when transferred it will pass in its own corpus the thing it represents without intimation.[56] If, for this purpose, a deed of transfer and not simple delivery of the document is required, the document is not a negotiable instrument;[57] and even in the case of documents which transfer the right by mere delivery they must, to be negotiable, be in a state in which this can be accomplished. Thus if a bill of exchange or cheque is so drawn as to require indorsement for its transference it is not negotiable until it has been indorsed.

The second characteristic is the more important. If a document is negotiable a valid title may be acquired to it, although it was stolen

---

[51] *Heritable Reversionary Co.* v. *Millar* (1892) 19 R. (H.L.) 43. In his speech Lord Watson refers to 'the well-known principle that a true owner who chooses to conceal his right from the public, and to clothe his trustee with all the *indicia* of ownership, is thereby barred from challenging rights acquired by innocent third parties for onerous consideration under contracts with his fraudulent trustee.' See also *Bank of Scotland* v. *Liquidators of Hutchison, Main & Co.*, 1914 S.C. (H.L.) 1.

[52] Bankruptcy (Scotland) Act 1985, s. 33(1).

[53] Bell's *Prin.*, §528.

[54] See generally Gow, *Mercantile Law*, pp. 394 *et seq.*

[55] *London Joint Stock Bank* v. *Simmons* [1891] 1 Ch. 270, *per* Bowen L.J. at p. 294; [1892] A.C. 201. See Gloag and Irvine's *Law of Rights in Security*, pp. 544 *et seq.*

[56] *Connal & Co.* v. *Loder* (1868) 6 M. 1095, *per* Lord Neaves.

[57] *London & County Banking Co.* v. *London & River Plate Bank* (1887) 20 Q.B.D. 232; 21 Q.B.D. 535.

from, or passed out of the possession of, the owner or was delivered to the holder without the owner's consent. 'The general rule of the law is, that where a person has obtained the property of another from one who is dealing with it without the authority of the true owner, no title is acquired as against that owner, even though full value be given, and the property be taken in the belief that an unquestionable title is being obtained, unless the person taking it can show that the true owner has so acted as to mislead him into the belief that the person dealing with the property had authority to do so. If this can be shown, a good title is acquired by personal estoppel[58] against the true owner. There is an exception to the general rule, however, in the case of negotiable instruments. Any person in possession of these may convey a good title to them, even when he is acting in fraud of the true owner, and although such owner has done nothing tending to mislead the person taking them.'[59]

This protection is given only to one who has taken the bill for value and in good faith.[60] A bona fide holder is one who takes the instrument honestly and without knowledge of any defect in the title of the transferor. Negligence or foolishness in not suspecting that there is something wrong in that title when there are circumstances which might lead to that suspicion is not inconsistent with good faith; but if suspicion or doubt is in fact created and the bill is taken without any inquiry, or if on inquiry the suspicion or doubt is not removed, the holder would not be in good faith.[61]

Documents may be made negotiable either by statute or by mercantile usage recognised by the law. But it is not within the power of private persons to give by stipulation this privilege to a document. Such a stipulation may be good as between the immediate parties, but it cannot affect the rights of subsequent holders so as to place these at the mercy of any thief who can find a bona fide purchaser or to give them a right to sue on the document.[62] 'Independently of the law merchant and of positive statute ... the law does not either in Scotland or in England enable any man by a written engagement to give a floating right of action at the suit of anyone into whose hands the writing may come and who may thus acquire a right of action better than the right of him under whom he derives title.'[63]

Among the class of British negotiable instruments are bills of exchange, cheques and promissory notes[64] (except in so far as they are

---

[58] i.e. personal bar.
[59] London Joint Stock Bank v. Simmons [1892] A.C. 201, per Lord Herschell at p. 215; Walker & Watson v. Sturrock (1897) 35 S.L.R. 26.
[60] Banque Belge v. Hambrouck [1921] 1 K.B. 321.
[61] Jones v. Gordon (1877) 2 App.Cas. 616, per Lord Blackburn; London Joint Stock Bank v. Simmons, supra, per Lord Herschell.
[62] Crouch v. Credit Foncier of England (1873) L.R. 8 Q.B. 374, per Lord Blackburn.
[63] Bovill v. Dixon (1856) 3 Macq. 1, per Lord Cranworth L.C.
[64] See Chap. 26, supra.

restrictively indorsed or have lost the character of negotiability through being overdue or otherwise), banknotes, exchequer bills and bonds (unless registered), treasury bills, dividend warrants, debenture bonds of a British company payable to bearer, scrip certificates to bearer for shares, and share warrants to bearer. The class is not, however, stereotyped; and if the court is satisfied that other documents have, by general usage of traders and merchants, come to be treated as negotiable instruments, it will recognise and give effect to this usage.[65] Post Office money orders and postal orders are not negotiable instruments.[66] A bill of lading is not strictly a negotiable instrument, as the transferee does not get a better title than the transferor;[67] nor are documents of title under the Factors Act. A deposit receipt is not a negotiable instrument.[68]

38.10 **Goodwill.**—The goodwill of a business was said by Lord Eldon to be 'nothing more than the probability that the old customers will resort to the old place.'[69] This is an important element in goodwill, but as a definition the statement is too narrow.[70] The goodwill of a business is the whole advantage, whatever it may be, of the reputation and connection of the firm. 'It is the connection formed, together with the circumstances, whether of habit or otherwise, which tend to make it permanent, that constitutes the goodwill of a business. It is this which constitutes the difference between a business just started, which has no goodwill attached to it, and one which has acquired a goodwill. The former trader has to seek out his customers from among the community as best he can. The latter has a custom ready made. He knows what members of the community are purchasers of the articles in which he deals, and are not attached by custom to any other establishment.[71]

Goodwill may be sold, and the vendor thereby bars himself from representing that he is continuing the old business; he therefore cannot use the firm name[72] or trade mark, nor can he solicit the customers of that business to transfer their custom to him.[73] The vendor may, however, set up for himself in the old trade under his own name, and even in close proximity to the premises in which the business he has sold

---

[65] *Goodwin* v. *Robarts* (1875) L.R. 10 Exch. 337; 1 App.Cas. 476; *Bechuanaland Exploration Co.* v. *London Trading Bank* [1898] 2 Q.B. 658.

[66] *Fine Art Society* v. *Union Bank of London* (1886) 17 Q.B.D. 705.

[67] Scrutton on *Charterparties and Bills of Lading* (19th ed.), p. 185; Carver's *Carriage by Sea* (13th ed.), § 1599.

[68] *Barstow* v. *Inglis* (1857) 20 D. 230; *Wood* v. *Clydesdale Bank*, 1914 S.C. 397. As to the nature of a deposit receipt, see *Dickson* v. *National Bank of Scotland*, 1917 S.C. (H.L.) 50.

[69] *Cruttwell* v. *Lye* (1810) 17 Ves. 335.

[70] *Trego* v. *Hunt* [1896] A.C. 7.

[71] *Trego* v. *Hunt, supra*, per Lord Herschell at p. 17; *Inland Revenue Comrs.* v. *Muller & Co's Margarine* [1901] A.C. 217, per Lord Macnaghten at p. 223.

[72] *Smith* v. *McBride & Smith* (1888) 16 R. 36.

[73] *Dumbarton Steamboat Co.* v. *Macfarlane* (1899) 1 F. 993; *Curl Bros.* v. *Webster* [1904] 1 Ch. 685.

is carried on; and he may deal with customers of the old business who come to him of their own accord without solicitation.[74] The executor carrying through a contract for the sale of a business concluded by the deceased was held not entitled to solicit the customers of that business.[75] Where a sale of the debtor's business is effected by the trustee in his sequestration or by a trustee for creditors, the debtor, it has been held, cannot be prevented from soliciting the customers of that business.[76] Where the firm name is sold alone and not as an element in the goodwill of the business, the ambit of the vendor's obligation is much more restricted, and no question of the goodwill of the business itself is involved.[77]

The Partnership Act 1890[78] provides that the mere receipt of part of the profits of a business by a person, in respect of the sale by him of the goodwill, does not make him a partner, but contains no other provision on the subject. If the matter is not dealt with in the contract of copartnery, the goodwill of the business is part of the assets of the firm, and, on its dissolution, any partner, or the representative of a deceased partner, can insist on its being sold.[79] A provision in a contract of copartnery whereby one partner undertakes not to carry on the same business after the dissolution of the firm is not a mere personal contract between the partners, but passes with the goodwill, and may be enforced by a purchaser thereof.[80]

In the case of a professional business depending on the personal qualities of the practitioner, the goodwill of the practice is not considered to have the value which belongs to the goodwill of a commercial business.[81]

Goodwill may be moveable or heritable. This is a question of fact depending on whether the goodwill is associated with the premises in which the business has been carried on or with the reputation of the trader.[82] In some cases both of these elements may be present, and if so, the goodwill is treated as partly heritable and partly moveable.[83]

Further Reading

Gow, *Mercantile Law* (1964).
Halliday, *Conveyancing Law and Practice in Scotland*, Vol. I (1985).

[74] *Re David & Matthews* [1899] 1 Ch. 378; but see para. 39.1, *supra* (passing off).
[75] *Boorne* v. *Wicker* [1927] 1 Ch. 667.
[76] *Walker* v. *Mottram* (1881) 19 Ch.D. 355; *Farey* v. *Cooper* [1927] 2 K.B. 384; *Melrose Drover* v. *Heddle* (1902) 4 F. 1120.
[77] *Barr* v. *Lions*, 1956 S.C. 59, *per* Lord President Clyde at p. 64.
[78] s. 2(3)(*e*).
[79] Bell's *Prin.*, § 379; *Re David & Matthews, supra.*
[80] *Townsend* v. *Jarman* [1900] 2 Ch. 698.
[81] *Bain* v. *Munro* (1878) 5 R. 416; *Rodger* v. *Herbertson*, 1909 S.C. 256; *Thatcher* v. *Thatcher* (1904) 11 S.L.T. 605; see *May* v. *Thomson* (1882) Ch.D. 705, *per* Jessel M.R. at p. 718.
[82] *Muirhead's Trs.* v. *Muirhead* (1905) 7 F. 496; *Graham* v. *Graham's Trs.* (1904) 6 F. 1015; *Hughes* v. *Assessor for Stirling* (1892) 19 R. 840.
[83] *Murray's Tr.* v. *McIntyre* (1904) 6 F. 588; *Assessor for Edinburgh* v. *Caira & Crolla*, 1928 S.C. 398.

CHAPTER 39

INTELLECTUAL PROPERTY

I. TRADE NAMES AND MARKS

39.1 **Passing Off.**—Apart from statute there can be no right of property in a name or mark;[1] but the common law has always recognised the right of a trader who uses a name or mark to prevent other parties from making use of it or of a colourable imitation of it in such a way as to mislead the public into thinking that the business carried on, or the goods sold, by these parties are his.[2] 'No man is entitled to represent his goods as being the goods of another man, and no man is permitted to use any mark, sign or symbol, device or other means whereby, without making a direct false representation himself to a purchaser who purchases from him, he enables such purchaser to tell a lie, or to make a false representation, to somebody else who is the ultimate customer.'[3] The 'get-up' of goods may constitute passing off.[4] In an action by a trader seeking to prevent the use by another of a name or device in connection with goods, it is incumbent on the pursuer to prove that that name or device has become so associated with the goods, made or sold by him as to denote in the market that they are his.[5] If the name is an invented or fancy word this proof is much easier than in the case of an ordinary word descriptive of the quality or place of manufacture of the article, but even such a descriptive word may acquire a secondary significance

---

[1] *Kinnell & Co.* v. *Ballantine & Sons*, 1910 S.C. 246, *per* Lord President Dunedin and Lord Skerrington.

[2] *Williamson* v. *Meikle*, 1909 S.C. 1272, *per* Lord Skerrington at p. 1278. The product of a particular industry may be protected: *Erven Warnink Besloten Vennootschap* v. *J. Townend & Sons (Hull) Ltd.* [1979] A.C. 731; *Bollinger (J.)* v. *Costa Brava Wine Co.* [1960] Ch. 262 (champagne); *Vine Products* v. *Mackenzie & Co.* [1969] R.P.C. 1 (sherry); *Walker (John) & Sons* v. *Henry Ost & Co.* [1970] 1 W.L.R. 917 (whisky); *John Walker & Sons* v. *Douglas McGibbon & Co.*, 1972 S.L.T. 128 (whisky); *Lang Brothers Ltd.* v. *Goldwell Ltd.*, 1982 S.L.T. 309 (whisky); *John Walker & Sons Ltd.* v. *Douglas Laing & Co. Ltd.*, 1993 S.L.T. 156; *William Grant & Sons Ltd.* v. *Glen Catrine Bonded Warehouse Ltd.*, 1995 G.W.D. 15–873 (whisky).

[3] *Singer Co.* v. *Loog* (1880) Ch.D. 395, 412; *Cellular Clothing Co.* v. *Maxton & Murray* (1899) 1 F. (H.L.) 29.

[4] *Haig & Co.* v. *Forth Blending Co.*, 1954 S.C. 35 (whisky bottle of peculiar shape protected); *Reckitt & Colman Products Ltd.* v. *Borden Inc.* [1990] 1 W.L.R. 491 (lemon-shaped container); *Taittinger S.A.* v. *Allbev Ltd.* [1994] 4 All E.R. 475 (champagne bottle).

[5] *Kinnell & Co.* v. *Ballantine & Sons*, 1910 S.C. 246.

as denoting an article made or sold by a particular trader so as to make its use without qualification by a rival trader misleading.[6] It is not necessary to prove fraud on the part of the defender[7] or that any member of the public has been actually deceived;[8] but it must be shown that the defender's use of the name or device is likely to deceive the public.[9] An individual cannot be restrained from carrying on business or selling his goods under his own name unless it appears from his conduct that he is seeking to take advantage of the similarity of his name with that of a rival trader for the purpose of passing off his own goods as those of his rival;[10] but a newly formed limited company may be prohibited from using a name which is liable to be confused with that of another established business in the same line of trade, although the name selected is, or incorporates, the personal name of one of the directors or shareholders.[11] Where a trader makes false representations as to his goods amounting to a fraud on the public, he is thereby disentitled to protection for the name used by him in regard to these goods.[12] A professional designation such as C.A. or W.S. may be protected from use by unqualified persons.[13]

39.2 Registration of Trade Marks.—While the right to protect a trade name is left to depend on the common law, trade marks have since 1875 (the date of the first Act[14]) been afforded further protection by a series of statutes. The present statutory provisions are contained in the Trade Marks Act 1994.[15] But these in no way affect the common law rights and remedies against anyone for passing off goods.[16] Under the Act,[17] a trade mark is defined as, 'any sign capable of being represented graphically which is capable of distinguishing goods or services of one undertaking from those of other undertakings'. And it may 'consist of words (including personal names), designs, letters, numerals or the shape of goods or their packaging'. Thus, if they can be represented

[6] *Reddaway* v. *Banham* [1896] A.C. 199; *Cellular Clothing Co.* v. *Maxton & Murray, supra.*
[7] *Singer Machine Manufacturers* v. *Wilson* (1877) 3 App.Cas. 376, *per* Earl Cairns L.C. at p. 391.
[8] *Kinnell & Co.* v. *Ballantine & Sons, supra.*
[9] *Dunlop Pneumatic Tyre Co.* v. *Dunlop Motor Co.*, 1907 S.C. (H.L.) 15.
[10] *Dunlop Pneumatic Tyre Co.* v. *Dunlop Motor Co.* (1906) 8 F. 1146, *per* Lord Kyllachy; *Reddaway* v. *Banham, supra, per* Lord Herschell; *Dorman & Co.* v. *Henry Meadows* [1922] 2 Ch. 332; *Jaeger* v. *Jaeger Co.* (1927) 44 R.P.C. 437.
[11] *John Haig & Co.* v. *John D.D. Haig*, 1957 S.L.T. (Notes) 36; *Kingston, Miller & Co.* v. *Thomas Kingston & Co.* [1912] 1 Ch. 575; see also para. 38.10, *infra* (goodwill).
[12] *Bile Bean Manufacturing Co.* v. *Davidson* (1906) 8 F. 1181.
[13] *Society of Accountants in Edinburgh* v. *Corporation' of Accountants* (1893) 20 R. 750.
[14] Trade Marks Registration Act 1875.
[15] This Act repealed the Trade Marks Act 1938, and implemented First Council Directive (89/104/EEC). For the 1994 Act, see Morcom, *A Guide to the Trade Marks Act 1994* (1994), and Groom and Ors, *U.K. Trade Marks Act 1994: A Practical Guide (1994)*. As to the 1938 Act, see Kerly's *Trade Marks and Trade Names* (12th ed., 1986).
[16] s. 2.
[17] s. 1(1).

graphically, smells and sounds, *e.g.* the roar of the M.G.M. lion,[18] can be trade marks.

The Act makes provision for the registration of trade marks in a register kept at the Patent Office.[19] By registration of his mark, the proprietor obtains a property right, entitling him to the rights and remedies under the Act, and is relieved of the burden, which rested on him under the common law, of establishing his title to the mark by proof of user.[20] No one now can recover damages for infringement of an unregistered trade mark.[21] The registration is for a period of ten years, but may be renewed for a period of ten years at a time.[22] A mark must be registered for particular goods, or services or classes of goods.[23]

In a change from the 1938 Act, the register, under the 1994 Act, is no longer divided into two parts: A and B, but is now a single register onto which trade marks will be entered in the prescribed manner.[24]

Provision is made for preventing the registration of marks on either: (a) absolute grounds,[25] which relate to the nature of the trade mark; or (b) relative grounds,[26] which are concerned with the trade mark's relationship with an earlier mark. Registration will be refused on absolute grounds on the basis that: the trade mark lacks a distinctive character;[27] that it merely indicates things like purpose, value, origin, time of production of goods or rendering of services;[28] that the trade mark consists exclusively of signs or indications which have become customary in the current language or practices of the trade;[29] or the trade mark is contrary to public policy or accepted morality or is likely to deceive the public.[30] Also, where a sign does not qualify as a trade mark (as defined above);[31] or a sign consists of a shape resulting from the nature of the goods or which is necessary to obtain a technical result or which gives substantial value to the goods,[32] the sign is not registerable. And where a trade mark application is made in bad faith, it will not be registered.[33]

[18] House of Lords Public Bill Committee, 2nd sitting, January 18, 1994, col. 33.
[19] s. 63; see also The Trade Mark Rules 1994 (S.I. 1994 No. 2583) rules 32–39.
[20] *Champagne Heidsieck et Cie Monopole Société Anonyme* v. *Buxton* [1930] 1 Ch. 330; *Boord & Son* v. *Thom & Cameron*, 1907 S.C. 1326, 1342.
[21] s. 2(2).
[22] ss. 42, 43.
[23] s. 34; see also rule 7 of, and Sched. 4 to, the Trade Marks Rules 1994 (S.I. 1994 No. 2583).
[24] s. 63; see also the Trade Mark Rules 1994 (S.I. 1994 No. 2583), rules 32–34.
[25] s. 3.
[26] s. 5.
[27] s. 3(1)(b).
[28] s. 3(1)(c).
[29] s. 3(3).
[30] s. 3(3).
[31] s. 3(1)(a).
[32] s. 3(4).
[33] s. 3(6); see also s. 3(5), regarding the circumstances concerning the non-registration of specially protected emblems, *e.g.*, Royal arms, under s. 4; s. 3(4), relating to illegality under United Kingdom Community law.

Refusal to register a trade mark under the relative grounds will arise, *inter alia*, where: (i) a trade mark is identical with an earlier trade mark[34] and the later trade mark relates to identical goods or services protected by the earlier trade mark;[35] (ii) a later trade mark is identical to the earlier trade mark and relates to similar goods or services as the earlier trade mark or the later trade mark is similar and relates to identical or similar goods or services and the later trade mark is likely to cause confusion to the public;[36] or (iii) a later trade mark is identical or similar to an earlier trade mark, although the later trade mark is to be registered regarding goods or services which are not similar, then, if the earlier trade mark has a reputation in the United Kingdom[37] and using the later trade mark would take unfair advantage of, or be detrimental to, the distinctive character or the repute of the earlier trade mark.[38] However, if the proprietor of the earlier trade mark or earlier rights consents to the use of the later trade mark, then registration will not be refused.[39]

39.3 Applications for Registration.—These are made to the registrar and are advertised.[40] Within three months of the advertisement, notice of opposition may be given by any person,[41] or where an application has been published, a person may make written observation as to a trade mark's registerability.[42] Subject to para. 39.2, once an application has been accepted without opposition (or where any opposition has been withdrawn or decided in the applicant's favour) the registrar must register the trade mark, unless the application was accepted in error; the registrar no longer has a discretion to refuse to accept any application. There is an appeal to an appointed person[43] or the court from any decision of the registrar.[44] A registration must be taken as valid after five years, unless the application for registration was in bad faith.[45]

39.4 Assignation of Registered Mark.—A registered mark can be assigned[46] either in whole or in part.[47] However, such an assignation must be in

---

[34] As defined in s. 6.

[35] s. 5(1).

[36] s. 5(2).

[37] Or the European Community if it is a Community trademark.

[38] s. 5(3). See also s. 5(4) concerning unregistered trademarks and earlier rights.

[39] s. 5(5).

[40] ss. 32, 38, 81. See also The Trade Marks Rules 1994 (S.I. 1994 No. 2583), especially rules 5, 11–15 and 65. Publication is in the Trade Marks Journal.

[41] s. 38(2).

[42] As defined in s. 77.

[43] s. 38(3).

[44] s. 76 defines decision to include "any act of the registrar in the exercise of a discretion vested in him by or under" the Act. An exception will be classification, see s. 34(2).

[45] s. 48.

[46] s. 24.

[47] s. 24(2).

writing and signed by the assignor or his agent.[48] Also, an assignation can be by way of security,[49] and a registered trade mark can be the subject of a security 'in the same way as other ... moveable property.'[50] Moreover, an assignation of a registered trademark is a 'registerable transaction' under the 1994 Act.[51] Consequently, a person other than the proprietor of the trade mark can be registered as the 'registered user' of it.[52] There are also provisions with respect to the rectification of, and removal of marks from, the register.[53] It is an offence punishable by fine for anyone to represent an unregistered mark as being registered or to make false representations concerning goods or services which are the subject of a registered trademark.[54]

II. PATENTS

39.5 Patents.—Patents are granted by the Sovereign in the exercise of the royal prerogative. The right which the patentee acquires by the grant is one of monopoly in an invention, enabling him to exclude others from manufacturing in a particular way, and using, that invention.[55] The foundation of the law is the English Statute of Monopolies[56]—extended to Scotland at the Union[57]—by which monopolies were declared to be illegal, but exception was made of 'letters-patent and grants of privilege for the term of fourteen years or under, hereafter to be made, of the sole working or making of any manner of new manufactures within this realm to the true and first inventor or inventors of such manufactures which others at the time of making such letters-patent and grants shall not use so as also they be not contrary to the law nor mischievous to the state by raising prices of commodities at home, or hurt of trade, or generally inconvenient.'[58]

The law is now contained in the Patents Act 1977[59] which implements the obligations of the United Kingdom under the Convention for the

[48] s. 24(3). As to execution of the assignation by the assignor, see s. 36B of the Companies Act 1985 (as amended by Sched. 4 to the Requirements of Writing (Scotland) Act 1995), and the aforesaid 1995 Act.
[49] s. 24(4).
[50] s. 24(5). See also s. 25(2)(c).
[51] s. 25(2)(a).
[52] ss. 25 and 28–31.
[53] ss. 64 and 46–47.
[54] s. 95.
[55] Bell, *Prin.*, § 1349; *Steers* v. *Rogers* (1893) 10 R.P.C. 245, *per* Lord Herschell; *Edwards & Co.* v. *Picard* [1909] 2 K.B. 903.
[56] 21 Jac. 1, c. 3.
[57] *Neilson* v. *Househill Coal and Iron Co.* (1842) 4 D. 470, *per* Lord Cunningham at p. 475; Bell's *Comm.*, i, 103.
[58] 21 Jac. 1, c. 3, s. 6.
[59] Certain provisions of the Patents Act 1949 still govern patents granted under that Act. Sections 86 and 87 of the 1977 Act, which give effect to the Community Patent Convention, are not yet in force. See also the Patents Rules 1990 (S.I. 1990 No. 2384, as amended by S.I. 1993 No. 2423).

European Patent for the Common Market, the Convention on the Grant of European Patents and the Patent Co-operation Treaty signed at Washington on June 19, 1970. The Act departs from much of the authority and usage of the prior law and decisions on the earlier statutes must be used with some caution; the 1977 Act must be primarily construed in the context of the three international agreements.[60] In addition to establishing a new 'domestic' patent system, the Act gives effect in the United Kingdom to European patents (U.K.), incorporates the provisions of the Common Market Convention into United Kingdom law, and provides for the treating of international applications under the 1970 Treaty as domestic applications.[61] The incorporation of the Common Market Convention involves the recognition in the United Kingdom of 'Community patents' granted by the European Patent Office.

In Scotland, proceedings relating primarily to patents are competent in the Court of Session only; the sheriff court has patent jurisdiction only in relation to incidental questions.[62] Judicial notice has to be taken of any decision of, or expression of opinion by, a court established under the three international agreements on any question arising under or in connection with one of the conventions;[63] it has been suggested that this is directed to evidentiary matters and does not give the rulings of such courts any greater status than they would otherwise possess.[64]

39.6 **Subject Matter of the Patent.**—Patents are granted for inventions and the first requirement is that the applicant has made an 'invention,' a term which is not defined.[65] The invention must be new, involve an inventive step and be capable of industrial application.[66] An invention is new if it does not form part of the state of the art; the state of the art being all matter which has at any time before the date of application for the patent been made available to the public in the United Kingdom or elsewhere by written or oral description, by use or in any other way.[67] An invention involves an inventive step if it is not obvious to a person skilled in the art.[68] An invention is capable of industrial application if it can be made or used in any kind of industry, including agriculture, but

---

[60] *Genentech Inc.'s Patent* [1989] R.P.C. 147. See *Vapocure Technologies Ltd.'s Appln.* [1990] R.P.C. 1, *per* Sir Denys Buckley at pp. 12–13.
[61] 1977 Act, Pt. II, as amended by Copyright, Designs and Patents Act 1988, Sched. 5, paras. 21–25.
[62] s. 98.
[63] s. 91(1)(c).
[64] *Genentech Inc.'s Patent, supra, per* Mustill L.J. at p. 266.
[65] *Genentech Inc.'s Patent, supra, per* Mustill L.J. at p. 262.
[66] s. 1(1).
[67] s. 2.
[68] s. 3; *Windsurfing International Inc.* v. *Tabun Marine (Great Britain) Ltd.* [1985] R.P.C. 59; *Hallen Co.* v. *Brabantia (U.K.) Ltd.* [1991] R.P.C. 195; *Shoketsu Kinzoku Kogyo KK's Patent* [1992] F.S.R. 184; *Mölnlycke A.B.* v. *Procter & Gamble Ltd. (No. 5)* [1992] F.S.R. 549, *per* Morritt J. at pp. 577—579.

methods of treatment or diagnosis practised on the human or animal
body are not capable of industrial application.[69] The following are not
inventions for purposes of the Act: a discovery,[70] scientific theory or
mathematical method; literary and other works which can be protected
by copyright; schemes, rules or methods for performing a mental act,
playing a game or doing business or a program for a computer; the
presentation of information.[71] A patent will not be granted for an
invention the publication or exploitation of which would be expected to
encourage offensive, immoral or anti-social behaviour, nor for animal or
plant varieties or biological processes for the production of animals or
plants other than micro-biological processes.[72] Behaviour is not regarded
as offensive, immoral or anti-social only because it is prohibited by
law.[73]

39.7   Grant of Patent.—An application for a patent may be made by any
person who claims to be the actual deviser of an invention to the
Comptroller-General of Patents, Designs and Trade Marks at the Patent
Office in London. The application must contain a request for the grant
of a patent and a specification describing the invention in a manner
clear enough and complete enough for the invention to be performed by
a person skilled in the art. The specification must also contain a claim or
claims which define the matter for which the applicant seeks
protection.[74] After publication in the journal published by the
comptroller, the application is referred by the comptroller to an
examiner who makes first a preliminary examination and search to
determine, if possible, whether the invention is new and involves an
inventive step.[75] Subsequently, on a request by the applicant, the
examiner makes a substantive examination and reports whether the
application complies with the requirements of the Act.[76]

Any person may make observations in writing to the comptroller on
the question of whether the invention is patentable and the comptroller
shall consider the observations.[77] If the examiner reports that the
application complies with the requirements of the Act, the comptroller
may, on payment of the prescribed fee, grant the patent.[78] Notice of the
grant is published in the journal as is the specification.[79]

---

[69] s. 4.
[70] As to what is required to make a discovery patentable, see *Chiron Corporation* v.
Organon Teknika Ltd. (No. 3) [1994] F.S.R. 202, *per* Aldous J. at p. 239.
[71] s. 1(2).
[72] s. 1(3).
[73] s. 1(4).
[74] s. 14.
[75] s. 17.
[76] s. 18.
[77] s. 21.
[78] s. 18(4).
[79] s. 24.

39.8 Term of Patent: Transmission.—The term during which the monopoly in the patent is secured to the inventor is now 20 years.[80] A patent is incorporeal moveable property[81] and may pass to the proprietor's representatives on his death or on his sequestration. It may be assigned and a security can be granted over it.[82] The person becoming entitled to a patent is required to register his title in the register of patents.[83] A licence may be granted under a patent for working the invention.[84] If a proprietor desires to make his patent available, as a matter of right, to any person seeking a licence and that on such terms as may be settled by agreement or, in default of agreement, by the comptroller, he may apply to the comptroller for an entry to be made in the register to the effect that licences are to be available as of right and the comptroller shall make that entry.[85] In certain circumstances compulsory licences may be granted.[86]

39.9 Revocation of Patent: Abuse.—The court or the comptroller may, on the application of any person, revoke a patent on any of the following grounds: that the invention was not patentable; that the grantee was not the only person entitled to it; that the specification does not disclose the invention clearly and completely enough; that the matter disclosed in the specification extends beyond that disclosed in the application; or that the protection conferred by the patent has been extended by an inadmissible amendment.[87] The grounds are also available as defences to an action for infringement. In patent disputes, the nature of the invention for which the patent was granted must be ascertained from the specification, which falls to be construed by the court.[88]

39.10 Infringement.—A person infringes a patent if, without the consent of the proprietor, he makes, disposes of, offers to dispose of, uses or

---

[80] s. 25. Under the 1949 Act the period was 16 years. In the case of medicinal products, there may be an extension for a period not exceeding five years: Council Regulation (E.E.C.) 1768/92; Patents (Supplementary Protection Certificate for Medicinal Products) Regulations 1992 (S.I. 1992 No. 3091); Patents (Supplementary Protection Certificate for Medicinal Products) Rules 1992 (S.I. 1992 No. 3162 as amended by S.I. 1993 No. 947).

[81] s. 31(2).

[82] s. 31(3).

[83] s. 32 (as substituted by Patents, Designs and Marks Act 1986, Sched. 1, para. 4). As to evidence, see s. 32(10).

[84] s. 31(4).

[85] s. 46.

[86] s. 48.

[87] s. 72; *Conoco Specialty Products (Inc.)* v. *Merpo Montassa Ltd.*, 1992 S.L.T. 444; *Assidoman Multipack Ltd. (formerly Multipack Wraparound Systems Ltd.)* v. *The Mead Corporation* [1995] F.S.R. 225; *Biogen Inc.* v. *Medeva plc* [1995] F.S.R. 4.

[88] See *Lyle & Scott* v. *Wolsey*, 1955 S.L.T. 322 ('Y-front' case), for Lord Hill Watson's observations on the construction of specifications and the function of expert witnesses. See also, as to the method of construction, *Catnic Components Ltd.* v. *Hill & Smith Ltd.* [1982] R.P.C. 237, *per* Lord Diplock at p. 242; *Improver Corporation* v. *Remington Consumer Products Ltd.* [1990] F.S.R. 181, *per* Hoffmann J. at p. 189; *Assidoman Multipack Ltd. (formerly Wraparound Systems Ltd.* v. *The Mead Corporation* [1995] F.S.R. 225 (and cases cited therein).

imports the product or keeps it, whether for disposal or otherwise, or, where the invention is a process, uses the process or offers it for use in the United Kingdom, or he disposes of, uses, imports, or keeps any product obtained directly by the process.[89] Infringement of the patent entitles the proprietor to interdict against the infringer, and also to damages[90] unless the latter proves that at the date of the infringement he was not aware, and had not reasonable grounds for supposing, that the patent existed.[91] The proprietor is entitled to an account of profits made by the infringer in lieu of damages.[92] Where infringement is widespread, he has been held entitled to damages on a royalty basis.[93] The defender may not only deny the infringement, but may counterclaim for revocation of the patent.[94]

III. DESIGNS

39.11 **Design Right.**—Design right is a property right which subsists in an original design,[95] a 'design' being the design of any aspect of the shape or configuration (internal or external) of the whole or part of an article.[96] A design is not original if it is commonplace in the design field in question at the time of its creation.[97] The right does not exist, however, in: (a) a method or principle of construction, (b) features of shape or configuration of an article which—(i) enable the article to be connected to, or placed in, around or against, another article so that either article may perform its function ('must fit'), or, (ii) are dependent upon the appearance of another article of which the article is intended by the designer to form an integral part ('must-match'), or (c) surface decoration.[98] Registration of the design is not necessary but the right does not subsist until an article has been made to the design or the design has been recorded in a 'design document,' *i.e.* any record of the design.[99] The design must also qualify for protection by reference to the citizenship or residence or seat of the designer or other owner.[1] The designer is the person who created the design.[2]

39.12 **Design Right: Ownership.**—The designer is the first owner of the design right unless either the design was created in pursuance of a commission,

---

[89] s. 60.
[90] s. 61. As to damages, see *United Horse Shoe Co.* v. *Stewart & Co.* (1888) 15 R. (H.L.) 45.
[91] s. 62(1).
[92] s. 61(2).
[93] *British Thomson-Houston Co.* v. *Charlesworth, Peebles & Co.*, 1923 S.C. 599.
[94] s. 74(1).
[95] Copyright, Designs and Patents Act 1988, s. 213(1).
[96] s. 213(2).
[97] s. 213(4); see also *C & H Engineering* v. *F. Klucznik & Sons Ltd.* [1992] F.S.R. 421, per Aldous J. at p. 428.
[98] s. 213(3).
[99] ss. 213(6), 263(1).
[1] ss. 213(5), 217–220.
[2] s. 214. As to joint designs, see s. 259.

in which case the person who commissioned it is the owner, or the design was created by an employee in the course of his employment, in which case the employer is the first owner of the right.[3] Where the design does not qualify for protection by reference to the designer, commissioner or employer, it may qualify if the first marketing of articles made to the design is by a qualifying person who is exclusively authorised to market them in the United Kingdom and it takes place there, elsewhere in the European Community or in another state to which the provision extends by order; that person is then the first owner of the right.[4] The design right is transmissible by assignation in writing, by testamentary disposition, or by operation of law as personal or moveable property.[5]

39.13 Design Right: Exercise.—The owner has the exclusive right to reproduce the design for commercial purposes by making articles to the design or by making a design document recording the design for the purpose of enabling such articles to be made.[6] Reproduction means copying the design so as to produce articles exactly or substantially to that design, and it may be direct or indirect.[7] The test as to whether an allegedly infringing article is made substantially to the pursuer's design is an objective one, 'to be decided through the eyes of the person to whom the design is directed.'[8] It is a primary infringement of the design right to do, without the licence of the owner, or authorise another person to do, anything which is the exclusive right of the owner.[9] It is a secondary infringement knowingly to import into the United Kingdom or possess for commercial purposes or sell or let for hire in the course of business articles made in infringement of the design right.[10] There are exceptions to the rights of the design owner where the act concerned is an infringement of copyright,[11] where a licence of right has been obtained[12] or where the design is used for the services of the Crown.[13] The remedies for infringement include: damages (which may be increased because of the flagrancy of the infringement or the benefit to the defender), interdict[14] and count reckoning and payment of profits.[15]

---

[3] s. 215.
[4] s. 220.
[5] s. 222.
[6] s. 226(1).
[7] ss. 226(2), (4); see also *C & H Engineering* v. *F. Klucznik & Sons Ltd., supra*, at p. 428.
[8] *C & H Engineering* v. *F. Klucznik & Sons Ltd., supra*, at p. 428.
[9] s. 226(3).
[10] ss. 227, 228.
[11] s. 236.
[12] s. 237.
[13] ss. 240–244.
[14] *Squirewood Ltd.* v. *H. Morris & Co. Ltd.*, 1993 G.W.D. 20–1239; noted by MacQueen, [1994] E.I.P.R. 86.
[15] ss. 229–233; Act of Sederunt (Copyright, Designs and Patents) 1990 (S.I. 1990 No. 380 as amended by S.I. 1994 No. 3066).

Damages are not to be awarded where the infringement was innocent in that the defender did not know, and had no reason to believe, that design right subsisted in the design.[16] A person aggrieved by groundless threats of infringement proceedings may obtain a declaration that the threats are unjustifiable, interdict against their continuance and damages in respect of loss sustained by the threats.[17] In the last five years of the design right term, any person is entitled to a licence as of right.[18] The Part of the Act may be extended to the Channel Islands, the Isle of Man or any colony and a country may be designated by order as one enjoying reciprocal protection under the Part.[19]

39.14 Design Right: Duration.—The design right expires 15 years from the end of the calendar year in which the design was first recorded or an article was first made to the design, whichever first occurred, or, if articles made to the design are made available for sale or hire within five years from the end of that calendar year, 10 years from the end of the calendar year in which that first occurred.[20]

39.15 Copyright and Design Right.—It is not an infringement of design right to do anything which is an infringement of the copyright in the same work.[21] It is not an infringement of any copyright in a design document or a model recording or embodying a design for anything other than an artistic work or a typeface to make an article to the design or to copy an article made to the design.[22] Where an artistic work has been exploited by making, by an industrial process, copies of the work and marketing them, the copyright is not infringed if, after 25 years from the end of the calendar year in which the articles were first marketed, the work is copied by making articles of any description, or doing anything for the purpose of making articles of any description; 'making by an industrial process' is defined by subordinate legislation which also excludes from this provision certain articles which are primarily of a literary or artistic character.[23] Copyright in an artistic work is not infringed by anything done by an assignee or licensee of the registered proprietor of a corresponding design in good faith, in reliance on the registration and without notice of any proceedings for cancellation or rectification of the registration.[24] In relation to an artistic work, copying includes making a copy in three dimensions of a two-dimensional work and the making of a copy in two dimensions of a three-dimensional work.[25]

[16] s. 233.
[17] s. 253.
[18] s. 237.
[19] ss. 255–256.
[20] s. 216.
[21] s. 236.
[22] s. 51(1).
[23] s. 52(2); Copyright (Industrial Process and Excluded Articles) (No. 2) Order 1989 (S.I. 1989 No. 1070).
[24] s. 53.
[25] s. 17(3).

39.16   Registered Designs.—Under the Registered Designs Act 1949 any person claiming to be the proprietor of any new or original design not previously published in the United Kingdom may apply to the comptroller to have it registered in the Register of Designs kept at the Patent Office.[26] 'Design' means 'features of shape, configuration, pattern or ornament applied to an article by any industrial process, being features which, in the finished article, appeal to, and are judged by, the eye, but does not include: (*a*) a method or principle of construction, or (*b*) features of shape or configuration of an article which—(i) are dictated solely by the function which the article has to perform, or (ii) are dependent upon the appearance of another article of which the article is intended by the author of the design to form an integral part.'[27] The comptroller may, subject to appeal to the Appeal Tribunal, refuse to register a design and is not required to register a design the use of which is, in his opinion, contrary to law or morality.[28] On registration the proprietor obtains a copyright in the design for five years, which may be extended for four further periods of five years.[29] As a result, the proprietor enjoys the exclusive right in the United Kingdom of making, importing, selling, hiring or otherwise using the article of registered design.[30]

IV. COPYRIGHT

39.17   Definition.—The law of copyright was restated and amended by Part I of the Copyright, Designs and Patents Act 1988.[31] A provision which corresponds to a provision of the previous law is not to be construed as departing from the previous law merely because of a change of expression; decisions under the prior law may be referred to for the purpose of establishing whether a provision departs from the prior law or otherwise for establishing the true construction of the Act.[32] Copyright is a property right subsisting in a 'copyright work.'[33] For copyright to subsist, the author of the work must be a qualifying person, that is, connected by citizenship, domicile, residence or incorporation with the copyright area[34] (the United Kingdom and other countries to

---

[26] Registered Designs Act 1949, ss. 1(1), 17(1); as to s. 1, see *R.* v. *Registered Designs Appeal Tribunal, ex. p. Ford Motor Co., The Times*, March 9, 1994. For an amended version of the Act, see Copyright, Designs and Patents Act 1988, Sched. 4.

[27] *Ibid.*, s. 1(3). See *Amp. Inc.* v. *Utilux Pty.* [1972] R.P.C. 103.

[28] *Ibid.*, ss. 3(3), 28, 43(1). See *Masterman's Design* [1991] R.P.C. 89.

[29] *Ibid.*, ss. 7(1), (2).

[30] *Ibid.*, s. 7(1).

[31] The Copyright (Computer Programs) Regulations 1992 (S.I. 1992 No. 3233) are intended to implement E.E.C. Council Directive No. 91/250/E.E.C. They amend ss. 3, 18, 21, 27, 29 and 296 of the 1988 Act and insert new ss. 50A-C and 296A.

[32] s. 172.

[33] s. 1(2).

[34] s. 154.

which the Act has been extended)[35] or the work must have been first published in the copyright area.[36] The owner of the copyright has the exclusive right to do certain specified acts in relation to the work.[37] The author of the work has certain 'moral rights.'[38]

39.18   Copyright Works.—Copyright works are: (a) original literary, dramatic, musical or artistic works, (b) sound recordings, films, broadcasts or cable programmes, and (c) the typographical arrangement of published editions.[39] 'Original' in this connection refers to the form or expression of thought and not to the thought expressed.[40] The material on which the author has worked may not be new, but the result of his skill and labour as applied to that material must be to produce an original work.[41] Nor need the expression be in a novel form so long as it is not copied from another work but originates from the author.[42] A literary work is any work, other than a dramatic or musical work, which is written, spoken or sung and includes a table or compilation and a computer program. A dramatic work includes a work of dance or mime. A musical work is a work consisting of music, exclusive of any words or action intended to be sung, spoken or performed with the music.[43] There is no copyright in a literary, dramatic or musical work until it is recorded in writing or otherwise.[44] An artistic work is: (a) a graphic work (including a painting, drawing, diagram, map, chart or plan and any engraving or similar work), photograph, sculpture or collage, irrespective of artistic quality, (b) a work of architecture being a building or a model for a building, or (c) a work of artistic craftsmanship.[45] Copyright in a literary, dramatic, musical or artistic work expires at the end of the period of 50 years from the end of the calendar year in which the author dies.[46] Copyright in a sound recording or film expires at the end of the period of 50 years from the end of the

---

[35] Copyright (Application to other Countries) (No. 2) Order 1989 (S.I. 1989 No. 1293). No orders as to dependent territories have been made under the 1988 Act (s. 157(2)) but the numerous orders made under the Copyright Act 1956 remain in force (Sched. 1, para. 36(2)).

[36] s. 155.

[37] s. 2(1).

[38] s. 2(2). See para. 39.33.

[39] s. 1(1).

[40] *Harpers* v. *Barry, Henry & Co.* (1892) 20 R. 133.

[41] *e.g. Joy Music* v. *Sunday Pictorial* [1960] 2 Q.B. 60.

[42] *Macmillan & Co.* v. *Cooper* (1924) 93 L.J. (P.C.) 113, approving the judgment of Peterson J., in *University of London Press* v. *University Tutorial Press* [1916] 2 Ch. 601, and Lord Kinloch's opinion in *Black* v. *Murray* (1870) 9 M. 341 at p. 355; *Leslie* v. *Young & Sons* (1894) 21 R. (H.L.) 57; *G.A. Cramp & Sons* v. *Frank Smythson* [1944] A.C. 329.

[43] s. 3(1).

[44] s. 3(2).

[45] s. 4(1). As to 'original literary work,' see *Exxon Corporation* v. *Exxon Insurance Consultants International Ltd.* [1982] Ch. 119. As to 'artistic craftsmanship,' see *George Hensher* v. *Restawile Upholstery (Lancs.)* [1976] A.C. 64.

[46] s. 12(1).

calendar year in which it was made, or, if it was released before the end of that period, 50 years from the end of the calendar year in which it was released;[47] in the case of a broadcast or cable programme it expires at the end of the period of 50 years from the end of the calendar year in which the broadcast was made or the programme was included in a cable programme service.[48] Copyright exists in the typographical arrangement of a published edition of the whole or any part of one or more literary, dramatic or musical works but not if it reproduces the typographical arrangement of a previous edition;[49] such copyright expires at the end of the period of 25 years from the end of the calendar year in which the edition was first published.[50]

39.19 Ownership of Copyright.—The author of a work is the person who creates it.[51] The author is the first owner of the copyright unless a literary, dramatic, musical or artistic work has been made by the author in the course of his employment in which case the employer is the owner of the copyright subject to any agreement to the contrary.[52] The copyright is transmissible by assignation, by testamentary disposition or by operation of law as moveable property.[53] A bequest of a document recording or embodying an unpublished work includes the copyright unless a contrary intention is indicated.[54] A licence granted by the owner is binding on his successors in title, except a purchaser in good faith for valuable consideration and without notice, actual or constructive, of the licence or a person deriving title from such a purchaser.[55] Where an organisation has as one of its main objects the negotiation or granting of licences as owner or agent for him, the terms of any licensing scheme may be referred to the Copyright Tribunal.[56]

39.20 The Restricted Acts.—The restricted acts are: (a) to copy the work which, in the case of a literary, dramatic, musical or artistic work, includes reproducing the work in any material form and storing it in any medium by electronic means, and, in the case of an artistic work, includes the making of a copy in three dimensions of a two-dimensional work and the making of a copy in two dimensions of a three-dimensional work;[57] (b) to issue copies of the work to the public by putting into circulation copies not previously put into circulation in the

---

[47] s. 13(1).
[48] s. 14(1).
[49] s. 8.
[50] s. 15.
[51] s. 9(1).
[52] s. 11.
[53] s. 90(1).
[54] s. 93.
[55] s. 90(4).
[56] ss. 116–123; Copyright Tribunal Rules 1989 (S.I. 1989 No. 1129).
[57] s. 17.

United Kingdom or elsewhere which, in the case of sound recordings and films includes any rental of copies to the public;[58] (c) to perform, show or play a literary, dramatic or musical work in public which includes the delivery of lectures, addresses, speeches and sermons;[59] (d) to broadcast the work or include it in a cable programme service;[60] (e) to make an adaptation of a literary dramatic or musical work or to do any of the previous acts in relation to an adaptation, an adaptation including a translation of a literary work, a conversion of a dramatic work to a non-dramatic work and vice versa, and an arrangement or transcription of a musical work.[61] To do these acts, or to authorise another to do them, without the licence of the owner of the copyright in the work is an infringement of the copyright.[62] There is a secondary infringement where infringing copies of the work are imported into the United Kingdom otherwise than for private and domestic use[63] and where a person, without the licence of the copyright owner, possesses in the course of business, sells, hires or exhibits infringing copies.[64]

39.21 **Permitted Acts.**—There are, however, many types of act which do not infringe copyright.[65] Fair dealing is allowed for purposes of private study and research, criticism and review.[66] Some incidental inclusion in another work is allowed.[67] Copying is allowed for educational purposes,[68] and for inclusion in anthologies.[69] Copyright is not infringed by anything done for purposes of parliamentary or judicial proceedings.[70] Spoken words may be reported as part of current events.[71] Public reading or recitation of a reasonable extract from a literary or dramatic work does not infringe if it is accompanied by a sufficient

---

[58] s. 18, as amended by S.I. 1992 No. 3233.

[59] s. 19.

[60] s. 20.

[61] s. 21.

[62] s. 16(2).

[63] s. 22.

[64] s. 23.

[65] ss. 28–76. It is not possible to deal with this matter in detail. Relevant statutory instruments are: Copyright (Recording for Archives of Designated Class of Broadcasts and Cable Programmes) (Designated Bodies) Order 1989 (S.I. 1989 No. 1011); Copyright (Recordings of Folksongs for Archives) (Designated Bodies) Order 1989 (S.I. 1989 No. 1012); Copyright (Sub-Titling of Broadcasts and Cable Programmes) (Designated Body) Order 1989 (S.I. 1989 No. 1013); Copyright (Material Open to Public Inspection) (International Organisations) Order 1989 (S.I. 1989 No. 1098); Copyright (Material Open to Public Inspection) (Marking of Copies of Maps) Order 1989 (S.I. 1989 No. 1099).

[66] ss. 29–30.

[67] s. 31; see *British Broadcasting Corporation* v. *British Satellite Broadcasting Ltd.* [1992] 1 Ch. 141.

[68] ss. 32, 34–36; Copyright (Educational Establishments) (No. 2) Order 1989 (S.I. 1989 No. 1068); Copyright (Application of Provisions Relating to Educational Establishments to Teachers) (No. 2) Order 1989 (S.I. 1989 No. 1067).

[69] s. 33.

[70] s. 45.

[71] s. 58.

acknowledgement.[72] There are special provisions as to libraries and archives.[73]

39.22 Remedies.—An infringement of copyright is actionable by the owner and he may obtain relief by way of damages, interdict and count reckoning and payment.[74] Additional damages may be awarded having regard to the flagrancy of the infringement and any benefit accruing to the defender by reason of the infringement.[75] Damages are not recoverable if the defender did not know, and had no reason to believe, that copyright subsisted in the work.[76] An owner may obtain an order for delivery up of infringing copies and any article specifically designed or adapted for making copies of the particular copyright work;[77] the order may be that the copies or article shall be forfeited to the copyright owner or destroyed.[78] Where infringing copies are found exposed or otherwise immediately available for sale or hire the copyright owner may seize and detain them at his own hand if he has given prior notice to the local police station; the right is subject to the obscure qualification that there may not be seized anything in the possession, custody or control of a person at a permanent or regular place of business of his, and force may not be used.[79] The owner of copyright in a literary, dramatic or musical work, or in a sound recording or film, may, by giving notice to the Commissioners of Customs and Excise, have the importation of infringing copies prohibited.[80] An exclusive licensee has rights and remedies concurrent with those of the copyright owner.[81] Various dealings with infringing copies are criminal offences.[82]

39.23 Moral Rights.—The author of a copyright work has certain moral rights which he retains even although he is no longer the owner of the copyright. The author of literary, dramatic, musical or artistic work, and the director of a film, has the right to be identifed as the author or director in specifed circumstances.[83] For example, the author of a literary work (other than words intended to be sung or spoken with music) or a dramatic work has the right to be identified whenever the

---

[72] s. 59.
[73] ss. 37–43; Copyright (Librarians and Archivists) (Copying of Copyright Material) Regulations 1989 (S.I. 1989 No. 1212).
[74] s. 96.
[75] s. 97(2).
[76] s. 97(1).
[77] s. 99.
[78] s. 114; Act of Sederunt (Copyright, Designs and Patents) 1990 (S.I. 1990 No. 380 as amended by S.I. 1994 No. 3066).
[79] s. 100; Copyright and Rights in Performances (Notice of Seizure) Order 1989 (S.I. 1989 No. 1006).
[80] s. 111; Copyright (Customs) Regulations 1989 (S.I. 1989 No. 1178).
[81] ss. 92, 101.
[82] ss. 107–110.
[83] s. 77(1). There are exceptions.

work is published commercially, performed in public, broadcast, or included in a cable service or whenever copies of a film or sound recording including the work are issued to the public.[84] The right must have been asserted by the inclusion of a statement in an assignation of the copyright or in a separate written instrument.[85] The second moral right is that the author or director has the right, in specifed circumstances, not to have his work subjected to derogatory treatment, that is, something which amounts to distortion or mutilation of the work or is otherwise prejudicial to the honour or reputation of the author or director.[86] In the case of a literary, dramatic or musical work the right is infringed by a person who publishes commercially, performs in public, broadcasts or includes in a cable programme a derogatory treatment of the work or issues to the public copies of a film or sound recording of such a treatment.[87] A person who commissions the taking of a photograph or the making of a film for private and domestic purposes has the right not to have the work issued to the public or exhibited in public.[88] A person has a right not to have a literary, dramatic, musical or artistic work falsely attributed to him as author.[89] The rights as to identification, derogatory treatment and privacy subsist so long as copyright subsists in the work;[90] the right as to false attribution continues for 20 years after the person's death.[91] Moral rights are not assignable[92] but do transmit on death.[93] Infringement of a moral right is actionable as a breach of statutory duty[94] but in the case of the right as to derogatory treatment the court may, if it thinks it is an adequate remedy, grant an interdict prohibiting the doing of the act unless a disclaimer is made dissociating the author from the treatment of the work.[95]

[84] s. 77(2).
[85] s. 78.
[86] s. 80(1). There are exceptions: ss. 81–82.
[87] s. 80(3).
[88] s. 85.
[89] s. 84.
[90] s. 86(1).
[91] s. 86(2).
[92] s. 94.
[93] s. 95.
[94] s. 103(1).
[95] s. 103(2).

CHAPTER 40

LANDOWNERSHIP

40.1 Introductory.—The law of heritable property is largely bound up with questions of conveyancing and planning law, which do not fall within the scope of this work. But as it is impossible to understand the questions dealt with in this chapter without some knowledge of the elementary principles of land tenure, a brief reference to these is necessary.

The cardinal feature of Scots conveyancing is the system of registration of titles to heritage. In 1617 there was instituted the Register of Sasines.[1] This is open to the public; and for the purpose of ascertaining the ownership of land and the burdens which have been imposed on it recourse must be had to this register. The Land Registration (Scotland) Act 1979 introduced a system of registration of interests in land[2] in a Land Register of Scotland which will gradually supersede the recording of deeds in the Register of Sasines.[3] A person who enters into a contract to purchase land has a right as against the seller to have the bargain implemented and may sue him for damages if he fails to implement it. But he has not a real right against all and sundry; he is not in fact the owner until the conveyance to him has been placed on the register. Hence if another party purchasing the same land under a later contract should first register the conveyance in his favour he would (in the absence of fraud or *mala fides*)[4] acquire a right to the land to the exclusion of the earlier purchaser.[5] So also, in order that a burden may form a charge on the land, no matter what changes occur in its ownership, it must appear on the register. The current form of security over land is the standard security which has superseded the bond and disposition in security.[6] The owner of land who has borrowed money binds himself to repay the loan and grants a standard security over the land, so that the lender may not only sue the borrower but may

---

[1] Registration Act 1617.

[2] 'Interest in land' is defined in s. 28 as 'any estate, interest, servitude or other heritable right in or over land, including a heritable security but excluding a lease which is not a long lease.'

[3] See statutory instruments issued under s. 30 for commencement orders.

[4] *Rodger (Builders) Ltd.* v. *Fawdry*, 1950 S.C. 483; 1950 S.L.T. 345.

[5] Halliday, *Conveyancing Law and Practice*, Vol. 1, §§ 1–10 *et seq.*; dicta in *Gibson* v. *Hunter Home Designs Ltd.*, 1976 S.C. 23; *Leeds Permanent Building Society* v. *Aitken Malone & Mackay*, 1986 S.L.T. 338; *Sharp* v. *Thomson*, 1994 S.L.T. 1068.

[6] Conveyancing and Feudal Reform (Scotland) Act 1970.

have recourse against the land for payment of his debt.[7] But unless the standard security appears on the register it would not form an effectual charge on the land as against a purchaser. On the other hand, if the standard security is registered, it will affect the lands, whoever may be the owner and whatever be the title by which he has acquired it.

A person who appears on the register as the owner of land is said to be infeft. In the earliest times, in conformity with the principle that delivery was the sole means of transmitting property, the transference of heritage was effected by the only possible form of delivery, namely, symbolical delivery. If heritable subjects were sold, appropriate symbols such as earth and stone for land, a clap and happer for a mill and a net for a salmon fishing, were handed over by the seller to the purchaser in the presence of witnesses. This constituted sasine. The transaction was then recorded in a deed known as an instrument of sasine which described the subjects and detailed the ceremony; and this instrument was registered in the Register of Sasines, thereby enabling the public to learn of the change in the ownership of the land. By this means the buyer became infeft, or, in other words, obtained a real right to the subjects. In course of time it was recognised that the important feature was the appearance of the transaction on the register. The cumbrous proceeding of delivering symbols dropped out. It came to suffice that the record (the instrument of sasine), although what was recorded in it had not actually taken place, should be entered in the register; and finally the record has disappeared and all that is necessary is that the deed of conveyance itself should be registered. Infeftment now depends on the registration of the deed transferring the land or registration of an interest in land. The purchaser of land is infeft when, and only when, his title is recorded[7a] or his interest registered; and the owner of a security over land, by registering the deed showing the existence of the security in the register, acquires a charge on the land effectual against all who may have rights of property in it. A floating charge which attaches to heritable property which has been sold but where the buyers have not yet registered the disposition in their favour, operates as a prior fixed security over the property[7b] in favour of the holder.

In dealing with the law of landownership, apart from conveyancing, it is proposed to consider the rights of the Crown, the regalia; the effects of possession of heritable property; the incidents of ownership, including

[7] For example, a statutory standard condition normally incorporated in the standard security empowers the creditor, upon the debtor's default, to sell the land in satisfaction of the debt. The creditor must exercise his rights *civiliter* and with proper regard to the interests of the debtor: *Armstrong.*, 1988 S.L.T. 255; see too *Dick* v. *Clydesdale Bank plc*, 1991 S.C. 365.

[7a] This principle was vigorously defended in *Sharp* v. *Thomson*, 1994 S.L.T. 1068 against the assertion that delivery of a feu disposition created a personal right of ownership in the purchasers of a flat. This decision has now been affirmed May 4, 1995.

[7b] *Sharp* v. *Thomson, supra.*

such matters as the law of minerals, game, natural rights and servitudes; common property and common interest; and time shares.

I. REGALIA

40.2 Regalia: *Majora* and *Minora*.—The rights of the Crown in heritable property fall into two classes. The first consists of those rights which the Crown holds in trust for the public and which cannot be alienated; the second, of proprietary rights which belong to the Crown without restriction either as to their exercise or as to their alienation. 'These two ideas [of sovereignty and of property in the Crown] are perfectly separate and distinct ... The Crown, if it has not granted it out, has a right of property in the foreshore which may be alienated, and also a right of sovereignty as guardian of the public interests for navigation, fishing, and other public uses which cannot be alienated.'[8] The inalienable rights are called *regalia majora*;[9] the others are the *regalia minora*. They are indeed distinct, but there are cases, *e.g.* the foreshore, in which, as the above quotation shows, they are both found existing in regard to the same object.

40.3 The Sea.—The sea below the foreshore and within the 12 mile limit belongs to the Crown in trust for the public rights of navigation and white fishing.[10] The Crown appears to be able to alienate the seabed,[11] but no right in it which, if exercised by the grantee, would interfere with the rights of the public, can be granted without the sanction of Parliament.[12]

40.4 The Foreshore.—The foreshore is the shore between the high and low water marks of ordinary spring tides.[13] In the foreshore the Crown has, as already noticed, a double right—a right of sovereignty and a right of property. In virtue of the former right the foreshore is vested in the Crown for the benefit of the public.[14] More than one public right is included. Of these, the two most important are the right of navigation

---

[8] *Smith* v. *Lerwick Harbour Comrs.* (1903) 5 F. 680, at p. 691.

[9] No title, deed, or document is required to establish the existence of these fundamental inalienable rights: *cf.* s. 28(1)(*g*) of the Land Registration (Scotland) Act 1979.

[10] *Gibson* v. *Lord Advocate*, 1975 S.C. 136; *Crown Estate Commissioners* v. *Fairlie Yacht Slip*, 1979 S.C. 156; *Walford* v. *Crown Estate Commissioners*, 1988 S.L.T. 377; *Walford* v. *David*, 1989 S.L.T. 876. For the extension of the limit from three miles to 12 miles see the Territorial Sea Act 1987, s. 1.

[11] *Shetland Salmon Farmers* v. *Crown Estate Commissioners*, 1991 S.L.T. 166; and see generally *Stair Memorial Encyclopaedia*, Vol. 21 (Sea and Continental Shelf).

[12] *Lord Advocate* v. *Wemyss* (1899) 2 F. (H.L.) 1, at pp. 8 and 9.

[13] *Agnew* v. *Lord Advocate* (1873) 11 M. 309; *Fisherrow Harbour Comrs.* v. *Musselburgh Real Estate Co.* (1903) 5 F. 387; and see generally *Stair Memorial Encyclopaedia*, Vol. 18 (Property: Landownership).

[14] See *Burnet* v. *Barclay*, 1955 J.C. 34; Smith, *Short Commentary*, p. 64.

and the right of white fishing. The former includes the right to anchor, to load and discharge goods, to embark and disembark, and to take in ballast.[14a] The latter includes the right to dry nets and (with the exception of oysters and mussels which belong to the Crown[15]) to take shellfish.[16] Both these rights are inalienable by the Crown.[17] In addition, the public probably has a right to go on the foreshore for recreation.[18]

The foreshore itself, however, may be alienated, and an adjacent proprietor is held to own it if he has from the Crown either a specific grant of it, or a title habile to include it which has been followed by possession for the prescriptive period.[19] Such possession need not be, and indeed cannot be, such as to exclude the public entirely, for the rights of the public cannot be impaired.[20] An application to register an interest in land including a foreshore may result in rights to indemnity being excluded[21] and notification of the application being made to the Crown Estates Commissioners.[22] The owner has the exclusive use of taking sea-ware and other materials from the foreshore, provided he does nothing to hinder the public in the exercise of its rights.

40.5 Navigable Rivers.—Rivers which are tidal and navigable are regarded as part of, and subject to the same rule as, the sea. The solum belongs to the Crown, subject to the public rights of navigation and fishing.[23]

On the other hand, if the river is navigable but non-tidal, the solum belongs not to the Crown but to the riparian proprietors.[23a] The public have a right of navigation,[24] but no other rights in regard to the river. The banks are private property and cannot be used by the public except for purposes incidental to navigation.[25] The right of public navigation is

---

[14a] *Crown Estate Commissioners* v. *Fairlie Yacht Slip, supra.*

[15] *Parker* v. *Lord Advocate* (1904) 6 F. (H.L.) 37.

[16] Balfour's *Practicks*, 626; *Hall* v. *Whillis* (1852) 14 D. 324.

[17] *McDouall* v. *Lord Advocate* (1875) 2 R. (H.L.) 49.

[18] *Hope* v. *Bennewith* (1904) 6 F. 1004; *Mather* v. *Alexander*, 1926 S.C. 139 (erecting hut on foreshore); *Burnet* v. *Barclay, supra.* But see *Alfred F. Beckett* v. *Lyons* [1967] Ch. 449. For the powers of local authorities in regard to the seashore, see the Civic Government (Scotland) Act 1982, ss. 120–123; *cf. Mags. of Buckhaven & Methil* v. *Wemyss Coal Co.*, 1932 S.C. 201.

[19] Prescription and Limitation (Scotland) Act 1973, ss. 1(1) and (4) as amended by s. 10 of the Land Registration (Scotland) Act 1979. See Chap. 15 *supra*, and *Luss Estates Co.* v. *B.P. Oil Refinery Ltd.*, 1981 S.L.T. 97; 1982 S.L.T. 457; 1987 S.L.T. 201.

[20] *Marquis of Bute* v. *McKirdy & McMillan*, 1937 S.C. 93.

[21] A key feature of the system of registration of title is that a title which has been registered is guaranteed by an indemnity from the Keeper.

[22] Land Registration (Scotland) Act 1979, s. 14, the object being to alert the Commissioners to any title which has not yet been fortified by prescriptive possession.

[23] *Orr Ewing* v. *Colquhoun's Trs.* (1877) 4 R. (H.L.) 116; and see generally *Stair Memorial Encyclopaedia*, Vol. 25 (Water and Water Rights: Rivers).

[23a] See, *e.g.*, *Stirling* v. *Bartlett*, 1992 S.C. 523; 1993 S.L.T. 763.

[24] *Wills' Trs.* v. *Cairngorm Canoeing and Sailing School*, 1976 S.C. (H.L.) 30; *Scammell* v. *Scottish Sports Council*, 1983 S.L.T. 462; *Burton's Trs.* v. *Scottish Sports Council*, 1983 S.L.T. 418; *Stair Memorial Encyclopaedia*, Vol. 18 (Property: Landownership).

[25] *Leith-Buchanan* v. *Hogg*, 1931 S.C. 204.

not a servitude and cannot be lost through disuse.[26] It follows, from the right of navigation, that a member of the public can prevent any interference with the bed of the river which affects that right; but he has no title to object to any structure being put in the river unless it obstructs navigation. His right is one of passage,[27] and there may be many operations in a river to which an opposite heritor would have a title to object, but which are quite lawful in a question with the public.[28] The prevention of pollution in rivers is governed by Rivers (Prevention of Pollution) (Scotland) Acts 1951 and 1965.[29]

40.6 **Ferry: Port and Harbour.**—These rights are classed as regalia, though in certain respects they differ from the other regalia. They are rights belonging to the Crown, which may be acquired from it by grant or prescription.[30]

A right of ferry is an incorporeal heritable right.[31] It is the right to carry persons by water across a narrow sea, river or loch, from one definite place to another. The place is not necessarily confined to a particular spot, but may be a stretch of shore. It involves the right to charge a fee for services and to exclude others from carrying passengers within the limits of the ferry, and the duty of receiving any person for carriage at reasonable times. Neighbouring proprietors may keep boats for the ferrying of their own families and servants, but may not, by carrying strangers for hire, interfere with the right of ferry.[32] Ferries are the responsibility of local authorities.[33] A council may acquire, maintain and operate ferries; lease or hire ferries; make arrangements for their operation; fix fares and charges; and subsidise ferries from the local rates.

Harbours[34] are either private or public. The former belong to individuals and are used for their own purposes, and the public have no right to resort to them, except with the permission of the proprietor.[35] Public harbours are those which anyone may use on payment of the

---

[26] *Wills' Trs.* v. *Cairngorm Canoeing and Sailing School, supra.*

[27] *Scammell* v. *Scottish Sports Council, supra; Burton's Trs.* v. *Scottish Sports Council, supra.*

[28] *Orr Ewing* v. *Colquhoun's Trs., supra; Campbell's Trs* v. *Sweeney,* 1911 S.C. 1319.

[29] As amended by, *inter alia*, the Control of Pollution Act 1974, the Water (Scotland) Act 1980, the Water Act 1989, Sched. 25, and the Local Government etc. (Scotland) Act 1994. cf. *Lockhart* v. *National Coal Board,* 1981 S.L.T. 161 and para. 40.22, *infra.* See too the Water Act 1989, Sched. 23; the Prevention of Oil Pollution Act 1971: *John* v. *Wright,* 1980 J.C. 99; 1980 S.L.T. (Notes) 89; *Davies* v. *Smith,* 1983 S.L.T. 644.

[30] See *L.M. & S. Ry.* v. *Macdonald,* 1924 S.C. 835.

[31] *Baillie* v. *Hay* (1866) 4 M. 625; *Duke of Montrose* v. *Macintyre* (1848) 10 D. 896; and see, generally, Gordon, *Scottish Land Law,* paras. 10–23; *Stair Memorial Encyclopaedia,* Vol. 18 (Property: Landownership).

[32] *Weir* v. *Aiton* (1858) 20 D. 968.

[33] Local Government (Scotland) Act 1973, s. 153 as amended.

[34] See generally *Stair Memorial Encyclopaedia,* Vol. 11; Gordon, *Scottish Land Law,* Ch. 10.

[35] *Colquhoun* v. *Paton* (1859) 21 D. 996.

proper dues.[36] The right of port and harbour may be granted by the Crown to an individual[37] or a harbour trust[38] or a corporation,[39] and confers the right to exact dues.[40] The corresponding duty of the grantee of the right is to maintain the harbour so far as the dues received are sufficient for that purpose.[41] The Secretary of State has power to develop, maintain and manage harbours made by or maintained by him by virtue of an Act or order.[42] He may make loans to harbour authorities.[43] Local authorities have general responsibility for harbours.[44] They may acquire compulsorily any harbour in a poor state of repair, or a harbour whose maintenance is to be discontinued by its owner. The harbour trustees may remove unserviceable vessels from the harbour.[45]

40.7 Precious Metals: Forestry: Highways.—These subjects are pure *regalia minora*. They are part of the patrimony of the Crown, but they may be alienated, and the public has no rights in any of them. Precious metals are dealt with elsewhere.[46]

The chief privilege flowing from a right of forestry was that one-third of the value of cattle forfeited for straying into the forest went to the forester, the other two-thirds going to the Crown. The right is of no practical importance in modern times.[46a]

Highways are included in the regalia.[47] They belong to the Sovereign. The solum of a highway belongs, unless it has been acquired from him, to the proprietor of the lands, the highway being merely a right of passage over the soil.[48]

40.8 Salmon Fishings.—Salmon fishing is a separate feudal right, which is vested in the Crown. It is among the *regalia minora*,[49] and the right of

---

[36] But see the difficulties experienced by a member of the public in *Coutts* v. *J.M. Piggins Ltd.*, 1982 S.L.T. 213; 1983 S.L.T. 320.

[37] As in *Crown Estate Commissioners* v. *Fairlie Yacht Slip Ltd.*, 1979 S.C. 156.

[38] See Harbours (Scotland) Act 1982. In relation to the privatisation of the ports industry, see Ports Act 1991.

[39] *Earl of Stair* v. *Austin* (1880) 8 R. 183; *Macpherson* v. *Mackenzie* (1881) 8 R. 706; *Crown Estate Commissioners* v. *Fairlie Yacht Slip Ltd.*, 1979 S.C. 156.

[40] See, for example, *Aberdeen Harbour Board* v. *Irvin & Sons Ltd.*, 1980 S.L.T. (Sh.Ct.) 89.

[41] *Firth Shipping Co.* v. *Earl of Morton's Trs.*, 1938 S.C. 177.

[42] Harbours Development (Scotland) Act 1972.

[43] Harbours (Loans) Act 1972 as amended by the Transport Act 1981, Sched. 12.

[44] Local Government (Scotland) Act 1973, s. 154 as amended.

[45] *Peterhead Harbour Trs.* v. *Chalmers*, 1984 S.L.T. 130.

[46] *Infra*, para. 40.15.

[46a] For a review of the law relating to forestry management, see *Stair Memorial Encyclopaedia*, Vol. 11 (Forestry).

[47] Bank., I, iii, 4; II, i, 5; Ersk., II, vi, 17. There has been extensive legislation in relation to highways: see generally *Stair Memorial Encyclopaedia*, Vol. 20 (Roads).

[48] *Galbreath* v. *Armour* (1845) 4 Bell's Apps. 374; *Waddell* v. *Earl of Buchan* (1868) 6 M. 690.

[49] Except in Orkney and Shetland (*Lord Advocate* v. *Balfour*, 1907 S.C. 1360).

salmon fishing may, therefore, be granted by the Crown to a subject. The title is either an express grant of the salmon fishings[50] or a barony title[51] or a charter *cum piscationibus* coupled with possession for the prescriptive period.[52] The possession must, as a rule, be by fishing by net and coble, but fishing by rod may be enough,[53] at least in cases where fishing by net and coble is impossible.[54] Where a grant or lease of salmon fishing is made by the Crown, it carries with it, unless it is specifically limited, the exclusive right to fish by all lawful and legitimate means.[55]

If the owner of the salmon fishings owns the land on both banks he has the whole fishings. But if the banks are owned by different proprietors, the fishing rights depend on the terms of the titles. If each proprietor has a right of salmon fishing *ex adverso* of his lands, and the stream is broad enough to allow a clear sweep of the nets without crossing the *medium filum*, each proprietor must keep to his own half. Where the stream is not sufficiently broad to admit of this, the court will make the necessary arrangement.[56] These rules apply only if neither of the parties has established by immemorial possession a higher right.[57] Where the owner of a salmon fishings is not a riparian proprietor, the presumption is that he has a right to the whole fishings unless one of the riparian proprietors has an adverse right.[58] He has a right of access to the river and a right to moor boats, dry nets, fix posts, and do anything necessary for the exercise of his right, provided he pays due regard to the rights of the owner of the bank.[59]

Many statutes from the fourteenth century onwards have been passed to regulate salmon fishing. The exact terms of such of the older Acts as survive are not important, because they have been so much extended

---

[50] The conveyancing phrase 'parts and pertinents' does not include salmon fishing: *McKendrick* v. *Wilson*, 1970 S.L.T. (Sh.Ct.) 39.

[51] Land is held on a barony title when it is held direct from the Crown and has been erected by the grant *in liberam baroniam, i.e.* into a freehold barony. A grant of barony carries with it various special rights and advantages: *Lord Advocate* v. *Cathcart* (1871) 9 M. 744.

[52] Prescription and Limitation (Scotland) Act 1973, s. 1(1) and (4) as amended by s. 10 of the Land Registration (Scotland) Act 1979. (Note that the prescriptive period is usually 10 years, but 20 years when prescription is pled against the Crown); *cf. Maxwell* v. *Lamont* (1903) 6 F. 245; *Fothringham* v. *Passmore*, 1984 S.C. (H.L.) 96; 1984 S.L.T. 401; Tait's *Game and Fishing Laws of Scotland* (2nd ed.), p. 122; *Stair Memorial Encyclopaedia*, Vol. 18 (Property: Landownership).

[53] *Warrand's Trs.* v. *Mackintosh* (1890) 17 R. (H.L.) 13, at p. 23; *Maxwell* v. *Lamont, supra, per* Lord Kinnear.

[54] *Sinclair* v. *Thriepland* (1890) 17 R. 507.

[55] *Joseph Johnston & Son* v. *Morrison*, 1962 S.L.T. 322; *Walford* v. *Crown Estate Commissioners*, 1988 S.L.T. 377.

[56] See *Gay* v. *Malloch*, 1959 S.C. 110; *Fothringham* v. *Passmore*, 1984 S.C. (H.L.) 96; 1984 S.L.T. 401.

[57] *Earl of Zetland* v. *Tennent's Trs.* (1873) 11 M. 469; *Campbell* v. *Muir*, 1908 S.C. 387; *Fothringham* v. *Passmore, supra.*

[58] *Lord Monimusk* v. *Forbes* (1623) Mor. 14264.

[59] *Berry* v. *Wilson* (1841) 4 D. 139; *Middletweed Ltd.* v. *Murray*, 1989 S.L.T. 11 (right of access held not to include vehicular access).

and interpreted by decision that there is almost a second common law based on the early statutes. The current statutes are the Salmon Fisheries (Scotland) Act 1868,[60] the Salmon and Freshwater Fisheries (Protection) (Scotland) Act 1951,[61] the Sea Fish (Conservation) Act 1967,[62] the Freshwater and Salmon Fisheries (Scotland) Act 1976[63] and the Salmon Act 1986.[64] The Acts deal chiefly with three subjects: (1) close time for salmon; (2) prohibition of fixed engines and certain other methods of fishing;[65] and (3) restrictions on the erection of obstructions to the free passage of the fish up and down the river. The Secretary of State has now general superintendence of salmon fisheries except in the Tweed. The fisheries and the adjoining sea have been divided into districts, each district being under the charge of a district board elected by the fishery proprietors of the district.[66] Protection orders in relation to catchment areas of rivers may be made, and wardens appointed to secure compliance with the orders.[67] Water authorities have a general duty to maintain, improve, and develop the salmon fisheries in their areas.[68]

Under the 1986 Act the annual close time for each district is a continuous period of not less than 168 days.[69] No person may fish or take salmon during Sunday, and under the 1951 Act the weekly close time, except for rod and line, is from 6 p.m. on Friday to 6 a.m. on Monday.[70] The Secretary of State may vary the annual close time for any district on the application of the district board, or of two salmon fisheries proprietors.[71]

[60] See, for example, *The Fishmongers' Co.* v. *Bruce,* 1980 S.L.T. (Notes) 35. In *Brady* v. *Procurator Fiscal Stonehaven, The Times,* February 27, 1995, a bill of suspension against conviction for possession of 'unclean' and 'unseasonable' salmon under s. 20 of the 1868 Act was allowed. An 'unclean' fish is one which is exhausted after breeding or which has started spawning; an 'unseasonable' fish is one which has started spawning or was just about to spawn (*i.e.* gravid).

[61] As amended by the Water Act 1989, Sched. 17; and see, for example, *Anderson* v. *Laverock,* 1976 J.C. 9; *Lockhart* v. *Cowan,* 1980 S.L.T. (Sh.Ct.) 91; *Corbett* v. *MacNaughton,* 1985 S.L.T. 312.

[62] As amended by, *inter alia,* the Salmon and Freshwater Fisheries Act 1975; the Fisheries Act 1981; the Inshore Fishing (Scotland) Act 1984; and the Water Act 1989, Sched. 17.

[63] As amended by the Fisheries Act 1981, s. 38; and the Salmon Act 1986, Sched. 4.

[64] As amended by, *inter alia,* the Water Act 1989, Sched. 17, and the Water Consolidation (Consequential Provisions) Act 1991, Sched. 3.

[65] *Lockhart* v. *Cowan, supra; Salar Properties (U.K.)* v. *Annandale & Eskdale D.C.,* 1992 G.W.D. 7–381.

[66] *Cormack* v. *Crown Estate Commissioners,* 1985 S.C. (H.L.) 80; 1985 S.L.T. 426. Proprietors of salmon fishings may present a petition to have constituted a district fishery board: *Fraser, Petr.,* 1980 S.L.T. (Sh.Ct.) 70.

[67] 1976 Act, ss. 1 and 2.

[68] Water Act 1973, s. 40 as amended.

[69] 1986 Act, s. 6(1); and for further details, see Jauncey, *Fishing in Scotland* (2nd ed.), p. 10; Gordon, *Scottish Land Law,* para. 8–90 *et seq.;* Stair Memorial Encyclopaedia, Vol. 11, (Fisheries), para. 15; Scott Robinson, *The Law of Game, Salmon and Freshwater Fishing in Scotland.*

[70] 1951 Act, s. 13, as amended by regulations S.I. 1988 No. 390; see *Stair Encyclopaedia, op. cit.,* para. 17.

[71] ss. 6(3)–(6) and Sched. 1 of the 1986 Act.

Salmon fishing by cruives is lawful in rivers above the highest point at which the ebb and flow of the tide is perceptible, where the right is derived from an express grant of cruives by the Crown or from possession for the prescriptive period proceeding on a habile title from the Crown.[72] Except rod fishing, the only other lawful method of fishing for salmon in Scottish rivers, other than the tributaries of the Solway, is by net and coble.[73] Cruives have now practically disappeared. The tests of the legality of the method of fishing by net and coble are these: (1) That when the net is in the water it is constantly in motion; (2) that one end never leaves the hand of the fisherman; and (3) that the fish are surrounded by the whole net and drawn ashore with it.[74]

Obstructions are regulated by by-laws, which provide, *inter alia*, that no mill dam shall be so altered as to create a greater obstruction to the passage of fish than already existing, and that every dam, weir or cauld shall be provided with a salmon ladder.[75]

Salmon fishing in the Tweed and the Solway is regulated by special statutes.[76] The Esk is regulated by the Salmon and Fresh Water Fisheries Act 1975.[77]

The right of salmon fishing in the sea is obtained in the same way as the right of fishing in rivers, *i.e.* by Crown grant, express or implied.[78] The prohibition of fishing by fixed instruments does not extend to the seashore.[79] Stake nets, for example, are therefore legal. Fishing for salmon at sea is, however, now regulated by statute.[80] The import of live fish of the salmon family is prohibited,[81] and the Secretary of State may forbid the import of live fish which might compete with, displace, prey on or harm the habitat of any salmon.[82]

---

[72] See generally Gordon, *Scottish Land Law*, para. 8–99.

[73] Tait's *Game Laws*, p. 161; *Stair Encyclopaedia, op. cit.*, para. 11; Gordon, *op. cit.* para. 8–94 *et seq.*; Scott Robinson, *op. cit.* 1951 Act, s. 2(1).

[74] Tait's *Game Laws*, p. 179; *Stair Encyclopaedia, op. cit.*, para. 11; Gordon, *op. cit.* para. 8–94 *et seq.*; Scott Robinson, *op. cit. Hay* v. *Magistrates of Perth* (1863) 1 M. (H.L.) 41.

[75] *Stair Encyclopaedia, op. cit.*, para. 19.

[76] For example, Solway Fisheries Act 1804; Solway Salmon Fisheries Commissioners (Scotland) Act 1877: See *Salar Properties (U.K.)* v. *Annandale & Eskdale D.C.*, 1992 G.W.D. 7–381; *MacDougall* v. *Cochrane*, 1988 S.C.C.R. 179; *Stair Encyclopaedia, op. cit.*, paras. 40–45; Gordon, *op. cit.*, para 8–121 *et seq.*

[77] s. 39, as amended by Salmon Act 1986, s. 26; Water Act 1989, Scheds. 17 and 27; and Water Consolidation (Consequential Provisions) Act 1991, Sched. 1. See *Haddon* v. *Craig*, 1967 S.L.T. (Sh.Ct.) 25; *Stair Encyclopaedia, op. cit.*, para. 46; see, too, s. 141(4)(*b*) of the Water Act 1989 (National Rivers Authority's duties).

[78] *McDouall* v. *Lord Advocate* (1875) 2 R. (H.L.) 49.

[79] Tait's *Game Laws*, p. 162; Gordon, *op. cit.*, para. 8–103.

[80] Sea Fish (Conservation) Act 1967 as amended; Salmon and Migratory Trout (Prohibition of Fishing) (No. 2) Order 1972 (S.I. 1973 No. 207). See, too, the Inshore Fishing (Scotland) Act 1984, as amended by the Inshore Fishing (Scotland) Act 1994; and the Sea Fisheries (Wildlife Conservation) Act 1992; *Wither* v. *Cowie*, 1994 S.L.T. 363; 1990 S.C.C.R. 741; and *Stair Memorial Encyclopaedia*, Vol. 11, (Fisheries), para. 148 *seriatim*.

[81] Diseases of Fish Act 1937, s. 1 as amended by Diseases of Fish Act 1983, s. 1.

[82] Import of Live Fish (Scotland) Act 1978.

II. POSSESSION OF HERITAGE

40.9 **Effects of Possession.**—In the law of heritable property possession has three practical effects. First, a possessor has the right to maintain or recover possession by availing himself of the possessory remedies. Secondly, possession in good faith, even by one who has no valid title, gives the possessor certain advantages. Thirdly, possession is an essential factor in positive prescription. The last of those points has been considered elsewhere,[83] and only the two others need be noticed here.

40.10 **Possessory Remedies.**—These are of two kinds, according as they are designed to repel encroachment and retain possession or to recover possession which has been lost.[84] The remedy of interdict is designed to maintain the existing state of possession and to prevent any threatened or attempted disturbance of that possession. Removing is the remedy available for recovering possession which has been lost. In either case some prima facie title is required.[85] Infeftment is obviously the best of all titles, but a lease is sufficient,[86] or a title which, though not expressly including the subject, is prima facie applicable thereto.

The possession required must be for not less than seven years,[87] and it must be open, peaceful and exercised as a matter of right. Thus, if the assertion of a right is constantly challenged and active steps are taken to prevent its exercise (as, *e.g.* where fences are erected by the owner of property across a footpath over it which another or the public claim a right to use), the possession is not of the peaceful kind required.[88] Or if a person holds a subject under contract his possession will probably be ascribed rather to his right under the contract than to an independent right of possession.[89]

A judgment in a possessory action does not settle any question of heritable right. It decides merely that the existing state of possession is not to be inverted. The parties to the possessory action may have no title to raise questions of heritable right, and if they have a title and wish to have such questions settled, the appropriate process is an action of declarator or of reduction. But, standing a possessory judgment in his favour, the holder has the rights of a bona fide possessor,[90] and is entitled to retain possession until he is ousted by an action challenging his title on its merits.

---

[83] See Chap. 15, *supra.*
[84] Mackay's *Manual of Practice,* p. 176; Burn Murdoch on *Interdict,* p. 75.
[85] *Carson* v. *Miller* (1863) 1 M. 604, *per* Lord Justice-Clerk Inglis, at p. 611; *cf.* Stair, IV, iii, 47; *Watson* v. *Shields,* 1994 S.C.L.R. 819 (Sh. Ct.).
[86] *Galloway* v. *Cowden* (1884) 12 R. 578.
[87] *Colquhoun* v. *Paton* (1859) 21 D. 996.
[88] *McKerron* v. *Gordon* (1876) 3 R. 429.
[89] *Calder* v. *Adam* (1870) 8 M. 645.
[90] *Infra,* para. 40.12.

40.11 Bona Fide Possession.—A bona fide possessor is one who, though not in fact proprietor, believes himself proprietor on probable grounds and with a good conscience.[91] It is necessary that the possession should have been on a colourable title and in bona fide. An obvious case of a colourable title is one *ex facie* regular but which is subsequently reduced because granted *a non domino*. Of bona fides there is an excellent instance in the undernoted case,[92] where the holder took the advice of counsel as to his rights, and in accordance with the opinion continued to exercise the rights of a proprietor.

A bona fide possessor, however, is put in mala fide when the true owner vindicates his right. This may happen if the true owner produces clear and irrefutable evidence of his right. Otherwise, the possessor is put in mala fide only by the decree of a court. It depends on circumstances whether the judgment of a Lord Ordinary will have this effect. In a case of great difficulty the possessor may be protected until judgment in the Inner House, or even in some exceptional cases in the House of Lords.

40.12 Effects of Bona Fide Possession.—The effect of bona fides is threefold. In the first place it affords the possessor a defence to a demand by the true owner of the subject for restoration of the fruits drawn by the possessor. Under the strict rule of law one who has, without a valid title, been in possession and drawn the fruits of a subject might be required by the true owner to restore both the subject and these fruits. But where the possession has been held by a bona fide possessor he is allowed the benefit of an equitable plea in defence to the claim for restoration, the effect of which is that he is permitted to retain, not indeed the subject,[93] but the fruits which he has drawn.[94] Of this plea Stair observes that as it 'is in favour of the innocent possessor, so it is in hatred of the other party not pursuing his right.'[95]

Fruits while still growing belong to the owner of the soil, but when severed they become moveable and the property of the bona fide possessor.[96] In terms this applies to natural fruits, but the rule extends to industrial fruits, and to civil fruits, such as rents.[96] Everything severed while the possessor is in bona fide belongs to him.

The second advantage which accrues to a bona fide possessor is that he is entitled to recompense for improvements made by him on the subject possessed in the belief that he was enhancing the value of his own property. The true owner must repay him the amount of his

[91] Erskine, *Inst.* II, i, 25.
[92] *Huntly's Trs.* v. *Hallyburton's Trs.* (1880) 8 R. 50; see also *Menzies* v. *Menzies* (1863) 1 M. 1025.
[93] *Darling's Trs.* v. *Darling's Trs.,* 1909 S.C. 445.
[94] *Menzies* v. *Menzies* (1863) 1 M. 1025, *per* Lord Ardmillan.
[95] Stair, II, i, 24.
[96] *Duke of Roxburghe* v. *Wauchope* (1825) 1 W. & S. 41.

expenditure, in so far as, and to the extent to which, it has benefited the subjects. But, if a liferenter executes improvements on the subject liferented he has no such claim, as presumably he was led to do so for his own benefit while his right subsisted.[97]

Lastly there is no liability for violent profits. A possessor in bad faith is responsible for violent profits. 'Violent profits are profits acquired by violence—by an intruder without colour of law, who must account on the strictest footing.'[98] They include not only all the profits which the owner could have made if he had been in possession, but also all damage which the subject may receive at the hands of the possessor.[99] Violent profits in the case of houses and other urban subjects in burghs were customarily double the rent.[1]

III. INCIDENTS OF OWNERSHIP

40.13 **Right to Use Property.**—The right of property in land entitles the proprietor to make what use of it he pleases, subject only to such restrictions as may be imposed by the common law or by statute or by the necessity for observing the rights of his neighbours or of the public generally. In addition to such general restrictions he may also be limited in his right of use by the conditions of his title or by rights which have been created in favour of other persons.

Of the common law restrictions that which has probably most engaged the attention of the courts is the restraint laid upon a proprietor by the law of neighbourhood. The law acknowledges 'the undoubted right of the proprietor to the free and absolute use of his own property, but there is this restraint or limitation imposed for the protection of his neighbour, that he is not so to use his property as to create that discomfort or annoyance to his neighbour which interferes with his legitimate enjoyment.'[2] *Sic utere tuo ut alienum non laedas.* It is laid down by the institutional writers that a proprietor may be restrained from operations on his property, otherwise lawful, if these are *in aemulationem vicini, i.e.* for the sole purpose of inconveniencing or injuring his neighbour.[3] The presumption is that the proprietor is not acting emulously;[4] and, if the operations have been undertaken by him

---

[97] *Wallace* v. *Braid* (1900) 2 F. 754.

[98] *Houldsworth* v. *Brand's Trs.* (1876) 3 R. 304, *per* Lord Justice-Clerk Moncreiff.

[99] *Gardner* v. *Beresford's Trs.* (1877) 4 R. 1091, *per* Lord President Inglis; see *Inglis' Trs.* v. *Macpherson*, 1910 S.C. 46.

[1] Erskine, *Inst.* II, vi, 54; Bell, *Prin.*, § 1268 (c); *Jute Industries* v. *Wilson & Graham*, 1955 S.L.T. (Sh.Ct.) 46.

[2] *Fleming* v. *Hislop* (1886) 13 R. (H.L.) 43, *per* Lord Fitzgerald.

[3] Ersk., II, i, 2; Bankton, IV, xlv, 112; Bell's *Prin.* § 964. *Cf.* the German Code, § 226— 'The exercise of a right which can have no purpose except the infliction of injury on another is unlawful'; Smith, *Short Commentary*, p. 530; *More* v. *Boyle,* 1967 S.L.T. (Sh.Ct.) 38.

[4] Bankton, *supra.*

with a view to his own convenience or benefit, however inconsiderable, they cannot be restrained.[5] There is a frequent reference to 'this valuable rule of our law'[6] in the older cases.[7] But for dicta in *Mayor of Bradford* v. *Pickles*,[8] there would be no reason to doubt that it remained part of our law and it has since been affirmed.[9]

40.14 Right to Exclusive Possession.—The right of property in land extends, subject to what is said in the next paragraph, *a caelo usque ad centrum*. There are at common law no limits in the vertical direction except such as physical conditions impose.[10] A conveyance of land, therefore, in unqualified terms will give the disponee not merely a right to the surface but also to everything beneath the surface.[11] It follows from the exclusive nature of the right of property[12] that a proprietor is entitled to prohibit trespass on his lands. The legal remedy available to the proprietor against trespass is interdict, which will not, however, be granted in the absence of any actual trespass or of an explicit threat of trespass, or if there is no reasonable probability of a trespass being repeated.[13] But 'the exclusive right of a landowner yields wherever public interest or necessity requires that it should yield'[14] Thus property may be entered for the purpose of extinguishing a fire, in pursuit of a criminal, or by a constable for the purpose of ascertaining whether a crime or offence is being committed,[15] and a right to enter premises without the proprietor's permission may be conferred by statute.[16]

As the proprietor may prevent trespass on the surface of his lands, so may he prevent any encroachment below[17] or above the surface. Thus he has been held entitled to insist on the removal of a cornice on his neighbour's house which projected a few inches beyond the boundary;[18] he is not bound to submit to the branches of his neighbour's trees

---

[5] *Dunlop* v. *Robertson* (1803) Hume's Decs. 575; *Somerville* v. *Somerville* (1613) Mor. 12769. The doctrine applies only to active operations: *Graham* v. *Greig* (1838) 1 D. 171.

[6] *Ritchie* v. *Purdie* (1833) 11 S. 771, *per* Lord Gillies.

[7] These are collected in Rankine on *Land-Ownership*, p. 381, and *Encyclopaedia of Scots Law*, Vol. XII, p. 497. *Weir* v. *Aiton* (1858) 20 D. 968.

[8] [1895] A.C. 587, *per* Lord Watson at p. 597. But *cf. Young & Co.* v. *Bankier Distillery Co.* (1893) 20 R. (H.L.) 76 at p. 77.

[9] *Campbell* v. *Muir*, 1908 S.C. 387, especially *per* Lord President Dunedin at p. 393.

[10] *Glasgow City and District Ry.* v. *MacBrayne* (1883) 10 R. 894, *per* Lord McLaren at p. 899. But see para. 31.2, *supra*.

[11] See *Campbell* v. *McCutcheon*, 1963 S.C. 505.

[12] See para. 36.1, *supra*.

[13] Bell, *Prin.*, § 961; Rankine on *Land-Ownership*, p. 140; see also *Inverurie Mags.* v. *Sorrie*, 1956 S.C. 175.

[14] Bell, *Prin.*, § 956.

[15] *Shepherd* v. *Menzies* (1900) 2 F. 443; *Southern Bowling Club* v. *Ross* (1902) 4 F. 405.

[16] Thus the Health and Safety at Work etc. Act 1974, s. 20, authorises inspectors to enter upon premises without the permission of the owner; *cf. Skinner* v. *John G. McGregor (Contractors)*, 1977 S.L.T. (Sh.Ct.) 83; *Tudhope* v. *Laws*, 1982 S.L.T. (Sh.Ct.) 85; *Laws* v. *Keane*, 1983 S.L.T. 40; and see Gordon, *Scottish Land Law*, para. 13–15.

[17] *Davey* v. *Harrow Corporation* [1958] 1 Q.B. 60.

[18] *Milne* v. *Mudie* (1828) 6 S. 967; *Hazle* v. *Turner* (1840) 2 D. 886.

overhanging his ground, and may remove such branches;[19] he may prevent the jib of a crane passing over his property.[20] The court has an equitable power in exceptional circumstances to refuse to enforce a proprietor's right in a question of encroachment by a neighbouring proprietor.[21]

40.15   Minerals.[22]—Mines of gold and silver, and mines of lead of such fineness that three halfpennies of silver may be got out of the pound of lead, belong to the Crown.[23] The Crown, however, is not merely entitled, but is bound, when required, to make a grant of these precious minerals to the proprietor of the lands in which they are found in consideration of payment of a royalty.[24] Coal is vested in the British Coal Corporation, formerly the National Coal Board.[25] All other minerals belong to the owner of the land in which they are found. A lease of minerals differs from the ordinary lease of urban or agricultural subjects. 'The true nature of a mineral lease seems to be rather a grant of a temporary privilege—a privilege during a period of removing and appropriating so much of the substance of the minerals within a certain area as the grantee may be able or may choose to excavate, and that for a consideration or price calculated according either to the duration of the privilege or the amount appropriated.'[26] What is called a mineral lease is really, when properly considered, an out-and-out sale of a portion of the land.[27] The consideration under the lease is either rent or royalties (*i.e.* a payment on the amount of minerals won by the lessee) or it may be both. But the term 'rent' is figurative, as the payment is not for the use of the soil but for the consumption or taking away of part of it.[28] Agreement as to duration is an essential prerequisite of a valid lease of minerals.[29]

[19] *Halkerson* v. *Wedderburn* (1781) Mor. 10495; *Lemmon* v. *Webb* [1895] A.C. 1.

[20] *Brown* v. *Lee Constructions,* 1977 S.L.T. (Notes) 61; but see *Woollerton and Wilson* v. *Richard Costain* [1970] 1 W.L.R. 411.

[21] *Sanderson* v. *Geddes* (1874) 1 R. 1198; *Begg* v. *Jack* (1875) 3 R. 35; *Grahame* v. *Mags. of Kirkcaldy* (1882) 9 R. (H.L.) 91; *Wilson* v. *Pottinger,* 1908 S.C. 580; (1908) 15 S.L.T. 941; *Anderson* v. *Brattisanni's,* 1978 S.L.T. (Notes) 42.

[22] There has been much controversy as to whether particular substances such as freestone, whinstone, clay, oil-shale, are or are not minerals; see *N.B. Ry.* v. *Budhill Coal Co.,* 1910 S.C. (H.L.) 1; *Cal. Ry.* v. *Symington,* 1912 S.C. (H.L.) 9; *Borthwick Norton* v. *Paul,* 1947 S.C. 659; *Secretary of State for Scotland* v. *Assessor for Inverness-shire,* 1948 S.C. 334.

[23] Royal Mines Act 1424.

[24] Mines and Metals Act 1592; *Earl of Hopetown* v. *Officers of State* (1750) Mor. 13527; *Earl of Breadalbane* v. *Jamieson* (1875) 2 R. 826.

[25] Coal Industry Nationalisation Act 1946, s. 5; Coal Industry Acts 1987 and 1990; but the Coal Industry Act 1994 makes provision for a new regulatory body, the Coal Authority, and for the transfer of coal-mining activities to the private sector by means of licensed coal-working operations.

[26] *Fleeming* v. *Baird* (1871) 9 M. 730, *per* Lord Justice-Clerk Moncreiff.

[27] *Gowans* v. *Christie* (1873) 11 M. (H.L.) 1, 12.

[28] *Nugent* v. *Nugent's Trs.* (1899) 2 F. (H.L.) 21, 22.

[29] *Cumming* v. *Quartzag Ltd.,* 1980 S.C. 276; 1981 S.L.T. 205.

40.16   Minerals under Railways, the Foreshore, the Sea or Highways.—Special questions arise in regard to minerals thus situated.

When, towards the middle of the nineteenth century, the railways were being constructed, difficulties emerged in connection with land rights. If, under their powers as to the acquisition of land, no provision had been made as to the minerals, the railway companies would have found themselves compelled to take the minerals as included in the land; and, apart from other difficulties, as the value, or even the existence, of minerals was in many cases uncertain, it would have been impossible to fix a fair value for lands compulsorily acquired. The Railway Clauses Consolidation (Scotland) Act 1845 was passed to deal with this situation, and the statutory provisions are now contained in sections 70 to 78 of that Act, as amended by sections 15 to 17 of the Mines (Working Facilities and Support) Act 1923.[30] The railway is not to be entitled to minerals under the land purchased, except so much as must be dug out or carried away or used in its construction, unless it shall have been expressly purchased. With these exceptions all minerals are deemed to be excepted from the conveyance. If the party in right of the minerals lying under the 'area of protection' desires to work them, he must give notice to the railway and to the royalty owner (if any); and the railway has then the right to prevent the working of the minerals on paying compensation to the mine owner and the royalty owner. By the 'area of protection' is meant the area comprising any railway or works and such lateral distance therefrom on all or both sides thereof as is equal at each point along the railway to one-half the depth of the seam at that point, or 40 yards, whichever be the greater. Minerals under the foreshore belong to the Crown as owner of the foreshore, but may be alienated in favour of a subject, provided the rights of the public are not interfered with.[31] Subject to the permission of the local coast protection authority, the excavation of minerals on or under the seashore (other than minerals more than 50 feet below the surface) is prohibited.[32]

Minerals under the sea within the 12 mile limit also belong to the Crown. The opinion has been expressed that, in so far as they are capable of being worked without causing disturbance, they may be alienated in favour of a subject.[33]

Minerals under roads may be excavated by the owner. Road trustees and other authorities have no right to them, but may prevent workings which endanger the road.[34]

---

[30] See also the Mining Industry Act 1926, ss. 9, 24(1); Coal Industry Nationalisation Act 1946, s. 65; Railway and Canal Commission (Abolition) Act 1949; Mines (Working Facilities and Support) Act 1966; Mines (Working Facilities and Support) Act 1974; Town and Country Planning (Minerals) Act 1981.

[31] *Supra,* para. 40.4.

[32] Coast Protection Act 1949, s. 18; see *British Dredging (Services)* v. *Secretary of State for Wales and Monmouthshire* [1975] 1 W.L.R. 687.

[33] *Lord Advocate* v. *Wemyss* (1899) 2 F. (H.L.) 1, *per* Lord Watson.

[34] *Waddell* v. *Earl of Buchan* (1868) 6 M. 690.

40.17   Game.[35]—Game falls within the class of animals which are not the subject of property until appropriated.[36] 'If we were at liberty to go to the law of nature we perhaps might not see our way to draw a distinction between those birds and animals *ferae naturae* that are game and those that are not so. But the law of Scotland has always, or at least for a long period, recognised such a distinction.'[37] The various Game Acts are elsewhere[38] referred to, and each Act must be consulted to find what birds and animals are classed as game under it. There is no general definition, but hares, pheasants, partridges and grouse are included in all the Acts.

The right to kill game is an incident of the right of landed property; a privilege *sui generis*, which has nothing to do with the ordinary use of land.[39] A tenant as such has no right to take the game, since it is a right belonging to the proprietor alone.

The Game (Scotland) Act 1772[40] protects grouse from December 10 to August 12, blackgame from December 10 to August 20, partridges from February 1 to September 1, and pheasants from February 1 to October 1.

40.18   Fishing.[41]—Fish belong to no one while they are in their natural state, but if enclosed in a fish-pond they become the property of the person having right to, and enclosing them in, the pond.[42] The right of angling for trout in private streams is an accessory to the right of property in the adjoining lands,[43] and there is no common right of fishing for trout belonging to the public at large or to such members of the community as may have access to the water by virtue of a right of passage along the banks.[44] The same rule applies to lochs[45] and to rivers which are navigable but not tidal.[46] With regard to the rights of opposite proprietors, each has a right to fish up to the middle of the stream, and, at least in small rivers, each has a common interest in that part of the

---

[35] Tait's *Game and Fishing Laws of Scotland*, 2nd ed.; *Stair Memorial Encyclopaedia*, Vol. 11 (Game); Gordon, *Scottish Land Law*, Chap. 9; Scott Robinson, *The Law of Game, Salmon and Freshwater Fishing in Scotland* (1990).

[36] See para. 37.4, *supra*.

[37] *Welwood* v. *Husband* (1874) 1 R. 507, at p. 511.

[38] See paras. 41.26 and 41.33, *infra*.

[39] *Welwood* v. *Husband*, *supra*.

[40] As amended by the Protection of Birds Act 1954.

[41] Tait's *Game and Fishing Laws of Scotland*, 2nd ed.; Gordon, *Scottish Land Law*, Chap. 8. For salmon fishing, see para. 40.8, *supra*.

[42] *Copland* v. *Maxwell* (1871) 9 M. (H.L.) 1. The Theft Act 1607 provides that whosoever takes fish 'in proper stanks and lochs' shall be liable to a fine. The taking of fish from a stank is theft— *Pollok* v. *McCabe*, 1910 S.C. (J.) 23.

[43] See, for example, *East Lothian Angling Association* v. *Haddington Town Council*, 1980 S.L.T. 213, where an angling association with licences to fish granted by riparian proprietors, but with no real right or interest in the fishing as such, could not recover damages for injury to the fishing.

[44] *Fergusson* v. *Shirreff* (1844) 6 D. 1363.

[45] *Montgomery* v. *Watson* (1861) 23 D. 635.

[46] *Grant* v. *Henry* (1894) 21 R. 358.

river which flows between their estates.[47] Difficulties may arise where a river changes its course.[48]

IV. NATURAL RIGHTS OF PROPERTY

40.19 Natural Rights and Servitudes.—Ownership of property carries with it certain rights against, and obligations towards, owners and occupiers of neighbouring property. Some of these rights arise *ex lege* from the relative situations of the properties: these may be called natural rights. Other rights, which are created by prescription or agreement, express or implied, are known as servitudes, and are dealt with hereafter under that head.[49] The former are necessary for the comfortable enjoyment of property, and are real rights of the same nature as ownership itself. They are incidents of the title to the property. They may be modified by the operation of contract, express or implied, *e.g.* by a servitude; but they cannot properly be said to be discharged or extinguished by contract, seeing that, if the contractual superimposed right comes to an end, the original natural right revives in full force.[50]

Certain of these rights are sometimes described as natural servitudes, but it seems better to reserve the term servitude to denote rights which do not arise *ex lege*, but from grant or prescription.

Natural rights of property may be considered with reference to (a) the right of support to land; and (b) rights in water incidental to property in land.

40.20 Right of Support.—Land in general requires support both from below and from the surrounding land; if the necessary subjacent or adjacent support is withdrawn, it subsides with or without surface cracking. And here it is necessary to distinguish between land in its natural state and land carrying buildings. Obviously land carrying buildings requires greater support than it would if in its natural state, and a neighbouring owner may be bound to afford sufficient support for the land itself, but not bound to support the additional burden of the buildings.

An owner of land has an unqualified right to such support as is necessary to uphold the land in its natural state.[51] Questions regarding support generally arise where underlying supporting strata have been removed by mining.[52] 'If A conveys minerals to B reserving the

[47] *Arthur* v. *Aird,* 1907 S.C. 1170.
[48] *Annandale & Eskdale D.C.* v. *N.W. Water Authority,* 1978 S.C. 187; 1979 S.L.T. 266 (where the river was also part of the boundary between England and Scotland).
[49] See *infra,* para. 40.25.
[50] Rankine, *Land-Ownership,* p. 385.
[51] *Dalton* v. *Angus* (1881) 6 App.Cas. 740; *Bank of Scotland* v. *Stewart* (1891) 18 R. 957; *Stair Memorial Encyclopaedia,* Vol. 18 (Property: Landownership).
[52] For right of support for pipes laid under statutory authority, see *Edinburgh and District Water Trs.* v. *Clippens Oil Co.* (1900) 3 F. 156, and *Midlothian County Council* v. *N.C.B.,* 1960 S.C. 308; and for liability of the British Coal Corporation (National Coal Board) for damage caused by subsidence of workings vested in it, see Coal Industry Nationalisation Act 1946, s. 48(1); and the Coal Mining Subsidence Act 1991.

property of the surface, or if A conveys the surface to B reserving the
property of the minerals below it, A in the one case retains, and B in
the other gets, a right to have the surface supported unless the contrary
shall be expressly provided or shall appear by plain implication from the
terms of the conveyance.'[53] Where the right of support is not displaced
by provision or implication, and a subsidence occurs, it is an actionable
wrong, involving liability in damages independent of negligence; but this
liability is owed only to the landowner as an incident of ownership in
respect of damage to his property, and not to other parties for personal
injury.[54] Each fresh subsidence is a new wrong allowing of a further
action of damages, even though no further mining has taken place
between the earlier and the later subsidence.[55] This right to bring more
than one action of damages is not an exception to the general rule that
the whole damages resulting from one wrong must be sued for in one
action, for the ground of action in this case is not the mining but the
subsidence, and each fresh subsidence is a new and independent
infringement of the surface owner's rights.

Somewhat similar questions may arise between adjacent owners.
Where there is rock close to the surface, little adjacent support may be
necessary, but where the ground is friable considerable subsidence might
be caused by a neighbour digging or quarrying right up to the edge of
his property: in such a case the neighbour is bound to stop excavating at
such a distance from his boundary as will leave sufficient support for the
neighbouring land.

Where buildings are placed on the lands there can be no natural right
of support for the surface thus altered. In England the right of support
of buildings is regarded as of the nature of a servitude. In Scotland the
law is not so clearly developed. The right of support for buildings may
be acquired in various ways. Thus it may be obtained by express grant,
but it more usually arises from implied grant.[56] Where the ownership of
the minerals is severed from that of the surface after buildings have
been erected, it will be held that the mineral owner is bound to afford
sufficient support for the enjoyment of the surface with buildings as they
exist when the severance takes place, for parties cannot be held to have
contemplated that existing buildings were not to be supported. On the
other hand, it cannot be implied that the mineral owner has undertaken
to support and to be liable for damage to all buildings, however
extensive, which may afterwards be erected, for this might subject him
to heavy claims for damages in respect of property which the parties
never had in contemplation.[57] But if, at the time of the severance of the

---

[53] *White* v. *Wm. Dixon* (1883) 10 R. (H.L.) 45, *per* Lord Watson; *Cal. Ry.* v. *Sprot*
(1856) 2 Macq. 449; *Butterknowle Colliery Co.* v. *Bishop Auckland Industrial Co-operative
Co.* [1906] A.C. 305. The principles governing the decisions are applicable in both
England and Scotland; *Caledonian Ry.* v. *Sprot, supra* at p. 461; *Buchanan* v. *Andrew*
(1873) 11 M. (H.L.) 13 at p. 16.
[54] *Angus* v. *N.C.B.*, 1955 S.C. 175.
[55] *Darnley Main Co.* v. *Mitchell* (1886) 11 App.Cas. 127.
[56] *Dalton* v. *Angus, supra*, at pp. 792, 830.
[57] *Hamilton* v. *Turner* (1867) 5 M. 1086 at pp. 1095, 1099, 1100.

ownership of the minerals from that of the land, the land was conveyed expressly with a view to the erection of buildings or to any other use which might render increased support necessary, there is an implied right to such support as the contemplated use of such land requires.[58]

The right of the surface owner to support may, however, be modified by the terms of his title or by agreement. The mineral owner may be entitled to bring down the surface on payment of damages,[59] or even without paying damages.[60] The Mines (Working Facilities and Support) Act 1966[61] gives power to the Court of Session[62] to grant to a person having the right to work minerals various ancillary rights provided these are required for the proper and convenient working of the minerals. These ancillary rights include a right to let down the surface on payment of compensation.

The support due by the owner of a building to a contiguous building or to the upper storey of the same building is noticed under the heading of Common Interest.[63]

40.21 Rights in Water: Water not in a Definite Channel.[64]—Surface water, or water percolating through the ground, may be appropriated by the owner of the land where it is found. It cannot be conveyed as property separately from the land itself.[65] A neighbouring proprietor may have a right to object to the appropriation of water from a definite stream or water course, but until water has reached such a stream it is entirely at the disposal of the person in whose land it is found. So an owner may appropriate underground percolating water by sinking a well, notwithstanding that this may cause his neighbour's well to dry up; his neighbour has no right to object, even if he enjoyed for the prescriptive period the well now rendered useless.[66] But, in the general case, an owner desires not to appropriate but to get rid of surface water. Such water may drain directly into a stream, and in that case no difficulty arises. On the other hand it may drain naturally on to lower land owned

---

[58] *Caledonian Ry.* v. *Sprot* (1856) 2 Macq. 449; *North British Ry.* v. *Turners* (1904) 6 F. 900; *Dalton* v. *Angus, supra,* at p. 792.

[59] *Anderson* v. *McCracken Brothers* (1900) 2 F. 780.

[60] *Buchanan* v. *Andrew* (1873) 11 M. (H.L.) 13; *Bank of Scotland* v. *Stewart* (1891) 18 R. 957; *Pringle* v. *Carron Co.* (1905) 7 F. 820.

[61] As amended by the Mines (Working Facilities and Support) Act 1974, the Ancient Monuments and Archaeological Areas Act 1979; the Town and Country Planning (Minerals) Act 1981; and the Coal Industry Acts 1987 and 1990.

[62] Formerly the Railway and Canal Commissioners: Part I of the Mines (Working Facilities and Support) Act 1923, until s. 1 of the Railway and Canal Commission (Abolition) Act 1949 substituted the Court of Session.

[63] Para. 40.39, *infra;* and see *Lord Advocate* v. *Reo Stakis Organisation Ltd.,* 1982 S.L.T. 140.

[64] See Ferguson's *Law of Water and Water Rights of Scotland; Stair Memorial Encyclopaedia,* Vol. 18 (Property: Landownership); Vol. 25 (Water and Water Rights).

[65] *Crichton* v. *Turnbull,* 1946 S.C. 52.

[66] *Chasemore* v. *Richards* (1859) 7 H.L.C. 349; *Mayor of Bradford* v. *Pickles* [1895] A.C. 587; *Milton* v. *Glen-Moray Glenlivet Distillery Co.* (1898) 1 F. 135; *Bradford Corporation* v. *Ferrand* [1902] 2 Ch. 655; *Langbrook Properties* v. *Surrey County Council* [1970] 1 W.L.R. 161.

by a different proprietor, and in that case, the owner of the lower land is bound to receive it.[67] But the owner of the higher ground is not entitled to increase this burden on his neighbour by draining in such a way as to send down to the neighbouring land water which would not naturally run that way, or by sending down water artificially brought to the surface by pumping operations or conveyed from a distant stream.[68] It is otherwise in the case of ordinary agricultural drainage. This may alter the natural run-off of surface water, and may thereby considerably increase the burden on the adjacent owner. Nevertheless the latter is bound to receive it. It might be thought that the inferior owner should not be bound to suffer any increase of the natural burden, but it has long been settled that, as agricultural drainage is a necessary operation, the adjacent owner has no right to object to it and is bound to submit to the consequent alteration of the natural flow of water on to his land.[69] Provision for regulating such drainage on application to, and under the authority of, the sheriff is made by the Land Drainage (Scotland) Act 1930. The Secretary of State also has power to make schemes for the drainage of agricultural land.[70] The obligation of an inferior owner to receive the natural run-off may also arise in connection with mining. A mineowner is entitled to work his minerals right up to his boundary, although this may cause water to drain into adjacent workings. The neighbouring mineowner has no right to object to this; if he requires protection he must protect himself by leaving an adequate barrier of his own minerals.[71]

40.22   Streams.[72]—Once water has reached a watercourse, however small it may be[73] and whether it be above or below the surface, very different principles apply. Such water is no longer subject to the sole control of the owner on whose land it happens to be. All the riparian proprietors, from the source to the mouth of the stream, have a common interest in it, and are entitled to object if their particular interests are infringed. Members of the public have no right to interfere in any case except where a stream is navigable.[74]

The bed or alveus of a non-tidal stream belongs to the proprietor of the land through which it flows, and if the stream separates the lands of two proprietors, each is prima facie owner of the soil of the bed up to

---

[67] *Campbell* v. *Bryson* (1864) 3 M. 254; *Logan* v. *Wang (U.K.) Ltd.,* 1991 S.L.T. 580.
[68] *Young* v. *Bankier Distillery* (1893) 20 R. (H.L.) 76; contrast *Anderson* v. *Robertson,* 1958 S.C. 367. Different considerations arise where an artificial embankment has been constructed to protect land from the sea: *McLaren* v. *British Railways Board,* 1971 S.C. 182.
[69] *Campbell* v. *Bryson, supra.*
[70] Land Drainage (Scotland) Acts 1941 and 1958.
[71] *Durham* v. *Hood* (1871) 9 M. 474.
[72] For a discussion of the definition of 'stream,' see Gordon, *Scottish Land Law,* para. 7–25.
[73] *Cruikshanks & Bell* v. *Henderson,* 1791 Hume 506.
[74] See para. 40.5, *supra.*

the *medium filum*, or middle line, of the stream.[75] But although the bed of the stream may belong to a proprietor, he has no right to interfere with it in any way which may result in injury to the interest of any other riparian proprietor.[76] A proprietor may, however, acquire, by the operation of prescription, certain rights which prejudice other riparian proprietors.

Apart from fishing questions, an upper heritor is not concerned with the operations of a lower heritor except in so far as these cause, or are likely to cause, the water to regurgitate and prevent it from flowing freely away from the upper heritor's land.[77] But the position of the lower heritor exposes him to greater risk that his rights in the water may be prejudiced by the interference of the upper heritor with the quantity or quality of flow of the stream.

A riparian proprietor has a right to take water from the stream for what are known as the primary uses, *i.e.* drink for man and beast and ordinary domestic purposes, even though the result should be to exhaust the water altogether. He may be entitled to draw off water for other purposes, *e.g.* irrigation or manufacturing operations, but he can do so only if no other riparian proprietor's interest is thereby infringed.[78] 'A riparian proprietor is entitled to have the water of the stream on the banks of which his property lies flow down as it has been accustomed to flow down to his property, subject to the ordinary use of the flowing water by upper proprietors, and such further use, if any, on their part, in connection with their property as may be reasonable under the circumstances. Every riparian proprietor is thus entitled to the water of his stream in its natural flow without sensible diminution or increase, and without sensible alteration in its character or quality. Any invasion of this right causing actual damage, or calculated to found a claim which may ripen into an adverse right, entitles the party injured to the intervention of the Court.'[79] If the natural speed or direction of flow of the stream as it comes down to the lower proprietor's land is altered, this may injure him by requiring him to strengthen the banks of the stream in his property, or it may have the effect of altering the channel of the stream when it reaches him. So also if the natural flow of the stream is altered (*e.g.* if it is stored up and released at intervals), the inferior heritor who is injured by the resulting intermittent flow of the stream, may object.[80] But a lower heritor has in general no interest to object to an upper heritor diverting a part or even the whole of the

---

[75] *Menzies* v. *Marquess of Breadalbane* (1901) 4 F. 55; *cf. Stirling* v. *Bartlett*, 1992 S.C. 523; 1993 S.L.T. 763.

[76] *Morris* v. *Bicket* (1866) 4 M. (H.L.) 44; *Plean Precast Ltd.* v. *National Coal Board*, 1985 S.C. 77; *G.A. Estates Ltd.* v. *Caviapen Trustees Ltd.* (No. 1), 1993 S.L.T. 1037.

[77] *Hope* v. *Heriot's Hospital* (1878) 15 S.L.R. 400.

[78] *McCartney* v. *Londonderry & Lough Swilly Ry.* [1904] A.C. 301; *Young* v. *Bankier Distillery Co.* (1893) 20 R. (H.L.) 76, *per* Lord Macnaghten; *Rugby Joint Water Board* v. *Walters* [1967] Ch. 397.

[79] *Per* Lord Macnaghten in *Young* v. *Bankier Distillery Co., supra.*

[80] *Hunter & Aitkenhead* v. *Aiken* (1880) 7 R. 510.

stream, provided that the water is returned to the stream without sensible diminution in quantity or deterioration in quality before the stream reaches the property of the lower heritor.[81] Whilst obviously the natural overflow of a stream involves nobody in liability, an overflow of one which has been converted to use as a public sewer by, *e.g.* a local authority, may render the authority liable.[82]

A riparian proprietor has also an interest to prevent any interference with the stream by the proprietor of the land on the opposite side. No riparian proprietor is, even on his own portion of the alveus, entitled to do anything which prejudicially affects the common interest in the flowing water or from which such a result may reasonably be apprehended: any such operation may be prevented unless the court is satisfied that there is not, and will not at any future time be, any injury resulting from it.[83] A heritor is entitled to put an embankment on his own lands, if this is necessary to prevent their being flooded, although it has the effect of increasing the flood on the lands of the opposite heritor;[84] but he has no right to obstruct the regular channels through which the river flows in time of flood, even if these are dry at other times.[85] In a question with an opposite heritor an owner is not entitled to divert water for any purpose even though he returns it before the stream leaves his property, for any such diversion must diminish the stream flowing past the opposite heritor's property.[86]

A heritor may also prevent any operations which cause appreciable change in the quality of the water flowing past his property. Discharge of sewage or other matter into a stream is not prohibited at common law so long as no appreciable pollution results. Perhaps the most frequently adopted criterion of pollution is whether or not the addition of the material objected to unfits the water of the stream for use for any of the primary purposes, but this is not in all cases the proper test. An upper heritor's operations may leave the water fit to drink but may unfit it for some special use to which the lower heritor has been putting it, *e.g.* distilling: in such a case the lower heritor is entitled to object.[87] The fact that a certain amount of pollution may have already existed apart from the operations complained of does not entitle any heritor to increase the amount of pollution if such increased pollution causes any damage to lower heritors.[88] Some degree of pollution may have become legalised by continuing for the prescriptive period, and in that case the

---

[81] *Orr Ewing* v. *Colquhoun's Trs.* (1877) 4 R. (H.L.) 116, *per* Lord Blackburn at p. 127.

[82] See *Greyhound Racing Trust* v. *Edinburgh Corporation,* 1952 S.L.T. 35. See too the Control of Pollution Act 1974.

[83] *Morris* v. *Bicket, supra; Orr Ewing* v. *Colquhoun's Trs., supra, per* Lord Blackburn; *McGavin* v. *McIntyre Brothers* (1890) 17 R. 818, *per* Lord Trayner; *Kensit* v. *Great Eastern Ry.* (1884) 27 Ch.D. 122, *per* Cotton L.J.

[84] *Farquharson* v. *Farquharson* (1741) Mor. 12779; *Gerrard* v. *Crowe* [1921] A.C. 395.

[85] *Menzies* v. *E. Breadalbane* (1828) 3 W. & S. 235.

[86] *White & Sons* v. *White* (1906) 8 F. (H.L.) 41.

[87] *Young* v. *Bankier Distillery* (1893) 20 R. (H.L.) 76.

[88] *McIntyre Brothers* v. *McGavin* (1893) 20 R. (H.L.) 49.

heritor causing the pollution is entitled to continue his operations, but not to increase the amount of noxious matter which he discharges into the stream. The common law has, however, been substantially replaced on the question of river pollution by statutory provisions, the current ones being contained in the Rivers (Prevention of Pollution) (Scotland) Acts 1951 and 1965,[89] and the Control of Pollution Act 1974.[90] The 1951 Act[91] provided for the establishment of river purification boards with functions to prevent the pollution of rivers. It is an offence to cause[92] or knowingly to permit to enter controlled waters[93] any poisonous, noxious or polluting matter; to impede the proper flow of inland waters in a manner leading to a substantial aggravation of pollution; to permit to enter controlled waters any solid waste matter;[94] or to discharge, without the consent of the river pollution authority, trade or sewage effluent into controlled waters; or to discharge into controlled waters any matter other than trade or sewage effluent from a sewer.[95] Where any sewage effluent is discharged into controlled waters from any works or sewer vested in a local authority and the authority was bound to receive into the works or sewer matter included in the discharge, the authority may be guilty of an offence whether or not it caused or knowingly permitted the discharge.[96]

40.23   Lochs.—Lochs fall into two classes. First, there are those which are entirely surrounded by the lands of one proprietor. In that case the whole loch (water and solum) belongs to the owner of the surrounding land and is under his sole control. If a stream runs out of it, however, he is limited in his use of the loch by the necessity for respecting the rights of the riparian owners in the stream. Secondly, the loch may be one on which the lands of several owners abut. In this case there is a presumption of a joint right of property in all. The titles or the titles coupled with the state of possession may, however, be such as to give one owner the exclusive right.[97] When there are joint rights each proprietor has an exclusive right to the *solum* from his own shore up to the middle of the loch.[98] But he must not interfere with the enjoyment

---

[89] These Acts replaced the Rivers Pollution Acts 1876 and 1893.

[90] Pt. II.

[91] Now read with the Local Government (Scotland) Act 1973, s. 135, and the Local Government etc. (Scotland) Act 1994, s. 37.

[92] *Impress (Worcester)* v. *Rees* [1971] 2 All E.R., 357; *Alphacell* v. *Woodward* [1971] 2 All E.R. 910; *Price* v. *Cormack* [1975] 1 W.L.R. 988; *Lockhart* v. *N.C.B.,* 1981 S.L.T. 161.

[93] Defined in s. 30A of the 1974 Act (inserted by Sched. 23 of the Water Act 1989) as including watercourses and rivers.

[94] 1974 Act, s. 31, as substituted by Sched. 23 of the Water Act 1989; *cf. Gavin* v. *Ayr County Council,* 1950 S.C. 197.

[95] 1974 Act, s. 32, as substituted by Sched. 23 of the Water Act 1989 and amended by the Local Government etc. (Scotland) Act 1994, Scheds. 13 and 14.

[96] 1974 Act, ss. 32(2), (5), (6), as substituted by Sched. 23 of the Water Act 1989 and amended by the Local Government etc. (Scotland) Act 1994, Scheds. 13 and 14.

[97] *Scott* v. *Lord Napier* (1869) 7 M. (H.L.) 35.

[98] *Cochrane* v. *Earl of Minto* (1815) 6 Pat. 139.

by the other owners of their right to the water, which is common to all.[99] All proprietors have the right to sail and fish upon the loch, but the court may restrict or regulate the number of boats each proprietor may put on it.[1] The common law rights of owners of lands surrounding an artificial loch or reservoir are not clearly settled.[2] There are statutory provisions concerning pollution and damage arising from certain operations.[2]

V. SERVITUDES

40.24 Definition.—A '"servitude" is a burden on land or houses, imposed by agreement—express or implied—in favour of the owners of other tenements; whereby the owner of the burdened or "servient" tenement, and his heirs and singular successors in the subject, must submit to certain uses to be exercised by the owner of the other or "dominant" tenement; or must suffer restraint in his own use and occupation of the property. Presupposing those extensions or restraints of the exclusive or absolute right of use which naturally proceed from the situation of conterminous properties, a servitude is a further limitation of that right in favour of the owner of another subject.'[4]

Servitudes may be classified in various ways, but the classification of most practical importance is that which divides them into positive and negative servitudes. The quotation from Bell indicates the distinction between positive and negative. A positive servitude is one by which the owner of the dominant tenement is entitled to exercise certain rights over the servient tenement, and which is capable of possession in the sense of being actively exercised by the owner of the dominant tenement. Thus, a right of way or of access over the servient tenement is a positive servitude, as it enables the owner of the dominant tenement to pass over the servient tenement. On the other hand, a negative servitude consists in a restraint on the rights of the owner of the servient tenement and cannot be so possessed. A typical instance of this class is a servitude by which the owner of the servient tenement is restrained from building so as to injure the light of the dominant tenement.

The institutional writers also distinguish servitudes as urban and rural, and personal and praedial. Urban are such as relate to buildings (whether in the town or the country); rural to lands. The distinction between praedial and personal servitudes is of little practical importance

---

[99] *Menzies* v. *Macdonald* (1854) 16 D. 827; affd. 2 Macq. 463.

[1] *Menzies* v. *Wentworth* (1901) 3 F. 941.

[2] *Kilsyth Fish Protection Association* v. *McFarlane,* 1937 S.C. 757.

[3] See, *e.g.* the Control of Pollution Act 1974, ss. 30A–42, as substituted by Sched. 23 of the Water Act 1989 and amended by the Local Government etc. (Scotland) Act 1994, Scheds. 13 and 14; the Water (Scotland) Act 1980, s. 10; the Wildlife and Countryside Act 1981, s. 29 (see *North Uist Fisheries Ltd.* v. *Secretary of State for Scotland*, 1992 S.L.T. 333).

[4] Bell, *Prin.,* § 979.

as the only personal servitude is liferent,[5] and all other servitudes are praedial.

40.25   Characteristics of Servitudes.—A servitude exists for the benefit of the dominant tenement: it is a right annexed to that tenement, and no one can have any claim to a servitude except as proprietor of the tenement. It is inalienable and inseparable from the dominant tenement, and the proprietor cannot make it over to anyone not connected with that tenement or set up a right to it independently of the right to the tenement.[6] Moreover, it is for the use and benefit of the dominant tenement and not for purposes unconnected with that tenement. Hence a servitude of way in favour of one estate cannot be used for the benefit of another;[7] and a servitude of digging for slates and stones does not entitle the dominant owner to use his right for the purpose of selling the slates and stones to others.[8]

It is a further characteristic of servitudes that the burden imposed on the owner of the servient tenement is not to do anything active but merely to suffer the restraint of his rights involved in the servitude. Thus, as was pointed out in a leading case, an obligation on a vassal to provide and uphold a boat for the use of the superior could not be a servitude because it consisted *in faciendo* not *in patiendo*.[9] So also in the case of a servitude of way the owner of the servient tenement is under no obligation to repair the way.[10]

In the exercise of the servitude the owner of the dominant tenement must use his right *civiliter*, that is to say, in the way which, consistently with its enjoyment, is least burdensome to the servient tenement,[11] and the owner of the latter tenement may make use of his property as he pleases provided he respects the servitude right.[12] Hence, the owner of a moor, over which there exists a servitude of digging and winning peat, is free to plough the moor so long as he leaves what is sufficient for the servitude unploughed;[13] the proprietor of a stream subject to a servitude

---

[5] See para. 47.1, *infra*.

[6] *Drummond* v. *Milligan* (1890) 17 R. 316, *per* Lord McLaren; *Patrick* v. *Napier* (1867) 5 M. 683, *per* Lord President Inglis and Lord Ormidale. In *Irvine Knitters Ltd.* v. *North Ayrshire Co-operative Society Ltd.*, 1978 S.C. 109, where the original buildings (nos. 84–90) of the dominant tenement were demolished and new and more extensive buildings (nos. 78–106) were erected partly on the dominant tenement and partly on adjoining premises, it was held that the servitude of access continued to exist *quoad* nos. 84–90. See, too, *Alba Homes Ltd.* v. *Duell*, 1993 S.L.T. (Sh.Ct.) 49, where the dominant tenement was divided into two plots, and an additional house built on the second plot; and see generally *Stair Memorial Encyclopaedia*, Vol. 18 (Property: Landownership).

[7] *Scotts* v. *Bogles*, July 6, 1809, F.C.; *Irvine Knitters Ltd.* v. *North Ayrshire Co-operative Society Ltd.*, *supra*.

[8] *Murray* v. *Mags. of Peebles*, Dec. 8, 1808, F.C.

[9] *Tailors of Aberdeen* v. *Coutts* (1840) 1 Robin.App. 296, *per* Lord Corehouse at p. 310.

[10] *Allan* v. *MacLachlan* (1900) 2 F. 699.

[11] *Cf. dicta* in *Alvis* v. *Harrison*, 1991 S.L.T. 64 (H.L.).

[12] Erskine, *Inst.* II, ix, 34.

[13] *Watson* v. *Dunkennar Feuars* (1667) Mor. 14529.

of watering cattle may cover over the stream if he leaves open so much as is required for the use of the cattle;[14] and the proprietor of land over which is a servitude of footpath may erect swing gates across the path.[15]

40.26   Constitution of Servitudes.—As a general rule burdens on heritage do not affect singular successors unless they appear in the Register of Sasines or the Land Register of Scotland.[16] But this is not necessary in the case of servitudes; and heritage may be subject to a servitude although there is no reference to it in the titles of the dominant or of the servient tenement.[17] This being so, it has been held essential that they should be limited 'to such uses or restraints as are well established and defined, leaving others as mere personal agreements. What shall be deemed a servitude of a regular and definite kind is a secondary question, as to which the only description that can be given generally seems to be that it shall be such a use or restraint as by law or custom is known to be likely and incident to the property in question, and to which the attention of a prudent purchaser will in the circumstances naturally be called.'[18] But the class of servitudes is not rigid and stereotyped; and there is authority for the view that a burden on property which satisfies the requirements of the law as to the nature and conditions of a servitude may be allowed as a servitude, although there is no precedent specifically recognising it as such. 'The habits and requirements of life varying and extending with advancing civilisation, improved agriculture, and multiplying necessities, may render the introduction of a new servitude possible and legitimate. But it must, in my opinion, be of a truly praedial character, similar in nature and quality to the praedial servitudes which the law has already recognised.'[19] There are various modes in which servitudes may be created; and in this matter the distinction between positive and negative servitudes is of importance.

40.27   Express Grant or Reservation.—Both positive and negative servitudes may be created in this way,[20] and this is the only method of creating a

[14] *Beveridge* v. *Marshall*, Nov. 18, 1808, F.C.

[15] *Sutherland* v. *Thomson* (1876) 3 R. 485; *Orr Ewing* v. *Colquhoun's Trs.* (1877) 4 R. (H.L.) 116, at pp. 121, 137; *Drury* v. *McGarvie*, 1993 S.L.T. 987.

[16] *Supra*, para. 40.1.

[17] *Cf.* s. 3(2) of the Land Registration (Scotland) Act 1979 and s. 28(1)(*d*) defining a servitude as an 'overriding interest' (*i.e.* an interest in land which can exist as a real right without being recorded or registered).

[18] Bell, *Prin.*, 979; approved by Lord Watson in *N.B. Ry.* v. *Park Yard Co.* (1898) 25 R. (H.L.) 47; *Murray's Trs.* v. *Trs. for St. Margaret's Convent* (1906) 8 F. 1109, *per* Lord Kinnear; 1907 S.C. (H.L.) 8; *Marquis of Huntly* v. *Nicol* (1896) 23 R. 610, *per* Lord Kinnear.

[19] *Patrick* v. *Napier* (1867) 5 M. 683, *per* Lord Ardmillan; *Dyce* v. *Hay* (1849) 11 D. 1266, 1 Macq. 312, *per* Lord St. Leonards; *Harvey* v. *Lindsay* (1853) 15 D. 768, *per* Lord Ivory; Rankine, *Land-Ownership*, p. 419.

[20] Erskine, *Inst.*, II, ix, 35; *Inglis* v. *Clark* (1901) 4 F. 288; *Metcalfe* v. *Purdon* (1902) 4 F. 507; *Ferguson* v. *Tennant*, 1978 S.C. (H.L.) 19.

negative servitude.[21] The grant must be made in favour of the owner of the dominant tenement[22] by one who either at the time, or subsequently comes to be, owner of the servient tenement.[23] No servitude can be created by express reservation where the granter remains the owner of the alleged servient tenement.[24] As in the case of the other heritable rights, the grant must be contained in writing.[25] It may appear in the titles of the tenements or may be contained in a separate deed. It is not essential that it should appear in the Register of Sasines[26] or the Land Register of Scotland.[27]

But if it does not enter the Register, the grant of a positive servitude is not effectual against singular successors unless it is followed by possession, so that its existence may be advertised and purchasers put on their guard.[28] If there is possession for a continuous period of 20 years openly, peaceably and without any judicial interruption, and the possession was founded on and followed the execution of a deed which is sufficient in respect of its terms expressly to constitute the servitude, the validity of the servitude as so constituted becomes unchallengeable.[29] In the case of negative servitudes possession is not possible; and these occupy, therefore, a rather anomalous position, as their existence is not disclosed either on the Register or by any acts which may come to the knowledge of a purchaser. The court tends to interpret more strictly a servitude created by grant than one created by prescription.[30]

Besides express grant or reservation there are two other means by which positive servitudes may come into existence.

---

[21] Rankine, p. 426.

[22] *Safeway Food Stores* v. *Wellington Motor Company (Ayr)*, 1976 S.L.T. 53. The proprietor of the dominant tenement cannot *ex proprio motu* extend the benefit of the servitude to other properties, thus increasing the burden imposed on the servient tenement: *Irvine Knitters Ltd.* v. *North Ayrshire Co-operative Society Ltd.*, 1978 S.C. 109.

[23] *Stephen* v. *Brown's Trs.*, 1922 S.C. 136. It is impossible for one *pro indiviso* proprietor to constitute a servitude over property owned jointly with others without the express consent of those others: *Fearnan Partnership* v. *Grindlay*, 1990 S.L.T. 704. (The question of *pro indiviso* proprietorship was not discussed in the House of Lords: 1992 S.C. (H.L.) 38; 1992 S.L.T. 460).

[24] *Hamilton* v. *Elder*, 1968 S.L.T. (Sh.Ct.) 53.

[25] Requirements of Writing (Scotland) Act 1995, s. 1(2). A positive servitude may be constituted in the recorded title of either the dominant or the servient tenement: *Balfour* v. *Kinsey*, 1987 S.L.T. 144. If the deed constituting the grant has been lost, an action of proving the tenor may be necessary: *Crichton* v. *Wood*, 1981 S.L.T. (Notes) 66. It is a question of construction whether a servitude has in fact been constituted: *Fearnan Partnership* v. *Grindlay*, 1992 S.C. (H.L.) 38; 1992 S.L.T. 460 (right to graze cow held not to be a servitude).

[26] Bell, *Prin.*, § 994; *Cowan* v. *Stewart* (1872) 10 M. 735; *McLean* v. *Marwhirn Developments*, 1976 S.L.T. (Notes) 47.

[27] s. 3(2) and s. 28(1)(*d*) of the Land Registration (Sc.) Act 1979; *cf.* note 17, *supra*.

[28] Erskine, *Inst.*, II, ix, 3; *Campbell's Trs.* v. *Glasgow Corporation* (1902) 4 F. 752; and *cf.* dicta in *Balfour* v. *Kinsey*, 1987 S.L.T. 144; *Robertson* v. *Hossack*, 1995 S.L.T. 291.

[29] Prescription and Limitation (Scotland) Act 1973, s. 3(1).

[30] *Crawford* v. *Lumsden*, 1951 S.L.T. (Notes) 62 (reversing the Lord Ordinary: 1951 S.L.T. 64); *Moyes* v. *Macdiarmid* (1900) 2 F. 918; see also *Hunter* v. *Fox*, 1964 S.C. (H.L.) 95; *Robson* v. *Chalmers Property Investment Company*, 1965 S.L.T. 381; *Walker's Exrx.* v. *Carr*, 1973 S.L.T. (Sh.Ct.) 77; *McEachen* v. *Lister*, 1976 S.L.T. (Sh.Ct.) 38; *Irvine Knitters* v. *North Ayrshire Co-operative Society*, 1978 S.C. 109; *Alvis* v. *Harrison*, 1991 S.L.T. 64 (H.L.).

40.28 Implied Grant or Reservation.—The constitution of a servitude by implication may occur when the owner of a heritage severs it into two or more parts and alienates one or more of these parts. A, the proprietor of an estate, for example, dispones a portion to B and retains the other portion. B claims that, although there are no words in the disposition creating a servitude over the retained portion, such a servitude has been created by implication. This is a claim to a servitude constituted by implied grant.[31] On the other hand, the proprietor A may claim that the retained portion has by implication a servitude over the portion granted to B. This is a claim to a servitude constituted by implied reservation. These two cases are distinct, and are ruled by different considerations.

In the first case, where the claim is to an implied grant of servitude, the principle that 'when anything is granted all things are understood to be granted therewith that are necessary thereto'[32] applies, and, therefore, the grant will include such servitudes as are necessary for the use of the property. Hence, if the only means of access to the land disponed to B is over A's retained portion, a servitude of way over that portion will be implied, for 'it is of the essence of property in the soil that the proprietor should have access to and from it.'[33] But the law goes further than this. 'When two properties are possessed by the same owner and there has been a severance made of part from the other, anything which was used and was necessary for the comfortable enjoyment of that part of the property which is granted shall be considered to follow from the grant if there are the usual words in the conveyance. I do not know whether the usual words are essentially necessary; but where there are the usual words I cannot doubt that this is the law.'[34] It is not required that the servitude claimed should be so essential that the property could have no value without it; it is enough that it is necessary for 'the convenient and comfortable enjoyment of the property as it existed before the time of the grant.' Thus in *Ewart* v. *Cochrane* the owner of a tanyard and house with a garden adjoining it constructed a drain from the former to a cesspool in the garden, and thereafter sold the tanyard, retaining the house and garden. In a question between the persons who had come to be in right respectively of the two properties, it was held that the drain could not be removed, as there had passed by implication on the sale of the tanyard a right to keep the drain in the position which it occupied.

---

[31] See, *e.g. Rogano Ltd.* v. *British Railways Board*, 1979 S.C. 297, where it was argued that there had been an implied grant of a servitude of support by severance of land previously in one ownership. However where there has been an express grant of servitude, the possibility of an implied grant may be precluded: *McEachen* v. *Lister*, 1976 S.L.T. (Sh.Ct.) 38.

[32] Stair, II, vii, 6.

[33] *McLaren* v. *City of Glasgow Union Ry.* (1878) 5 R. 1042, *per* Lord Justice-Clerk Moncreiff; *Walton Bros.* v. *Mags. of Glasgow* (1876) 3 R. 1130; Stair, II, vii, 10.

[34] *Per* Lord Campbell in *Ewart* v. *Cochrane* (1861) 4 Macq. 117; see also *Wheeldon* v. *Burrows* (1879) 12 Ch.D. 31; *Gow's Trs.* v. *Mealls* (1875) 2 R. 729; *Costagliole* v. *English* [1969] C.L.Y. 1158.

A statute may create a servitude right by implication.[35] It is more difficult to establish that a servitude has been impliedly reserved. 'If the grantor intends to reserve any right over the tenement granted, it is his duty to reserve it expressly in the grant.'[36] This is the general rule. There is an admitted exception where the servitude is one of necessity in the sense that the retained property would be useless without it, as, *e.g.* a way forming the only access to the property; but it is not enough for this purpose to show merely that the servitude claimed as reserved is necessary for the comfortable enjoyment of the reserved portion.[37] If English authorities can be relied on—and there has been frequent reference to these in the Scottish cases—a servitude by implied reservation is allowed where there are reciprocal rights as between the property conveyed and the property retained, as in the case of two adjoining houses originally built together by a common owner and dependent each on the other for support,[38] and it is said that 'the law will readily imply the grant or reservation of such easements as may be necessary to give effect to the common intention of the parties to a grant of real property, with reference to the manner or purposes in and for which the land granted or some land retained by the grantor is to be used. But it is essential for this purpose that the parties should intend that the subject of the grant or the land retained by the grantor should be used in some definite and particular manner. It is not enough that the subject of the grant or land retained should be intended to be used in a manner which may or may not involve this definite and particular use.'[39]

If a positive servitude has been possessed for a continuous period of 20 years, openly, peaceably and without any judicial interruption, and the possession was founded on, and followed the execution of, a deed which is sufficient in respect of its terms by implication to constitute the servitude, then on the expiry of the 20 years the validity of the servitude as so constituted becomes unchallengeable, except on the ground that the deed is *ex facie* invalid or was forged.[40]

40.29   Prescription.—Negative servitudes cannot be acquired or constituted by prescription, and the mere enjoyment of a state of things existent on a neighbour's estate for the prescriptive period does not give a right to demand its continuance or to prohibit its being altered.[41] A positive servitude on the other hand may be constituted by prescription. If a

---

[35] *Central Regional Council* v. *Ferns*, 1979 S.C. 136 (Water (Scotland) Act 1946).

[36] *Shearer* v. *Peddie* (1899) 1 F. 1201.

[37] *Murray* v. *Medley*, 1973 S.L.T. (Sh.Ct.) 75.

[38] See Rankine, *Land-Ownership*, p. 438; *Union Lighterage Co.* v. *London Graving Dock Co.* [1902] 2 Ch. 557; see also *Ferguson* v. *Campbell*, 1913 1 S.L.T. 241.

[39] *Pwllbach Colliery Co.* v. *Woodman* [1915] A.C. 634, per Lord Parker; *Cory* v. *Davies* [1923] 2 Ch. 95; *Wong* v. *Beaumont Property Trust* [1965] 1 Q.B. 173.

[40] Prescription and Limitation (Scotland) Act 1973, s. 3(1).

[41] Rankine, p. 426; *Anderson* v. *Robertson*, 1958 S.C. 367; but see *McLaren* v. *British Railways Board*, 1971 S.C. 182.

positive servitude has been possessed for a continuous period of 20 years openly, peaceably and without judicial interruption, the existence of the servitude as so possessed becomes unchallengeable.[42] Infeftment in the dominant tenement is no longer a prerequisite, possession alone being sufficient.[43]

The acts of possession must be overt in the sense that they must in themselves be of such character or be done in such circumstances as to indicate unequivocally to the proprietor of the servient tenement the fact that a right [44] is asserted and the nature of that right; and it must be shown that they either were known or ought to have been known, to the owner of the servient tenement or to the persons to whom he entrusted the charge of his property.[45]

Where a servitude is thus acquired, the possession affords the measure of the right acquired. *Tantum praescriptum quantum posses-sum*[46] (there is only prescription in so far as there has been possession). According to Erskine, however, a servitude by prescription may sometimes justly be extended beyond former usage; but the extension would apparently be admitted only where it was such a development of the use as might be held to be involved in the possession.[47]

40.30 Extinction of Servitudes.—A servitude may be extinguished in one or other of the following six ways: (1) By a change of circumstances. Thus, if land is acquired under compulsory powers, it is taken free of all servitudes unless it be otherwise provided in the special Act authorising its acquisition.[48] So also, if either the dominant or the servient tenement is destroyed, the servitude is extinguished, for in that case nothing remains to be the subject of a servitude. But, if the dominant is only temporarily rendered unfit for the servitude, the servitude is suspended for the time but is not extinguished.[49] (2) It may be extinguished *confusione, i.e.* by both tenements passing into the ownership of the same person, for when one person is the absolute owner of two estates it is impossible to speak of his having, in respect of his ownership and possession of one of them, any rights over the other. *Res sua nemini servit* (no one can have a servitude over his own property).[50] If the tenements thereafter come to belong to different persons, the servitude does not thereupon revive, but requires to be constituted *de novo*.[51]

---

[42] 1973 Act, s. 3(2). See Chap. 15.

[43] 1973 Act, s. 3(4).

[44] *Middletweed Ltd.* v. *Murray*, 1989 S.L.T. 11 (vehicular access allowed as a privilege, not a right).

[45] *McInroy* v. *Duke of Atholl* (1891) 18 R. (H.L.) 46, *per* Lord Watson; *McGregor* v. *Crieff Co-operative Society*, 1915 S.C. (H.L.) 93; *cf. Diment* v. *N.H. Foot* [1974] 1 W.L.R. 1427.

[46] *Kerr* v. *Brown*, 1939 S.C. 140.

[47] Erskine, *Inst.*, II, ix, 4; Rankine, *Land-Ownership*, p. 50.

[48] *Magistrates of Oban* v. *Callander and Oban Ry.* (1892) 19 R. 912.

[49] Erskine, *Inst.*, II, ix, 37.

[50] *Baird* v. *Fortune* (1861) 4 Macq. 127, *per* Lord Cranworth; *Donaldson's Trs.* v. *Forbes* (1839) 1 D. 449.

[51] Erskine, *supra*: *Union Bank* v. *Daily Record* (1902) 10 S.L.T. 71.

There is an exception to this in the case where the estates are held on distinct titles, and a separation of the titles, independently of the will of the proprietor, may be anticipated;[52] as, for example, where one estate is held under an entail and the other in fee-simple, or where they are held under entails with different destinations. It has already been shown that on the severance of the unity of a property a servitude may be impliedly granted or reserved.[53] (3) It may be renounced by the proprietor of the dominant tenement. (4) It may be lost through the operation of the negative prescription. And here it is necessary to attend to the distinction between the two classes of servitude. As a positive servitude entitles the owner of the dominant tenement to exercise certain rights over the servient tenement, it will be lost by mere non-exercise of these for 20 years.[54] This period will run from the midnight following upon the last occasion on which the dominant owner exercised his right.[55] But in the case of a negative servitude, as there is no active use of these by the dominant owner but merely a restraint laid on the servient owner, there is no room for prescription unless the latter does something which is inconsistent with the restraint laid upon him. Thus the owner of land subject to the servitude *altius non tollendi* cannot plead that it has been lost by prescription unless he has erected buildings in contravention of the servitude; but, if he has done so, prescription will operate if the contravention has remained unchallenged for a period of 20 years since its date.[56] The operation of prescription will not be averted by the fact that the servitude appears in the title of the servient tenement.[57] (5) A servitude may also be lost if there is conduct on the part of the dominant owner showing an intention to relinquish it or of such a nature as to raise a plea of personal bar, by acquiescence or otherwise, against its enforcement.[58] (6) A servitude may be discharged by the Lands Tribunal where changes in the neighbourhood have made the servitude unreasonable or inappropriate,[59] or where the existence of the servitude impedes some reasonable use of the land.[60]

40.31 Particular Servitudes.—The nature of the servitudes recognised by the institutional writers may be briefly indicated. They may be grouped

---

[52] Bell, *Prin.*, § 997; *Donaldson's Trs.* v. *Forbes* (1839) 1 D. 449.

[53] *Supra*, para. 40.28; see *Walton Bros.* v. *Mags. of Glasgow* (1876) 3 R. 1130, *per* Lord President Inglis.

[54] Prescription and Limitation (Scotland) Act 1973, ss. 3(5) and 7; see Chap. 15; *cf. Walker's Exrx.* v. *Carr*, 1973 S.L.T. (Sh.Ct.) 77.

[55] 1973 Act, ss. 8, 14.

[56] 1973 Act, ss. 7, 3(5); *cf.* Erskine, *supra*; *Wilkie* v. *Scott* (1688) Mor. 11189.

[57] *Graham* v. *Douglas* (1735) Mor. 10745. Only a real right of ownership in land is imprescriptible: 1973 Act, Sched. 3, para. (*a*).

[58] Bell, *Prin.*, §999; Rankine, *Land-Ownership*, pp. 441; *Mags. of Rutherglen* v. *Bainbridge* (1886) 13 R. 745; see also *Millar* v. *Christie*, 1961 S.C. 1.

[59] Conveyancing and Feudal Reform (Scotland) Act 1970, s. 1; see *e.g. Devlin* v. *Conn*, 1972 S.L.T. (Lands Tr.) 11, and see generally J.M. Halliday, *The Conveyancing and Feudal Reform (Scotland) Act 1970* (2nd ed.), §2.4.

[60] 1970 Act, s. 1; see *e.g. Orsi* v. *McCallum*, 1980 S.L.T. (Lands Tr.) 2.

under the headings of urban and rural servitudes.[61] The third of the urban servitudes (Light or Prospect) is negative: the others are all positive servitudes.

40.32 Urban Servitudes.—These are support, stillicide, and light or prospect.

(1) Support includes the servitudes known in the Civil law as *tigni immittendi* and *oneris ferendi*. The former is the right to let a beam or other structural part of the dominant building into the wall of the servient tenement and to keep it there; the second is the right to have a building supported.[62] These servitudes are noticed by the institutional writers, but there is little to be found in the reported decisions regarding them.[63]

(2) Stillicide. No proprietor can build so as to throw the rainwater falling from his own house immediately upon his neighbour's ground; but this servitude of stillicide or eavesdrop entitles him to do so.[64]

(3) Light or Prospect. The negative servitudes *non aedificandi, altius non tollendi*, and *non officiendi luminibus* restrain proprietors from building on their ground, or from raising their buildings beyond a certain height, or from building so as to hurt the light or prospect of the dominant tenement. The institutional writers refer also to another form of servitude of light which prevents the making in the servient tenement of windows and other openings which would interfere with a neighbour's privacy.[65]

40.33 Rural Servitudes.—These include way, aquaehaustus, aqueduct, pasturage and fuel, feal and divot.

(1) Way. The way may be a footpath, a horse road or a carriage road, and the terms of the grant or the extent of possession during the prescriptive period will determine to which category the way belongs.[66] The more burdensome servitude will include the less.[67] The destination of the road may impose a limitation on its use by confining it to traffic for certain purposes, as in the case of a church road or a road to a market,[68] but the opinion has been expressed that, if a servitude of way

---

[61] Note, however, Rankine's comment in *Land-Ownership* (4th ed.) at p. 446: 'The distinction of the Roman law between rural and urban servitudes, though adopted by all writers on Scots law, is of no practical value. The only divisions which point to real differences in the nature of the rights are those, already noticed, between positive and negative; continuous and discontinuous; apparent and non-apparent.'

[62] Erskine, *Inst.* II, ix, 7; Bell, *Prin.,* § 1003; Rankine, *Land-Ownership,* p. 656.

[63] *Murray* v. *Brownhill* (1715) Mor. 14521; *Troup* v. *Aberdeen Heritable Securities Co.,* 1916 S.C. 918. A more recent decision is *Rogano Ltd.* v. *British Railways Board,* 1979 S.C. 297.

[64] Stair, II, vii, 7; Erskine, *Inst.,* II, ix, 9; Bell, *Prin.,* § 1004.

[65] Stair, II, vii, 9; Erskine, *Inst.,* II, ix, 10; Bell, *Prin.,* §§ 1005–7; Rankine, p. 461.

[66] Prescription and Limitation (Scotland) Act 1973, s. 3(2); *cf.* Stair, II, vii, 10; Erskine, *Inst.,* II, ix, 12; Bell, *Prin.,* § 1010; *Malcolm* v. *Lloyd* (1886) 13 R. 512, *per* Lord President Inglis; *Alvis* v. *Harrison,* 1991 S.L.T. 64 (H.L.).

[67] Stair, *supra.*

[68] *Cf.* for example, *Gray* v. *MacLeod,* 1979 S.L.T. (Sh.Ct.) 17.

is acquired by prescription, there is no restraint on its use by the dominant tenement as a road of one or other of the above descriptions by reference to the purpose of the traffic passing over it; the road may be used generally by the dominant owner irrespective of whether the traffic is for agricultural or building or any other particular purpose.[69] As has been already noticed, the owner of the servient tenement is not bound to repair the road, and he may erect on it gates so long as these do not interfere with the enjoyment of the servitude.[70] The servient owner has, in the case of a way acquired by prescription, been allowed to alter its line where the new line would be equally convenient to the dominant owner, but this is not possible where the servitude has been constituted by a grant in which the line of road has been laid down.[71]

(2) Aquaehaustus gives the right to take water from or to water cattle at a well or stream in the servient tenement. It involves the right of access by the dominant owner and a right to clean out or repair the well.[72]

(3) Aqueduct is the right to convey water by pipes or canals through the servient tenement.[73] The duty of maintaining the aqueduct in proper condition is on the dominant owner, and he is entitled to access to it for this purpose.[74] Similar to this servitude is that of a dam or damhead by which one acquires a right of gathering water on his neighbour's land and of building banks or dykes for containing the water.[75]

(4) Pasturage is the right to feed cattle or sheep on another's ground or on a common.[76] It is usually found as a right enjoyed in common with others. If the extent of the right is not expressly defined, it is the amount of stock the servient tenement can winter.[77] The servient owner is entitled to use the surplus pasturage. The dominant owner may interdict the servient owner from carrying out operations which might damage the pasture or detract from the value of the servitude even where the dominant owner is not in fact exercising the right of pasturage.[78]

---

[69] *Carstairs* v. *Spence,* 1924 S.C. 380, *per* Lord President Clyde.

[70] *Supra,* para 40.25. But see *Lanarkshire Water Board* v. *Gilchrist,* 1973 S.L.T. (Sh.Ct.) 58.

[71] *Hill* v. *Maclaren* (1879) 6 R. 1363; *Moyes* v. *Macdiarmid* (1900) 2 F. 918; Bell, *Prin.,* § 1010.

[72] Erskine, *Inst.,* II, ix, 13; Bell, *Prin.,* § 1011; Rankine, *Land-Ownership,* pp. 571 *et seq.*

[73] See, *e.g. More* v. *Boyle,* 1967 S.L.T. (Sh.Ct.) 38.

[74] The owner of the servient tenement has a duty not to obstruct the enjoyment of the dominant owner of his rights, and not to interfere with or render more expensive the rights of the dominant owner to access to the water: *Central Regional Council* v. *Ferns,* 1979 S.C. 136.

[75] Erskine, *supra.*

[76] Stair, II, vii, 14; Erskine, II, ix, 14; Bell, *Prin.,* § 1013; Rankine, p. 454; *Fraser* v. *S. of State for Scotland,* 1959 S.L.T. (Notes) 36; *Fearnan Partnership* v. *Grindlay,* 1992 S.L.T. 460 (H.L.) (circumstances in which held that no servitude had been constituted).

[77] *L. Breadalbane* v. *Menzies* (1741) 5 Br. Supp. 710; but see *Ferguson* v. *Tennant and Ors.,* 1978 S.C. (H.L.) 19; 1978 S.L.T. 165.

[78] *Ferguson* v. *Tennant and Ors., supra.*

(5) Fuel, feal and divot is a servitude which gives the right to cut and remove peat for fuel and turf for fences.[79]

Other servitudes which have been recognised are the right to use ground for the purpose of bleaching clothes,[80] and of taking stone from the servient for the use of the dominant tenement.[81]

40.34 Public Right of Way.—This differs from the servitude of way in that it exists for the benefit of the public and may be vindicated by a member of the public. A servitude of way, on the other hand, is for the use and benefit of the dominant tenement alone, and it is only the proprietor of that tenement who has a title to sue in regard to it.[82]

A public right of way is a right in the public to pass from one public place to another public place.[83] And the road must follow a definite route.[84] 'It will not do for people to enter the ground of a proprietor, and walk about in it as much as they choose, and come out where they entered. That will not make a right of way. The line of road must be a marked line. Persons will never make a line of footpath by straying in fifty different lines over a man's property.'[85] Like a servitude of way, it may be a footpath, a horse road or a carriage road,[86] or indeed a motor road.[87]

This right of way may be acquired by grant, but almost invariably it has been created by possession or use for the prescriptive period of 20 years.[88] The use must be by the public, and not such as can be reasonably ascribed to a private servitude; it must be of such a character as to indicate that a right to use the track is asserted, for a use which is due to the permission or tolerance of the proprietor will not suffice; and it must be continuous, open and peaceable and without any judicial interruption. The amount of unrestricted public use which must be proved varies with circumstances; in a thinly populated district use by a

---

[79] Stair, II, vii, 13; Bell, *Prin.*, § 1014; Rankine, p. 456.

[80] *Home* v. *Young* (1846) 9 D. 286.

[81] *Murray* v. *Mags. of Peebles*, Dec. 8, 1808 F.C.

[82] *Thomson* v. *Murdoch* (1862) 24 D. 975, *per* Lord Deas; *Jenkins* v. *Murray* (1866) 4 M. 1046, *per* Lord Curriehill.

[83] *Campbell* v. *Lang* (1853) 1 Macq. 451; *Young* v. *Cuthbertson* (1854) 1 Macq. 455; *Marquis of Bute* v. *McKirdy & McMillan*, 1937 S.C. 93 (foreshore); *Love-Lee* v. *Cameron*, 1991 S.C.L.R. 61.

[84] *Mackintosh* v. *Moir* (1871) 9 M. 574; (1872) 10 M. 517.

[85] *Jenkins* v. *Murray, supra, per* Lord Curriehill.

[86] *Mackenzie* v. *Bankes* (1868) 6 M. 936.

[87] *Smith* v. *Sexton*, 1927 S.N. 92.

[88] Prescription and Limitation (Scotland) Act 1973, s. 3(3). See, *e.g. Richardson* v. *Cromarty Petroleum Co. Ltd.*, 1982 S.L.T. 237; *Cumbernauld & Kilsyth D.C.* v. *Dollar Land (Cumbernauld) Ltd.*, 1993 S.L.T. 1318 (H.L.); and Chap. 15, *supra*. Thus public rights of way usually come into existence without any title, deed or document which could be ascertained by a search in the registers: *cf.* s. 28(1)(g) of the Land Registration (Scotland) Act 1979, defining a public right of way as an 'overriding interest' (*i.e.* an interest in land which can exist as a real right without being recorded or registered).

small number of persons may be sufficient.[89] If the right of way is established, the use is not limited to passage from one end to the other; a member of the public is entitled to use it for part of its course, as *e.g.* for the purpose of reaching his own property.[90] As in the case of a servitude road, the proprietor of the lands over which the way runs is not debarred from dealing with his property in any lawful manner which does not interfere with the right of the public.[91]

A right of way constituted by use will be lost by disuse for the prescriptive period,[92] or it may be in a shorter period if the proprietor without challenge openly carries out operations on his land which make the use of the way impossible.[93]

An action for vindication of a right of way may be brought by any member of the public,[94] or by a local authority.[95] When the question of the existence of a particular right of way has been properly raised and decided, the decision is *res judicata* in any subsequent action even when raised by a different party. So also an action of declarator that there is no right of way may be defended by any member of the public or by the local authority,[96] and here also a judgment will be *res judicata*. The same result follows if the action is raised or defended by a society formed to defend rights of way.[97] The owner of land traversed by a public right of way has been held to owe a duty of care to the users thereof.[98]

VI. COMMON PROPERTY AND INTEREST

40.35 **Nature of Right.**—Property may be vested in two or more persons either jointly or in common. Where property is held jointly the owners have no separate estates but only one estate vested in them *pro indiviso*, not merely in respect of possession but also in respect of the right of property. The right of a joint owner accresces on his death to the others and cannot be alienated or disposed of either *inter vivos* or *mortis causa*. Instances of this mode of holding are found in the ownership of trustees, the rights of members in the property of a club, and joint liferents.

---

[89] *Macpherson* v. *Scottish Rights of Way Society* (1888) 15 R. (H.L.) 68; *Richardson* v. *Cromarty Petroleum Co. Ltd., supra.* For a decision involving an urban area, see *Strathclyde (Hyndland) Housing Society Ltd.* v. *Cowie*, 1983 S.L.T. (Sh.Ct.) 61.

[90] *McRobert* v. *Reid*, 1914 S.C. 633.

[91] *Reilly* v. *Greenfield Coal and Brick Co.*, 1909 S.C. 1328, *per* Lord President Dunedin at p. 1338; *Midlothian D.C.* v. *McKenzie*, 1985 S.L.T. 36 (a landowner has to justify anything whch restricts the unobstructed use of a public right of way).

[92] 1973 Act, s. 8.

[93] Rankine, *Land-Ownership*, p. 337.

[94] *Potter* v. *Hamilton* (1870) 8 M. 1064.

[95] Local Government (Scotland) Act 1973, ss. 189, 235 as amended by the Local Government etc. (Scotland) Act 1994.

[96] *Cf. Alston* v. *Ross* (1895) 23 R. 273; *Alexander* v. *Picken*, 1946 S.L.T. 91.

[97] *Macfie* v. *Scottish Rights of Way Society* (1884) 11 R. 1094.

[98] *Johnstone* v. *Sweeney*, 1985 S.L.T. (Sh.Ct.) 2.

In the case of property held in common each proprietor has a title to his own share which he may alienate or burden[99] by his separate act. On the death of one of the common owners his share will pass under his will or transmit to his heirs.[1] Examples of this holding include that of heirs-portioners under the former law of intestate succession,[2] and disponees in a disposition granting property to 'A and B.'[3]

40.36 Management of Common Property.—All the proprietors are entitled to a voice in the management of the property, and no one of them has a right to a greater measure of control than another. Any one of them may, therefore, prevent any alteration of the condition of the property or any 'extraordinary use' of the subject,[4] and the purported creation of a right of servitude over the property at the instance of one owner will be null if the others do not consent.[5] The rule is: *in re communi melior est conditio prohibentis* (in common property the objector is in the better position). An exception to this rule is admitted in regard to necessary operations in rebuilding and repairing; these are not to be stopped by the opposition of any of the owners.[6]

It is also a general, although not a universal, rule that all the proprietors must concur in actions against other parties relative to the common property.[7] One proprietor alone has no title to bring a declarator of property in regard to the subjects, for a decree in the action would not be *res judicata* as against the other common proprietors;[8] nor can one prosecute an action of removing against a tenant possessing under a lease granted by all.[9] But any one of the proprietors may take proceedings for the purpose of protecting the subject from encroachment or trespass.[10]

Where one common owner without the agreement of the others enjoys sole occupation of the subjects, recompense is not an appropriate

---

[99] *McLeod* v. *Cedar Holdings Ltd.*, 1989 S.L.T. 620.

[1] *Cargill* v. *Muir* (1837) 15 S. 408, *per* Lord Moncreiff; *Johnston* v. *Craufurd* (1855) 17 D. 1023, *per* Lord Curriehill; *Schaw* v. *Black* (1889) 16 R. 336, *per* Lord Shand. On the distinction between common property and joint property see *Magistrates of Banff* v. *Ruthin Castle Ltd.*, 1944 S.C. 36 at p. 64; *Munro* v. *Munro*, 1972 S.L.T. (Sh.Ct.) 6; Smith, *Short Commentary*, p. 479; Gordon, *Scottish Land Law*, para. 15–09 *et seq.*; K.G.C. Reid, 'Common Property: Clarification and Confusion,' 1985 S.L.T. (News) 57; *Stair Memorial Encyclopaedia*, Vol. 18 (Property: Landownership, para. 17 *et seq.*).

[2] See para. 42.3, of the 9th edition of this work.

[3] See Gordon, *Scottish Land Law*, para. 15–10 *et seq.*; *Steele* v. *Caldwell*, 1979 S.L.T. 228; *Smith* v. *MacKintosh*, 1988 S.C. 453; 1989 S.L.T. 148; *Stair Memorial Encyclopaedia*, Vol. 18 (Property: Landownership, para. 17 *et seq.*).

[4] Bell, *Prin.*, § 1075; *cf. Bailey's Exrs.* v. *Upper Crathes Fishing Ltd.*, 1987 S.L.T. 405.

[5] *W.V.S. Office Premises* v. *Currie*, 1969 S.C. 170.; *Fearnan Partnership* v. *Grindlay*, 1992 S.C. (H.L.) 38; 1992 S.L.T. 460.

[6] Bell, *Prin., supra; Deans* v. *Woolfson*, 1922 S.C. 221.

[7] *Lade* v. *Largs Bakery Co.* (1863) 2 M. 17, *per* Lord Deas.

[8] *Millar* v. *Cathcart* (1861) 23 D. 743.

[9] Erskine, *Inst.*, II, vi, 53; *Aberdeen Station Committee* v. *N.B. Ry* (1890) 17 R. 975, at p. 984.

[10] *Warrand* v. *Watson* (1905) 8 F. 253; *Aberdeen Station Committee* v. *N.B. Ry., supra*, at pp. 981 and 984.

remedy in a dispute between them.[11] Agreement to such occupation does not constitute a lease.[12] Where common property is a matrimonial home,[13] either spouse may seek the court's authority to carry out non-essential repairs or improvements appropriate for the reasonable enjoyment of the spouse's occupancy rights.[14] The court may apportion any expenditure incurred between the spouses.[15] The court may also pronounce an exclusion order against one spouse,[16] or otherwise regulate their rights of occupancy.[17]

40.37 **Division of the Property**—No one is bound to remain indefinitely associated with another or others in the ownership of common property. Any one of the proprietors may, even against the wish of the others, insist on a division of the property.[18] This right to have the property divided is a necessary incident of common property, and it is in law impossible to create common property and at the same time to exclude this right.[19] But the right must be exercised with due regard to the interests of all the proprietors. While the right of the proprietor who wishes to terminate the community is to have the subject divided,[20] where division is impracticable or would entail a sacrifice to an appreciable extent of the interests of the parties (as was found in the case of a feuing estate), a sale of the whole and division of the price will be ordered.[21] An action of ejection by one common owner against another is probably incompetent[22] except where associated with division and sale.[23]

[11] *Denholm's Trs.* v. *Denholm*, 1984 S.L.T. 319; Gordon, *Scottish Land Law*, para. 15–27.

[12] *Barclay* v. *Penman*, 1984 S.L.T. 376; *cf.* dicta in *Bell's Exrs.* v. *Inland Revenue*, 1987 S.L.T. 625, *per* the Lord President at p. 628D–F; but see also Gordon, *Scottish Land Law*, para. 15–27.

[13] s. 22 of the Matrimonial Homes (Family Protection) (Scotland) Act 1981 (c. 59), as amended by the Law Reform (Misc. Provs.) (Scotland) Act 1985, s. 13.

[14] 1981 Act, s. 2(4)(*a*); and see Chap. 48, *infra*.

[15] 1981 Act, s. 2(4)(*b*).

[16] 1981 Act, s. 4, as amended.

[17] 1981 Act, s. 3.

[18] *Brock* v. *Hamilton* (1852) 19 D. 701; *Anderson* v. *Anderson* (1857) 19 D. 700; *Upper Crathes Fishings Ltd.* v. *Bailey's Exrs.*, 1991 S.C. 30; 1991 S.L.T. 747; *Farquharson* v. *Farquharson*, 1991 G.W.D. 5–271; *Langstane (SP) Housing Association Ltd.* v. *Davie*, 1994 S.C.L.R. 158 (action for recovery of possession held incompetent); and see generally Gordon, *Scottish Land Law*, para. 15–24 *seriatim*; *Stair Memorial Encyclopaedia*, Vol. 18 (Property: Landownership, para. 32).

[19] *Grant* v. *Heriot's Trust* (1906) 8 F. 647, at p. 658.

[20] *Morrison* v. *Kirk*, 1912 S.C. 44; *Williams* v. *Cleveland and Highland Holdings Ltd.*, 1993 S.L.T. 398.

[21] *Brock* v. *Hamilton, supra; Thom* v. *Macbeth* (1875) 3 R. 161; *Campbells* v. *Murray*, 1972 S.L.T. 249 (sale by private bargain competent); *Scrimgeour* v. *Scrimgeour*, 1988 S.L.T. 590 (competent to grant warrant to a wife to purchase her husband's one-half share at the open market price fixed by a reporter); *Berry* v. *Berry (No. 2)*, 1989 S.L.T. 292; *The Miller Group Ltd.* v. *Tasker*, 1993 S.L.T. 207; *Grieve* v. *Morrison*, 1993 S.L.T. 852. The division need not necessarily be an equal one: see, *e.g.*, *Ralston* v. *Jackson*, 1994 S.L.T. 771.

[22] *Price* v. *Watson*, 1951 S.C. 359.

[23] *Barclay* v. *Penman, supra*.

In an action at the instance of one spouse for the division and sale of a matrimonial home owned by the spouses in common decree may, in the discretion of the court, be refused or postponed for such period as the court may consider reasonable or granted subject to such conditions as it may prescribe.[24] In exercising that discretion the court is to have regard to all the circumstances of the case and, in particular, to the conduct of the spouses, their needs and resources, the needs of any child of the family, any business use of the home and whether the spouse seeking decree has offered suitable alternative accommodation to the other spouse. As these provisions apply only to an action between spouses they cannot be invoked after the dissolution of the marriage, but there is no limitation on the length of any period of postponement.[25] An action of division and sale may also be sisted pending the outcome of an application by one spouse for an order for the transfer of the property of the matrimonial home.[26]

40.38 Commonty: Runrig.—Commonty[27] is a species of common property, once highly important, but now almost extinct, held as an accessory of the private estates of the commoners. Originally it was regarded as of value only for pasturage and other uses of the surface, but it has been held to carry right to the minerals. Difficulty has been experienced in distinguishing this right from a servitude of pasturage. In questions as to the uses to which a commonty may be put, the rule *melior est conditio prohibentis* applies, and nothing which is not sanctioned by usage may be done without the consent of all the commoners.[28] No action of division of commonty lands was competent till the Division of Commonties Act 1695 (c. 38), whereby it is enacted 'that all commonties, except the commonties belonging to the King and royal burghs may be divided at the instance of any having interest by summons raised against all concerned before the Lords of Session who are hereby empowered ... to value and divide the same according to the value of the rights and interests of the several parties concerned.' Under the statute where the commonty is divided among the common proprietors each receives a share of the commonty next to, and corresponding to the value of, his lands.[29] Where the value of the subjects in dispute is small, the action may be brought in the sheriff court.[30]

[24] Matrimonial Homes (Family Protection) (Scotland) Act 1981, s. 19; *Hall* v. *Hall,* 1987 S.L.T. (Sh.Ct.) 15; *Berry* v. *Berry,* 1988 S.L.T. 650. Ss. 7 and 9(2) of the 1981 Act do not apply to actions of division and sale: *Dunsmore* v. *Dunsmore,* 1986 S.L.T. (Sh.Ct.) 9.
[25] *Crow* v. *Crow,* 1986 S.L.T. 270.
[26] *Rae* v. *Rae,* 1991 S.L.T. 454; (contrast with the previous law: *Dickson* v. *Dickson,* 1982 S.L.T. 270).
[27] See Gordon, *Scottish Land Law,* para. 15–20 *et seq.*
[28] *Campbell* v. *Campbell,* Jan. 24, 1809 F.C.; *Innes* v. *Hepburn* (1859) 21 D. 832.
[29] See *Macandrew* v. *Crerar,* 1929 S.C. 699.
[30] Sheriff Courts (Scotland) Act 1907, s. 5.

Runrig lands are those which are in alternate or intermixed patches and belong to different proprietors. The Runrig Lands Act 1695 (c. 23) authorises the division of such lands.[31]

40.39   **Common Interest.**—In a passage[32] which has been accepted as an authoritative exposition of the meaning of this term[33] Bell says that 'a species of right differing from common property takes place among the owners of subjects possessed in separate portions but still united by their common interest. It is recognised in law as "common interest." It accompanies and is incorporated with the several rights of individual property. In such a case a sale or division cannot resolve the difficulties which may arise in management, but the exercise and effect of the common interest must, when dissensions arise, be regulated by law or equity.' Riparian proprietors have a common interest in the water of the stream.[34] Where a square is laid out in a town with a central garden for the use of the owners of the houses forming the square, these, in the general case, have a common interest in the garden, although they may have no right of property in it.[35] Feuars or neighbouring owners may have a common interest in a passage giving a common access or in a boundary wall or in an area reserved for light or common use.[36] But it is in the case of flatted houses that the most frequent illustration of this interest is to be found.

40.40   **Flatted Houses.**—Where different floors or storeys of the same house belong to different persons, there is no common property among the proprietors of the several floors or storeys, but the respective rights of property in them are qualified by the common interest of all. The titles may contain express provision as to the rights and obligations of the proprietors, but, apart from such provision, the law of the tenement is as follows:[37] The owners of the lower storeys must uphold them for the support of the upper; and the owner of the highest storey must uphold it as a cover for the lower. But there is no absolute duty of support or protection, and to establish liability to make reparation the relevant

---

[31] For fuller particulars as to commonty and runrig see Rankine, *Land-Ownership*, pp. 598 *et seq.*; Bell, *Prin.*, §§ 1087–99; Gordon, *Scottish Land Law*, para. 15–52 *seriatim*.

[32] *Prin.*, § 1086.

[33] See *Grant* v. *Heriot's Trust* (1906) 8 F. 647, at p. 658; *Smith* v. *Giuliani*, 1925 S.C. (H.L.) 45, at p. 57; *Fearnan Partnership* v. *Grindlay*, 1992 S.C. (H.L.) 38; 1992 S.L.T. 460; Gordon, *Scottish Land Law*, para. 15–31 *seriatim*.

[34] See para. 40.22, *supra*.

[35] *George Watson's Hospital* v. *Cormack* (1883) 11 R. 320; *Grant* v. *Heriot's Trust*, *supra*.

[36] *Mackenzie* v. *Carrick* (1869) 7 M. 419; *Grant* v. *Heriot's Trust, supra; Thom.* v. *Hetherington*, 1987 S.C. 185; 1988 S.L.T. 724 (a decision which provoked a Scottish Law Commission Consultation Paper, *Mutual Boundary Walls*: see 1992 S.L.T. (News) 199). As to the common interest of the inhabitants of a burgh in a street and the space above it, see *Donald & Sons* v. *Esslemont & Macintosh*, 1923 S.C. 122.

[37] *Smith* v. *Giuliani*, 1925 S.C. (H.L.) 45; and see *Wells* v. *New House Purchasers*, 1964 S.L.T. (Sh.Ct.) 2; Gordon, *Scottish Land Law*, para. 15–35 *et seq*; *Stair Memorial Encyclopaedia*, Vol. 18 (Property: Landownership).

proprietor must be shown to have been negligent.[38] The roof belongs to the owner of the highest storey, but he may be compelled to keep it in repair and to refrain from injuring it. If that storey is divided among several proprietors, each must uphold that portion of the roof which covers his property.[39] A local Act which requires owners of roofs to repair them does not apply to the owners of the lower storeys where there are no provisions in the titles imposing that duty on them.[40] A garret may not without consent be converted into an attic storey.[41] The solum on which the flatted house is erected, the area in front, and the back ground are presumed to belong to the owner of the lowest floor, or to the owners thereof severally, subject to the common interest of the other proprietors to prevent injury to their flats, especially by depriving them of light.[42] The external walls belong to each owner in so far as they enclose his flat;[43] but the other owners can prevent operations on them which would endanger the security of the tenement. The gables are common to the owner of each flat, so far as they bound his property, and to the owner of the adjoining house, but he and the other owners in the tenement have cross-rights of common interest to prevent injury to the stability of the building.[44] The floor and ceiling of each flat are divided in ownership by an imaginary line drawn through the middle of the joists; they may be used for the ordinary purposes, but may not be weakened or exposed to unusual risk from fire.[45] The common passages and stairs are the common property of all to whose premises they form an access, and the walls which bound them are the common property of these persons and the owners on their further side.[46]

40.41 Common Gables.—For the purpose of economising space a gable may be built originally, or may come afterwards to stand, on a boundary. It may be, or may be held to have been, erected one-half on each side of the boundary so as to accommodate the houses erected, or to be erected, on each side. The right to encroach beyond the boundary is founded on the custom of burghs and of other populous places where houses are erected streetwise. Much discussion has arisen with regard to the right of the first builder and his successors in the ownership to recover one-half of the cost from the owner of the adjoining stance. It seems to be settled that, in the absence of stipulation to the contrary,

---

[38] *Thomson* v. *St. Cuthbert's Co-operative Association,* 1958 S.C. 380; *Kerr* v. *McGreery,* 1970 S.L.T. (Sh.Ct.) 7; *Doran* v. *Smith,* 1971 S.L.T. (Sh.Ct.) 46.
[39] *Sanderson's Trs.* v. *Yule* (1897) 25 R. 211.
[40] *Duncan Smith & McLaren* v. *Heatly,* 1952 J.C. 61; see also *Musselburgh Town Council* v. *Jameson,* 1957 S.L.T. (Sh.Ct.) 35.
[41] *Sharp* v. *Robertson* (1800) Mor. 'Property' App. No. 3; *Watt* v. *Burgess' Tr.* (1891) 18 R. 766.
[42] *Boswell* v. *Mags. of Edinburgh* (1881) 8 R. 986.
[43] See for example *Anderson* v. *Brattisani's,* 1978 S.L.T. (Notes) 42.
[44] *Gellatly* v. *Arrol* (1863) 1 M. 592. See *Todd* v. *Wilson* (1894) 22 R. 172.
[45] *McArly* v. *French's Trs.* (1883) 10 R. 574.
[46] Rankine, *Land-Ownership,* p. 677.

this right cannot be enforced till the adjacent owner for the time being actually begins to make use of the wall. Each of the parties has a right of property in his own share while each has a common interest in the whole.[47] The customary uses to which the gable may be put are mainly the insertion of joists, dooks, fireplaces and chimneys, and the binding into it of front and back walls.[48] A fence or division wall cannot, without agreement, be converted into a house gable.[49]

40.42   March-Fences and Division Walls.—Under the March Dykes Act 1661 (c. 41),[50] a proprietor of lands is enabled to compel the owner of conterminous lands to bear half the expense of erecting, repairing, or where necessary re-building[51] the march dyke or fence between their lands. The Act applies only to lands exceeding five or six acres.[52] The fence must be advantageous to both proprietors, but the advantage need not be equal;[53] and the court will refuse an application under the Act if the circumstances are such as to make the pursuer's demand oppressive or unfair.[54] The application is usually made in the sheriff court, but the jurisdiction of the Court of Session is not excluded.[55] The neighbouring proprietor cannot be made liable for the expense of the fence unless he has given his consent to its erection or has been made a party to proceedings under the Act.[56]

The Act has been supplemented by the March Dykes Act 1669 (c. 17), dealing with straightening of the marches. 'Where the marches are crooked and unequal' or unfit for a dyke or ditch, the sheriff, on application by the proprietor of the lands, is empowered to visit the marches, to adjudge, where necessary, parts of one estate to the other, and where the parts transferred *hinc inde* are not of equal value 'to decern what remains uncompensed of the price to the party to whom the same is wanting.' It is imperative that the sheriff should visit the marches.[57] As in the case of applications under the earlier Act, the

---

[47] *Jack* v. *Begg* (1875) 3 R. 35; *Glasgow Royal Infirmary* v. *Wylie* (1877) 4 R. 894; *Berkeley* v. *Baird* (1895) 22 R. 372; *Robertson* v. *Scott* (1886) 13 R. 1127; *Baird* v. *Alexander* (1898) 25 R. (H.L.) 35; *Wilson* v. *Pottinger,* 1908 S.C. 580; and see Gordon, *Scottish Land Law,* para. 4–37; Law Commission Consultation Paper, *Mutual Boundary Walls:* 1992 S.L.T. (News) 199; *Stair Memorial Encyclopaedia,* Vol. 18 (Property: Landownership).

[48] *Lamont* v. *Cumming* (1875) 2 R. 784.

[49] *Grahame* v. *Mags. of Kirkcaldy* (1882) 9 R. (H.L.) 91.

[50] Stair, II, iii, 75; Erskine, *Inst.* II, vi, 4; Bankton, i, x, 153–4; Rankine, *Land-Ownership,* pp. 613 *et seq*; Gordon, *Scottish Land Law,* para. 4–46 *et seq.*; *Stair Memorial Encyclopaedia,* Vol. 18 (Property: Landownership).

[51] *Paterson* v. *MacDonald* (1880) 7 R. 958.

[52] *Penman* v. *Douglas* (1739) Mor. 10481; *Secker* v. *Cameron,* 1914 S.C. 354.

[53] *Blackburn* v. *Head* (1904) 11 S.L.T. 521, *per* Lord Kyllachy.

[54] *Earl of Peterborough* v. *Garioch* (1784) Mor. 10497; *Secker* v. *Cameron, supra.*

[55] *Pollock* v. *Ewing* (1869) 7 M. 815. In this case and in *Graham* v. *Irving* (1899) 2 F. 29, the application of the Act where the estates were bounded by a stream or burn was considered; see Rankine, *Land-Ownership,* p. 615.

[56] *Ord* v. *Wright* (1738) Mor. 10479.

[57] *Lord Advocate* v. *Sinclair* (1872) 11 M. 137. See *Earl of Kintore* v. *Earl of Kintore's Trs.* (1886) 13 R. 997, as to the sheriff's powers under the Act.

court will refuse an application which would result in oppression or unfairness.

Without having recourse to these statutes adjoining heritors may agree to erect a fence at the common expense; or it may be that, without express agreement, a fence has been recognised and treated as a march-fence; and in such cases there is a common obligation on the part of the heritors to maintain and repair it.[58] In the case of such fences, and also of mutual division walls, questions may arise of whether the wall or fence is common property or is owned by each proprietor, usually *ad medium filum*, in so far as built on his ground. The latter appears to be the better view where there are no special considerations pointing to the contrary.[59] The property in the fence or wall is then subject to a right of common interest but each proprietor has a right to build or otherwise carry out operations *in suo* on or against his part of the wall provided there is no significant harm to the structure of the wall or other infringement of the common interest.[60] If, on the other hand, the wall is regarded as common property, the right of division and sale normally incident to such property is excluded.[61]

VII. TIME SHARES

40.43   **Time-Shares.**—Heritable property may be vested in one owner, who sells rights of occupancy for certain periods to other individuals.[62] Such arrangements are known as time-shares. The nature and effect of the rights granted depend upon the terms of the particular contract. Generally, the holder of a time-share may sell it to another, or gift or bequeath or otherwise dispose of it, as incorporeal property.[63] A time-share could take the form of a lease. Recent legislation offers protection to persons entering into time-share agreements.[64]

Further Reading

Gordon, *Scottish Land Law* (1989).
Halliday, *Conveyancing Law and Practice* (1984).
Jauncey, *Fishing in Scotland* (2nd ed., 1984).
Rankine, *Land-Ownership* (4th ed., 1909).
Scott Robinson, *The Law of Game, Salmon and Freshwater Fishing in Scotland* (1990).
Stair Memorial Encyclopaedia, Vol. 11 (Fisheries, Forestry, Harbours); Vol. 14 (Mines and Quarries); Vol. 18 (Property: Landownership); Vol. 20 (Roads); Vol. 21 (Sea and Continental Shelf); Vol. 25 (Water and Water Rights).
Tait, *Game Laws* (2nd ed., 1928).

[58] *Strang* v. *Steuart* (1864) 2 M. 1015.
[59] Rankine, pp. 620–621 and 636–637; *Thom* v. *Hetherington*, 1987 S.C. 185; 1988 S.L.T. 724.
[60] *Gray* v. *MacLeod*, 1979 S.L.T. (Sh.Ct.) 17; *Gill* v. *Mitchell*, 1980 S.L.T. (Sh.Ct.) 48; *Thom* v. *Hetherington*, *supra*.
[61] Rankine, *ibid.*
[62] Gordon, *Scottish Land Law*, paras. 15–08, 19–13.
[63] The contract may impose certain restrictions on disposal.
[64] Timeshare Act 1992 (c. 35).

CHAPTER 41

LEASES

The common law of leases, for social and economic reasons, has for many years been substantially eclipsed by statute, especially with regard to the security of the tenant's tenure and the amount of rent which he can be required to pay. Few lettings in town or country are now unaffected by statutory codes and those of residential property and agricultural land are particularly closely controlled. The common law is still, nevertheless, of importance, and it and those statutory provisions of general application are dealt with first in this chapter. Thereafter the codes dealing with agricultural holdings, landowners and crofters, and dwelling-houses and shops will be summarised.

I. GENERAL LAW

41.1 Nature of Contract.—The contract of lease is one whereby certain uses, or the entire possession and control of lands, houses or other heritable subjects are given to the tenant for a return, known as rent or lordship, in money or goods. The analogous contract in the case of moveables is that of hire. A mineral lease, since it involves a conveyance of part of the subjects and not merely of their fruits, is in substance a sale; but it has been uniformly treated, in questions as to the incidents implied in the contract, as falling under the law of leases.[1] A right to the use of a heritable subject, where no possession of any specific part is given, *e.g.* a right to exhibit advertisements on the walls of a building, is a contract which does not fall under the law of leases.[2] The right to possession conferred by the contract must be exclusive.[3] Where an employee is given the occupancy of a house the contract, unless the provisions are exceptional,[4] will be regarded as a contract of service and not as a

---

[1] A power to grant leases does not generally import a power to grant leases of minerals which have not previously been let: *Campbell* v. *Wardlaw* (1883) 10 R. (H.L.) 65; *Nugent's Trs.* v. *Nugent* (1898) 25 R. 475.

[2] *U.K. Advertising Co.* v. *Glasgow Bag-Wash Co.*, 1926 S.C. 303; but see *Brador Properties Ltd.* v. *British Telecommunications plc*, 1992 S.L.T. 490; 1992 S.C.L.R. 119. The question whether a bargain about the use of land is a lease or not has been discussed in land valuation cases: *e.g. Magistrates of Perth* v. *Assessor for Perth*, 1937 S.C. 549; *L.N.E.R. Ry.* v. *Assessor for Glasgow*, 1937 S.C. 309.

[3] *Chaplin* v. *Assessor for Perth*, 1947 S.C. 373.

[4] See *Dunbar's Trs.* v. *Bruce* (1900) 3 F. 137; *Carron Co.* v. *Francis*, 1915 S.C. 872.

lease,[5] and the employee a 'service occupier' and not a tenant; but for this to be so the employee's residence in the house must be ancillary and necessary to the performance of his duties.[6] Where a person is permitted to occupy premises as an act of grace or friendship, and the intention to create a tenancy is not present, the right conferred on him may be construed as a mere licence to occupy, and not a lease.[7] There are four cardinal elements in a lease, the parties,[8] the subjects, the rent and the duration; in the absence of *consensus in idem* as to these elements, or at least the first three, there will be no lease.[9] The occupant of a house or other subject belonging to another is, however, presumed to occupy as tenant and though no direct obligation to pay rent is proved is bound to pay the annual value of the subject to the proprietor.[10] There is probably no limit of the time for which subjects may be let, but if no term be expressed the contract will be treated as a lease for a year only, and not in perpetuity.[11] Leases for not more than one year do not require to be constituted by writing, nor are there restrictions on the manner whereby they may be proved. Parole evidence is sufficient, and evidence of actings may be enough to lead to the inference that such a lease has been granted.[12] The necessity of writing in the case of leases for more than a year has already been considered.[13]

---

[5] *Sinclair* v. *Tod*, 1907 S.C. 1038. As a service occupier he is not entitled to security of tenure or rent protection under the Rent Acts: see *Marquis of Bute* v. *Prenderleith*, 1921 S.C. 281.

[6] *Cairns* v. *Innes*, 1942 S.C. 164; *MacGregor* v. *Dunnett*, 1949 S.C. 510, *per* Lord President Cooper at p. 514; *Cargill* v. *Phillips*, 1951 S.C. 67.

[7] *Commissioners of H.M. Works* v. *Hutchison*, 1922 S.L.T. (Sh.Ct.) 127; *Scottish Residential Estates Development Co. Ltd.* v. *Henderson*, 1991 S.L.T. 490; but see too *Brador Properties Ltd.* v. *British Telecommunications plc*, 1992 S.C. 12; 1992 S.L.T. 490, Paton & Cameron, *Landlord and Tenant*, p. 12; *cf. Heslop* v. *Burns* [1974] 1 W.L.R. 1241. See also *Stirrat* v. *Whyte*, 1967 S.C. 265, where fields were let for a rotation of cropping on condition that the let should terminate in the event of the sale of the farm at any time.

[8] A landlord may grant a valid lease to a group of persons, including himself *qua* tenant: *Pinkerton* v. *Pinkerton*, 1986 S.L.T. 672. *Quaere*, however, whether *pro indiviso* proprietors can competently grant a lease to one of their number: *Bell's Exrs.* v. *Inland Revenue*, 1986 S.C. 252; 1987 S.L.T. 625; *Clydesdale Bank plc* v. *Davidson*, 1994 S.C.L.R. 828 (Sh.Ct.); Gordon, *Scottish Land Law*, paras. 15–15, 19–06. Note too the decision in *Kildrummy (Jersey) Ltd.* v. *Inland Revenue Commissioners*, 1991 S.C. 1; 1992 S.L.T. 787, where a lease granted by a married couple to a company (which had undertaken by deed of trust to hold the subjects as nominee in trust for the couple) was held a nullity as being an attempt by the couple to enter into a contract with themselves for their own benefit.

[9] *Gray* v. *Edinburgh University*, 1962 S.C. 157; *Erskine* v. *Glendinning* (1871) 9 M. 656; *Trade Development Bank* v. *David W. Haig (Bellshill)*, 1983 S.L.T. 510 *per* Lord President Emslie at p. 514; *Shetland Islands Council* v. *B.P. Petroleum Development Ltd.*, 1990 S.L.T. 82, 1989 S.C.L.R. 48; *Scottish Residential Estates Development Co. Ltd.* v. *Henderson*, 1991 S.L.T. 490; Gordon, *Scottish Land Law*, paras. 19–06 *et seq.*

[10] *Glen* v. *Roy* (1882) 10 R. 239.

[11] *Dunlop* v. *Steel Co. of Scotland* (1879) 7 R. 283; *Gray* v. *Edinburgh University*, *supra*; *Tom Dickson Cameras (Glasgow) Ltd.* v. *Scotfilm Laboratories Ltd.*, 1987 G.W.D. 31–1152.

[12] *Morrison-Low* v. *Paterson*, 1985 S.C. (H.L.) 49; 1985 S.L.T. 255, *per* Lord Keith of Kinkel; distinguished in *Strachan* v. *Robertson-Coupar*, 1989 S.C. 130.

[13] Para. 8.2, *supra*.

41.2 Lease as a Real Right.—At common law a lease was merely a personal contract, binding on the lessor and his representatives, not upon his singular successors as purchasers or creditors; the tenant thus had no security of tenure against the lessor's singular successor, who could repudiate the lease. This was altered by the Leases Act 1449, whereby, when its provisions, as interpreted by decisions, are complied with, a real right in the subjects let is obtained by the tenant. The Act is applicable to leases of lands, houses, mines, and salmon fishing, but not to leases of shootings, which are not capable of being created separate tenements; such lettings, consequently, are not binding in a question with a singular successor.[14] It has been extended to any contract in writing for a consideration and for a period of not less than a year whereby an owner of land to which a right of fishing for freshwater fish in any inland waters pertains or the occupier of such a right authorises another person so to fish.[15] The conditions required to bring a lease within the purview of the Leases Act, and so make it binding on singular successors, are (1) that the lease (if for more than a year) must be in writing; (2) that there must be a specific continuing rent[16]; (3) that there must be an ish, or term of expiry; and (4) that the tenant must have entered into possession, possession being the equivalent of sasine in the feudal system.[17] Leases in perpetuity, therefore, though valid in a question with the lessor, are not binding on his singular successors. There is probably no limit to the number of years for which a lease, valid against singular successors, may be granted, but where the lease is for a definite period, with a continual option to the tenant to demand a new lease on the expiry of the old, the arrangement is binding on a singular successor only for the period current at the commencement of his interest.[18] The rent must not be illusory, a term never more exactly interpreted, but it is no objection, providing there is a continuing rent, that a capital sum, known as a grassum, has been taken at the beginning of the lease.[19]

41.3 Real and Personal Conditions.—When a lease falls within the provisions of the Leases Act 1449, all its ordinary conditions are binding on singular successors. But there may be conditions which are not *inter naturalia* of the lease, that is, provisions which have reference to the private relations of the contracting parties, and not to their general

---

[14] *Birbeck* v. *Ross* (1865) 4 M. 272. A lease of, *e.g.* a deer forest, where the tenant has the exclusive occupation of the lands themselves is not a lease of shootings: *Farquharson* (1870) 9 M. 66.

[15] Freshwater and Salmon Fisheries (Scotland) Act 1976, s. 4.

[16] *Mann* v. *Houston*, 1957 S.L.T. 89.

[17] Bell, *Prin.*, § 1190. An incoming tenant who in advance of the term is allowed to perform certain acts on the ground may not have possession for the purpose of the Act: *Millar* v. *McRobbie*, 1949 S.C. 1.

[18] See *Bisset* v. *Magistrates of Aberdeen* (1898) 1 F. 87.

[19] Bell, *Prin.*, § 1201; See *Mann* v. *Houston, supra.*

relations as landlord and tenant. By such provisions a singular successor of the landlord is not bound. Examples are a provision under which rent is to be ascribed to payment of a prior debt,[20] or a provision that a deduction from the rent is to be made for services to be rendered by the tenant,[21] or a provision, in a lease for 999 years, under which the landlord undertook to grant a feu on demand,[22] or a personal arrangement permitting a change of use.[23]

Obligations which would be binding on a singular successor of the landlord are not necessarily binding on a succeeding heir of entail. They may fail, not because they are exceptional or personal obligations not *inter naturalia* of the lease, but because if they were allowed to transmit they would, by burdening the succession, contravene the fetters of the entail. Thus although an obligation to pay for improvements executed by the tenant,[24] or to take over sheep stock at valuation, transmits against singular successors,[25] neither was held to be binding on a succeeding heir of entail.[26] Under the Entail (Scotland) Act 1914, however, an obligation to take over sheep stock contained in a lease granted by an heir of entail in possession is now binding on succeeding heirs of entail.[27]

**41.4	Long leases.**—In the case of leases of lands and heritages in Scotland for a period exceeding 20 years, an equivalent to possession as a means of obtaining a real right is afforded by the Registration of Leases (Scotland) Act 1857.[28] The Act provides that such leases[29] may be recorded in the Register of Sasines, but if the lands and heritages are situated in an area in respect of which the provisions of the Land Registration (Scotland) Act 1979 have come into operation the only means of obtaining the real right will now be by registration of the lease in the Land Register.[30] When recorded or registered as the case may be such leases are effectual against the singular successors of the lessor, even though the lessee has not entered into possession. The Act in effect provided an alternative to feuing, where that, for technical

---

[20] Bell, Prin., § 1202.

[21] *Ross* v. *Duchess of Sutherland* (1838) 16 S. 1179. See also *Montgomery* v. *Carrick* (1848) 10 D. 1387.

[22] *Bisset* v. *Magistrates of Aberdeen* (1898) 1 F. 87.

[23] *B.P. Oil Ltd.* v. *Caledonian Heritable Estates Ltd.*, 1990 S.L.T. 114.

[24] *Stewart* v. *McRa* (1834) 13 S. 4.

[25] *Panton* v. *Mackintosh* (1903) 10 S.L.R. 763.

[26] *Moncrieff* v. *Tod & Skene* (1825) 1 W. & S. 217 (improvements); *Gillespie* v. *Riddell*, 1908 S.C. 628, affd. 1909 S.C. (H.L.) 3 (sheep stock). Compare *Jolly's Exx.* v. *Viscount Stonehaven*, 1958 S.C. 635.

[27] s. 5.

[28] As amended by the Conveyancing (Scotland) Act 1924, s. 24, by the Long Leases (Scotland) Act 1954, s. 26, by the Land Tenure Reform (Scotland) Act 1974, Sched. 6, and by the Law Reform (Misc. Provs.) (Scotland) Act 1985, s. 3.

[29] Including leases of shootings: *Palmer's Trs.* v. *Brown*, 1989 S.L.T. 129; 1988 S.C.L.R. 499.

[30] s. 3(3).

reasons, *e.g.* an entail or a prohibition of sub-feuing, was impossible, which could afford similar security to the person in enjoyment of the right or his assignee. The requirements for a valid recording in the Register of Sasines of a lease under the 1857 Act[31] are (1) that the lease must be executed in a probative writing and (2) that the period of the lease must exceed 20 years, failing which there must be an obligation to renew the lease so as to endure for a period exceeding that number of years. The statutory requirements for registration in the Land Register are essentially the same, although the wording differs to some extent.[32] Prior to the amendments made by the 1974 Act the period of the lease required to be at least 31 years, and the subjects let, except in the case of a lease of mines and minerals, required not to exceed 50 acres in extent. On the other hand, no rent is necessary, and no definite ish is required. The particular value of the Act is that it enables the lessee of a registered lease to borrow on the security of the lease by conferring an effectual real right on his assignee in security without relinquishing possession to him. Such leases may be assigned absolutely or in security. The Act provides forms of deeds for executing such assignations,[33] but the grant of a right under a lease by way of a heritable security requires now to take the form of a standard security.[34] Real conditions may be created when such leases are assigned to the same effect as if the assignee had been a grantee of the lease.[35] Obligations created in registered leases may be varied or discharged by the Lands Tribunal under the Conveyancing and Feudal Reform (Scotland) Act 1970.[36] The sheriff has power to grant a renewal of a long lease where the landlord has failed to renew it in implement of an obligation to do so.[37] This power is available in cases where the landlord has failed to renew the lease having been given written notice by the tenant that he requires the landlord to do so, and in cases where the landlord is unknown or cannot be found.[38]

Prior to September 1, 1974 it was permissible to provide in leases of long duration for the payment of a casualty on events such the assignation of the lease to a singular successor,[39] but it is now no longer lawful to stipulate for the payment of any casualty.[40] It remains permissible, however, to stipulate for review of rent or a periodical variation of rent on terms prescribed in the lease.

---

[31] ss. 1 and 17, as amended by 1974 Act, Sched. 6, paras. 1 and 4.

[32] 1979 Act, s. 28(1), as amended.

[33] Schedules; and see 1924 Act, s. 24; *Crawford* v. *Campbell*, 1937 S.C. 596.

[34] Conveyancing and Feudal Reform (Scotland) Act 1970, ss. 9(3), 32, Sched. 8.

[35] Law Reform (Misc. Provs.) (Scotland) Act 1985, s. 3.

[36] 1970 Act, ss. 1, 2(6); *McQuiban* v. *Eagle Star Insurance Company*, 1972 S.L.T. (Lands. Tr.) 39.

[37] 1985 Act, s. 2 (inserting s. 22A in the Land Registration (Scotland) Act 1979).

[38] 1979 Act, s. 22A(7).

[39] *e.g. Crawford* v. *Campbell, supra.*

[40] Land Tenure Reform (Scotland) Act 1974, s. 16.

41.5 Limitation on Residential Use of Property Let under Long Leases.—The Land Tenure Reform (Scotland) Act 1974[41] provides for the prohibition of the imposition in deeds executed after the commencement of that Act of any feuduty, ground annual or other periodical payment and for the right to redeem, and in certain circumstances redemption by law of, such payments in deeds executed before that date. This reform was thought likely to result in more extensive use of long leases. Accordingly, while long leases of industrial or commercial property are not affected, the Act has introduced limitations upon the residential use of property let under long leases. It is a condition of every long lease executed after September 1, 1974 that no part of the property which is subject to the lease shall be used as or as part of a private dwelling-house.[42] An exception is made in the case of use as a private dwelling-house which is ancillary to the use of the remainder of the subjects let for other purposes, where it would be detrimental to the efficient use of the remainder of the subjects if the ancillary use did not occur on that property.[43] Caravan sites, agricultural holdings, small landholdings and crofts are also exempted from the prohibition.[44] 'Long lease' for this purpose is defined as meaning any grant of a lease or a liferent or other right of occupancy granted for payment subject to a duration which could extend for more than 20 years, or if there is to be liability to make some payment or perform some other obligation if renewal so as to extend the period for more than 20 years is not effected.[45] If a breach of the statutory prohibition occurs, the lessor may give notice to the lessee to terminate the use which constitutes the breach within 28 days.[46] If the lessee does not do so within that period the lessor may raise an action of removing to terminate the lease, but the lessee may avoid the consequences by ceasing the use at any time before decree is extracted.[47] If it is proved that the lessor has either expressly or by his actings approved of the use which contravenes the statutory prohibition the lessee is not subject to immediate removal, but the remaining duration of the lease is restricted so as not to continue for more than 20 years.[48] This defence is available only to a lessee who is actually occupying the subjects, but provision is made to enable a sub-lessee to be sisted in the action and to plead the defence if the use has been approved by the lessor in his sub-lease.[49] Provision is also made for the intimation of the action to heritable

---

[41] Pt. I.
[42] s. 8, as amended by Law Reform (Misc. Provs.) (Scotland) Act 1985, s. 1; see, as to the meaning of this expression, *Brown* v. *Crum Ewing Trs.*, 1918 1 S.L.T. 340; *Assessor for Lothian Region* v. *Viewpoint Housing Association*, 1983 S.L.T. 479.
[43] s. 8(3).
[44] s. 8(5).
[45] s. 8(4).
[46] s. 9(1).
[47] ss. 9(3), (6).
[48] s. 9(4).
[49] ss. 10(3)–(5).

creditors, who may seek to be sisted in the action and plead any defence which could be pleaded by the defender.[50]

41.6 **Tenants-at-will.**—A tenancy-at-will is an anomalous type of holding which has become established by custom and usage in certain parts of Scotland, particularly in fishing and rural villages of the north-east coast, in Highland villages and a mining village in Lanarkshire.[51] The system is that the tenant rents land from the landowner for building a house, but obtains no formal title to the land. A ground rent is paid in respect of the land, and the right to occupy the land and the building or buildings which have been placed on it changes hands by means of a simple receipt for the price and intimation of the change of tenant to the landlord or the factor of the estate. If the tenant fails to pay the rent the house reverts to the landlord, who sells it in order to recover the arrears of rent. The informality of this kind of holding carries with it certain disadvantages, particularly due to the fact that the tenant-at-will, not having a recorded title, cannot normally borrow on the security of his house and has no contractual right to demand a formal title. His position has, however, been recognised by statute and improved upon in two important respects. He is treated as if he were the owner of the house for the purpose of obtaining an improvement grant from the local authority.[52] And he is now entitled to acquire his landlord's interest in the land which is subject to the tenancy-at-will and to obtain a conveyance of it upon payment to him of compensation of an amount fixed, failing agreement, by reference to a statutory formula together with the expenses reasonably and properly incurred by the landlord in conveying his interest.[53] Disputes as to whether a person is a tenant-at-will,[54] the extent or boundaries of the land, the value of any tenancy land, expenses and what are the appropriate terms and conditions subject to which the landlord's interest in the tenancy land is to be conveyed are determined by the Lands Tribunal, which also has powers to deal with the case where the landlord is unknown or cannot be found.[55] If the landlord fails to convey his interest or is unknown or cannot be found a conveyance may be obtained by application to the sheriff.[56] Provision is also made with reference to heritable securities over tenancy land, whereby the heritable creditor is entitled to be a party to an application to the Lands Tribunal for the determination of disputes, and the tenancy land may be disburdened of the security if the heritable creditor fails to do so or is unknown and cannot be found.[57]

---

[50] s. 10(2).

[51] Paton and Cameron, pp. 68–69.

[52] See definition of 'owner' in Housing (Scotland) Act 1987, ss. 246, 338.

[53] Land Registration (Scotland) Act 1979, s.20: see generally Gordon, *Scottish Land Law*, paras. 19–104.

[54] *Ferguson* v. *Gibbs*, 1987 S.L.T. (Lands Tr.) 32; *MacLean's Exr.* v. *Kershaw*, 1993 S.L.C.R. 145.

[55] ss. 21(1), (2).

[56] ss. 21(3), (4).

[57] s. 22.

41.7 Rights of Tenant.—The tenant's principal right is to be placed in full possession of the subjects let, and to be allowed to remain there for the duration of the lease. In agricultural and urban leases alike, although not in the case of leases of minerals, there is an implied warranty that the subjects are reasonably fit for the purpose for which they are let.[58] There is, however, no general implication of fitness for any particular business which the tenant may desire to carry on there, the presumption being that the tenant has satisfied himself of the suitability of the subjects for his own purposes.[59] In agricultural leases the landlord is under an implied obligation to put the houses, offices and fences into 'tenantable repair,' in other words into such a condition that they will last, with reasonable care, for the period of the lease.[60] During the lease the obligation lies on the tenant to keep up and repair the buildings and fences on the farm so that they are in the same tenantable condition at the ish; but he is not liable for extraordinary repairs rendered necessary by *damnum fatale* or natural wear and tear.[61] In the case of urban subjects, however, the obligation to repair lies at common law, in default of stipulations to the contrary, upon the landlord.[62] The obligation is to uphold the subjects during the currency of the lease in a tenantable or habitable condition, and wind and watertight so that they will be proof against the ordinary attacks of the elements,[63] but he is not liable for defects due to *damnum fatale* or which arise out of failures by third parties to perform their obligations. His obligation is not a warranty to the tenant that no disrepair will occur, nor is there an absolute duty to keep the subjects free from defects; it amounts to an undertaking to put matters right on receiving notice of their existence, and there is no breach until a particular defect is brought to his notice and he fails to remedy it. Landlords have accordingly been held not to be liable in damages for injury sustained by the tenant owing to a chance defect arising during the currency of the lease.[64] The obligation is confined to the maintenance of the subjects let, and the landlord is not in breach of it if damage occurs within them caused by defects in property which lies beyond the curtilage of the subjects.[65]

---

[58] Ersk., II, vi, 39; Rankine, *Leases* (3rd ed.), pp. 241, 249; Gordon, *Scottish Land Law*, paras. 19–181 *et seq.*

[59] *Glebe Sugar Refining Co.* v. *Paterson* (1900) 2 F. 615; *Paton* v. *MacDonald*, 1973 S.L.T. (Sh.Ct.) 85.

[60] *Davidson* v. *Logan*, 1908 S.C. 350; *Christie* v. *Wilson*, 1915 S.C. 645 (water supply). As to houses, see *Reid* v. *Baird* (1876) 4 R. 234; *Wolfson* v. *Forrester*, 1910 S.C. 675.

[61] *Johnstone* v. *Hughan* (1894) 21 R. 777.

[62] Rankine, *Leases*, p. 241; Ersk., II, vi, 43.

[63] *Wolfson* v. *Forrester*, 1910 S.C. 675, *per* Lord President Dunedin at p. 680; see also *Reid* v. *Baird* (1876) 4 R. 234; *McGonigal* v. *Pickard*, 1954 S.L.T. (Notes) 62; *Gunn* v. *N.C.B.*, 1982 S.L.T. 526 (dampness); *McLaughlin* v. *Inverclyde D.C.*, 1986 G.W.D. 2–34 (Sh.Ct.) (alleged water penetration); *McArdle* v. *City of Glasgow D.C.*, 1989 S.C.L.R. 19 (Sh.Ct.) (dampness); *Morrison* v. *Stirling D.C.*, 1991 G.W.D. 12–714 (dampness).

[64] *Hampton* v. *Galloway* (1899) 1 F. 501; *Dickie* v. *Amicable Property Investment Co.*, 1911 S.C. 1079; *North British Storage Co.* v. *Steele's Trs.*, 1920 S.C. 194.

[65] *Golden Casket (Greenock)* v. *B.R.S. (Pickfords)*, 1972 S.L.T. 146.

The Housing (Scotland) Act 1987[66] provides that in the case of houses let where no rent is payable, or the rent payable is less than that specified by order made by the Secretary of State, there shall be implied an undertaking that the house will be kept by the landlord during the tenancy in all respects reasonably fit for human habitation. In the case of leases of houses for a period of less than seven years the landlord is required by that Act[67] to keep in repair the structure and exterior of the house, including drains, gutters and external pipes, and in repair and proper working order the installations in the house for the supply of water, gas, electricity and sanitation, and for space heating or heating water; contracting out of this statutory obligation may only be done with the concurrence of the sheriff.[68] The landlord's obligations, conventional, statutory or at common law, carry with them a liability to any persons who or whose property may be on the premises for any injury or damage arising to them as a result of any failure on his part to perform them.[69]

The obligation of upkeep is subject to the law of *rei interitus*, and therefore the accidental destruction of a house puts an end to the obligation on either side.[70] Total destruction of the subjects of lease, without fault, has the effect of putting an end to the contract and liberating both landlord and tenant from its obligations.[71] In the case of partial injury it is a question of degree whether the tenant is entitled to abandon the lease.[72] If not, or if he does not choose to do so, he is entitled to claim a proportionate deduction, or abatement, from the rent.[73] A landlord is under no implied obligation to abstain from using other property in competition with the business carried on by the tenant.[74] If by alterations or repairs on other property he interferes with the tenant's interests, he will be liable, even although there is no proof that the work in question was not carried out with reasonable care, for

[66] Sched. 10, para. 1 (as amended by the Housing (Scotland) Act 1988, Sched. 8). The original statutory provision, s. 6(1) of the Housing (Scotland) Act 1966, has been construed in a decision upon the same provision in an English Act as involving the necessity of notice to the landlord of any defect: *Morgan* v. *Liverpool Corporation* [1927] 2 K.B. 131.

[67] Sched. 10, paras. 3 and 4; and cf. *Kilna* v. *Cumbernauld Development Corporation*, 1988 G.W.D. 32–1379 (Sh.Ct.) (dealing with earlier provision, s. 8 of Housing (Scotland) Act 1966).

[68] Sched. 10, para. 5; *Little* v. *City of Glasgow D.C.*, 1988 S.C.L.R. 482 (Sh.Ct.).

[69] Occupier's Liability (Scotland) Act 1960, s. 3; see also *Haggarty* v. *Glasgow Corporation*, 1964 S.L.T. (Notes) 54; *Lamb* v. *Glasgow D.C.*, 1978 S.L.T. (Notes) 64; *Morrison* v. *Stirling D.C.*, 1991 G.W.D. 12–714.

[70] *Cameron* v. *Young*, 1908 S.C. (H.L.) 7. See, too, para. 12.5 supra. As to the case where a house is rendered unfit to live in by reason of war damage, see the War Damage to Land (Scotland) Act 1941.

[71] Stair, I, xv, 2; *Duff* v. *Fleming* (1870) 8 M. 769; *Cantors Properties (Scotland)* v. *Swears & Wells*, 1978 S.C. 310.

[72] *Allan* v. *Markland* (1882) 10 R. 383.

[73] *Muir* v. *McIntyre* (1887) 14 R. 470; *Sharp* v. *Thomson*, 1930 S.C. 1092.

[74] *Craig* v. *Millar* (1888) 15 R. 1005.

any structural damage, and for injury to the tenant's effects or interference with his business, but not for injury resulting merely from noise, vibration or temporary interference with access.[75] A tenant, as the occupier, normally pays the rates, but in the case of a furnished letting, in a question between himself and the landlord, the landlord is by custom bound to relieve the tenant of this liability in the absence of express stipulation to the contrary.[76]

41.8 Rights of Public Sector Tenants: Secure Tenancies and the Right to Purchase.—The Housing (Scotland) Act 1987[77] provides tenants of dwelling-houses in the public sector with a series of important rights. Most important of all is the right of the tenant of a dwelling-house let under a secure tenancy[78] to purchase the dwelling-house.[79] This right is available to the tenant once he has been in occupation for not less than two years[80] and where the landlord is a local authority, a new town development corporation, the Scottish Special Housing Association, Scottish Homes, the Housing Corporation, a registered housing association, a housing co-operative, or a police or fire authority.[81]

---

[75] *Huber* v. *Ross*, 1912 S.C. 898; and *cf. Chevron Petroleum (U.K.) Ltd.* v. *Post Office*, 1986 S.C. 291; 1987 S.L.T. 588; 1987 S.C.L.R. 97 (whether derogation of grant by landlord).

[76] *Macome* v. *Dickson* (1868) 6 M. 898; *Sturrock* v. *Murray*, 1952 S.C. 454.

[77] (c.26) Pt. III, consolidating and amending *inter alia* the Tenant's Rights etc. (Scotland) Act 1980 which introduced secure tenancies and the right to purchase. The 1987 Act was itself further amended by the Housing (Scotland) Act 1988, the Leasehold Reform, Housing and Urban Development Act 1993, and the Local Government etc. (Scotland) Act 1994. See, generally, commentary by Paul Q. Watchman, *The Housing (Scotland) Act 1987* (1991); C.M.G. Himsworth, *Housing Law in Scotland* (4th ed., 1994); Gordon, *Scottish Land Law*, para. 19–106.

[78] For the meaning of 'secure tenancy' see s. 44 and Sched. 2 of the 1987 Act; and see also *Kinghorn* v. *Glasgow D.C.*, 1984 S.L.T. (Lands Tr.) 9; *Thomson* v. *City of Glasgow D.C.*, 1986 S.L.T. (Lands Tr.) 6 (apartment in council hostel); *Campbell* v. *Western Isles I.C.*, 1989 S.L.T. 602 (missive of let failing to specify that letting on temporary basis); *Miller* v. *Falkirk D.C.*, 1990 S.L.T. (Lands Tr.) 111 (applicant tenant of two houses); *MacDonald* v. *Strathclyde D.C.*, 1990 S.L.T. (Lands Tr.) 10 (schoolhouse); *Walker* v. *Strathclyde R.C.*, 1990 S.L.T. (Lands Tr.) 17 (house within curtilage of school).

[79] A tenant required in terms of his contract of employment to occupy the house for the better performance of his duties may not be eligible to purchase: *Campbell* v. *City of Edinburgh D.C.*, 1986 S.C. 153; 1987 S.L.T. 51; *Forbes* v. *City of Glasgow D.C.*, 1988 G.W.D. 31–1330 (parks department employees); *McKay* v. *Livingston Development Corporation*, 1990 S.L.T. (Lands Tr.) 54 (security duties); *De Fontenay* v. *Strathclyde R.C.*, 1990 S.L.T. 605; *Little* v. *Borders R.C.*, 1990 S.L.T. (Lands Tr.) 2; *McTurk* v. *Fife R.C.*, 1990 S.L.T. (Lands Tr.) 49 (school janitor); *Jack* v. *Strathclyde R.C.*, 1992 S.L.T. (Lands Tr.) 28. Note also that a right of pre-emption contained in the title deeds may restrict the secure tenant's right to purchase: *Ross and Cromarty D.C.* v. *Patience*, 1994 S.C.L.R. 779.

[80] s. 61(2)(c); for the meaning of 'occupation' see s. 61(10); *McLoughlin's C.B.* v. *Motherwell D.C.*, 1994 S.L.T. (Lands Tr.) 31; *Beggs* v. *Kilmarnock and Loudoun D.C.*, 1995 G.W.D. 12–687.

[81] ss. 44(2), 61(2); Local Government etc. (Scotland) Act 1994, Sched. 13, para. 152 (to be brought into force by statutory instrument). But see also s. 43(3) of the Housing (Scotland) Act 1988: no further secure tenancies with housing associations, subject to transitional provisions; see *Milnbank Housing Association Ltd.* v. *Murdoch*, 1995 S.L.T. (Sh.Ct.) 11.

Detailed provisions are made for the procedure to be adopted by purchasing tenants and their landlords, for the conditions to be attached to the sale,[82] and for the price to be paid which includes the right to obtain substantial discounts from the purchase price by reference to the length of time for which the tenant or his spouse has been in occupation of housing in the public sector.[83] The statutory right to buy cannot be excluded by contract,[84] nor can the landlord impose financial penalties or other conditions which might discourage a tenant from buying.[85] Where a tenant dies after concluding missives, but before delivery of the disposition, his executors may enforce the missives.[86] Loans are available to tenants who have applied for and been unable to obtain a sufficient building society loan to enable them to exercise this right.[87] A 'rent to loan' scheme provides a further method of financing a purchase.[87a] The Act also provides public sector tenants with security of tenure by restricting the circumstances in which a secure tenancy may be brought to an end. A secure tenancy may not be brought to an end except where the tenant consents to this either by written agreement with the landlord or by giving four weeks notice to the landlord,[88] or where he dies leaving no qualified person to succeed him,[89] or where, if

[82] See, for example, *Forsyth* v. *Scottish Homes*, 1990 S.L.T. (Lands Tr.) 37 (deletion of conditions relating to repair work); *MacDonald* v. *Strathclyde R.C.*, 1990 S.L.T. (Lands Tr.) 10 (insertion of conditions relating to emergency egress); *McLuskey* v. *Scottish Homes*, 1993 S.L.T. (Lands Tr.) 17 (liability for maintenance of common parts); *City of Glasgow D.C.* v. *Doyle*, 1993 S.L.T. 604 (possible condition that the subjects to be conveyed would be less than the subjects let); *Ross and Cromarty D.C.* v. *Patience*, 1994 S.C.L.R. 779.
[83] s. 61 *et seq.* (Note that in the event of resale within three years, repayment of the discount may be necessary: ss. 72, 73; *Clydebank D.C.* v. *Keeper of the Registers of Scotland*, 1994 S.L.T. (Lands Tr.) 2). See generally *Keay* v. *Renfrew D.C.*, 1982 S.L.T. (Lands Tr.) 33; *Motherwell D.C.* v. *Gliori*, 1986 S.C. 189; 1986 S.L.T. 445; *McGroarty* v. *Stirling D.C.*, 1987 S.L.T. 85; *City of Edinburgh D.C.* v. *Davis*, 1987 S.L.T. (Sh.Ct.) 33. As to "occupation" for the purposes of calculating the discount, see *Drummond* v. *City of Dundee D.C.*, 1993 G.W.D. 26–1637; *Kelly* v. *City of Dundee D.C.*, 1994 S.L.T. 1268. A further right to abatement of the price on the ground of the landlord's default was introduced by the Leasehold Reform, Housing and Urban Development Act 1993, ss. 144 and 145.
[84] s. 61(1).
[85] s. 75. *Lord Advocate* v. *City of Glasgow D.C.*, 1990 S.L.T. 721; *Brookbanks* v. *Motherwell D.C.*, 1988 S.L.T. (Lands Tr.) 72; *Wingate* v. *Clydebank D.C.*, 1990 S.L.T. (Lands Tr.) 71.
[86] *Cooper's Exrs.* v. *City of Edinburgh D.C.*, 1990 S.L.T. 621; 1991 S.L.T. 518 (H.L.); *Jack's Exrx.* v. *Falkirk D.C.*, 1992 S.L.T. 5.
[87] s. 216.
[87a] By means of an initial capital payment, followed by regular payments representing deferred financial commitment: ss. 62A, 73A–73D of the 1987 Act as amended by the Leasehold Reform, Housing and Urban Development Act 1993, ss. 141 to 143.
[88] ss. 46(1)(c), (f).
[89] s. 46(1)(a); for the meaning of 'qualified person' see s. 52(2); *Cooper's Exrs.* v. *City of Edinburgh D.C.*, 1991 S.C. (H.L.) 5; 1991 S.L.T. 518 (missives concluded prior to the death of qualified person enforceable by deceased's executors); *Hamilton D.C.* v. *Lennon*, 1990 S.C. 230; 1990 S.L.T. 533 (nephew caring for relative not a joint tenant); *Roxburgh D.C.* v. *Collins*, 1991 S.L.T. (Sh.Ct.) 49; 1991 S.C.L.R. 575 (Sh.Ct.) (son living and working elsewhere); and see Gordon, *Scottish Land Law*, paras. 19–50.

there is a qualified person, that person declines the tenancy or subsequently dies,[90] or where the dwelling-house has ceased to be occupied,[91] or by an order for possession granted by the sheriff.[92] Secure tenants are also given the right to a written lease which embodies the terms of the tenancy,[93] the right to sub-let with the landlord's consent which shall not be unreasonably withheld[94] and, also with consent, to carry out alterations and improvements to the house.[95] In certain circumstances, an approved private sector landlord may acquire, from a public sector landlord, houses occupied by secure tenants.[96] Tenants retain their right to buy, but have the lesser security of tenure available under the assured tenancy regime.[97]

41.9 Protection against Harassment and Eviction.—The tenant, as a residential occupier, is protected by the Rent (Scotland) Act 1984[98] and the Housing (Scotland) Act 1988[99] against harassment by any person, including the landlord, which is intended to induce him to give up the occupation of the premises or any part of them, or to refrain from exercising any right or pursuing any remedy to which he is entitled in respect of the premises. Where the tenancy has come to an end and the occupier continues to reside in the premises he has the right not to be ejected without a court order;[1] the landlord's proper course is to apply to the court for a warrant for his ejection, and if he attempts to eject the occupier at his own hand he may be liable in damages for wrongous ejection[2] as well as to the criminal penalty provided by the 1984 Act.[3]

The Sex Discrimination Act 1975, section 30, and the Race Relations Act 1976, section 21, make discrimination unlawful in the letting of

---

[90] s. 46(1)(*b*); see too s. 52 *et seq.*

[91] s. 46(1)(*d*); see too abandonment by tenant: ss. 49–51.

[92] s. 46(1)(*e*); for the grounds on which such an order may be made see s. 48 and Sched. 3, Pt. I; *Scottish Special Housing Association* v. *Lumsden*, 1984 S.L.T. (Sh.Ct.) 71; *Charing Cross & Kelvingrove Housing Association* v. *Kraska*, 1986 S.L.T. (Sh.Ct.) 42; *Monklands D.C.* v. *Johnstone*, 1987 S.C.L.R. 480; *City of Glasgow D.C.* v. *James Brown*, 1988 S.C.L.R. 679 (Sh.Ct.); *Midlothian D.C.* v. *Brown*, 1991 S.L.T. (Sh.Ct.) 80; 1990 S.C.L.R. 765 (Sh.Ct.); *Midlothian D.C.* v. *Drummond*, 1991 S.L.T. (Sh.Ct.) 67; *Renfrew D.C.* v. *Inglis*, 1991 S.L.T. (Sh.Ct.) 83; 1992 S.C.L.R. 30 (Sh.Ct.); *City of Glasgow D.C.* v. *Erhaiganoma*, 1993 S.C.L.R. 592.

[93] ss. 53, 54.

[94] ss. 55, 56.

[95] ss. 57–60.

[96] Pt. III of the Housing (Scotland) Act 1988 (c.43); and see, e.g., *Waverley Housing Trust Ltd.* v. *Roxburgh D.C.*, 1995 S.L.T. (Lands Tr.) 2.

[97] See the annotations to the Housing (Scotland) Act 1988 by P. Robson, *Scottish Current Law Statutes 1988*, Vol. 4; and para 41.46 *infra.*

[98] ss. 22(2) and (2A).

[99] ss. 36–38 of the 1988 Act.

[1] ss. 22, 23 of the 1984 Act, and s. 23A (inserted by the Housing (Scotland) Act 1988, s. 40); *cf. N.C.B.* v. *McInnes*, 1968 S.C. 321.

[2] See Rankine, *Leases*, p. 592; *Cairns* v. *Innes*, 1942 S.C. 164; s. 36 of the Housing (Scotland) Act 1988.

[3] s. 22, as amended by s. 38 of the Housing (Scotland) Act 1988.

premises, in affording access to facilities in premises let, and in evicting tenants.[4]

41.10 **Tenant's Remedies.**—If the subjects are at the outset to a material extent unfit for their purpose, the tenant may refuse to enter into possession and claim damages.[5] He has the same remedy where the subjects are advertised as possessing certain qualities or advantages which they do not possess.[6] If, during the currency of the lease, the landlord should fail to execute repairs, with the result that the subjects become unfit for their purpose, the tenant may abandon the lease. If he proposes also to claim damages he is probably bound to give immediate notice; if not, and the landlord accepts his renunciation, a compromise between the parties, involving an abandonment of the tenant's claim for damages, will be inferred.[7] The question whether a tenant may abandon the lease depends upon the materiality of the defects, which admits of no rule more definite than that both parties must behave reasonably in the matter.[8] Short of abandoning the lease, the tenant may find a remedy in damages,[9] or in the retention of his rent. This right has been rested on the principle that payment of rent, and furnishing a subject in the condition agreed upon, expressly or impliedly, are the correlative obligations in a mutual contract, and therefore that any material failure on the part of the landlord justifies the tenant in the exercise of a right of retention.[10] A defect will more readily be held to be material, especially in the case of failure to carry out improvements, in the later than in the earlier years of the lease.[11] An offer to consign the rent is an element in favour of the tenant's case, but is not *per se* a good answer to a demand for payment.[12] The fact that the tenant has paid certain instalments of the rent while the defects of which he complains were obvious does not bar an ultimate plea of retention.[13] It is a question of circumstances whether the payment of rent without objection will bar an

---

[4] *Alexander* v. *Home Office* [1988] 1 W.L.R. 968; [1988] I.R.L.R. 190 (C.A.).

[5] *Critchley* v. *Campbell* (1884) 11 R. 475.

[6] *Brodie* v. *McLachlan* (1900) 8 S.L.T. 145.

[7] *Lyons* v. *Anderson* (1886) 13 R. 1020.

[8] *McKimmie's Trs.* v. *Armour* (1899) 2 F. 156 (house had become insanitary). Note that destruction of the subjects, such as by accidental fire, puts an end to the lease altogether: see para. 41.25, *infra*.

[9] See, for example, *Morrison* v. *Stirling D.C.*, 1991 G.W.D. 12–714. Continued occupation in the knowledge that a house is in a dangerous state may, on the principle of *volenti non fit injuria*, bar a claim for damages: *Dickie* v. *Amicable Property Investment Co.*, 1911 S.C. 1079; *Mullen* v. *C.C. of Dunbarton*, 1933 S.L.T. 185; *Proctor* v. *Cowlairs Co-operative Society*, 1961 S.L.T. 434.

[10] *Christie* v. *Birrells*, 1910 S.C. 986; *Earl of Galloway* v. *McConnell*, 1911 S.C. 846; *Haig* v. *Boswall-Preston*, 1915 S.C. 339; *Finland & Mitchell* v. *Howie*, 1926 S.C. 319; *Renfrew D.C.* v. *Gray*, 1987 S.L.T. (Sh.Ct.) 70; for a discussion of the principle of mutuality in relation to lease, see Paton & Cameron, *Landlord and Tenant*, p. 90; *Edmonstone* v. *Lamont*, 1975 S.L.T. (Sh.Ct.) 57.

[11] *Bowie* v. *Duncan* (1807) Hume 839.

[12] *Earl of Galloway* v. *McConnell, supra*.

[13] *Haig* v. *Boswall-Preston, supra*.

ultimate claim for damages for defects existing during the period for which the rent was paid.[14] It is open to the parties to agree that the tenant shall not withhold payment of the rent.[15]

41.11 Obligations of Tenant.—A tenant is bound to enter into possession, to occupy and use the subjects. The tenant of an hotel, who had shut it up in the interests of a rival house of which he had obtained a lease, was found liable in damages for breach of a material condition.[16] A landlord was held entitled to terminate a lease on the same ground when the tenant who had undertaken to reside on the farm leased was sent to prison for a substantial period.[17] In his occupation and use he is bound to exercise reasonable care. Thus damages were held to be due for injury caused by burst pipes, in a case where a tenant had left the house in winter without turning off the water or giving notice to the landlord.[18] In the cases where the landlord has a right of hypothec the tenant is bound to plenish or stock the subjects, and the obligation may be enforced by a replenishing order in the sheriff court.[19] The tenant may not invert the possession, by utilising the subjects for some purpose other than that for which they were let. So the tenant of a farm is not entitled to use it as a posting station;[20] a priest may not erect, in premises let as his residence, wooden huts for the accommodation of evicted tenants.[21] On the other hand the tenant of a furnished house may alter the position of the furniture or pictures;[22] the tenant of a shop may sell his stock by auction.[23] The tenant is also bound to pay rent when it becomes due. A tenant may have certain duties of care on the expiry of a lease.[24]

41.12 Rent: Hypothec; Rent Reviews.—A landlord has the ordinary remedies of a creditor for the recovery of his rent. He may raise an action for payment of the rent even if the tenant has purported to renounce the lease and is no longer in possession of the subjects, so that by suing for the outstanding rent he is seeking implement of only one of the obligations incumbent upon the tenant under the lease.[25] In certain subjects he has, in addition, a right in security known as hypothec which he may put in force by the process known as landlord's sequestration.

[14] *Ramsay* v. *Howison*, 1908 S.C. 697. Opinion of Lord Salveson in *Haig* v. *Boswall-Preston, supra.*
[15] *Skene* v. *Cameron*, 1942 S.C. 393.
[16] *Graham* v. *Stevenson* (1792) Hume 781. See *Smith* v. *Henderson* (1897) 24 R. 1102.
[17] *Blair Trust Co.* v. *Gilbert*, 1940 S.L.T. 322; affd., 1941 S.N. 2.
[18] *Mickel* v. *McCoard*, 1913 S.C. 896.
[19] *Whitelaw* v. *Fulton* (1871) 10 M. 27; *Wright* v. *Wightman* (1875) 3 R. 68.
[20] *Baillie* v. *Mackay* (1842) 4 D. 1520.
[21] *Kehoe* v. *Marquis of Lansdowne* [1893] A.C. 451.
[22] *Miller* v. *Stewart* (1899) 2 F. 309.
[23] *Keith* v. *Reid* (1870) 8 M. (H.L.) 110; *Morrison* v. *Forsyth*, 1909 S.C. 329 (clearance sale).
[24] See, for example, *Fry's Metals Ltd.* v. *Durastic Ltd.*, 1991 S.L.T. 689.
[25] *Salaried Staff London Loan Co.* v. *Swears & Wells*, 1985 S.C. 189; 1985 S.L.T. 326.

At common law a general incident of the contract of lease, the landlord's hypothec was abolished in 1880 as to all subjects let for agriculture or pasture and exceeding two acres in extent.[26] It was also excluded, by the House Letting and Rating Act 1911, in all lets to which that Act applied, from all bedding material and all implements of trade used by the occupier or a member of his family, and also from all such furniture as the occupier might select, to the value of £10, according to the sheriff officer's valuation.[27] That Act has, however, now been repealed,[28] and these exclusions no longer apply.[29] In a case where the hypothec has been abolished a landlord has no preference over any other creditor.[30]

It is common in the case of leases of longer duration for the lease to contain a clause providing for the review of rent at regular intervals, such as every five years. A time limit may be set by the clause as to when an application for review of the rent may be made, but as a general rule time will not be treated as of the essence so to bar a late application for review unless there is some special reason for doing so such as an express statement to this effect in the clause.[31] Acceptance of rent without qualification or explanation may be sufficient, however, to imply that the landlord has abandoned and thus waived his right to seek a review.[32]

41.13 Invecta et Illata.—In cases where hypothec still exists, mainly in leases of houses, shops, mines and market gardens, the hypothec covers the ordinary equipment, the furniture in a house, the stock-in-trade in a shop. The subjects covered are known as the *invecta et illata*. At common law, certain items are exempt.[33] The category of exempt items was extended by the Debtors (Scotland) Act 1987:[34] family clothing, tools of trade, medical aids, books, toys, articles reasonably required for the care or upbringing of the children, and certain household furniture and fittings, are all exempt.[35] The hypothec may cover goods brought to

[26] Hypothec Abolition (Scotland) Act 1880. See Rankine, *Leases*, pp. 371–372.
[27] s. 10.
[28] Local Government (Scotland) Act 1973, Sched. 29.
[29] But see now the Debtors (Scotland) Act 1987: para. 41.13, *infra*.
[30] *McGavin* v. *Sturrock's Trs.* (1891) 18 R. 576.
[31] *United Scientific Holdings* v. *Burnley B.C.* [1978] A.C. 904; *Scottish Development Agency* v. *Morrisons Holdings Ltd.*, 1986 S.L.T. 59; *Yates, Petr.*, 1987 S.L.T. 86; *Leeds Permanent Pension Scheme Trs.* v. *William Timpson*, 1987 S.C.L.R. 571; *Legal and Commercial Properties Ltd.* v. *Lothian R.C.*, 1988 S.L.T. 463; 1988 S.C.L.R. 201; *Visionhire Ltd.* v. *Britel Fund Trs. Ltd.*, 1991 S.L.T. 883 (I.H.); 1992 S.C.L.R. 236 (I.H.).
[32] *Banks* v. *Mecca Bookmakers (Scotland)*, 1982 S.C. 7; 1982 S.L.T. 150.
[33] For example, money, bonds, bills and tenant's clothes (Bell, *Prin.*, § 1276); the tenant's tools of trade, by analogy with the law relating to other forms of diligence (*Macpherson* v. *Macpherson's Tr.* (1905) 8 F. 191; Rankine, *Leases* (3rd. ed., p. 374).
[34] (c.18) s. 99, applying ss. 16, 23 and 26 of the 1987 Act to hypothec and sequestration for rent. Note that only articles 'belonging to a debtor' may be exempt in terms of the 1987 Act.
[35] See s. 16; Wilson, *Debt* (2nd ed.), paras. 7.12, 16.3; commentary by D.I. Nichols in *Scottish Current Law Statutes 1987*, Vol. I. The categories in s. 16(2) may be varied by regulations.

the premises, though they do not belong to the tenant, as in the case of hired furniture.[36] It has been held that the hypothec applies whether the whole of the tenant's plenishing, or merely a single article,[37] is obtained on hire or hire-purchase, though not where the subjects are let furnished and an additional article is obtained on hire.[38] It is doubtful whether the right of hypothec over hired furniture is affected by notice given to the landlord before it is placed in the house.[39] Goods in a shop on sale or return present another doubtful case.[40] An agreement between the owner of the article and the tenant to exclude the article from the landlord's hypothec will not be effective against the landlord unless he has been informed of the agreement.[41] Hypothec does not cover goods belonging to the tenant which are on the premises for a purpose merely temporary, such as goods sent to be repaired, or for exhibition.[42] Nor does it cover goods which are the property of a member of the tenant's family, or of a lodger.[43] Goods of a sub-tenant, however, may be sequestrated for the rent due by the principal tenant, and also for the rent due by the sub-tenant himself.[44] If no steps are taken to enforce the hypothec it does not preclude the sale and removal of articles forming part of the *invecta et illata*, but if sequestration is used before an article sold has been removed the landlord's right is preferable to that of the purchaser, even although the property in the thing sold may have passed at the time of the sale.[45] In a sale under sequestration the owner of property attached as *invecta et illata* may insist that the tenant's goods shall be sold first.[46]

41.14 Hypothec: Rents Covered.—Hypothec secures one year's rent, not prior arrears.[47] It falls if not put in force by sequestration within three months of the last term of payment. It is the usual practice to sequestrate for the rent actually due and in security of that to become due at the next term.

The right of a landlord to sequestrate for rent is not affected by the sequestration of the tenant.[48] He is, however, subject to certain preferable claims, which must be met as far as the proceeds of the

[36] *McIntosh* v. *Potts* (1905) 7 F. 765; *Nelmes* v. *Ewing* (1883) 11 R. 193.

[37] *Dundee Corporation* v. *Marr*, 1971 S.C. 96.

[38] *Edinburgh Albert Building Co.* v. *General Guarantee Corporation*, 1917 S.C. 239.

[39] See Rankine, *Leases*, p. 375.

[40] Stewart, *Diligence*, p. 470; Rankine, *Leases*, p. 377.

[41] *Jaffray* v. *Carrick* (1836) 15 S. 43; *Dundee Corporation* v. *Marr, supra.*

[42] *Pulsometer Co.* v. *Gracie* (1887) 14 R. 316.

[43] *Bell* v. *Andrews* (1885) 12 R. 961; *cf.* goods which had been transferred to a third party: *Rossleigh Ltd.* v. *Leader Cars Ltd.*, 1987 S.L.T. 355.

[44] *Steuart* v. *Stables* (1878) 5 R. 1024.

[45] *Ryan* v. *Little*, 1910 S.C. 219.

[46] *McIntosh* v. *Potts* (1905) 7 F. 765; Gordon, *Scottish Land Law*, para. 19–174 and cases therein cited.

[47] *Young* v. *Welsh* (1833) 12 S. 233.

[48] Bankruptcy (Scotland) Act 1985, s. 33(2); nor by the appointment of a receiver: *Grampian Regional Council* v. *Drill Stem (Inspection Services)*, 1994 S.C.L.R. 36 (Sh.Ct).

invecta et illata, when ultimately sold, suffice. Certain preferable claims have been recognised at common law.[49]

41.15 **Sequestration.**—Sequestration for rent is exclusively a sheriff court process.[50] The ordinary course of procedure is that a warrant to sequestrate is granted on an *ex parte* statement, the goods are inventoried and valued by a sheriff officer, and ultimately sold, under a separate warrant from the sheriff, by auction. After they have been inventoried the goods are *in manibus curiae*, and anyone who removes them, be he the tenant, a purchaser, or another creditor, must, if in good faith, account for their value, and, if in bad faith, is liable for the rent.[51]

41.16 **Right of Retention under Hypothec.**—Without applying for sequestration a landlord may interdict the removal of the *invecta et illata*, and, if they have been removed, may obtain a warrant to have them brought back. It has been held that such a warrant should not be pronounced without intimation to the tenant, except for some exceptional reason specified in the judgment.[52] Interdict and recovery of goods constitute exceptional remedies, and the landlord will be liable in damages, either if the statement on which he obtains authority proves untrue,[53] or if there is a genuine dispute as to the rent and the circumstances render extreme measures unnecessary.[54]

41.17 **Rent: Legal and Conventional Terms.**—The terms of payment of rent are usually expressly agreed as between landlord and tenant in the lease. But in a question in the succession of the landlord or, if the landlord sells the subjects let, between him and the purchaser, the allocation of the rents may depend, in agricultural or pastoral leases,[55] on the legal and not on the conventional terms. The legal terms, in farms primarily arable, and where the tenant's entry is at Martinmas, are the Whitsunday and Martinmas[56] following the term of entry. In a pastoral farm, with entry at Whitsunday, the first half-year's rent is legally due at entry, the second at the following Martinmas.[57] The underlying theory is

---

[49] See Gloag and Irvine, *Rights in Security*, pp. 424, 425.

[50] *Duncan* v. *Lodijensky* (1904) 6 F. 408; *cf.* specific provisions that the leave of the sheriff is required before doing diligence for rent in the context of protected, statutory and assured tenancies: s. 110 of the Rent (Scotland) Act 1984, and s. 29 of the Housing (Scotland) Act 1988.

[51] Bell, *Prin.*, § 1244.

[52] *Johnston* v. *Young* (1890) 18 R. (J.) 6; *Jack* v. *Black*, 1911 S.C. 691.

[53] *Jack* v. *Black, supra*; *Shearer* v. *Nicholl*, 1935 S.L.T. 313.

[54] *Gray* v. *Weir* (1891) 19 R. 25.

[55] These rules do not apply to the rents of residential property, which accrue *de die in diem*: *Butter* v. *Foster*, 1912 S.C. 1218.

[56] In terms of the Term and Quarter Days (Scotland) Act 1990, Whitsunday and Martinmas signify May 28 and November 28 respectively, unless otherwise defined in the lease: see *Provincial Insurance plc* v. *Valtos Ltd.*, 1992 S.C.L.R. 203 (Sh.Ct.).

[57] See opinion of Lord Johnstone in *Butter, supra*, at p. 1224; *Baillie* v. *Fletcher*, 1915 S.C. 677.

that rent is not due legally (though it may be conventionally) until the tenant has had the benefit of the crop. Rents conventionally payable before the legal term are known as forehand; payable later, as backhand. The legal terms rule in allocating rents between the heir of a landlord and his executor, and also between a fiar and the representatives of the liferenter, except when the rent is forehand, when the conventional terms rule. The executor is entitled to all backhand rents which were legally due for the term preceding the landlord's death, and also, under the Apportionment Act 1870, to a share of the next term's rent corresponding to the number of days by which the deceased survived that term.[58] In the case of a sale, in the absence of any express provision, the purchaser is entitled to the rents to become due for the possession following his term of entry, according to the legal and not the conventional terms, except in the case of forehand rents, in which case he is entitled to the rents payable at the conventional terms following the term of entry.[59]

41.18 Assignability: Subletting.—A lease may or may not be assignable. Where there is no express provision in the lease an exclusion of the power to assign or sublet will be implied at common law in accordance with the principle of *delectus personae*, subject to certain exceptions. Judicial or legal assignees are not excluded. Leases of unfurnished urban subjects, in town or country, may be assigned, for here the element of *delectus personae* is less strong.[60] Leases of rural subjects may also be assigned where they are for an extraordinary duration, on the basis that such a lease amounts in effect to a right of property.[61] Rural leases of ordinary duration, however, *i.e.* farm leases whether arable or pastoral, leases of shootings and fishings, are according to the general rule, not assignable.[62] Subletting follows the same rules.[63] A provision (once common in mining leases) that the tenant shall not assign without the landlord's consent gives the landlord an absolute right to refuse, or to impose conditions.[64] A clause frequently used provides that the landlord's consent to assignation should not be unreasonably withheld.[65]

---

[58] *Campbell* v. *Campbell* (1849) 11 D. 1426; *Balfour-Kinnear* v. *Inland Revenue*, 1909 S.C. 619.

[59] Titles to Land Consolidation Act 1868, s. 8; *Baillie* v. *Fletcher*, 1915 S.C. 677.

[60] *Robb* v. *Brearton* (1895) 22 R. 885; Rankine, *Leases*, p. 175.

[61] Rankine, *Leases*, p. 173; *Bain* v. *Mackenzie* (1896) 23 R. 528, at 532, *per* Lord Kinnear.

[62] Bell, *Prin*, § 1214; *Mackintosh* v. *May* (1895) 22 R. 345.

[63] Bell, *Prin.*, § 1216; Gordon, *Scottish Land Law*, para. 19–32 *et seq.*

[64] *Marquis of Breadalbane* v. *Whitehead* (1893) 21 R. 138; *Lousada & Co. Ltd.* v. *J.E. Lesser (Properties) Ltd.*, 1990 S.C. 178; 1990 S.L.T. 823 (suspensive condition). See, however, as to discrimination by withholding consent on grounds of sex or race, Sex Discrimination Act 1975, ss. 31–32; Race Relations Act 1976, s. 24.

[65] See, for example, *Renfrew D.C.* v. *A.B. Leisure (Renfrew) Ltd.*, 1988 S.L.T. 635; 1988 S.C.L.R. 512; sequel in 1990 S.C.L.R. 375; *Brador Properties Ltd.* v. *British Telecommunications plc*, 1992 S.C. 12; and Gordon, *Scottish Land Law*, para. 19–27.

Prior to the Land Tenure Reform (Scotland) Act 1974 a proprietor who had granted a lease to a tenant could not interpose another party as tenant so as to degrade the first lessee into the position of a sub-tenant.[66] It is, however, now competent, and deemed always to have been competent, for a lessor during the subsistence of the lease to grant a lease of or including his interest in the whole or part of the land already let, whether for a longer or shorter period or for the same duration as the lease already granted.[67] Such a grant is now effectual for all purposes as a lease of land.

41.19 Effects of Assignation.—The assignation of a lease is completed, in questions between the landlord, the tenant and the assignee, by intimation to the landlord.[68] While a sub-lease involves no change of tenant so far as the landlord is concerned and the original tenant continues bound to implement the obligations of the lease, an assignation involves the substitution of the assignee as the sole tenant. The result is that the cedent disappears and has no further rights or obligations after the date of entry, while the assignee incurs liability to the landlord for all future rents, and also probably for arrears.[69] There is no rule to preclude the assignation of an unprofitable lease, if assignable, to a person of no means. A sub-let, on the other hand, does not bring the sub-tenant into any contractual relations with the landlord, does not involve him in any liability for rent, or affect the liability of the tenant.[70] In questions in the bankruptcy of a tenant an assignation, though followed by intimation to the landlord, does not complete the right of the assignee in a question with the trustee in the sequestration. For that, actual possession is required,[71] unless the lease is registered under the Registration of Leases (Scotland) Act 1857, in which case the assignation may be effectually completed by registration in the forms provided by the Act.[72]

41.20 Transfer of Tenancy of Matrimonial Home.—Prior to 1981 a lease of premises occupied by a husband and wife as their matrimonial home which had been granted in favour of one spouse gave no right of occupation to the other spouse. The Matrimonial Homes (Family

[66] *Wilson* v. *Wilson* (1859) 21 D. 309, *per* Lord Justice-Clerk Inglis at p.312.
[67] 1974 Act, s.17.
[68] *Inglis* v. *Paul* (1829) 7 S. 469; and see *Smith* v. *Place D'Or 101 Ltd.*, 1988 S.L.T. (Sh.Ct.) 5 (circumstances in which held that delivery of a formal deed of assignation was not necessary in addition to intimation to render the assignation effective).
[69] *Skene* v. *Greenhill* (1825) 4 S. 25; *Burns* v. *Martin* (1887) 14 R. (H.L.) 20, opinion of Lord Watson.
[70] Bell, *Prin.*, § 1252. As to possible endurance of sub-lessee's right of possession beyond termination of head lease, see Gordon, *Scottish Land Law*, para. 19–34.
[71] *Ramsay* v. *Commercial Bank* (1842) 4 D. 405.
[72] ss. 2, 16, as amended by the Land Tenure Reform (Scotland) Act 1974, Sched. 6; see para. 41.4, *supra*.

Protection) (Scotland) Act 1981[73] however, introduced an important change in the law as to the rights of occupancy of spouses[74] in the matrimonial home. A spouse who is neither the owner nor the tenant of it now has the right, if in occupation, to continue to occupy the matrimonial home and, if not in occupation, to enter into and take occupation of it.[75] In addition the Act contains a provision which enables the court to make an order transferring the tenancy of the matrimonial home from one spouse to the other.[76] The effect of such an order is to vest the tenancy in the other spouse without intimation to the landlord, subject to all the liabilities under the lease other than for any arrears of rent for the period prior to the making of the order which remain the liability of the spouse who was originally entitled to the house.[77] Where both spouses are joint or common tenants of the matrimonial home the court may, on the application of one of them, make an order vesting the tenancy in that spouse solely, subject to the payment by the applicant to the other spouse of such compensation as seems just and reasonable.[78] Some protection for the interests of the landlord is afforded by the fact that the court is required to have regard to the suitability of the applicant to become the tenant or sole tenant of the house as the case may be and to his or her capacity to perform the obligations under the lease.[79] A copy of the application must also be served on the landlord and the court must give him an opportunity of being heard by it before making an order transferring the lease.[80] Certain types of lease are excluded from this procedure altogether.[81] It is not competent for an application to be made where the matrimonial home is or is part of an agricultural holding or is let under a long lease. Nor is it competent where the premises are let to the spouse by his or her employer as an incident of employment and the lease is subject to a requirement that the spouse must reside therein, or if the spouses are joint or common tenants that they must both reside there. There are exceptions also in the case of premises which are on or pertain to a croft or the subject of a cottar or the holding of a landholder or statutory small tenant or are part of the tenancy land of a tenant-at-will, but these do not apply where both spouses are joint or common tenants of the matrimonial home. Other methods whereby a tenancy may be transferred from one spouse to another remain competent, but the advantage of the statutory procedure is that an order for transfer may

---

[73] As amended by the Law Reform (Misc. Provs.) (Scotland) Act 1985, s. 13.

[74] As to cohabiting couples, see s. 18 of the 1981 Act.

[75] s. 1. The spouse's rights to continue occupying or to enter and occupy include the right to do so together with any child of the family: s. 1(1A).

[76] s. 13, as amended by the Family Law (Scotland) Act 1985 (c.37), Sched. 1.

[77] s. 13(5).

[78] s. 13(9).

[79] s. 13(3).

[80] s. 13(4).

[81] See ss. 13(7) and (10).

be obtained irrespective of whether the other spouse or the landlord is willing to consent to it.

41.21 Sale by Landlord.—When lands subject to a lease are sold, the original landlord, and his executors after his death, remain liable on all obligations which do not transmit against the purchaser.[82] Whether he remains liable on obligations which do transmit is not fully settled, but the law probably is that he remains liable on all obligations to pay money, such as an obligation to pay for improvements executed by the tenant, but that the purchaser alone is liable for upkeep and repairs.[83]

41.22 Bankruptcy of Tenant.—Except under an express provision, bankruptcy of the tenant does not put an end to the lease.[84] Whether a lease is assignable voluntarily or not it will pass, in the absence of an express provision to the contrary, to the trustee in sequestration of the tenant.[85] The trustee is never bound to adopt the lease. If he does, he incurs personal liability not only for the rent, but for arrears.[86] He is entitled to a reasonable time to consider the question, and temporary intromissions with the subjects, for the purpose of realising the bankrupt's effects, will not readily be construed as precluding ultimate rejection.[87] A conventional exclusion of the right of a trustee in sequestration is construed as giving the landlord an option to refuse, and cannot be founded on by the bankrupt.[88]

41.23 Succession to Tenant.—Prior to the assimilation of heritable and moveable succession by the Succession (Scotland) Act 1964,[89] a lease was heritable in the succession to a deceased tenant, and vested on his intestacy in his heir-at-law. It now vests in the tenant's executor by virtue of the confirmation,[90] and the right to succeed, unless carried by a destination in the lease[91] or by a valid testamentary bequest, passes to his heirs in intestacy. To avoid cases where, because the deceased tenant has made no valid bequest of the lease or it has not been accepted by the legatee, a lease might otherwise require to be divided among several of the heirs in intestacy, the Act extended to the executor a limited power to assign the lease; this power may be exercised notwithstanding

---

[82] *Gardiner* v. *Stewart's Trs.*, 1908 S.C. 985; *Riddell's Exrs.* v. *Milligan's Exrs.*, 1909 S.C. 1137. As to sales by public sector landlords, see Pt. III of the Housing (Scotland) Act 1988.

[83] *Walker* v. *Masson* (1857) 19 D. 1099.

[84] *Dobie* v. *Marquis of Lothian* (1864) 2 M. 788; Rankine, *Leases*, p. 693.

[85] Bell, *Prin.*, § 1216. As to the trustee's right to dispose of growing crops, see *McKinley* v. *Hutchinson's Tr.*, 1935 S.L.T. 62.

[86] *Dundas* v. *Morison* (1857) 20 D. 225.

[87] *McGavin* v. *Sturrock's Tr.* (1891) 18 R. 576.

[88] *Dobie* v. *Marquis of Lothian* (1864) 2 M. 788.

[89] s. 1.

[90] ss. 14, 36(2); see *Cormack* v. *McIldowie's Exrs.*, 1975 S.C. 161; 1975 S.L.T. 214.

[91] See Gordon, *Scottish Land Law*, para. 19–39.

a prohibition of assignation in the lease, whether this be express or implied.[92] He may transfer the lease under this statutory power to any one of the deceased's heirs in intestacy,[93] or in or towards the satisfaction of a claim by a person entitled to legal or prior rights out of the deceased's estate; but, where he has to rely on this power, he may not transfer the lease to anyone else without the consent of the landlord. The power must be exercised within a period of one year, or such longer period as may be fixed by agreement or failing agreement by the sheriff on summary application by the executor.[94] Failure to obtain confirmation to the deceased tenant's interest and to transfer it within that period will result in termination of the lease.[95] As a gratuitous trustee the executor is subject to the common law prohibition against acting as *auctor in rem suam*, and if he transfers the lease to himself he will be liable to the consequences in law of breach of that prohibition.[96]

Unless the lease could be assigned *inter vivos* the tenant had no power at common law to bequeath his lease so as to compel the landlord to accept his legatee,[97] although if the landlord accepts the legatee as tenant the bequest will be effective.[98] The 1964 Act, however, conferred on the tenant a limited right of bequest in cases where a prohibition of assignation was merely implied. Provided there is no express prohibition, the tenant may validly bequeath the lease to any one of the persons who would have been entitled to succeed to it as his intestate heirs.[99] A slightly wider right of bequest was afforded by the Agricultural Holdings and Crofters Acts, which is unaffected by this provision of the 1964 Act.[1] In the case of dwelling-houses which are subject to the Rent Acts certain persons are entitled to succeed to the lease to the extent of remaining in the house by virtue of the Acts on the death of the tenant, independently of any rights at common law. One transmission of the right to remain in occupation may occur; thereafter, in the case of a contractual tenancy, the normal law of succession will operate.[2]

41.24   Termination: Notice.—A lease comes to an end if either party gives notice within a certain period before the term fixed for its expiry. Such

---

[92] ss. 16(1), (2).
[93] *MacLean* v. *MacLean*, 1988 S.L.T. 626.
[94] s. 16(3).
[95] *Lord Rotherwick's Trs.* v. *Hope*, 1975 S.L.T. 187; *Morrison-Low* v. *Paterson*, 1985 S.C. (H.L.) 49; 1985 S.L.T. 255, *per* Lord Keith of Kinkel.
[96] *Inglis* v. *Inglis*, 1983 S.C. 8; 1983 S.L.T. 437; *cf.* para. 46.12, *infra*.
[97] See Hunter, *Landlord and Tenant*, i, p. 237; *Bain* v. *Mackenzie* (1896) 23 R. 528; *Reid's Trs.* v. *Macpherson*, 1975 S.L.T. 101.
[98] *Kennedy* v. *Johnstone*, 1956 S.C. 39, *per* Lord Sorn at p. 47.
[99] s. 29(1).
[1] s. 29(2); see, generally, Gordon, *Scottish Land Law*, para. 19–42 *et seq.*
[2] See *infra*, para. 41.52.

notice is necessary because in its absence the relationship of landlord and tenant is continued by tacit relocation.[3] The lease is then renewed, not for the original term but for a year, and from year to year thereafter. The legal effect of tacit relocation is that all the stipulations and conditions of the original contract remain in force, so far as these are consistent with a lease from year to year; an option to renew a lease for a longer period will not be exercisable during tacit relocation.[4] In the case of an urban lease, verbal notice within the necessary period by either party of intention to terminate the contract is sufficient to prevent the setting in of tacit relocation.[5] Where there are joint tenants, to exclude tacit relocation, a notice of removal by one of them will be enough.[6] If, having served notice to quit, the landlord continues regularly and without reservation to accept rent from the tenant he may be held to have departed from the notice or to be barred from insisting on it, so that a new lease will arise by tacit relocation.[7] If on the expiry of the contractual term the tenant remains in possession after notice to quit, he is in the position of an intruder without title, and may be liable for violent profits.[8] The landlord's remedy in order to recover possession from the tenant is to raise an action of removing against him.[9]

In order to be effective, the landlord's notice to quit, or the tenant's notice of removal, must be served so as to give due notice to the other party. The period of notice required is laid down by statute and varies according to the type of lease. The leading provisions may be summarised as follows:[10]

  (a) in the case of lands exceeding two acres in extent, written notice must be given, failing an agreement to the contrary, not less than one or more than two years before the ish;[11] where the lease is from year to year, however, or for any other period less than three years, the minimum period is six

[3] See para. 14.22, *supra*; unless the lease expressly excludes tacit relocation; *MacDougall* v. *Guidi*, 1992 S.C.L.R. 167 (Sh.Ct.). Note also A.G.M. Duncan, 'Tacit Relocation in Leases,' 1978 S.L.T. (News) 157.
[4] *Commercial Union Assurance Co.*, 1964 S.C. 84; 1964 S.L.T. 62.
[5] See Rankine, *Leases*, p. 574; *Craighall Cast Stone Co.* v. *Wood Bros.*, 1931 S.C. 66.
[6] *Smith* v. *Grayton Estates*, 1960 S.C. 349.
[7] See Gloag, *Contract*, p. 735; *Milner's C.B.* v. *Mason*, 1965 S.L.T. (Sh.Ct.) 56.
[8] See para. 14.22, *supra*. For an example of an ejection and caution for violent profits, see *Middleton* v. *Booth*, 1986 S.L.T. 450; and for an action of removing and caution for violent profits, see *Imperial Hotel (Glasgow) Ltd.* v. *Brown*, 1990 S.C.L.R. 86 (Sh.Ct.).
[9] For procedure in actions of removing, see Sheriff Courts (Scotland) Act 1907, Sched. 1 (as amended), rr. 34.5–34.10 (formerly rr. 103–107); such actions are subject to the summary cause procedure: Sheriff Courts (Scotland) Act 1971, s. 35 as amended by the Law Reform (Misc. Provs.) (Scotland) Act 1985, s. 18 and Sched. 2. Note the special provisions for the protection of agricultural employees and their families occupying tied houses in Rent (Scotland) Act 1984, s. 24.
[10] See, for a full statement, Paton and Cameron, *Landlord and Tenant*, pp. 262 *et seq.*
[11] 1907 Act, s. 34(*a*).

months.[12] Where the lease is one of agricultural or pastoral land and falls within the Agricultural Holdings Act the period of notice, of not less than one or more than two years, is fixed by law and cannot be varied by agreement; this period applies in all cases, including leases from year to year, except where the lease is for a period of less than year to year.[13]

(b)   in the case of houses or land not exceeding two acres in extent, fishings and shootings, the period of notice prescribed, unless otherwise agreed, is a minimum of 40 days before May 15 or November 11[14] according to the term at which the tenancy is to end;[15] where the subjects are let for a period not exceeding four months the period of notice must be one third of the full duration of the lease.[16] These requirements are reinforced by a general provision with regard to dwelling-houses now contained in the Rent (Scotland) Act 1984,[17] which cannot be varied by agreement, that a minimum of four weeks' notice must be given in all cases where a notice to quit is required. The notice must be given four weeks before the date when it is to take effect, which means that the period of notice should be calculated with reference to the date of the ish.[18]

In the case of leased premises in respect of which a closing order or the like has been made, either the landlord or the tenant may apply to the sheriff for an order determining the lease.[19]

If an executor, to whom a lease has devolved in intestacy, is satisfied that he cannot dispose of the lease according to law or has in fact not done so within a period of one year from the date of the deceased tenant's death, or such longer period as may be fixed by agreement or failing agreement by the sheriff on summary application by the executor, he or the landlord may, by giving due notice, terminate the lease altogether.[20] An application by executors for an extension of the one

[12] 1907 Act, s. 34(b).

[13] Agricultural Holdings (Scotland) Act 1991, s. 21; see *Kildrummy (Jersey) Ltd.* v. *Calder*, 1994 S.L.T. 888; and also para. 41.30 *infra*.

[14] *Quaere* whether s. 1(2)(a) of the Term and Quarter Days (Scotland) Act 1990 affects s. 37 of the Sheriff Courts (Scotland) Act 1907.

[15] Sheriff Courts (Scotland) Act 1907, s. 37, but see *MacDougall* v. *Guidi*, 1992 S.C.L.R. 167 (Sh.Ct.) where 40 days' notice held unnecessary in a lease which expressly excluded tacit relocation; note that, under s. 38, notice to quit is obligatory, where the lease is for a period less than one year, only in the absence of express stipulation. See also Removal Terms (Scotland) Act 1886, s. 4, and note the effect of the Term and Quarter Days (Scotland) Act 1990, particularly s. 1(2)(a).

[16] 1907 Act, s. 38, and 1886 Act, s. 5, both as amended by Rent (Scotland) Act 1971, Sched. 18, Pt. II.

[17] s. 112; see *Schnabel* v. *Allard* [1967] 1 Q.B. 627.

[18] *Hamilton D.C.* v. *Maguire*, 1983 S.L.T. (Sh.Ct.) 76.

[19] Housing (Scotland) Act 1987, s. 322.

[20] Succession (Scotland) Act 1964, ss. 16(3), (4).

year period was held to be incompetent when it was not made until after one year after the deceased tenant's death, notice of termination of the lease having been given in the meantime by the landlord.[21]

41.25 Termination: Irritancies.—Although a lease is normally terminated by a notice to quit or of removal, it may also be brought to an end before the date of its natural expiration by the destruction of the subjects,[22] or their acquisition in whole or part by a third party acting under compulsory powers,[23] or because there is no one left who can claim to be a tenant, as where a lease was granted in favour of a partnership and the partnership has been dissolved by death.[24] The lease itself may contain provisions for its premature termination, known as breaks, in favour of either party or both, that in the option of the tenant being a power to renounce and that in favour of the landlord being a power to resume.[25] A power in favour of the landlord to resume for planting woodlands is common in agricultural leases.[26] The landlord may also consent to a renunciation of the subjects by the tenant before the ish.

A lease may also be terminated before the date of its natural expiration by the enforcement of an irritancy,[27] legal or conventional, in which case the tenant's right to occupy the subjects will be forfeited or annulled.[28] The legal irritancies relate solely to non-payment of rent. An irritancy is recognised at common law, and enforceable only by an extraordinary action of removing in the Court of Session, in all cases where two years' rent is unpaid.[29] There is no other legal irritancy in urban subjects. In subjects falling under the Agricultural Holdings Act 1991, where six months' rent is due and unpaid, the landlord may raise an action in the sheriff court concluding for the removal of the tenant at

[21] *Gifford* v. *Buchanan*, 1983 S.L.T. 613.
[22] *Duff* v. *Fleming* (1870) 8 M. 769; *Cantors Properties (Scotland)* v. *Swears & Wells*, 1978 S.C. 310.
[23] *Mackeson* v. *Boyd*, 1942 S.C. 56.
[24] *Inland Revenue* v. *Graham's Trs.*, 1971 S.C. (H.L.) 1; *Jardine-Paterson* v. *Fraser*, 1974 S.L.T. 93.
[25] Rankine, *Leases*, p. 527; Paton & Cameron, *Landlord and Tenant*, p. 242.
[26] *Sykes and Edgar*, 1974 S.L.T. (Land Ct.) 4; *Fothringham* v. *Fothringham*, 1987 S.L.T. (Land Ct.) 10; and see para. 41.30, *infra*.
[27] The word 'irritancy' means forfeiture: see *Dorchester Studios (Glasgow)* v. *Stone*, 1975 S.C. (H.L.) 56, *per* Lord Fraser of Tullybelton at p. 74. As to procedure and content of notice of irritancy, see *C.I.N. Properties Ltd.* v. *Dollar Land (Cumbernauld) Ltd.*, 1992 S.C. (H.L.) 104; 1992 S.L.T. 669. Note that where one landlord has disponed the property to another, assignation of the notice of irritancy may be required: *Life Association of Scotland* v. *Blacks Leisure Group*, 1989 S.L.T. 674.
[28] Where a tenant remains in bona fide possession after the irritancy, he may be liable to pay a reasonable rent: *H.M.V. Fields Properties Ltd.* v. *Skirt n' Slack Centre of London Ltd.*, 1986 S.C. 114; 1987 S.L.T. 2. If payment is offered after the irritancy, a landlord should take care to avoid acts amounting to either waiver of the notice of irritancy, or oppression: *H.M.V. Fields Properties Ltd.* v. *Bracken Self Selection Fabrics Ltd.*, 1991 S.L.T. 31; 1990 S.C.L.R. 677; *C.I.N. Properties Ltd.* v. *Dollar Land (Cumbernauld) Ltd.*, 1992 S.L.T. 211 (I.H.).
[29] Erskine, II, vi, 44. As to the construction of irritancies, see para. 13.19, *supra*.

the next term of Whitsunday or Martinmas.[30] Conventional irritancies[31] are unlimited in number and may be used to underwrite a variety of obligations; usually they cover non-payment of rent and the various forms of insolvency. A landlord who enforces an irritancy cannot also claim damages for the premature determination of the lease.[32] Whatever may be the terms in which a conventional irritancy is expressed, it is construed as giving the landlord an option to avoid the lease, not as giving the defaulting tenant a right to abandon it.[33]

Legal irritancies may be purged at any time before decree is pronounced. The common law rule was that conventional irritancies could not be purged unless they merely expressed the irritancy which the law would infer. Once incurred they were strictly enforced,[34] and while power was reserved to the court to prevent oppressive use or abuse of the irritancy[35] the circumstances in which this could be exercised were so closely defined as to provide the tenant with no relief if it was his own inadvertence which led to the irritancy being incurred.[36] The position as regards conventional irritancies has now been modified by the Law Reform (Miscellaneous Provisions) (Scotland) Act 1985.[37] A distinction is drawn for this purpose between pecuniary obligations on the one hand and non-pecuniary obligations and changes in the tenant's circumstances on the other. The landlord is not entitled to rely on a provision for irritancy in the event of the tenant's failure to pay rent or make any other payment on or before the due date or within a stipulated period unless he has served a notice on the tenant after the date when the payment became due requiring him to make payment of the sum which he has failed to pay together with interest within the period, being not less than 14 days, which is specified in the notice and stating that if he does not do so the lease may be terminated.[38] If the tenant fails to make payment within the specified

[30] 1991 Act, s. 20: in terms of the Term and Quarter Days (Scotland) Act 1990, Whitsunday and Martinmas signify May 28 and November 28 respectively, unless the lease provides otherwise; see *Provincial Insurance plc* v. *Valtos Ltd.*, 1992 S.C.L.R. 203 (Sh.Ct.).

[31] As to purging of conventional irritancies, see *McDouall's Trs.* v. *MacLeod*, 1949 S.C. 593.

[32] *Buttercase* v. *Geddie* (1897) 24 R. 1128; *H.M.V. Fields Properties Ltd.* v. *Skirt n' Slack Centre of London Ltd.*, 1986 S.C. 114; 1987 S.L.T. 2.

[33] *Bidoulac* v. *Sinclair's Tr.* (1889) 17 R. 144.

[34] Note however the limited protection where the lease is vested in an executor: Succession (Scotland) Act 1964, s. 16(7).

[35] See *Lucas's Exrs.* v. *Demarco*, 1968 S.L.T. 89; *C.I.N. Properties Ltd.* v. *Dollar Land (Cumbernauld) Ltd.*, 1992 S.C. (H.L.) 104; 1992 S.L.T. 669.

[36] *Dorchester Studios (Glasgow)* v. *Stone*, 1975 (H.L.) 56; *H.M.V. Fields Properties* v. *Skirt n' Slack Centre of London*, 1982 S.L.T. 477; 1987 S.L.T. 2; *H.M.V. Fields Properties* v. *Tandem Shoes*, 1983 S.L.T. 114.

[37] ss. 4–7. The 1985 Act came into force on October 30, 1985, and applies to all leases, whether entered into before or after the Act, except leases of land used wholly or mainly for residential purposes; agricultural holdings; and holdings of crofter, cottars, small landholders or statutory small tenants, in which cases there is other protection for tenants. It is impossible to contract out of the 1985 Act: s. 6(1).

[38] s. 4.

time limit the irritancy is no longer purgeable and the strict rules of the common law apply.[39] So far as the non-pecuniary obligations and changes in the tenants' circumstances such as liquidation or insolvency are concerned, the landlord is not entitled to rely on a provision for irritancy in that event if in all the circumstances of the case a fair and reasonable landlord would not seek to do so, regard being had to whether a reasonable opportunity has been afforded to the tenant to remedy the breach if it was capable of being remedied within reasonable time.[40]

41.26   Ground Game.—An agricultural tenant, if there is no stipulation to the contrary in his lease, may kill rabbits, and may authorise anyone else to do so.[41] Under the Ground Game Act 1880, an occupier of land has the right, declared to be 'incident to and inseparable from his occupation of the land,' and of which he cannot deprive himself by any contract,[42] to kill hares and rabbits. This right may be exercised by the occupier himself, or, with his authority in writing, by members of his household resident on the land, persons in his ordinary employment, and one other person bona fide employed for reward;[43] the occupier and the owner or any other person having the right to kill or take game on the land may make an agreement for the joint execution, or the execution for their joint benefit, of that right otherwise than by the use of firearms.[44] Only the occupier and one other person authorised in writing may use firearms,[45] except where authorisation of additional persons is sanctioned by the Secretary of State.[46] There are limitations as to the period of the year during which the occupier's right to kill ground game with firearms may be exercised.[47] It is a criminal offence for anyone to use firearms for the purpose of killing ground game between the expiration of the first hour after sunset, and the commencement of the last hour before sunrise, or to employ poison.[48] The use of spring traps is closely regulated, and it is an offence to use traps other than those approved, or to use them in an unapproved manner, or, except under licence, to use them elsewhere than in a rabbit hole.[49]

---

[39] *C.I.N. Properties Ltd.* v. *Dollar Land (Cumbernauld) Ltd.*, 1992 S.C. (H.L.) 104; 1992 S.L.T. 669.

[40] s. 5; and see dicta of Lord Justice-Clerk Ross in the Inner House in *C.I.N. Properties Ltd.* v. *Dollar Land (Cumbernauld) Ltd.*, 1992 S.L.T. 211, and in the House of Lords, Lord Jauncey (common law rules and oppression); see also *Blythswood Investments (Scotland) Ltd.* v. *Clydesdale Electrical Stores Ltd. (in receivership)*, 1995 S.L.T. 150 ("fair and reasonable landlord").

[41] *Crawshay* v. *Duncan*, 1915 S.C. (J.) 64.

[42] 1880 Act, s. 3; *Sherrard* v. *Gascoigne* [1900] 2 Q.B. 279.

[43] s. 1; *Stuart* v. *Murray* (1884) 12 R. (J.) 9; *Niven* v. *Renton* (1888) 15 R. (J.) 42.

[44] Agriculture (Scotland) Act 1948, s. 48(4).

[45] 1880 Act, s. 1(1)(a).

[46] See 1948 Act, s. 48(2); Pests Act 1954.

[47] 1880 Act, s. 1(3), as amended by 1948 Act, s. 48(1).

[48] Hares (Scotland) Act 1848, s. 4; 1880 Act, s. 6, as amended by Pests Act 1954.

[49] 1948 Act, s. 50, as amended by Pests Act 1954, s. 10.

II. AGRICULTURAL HOLDINGS[50]

41.27 Agricultural Holdings Acts.—At common law a tenant who made improvements on the subjects let had no claim for compensation against the landlord, the legal presumption being that he made the improvements in the hope of recouping himself during the remaining years of the lease.[51] While this remains the law in urban leases, a series of statutes have introduced a right to compensation in the case of agricultural holdings with the object of encouraging the tenant to farm well and to make the necessary improvements to his holding. The code relating to agricultural holdings is contained principally in the Agricultural Holdings (Scotland) Act 1991,[52] although the rules of good husbandry and good estate management are still to be found in the Agriculture (Scotland) Act 1948. The 1991 Act was a consolidating measure, and decisions under earlier enactments[53] remain of importance. Besides conferring on the tenant important compensation rights, the legislation has afforded him substantial security of tenure and regulates closely the rights and obligations of each party under the lease. The Act recognises only one type of tenant, that is, the tenant entitled to claim the benefit of the statutory provisions in favour of agricultural tenants;[54] and contracting out of the statutory provisions is widely prohibited.[55]

41.28 Agricultural Holding: Meaning.—The 1991 Act defines the term 'agricultural holding' as 'the aggregate of the agricultural land comprised in a lease, not being a lease under which the land is let to the tenant during his continuance in any office, appointment or employment held under the landlord.'[56] 'Agricultural land' is itself defined[57] as meaning 'land used for agriculture for the purposes of a trade or business' including any other land which may be designated as agricultural land by the Secretary of State under the 1948 Act.[58] The definition of the word 'agriculture' in the 1991 Act is comprehensive and covers every kind of

---

[50] See Gill, *Law of Agricultural Holdings in Scotland* (2nd ed., 1990); annotations to the 1991 Act by A.G.M. Duncan in *Scottish Current Law Statutes*, 1991, Vol. 3; and article by A.G.M. Duncan, 'The Agricultural Holdings (Scotland) Act 1991,' 1992 S.L.T. (News) 1. For a convenient statement of the current legislation, see *Parliament House Book*, Division L.

[51] *Walker* v. *McKnight* (1886) 13 R. 599.

[52] (c.55). The Act came into force on September 25, 1991.

[53] Esp. Agricultural Holdings (Scotland) Act 1923; Smallholders and Agricultural Holdings (Scotland) Act 1931; Agriculture (Scotland) Act 1948; Agricultural Holdings (Scotland) Act 1949, as amended by the Agriculture Act 1958, the Agriculture (Miscellaneous Provisions) Acts 1968 and 1976, and the Agricultural Holdings (Amendment) (Scotland) Act 1983.

[54] *cf. Dalgety's Trs.* v. *Drummond*, 1938 S.C. 709.

[55] *e.g.* ss. 3, 48 and 53 of the 1991 Act.

[56] s. 1(1).

[57] s. 1(2).

[58] Under s. 86(1) of the 1948 Act.

horticultural and farming activity.[59] 'Lease' is defined as meaning 'a letting of land for a term of years, or for lives, or for lives and years, or from year to year.'[60]

41.29 **Incidents of Lease.**—*Minimum Term.*— The Act contains a general restriction on letting agricultural land for less than from year to year; unless the lease was entered into for grazing or mowing only for a specified period of the year, or was granted by a person who is himself a tenant for a shorter period than from year to year, such a lease, in the absence of the prior approval of the Secretary of State, will be treated, with the necessary modifications, as if it were a lease from year to year.[61] When the ish is reached the lease is held to be continued in force from year to year by tacit relocation until notice to terminate is given by either party.[62]

Written Lease.—Where there is no written lease[63] embodying the terms of a tenancy, either party may require the other to enter into a written agreement for this purpose.[64] Where a written lease has been entered into but it does not contain any one or more of the matters specified in Schedule 1[65] to the 1991 Act or is inconsistent with it or with the provisions of section 5 as to the liability for the maintenance of fixed equipment, a similar request may be made.[66] If parties are unable to agree the matter may be referred to arbitration.

Liability for Maintenance.—The Act deems[67] the incorporation in every lease of an undertaking by the landlord to put the fixed equipment on the holding into a thorough state of repair, and to provide

[59] s. 85(1) of the 1991 Act.

[60] s. 85(1); see *Stirrat* v. *Whyte*, 1967 S.C. 265, for an example of a let which was held not to be a lease within the meaning of this definition. See also *Morrison-Low* v. *Paterson*, 1985 S.C. (H.L.) 49; 1985 S.L.T. 255, in which it was held that evidence of actings was sufficient to justify the inference that a lease had been granted for not more than a year and thus from year to year for the purposes of the Act; *Pickard* v. *Ritchie*, 1986 S.L.T. 466 (averments of actings insufficient to support inference of a lease); *Strachan* v. *Robertson-Coupar*, 1989 S.L.T. 488 (an arrangement not amounting to a lease); *Dickson* v. *MacGregor*, 1992 S.L.T. (Land Ct.) 83 (complications arising from formation of a limited partnership); *Commercial Components (U.K.) Ltd.* v. *Young*, 1993 S.L.T. (Sh.Ct.) 15 (facts and circumstances not capable of supporting inference of lease).

[61] s. 2; see *Gairneybridge Farm and King*, 1974 S.L.T. (Land Ct.) 8; *N.C.B.* v. *Drysdale*, 1989 S.C. 217; 1989 S.L.T. 825.

[62] s. 3; see *Smith* v. *Grayton Estates*, 1960 S.C. 349; *Morrison* v. *Rendall*, 1986 S.C. 69, dicta at p. 73 (also *sub nom. Morrison's Exrs.* v. *Rendall*, 1986 S.L.T. 227, dicta at p. 230G-H).

[63] As to meaning of 'lease in writing,' see *Grieve* v. *Barr*, 1954 S.C. 414.

[64] 1991 Act, s. 4(1)(*a*).

[65] These matters are: (i) the names of the parties, (ii) particulars of the holding, with reference to a map or plan, (iii) the term of the lease, (iv) the rent and the dates on which payable, (v) certain undertakings by the parties relating to damage to buildings and the destruction of harvested crops.

[66] 1991 Act, s. 4(1)(*b*).

[67] *Ibid.*, s. 5.

the necessary buildings and other equipment. The landlord is also bound
to make such replacement or renewal as may be rendered necessary by
natural decay or by fair wear and tear. The tenant's liability is limited to
an undertaking to maintain the equipment in a state of good repair, fair
wear and tear excepted.

Variation of Rent.—The Act enables either party to seek a variation
of the contractual rent; he may serve a written demand on the other
party for a reference of the matter to arbitration.[68] The rent properly
payable in respect of the holding for this purpose is normally the rent at
which, having regard to the terms of the lease but not to the personal
circumstances of the tenant,[69] the holding might reasonably be expected
to be let in the open market.[70] But the arbiter is directed to take
account of certain other factors in arriving at the appropriate rent if he
considers that the evidence available to him is insufficient to enable him
to determine the open market rent or if the open market for rents for
comparable subjects in the surrounding area is distorted by scarcity of
lets or other factors.[71] The award of an arbiter who has been appointed
by the Secretary of State or by the Land Court is subject to appeal to
the Land Court on any question of law or fact, including the amount of
the award itself.[72] A review of the rent by this process may be obtained
at intervals of not less than three years.[73] The landlord, where he has
carried out certain specific improvements, has an absolute right to
increase the rent by an amount equal to the increase in the rental value
of the holding attributable to the carrying out of the improvements[74];
the increase operates from the date of completion and the landlord must
serve notice in writing on the tenant.

Pactional Rent.—A provision in a lease for penal or pactional rent,
i.e. for payment of a fixed sum as damages for any breach of its
conditions, is not binding. The landlord, in spite of the existence of such
a clause in the lease, must prove the actual damage which he has
sustained in consequence of the tenant's breach of the conditions of the
lease.[75]

---

[68] *Ibid.*, s. 13. Parties cannot contract out of that section: *cf. Moll* v. *Macgregor*, 1990
S.L.T. (Land Ct.) 59; 1991 S.L.C.R. 1, 173 (a decision relating to earlier legislation: s. 7
of the 1949 Act).

[69] The decision in *Guthe* v. *Broatch*, 1956 S.C. 132, is thus superseded.

[70] s. 13(3); certain other factors relating to improvements and dilapidations are also to
be disregarded: ss. 13(5) and (7); *Broadland Properties Estates Ltd.* v. *Mann*, 1994 S.L.T.
(Land Ct.) 7 (allocated milk quota not an improvement).

[71] See s. 13(4); *Aberdeen Endowments Trust* v. *Will*, 1985 S.L.T. (Land Ct.) 23.

[72] s. 61(2); *e.g. Earl of Seafield* v. *Stewart*, 1985 S.L.T. (Land Ct.) 35. As to the
appointment of an arbiter, failing agreement between the parties, see Sched. 7 and
ss. 63–64. Note that the matter may be determined instead by the Land Court at first
instance if the parties so agree: s. 60.

[73] s. 13(8).

[74] 1991 Act, s. 15.

[75] *Ibid.*, s. 48.

Freedom of Cropping.—A tenant may practise any system of cropping arable lands, and may dispose of the produce of the farm other than manure produced on it as he pleases, notwithstanding any provision of the lease or local custom which may bind him to some particular method of cultivation.[76] This provision does not apply to the last year of the lease, nor, in leases from year to year, to the year before the tenant leaves; and it does not apply to land in grass which is to be retained in that condition throughout the tenancy.[77] On the other hand, the tenant must make provision against the deterioration of the holding; and, in the case of crops sold contrary to the provisions of the lease or to local custom, must return to the holding the full equivalent manurial value thereof. The landlord is entitled to obtain an interdict to restrain the exercise of the tenant's freedom of cropping if he allows the holding to deteriorate, and to damages for his failure in these duties. After notice to terminate has been given, the tenant may not remove any manure or compost unless and until he has given the landlord or the incoming tenant a reasonable opportunity to purchase it at its fair market value.[78]

Fixtures.—It is provided that any engine, machinery, fencing or other fixture affixed to a holding by a tenant, and any building erected by him for which he is not entitled to compensation, and which is not affixed or erected in pursuance of some obligation, or in substitution for some fixture or building belonging to the landlord, shall be the property of the tenant and removable by him before, or within six months after, the termination of the lease. The right of removal is conditional on the tenant having paid all rent owing by him, and satisfied his other obligations in respect of the holding. In removal no avoidable damage to other buildings must be done, and all damage done must be made good. The tenant must give one month's notice in writing of his intention to remove a fixture or building, and the landlord may elect to purchase it at a price which is the equivalent of the fair value to an incoming tenant.[79]

Record of Holding.—Either landlord or tenant may at any time require the making of a record of the condition of the fixed equipment on and of the cultivation of the holding;[80] the tenant may also require the making of a record of the existing improvements carried out by him for which he, with the consent in writing of his landlord, has paid compensation to an outgoing tenant, and of any fixtures or buildings which he is entitled to remove. Such record will, where required, be made by a person appointed by the Secretary of State, and the cost, unless otherwise agreed, will be borne equally by the parties. In leases

[76] *Ibid.*, s. 7(1).
[77] s. 7(5).
[78] s. 17.
[79] s. 18.
[80] s. 8.

entered into after the Act of 1949, however, a record of the condition of the fixed equipment must be made forthwith.[81] The existence of such a record is a prerequisite to any claim by the tenant for compensation for continuous good farming, and to any claim by the landlord for compensation for deterioration.[82]

41.30 **Notice to Quit and Removal.**—Where a tenant is six months in arrear with his rent, the landlord may raise an action in the sheriff court for his removal at the next term of Martinmas or Whitsunday.[83] Decree of removal and ejection of the tenant may follow, unless the tenant pays the arrears due by him or finds caution for them to the sheriff's satisfaction. A lease terminated in this way is treated[84] as if it had expired naturally at that term, and the tenant will be entitled to the usual away-going rights.[85]

Where a tenancy is to be terminated otherwise than of consent at the expiry of the stipulated period for the endurance of the lease, notice to quit or of removal must be given.[86] In order to be effective, such notice[87] must be given not less than one or more than two years before the expiry of the lease, notwithstanding any contractual provision to the contrary;[88] failing such notice, the lease is renewed by tacit relocation from year to year. Where notice is served on the tenant, he may within one month serve a counter-notice on the landlord.[89] This has the effect of restricting the operation of the notice to quit to cases where the landlord can obtain the consent of the Land Court, except in certain special circumstances,[90] *e.g.* where the notice is given by reason of the

---

[81] s. 5 (of the 1991 Act).

[82] ss. 44–47.

[83] s. 20(1). Under the Term and Quarter Days (Scotland) Act 1990, s.1(1)(*a*) and 2(*a*), the terms Whitsunday and Martinmas signify May 28 and November 28 respectively; see also *Austin* v. *Gibson*, 1979 S.L.T. (Land Ct.) 12; *Provincial Insurance plc* v. *Valtos Ltd.*, 1992 S.C.L.R. 203.

[84] s. 20(2).

[85] *Quaere* whether the tenant would be entitled to compensation for disturbance and reorganisation: see *Scottish Current Law Statutes*, Vol. 3, annotations to 1991 Act, A.G.M. Duncan; and article 'The Agricultural Holdings (Scotland) Act 1991,' A.G.M. Duncan, 1992 S.L.T. (News) 1, at p. 2.

[86] s. 21(1); *Morrison* v. *Rendall*, 1986 S.C. 69, *sub nom. Morrison's Exrs.* v. *Rendall*, 1986 S.L.T. 227 (precursor of s. 21(1).) *Quaere* whether tenant's unilateral renunciation effective: Gill, *Law of Agricultural Holdings in Scotland*, (2nd ed.), para. 250. The landlord's right to remove a tenant whose estate has been sequestrated, or who has incurred an irritancy under the lease, remains unaffected: s. 21(6).

[87] See Removal Terms (Scotland) Act 1886, s. 6; Sheriff Courts (Scotland) Act 1907, ss. 36, 37 and Form H2 (formerly Form L); Term and Quarter Days (Scotland) Act 1990. As to the effect of deviation from the requirements of the prescribed Form, see *Rae* v. *Davidson*, 1954 S.C. 361; *Callander* v. *Watherston*, 1970 S.L.T. (Land Ct.) 13; *Mackie* v. *Gardner*, 1973 S.L.T. (Land Ct.) 11; *Gemmell* v. *Andrew*, 1975 S.L.T. (Land Ct.) 5; *Taylor* v. *Brick*, 1982 S.L.T. 25; *Morrison's Exrs.* v. *Rendall*, 1989 S.L.T. (Land Ct.) 89. As to the need for writing, see s. 21(3)(*a*) and *Morrison* v. *Rendall*, 1986 S.C. 69 (*sub nom. Morrison's Exrs.* v. *Rendall*, 1986 S.L.T. 227).

[88] s. 21(3); *Duguid* v. *Muirhead*, 1926 S.C. 1078.

[89] Under s. 22.

[90] s. 22(2); the tenant may take any question arising under this subsection to arbitration: s. 23.

tenant's apparent insolvency,[91] or on the issue within the last nine months by the Land Court of a certificate of bad husbandry,[92] or because the tenant has failed to comply with a demand in writing to remedy a breach of any term or condition of his tenancy,[93] or where the tenant has acquired right to the lease by succession or as a legatee,[94] and in each case it is stated in the notice to quit that it is given by reason of these circumstances.

The Land Court may only give their consent, where it is required, to the operation of a notice to quit if they are satisfied as to one or more of the following reasons, which the landlord must specify in his application:[95]

    (a)   that the carrying out of the purpose for which the landlord proposes to terminate the tenancy is desirable in the interests of good husbandry;

    (b)   that its carrying out is desirable in the interests of sound management of the estates of which it forms part;[96]

    (c)   that its carrying out is desirable for the purposes of agricultural research, experiments, etc.;

    (d)   that greater hardship would be caused by withholding than by giving consent to the operation of the notice;[97] or

    (e)   that the landlord's purpose is to employ the land for use other than for agriculture.

Further protection is afforded to the tenant by section 24(2) which provides that the Land Court may withhold their consent, even if they are satisfied as to one or more of these reasons, if it appears to them that a fair and reasonable landlord would not insist on possession.[98] An application to the Land Court for the granting of consent is competent in cases where the notice to quit has been served without prejudice to

---

[91] s. 22(2)(*f*).

[92] ss. 22(2)(*c*) and 26. For the rules of good husbandry, see s. 85(2) of the 1991 Act, referring to the Agriculture (Scotland) Act 1948, Sched. 6; *Austin* v. *Gibson, supra; Luss Estates Co.* v. *Firkin Farm Co.*, 1985 S.L.T. (Land Ct.) 17; *Cambusmore Estate Trs.* v. *Little*, 1991 S.L.T. (Land Ct.) 33.

[93] s. 22(2)(*d*), subject, however, in the case of a breach relating to fixed equipment to the special provisions of ss. 32 and 66. Note that the rights afforded by sub-heads (*c*) and (*d*) (formerly sub-heads (*d*) and (*e*)) are mutually exclusive: *Macnabb* v. *Anderson*, 1955 S.C. 38.

[94] s. 22(2)(*g*). Note that special provisions apply in the case of tenancies acquired by succession or as legatees by near relatives, for the termination of which the consent of the Land Court *is* required: see para. 41.35, *infra*.

[95] s. 24(1) and see s. 24(2)—consent to be withheld if a 'fair and reasonable landlord' would not insist on possession. See, too, *Altyre Estate Trs.* v. *McLay*, 1975 S.L.T. (Land Ct.) 12.

[96] See *Gemmell* v. *Andrew, supra*; *Prior* v. *J. & A. Henderson*, 1984 S.L.T. (Land Ct.) 51; the reference is to the landlord's own estate, not land which has passed into other hands: *Smoor* v. *Macpherson*, 1981 S.L.T. (Land Ct.) 25.

[97] As to the evidence required to show greater hardship, see *Somerville* v. *Watson*, 1980 S.L.T. (Land Ct.) 14; *Hutchison* v. *Buchanan*, 1980 S.L.T. (Land Ct.) 17; *Clamp* v. *Sharp*, 1986 S.L.T. (Land Ct.) 2.

[98] ss. 24(1) and (2); *Altyre Estate Trs.* v. *McLay*, 1975 S.L.T. (Land Ct.) 12.

other proceedings in some other court, such as an action for declarator
and removing in the sheriff court on the ground that the lease has
expired; but it may be appropriate for the application in the Land Court
to be sisted pending the outcome of the other proceedings.[99] Since the
Land Court has no jurisdiction to adjudicate on questions as to whether
or not the holding is an agricultural holding under the 1991 Act, any
such question will require to be referred to the sheriff court or to the
Court of Session and the application sisted until it has been decided
there.[1] A landlord may have a power of resumption for building,
planting, feuing or other non-agricultural purposes. When exercising
such a power, the normal rules relating to notices to quit do not apply.[2]

41.31 Compensation to Tenant for Improvements: Arbitration.—A tenant is
entitled on quitting the holding, to compensation for certain improvements.[3] The rules relating to the improvements for which
compensation may be claimed are set out in sections 33 to 39 of the
1991 Act and Schedules of some complexity. Schedules 3 to 6, to which
reference must be made, enumerate the improvements and they are
classified (a) according to the dates when they were begun, and (b)
according as they call or do not call for the consent of or notice to the
landlord. It should be noted that a landlord, if the holding has
deteriorated through the failure of the tenant to cultivate according to
the rules of good husbandry, may claim compensation in his turn.[4] In
the cases of leases entered into after certain dates no claim is good
unless a record of the condition of the holding has been made. The
amount of compensation will be ascertained, in default of agreement, by
arbitration.[5] In fixing compensation for improvements the arbiter is to
give such sum as fairly represents the value of the improvement to an
incoming tenant[6] and is bound in certain cases to take into account any
benefit which the landlord has given or allowed in consideration of the
tenant executing the improvement.[7] It was held[8] that no compensation
was due if the tenant was expressly bound to execute the improvement
in question, but this is no longer the law except as to leases before
January 1, 1921.[9] In general, contracting out of the compensation
provisions of the Act is not allowed.[10]

---

[99] *Eagle Star Insurance Co.* v. *Simpson*, 1984 S.L.T. (Land Ct.) 37; *Prior* v. *J. & A. Henderson, supra.*
[1] *Allan-Fraser's Trs.* v. *Macpherson*, 1981 S.L.T. (Land Ct.) 17.
[2] Agricultural Holdings (Scotland) Act 1991, s. 21(7). See, generally, Gordon, *Scottish Land Law*, para. 19–53.
[3] s. 33 *et seq.*
[4] ss. 45–48.
[5] See Sched. 7 of the 1991 Act for provisions regulating arbitration.
[6] s. 36.
[7] See s. 36(2).
[8] *Earl of Galloway* v. *McClelland*, 1915 S.C. 1062.
[9] s. 34(2).
[10] s. 53(1); *Young* v. *Oswald*, 1949 S.C. 412 was decided on the very different wording of the Act of 1923 and is of doubtful application.

Arbitration is the method by which all claims of whatever nature by the tenant or the landlord[11] arising under the Act or on or out of the termination of the holding are to be settled.[12] For example, either party may obtain a review of the rent by serving on the other a demand for a reference to arbitration of the question what rent should properly be payable in respect of the holding.[13] A general reference to arbitration, as to 'any question or difference between the landlord and the tenant,' except a question or difference as to liability for rent, is made by the Act to cover cases for which no express provision is made.[14] Where the question or difference relates to a demand in writing served on the tenant by the landlord requiring the tenant to remedy a breach of any term or condition of the tenancy by the doing of any work of provision, repair, maintenance or replacement of fixed equipment, the arbiter has power to modify that demand.[15] An arbiter acting under the Act may at any stage in the proceedings *ex proprio motu* state a case on a question of law for the opinion of the sheriff, and either party may apply to the sheriff to direct the arbiter to do so.[16] The sheriff's opinion, once given, is binding upon the arbiter,[17] but there is a final right of appeal to the Court of Session.[18] In statutory rent review cases, but only where the arbiter has been appointed by the Secretary of State or by the Land Court, either party to the arbitration has the right to appeal to the Land Court on any question of law or fact including the amount of the award.[19]

41.32 **Compensation to Tenant for Disturbance.**—When a landlord gives notice to quit (or the tenant gives a counter-notice under section 22) and the tenant leaves the holding, he is entitled to compensation for disturbance,[20] unless section 43(2) applies. The minimum amount is one year's rent; the maximum on proof of additional loss directly attributable to his removal, two years' rent.[21] Written notice of an intention to make a claim must be given to the landlord within two months of the termination of the tenancy even where the claim is restricted to the minimum.[22] The notice of intention to claim must

---

[11] As to meaning of landlord, see s. 85(1) and Gill, *Law of Agricultural Holdings in Scotland* (2nd ed.), paras. 30–36.

[12] s. 60–61. As to appointment of arbiter, see Sched. 7; *Chalmers Property Investment Co.* v. *MacColl*, 1951 S.C. 24. Note that, if both parties agree, recourse may be made to the Land Court instead of to arbitration: s. 60(2).

[13] s. 13(1); see para. 41.29, *supra.*

[14] s. 60(1): *cf. Brodie* v. *Ker*, 1952 S.C. 216; *Cormack* v. *McIldowie's Exrs.*, 1974 S.L.T. 178 (reported further 1975 S.C. 161; 1975 S.L.T. 214); *Craig, Applicant*, 1981 S.L.T. (Land Ct.) 12, as to the limits of this jurisdiction.

[15] s. 66.

[16] Sched. 7, para. 20.

[17] *Mitchell-Gill* v. *Buchan*, 1921 S.C. 390.

[18] Sched. 7, para. 21.

[19] s. 61(2).

[20] s. 43(1).

[21] s. 43(4).

[22] s. 62.

specify the nature of the claim. There is sufficient specification if the notice refers to the statutory provision, custom or term of an agreement under which the claim is made.[23]

Where he is entitled to compensation for disturbance, the tenant is in certain cases entitled under sections 54 to 55 of the 1991 Act to payment in addition of a sum to assist in the reorganisation of his affairs, being a sum equal to four times the annual rent or an appropriate proportion in the case of part of a holding.[24] No such sum is payable, however, if the tenancy is terminated by virtue of a notice to quit which contains a statement,[25] and, if an application is made to the Land Court for consent to the operation of the notice, the court is satisfied that the carrying out of the purpose for which the landlord proposes to terminate the tenancy is desirable on one or other of a number of grounds set out in section 24 of the Act. These grounds relate to good husbandry, sound management of the estate of which the holding forms part, agricultural research, and to the fact that the landlord will suffer hardship unless the notice to quit has effect.[26] The right to an additional payment is also excluded in cases where the tenancy is terminated by notice to quit served on a tenant who has acquired right to the lease by succession or as a legatee.[27]

41.33 **Compensation for Damage by Game.**—A tenant is entitled to compensation for damage by game (*i.e.* deer, pheasants, partridges, grouse, black game) provided that the amount of damage done exceeds 12 pence per hectare of the area affected, and that the tenant has not permission in writing to kill the game in question.[28] Provision is made for timely notice to the landlord of a claim under this head.[29] A shooting tenant is bound to indemnify the landlord against claims for such compensation.[30] It has been held to be no objection to a claim that the damage was done by black game coming from another property and at a season of the year when it was unlawful to kill them.[31] When a tenant has permission from the landlord to kill any of the enumerated kinds of game, no claim for compensation in respect of damage by game of that kind is competent.[32]

---

[23] s. 62(3); Gill, *op. cit.*, para. 430.
[24] This is a fixed payment, regardless of actual loss: *Copeland* v. *McQuaker*, 1973 S.L.T. 186.
[25] As to this requirement, see s. 55, and *Barnes-Graham* v. *Lamont*, 1971 S.C. 170; *Copeland* v. *McQuaker, supra.*
[26] 1991 Act, s. 24(1); s. 55(1). Note however that s. 55(1) does not apply if the reasons given by the Land Court for consent to the operation of the notice include or would have included the reason that the landlord's purpose is to employ the land for use other than agriculture: see s. 55(2).
[27] s. 55(2)(*b*).
[28] s. 52.
[29] s. 52(2); and *cf. Earl of Morton's Trs.* v. *Macdougall*, 1944 S.C. 410.
[30] s. 52(4).
[31] *Thomson* v. *Earl of Galloway*, 1919 S.C. 611.
[32] *Ross* v. *Watson*, 1943 S.C. 406.

41.34 Bequest of Lease: Succession.—The tenant of a holding may, unless his power to do so is expressly excluded by the lease,[33] bequeath his lease, under section 11 of the 1991 Act, to his son-in-law or daughter-in-law or to any one of the persons who would be, or would in any circumstances have been, entitled to succeed to the estate on his intestacy.[34] The legatee must intimate the bequest to the landlord within 21 days of the tenant's death or, if he is prevented by some unavoidable cause from giving such notice within that period, as soon as practicable thereafter. By doing so he accepts the lease, which then becomes binding upon both as from the date of the deceased's death unless the landlord, within one month of intimation being made, gives a counter-notice to the legatee that he objects to receiving him as tenant. If such objection is made, the legatee may apply to the Land Court for an order declaring him to be tenant under the lease, which the Land Court must grant unless a reasonable ground of objection is established by the landlord.[35] If the legatee refuses the bequest or is rejected, the right to the lease will be treated as intestate estate of the deceased tenant, and will pass accordingly.[36] A legatee who accepts the bequest but fails to give timeous notification of his acceptance has no right to possess, nor does any other person who claims right to the lease by transfer of the tenant's interest to him.[37] The acquirer of such a lease, that is to say any person to whom the lease is transferred under section 16 of the Succession (Scotland) Act 1964,[38] must also within 21 days notify the landlord, who may again give a counter-notice, remitting the matter to the Land Court.[39] As in the case of a bequest, time is of the essence and an acquirer who fails to give notice within 21 days will have no right to possess under the lease.[40] A person who is a near relative of the deceased tenant and has acquired right to the lease of an agricultural holding under section 16 of the 1964 Act or as a legatee under section 11 of the 1991 Act is subject to the special provisions which the 1991 Act provides for the termination of tenancies acquired by succession.[41]

41.35 Termination of Tenancies Acquired by Succession.—A near relative of the deceased tenant who has acquired right to the lease of the holding under section 16 of the 1964 Act or as a legatee under section 11 of the 1991 Act is in a privileged position as regards termination of the lease on its expiry as compared with other such successors. In the case of

[33] *Kennedy* v. *Johnstone*, 1956 S.C. 39.
[34] s. 11(1); Gordon, *Scottish Land Law*, para. 19–42.
[35] s. 11(6). Such a ground must be personal to the heir; *e.g. Reid* v. *Duffas Estate*, 1955 S.L.C.R. 13.
[36] s. 11(8).
[37] *Coats* v. *Logan*, 1985 S.L.T. 221.
[38] See para. 41.23, *supra*.
[39] s. 12; as to the notice to be given by the acquirer to the landlord, see *Garvie's Trs.* v. *Garvie's Tutors*, 1975 S.L.T. 94.
[40] *Coats* v. *Logan*, *supra*.
[41] 1991 Act, s. 25.

other successors the landlord is able to terminate the tenancy on the expiry of the lease by notice to quit without the consent of the Land Court.[42] In the case of near relatives, however, a category which is confined to the deceased tenant's spouse or child (including an adopted child),[43] the consent of the Land Court is required to the operation of the notice to quit and the grounds on which it is given must be specified in the notice.[44] The grounds for consent differ from those which apply in other cases where the Land Court's consent to the operation of a notice to quit is required,[45] and different grounds apply depending upon whether the tenancy was let before January 1, 1984 or on or after that date.[46] Where the holding was let before January 1, 1984 consent must be given if the Land Court are satisfied (1) that the tenant has neither sufficient training in agriculture nor sufficient experience in the farming of land to enable him to farm the holding with reasonable efficiency, (2) that the holding is not capable of providing full-time employment for an individual occupying it and at least one other man and the landlord proposes to amalgamate it with other land,[47] or (3) that the tenant is the occupier of other agricultural land which he has occupied since before the deceased tenant's death and which is capable of providing full-time employment for himself and at least one other man.[48] Where the holding was let on or after that date, there is a further ground, namely that the tenant does not have sufficient financial resources to enable him to farm the holding with reasonable efficiency, and the ground about insufficient training and experience is modified to enable account to be taken of the fact that the tenant is already engaged on a suitable course of training in agriculture. There is one other important difference, namely, that, except in the case of the ground involving amalgamation of holdings, the onus is on the successor tenant to satisfy the Land Court that the circumstances are not as specified in the landlord's notice to quit.[49] The general rule which applies in all other cases where the Land Court's consent is required is that the onus is on the landlord to satisfy the Land Court as to the grounds of his application.[50] The effect of these differences is that it is likely to be easier for a landlord to obtain consent and thus terminate the tenancy where the holding was let on or after January 1, 1984.

[42] s. 22(2)(g).
[43] s. 25(5) and Sched. 2, Pt. III.
[44] s. 25; and see article by R.D. Sutherland, 'Unforeseen Consequences of the Agricultural Holdings (Scotland) Act 1991', 1993 S.L.T. (News) 351.
[45] See para. 41.30 supra.
[46] Sched. 2, Pts. I and II.
[47] As to the meaning of 'amalgamation,' see Mackenzie v. Lyon, 1984 S.L.T. (Land Ct.) 30.
[48] 'Occupier' in this context means occupier as an individual and not as a partner in a firm which is the owner or tenant of other land: Haddo House Estate Trs. v. Davidson, 1984 S.L.T. (Land Ct.) 14.
[49] s. 25(3)(b).
[50] McLaren v. Lawrie, 1964 S.L.T. (Land Ct.) 10.

III. LANDHOLDERS AND CROFTERS

41.36 Small Landholders Acts.—A substantial proportion of agricultural and pastoral land in Scotland does not fall under the Agricultural Holdings Acts, but is dealt with, as landholders' holdings or as crofts, by separate statutory provisions. These holdings are lettings of agricultural land which do not exceed 20 hectares whatever the rent, or do not exceed £50 in rent, whatever the area; in the case of crofts the maximum area, whatever the rent, is 30 hectares. These lettings were originally brought under statutory control by the Crofters Holdings (Scotland) Act 1886, which applied only in the crofting counties.[51] That Act was amended by the Small Landholders (Scotland) Act 1911, which extended the statutory protection to similar holdings throughout the country; the 1911 Act was itself amended by the Land Settlement (Scotland) Act 1919, and the Small Landholders and Agricultural Holdings (Scotland) Act 1931. In 1955 the separate category of crofters was reinstituted in the crofting counties only by the Crofters (Scotland) Act 1955.[52]

The 1911 Act established the Scottish Land Court,[53] which superseded the Crofters Commission operating under the 1886 Act. A new Crofters Commission was set up by the 1955 Act for administrative purposes, but the Land Court continues to have jurisdiction over crofters as well as landholders in judicial matters, and it has important functions with regard to agricultual holdings.[54] The Land Court is final on all questions of fact, but may *ex proprio motu*, and must, on the application of either party, state a case on a question of law to either Division of the Court of Session. There is no appeal to the House of Lords.[55] The powers and jurisdiction of the Land Court lie solely within the limits which statute has laid down, and questions which it has no jurisdiction to decide require to be determined in the ordinary courts.[56] An order or determination of the Land Court may be enforced as if it were a decree of the sheriff having jurisdiction in the area in which the order or determination is to be enforced.[57]

41.37 Landholders: Meaning.—The Small Landholders Acts apply to agricultural holdings,[58] other than market gardens,[59] outside the crofting

---

[51] The former counties of Argyll, Caithness, Inverness, Orkney, Ross and Cromarty, Sutherland and Zetland: see now s. 61(1) of the Crofters (Scotland) Act 1993.

[52] See para. 41.40, *infra*.

[53] s. 24; see now the Scottish Land Court Act 1993; and see para. 2.8, *supra*.

[54] See *supra*, paras. 41.30, 41.32, 41.34.

[55] s. 1 of the Scottish Land Court Act 1993. As to members' tenure of office, see *Mackay and Esslemont* v. *Lord Advocate*, 1937 S.C. 860.

[56] *Garvie's Trs.* v. *Still*, 1972 S.L.T. 29; *Eagle Star Insurance Co. Ltd.* v. *Simpson*, 1984 S.L.T. (Land Ct.) 37.

[57] Scottish Land Court Act 1993, Sched. 1.

[58] See para. 41.28, *supra*.

[59] See *Grewar* v. *Moncur's C.B.*, 1916 S.C. 764.

counties,[60] which are holdings under the 1911 Act, that is holdings which were, in April 1912, let at a rent not exceeding £50 or did not, exclusive of common grazings, exceed 20 hectares in extent.[61] The provisions of the 1911 Act extended to existing holdings held under the 1886 Act, new holdings registered under the 1911 Act,[62] and holdings held by tenants under an existing lease from year to year.[63] The tenants in the last category, existing yearly tenants, are required, in order to qualify under the Act, to reside on or within three kilometres of the holding, and to cultivate the holding themselves or with members of their family, with or without hired labour.[64] It is also necessary, in order to qualify as a 'landholder' and so benefit fully under the Act, that the tenant or his predecessor in the same family should have provided or paid for the whole or greater part of the buildings and permanent improvements without receiving payment for them from the landlord or his predecessor in title;[65] if the existing yearly tenant did not fulfil this latter requirement, he became a 'statutory small tenant.'[66] Tenants under an existing lease for more than a year who qualified under the 1911 Act became landholders or statutory small tenants on the expiry of the period of the contractual lease.[67]

Grass parks, let for the purposes of a business not primarily agricultural, are excluded;[68] so are subjects let 'to any innkeeper or tradesman placed in the district by the landlord for the benefit of the neighbourhood.'[69] It has been held where the subjects would have been a holding under the Acts but for the existence of a second house, which was not used for the purpose of the holding but for letting in summer, that this house might be excised and the statutory provisions applied to the rest of the holding.[70] Occupants of land for less than a year, and persons who did not satisfy the conditions as to residence and cultivation, are not within the Act. If, however, a tenant became either a landholder or a statutory small tenant on the Act of 1911 coming into operation, he does not lose his rights as such by a subsequent agreement with the landlord under which he accepts a lease for less than a year.[71]

---

[60] Holdings in these counties (see n. 51, *supra*) are regulated by the Crofters (Scotland) Act 1993; see *infra*, para. 41.40.

[61] 1911 Act, s. 26, as amended by Agriculture (Adaptation of Enactments) (Scotland) Regulations 1977 (S.I. 1977 No. 2007). See *Malcolm* v. *McDougall*, 1916 S.C. 283.

[62] s. 7, as amended by Land Settlement (Scotland) Act 1919, s. 9, and S.I. 1977 No. 2007.

[63] s. 2(1).

[64] s. 2(1) (ii), as amended by Agriculture (Adaption of Enactments) (Scotland) Regulations 1977.

[65] s. 2(1) (iii), proviso (a).

[66] See *infra*, para. 41.39.

[67] s. 2(1)(iii).

[68] 1911 Act, s. 26(3)(g).

[69] 1886 Act, s. 33. See *Stormonth-Darling* v. *Young*, 1915 S.C. 44; *Taylor* v. *Fordyce*, 1918 S.C. 824. Section 33 was repealed so far as applying to the crofting counties by Sched. 7 of the Crofters (Scotland) Act 1993.

[70] *McNeil* v. *Duke of Hamilton's Trs.*, 1918 S.C. 221.

[71] *Clelland* v. *Baird*, 1923 S.C. 370.

41.38 **Tenure of Landholder.**—The following are the main provisions regulating the tenure of a landholder, and these are not affected by any agreement to the contrary:—

Fair Rent.—While the Acts fixed the rent at its existing level, parties were left free to negotiate a new rent by agreement. Failing agreement, application may be made by either party to the Land Court to fix a fair rent. The Land Court may cancel arrears of rent, in whole or part, where it considers it reasonable to do so.[72] Once the rent has been fixed it cannot be altered, except by agreement, for the next seven years. The Land Court is directed, in fixing a fair rent, to consider all the circumstances of the case, holding, and district.[72] It has been held that they should take into consideration any special circumstances affecting the holding, *e.g.* on the one hand, its suitability for summer letting,[73] on the other, its liability to damage from game or deer.[74] But they may not take into consideration the fact that the tenant has incurred the burden of a loan from his landlord to enable him to build a house on the holding.[75]

Security of Tenure.—The landholder cannot be removed from his tenancy except on certain clear grounds specified in the Acts, termed statutory conditions. These include non-payment of rent for a year or more; failure to cultivate the holding; execution of a deed purporting to assign the holding; sub-letting; apparent insolvency or execution of a trust deed for the benefit of his creditors; opening a public-house without the landlord's consent.[76]

Resumption by Landlord: Renunciation.—The landlord has the right, on making application to the Land Court, and on making such compensation as that court may determine, to resume possession of the holding 'for some reasonable purpose, having relation to the good of the holding or of the estate.'[77] Building, feuing, and planting are among the grounds expressly specified. The landlord's intention to reside on the holding is not a ground of resumption of possession.[78] A landholder may renounce his holding on giving one year's notice to the landlord.[79]

Compensation for Improvements.—On renunciation, or on being removed from the holding, the tenant is entitled, in addition to his

---

[72] 1886 Act, s. 6.
[73] *McNeil* v. *Duke of Hamilton's Trs.*, 1918 S.C. 221.
[74] *McKelvie* v. *Duke of Hamilton's Trs.*, 1918 S.C. 301.
[75] *Dept. of Agriculture* v. *Burnett*, 1937 S.L.T. 292.
[76] 1886 Act, ss. 1 and 3; 1911 Act, s. 10.
[77] 1886 Act, s. 2; 1911 Act, s. 19, and, as to statutory small tenant, s. 32(15). See *Whyte* v. *Stewart*, 1914 S.C. 675.
[78] Small Landholders, etc., Act 1931, s. 8.
[79] 1886 Act, s. 7; 1911 Act, s. 18; Gordon, *Scottish Land Law*, para. 19–56.

rights under the Agricultural Holdings Acts,[80] to compensation for any permanent improvements, if suitable to the holding, executed or paid for by himself or a predecessor in the same family, and not made in obedience to a specific obligation in writing.[81] The compensation is fixed, failing agreement, by the Land Court; this forms an important part of the court's work.

Assignation: Sub-letting.—A landholder has in general no power to assign his holding. But if he is unable to work the holding through age or infirmity, he may apply to the Land Court for power to assign it to his son-in-law or to any person who would succeed him on intestacy.[82] He has no power, without the landlord's consent, to subdivide the holding or to sub-let it, except to 'holiday visitors'[83] or, probably, for a period less than a year.[84] Unless he is a new holder established by the Board of Agriculture, now the Secretary of State for Scotland, he is not entitled to erect a new house on his holding, except in substitution for one already existing; a new holder may do so with the consent of the landlord and the Secretary of State.[85]

Succession.—The landholder may bequeath his holding to his son-in-law or to any one of the persons who would be, or would in any circumstances have been, entitled to succeed to his estate on his intestacy; otherwise a holding passes to the tenant's executor on his death according to the law of intestate succession.[86]

Provisions are made for the compulsory enlargement of holdings,[87] for the rights of a landlord in the event of a vacancy in a holding,[88] for the regulation of common grazing,[89] and for a record, by the Land Court, as to the state of the holding.[90]

41.39 **Statutory Small Tenants.**—A statutory small tenant is a person who would have been a landholder but for the fact that the whole or greater part of the buildings and permanent improvements were not provided by him nor by any predecessor in the same family.[91] Save as provided by section 32 of the Act of 1911, the provisions of the Acts do not apply to him. Under that section he is entitled, notwithstanding any agreement to

[80] *Supra*, para. 41.31.
[81] 1886 Act, s. 8.
[82] 1911 Act, s. 21, as amended by Succession (Scotland) Act 1964, Sched. 2, para. 15.
[83] 1886 Act, s. 1(4); 1911 Act, s. 10.
[84] *McNeil* v. *Duke of Hamilton's Trs.*, 1918 S.C. 221.
[85] 1886 Act, s. 1(4); 1911 Act, s. 10(2).
[86] 1886 Act, s. 16(*h*) and 1911 Act, s. 21, as amended by Succession (Scotland) Act 1964, Sched. 2, paras. 9 and 15.
[87] 1886 Act, s. 11; 1911 Act, s. 16, as amended by 1919 Act, s. 11, 1931 Act, s. 7, and S.I. 1977 No. 2007.
[88] 1911 Act, s. 17.
[89] 1911 Act, s. 24.
[90] Small Landholders, etc., Act 1931, s. 10.
[91] See 1911 Act, s. 2(1)(iii), proviso (b).

the contrary,[92] to obtain, on application to the Land Court, a renewal of his tenancy at the expiry of the lease, unless the landlord can satisfy the court that there is a reasonable objection to him. Either he or the landlord may apply to the court to fix an 'equitable' rent. An equitable rent is one which would be equitable as between a willing lessor and a willing lessee, but allowing no rent in respect of improvements made by the tenant or his predecessors in title and for which no payment has been received. Unless the lease permits, he has no power to assign his lease.[93] The landlord has power to resume the subjects under the same conditions as those specified for resumption in the case of a landholder,[94] and the statutory small tenant is entitled in the event of a resumption to the like compensation as would be payable under the Agricultural Holdings Acts to a tenant on whom a notice to quit has been served.[95] The 1931 Act gave the statutory small tenant the option, on giving notice to the landlord, of converting his tenure into that of a landholder, and becoming entitled to all the consequent rights and privileges.[96]

41.40 **The Crofters Acts.**—The category of crofters, and with it the Crofters Commission, were reintroduced to the crofting counties by the Crofters (Scotland) Act 1955.[97] The effect of the Act was to substitute in these counties a fresh code of law for that which had applied to landholders and statutory small tenants; the distinction between landholders and statutory small tenants was abolished. The statutory rights to a fair rent, security of tenure and compensation for permanent improvements, first introduced by the Crofters Holdings (Scotland) Act 1886, remain the basis of crofting tenure. The Crofters (Scotland) Act 1993 consolidated and to some extent amended the legislation relating to crofting.[98]

A croft is defined[99] as a holding in the crofting counties which was a landholder's or a statutory small tenant's holding immediately before the 1955 Act came into operation; or which was, before the 1961 Act came into operation, constituted a croft by the registration of an order of the

---

[92] See *Clelland* v. *Baird*, 1923 S.C. 370.

[93] 1911 Act, s. 32(1). As to succession, see Gordon, *Scottish Land Law*, para. 19–46 *et seq.*

[94] s. 32(15).

[95] 1931 Act, s. 13; Agricultural Holdings (Scotland) Act 1991, ss. 54 and 59.

[96] 1931 Act, s. 14; see also 1911 Act, s. 32(11).

[97] Amended by Crofters (Scotland) Act 1961, Crofting Reform (Scotland) Act 1976, and Crofter Forestry (Scotland) Act 1991. See now the consolidating Crofters (Scotland) Act 1993 (c. 44). The crofting counties are the former counties of Argyll, Caithness, Inverness, Orkney, Ross and Cromarty, Sutherland and Zetland: see s. 61(1) and n.51, *supra*.

[98] The 1993 Act (c. 44) came into force (with the exception of s. 28) on January 5, 1994. There are transitional provisions in Sched. 6. The Act implemented most of the recommendations of the Scottish Law Commission in their Report Cm.2187. Contracting out of the Act is limited: s. 5(3). Subsequent statutory references are to the 1993 Act, unless otherwise indicated.

[99] s. 3; as to whether rights in pasture or grazing land held by the tenant form part of the croft, see s. 3(4) and (5). See also *Ross* v. *Graesser*, 1962 S.C. 66; *Stornoway Trust* v. *Mackay*, 1989 S.L.T. (Land Ct.) 36.

Land Court authorising the registration of the tenant as a crofter under that Act;[1] or which the Secretary of State has directed shall be a croft;[2] or a holding entered in the Register of Crofts by the Crofters Commission in accordance with their decision under section 15(4) of the 1955 Act where neither landlord nor tenant, having been notified of the decision, successfully challenged it.[3] A croft may be enlarged by the addition of non-crofting land by agreement of the owner and the crofter so long as the enlarged area, exclusive of any common pasture or grazing land held therewith, does not exceed 30 hectares and the combined rent does not exceed £100.[4] The Crofters Commission may in certain circumstances authorise the enlargement of a holding which exceeds these limits.[5]

The function of the Crofters Commission is to reorganise, develop and regulate crofting in the crofting counties and to promote the interests of crofters.[6] The Commission's sphere of action is primarily administrative, and jurisdiction over legal matters, which may be referred to them by the parties themselves or by the Commission, remains with the Land Court.[7]

41.41 Crofting Tenure.—Every tenancy of a croft is subject to the statutory conditions set out in Schedule 2 to the Crofters (Scotland) Act 1993, which include timeous payment of rent, cultivation and maintenance of the croft, and allowing the landlord to take minerals,[7a] water, timber and peats, and to exercise certain other rights. Applications for the fixing of a fair rent for the croft are made to the Land Court, and the fair rent is determined on a consideration of all the circumstances including the croft, the district, and any permanent or unexhausted improvements on the croft executed or paid for by the crofter or his predecessors.[8] Further provisions regulate the resumption of a croft by the landlord,[9] the renunciation of the tenancy by the crofter,[10] and the

---

[1] Under 1955 Act, s. 4, repealed by 1961 Act, Sched. 3.

[2] Under 1961 Act, s. 2(1), which ceased to have effect in terms of the 1976 Act, Sched. 2, para. 17. Both the 1961 Act and the 1976 Act were repealed by the Crofters (Scotland) Act 1993.

[3] s. 3(1)(e) of the 1993 Act. A holding, unless qualifying in terms of s. 3, may lack the necessary legal attributes to be a croft despite an existing entry in the Register of Crofts: *Palmer's Trs.* v. *Crofters Commission*, 1990 S.L.T. (Land Ct.) 21.

[4] s. 4(1).

[5] s. 4(1) and (2).

[6] s. 1.

[7] ss. 2 and 53.

[7a] *Strathern* v. *MacColl*, 1992 S.C. 339.

[8] s. 6.

[9] ss. 20 and 21 of the 1993 Act; see also s. 21(1) (decrofting in the event of resumption); Gordon, *Scottish Land Law*, para. 19–54; *Portman Trs.* v. *Macrae*, 1971 S.L.T. (Land Ct.) 6; *Wester Ross Salmon Ltd.* v. *Maclean*, 1986 S.L.T. (Land Ct.) 11. Resumptions will normally be authorised only where the purpose for which this is sought is likely to be put into effect in the near future: *Cameron* v. *Corpach Common Graziers*, 1984 S.L.T. (Land Ct.) 41.

[10] s. 7.

compensation payable in either event.[11] The crofter has security of
tenure, but he may be removed by the Land Court on the landlord's
application where one year's rent remains unpaid or one of the statutory
conditions of tenure[12] has been broken.[13] The crofter may not sub-let
his croft without the Commission's consent except to holiday visitors,[14]
nor may he assign it to a member of his family unless the landlord,
whomfailing the Commission has given written consent,[15] nor may he
subdivide it without the consent of the Commission and the landlord.[16]
The crofter may bequeath the croft to any member of his family, but a
bequest of it to anyone else without the Commission's approval will be
invalid.[17] In a case of intestacy, or the failure of a bequest, the right to
the croft is treated as intestate estate of the deceased crofter in
accordance with Part I of the Succession (Scotland) Act 1964.[18] If the
executor fails within three months to furnish to the landlord particulars
of the transferee under section 16(2) of the 1964 Act, the Commission
may give notice to potential claimants requiring them to intimate to the
Commission within a certain time; then, after a mandatory consultation
with any executor of the deceased crofter, may nominate a person as
successor to the tenancy of the croft.[19] Alternatively the Commission
may declare the croft vacant.[20] The landlord is obliged to accept the
transferee or the person nominated by the Commission as successor to
the tenancy of the croft.[21]

41.42 Cottars.—A cottar is defined as being the occupier of a dwelling-house
situated in the crofting counties with or without land who pays no rent,
or the tenant from year to year of a dwelling-house situated in those
counties who resides therein and pays an annual rent not exceeding £6
whether with or without garden ground but without arable or pasture
land.[22] Under the 1993 Act a cottar who, if not paying rent, is removed
from his dwelling and any land or buildings occupied by him in

[11] ss. 30 to 35: compensation to the crofter in respect of permanent improvements, and
compensation to the landlord in respect of deterioration or damage. Interest on
compensation may be awarded. In addition to compensation, a crofter may be entitled to
a share in the value of the land where the land has been resumed: s. 21 of the 1993 Act;
MacKenzie v. *Barr's Trs.*, 1993 S.L.T. 1228.
[12] See list in Sched. 2 to the 1993 Act.
[13] ss. 5, 26; see, for example, *Burton Property Trust* v. *MacRae*, 1989 S.L.C.R. 34;
Cheyne v. *Hunter*, 1989 S.C.L.R. 38.
[14] ss. 27, 29 and Sched. 2, para. 6.
[15] s. 8, and Sched. 2, para. 2. Assignation to a person other than a member of the
family is possible only with the Commission's written consent.
[16] s. 9 and Sched. 2, para. 7.
[17] ss. 10(1).
[18] ss. 10(5) and 11.
[19] s. 11(4) and (5).
[20] s. 11(8).
[21] s. 11(6).
[22] s. 12(5); as to the difference between a non-rent paying cottar and a squatter, see
Duke of Argyll's Trs. v. *MacNeill*, 1983 S.L.T. (Land Ct.) 35; and see also *Philips* v.
Macphail, 1994 S.L.T. (Land Ct.) 27.

connection therewith, or, if paying rent, renounces his tenancy or is removed, is entitled to compensation for permanent improvements.[23] Failing agreement the amount of compensation payable is fixed by the Land Court in the same manner as for crofters.[24]

41.43 **Rights of Acquisition.**—The Crofting Reform (Scotland) Act 1976 introduced important new rights in favour of crofters and cottars. A crofter now has the right, failing agreement with the landlord, to apply to the Land Court to acquire croft land tenanted by him.[25] He has an absolute right subject to such terms and conditions as the Land Court may determine to a conveyance of the site of the dwelling-house on or pertaining to his croft including the building thereon and garden ground, and a cottar has the same right to a conveyance of the site of the dwelling-house occupied by him.[26] It is in the discretion of the Land Court whether or not to make an order authorising the crofter to acquire croft land, but they are directed not to make such an order where they are satisfied that to do so would cause a substantial degree of hardship to the landlord or that the acquisition would be substantially detrimental to the sound management of the estate.[27] Failing agreement, the consideration payable in respect of the acquisition of croft land and the conveyance of the site of the dwelling-house, and the terms and conditions to be imposed, are to be determined by the Land Court.[28] Provision is made for the repayment to the landlord or his representative of part of the consideration if the former crofter or a member of his family disposes of the croft land or any part of it other than by lease for crofting or agricultural purposes at any time within five years.[29] Where a crofter has purchased his landlord's interest and wishes to let the croft to his son, a new lease is required and alteration of the entry in the Register of Crofts is insufficient.[30] Finally a crofter now has, in addition to his right to any compensation, the right to a share in the value of any part of his croft which is resumed by the landlord or is acquired by an authority possessing compulsory powers.[31]

---

[23] s. 36(1).

[24] s. 36(2).

[25] ss. 12(1) and 25(4) of the 1993 Act. The sale should be effected by a disposition rather than by feu charter unless there are special conditions requiring special means of enforcement: *Fulton* v. *Noble*, 1983 S.L.T. (Land Ct.) 40. As to the meaning of 'croft land', see s. 12(3); *MacMillan* v. *MacKenzie*, 1995 S.L.T. (Land Ct.) 7; *MacKenzie* v. *Barr's Trs.*, 1993 S.L.T. 1228, at p. 1237.

[26] ss. 12(2), (4) and 16; see *Campbell* v. *Duke of Argyll's Trs.*, 1977 S.L.T. (Land Ct.) 22.

[27] s. 13, see *Geddes* v. *Gilbertson*, 1984 S.L.T. (Land Ct.) 55.

[28] ss. 14, 15; *Ferguson* v. *Ross Estates*, 1977 S.L.T. (Land Ct.) 19; *Cameron* v. *Duke of Argyll's Trs.*, 1981 S.L.T. (Land Ct.) 2; *Macleod's Exr.* v. *Barr's Trs.*, 1989 S.C. 72; 1989 S.L.T. 392.

[29] s. 14(3). As to the meaning of 'disposes of,' see *Whitbread* v. *MacDonald*, 1992 S.C. 479; 1992 S.L.T. 1144.

[30] *Sutherland* v. *Sutherland*, 1986 S.L.T. (Land Ct.) 22.

[31] ss. 21, 37; *MacRae* v. *Secretary of State*, 1981 S.L.T. (Land Ct.) 18.

41.44 **Administration of Crofting.**—The Crofters Commission is given wide powers to enable it to perform its function of promoting the welfare and development of the crofting communities. It has the duty of compiling a Register of Crofts,[32] and of exercising a general supervision over common grazings.[33] Where a croft becomes vacant, the landlord must give notice of the fact to the Commission, and may only re-let it with the Commission's consent.[34] If the landlord fails to take steps to re-let it, the Commission may step in and re-let it themselves on his behalf;[35] in certain cases where the croft has become vacant the Commission has power to direct that it cease to be a croft.[36] Where the crofter is an absentee, that is, is not resident on or within 16 kilometres of the croft, the Commission may, where this is in the general interest of the community, terminate his tenancy; in such circumstances a dispossessed crofter may be entitled to, or liable for, compensation.[37] The Commission have power to prepare reorganisation schemes, re-allocating land in a manner conducive to its proper and efficient use; if a scheme is confirmed by the Secretary of State, the Commission must put it into effect.[38]

IV. DWELLING HOUSES AND SHOPS

41.45 **General.**—The statutory code relating to tenancies of dwelling-houses is now contained in the Housing (Scotland) Act 1988 and the Rent (Scotland) Act 1984. The 1988 Act is intended gradually to supersede previous legislation,[39] and in particular the 1984 Act. The main purposes of the Acts have always been to provide for the security of tenure of tenants of certain dwelling-houses by restricting the landlord's right to remove them at the end of the lease, and to control or regulate the amount of rent which the tenant can be required to pay. The 1988 Act weakens security of tenure and restricts the circumstances in which rent may be regulated. The Acts also contain provisions prohibiting the charging of premiums by a landlord, and giving power to the court in

---

[32] s. 41.
[33] ss. 47–52.
[34] s. 23.
[35] s. 23(5).
[36] s. 24(2) and (3), and 22(11) (decrofting applicable to part of a croft); see also *Gray* v. *Crofters Commission*, 1980 S.L.T. (Land Ct.) 2; *MacColl* v. *Crofters Commission*, 1986 S.L.T. (Land Ct.) 4.
[37] ss. 22, 30 and 34.
[38] ss. 38, 39 and Sched. 4.
[39] The principal Acts were the Rent (Scotland) Act 1920, the Rent Restriction Act 1923, the Rent Restriction Act 1933, the Increase of Rent and Mortgage Interest (Restrictions) Act 1938, the Rent Restriction Act 1939, the Housing (Repairs and Rents) (Scotland) Act 1954, the Rent Act 1957, the Rent Act 1965, the Rent (Scotland) Act 1971, the Rent Act 1974, and the Tenants' Rights, Etc. (Scotland) Act 1980. The principal Acts relating to furnished lettings were the Rent of Furnished Houses (Scotland) Act 1943 and the Landlord and Tenant (Rent Control) Act 1949.

certain cases to mitigate hardship to a landlord who is the debtor in a heritable security.

The legislation is notoriously complicated, and has been said to bristle with difficulties.[40] For political and economic reasons the extent and pattern of control have fluctuated considerably since legislation on this subject was first introduced. The Act of 1920 consolidated a series of earlier Acts which had been passed between 1915 and 1919. It provided for a system of control of rents, security of tenure and control of heritable securities and it applied to the majority of dwelling-houses which were let unfurnished to tenants. The Acts of 1923, 1933 and 1938, while taking many of the more valuable dwelling-houses out of control, extended and amended the provisions of the 1920 Act relating to security of tenure. The Act of 1939 reimposed control over a wide range of dwelling-houses let unfurnished, and introduced, in relation to those houses which had been newly controlled by it, a separate system to be applied in order to assess the limit of recoverable rent. The Act of 1957 decontrolled many dwelling-houses which were at the time subject to control, but the situation was again reversed by the Act of 1965 which not only brought into protection most of the houses which had been decontrolled by the 1957 Act but also introduced a new form of rent regulation and made a number of amendments to the system of security of tenure. The protection of tenants of dwelling-houses let furnished originated from the Act of 1943, which introduced a system whereby reasonable rents for the dwelling-houses might be assessed by a Rent Tribunal and registered. The Act of 1949 introduced a measure of security of tenure to tenants who chose to take advantage of the provisions of the 1943 Act as to rent. The Act of 1971 preserved the distinction which then existed between dwelling-houses let unfurnished on the one hand and those let furnished on the other, but this distinction was removed by the Act of 1974. The Act of 1980 removed the distinction which had existed since 1965 between controlled tenancies on the one hand, being those tenancies which were still covered by the system of rent control which was contained in the Acts prior to that date, and regulated tenancies on the other by providing for all remaining controlled tenancies to be converted to regulated tenancies. It also introduced a new category known as the short tenancy, under which on compliance with certain conditions the landlord can be assured of recovering possession on the expiry of the stipulated period of the lease.

The provisions of the Housing (Scotland) Act 1988 and the Rent (Scotland) Act 1984 are too complicated to state here in detail, and reference must be made to the specialist textbooks and to the relevant legislation.[41] What follows is merely a statement in outline of the main

[40] See the collection of epithets in the preface to Megarry, *The Rent Acts* (10th ed. 1967).

[41] Esp. *Stair Memorial Encyclopaedia*, Vol. 13; Megarry, Rent Acts (11th ed.); Fraser, *The Rent Acts in Scotland* (2nd ed., 1952) is now substantially out of date. For a convenient statement of the current legislation and references to the relevant statutory

features of the current legislation. The main essential is to understand which tenancies are and which are not assured or protected, and the categories into which these tenancies have been divided.

41.46 **Assured Tenancies.**—Assured tenancies[42] were introduced by the Housing (Scotland) Act 1988,[43] and are available only to persons becoming tenants after the Act came into force. Existing protected tenancies continue as such, with all the rights attaching thereto.[44] There are two types of assured tenancy: (a) the 'assured tenancy' which provides some security of tenure but no recourse to the rent registration service;[45] and (b) the fixed term 'short assured tenancy,' where there is no security of tenure, but there may be a right to have the rent reduced.

(a) Assured Tenancies.—An assured tenancy is a tenancy[46] under which a house is let as a separate dwelling[47] where the tenant[48] is an individual[49] and the house is his only or principal home.[50] There is security of tenure.[51] There can be no order for possession while the contract runs, unless the tenancy agreement specifically makes provision for termination on one of a number of grounds, such as a pre-existing heritable security and repossession by the lender, or three months' arrears of rent.[51] Existing rights of protection against unlawful eviction and harassment[52] are augmented by the 1988 Act.[53] It is also an offence to require premiums or advance payment of rent in respect of an assured tenancy.[54]

instruments, see *Parliament House Book*, Division L; see also the annotations to the Housing (Scotland) Act 1988 in *Scottish Current Law Statutes 1988*, Vol. 4, where a more complete review of the legislation and case law is to be found.

[42] See, generally, Gordon, *Scottish Land Law*, paras. 19–72 et seq.; annotations by P. Robson to the 1988 Act in *Scottish Current Law Statutes 1988*, Vol. 4; and article, T. Mullen, 'The Housing (Scotland) Act 1988: Private Sector Rented Accommodation,' 1989 S.L.T. (News) 245.

[43] (c.43), as amended by the Housing Act 1988. Pt. II of the Act came into force on January 2, 1989.

[44] Sched. 4, para. 13. For protected tenancies (private sector) see para. 41.47, *infra*. For secure tenancies (public sector) see para. 41.8, *supra*.

[45] As to rent registration, see para. 41.50, *infra*.

[46] Other than an excluded tenancy: see s. 12(2) and Sched. 4 of the 1988 Act. Examples of excluded tenancies are: tenancies at low rents; tenancies of shops and agricultural land; lettings to students and holiday lettings.

[47] Note special provisions relating to shared living accommodation occupied along with separate accommodation: ss. 14, 21: sub-let accommodation: ss. 15, 28; and houses let together with other land: s. 13.

[48] Or at least one of the joint tenants: s. 12(1)(*b*).

[49] See difficulties arising in *Ronson Nominees* v. *Mitchell*, 1982 S.L.T. (Sh.Ct.) 18; *Hilton* v. *Plustitle*, [1989] 1 W.L.R. 149; [1988] 3 All E.R. 1051.

[50] s. 12(1)(*b*).

[51] s. 18(6) and Sched. 5. Note that the landlord has a duty to provide the tenant with a written tenancy document and a rent book: s. 30.

[52] ss. 22–23 of the Rent (Scotland) Act 1984.

[53] ss. 36–38 of the 1988 Act. ss. 36 and 37 deal with unlawful eviction. s. 38 inserts s. 22(2A) in the 1984 Act (offence if the landlord does acts calculated to interfere with the peace or comfort of the tenant, or if he withdraws services reasonably required for the occupation of the tenant).

[54] s. 27 of the 1988 Act.

When the contractual tenancy terminates and the tenant remains in possession, a statutory assured tenancy comes into being.[55] The statutory assured tenancy comprises all the rights and obligations of the original agreement.[56] The terms of the statutory assured tenancy may subsequently be adjusted,[57] and the rent may be increased.[58] The landlord cannot bring the statutory tenancy to an end unless he establishes one or more of the grounds in Schedule 5, and obtains an order from a sheriff in terms of Part II of the 1988 Act.[59] Some grounds result in the mandatory granting of a possession order.[60] Other grounds entitle the sheriff to exercise discretion, as he must be satisfied not only that the ground has been established, but also that it is reasonable to make an order for possession.[61]

(b) Short Assured Tenancies.—A short assured tenancy is an assured tenancy for a minimum term of six months, in respect of which a notice in the prescribed form has been served.[62] The tenant may apply to the rent assessment committee for a determination of the rent.[63] The landlord has an automatic right to recover possession at the end of the term of the tenancy, provided that he has given at least two months notice that he requires possession of the house.[64] The sheriff has no discretion to refuse to grant recovery of possession. In addition, the landlord can regain possession by establishing any of the assured tenancy repossession grounds.[65] Where a short assured tenancy comes to an end, and there is tacit relocation or a new contractual tenancy of the

---

[55] s. 16.

[56] Except for rights and obligations relating to termination by the landlord or the tenant; and certain provisions for increases in rent: s. 16(1); and unless the terms of the original tenancy either specifically permitted or prohibited assignation or sub-letting, there is an implied term in the statutory assured tenancy that assignation or sub-letting would require the landlord's consent: s. 23.

[57] s. 17 (which specifically excludes adjustment of the amount of the rent).

[58] ss. 24 and 25. It is the landlord who initiates proceedings: the tenant can only respond to the landlord's initiatives, by, for example, referring the proposed increase to a rent assessment committee. See Gordon, *Scottish Land Law*, para. 19–154 *et seq.*

[59] ss. 16(2), 18, 19 and 20. In certain circumstances a tenant may be entitled to removal expenses: s. 22.

[60] s. 18(3); Sched. 5, Pt. I: grounds include—premises required by landlord as his only or principal home; pre-existing heritable security and repossession by lender; holiday let; student letting (period not exceeding 12 months); occupation required for a minister; demolition or reconstruction work; death of former tenant; three months' rent arrears. For notices to be given, see s. 19 and Sched. 5, Pt. IV.

[61] s. 18(4); Sched. 5, Pt. II: grounds include—suitable alternative accommodation available for tenant (and see Sched. 5, Pt. III); tenant's own notice to quit; persistent delays in payment of rent; rent arrears; breach of tenant's obligations; deterioration in subjects due to tenant's neglect; nuisance, or immoral or illegal use; deterioration of furniture owing to tenant's ill-treatment; tenant's employment ceasing when tied accommodation.

[62] s. 32: *i.e.* a notice to the effect that the tenancy is a short assured tenancy: *cf.* S.I. 1988 No. 2109. The actual length of the tenancy need not in fact be 'short.'

[63] s. 34: see too s. 32(5); Gordon, *Scottish Land Law*, para. 19–156 *seriatim.*

[64] s. 33.

[65] s. 33(1); Sched. 5.

same or substantially the same premises, then such a tenancy is also a short assured tenancy.[66]

The 1988 Act provides for one statutory transmission only. Where a tenant under an assured tenancy dies, his spouse or cohabitee becomes entitled to a statutory assured tenancy.[67] Ground 7 of Schedule 5[68] does not apply where a spouse or cohabitee succeeds under section 31 or under the will or intestacy of a tenant.

41.47   Protected Tenancies.[69]—The definition of the expression 'protected tenancy' in the 1984 Act[70] takes the form of providing that every tenancy under which a dwelling-house is let as a separate dwelling is a protected tenancy, and then excepting certain specific tenancies from this description. These exceptions are as follows—

(a)   Where the rateable value of the dwelling-house exceeded £200 on March 23, 1965, or exceeded that figure when a rateable value was first shown on the valuation roll[71] unless it was first shown on the valuation roll on or after April 1, 1978, in which case the upper limit is £1,600;[72]

(b)   Where either no rent is payable under the tenancy or the rent payable is less than two-thirds of the rateable value on March 23, 1965 or when first shown on the valuation roll;[73]

(c)   Where the dwelling-house is *bona fide* let at a rent which includes payments in respect of board or attendance,[74] provided in the case of attendance that the amount of the rent attributable to it forms a substantial part of the whole rent;[75]

(d)   Where the tenancy is granted by an educational institution to a person who is pursuing or intends to pursue a course of study provided by that institution;[76]

[66] s. 32(3)—whether or not it is a tenancy for at least six months, and whether or not a notice has been served.

[67] s. 31. The house must have been the spouse/cohabitee's principal home immediately before the tenant's death. The right of succession does not apply where the deceased tenant had himself acquired the tenancy by succession.

[68] Permitting repossession by the landlord within 12 months where the tenancy devolves under the will or intestacy of the former tenant.

[69] See generally A.G.M. Duncan & J.A.D. Hope, *The Rent (Scotland) Act 1984* (1986). Following upon the Housing (Scotland) Act 1988, there will be no new protected tenancies, except in special transitional cases (s. 42 of the 1988 Act), and in the case of short tenancies (s. 42(2), and para. 41.48, *infra*). Pre-existing protected tenancies continue: Sched. 4, para. 13 of the 1988 Act.

[70] s. 1(1).

[71] ss. 1(1)(a), 7.

[72] The limit was formerly £600, and was increased by S.I. 1985 No. 314: See Gordon, *Scottish Land Law*, para. 19–67.

[73] s. 2(1)(a); see *Thomson* v. *Lann*, 1967 S.L.T. (Sh.Ct.) 76; *Fennel* v. *Cameron*, 1968 S.L.T. (Sh.Ct.) 30.

[74] s. 2(1)(b); *Gavin* v. *Lindsay*, 1987 S.L.T. (Sh.Ct.) 12.

[75] s. 2(4); as to the meaning of 'substantial', see *Marchant* v. *Charters* [1977] 1 W.L.R. 1181.

[76] s. 2(1)(c).

(e)   Where the purpose of the tenancy is to let the house for a holiday;[77]

(f)   Where the dwelling-house is let together with land other than the site of the dwelling-house;[78]

(g)   Where the tenancy has been granted by the Crown, a local authority, a housing corporation, a housing association or certain other public bodies;[79]

(h)   Premises which consist of or comprise premises licensed for the sale of exciseable liquor;[80] and

(i)   Where the landlord's interest belongs to a resident landlord, *i.e.* if the dwelling-house forms part only of a building, the tenancy was granted by a person who occupied as his residence another dwelling-house which also forms part of that building, and the landlord has at all times since it was granted continued to occupy another dwelling-house there as his residence.[81]

Furnished tenancies, where the amount of rent attributable to the use of furniture was substantial, were previously excluded from the Rent Acts, although furnished tenants could apply to the Rent Tribunal to fix a reasonable rent and were afforded a limited security of tenure in the event of service of a notice to quit.[82] The full protection of the Rent Acts was, however, extended to these tenancies by the Rent Act 1974,[83] and they now fall within the definition of protected tenancy unless excluded from it by one or other of the exceptions listed above.

The expression 'tenancy' is defined[84] as including a sub-tenancy, but the right to possession conferred upon the tenant must be exclusive and a right which amounts merely to a licence to occupy will be excluded from protection under the Acts.[85] Similarly a service occupier, whose occupancy of the dwelling-house is attributable not to a lease but to his contract of service, is not protected.[86] The term dwelling-house for this purpose covers, as well as self-contained dwelling-houses, part of a house if let as a separate dwelling, even if it amounts only to a single room;[87] but it does not cover the lease of a house which contains a

---

[77] s. 2(1)(d).

[78] s. 2(1)(e); see also s. 1(3); *Campbell* v. *McQuillan*, 1983 S.C. 35.

[79] ss. 1(1)(c), 4, 5. But note that a rent limit for dwelling-houses let by housing associations and the Housing Corporation is provided by Pt. VI of the Act, ss. 55–61, although s. 69 of the Housing (Scotland) Act 1988 restricts the definition of 'housing association,' and ss. 43(1)(a) and (2) takes housing association tenancies out of Pt. VI of the 1984 Act.

[80] s. 10(1).

[81] ss. 1(1)(d) and 6. *Cf. Barnett* v. *O'Sullivan*, [1994] 1 W.L.R. 1667 (relating to the equivalent English provision).

[82] 1943 Act, s. 2(1) and 1949 Act, ss. 11 and 17; see *infra*, para. 41.54.

[83] s. 1.

[84] s. 115(1) of the Rent (Scotland) Act 1984.

[85] *Commissioners of H.M. Works* v. *Hutchison*, 1922 S.L.T. (Sh.Ct.) 127; *Heslop* v. *Burns* [1974] 1 W.L.R. 1241; *Marchant* v. *Charters, supra*; *cf. Street* v. *Mountford* [1985] A.C. 809.

[86] *Cairns* v. *Innes*, 1942 S.C. 164; *MacGregor* v. *Dunnett*, 1949 S.C. 510; *Cargill* v. *Phillips*, 1951 S.C. 67.

[87] s. 1(1); *Neale* v. *Del Soto* [1945] K.B. 144; *Cole* v. *Harris* [1945] K.B. 474.

number of units of habitation within it.[88] Premises do not lose their character as a dwelling-house merely because part of the house is used for business purposes, provided that the main use can be said to be residential occupation.[89] The premises must, however, be such as would within accepted principles be held to be a dwelling-house for the purposes of the Acts.[90] Where any retail trade or business is carried on from the house so as to bring the premises within the definition of 'shop' for the purposes of the Tenancy of Shops (Scotland) Act 1949, the tenancy will not be a regulated tenancy.[91] Unless he retains possession of the dwelling-house as his residence the tenant will not be entitled to the protection of the Acts.[92] Since the whole policy of the Acts is to protect the home, a tenant who ceases to reside in the premises to any substantial extent loses protection even though he may continue to use the premises for other purposes.[93] Where the tenant is a company, which by its nature is incapable of being in physical occupation of a dwelling-house, it is entitled to the benefit of the Acts so far as regards the rent but cannot obtain security of tenure as a statutory tenant when the contractual tenancy comes to an end.[94]

41.48 Regulated, Statutory and Short Tenancies.—

(a) Regulated Tenancies.—The Rent Act 1965, which introduced a new pattern of rent regulation, made it necessary to distinguish between the categories of controlled and regulated tenancies. Controlled tenancies were those tenancies which were still covered by the system of rent control which was contained in the Acts prior to 1965. The category of regulated tenancy, which was introduced by the 1965 Act,[95] comprised all other tenancies of dwellings whose rateable value on March 23, 1965 did not exceed £200. A house fell into this category as it became decontrolled on being relet to a new tenant.[96] Similarly, where a house was released from control on a second transmission from a controlled tenant, it became a regulated tenancy.[97] This distinction is now of historical interest only, however, because the Tenants' Rights, Etc. (Scotland) Act 1980 provided that all remaining controlled tenancies should cease to be controlled tenancies and become regulated

[88] *Horford Investments* v. *Lambert* [1976] Ch. 39; *St. Catherine's College* v. *Dorling* [1980] 1 W.L.R. 66.
[89] *Cargill* v. *Phillips, supra; Cowan & Sons* v. *Acton*, 1952 S.C. 73.
[90] *Maunsell* v. *Olins* [1975] A.C. 373; *Horford Investments* v. *Lambert* [1976] Ch. 39.
[91] s. 10(2); see *infra*, para. 41.56.
[92] s. 3(1); *Menzies* v. *Mackay*, 1938 S.C. 74; *Cowan & Sons* v. *Acton, supra; Langford Property Co.* v. *Tureman* [1949] 1 K.B. 29.
[93] *Stewart* v. *Mackay*, 1947 S.C. 287, *per* Lord President Cooper at p. 293.
[94] *Hiller* v. *United Dairies (London)* [1934] 1 K.B. 57; *Ronson Nominees* v. *Mitchell*, 1982 S.L.T. (Sh.Ct.) 18.
[95] 1965 Act, s. 1(4).
[96] 1971 Act, Sched. 2, paras. 1(*c*), 4.
[97] 1971 Act, Sched. 2, para. 5; see *infra* para. 41.52.

tenancies.[98] For the purposes of the 1984 Act a tenancy is a regulated tenancy if it is a protected or statutory tenancy.[99]

(b) Statutory Tenancies.—The Act draws a distinction between the tenant who occupies under a contract or a relocated contract and the tenant who remains in occupation after the expiry of the lease by virtue of the Rent Acts. The tenant in the former case is called a protected tenant, and his tenancy is a protected tenancy for so long as he is entitled to retain possession of the dwelling-house under a contractual tenancy.[1] After the protected tenancy has come to an end the person who immediately before that termination was the protected tenant of the dwelling-house is, for so long as he retains possession of it, the statutory tenant of the dwelling-house and his tenancy is called a statutory tenancy.[2] The transition from a protected tenancy to a statutory tenancy takes place where the tenant has invoked the protection of the Acts in answer to a notice to quit and his contractual right to occupancy has otherwise ceased. If no notice to quit is served the tenant will continue in occupation as a protected tenant under tacit relocation.

(c) Short Tenancies.—In order to encourage landlords to make accommodation available for letting the 1980 Act introduced a new category of tenancy, known as the short tenancy, as to which the landlord is assured of recovery of possession when the lease comes to an end. A tenancy falls within this category if (a) the tenant was not already a protected or statutory tenant of the dwelling-house before its creation, (b) it is for a specified period of not less than one nor more than five years, (c) it does not contain any provision whereby the landlord may terminate the tenancy before the expiry of that period other than for non-payment of rent or for breach of any other obligation of the tenancy, (d) before its creation the landlord has served on the tenant a notice in writing informing him that the tenancy will be a short tenancy and (e) a fair rent has already been registered for the dwelling-house or an application for its registration is made within 14 days after the commencement of the tenancy.[3]

41.49 Recoverable Rent.—The rent that can be recovered from the tenant during contractual periods is limited by what is called the contractual rent limit.[4] The amount of any excess over that limit is irrecoverable from the tenant, notwithstanding anything in any agreement.[5] Where a

[98] 1980 Act, s. 46.
[99] 1984 Act, s. 8. Where rent is payable weekly, the tenant is entitled to a rent book: s. 113.
[1] s. 1(1).
[2] s. 3(1); see also *Jessamine Investment Co.* v. *Schwartz* [1978] Q.B. 264.
[3] s. 9(1). It is still possible to grant new short tenancies: s. 42(2) of the Housing (Scotland) Act 1988.
[4] s. 28.
[5] s. 28(1); *North* v. *Allan Properties (Edinburgh) Ltd.*, 1987 S.L.T. (Sh.Ct.) 141; 1987 S.C.L.R. 644 (Sh.Ct.).

rent for the dwelling-house has been registered, the rent so registered is the contractual rent limit;[6] until registration has taken place the only limit on the rent which can be recovered during contractual periods is that upon which the parties have agreed. The limit on the rent which is recoverable during statutory periods is set by the registered rent, or if registration has not yet taken place by the amount of rent which was recoverable for the last contractual period, subject to certain adjustments which are permitted with respect to charges for the provision of services or the use of furniture.[7] Where the rent is payable weekly, the landlord is required to provide a rent book.[8]

41.50 Registration of Rent.—The 1965 Act introduced machinery for the determination of fair rents for tenancies by local rent officers and rent assessment committees, and for their registration.[9] Either party or both may apply to the rent officer to fix a fair rent for the dwelling-house. When fixed, the fair rent forms the basis for the figure which is registered by the rent officer for the house; the registered rent becomes the rent limit, an amount in excess of which will be irrecoverable from the tenant.[10] The term 'fair rent' is not defined, but certain guide lines are set,[11] for instance, that regard should be had to all the circumstances other than circumstances personal to the parties themselves, that the rent officer or rent assessment committee as the case may be should apply their knowledge and experience of current rents of comparable property in the area, that it should be assumed that there is no substantial shortage of accommodation for letting in the locality and that improvements carried out by the tenant should be disregarded.[12] Regard must be had therefore to current market rents, making such adjustment as may be necessary to take account of scarcity.[13] Since a fair rent should be fair to the landlord as well as to the tenant, a fair return to the landlord on the capital value of the property is also a relevant and necessary consideration to be taken into account.[14] In considering the capital value of the house the fact that there is a sitting tenant with a right to possess the house is a personal circumstance to which regard must not be had.[15] Subject to these considerations the appropriate method or methods of valuation will depend on the circumstances.[16]

[6] s. 28(2).
[7] ss. 29 and 31.
[8] s. 113.
[9] See now 1984 Act, Pt. V, ss. 43–54. Pt. V was amended by the Deregulation and Contracting Out Act 1994, Sched. 16. See also *Western Heritable Investment Co. Ltd.* v. *Inglis*, 1978 S.C. 304.
[10] ss. 28, 29, 49.
[11] See s. 48; *Western Heritable Investment Co. Ltd.*, Applicants, 1992 G.W.D. 26–1497.
[12] See *Stewart's J.F.* v. *Gallacher*, 1967 S.C. 59.
[13] *Learmonth Property Investment Co.* v. *Aitken*, 1970 S.C. 223; *Western Heritable Investment Co.* v. *Husband*, 1983 S.C. (H.L.) 60; 1983 S.L.T. 578.
[14] *Learmonth Property Investment Co.* v. *Aitken, supra*; *Skilling* v. *Arcari's Exrx.*, 1974 S.C. (H.L.) 42.
[15] *Skilling* v. *Arcari's Exrx., supra*.
[16] *Albyn Properties* v. *Knox*, 1977 S.C. 108; 1977 S.L.T. 41.

The fair rent may, in the first place, be agreed between the parties themselves, and a joint application made on that basis to the rent officer.[17] Alternatively, applications for registration may be made by one party only, and the other may or may not lodge objections as he pleases. In either case the rent officer has an overriding discretion as to the amount which is fair in the circumstances; where objections are raised, or he is not satisfied as to the figure applied for, he may himself determine the appropriate figure, after consultation with the parties. Either party then has the right to appeal against his decision to the rent assessment committee, whose decisions are final in fact but not on points of law. The committee are bound to observe the rules of natural justice,[18] and it is their duty not merely to inform the parties of the result of their deliberations but also to give reasons for their decision.[19] A certificate of fair rent may be sought in advance by a person intending to provide a dwelling-house by the erection or conversion of premises, or to make improvements in a dwelling-house, or to let a house as a regulated tenancy which is not subject to such a tenancy at the time.[20] The certificate, obtainable on application to the rent officer, specifies the rent which would in the rent officer's opinion be a fair rent under a regulated tenancy of the dwelling-house, or if the contemplated work were carried out, and thus provides a valuable indication of the return which the prospective landlord can expect on his expenditure.

The opportunities for variation of the registered rent are stated more broadly than in the case of the restrictions on rent imposed by earlier Acts. Entries may be made in the register which will enable the landlord to vary the rent in respect of naturally fluctuating expenditure incurred by him in connection with the tenancy, such as in relation to the use of furniture or the provision of services, without further recourse to the rent officer.[21] Otherwise the registered rent remains fixed for three years. Any application for variation of the figure by either party within that period will only be entertained on the ground that owing to some change of circumstance the registered rent no longer represents a fair rent for the dwelling house,[22] except that a landlord alone may make an application within the last three months of the three-year period. After three years an application for variation can be made by either party alone for a new consideration of the fair rent, when once again the whole circumstances, including any improvements made in the mean-time, will be taken into account.

[17] For procedure in applications to rent officers, see s. 46 and Sched. 5; see also Gordon, *Scottish Land Law*, paras. 19–148 *et seq.*

[18] *Learmonth Property Investment Co.* v. *Aitken, supra.*

[19] *Albyn Properties* v. *Knox, supra.*

[20] s. 47 and Sched. 6.

[21] s. 49. (Note that subss., (4) and (5) were repealed by the Housing (Scotland) Act 1988, s. 72 and Sched. 10.)

[22] s. 46(3); see *London Housing and Commercial Properties* v. *Cowan* [1977] Q.B. 148.

41.51 Security of Tenure.—While the contract of tenancy exists and the tenant continues to occupy the premises as a contractual tenant he has security of tenure under his contract; he cannot be ejected by his landlord except for a breach of the conditions of the lease, and he does not need the protection of the Acts. But, when the contractual tenancy is terminated, the Rent Acts will enable the tenant to retain possession of the dwelling-house, whatever contractual undertaking he may have made to remove as a statutory tenant, provided he continues personally to occupy the house as his residence.[23] Unless he voluntarily gives up possession of the house, he may only be removed by decree of removal granted by the court. The court[24] may not make an order for possession of a house which is let on a protected tenancy or is subject to a statutory tenancy except on certain conditions.[25] These are (1) that it considers it reasonable to make such an order[26] and (2) either that suitable alternative accommodation[27] is available for the tenant or will be available for him when the order in question takes effect, or that the landlord can establish that his application falls within any of the Cases set out in Part I of Schedule 2 to the 1984 Act. There are a number of additional Cases, set out in Part II of Schedule 2, in which if the landlord can establish his right to possession at common law the court must order possession.[28]

The Cases listed in Part I of the Schedule, being the grounds on which the court has a discretion whether or not to make an order for possession, are in summary as follows: (1) non-payment of rent, or breach of an obligation of the tenancy; (2) conduct on the part of the occupiers of the dwelling-house which is a nuisance to adjoining occupiers, or its use for an illegal or immoral purpose; (3) deterioration of the condition of the dwelling-house owing to neglect or default on the part of the tenant, any person residing with him or his sub-tenant; (4) deterioration of the condition of any furniture provided for use under the tenancy owing to ill treatment by the tenant, any person residing with him or his sub-tenant; (5) steps taken by the landlord in consequence of a notice to quit given by the tenant; (6) unauthorised assignation or sub-letting by the tenant; (7) requirement of the dwelling-house by the landlord for occupation as a residence for his employee; (8) requirement[29] of the dwelling-house by the landlord for occupation as a residence for himself or certain members of his family, provided the landlord did not become landlord of the dwelling-house by purchase after certain dates[30]; (9) rent charged by the tenant for sub-letting of

[23] See paras. 41.47, *supra.*
[24] Normally the sheriff: see s. 102.
[25] s. 11(1).
[26] See *Smith* v. *Poulter* [1947] K.B. 339; *Barclay* v. *Hannah*, 1947 S.C. 245.
[27] *Turner* v. *Keiller*, 1950 S.C. 43; see also Sched. 2, Pt. IV; *Hill* v. *Rochard* [1983] 1 W.L.R. 478.
[28] s. 11(2).
[29] As to requirement, see *Kennealy* v. *Dunne* [1977] Q.B. 837.
[30] Note, however, that the court is directed not to make the order if greater hardship would be caused by granting it than by refusing to do so: s. 11(3) and Sched. 2, Pt. III; see also *Kerr* v. *Gordon*, 1977 S.L.T. (Sh.Ct.) 53.

any part of the dwelling-house in excess of the rent recoverable under the Act; (10) overcrowding, where the tenant has failed to take reasonable steps to alleviate the situation. The court has a general discretion to adjourn the application, sist the action, suspend execution of the order for possession or postpone the date of for such periods and on such terms as it thinks fit.[31]

The Cases listed in Part II of the Schedule are those in which the court is directed to make an order for possession if the circumstances of the Case are established.[32] They are in summary as follows: (11) requirement of the dwelling-house by the owner-occupier for occupation as a residence for himself or a member of his family[33]; (12) requirement of the dwelling-house for occupation by himself or by a member of his family by a person who acquired the house with a view to occupying it as his residence after his retirement; (13) where the dwelling-house had been the subject of a holiday letting and is let out of season for a specified period not exceeding eight months; (14) where the dwelling-house has been the subject of a student letting and is let out on another tenancy between student lettings for a specific period not exceeding 12 months; (15) where the dwelling-house was let on a short tenancy,[34] on the termination of that tenancy; (16) requirement of the dwelling-house for occupation by a minister or full-time lay missionary; (17) requirement of the dwelling-house by the landlord for occupation by a person employed by him in agriculture; (18) as Case 17, where an amalgamation has been carried out under the provisions of the Agriculture Act 1967; (19) requirement of the dwelling-house by the landlord for occupation by a person responsible for the control of the farming of any part of the land or by a person employed by him in agriculture, in certain situations where neither Case 17 nor Case 18 would apply; (20) where the dwelling-house has been designed or adapted for use by a person with special needs, is no longer occupied by such a person and the landlord requires it for occupation by a person who has such special needs; and (21) where the dwelling-house was occupied by a person who at the time when he acquired it was a member of the regular armed forces of the Crown, and he requires it for his residence. In all of these Cases the tenant must be warned in writing at the outset that the relevant provisions of the 1984 Act may be invoked by the landlord, although in some of them the court has a discretion to dispense with this requirement if it is of opinion that it is just and equitable to make an order for possession.[35]

41.52 Transmission on Death.—The persons who are protected by the Rent Acts are spoken of in the Acts as tenants. The expression 'tenant' is

[31] s. 12.
[32] ss. 11(2), 12(5).
[33] See *Tilling* v. *Whiteman* [1980] A.C. 1; *Kennealy* v. *Dunne, supra.*
[34] For definition of 'short tenancy,' see s. 9(1).
[35] Cases 11, 12.

defined[36] as including a statutory tenant, and this expression in turn includes statutory tenants by succession.[37] If the dwelling-house was the only or principal home of the original tenant's spouse at the time of the tenant's death, that spouse is the statutory tenant by succession so long as he or she retains possession of the dwelling-house without being entitled to do so under a contractual tenancy.[38] If the tenant leaves no such spouse, the statutory tenant by succession will be such member of the tenant's family as may be decided by agreement between the parties, or in default of agreement by the sheriff,[39] provided that member was residing with the tenant for not less than six months immediately before his death. The effect of these provisions is to confer a right on the tenant's successor to remain in occupation of the dwelling-house after the tenant's death; this is the case whether the deceased was a contractual or a statutory tenant,[40] and no formal claim is required.

Prior to the 1965 Act it was the rule that only one statutory transmission could take place,[41] and then only in favour of one person.[42] The 1965 Act and subsequent legislation provided for a further transmission to a second successor, similarly qualified, who is entitled to remain in occupation on the first successor's death.[43] The Housing (Scotland) Act 1988[44] reverted to one statutory successor: only a spouse or cohabitee may be statutory tenant by succession as 'first successor' although other members of the family[45] may acquire a statutory assured tenancy. There is no second succession on the death of the first successor, but there may be a statutory assured tenancy.[46]

A statutory tenancy is regarded as a purely personal right, which cannot be assigned; a statutory tenant cannot bequeath his right to occupancy by will, nor will it transmit on his intestacy to his executor.[47] Where the contractual tenancy still subsists at the tenant's death, however, the right to occupy the house under the lease may pass under the deceased's will or to his executor; in such a case, in view of the provisions for statutory transmission, complicated situations can arise. Where the heir and the person who would be entitled to occupy the house as a successor are one and the same person, he will be presumed

---

[36] s. 115(1).

[37] s. 3(1)(b); Sched. 1.

[38] Sched. 1, para. 2.

[39] Sched. 1, para. 3; see *Williams* v. *Williams* [1970] 1 W.L.R. 1530. As to the expression 'family,' see *Dyson Holdings* v. *Fox* [1976] Q.B. 503; *Joram Developments* v. *Sharratt* [1979] 1 W.L.R. 928 (H.L.).

[40] s. 3(1)(b); *Moodie* v. *Hosegood* [1952] A.C. 61; *Walker* v. *McArdle*, 1952 S.L.T. (Sh.Ct.) 60.

[41] *Joint Properties* v. *Williamson*, 1945 S.C. 68; *Campbell* v. *Wright*, 1952 S.C. 240.

[42] *Dealex Properties* v. *Brooks* [1966] 1 Q.B. 542.

[43] 1984 Act, Sched. 1, paras. 5–7.

[44] See the Rent (Scotland) Act 1984, s. 3 and Sched. 1, as amended by the Housing (Scotland) Act 1988, s. 46 and Sched. 6; and see Gordon, *Scottish Land Law*, para. 19–49.

[45] If resident with the original tenant: 1984 Act, Sched. 1A, para. 3.

[46] See the 1984 Act, Sched. 1A, paras. 5 and 6; and s. 3A(2) and Sched. 1B. As to assured tenancies, see para 41.46, *supra*.

[47] *Lovibond & Sons* v. *Vincent* [1929] 1 K.B. 687.

to occupy the house as a successor and not as a contractual tenant, unless he intimates to the landlord the fact that he has inherited the lease.[48] The mere payment and acceptance of rent from a contractual tenant's widow will not of itself constitute a fresh contractual tenancy in her favour where her occupancy can be attributed to a succession under the Acts.[49] If the person to whom the lease would pass by testate or intestate succession is not the same as the successor, the heir's rights and obligations are suspended while the successor continues to occupy the house.[50] While the contractual tenancy is suspended, however, the landlord still has the right to terminate the lease at the ish, and it is recommended that this be done to prevent an eventual succession by the deceased tenant's heir.[51]

41.53 Termination of Statutory Tenancy: Release from Rent Regulation.— Generally speaking, so long as the statutory tenant continues to occupy the dwelling-house he will continue to be protected by the Acts. He will, however, lose the right to protection if he voluntarily surrenders possession of the house,[52] or fails to use the house as his residence, or if the house ceases to exist. His tenancy will come to an end if he accepts a new contractual tenancy from the landlord, or, it is thought, agrees to a rent which is less than two-thirds of the relevant rateable value of the house. It will also be terminated where decree of removal is granted by the sheriff,[53] or where, by reason of a change in the law or the scope of the Acts, the statutory protection ceases to apply to the dwelling-house. Under current legislation, the 1984 Act provides[54] for the release from rent regulation of houses of any class or description on the making of an order to that effect by the Secretary of State. Where such an order is made, transitional provisions may be included to avoid or mitigate hardship to existing tenants.[55]

41.54 Part VII Contracts.—Under the Rent of Furnished Houses Control (Scotland) Act 1943, rent tribunals were set up to fix, on application, reasonable rents for furnished lettings; and the Landlord and Tenant (Rent Control) Act 1949 extended the 1943 Act by introducing provisions which were designed to afford a limited measure of security of tenure to tenants of furnished houses. The existence of a separate code for furnished lettings was, however, a source of confusion and possible abuse, and the opportunity was taken when the category of

---

[48] *Grant's Trs.* v. *Arrol,* 1954 S.C. 306.
[49] *Campbell* v. *Wright,* 1952 S.C. 240.
[50] *Moodie* v. *Hosegood, supra.*
[51] See Fraser, *The Rent Acts in Scotland,* pp. 8–9.
[52] Note, however, protection against harassment, 1984 Act, s. 22(2)(*a*).
[53] See para. 41.51, *supra.*
[54] s. 95, as amended by the Housing (Scotland) Act 1988, Sched. 10; *cf. re* Pt. VII contracts, s. 64(3).
[55] s. 95(2); *cf.* 1957 Act, Sched. 4, for transitional provisions applicable to de-control under that Act.

regulated tenancy was introduced in 1965 to exclude furnished lettings which were also regulated tenancies from this system. There remained some overlap in protection as regards those furnished lettings which also qualified as controlled tenancies, but this disappeared when the category of controlled tenancy was finally removed by the Tenants' Rights, Etc. (Scotland) Act 1980.[56] The Rent Tribunals were abolished at the same time and their functions were transferred to the Rent Assessment Committees.[57] While therefore the legislation which has been re-enacted in Part VII of the Rent (Scotland) Act 1984[58] has its origins in the system which was set up to deal with furnished lettings separately from the main stream of control, it now has a much more limited effect. As a result of the Housing (Scotland) Act 1988, no new Part VII contracts can be entered into.[59]

Part VII contracts are contracts whereby one person grants to another the right to occupy as a residence a house or part of a house in consideration of a rent which includes payment for the use of furniture or for services.[60] Where, however, the house is subject to a regulated tenancy, Part VII of the Act is expressly excluded.[61] There are certain other express exclusions: a letting is not subject to Part VII if the contractual rent includes a substantial element attributable to board[62] or if the interest of the lessor belongs to a government department[63]; a right to occupy a house or part of a house for a holiday is not to be treated as a right to occupy it as a residence[64]; and an owner-occupier who grants to another person a right to occupy his house which is a Part VII contract and gives the requisite written notice to that person may recover possession when he requires the house again as his residence without the intervention of the Rent Assessment Committee.[65] Part VII of the 1984 Act applies within the same limits of rateable value as are set for protected tenancies[66]; that is where the rateable value of the house in question on March 23, 1965 or when a rateable value was first shown for it on the valuation roll did not exceed £200, unless it was first shown in the valuation roll on or after April 1, 1978, in which case the upper limit is £1,600.[67]

Since furnished tenancies have now been brought within the full protection of the Rent Acts and where appropriate fall within the

[56] s. 46.
[57] s. 52.
[58] 1984 Act, ss. 62–81.
[59] Housing (Scotland) Act 1988, s. 44, subject to certain exceptions for transitional cases.
[60] s. 63(1). Where the rent is payable weekly, a tenant is entitled to a rentbook and written conditions: s. 79.
[61] s. 63(3)(*d*).
[62] s. 63(3)(*c*).
[63] s. 63(3)(*a*); *McLaughlin* v. *Greater Glasgow Health Board*, 1989 S.L.T. 793.
[64] s. 63(6).
[65] s. 73.
[66] *cf.* s. 1(1).
[67] s. 64(1). Limit formerly £600: increased by S.I. 1985 No. 314.

definition of regulated tenancy,[68] they no longer as a general rule fall within Part VII of the 1984 Act except where there is a resident landlord.[69] On the other hand a tenancy which is precluded from being a protected tenancy by virtue only of the fact that there is a resident landlord is treated as a Part VII contract even although the rent may not include payment for the use of furniture or for services.[70] Resident landlord lettings have therefore replaced furnished lettings as the main concern of this part of the legislation. It also extends to other cases where protection is not available, *e.g.* where the tenant shares accommodation with his landlord,[71] where the right to occupy in consideration of a rent which includes payment for the use of furniture is a licence and not a tenancy,[72] where there is substantial attendance,[73] where the rent includes any payment in respect of board,[74] where there is a furnished tenancy but at a rent too low for it to be a protected tenancy,[75] or where there is a student letting which includes payment for furniture or services.[76] There must, however, be a subsisting contract as at the date of reference to the Rent Assessment Committee.[77]

Rent control is effected by a reference of the contract by either party to the Rent Assessment Committee. In this context the Committee acts as a tribunal of first instance, as distinct from the appellate role which it has with regard to the determination of rents for regulated tenancies. The Committee may, on consideration of the case, approve the rent payable under the contract, or reduce it to such sum as they may in all the circumstances think reasonable, or dismiss the application.[78] Once fixed, the rent is entered on a register kept by the Committee, and becomes the limit beyond which any payment in excess is irrecoverable;[79] it may be varied on the application of either party on proof of change of circumstances.[80] The rent fixed by the Committee must not be lower than any amount which has been registered for the house as the rent recoverable under a regulated tenancy under Part V of the 1984 Act.[81]

Security of tenure of a temporary nature is available to the lessee under a Part VII contract on the service on him of a notice to quit.[82] In this case a distinction is drawn between Part VII contracts which were

[68] See para. 41.47, *supra*.
[69] s. 6.
[70] s. 98.
[71] s. 96.
[72] *cf. Luganda* v. *Service Hotels* [1969] 2 Ch. 209.
[73] ss. 2(1)(*b*), (4).
[74] s. 2(1)(*b*).
[75] s. 2(1)(*a*).
[76] s. 2(1)(*c*).
[77] *R.* v. *City of London, etc. Rent Tribunal, ex p. Honig* [1951] 1 K.B. 641.
[78] ss. 65 (as amended by s. 68 of the Housing (Scotland) Act 1988), 66.
[79] ss. 67, 69.
[80] s. 66(4).
[81] s. 66(2).
[82] ss. 71–74.

entered into before December 1, 1980 and those entered into on or after that date. In the former case the system which was originally set up to deal with furnished lettings applies, whereby if an application has already been made to the Committee to fix or reconsider the rent, a subsequent notice to quit will not have effect before the expiry of six months after the Committee's decision, unless the Committee sees fit in the circumstances to substitute a shorter period; an application made after the service of the notice will also entitle the lessee to this extension of notice.[83] Thereafter, unless the Committee has substituted a shorter period, further extensions of not more than six months at a time may be granted.[84] In the case of Part VII contracts entered into on or after December 1, 1980 the power to grant a postponement of the operation of a notice to quit is vested in the sheriff and the period of postponement is limited to three months.[85] Because this mechanism for protecting the lessee in occupation after the expiry of the lease operates only by means of extensions of periods of notice on a reference to the Committee, it has been held not to apply where the contract is terminated by the expiration of a fixed period.[86] Owner-occupiers who have previously occupied the dwelling-house as a residence are able to exclude these provisions for security of tenure in advance when granting the right to occupy under a Part VII contract to another person, with the result that they will be able to obtain vacant possession at once upon the expiration of the period stated in the notice to quit.[87]

41.55 Tenancies under Shared Ownership Agreements.—Tenancies under shared ownership agreements[88] are excluded from regulation under the Rent (Scotland) Act 1984; nor do they qualify as assured tenancies.[89]

41.56 Tenancy of Shops.—Security of tenure for the tenant of a shop is afforded by the Tenancy of Shops (Scotland) Acts 1949 and 1964. The expression 'shop' is defined in the 1949 Act as including any shop within the meaning of the Shops Acts,[90] that is, any premises where any retail trade or business is carried on.[91] The Act has been held not to apply to sub-tenants of a shop;[92] and a tenant who occupies premises which fall

---

[83] s. 71(1).
[84] s. 72.
[85] s. 76.
[86] *Langford Property Co.* v. *Goodman* [1954] 163 Estates Gazette 324 (Q.B.); see also *Schnabel* v. *Allard* [1967] 1 Q.B. 627, *per* Lord Denning M.R., at p. 1298. Note, however, that under the Sheriff Courts (Scotland) Act 1907, ss. 37 and 38, a notice to quit is mandatory where a house is let for a period of a year or more.
[87] s. 73.
[88] Such as contracts with non-profit housing associations, whereby the occupier buys a percentage of the equity in his home and pays rent for the remainder: *cf. Link Housing Association* v. *McCandless*, 1990 G.W.D. 39–2270.
[89] s. 47 of the Housing (Scotland) Act 1988.
[90] s. 3(2).
[91] See *Golder* v. *Thos. Johnstons (Bakers)*, 1950 S.L.T. (Sh.Ct.) 50; *Thom* v. *B.T.C.*, 1954 S.L.T. (Sh.Ct.) 21; *Wright* v. *St. Mungo Property Co.* (1955) 71 Sh. Ct. Rep. 152; *King* v. *Cross Fisher Properties*, 1956 S.L.T. (Sh.Ct.) 79.
[92] *Ashley Wallpaper Co.* v. *Morrisons Associated Cos.*, 1952 S.L.T. (Sh.Ct.) 25.

within the 1949 Act cannot claim the protection of the Rent Acts as the tenant of a regulated tenancy.[93]

Where the tenant has been given notice of the termination of his tenancy and he is unable to obtain a renewal of it on terms which are satisfactory to him, he may apply to the sheriff for a renewal of the tenancy, provided that he does so within 21 days after the service of the notice and before it takes effect.[94] Where such an application is made, the sheriff may grant a renewal for such period not exceeding one year, at such rent and on such conditions as he thinks reasonable.[95] Thereafter a new lease is deemed to take effect, and the landlord's notice to quit is treated as having lapsed.[96] The tenant may apply for further renewals, having the same right to do so as if the tenancy had been renewed by agreement between the parties.[97] Applications are conducted and disposed of under the summary cause procedure, and the sheriff's decision is final.[98]

Where he thinks it reasonable to do so, the sheriff has power to dismiss the tenant's application. He may in any event not renew the tenancy if he is satisfied as to certain grounds for a termination specified in the Act.[99] For instance, a tenant will not be able to obtain a renewal where he is in breach of a material condition of the lease, where he has refused an offer by the landlord of reasonable alternative accommodation on terms and conditions which the sheriff thinks reasonable, or if it can be shown by the landlord that greater hardship would be caused by renewing the tenancy than by refusing to do so.[1]

Further Reading

Duncan, A.G.M., *The Agricultural Holdings (Scotland) Act 1991* (1991).
Fraser, *Rent Acts in Scotland* (2nd ed., 1952).
Gill, *Law of Agricultural Holdings in Scotland* (2nd ed., 1990).
Gordon, *Scottish Land Law* (1989).
Graham, K.H.R., *Scottish Land Court, Practice and Procedure.*
Himsworth, C.M.G., *Housing Law in Scotland* (4th ed., 1994).
Hunter, *Landlord and Tenant* (4th ed., 1876).
MacCuish & Flyn, *Crofting Law* (1990).
Megarry, *Rent Acts* (11th ed., 1988).
Paton and Cameron, *Landlord and Tenant* (1967).
Rankine, *Leases* (3rd ed., 1916); Scott, *Law of Smallholdings* (1933).
Robson, P., *Residential Tenancies* (1994).
Ross & McKichan, *Drafting and Negotiating Commercial Leases in Scotland* (2nd ed., 1993).
Ross & P.Q. Watchman, *The Housing (Scotland) Act 1987* (1991).
Stair Memorial Encyclopaedia, Vol. 1 (Agriculture: Crofting and Smallholdings); Vol. 13 (Landlord and Tenant).

[93] 1984 Act, s. 10(2).
[94] 1949 Act, s. 1(1).
[95] *Ibid.*, s.1(2); *McMahon* v. *Associated Rentals Ltd.*, 1987 S.L.T. (Sh.Ct.) 94; *Robertson* v. *Bass Holdings Ltd.*, 1993 S.L.T. (Sh.Ct.) 55.
[96] *Scottish Gas Board* v. *Kerr's Trs.*, 1956 S.L.T. (Sh.Ct.) 69.
[97] 1949 Act, s. 1(4).
[98] *Ibid.*, s. 1(7), as amended by Sheriff Courts (Scotland) Act 1971, Sched. 1.
[99] *Ibid.*, s. 1(3).
[1] See *Craig* v. *Saunders & Connor*, 1962 S.L.T. (Sh.Ct.) 85; *Jalota* v. *Salvation Army Trustee Co.*, 1994 G.W.D. 12–770.

PART VII—SUCCESSION

CHAPTER 42

LEGAL RIGHTS OF SPOUSES AND ISSUE

42.1 THE following two chapters deal with the law of succession; but before entering on this subject it is necessary to notice the legal rights of the surviving spouse and issue of a deceased person in his or her estate. Although this chapter is principally concerned with the present state of the law, it is necessary to note certain aspects of the law as it existed in respect of deaths occurring before September 10, 1964, when the Succession (Scotland) Act 1964 took effect. In the case of deaths before that date the legal rights which could be claimed were: (1) terce and courtesy, legal rights of liferent accruing to a widow and widower respectively in the heritable estate of the deceased spouse; (2) *jus relictae* and *jus relicti*, the share of moveables accruing to a widow and widower respectively; and (3) legitim, or bairn's part, which was the portion of moveables falling to the surviving children. As a result of the changes introduced by the 1964 Act in respect of deaths on or after that date the only legal rights now available are those exigible from moveables, the rights of terce and courtesy having been abolished[1] in the case of deaths occurring on or after September 10, 1964, and the right to claim legitim now extends to the issue of predeceasing children.[2] By the Law Reform (Miscellaneous Provisions) (Scotland) Act 1968 illegitimate children and their issue[3] were given the right to claim legitim but because of the definition given to 'issue' illegitimate children of a predeceasing child, whether or not that child was legitimate, and others who were not 'lawful issue' had no right to legitim. Distinctions of relationship based on whether or not a person's parents were married are, however, abolished by the Law Reform (Parent and Child) (Scotland) Act 1986.[4] Accordingly, children and issue of predeceasing children now have a right to legitim from the estate of an ancestor dying on or after the commencement of the Act whether or not they were born in wedlock and whether or not they trace their descent through lawful relationship.

---

[1] Succession (Scotland) Act 1964, s. 10(1); references in any other enactment to terce or courtesy no longer have effect: Sched. 2, para. 2. For an account of these rights, see the 9th ed. of this book, para 41.3.

[2] 1964 Act, s. 11.

[3] ss. 2 and 3 and Sched. 1, paras. 3, 4, 5 and 7.

[4] s. 1.

42.2 Nature of the Rights.—Certain characteristics are common to all of these rights. They are not strictly rights of succession, but rather are claims in the nature of debts due from the deceased's estate. The claimants cannot, however, compete with creditors of the deceased; their claims attach to the free moveable estate remaining after these debts have been met,[5] and, in a case of intestacy, after satisfaction of the prior rights of a surviving spouse.[6] The spouse, parent or grandparent, as the case may be, remains free to deal with his property in his lifetime. During his life he may defeat or diminish the claims on his moveable estate by converting it in whole or in part into heritage; similarly, by selling his heritage and investing the proceeds, he could defeat or diminish the claims of a surviving spouse on it; or he may alienate his estate (either gratuitously or for onerous consideration) so as to leave nothing to meet the claims. But he cannot defeat or diminish the claims by any testamentary or *mortis causa* disposition, and his will can receive effect only after they have been satisfied. If a deed of alienation, although appearing *ex facie* to divest him of property in his lifetime, in fact leaves it under his command, or, if there is any trust or understanding whereby the benefit of the property is retained by him or he is entitled to call for its re-conveyance to him, it will not be effectual to exclude the claims of the spouse and issue.[7] This is so, for example, if the fruits or income of the property are to be paid to him or applied for his benefit. But, as rights of fee and liferent are recognised by the law as distinct interests, it is competent to exclude the claims by a deed alienating the property notwithstanding that a liferent is reserved to the grantor.[8] The mere circumstance that the deed was executed for the express purpose of shutting out the legal claims will not render it ineffectual;[9] and the fact that the beneficial right may in certain circumstances revert to the grantor of the deed does not make the deed revocable so long as the circumstances do not arise.[10] A person claiming legal rights may be required to elect between those rights and a testamentary provision.[11]

In the past a spouse's legal rights might be claimed on divorce. The 1964 Act abolished that system, and introduced a more flexible arrangement whereby financial provision was made at the discretion of

---

[5] *Naismith* v. *Boyes* (1899) 1 F. (H.L.) 79, *per* Lord Watson at pp. 81, 82, applied in *Petrie's Trs.* v. *Manders's Trs*, 1954 S.C. 430; *Russel* v. *Att.-Gen.*, 1917 S.C. 28; *Cameron's Trs.* v. *MacLean*, 1917 S.C. 416.

[6] 1964 Act, s. 10(2); see paras. 43.2 and 43.4, *infra*.

[7] Fraser on *Husband and Wife*, ii, 1000; Bell, *Prin.*, §§ 1584, 1585; *Lashley* v. *Hog* (1804) 4 Pat. 581; *Nicolson's Assignee* v. *Hunter*, March 3, 1841, F.C.; *Buchanan* v. *Buchanan* (1876) 3 R. 556; *Drysdale's Trs.* v. *Drysdale*, 1940 S.C. 85.

[8] *Collie* v. *Pirie's Trs.* (1851) 13 D. 506.

[9] *Boustead* v. *Gardner* (1879) 7 R. 139; *Skinner* v. *Beveridge* (1872) 10 S.L.R. 12; *Scott* v. *Scott*, 1930 S.C. 903; *Campbell* v. *Campbell's Trs.*, 1967 S.L.T. (Notes) 30.

[10] See *Scott* v. *Scott, supra, per* Lord President Clyde at pp. 915–916; also *Campbell* v. *Campbell's Trs., supra.*

[11] See *infra*, para. 42.7; paras. 44.33 to 44.35.

the court. That system now obtains in a modified form under which the court's discretion is subjected to certain mandatory principles.[12]

42.3 Legal Rights in Moveable Estate.—The rights which are available to the surviving spouse and issue of a deceased person out of his moveable estate are full rights of fee. These are *jus relictae* and *jus relicti*, in the case of the widow and widower respectively, and legitim, which is the portion of moveables falling to issue.

In the computation of the proportion of the free moveable estate falling to each of these rights, the deceased's moveables are divided in two or three parts according to whether he died survived only by his spouse or only by issue, on the one hand, or by both spouse and issue, on the other.[13] The possible units are: (1) the surviving spouse's share (*jus relictae* or *jus relicti* as the case may be); (2) the share falling to issue (legitim); and (3) the dead's part, which is free to pass under the deceased's will or, in a case of intestacy, according to the ordinary rules of succession. If the deceased is survived by his spouse and by issue, the moveables fall to be divided into three parts, one-third passing to each unit.[14] If he is survived by his spouse only and not by issue, or by issue only, the division is into two, one half going to the dead's part and the other passing as a legal right to the spouse or issue as the case may be. If the deceased is survived by neither spouse nor issue, there are, of course, no legal rights, and the whole of his free moveable estate will fall to be dealt with as dead's part.

The right to *jus relictae* or *jus relicti* and to legitim vests on the death of the spouse or ancestor. The amount of the shares of the free moveable estate due in virtue of these rights is determined according to the value of that estate as at that time,[15] except that, if there has been realisation of the estate in ordinary course, it is the actual realised value and not the estimate as at the date of death which determines the amount of the estate for the purpose of calculating the legal rights.[16] It is the free moveable estate actually left by the deceased which is valued for this purpose and so where a partner's contingent right to the goodwill of a partnership was, in terms of the partnership agreement, extinguished on his death, it was held that the value of the goodwill did not require to be taken into account in determining the fund available for payment of legal rights.[17] It has been decided that a discretionary death gratuity paid after death to personal representatives must, however, be brought into account in the computation of legal rights,[18]

[12] See para. 48.27, *infra*; Family Law (Scotland) Act 1985.
[13] See table set out in Meston, *op. cit.*, App. 1, reproduced in *Parliament House Book*, Division M.
[14] See Succession (Scotland) Act 1964, s. 11(4).
[15] *Gilchrist* v. *Gilchrist's Trs.* (1889) 16 R. 1118; *Russel* v. *Att.-Gen.*, 1917 S.C. 28; see also *Milne* v. *Milne's Trs.*, 1931 S.L.T. 336.
[16] *Alexander* v. *Alexander's Trs.*, 1954 S.C. 436.
[17] *Ventisei* v. *Ventisei's Exrs.*, 1966 S.C. 21.
[18] *Beveridge* v. *Beveridge's Exrx.*, 1938 S.C. 160.

but that income falling into intestacy through the operation of the Thellusson Act (or subsequent legislation against accumulations) is excluded.[19] Sums lent on heritable security, although now moveable in the general succession of the creditors, are heritable for the purposes of legal rights, as also are ground annuals, and are not included in the computation of the estate for the purpose of their ascertainment.[20] Personal bonds bearing interest, although made moveable by the Bonds Act 1661 (c. 32), as regards the general succession and legitim, remained heritable *quoad jus relictae* and *jus relicti*, but are now moveable as regards these rights also.[21] Claims to *jus relictae, jus relicti* or legitim may be extinguished by the long negative prescription, and it seems that the plea of *non valens agere* formerly competent[22] in certain cases may no longer be available.[23]

In competition with creditors the spouse and issue have no right to any part of the estate which is required to meet the debts of the deceased. But in a question of the incidence of a debt as between the heritable and the moveable estate, only moveable debts may be deducted, the principle being that in fixing the amount of the legal claims there can be deducted only those debts which, had they been assets and not liabilities of the deceased, would have gone to increase the amount of these claims.[24] Among such deductions are funeral charges, the expense of confirming and realising the estate,[25] estate duty,[26] and ante-nuptial marriage contract provisions.[26] There is authority for saying that a 'rational' or reasonable provision to a widow may diminish the legitim fund, and that a similar provision to children may diminish the *jus relicti* or *jus relictae*, if these provisions are made in *inter vivos* deeds notwithstanding that their operation is suspended till the grantor's death.[27]

42.4 ***Jus Relictae: Jus Relicti.***—By virtue of these rights the widow or widower, as the case may be, is entitled either to one-half or one-third of the free moveable estate, depending on whether there are issue to take legitim. The right of the widower to *jus relicti* was introduced by

---

[19] *Lindsay's Trs.* v. *Lindsay*, 1931 S.C. 586. For Thellusson Act, see para. 44.31, *infra.*

[20] Titles to Land Consolidation (Scotland) Act 1868, s. 117, as amended by Succession (Scotland) Act 1964, s. 34 and Sched. 3.

[21] Conveyancing (Scotland) Act 1924, s. 22; see para. 36.10, *supra.*

[22] *Campbell's Trs.* v. *Campbell's Trs.*, 1950 S.C. 48; *Pettigrew* v. *Harton*, 1956 S.C. 67; cf. *Mill's Trs.* v. *Mill's Exrs.*, 1965 S.L.T. 375, a case of intestacy supervening.

[23] The disappearance of this plea seems to follow the repeal of the older prescription statutes by the Prescription and Limitation (Scotland) Act 1973. See Walker, *The Law of Prescription and Limitation in Scotland* (4th ed.), pp. 64, 83; para. 16.10, n.54, *supra.*

[24] See Conveyancing (Scotland) Act 1924, s. 22.

[25] *Russel* v. *Att.-Gen.*, 1917 S.C. 28. As to mourning and aliment to the widow, see *Baroness de Blonay* v. *Oswald's Reps.* (1863) 1 M. 1147; *McIntyre* v. *McIntyre's Trs.* (1865) 3 M. 1074; *Griffiths' Trs.* v. *Griffiths*, 1912 S.C. 626.

[26] Inheritance tax is now deductible as previously was estate duty.

[26a] *Bell* v. *Bell* (1897) 25 R. 310.

[27] Fraser, *Husband and Wife*, ii, 1011; Bell, *Prin.*, § 1585; *Lawrie* v. *Edmond's Trs.* (1816) Hume 291; *McLeod* v. *Love*, 1914 S.C. 983.

the Married Women's Property (Scotland) Act 1881,[28] which enacts that the husband shall take the same share and interest in his wife's moveable estate which is taken by a widow in her deceased husband's moveable estate, and subject to the same rules 'in relation to the nature and amount of such share and interest and the exclusion, discharge or satisfaction thereof, as the case may be.' The Act does not affect contracts between spouses made either before or during the marriage.[29] These rights are available to a surviving spouse only, and a decree of judicial separation pronounced in favour of a wife precludes a claim for *jus relicti* on her death.[30]

42.5 **Legitim.**—As in the case of *jus relictae* and *jus relicti*, legitim is either one-third or one-half of the ancestor's moveable estate; one-third if there is a surviving spouse entitled to his or her legal rights, and one-half if there is no surviving spouse or if his or her legal rights have been renounced.

The right to claim legitim was, prior to the 1964 Act, limited to the surviving children of the deceased; it was divided equally among those children, including posthumous children, who were not forisfamiliated. 'By a child forisfamiliated is to be understood one who, by having already received from his father his share of the legitim, and discharged it, or by his renouncing it even without real satisfaction, is no longer accounted a child in the family and is therefore excluded from any further share of it.'[31] The 1964 Act introduced to claims for legitim in respect of deaths on or after September 10, 1964, the principle of representation, which had hitherto only applied to the intestate succession to moveable estate.[32] Accordingly, where a person dies predeceased by a child who has left issue, however remote, who survive the deceased, and the child would, if he had survived the deceased, have been entitled under any rule of law to legitim out of the deceased's estate, such issue have the like right to legitim as the child would have had if he had survived the deceased. Division among such issue, if more than one, is *per stirpes* at the level of the class nearest in degree to the deceased of which there are surviving members.[33] For all purposes relating to the succession to any person who has died on or after September 10, 1964 (whether testate or intestate), adopted children are treated as children of the adopter, and as such are entitled to claim legitim from his moveable estate or represent the adopting parent in a claim for legitim to which he would have been entitled by survivance.[34]

---

[28] s. 6.

[29] *Murray's Trs.* v. *Murray* (1901) 3 F. 820.

[30] Conjugal Rights (Scotland) Amendment Act 1861, s. 6.

[31] Erskine, *Inst.*, III, ix, 23; see *infra*, paras. 42.6, 42.7.

[32] Succession (Scotland) Act 1964, s. 11(1), as amended by Law Reform (Parent and Child) (Scotland) Act 1986.

[33] 1964 Act, s. 11 (2) as amended.

[34] 1964 Act, s. 23 (1).

The only circumstances in which an adopted child now has a claim for legitim against the estate of a natural parent are when that parent died on or after September 10, 1964, and the adoptive parent or parents died before that date.[35] Illegitimate children may now claim legitim as, in the event of their dying before the parent from whose estate the legitim is claimed, may their issue.[36]

42.6 Collation _Inter Liberos_.[37]—This doctrine is designed to preserve equality among the claimants on the legitim fund. 'Collation' is in Scots law a technical term meaning 'the right which belongs to persons interested in a succession to have the particular part of the estate in which one of them has acquired a separate right thrown into the common fund in order to provide an equal division of the whole.'[38] If a child entitled to legitim has received advances from the parent in his lifetime, these must (as a general rule) be collated by that child when the fund comes to be distributed among the issue; the effect of this is that the advances are brought in to augment the total amount of the legitim fund and are then, in its division, set against the share of the fund falling to that child. This principle now applies to legitim claims made not only by children but also by remoter issue representing deceased children. Such issue must collate any advances made to them by the person whose estate is being distributed, and also the appropriate proportion of any advances made to the person whom they represent.[39] Whether a provision does or does not fall to be collated depends on its nature and the circumstances in which it is made.[40] Advances 'made for the purpose of setting the child up in trade or for a settlement in the world or for a marriage portion' must be collated.[41] On the other hand, sums lent to the descendant are not the subject of collation, as these are, like other debts, due to the whole estate (and not merely to the legitim fund) and recoverable for its behoof;[42] nor are payments by way of remuneration for services rendered by the descendant,[43] or made by the ancestor in discharge of his natural duty to maintain and educate the descendant.[44] There is no ground for requiring the collation of a provision of a heritable right[45] or of a legacy to the descendant, as these do not affect the legitim fund,[46] heritable subjects not being included in

---

[35] Law Reform (Misc. Provs.) (Scotland) Act 1966, s. 5.

[36] See para. 42.1 and n. 2, _supra_.

[37] See McLaren, i, 316 _et seq._

[38] _Young_ v. _Young's Trs._, 1910 S.C. 275, _per_ Lord Kinnear at p. 288.

[39] See 1964 Act, s. 11(3).

[40] Stair, III, viii, 45; Erskine, _Inst._, III, ix, 24; _Duncan_ v. _Crichton's Trs._, 1917 S.C. 728.

[41] Bell, _Prin._, § 1588.

[42] _Webster_ v. _Rettie_ (1859) 21 D. 915.

[43] _Minto_ v. _Kirkpatrick_ (1833) 11 S. 632.

[44] Erskine, _Inst._, III, ix, 24.

[45] Erskine, _Inst._, III, ix, 25.

[46] _Ibid._

that fund and legacies being due only from the dead's part after that fund has been fixed. It has been held that a provision for a child in a marriage contract which contains no reference to discharge of legal rights must be collated if that child is to participate in the legitim fund.[47] Although an advance is of such a nature that it would fall to be collated, collation is excluded if it appears that it was the ancestor's intention that the descendant should have the advance in addition to a share of the legitim.[48]

Collation *inter liberos* arises only between children or issue of predeceasing children claiming legitim. If there is only one claimant for legitim, neither the other descendants of the deceased who have accepted provisions in lieu of legitim nor the testator's trustees have any title to insist that that claimant shall collate advances; nor, on the other hand, can that claimant require the other descendants, who are not claiming legitim, to collate advances received by them.[49] So also there is no place for collation in a question between issue and the surviving spouse.[50] A parent may, however, bargain with a child receiving an advance, that the advance is to be taken as a payment to account of that child's share of legitim, so as to entitle the parent's executors to set off the amount of the advance in accounting to that child or his issue for his legitim.[51]

42.7 Satisfaction of Legal Rights.—Where advances made by the deceased during his lifetime require to be collated *inter liberos*, these will satisfy, in whole or part, the recipient's claim to legitim. But a spouse or descendant may also be required to elect between a legacy made in his favour by the deceased and the legal rights themselves, where the legacy is made in lieu or satisfaction of the legatee's legal rights. In accordance with the principle of approbate and reprobate the legatee cannot take both such a legacy and his legal rights, but must elect between them. If he chooses to take the legacy, he forfeits his legal rights, which are held to have been satisfied by the testamentary provision; if he takes his legal rights, he loses the legacy.[52]

Formerly the legacy, for this principle to operate, required to be expressly stated to be in lieu of legal rights; if this was not so, a claim for legal rights did not necessarily involve a complete forfeiture of the testamentary provisions.[53] In the case of testamentary dispositions made on or after September 10, 1964, however, in which provision is made in

---

[47] *Elliot's Exrx.* v. *Elliot*, 1953 S.C. 43. Note that legitim may no longer be discharged by an ante-nuptial marriage contract: Succession (Scotland) Act 1964, s. 12; *infra*, para. 42.8.

[48] Erskine, *Inst.*, III, ix, 24; *Douglas* v. *Douglas* (1876) 4 R. 105.

[49] *Coats' Trs.* v. *Coats*, 1914 S.C. 744; *Gilmour's Trs.* v. *Gilmour*, 1922 S.C. 753.

[50] Erskine, *Inst.*, III, ix, 25.

[51] *Young* v. *Young's Trs.*, 1910 S.C. 275; see also *Gilmour's Trs.* v. *Gilmour, supra*.

[52] See further, paras. 44.32 to 44.35, *infra*.

[53] Para. 44.35 *infra*.

favour of the spouse or any issue of the testator, a declaration that it is made in full and final satisfaction of legal rights will, in the absence of an express provision to the contrary, be implied.[54] A claim for legal rights does not involve forfeiture of testamentary provisions in favour of issue of the claimant unless these provisions are dependent on the forfeited right of the claimant.[55]

By accepting the testamentary provision a spouse or descendant is not necessarily barred from claiming legal rights in any estate which has fallen into intestacy, or may subsequently do so; the bar operates only in so far as the claim for legal rights conflicts with the testamentary settlement.[56] But an express discharge of legal rights in absolute and unqualified terms excludes the right to claim legal rights out of estate falling into intestacy.[57]

The acceptance of a testamentary provision in lieu of legal rights, unlike a prior discharge thereof, benefits the dead's part, out of which the testamentary provision is paid.[58]

42.8 Prior Discharge of Legal Rights.—Legal rights may be discharged during the lifetime of the ancestor or spouse by the person prospectively entitled thereto. In the case of spouses, the ante-nuptial contract may contain a renunciation of *jus relictae* and *jus relicti*. This is usually done by express words of discharge,[59] but, even without such words, a settlement in the contract of the whole estate which may belong to the settlor at the date of his death on his spouse, being inconsistent with the assertion of such a claim, will exclude it.[60] Acceptance by a wife in her husband's lifetime of a liferent provided to her in a post-nuptial contract or other deed will exclude her claim to *jus relictae* out of the fund burdened with the liferent, because the acceptance of a liferent is inconsistent with a claim to carry off part of the fee.[61] In the case of children it was possible, prior to the 1964 Act, for intending spouses to discharge prospectively the right of any child of the marriage to claim legitim, even if the provision in favour of children in the ante-nuptial marriage contract was made in such a way that some of them would

---

[54] 1964 Act, s. 13. *Munro's Trs.*, 1971 S.C. 280. 'Any issue of the testator' includes any illegitimate children of the testator and issue of any such children (Law Reform (Misc. Provs.) (Scotland) Act 1968, s. 3, Sched. 1, para. 6 and now Law Reform (Parent and Child) (Scotland) Act 1986, s. 1).

[55] *Munro's Trs., supra.*

[56] *Naismith* v. *Boyes* (1899) 1 F. (H.L.) 79; *Petrie's Trs.* v. *Manders's Tr.*, 1954 S.C. 430. But note that income falling into intestacy through the operation of the Thellusson Act (or subsequent legislation against accumulations) is not subject to legal rights: *Lindsay's Trs.* v. *Lindsay*, 1931 S.C. 586; see para. 44.31, *infra.*

[57] *Melville's Trs.* v. *Melville's Trs.*, 1964 S.C. 105; contrast *Petrie's Trs., supra.*

[58] See further, para. 42.8, *infra.*

[59] *Maitland* v. *Maitland* (1843) 6 D. 244.

[60] McLaren, i, 136; *Home* v. *Watson* (1757) 5 Brown's Supp., 330; *Fisher's Trs.* v. *Fisher* (1844) 7 D. 129.

[61] *Riddel* v. *Dalton* (1781) Mor. 6457; *Edward* v. *Cheyne* (1888) 15 R. (H.L.) 33; *Smart* v. *Smart*, 1926 S.C. 392.

take no benefit from it.[62] Where the trust constituted under such an ante-nuptial contract was brought to an end during the lifetime of the parties it was held that the termination of the trust did not by operation of law revive legal rights.[63] Since the 1964 Act, however, the right of a child or remoter issue cannot be discharged without that person's consent; nothing contained in an ante-nuptial marriage contract executed on or after September 10, 1964 will operate so as to exclude that right.[64] Where provisions are made in his favour, the child or his issue will have the usual right to elect between these testamentary provisions and the right to legitim; in other words, it is now a question only of satisfaction, no longer of prior discharge. A descendant may, should he himself desire to do so, renounce his right to claim legitim during the ancestor's lifetime, if it is made clear in the deed that this is his intention; ambiguous expressions will not be construed as having this effect.

The effect of a prior discharge of legal rights is that the grantor of the discharge is treated as dead. If a spouse has during the marriage renounced his or her legal right, then the estate of the predeceaser is divisible equally between dead's part and legitim, or, if there are no issue entitled to legitim, the whole is dead's part.[65] In the case of legitim, if one child has discharged his right, the entire fund is divided among the other claimants just as if that child had predeceased the parent; and if all the children have discharged their rights, the moveable estate becomes divisible equally between *jus relicti* or *jus relictae* and dead's part; or, if the claim for these rights is not exigible, the whole becomes dead's part.

42.9   Exclusion from Legal Rights: Unlawful Killing.—A person who has unlawfully killed is excluded from participation in legal rights exigible against his victim's estate on the same principles and subject to the same reliefs as are applicable to testate and intestate succession.[66]

Further Reading

Clive, *Husband and Wife* (3rd ed., 1992).
Fraser, *Husband and Wife* (2nd ed., 1876).
Macdonald, *Succession* (2nd ed., 1994).
McLaren, *Wills and Succession* (3rd ed., 1894 and Supplement, 1934).
Meston, *Succession (Scotland) Act 1964* (3rd ed., 1982).
Stair Memorial Encyclopaedia, Vol. 25.

[62] *e.g., Galloway's Trs.* v. *Galloway*, 1943 S.C. 339.
[63] *Callender* v. *Callender's Trs.*, 1972 S.C. (H.L.) 70. There might, however, be revival of legal rights if the deed terminating the trust showed an intention to that effect.
[64] 1964 Act, s. 12.
[65] Erskine, *Inst.*, III, ix, 20. Under the common law rule that donations between spouses were revocable, a spouse might revoke a discharge of legal rights if it was in effect a donation to the other spouse (see Fraser, *Husband and Wife*, ii, 927), but that rule was abrogated by the Married Women's Property (Scotland) Act 1920, s. 5. That Act has now been repealed by the Family Law (Scotland) Act 1985, s. 24 of which provides, however, that marriage shall not of itself affect the respective rights of spouses in relation to their property.
[66] See para. 43.6, *infra*.

CHAPTER 43

INTESTATE SUCCESSION

43.1 **Presumption of Life.**—At common law a person is, in the absence of proof of his death, presumed to continue in life for a reasonable time.[1] No precise period has been fixed, but Stair speaks of 80 or 100 years.[2] In cases where evidence was adduced which satisfied the court that the explanation of the disappearance of a missing person was his death, he has been presumed to be dead although under that age.[3] Where a number of persons perished in a common calamity, there was, prior to the Succession (Scotland) Act 1964, no presumption based on age or sex as to which was the last survivor.[4] The general rule which was introduced by that Act for the purposes of succession is now that, where two persons have died in circumstances indicating that they died simultaneously or rendering it uncertain which of them survived the other, the younger person is presumed to have survived the elder;[5] but this rule is subject to two exceptions. Where the two persons were husband and wife, there is a presumption that neither survived the other;[6] the result is that the husband, having failed to survive, fails to qualify as a beneficiary in the division of the wife's estate, and vice versa. This exception is intended to avoid situations in which the estate of the elder spouse would pass to the younger and then to the younger spouse's relatives to the exclusion of those of the elder, which might be contrary to the wishes of the elder spouse. The other exception to the general rule arises where the elder person has left a testamentary provision which contains a provision in favour of the younger, whom failing in favour of a third person; if the younger person has died intestate the effect of the survivorship clause is preserved, so as to prevent the legacy passing to the younger person's relatives against the declared wishes of the elder, by a presumption, for the purposes of that provision only, that the elder person survived the younger.[7] No

---

[1] Dickson on *Evidence*, § 116; Stevenson's *Presumption of Life* (1893); *Greig* v. *Merchant Co. of Edinburgh*, 1921 S.C. 76.

[2] IV, xlv, 17.

[3] *Greig* v. *Merchant Co. of Edinburgh, supra.*

[4] *Drummond's J.F.* v. *H.M. Advocate*, 1944 S.C. 298; applied in *Ross's J.F.* v. *Martin*, 1955 S.C. (H.L.) 56.

[5] s. 31(1)(*b*).

[6] s. 31(1)(*a*).

[7] s. 31(2).

presumption arises for consideration if there is proof that one person survived the other and such proof may be on a balance of probabilities.[8]

A statutory presumption of death which applied where a person had disappeared and had not been heard of for seven years or more was introduced by the Presumption of Life Limitation (Scotland) Act 1881[9] and it substantially reduced the importance of, although it did not supplant, the common-law rule. Both the common law and the previous statutory provisions have now been replaced by the Presumption of Death (Scotland) Act 1977 which provides for the granting of declarator of death if the court is satisfied on a balance of probabilities that a person who is missing:

(1) has died, or
(2) has not been known to be alive for a period of at least seven years.[10]

The court in granting declarator must find the date and time of death. If that is uncertain it will be taken to be the end of the period to which the uncertainty relates or, where the missing person has not been known to be alive for a period of seven years or more, the end of the day occurring seven years after the date on which he was last known to be alive.[11] The court may also determine the domicile of the missing person at his death and any question relating to an interest in property arising as a consequence of his death, and may appoint a judicial factor on his estate.[12] At the expiry of the time for appeal or, if an appeal is made, on the refusal or withdrawal of the appeal, the decree of declarator is conclusive of all the matters contained in it and effective against any person and for all purposes including the acquisition of rights to or in property belonging to any person.[13] The decree may, nonetheless, be afterwards varied or recalled[14] (e.g. where the missing person reappears or fresh evidence pointing to a different date of death comes to light) but such variation or recall affects property rights only if the application for variation or recall is made within five years of the date of decree.[15] If the application is within that time, the court may make such order in relation to property rights as it considers fair and reasonable in all the circumstances of the case. The order does not, however, affect income accruing between the date of decree and the date of variation or recall,

[8] *Lamb* v. *Lord Advocate*, 1976 S.C. 110.
[9] This Act was repealed and replaced by the Presumption of Life Limitation (Scotland) Act 1891, which remained in force until repealed by the 1977 Act. See *Barr* v. *Campbell*, 1925 S.C. 317, as to the effect of a decree under the Act on the construction of a trust disposition and settlement.
[10] Act, s. 1.
[11] *Ibid.*, s. 2(1).
[12] *Ibid.*, s. 2(2).
[13] *Ibid.*, s. 3.
[14] *Ibid.*, s. 4.
[15] *Ibid.*, s. 5.

nor does it affect rights acquired by third parties in good faith and for value. If no order is made, property rights remain unaffected by the recall or variation of the decree. In considering what order should be made the court must, so far as practicable in the circumstances, have regard to restricting any rights which, as a result of the order, emerge under a trust, to rights in undistributed property plus the value, as at the date of distribution, of rights in property which has been distributed. The court must also have regard, if the facts in respect of which the decree was varied or recalled justify such a course, to the repayment to an insurer of any capital sum paid as a result of the decree. Trustees are required, on the granting of decree of declarator, to effect insurance against any claims which may arise if the decree is varied or recalled and insurers may, before paying any capital sum as a result of a decree of declarator, require the payee to effect insurance against any claim which the insurer may have in the event of variation or recall.

43.2 Succession on Death.—On the death of a person his property, so far as it is not regulated by deed, devolves on his heir or heirs according to the rules of intestate succession; but it is only to the balance after deduction of legal and prior rights, referred to as the free estate, that the rules of succession apply. There are, in effect, three sets of rules of division, which require to be considered in turn. First, after the debts and other liabilities of the estate have been met, the prior rights of a surviving spouse, if any, must be satisfied.[16] There then fall to be deducted from any moveable estate which remains such legal rights as may be due to the surviving spouse or to issue.[17] The final division of the balance of the deceased's moveable and heritable estate is made according to the rules of intestate succession applicable to the free estate.[18] The extent of the free estate will thus vary from case to case; where the intestate died survived by neither spouse nor issue no prior or legal rights will arise, and the rules of succession will apply to the whole of his estate after payment of debts, whereas in other cases all or most of the deceased's estate may be exhausted by the rights of his surviving spouse and issue. Those who succeed to property on the owner's death, whether by testate or intestate succession, are called universal successors, in contradistinction to singular successors who acquire the property of the owner in his lifetime by singular title, such as contract, conveyance or diligence.

Under the common law only those of legitimate relationship were entitled to succeed on intestacy. Limited exceptions were introduced by the Legitimacy Act 1926[19] and substantially re-enacted in the Succession

---

[16] *Infra*, para. 43.4.

[17] See previous chapter.

[18] For a convenient table of the three rules of division, see Meston, *Succession (Scotland) Act 1964* (3rd ed.), App. 1, pp. 97 *et seq.*, reproduced in the *Parliament House Book*, Division M.

[19] s. 9; replaced by 1964 Act.

(Scotland) Act 1964. A more radical change was, however, effected, by way of amendment of the 1964 Act, by the Law Reform (Miscellaneous Provisions) (Scotland) Act 1968 which, so far as succession to, and legal rights in, their parents' estate and succession by parents to the estates of their children were concerned, equiparated illegitimate with legitimate children.[20] Beyond that, there was, however, under the 1968 Act, no succession through illegitimate relationship and, accordingly, an illegitimate child still could not represent its predeceasing parent in a succession opening after the parent's death.[21] Illegitimate children were therefore excluded from succession by representation to, for example, their grandparents' estate. For the purposes of succession to the estate of an illegitimate person, that person was presumed not to be survived by his father unless the contrary was shown.[22] The Law Reform (Parent and Child) (Scotland) Act 1986, which supersedes the 1968 Act, now provides that the fact that a person's parents are not or have not been married to one another shall be left out of account in establishing the legal relationship between that person and any other person and that any such relationship shall have effect as if the parents were or had been married to one another.[23] As a result of that provision and of amendments[24] made to the 1964 Act any distinction for the purposes of succession is abolished between a legitimate and an illegitimate child and between ascendants, collaterals and issue who trace their relationship to the deceased through legitimate relationships and those who rely on illegitimate relationships. Certain rules for the presumption of paternity are laid down[25] but there is no longer any presumption that a child born out of wedlock is not survived by his father. The Act does not apply to the succession to the estate of anyone who died before its commencement.[26]

Under the previous law an adoption order did not deprive the adopted child of his rights in succession to the estate of his natural parents, nor did he acquire any in the estate of the adopter.[27] The 1964 Act[28] reversed this position in relation to the succession to any person who died on or after September 10, 1964, and provides that an adopted person is to be treated for all purposes of succession as a child of the adopter, and not as the child of any other person. He is entitled to legitim, and to represent his adopter as one of his issue. The only circumstance in which an adopted person is entitled to succeed to the

[20] ss. 1, 2 and 3 and Sched. 1.
[21] 1964 Act, s. 4(4) as amended by 1968 Act, s. 1.
[22] *Ibid.*, s. 4(3).
[23] s. 1(1).
[24] Scheds. 1 and 2.
[25] s. 5.
[26] s. 9(1)(*d*).
[27] Adoption Act 1958, s. 18.
[28] s. 23(1).

estate of his natural parent, or to claim legitim in that estate, when that parent died on or after September 10, 1964, is where the adoptive parent or parents died before that date.[29] In relation to his collaterals an adopted person adopted by two spouses jointly is treated as a brother or sister of the full blood of any other child or adopted child of both spouses. In any other situation where the relationship between an adopted child and another child or adopted child of the adopter is in issue the children are treated as brothers or sisters of the half blood only.[30]

Where there are no relatives entitled to succeed to the intestate estate, it falls to the Crown as *ultimus haeres*.[31]

The Scottish rules of succession apply to the moveable estate of a person who dies domiciled in Scotland, and to the devolution of immoveable property situated in Scotland whatever the domicile of the deceased.

43.3   The Succession (Scotland) Act 1964.—The law of intestate succession in Scotland was extensively altered by the 1964 Act, which introduced with respect to deaths on or after September 10, 1964 changes which had long been thought overdue.[32] The most fundamental change was the assimilation, after the satisfaction of prior and legal rights, of the deceased's heritable and moveable estate for the purposes of succession. The rules which now fall to be applied without distinction as between heritage and moveables are similar to those which regulated the division of moveables under the previous law, but with wider possibilities of representation; thus all the persons in the class nearest in degree to the deceased, or their representatives *per stirpes*, share equally in the whole free estate. With the disappearance of the heir-at-law the doctrine of collation *inter haeredes* was rendered unnecessary. The special characteristics of certain items are preserved by their exclusion from the Act; the previous law still regulates the succession to titles, honours, and coats of arms.[33] Significant improvements were made in the position of the surviving spouse, both as regards prior rights and in the succession to the free estate in which previously she took no part. In the line of ascent and the collateral line the emphasis on the blood tie was removed

---

[29] Law Reform (Misc. Provs.) (Scotland) Act 1966, s. 5.

[30] 1964 Act, s. 24.

[31] Stair, IV, xiii, 1; Erskine, *Inst.*, III, x, 2; *Rutherford* v. *Lord Advocate*, 1932 S.C. 674; Law Reform (Misc. Provs.) (Scotland) Act 1940, s. 6; Succession (Scotland) Act 1964, s. 7.

[32] See Meston, *op. cit.*, pp. 7–9. For an account of the prior law, see the 9th ed. of this work, para. 42.3.

[33] 1964 Act, s. 37(1); note that the exclusion extends to the Act as a whole, including its provisions as to adopted children. The exclusion also extends to the provisions of the Law Reform (Parent and Child) (Scotland) Act 1986 by which distinctions on the ground of illegitimate as opposed to legitimate relationship are abolished and consequential amendments made to the 1964 Act. In questions of succession to titles, honours and coats of arms the assimilation of illegitimate to legitimate status does not therefore apply.

by equating the rights of the mother and her relations with those of the father, and of the collaterals of the half-blood uterine with those consanguinean.

The law as regulated by the Act will now be considered in more detail.

43.4   Surviving Spouse's Prior Rights.—Where the deceased died intestate, but only then, the surviving spouse is entitled to certain valuable rights in the other's estate, known as prior rights.[34] *Quoad* these rights the surviving spouse ranks next after the creditors of the deceased, and the rights must be satisfied before the estate becomes available to the claimants for legal rights and intestate heirs.[35] Intestacy for this purpose arises where the deceased leaves the whole or any part of his estate undisposed of by testamentary disposition;[36] and in a case of partial intestacy the surviving spouse is only entitled to receive prior rights out of the intestate part of the estate. There are two separate rights, under section 8 of the 1964 Act to the dwelling-house with furniture and plenishings, and under section 9 to a financial provision out of the remainder of the intestate estate.

The right under section 8 falls into two parts. As far as the dwelling-house is concerned, the surviving spouse is entitled to receive the deceased's interest in the house, including any garden or other ground attached, in which the surviving spouse was ordinarily resident at the date of the intestate's death[37] up to a value of £110,000; it is not a requirement that the deceased should have been resident in the house at his death. The interests available to the surviving spouse under this right are those of ownership or of tenancy under a lease, other than one to which the Rent Acts[38] apply, subject in either case to any heritable debts secured over the interest.[39] If the surviving spouse was ordinarily resident in more than one house an interest in which is included in the deceased's intestate estate, he or she has the right to elect within six months of the intestate's death which one to take under this section.[40] If the value of the interest in the house exceeds £110,000, the surviving spouse is entitled instead to a payment of £110,000 in cash; if it is less, the entitlement is to the interest in the house itself, with two exceptions

---

[34] Note that a decree of judicial separation obtained by a wife extinguishes all the rights of the husband in her intestate succession: Conjugal Rights (Scotland) Amendment Act 1861, s. 6.

[35] See 1964 Act, ss. 1(2), 10(2).

[36] s. 36(1). There may, therefore, be an intestacy where the sole beneficiary under a will renounces his or her rights (*Kerr, Petr.*, 1968 S.L.T. (Sh.Ct.) 61; *Munro's Trs. v. Munro*, 1971 S.C. 280).

[37] s. 8(4) and s. 8(1), as amended by the Succession (Scotland) Act 1973, s. 1, Prior Rights of Surviving Spouse (Scotland) Order 1993 (S.I. 1993 No. 2690).

[38] See para. 33.45, *supra*; for statutory transmission on death under the Rent Acts see para. 33.51, *supra*.

[39] s. 8(6)(*d*).

[40] Proviso to s. 8(1).

where the entitlement is to the value of the interest only. These exceptions arise where the house forms only part of the subjects comprised in one tenancy of which the intestate was the tenant, or where it forms the whole or part of subjects falling into the intestate estate used by him for carrying on a trade, profession or occupation and the likelihood is that the value of the estate as a whole would be substantially diminished if the house were to be disposed of otherwise than with the assets of that trade, profession or occupation.[41] The second right under section 8 is to the furniture and plenishings falling within the deceased's intestate estate, up to a maximum of £20,000.[42] This is an entirely independent right, which exists even if the dwelling-house in which they are contained does not fall within the deceased's intestate estate. It is expressly provided[43] that the term 'furniture and plenishings' does not include any article or animal used at the date of the intestate's death for business purposes, or money or securities for money, or any heirloom. Where the intestate estate comprises the furniture and plenishings of two or more dwelling-houses, the surviving spouse is limited to the furniture and plenishings of any one of them; the right to elect must be exercised within six months, and is in no way dependent on the right to elect between the dwelling-houses themselves.

The right to a financial provision out of the intestate estate under section 9 is exigible only after the claims under section 8 have been satisfied. If the intestate was survived by lawful issue in whatever degree, the right is to the sum of £30,000 out of the remainder of the intestate estate; if no issue survive the intestate the sum is £50,000, with interest in each case at the rate of seven per cent. per annum.[44] If the surviving spouse is entitled to receive any payment or benefit, other than a bequest of the house or furniture, by virtue of a testamentary disposition out of the deceased's estate, the amount or value of the legacy must be deducted from the appropriate figure due under section 9. If the intestate estate is less than the amount which the surviving spouse is entitled to receive, the right is to a transfer of the whole of that estate; in some cases, therefore, the whole of the balance of the intestate estate may pass to the surviving spouse under this right, leaving nothing upon which the legal rights of issue or the rules of succession to the free estate can operate. If the estate exceeds the entitlement, there is a division of the entitlement among the heritage and moveable property respectively in proportion to the respective amounts of those parts so that a proper balance is preserved prior to the deduction from the moveables of legal rights.[45]

[41] s. 8(2).
[42] s. 8(3), amended as set out in n. 37 *supra*.
[43] See s. 8(6)(*b*).
[44] s. 9(1), amended as set out in n. 37 *supra*.
[45] s. 9(3); see previous chapter.

43.5 Order of Succession to the Free Estate.[46]—The free estate is that part of the intestate's estate which remains after the deduction of prior and legal rights. The order of succession to this part is set out in section 2 of the 1964 Act, by means of a statutory list. This list follows, broadly speaking, the same general pattern as that which applied under the previous law; those who are nearer in relationship to the intestate and so higher on the list are preferred to and exclude those lower down. Separate sections[47] deal with representation, and the division of the intestate estate among those entitled to it. Representation is applied throughout the succession, except in relation to a parent or spouse of the intestate. The division is equally *per capita* among those who are in the same degree of relationship to the intestate, while the representatives of predeceasing members of that class take *per stirpes*. The entitlement of a representative to participate must be determined at the date of death of the deceased; there is no provision by which an heir in intestacy dying during the administration of the deceased's estate can be represented by issue.[48]

In the first instance the succession descends to the surviving children of the intestate, including adopted children, and the issue of predeceasing children. Failing issue the succession opens to collaterals or their issue; if the intestate is survived by one or both of his parents, the parent or parents equally have right at this stage to participate to the extent of one-half of the free intestate estate. Failing issue of collaterals of the whole blood, collaterals of the half blood are entitled to succeed, without distinction between those related through the mother (uterine) and those related through the father (consanguinean).[49] Failing collaterals the succession passes to the parents, who are entitled to share the whole available estate between them; if only one survives, the whole free estate goes to the survivor. In the absence of any prior relative—that is, issue, collaterals or parents—of the intestate, the succession passes to the surviving spouse; in such a situation, there being no issue to take legitim, the surviving spouse would be entitled to take the entire intestate estate after payment of the deceased's debts. Failing a surviving spouse, the succession opens to ascendants, the relatives of the intestate's mother being placed on an equal footing with those of the father. The succession passes in the first instance to uncles or aunts of the intestate, then to grandparents, and then to collaterals of grandparents. Finally, it passes to remoter ancestors of the intestate of whatever degree, before falling to the Crown as *ultimus haeres*.[50]

43.6 Exclusion from Succession: Unlawful Killing.—By a rule of public policy no one can succeed to the estate of a person whom he has unlawfully

---

[46] See Meston, *op. cit.*, App. 2, for examples of the division of particular estates.
[47] ss. 5, 6.
[48] *MacLean* v. *MacLean*, 1988 S.L.T. 626.
[49] s. 3.
[50] s. 7.

killed. The principle is that the perpetrator of a crime is not to be allowed to profit by his own wrong. Negligence short of the standard required for culpable homicide probably does not bring the rule into operation but the degree of moral culpability need not be high.[51] In cases other than murder the court may, however, modify the effect of the rule if it is satisfied that the justice of the case so requires when regard is had to the conduct of the offender and of the deceased and to such other circumstances as appear to be material.[52] The power to modify does not, however, extend to excluding the rule entirely.[53]

43.7   Vesting of the Right of Heirs in Intestacy.—At common law the succession, unlike legal rights,[54] did not vest in the heir-at-law or next of kin by their mere survivance of the intestate. The heir-at-law acquired no transmissible right in the lands until he took the appropriate steps to establish his right; this he might do by service, that is, by means of proceedings in which, on proving his right of succession, he obtained a decree of court serving him as heir, or in certain cases by applying to the superior of the lands and obtaining from him a writ acknowledging his right as heir. The common-law rule with regard to heritage was altered by the Conveyancing (Scotland) Act 1874, which provided that a personal right to every estate in land descendible to heirs should thereafter, without service or other procedure, vest in the heir entitled to succeed thereto by his survivance of the person to whom he was entitled to succeed.[55] The heir-at-law was thus enabled immediately to dispose of the estate, and it would transmit on his death to his heir or representative. The procedures of service and acknowledgement remained in use as the means whereby the heir completed title and acquired a real right in the heritage, but they were no longer necessary in order to give him a personal right. In the same way, at common law confirmation was necessary, although certain exceptions were allowed,[56] before vesting took place in the next-of-kin; if the next-of-kin died before confirmation was expede, the right opened to those who were next in the order of succession. This common-law rule was altered by the Confirmation of Executors Act 1823,[57] to the effect of giving the heirs *in mobilibus* a vested right in the succession immediately on the death of the intestate. Accordingly, since that date, although confirmation remains necessary for the purpose of conferring on the executor a title to recover and administer the estate, it has not been required in

[51] *Smith, Petr.*, 1979 S.L.T. (Sh.Ct.) 35.
[52] Forfeiture Act 1982; *Paterson, Petr.*, 1986 S.L.T. 121.
[53] *Cross, Petr.*, 1987 S.L.T. 384, where operation of the rule was modified entirely in relation to heritage and to the extent of 99 per cent. in relation to moveable estate.
[54] See Bell, *Lectures on Conveyancing*, p. 1139.
[55] s. 9; *McAdam v. McAdam* (1879) 6 R. 1256.
[56] These are given in Erskine, III, ix, 30, and McLaren, *Wills and Succession*, ii, 1604.
[57] s. 1; *Webster v. Shiress* (1878) 6 R. 102.

order to enable an heir to transmit his right to assignees or creditors, or to his legal representatives.[58]

The assimilation of heritage and moveables effected by the 1964 Act[59] extends to the administration and winding up of the deceased's estate; and the previous arrangements for moveables now apply, with modifications, to the whole estate without distinction between heritable and moveable property.[60] Thus the whole of the deceased's estate,[61] whether he died testate or intestate, vests in his executor by virtue of the confirmation. But the right of the intestate's heirs to participate in the estate vests, by virtue of the 1823 Act, by their survivance of the intestate.[62]

43.8 Incidence of Liabilities.—The whole of the deceased's estate is liable for his debts, even before the deduction of legal rights.[63] Formerly a creditor could sue either the heir-at-law or the executor,[64] but as between the heir and the executor the rule was that the former was liable in debts which were heritable or secured over heritage, and the latter in those that were moveable.[65] Hence, an heir who was required to pay a moveable debt had a right of relief against the executor, and the executor paying a heritable debt was entitled to relief from the heir.[66] Although the heir-at-law and the distinction between heritable and moveable for the purposes of succession to the free estate have disappeared, the 1964 Act expressly saved[67] the existing law whereby particular debts fall to be paid out of a particular part of the estate. The incidence of liabilities remains of significance in computing the moveable estate for the purposes of legal rights.

The moveable estate is liable under personal contracts entered into by the deceased. If, therefore, the deceased has concluded a contract for the purchase of lands, but dies before obtaining a disposition, the lands fall into the estate as heritage, but the price is payable out of moveables.[68] On the other hand, if the deceased has sold heritage but dies before granting a disposition, the contract must be implemented, but the price received will fall to be added to the moveable estate.[69]

[58] *Frith* v. *Buchanan* (1837) 15 S. 729; *Elder* v. *Watson* (1859) 21 D. 1112. For confirmation of executors, see para. 45.3, *infra*.
[59] Succession (Scotland) Act 1964, s. 1(1).
[60] s. 14(1).
[61] Note however the exceptions in s. 37(1).
[62] See *Webster* v. *Shiress, supra, per* Lord Justice-Clerk Moncreiff at p. 106.
[63] See *Naismith* v. *Boyes* (1899) 1 F. (H.L.) 79, *per* Lord Watson at p. 82.
[64] *British Linen Co.* v. *Lord Reay* (1850) 12 D. 949; *Carnousie* v. *Meldrum* (1630) Mor. 5204.
[65] Erskine, III, ix, 48; *Duncan* v. *Duncan* (1882) 10 R. 1042.
[66] Act 1503, c. 76; Erskine, III, ix, 48.
[67] s. 14(3).
[68] *Ramsay* v. *Ramsay* (1887) 15 R. 25; *Fairlie's Trs.* v. *Fairlie's Curator Bonis*, 1932 S.C. 216, *per* Lord President Clyde at p. 220.
[69] *Chiesley* (1704) Mor. 5531; *Heron* v. *Espie* (1856) 18 D. 917; *McArthur's Exrs.* v. *Guild*, 1908 S.C. 743.

Liability attaches to heritage where the estate is liable under a heritable security, for such securities remain heritable *quoad* the debtor's succession,[70] and also for annuities granted by the deceased as these are heritable rights.[71]

In the case of testate succession the same rules hold as to the incidence of liabilities unless the testator has evinced a different intention. If trustees are directed to convey heritage burdened with debt to a beneficiary, that beneficiary is liable in the debt, and a general clause directing the trustees to pay all debts is not sufficient to relieve the beneficiary.[72] It is not clear whether this rule applies to the case of a bequest of a specific moveable subject which has been pledged or assigned in security by the testator.[73]

Further Reading

Macdonald, *An Introduction to the Scots Law of Succession* (1990).
McLaren, *Wills and Succession* (3rd ed., 1894 and Supplement, 1934).
Meston, *Succession (Scotland) Act 1964* (3rd ed., 1982).
Stair Memorial Encyclopaedia, Vol. 25.

---

[70] *Bell's Trs.* v. *Bell* (1884) 12 R. 85.
[71] *Breadalbane's Trs.* v. *Jamieson* (1873) 11 M. 912. See para. 36.11, *supra*.
[72] *Douglas's Trs.* v. *Douglas* (1868) 6 M. 223; *Macleod's Trs.* (1871) 9 M. 903.
[73] *Stewart* v. *Stewart* (1891) 19 R. 310; *Heath* v. *Grant's Trs.*, 1913 S.C. 78; *Reid's Trs.*
v. *Dawson*, 1915 S.C. (H.L.) 47, *per* Lord Dunedin at p. 50.

CHAPTER 44

TESTATE SUCCESSION

44.1 A will is a declaration of what a person wishes to be done with his estate after his death.[1] In order that the declaration may be effectual the law (with an important exception[2]) requires that it shall be expressed in writing executed in certain prescribed modes, but otherwise allows almost complete freedom of testamentary disposition. A certain degree of restriction is imposed by the existence of the legal rights of spouses and issue[3] and, as will hereafter be noticed,[4] there are purposes to which, on grounds of public policy, the law will not permit property to be devoted by testamentary deed.

It is essential to the validity of a will that the testator had sufficient capacity to test, and that it satisfies the requirements of the law in point of form.[5]

44.2 Capacity to Test: Reduction of Will.—Children under 12 have no capacity to test. A person of or over the age of 12 has testamentary capacity, which includes the capacity to exercise by testamentary writing any power of appointment.[6] A married woman can, and always could, test without her husband's consent.[7]

A testament executed by a person who was at the time insane is ineffectual. It is necessary to the exercise of the power of testing that the testator should be capable of comprehending the nature and effect of the testamentary act; and, in the absence of such capacity, the deed is null. If a person who is insane has a lucid interval, a will made in that interval may be sustained.[8] Where there is no general insanity on the part of the testator but merely delusions, it must appear that these delusions influenced the dispositions made in the will in order to deprive them of effect.[9] The law also recognises the existence of a state known

---

[1] Erskine, *Inst.*, III, ix, 5.

[2] *Infra*, para. 44.3.

[3] See Chap. 42, *supra*; note that a surviving spouse's prior rights emerge only in a case of intestacy: para. 43.4, *supra*.

[4] Para. 44.30, *infra*.

[5] As to formal validity of wills executed furth of Scotland, see Wills Act 1963, ss. 1, 2.

[6] Age of Legal Capacity (Scotland) Act 1991, s. 2(2).

[7] McLaren, *Wills and Succession*, i, 261 (in this chapter cited as McLaren).

[8] *Nisbet's Trs.* v. *Nisbet* (1871) 9 M. 937; *cf. Muirden* v. *Garden's Exrs.*, 1981 S.L.T. (Notes) 9.

[9] *Sivewright's Trs.* v. *Sivewright*, 1920 S.C. (H.L.) 63; *Ballantyne* v. *Evans* (1886) 13 R. 652.

as facility, in which, while there is no incapacity to test, there is such weakness or pliability as exposes the testator to improper practices and solicitations by interested parties.[10] This facility may be due to natural disposition, or to old age, or to ill-health. It is not in itself fatal to the will; but, if, in addition, either fraud or circumvention has been used to impetrate the will, it will be reduced.[11]

Apart from cases of mental weakness, a will may be set aside on the ground that it was executed under error induced by misrepresentation,[12] or was obtained by undue influence (that is, an influence exercised by fraud or coercion[13]). The law regards with grave suspicion a will in favour of the solicitor who prepared it, and requires that he shall clear himself from the suspicion that it was got by deception or undue influence or that the testator did not know what he was about when making the will.[14] Preparation of a will by a prospective beneficiary who is not a law agent is less objectionable, being at most a suspicious circumstance.[15]

44.3 Execution of Wills.—With effect from August 1, 1995 new rules relating to the execution of wills and other testamentary documents will come into effect.[16] The rules do not apply to wills executed before that date, in relation to which the rules set out in this paragraph continue to have effect.[17] Wills and legacies must be in writing,[18] and the writing must be (1) a deed subscribed[19] and attested in accordance with the rules as to the execution of deeds,[20] or (2) a holograph writing, *i.e.* a document in the handwriting of, and signed by, the testator; or (3) a document to

---

[10] *Morrison* v. *Maclean's Trs.* (1862) 24 D. 625.

[11] *McDougal* v. *McDougal's Trs.*, 1931 S.C. 102; *cf. West's Trs.* v. *West*, 1980 S.L.T. 6; as to fraud and circumvention in the law of contract, see *Mackay* v. *Campbell*, 1966 S.L.T. 329; 1967 S.L.T. 337 (H.L.).

[12] *Munro* v. *Strain* (1874) 1 R. 522.

[13] *Weir* v. *Grace* (1899) 2 F. (H.L.) 30, *per* Lord Halsbury at p. 31; *Forrest* v. *Low's Trs.*, 1907 S.C. 1240, *per* Lord Kinnear at p. 1256; 1909 S.C. (H.L.) 16; *Williams* v. *Philip* (1907) 15 S.L.T. 396; see also *McKechnie* v. *McKechnie's Trs.*, 1908 S.C. 93; *Gray* v. *Binny* (1879) 7 R. 332; *Ross* v. *Gosselin's Exrs.*, 1926 S.C. 325.

[14] *Stewart* v. *McLaren*, 1920 S.C. (H.L.) 148; *Forrest* v. *Low's Trs.*, *supra; Weir* v. *Grace, supra.*

[15] *Tiarks* v. *Paterson*, 1992 G.W.D. 23–1328.

[16] Requirements of Writing (Scotland) Act 1995; see Chap. 6, *supra*; and Rennie and Cusine, The *Requirements of Writing* (1995).

[17] *Ibid.*, s. 14(3).

[18] Note that there are statutory provisions as to the disposal by a member of a registered Friendly Society of sums payable by the Society and not exceeding a prescribed limit (Friendly Societies Act 1974, s. 66; *Morton* v. *French*, 1908 S.C. 171) and as to sums, under the same limit, by members of Industrial and Provident Societies. As to nominations by depositors of sums in the National Savings Bank, see National Savings Bank Act 1971, s. 8.

[19] See *Baird's Trs.* v. *Baird*, 1955 S.C. 286; *Ferguson*, 1959 S.C. 56.

[20] See above.

which the testator has appended in his own handwriting[21] the words 'adopted as holograph' or similar words. Where the testator is blind or cannot write, the deed may be executed on his behalf by a notary, law agent, justice of the peace or parish minister (or his assistant or successor) acting as notary within his own parish.[22] It is not essential to the validity of the will that this procedure be followed; a blind person may sign a will himself and, provided it is *ex facie* valid, the onus will be on any party challenging the deed to show that the testator did not comprehend its terms.[23]

In holograph documents of a testamentary character subscription by the granter is essential to satisfy the requirements of a completed testamentary act.[24] Subscription by initials or by Christian name alone or by a familiar or pet name has been held to be sufficient if that was the writer's ordinary method of signing comparable communications or can on other grounds be taken as indicating that what is written above the subscription is the concluded expression of the writer's intention.[25] If a number of writings can be read together as one document they are sufficiently authenticated by subscription of the last of them.[26] There must, however, be subscription, and it will not do to sign the deed in the middle,[27] in the margin[28] or on the back.[29] It is enough for the validity of the deed that the essential parts should be holograph; if a portion only of the document is written by the testator, as where a printed form of will is filled up, that portion will be allowed effect provided that it is in itself and apart from the other parts of the document sufficient to constitute a testamentary disposition.[30] A testamentary writing has been held to be holograph when it was typed by the granter, that being his method of writing,[31] but the document must *in gremio* state that it was typed by the granter.[32] A statement in the writing that it is holograph of the granter has no evidential value unless the subscription is admitted or proved to be genuine;[33] and proof

---

[21] But see *McBeath's Trs.* v. *McBeath*, 1935 S.C. 471.

[22] Conveyancing (Scotland) Act 1924, s. 18. See *Finlay* v. *Finlay's Trs.*, 1948 S.C. 16; *Hynd's Tr.* v. *Hynd's Trs.*, 1954 S.C. 112; 1955 S.C. (H.L.) 1; *McIldowie* v. *Muller*, 1979 S.C. 271. See para. 12.5, *supra*.

[23] *Duff* v. *Earl of Fife* (1823) 1 Shaw's App. 498.

[24] *Taylor's Executrices* v. *Thom*, 1914 S.C. 79; *McLay* v. *Farrell*, 1950 S.C. 149; *Lorimer's Exr.* v. *Hird*, 1959 S.L.T. (Notes) 8.

[25] *Speirs* v. *Home Speirs* (1879) 6 R. 1359; *Draper* v. *Thomason*, 1954 S.C. 136; *Rhodes* v. *Peterson*, 1971 S.C. 56; *cf. Jamieson's Exrs.*, 1982 S.C. 1.

[26] *Lowrie's J.F.* v. *McMillan, etc.*, 1972 S.L.T. 159.

[27] *McLay* v. *Farrell, supra.*

[28] *Robbie* v. *Carr*, 1959 S.L.T. (Notes) 16.

[29] *Boyd* v. *Buchanan*, 1964 S.L.T. (Notes) 108.

[30] *Bridgeford's Exr.* v. *Bridgeford*, 1948 S.C. 416; *Tucker* v. *Canch's Tr.*, 1953 S.C. 270; *Gillies* v. *Glasgow Royal Infirmary*, 1960 S.C. 438. See also *Ayrshire Hospice, Petrs.*, 1993 S.L.T. (Sh.Ct.) 75.

[31] *McBeath's Trs.* v. *McBeath, supra.*

[32] *Chisholm* v. *Chisholm*, 1949 S.C. 434.

[33] *Harper* v. *Green*, 1938 S.C. 198.

of genuineness is now a prerequisite for confirmation of executors nominate under a holograph will.[34]

Writings which are not in themselves capable of effect may be validated by adoption. Thus if the testator appends to an informal document a signed note in his own handwriting adopting the document as holograph, it will thus be made effectual.[35] This is the case also if the testator in a properly executed deed refers to, and adopts, prior informal writings; and it will be sufficient for this purpose if the later deed, without expressly adopting the earlier writings, recognises them and demonstrates that the testator intended that they should form part of his will.[36] Moreover, a testator may by anticipation provide in his settlement that future writings, although neither tested nor holograph, or even, it may be, unsigned,[37] shall be received as valid, and a direction of this kind imparts to writings which come within the description given in the settlement the same efficacy as if they actually formed part of that deed.[38] But if the testator has directed that the future writings are to be 'under my hand,' a writing to be effective must be subscribed, unless he has made it plain that it need not be so.[39] Unauthenticated alterations to a duly executed will are generally inoperative but it has been observed that there may be circumstances in which they can receive effect if they are shown to have been made before execution.[40]

44.4 **Other Writings with Testamentary Effect.**—Besides deeds which are in their nature *mortis causa*, other deeds may contain provisions which are regarded as testamentary. An instance is to be found in marriage contracts. Provisions in these conceived in favour of parties who are to take on the death or failure of the spouses and issue of the marriage are generally treated as testamentary and, therefore, revocable.[41] Again, a special destination in the title to heritage will carry the property on the death of the proprietor to the person named in the destination. If a party acquiring property in his own right chooses to take the title in such terms as to himself and A or the survivor of them, this will operate

[34] See 1964 Act, s. 21; an affidavit by each of two persons that the writing and signature are in the testator's handwriting is sufficient.

[35] *Gavine's Tr.* v. *Lee* (1883) 10 R. 448; *Macphail's Trs.* v. *Macphail*, 1940 S.C. 560; *Hogg's Exr.* v. *Butcher*, 1947 S.N. 141, 190.

[36] *Callander* v. *Callander's Trs.* (1863) 2 M. 291; *Cross's Trs.* v. *Cross*, 1921 1 S.L.T. 244.

[37] As in *Crosbie* v. *Wilson* (1865) 3 M. 870; *Taylor's Executrices* v. *Thom*, *supra*, per Lord Skerrington.

[38] *Lowson* v. *Ford* (1866) 4 M. 631, *per* Lord Cowan.

[39] *Waterson's Trs.* v. *St. Giles Boys' Club*, 1943 S.C. 369, overruling *Ronald's Trustees* v. *Lyle*, 1929 S.C. 104. See too *Russell's Exr.* v. *Duke*, 1946 S.L.T. 242 (list of bequests on one side of used envelope and signature on other held a valid will).

[40] *Syme's Exrs.* v. *Cherrie*, 1986 S.L.T. 161.

[41] See *Lord Advocate* v. *Stewart* (1906) 8 F. 579, at p. 589; *Barclay's Trs.* v. *Watson* (1903) 5 F. 926; and *Law, Petr.*, 1962 S.C. 500.

as a nomination of A as successor to that party in the right to the property.[42] Although such destinations may have certain testamentary effects they are not, however, strictly writings of a testamentary character[43] and so where the property which is the subject of a special destination in favour of A and B and the survivor has been provided solely by A, B's share passes to A on B's death by reversion and unburdened by B's debts. It is not affected by any testamentary act of B or part of his estate passing by succession.[44] And the same effect is allowed to special destinations occurring in documents of title, such as bonds, debentures, certificates of debt, and stock or share certificates of public companies.[45] On the other hand, no such effect is given to the terms of deposit-receipts; a deposit-receipt cannot operate as a will[46] and instructions attached to or written on a deposit-receipt do not receive testamentary effect unless they are indicative of an intention to bequeath.[47]

44.5 Intention to Test.—The law does not require that a will shall be in any particular form or that it shall be expressed in technical language. However imperfect the language, a document will receive effect as a will if it can fairly be construed as meaning that the author intended thereby to bequeath his estate in whole or in part.[48] A letter to the intended beneficiary may have this effect.[49] On the other hand, a mere list of names and sums of money is not sufficient for this purpose.[50]

If on the face of a writing there be something which raises a doubt whether it was meant to be a testament or, on the other hand, merely a memorandum or note of instructions for the preparation of a formal deed, evidence will be admitted for the purpose of determining the character of the writing. Thus, in *Munro* v. *Coutts*[51] a testator, who had executed a formal settlement, sent to his agent a letter containing a holograph signed document beginning 'I wish a codicil to be made to my last will and settlement in the following manner,' and containing a number of bequests. There being doubt regarding this document, extrinsic evidence was admitted; and, on considering the terms of the correspondence between the testator and his agent and the other facts

---

[42] *Dennis* v. *Aitchison*, 1923 S.C. 819, *per* Lord President Clyde at p. 824; 1924 S.C. (H.L.) 122. Contrast contractual destinations, para. 44.9, *infra*.

[43] *Hay's Tr.* v. *Hay's Trs.*, 1951 S.C. 329, *per* Lord President Cooper at p. 333.

[44] *Barclays Bank* v. *McGreish*, 1983 S.L.T. 344.

[45] *Connell's Trs.* v. *Connell's Trs.* (1886) 13 R. 1175; *Dennis* v. *Aitchison*, 1924 S.C. (H.L.) 122; *Drysdale's Trs.* v. *Drysdale*, 1922 S.C. 741; *Duff's Trs.* v. *Phillips*, 1921 S.C. 287.

[46] *Dinwoodie's Exr.* v. *Carruthers' Exr.* (1895) 23 R. 234.

[47] *Gray's Trs.* v. *Murray, etc.*, 1970 S.L.T. 105.

[48] *Colvin* v. *Hutchison* (1885) 12 R. 947; *Draper* v. *Thomason*, 1954 S.C. 136.

[49] *Rhodes* v. *Peterson, supra*.

[50] *Waddell's Trs.* v. *Waddell* (1896) 24 R. 189; *Cameron's Trs.* v. *Mackenzie*, 1915 S.C. 313.

[51] (1813) 1 Dow 437.

proved, the House of Lords came to the conclusion that the document, although not defective in form, was intended to be no more than instructions to the agent and not a final testamentary writing. The same conclusion has been reached in cases where the doubt as to the effect of the document was created by the language of a letter with which the document was forwarded to the writer's law agent.[52] The effect of a title or heading placed on a deed may be such as to cast doubt on the deed, and to allow of evidence as to the circumstances attending its execution. The fact that a writing, which was in other respects a perfect will, was headed 'Notes of Intended Settlement,' was held, where the evidence was inconclusive, not sufficient to deprive the writing of effect.[53] But deeds entitled 'Drafts' have been rejected.[54] The document must evince a present concluded testamentary intention.[55]

44.6 Revocability of Will.—A will is in its nature revocable at any time by the testator. It matters not that the will has been delivered; and a statement in a testamentary deed that it is irrevocable is of no effect. A person may, however, bind himself to leave his estate by will to another; and in that case a will made in contravention of the contract or promise may be reduced.[56]

44.7 Revocation of Will.—A will may be revoked in whole or in part in various ways. Thus (1) the testator may destroy, or tear up, the deed or may obliterate or cancel the writing. When it is shown that a man duly executed a will and had it at one time in his custody, but it is not forthcoming at his death, the presumption will be that he destroyed it *animo revocandi*.[57] But, if it be shown that the destruction or obliteration occurred without *animus revocandi* on the part of the testator, as, *e.g.* if it were accidental or were due to insanity, or were done without his consent, the will would not be revoked.[58] Unauthenticated cancellations are of no effect, unless they render the original indecipherable[59] but the authenticated cancellation of a residue clause has been held to be valid, notwithstanding the apparent misapprehension of the testator that there would be no residue.[60] Where a second

[52] *Young's Trs.* v. *Henderson*, 1925 S.C. 749; *MacLaren's Trs.* v. *Mitchell & Brattan*, 1959 S.C. 183.
[53] *Hamilton* v. *White* (1882) 9 R. (H.L.) 53.
[54] *Sprot's Trs.* v. *Sprot*, 1909 S.C. 272; *Forsyth's Trs.* v. *Forsyth* (1872) 10 M. 616.
[55] *Jamieson's Exrs.*, 1982 S.C. 1.
[56] *Curdy* v. *Boyd* (1775) M. 15946; *Paterson* v. *Paterson* (1893) 20 R. 484; *Smith* v. *Oliver*, 1911 S.C. 103, *per* Lord President Dunedin at p. 111. The promise can be proved only by writ or oath; *Gray* v. *Johnston*, 1928 S.C. 659.
[57] *Bonthrone* v. *Ireland* (1883) 10 R. 779, *per* Lord Young at p. 790; *Clyde* v. *Clyde*, 1958 S.C. 343.
[58] Bell, *Prin.*, § 1866; McLaren, i, 409; *Fotheringham's Trs.* v. *Reid*, 1936 S.C. 831.
[59] *Manson* v. *Edinburgh Royal Institution*, 1948 S.L.T. 196; *Hogg's Exr.* v. *Butcher*, 1947 S.N. 141, 190.
[60] *Thomson's Trs.* v. *Bowhill Baptist Church*, 1956 S.C. 217.

will was executed by a testatrix and an earlier one destroyed in accordance with professional practice by her solicitor, and later it was found that the second was invalid, it was held that the earlier will had not been revoked by its destruction, but that its effective revocation was conditional upon the valid execution of a later will.[61] (2) He may revoke the will by a subsequent testamentary writing. This may be express, the testator declaring that earlier wills are revoked; but even an express general revocation of prior wills does not necessarily revoke a bequest of a specific subject, at least if it is contained in a separate writing delivered to the beneficiary.[62] Revocation may be implied from the circumstance that the two deeds are inconsistent, in which case the later deed will prevail. A universal settlement of the testator's estate effected by the later deed will have that result.[63] A will which has other characteristics of a universal settlement may not be so regarded if it lacks a residue clause.[64] It is only in so far as the two deeds are inconsistent that the earlier one is revoked by implication; and if the two are only partially inconsistent, there is revocation only to the extent of that inconsistency. In so far as the deeds can be brought into harmony, they will be read as together forming the testator's will.[65] Where a testamentary writing has been revoked by a subsequent testamentary writing which is itself cancelled by the testator, the general rule is that the earlier will revive and receive effect as if it had never been revoked; but it has been suggested that this rule may, in certain circumstances, suffer exception.[66]

44.8 *Conditio si Testator sine Liberis Decesserit.*—A settlement which makes no provision for children *nascituri* is presumed to be revoked by the subsequent birth of a child whether legitimate or illegitimate[67] to the testator. This presumption rests upon the supposition that in the altered circumstances the testator would not have desired that his will should remain in force; and the presumption may be rebutted by circumstances showing his intention that the will should stand notwithstanding the birth of the child.[68] The strongest case for the application of this rule is

[61] *Cullen's Exr.* v. *Elphinstone*, 1948 S.C. 662.

[62] *Clark's Exr.* v. *Clark*, 1943 S.C. 216.

[63] *Macrorie's Exrs.* v. *McLaren*, 1984 S.L.T. 271; *Dick's Trs.* v. *Dick*, 1907 S.C. 953; *Bertram's Trs.* v. *Matheson's Trs.* (1888) 15 R. 572.

[64] *Duthie's Exr.* v. *Taylor*, 1986 S.L.T. 142.

[65] *Stoddart* v. *Grant* (1852) 1 Macq. 163; *Scott* v. *Sceales* (1864) 2 M. 613; *Gordon's Executor* v. *Macqueen*, 1907 S.C. 373; *Mitchell's Administratrix* v. *Edinburgh Royal Infirmary*, 1928 S.C. 47; *Morton's Exr., Petr.*, 1985 S.L.T. 14.

[66] See *Bruce's J.F.* v. *Lord Advocate*, 1964 S.L.T. 316; 1968 S.L.T. 242; 1969 S.L.T. 337; 1969 S.C. 296; *cf. Scott's J.F.* v. *Johnston*, 1971 S.L.T. (Notes) 41.

[67] Formerly, Law Reform (Misc. Provs.) (Scotland) Act 1968, ss. 6(2) and (3) and now Law Reform (Parent and Child) (Scotland) Act 1986, s. 1. The birth of an illegitimate child does not have this effect in the case of a deed executed before November 25, 1968.

[68] *Elder's Trs.* v. *Elder* (1895) 21 R. 704, 22 R. 505; *Millar's Trs.* v. *Millar* (1893) 20 R. 1040; *Stuart Gordon* v. *Stuart Gordon* (1899) 1 F. 1005.

that of a testator who was childless when the will was made and died without having a reasonable opportunity of altering it. But it is not enough to displace the presumption that there were children in life at the date of the will[69] or that the testator survived the birth of the child for a considerable period without revising the will.[70] If the will is revoked, it is revoked *in toto*, but earlier wills expressly revoked by it are not revived.[71] If, however, the revocation of the earlier will was merely by implication, as in the case of a universal settlement, the earlier will becomes operative on the revocation of the later will by a subsequent birth.[72] The right to found on the *conditio* is personal to the after-born child, and no other party can challenge the will on this ground.[73]

44.9   Revocation of Special Destinations.—As has been pointed out above,[74] a special destination may have testamentary effect. There are cases in which such a destination is contractual as between the parties who have created it, so as to exclude the possibility of testamentary revocation except by their joint consent.[75] Where both A and B have contributed jointly to the purchase of property of which the title is taken in name of A and B and the survivor, A and B are each free to deal with their respective shares by *inter vivos* deed.[76] When property is held in joint names, each party having contributed an equal share of the purchase price, a special destination cannot be revoked by testamentary deed.[77] If one of the parties has paid the whole purchase price, he is entitled to revoke the special destination *quoad* his own share.[78] If, however, the disposition narrates that the purchase price was paid in equal shares, extrinsic evidence to show that it was in fact paid by one party is inadmissible,[79] unless both parties agree that the narrative is inaccurate.[80] Where there is no contractual element in a special destination, it may be expressly or impliedly revoked by testamentary deed. It cannot, however, be impliedly revoked by a testamentary deed executed on or after September 10, 1964. By statute such a deed is only effective to evacuate a special destination if it contains a specific reference to the

---

[69] *Knox's Trs.* v. *Knox*, 1907 S.C. 1123.

[70] *Nicolson* v. *Nicolson's Tutrix*, 1922 S.C. 649; *Rankin* v. *Rankin's Tutor* (1902) 4 F. 979.

[71] *Crown* v. *Cathro* (1903) 5 F. 950; *Elder's Trs.* v. *Elder* (1895) 22 R. 505.

[72] *Nicolson* v. *Nicolson's Tutrix, supra*; McLaren, Supplement, p. 106.

[73] *Stevenson's Trs.* v. *Stevenson*, 1932 S.C. 657.

[74] Para. 44.4, *supra*.

[75] *Renouf's Trs.* v. *Haining*, 1919 S.C. 497.

[76] *Steele* v. *Caldwell*, 1979 S.L.T. 228, followed in *Smith* v. *MacKintosh*, 1989 S.L.T. 148.

[77] *Perrett's Tr.* v. *Perrett*, 1909 S.C. 522; *Chalmers' Trs.* v. *Thomson's Exrx.*, 1923 S.C. 271; and see *Shand's Trs.* v. *Shand's Trs.*, 1966 S.L.T. 306; *Marshall* v. *Marshall's Exr.*, 1987 S.L.T. 49.

[78] *Brown's Trs.* v. *Brown*, 1943 S.C. 488; *Hay's Tr.* v. *Hay's Trs.*, 1951 S.C. 329.

[79] *Gordon-Rogers* v. *Thomson's Exrs.*, 1988 S.L.T. 618.

[80] As in *Hay's Tr., supra*.

destination and a declared intention on the part of the testator to evacuate it.[81] In determining the effect on a special destination of a testamentary deed executed prior to September 10, 1964, which makes no specific reference to that destination, the following principles apply: (a) If a testator holds property on a destination created by a third party, that destination is presumed to be revoked by a general settlement of the testator which is dated after the destination and is inconsistent with the terms thereof.[82] (b) If a testator holds property on a destination created by him in favour of himself and another or others after the date of his testamentary general settlement, the terms of that destination must receive effect as the last expression of the testator's intention in relation to that property.[83] (c) If the special destination was granted by the testator in favour of himself and others before he made his will, there is a presumption that it was not revoked by the subsequent general settlement.[84] The destination and the settlement must be read together as expressions of the testator's intention. If, therefore, the purposes of the settlement are irreconcilable with the terms of the destination, the presumption is rebutted and the destination is held to have been revoked by implication.[85] But a clause in the subsequent settlement which revokes all prior testamentary writings without reference to special destinations will not *per se* revoke a prior destination made by the testator, because a special destination is not a writing of a testamentary nature, although it may have testamentary effect.[86]

44.10 Mutual Wills.—A mutual settlement is a deed in which two or more parties give directions as to the disposal of their estates after their deaths. The question which has most commonly arisen in regard to this unfortunate form of deed is whether it is contractual, so as to debar the survivor of the parties from altering it as regards his or her estate after the death of the other party or parties, or is merely testamentary, leaving the survivor free to do so. The decisions show that this question must be solved on the terms of the particular deed, but the following rules may be extracted: (1) As a rule a mutual settlement is no more than two wills contained in one deed, and as wills are revocable, the

---

[81] Succession (Scotland) Act 1964, s. 30; *Stirling's Trs.*, 1977 S.L.T. 229; *Marshall v. Marshall's Exr.*, supra.

[82] *Thoms v. Thoms* (1868) 6 M. 704.

[83] *Perrett's Trs.*, supra.

[84] *Campbell v. Campbell* (1880) 7 R. (H.L.) 100; *Perrett's Trs.*, supra, per Lord President Dunedin at p. 527.

[85] *Perrett's Trs.*, supra, and *Dennis v. Aitchison*, 1924 S.C. (H.L.) 122; see also *Brown's Trs. v. Brown* and *Hay's Tr. v. Hay's Trs.*, supra, where the settlements expressly included the conveyance of all estate held under special destinations.

[86] *Murray's Exrs. v. Geekie*, 1929 S.C. 633. Note that, on implied revocation, this case is distinguishable from *Brown's Trs.* and *Hay's Trs.*, supra, because there is here no express reference in the dispositive clause of the settlement to estate held under special destinations.

survivor may revoke the deed *quoad* his own estate; (2) where the parties are spouses, it is easier to hold that the provisions in favour of the spouses themselves or their children are contractual than it is in the case of provisions in favour of other parties; (3) the survivor may be debarred from altering the deed notwithstanding that, under its terms, he is given the fee of the whole estate,[87] but it is more difficult to hold that this is so in that case than where his interest in the estate of the predecessor is limited to a liferent.[88] If there is a clause in the deed dealing with revocation by the parties or the survivor, the terms in which it is expressed have great weight in determining the character of the deed.[89] It is very difficult to establish that a mutual will is irrevocable *stante matrimonio*.[90]

44.11 Interpretation of Wills: Extrinsic Evidence.[91]—In construing a testamentary deed it is the object of the court to ascertain and give effect to the intention of the testator. That intention is to be collected from the language of the deed read in the light of those circumstances (such as the state of the testator's family and property) known to the testator and with reference to which he has written his deed;[92] and it is not permissible to search for his intention apart from the terms of his deed. Evidence of the testator's own opinion of the effect of his will is imcompetent,[93] and it is doubtful whether revoked writings can be used as an aid to construction.[94]

The cases in which extrinsic evidence in aid of the interpretation of a will is admitted are all of an exceptional nature. The rules on this point may be summarised thus.[95] (a) A testator is always presumed to use words in their strict and primary acceptation, unless it appears from the context that he has used them in a different sense. (b) In the absence of such a context, the words must have their strict and primary sense if, so interpreted, they are sensible with reference to extrinsic circumstances; if not so sensible, extrinsic evidence is admitted. (c) If the characters in which a will is written need deciphering, or the language requires to be translated, evidence is admitted to declare what the characters are or to

---

[87] As in *Duthie* v. *Keir's Exr.*, 1930 S.C. 645.

[88] *United Free Church of Scotland* v. *Black*, 1909 S.C. 25; *Lawrie's Exrs.* v. *Haig*, 1913 S.C. 1159; *Corrance's Trs.* v. *Glen* (1903) 5 F. 777.

[89] *Lawrie's Exrs.* v. *Haig* and *Duthie* v. *Keir's Exr.*, *supra*; *Craig's Trs.* v. *Craig's Trs.*, 1927 S.C. 367; *Thomson's Trs.* v. *Lockhart*, 1930 S.C. 674, at p. 678.

[90] During the existence of the marriage: *Saxby* v. *Saxby's Exrs.*, 1952 S.C. 352.

[91] See Walkers, *Evidence*, Chap. XXI.

[92] *Trs. of the Free Church of Scotland* v. *Maitland* (1887) 14 R. 333; *Hannay's Trs.* v. *Keith*, 1913 S.C. 482; *Dunsmure* v. *Dunsmure* (1879) 7 R. 261, *per* Lord Gifford.

[93] *Devlin's Trs.* v. *Breen*, 1945 S.C. (H.L.) 27.

[94] *Devlin's Trs.*, *supra*, at p. 32.

[95] The rules are formulated in Sir James Wigram's book on *Extrinsic Evidence in Aid of the Interpretation of Wills* (5th ed., 1914), and are quoted in McLaren, i, 374. For an example of a case in which the context in which a word was used required its being given a meaning other than its strict and primary acceptation see *Yule's Trs.*, 1981 S.L.T. 250 ('child' interpreted as meaning 'grandchild').

inform the court of the meaning of the language. (d) For the purpose of determining the object of the testator's bounty or the subject of disposition or the quantity of interest given, the court may inquire into all the material facts as to the person or property or the circumstances of the testator and his family and affairs. In accordance with the maxim, *falsa demonstratio non nocet dummodo constet de persona (re)*, a mistake in the description of the subject or object is not fatal to the bequest, and extrinsic evidence is admissible in order to determine the person or thing intended. Thus, where a legacy was bequeathed to 'William Keiller, confectioner, Dundee,' and there was no such person, the court allowed evidence in order to determine whether the legatee was William Keiller, a confectioner in Montrose, or James Keiller, a confectioner in Dundee.[96] Where, however, there is no ambiguity, parole evidence of the testator's intention will not be admitted to give an enlarged meaning to a description which is capable of application in its terms.[97] Evidence of statements by the testator as to his intention is not allowed except in one case, namely, where the description of the legatee, or of the thing bequeathed, is equally applicable in all its parts to two persons, or to two things.[98] If, after all competent evidence has been received, the subject or object of the legacy is uncertain it will fail on the ground of uncertainty.[99]

Where two clauses of a settlement are contradictory and cannot be reconciled, then, in the absence of any reason for preferring the one to the other, the later will receive effect as presumably embodying the latest expression of the testator's intention.[1]

44.12 Testamentary Disposition of Heritage.—Prior to the Titles to Land Consolidation (Scotland) Act 1868, there could be no valid testamentary disposition of heritage unless it was in the form of a conveyance *de praesenti* taking effect at death, and the word 'dispone' had to be used.[2] But by section 20 of that statute it is enacted that the succession to lands may be settled by testamentary deed and that the word 'dispone' need not be used; it is enough if the deed contains, with reference to lands, 'any word or words which would, if used in a will or testament with reference to moveables, be sufficient to confer upon the executor of the grantor, or upon the grantee or legatee of such moveables, a right to claim and receive the same.'

[96] *Keiller* v. *Thomson's Trs.* (1826) 4 S. 724; *Macfarlane's Trs.* v. *Henderson* (1878) 6 R. 288; *Johnstone's Exrs.* v. *Johnstone* (1902) 10 S.L.T. 42; *Cathcart's Trs.* v. *Bruce*, 1923 S.L.T. 722. Cf. also *Shairp* v. *Henderson*, 1930 S.L.T. 743.

[97] *Fortunato's J.F.* v. *Fortunato*, 1981 S.L.T. 277.

[98] *Charter* v. *Charter* (1874) L.R. 7 H.L. 364, *per* Earl Cairns L.C.; *Re Ray* [1916] 1 Ch. 461.

[99] See para. 44.13, *infra*.

[1] McLaren, i, 354.

[2] *Kirkpatrick's Trs.* v. *Kirkpatrick* (1874) 1 R. (H.L.) 37; *Duke of Argyll* v. *Riddell*, 1912 S.C. 694, *per* Lord President Dunedin at p. 741.

44.13 Uncertainty: Delegation of Power of Testing.—If it is impossible, on the construction of the deed, to ascertain the subject matter, or the object, of the bequest, the legacy will fail from uncertainty.[3] This ground of objection has been much considered in connection with cases in which a testator places his estate in the hands of trustees with a power to them to select the beneficiaries. The law does not admit of the delegation of the power of testing. A direction, therefore, to trustees to dispose of the testator's estate as they think proper is ineffectual.[4] But, on the other hand, a testator may confer on his trustees, or on a selected individual, power to choose the beneficiaries from among a class of persons or objects and, provided this class be sufficiently definite, the bequest will be sustained.[5] If the class is not a definite one,[6] or if the testator omits to appoint a trustee or executor,[7] the testator's directions will fail on the ground of uncertainty.

44.14 Residue: Intestacy.—In well-drawn testaments the bequest of legacies is usually followed by a clause disposing of the residue of the testator's estate. Residue comprises the whole of the testator's estate, capital and income, not required for the antecedent purposes of the testamentary deed or deeds.[8] The residuary legatee is regarded by the law as taking the estate subject to the burden of the prior purposes of the will;[9] and if, and to the extent to which, a legacy fails, the subject of the legacy enures to residue. If the residue is given at the testator's death, it matters not that the failure of the legacy is not ascertained until a later date, the subject will fall to the residuary legatee. When a testator makes a bequest of the 'free residue' of his estate, and legal rights are claimed, these as well as debts and legacies are prima facie to be deducted before the 'free residue' is ascertained.[10]

The right of the heirs *ab intestato* is displaced only in so far as the estate is effectually disposed of in favour of others. If, therefore, there be no residuary bequest, the subject of any testamentary disposition which fails of effect will fall into intestacy; and similarly, if the residuary bequest fails, the residue to the extent of that failure will devolve on the heirs *ab intestato*. These heirs are ascertained at the date of the

---

[3] McLaren, i, 349; *Magistrates of Dundee* v. *Morris* (1858) 3 Macq. 134, *per* Lord Wensleydale; *Robertson's J.F.* v. *Robertson*, 1968 S.L.T. 32.

[4] *Bannerman's Trs.* v. *Bannerman*, 1915 S.C. 398, *per* Lord Skerrington; *Anderson* v. *Smoke* (1898) 25 R. 493; *Wood* v. *Wood's Exrx.* 1995 S.L.T. 563.

[5] See *Crichton* v. *Grierson* (1828) 3 W. & S. 323, and *Hill* v. *Burns* (1826) 2 W. & S. 80, and cases there cited. See para. 44.29, *infra.*

[6] As in *Blair* v. *Duncan* (1901) 4 F. (H.L.) 1; *Turnbull's Trs.* v. *Lord Advocate*, 1918 S.C. (H.L.) 88. The cases are discussed in *Reid's Trs.* v. *Cattanach's Trs.*, 1929 S.C. 727. As to the effect of a bequest for 'charitable' purposes see para. 46.17, *infra.*

[7] *Angus' Exrx.* v. *Batchan's Trs.*, 1949 S.C. 335.

[8] *Sturgis* v. *Campbell* (1865) 3 M. (H.L.) 70, *per* Lord Westbury.

[9] *Storie's Trs.* v. *Gray* (1874) 1 R. 953.

[10] *Samson* v. *Raynor*, 1928 S.C. 899.

testator's death and acquire right then to any portion of the estate which may be found not to have been disposed of.[11]

44.15 Classification of Legacies.—Legacies may be classified as general or special.[12] A general legacy is one in which the subject given is 'bequeathed indefinitely without any character distinguishing it from others of the same kind belonging to the deceased,'[13] as, *e.g.* a sum of money or a certain quantity or amount of things falling under some generic description. In this case the legatee has no more than a right of personal action against the executor or trustee for implement of the legacy. A special legacy, on the other hand, is the bequest of a determinate subject: 'where some individual is left'[14] as, *e.g.* a certain horse, or a debt due to the testator by a particular person, or some particular investment belonging to the testator. This has the effect of a *mortis causa* assignation to the legatee, who may bring an action against any person in possession of the subject after the death of the testator in order to compel him to make it forthcoming; and, although the executor must be called in this action, this is only to obviate the risk of the subject being carried off by the legatee, while the rest of the testator's estate may be insufficient to pay his debts so that the subject of the specific legacy is required for this purpose.[15] Demonstrative legacies are those in which the testator indicates the source from which the legacy is to be provided.[16] Where the legacy takes this form, the question may arise whether it is dependent on the existence or sufficiency of the funds denoted as the source of payment, or whether the legatee has, in the event of these funds disappearing or proving insufficient, a claim against the general estate of the testator. Thus in *Douglas's Exrs.*[17] the testator bequeathed sums of money 'to be paid out of the arrears of income due to me from the Monteath trust estate,' and, these arrears being insufficient, it was held that the balance must be made up out of the residue of the estate.

44.16 Ademption of Special Legacies.—Where the subject of a special legacy has ceased to form part of the testator's estate at the date of his death the legacy is adeemed, and nothing is due to the legatee. The intention of the testator is not considered in this matter. The only inquiries necessary are (a) whether the legacy is a special one, and, if so (b) whether the thing bequeathed does or does not remain part of the testator's estate.[18] Thus, if the testator has alienated the thing

[11] *Lord* v. *Colvin* (1865) 3 M. 1083.
[12] Erskine, III, ix, 11; Bell, *Prin.*, §§ 1876, 1877; McLaren, i, 575.
[13] Erskine, III, ix, 13.
[14] Stair, III, viii, 38.
[15] Erskine and Bell, *supra*.
[16] McLaren, i, 575.
[17] (1869) 7 M. 504.
[18] *McArthur's Exrs.* v. *Guild*, 1908 S.C. 743, *per* Lord Kinnear.

bequeathed, or if it has perished, or if a debt due to the testator and bequeathed by him has been paid up in his lifetime,[19] or if an investment bequeathed has been realised and the money reinvested,[20] or if money in a particular bank is bequeathed and the account is transferred to another bank,[21] or if heritage bequeathed has been taken from him under compulsory powers,[22] in all these cases the legacy is adeemed. But it is not adeemed where the testator has transferred the subject of the legacy but at the testator's death something remains to be done to perfect the transferee's title.[23] Where the subject of bequest is shares in a company, and these shares are subdivided or converted into stock or otherwise altered by the act of the company, it seems that there is no ademption if the change is in name or form only, and the subject remains substantially the same at the testator's death.[24] The test is whether the subject of the testator's bequest has remained substantially the same thing at his death; if it has, there is no ademption.[25]

44.17 Abatement of Legacies.—If the testator's estate should prove insufficient to satisfy in full all his bequests, the classification of these is of importance, because on this depends the order in which they shall abate. A testator may provide for this contingency in his will, but in the absence of such a provision, the following rules hold. The residuary legatees have no right to receive anything until the prior legacies are paid in full. As between these prior legatees, a special legatee is entitled to be paid his legacy in full though nothing should remain for the general legatees. General legacies abate equally.[26] The order or numbering of the legacies does not give an earlier legacy priority over a later.[27]

44.18 Cumulative and Substitutional Legacies.—Testamentary writings may contain more than one legacy to the same legatee, so that a doubt arises whether he is entitled to one only or to both. The testator may make his intention on this point clear by an express provision; and in all cases the court will examine his deed or deeds for the purpose of discovering indications of what was intended. It may be said that differences in the

---

[19] *Cobban's Exrs.* v. *Cobban*, 1915 S.C. 82; *Pagan* v. *Pagan* (1838) 16 S. 383.

[20] *Anderson* v. *Thomson* (1877) 4 R. 1101; *Maclean* v. *Maclean's Exrx.*, 1908 S.C. 838. See also *Thomson's Trs.* v. *Lockhart*, 1930 S.C. 674.

[21] *Ballantyne's Trs.* v. *Ballantyne's Trs.*, 1941 S.C. 35, distinguished in *Re Dorman (Deceased)* [1994] 1 W.L.R. 282.

[22] *Chalmers* v. *Chalmers* (1851) 14 D. 57.

[23] *Tennant's Trs.* v. *Tennant*, 1946 S.C. 420.

[24] *Macfarlane's Trs.* v. *Macfarlane*, 1910 S.C. 325; *Re Clifford* [1912] 1 Ch. 29; *Re Leeming* [1912] 1 Ch. 828.

[25] *Ogilvie Forbes' Trs.* v. *Ogilvie Forbes*, 1955 S.C. 405, *per* Lord President Clyde at p. 411.

[26] Erskine, *Inst.*, III, ix, 12; McLaren, i, 586.

[27] *McConnel* v. *McConnel's Trs.*, 1931 S.N. 31.

bequests will be favourable to the claim that both are due as, for example, where a motive is stated for the one bequest which is not stated as to the other.[28] Assuming, however, that the testator's intention cannot be ascertained, there are certain well-settled rules or presumptions which will be applied. A distinction is taken between legacies to the same legatee left in the same deed and legacies left in separate deeds. In the first case, *i.e.* where the legacies are contained in the same writing, when exactly the same amount is given twice, the presumption is that this is a mere repetition arising from some mistake or forgetfulness.[29] On the other hand, where the legacies are not of the same amount, they are presumed to be cumulative. Where the same amount is bequeathed to the same legatee in two distinct testamentary writings, both legacies are presumed to be due,[30] and *a fortiori* this is also so where the legacies are of different amounts.[31] These rules proceed on the assumption that both writings are operative and that the second does not revoke or supplant the earlier.[32]

44.19 *Legatum Rei Alienae*.—Whether effect can be given to the bequest of a subject which does not belong to the testator depends upon his knowledge. If he knew that the subject did not belong to him then, as it is not to be supposed that the testator intended a derisory bequest, effect is given to the legacy by requiring the executor to purchase the subject for the legatee or, if it cannot be purchased, to pay its value to him. But if the testator believed the subject to be his own (which is presumed to be the case until the contrary is proved), then the legacy fails; for it may be assumed that he would not have made the bequest had he been aware that the subject did not belong to him.[33]

44.20 **Terms Descriptive of Legatee.**—The meaning of such terms depends in each case on the context in which they appear, but some of the more frequent of them have acquired a recognised prima facie meaning in legal interpretation. Thus the word 'issue' includes all direct descendants,[34] unless the context demands a more restricted meaning;[35] and 'children' does not normally include grandchildren.[36] In the case of a gift to a class of relatives followed by a provision that in the event of the predecease of any of such relatives the issue is to take, the issue of one

---

[28] *Horsburgh* v. *Horsburgh* (1848) 10 D. 824.
[29] But see *Gillies* v. *Glasgow Royal Infirmary*, 1960 S.C. 438, where legatee appeared twice in residue clause.
[30] *McLachlan* v. *Seton's Trs.*, 1937 S.C. 206.
[31] *Hooley* v. *Hatton* (1773) 1 Brown's Chancery Cases 390; *Royal Infirmary of Edinburgh* v. *Muir's Trs.* (1881) 9 R. 352; *Fraser* v. *Forbes' Trs.* (1899) 1 F. 513.
[32] *Beattie* v. *Thomson* (1861) 23 D. 1163.
[33] Erskine, *Inst.*, III, ix, 10; *Meeres* v. *Dowell's Exr.*, 1923 S.L.T. 184.
[34] *Stewart's Trs.* v. *Whitelaw*, 1926 S.C. 701; *Murray's Trs.* v. *Mackie*, 1959 S.L.T. 129.
[35] See *Stirling's Trs.* v. *Legal and General Assurance Soc.*, 1957 S.L.T. 73, and cases cited therein.
[36] *Adam's Exrx.* v. *Maxwell*, 1921 S.C. 418; *cf. Lindsay's Trs.*, 1954 S.L.T. (Notes) 51.

who predeceases the making of the will does not take.[37] When a bequest is made to 'heirs,' the rule prior to the Succession (Scotland) Act 1964 was that the heir-at-law was entitled to the subject if it was heritable, the heirs *in mobilibus* if it was moveable, and, if it was mixed, the heritage went to the heir-at-law and the moveable portion to the heirs *in mobilibus*,[38] but this distinction does not apply to bequests to 'heirs' made on or after September 10, 1964.[39] Further it is thought that, in the absence of clear indication to the contrary, a reference in a private deed to the 'heir' or 'heirs' of a person dying on or after September 10, 1964, must be construed as a reference to those entitled to succeed on intestacy under the 1964 Act;[40] prima facie such a bequest must be construed as a reference to those who have rights of succession in that person's estate, and the heirs of that person cannot be ascertained until he dies.[41] However, 'heirs' has a different meaning from 'next-of-kin': the former does, the latter does not, include the heirs who come in by representation.[42] Where the bequest is made to a person's 'heirs and executors' this expression is held to mean heirs in intestacy, and executors-nominate are not included.[43] The term 'blood relations' covers all those who can show a traceable relationship by blood, and is not restricted to next-of-kin.[44] 'Assignees' in a destination-over means those to whom the legatee may have assigned the subject, provided he acquires a vested right, but not otherwise.[45] When a testator makes a bequest in favour of his own heirs or next-of-kin, these are normally ascertained at the date of his death.[46] When terms of relationship are used to point out the legatee, the common law rule is that only legitimate relations, as a general rule, take and that the words 'child,' 'children' and 'issue' are not normally to be interpreted so as to include illegitimate children.[47] In respect of all deeds executed and

---

[37] *McKinnon's Trs.* v. *Brownlie,* 1947 S.C. (H.L.) 27.

[38] *Blair* v. *Blair* (1849) 12 D. 97; *Grant's Trs.* v. *Slimon,* 1925 S.C. 261. For an unusual case of applying the rules of heritable succession to a bequest of moveables see *Paton's Trs.* v. *Paton,* 1947 S.C. 250.

[39] Succession (Scotland) Act 1964, s. 1(1); but note exceptions in s. 37(1).

[40] Note that the 1964 Act, Sched. 2, paras. 1 and 2, expressly provide that references in any enactment to the heir-at-law or heirs of a deceased person are to be construed as references to the persons who are entitled by virtue of that Act to succeed on intestacy to that person's estate.

[41] See *Black* v. *Mason* (1881) 8 R. 497, *per* Lord President Inglis at p. 500; McLaren, ii, pp. 757, 762.

[42] *Gregory's Trs.* v. *Alison* (1889) 16 R. (H.L.) 10; *Steedman's Trs.* v. *Steedman,* 1916 S.C. 857; *Borthwick's Trs.* v. *Borthwick,* 1955 S.C. 227. See para 43.5, *supra.*

[43] *Lady Kinnaird's Trs.* v. *Ogilvy,* 1911 S.C. 1136, but see also *Scott's Exrs.* v. *Methven's Exrs.* (1890) 17 R. 389, and *Montgomery's Trs.* v. *Montgomery* (1895) 22 R. 824.

[44] *Cuninghame* v. *Cuninghame's Trs.,* 1961 S.C. 32.

[45] *Bell* v. *Cheape* (1845) 7 D. 614.

[46] *Anderson's Trs.* v. *Forrest,* 1917 S.C. 321; *Grant's Trs.* v. *Crawford's Tr.,* 1949 S.L.T. 374; but see Henderson, *Vesting,* pp. 228–229, and at pp. 92–97, for bequests to heirs of legatees.

[47] *Scott's Trs.* v. *Smart,* 1954 S.C. 12.

provisions made on or after November 25, 1968 it is, however, now provided by statute that the descriptive term is, unless the contrary intention appears, to be taken to include illegitimate relations[48] and references to 'children' and 'issue' and other references descriptive of relationship are to be interpreted accordingly. Those who, because of illegitimate relationship would not have been entitled to inherit as the law stood when a testator died, cannot benefit from a change in the law attributing to them the status of legitimacy which takes place before the estate vests.[49] For all purposes relating to the succession to a deceased person, an adopted person is to be treated as the child of the adopter;[50] this provision extends to deeds executed before as well as after the making of an adoption order.[51] It is also provided that in a deed executed after the making of an adoption order and on or after September 10, 1964, any reference to the child or children of the adopter is, unless the contrary intention appears, to be construed as including a reference to the adopted person and similarly any reference to a person related to the adopted person is to be construed as if the latter were a child of the adopter.[52] It has been held that the latter provision is designed only to apply where a deed has been executed by a granter in knowledge both of the statutory equality of adopted children and of the existence of an adoption order.[53] There is no presumption in Scotland, where the word 'wife' is used in a testamentary family provision, in favour of the wife who existed at the date of the will;[54] but a testamentary provision may be construed as made in favour of a person in her capacity as the testator's wife, in which case divorce subsequent to the date of the will will disqualify her from taking it.[55] A bequest to 'dependants' has been held to be void from uncertainty.[56]

44.21 Interest of Legatee: Destinations-Over.—Under the more usual forms of bequest the benefit conferred on the legatee is an annuity or an interest in liferent or in fee in the subject of the bequest. It is now clear that an interest intermediate between fee and liferent is a conception which the

---

[48] Formerly, Law Reform (Misc. Provs.) (Scotland) Act 1968, ss. 5 and 22(5) and now Law Reform (Parent and Child) (Scotland) Act 1986, s. 1(2). As to legitimated persons see para. 49.4, *infra*, and Legitimation (Scotland) Act 1968, ss. 2, 3 and 8, applied in *Russell* v. *Wood's Trs.*, 1987 S.L.T. 503.

[49] *Wright's Trs.* v. *Callender*, 1993 S.L.T. 556.

[50] Succession (Scotland) Act 1964, s. 23(1). Note that where the adopter died before September 10, 1964, and the natural parent died on or after that date, the adopted child retains his rights of succession to the estate of his natural parent; Law Reform (Misc. Provs.) (Scotland) Act 1966, s. 5.

[51] *Salvesen's Trs., Petrs.*, 1992 S.C.L.R. 729.

[52] 1964 Act, s. 23(2); *mortis causa* deeds are deemed for the purposes of this provision to have been executed on the adopter's death.

[53] *Salvesen's Trs., supra.*

[54] *Burn's Trs., Petrs.*, 1961 S.C. 17. *Cf. Couper's J.F.* v. *Valentine*, 1976 S.L.T. 83.

[55] *Pirie's Trs.* v. *Pirie*, 1962 S.C. 43; but see as to 'fiancée,' *Ormiston's Exr.* v. *Laws*, 1966 S.L.T. 110.

[56] *Robertson's J.F.* v. *Robertson*, 1968 S.L.T. 32.

law does not recognise.[57] Certain forms of bequest raise a doubt as to the legatees entitled to take. A direction that residue shall 'be equally divided between my nephews and nieces and their children' may mean either that nephews and nieces and their children are to take equal shares or that each nephew and niece is to take an equal share, the children of any predeceaser taking their parent's share. In *Clow's Trustees* v. *Bethune*,[58] after considerable diversity of judicial opinion, the decision was for the latter construction, and the case illustrates the relevant considerations.

Destinations-over are frequently attached to bequests, *e.g.* to A, whom failing B. Here A is the institute and B may be either a conditional institute or a substitute. If the former then, if and when A acquires right to the legacy, the destination-over to B at once flies off. But this is not so if B is a substitute. B will take in succession to A on his death if the substitution is not defeated by A.[59] A has the unrestricted right of fee and may after acquiring right to the subject consume it or dispose of it by either *inter vivos* or *mortis causa* deed thus defeating the substitution; but, if the substitution is not defeated, the subject will pass to B on A's death. A substitution includes a conditional institution so that, where B is called as a substitute he will take in place of A if A does not acquire right to the subject. Although it is possible to have a substitution in moveables,[60] there is a very strong presumption against this.[61] On the other hand, where the subject is heritage the presumption is that the destination is a substitution,[62] though the presumption may yield to the terms of the will.[63] The fact that a disposition of estate is made after the death of a legatee will not suffice to restrict his interest to a liferent if there are no other features of the deed pointing to this restriction.[64]

44.22 Vesting of Legacies.—A legacy is said to vest in a legatee when he acquires right to it. It then becomes his property; he may dispose of it by *inter vivos* or *mortis causa* deed; it may be made available to meet his debts; and on his death intestate it will transmit as part of his estate. It is not necessary that the legatee should be entitled to payment or

---

[57] *Cochrane's Exrx.* v. *Cochrane*, 1947 S.C. 134, overruling *Heavyside* v. *Smith*, 1929 S.C. 68. Followed in *Innes' Trs.* v. *Innes*, 1948 S.C. 406.

[58] 1935 S.C. 754; and see *Boyd's Trs.* v. *Shaw*, 1958 S.C. 115, where a destination-over to issue of a named beneficiary 'equally amongst them' was similarly construed.

[59] McLaren, *Wills*, p. 623; *Cochrane's Exrx.* v. *Cochrane, supra.*

[60] *Dyer* v. *Carruthers* (1874) 1 R. 943.

[61] *Crumpton's J.F.* v. *Barnardo's Homes*, 1917 S.C. 713, *per* Lord President Strathclyde; *Greig* v. *Johnstone* (1833) 6 W. & S. 406.

[62] *Watson* v. *Giffen* (1884) 11 R. 444. There may be indefeasible clauses of return in favour of the grantor of the deed or his heirs but the instances of this in modern cases are not numerous—see *Robertson* v. *Hay-Boyd*, 1928 S.C. (H.L.) 8.

[63] *Simpson's Trs.* v. *Simpson* (1889) 17 R. 248.

[64] *Turner's Trs.* v. *Turner*, 1961 S.L.T. 319.

possession of the legacy, for vesting may, and often does, take place although the legatee has no right to possession. Nor are the circumstances that the bequest is made through the instrumentality of a trust, or that it is subject to a liferent or annuity, inconsistent with immediate vesting in the fiar.[65] Thus, if trustees are directed to hold a fund for A in liferent and, on his death, to hold it for or pay it to B, B will acquire a vested interest on the death of the testator.[66] Nor will a power in the trustees to encroach on capital operate so as to postpone vesting of the capital in the legatees.[67]

The date of vesting is to be determined in accordance with the testator's intention as disclosed in his testament. This is the governing principle, and the further rules which have been developed in the course of the decisions are all subject to this qualification, that they must yield to clear expressions of the testator's intention.[68] There is sometimes inserted in a testament an explicit declaration as to the time at which a legacy is to vest, and this usually settles the question, but not invariably, for such a declaration has been disregarded where it was irreconcilable with the terms of the bequest[69] and indeed it has been observed that the courts have in general shown little enthusiasm for artificial vesting dates.[70] There are also two general considerations which influence the court. In the first place, there is a presumption in favour of early vesting; that is to say, in a case of doubt the court is favourable to that construction which will give the legatee a vested interest at the earliest date. As a will cannot come into effect until the testator's death, there can be no vesting prior to that time; and the presumption is, therefore, for vesting *a morte testatoris*.[71] Secondly, where a testator purports to dispose of his whole estate, the court is disinclined to adopt a construction which will involve total or partial intestacy, although it may be compelled to do so.[72]

The question must always depend mainly on the terms in which the particular bequest is made. If it be given to the legatee unconditionally, vesting will take place immediately. A legacy which is payable on a *dies certus*, *i.e.* a time or event which must arrive sooner or later (as, *e.g.* the death of a liferenter or other person), is regarded as an unconditional

---

[65] *Carleton* v. *Thomson* (1867) 5 M. (H.L.) 151; *Wemyss's Trs.* v. *Wemyss*, 1994 G.W.D. 11–702.

[66] Henderson on *Vesting*, p. 24; *Whitelaw's Trs.* v. *Whitelaw's Trs.*, 1981 S.L.T. 94.

[67] *MacGregor's Trs.* v. *MacGregor*, 1958 S.C. 326.

[68] *Carleton* v. *Thomson, supra; Bowman* v. *Bowman* (1899) 1 F. (H.L.) 69, *per* Lord Halsbury L.C.; *Barclay's Tr.* v. *Inland Revenue*, 1975 S.C. 1.

[69] See *Croom's Trs.* v. *Adams* (1859) 22 D. 45.

[70] See *Carruther's Trs.* v. *Carruthers' Trs.*, 1949 S.C. 530, *per* Lord President Cooper at p. 545. This case is concerned with an attempt, by the application of the maxim *quod fieri debet infectum valet* (what ought to be done avails although not done) to frustrate a testator's express direction as to vesting.

[71] *Carleton* v. *Thomson, supra; Taylor* v. *Gilbert's Trs.* (1878) 5 R. (H.L.) 217, *per* Lord Blackburn.

[72] See *Cummings* v. *Gillespie's Exrs.*, 1994 G.W.D. 36–2158.

legacy.[73] On the other hand, if it is uncertain whether the event contemplated will ever happen, it cannot be known in the meantime whether the legacy will ever become due, and, in accordance with the maxim *dies incertus pro conditione habetur*, (an uncertain day is regarded as a condition) the legacy is regarded as conditional.[74]

44.23 **Vesting of Conditional Bequests.**—In the case of conditional legacies a distinction is drawn between suspensive (precedent) and resolutive (subsequent) conditions.[75] The former operate to prevent vesting until the fulfilment of the condition, the latter do not prevent vesting, but render it liable to be defeated if the event occur—that is, there is vesting subject to defeasance. There is little trace of the doctrine of vesting subject to defeasance in regard to legacies prior to the decision of the House of Lords in *Taylor* v. *Gilbert's Trs.*,[76] but since then the doctrine has been considerably developed. As a general rule, conditions which are personal to the legatee have the effect of suspending vesting *pendente conditione*. The more usual of such conditions are those relating to the age of the legatee, or to his survivance of some time or event. If a testator leaves a bequest, or directs his trustees to pay a legacy, to A in the event of his attaining majority, there is no vesting in A while he is under 18. In this case the condition as to age is adjected to the substance of the gift: A becomes the object of the testator's bounty only when he reaches the age of 18. But if a bequest takes the form of a bequest to A with a provision that it is to be paid to him when he attains majority the bequest will vest in A at once although he is not major. The gift here is made without qualification, and the provision as to majority refers to payment, and was presumably introduced only for the protection of A while he is under age.[77]

Where the qualification of the legacy consists of words of survivorship (to A, B and C and the survivors or survivor of them), the vesting of the legacy will depend on the determination of the time to which these words refer. The testator may point out the time or event which the legatee must survive in order to acquire right to the legacy. Where he fails to do so, the rule laid down in the leading case of *Young* v. *Robertson*[78] is as follows: The words of survivorship are to be referred to the period appointed by the settlement for payment or distribution of the subject matter of the gift. If a testator gives a sum of money or the residue of his estate to be paid or distributed among a number of persons and refers to the contingency of any one or more of them dying,

---

[73] See, *e.g., Mowbray's Trs.* v. *Mowbray's Exr.*, 1931 S.C. 595; *Fraser's Trs.* v. *Cunninghame*, 1928 S.L.T. 425.

[74] McLaren, ii, 783, 796; see Lord Skerrington's opinion in *Wylie's Trs.* v. *Bruce*, 1919 S.C. 211, at p. 240.

[75] See above.

[76] (1878) 5 R. (H.L.) 217.

[77] *Alves' Trs.* v. *Grant* (1874) 1 R. 969; *Wemyss's Trs.* v. *Wemyss*, 1994 G.W.D. 11–702.

[78] (1862) 4 Macq. 314.

and then gives the estate or the money to the survivor in that simple form of gift which is to take effect immediately on the death of the testator, the period of distribution is the period of death, and accordingly the contingency of death is to be referred to the interval of time between the date of the will and the death of the testator. Vesting in this case will take place *a morte testatoris*. On the other hand, if the testator gives a liferent in a sum of money or in the residue of his estate, and at the expiration of that liferent directs the money to be paid or the residue to be divided among a number of objects, and then refers to the possibility of some one or more of those persons dying, without specifying the time, and directs in that event the payment or distribution to be made among the survivors, it is understood by the law that he means the contingency to extend over the whole period of time that must elapse before the payment or distribution takes place. The result, accordingly, is that in such a case the survivors are to be ascertained in like manner by a reference to the period of distribution, namely the expiration of the liferent; and vesting is, therefore, suspended till that event.[79] A survivorship clause may, however, be so worded, notwithstanding the subsistence of a liferenter, as to import only survivorship of the legatees *inter se*; in that event vesting is suspended until only the survivor is left, and the right then vests in him whether or not he survives the liferenter.[80] But this doctrine of 'intermediate' vesting cannot, it is thought, be extended to a case where the fee is destined to more than two persons and the words 'survivors or survivor' are used.[81]

A similar rule holds in regard to destinations-over (to A, whom failing to B). When trustees are directed to pay a legacy to a beneficiary on the occurrence of an event and, failing him, to another or to other persons, then, if he does not survive that event, he takes no right under the settlement.[82] In the case of a simple bequest without postponement of payment, the destination-over is read as providing for the contingency of the legatee's predeceasing the testator, and as the destination-over ceases to be operative on the testator's death, the legacy vests at that date; but if the legacy is to be paid at a subsequent date, there is no vesting till that date. A destination-over to another person *nominatim* may take the form of a bequest to 'A whom failing B,' or to 'A or B.' At one time it was thought that the general rule did not apply where the persons called under the destination-over were described as the heirs of the institute, but it is now settled that under a destination-over to heirs

---

[79] *Laing's Trs.*, 1965 S.L.T. 215; *cf. Stirling's Trs.*, 1977 S.L.T. 229. Forfeiture of the liferent on the liferenter's election to claim legal rights does not accelerate vesting (*Muirhead* v. *Muirhead* (1890) 17 R. (H.L.) 45; *Munro's Trs.*, 1971 S.C. 280).

[80] *Lindsay's Trs.* v. *Sinclair* (1885) 12 R. 964; *Macfarlane's Trs.* v. *Macfarlane's Curator Bonis*, 1934 S.C. 476.

[81] *Playfair's Trs.* v. *Stewart's Trs.*, 1960 S.L.T. 351.

[82] *Bryson's Trs.* v. *Clark* (1880) 8 R. 142.

vesting is suspended. Hence, if a legacy is bequeathed on the expiry or termination of a liferent to A or his heirs, it vests in A only at the death of the liferenter;[83] vesting will not be accelerated by a renunciation of the liferent by the liferenter before that date[84] and, unless provision has been made for its disposal, income in the intervening period will fall into intestacy.[85] But such a renunciation, coupled with the valid exercise by the liferenter of a power to appoint the fee by *inter vivos* deed, will enable immediate payment of the capital to be made to the appointee.[86]

The rule as to the effect of words of survivorship or a destination-over on vesting in the legatee called in the first place is well settled. Somewhat different considerations affect the vesting in the person or persons called on that legatee's failure. If a testator directs his trustees to hold his estate for a person in liferent, and on his death, to divide it among such of certain persons as may then be alive, the issue of any of these who may predecease being entitled to their parent's share, do the issue of one who predeceases the liferenter take a vested right on their parent's death or is vesting in them suspended (as in the case of their parent) until the death of the liferenter? Or, if the bequest on the termination of the liferent be to A, whom failing to B, and A predeceases the liferenter, does B acquire a vested interest on A's death although he (B) may subsequently also predecease the liferenter? In a well-drawn settlement this should be made clear; but in the absence of express provision the question will depend on whether the conditions which affect the institute are by implication to be held to affect also the conditional institute. As a rule, if the gift-over to the issue of the legatee is substitutional the condition of survivance of the termination of the liferent expressed with reference to the parent is held to apply to the issue also,[87] but if the gift to the issue is an original one, they may acquire a vested right notwithstanding that they predecease the liferenter.[88]

44.24 Vesting Subject to Defeasance.[89]—There are three types of cases in which the application of this doctrine is now definitely recognised, and beyond which it will not readily be extended.[90]

---

[83] *Wylie's Trs.* v. *Bruce*, 1919 S.C. 211; *Mackenzie's Trs.* v. *Georgeson*, 1923 S.C. 517.

[84] *Middleton's Trs.* v. *Middleton*, 1955 S.C. 51; *Chrystal's Trs.* v. *Haldane*, 1960 S.C. 127. Distinguish *Hurll's Trs.* v. *Hurll*, 1964 S.C. 12 (forfeiture).

[85] *Buyers' Trs. and Nunan*, 1981 S.C. 313, *sub nom. Collie and Buyers*, 1981 S.L.T. 191, overruling on this point *Middleton's Trs.* v. *Middleton, supra*.

[86] *Stainton* v. *Forteviot Trust*, 1948 S.C. (H.L.) 115; *Neame* v. *Neame's Trs.*, 1956 S.L.T. 57; and see para. 44.29, *infra*.

[87] *Todd's Trs.* v. *Todd's Exrx.*, 1922 S.C. 1; *Banks' Trs.* v. *Banks' Trs.*, 1907 S.C. 125.

[88] *Campbell's Tr.* v. *Dick*, 1915 S.C. 100; but see *Robertson's Trs.* v. *Mitchell*, 1930 S.C. 970, *per* Lord President Clyde at p. 976.

[89] See Henderson on *Vesting*, and Smith, *Short Commentary*, pp. 436 *et seq.*

[90] Approved *per* Lord Reid in *Barclay's Tr.* v. *Inland Revenue*, 1975 S.C. 1 at p. 14. The word 'readily' is to be stressed (*ibid.*).

(1) 'For A in liferent and his issue in fee, whom failing to B.'—If trustees are directed to hold a fund for A in liferent and for his or her issue in fee, and failing issue of A, then for B in fee, B will, if there are no such issue in existence at the testator's death, take a vested right subject to defeasance if A subsequently has issue.[91] Should A never have issue, B's right is treated as having been from the first absolute, and it matters not that he predeceases the liferenter. On the other hand, if the bequest to A's issue comes into effect, B's right is wholly defeated. It is a condition of immediate vesting in B that his right can only be defeated by A having a child.[92] If the destination-over to B is framed so as to take effect on the death of A without leaving issue, the fee remains vested in B unless A is survived by issue.[93] If, however, the gift to B is qualified by conditions which in themselves suspend vesting, as, for example, by a destination-over to his heirs or to another person *nominatim* (*e.g.* to A in liferent and his issue in fee, whom failing to B, whom failing to C), or by words which show that his survivance of the expiry of the liferent is required, there is no room for vesting in him prior to that event, because the gift to B is not solely dependent upon A having no issue; in other words, it is subject to a double contingency.[94] But a contingency that issue may emerge to several liferenters (*e.g.* to A in liferent and his issue in fee, whom failing to B in liferent and his issue in fee, whom failing to C) is not such a double contingency as will suspend vesting in the ultimate beneficiary, C.[95]

(2) 'For A in fee, with a direction to hold for A in liferent and his issue in fee.'—If a bequest be made to A with a further direction that the trustees shall hold for him in liferent and for his issue in fee, it has been held in a series of cases that the fee will remain with A if he has no issue.[96] The ground for this construction is that the testator, having made a gift to A, is not to be taken to have intended by the further direction to revoke that gift, but rather to subordinate it to the bequest to the issue. In the event of there being issue, A's right is reduced to a liferent out of favour to the issue who are to have the fee; but if there are no issue, then A is to remain in enjoyment of the fee. It is essential in this case that there should be language sufficient to confer a right of fee upon A, for if, on the construction of the deed, it appears that

[91] *Taylor* v. *Gilbert's Trs.* (1878) 5 R. (H.L.) 217.
[92] *Steel's Trs.* v. *Steel* (1888) 16 R. 204.
[93] *Gregory's Trs.* v. *Alison* (1889) 16 R. (H.L.) 10. Note that in *Taylor* v. *Gilbert's Trs.*, *supra*, vesting in A's issue was dependent upon one or more of them (a) surviving A and (b) attaining majority. See also *Munro's Tr.* v. *Monson*, 1962 S.C. 414.
[94] *Lees' Trs.* v. *Lees*, 1927 S.C. 886; *Nicolson's Trs.* v. *Nicolson*, 1960 S.C. 186.
[95] *Taylor* v. *Gilbert's Trs.*, *supra*; *G.'s Trs.* v. *G.*, 1937 S.C. 141; *Moss's Tr.* v. *Moss's Trs.*, 1958 S.C. 501.
[96] *Tweeddale's Trs.* v. *Tweeddale* (1905) 8 F. 264; *Donaldson's Trs.* v. *Donaldson*, 1916 S.C. (H.L.) 55; *Aitken's Trs.* v. *Aitken*, 1921 S.C. 807; *Livingston's Trs.* v. *Livingston's Trs.*, 1939 S.C. (H.L.) 17. Distinguished in *Riddoch's Trs.* v. *Calder's Trs.*, 1947 S.C. 281, where there was held to be initial gift of fee; *cf. Scott's Trs.* v. *De Moyse-Bucknall's Trs.*, 1978 S.C. 62.

nothing more than a liferent was in any circumstances given to him, the doctrine is inapplicable.[97]

(3) 'For A in liferent and B in fee, whom failing to B's issue.'—If trustees are directed to hold a fund for behoof of a legatee with a provision that, if he predeceases the expiry of a liferent or other event leaving issue, such issue shall take their parent's share, the legatee will take a vested right subject to defeasance if he predecease the event and leave issue. If he does not so predecease (whether he has issue or not), or if he predecease but does not leave issue, his right is not defeated. The only event on which divestiture of his right takes place is if he does predecease and is survived by issue.[98]

In all these cases there is this common feature, that the legatee's interest is liable to be defeated only by the contingency that there may be issue born to the liferenter or legatee. There are, however, other cases of rather exceptional nature and not capable of classification, in which vesting subject to defeasance has been held to take place.[99]

44.25   Vesting of Class-Gifts.—The general rule is that (unless the will provides otherwise) those members only who are in existence when the time appointed for payment of the bequest arrives are entitled to participate in it. Hence, under a simple bequest to the children of A, where there is nothing to postpone payment beyond the testator's death, the children then alive take the bequest to the exclusion of children born later.[1] A child *in utero* is treated as if already born.[2]

But if the time of payment is postponed as, for example, if the gift be to A in liferent and to his children in fee, all the children who are born prior to the death of the liferenter are included.[3] In this case the gift vests in the children alive at the testator's death, or if there are none, in the child first born, subject to partial defeasance to the extent necessary to allow of children born later receiving equal shares.[4] The fact that the

[97] *Muir's Trs.* v. *Muir's Trs.* (1895) 22 R. 553; *Nicol's Trs.* v. *Farquhar*, 1918 S.C. 358; *Smith's Trs.* v. *Clark*, 1920 S.C. 161.

[98] *Allan's Trs.* v. *Allan*, 1918 S.C. 164; *Gibson's Trs.* v. *Gibson*, 1925 S.C. 477; and see *Coulston's Trs.* v. *Coulston's Trs.*, 1911 S.C. 881, where two contingencies were held to be alternative and not cumulative so as to suspend vesting.

[99] See, *e.g. Yule's Trs.* v. *Deans*, 1919 S.C. 570, *per* Lord Skerrington; *McCall's Trs.* v. *McCall*, 1957 S.L.T. (Notes) 16; *Martin's Trs.* v. *Milliken* (1864) 3 M. 326; *Bruce's Trs.* v. *Bruce's Trs.* (1898) 25 R. 796.

[1] *Stopford Blair's Exrs.* v. *Heron Maxwell's Trs.* (1872) 10 M. 760; *Hayward's Exrs.* v. *Young* (1895) 22 R. 757; *Wood* v. *Wood* (1861) 23 D. 338, *per* Lord Cowan. Where the bequest is to children, illegitimate children are included in the class unless the contrary intention appears (Law Reform (Misc. Provs.) (Scotland) Act 1968, s. 5—applicable only to deeds executed on or after November 25, 1968—and see now Law Reform (Parent and Child) (Scotland) Act 1986, s. 1).

[2] *Cox's Trs.* v. *Cox*, 1950 S.C. 117.

[3] *Hickling's Trs.* v. *Garland's Trs.* (1898) 1 F. (H.L.) 7, *per* Lord Davey; *Christie* v. *Wisely* (1874) 1 R. 436; *Ross* v. *Dunlop* (1878) 5 R. 833; *Potter's Trs.* v. *Allan*, 1918 S.C. 173; *Murray's Tr.* v. *Murray*, 1919 S.C. 552.

[4] *Douglas* v. *Douglas* (1864) 2 M. 1008; *Carleton* v. *Thompson* (1867) 5 M. (H.L.) 151.

class is liable to be enlarged does not suspend the vesting. Where the bequest is to children, as and when they respectively attain majority and the shares are then to be paid over, it has been held that the bequest is limited to the children alive when the eldest child reaches majority and so becomes entitled to demand payment of his share, as otherwise the share to be paid to the eldest child could not be fixed.[5]

In the case of *Hickling's Trs. v. Garland's Trs.*[6] the testator directed his trustees to hold a sum for a daughter in liferent, and on her death leaving issue to divide it among her issue. On the daughter's death two children were alive and two had predeceased her. It was held that the sum had vested in all four children. The bequest was dependent on the contingency of the daughter leaving, that is being survived by, children; but that contingency was not imported into the description of the class so as to confine the gift to those children who survived their mother. If, through the survivance of certain members of the class the bequest came into effect, it operated in favour of all the members of the class. It is otherwise if the bequest is so framed as to show that only those children who survive the contingency are meant to share in the fund, or if there is a destination-over in the case of the liferenter dying without leaving issue.[7]

44.26 **Division *Per Capita* or *Per Stirpes*.**—Where a bequest is made to a number of individuals, although there are no words indicating the share to be taken by each, there is no room for doubt as to the mode of division: each will take an equal share. But if the legatees are called under a term or terms descriptive of a group, there may be doubt as to whether the fund is to be divided among all the beneficiaries as individuals (*per capita*) or according to the group or groups (*per stirpes*). It is clear that under a gift of residue to the children of A and the children of B either the family division may be disregarded so that each child of the two families receives an equal share, or the residue may be divided into halves and one-half distributed among the members of each family. It is within the power of the testator to use expressions which will remove all doubt on this point. The general presumption is in favour of *per capita* distribution, unless the language of the will or the frame of the bequest indicates the other mode of division.[8] There is, however, a presumption that where a bequest is given severally to parties in liferent and their issue in fee, the connection between the liferent and the fee implies stirpital division of the fee.[9]

[5] *Scott's Trs. v. Scott*, 1909 S.C. 773.

[6] (1898) 1 F. (H.L.) 7; *cf. Primrose's Trs. v. Gardiner, etc.*, 1973 S.L.T. 238.

[7] *Graham's Trs. v. Lang's Trs.*, 1916 S.C. 723; *Craik's Trs. v. Anderson*, 1932 S.C. 61.

[8] McLaren, ii, 780; *Hay Cunningham's Trs. v. Blackwell*, 1909 S.C. 219; *Robertson's Trs. v. Horne*, 1921 S.C. 817; *Campbell's Trs. v. Welsh*, 1952 S.C. 343; *cf. Boyd's Tr. v. Shaw*, 1958 S.C. 115; *Bailey's Trs. v. Bailey*, 1954 S.L.T. 282.

[9] *Home's Trs. v. Ramsay* (1886) 12 R. 314, *Bailey's Trs. v. Bailey, supra, Primrose's Trs. v. Gardiner, supra.*

44.27   Accretion.—Another question which may arise in regard to a legacy in favour of a number of legatees is whether the legacy is joint or several. If the legacy be given to the legatees jointly or without words importing that they are to take separate shares then, if any of these die without acquiring a vested right, the survivors will be entitled to the whole of the fund or subject bequeathed. A legacy to A and B simply will, if A predecease the testator, give B right to the whole of that sum.[10] But if words of severance, such as 'equally' or 'share and share alike,' are used, accretion is excluded, and the share of a predeceaser will, in the case of a legacy, fall into residue (if there be a residuary bequest), or in the case of residue, lapse into intestacy. The rule has been authoritatively stated in these terms: 'When a legacy is given to a plurality of persons named or sufficiently described for identification "equally among them," or "in equal shares," or "share and share alike," or in any other language of the same import, each is entitled to his own share and no more, and there is no room for accretion in the event of the predecease of one or more of the legatees. The rule is applicable whether the gift is in liferent or in fee to the whole equally, and whether the subject of the bequest be residue or a sum of fixed amount or corporeal moveables. The application of this rule may, of course, be controlled or avoided by the use of other expressions by the testator importing that there shall be accretion in the event of the predecease of one of more of the legatees.'[11] The most important exception to this rule occurs in bequests to a class, where notwithstanding the use of such terms as 'equally,' 'share and share alike,' the share of a predeceaser accresces to the survivors.[12]

If it is intended that accrescing shares shall be subject to the same conditions as the original share, as, *e.g.* where the original shares are settled on the beneficiaries in liferent, this should be made clear in the settlement, as there is no implication that the conditions apply to more that the original gift. Where the issue of the predeceaser take by virtue of the *conditio si institutus sine liberis decesserit* or a clause calling issue, it is only the parent's original share and not what would have accresced to him had he survived that can, as a general rule, be claimed by the issue, unless the will provides otherwise,[13] or adherence to the rule would result in intestacy.[14] In respect of provisions made on or after November 25, 1968 accretion operates for the benefit of an illegitimate person or of a person whose right is traceable through an illegitimate

---

[10] Stair, III, viii, 27; *Andrew's Exrs.* v. *Andrew's Trs.*, 1925 S.C. 844.

[11] *Paxton's Trs.* v. *Cowie* (1886) 13 R. 1191; applied in *Cochrane's Trs.* v. *Cochrane*, 1914 S.C. 403; *White's Trs.*, 1957 S.C. 322; *Fraser's Trs.* v. *Fraser*, 1980 (S.L.T.) 211; but see *Young's Trs.* v. *Young*, 1927 S.C. (H.L.) 6 and *Mitchell's Trs.* v. *Aspin*, 1971 S.L.T. 166.

[12] *Muir's Trs.* v. *Muir* (1889) 16 R. 954; *Roberts' Trs.* v. *Roberts* (1903) 5 F. 541.

[13] *Henderson* v. *Henderson* (1890) 17 R. 293; *Young* v. *Robertson* (1862) 4 Macq. 337; *Crosbie's Trs.* v. *Crosbie*, 1927 S.C. 159; *Miller's Trs.* v. *Brown*, 1933 S.C. 669.

[14] *Beveridge's Trs.* v. *Beveridge*, 1930 S.C. 578.

person as it would for someone who is legitimate, unless the contrary intention appears.[15]

44.28 ***Conditio si Institutus sine Liberis Decesserit.***[16]—In certain cases this condition is read into a bequest, including a bequest of revenue.[17] The effect is that, if the legatee die without acquiring a vested interest leaving issue,[18] the issue (although they are not mentioned in the will) have right to the legacy in preference (as the case may be) to the conditional institute, or the residuary legatee, or the heirs *ab intestato* of the testator. In the case of a bequest of income it applies so as to enable the payment of income to the issue of a beneficiary who before his death has entered into and enjoyed the bequest.[19] It is applicable only to bequests by a testator to his own descendants or to his nephews and nieces,[20] including those whose relationship to him is illegitimate,[21] but not to a step-child;[22] and where the legatees are nephews or nieces it is necessary that the testator should by the terms of his will have placed himself *in loco parentis* to them, which means that he should have made a settlement in their favour similar to that which a parent might be supposed to make.[23] In such circumstances the presumption is that the *conditio* applies, in the absence of a contrary intention expressed or clearly implied in the deed itself or in other operative testamentary writings.[24] These limits to its application are now settled; but within these limits it is always a question of construction whether in any particular case the *conditio* is to be admitted.[25] It is favourable to its admission that the settlement is a universal one, that the beneficiaries are a class, and that the provision is of the nature of a family settlement.[26] On the other hand, the *conditio* does not apply if the bequest proceeds purely from *delectus personae* apart from the fact of relationship;[27] and, as its justification is the presumption that the failure to mention issue was due to the testator having overlooked the contingency of the legatee's predecease leaving issue, it does not apply if

---

[15] Formerly Law Reform (Misc. Provs.) (Scotland) Act 1968, ss. 6(1)(*b*), 6(3) and 22(5) and now Law Reform (Parent and Child) (Scotland) Act 1986, s. 1(2).

[16] McLaren, i, Chap. XL; Henderson on *Vesting*, Chap. XVII.

[17] *Pattinson's Trs.* v. *Motion*, 1941 S.C. 290.

[18] Including, in provisions made on or after November 25, 1968, illegitimate issue (Law Reform (Misc. Provs.) (Scotland) Act 1968, ss. 6(1)(*a*), 6(3) and 22(5); Law Reform (Parent and Child) (Scotland) Act 1986, s. 1).

[19] *Reid's Trs.* v. *Reid etc.*, 1969 S.L.T. (Notes) 4.

[20] *Hall* v. *Hall* (1891) 18 R. 690.

[21] Except in provisions made before November 25, 1968. See n. 18, *supra*.

[22] *Sinclair's Trs.* v. *Sinclair*, 1942 S.C. 362.

[23] *Bogie's Trs.* v. *Christie* (1882) 9 R. 453. See *Waddell's Trs.* v. *Waddell* (1896) 24 R. 189 and *Alexander's Trs.* v. *Paterson*, 1928 S.C. 371.

[24] *Knox's Exr.* v. *Knox*, 1941 S.C. 532; *Devlin's Trs.* v. *Breen*, 1945 S.C. (H.L.) 27, *per* Lord Thankerton at p. 35; *Reid's Trs.* v. *Reid*, 1960 S.L.T. (Notes) 5.

[25] *Devlin's Trs.*, *supra*, at p. 32.

[26] *Blair's Exrs.* v. *Taylor* (1876) 3 R. 362; *Devlin's Trs.*, *supra*.

[27] *Keith's Trs.* v. *Keith* (1908) 16 S.L.T. 390.

the terms of the will afford evidence that this is not so; and such evidence is found where the testator in other legacies has made express provision for the issue of predeceasing legatees.[28] It applies although the parent was called as a conditional institute,[29] but it cannot apply if the legatee was dead when the will was executed.[30] It admits the issue of a legatee who has either predeceased the testator or died after the testator without having acquired a vested right.[31] It applies in marriage contracts as well as in testamentary deeds,[32] but not in the case of any other *inter vivos* deed.[33] As already mentioned, the issue take only the parent's original share.[34]

44.29   **Powers.**—A power or faculty is an authority reserved by or conferred upon a person to dispose, either wholly or partially, of property either for his own benefit or for that of others.[35] Such powers may be general, by which is meant a power to dispose of the property at pleasure, or special, by which is meant a more limited power. The typical instance of a special power is that of appointing a fund among members of a specified class. The person from whom the power issues is known as the donor of the power and the recipient as the donee of the power.

Where a person settles his property, or takes a disposition, in favour of himself in liferent and at the same time reserves to himself a general power of disposing of the property, this is equivalent to a fee. He has right to the property independently of the settlement or disposition, and if he reserves to himself the enjoyment of the fruits of the property and the power to dispose of the property at pleasure, he remains substantially the proprietor.[36] In that situation he is both donor and donee of the power and is outwith the ambit of the ordinary rule that the donee of a power cannot delegate the exercise thereof.[37]

[28] *Greig* v. *Malcolm* (1835) 13 S. 607; *McNab* v. *Brown's Trs.*, 1926 S.C. 387, approved in *Paterson* v. *Paterson*, 1935 S.C. (H.L.) 7. See *Alexander's Trs.* v. *Paterson, supra*, and *Reid's Trs.* v. *Reid, supra*.

[29] *Greig's Trs.* v. *Simpson*, 1918 S.C. 321.

[30] *Rhind's Trs.* v. *Leith* (1866) 5 M. 104; *Low's Trs.* v. *Whitworth* (1892) 19 R. 431; but see *Miller's Trs.* v. *Miller*, 1958 S.C. 125 (*conditio* applied where the bequest was confirmed by a codicil executed after the institute's death).

[31] *Young* v. *Robertson* (1862) 4 Macq. 337, *per* Lord Chancellor (Westbury) at p. 340; *Grant* v. *Brooke* (1882) 10 R. 92; *Alexander's Trs.* v. *Paterson, supra; cf. Mitchell's Exrs.* v. *Gordon's J.F.*, 1953 S.C. 176, where Lord President Cooper suggested, *obiter*, that its applicability was dependent upon the institute predeceasing the testator; *sed contra*: *McGregor's Trs.* v. *Gray*, 1969 S.L.T. 355.

[32] *Hughes* v. *Edwardes* (1892) 19 R. (H.L.) 33.

[33] *Halliday* (1869) 8 M. 112; *Crichton's Tr.* v. *Howat's Tutor* (1890) 18 R. 260; *Trs. of Gwendolen Beatrice Thomson's Trust*, 1963 S.C. 141.

[34] *Supra*, para. 44.27.

[35] Farwell on *Powers* (3rd ed., 1916), p. 1. The subject of Powers is treated in McLaren on *Wills and Succession*. The English books are Farwell on *Powers* (3rd ed.), and Sugden (Lord St. Leonards) on *Powers* (8th ed., 1861).

[36] *Morris* v. *Tennant* (1855) 27 Sc. Jur. 546; 30 Sc. Jur. 943; *Baillie* v. *Clark*, Feb. 23, 1809, F.C.

[37] *Cuninghame* v. *Cuninghame's Trs.*, 1961 S.L.T. 194, *per* Lord Ordinary (Mackintosh) at p. 197, and Lord President Clyde at p. 201; *Monies* v. *Monies*, 1939 S.C. 344.

If the donor confers on the donee a liferent with a power of disposal, both in unqualified terms, that is a gift of the fee,[38] and the donee may demand immediate payment or conveyance thereof. But if the liferent is declared to be alimentary, whatever may be the extent of the power,[39] or, although the liferent be unqualified, if the power is to be exercised in a particular manner, as by will or *mortis causa* deed only, or otherwise falls short of a general power, in either case the donee of the power is not in right of the fee of the property.[40]

The power must be exercised in accordance with the terms on which it is given. If the deed which confers it prescribes that it shall be exercised by will, it cannot be exercised by an *inter vivos* deed; but a power to appoint by 'any writing under her hand' has been held wide enough to include *inter vivos* as well as testamentary deeds.[41] A mere reference in the power to the death of the donee of it, *e.g.* the postponement of payment to the fiars until the expiry of the donee's liferent, does not restrict him to choosing persons who survive him as the objects of the power, or suspend the vesting of indefeasible interests in the person chosen until the death.[42] In that event the power may be validly exercised by *inter vivos* deed. In interpreting a power there is no presumption that the objects should be the persons who would take failing its exercise.[43] It is not necessary to support a deed as an exercise of a power that it should make reference to the power; if there is no such reference, it becomes a question on the terms of the deed whether the donee intended to exercise the power.[44] It has long been recognised that words of general conveyance in a settlement are, unless a contrary intention appears, to be construed as including any estate which the testator had power to dispose of in any manner he might deem proper.[45] Thus, in *Hyslop* v. *Maxwell's Trs.*,[46] a power given by a testator to his niece, who enjoyed the liferent of a sum under his will, to dispose of that sum by will or deed after her death as she might think fit, was held to be exercised by her general settlement although it made no reference to the power and was executed before the death of the testator. As the power in this case was a general one, it fell under the rule. It is not yet finally settled whether a special power is to be held to be exercised by a general settlement which does not notice the power or purport to include property subject to disposal by the testator,[47] but the prevailing

[38] *Rattray's Trs.* v. *Rattray* (1899) 1 F. 510; *Mackenzie's Trs.* v. *Kilmarnock's Trs.*, 1909 S.C. 472; *Baird* v. *Baird's Trs.*, 1956 S.C. (H.L.) 93.

[39] *Ewing's Trs.* v. *Ewing*, 1909 S.C. 409.

[40] *Alves* v. *Alves* (1861) 23 D. 712; *Howe's Trs.* v. *Howe's J.F.* (1903) 5 F. 1099.

[41] *Stirling's Trs.* v. *Legal & General Assurance Soc.*, 1957 S.L.T. 73.

[42] *Stainton* v. *Forteviot Trust*, 1948 S.C. (H.L.) 115; *Neame* v. *Neame's Trs.*, 1956 S.L.T. 57.

[43] *Stainton* v. *Forteviot Trust, supra.*

[44] *Smart* v. *Smart*, 1926 S.C. 392.

[45] *Bray* v. *Bruce's Exrs.* (1906) 8 F. 1078.

[46] (1834) 12 S. 413.

[47] *Alexander's Trs.* v. *Alexander's Trs.*, 1917 S.C. 654; but see *Tarratt's Trs.* v. *Hastings* (1904) 6 F. 968.

opinion is that it is.[48] The law to be applied to determine whether or not a power has been validly exercised by a testamentary writing is that of the domicile of the donee at the date of his death.[49]

The exercise of a power is open to objection if it amounts to what is termed a fraud on the power[50] or is *ultra vires*. The term 'fraud' in this connection does not denote dishonest or immoral conduct on the part of the appointer; it means that the power has been exercised for a purpose, or with an intention, beyond the scope of, or not justified by, the deed creating the power.[51] Thus, it is a fraudulent exercise if the donee of a special power makes an appointment with the intention of benefiting himself or some other person not an object of the power;[52] or if the fund subject to the special power is appointed wholly to one object of the power in consequence of a bribe.[53] So also a parent cannot in exercising a power of appointing a fund among his children bargain with them for the purchase by him of other interests belonging to them.[54] But where the donee's purpose and intention in making the appointment was to benefit the objects of the power, the mere presence of an incidental benefit to himself, *e.g.* under an arrangement for the variation of trust purposes, will not be sufficient to constitute a fraud on the power.[55] Appointments in fraud of the power are voidable at the instance of an interested object of the power but challenge may be barred by homologation.[56]

The rule as to an *ultra vires* exercise has been thus stated: 'If you cannot disconnect that which is imposed by way of condition or mode of enjoyment from the gift, the gift itself may be found to be involved in conditions so much beyond the power that it becomes void. But where that is not so, where you have a gift to an object of the power, and where you have nothing alleged to invalidate the gift but conditions which are attempted to be imposed as to the mode in which that object of the power is to enjoy what is given to him, then the gift may be valid and take effect without reference to those conditions.'[57] In the case of a power to apportion a fund among a class, it is, since the Powers of Appointment Act 1874 (which alters the former law), no longer an objection to the exercise that certain members of the class are omitted

---

[48] *Burns' Trs.* v. *Burns' Trs.*, 1935 S.C. 905; *Gemmell's Trs.* v. *Shields*, 1936 S.C. 717.

[49] *Drurie's Trs.* v. *Osborne*, 1960 S.C. 444.

[50] McLaren, ii, 1107; Farwell on *Powers*, 457.

[51] Per Lord Parker in *Vatcher* v. *Paull* [1915] A.C. 372, at p. 378; *Re Simpson* [1952] Ch. 412.

[52] *Stein* v. *Stein* (1826) 5 S. 101; *Craig* v. *Craig's Trs.* (1904) 12 S.L.T. 136, 620; *Dick's Trs.* v. *Cameron*, 1907 S.C. 1018.

[53] *Re Wright* [1920] 1 Ch. 108.

[54] *Smith Cunninghame* v. *Anstruther's Trs.* (1872) 10 M. (H.L.) 39.

[55] *Pelham Burn, Petr.*, 1964 S.C. 3.

[56] *Callander* v. *Callander's Exr.*, 1976 S.L.T. 10., *Colquhoun's Trs.* v. *Marchioness of Lorne's Trs.*, 1990 S.L.T. 34.

[57] *McDonald* v. *McDonald's Trs.* (1875) 2 R. (H.L.) 125, *per* Earl Cairns L.C.; *Dalziel* v. *Dalziel's Trs.* (1905) 7 F. 545, *per* Lord Dunedin; *Re Holland* [1914] 2 Ch. 595.

or receive only illusory shares; the whole of the fund may validly be appointed to one of the class. But in so far as the exercise purports to give any share of the fund to one who is not a member of the class it is bad.[58] A power to apportion under restrictions and conditions is validly exercised by a gift of liferent of a share with an unqualified power of testamentary disposal, or by a gift of a share to one member of the class in liferent and to another in fee.[59] If the deed should appoint the fund to the children on condition that they forgive a certain debt or pay a certain sum, the condition could be severed from the substance of the appointment with the result that the deed would be good as an appointment to the children, and the condition would be treated as void.[60] Partial invalidity in the exercise of a power is not necessarily fatal to the whole exercise. The question is whether the appointer, if aware of the partial invalidity, would have left the rest of the appointment as it stands.[61]

The existence of a power of appointment over a fund bequeathed to a class does not suspend vesting in the members of the class; they take a right to an equal share of the fund, which may be defeated in whole or in part by an exercise of the power.[62] If the power is not exercised, or if the exercise is wholly invalid, the members of the class remain vested in equal shares of the fund.[62a] The donee of a power may validly bind himself that he will not exercise the power so as to exclude or reduce below a certain amount the share of an object of the power. A liferent and power of disposal may be renounced, whereupon the fee vests in the objects in terms of the deed creating the power.[63]

44.30 Ineffectual Conditions and Directions: Repugnancy.—If a bequest is made subject to a condition which is in its nature impossible, uncertain,[64] illegal, or *contra bonos mores*, the condition is held *pro non scripto*, and the bequest is effectual.[65] Thus, a legacy given *ob turpem*

---

[58] See, *e.g. Moubray's Trs.* v. *Moubray*, 1929 S.C. 254, where the earlier cases are reviewed, and *Colquhoun's Trs., supra.* Illegitimate persons are taken to be proper objects of a special power of appointment created by deed executed on or after November 25, 1968 unless the contrary appears (formerly, Law Reform (Misc. Provs.) (Scotland) Act 1968, ss. 5(3) and 22(5) and now Law Reform (Parent and Child) (Scotland) Act 1986, s. 1(2)).

[59] *Moubray's Trs.* v. *Moubray*, 1929 S.C. 254; *Gemmell's Trs.* v. *Shields*, 1936 S.C. 717; *Angus's Trs.* v. *Monies*, 1939 S.C. 509.

[60] Farwell on *Powers*, p. 343.

[61] *Coat's Trs.* v. *Tillinghast*, 1944 S.C. 466; *Monies* v. *Monies*, 1939 S.C. 344; *Middleton's Trs.* v. *Borwick*, 1947 S.C. 517; *Torrance's Trs.* v. *Weddel*, 1947 S.C. 91; *Cathcart's J.F.* v. *Stewart*, 1948 S.C. 456; *Maclaren's Trs.* v. *Wilkie*, 1948 S.C. 652; *Wight's Trs.* v. *Milliken*, 1960 S.C. 137; *Ford's Trs.* v. *Calthorpe, etc.*, 1971 S.C. 115.

[62] *Sivright* v. *Dallas* (1824) 2 S. 643; *Watson* v. *Majoribanks* (1837) 15 S. 586; *Romanes* v. *Riddell* (1865) 3 M. 348.

[62a] *Wemyss's Trs.* v. *Wemyss*, 1994 G.W.D. 11–702.

[63] *Lawson* v. *Cormack's Trs.*, 1940 S.C. 210.

[64] In *Veitch's Exr.* v. *Veitch*, 1947 S.L.T. 17, a condition that the legatee 'occupy' a house was held not to be uncertain. See also *Hood* v. *Macdonald's Trs.*, 1949 S.C. 24.

[65] Bell, *Prin.*, § 1785; McLaren, i, 600.

causam,[66] or subject to a condition amounting to an absolute and general restraint of marriage by the legatee[67] or to a wife on condition that she ceases to live with her husband,[68] or to a young child on condition that he shall not reside with his parents (of unobjectionable character),[69] receives effect as an unconditional legacy as these conditions are not sanctioned by the law; and testamentary directions requiring that the testator's estate should be disposed of in an unreasonable manner which conferred no benefit on any person or on the public have been refused effect as involving an abuse of the power of testation.[70] A legacy to an enemy alien remains legally incapable of payment during the war.[71]

Further, on the ground 'that an act which, if done, can be at once undone by the person having an interest, will not be directed by the Court to be done,' it has been held in a series of cases that if trustees are directed to purchase an annuity payable to a person, that person (seeing that he could sell the annuity if it were purchased) may claim the purchase price of the annuity in lieu of it.[72] And where a vested, unqualified, and indefeasible right of fee in a bequest is given in a trust disposition and settlement to a beneficiary of full age, he is entitled to payment of the bequest notwithstanding any direction to the trustees to retain the capital and to pay over the income to him or to apply the capital or income in some way for his behoof.[73] Such a direction is considered to be repugnant to the right of fee vested in the beneficiary and, therefore, nugatory. But it is otherwise if there are other trust purposes which require that the subject of the bequest shall be retained by the trustees, or if the trustees are not merely directed to retain the bequest but are given power in their discretion to withdraw the fee from the beneficiary and to settle the bequest on him in liferent and on others in fee.[74] In such circumstances the beneficiary cannot put an end to the trust management.

44.31 The Thellusson Act.—By the Accumulations Act 1800 (commonly known as the Thellusson Act), the legislature interposed to check the

---

[66] For an immoral consideration: *Johnston* v. *McKenzie's Exrs.* (1835) 14 S. 106; *Young* v. *Johnston & Wright* (1880) 7 R. 760.

[67] *Ibid.*; *Sturrock* v. *Rankin's Trs.* (1875) 2 R. 850; *Aird's Exrs.* v. *Aird*, 1949 S.C. 154.

[68] *Wilkinson* v. *Wilkinson* (1871) L.R. 12 Eq. 604.

[69] *Grant's Trs.* v. *Grant* (1898) 25 R. 929; *Fraser* v. *Rose* (1849) 11 D. 1466.

[70] *Aitken's Trs.* v. *Aitken*, 1927 S.C. 374; *Lindsay's Exr.* v. *Forsyth*, 1940 S.C. 568; *McCaig* v. *The University of Glasgow*, 1907 S.C. 231; *McCaig's Trs.* v. *Lismore United Free Kirk Session*, 1915 S.C. 426; *Sutherland's Trs.* v. *Verschoyle*, 1968 S.L.T. 43.

[71] *Weber's Trs.* v. *Riemer*, 1947 S.L.T. 295.

[72] *Dow* v. *Kilgour's Trs.* (1877) 4 R. 403; *Dempster's Trs.* v. *Dempster*, 1921 S.C. 332; contrast *Branford's Trs.* v. *Powell*, 1924 S.C. 439.

[73] *Yuill's Trs.* v. *Thomson* (1902) 4 F. 815; *Miller's Trs.* v. *Miller* (1890) 18 R. 301; *Dowden's Trs.* v. *Governors of Merchiston Castle School*, 1965 S.C. 56; *Smith's Tr.* v. *Michael*, 1972 S.L.T. 89; *Graham* v. *Graham's Trs.*, 1927 S.C. 388; contrast *Ford's Trs.* v. *Ford*, 1940 S.C. 426, where the later direction disposed of the fee.

[74] *Chamber's Trs.* v. *Smiths* (1878) 5 R. (H.L.) 151.

mischief which, it was anticipated, might arise from directions for the accumulation of income for prolonged periods. By that statute accumulation of income was prohibited beyond one or other of four periods. The 1800 Act was re-enacted with modifications by the Trusts (Scotland) Act 1961;[75] and, by the Law Reform (Miscellaneous Provisions) (Scotland) Act 1966,[76] two further periods were added in respect of deeds taking effect after August 3, 1966 bringing the total number of periods now available to six. These are: (1) the life of the grantor of the deed; (2) a term of 21 years from the death of the grantor; (3)[77] a term of 21 years from the date of the deed;[78] (4)[79] the duration of the minority[80] or respective minorities of any person or persons living or *in utero* at the date of the deed; (5) the duration of the minority or respective minorities of any person or persons living or *in utero* at the death of the grantor; and (6) the duration of the minority or respective minorities of any person or persons who, under the terms of the deed directing accumulation, would for the time being, if of full age, be entitled to the rents or income directed to be accumulated.

Of these, period (1) can, by definition, only apply in the case of *inter vivos* deeds under which accumulation is directed during the grantor's lifetime;[81] but that period will not operate so as to prevent accumulation under periods (3), (4) or (6) continuing beyond the date of the grantor's death.[82] With this exception, however, the periods are alternative, not cumulative, and it is not permissible to add one period to another.[83] Period (6) is available in a case where an accumulation is directed from a period subsequent to the date of the grantor's death,[84] it not being required that the minor should be in life at that date.[85] But where the direction is to accumulate income from the date of the grantor's death, the restriction under periods (2) or (5) will apply, whether or not accumulation has in fact taken place during that period.[86]

The statutory restrictions are not confined to cases in which accumulation of income is expressly directed. If a settlement is so

[75] s. 5.

[76] s. 6.

[77] This period was added by the 1966 Act.

[78] As to whether an arrangement under the Trusts (Scotland) Act 1961 may amount to a new settlement so as to introduce a new *terminus a quo*, see *Aikman, Petr.*, 1968 S.L.T. 137.

[79] *Ibid.*

[80] *i.e.* the period during which a person is under the age of 18—Age of Majority (Scotland) Act 1969, ss. 1(1) and (2).

[81] *Stewart's Trs.* v. *Stewart*, 1927 S.C. 350; *Union Bank* v. *Campbell*, 1929 S.C. 143.

[82] 1961 Act, s. 5(4); 1966 Act, s. 6(1) proviso. It is, however, essential that, where under an *inter vivos* deed an accumulation period has begun during the life of the granter, any additional period beyond the granter's death should be a period 'directed' by the granter (*McIver's Trs.* v. *Inland Revenue*, 1974 S.L.T. 202).

[83] *Union Bank* v. *Campbell, supra.*

[84] See *Carey's Trs.* v. *Rose*, 1957 S.C. 252.

[85] *Re Cattell* [1914] 1 Ch. 177.

[86] *Campbell's Trs.* v. *Campbell* (1891) 18 R. 992; *Carey's Trs.* v. *Rose, supra.*

framed that accumulation of income beyond the permitted period necessarily results, the Act will apply. Thus, where trustees were directed to convey the residue of the testator's estate to the children of M, and at the expiry of 21 years from the testator's death M was alive but had no children, it was held that, while it was the duty of the trustees within that period to accumulate the income for behoof of the residuary legatees, the income thereafter accruing could not be accumulated.[87] The statutory restrictions apply also in a case where the power to accumulate is merely discretionary, and there is no duty to exercise it.[88]

While the statutes put an end to accumulation after the prescribed periods, they do not otherwise affect the dispositions of the deed.[89] The deed is to be read as if it had expressly declared that the accumulation directed should then end, and for the rest it receives effect exactly as it stands.

The 1961 Act provides that the income directed to be accumulated contrary to its provisions shall 'go to, and be received by, the person or persons who would have been entitled thereto if such accumulation had not been directed.'[90] Accordingly, if there is a present gift of the income-bearing subject and the direction for accumulation is merely a burden on that gift, so that apart from it the legatee would have taken the income, the income released by the statute will go to the legatee.[91] On the other hand, if the gift is a future one, the statute does not operate to accelerate or enlarge the right of the legatee.[92] Thus, if the gift is to be made over to the legatee at the termination of an annuity, any income accruing during the annuitant's lifetime, but after the period of 21 years from the testator's death, will not go to the legatee.[93] If the subject of the gift were residue, the income in that case would fall into intestacy.[94] Renunciation of a liferent would have the same effect. Where the income is that accruing on a legacy, the result of the statute is that the income will fall into residue if there be a residuary bequest

---

[87] *Lord* v. *Colvin* (1860) 23 D. 111; *Barbour* v. *Budge*, 1947 S.N. 100. See also *Gibson's Trs.*, 1963 S.C. 350.

[88] 1966 Act, s. 6(2).

[89] *Elder's Trs.* v. *Treasurer of the Free Church of Scotland* (1892) 20 R. 2, *per* Lord Kyllachy; *Maxwell's Trs.* v. *Maxwell* (1877) 5 R. 248, *per* Lord Justice-Clerk Moncreiff; *Landale's Trs.* v. *Overseas Missionary Fellowship*, 1982 S.L.T. 158.

[90] 1961 Act, s. 5(3).

[91] *Maxwell's Trs.* v. *Maxwell, supra; Mackenzie* v. *Mackenzie's Trs.* (1877) 4 R. 962; *Stewart's Trs.* v. *Whitelaw*, 1926 S.C. 701; McLaren, i, 313.

[92] *Russell's Trs.* v. *Russell*, 1959 S.C. 148; *cf. Young's Trs.* v. *Chapelle, etc.*, 1971 S.L.T. 147.

[93] *Smith* v. *Glasgow Royal Infirmary*, 1909 S.C. 1231; *Wilson's Trs.* v. *Glasgow Royal Infirmary*, 1917 S.C. 527; *Pyper's Trs.* v. *Leighton*, 1946 S.L.T. 255; *cf. Dowden's Trs.* v. *Governors of Merchiston Castle School*, 1965 S.C. 56.

[94] *Elder's Trs.*, and *Wilson's Trs., supra; Carey's Trs.* v. *Rose*, 1957 S.C. 252. Legal rights are not claimable out of the income thus brought into intestacy: *Lindsay's Trs.* v. *Lindsay*, 1931 S.C. 586.

which by means of present gift gives to the residuary legatee everything not otherwise disposed of (and its terms allow of the income being paid away, for the retention of the income for behoof of residuary legatees would be equivalent to accumulation) or, otherwise, into intestacy.[95] A person in whom a fund has vested subject to defeasance is not entitled to the income under the statutory provision as the right of fee is not absolute.[96]

The Accumulations Act 1892 prohibits the accumulation of income by will for the purchase of land only.[97]

44.32 Limitation on the Creation of Liferents.—The Law Reform (Miscellaneous Provisions) (Scotland) Act 1968[98] provides that where, by any deed executed on or after November 25, 1968, there is created a liferent interest in any property, that interest is converted into a right of fee if anyone of full age becomes entitled to it who was not living or *in utero* at the date of the coming into operation of the deed.[99] In the case of someone not of full age, the conversion into a right of fee is postponed until he attains majority and is subject to the proviso that he should then still be entitled to the liferent interest. The conversion does not affect rights created independently of the deed or rights of security holders or superiors of heritable property. These provisions re-enact with some variations the substance of provisions of the Trusts (Scotland) Act 1921[1] and the Entail Amendment Act 1848[2] which continue to apply to liferent interests created by deeds executed before November 25, 1968. Under the latter Act which applies to heritage, whereas the 1921 Act applies to moveables, there is no automatic conversion into a right of fee but the liferenter is enabled, if he so chooses, to acquire the fee by petitioning the court for that purpose.[3] The section does not apply to annuities.[4]

44.33 Approbate and Reprobate or Election.—The doctrine known in Scots law as approbate and reprobate is the same as that of election in the law of England. It has been authoritatively stated in these terms: 'It is

[95] *Smith* v. *Glasgow Royal Infirmary, supra, per* Lord President Dunedin at p. 1236; *Cathcart's Trs.* v. *Foresterhill Hospital*, 1977 S.L.T. 114.
[96] *Russell's Trs.* v. *Russell, supra, per* Lord President Clyde and Lord Russell (*obiter*).
[97] *Robertson's Trs.* v. *Robertson's Trs.*, 1933 S.C. 639.
[98] s. 18.
[99] A *mortis causa* deed comes into operation on the death of the testator and the execution or coming into operation of a special power of appointment is referable to the date of execution or, as the case may be, coming into operation of the deed creating the power (s. 18(5)).
[1] s. 9; Conveyancing (Scotland) Act 1924, s. 45.
[2] s. 48.
[3] *Crichton-Stuart's Tutrix*, 1921 S.C. 840, *per* Lord President Clyde; *Earl of Moray, Petr.*, 1950 S.C. 281.
[4] *Drybrough's Tr.* v. *Drybrough's Tr.*, 1912 S.C. 939.

equally settled in the law of Scotland and of England that no person can accept and reject the same instrument. If a testator gives his estate to A and gives A's estate to B, Courts of Equity hold it to be against conscience that A should take the estate bequeathed to him and at the same time refuse to effectuate the implied condition in the will of the testator. The Court will not permit him to take that which cannot be his but by virtue of the disposition of the will and at the same time to keep what by the same will is given or intended to be given to another person.'[5] In the leading modern case,[6] children taking provisions made by a testatrix out of her own estate claimed also to be entitled to challenge her appointment of a fund made in the same deed and to take that fund as in default of valid appointment; but the court, applying the doctrine, held that acceptance of one part of the deed was inconsistent with rejection of another part.

The most familiar illustration of the doctrine is to be found in cases where a bequest is made to a spouse or descendant who has a legal right in the estate of the testator.[7] A descendant or spouse cannot be deprived of that right by testament,[8] but he or she may be required to elect between it and a testamentary provision. A case for election will arise if a provision in a testament is made with an express declaration that it is given in satisfaction of the legal rights,[9] or if the provision is contained in a universal settlement, for a legatee cannot, by claiming under a deed which was intended to dispose of the whole estate, approbate it and at the same time reprobate it by withdrawing a portion of the estate to meet his or her legal rights.[10] On the other hand, if the settlement is a partial one and disposes only of dead's part, a claim for legal rights would not disturb it, and, therefore, children or their issue might take both these rights and provisions under the deed.[11]

44.34   Conditions of Election.—It is stated by Lord President Inglis, in *Douglas's Trs.* v. *Douglas*,[12] 'that, to make a proper case of election, the facts of the case must be such as to satisfy three conditions. In the first place, I think the party who is put to his election must have a free choice, and that whichever alternative he chooses, he shall have a right absolutely to that which he has chosen, without the possibility of his right being interfered with or frustrated by the intervention of any third

---

[5] *Per* Lord Eldon in *Ker* v. *Wauchope* (1819) 1 Bligh 1.

[6] *Crum Ewing's Trs.* v. *Bayly's Trs.*, 1911 S.C. (H.L.) 18.

[7] The issue of predeceasing children now share in the division of legitim: Succession (Scotland) Act 1964, s. 11.

[8] See para. 42.2, *supra*.

[9] Such a declaration is implied in all testaments made on or after September 10, 1964: Succession (Scotland) Act, s. 13 as amended by the Law Reform (Misc. Provs.) (Scotland) Act 1968, s. 3 and Sched. 1, para. 6.

[10] *Henderson* v. *Henderson* (1782) Mor. 8191; McLaren, i, 139.

[11] *White* v. *Finlay* (1861) 24 D. 38; McLaren, i, 140.

[12] (1862) 24 D. 1191, at p. 1208; *Brown's Trs.* v. *Gregson*, 1920 S.C. (H.L.) 87.

party. In the second place, the necessity of making the election must arise from the will, express or implied, of someone who has the power to bind the person put to his election. And, in the third place, the result of the election of one or other of the alternatives must be to give legal effect and operation to the will so expressed or implied.' In making an election a person should have information as to the alternative rights open to him; and there are numerous cases in which an election made in ignorance or in circumstances which show that it does not represent a free and deliberate choice, has been held not to be binding.[13]

44.35 **Equitable Compensation: Forfeiture.**—A person who elects to claim against a will (*e.g.* a spouse or descendant enforcing legal rights) loses, in any event, any benefit given him by the will so far as is necessary to indemnify those who have been prejudiced by his election, by restoring to the estate what has been taken as *jus relictae* or legitim. Thus, in *Macfarlane's Trs.* v. *Oliver*,[14] a testator directed his trustees to hold his whole estate for behoof of his son and daughter equally in liferent and for their issue respectively in fee. The daughter having claimed her legitim, the trustees accumulated the share of income which would have been payable to her as liferentrix until it reached a sum which enabled them to make good to her brother and to the grandchildren the loss occasioned to them by her claim of legitim; and it was held that, compensation having thus been made, the daughter was entitled to the future income of the share bequeathed to her and her children. But if a conventional provision is made for a spouse or child on the express condition that it is to be taken in satisfaction of her or his legal rights, the assertion of these rights normally involves total forfeiture of the provision. In testamentary settlements executed prior to September 10, 1964, the doctrine of equitable compensation operates in the absence of a clause of satisfaction; but such a clause is now implied in all wills made on or after that date.[15] Accordingly, a claim for legal rights will result in forfeiture of all provisions made for the claimant in such a deed unless the will contains a statement to the contrary. Not infrequently the provision in favour of a child is in the form of a liferent to him and the fee to his issue or a destination-over of the liferent to his spouse. Where the clause of satisfaction includes also a provision for forfeiture, it may expressly declare the forfeiture of their rights as well as those of the claimant; but if it does not, the fate of their rights depends on whether there is a separate and independent gift to them. If there is, their rights

---

[13] See *Inglis* v. *Breen* (1890) 17 R. (H.L.) 76; *Stewart* v. *Bruce's Trs.* (1898) 25 R. 965; *Dawson's Trs.* v. *Dawson* (1896) 23 R. 1006; *Walker* v. *Orr's Trs.*, 1958 S.L.T. 220.

[14] (1882) 9 R. 1138. And see *Thomson's Trs.* v. *Thomson*, 1946 S.C. 399.

[15] Succession (Scotland) Act 1964, s. 13, as amended by the Law Reform (Parent and Child) (Scotland) Act 1986, Sched. 2. See formerly, Law Reform (Misc. Provs.) (Scotland) Act 1968, s. 3 and Sched. 1, para. 6; *Munro's Trs.*, 1971 S.L.T. 33; 1971 S.C. 280.

are not forfeited;[16] but if there is not, and on a construction of the deed it appears that the right of the issue or spouse is dependent on the liferent taking effect, forfeiture of their right is involved in the child's election to take legitim.[17] Where the clause of satisfaction does not contain an express forfeiture, it is doubtful whether forfeiture of the conventional provision by any person other than the actual claimant will be inferred.[18] Where there is forfeiture, any balance of the forfeited provision after indemnification falls either into residue or into intestacy. It falls into intestacy if the provision was itself a gift of residue or part thereof, into residue if the provision was one of the prior purposes such as a legacy.[19] Thus, a son claiming legitim may in the end take the balance of a gift or residue *qua* heir in intestacy.[20] If, however, a forfeiture clause is combined with a destination-over in the event of forfeiture and the destination-over fails, *e.g.* because there is no one to take under it, the forfeiture does not take effect.[21]

44.36 Satisfaction of Legitim.—As was shown in Chapter 42,[22] a descendant's discharge of legitim *in the ancestor's lifetime* is equivalent in its effect to the descendant's death. It is otherwise when a descendant elects *after the ancestor's death* to accept a bequest in place of legitim. When a parent dies the right to legitim vests, and each child (or the issue of a predeceasing child) becomes a creditor with a claim on the executory for his or her share; and, if the child chooses rather to accept the bequest than to demand legitim, the debt to that child is extinguished. But the extinction of the debt benefits, not the legitim claimants, but the dead's part out of which the accepted bequest has been paid.[23]

A declaration by a testator that a legacy is given in satisfaction of legal rights will debar a legatee accepting the legacy from advancing any claim for these which conflicts with the scheme of the testator's settlement.[24] Whether the declaration has or has not a wider effect is a question of circumstances. The declaration may be read as intended to exclude such claims only in so far as necessary for the protection of the settlement. If this is so, then the legatee will not be debarred from

---

[16] *Fisher* v. *Dixon* (1831) 10 S. 55, affd. 6 W. & S. 431; *Jack* v. *Marshall* (1879) 6 R. 543; *Brown's Trs.* v. *Gregson*, 1916 S.C. 97; *Hurll's Trs.* v. *Hurll*, 1964 S.C. 12; *Munro's Trs., supra.* See also *Ballantyne's Trs., Petrs.*, 1992 S.C.L.R. 889, where forfeiture of the rights of issue did not prevent their succession as conditional institutes under another provision of the will.

[17] *Campbell's Trs.* v. *Campbell* (1889) 16 R. 1007; *McCaull's Trs.* v. *McCaull* (1900) 3 F. 222; *Ballantyne's Trs.* v. *Ballantyne*, 1952 S.C. 458; *McCartney*, 1951 S.C. 504.

[18] See *Nicolson's Trs.* v. *Nicolson*, 1960 S.C. 186, *per* Lord President Clyde at p. 193; *Hurll's Trs., supra, per* Lord Justice-Clerk Grant, at p. 19.

[19] *Wingate* v. *Wingate's Trs.*, 1921 S.C. 857.

[20] As in *Tindall's Trs.* v. *Tindall*, 1933 S.C. 419.

[21] *Macnaughton* v. *Macnaughton's Trs.*, 1954 S.C. 312.

[22] *Supra*, para. 42.8.

[23] *Fisher's Trs.* v. *Dixon* (1842) 2 D. 1121; *per* Lord Fullerton, affd. 2 Bell's App.63.

[24] See n. 8 *supra*, and para. 44.33, *supra*.

asserting his or her legal rights against any portion of the estate which may fall into intestacy. Thus where a testator bequeathed a liferent of his estate to his widow in lieu of her legal rights and the residue to his children and, by reason of the death of all the children, the estate fell into intestacy, it was held that the widow's acceptance of the liferent did not exclude her claim for her legal rights from the intestate estate.[25] But if it appears that the declaration was meant to safeguard the interests not only of the beneficiaries under the settlement but of the heirs *ab intestato* also, then the claim for legal rights would be completely debarred.[26]

44.37 Exclusion from Succession; Unlawful Killing.—A person who has unlawfully killed is excluded from participation in his victim's testate estate and from the benefit of donations *mortis causa* on the same principles and subject to the same reliefs as are applied to succession on intestacy and participation in legal rights.[27] Such exclusion will normally result in the estate bequeathed to the killer falling into intestacy. Suggestions that forfeiture leads to the killer being treated as having predeceased the victim are unsound.[28]

44.38 Donation *Mortis Causa*.—This was defined by Lord President Inglis in *Morris* v. *Riddick*[29] as 'conveyance of an immoveable or incorporeal right, or a transference of moveables or money by delivery, so that the property is immediately transferred to the grantee, upon the condition that he shall hold for the grantor so long as he lives, subject to his power of revocation, and, failing such revocation, then for the grantee on the death of the grantor.' It has been said[30] that three essentials must occur: (1) the donor must act in contemplation of his death, (2) the subject of the donation must be delivered to the donee, and (3) the donor must manifest his intention to make in favour of the donee a *de praesenti* gift consistent with the double resolutive condition stated above. Where there has been no delivery of the subject said to have been gifted, there is difficulty in establishing donation; but it has been laid down in a series of cases that delivery is not in all circumstances indispensable. In the case of a document such as a deposit-receipt[31] the

---

[25] *Naismith* v. *Boyes* (1899) 1 F. (H.L.) 79; *McGregor's Trs.* v. *Kimbell*, 1911 S.C. 1196; contrast *Sim* v. *Sim* (1902) 4 F. 944. *Naismith* applied: *Petrie's Trs.* v. *Manders's Tr.*, 1954 S.C. 430.

[26] *Ibid.*

[27] See para. 43.6, *supra.*

[28] *Hunter's Exrs., Petrs.*, 1992 S.L.T. 1141.

[29] (1867) 5 M. 1036.

[30] *Macpherson's Exrx.* v. *Mackay*, 1932 S.C. 505, *per* Lord President Clyde at p. 513; see also *Graham's Trs.* v. *Gillies*, 1956 S.C. 437, at p. 448 and *Forrest-Hamilton's Tr.* v. *Forrest-Hamilton*, 1970 S.L.T. 338.

[31] 'There must be delivery or its equivalent in the case of cash or bank notes'—Lord Mackenzie in *Hutcheson's Exr.* v. *Shearer*, 1909 S.C. 15; see also *Crosbie's Trs.* v. *Wright* (1880) 7 R. 823, *per* Lord Deas.

fact that it was not delivered to the person alleging donation will not prevent the donation being effectual, if the intention to make it is otherwise established,[32] but there must be an equivalent to delivery.[33] There is, as in the case of donation *inter vivos*, a presumption against donation which has to be overcome.[34]

The effect of the donation is that the right of property in the subject passes at once to the donee. But during the lifetime of the donor that right is only a qualified one. Not only is the gift revocable by the donor, but it falls by the donee's predecease.[35] While the gift must have been made in contemplation of the donor's death, it is not required that he should have been under an immediate apprehension of death: and, although the gift may have been made at a time when he was dangerously ill, it is not *ipso facto* revoked by his recovery.[36]

Donations *mortis causa* 'savour much indeed of legacies.'[37] Thus, they remain under the power of the donor during his lifetime, and it is only on his death that the donee acquires an effectual right,[38] they are chargeable with the donor's debts if there is a deficiency of funds for their payment; and they do not affect the legal rights of the donor's spouse or issue.[39] But they differ from legacies in respect that there is an immediate, though conditional, transference of property and that, however valuable the gift may be, it does not require to be constituted by writing but may be proved by parole evidence. 'Where they become good by the grantor's death, they are effectual against his heir or executor in the same manner as other deeds delivered at the date,' and the donee is entitled to the subject of the gift although nothing is left for the legatees.[40]

Further Reading

Henderson, *Principles of Vesting* (2nd ed., 1938).
Macdonald, *Succession* (2nd ed., 1994).
McLaren, *Wills and Succession* (3rd ed., 1894 and Supplement, 1934).
Murray, *Law of Wills in Scotland*.
Stair Memorial Encyclopaedia, Vol. 25.

---

[32] *Carmichael* v. *Carmichael's Exrx.*, 1920 S.C. (H.L.) 195, at pp. 203 and 205; *Scott's Trs.* v. *Macmillan* (1905) 8 F. 214; *Macfarlane's Trs.* v. *Miller* (1898) 25 R. 1201, and cases there cited; *Macpherson's Exrx.* v. *Mackay*, 1932 S.C. 505; *Graham's Trs.* v. *Gillies, supra.* Contrast the case of an *inter vivos* donation, *Brownlee's Exrx.* v. *Brownlee*, 1908 S.C. 232.

[33] *Gray's Trs.* v. *Murray, etc.*, 1970 S.L.T. 105.

[34] *Macpherson's Exrx.* v. *Mackay, supra.*

[35] See *Morris* v. *Riddick, supra*; *Lord Advocate* v. *Galloway* (1884) 11 R. 541.

[36] *Blyth* v. *Curle* (1885) 12 R. 674.

[37] Bankton, I, ix, 16.

[38] *Ibid.*

[39] *Morris* v. *Riddick, supra.*

[40] Bankton, I, ix, 18; *Morris* v. *Riddick, supra, per* Lord Deas at p. 1044.

CHAPTER 45

EXECUTORS AND JUDICIAL FACTORS

I. EXECUTORS

45.1 Vitious Intromission—The title to ingather and distribute the estate, both heritable and moveable,[1] of a deceased person belongs to the executor nominated by the deceased, or appointed by the court, and in either case authorised to do so by confirmation by the court. An unauthorised intromitter may incur liability for the whole debts of the deceased, even if there was no fraudulent intention.[2] But the court has regard to the character and circumstances of the intromission and may relieve the vitious intromitter of the penal consequences of his actings. Thus, if the intromitter had a probable title for intromitting, *e.g.* if he was general disponee of the deceased (although this is not a competent title to intermeddle with the estate without confirmation), or if the circumstances show that he acted in good faith, he may escape universal liability.[3] Intromission either necessary or *custodiae causa* (for the sake of custody) by the wife and children of the deceased holding possession for the purpose of preserving the estate for the benefit of all concerned, does not infer liability; and there is clearly no place for it if the goods intermeddled with did not belong to the deceased.[4]

This rule was introduced for the benefit of creditors of the deceased and it is not available as a ground of action to heirs or legatees.[5] It cannot be pleaded against the heirs of a deceased vitious intromitter, the heir being liable only in so far as he is *lucratus* through succession to the intromitter. Where several are concerned in the intromission, each is liable *in solidum* and may be sued without calling the others; but the intromitter who pays the debt has relief against his fellow-intromitters. An intromitter who confirms before action is brought against him, or within a year and day, thereby subjecting himself to liability to account,

---

[1] Succession (Scotland) Act 1964, s. 14(1). Note that the executor had no title to ingather heritage in the case of persons dying before September 10, 1964.
[2] *Forbes* v. *Forbes* (1823) 2 S. 395; *Wilson* v. *Taylor* (1865) 3 M. 1060.
[3] *Adam* v. *Campbell* (1854) 16 D. 964; *Simpson* v. *Barr* (1854) 17 D. 33; *Greig* v. *Christie*, 1908 S.C. 370.
[4] *Greig* v. *Christie, supra.*
[5] Erskine, *Inst.,* III, ix, 54.

purges the vitiosity of his prior intromissions; but confirmation merely as executor-creditor[6] does not suffice for this purpose.[7]

45.2 Appointment of Executor.—An executor is appointed: (*a*) either expressly or impliedly by the deceased (executor-nominate), or (*b*) by the court (executor-dative). With regard to (*a*), the persons who may be executors are, in order: (*i*) the executor nominated[8] by the deceased; or failing such an appointment, (*ii*) the testamentary trustees; or failing them, (*iii*) any general disponee or universal legatory or residuary legatee.[9]

Where the deceased dies intestate or there is no executor-nominate, the executor is appointed by the decerniture of the sheriff on an application for this purpose. The court in which the application should be made is that of the sheriffdom in which the deceased was domiciled, or, if he had no domicile in Scotland or no fixed domicile, in the Sheriff Court of Edinburgh as the *commune forum*. The order of preference[10] observed in making the appointment is: (1) next-of-kin and, if these do not claim, the representatives of next-of-kin who have died after the deceased but before confirmation is expede;[11] (2) the widow; (3) the children or descendants of such persons as would have been next-of-kin had they survived the deceased but who have predeceased him; (4) creditors; (5) legatees; and (6) the procurator fiscal of court or a judicial factor. Where the father or mother of the deceased have right to a share of the estate, they rank *pari passu* with the next-of-kin in competition for the office.[12] The husband, if he is entitled to *jus relicti*, has right to the office, but not in competition with his wife's next-of-kin.[13] Where the deceased has died intestate but is survived by a spouse, and the intestate estate is less than the amount which the surviving spouse is entitled to receive under prior rights, the surviving spouse has the right to be appointed executor;[14] otherwise the preference of the surviving spouse's right to the office will depend on the extent to which the deceased's estate exceeds the value of these rights.[15] An executor appointed by the court is known as an executor-dative. All applicants having an equal right in the estate are entitled to be conjoined in the office. It is not settled to what extent the court is entitled to take into consideration the capacity or incapacity of an applicant.[16]

---

[6] See para. 45.5, *infra*.
[7] Erskine, *Inst.*, III, ix, 52.
[8] *Tod*, (1890) 18 R. 152.
[9] Executors (Scotland) Act 1900, s. 3.
[10] See Currie, *Confirmation of Executors*, pp. 98 *et seq.*
[11] Confirmation of Executors (Scotland) Act 1823, s. 1; Succession (Scotland) Act 1964, s. 5(2).
[12] *Webster* v. *Shiress* (1878) 6 R. 102; *Muir* (1876) 4 R. 74.
[13] *Campbell* v. *Falconer* (1892) 19 R. 563.
[14] 1964 Act, s. 9(4). See para. 42.5, *supra*.
[15] Currie, *op. cit.*, p. 108.
[16] *Crolla*, 1942 S.C. 21.

45.3 Confirmation of Executors.—The appointment of a person as executor does not in itself confer on him authority to intromit with the estate of the deceased. In order to obtain such authority, he must expede confirmation, that is, he must apply for, and obtain from the sheriff, a sentence or decree authorising him to 'uplift, receive, administer and dispose of' the estate and to act in the office of executor; and an executor who intromits with the estate without confirmation is a vitious intromitter.[17] Confirmation in favour of an executor-nominate is called a testament-testamentar; in favour of an executor-dative a testament-dative. The office of executor is purely administrative.[18]

As a condition of confirmation, an executor-dative must find caution to make the estate forthcoming to parties interested, but this is not required in the case of an executor-nominate or a spouse who has right to the whole intestate estate and is executor-dative.[19] All executors must give up on oath a full and true inventory of the whole estate, heritable and moveable, known to have belonged to the deceased, including property outwith Scotland.[20] A confirmation noting the Scottish domicile of the deceased is treated for purposes of the law of England and Wales as a grant of representation to the executors named therein in respect of the property of which in terms of the confirmation they are executors.[21] There is a corresponding provision for Northern Ireland.[22]

Confirmation to part only of the estate known to exist is prohibited by statute (except in the case of an executor-creditor) and is of no effect.[23] If an executor discovers that any part of the estate has been omitted or undervalued, he may by an eik have the same confirmed in addition to the estate orginally confirmed; and it is also open to a creditor or other party interested to apply for confirmation *ad omissa vel male appretiata* (to items omitted or undervalued). On such an application, if there has been no fraud on the part of the original executor, the sheriff will ordain the omitted subjects or the difference in value to be added to the original confirmation, or, if there be fraud, will grant a confirmation of the subjects to the exclusion of the original executor.

45.4 Confirmation in Small Estates.—Modern statutes have introduced a simple mode of obtaining confirmation in small estates. Where the value

---

[17] *Cunningham & Bell* v. *McKirdy* (1827) 5 S. 315.

[18] *Smart* v. *Smart*, 1926 S.C. 392.

[19] Confirmation of Executors (Scotland) Act 1823, s. 2 (amended by Law Reform (Misc. Provs.) (Scotland) Act 1980, s. 5); Succession (Scotland) Act 1964, s. 20, proviso. See *Harrison* v. *Butters*, 1969 S.L.T. 183.

[20] Probate and Legacy Duties Act 1808, s. 38. It is competent to include in the inventory of the estate of a person dying domiciled in Scotland any real estate of the deceased in England and Wales or Northern Ireland: Administration of Estates Act 1971, s. 6.

[21] Administration of Estates Act 1971, s. 1.

[22] s. 2.

[23] Confirmation of Executors (Scotland) Act 1823, s. 3; *Elder* v. *Watson* (1859) 21 D. 1122.

of the whole estate of the deceased does not exceed £17,000, an application may be made to the sheriff clerk, who fills up an inventory, takes the applicant's oath thereto, gets caution, if necessary, and expedes confirmation for a small fee. This procedure applies to both testate and intestate estates.[24]

There are statutory provisions permitting payments of certain kinds and under a specific amount without the exhibition of confirmation.[25]

45.5 Executor-Creditor.—A creditor may sue the executor who has confirmed to the debtor's estate to make payment of the debt. If there has been no confirmation, the creditor may apply for the office and may be confirmed as executor-creditor; and, when one creditor so applies, every co-creditor may apply to be conjoined with him in the office. This confirmation is truly a form of diligence[26] and, as the creditor resorts to it solely for his own behoof, he is not required to confirm to more than the amount of his debt.

Confirmation is, however, available only to a creditor whose debt has been constituted by decree during the debtor's lifetime. If the debt is not so established, the procedure open to the creditor is to charge the next-of-kin to confirm. These may renounce the succession within 20 days after the charge, and if they fail to do so, they become liable, as vitious intromitters, for the debt. Should the next of kin renounce the succession, the charger may constitute his debt and obtain a decree *cognitionis causa* (for the sake of constituting) against the *haereditas jacens* (the vacant estate) and, having thus constituted the debt, may obtain confirmation as executor-creditor.[27]

45.6 Effect of Confirmation.—Every part of the deceased's estate, heritable and moveable, falling to be administered under the law of Scotland, to which confirmation has been obtained, vests for the purposes of administration in the executor by virtue of the confirmation;[28] the confirmation confers on him full power to ingather, administer and dispose of the estate contained in the inventory. Before confirmation, an

---

[24] Intestates' Widows and Children (Scotland) Act 1875; Small Testate Estates (Scotland) Act 1876, as amended by Confirmation to Small Estates (Scotland) Act 1979, s. 1; Confirmation to Small Estates (Scotland) Order 1989 (S.I. 1989 No. 289); Currie, *Confirmation of Executors*, pp. 223 *et seq.*

[25] Administration of Estates (Small Payments) Act 1965, Sched. 1; Administration of Estates (Small Payments) (Increase of Limit) Order 1984 (S.I. 1984 No. 539).

[26] *Smith's Trs.* v. *Grant* (1862) 24 D. 1142, at p. 1169.

[27] Erskine, *Inst.*, III, ix, 34–35; Stewart on *Diligence*, p. 441; *Smith* v. *Tasker*, 1955 S.L.T. 347; *Stevens* v. *Thomson*, 1971 S.L.T. 136. It may be noted that under s. 11A of the Judicial Factors (Scotland) Act 1889 (added by the Bankruptcy (Scotland) Act 1985, s. 75(1), Sched. 7, para. 4), where a deceased party has left no settlement appointing trustees or other parties having power to manage his estate, or in the event of such parties not accepting or acting, a judicial factor may be appointed on the application of a creditor of the deceased or any person having an interest in the succession. This provision is applicable as well to solvent as to insolvent estates.

[28] Succession (Scotland) Act 1964, s. 14(1).

executor may indeed sue for a debt due to the deceased;[29] but, without it, he cannot obtain an extract of decree for, or enforce, payment or grant an effectual discharge of, the debt. A debtor of the deceased is not bound to pay his debt to anyone except an executor who has confirmed to it;[30] and, if he chooses to pay to anyone else, this does not discharge him of his debt in a question with the executor who has confirmed. The executor alone has a title to sue those indebted to the deceased. Except in very special circumstances, an heir or residuary legatee has no such title;[31] but, if the executor is unwilling to raise an action against a debtor and the legatee desires to do so, he may require the executor to give him the use of his name as pursuer of the action on condition of securing the executor against any risk of liability for the expenses of the action.

The confirmation itself, in the case of deaths on or after September 10, 1964, constitutes a valid title in the executor to the heritage contained in the inventory to it, and which has vested in him thereunder.[32] The executor may then transfer the heritage to the beneficiary entitled thereto by means of a statutory form of docket which is endorsed on the confirmation.[33] A person who in good faith and for value subsequently acquires title to any interest in the heritage which was vested in the executor directly or indirectly, whether from the executor himself or from a person deriving title from the executor, is protected under the Succession (Scotland) Act 1964, in that no challenge may be made to that title on the ground that the confirmation was reducible or has been reduced, or that the title should not have been transferred to the person deriving title from the executor.[34]

45.7 Duties of the Executor.—The executor is not, in a question with creditors, to be regarded as a trustee for their behoof. He is proprietor of the executry burdened with the debts chargeable against it. As the deceased was debtor to his creditors, so is the executor who comes in his place, with this limitation, that the executor's liability does not extend beyond the estate committed to his charge. The executor is *eadem persona cum defuncto* (the same person as the deceased).[35]

---

[29] *Chalmers' Trs.* v. *Watson* (1860) 22 D. 1060; *Bones* v. *Morrison* (1866) 5 M. 240; *Mackay* v. *Mackay*, 1914 S.C. 200.
[30] *Fraser* v. *Gibb* (1784) Mor. 3921; *Buchanan* v. *Royal Bank of Scotland* (1843) 5 D. 211.
[31] *Morrison* v. *Morrison's Exr.*, 1912 S.C. 892.
[32] s. 15(1). The inventory to the confirmation must contain such a description of the heritage as will be sufficient to identify the property or interest therein as a separate item in the estate: Act of Sederunt (Confirmation of Executors Amendment) 1966 (S.I. 1966 No. 593).
[33] s. 15(2); Sched. 1. The docket may be used as a link in title in any deduction of title.
[34] s. 17.
[35] *Globe Insurance Co.* v. *Scott's Trs.* (1849) 7 Bell's App. 296; *Stewart's Trs.* v. *Stewart's Exr.* (1896) 23 R. 739; *Mitchell* v. *Mackersy* (1905) 8 F. 198; *Tait's Exrx.* v. *Arden Coal Co.*, 1947 S.C. 100; *Murray's J.F.* v. *Thomas Murray & Sons (Ice Merchants) Ltd.*, 1992 S.L.T. 824. See also Succession (Scotland) Act 1964, s. 19.

Under the common law, an executor might pay creditors according to the rule applicable to diligence, *prior tempore potior jure* (prior in time, preferable in right). Creditors who lived at a distance or who were late in learning of their debtor's decease were thus liable to be prejudiced; and, accordingly, in order to provide a remedy for this, the Act of Sederunt of February 28, 1662 was passed. By this Act, all creditors using legal diligence by citation of the executors or by obtaining themselves confirmed executors-creditors, or citing other executors-creditors, within six months after their debtor's death, come in *pari passu* with those who have used more timely diligence. Hence, an executor cannot be compelled to pay away any part of the estate until after the expiry of the six months, nor (unless the solvency of the estate is assured) is he in safety to do so, seeing that until that period has elapsed it cannot be known for certain how many creditors may have claims on the fund in his hands. There is an exception in the case of privileged debts, *i.e.* debts which have preference over all other debts and must in any case be paid, under which term are included deathbed and funeral expenses, mourning for the widow and family, the expenses of administering the deceased's estate and, probably, debts which would be preferred in sequestration.[36]

After the expiry of the six months, the executor may proceed to pay *primo venienti* (to the first who comes along) and is not answerable for so doing to creditors who appear afterwards. This rule protects executors acting fairly in the discharge of their duties; but there may be circumstances, *e.g.* if it became plain that the estate was insolvent, in which it would not be proper for the executor to pay off certain debts without regard to the claims of other creditors.[37] Even after the period of six months has expired a creditor citing the executor while funds remain in his hands is entitled to participate in the division of these funds.[38] Where the validity of a creditor's claim is doubtful, the executor may require the creditor to constitute it by decree.[39]

After the claims of creditors have been met, it is the executor's duty (unless he himself is alone interested in the estate) to account for and distribute what remains of the estate to those who have right to it. These parties are not entitled to receive any benefit from the estate until the claims of creditors have been satisfied; and, if, in the knowledge that there are outstanding debts, the executor chooses to distribute the whole estate to the beneficiaries, he may be made personally liable to an unsatisfied creditor, unless the latter has consented to the payment or

[36] Erskine, III, ix, 43; *Barlass's Trs.,* 1916 S.C. 741; Bankruptcy (Scotland) Act 1985, s. 51, Sched. 3.

[37] *Taylor & Fergusson* v. *Glass's Trs.,* 1912 S.C. 165, *per* Lord Dunedin; *Stewart's Trs.* v. *Evans* (1871) 9 M. 810.

[38] *Russel* v. *Simes* (1790) Bell's Oct. Cases 217.

[39] *McGaan* v. *McGaan's Trs.* (1883) 11 R. 249, *per* Lord President Inglis.

has so acted as to be personally barred from objecting to the executor's conduct.[40]

The Succession (Scotland) Act 1964 provides that an adopted person is to be treated for the purposes of succession as the child of the adopter; but an executor is not obliged, before distributing the estate, to check whether an adoption order has been made which would entitle a person to an interest in the estate.[41] Similarly, the executor is not obliged to ascertain whether an illegitimate person exists, or has existed, the fact of whose existence is relevant to the distribution of the estate or whether any paternal relative of an illegitimate person exists who may have an interest in the estate.[42] Where an interest in a lease forms part of the deceased's estate at his death in relation to which the deceased has not made a valid bequest or has made a bequest which has failed, the executor is entitled to transfer it, without the consent of the landlord, to any of the persons having rights of succession on intestacy in or towards the satisfaction of that person's claim.[43]

Although the office of the executor is distinct from that of trustee, both are governed by the general principles which apply to the administration of an estate by one person for behoof of others. In formal testamentary deeds trustees are usually also nominated executors, and in this case it is not easy to mark the point of differentiation between the respective duties of the two offices. Executors-nominate, as defined in the Executors (Scotland) Act 1900, are included in the definition of trustee for the purposes of the Trusts (Scotland) Acts 1921[44] and 1961,[45] and this definition was extended by the Succession (Scotland) Act 1964[46] so as to include executors-dative. Thus, executors have the same powers, privileges and immunities and are subject to the same obligations, limitations and restrictions as gratuitous trustees under those Acts,[47] except that an executor-dative does not have power to resign or to assume new trustees.

Removal of an executor from office for failure to co-operate with another executor in the administration, whilst a great rarity, is illustrated in at least one reported case.[48]

45.8 Failure of Executors by Death: Confirmation *ad non executa*.—Executry is an office and does not descend to heirs. Where, therefore, there is but one executor, the office dies with him; if there are two or more, it

---

[40] *Lamond's Trs.* v. *Croom* (1871) 9 M. 662; *Heritable Securities Investment Association* v. *Miller's Trs.* (1893) 20 R. 675; *Campbell* v. *Lord Borthwick's Trs.*, 1930 S.N. 156.

[41] See s. 24(2).

[42] Law Reform (Misc. Provs.) (Scotland) Act 1968, s. 7 (as amended by Law Reform (Parent and Child) (Scotland) Act 1986, Sched. 1).

[43] 1964 Act, s. 16; see para. 33.23, *supra*.

[44] s. 2.

[45] s. 6.

[46] s. 20.

[47] See in particular 1921 Act, ss. 4 and 5; 1961 Act, ss. 2 and 4.

[48] *Wilson* v. *Gibson*, 1948 S.C. 52.

accrues to the survivor. The Executors (Scotland) Act 1900 contains provisions for the cases: (a) where any sole or last surviving trustee or executor has died with any property (heritable or moveable) in Scotland vested in him as trustee or executor; and (b) where a confirmation has become inoperative by the death or incapacity of all the executors in whose favour it has been granted. In the first case, the executor of the sole or last surviving trustee or executor may confirm, and this will enable him to recover and transfer the property;[49] in the second case, no title to intromit with the estate confirmed transmits to representatives of the executors, but confirmation *ad non executa* (to matters in respect of which an executry has not been completed) may be granted to those parties to whom confirmations *ad omissa* are granted and is a sufficient title to continue and complete the administration of the estate.[50]

It has never been in use for an executor to obtain a discharge, for there could be no discharge until the administration of the estate was completed, and after the whole estate has been administered, the executor's office has terminated and no discharge is needed.[51]

II JUDICIAL FACTORS

45.9 Grounds of Appointment.—The Court of Session has for a long time, in the exercise of the *nobile officium*, been able to appoint judicial factors to manage and administer estates in cases where this is necessary to afford protection against loss or injustice which cannot be prevented by means of the ordinary legal remedies. No limit can be set to the circumstances in which this power may be exercised;[52] but the more familiar instances of such appointments are: (1) The appointment of a factor on a trust estate, as, *e.g.* where there is a total failure of trustees, or there has been misconduct on their part, or where there is a deadlock in the administration of the trust.[53] (2) The appointment of a factor on the estate of a deceased person on the application of a creditor or a person interested in the succession of the deceased.[54] (3) The

---

[49] s. 6. If a note of property in England and Wales or Northern Ireland held in trust by a deceased person dying domiciled in Scotland is set forth in the inventory and is contained in, or appended to, the confirmation of Scottish estate which notes the domicile, the confirmation has the effect of a grant of representation in those countries in relation to the property specified in the note: Administration of Estates Act 1971, s. 5.

[50] s. 7.

[51] Erskine, III, ix, 47; *Johnston's Executor* v. *Dobie*, 1907 S.C. 31.

[52] *Leslie's J.F.*, 1925 S.C. 464. The sheriff now has the power to appoint judicial factors: Judicial Factors (Scotland) Act 1880, s. 4 (amended by Law Reform (Misc. Provs.) (Scotland) Act 1980, s. 14(1)(*b*).) Act of Sederunt (Judicial Factors Rules) 1992 (S.I. 1992 No. 272) (amended by Act of Sederunt (Judicial Factors Rules) (Amendment) 1994 (S.I. 1994 No. 2354)). There cannot now be appointment of a factor *loco tutoris*: Age of Legal Capacity (Scotland) Act 1991, s. 5(4).

[53] See, *e.g. Stewart* v. *Morrison* (1892) 19 R. 1009.

[54] Judicial Factors (Scotland) Act 1889, s. 11A (added by Bankruptcy (Scotland) Act 1985, s. 75(1), Sched. 7, para. 4). Act of Sederunt (Judicial Factors Rules) 1992 (S.I. 1992 No. 272), Pt. II.

appointment of a *curator bonis* to persons who, by reason of mental or physical incapacity, are unable to manage, or provide for the management of, their property.[55] (4) The appointment of a factor *loco absentis* on the property of an absent person either where he is ignorant of his interests, or these are unprotected, or where the interests of third parties require that the appointment shall be made.[56] (5) The appointment of a factor on partnership estates.[57] (6) The appointment of a factor on property which is the subject of judicial competition, where circumstances render it expedient that provision should be made in this way for the custody of the estate pending the issue of litigation. Factors may also be appointed on estates held *pro indiviso* in certain cases where the co-proprietors are unable to agree in regard to its administration,[58] and, on the application of the liferenter and fiduciary fiar, where the fee of the estate has been conveyed to a person in liferent and in fee to persons who are, when the conveyance comes into operation, unborn or incapable of ascertainment.[59]

45.10   Sequestration of Estate.—In addition to appointing a judicial factor, the court may sequestrate the estate. Sequestration is defined by Bell[60] as 'a judicial assumption by the court of the possession of property which is in competition before it, that it may be placed in the custody of a neutral person, accountable in court for his management, and sufficiently responsible, in order to be preserved and properly managed, for the benefit of those who shall be preferred in the competition.' It may be resorted to in cases where the court deems it necessary that the person in possession of property shall be superseded as regards its custody and management.

45.11   Duties and Powers of Factor.—A judicial factor is an officer of court, not subject to the control of parties,[61] and his duties are largely regulated by statutes and Acts of Sederunt.[62] He must find caution for the due performance of the office, and must lodge with the Accountant

[55] Para. 47.24, *infra.* As to the nature of the office of *curator bonis*, see *I.R.* v. *McMillan's Curator Bonis*, 1956 S.C. 142; *Fraser* v. *Paterson (No. 2)*, 1988 S.L.T. 124 (O.H.).

[56] Stair, IV, 1, 28; Bell's *Prin.*, § 2120; *Peterson & Co.* (1851) 13 D. 951.

[57] *Dickie* v. *Mitchell* (1874) 1 R. 1030; *Carabine* v. *Carabine*, 1949 S.C. 521; see para., 24.29, *supra.* For appointment on the estate of a company, see *Fraser, Petr.*, 1971 S.L.T. 146.

[58] *Bailey* v. *Scott* (1860) 22 D. 1105; *Allan* (1898) 36 S.L.R. 3; 6 S.L.T. 152.

[59] 1921 Act, s. 8(2); *Napier* v. *Napiers*, 1963 S.L.T. 143; see also *Gibson*, 1967 S.L.T. 150.

[60] *Comm.* ii, 244.

[61] *McCulloch* v. *McCulloch*, 1953 S.C. 189.

[62] Act of Sederunt, February 13, 1730; Judicial Factors Act 1849 (Pupils Protection Act); Judical Factors (Scotland) Act 1880; Judicial Factors (Scotland) 1889; Trusts (Scotland) Act 1921; Trusts (Scotland) Act 1961; Trustee Investments Act 1961; Rules of Court (1994), Ch. 61 and rr. 72.5–72.6; Act of Sederunt (Appointment of Judicial Factors) 1967.

of Court a rental of the lands and an inventory of the moveable property belonging to the estate. He administers the estate under the superintendence of the Accountant, who may make such orders as he considers proper,[63] and with whom the factor must lodge annual accounts.

By virtue of the definitions of 'trustee' and 'judicial factor' in the Trusts (Scotland) Act 1921,[64] as amended by the Trusts (Scotland) Act 1961,[65] the provisions of these Acts extend to any person holding a judicial appointment as a factor or curator on another person's estate.[66] Accordingly, judicial factors may exercise the general powers conferred on trustees by section 4 of the 1921 Act where such an exercise would not be at variance with the terms or purposes of the trust; and where the factor desires to do something which would be at variance with the terms or purposes of his appointment he may apply to the court for special powers under section 5.[67] The function of a judicial factor is, generally speaking, to conserve and manage the estate under his charge, and it may not be easy to decide whether the exercise of a particular power, e.g. to sell or purchase heritage, would be at variance with his appointment; each case must be decided on its own facts, and in a case of doubt a petition for special powers would be justified.[68] In the case of the powers specified in section 2(1) of the Trusts (Scotland) Act 1961, the factor can apply to the Accountant of Court for consent to the doing of the act.[69] The Accountant can, in limited circumstances, authorise encroachment upon capital.[70] Section 2 of the 1961 Act, which guarantees the validity of any title acquired by a person who enters into a transaction with trustees purporting to act under section 4 of the 1921 Act, extends to judicial factors; and a purchaser of heritage from a factor need not look behind the purported exercise of the power under that section.[71]

The voluntary acts of a judicial factor in the administration of the estate, as, for example, the sale of heritage, do not affect the rights of succession to the estate, although it is otherwise where the act was a necessary one.[72] In the case of a trust estate, the judicial factor takes

---

[63] 1849 Act, ss. 19 and 20.
[64] s. 2.
[65] s. 4.
[66] Esp. 1921 Act, ss. 2, 4, 5; 1961 Act, ss. 2, 4, See para. 46.11, *infra.*
[67] *Tennent's J.F.* v. *Tennent*, 1954 S.C. 215.
[68] *Cunningham's Tutrix*, 1949 S.C. 275; *Bristow*, 1965 S.L.T. 225; see also *Murray's J.F.* v. *Thomas Murray & Sons (Ice Merchants) Ltd.*, 1992 S.L.T. 824, *per* Lord Justice-Clerk Ross at p. 830 and Lord Cullen at pp. 835I–836B.
[69] 1961 Act, ss. 2(3)–(6) (added by Law Reform (Misc. Provs.) (Scotland) Act 1980, s. 8).
[70] *Broadfoot's C.B., Noter*, 1989 S.L.T. 566.
[71] See further, para. 46.11, *infra.*
[72] *Moncrieff* v. *Miln* (1856) 18 D. 1286; *Macfarlane* v. *Greig* (1895) 22 R. 405; *Macqueen* v. *Tod* (1899) 1 F. 1069; *McAdam's Exr.* v. *Souters* (1904) 7 F. 179; *Macfarlane's Trs.* v. *Macfarlane*, 1910 S.C. 325.

the place of the trustees and administers the estate in accordance with the provisions of the trust.[73] He has no higher powers than those allowed by the truster to the trustees.[74] He may do what the truster has directed shall be done,[75] and may even in certain cases exercise discretionary powers conferred on the trustees.[76]

At the conclusion of his administration, the judicial factory may obtain a discharge on presenting a petition for that purpose to the court,[77] or, where the factory has terminated by its recall or the death or coming of age of the ward or by reason of the exhaustion of the estate, by obtaining a certificate from the Accountant of Court.[78]

Further Reading

Currie, *Confirmation of Executors* (8th ed., 1993).
Irons, *Judicial Factors* (1908).
McLaren, *Wills and Succession* (3rd ed., 1894, and Supplement, 1934).
Thoms, *Judicial Factors* (2nd ed., 1881).
Walker, *Judicial Factors* (1974).
Wilson and Duncan, *Trusts, Trustees and Executors* (1975).

[73] *Orr Ewing* v. *Orr Ewing's Trs.* (1884) 11 R. 600, *per* Lord President Inglis at p. 627; *Browning's Factor* (1905) 7 F. 1037, *per* Lord Johnston.
[74] He does not have the powers of investment conferred on the trustees and, unless wider powers are granted by the court, he must administer the estate in accordance with the Trustee Investments Act 1961: *Carmichael's J.F.* v. *Accountant of Court*, 1971 S.C. 295.
[75] *Stirling's J.F.*, 1917 1 S.L.T. 165.
[76] See *infra*, para. 46.11; *Leith's J.F.* v. *Leith*, 1957 S.C. 307.
[77] *Campbell* v. *Grant* (1870) 8 M. 988.
[78] Judicial Factors Act 1849, s. 34A (inserted by Law Reform (Misc. Provs.) (Scotland) Act 1990, s. 67); Rules of Court 61.31(1)–61.32.

CHAPTER 46

TRUSTS

46.1 General.—The doctrine of trusts has long been familiar to Scots lawyers, but no detailed treatment of this subject is to be found in the institutional writers. In the nineteenth century a great development, in which the influence of English law may be traced, took place in this branch of the law; and between 1861 and 1910 various statutes dealing with the administration of trusts were passed. These were all repealed by the Trusts (Scotland) Act 1921, which, as amended by the Trusts (Scotland) Act 1961, is the statute now in force. Many of the sections of the 1921 Act merely re-enact (in some cases with amendments) the provisions of the earlier statutes; but it also contains new sections which made important alterations to the former law. These Acts are not confined in their application to trustees in the strict sense of the term, for section 2 of the 1921 Act defines 'trustee' as including 'any trustee *ex officio*, executor-nominate, tutor, curator, guardian (including a father or mother acting as guardian of a child under the age of 16 years),[1] and judicial factor.'[2] The Acts do not, however, apply to trusts constituted by a public general statute.[3]

46.2 The Trustee.—Erskine speaks of a trust as 'of the nature of depositation, by which a proprietor transfers to another the property of the subject intrusted, not that it should remain with him, but that it may be applied to certain uses for the behoof of a third party.'[4] This is an apt description of a familar form of trust, but as a definition it is not sufficiently comprehensive.[5] A trust, for instance, may arise by implication of law as well as by express constitution, and a person may

---

[1] As amended by Age of Legal Capacity (Scotland) Act 1991, Sched. 1.

[2] As to judicial factors, see para. 45.9, *supra*. Executors-dative are now included: Succession (Scotland) Act 1964, s. 20. Where a policy of assurance vests in trust by virtue of the Married Women's Policies of Assurance (Scotland) Act 1880, s. 2, the trust is a trust, and the person in whom the policy vests is a trustee, within the meaning of the Trusts (Scotland) Act 1921: Married Women's Policies of Assurance (Scotland) (Amendment) Act 1980, s. 2(1).

[3] *Board of Management for Edinburgh Royal Infirmary, Petrs.*, 1959 S.C. 393.

[4] Erskine, *Inst.*, III, i, 32.

[5] On the other hand, Lord Westbury's statement in *Fleeming v. Howden* (1868) 6 M. (H.L.) 113, at p. 121, that 'an obligation to do an act with respect to property creates a trust' is too general; see *Bank of Scotland v. Liquidators of Hutchison, Main & Co.*, 1914 S.C. (H.L.) 1.

find himself bound as a trustee without his assent or even against his wishes.[6] But Erskine's statement is useful as directing attention to what is of the essence of the position of a trustee, namely, that, while he has the legal title to the property held in trust, he is under an obligation to use his powers as legal owner for the benefit of some person other than himself (or it may be for a number of persons of whom he is one) or for some object not his own. The title to the property affected by the trust belongs to the trustee. 'The property of the thing intrusted, be it in land or in moveables, is in the person of the intrusted, else it is not proper trust.'[7] However, the trustee, as such, does not enjoy the benefits derived from proprietorship, but must hold and apply the property for the purposes of the trust.

46.3   The Beneficiary: Conversion.—The person or persons for whose benefit the trust exists are known as the beneficiary or beneficiaries;[8] and their interest is termed the beneficial interest or *jus crediti*. This beneficial interest may (subject to the trustee's right to possess and administer the trust in terms of the truster's directions) be transmitted by the beneficiary's deed or attached by his creditors; and, if the beneficiary dies vested in the beneficial interest, it will form part of his estate to be disposed of in terms of his testamentary or other deeds, or in accordance with the law of intestate succession.

In these circumstances, a question may arise as to the character of the beneficial interest, whether it is heritable or moveable. This will depend upon the nature of the subject held in trust, for the *jus crediti* partakes of the nature and quality of that subject. But in this matter, the nature of the subject and, consequently, of the beneficial interest, may be affected by the provisions of the trust deed. If the truster has *directed* his trustees to sell the heritable property which is the subject of the trust and to make over the proceeds to the beneficiaries, then, as the truster's intention is that the beneficiaries shall receive not the heritage but the proceeds, the right of the beneficiaries is regarded as moveable, whether the sale has, or has not, been effected. This is known as constructive conversion. If, on the other hand, there is given to the trustees merely a *power* to sell, then, until that power is exercised, there is no conversion. So also if the right to sell is to arise only in the case of necessity, or is limited to particular purposes, as, for example, to pay debts, or is not indispensable to the execution of the trust, then unless the necessity arises and is acted on, or after the particular purposes are answered, or if the sale is not indispensable, there is no change in the quality of the

---

[6] See, *e.g. Stevenson* v. *Wilson*, 1907 S.C. 445; *National Bank of Scotland Nominee Co.* v. *Adamson*, 1932 S.L.T. 492.

[7] Stair, I, xiii, 7. See also *Inland Revenue* v. *Clark's Trs.*, 1939 S.C. 11; *Parker's Trs.* v. *Inland Revenue*, 1960 S.C. (H.L.) 29; *Johnston* v. *Macfarlane*, 1985 S.L.T. 339.

[8] In English law, the beneficiary is known also as the *cestui que trust*.

subjects.[9] The sale of heritage authorised by the court on the ground of expediency will not effect conversion if this was not the truster's intention.[10]

If the effect of the directions in the trust deeds is constructively to convert the property, the beneficiaries (if capable of electing) may nevertheless, before there has been actual conversion, elect to take the property in its existing state. Thus, for example, where trustees, who are directed to sell heritage and pay the proceeds to A, have not effected a sale, it is open to A to intimate his intention to take the heritage rather than its price; and, as he could at once reinvest the price in the purchase of heritage, it would be futile to insist on a sale being carried out by the trustees. This is known as re-conversion. The election may be express or may be inferred from circumstances. It has been said that in order to effect re-conversion there must be either an overt act by the party in right of the succession or such lapse of time as, coupled with surrounding circumstances, imports unequivocally a determination to take the property as it stands.[11]

Where there is a direction in a will for conversion, this direction is held to have been given for the purposes of the will. It takes effect, so far as is necessary, to carry out these purposes. If, and in so far as, these purposes fail, the rights of those who are entitled to the estate independently of the will are not affected by the direction. The heir-at-law was entitled to the heritage which belonged to the testator unless it was effectually alienated in favour of others, and his right was not displaced merely by a direction to convert the heritage into moveable property. In *Cowan* v. *Cowan*[12] a testator directed his trustees to realise the whole estate but, beyond giving certain legacies, did not dispose of it in favour of anyone. The estate, therefore, fell into intestacy. It was held that the funds must be divided between the heir-at-law and the heirs *in mobilibus* in the proportions in which they had been derived from the heritable and moveable estate respectively as at the testator's death.

46.4   Constitution of the Trust.—A trust may be constituted either by the act of the truster or by operation of law. No technical language is required for the creation of a trust.[13] A bequest to a person followed by precatory words expressive of the testator's wish or recommendation or confidence that the legatee will apply the subject bequeathed for behoof of other persons may be regarded as imposing a trust for this purpose

---

[9] *Buchanan* v. *Angus* (1862) 4 Macq. 374; *Sheppard's Trs.* v. *Sheppard* (1885) 12 R. 1193; see also *Taylor's Trs.* v. *Tailyour,* 1927 S.C. 288.
[10] *Taylor's Trs.* v. *Tailyour, supra.*
[11] *Bryson's Tr.* v. *Bryson,* 1919 2 S.L.T. 303, *per* Lord Sands; *Hogg* v. *Hamilton* (1877) 4 R. 845; McLaren i, 237; *Mackintosh's Exr.* v. *Mackintosh,* 1925 S.L.T. 674.
[12] (1887) 14 R. 670; *McConochie's Trs.* v. *McConochie,* 1912 S.C. 653.
[13] *Gillespie* v. *City of Glasgow Bank* (1878) 6 R. (H.L.) 104, *per* Earl Cairns L.C. at p. 107; *Leitch* v. *Leitch,* 1927 S.C. 823.

on the legatee. Whether in such a case there is a trust depends on the intention of the testator as disclosed in the language of the bequest; and if it appears that that language, although not in form imperative, was intended to impose a duty on the legatee he will be deemed to be a trustee. A trust created in this way is known as a precatory trust.[14]

Where the purposes of a private trust[15] fail, either in whole or in part, or if the purposes do not exhaust the trust estate, then the estate, or so much of it as is not required for the trust purposes, must be accounted for to the creator of the trust or his representatives. In the case of a *mortis causa* trust, the truster being dead, the estate not required for the purposes of the trust will fall to be disposed of as part of the deceased's estate and will belong to his representatives or heirs; for example, if a testator by his trust-disposition and settlement conveys his estate to trustees with directions to settle the estate on his children and dies without leaving issue, the estate, in that event, would have to be accounted for to his heirs *ab intestato*. Where, on the other hand, the trust is an *inter vivos* one, the truster retains a reversionary interest in the trust estate, which is called the 'radical right' in the property. The truster is divested of his right in the funds conveyed in trust only in so far as these are required for carrying out the trust purposes; to the extent to which they are not so required they belong to the truster and are subject to his disposition. Thus, if in a marriage contract or other trust deed, funds are settled on the truster's issue, and there are no issue, then, in the absence of any further trust purpose, the funds revert to the truster.[16] Where the trustees fail, the truster, in virtue of his radical right, may appoint new trustees.[17]

46.5 Revocability of Trust.—An *inter vivos* trust may, or may not, be revocable by the truster. If the trust is set up voluntarily for the purpose merely of the administration of the estate for behoof of the truster, or if there are no other beneficiaries in existence, or if all the purposes in favour of these other beneficiaries are of a testamentary nature and are to take effect only on the truster's death, the trust is revocable. On the other hand, if the deed confers rights (and not mere *spes successionis* (hopes of succession)) on other parties, although these rights may not be vested but may be subject to contingencies, the terms of the deed thus show that it was intended that the trustees should hold the estate against the truster and the deed is regarded as irrevocable.[18] The question

[14] McLaren, i, 345; *Garden's Exr.* v. *More*, 1913 S.C. 285.

[15] See para. 46.18, *infra* as to public trusts.

[16] *Smith* v. *Stuart* (1894) 22 R. 130; *Montgomery's Trs.* v. *Montgomery* (1895) 22 R. 824; *Higginbotham's Trs.* v. *Higginbotham* (1886) 13 R. 1016.

[17] *Glentanar* v. *Scottish Industrial Musical Association*, 1925 S.C. 226.

[18] *Walker* v. *Amey* (1906) 8 F. 376; *Scott* v. *Scott*, 1930 S.C. 903; *Ross* v. *Ross's Trs.*, 1967 S.L.T. 12 (O.H.); *Campbell* v. *Campbell's Trs.*, 1967 S.L.T. (Notes) 30; *Bulkeley-Gavin's Trs.* v. *Bulkeley-Gavins's Trs.*, 1971 S.C. 209; *Lawrence* v. *Lawrence's Trs.*, 1974 S.L.T. 174; *Milligan* v. *Ross*, 1994 S.C.L.R. 430. See para. 46.6, *infra*.

depends, however, on the terms and purposes of the trust deed, and *in dubio* a declaration that it is irrevocable will probably be decisive.[19] A marriage contract may contain testamentary provisions which are always revocable, notwithstanding that the deed is declared to be irrevocable.[20] A truster may make himself the sole trustee of his own property but to make the trust irrevocable he must do something equivalent to delivery or transfer of the trust fund. Intimation to one of several beneficiaries will make the whole trust irrevocable;[21] as will, apparently, intimation to someone who was regarded as acting on behalf of the beneficiaries.[22] It has been held that the trust assets must be in existence at the time of intimation.[23]

46.6 Variation of Trusts.—At common law the powers of varying the purposes of a trust once it had taken effect, and where, in the case of *inter vivos* trusts, it could not be revoked by the truster, were very limited. Where all the beneficiaries interested in the estate concur in asking the trustees to denude at a date prior to that contemplated by the truster, and if they are all legally capable of giving their consent, the trustees are bound to do so on being exonered and discharged.[24] But where by reason of nonage or otherwise one or more of the beneficiaries was incapable of giving his consent, or where there was a contingent right in unborn issue, the concurrence of all those interested in the trust estate could not be obtained. Furthermore, where one of the interests was an alimentary right properly constituted,[25] and accepted,[26] it could not at common law be renounced by the beneficiary as part of such an arrangement. The Trusts (Scotland) Act 1921 empowered the court to authorise trustees to do certain acts although these were at variance with the terms or purposes of the trust, where expedient for its execution.[27] But it was not until the Trusts (Scotland) Act 1961 that it became possible to surmount the common-law obstacles to the formal variation of the purposes of the trust themselves.

Section 1 of the 1961 Act affords machinery whereby the court may give effective approval to the variation of trust purposes on behalf of

---

[19] *Scott* v. *Scott, supra.*

[20] *Barclays' Trs.* v. *Watson* (1903) 5 F. 926; *Law,* 1962 S.C. 500.

[21] *Allan's Trs.* v. *Lord Advocate,* 1971 S.C. (H.L.) 45.

[22] *Clark's Trs.* v. *Inland Revenue,* 1972 S.C. 177.

[23] *Export Credits Guarantee Department* v. *Turner,* 1979 S.C. 286; *Clark Taylor & Co. Ltd. and Quality Site Development (Edinburgh) Ltd.,* 1981 S.C. 111; *Tay Valley Joinery Ltd.* v. *C.F. Financial Services Ltd.,* 1987 S.L.T. 207; *Balfour Beatty Ltd.* v. *Britannia Life Ltd.,* 1994 G.W.D. 5–228. *Cf.* Reid, 1986 S.L.T. (News) 177.

[24] See *Earl of Lindsay* v. *Shaw,* 1959 S.L.T. (Notes) 13, *per* Lord Justice-Clerk Thomson. As to rectification of an *inter vivos* trust deed which does not accurately express the intention of the grantor, see Law Reform (Misc. Provs.) (Scotland) Act 1985, s. 8.

[25] Para. 47.10, *infra.*

[26] A renunciation before entering into enjoyment of the alimentary liferent is effective: *Douglas-Hamilton* v. *Duke and Duchess of Hamilton's Trs.,* 1961 S.C. 205.

[27] s. 5; see *infra,* para. 46.11.

beneficiaries[28] who, owing to nonage[29] or other incapacity, are incapable of assenting thereto, and may also authorise the variation or revocation of alimentary provisions. This machinery is invoked by means of a petition presented to the Inner House of the Court of Session by the trustees or any of the beneficiaries.[30] Subsection (1) enables the court to grant approval of an arrangement varying or revoking all or any of the trust purposes, or enlarging the powers of the trustees of managing or administering the estate,[31] on behalf of: (a) any of the beneficiaries who by reason of nonage or other incapacity cannot assent, or (b) any person who may become a beneficiary at a future date,[32] or (c) any person as yet unborn; it is a condition of its granting approval that the court should be of the opinion that the carrying out of the arrangement would not be prejudicial to the persons on behalf of whom its approval is sought.[33] The interests of such persons may be protected by insurance.[34] This may not be necessary if the liferenter has a power to appoint the fee which includes power to fix the date of vesting of the appointed shares,[35] or to protect negligible interests of remote beneficiaries.[36]

Under subsection (4), the court may authorise an arrangement whereby alimentary provisions are varied or revoked and, it may be, replaced by other provisions which may dispose of the whole or part of the capital of the trust estate; but such an authorisation may be granted only if the arrangement is approved either by the alimentary beneficiary or by the court on his behalf under subsection (1) and the court is satisfied that the carrying out of the arrangement would be reasonable, having regard to the whole income of the alimentary beneficiary and any other material factors.[37] Applications under subsection (4) have been refused as unnecessary on the following grounds: (a) that a liferenter

[28] See s. 1(6); *Countess of Lauderdale*, 1962 S.C. 302. The powers of the court under the Act are exercisable in relation to any trust under the Married Women's Policies of Assurance (Scotland) Act 1880: Married Women's Policies of Assurance (Scotland) (Amendment) Act 1980, s. 4.

[29] For purposes of the 1961 Act a person who is of, or over, the age of 16 years, but has not attained the age of 18 years, is deemed to be incapable of assenting: s. 1(2) (as amended by Age of Legal Capacity (Scotland) Act 1991, Sched. 1, para. 27).

[30] See the following cases for judicial observations on this procedure: *Colville*, 1962 S.C. 185; *Robertson*, 1962 S.C. 196; *Gibson's Tr.*, 1962 S.C. 204; *Findlay*, 1962 S.C. 210; *Tulloch's Trs.*, 1962 S.C. 245; also *Clarke's Trs.*, 1966 S.L.T. 249, *re* jurisdiction. Note that a declaration of irrevocability in an *inter vivos* trust deed does not preclude variation of its terms under this section: *Ommaney*, 1966 S.L.T. (Notes) 13.

[31] *Henderson, Petr.*, 1981 S.L.T. (Notes) 40.

[32] See *Buchan, Petr.*, 1964 S.L.T. 51; *Allan, Petrs.*, 1991 S.L.T. 202.

[33] The introduction of additional beneficiaries in a discretionary trust is prejudicial to the existing beneficiaries; *Margaret Jean Patricia Pollok-Morris*, 1969 S.L.T. (Notes) 60. As to prejudice to the beneficiaries, see also *John Sutherland Aikman*, 1968 S.L.T. 137.

[34] See *Robertson, supra*; *cf. Young's Trs.*, 1962 S.C. 293, where no insurance proposed and petition refused. Alternatively, an appropriate fund may be set aside.

[35] See *Colville, supra*, and *Dick*, 1963 S.C. 598.

[36] *Phillips*, 1964 S.C. 141.

[37] *Gibson's Tr.*, 1962 S.C. 204; *Dick, supra, per* Lord President Clyde at p. 602; *cf. Bergius' Trs., Petrs.*, 1963 S.C. 194, where liferent was contingent and application refused.

was entitled *ex proprio motu* to renounce a contingent alimentary liferent;[38] (b) that the liferent had ceased to be alimentary;[39] and (c) that the liferent created by a wife in favour of herself by a post-nuptial marriage contract was not a valid alimentary liferent.[40] The court will approve and authorise an arrangement under this section, which is only made possible by the exercise of a power of appointment, so long as the donee does not obtain any exclusive advantage thereby.[41]

46.7   Proof of Trust.—In the case of testamentary trusts, the existence and terms of the trust are almost invariably to be found recorded in some writing. But in *inter vivos* transactions, there may be cases of trust which are not in writing. A person may convey his estate to another in absolute terms but under a verbal agreement that it is to be held in trust; or property may be purchased by one party and by arrangement the title may be taken in the name of another who is to hold it not for his own benefit but for the benefit of the purchaser or subject to his directions. In such cases, the ostensible owner of the property is truly merely a trustee for another. At common law, trusts could be established by parole evidence; this was altered by the Blank Bonds and Trusts Act 1696 (c.25).[42] However, this Act has now been repealed by the Requirements of Writing (Scotland) Act 1995[43] and the common law position restored.

46.8   Trusts Arising by Operation of Law.—Besides those cases in which a trust is constituted either expressly or impliedly by the actings of parties, there are circumstances in which the law imposes on a person the duties and liabilities which attach to a trustee expressly appointed. The trust in such cases arises by operation of law. Thus, where a trustee has acquired any property or benefit which (although not part of the estate to which the trust under which he acts expressly attaches) he is not entitled to retain for his own benefit but must communicate to the beneficiaries under that trust, he is regarded as holding this property or benefit subject to a trust for behoof of these beneficiaries.[44] Similarly, a stranger to the trust, who obtains property belonging to the trust in circumstances which do not permit of his withholding it from the beneficiaries under the trust, is regarded as a trustee, *i.e.* as subject to

---

[38] *Findlay*, 1962 S.C. 210; *Smillie*, 1966 S.L.T. 41.
[39] *Strange*, 1966 S.L.T. 59; *Pearson*, 1968 S.C. 8; see also *Law, Petr.*, 1962 S.C. 500, where the liferent had ceased to be alimentary on the death of the husband and the other provisions of an ante-nuptial marriage contract for which approval of variation was sought were testamentary and revocable by the wife. Cf. *Sutherland, Petr.*, 1968 S.C. 200.
[40] *Cargill, Petr.*, 1965 S.C. 122.
[41] *Pelham Burn, Petr.*, 1964 S.C. 3.
[42] The occasion of this statute was the litigation between *Higgins* and *Callender* in (1696) Mor. 16182.
[43] Sched. 5.
[44] See *Laird* v. *Laird* (1858) 20 D. 972. See *infra*, para. 46.12.

the duty of restoring it to the trust.[45] In both of these cases, the trust is known as a 'constructive' trust and is created by the operation of the law and not by any intention on the part of the parties concerned that a trust shall be constituted. It is, however, to trusts expressly or impliedly constituted that the great body of trust law relates; and it is to such trusts that attention is mainly devoted in the following sections of this chapter.

46.9 Acceptance of Office: Assumption and Resignation of Trustees.—No one can be compelled to accept office as a trustee. Acceptance may be proved in any form—by written or verbal acceptance—and may be inferred from the fact that the person has acted as trustee. It is a question of fact whether the office has or has not been accepted.

The estate and office vest in the trustees jointly where more than one is appointed; and, in the absence of anything to the contrary in the trust deed, the right of survivorship is implied; so that if a trustee dies, the ownership and administration of the trust remain with the survivors. The law reads into all trusts (unless the contrary be expressed) a provision that a majority of the accepting and surviving trustees shall be a quorum.[46] There is also tacitly included a power to the trustee, if there be only one, or to the quorum, to assume new trustees;[47] and a statutory form of assumption which may be used for the assumption of new trustees is given in the 1921 Act.[48]

There is further included in all trusts, unless the contrary is expressed in the trust deed, a power to any trustee to resign office. But a sole trustee is not entitled to resign unless he has assumed new trustees who have accepted office, or new trustees or a judicial factor have been appointed by the court.[49] A conveyance to named persons and the heir of the last survivor as trustees entitles the heir to act as trustee.[50] Moreover, a trustee who has accepted a legacy bequeathed on condition that he accepts office or who is appointed on the footing of receiving remuneration for his services, may not resign unless it is otherwise provided in the trust deed; but such trustees may apply to the court for authority to resign. The effect of resignation is that the resigning trustee is divested of the trust estate, which thereupon accrues to the remaining trustees without the necessity for any conveyance thereof.[51] If the trustee who resigns, or the representatives of a deceased trustee, cannot

---

[45] See, for example, *Huisman* v. *Soepboer*, 1994 S.L.T. 682.

[46] Trusts (Scotland) Act 1921, s. 3(c).

[47] *Ibid.*, s. 3(b). It seems that a sole trustee can resign after assuming one new trustee: *Kennedy, Petr.*, 1983 S.L.T. (Sh.Ct.) 10.

[48] Trusts (Scotland) Act 1921, s. 21.

[49] *Ibid.*, s. 3(a); see also s. 19. At common law, trustees had no power to resign.

[50] *Glasgow Western Infirmary* v. *Cairns*, 1944 S.C. 488. See as to the machinery for formal recognition of the character of the heir, *Harry J.C.R. Skinner, Petr.*, 1976 S.L.T. 60.

[51] 1921 Act, s. 3(a); see also s. 20.

obtain a discharge from the remaining trustees and the beneficiaries refuse, or are unable, to grant a discharge, a petition may be presented to the court for a judicial discharge.[52] And where the body of trustees are unable otherwise to get exoneration they may, for this purpose, bring an action of multiplepoinding—the rule which requires double distress as the ground of this action being in this case relaxed.[53]

46.10   Removal of Trustees.—Under the common law, the court has power to remove a trustee from office. But the court is reluctant to exercise this power unless the trustee has been guilty of malversation of office or has shown by his conduct that he is unfit to discharge its duties;[54] in cases where there has been merely disagreement between the trustees, or the trustee has in good faith committed some irregularity or breach of trust, these circumstances have not been deemed sufficient to require that the trustee should be removed.[55] There is statutory provision for the cases where a trustee is either insane or incapable of acting by reason of mental or physical disability, or has been absent from the United Kingdom continuously for a period of at least six months.[56] In the case of incapacity it is enacted that the trustee shall be removed on the application of a co-trustee or beneficiary or anyone interested in the trust estate; and on a like application, the absent trustee may be removed.

In the case of such disability, or absence of the person who is the sole trustee, or where trustees cannot be assumed under a trust deed, the court may, in terms of section 22 of the 1921 Act, appoint a new trustee. This section comprehends all cases in which the trust cannot be kept up by means of powers within the trust deed.[57] A trust does not fail although all the trustees nominated in the trust deed should decline office or become unable to act; and under the common law, the court could, where necessary, appoint a trustee.[58] The statutory power does not exclude this power.[59] The court has also power to appoint a judicial factor on a trust estate, who administers the estate under the supervision of the Accountant of Court and in accordance with the provisions of the Judicial Factors Acts.[60]

---

[52] *Ibid.*, s. 18.

[53] *Taylor* v. *Noble* (1836) 14 S. 817; McLaren's *Court of Session Practice*, 666.

[54] *Cherry* v. *Patrick*, 1910 S.C. 32; *Stewart* v. *Chalmers* (1904) 7 F. 163; *MacGilchrist* v. *MacGilchrist's Trs.*, 1930 S.C. 635.

[55] *Gilchrist's Trs.* v. *Dick* (1883) 11 R. 22; *Hope* v. *Hope* (1884) 12 R. 27. In *Taylor*, 1932 S.C. 1, where there was a deadlock owing to the two trustees disagreeing, the court appointed an additional trustee.

[56] 1921 Act, s. 23. The application may now be made in the sheriff court: Law Reform (Misc. Provs.) (Scotland) Act 1980, s. 13.

[57] *Graham* (1868) 6 M. 958, *per* Lord President Inglis.

[58] *Campbell* v. *Campbell* (1752) Mor. 16203; *Grant* (1790) Mor. 7454.

[59] *McAslan* (1841) 3 D. 1263; *Glasgow* (1844) 7 D. 178; *Aikman* (1881) 9 R. 213; *Lamont* v. *Lamont*, 1908 S.C. 1033.

[60] See *infra*, para. 45.9.

46.11   Administration of the Trust: Powers and Duties of Trustees.—It is the duty of the trustee to administer the estate in accordance with the directions given by the truster. He must do what he is enjoined to do so far as it is lawful and possible. He may do what he is authorised by the truster to do; and he must refrain from doing what the truster has forbidden him to do. In many respects his duty coincides with that of an executor: thus, he is bound to ingather the estate with due dispatch, pay the debts of the truster, and when the time for distribution of the estate arrives distribute it as may be directed in the deed.

Certain general powers are conferred on trustees by section 4 of the Trusts (Scotland) Act 1921.[61] These powers, which may be exercised where such acts are 'not at variance with the terms or purposes of the trust,'[62] include, *inter alia*, those of selling,[63] feuing, excambing or granting leases of any duration of the heritable estate; of borrowing money on the security of the trust estate; and of acquiring with the trust funds any interest in residential accommodation reasonably required to enable the trustees to provide a suitable residence for occupation by any of the beneficiaries.[64] Where the trustees enter into a transaction in the purported exercise of certain of these powers, in particular with regard to heritage, the validity of the transaction and of any title acquired by the second party under it cannot be challenged by the second party or any other person on the ground that the act in question was in fact at variance with the terms or purposes of the trust;[65] a purchaser of heritage from trustees, for example, is completely protected by this provision and need not look behind the purported exercise of the power under section 4. But this provision affords only a limited protection to the trustees themselves, for it leaves open any question of liability between them and co-trustees or the beneficiaries.[66] Where the trustees wish to exercise any of the powers listed in section 4 but the act in question would or might be at variance with the terms or purposes of the trust, they may present an application to the court under section 5; under that section the court is empowered to grant authority to the trustees to do any of these acts notwithstanding that such act is at variance with the terms or purposes of the trust, on being satisfied that such act is, in all the circumstances, expedient for the execution of the trust.[67] It is also provided that the court may, under certain

---

[61] As amended by the 1961 Act, s. 4.

[62] See, as to the meaning of this expression, *Marquis of Lothian's C.B.*.., 1927 S.C. 579, at p. 585; *Leslie's J.F.*, 1925 S.C. 464; *Cunningham's Tutrix*, 1949 S.C. 275; *Christie's Trs.*, 1946 S.L.T. 309; *Bristow*, 1965 S.L.T. 225.

[63] See, for example, *Mauchline, Petr*, 1992 S.L.T. 421, *per* Lord Prosser at p. 424.

[64] s. 4(*ee*), added by 1961 Act.

[65] 1961 Act, s. 2(1).

[66] 1961 Act, s. 2(2) (as substituted by Law Reform (Misc. Provs.) (Scotland) Act 1980, s. 8); see *Barclay (Mason's C.B.)*, 1962 S.C. 594.

[67] This section does not apply to trusts constituted by private or local Acts of Parliament; see *Church of Scotland General Trustees*, 1931 S.C. 704.

circumstances, authorise an advance of part of the capital of a fund destined either absolutely or contingently to beneficiaries who are not of full age.[68]

In certain cases too, trustees who desire to exercise powers which neither the settlement[69] nor the statute provides may apply for authority to the court in the exercise of the *nobile officium*, as, for example, for authority to make advances to major beneficiaries.[70] Cases of this kind are exceptional and cannot be classified; but the *nobile officium* has been exercised to supply the deficiency 'where something administrative or executive is wanting in the constituting document to enable the trust purposes to be effectually carried out,'[71] or where there was an obvious *casus improvisus* (unforeseen situation) under the scheme of the trust or to relieve the trust of conditions which made it unworkable or tended to defeat its purpose,[72] or, in the case of trusts subject to the jurisdiction of a foreign court, to facilitate by means of an auxiliary jurisdiction the carrying out of an order of the foreign court.[73] Trustees have no power to buy heritage, other than as residential accommodation for the use of the beneficiaries,[74] unless given by the trust instrument, but, in very special circumstances, they may be given power through the *nobile officium*.[75] While the court has power in the exercise of the *nobile officium* to give retrospective sanction to *ultra vires* acts of administration by trustees, this power will be exercised only in exceptional circumstances and for compelling reasons;[76] and, where the trustees have acted contrary to the express terms of the trust or an interlocutor of the court, retrospective approval will usually be refused.[77] If trustees, or any one of their number, desire to place the trust under the administration of the Accountant of Court, an application may be made to the court for this purpose.[78] The superintendence of the Accountant is limited, however, to the administration of the trust in so far as it relates to the investment of the trust funds and the distribution thereof among the creditors interested and the beneficiaries under the trust.[79]

[68] 1921 Act, s. 16; *Macfarlane v. Macfarlane's Trs.*, 1931 S.C. 95; *Criag's Trs.*, 1934 S.C. 34; *Anderson's Trs.*, 1957 S.L.T. (Notes) 5.
[69] *Moss's Trs.*, 1952 S.C. 523.
[70] *Frew's Trs.*, 1932 S.C. 501; *Craig's Trs.*, supra.
[71] *Anderson's Trs.*, 1932 S.C. 226.
[72] *Hall's Trs.* v. *McArthur*, 1918 S.C. 646; see also observations in *Gibson's Trs.*, 1933 S.C. 190.
[73] *Lipton's Trs.*, 1943 S.C. 521; *Campbell-Wyndham-Long's Trs.*, 1951 S.C. 685.
[74] 1921 Act, s. 4(ee), added by 1961 Act.
[75] *Fletcher's Trs.*, 1949 S.C. 330.
[76] *Dow's Trs.*, 1947 S.C. 524; *East Kilbride District Nursing Assn.*, 1951 S.C. 64; *Horne's Trs.*, 1952 S.C. 70 (application in each case refused).
[77] But see *Campbell-Wyndham-Long's Trs.*, 1962 S.C. 132.
[78] 1921 Act, s. 17.
[79] *Coulson* v. *Murison's Trs.*, 1920 S.C. 322 (the law as to the competency of an application by one trustee is now altered); *Liddell's Trs.* v. *Liddell*, 1929 S.L.T. 169; *Donaldson's Trs.*, 1932 S.L.T. 463.

Trustees under a trust deed (as defined by the Trusts (Scotland) Act 1921[80]) may obtain from the court directions on questions relating to the investment, distribution, management or administration of the trust estate, or as to the exercise of any power vested in, or as to the performance of any duty imposed on, them.[81]

Where discretionary powers are conferred on trustees the court cannot, unless definite and precise averments of bad faith can be made, review or even examine the grounds on which trustees have exercised their discretion.[82] The question whether the discretionary powers are given only to the original trustees or, on the other hand, can be exercised by assumed trustees, depends on the terms of the deed, but the tendency of the recent decisions is to hold that they may be so exercised unless they are given in terms which clearly disclose a *delectus personae*.[83] Where a power of selection amongst charities is not expressly or impliedly given to named trustees personally, it may probably be exercised by assumed trustees, but not by a judicial factor, between whom and the testator there is no real nexus.[84]

46.12 *Auctor in Rem Suam.*—Apart from what is to be found in the trust deed or in the statutory provisions, there are certain principles recognised by the common law as regulating the administration of trusts and binding all trustees. Thus it has long been established that the trustee must not be *auctor in rem suam*; that is to say, he must not place himself in a situation in which his interest as an individual may conflict with his duty as a trustee.[85] It is a rule of universal application that a person having fiduciary duties to discharge (as, for example, an executor, guardian, judicial factor, agent, promoter or director of a company as well as a trustee in the strict sense) is not allowed to enter into engagements in which he has, or can have, a personal interest conflicting, or which may possibly conflict, with the interest of those whom he is bound to protect; and so strictly is this principle enforced that no question is allowed to be raised as to the fairness or unfairness of a contract so entered into.[86] It is not necessary to prove that the trustee obtained some advantage in the transaction. 'It is quite enough

---

[80] In *Leven Penny Savings Bank, Petrs.*, 1948 S.C. 147, the petitioning trustees failed to bring their trust within the definition.

[81] Court of Session Act 1988, s. 6(vi); Rules of Court (1994) rr. 63.4–63.6; *Peel's Tr.* v. *Drummond*, 1936 S.C. 786.

[82] *MacTavish* v. *Reid's Trs.*, (1904) 12 S.L.T. 404.

[83] *Angus's Exrx.* v. *Batchan's Trs.*, 1949 S.C. 335; but see *Leith's J.F.* v. *Leith*, 1957 S.C. 307.

[84] *Ibid.*

[85] *Aberdeen Ry.* v. *Blaikie Brothers* (1854) 1 Macq. 461. See also *The York Buildings Co.* v. *Mackenzie* (1795) 3 Pat. 378; *Hamilton* v. *Wright* (1842) 1 Bell's App. 574; *Huntington* v. *Henderson* (1877) 4 R. 295, *per* Lord Young; *Wright* v. *Morgan* [1926] A.C. 788; *Sarris* v. *Clark*, 1995 S.L.T. 44. The principle applies to an executor-dative by virtue of Succession (Scotland) Act 1964, s. 20: *Inglis* v. *Inglis*, 1983 S.C 8.

[86] *Aberdeen Ry.* v. *Blaikie Brothers*, *supra*, *per* Lord Cranworth L.C. at p. 471.

that the thing which he does has a tendency to injure the trust, a tendency to interfere with his duty,'.[87]

Hence, under this rule, a sale of trust property by trustees to, or a loan by them to, one of their number (however fair the terms of the transaction may have been) are all open to challenge at the instance of the beneficiary.[88] The transaction is not void, but is voidable.[89] The rule is not, however, extended to the case of a trustee buying from a beneficiary his interest in the trust property. A trustee is not forbidden from doing this, but the law casts upon him the onus of proving that he gave full value and that all necessary information was afforded to the beneficiary at the time of the sale.[90]

It is also settled that a trustee may not make profit out of his office, unless this is authorised (either expressly or impliedly) by the truster or agreed to by all the beneficiaries.[91] If a trustee, for example, acts as solicitor or factor for the trust, or manages a business on its behalf, he is not entitled to any remuneration for his services unless such authority or consent is given.[92] Nor is a trustee permitted to make profit for himself by means of his office. Whenever a person holding a fiduciary position gains, by reason of availing himself of that position, any advantage he must communicate that advantage to the trust. As already mentioned, the law regards him as holding the advantage as constructive trustee for behoof of the beneficiaries.[93] Thus in *Wilsons* v. *Wilson*[94] a tutor who renounced the lease of a farm held for behoof of the pupils, and obtained a lease in his own name was held bound to account to the pupils for all the profits which he had obtained from the farm under the lease in his own favour. In *Magistrates of Aberdeen* v. *University of Aberdeen*,[95] the town council purchased from themselves certain lands which they held as trustees. Afterwards they applied to the Crown for a grant of the salmon fishing opposite these lands on the representation that they were the owners of these lands, and obtained the grant. It was decided that the town council still held the lands in trust, and that moreover, as they had obtained the grant of the fishing in virtue of their

---

[87] *Ibid.*

[88] *Ritchies* v. *Ritchies' Trs.* (1888) 15 R. 1086; *Croskery* v. *Gilmour's Trs.* (1890) 17 R. 697; *Johnston* v. *MacFarlane*, 1987 S.L.T. 593; *Clark* v. *Clark's Exrs.*, 1989 S.L.T. 665. A creditor of the beneficiary is also entitled to challenge the transaction—*Meff* v. *Smith's Trs.*, 1930 S.N. 162.

[89] *Fraser* v. *Hankey & Co.* (1847) 9 D. 415.

[90] *Dougan* v. *Macpherson* (1902) 4 F. (H.L.) 7.

[91] *Sleigh* v. *Sleigh's J.F.*, 1908 S.C. 1112; *A.B.'s Curator Bonis*, 1927 S.C. 902; *Williams* v. *Barton* [1927] 2 Ch. 9; *Sarris* v. *Clark*, 1992 S.L.T. 44, in which it was held that the doctrine did not apply where the truster, having foreseen a possible conflict, still appointed a person a trustee.

[92] *Mackie* v. *Mackie's Trs.* (1875) 2 R. 312; *Mills* v. *Brown's Trs.* (1901) 3 F. 1012. If a truster empowers his trustees to appoint one of their number as law agent, this implies that he may be remunerated by the trust; *Lewis' Trs.* v. *Pirie*, 1912 S.C. 574.

[93] See para. 46.8, *supra*.

[94] (1789) Mor. 16376. See also *McNiven* v. *Peffers* (1868) 7 M. 181.

[95] (1877) 4 R. (H.L.) 48.

possession of these lands, they were bound to hold the fishing as trustees for the benefit of the trust.

So, if the trustee in breach of his duty employs funds belonging to the trust in trade, although any loss thereby incurred must be made good by him to the estate, any profit earned may be claimed by the beneficiaries; it is not enough that he makes the funds forthcoming with any interest that might have been obtained from proper trust investments.[96]

The law requires further that the trustee shall act in the administration of the trust with a due measure of prudence and diligence. He is bound to exercise that degree of diligence in the exercise of his office which a man of ordinary prudence would exercise in the management of his own private affairs.[97] His responsibility is tested by this average standard and not by reference to the intelligence or prudence exhibited by the particular trustee in the management of his own affairs. If the trustee fails to administer the estate with the required degree of care he is guilty of negligence and may be liable for loss occasioned through his negligence.

46.13   Investment of Trust Funds.—One of the usual duties of trustees is to find suitable investments for the trust funds. Trust deeds commonly contain clauses specifying the investments which the trustees may make; sometimes it is provided that the trustees may retain stocks in which the truster has already invested, and a general power to do so authorises the trustees to keep these stocks.[98] General provision is also made by the Trustee Investments Act 1961 for the investment by trustees of the trust funds in their hands unless specially prohibited by the constitution or terms of the trust;[99] the powers contained in the Act are in addition to, and not in derogation from, any special power of investment which may otherwise have been conferred on the trustees.[1] The Act divides the investments in which the trustees have authority to place the funds into three categories:[2] (a) narrower-range investments not requiring advice (e.g. national savings certificates); (b) narrower-range investments requiring advice (e.g. gilt-edged and certain other fixed-interest securities, debentures and other deposits); and (c) wider-range investments (which always require advice, and include equity shares and

[96] *Cochrane* v. *Black* (1855) 17 D. 321; *Laird* v. *Laird* (1855) 17 D. 984; (1858) 20 D. 972.

[97] *Buchanan* v. *Eaton*, 1911 S.C. (H.L.) 40; *Raes* v. *Meek* (1889) 16 R. (H.L.) 31; *Knox* v. *MacKinnon* (1888) 15 R. (H.L.) 83; *Tibbert* v. *McColl*, 1994 S.L.T. 1277.

[98] *Robinson* v. *Fraser's Trs.* (1881) 8 R. (H.L.) 127, *per* Lord Watson at p. 138.

[99] See s. 1(3). Regulations may be made extending the investment powers of trustees of a charitable trust: Charities Act 1992, ss. 38, 39. A provision in any instrument or enactment which authorises investment in units of a security is deemed to authorise investment in units of any uncertificated security which, if the security had been in certificated form, would have been an authorised investment: Uncertificated Securities Regulations 1992 (S.I. 1992 No. 225), reg. 50.

[1] s. 3 and Second Sched.

[2] First Sched.

shares in building societies). Where advice is required, trustees must obtain and consider proper advice given or confirmed in writing by a person who is reasonably believed to be qualified to give such advice by his ability and experience of financial matters.[3] When the trustees wish to place trust funds in wider-range investments, they must divide the trust estate into two parts of equal value as at the time of the division. The first part must be confined to narrower-range investments, and while property falling into the second part may be invested in wider-range investments, the division is permanent; no transfer may be made from one part of the fund to the other unless a compensating transfer is made at the same time.[4] The investments mentioned in the trust deed and those mentioned in the statute (unless excluded by the trust deed) are authorised investments. The court will normally refuse to widen trustees' powers of investment, in the course of a variation by means of a *cy près* scheme, beyond those authorised in the original deed and by the statute.[5]

It is the duty of trustees to confine themselves to these authorised investments;[6] to make investments outside them is a breach of trust. But their duty goes further than this. Within the class of authorised investments they must exercise discretion in selecting their investments, and must avoid those which are attended with hazard.[7] If a trustee makes the investment negligently or in bad faith he will be held responsible for loss thereby occasioned to the trust estate. In the exercise of his powers of investment under the statute, it is the trustee's duty to have regard to the need for diversification of investments, and to the suitability of proposed investments to the particular trust, and to obtain and consider advice where it is required.[8] And it has been clearly laid down that, despite directions by a settlor to retain investments, it is the duty of trustees, where necessary for the safety of the trust, to sell those investments.[9]

In the case of loans on the security of heritage a trustee is not chargeable with breach of trust by reason only of the proportion borne by the amount of the loan to the value of the property at the time of the loan, provided: (a) that the trustee acted upon a report as to the value of the property made by an able, practical valuator instructed and employed independently of any owner of the property, and (b) that the amount of the loan by itself or in combination with prior or *pari passu*

---

[3] s. 6(4), (5).
[4] s. 2.
[5] *Mitchell Bequest Trs.*, 1959 S.C. 395.
[6] *Learoyd* v. *Whiteley* (1887) 12 App.Cas. 727, *per* Lord Watson at p. 733; *Brownlie* v. *Brownlie's Trs.* (1879) 6 R. 1233, *per* Lord President Inglis at p. 1236.
[7] *Ibid.*
[8] Trustee Investments Act 1961, s. 6; see *Nestle* v. *National Westminster Bank plc* [1993] 1 W.L.R. 1260 Cf. *Nestle, supra*, with *Tibbert* v. *McColl*, 1994 S.L.T. 1277 on the onus of proving loss for breach of trust by a trustee.
[9] *Thomson's Trs.* v. *Davidson*, 1947 S.C. 654.

loans does not exceed two-thirds of the reported value.[10] If a heritable security for money lent by a trustee would have been a proper investment for a lower sum than was advanced by him, the trustee is liable only for the excess with interest.[11]

46.14 Breach of Trust: Beneficiary's Remedies.—A trustee who has been guilty of a breach of trust may be required to make good all the loss thereby occasioned to the estate. Where the breach consists of an unauthorised investment of trust funds, the beneficiaries may either adopt the investment or may repudiate it and have the sum invested restored to the trust with interest. If the breach consists of the employment of the trust funds for his private purposes, the trustee may be required to account for the capital and also, at the option of the beneficiary, either for the profit he has made by its use, or for interest at a rate fixed by the court.[12] For breach of trust the trustees are jointly and severally liable, and one or more of them may be sued without calling all of them.[13]

Moreover, the beneficiary has a right to 'follow the trust property' as against the trustees or his creditors or others claiming through him; that is to say, if the trustee has, in breach of his trust, parted with trust property—whether it be money or specific items—or has converted it into some other form, that property, or the property into which it has been converted, may be claimed as belonging to the trust. 'All property belonging to a trust, however much it may be changed or altered in its nature or character, and all the fruits of such property, whether in its original or in its altered state, continues to be subject to, or affected by, the trust'.[14] There are, however, limitations on this right to follow the property. It cannot be asserted against one who has acquired the property for value in good faith and without notice of the trust;[15] and it is necessary that the property which the beneficiary claims to follow can be traced and identified either as having been acquired with, or as representing, the original trust estate or some part of it.[16]

[10] 1921 Act, s. 30; *Boyd* v. *Greig*, 1913 1 S.L.T. 398; *Shaw* v. *Cates* [1909] 1 Ch. 389.
[11] 1921 Act, s. 29.
[12] *Douglas* v. *Douglas's Trs.* (1864) 2 M. 1379; *Cochrane* v. *Black* (1855) 17 D. 321; *Laird* v. *Laird* (1885) 17 D. 984.
[13] *Allen* v. *McCombie's Trs.*, 1909 S.C. 710.
[14] *Pennell* v. *Deffel* (1853) 4 De G.M. & G. 372, *per* Turner L.J. at p. 388; *Re Hallett's Estate* (1879) 13 Ch.D. 696; *Sinclair* v. *Brougham* [1914] A.C. 398; *Banque Belge* v. *Hambrouk* [1921] 1 K.B. 321; *Taylor* v. *Forbes & Co.* (1830) 4 W. & S. 444; *Magistrates of Airdrie* v. *Smith* (1850) 12 D. 1222. See also *Aluminium Industrie Vasssen B.V.* v. *Romalpa Aluminium* [1976] 1 W.L.R. 676.
[15] *Somervail* v. *Redfearn* (1813) 1 Dow 50 (the facts of which are stated in para. 38.8, *supra*); *London & Canadian Loan and Agency Co.* v. *Duggan* [1893] A.C. 506; see also *Thomson* v. *Clydesdale Bank* (1893) 20 R. (H.L.) 59; *Bertram Gardner & Co.'s Tr.* v. *King's Remembrancer*, 1920 S.C. 555, *per* Lord Skerrington at p. 562. See also Trusts (Scotland) Act 1961, s. 2(1), for sale of heritage at variance with the terms or purposes of the trust; para. 46.11, *supra*.
[16] *Re Hallett's Estate, supra*; Bell, *Comm.*, i, 286, 295, 296; *James Roscoe (Bolton) Ltd.* v. *Winder* [1915] 1 Ch. 62.

So, if a trustee mixes the trust funds with his own money, the court will separate the trust from the private moneys and will award the former specifically to the beneficiaries. This principle has been applied to those in a fiduciary position, although not trustees in the ordinary sense. Thus, where a law agent, who had, without the knowledge of his client, sold shares which she had entrusted to him and lodged the price in his bank account, subsequently became bankrupt, a sum equivalent to the amount of the price of the shares was, by order of the court, taken out of the sequestration and restored to the client.[17]

Where trust moneys are thus mixed with the trustee's private funds, and the trustee thereafter draws cheques on the account for his own purposes, the rule of *Clayton's Case*[18] does not apply in a question between the trustee and the beneficiary. Although the trust funds may have been paid in first, it is assumed that the trustee meant to act honestly and he is taken to have drawn out his own money rather than that belonging to the trust,[19] unless the circumstances exclude this assumption, as in the case where, after the trust funds are paid into a bank, the whole of the moneys in the bank account are drawn out before further money is paid in.[20]

46.15 Breach of Trust: Protection to Trustees against Liability therefor.— There is not infrequently to be found in trust deeds a clause designed to alleviate the responsibility of the trustees in the administration of the estate. Thus, in the case of *Knox* v. *Mackinnon*[21] it was declared that the trustees 'should not be liable for omissions, errors or neglect of management, nor *singuli in solidum*, but each shall be liable for his own actual intromissions only.' It was held that clauses of this kind do not protect against positive breach of duty. Lord Watson observed: 'I see no reason to doubt that a clause conceived in these or similar terms will afford a considerable measure of protection to trustees who have bona fide abstained from closely superintending the administration of the trust or who have committed mere errors of judgment while acting with a single eye to the benefit of the trust and of the persons whom it concerns; but it is settled in the law of Scotland that such a clause is

---

[17] *Jopp* v. *Johnston's Tr.* (1904) 6 F. 1028; *Macadam* v. *Martin's Tr.* (1872) 11 M. 33; see also *Southern Cross Commodities Property Ltd.* v. *Martin*, 1991 S.L.T. 83, *per* Lord Milligan especially at p. 85 A–D; *Att. Gen. for Hong Kong* v. *Reid* [1994] 1 A.C. 324 (P.C.).

[18] See para. 15.7, *supra*.

[19] *Re Hallett's Estate, supra*.

[20] *James Roscoe (Bolton) Ltd.* v. *Winder* [1915] 1 Ch. 62; *Re Stenning* [1895] 2 Ch. 433; see also *Re. Goldcorp Exchange Ltd. (In Receivership)* [1995] 1 A.C. 74; *Bishopgate Investment Management Ltd.* v. *Homan* [1995] Ch. 211; and *Style Financial Services Ltd.* v. *Bank of Scotland*, 1995 G.W.D. 14–761, which provide that where a *mala fides* fiduciary's bank account is overdrawn, the misappropriated trust money cannot be traced: as there is no fund to trace.

[21] (1888) 15 R. (H.L.) 83; *Ferguson* v. *Paterson* (1900) 2 F. (H.L.) 37; see also *Inglis*, 1965 S.L.T. 326.

ineffectual to protect a trustee against the consequences of *culpa lata*, or of gross negligence on his part, or of any conduct which is inconsistent with bona fides. I think it is equally clear that the clause will afford no protection to trustees who, from motives however laudable in themselves, act in plain violation of the duty which they owe to the individuals beneficially interested in the funds which they administer.'

The 1921 Act contains the following provisions relative to the protection of the trustees. By section 3 it is provided that all trusts, unless the contrary be expressed, shall be held to include a provision that each trustee shall be liable only for his own acts and intromissions and shall not be liable for the acts and intromissions of co-trustees and shall not be liable for omissions; but this section does not afford protection to a trustee who neglects his duties or who authorises or acquiesces in breaches of trust committed by his co-trustees.

Again, where a trustee has committed a breach of trust at the instigation or request or with the consent in writing of a beneficiary, it is provided that the court may, if it thinks fit, order that all or any part of the interest of that beneficiary shall be applied in indemnifying the trustee.[22] This section does not give the trustee a right to be indemnified but leaves the matter to the decision of the court; and to raise a case for indemnity the beneficiary must have known the facts which made what was done a breach of trust and his concurrence must have been 'clear and direct.'[23]

Lastly, the 1921 Act introduced two new provisions borrowed from the law of England.[24] If it appears to the court that a trustee who has committed a breach of trust has acted honestly and reasonably and ought fairly to be excused for the breach of trust, then the court may relieve the trustee from personal liability;[25] and a trustee is not liable for breach of trust merely by continuing to hold an investment which has ceased to be an authorised investment.[26]

The following obligations of a trustee are imprescriptible: (a) the obligation to produce accounts of his intromissions with any of the trust property; (b) the obligation to make reparation or restitution in respect of any fraudulent breach of trust to which the trustee was party or was privy; (c) the obligation to make furthcoming to any person entitled thereto any trust property, or the proceeds of any such property, in the possession of the trustee, or to make good the value of any such property previously received by the trustee and appropriated to his own use.[27] The obligation of a third party to make furthcoming to any party

[22] 1921 Act, s. 31.
[23] *Henderson* v. *Henderson's Trs.* (1900) 2 F. 1295.
[24] These provisions now appear in ss. 4 and 61 of the Trustee Act 1925.
[25] s. 32; *Clarke* v. *Clarke's Trs.*, 1925 S.C. 693; *Re Allsop* [1914] 1 Ch. 1.
[26] s. 33; *Re Pauling's Settlement Trusts (Younghusband* v. *Coutts & Co.)* [1964] 1 Ch. 303.
[27] Prescription and Limitation (Scotland) Act 1973, Sched. 3.

entitled thereto any trust property received by the third party otherwise than in good faith and in his possession is also imprescriptible. It would seem that a trustee's obligation to make reparation for an *ultra vires* or negligent breach of trust is subject to the quinquennial prescription.[28]

46.16 Trustees: Liability to Creditors.—For debts incurred by the truster trustees are not liable beyond the amount of the trust estate. But if the trustees contract debts or incur liabilities in the course of their administration, they are personally liable for these in a question with the creditors, unless the creditors transacted with them on the terms that the trust estate alone was to be responsible. Accordingly, if trustees choose to continue the truster's, or enter into another, business, they are personally liable to the trade creditors;[29] and if they conduct an unsuccessful litigation they are, as a general rule, so liable in expenses to the successful litigant.[30] But in entering into a contract it is open to the trustees in the general case to stipulate that the trust estate alone shall be liable, and this stipulation may be effectual. Thus in one case[31] where trustees borrowed money on a heritable bond in which they bound themselves 'as trustees' it was held that their liability was limited to the amount of the trust estate. The nature of the transaction may, however, be such as to prevent any effective limitation of their liability, as is exemplified in the case of trustees being registered as the proprietors of shares of a company incorporated under the Companies Acts. As shareholders, the trustees are and must be personally liable, for it is not within the power of a company to differentiate between those shareholders who are trustees and those who are not, to the effect of enabling the former to hold on any other terms than would apply if the holders were individuals holding for their own behoof.[32] In Scotland trusts may be noticed in the register of the company,[33] but notice of the trust, while it may be useful as earmarking the shares for the trust, does not affect the liability of the trustees. While the trustees as shareholders are personally liable, they are entitled to be indemnified out of the trust estate, unless they were in breach of trust in holding the shares.[34]

Executors are enabled to tranfers shares belonging to the deceased without being registered as the holders of the shares, and may thus avoid incurring the risk of personal liability.[35]

---

[28] *Ibid.*, Sched. 1, para. 1(*d*). See *Hobday* v. *Kirkpatrick's Trs.*, 1985 S.L.T. 197.

[29] *Ford & Sons* v. *Stephenson* (1888) 16 R. 24.

[30] *Anderson* v. *Anderson's Tr.* (1901) 4 F. 96.

[31] *Gordon* v. *Campbell* (1842) 1 Bell's App. 428; see *Brown* v. *Sutherland* (1875) 2 R. 615.

[32] *Lumsden* v. *Buchanan* (1865) 3 M. (H.L.) 89; *Muir* v. *City of Glasgow Bank* (1879) 6 R. (H.L.) 21.

[33] This is not permitted in the case of companies registered in England and Wales: Companies Act 1985, s.360.

[34] *Buchan* v. *City of Glasgow Bank* (1879) 6 R. (H.L.) 44; *Wishart* v. *City of Glasgow Bank* (1879) 6 R. 1341, *per* Lord Shand.

[35] Companies Act 1985, s. 183(3).

46.17 Public and Charitable Trusts.—While the court has jurisdiction over the administration of all trusts, it exercises wider powers over trusts instituted for the benefit of the public, frequently described as 'charitable.'[36] The law of Scotland makes no precise definition of the expression 'charity' in this context; 'charitable trust' is merely a convenient general term. 'There is no distinction either as to construction or principles of administration between gifts to charitable trusts, properly so called, and gifts to purposes which, though not charitable, are lawful and useful. The true distinction is between private trusts or bequests, in which only individuals named or designed can claim an interest, and those which are intended for the benefit of a section of the public, and which may be enforced by *popularis actio*.'[37] This statement of the law[38] was accepted in *Anderson's Trs.* v. *Scott*,[39] and, therefore, in considering earlier decisions and dicta as to the powers of the court over 'charitable' trusts, the term 'charitable' must now, it would appear, be understood as including public trusts in general and not those only which are eleemosynary.

But although, according to this decision, no distinction need be drawn between charitable and public trusts as regards the jurisdiction of the court, the terms 'charitable' and 'public' have by no means the same effect when used by a testator to describe the objects of his bounty. If a testator leaves his estate to trustees in trust to divide it among such 'charitable' purposes as they may think proper, the descriptive word 'charitable' is, out of favour for charities,[40] held by itself to denote a sufficiently definite class of beneficiaries, and the gift is sustained. On the other hand, if the purposes are described merely as 'public,' this description is held to be so vague as to invalidate the bequest. Instructions to trustees to divide the estate among 'charitable or public,'[41] 'charitable or religious'[42] and 'charitable or social'[43] objects have been held void from uncertainty in respect that two classes of beneficiaries were favoured, and that the words 'public,' 'religious' and 'social' used without further detail to describe the second class were too vague a direction to receive effect. But a conjunction of the words

---

[36] *Dundas* (1869) 7 M. 670, *per* Lord President Inglis.

[37] *i.e.*, an action on behalf of the public. Any person possessing an interest, either existing or contingent, under the trust purposes of the trust has a title to enforce its due execution; *Ross* v. *Governors of Heriot's Hospital* (1843) 5 D. 589; *Murray* v. *Lord Cameron*, 1969 S.L.T. (Notes) 76.

[38] In McLaren, *Wills and Succession*, ii, 917.

[39] 1914 S.C. 942.

[40] *Magistrates of Dundee* v. *Morris* (1858) 3 Macq. 134.

[41] *Blair* v. *Duncan* (1901) 4 F. (H.L.) 1; *Turnbull's Trs.* v. *Lord Advocate*, 1918 S.C. (H.L.) 88; *Campbell's Trs.* v. *Campbell*, 1921 S.C. (H.L.) 12; *Reid's Trs.* v. *Cattanach's Trs.*, 1929 S.C. 727. There are numerous decisions as to the effect of various forms of bequest.

[42] *Macintyre* v. *Grimond's Trs.* (1905) 7 F. (H.L.) 90; but see *Brough* v. *Brough's Trs.*, 1950 S.L.T. 117; and para. 44.13, *supra*.

[43] *Rintoul's Trs.* v. *Rintoul*, 1949 S.C. 297; contrast *Milne's Trs.* v. *Davidson*, 1956 S.C. 81.

'charitable' and 'benevolent' does not impair the peculiar virtues of 'charitable.'[44] If the trust purposes are in themselves uncertain, the fact that the benefit of the trust is confined to a particular locality will not save the trust.[45] And a gift to 'charities' generally will fail if the testator does not appoint a particular person as trustee or executor to make a choice.[46]

Neither of the questions discussed above requires a precise definition of the word 'charitable,' which is treated as being sufficiently specific in itself. It is a different matter, however, where the construction of income tax statutes is concerned. In *Baird's Trs.* v. *Lord Advocate*[47] an attempt was made to achieve a definition of 'charitable purposes' in a taxing statute so as to produce uniformity between England and Scotland; but the court refused in that case to apply the technical definition of English law, and insisted that the words should be given their popular and ordinary meaning. It was laid down in *Baird's Trs.* that in their popular meaning the words were confined to the relief of poverty; but this definition has in most subsequent cases been considered to be too narrow.[48] In *Income Tax Commissioners* v. *Pemsel*,[49] Lord Watson[50] pointed out that the word 'charity' has been employed in the legislative language of the Scottish Parliament, and of the British Parliament when legislating for Scotland, in substantially the same sense as that in which it had been interpreted by the English courts; and it was held that for the purposes of the Income Tax Acts 'charitable purposes' should be given the technical meaning of English law,[51] based on the statute of Elizabeth and the decisions of the Court of Chancery. Finally, in *Inland Revenue* v. *Glasgow Police Athletic Association*[52] it was emphasised that for tax purposes the English law of

[44] *Wink's Exrs.* v. *Tallent*, 1947 S.C. 470; Lord Keith (p. 484) treats the words as synonymous. See also *Pomphrey's Trs.* v. *Royal Naval Benevolent Trust*, 1967 S.L.T. 61, *per* Lord Fraser at p. 63.

[45] *Turnbull's Trs.* v. *Lord Advocate, supra*; *Harper's Trs.* v. *Jacobs*, 1929 S.C. 345.

[46] *Angus's Exrx.* v. *Batchan's Trs.*, 1949 S.C. 335. *Cf. Guild* v. *Bladen* (O.H.), 1987 S.C.L.R. 221.

[47] (1888) 15 R. 682.

[48] *Anderson's Trs.* v. *Scott*, 1914 S.C. 942; *Allan's Exr.* v. *Allan*, 1908 S.C. 807, *per* Lord Kinnear; see Lord Halsbury's and Lord Davy's speeches in *Blair* v. *Duncan* (1901) 4 F. (H.L.) 1; *Chalmers' Trs.* v. *Turriff School Board*, 1917 S.C. 676, *per* Lord Justice-Clerk Dickson; *Wink's Exrs.* v. *Tallent*, 1947 S.C. 470, *per* Lord President Cooper.

[49] [1891] A.C. 531; see also *Jackson's Trs.* v. *Inland Revenue*, 1926 S.C. 579; *Inland Revenue* v. *Glasgow Musical Festival Association*, 1926 S.C. 920; *Scottish Woollen Technical College* v. *Inland Revenue*, 1926 S.C. 934.

[50] At pp. 558, 560.

[51] In *Pemsel's Case* Lord Macnaghten, with reference to English law, observes: ' "Charity," in its legal sense, comprises four principal divisions: trusts for the relief of poverty; trusts for the advancement of education; trusts for the advancement of religion; and trusts for other purposes beneficial to the community, not falling under any of the preceding heads.' But this does not mean that all trusts which are beneficial to the community are regarded in English law as charitable—*Att.-Gen.* v. *National Provincial Bank* [1924] A.C. 262.

[52] 1953 S.C. (H.L.) 13.

charities is part of the law of Scotland and not foreign law. The position is the same in deciding whether an organisation is established 'for charitable purposes only' so as to be entitled to rating relief on the subjects it occupies.[53] But the limited and technical meanings given to the words in *Baird's Trs.* v. *Pemsel* have never been applied in a question as to the construction or administration of a Scottish testamentary trust.[54]

The general principles of trust administration[55] are as applicable to public as to private trusts, and the definition of trust in the Trusts (Scotland) Act 1921 is so drawn as to include both types. There are, however, certain principles which are peculiar to public trusts. The court is said to apply a more lenient standard in its dealing with those who administer a trust of this kind than with private trustees. It does not press severely on them if in good faith they err in their management of the trust, and if their administration, although mistaken, has been honest and unconnected with any corrupt practice, they will not be punished for their actions in the past.[56] If the annual income of a public trust does not exceed £1,000 the trustees may, in certain circumstances, and after following prescribed procedure, expend capital of the trust notwithstanding any prohibition in the trust deed.[57] But the most striking distinction between public and private trusts is to be found in the power which the court possesses to act on the principle of *cy près* in the case of trusts of the former description.

46.18 *Cy Près.*—Where the intention of the founder of a charitable or public trust cannot be carried into effect in the precise manner directed by him, it is within the power of the court to direct that the funds shall be applied in a manner as nearly akin as possible to that directed. The principle has been authoritatively stated in these terms: 'In both countries (England and Scotland) this principle has prevailed, namely, that there shall be a very enlarged administration of charitable trusts. You look to the charity which is intended to be created—that is to say, the benefit of the beneficiary—and you distinguish between the charity and the means which are directed to the attainment of that charity. Now the means of necessity vary from age to age ... and the Courts of Equity have always exercised the power of varying the means of carrying out the charity from time to time, according as by that variation

[53] See Local Government (Financial Provisions, etc.) (Scotland) Act 1962, s. 4(10) as amended; *Scottish Burial & Cremation Society* v. *Glasgow Corporation*, 1967 S.C. (H.L.) 116.
[54] *Anderson's Trs.* v. *Scott, supra; Wink's Exrs.* v. *Tallent, supra,* per Lord Keith at p. 482.
[55] See paras. 46.11, *et seq.* The provisions of the Trustee Investments Act 1961 may be varied by regulations in their application to trusts which are 'charities' (see para. 46.20): Charities Act 1992, ss. 38–39.
[56] *Andrews* v. *Ewart's Trs.* (1886) 13 R. (H.L.) 69.
[57] Law Reform (Misc. Provs.) (Scotland) Act 1990, s. 11.

they can secure more effectually the great object of the charity, namely, the benefit of the beneficiary.'[58] According to this doctrine, known as *cy-près* or approximation, the court has power to vary the means by the substitution for a particular form of charity of another form approximating as closely as may be to the old one; but the court cannot change a charity, or sanction the application of the funds to a wholly different purpose. Some cases disclose a strict approach to the question whether there has been failure so as to admit of a *cy près* scheme, and it has been said that it is not a legitimate ground for the application of the doctrine that, through the changing circumstances of society, the administration of a charity has become increasingly arduous and discouraging in its results.[59] On the other hand, the court has shown itself ready to exercise its power in a case of strong expendiency falling short of impossibility of performance, where it is clear that the circumstances of the trust or the arrangements for its administration are such that its carrying out would be seriously hampered unless the means were varied.[60]

This principle is not, however, applicable in all cases where there is a charitable bequest; in the case of bequests which lapse before they take effect, there must be, either expressed or implied, a general charitable intention. In *Burgess's Trs.* v. *Crawford*[61] Lord President Dunedin distinguished between three classes of bequest. The first is where there is a gift for a charitable pupose, but the means by which it is to be carried out are not indicated; here the court will, out of the favour which it has always shown to charitable bequests, supply the means *cy près* so as to enable the purpose to be carried out.[62] The second class is where there is a gift to a society or institution which does not exist and never has existed, in which case, from the mere nonexistence of the object, there is spelled out a general charitable intention.[63] The third class is that in which the gift is in form made to a particular charitable institution which has ceased to exist, or for a particular purpose which cannot be effected; here the question arises in each case whether, on a fair construction of the deed, there is a general charitable intention with

---

[58] *Clephane* v. *Magistrates of Edinburgh* (1869) 7 M. (H.L.) 7, at p. 15; see also *Trs. of Carnegie Park Orphanage* (1892) 19 R. 605, and *Grigor Medical Bursary Fund Trs.* (1903) 5 F. 1143, *per* Lord McLaren; *Gibson's Trs.*, 1933 S.C. 190.

[59] *Glasgow Domestic Training School*, 1923 S.C. 892, *per* Lord President Clyde at p. 895; *Scotstown Moor Children's Camp*, 1948 S.C. 630.

[60] *Gibson's Trs.*, *supra*; *Glasgow Y.M.C.A.*, 1934 S.C. 452, *per* Lord Blackburn at p. 458; *Clutterbuck, Petr.*, 1961 S.L.T. 427; *Magistrates of Forfar, Petrs.*, 1975 S.L.T. (Notes) 36.

[61] 1912 S.C. 387, following Lord Herschell's opinion in *Re Rymer* [1895] 1 Ch. 19; see also *Cumming's Exr.* v. *Cumming*, 1967 S.L.T. 68, *per* Lord Avonside at p. 69.

[62] e.g. *Ballingall's J.F.* v. *Hamilton*, 1973 S.L.T. 236.

[63] e.g. *Tod's Trs.* v. *The Sailors' & Fishermen's Orphans' and Widows' Society*, 1953 S.L.T. (Notes) 72; *Pomphrey's Trs.* v. *Royal Naval Benevolent Trust*, 1967 S.L.T. 61; *Cumming's Exr.*, *supra*. Cf. *MacTavish's Trs.* v. *St. Columba's High Church*, 1967 S.L.T. (Notes) 50, where the expression of intention failed for uncertainty.

a direction as to the method in which that intention is to be effected,[64] or whether the gift is meant only for that particular institution[65] or that particular purpose.[66] If it is the latter, the doctrine of *cy près* has no place, and the gift fails with the failure of the institution or purpose. In *Burgess's Trs.*[67] the court, applying these rules, held that a bequest for the purpose of establishing an industrial school for females, which had become impossible of fulfilment owing to supervening legislation, lapsed as no intention beyond this particular object was disclosed in the settlement.

There is, however, an important difference between the cases discussed above, where there is a failure before the trust opens, and those where the failure occurs after the bequest has actually taken effect[68] in favour of a charity.[69] In the latter case it is not necessary to consider whether or not there is a general charitable intention. Although the trust or bequest may be for a particular charitable institution, the court will not allow the trust to lapse because of the subsequent failure of the object. The funds will in such a case be applied under a *cy près* scheme, unless a resulting trust or destination-over is brought into effect by the lapse.[70]

Where the principle of *cy près* falls to be applied, this is done by means of a scheme for the administration of the trust settled by the court.[71] The power of sanctioning the settlement of a scheme belongs to the *nobile officium*, and is exercisable only by the Inner House of the Court of Session.[72] It must be borne in mind that where a truster's directions are sufficient to enable trustees to prepare a scheme for themselves and where it is not impracticable to carry them out and there is no lack of machinery prescribed by the truster, it is unnecessary for the trustees to apply to the court at all.[73]

46.19 Statutory Reorganisation.—Under statute there is an alternative means of reorganising a public trust. The Court of Session (or if the Lord

---

[64] *e.g. Macrae's Trs.*, 1955 S.L.T. (Notes) 33; *Shorthouse's Trs.* v. *Aberdeen Medico-Chirurgical Society*, 1977 S.L.T. 148.

[65] *e.g., Connell's Trs.* v. *Milngavie District Nursing Association*, 1953 S.C. 230; *Fergusson's Trs.* v. *Buchanan*, 1973 S.L.T. 41.

[66] *e.g., Burgess's Trs., supra; Pennie's Trs.* v. *R.N.L.I.*, 1924 S.L.T. 520; *Tait's J.F.* v. *Lillie*, 1940 S.C. 534; *Hay Memorial J.F.* v. *Hay's Trs.*, 1952 S.C. (H.L.) 29; *McRobert's Trs.* v. *Cameron*, 1961 S.L.T. (Notes) 66.

[67] 1912 S.C. 387.

[68] As to failure to take effect, see *Cuthbert's Trs.* v. *Cuthbert*, 1958 S.C. 629; *Edinburgh Corporation* v. *Cranston's Trs.*, 1960 S.C. 244.

[69] *Anderson's Trs.* v. *Scott*, 1914 S.C. 942; *Re Slevin* [1891] 2 Ch. 236; *Davidson's Trs.* v. *Arnott*, 1951 S.C. 42.

[70] *Youngs's Trs.* v. *Deacons of the Eight Incorporated Trades of Perth* (1893) 20 R. 778; see also *Clarke* v. *Ross*, 1976 S.L.T. (Notes) 62.

[71] For procedure, see *Forrest's Trs.* v. *Forrest*, 1960 S.L.T. 88.

[72] See Trusts (Scotland) Act 1921, s. 26; *Ossington's Trs.*, 1966 S.L.T. 19; *Smart, Petrs.*, 1993 S.C.L.R. 958.

[73] *Robertson's Trs.*, 1948 S.C. 1; *Galloway* v. *Elgin Magistrates*, 1946 S.C. 353.

Advocate so appoints, the sheriff court where the annual trust income does not exceed a specified sum)[74] may, on the application of the trustees, approve a scheme for the variation or reorganisation of the trust purposes if it is satisfied:[75] (a) that the trust purposes, whether in whole or in part, have been fulfilled as far as it is possible to do so or can no longer be given effect to, whether in accordance with the directions or spirit of the trust deed or other document constituting the trust or otherwise; or (b) that the trust purposes provide a use for only part of the property available under the trust;[76] or (c) that the trust purposes were expressed by reference to: (*i*) an area which has since ceased to have effect for the purpose described expressly or by implication in the trust deed or (*ii*) a class of persons or area which has ceased to be suitable or appropriate, having regard to the spirit of the trust deed, or as regards which it has ceased to be practicable to administer the property available under the trust; or (d) that the purposes, in whole or in part, have, since the constitution of the trust, (*i*) been adequately provided for by other means, or (*ii*) have ceased to be such as would enable the trust to be recognised as a charity, or (*iii*) have ceased in any other way to provide a suitable and effective method of using the property available under the trust, having regard to the spirit of the trust deed.[77] Before approving the scheme, the court must be satisfied that the proposed purposes will enable the resources of the trust to be applied to better effect consistently with the spirit of the trust deed, having regard to changes in social and economic conditions since the time when the trust was constituted.[78] The scheme may provide for the transfer of the trust assets to another public trust, with or without a change in the purposes of the other trust or for the amalgamation of the trust with one or more public trusts.[79]

Where the annual income of a public trust does not exceed £5,000, and a majority of the trustees are of the opinion that any of (a) to (d) above apply in relation to the trust, they may determine that, to enable the resources of the trust to be applied to better effect consistently with the spirit of the trust deed, the trust purposes should be modified or the whole assets should be transferred to another public trust or that the trust should be amalgamated with one or more public trusts.[80] Where it has been determined that the purposes should be modified, the trustees may pass a resolution that the trust deed be modified by substituting

---

[74] Law Reform (Misc. Provs.) (Scotland) Act 1990, s. 9(5). No order has yet been made.

[75] Law Reform (Misc. Provs.) (Scotland) Act 1990, s. 9(1); *Smart Petrs.*, 1993 S.C.L.R. 958.

[76] As to the requirements of s. 9(1)(b), see *Smart Petrs.*, 1993 S.C.L.R. 958, *per* Lord President Hope (sitting in the Outer House) at p. 961 E–F.

[77] As to the requirements of s. 9(1)(d)(iii), see *Smart Petrs.*, *supra*, at pp. 961–962.

[78] s. 9(2).

[79] s. 9(3).

[80] s. 10(2).

new trust purposes.[81] The new purposes must not be so dissimilar in character to the purposes set out in the original trust deed that the modification would constitute an unreasonable departure from the spirit of the deed.[82] Before passing the resolution, the trustees must have regard to the circumstances of any locality to which the trust purposes relate and to the extent to which it may be desirable to achieve economy by amalgamating two or more trusts.[83] If the trust is a recognised charity, they must also ensure that the new purposes will enable the trust to continue to be granted tax exemption as a charity.[84] Where the trustees have determined that the assets should be transferred, they may pass a resolution that the trust be wound up and that the assets be transferred to another trust the purposes of which are not so dissimilar as to be an unreasonable departure from the spirit of the trust deed of the trust being wound up.[85] Before passing the resolution, the trustees must again have regard to the circumstances of any relevant particular locality, ensure the continuance of any tax exemption and ascertain that the trustees of the transferee trust will consent to the transfer of the assets.[86] Where the trustees determine that the trust should be amalgamated with another, they may pass a resolution that the trust will be amalgamated with one or more other trusts so that the purposes of the amalgamated trust will not be so dissimilar in character to those of the original trust as to constitute an unreasonable departure from the spirit of the trust deed.[87] Before passing the resolution the trustees must have regard to the circumstances of any relevant particular locality, ensure the continuance of any tax exemption and ascertain that the trustees of the other trust or trusts agree to such an amalgamation.[88] The resolutions cannot be acted upon until after an interval to allow for advertisement, the making of objections by interested persons and notification to the Lord Advocate.[89] The Lord Advocate may direct the trust not to proceed with the implementation of the resolution.[90]

46.20 **Charities.**—Rather oddly, charities in Scotland are defined by recognition by the Commissioners of Inland Revenue for purposes of exemption from tax.[91] A 'recognised body' is a body to which the Commissioners have intimated that it will be given relief under section

---

[81] s. 10(3).
[82] s. 10(4).
[83] s. 10(5).
[84] s. 10(6).
[85] s. 10(8).
[86] s. 10(9).
[87] s. 10(10).
[88] s. 10(11).
[89] ss. 10(12), (13). See also the Public Trusts (Reorganisation) (Scotland) (No. 2) Regulations 1993 (S.I. 1993 No. 2254), made pursuant to s. 10(13).
[90] s. 10(14).
[91] Law Reform (Misc. Provs.) (Scotland) Act 1990, s. 1.

505 of the Income and Corporation Taxes Act 1988[92] in respect of its income which is applicable and is applied to charitable purposes only, being a body which is established under the law of Scotland or which is managed or controlled wholly or mainly in or from Scotland.[93] A non-recognised body is a body which is neither a recognised one nor one which is registered or exempt from registration in England and Wales under the Charities Act 1960.[94] A recognised body is entitled to describe itself as 'a Scottish charity.'[95] A non-recognised body is not entitled to represent itself or hold itself out as a charity and may, at the instance of the Lord Advocate, be interdicted from doing so.[96] A recognised body must provide to any person who requests it, on payment of a reasonable charge, a copy of the trust deed or other document constituting the body, which describes the nature of the body and of its charitable purposes.[97] The persons concerned with the management and control of a recognised body must keep accounting records and prepare annual accounts and an annual report.[98] The Lord Advocate has powers to investigate the affairs of recognised bodies and to suspend persons concerned with their management or control; in certain circumstances, he can apply to the court for the exercise of a wide range of powers in relation to a recognised body, including the appointment *ad interim* of a judicial factor to manage its affairs.[99] These provisions do not apply to religious bodies designated by the Secretary of State.[1] The trustees of a recognised body, failing whom the Lord Advocate, can appoint additional trustees so that the number is not less than three.[2] The Lord Advocate can petition for the winding up of a recognised body which is a company.[3] An official known as 'the Scottish charities nominee' has powers to transfer the dormant bank account of a recognised body to another recognised body; where the amount at credit of the account exceeds £5,000 this can be done only if the Lord Advocate is not proposing to take any other action.[4]

Further Reading

Mackenzie Stuart, *Law of Trusts* (1932).
McLaren, *Wills and Succession* (3rd ed., 1894 and supplement, 1934).
Menzies, *Trustees* (2nd ed., 1913).
Norrie and Scobbie, *Trusts* (1991).
Wilson and Duncan, *Trusts, Trustees and Executors* (1975).

[92] cf. *William Muir (Bond 9) Ltd. Employees ShareScheme Trs.* v. *Inland Revenue Commissioners*, 1995 S.L.T. 225, in which it was held that income had not been "applied for charitable purposes".
[93] s. 1(7).
[94] s. 2.
[95] s. 1(7).
[96] s. 2.
[97] s. 1(5).
[98] s. 5.
[99] ss. 6, 7.
[1] s. 3(3). See the Charities (Designated Religious Bodies) (Scotland) Order 1993 (S.I. 1993 No. 2774).
[2] s. 13.
[3] s. 14.

CHAPTER 47

LIFERENT AND FEE

47.1 **Nature of Liferent: Annuities.**—A liferent is a right to use and enjoy a subject during life without destroying or wasting its substance (*salva rei substantia*).[1] It is described in the institutional writers as a personal servitude, the only personal servitude known in our law;[2] but in modern times the tendency is to regard it as a separate right or interest in property. It is to be distinguished from an annuity. An annuity is a right to receive from year to year a certain sum, and it is not necessarily limited to the lifetime of the recipient, for it may be given for a number of years or even in perpetuity.[3] A liferenter can claim only the fruits of the subject liferented, whereas an annuitant is entitled to the amount of his annuity, and (unless the deed creating it shows that it is to be charged on income only) can exact payment out of capital if the income falls short.[4]

The law does not recognise an interest intermediate between those of liferent and of fee,[5] which is the full and unlimited right in the capital or the subject itself.[6]

47.2 **Creation of Liferents by Constitution and Reservation: Limitations.**—Liferents were formerly divided into legal liferents or those 'constituted by the law,'[7] namely, terce and courtesy,[8] and conventional liferents 'constituted by the deeds of men';[9] but with the abolition of terce and courtesy[10] this distinction is now obsolescent. Conventional liferents may be created by reservation or constitution. A liferent by reservation is that which a proprietor reserves to himself when conveying the fee to another. In the case of heritage no title to a

---

[1] Stair, II, vi, 4; Erskine, *Inst.,* II, ix, 39.
[2] Erskine, *supra*; *Patrick* v. *Napier* (1867) 5 M. 683, *per* Lord President Inglis at p. 699.
[3] *Fleming* v. *Reuther's Exrs.,* 1921 S.C. 593; see also *Reid's Exrx.* v. *Reid*, 1944 S.C. (H.L.) 25.
[4] *Kinmond's Trs.* v. *Kinmond* (1873) 11 M. 381; *Knox's Trs.* v. *Knox* (1869) 7 M. 873; *Colquhoun's Trs.* v. *Colquhoun*, 1922 S.C. 32.
[5] See paras. 44.21 and 44.30, *supra*; *Cochrane's Exrx.* v. *Cochrane*, 1947 S.C. 134; Smith, *Short Commentary*, p. 487.
[6] As to 'fiduciary fee,' see Bell, *Prin.*, §§ 1713–1715; see also Trusts (Scotland) Act 1921, s. 8(2).
[7] Stair, II, vi, 2.
[8] See para. 42.1, *supra*.
[9] Stair, *supra*.
[10] Succession (Scotland) Act 1964, s. 10(1).

841

reserved liferent requires to be completed, for the grantor's former title to the land (which included the right to its fruits) still subsists as to the reserved liferent.[11] A liferent by constitution is one created by the proprietor in favour of another, with or without a grant of the fee to others; familiar instances of such liferents are those created in testamentary deeds.

There are statutory limitations on the creation of liferents in favour of persons who are not living nor *in utero* at the time when the deed creating the liferent comes into operation.[12]

47.3   Proper and Beneficiary Liferents.—A liferent may be constituted by a direct disposition or gift of a subject to a liferenter and fiar without the interposition of a trust. A liferent of this kind has been termed a proper liferent.[13] The possession belongs to the liferenter, who may hold either by himself or his servants; and the rights pertaining to the liferenter in a question with the fiar are determined by the law.[14] If the subjects should be destroyed or damaged through the fault of another the liferenter is entitled to damages for the loss he has sustained as a proper liferenter but cannot also claim damages for the cost of alternative accommodation.[15] Proper liferents were more common in former times, and it is to such liferents that the attention of the institutional writers appears to have been mainly devoted. In modern times, the advantages of a trust as obviating certain conveyancing difficulties in regard to the lodgement of the fee, and also as securing impartial administration as between the liferenter and the fiar, have led to the adoption in most cases of trust machinery. Where a subject is placed in the hands of trustees with directions to pay the income to one beneficiary and to hold the fee for another, the first of these has what has been termed a beneficiary liferent; he has not a direct right in the subjects, but a *jus crediti* under the trust.[16] Where the bequest takes the form of a direction to trustees to pay the income of a trust estate to a beneficiary, the terms of the deed may show that the income was intended to comprise either more or less than would have fallen to a proper liferenter.[17] If, however, there is given a liferent *simpliciter*, it has been laid down that the obligations resting on the liferenter are the same whether the liferent is given directly or through the medium of a trust.[18]

A proper liferent cannot be constituted over fungibles which perish in use, but may be constituted over subjects which, though they wear out

[11] Erskine, *Inst.*, II, ix, 42.
[12] See para. 44.32, *supra*.
[13] Erskine, *Inst.*, II, ix, 56; *Inland Revenue* v. *Wemyss*, 1924 S.C. 284; *De Robeck* v. *Inland Revenue*, 1928 S.C. (H.L.) 34, *per* Lord Dunedin; *Miller* v. *Inland Revenue*, 1930 S.C. (H.L.) 49, *per* Lord Dunedin.
[14] *Ferguson* v. *Ferguson's Trs.* (1877) 4 R. 532, *per* Lord President Inglis.
[15] *MacLennan* v. *Scottish Gas Board*, 1985 S.L.T. 2.
[16] *Ker's Trs.* v. *Justice* (1868) 6 M. 627.
[17] *Miller's Trs.* v. *Miller*, 1907 S.C. 833, *per* Lord McLaren.
[18] *Johnstone* v. *Mackenzie's Trs.*, 1912 S.C. (H.L.) 106, at p. 109.

in time, yet waste by such slow degrees that they may continue fit for use for the full course of an ordinary life.[19] In *Rogers* v. *Scott*[20] it was held that the effect of a direction to trustees to allow the testator's widow the liferent of his farm and stock was to place on her the obligation to maintain the stock and leave it substantially of the same description, value and extent as it was when she received it. Where a liferent of a house along with its furniture is given, it has been held that the furniture, as an accessory to the possession of the house, cannot be removed from the house and used elsewhere.[21]

47.4 Capital or Income.—The liferenter is entitled to the fruits of the subject but not to anything which is part of the corpus or capital. As between the liferenter and the fiar, a receipt will fall to, and a charge will be borne by, one or other according as these are of the nature of capital or of income. Although no general rule can be laid down, certain tests have been suggested for use in determining to which category a receipt or charge belongs. In *Ross's Trs.* v. *Nicoll*[22] Lord McLaren observed: 'In general I should be disposed to hold that every payment to be made from a trust estate which does not involve a diminution of capital ought to be regarded as a payment out of income, whether that payment is made yearly or half-yearly or periodically at longer intervals. All such payments when made to the trust estate are to be regarded as part of the profit as distinguished from the corpus of the estate, and therefore, fall to be made over from the estate to the person who is beneficially entitled to the income.' Another suggested criterion (which is only a rough one and not decisive in every case) is 'that capital expenditure is a thing that is going to be spent once and for all, and income expenditure is a thing that is going to recur every year.'[23] Apart from such general considerations, there is a series of cases regarding timber and minerals which not only rule the right of the liferenter as to these but have been referred to as affording guidance by analogy in questions as to items of receipt or expenditure of a different kind.[24]

47.5 Rights in Timber.—The wood growing on an estate belongs as part of the corpus to the fiar. He has the right to thinnings and to all trees blown down in an 'extraordinary storm'; and he may cut wood but not so as to interfere with the amenity and shelter of an estate and thus affect the liferenter's enjoyment of it.[25] The liferenter, on the other

---

[19] Erskine, *Inst.,* II, ix, 40; *Miller's Trs.* v. *Miller, supra.*
[20] (1867) 5 M. 1078.
[21] *Cochran* v. *Cochran* (1755) Mor. 8280; 2 Bell's *Illustrations*, p. 141.
[22] (1902) 5 F. 146.
[23] *Vallambrosa Rubber Co.* v. *Farmer*, 1910 S.C. 519, *per* Lord President Dunedin; *British Insulated and Helsby Cables* v. *Atherton* [1926] A.C. 205, *per* Viscount Cave L.C. and Lord Atkinson.
[24] See, *e.g.* in *Davidson's Trs.* v. *Ogilvie*, 1910 S.C. 294 (copyright royalties).
[25] *Dickson* v. *Dickson* (1823) 2 S. 152; *Tait* v. *Maitland* (1825) 4 S. 247.

hand, is entitled to ordinary windfalls and, in the case of copse-wood cut periodically on reaching maturity, he has the benefit of the cutting when the proper time for it arrives. He may also cut wood at the sight of the fiar for repairing fences and other purposes of the estate.[26]

47.6 Rights in Minerals.—The returns from mineral workings are not strictly fruits of the soil which could be claimed as such by a liferenter, but 'if the owner of the soil, the fiar, creates a mineral estate by working or letting a particular seam of minerals, he thereby brings the proceeds of the minerals so worked or let within the category of fruits and within the right of usufruct.'[27] Accordingly, it is settled that a gift of liferent or direction to trustees to pay the income of the estate to a beneficiary includes the rents and royalties from mines either worked, or let although not worked, in the lifetime of the grantor or truster. On the other hand, returns from mines opened by his trustees after his death are not included unless the truster has directed his trustees to work the minerals.[28]

47.7 Bonuses: Price of Shares.—Where the subject liferented comprises shares in a company the dividends on these declared in the liferenter's lifetime are payable to him.[29] If a company, which has power under its constitution to increase its capital, pays a bonus out of accumulated profits which have been carried to reserve, it will depend on the action of the company whether the bonus falls to the liferenter or to the fiar. The accepted rule is that 'when a testator or settlor directs or permits the subject of his disposition to remain as shares or stock in a company, which has the power either of distributing its profits as dividend or of converting them into capital, and the company validly exercises this power, such exercise of its power is binding on all persons interested under him, the testator or settlor, in the shares, and consequently what is paid by the company as dividend goes to the tenant for life,[30] and what is paid by the company to the shareholder as capital, or appropriated as an increase of the capital stock in the concern, enures to the benefit of all who are interested in the capital.'[31] A cash payment out of accumulated profits prima facie belongs to the liferenter.[32] But in

[26] *Macalister's Trs. v. Macalister* (1851) 13 D. 1239.
[27] *Campbell v. Wardlaw* (1883) 10 R. (H.L.) 65, *per* Lord Watson.
[28] *Ranken's Trs. v. Ranken*, 1908 S.C. 3; *Naismith's Trs. v. Naismith*, 1909 S.C. 1380; *Campbell v. Wardlaw, supra*.
[29] *Re Wakley* [1920] 2 Ch. 205; *Re Marjoribanks* [1923] 2 Ch. 307. But there may be a question of apportionment as regards current dividends.
[30] This is the English equivalent of liferenter.
[31] *Bouch v. Sproule* (1885) 29 Ch.D. 635, at p. 653; approved L.R. 12 App.Cas. 385, at p. 397; *Blyth's Trs. v. Milne* (1905) 7 F. 799; *Howard's Trs. v. Howard*, 1907 S.C. 1274; *Hill v. Permanent Trustee Corporation* [1930] A.C. 720. The question was also discussed in connection with super-tax; see *Inland Revenue Commissioners v. Blott* [1921] 2 A.C. 171; *Inland Revenue Commissioners v. Fisher's Exrs.* [1926] A.C. 395.
[32] *Forgie's Trs. v. Forgie*, 1941 S.C. 188.

cases where a company declares a bonus and at the same time offers its shareholders additional shares to be paid up to an amount equivalent to the bonus, it is a question of fact, looking to the form and substance of the particular transaction, whether the real intention of the company was to distribute cash or to capitalise the profits by effecting a distribution of shares. Unless the fund from which the payment is made has been in fact capitalised the payment is income and falls to the liferenter, and a mere statement by the company that the payment is made as a capital payment will not alter its character.[33]

In the less usual case of companies which have no power to increase their capital, if the company accumulates profits and uses them for capital purposes, it may be regarded as having appropriated the profits to capital, so as to make the distribution of them among the shareholders a distribution of capital.[34]

When company shares belonging to a liferented estate are sold in the interval between two dividends, the liferenter is entitled to the portion of the price paid in respect of such part of the future dividend as has accrued at the date of the sale, but this portion is to be estimated in accordance with the dividend expected at the date of the sale and not with the dividend ultimately paid.[35]

47.8 Burdens Affecting Liferent.—Liferenters bear the annual and ordinary burdens on the subjects, such as feu-duties, taxes, repairs,[36] the premiums for insurance against fire,[37] and interest on bonds charged on the property.[38] They are not answerable for ordinary wear and tear, nor for loss due to accident or *vis major*. While ordinary repairs are chargeable against revenue, the cost of extraordinary repairs or of rebuilding or of executing work of a permanent nature the benefit of which will at the expiry of the liferent accrue to the fiars is chargeable against capital.[39]

47.9 Right of Occupancy.—This is to be distinguished from a liferent. In *Clark* v. *Clark*[40] a testator directed his trustees to give 'the use of' his house to his widow, and it was held that she had not a liferent of, but a

[33] *Re Bates* [1928] Ch. 682; *Hill* v. *Permanent Trustee Corporation, supra.*
[34] *Bouch* v. *Sproule, supra.* There are also a number of decisions as to casualties, of which *Macdougall's Factor* v. *Watson,* 1909 S.C. 215; *Edgar's Trs.* v. *Edgeware,* 1915 S.C. 175; and *Stewart's Trs.* v. *Stewart,* 1931 S.C. 691, are the most recent. In view of the Feudal Casualties (Scotland) Act 1914, it is unnecessary to do more than refer to these.
[35] *McLeod's Trs.* v. *McLeod,* 1916 S.C. 604; *Cameron's Factor* v. *Cameron* (1873) 1 R. 21.
[36] *Johnstone* v. *Mackenzie's Trs.,* 1912 S.C. (H.L.) 106; Erskine, II, ix, 61; Bell, *Prin.,* § 1061.
[37] *Brown* v. *Soutar & Meacher* (1870) 8 M. 702; *Glover's Trs.* v. *Glover,* 1913 S.C. 115.
[38] *Glover's Trs.* v. *Glover, supra.*
[39] *Shaw's Trs.* v. *Bruce,* 1917 S.C. 169; *Preston* v. *Preston's Trs.* (1853) 15 D. 271; *Templeton* v. *Mags. of Ayr,* 1912 1 S.L.T. 421.
[40] (1871) 9 M. 435.

right to occupy, the house; and being merely an occupant she had no right to let it but, on the other hand, was liable only for rates and assessments in respect of occupancy and not for those burdens such as feu-duty, repairs or landlord's taxes which fall upon a liferenter. Whether a liferent of a house or this more limited right is given depends on the language used by the testator, but it has been thought to point to a gift of liferent that under the testator's directions no funds are left in the hands of the trustees to meet the annual burdens on the house.[41]

47.10 **Alimentary Liferents.**—A provision for the aliment of an individual is from its nature personal to him and not assignable by him or attachable by his creditors.[42] No man can effectually make an alimentary provision in favour of himself, for it is against the policy of the law that a person should have the beneficial enjoyment of his property and yet put it beyond the reach of his creditors.[43] Nor is it possible to make a right of fee alimentary;[44] if, therefore, trustees are directed to hold a subject or fund for, or to make it over to, a beneficiary in fee, any declaration that it is alimentary is of no effect. But a person may confer on another a liferent or annuity on the condition that it is to be alimentary. The proper mode of effecting this is to declare expressly that what is given is alimentary; but equivalents have been admitted as, *e.g.* where the right was declared to be exclusive of the beneficiary's acts and deeds and the diligence of creditors[45] or for his maintenance and support.[46] A mere exclusion of the rights of creditors without any restraint on the beneficiary's power to assign is ineffectual.[47] Further, in order to make the right alimentary, there must be a continuing trust under which the trustees are empowered to retain in their hands the subject out of which the liferent or annuity is given.[48] Formerly, however, the law recognised

---

[41] The cases are reviewed in *Johnstone* v. *Mackenzie's Trs., supra*; *Milne's Trs.* v. *Milne*, 1920 S.C. 456; see also *Montgomerie-Fleming's Trs.* v. *Carre*, 1913 S.C. 1018; and *Countess of Lauderdale*, 1962 S.C. 302.

[42] Stewart, *Diligence*, p. 93. The English equivalent of a wife's alimentary liferent, the 'restraint upon anticipation,' has been abolished; Married Women (Restraint upon Anticipation) Act 1949. The protection has been held to apply only to the extent of a reasonable provision for the beneficiary, the excess being open to diligence: *Livingstone* v. *Livingstone* (1886) 14 R. 43.

[43] 'That were to impose a condition contrary to law, that a man should at the same time be fiar, and yet not have power to affect the fee.'—*Creditors of Primrose* v. *Heirs* (1744) Mor. 15501, at p. 15504; *Kennedy* v. *Kennedy's Trs.*, 1953 S.C. 60; but see *infra* for ante-nuptial settlement by a woman.

[44] *Wilkie's Trs.* v. *Wight's Trs.* (1893) 21 R. 199, *per* Lord Rutherfurd Clark: *Watson's Trs.* v. *Watson*, 1913 S.C. 1133; *Miller* v. *Miller's Trs.*, 1953 S.L.T. 225.

[45] *Dewar's Trs.* v. *Dewar*, 1910 S.C. 730; see also Stewart, *Diligence*, p. 95. An interesting and instructive decision is that in *Textile Pensions Trust* v. *Custodian of Enemy Property*, 1947 S.C. 528.

[46] *Arnold's Trs.* v. *Graham*, 1927 S.C. 353; followed in *Miller* v. *Miller's Trs.*, 1953 S.L.T. 225.

[47] *Douglas, Gardner & Mill* v. *Mackintosh's Trs.*, 1916 S.C. 125.

[48] *Forbes's Trs.* v. *Tennant*, 1926 S.C. 294. As to alimentary rights in a question with creditors, see para. 53.10, *infra*.

one exception to the rule that prohibits any person from settling money so as to secure the income to himself and at the same time place it beyond the reach of his creditors, namely, that a woman might in her ante-nuptial marriage contract create an alimentary interest in her own favour in property derived from herself or from her father's estate.[49] This alimentary protection, which continued during the subsistence of the marriage but terminated with the dissolution of the marriage unless effective provision had been made in the deed constituting the liferent for the continuation of its alimentary character thereafter,[50] has now been abolished.[51]

An alimentary liferent, once accepted,[52] cannot be assigned or discharged nor can the administration of the trustees in whom the liferented subject is vested be terminated by any act or deed of the liferenter.[53] Moreover, if the liferenter acquires the fee of the subjects, his alimentary liferent does not merge in the fee; but the liferent and fee continue to subsist as separate rights. Hence, where a widower, who had, under his marriage contract, an alimentary liferent in his wife's estate, became entitled under her will to the fee it was held that he could not compel the marriage contract trustees to denude in his favour.[54]

It was formerly the rule that, even where a liferent provision made by a married woman in her ante-nuptial contract in her own favour out of her own funds was not declared to be alimentary, she could not, during the marriage, bring that provision to an end.[55] But in *Beith's Trs.* v. *Beith*[56] this authority was held to have been superseded as a result of supervening legislation as to the status and capacity of married women; and a married woman who had no issue and was admittedly past the age of child-bearing was held entitled to demand repayment of the funds provided by her, although her husband was still alive. There is no room for the extension of that decision to a case where the liferent is alimentary;[57] but under the Trusts (Scotland) Act 1961[58] the court may

---

[49] *Dempster's Trs.* v. *Dempster*, 1949 S.C. 92; *Sturgis's Tr.* v. *Sturgis*, 1951 S.C. 637; *Martin* v. *Bannatyne* (1861) 23 D. 705; see also *Neame* v. *Neame's Trs.*, 1956 S.L.T. 57; *Strange, Petr.*, 1966 S.L.T. 59.
[50] *Dempster's Trs., supra; Sturgis's Tr., supra; Pearson, Petr.*, 1968 S.C. 8; *Sutherland, Petr.*, 1968 S.C. 200.
[51] Law Reform (Husband and Wife) (Scotland) Act 1984, s. 5(1)(a).
[52] *Douglas-Hamilton* v. *Duke and Duchess of Hamilton's Trs.*, 1961 S.C. 205; as to a testamentary provision, see *Ford* v. *Ford*, 1961 S.C. 122.
[53] *White's Trs.* v. *White* (1877) 4 R. 786; *Hughes* v. *Edwardes* (1892) 19 R. (H.L.) 33; *Cuthbert* v. *Cuthbert's Trs.*, 1908 S.C. 967; *Coles, Petr.*, 1951 S.L.T. 308; *Kennedy* v. *Kennedy's Trs.*, 1953 S.C. 60. But see para. 46.6, *supra.*
[54] *Main's Trs.* v. *Main*, 1917 S.C. 660; *Howat's Trs.* v. *Howat*, 1922 S.C. 506; *Anderson's Trs., Petrs.*, 1932 S.C. 226.
[55] *Menzies* v. *Murray* (1875) 2 R. 507.
[56] 1950 S.C. 66.
[57] *Kennedy* v. *Kennedy's Trs.*, 1953 S.C. 60; *Chrystal's Trs.* v. *Haldane*, 1960 S.C. 127.
[58] s. 1(4); see para. 46.6, *supra.*

now, if certain conditions are satisfied, authorise an arrangement varying or revoking an alimentary liferent and making new provisions in its place.

47.11 Transmission and Extinction of Liferents.—Where the liferent is not alimentary, it may be transmitted by the liferenter to another by means of an assignation followed by intimation. The assignee will then become entitled to the fruits and income of the liferented subjects in place of the liferenter. 'The proper right of liferent is intransmissible, *ossibus usufructuarii inhaeret*. When the profits of the liferented subject are transmitted to another, the right becomes merely personal, for it entitles the assignee to the rent, not during his own life, but his cedent's, and is therefore carried by simple assignation without seisin.'[59]

A liferent is extinguished by the liferenter's death, by consolidation with the fee where the liferent and fee come to be vested in the same individual, unless the liferent is alimentary, and by discharge by the liferenter. Where a deed provides for the destination of the fee on the lapse or expiry of a liferent, failure to take the liferent by the person entitled to it may constitute a lapse.[60]

47.12 Apportionment of Income.—Under the common law, while the interest of money and the profits of subjects 'arising from continual daily labour' (such as 'fishings, collieries, saltworks') were held to vest *de die in diem*, annuities, rents and payments connected with land did not vest till the term of payment arrived.[61] Accordingly, if an annuitant entitled to an annuity payable at the usual terms for the preceding half-year died between terms, his representative could claim no part of the payment due at the next term after his death, although that might have taken place on the day preceding the term. But the common law has been altered by statute. The Apportionment Act 1870 (which superseded an Act passed in 1834), provides that all rents, annuities (which include salaries and pensions), dividends (including bonuses) and other periodical payments in the nature of income 'shall, like interest on money lent, be considered as accruing from day to day, and shall be apportionable in respect of time accordingly.' The Act applies equally to the liability to make, as to the right to receive, such payments.[62] The dividends to which it applies are those of public companies which include all companies registered under the Companies Acts;[63] the profits of a partnership do not fall under the Act.[64] A bonus, although

[59] Erskine, *Inst.*, II, ix, 24; *Ker's Trs.* v. *Justice* (1868) 6 M. 627, *per* Lord Curriehill.
[60] *Whitelaw's Trs.* v. *Whitelaw's Trs.*, 1981 S.L.T. 94.
[61] Erskine, *Inst.*, II, ix, 64–66; Bell's *Comm.*, ii, 8; see also *Balfour's Exrs.* v. *Inland Revenue*, 1909 S.C. 619.
[62] *Learmonth* v. *Sinclair's Trs.* (1878) 5 R. 548; *Bishop of Rochester* v. *Le Fanu* [1906] 2 Ch. 513.
[63] *Re Lysaght* [1898] 1 Ch. 115; *Re White* [1913] 1 Ch. 231.
[64] *Jones* v. *Ogle* (1872) L.R. 8 Ch. 192; *Re Cox's Trusts* (1878) 9 Ch.D. 159.

occasional and not periodical, is apportionable;[65] but payments by a company to its shareholders which are not declared or expressed to be made in respect of some definite period have been held not to be so, as they cannot be considered as accruing from day to day.[66] Independently of the statute it has been held that where a testator directs his trustees to pay to a liferenter the free income of the *universitas* of a mixed estate, this is to be regarded as equivalent to the gift of the income from a fund and accordingly that the right to the income vests *de die in diem*.[67]

The Act does not apply to sums payable under policies of assurance[68] or to any case in which it is expressly stipulated that no apportionment shall take place.[69] Thus, where a testator bequeathed shares in a company with the declaration that these should carry the dividend accruing thereon at the testator's death[70] or that the dividends should be paid to the legatee as received,[71] apportionment was held to be excluded for the benefit of the legatee. The Act will not, however, be excluded merely by inference.[72]

Further Reading

Dobie, *Manual of the Law of Liferent and Fee* (1941).
McLaren, *Wills and Succession* (3rd ed., 1894 and Supplement 1934).
Rankine, *Landownership* (4th ed., 1909).

---

[65] *Re Griffiths* (1879) 12 Ch.D. 655.
[66] *Re Jowitt* [1922] 2 Ch. 442.
[67] *Andrew's Trs.* v. *Hallett*, 1926 S.C. 1087, and cases there cited.
[68] s. 6. In *Inland Revenue* v. *Henderson's Exrs.*, 1931 S.C. 681, it was held that the Act did not apply in a question as to income tax.
[69] s. 7.
[70] *Re Lysaght, supra.* See *Re Edwards* [1918] 1 Ch. 142.
[71] *Macpherson's Trs.* v. *Macpherson*, 1907 S.C. 1067.
[72] *Tyrell* v. *Clark* (1852) 2 Drewry 86.

CHAPTER 48

48.1 **Marriage** is said by Erskine[1] to be truly a contract; but although this is true in the sense that it is founded on the consent of the parties, it is much more than a contract. It differs indeed in many important respects from other contracts. Thus, the conditions of marriage and the rights and duties created by it are not left to be regulated by the parties, nor can it be dissolved at their pleasure; and it affects the status both of the parties and of their issue. Hence it is recognised that the general rules of the law of contract cannot be applied indiscriminately to the relationship of marriage.[2]

48.2 **Impediments to Marriage in General.**—Under the common law a pupil could not marry, although if the married pair cohabited after puberty this gave force to the marriage.[3] But the Age of Marriage Act 1929[4] enacted that a marriage between persons either of whom is under the age of 16 is void. So also there can be no valid marriage if one of the parties was at the time of the marriage, by reason of insanity[5] or intoxication,[6] incapable of understanding the nature of the engagement entered into. Moreover, although a party may appear to have consented to marriage, yet, if it be proved that, through error, fraud, duress or design,[7] there was no true consent to marry, or to marry the other party to the ceremony[7a], the marriage will be declared null.[8] Family pressure can be of such force as to amount to duress excluding consent.[9] But the error or influence must be such as to exclude the consent to marriage; error, however grave, inducing the marriage, but not excluding such

[1] *Inst.*, I, vi, 2; and see Walton, *Husband and Wife* (3rd ed., 1951), Chap. 1.
[2] *Lang* v. *Lang*, 1921 S.C. 44, and see *Scott* v. *Kelly*, 1992 S.L.T. 915, where averments of facility and circumvention and of undue influence were held irrelevant in an action of declarator of nullity of marriage.
[3] Erskine, *Inst.*, I, vi, 3; Fraser, I, 53.
[4] Now Marriage (Scotland) Act 1977, s. 1.
[5] Erskine, *Inst.*, I, vi, 2; *Park* v. *Park*, 1914 1 S.L.T. 88; *Graham* v. *Graham* (1907) 15 S.L.T. 33.
[6] *Johnson* v. *Brown* (1823) 2 S. 495, and in Férgusson's *Consistorial Law*, p. 229.
[7] *Orlandi* v. *Castelli*, 1961 S.C. 113.
[7a] As in *Militante* v. *Ogunwomoju* [1993] 2 F.C.R. 355.
[8] See Clive, pp. 84–97 on lack of true consent.
[9] *Mahmood* v. *Mahmood*, 1993 S.L.T. 589; *Mahmud* v. *Mahmud*, 1994 S.L.T. 599.

consent, does not afford ground for annulling it. Thus, the fact that a wife has either concealed from her husband that she was pregnant at the date of the marriage or has induced him to marry her by fraudulently stating that her condition was due to him does not entitle him to have the marriage declared null.[10] The fact that one party is disabled by a rule of his religion from entering into the marriage does not render it void.[11] If consent be given, marriage is thereby perfected although the parties may never cohabit. *Consensus non concubitus facit matrimonium.*

48.3 **Forbidden Degrees.**—Marriage is forbidden within certain degrees of relationship. These are now defined by the Marriage (Scotland) Act 1977, but it is necessary to consider the law in force prior thereto, as it continues to govern the validity of all marriages contracted before January 1, 1978.

(a) *Marriages before January 1, 1978.*

Two modes of computing the degrees of relationship require to be considered for this purpose. By the Roman law method of calculation, which differs from that of the Canon law in this respect, the relationship in the collateral line between two persons is computed by counting from one to the common ancestor and thence downwards to the other party: thus uncle and nephew are held to be related in the third degree, and first cousins[12] in the fourth degree. By Canon law it is computed by counting from either of the parties to the common ancestor and, where the parties are not equally removed from that ancestor, the longer line of descent from him is taken: thus uncle and nephew are held to be related in the second degree (the nephew being two degrees removed from his grandfather) as also are first cousins. By the Act 1567, c. 15[13] (which refers to the eighteenth chapter of the Book of Leviticus), it was enacted that seconds in blood—by which was meant first cousins according to the computation of the Canon law—and all more distantly related might lawfully marry, and no distinction was made between the full blood and the half blood. Further, the same degrees as were forbidden in consanguinity (relationship between parties descended from a common ancestor) were forbidden in affinity (the relationship between one of the married parties and the blood relations of the other).[14] Marriage was moreover forbidden, by an extension beyond the terms of the Act, where the relationship of blood or affinity was, no matter how remote the degree, such that one of the parties might be deemed to

---

[10] *Lang* v. *Lang*, 1921 S.C. 44. See *MacDougall* v. *Chitnavis*, 1937 S.C. 390. *Contra* in England: Matrimonial Causes Act 1973, s. 12(*f*).

[11] *MacDougall* v. *Chitnavis, supra.* But religious belief regarding the prerequisites of marriage may preclude consent; *Mahmud* v. *Mahmud*, 1977 S.L.T. (Notes) 17; *Akram* v. *Akram*, 1979 S.L.T. (Notes) 87. As to capacity and conflict of laws, see Clive, Chap. 9, and *Bliersbach* v. *McEwen*, 1959 S.C. 43.

[12] Sometimes known as 'cousins-german'.

[13] Applied in *H.M. Advocate* v. *Martin & Aikman*, 1917 J.C. 8.

[14] *Purves' Trs.* v. *Purves* (1895) 22 R. 513.

stand *in loco parentis* to the other, as grand uncle and grand niece.[15] On these rules exceptions were engrafted by various Acts which were repealed and re-enacted to permit marriage after divorce by the Marriage (Enabling) Act 1960,[16] which permitted marriage between a man and a woman who was the sister, aunt or niece of the whole or half blood of a former wife of his (whether she was living or not) and between a man and a woman who was formerly the wife of his brother, uncle or nephew of the whole or half blood (whether living or not), provided that such a marriage was not invalid by the law of the domicile of either party thereto. Illegitimate relationship within the second degree was equally with legitimate a bar to marriage,[17] but the prohibition which depended on the fact that one of the parties stood *in loco parentis* to the other was based on a legal fiction and did not extend to cases where the relationship was merely a natural one.[18] For the purpose of the law relative to marriage the adopter of a child and the child itself were deemed to be within the prohibited degrees of consanguinity and that notwithstanding a subsequent adoption of the child by another.[19]

(b) *Marriages on or after January 1, 1978.*

For these marriages the previous law on forbidden degrees is replaced by a statutory code which includes an exhaustive list of relationships within which parties may not marry.[20] The effect is that marriage is forbidden between parties related within the third degree of consanguinity whether in direct line of ascent and descent or, according to the Roman law (not the Canon law) method of calculation, in the collateral line. As before, no distinction is made in consanguineous relationships between the full blood and the half blood.[21] In affinity the prohibition is confined to relationships within the second degree of ascent and descent and within that degree no longer extends to marriages with a grandparent of a former spouse or a former spouse of a grandchild.[22] The only marriages now prohibited where the relationship is by affinity are therefore those with the former spouse of a grandparent or with the grandchild of a former spouse, and between persons related in the first degree. In certain circumstances, however, such marriages may be allowed. Marriage with the former spouse of a parent or grandparent, or

---

[15] Erskine, *Inst.* I, vi, 9.

[16] Now repealed but still applicable to marriages before January 1, 1978.

[17] *Robertson* v. *Channing,* 1928 S.L.T. 376. See Clive (2nd ed.), p. 91 and Clive and Wilson (1st ed.), pp. 89–90, *sed contra* Fraser, i, pp. 131–132. Opinions were reserved in *Philp's Trs.* v. *Beaton, infra.*

[18] *Philp's Trs.* v. *Beaton,* 1938 S.C. 733.

[19] Adoption Act 1958, s. 13(3); *cf.* Adoption Act 1950, s. 10(1), Adoption of Children Act 1949, s. 11(1).

[20] Marriage (Scotland) Act 1977, ss. 2 and 27(3). Sched. 1 contains an exhaustive list of the forbidden relationships, to which reference should be made.

[21] s. 2(2)(*a*).

[22] s. 2 and Sched. 1, as amended by the Marriage (Prohibited Degrees of Relationship) Act 1986.

with the child or grandchild of a former spouse, is permitted if both parties are aged 21 or over at the time of the marriage and the younger party has not at any time before becoming 18 lived in the same household as the other party and been treated by him as a child of his family.[23] Marriage with the parent of a former spouse or the former spouse of a child can only take place if both parties are 21 or over and, in the case of marriage with the parent of a former spouse, both the former spouse and the other parent of the former spouse have died or, in the case of marriage with the former spouse of a child, both the child and the other parent of the child have died.[24] Both in consanguinity and affinity the relationship exists although traced through or to any person whose parents were not married to one another.[25] The law on adoptive relationships is unchanged.

48.4 Subsisting Prior Marriage.—A marriage with one who is at the time married to a third party is *ipso jure* null, although either, or both, of the contracts are irregular.[26]

48.5 Impotency.—Where either of the parties, being of suitable age, is incapable of sexual intercourse, the marriage may be declared null.[27] It is not essential that there should be structural incapacity; invincible repugnance may amount to impotency. Impotency is not, however, an absolute bar to marriage, but only affords ground on which it may be annulled;[28] and there may be circumstances which so plainly imply a recognition of the existence and validity of the marriage by the complaining spouse as to make it inequitable and contrary to public policy that he or she should be permitted to impugn it.[29] The defender in the action is entitled to an opportunity of undergoing remedial medical treatment.[30] The action may be brought by the impotent spouse on the ground of his own irremediable impotency.[31] It has been held that an action of declarator of nullity on the ground of impotency was not out of time 24 years after the pretended marriage.[32]

[23] s. 2(1A).
[24] s. 2(1B).
[25] 1977 Act, s. 2(4).
[26] See Clive, pp. 76–77; Marriage (Scotland) Act 1977, s. 2(3)(b).
[27] G. v. G., 1924 S.C. (H.L.) 42. See discussion in Clive, pp. 100–105. As to what does and does not constitute physical consummation, see *Baxter* v. *B.* [1948] A.C. 274; *Cackett* v. *C.* [1950] P. 253; *W.* v. *W.* [1967] 1 W.L.R. 1554 and *J.* v. *J.*, 1978 S.L.T. 128.
[28] See *Administrator of Austrian Property* v. *Von Lorang*, 1926 S.C. 598, *per* Lord President Clyde at p. 616; 1927 S.C. (H.L.) 80; *S.G.* v. *W.G.*, 1933 S.C. 728; as to onus, see *M.* v. *W. or M.*, 1966 S.L.T. 152.
[29] *C.B.* v. *A.B.* (1885) 12 R. (H.L.) 36, *per* Lord Selbourne L.C. at p. 38, Lord Watson at p. 45; *L.* v. *L.*, 1931 S.C. 477; *A.B.* v. *C.B.*, 1961 S.C. 347. A.I.H. and adoption of children generally have this effect (see Clive, pp. 103–104).
[30] *W.Y.* v. *A.Y.*, 1946 S.C. 27.
[31] *S.* v. *F.*, 1945 S.C. 202; *H.* v. *H.*, 1949 S.C. 587.
[32] *Allardyce* v. *A.*, 1954 S.C. 419. See this case too on the subject of expenses in an action of nullity.

48.6   Constitution of Marriage: Regular Marriage.—A marriage is regular or irregular according to its mode of constitution. A regular marriage may be either a religious or a civil marriage.[33] In either case each party to the marriage must submit to the registrar of the district in which the marriage is to be solemnised a notice of intention to marry accompanied by a birth certificate, and where either party has previously been married, evidence of the dissolution of the previous marriage.[34] There are special provisions where a party to a marriage intended to be solemnised in Scotland is residing in another part of the United Kingdom or is not domiciled in any part of the United Kingdom and also for marriages outside Scotland where a party resides in Scotland.[35] After receipt of the notice, the registrar, if satisfied that there is no legal impediment, or if so informed by the Registrar General, issues a marriage schedule which is the authority for the solemnisation of the marriage.[36] The schedule may not, however, be issued before the expiry of fourteen days from receipt of the notice unless on the written request of a party to the marriage and with the authority of the Registrar General.[37]

At any time before the solemnisation of a marriage any person may submit an objection in writing to the registrar.[38] Where the objection relates to a matter of misdescription or inaccuracy the registrar may, with the approval of the Registrar General, make any necessary correction. In any other case he must, pending consideration of the objection by the Registrar General, suspend the completion or issue of the marriage schedule or, if a marriage schedule has already been issued for a religious marriage, notify the celebrant of the objection and advise him not to solemnise the marriage.[39] If the Registrar General is satisfied, on consideration of an objection, that there is a legal impediment to the marriage he must direct the registrar to take all reasonable steps to ensure that the marriage does not take place. If, on the other hand, he is satisfied that there is no legal impediment, he must so inform the registrar and the marriage schedule may then be completed and issued, if that has not already been done, so that the marriage may proceed.[40] There is a legal impediment for this purpose where the parties to the marriage are within the forbidden degrees of relationship or are of the same sex or where either of them (a) is already married, (b) will be under the age of 16 on the date of the solemnisation of the intended marriage, (c) is incapable of understanding the nature of a marriage ceremony or of consenting to

[33] Marriage (Scotland) Act 1977, s. 8.
[34] *Ibid.*, s. 3(1).
[35] ss. 3(4) and (5) and (7).
[36] s. 6.
[37] s. 6(4).
[38] s. 5(1).
[39] s. 5(2).
[40] ss. 5(3) and 6(1).

marriage, or (d) is not domiciled in Scotland and his marriage in Scotland to the other party would be void *ab initio* according to the law of his domicile.[41]

A religious marriage may be solemnised by a minister of the Church of Scotland, a minister, clergyman, pastor or priest of a religious body prescribed by regulations, or other approved celebrant.[42] The marriage schedule must be produced to the celebrant and the parties to the marriage and two witnesses (who must be persons professing to be 16 years or over) must be present. Where the celebrant belongs to the Church of Scotland or a prescribed religious body, the marriage must be in accordance with a form recognised as sufficient by the church or body to which the celebrant belongs.[43] In any other case, the statutory requirement is that the form of solemnisation must include a declaration by the parties, in the presence of each other, the celebrant and the witnesses, that they accept each other as husband and wife and a declaration thereafter by the celebrant that they are husband and wife.[44]

A civil marriage is solemnised by an authorised registrar. No form is prescribed.[45] A marriage schedule must be available and the parties and witnesses must be present.[46]

It is an offence for anyone, who is not within the classes of persons authorised under the Act to solemnise marriages, to conduct a marriage ceremony in such a way as to lead the parties to believe that he is solemnising a valid marriage, or for the celebrant of a religious marriage to solemnise it without at the time having the marriage schedule available to him, or for either the celebrant of a religious marriage or an authorised registrar to solemnise a marriage without both parties being present.[47] Provided both parties were present at the marriage ceremony and the marriage has been registered, its validity is not to be questioned in any legal proceedings on the ground of failure to comply with a requirement or restriction imposed by the Act.[48] This provision does not save a marriage which has not been registered; thus, where parties had failed to comply with the necessary formalities, with the consequence that no schedule was available and registration could not take place, the marriage was void.[49]

48.7 Irregular Marriage.—Before 1940 an irregular marriage might be constituted by any one of three modes: (1) declaration *de praesenti*, *i.e.*

[41] s. 5(4).
[42] s. 8(1). See also Marriage (Prescription of Religious Bodies) (Scotland) Regulations 1977 (S.I. 1977 No. 1670).
[43] s. 14(*a*).
[44] ss. 14(*b*) and 9(3).
[45] s. 8(1).
[46] s. 19(2).
[47] s. 24.
[48] s. 23A as inserted by the Law Reform (Misc. Provs.) (Scotland) Act 1980, s. 22(1)(*d*).
[49] *Saleh* v. *Saleh*, 1987 S.L.T. 633.

consent to marriage there and then; (2) promise *subsequente copula*; and (3) cohabitation with habit and repute. No marriage can be contracted by the first two modes since July 1, 1940,[50] but the law relating to them may remain of importance for some time to come as questions of legitimacy and rights of succession may depend on the validity of an irregular marriage contracted many years before.[51] The statement of the law relating to all three modes is therefore retained, although only the third is now valid.

48.8 Declaration *de Praesenti*.—Declaration *de praesenti* meant the consent by the parties to present marriage.[52] It was sufficient that such consent be proved to have been given, whether in writing or orally, although no witnesses were present[53] and although the actual time and place at which the consent was given were not proved.[54] But the court had to be satisfied that the parties truly intended to contract marriage. Hence, although there was a writing expressing the parties' consent to marriage, the question might arise whether it was drawn up for the purpose of marriage or for some other purpose and, if so, the court would investigate the whole facts of the case, including the circumstances in which the consent was given and the subsequent conduct of the parties, in order to determine whether there was truly consent to present marriage.[55] But a person who had signed a mutual declaration of marriage was not allowed to plead that he had signed it with a mental reservation, where his conduct induced the other party to believe that he was consenting to marriage.[56] No such marriage was valid unless one of the parties had his or her usual place of residence in Scotland or had lived in Scotland for 21 days preceding the marriage.[57]

48.9 Promise *Subsequente Copula*.—Here there was promise of marriage, followed by intercourse permitted upon the faith of the promise.[58] The promise could not be proved by parole evidence. At one time it was established that the promise might be proved by writ or oath,[59] but in

---

[50] Marriage (Scotland) Act 1939, s. 5 now repealed; Marriage (Scotland) Act 1939 (Commencement) Order 1940. *Cf.* Marriage (Scotland) Act 1977, s. 21, which makes provision for the registration of decrees of declarator of such marriages.

[51] 1939 Act, s. 8.

[52] *Dalrymple* v. *Dalrymple* (1811) 2 Haggard 54; *Walker* v. *Macadam* (1813) 1 Dow 148, 5 Pat. 675; Clive, pp. 39–43.

[53] *Dysart Peerage Case* (1881) 6 App.Cas. 489; *Petrie* v. *Petrie*, 1911 S.C. 360; Fraser, i, 295.

[54] *Leslie* v. *Leslie* (1860) 22 D. 993.

[55] *Davidson* v. *Davidson*, 1921 S.C. 341; *Imrie* v. *Imrie* (1891) 19 R. 185; *Dunn* v. *Dunn's Trs.*, 1930 S.C. 131; *Courtin* v. *Elder*, 1930 S.C. 68.

[56] *Duran* v. *Duran* (1904) 7 F. 87.

[57] Marriage (Scotland) Act 1856, s. 1 (repealed by Marriage (Scotland) Act 1939, s. 8); see *Gray* v. *Gray*, 1941 S.C. 461.

[58] See Clive, pp. 43–48.

[59] Fraser, i, 386; Bell's *Prin.*, § 1518; Dickson on *Evidence*, § 545.

Longworth v. *Yelverton*[60] the opinion was expressed in the House of Lords that section 36 of the Court of Session Act 1830 made reference to the defender's oath incompetent. Where the promise was to be proved by writ, the writing need not contain an express promise: it was sufficient that there could be collected from its terms that a promise was given.[61] There was no limitation on the mode of proof of intercourse. It must have been allowed on the faith of the promise, otherwise there was no marriage; but if it followed the promise this would generally be presumed.[62] This presumption, however, and the presumption that there was present consent to marriage might be rebutted as, *e.g.* by some inference to be drawn from the subsequent conduct of the parties.[63] It was formerly suggested that a declarator was necessary to constitute the marriage, but it was latterly settled that the promise and intercourse in reliance on it in themselves constituted the marriage.[64] It was not, however, recognised by the law until it had been judicially affirmed, but once affirmed the marriage dated from the intercourse.[65] The declarator might be brought at the instance of the man[66] or of a child of the parties.[67]

48.10 Cohabitation with Habit and Repute.[68]—This is the only form of irregular marriage now recognised by the law. The consent by which marriage is constituted may be proved by the cohabitation, or living together at bed and board, of a man and woman who are generally reputed husband and wife. The repute must be general and consistent, so preponderating as to leave no substantial doubt.[69] The fact that the cohabitation was at the outset adulterous is not fatal to the constitution of marriage by continuance of the cohabitation with repute after the parties become free to marry;[70] nor is the fact that at the beginning of the cohabitation there was no intention of marriage.[71] The consent to marriage may be proved by cohabitation with habit and repute where spouses have previously been married to one another and divorced.[72] But, although there have been the requisite cohabitation and repute,

[60] (1867) 5 M. (H.L.) 144.
[61] *Ross* v. *Macleod* (1861) 23 D. 972; *Lindsay* v. *Lindsay*, 1927 S.C. 395.
[62] *Morrison* v. *Dobson* (1869) 8 M. 347; *Maloy* v. *Macadam* (1885) 12 R. 431.
[63] *N.* v. *C.*, 1933 S.C. 492.
[64] *Mackie* v. *Mackie*, 1917 S.C. 276.
[65] *N.* v. *C., supra, per* Lords Sands and Morison.
[66] *Hardie* v. *Boog*, 1931 S.L.T. 198; see *Lindsay* v. *Lindsay, supra.*
[67] *X.* v. *Y.*, 1921 1 S.L.T. 79.
[68] See Clive, pp. 48–67.
[69] See *Petrie* v. *Petrie*, 1911 S.C. 360, *per* Lord Johnston at p. 367; *Hamilton* v. *Hamilton* (1839) 2 D. 89, *per* Lord Fullerton; *cf. Donnelly* v. *Donnelly's Exr.*, 1992 S.L.T. 13, where there was some division in the repute.
[70] *Campbell* v. *Campbell* (1867) 5 M. (H.L.) 115; *De Thoren* v. *Wall* (1876) 3 R. (H.L.) 28. *Cf. Low* v. *Gorman*, 1970 S.L.T. 356.
[71] *Hendry* v. *Lord Advocate*, 1930 S.C. 1027; see also *A.B.* v. *C.D.*, 1957 S.C. 415, cohabitation after void marriage.
[72] *Mullen* v. *Mullen*, 1991 S.L.T. 205.

there is no marriage if it be shown that the parties had not in fact any matrimonial intention.[73] In most of the cases in which marriage has been thus established the cohabitation has continued for a considerable period.[74] A period of cohabitation lasting only 11 months has, however, been held to be sufficient;[75] there is no minimum period which must elapse.[75a]

48.11 Registration of Marriages.—In the case of religious marriages there is a statutory provision requiring that the marriage schedule be signed by the parties, the witnesses and the celebrant and transmitted to the district registrar within three days of the marriage. The registrar must then cause particulars of the marriage to be entered in the register of marriages.[76] Similar provisions apply to a civil marriage.[77] Irregular marriages are registered following intimation to the Registrar General by the Principal Clerk of Session of the decree of declarator.[78]

48.12 Legal Effects of Marriage: Adherence.—It is the duty of spouses to adhere to each other. The traditional view, supported by some judicial authority, was that the right of regulating the household belonged to the husband as its head, that he had therefore the right to fix the place of residence of the spouses and that, in the absence of just cause absolving her from that duty,[79] the wife must follow her husband wherever he was.[80] That is no longer the law.[81] Formerly, a spouse might exclude the other from his or her house but might, at any rate in the case of the husband, put himself in desertion by doing so.[82] Residence within the matrimonial home is, however, now protected by the Matrimonial Homes (Family Protection) (Scotland) Act 1981.[83] The court cannot, however, compel a spouse to adhere. In modern practice actions for adherence had become virtually unknown,[84] except when aliment was also sought and they were abolished in 1984.[85] Breach of the duty of

---

[73] *Bairner* v. *Fels*, 1931 S.C. 674; *Mackenzie* v. *Scott*, 1980 S.L.T. (Notes) 9.
[74] Fraser, i, 400; *Wallace* v. *Fife Coal Co.*, 1909 S.C. 682. A modern case, mainly concerned with assessing the evidence available, is *Nicol* v. *Bell*, 1954 S.L.T. 314 (cohabitation for 22 years).
[75] *Shaw* v. *Henderson*, 1982 S.L.T. 211.
[75a] *Kamperman* v. *MacIver*, 1994 S.L.T. 763.
[76] Marriage (Scotland) Act 1977, s. 15.
[77] *Ibid.*, ss. 19(3) and (4).
[78] *Ibid.*, s. 21.
[79] As to which, see para. 48.23, *infra.*
[80] *Stewart* v. *Stewart*, 1959 S.L.T. (Notes) 70.
[81] Law Reform (Husband and Wife) (Scotland) Act 1984, s. 4.
[82] *MacLure* v. *MacLure*, 1911 S.C. 200; *Millar* v. *Millar*, 1940 S.C. 56. In *Burgess* v. *Burgess*, 1969 S.L.T. (Notes) 22, it was accepted, apparently without hesitation, that a wife who excluded her husband from the matrimonial home was in desertion. Under the law as it then stood, however, a wife ordinarily had no obligation to aliment her husband and so no obligation to provide a home.
[83] See para. 48.16.
[84] But see *Stirling* v. *Stirling*, 1971 S.L.T. 322.
[85] Law Reform (Husband and Wife) (Scotland) Act 1984, s. 2(1).

adherence is recognised as a ground for divorce;[86] and the courts will not lend their aid to enforce a contract for voluntary separation.[87] Such contracts are revocable by either spouse at any time.[88] A revocation is not effectual unless the party seeking to revoke is genuinely willing to adhere.[89] The contract may be revoked by deed or letter or by the institution of an action of divorce or separation, and falls if the parties resume cohabitation. If parties have been living separately under a contract of separation, the court will grant decree for arrears of aliment which have become due in terms of the contract in the past but not for aliment in the future.[90]

The law formerly refused an action of reparation by one spouse against the other on the ground of the intimate relationship between them, but each may now sue the other in respect of a wrongful or negligent act or omission;[91] and a spouse may sue the other's employer for damages on the basis of vicarious liability.[92] An action of removing by one spouse against the other is competent, if they stand in the relation of landlord and tenant,[93] and an action based on contract is also competent.[94]

48.13 **Aliment.**—At common law a husband was bound to aliment his wife if she was willing to live with him,[95] even if she was a confessed adulteress.[96] The amount of aliment which would be awarded by the court depended on the rank and manner of life of the spouses.[97] The Married Women's Property (Scotland) Act 1920[98] for the first time placed on a wife, who had a separate estate or had separate income more than reasonably sufficient for her own maintenance, the obligation of providing her husband with maintenance if he was unable to maintain

[86] See para. 48.24, *infra.*
[87] *Macdonald* v. *Macdonald's Trs.* (1863) 1 M. 1065.
[88] Erskine, *Inst.*, I, vi, 30; Fraser, ii, 911 *et seq.*; *Drummond* v. *Rollock* (1624) Mor. 6152; *Macdonald* v. *Macdonald's Trs., supra.*
[89] *Palmer* v. *Bonnar*, 25 January 1812, F.C.; *Hood* v. *Hood* (1871) 9 M. 449; *Dickson* v. *Hunter* (1831) 5 W. & S. 458, *per* Lord Brougham L.C.
[90] *Livingston* v. *Begg* (1777) Mor. 6153; *Bell* v. *Bell*, 22 February 1812, F.C.; *Hood* v. *Hood, supra.*
[91] Law Reform (H. & W.) Act 1962, s. 2.
[92] *Webb* v. *Inglis*, 1958 S.L.T. (Notes) 8.
[93] *Millar* v. *Millar*, 1940 S.C. 56; see *Labno* v. *Labno*, 1949 S.L.T. (Notes) 18 *re* ejection.
[94] *Horsburgh* v. *Horsburgh*, 1949 S.C. 227.
[95] *Beveridge* v. *Beveridge*, 1963 S.C. 572.
[96] *Donnelly* v. *Donnelly*, 1959 S.C. 97.
[97] Erskine, *Inst.*, I, vi, 19; *Thomson* v. *Thomson* (1890) 17 R. 1091; *Scott* v. *Scott* (1894) 21 R. 853; and see *Alexander* v. *Alexander*, 1957 S.L.T. 298, where the husband's regular expenditure of capital was taken into account.
[98] s. 4. The earlier Acts are: Conjugal Rights (Scotland) Amendment Act 1861, and the amending Act of 1874; Married Women's Property (Scotland) Act 1877; Married Women's Policies of Assurance (Scotland) Act 1880; Married Women's Property (Scotland) Act 1881. See *Beith's Trs.* v. *Beith*, 1950 S.C. 66. for an interesting review of the changes and their effects.

himself. Aliment of spouses is now regulated by the Family Law (Scotland) Act 1985 under which each spouse owes an obligation of aliment to the other.[99] The obligation is to provide such support as is reasonable in the circumstances having regard to the needs and resources of the parties, their earning capacities and all the circumstances of the case.[1] As only very limited tax relief is now available to those paying aliment,[2] it is more appropriate when computing their resources to consider income net of tax.[3] Among the circumstances of which the court may, if it thinks fit, take account are any support, financial or otherwise, which an obligant gives, whether or not under an alimentary obligation, to a person whom he maintains as a dependant in his household.[4] On the other hand no account is to be taken of any conduct of a party unless it would be manifestly inequitable to leave it out of account.[5] The parents of a person under 18 years of age or, in some circumstances, under 25, have an obligation of aliment which, if that person be married, is concurrent with the obligation owed by his or her spouse.[6] There is no fixed order of liability in such cases but the court, in deciding the amount of any aliment to be paid by one of the obligants is to have regard, among the other circumstances of the case, to the obligation owed by the others.[7]

A claim for aliment only may be brought in the Court of Session or in the sheriff court and, unless the court considers it inappropriate, a claim for aliment may be made in proceedings for divorce, separation or declarator of marriage or of nullity, or relating to orders for financial provision or concerning rights and obligations in relation to children or concerning parentage or legitimacy or proceedings of any other kind where the court considers it appropriate to include a claim for aliment.[8] Where such a claim is made, the court also has power to award interim aliment.[8a] An action or claim is competent although the claimant is living in the same household as the defender.[9] It is a defence that the defender has made an offer, which it is reasonable to expect the person concerned to accept, to receive that person into his household and to fulfil the obligation of aliment.[10] In considering the reasonableness of an offer, the court is to have regard to any conduct, decree or other circumstances which appear to be relevant but an agreement by husband

---

[99] s. 1(1).

[1] ss. 1(2) and 4.

[2] See Income and Corporation Taxes Act 1988, s. 347B.

[3] *Wiseman* v. *Wiseman,* 1989 S.C.L.R. 757; *Pryde* v. *Pryde,* 1991 S.L.T. (Sh.Ct.) 26; *cf. MacInnes* v. *MacInnes,* 1990 G.W.D. 13–690.

[4] s. 4(3)(a). *Pryde* v. *Pryde, supra.*

[5] s. 4(3)(b).

[6] s. 1(1). See para. 49.7, *infra.*

[7] s. 4(2).

[8] s. 2.

[8a] s. 6(1).

[9] s. 2(6).

[10] s. 2(8).

and wife to live apart is not of itself to be regarded as making it unreasonable to expect an offer to be accepted.[11]

In granting decree in an action for aliment, the court may backdate its award,[11a] but such backdating does not affect any award of interim aliment.[11b] A decree for aliment may be varied or recalled if there has been a material change of circumstances;[12] demonstrating that the earlier award was made on information which turned out to be incorrect or incomplete does not constitute a change of circumstances.[12a] On a material change of circumstances a person who has entered into an agreement to pay aliment may apply to the court for variation of the amount or termination of the agreement.[13] Before such an application can be made, however, an obligation of aliment must continue to be owed under the Act; the right to seek a variation does not extend to couples who are cohabiting or are divorced.[13a] Variations of awards, including those made in actions brought before the commencement of the 1985 Act, may be backdated, but the power to backdate variations does not extend to the variation of an agreement;[14] nor to variation of awards of interim aliment.[15] Any provision in an agreement which purports to exclude liability for future aliment or restrict the right to claim aliment is of no effect unless it was fair and reasonable in all the circumstances of the agreement when it was entered into.[16]

48.14 *Jus Mariti.*—The effect of marriage under the common law on the position and property of the wife was profoundly modified by a series of statutes beginning in the middle of last century and concluding with the above-mentioned Act of 1920.[16a] Many points formerly of importance have ceased to be of more than historical interest, and are, therefore, not dealt with in the succeeding paragraphs.

Of the rights accruing to the husband on marriage, the most important was the *jus mariti*. This was the right of property in the wife's moveable estate vested by law in the husband. Marriage had the effect of an assignation to him of the whole moveable estate belonging to the wife at the date of the marriage or which she might acquire during its subsistence. The husband became *ipso jure* owner of this property; he might sell or dispose of it at his pleasure; and his creditors might attach it for his debts.[17] But the *jus mariti* might be excluded by a renunciation

---

[11] s. 2(9).
[11a] s. 3(1)(c).
[11b] *McColl* v. *McColl*, 1993 S.L.T. 617.
[12] s. 5(1).
[12a] *Walker* v. *Walker*, 1995 S.L.T. 375.
[13] s. 7(2).
[13a] *Drummond* v. *Drummond*, 1995 G.W.D. 11–587.
[14] *Ellerby* v. *Ellerby*, 1991 S.C.L.R. 608.
[15] *McColl, supra.*
[16] s. 7(1).
[16a] See n. 98, *supra.*
[17] *Fraser* v. *Walker* (1872) 10 M. 837.

or discharge in an ante-nuptial marriage contract; and a provision in a conveyance or bequest of property to a wife by a third party that it should belong to the wife exclusive of the *jus mariti* was effectual. There were also certain goods known as paraphernalia which did not fall under the right; these consisted of the wife's wearing apparel, her personal ornaments, the receptacles in which these were kept, and things given to her as paraphernalia by the husband at or before marriage.[18]

Since the husband became entitled to the wife's moveable estate, he was liable for the whole of the moveable debts contracted by her before the marriage. This liability, originally unlimited, was by the Married Women's Property (Scotland) Act 1877 limited to the property received by the husband from or in right of his wife at, before or after the marriage. That provision was repealed by the Law Reform (Husband and Wife) (Scotland) Act 1984[19] which, however, enacts that a husband shall not be liable, by reason only of being her husband, for any debts incurred by his wife before marriage. By the Married Women's Property (Scotland) Act 1881, the *jus mariti* was abolished in the case of marriages contracted after the date of the passing of the Act, July 18, 1881.

48.15 *Jus Administrationis*: **Wife's Obligations.**—Under the common law the husband became curator of the wife, and his consent to her acts in regard to her property was necessary. In the case of property falling under the *jus mariti*, the husband as owner might dispose of it as he pleased; but where that right did not apply (as in the case of heritable property), or where it was excluded, the *jus administrationis* had the effect of disabling the wife from effectually disposing of it without her husband's consent. All obligations undertaken by a wife without her husband's consent were (with some exceptions) null;[20] and all personal obligations, even if undertaken with his concurrence, were (again with some exceptions) also null.[21] With some minor exceptions the wife could not sue without her husband being conjoined as her curator, and, if she were sued, it was necessary that he should be called along with her as a defender.

In these matters the Act of 1920 effected a radical alteration of the law. A married woman was no longer under the curatory of her husband;[22] the *jus administrationis* was wholly abolished, and she had the same power of disposing of her estate as if she were unmarried; she was capable of entering into contracts and incurring obligations, and

---

[18] Erskine, *Inst.*, I, vi, 15; Fraser, i, 770.

[19] s. 6.

[20] Erskine, *Inst.*, I, vi, 20–24; Fraser, i, 519, 802.

[21] Erskine, *Inst.*, I, vi, 25; *Harvey* v. *Chessels* (1791) Bell's *Cases,* 255; *Jackson* v. *MacDiarmid* (1892) 19 R. 528; *Galbraith* v. *Provident Bank* (1900) 2 F. 1148.

[22] The 1920 Act (s. 2) provided that a minor wife was under the curatory of her husband during her minority but that provision was repealed by the Law Reform (Husband and Wife) (Scotland) Act 1984, s. 3.

might sue and be sued, as if she were unmarried, and her husband was no longer liable under contracts or obligations entered into or incurred by her on her own behalf. If the wife was deserted by, or living apart from, her husband, her contracts for the supply of goods to herself or her children bound her estate, but without prejudice to the right of the creditor to recover the price from the husband if he would have been liable under the former law. Finally, the Family Law (Scotland) Act 1985, which repeals the 1920 Act,[23] provides that marriage shall not of itself affect the respective rights of parties to a marriage in relation to their property nor shall it affect their legal capacity.[24]

48.16 Rights in the Matrimonial Home.—The effect of the abolition of the *jus mariti* and the *jus administrationis* was that, with the exception of certain rights which might emerge on death or divorce, marriage had little effect on the property rights of spouses. Unless they chose to create joint property rights each remained owner of his or her separate estate including any property acquired after marriage. In principle that is still the law.[25] Substantial practical modifications have, however, been introduced in relation to the matrimonial home by the Matrimonial Homes (Family Protection) (Scotland) Act 1981. That Act confers rights of occupancy in the matrimonial home on a 'non-entitled spouse' (*i.e.* the other spouse, where one spouse is entitled, by virtue of ownership or tenancy or permission given by a third party, to occupy the matrimonial home).[26] As occupancy rights can only be held by 'a spouse', the scheme of the Act does not extend beyond the grant of decree of divorce;[27] power to make analogous orders on the grant of decree of divorce is contained in the Family Law (Scotland) Act 1985.[28] Certain provisions of the 1981 Act are extended to a cohabiting couple.[28a] The rights conferred by the 1981 Act comprehend a right to continue in an existing occupation and to enter into and occupy the matrimonial home where the non-entitled spouse is not already in occupation; they may be exercised together with any child of the family.[29] The non-entitled spouse may renounce his or her rights but only in relation to a particular matrimonial home or intended matrimonial home and only if he or she affirms before a notary public that the renunciation is made freely and without coercion of any kind.[30] Matrimonial home is defined as meaning any house, caravan, houseboat or other structure provided or made available by one or both of the spouses as a family residence (or which, having been provided or made

[23] s. 28 and Sched. 2.
[24] s. 24.
[25] See Family Law (Scotland) Act 1985, s. 24.
[26] s. 1.
[27] s. 5(1)(*a*).
[28] s. 14(2)(*d*).
[28a] s. 18.
[29] s. 1(1A).
[30] s. 1(6).

864 HUSBAND AND WIFE

available by one or both of the spouses, has become a family residence).[31] It does not include a home provided by one spouse as his separate residence.[32]

If the entitled spouse refuses to allow the non-entitled spouse to exercise his right to enter and occupy the matrimonial home, that right may be exercised only with leave of the court.[33] Either spouse may apply to the court for an order declaring, enforcing or restricting occupancy rights or regulating their exercise or protecting the rights of the applicant spouse in relation to the other spouse.[34] If it appears that the application relates to a matrimonial home, the court must make an order declaring the rights of the applicant spouse, if applied for,[35] and otherwise is to make such order in relation to the application as appears to it just and equitable having regard to all the circumstances of the case including the conduct of the spouses, their respective needs and financial resources, the needs of any child of the family, the use of the matrimonial home in relation to any trade, business or profession of either spouse, and whether the entitled spouse has offered suitable alternative accommodation to the non-entitled spouse.[36] The court also has power to regulate the possession or use of furniture and plenishings in the matrimonial home.[37]

An order enforcing, restricting, regulating or protecting occupancy rights is not to have the effect of excluding the non-applicant spouse from the matrimonial home.[38] Either spouse may, however, apply to the court for an exclusion order suspending the occupancy rights of the other spouse.[39] The court is to make such an order if that is necessary for the protection of the applicant or any child of the family from any conduct or threatened or reasonably apprehended conduct of the non-applicant spouse which would be injurious to the physical or mental health of the applicant or child unless it appears to the court that the making of an order would be unjustified or unreasonable having regard to all the circumstances.[40] An exclusion order terminates on decree of divorce being pronounced.[41] Where the parties have been cohabitees, an

---

[31] s. 22.
[32] Ibid.
[33] s. 1(3).
[34] s. 3(1).
[35] There is authority for the view that a declarator under s. 3(1) is a necessary precondition for the obtaining of the other orders listed in s. 3: Welsh v. Welsh, 1987 S.L.T. (Sh.Ct.) 30.
[36] s. 3(3).
[37] s. 3(2). In Welsh supra it was held that it remains competent to pronounce an interdict at common law against the removal of furniture and plenishings.
[38] s. 3(5).
[39] s. 4.
[40] s. 4. The circumstances to be considered include the various matters noticed above in relation to orders enforcing or restricting occupancy rights, etc. (ss. 3(3)(a) to (8)). For factors influencing the granting of an interim exclusion order see Bell v. Bell, 1983 S.L.T. 224; Smith v. Smith, 1983 S.L.T. 275; Colagiacomo v. Colagiacomo, 1983 S.L.T. 559; Brown v. Brown, 1985 S.L.T. 376; McCafferty v. McCafferty, 1986 S.L.T. 650.
[41] s. 5(1)(a).

application may be made for the granting of occupancy rights.[41a] If such an order is in force, or if the parties are entitled or permitted by a third party to occupy the house concerned, other orders regarding occupancy rights, or an exclusion order, may be pronounced without it being necessary for the parties to continue to cohabit.[41b] It has also been observed that the parties need not be living together at the time when a grant of occupancy rights is sought, the only necessity being that the parties were cohabiting at the date of the conduct giving rise to the application.[41c]

The continued exercise by a non-entitled spouse of his occupancy rights is not to be prejudiced by reason only of any dealing by the entitled spouse relating to the home and a third party is not by reason of such dealings entitled to occupy the matrimonial home or any part of it.[42] There are certain situations in which this protection does not apply. The principal exclusions are where the non-entitled spouse has, in the required form,[43] consented to the dealing or renounced his or her occupancy rights or, where a sale to a third party has occurred, the third party has acted in good faith and there was exhibited to him by the seller either an affidavit that, at the time of the dealing, the property was not a matrimonial home in relation to which a spouse of the seller had occupancy rights, or an *ex facie* valid renunciation or consent by the non-entitled spouse.[44] Where both spouses are 'entitled' spouses, the rights of each are also protected[45] and the court has power to refuse division and sale of the matrimonial home.[46] Provision is made for dispensing with consent to dealing, for protection of occupancy rights against arrangements intended to defeat them and for transfer of tenancies.[47] Any interlocutor pronounced by the court dispensing with the consent of the non-entitled spouse must, however, relate to a specific proposed dealing; dispensation cannot, therefore, be obtained without production to the court of information regarding such a dealing.[48]

48.17 Wife's *Praepositura*: Housekeeping Allowance: Household Goods.—Where spouses were living together the wife was at common law presumed to be *praeposita negotiis domesticis*,[49] and, as such,

---

[41a] s. 18(1).
[41b] *Armour* v. *Anderson*, 1994 S.L.T. 1127.
[41c] *Ibid.*
[42] s. 6.
[43] Prescribed by S.I. 1982 No. 971—consent can be either narrated *in gremio* of a deed effecting the deal signed by the consenter, or given in a separate deed.
[44] s. 6(3).
[45] s. 9.
[46] s. 19; see para. 40.15.
[47] ss. 7 and 11 to 13. On transfer of tenancy see *McGowan* v. *McGowan*, 1986 S.L.T. 112.
[48] *O'Neill* v. *O'Neill*, 1987 S.L.T. (Sh.Ct.) 26; *Fyfe* v. *Fyfe*, 1987 S.L.T. (Sh.Ct.) 38.
[49] 'Entrusted with the charge of domestic affairs.'

authorised to pledge her husband's credit for the price of goods necessary for the family (such as food, clothing, medical attendance and furniture) purchased by her.[50] This presumption rested on the fact that the ordering of household necessities was usually entrusted to the wife; and where the house of a widower was managed by his daughter, the father was on similar grounds held liable on contracts for such goods entered into by the daughter.[51] The goods had to be of the kind suitable to the husband's position in life; and if the tradesman supplied the goods in reliance upon the wife's credit alone, he could not hold the husband liable. The legal presumption of the wife's *praepositura* has now been abolished. A married woman is no longer as a matter of law to be presumed to have been placed by her husband in charge of his domestic affairs.[52] A mandate may, however, be implied from circumstances or a husband may give his wife express authority to make contracts on his behalf, in which case he will be liable, on the ordinary principles of agency, on contracts within the scope of the authority conferred.

The common law rule was that a husband might at his pleasure terminate the *praepositura*. He might do so formally by means of inhibition or, without resorting to inhibition, he might, by notification to a tradesman, free himself from liability to that tradesman. Procedure by inhibition has been abolished.[53]

At common law, a wife was bound to account to her husband for her intromissions with money received as *praepositura*,[54] but the Married Women's Property Act 1964 altered the law that savings made by the wife from such money remained the husband's property.[55] The Act provided that money derived from any allowance made by the husband for the expenses of the matrimonial home or for similar purposes, or property acquired out of such money, should, in the absence of agreement to the contrary, be treated as belonging to the husband and wife in equal shares. This was judicially construed as embracing football pool prize money won by a wife whose husband averred that she had taken the stake money from her housekeeping allowance.[56] The 1964 Act has now been superseded by the Family Law (Scotland) Act 1985 which provides that if any question arises (whether during or after a marriage) as to the right of a party to a marriage to money derived from any allowance made by either party for their joint household expenses or for similar purposes, or to any property acquired out of such money, the money or property shall, in the absence of any agreement to the

---

[50] Erskine, *Inst.*, I, vi, 26.

[51] *Hamilton* v. *Forrester* (1825) 3 S. 572; see also *Debenham* v. *Mellon* (1880) 6 App.Cas. 24.

[52] Law Reform (Husband and Wife) (Scotland) Act 1984, s. 7.

[53] *Ibid.*

[54] *Ireland* v. *Ireland*, 1954 S.L.T. (Notes) 13.

[55] See *Preston* v. *Preston*, 1950 S.C. 253, and cases cited therein.

[56] *Pyatt* v. *Pyatt*, 1966 S.L.T. (Notes) 73.

contrary, be treated as belonging to each party in equal shares.[57] Moreover, in any question as to the respective rights of ownership in any household goods obtained in prospect of or during the marriage, other than by gift or succession from a third party, there is a presumption, unless the contrary is proved, that each spouse has a right to an equal share in the goods.[58]

48.18 Donations between Spouses.—Under the common law a donation by one spouse to the other during marriage was revocable by the donor. This is no longer so.[59]

48.19 Policies of Assurance.—By the Married Women's Policies of Assurance (Scotland) Act 1880 passed before the abolition of the *jus mariti* and *jus administrationis*, a married woman was enabled to effect a policy on the life of herself or her husband for her separate use and exclusive of these rights. The statute also contains a provision now of more practical importance that a policy, effected by a married man on his own life and expressed on the face of it to be for the benefit of his wife or children or both, shall be deemed a trust for these. 'Children' includes adopted children.[60] Delivery of the policy is not required,[61] as it is enacted that when effected it is to vest in the husband and his representatives, or any other trustee nominated, in trust for the purposes so expressed, 'and shall not otherwise be subject to his control, or form part of his estate, or be liable to the diligence of his creditors, or be revocable as a donation, or reducible on any ground of excess or insolvency.' If, however, the policy was effected with intent to defraud creditors, or if the person insured is made bankrupt within two years from its date, the creditors are entitled to repayment of the premiums out of the proceeds of the policy.[62] Any right to bring a statutory challenge of a gratuitous alienation is expressed to be without prejudice to the operation of section 2.[63] The 1880 Act has been held to apply to a policy taken out by a widower for behoof of his children,[64] and to an endowment policy under which the sum was payable at a fixed date to the husband, whom failing his widow, where the husband had predeceased that date.[65] The trust is for the interest of the wife or children as that interest is expressed in the policy; it may be an interest vesting at once in the

[57] s. 26.
[58] s. 25.
[59] Married Women's Property (Scotland) Act 1920, s. 5 now repealed by Family Law (Scotland) Act 1985, s. 28 and Sched. 2. See also 1985 Act, s. 24.
[60] Adoption (Scotland) Act 1978, s. 39.
[61] *Jarvie's Trs.* v. *Jarvie's Trs.* (1887) 14 R. 411.
[62] s. 2.
[63] Bankruptcy (Scotland) Act 1985, s. 34(7).
[64] *Kennedy's Trs.* v. *Sharpe* (1895) 23 R. 146. It does not apply to a policy taken out by an unmarried man for his future wife on the eve of his marriage: *Coulson's Trs.* v. *Coulson* (1901) 3 F. 1041, *per* Lord Justice-Clerk Macdonald.
[65] *Chrystal's Trs.* v. *Chrystal,* 1912 S.C. 1003.

beneficiaries or, on the other hand, contingent on their surviving the husband.[66] If the interest has vested in the wife, then although she predeceases her husband, the proceeds of the policy on his death will form part of her estate,[67] but his estate is entitled to receive out of the proceeds of the policy repayment of the amount of the premiums paid since the wife's death.[68] The policy may be surrendered by the trustee with, and it may be even without, the consent of the beneficiary,[69] but the trust created by the policy cannot *stante matrimonio* be revoked or put an end to by the husband even with the consent of his wife and children.[70] By the Married Women's Policies of Assurance (Scotland) (Amendment) Act 1980 trustees are given wide powers of dealing with the policy so far as not at variance with the terms or purposes of the trust[71] and beneficiaries are empowered, subject to the terms of the policy to assign their interest or renounce it.[72] The powers of approval and authorisation of trust variation given to the court by the Trusts (Scotland) Act 1961 are exercisable in relation to any trust constituted by section 2 of the 1880 Act[73] and the terms of settlement of the policy may now be varied or set aside by the court on divorce.[74]

48.20 **Judicial Separation.**—The grounds recognised by the common law as entitling a spouse to a decree of judicial separation were adultery and cruelty. The Licensing (Scotland) Act 1903[75] added a third ground, namely, habitual drunkenness, by which was meant such drunkenness as rendered the person 'at times dangerous to himself or herself or others or incapable of managing himself or herself and his or her affairs.' The grounds justifying judicial separation are, however, now equiparated with the grounds for divorce.[76]

48.21 **Dissolution of Marriage.**—By the law of Scotland marriage cannot be dissolved till death, except by divorce. Until January 1, 1977 the grounds of divorce were adultery, wilful desertion, incurable insanity, cruelty, sodomy and bestiality. Divorce for adultery was introduced at the Reformation and rested on common law. Wilful desertion was first enacted as a ground of divorce in 1573 and re-enacted by the Divorce

---

[66] *Chrystal's Trs.* v. *Chrystal, supra,* per Lord Johnston.
[67] *Cousins* v. *Sun Life Assurance Society* [1933] 1 Ch. 126.
[68] *Bilham* v. *Smith* [1937] 1 Ch. 636.
[69] *Schumann* v. *Scottish Widows' Fund* (1886) 13 R. 678; Married Women's Policies of Assurance (Scotland) (Amendment) Act 1980, s. 2(2)(*f*).
[70] *Scottish Life Assurance Co.* v. *Donald* (1901) 9 S.L.T. 348; *Edinburgh Life Assurance Co.* v. *Balderston,* 1909 2 S.L.T. 323; *cf. Barras* v. *Scottish Widows' Fund* (1900) 2 F. 1094.
[71] s. 2(2).
[72] s. 3.
[73] s. 4.
[74] Family Law (Scotland) Act 1985, ss. 14(2)(*h*) and (6).
[75] s. 73. See *Cox* v. *Cox,* 1942 S.C. 352; *Hutchison* v. *Hutchison,* 1945 S.C. 427; and *Rooney* v. *Rooney,* 1962 S.L.T. 294.
[76] Divorce (Scotland) Act 1976, s. 4.

(Scotland) Act 1938 which also added the other four grounds. The previous grounds of divorce are, however, all now abolished by the Divorce (Scotland) Act 1976 which purports to substitute irretrievable breakdown of marriage as the sole ground of divorce. The question of jurisdiction in divorce and other consistorial causes has already been considered.[77] In such actions, if the defender cannot be found, there must be edictal service and also service on the older children[78] of the marriage and on one or more of the next-of-kin, if these are known and are resident in the United Kingdom. Such persons may apply for leave to lodge defences.[79] Decree will not be granted if there is collusion between the parties,[80] and collusion is a ground for reducing a decree but the requirement that the pursuer take the oath of calumny, swearing that there has been no collusive agreement with the defender, has been abolished.[81] It is competent in this connection for the Lord Advocate to appear and lead proof.[82] Collusion means 'permitting a false case to be substantiated or keeping back a just defence.'[83] 'Mutual desire that a decree ... should be obtained, and mutual action to facilitate this end, are not collusion, if there be no fabrication or suppression.'[84] In all consistorial actions the facts must be proved.[85] The evidence must consist of or include evidence other than that of a party to the marriage,[86] unless the action satisfies the criteria set out in the Evidence in Divorce Actions (Scotland) Order 1989.[87] In proof of adultery, although a confession by a wife, supported by an extract birth certificate purporting to be signed by herself and a paramour, has been held insufficient,[88] and the practice of leading evidence from only the defender and his paramour has been disapproved,[89] the evidence of the defender and his paramour,[90] or even of the paramour alone,[91] can be sufficient. A finding of adultery in any previous proceedings and, in relation to the other grounds of divorce, an extract decree of separation if granted to the pursuer on substantially the same facts, may afford sufficient proof provided the evidence of the pursuer is also received.[92]

[77] Courts and Jurisdiction, Chap. 2, *supra*.
[78] Boys of 14 or over and girls of 12 or over.
[79] Rule of Court 49.16; Sheriff Court Rule 11A(6).
[80] See *Cooper* v. *Cooper*, 1987 S.L.T. (Sh.Ct.) 37; *cf. Sinclair* v. *Sinclair*, 1986 S.L.T. (Sh.Ct.) 54.
[81] 1976 Act, s. 9.
[82] Court of Session Act 1988, s. 19.
[83] *Walker* v. *Walker*, 1911 S.C. 163; *Fairgrieve* v. *Chalmers*, 1912 S.C. 745.
[84] *Administrator of Austrian Property* v. *Von Lorang*, 1926 S.C. 598, *per* Lord Sands at p. 628; 1927 S.C. (H.L.) 80. See *Riddell* v. *Riddell*, 1952 S.C. 475.
[85] Civil Evidence (Scotland) Act 1988, s. 8(1).
[86] *Ibid.*, s. 8(3).
[87] S.I. 1989 No. 582—straightforward undefended cases on the grounds of non-cohabitation where there are no children under 16 and no financial claims are made.
[88] *MacKay* v. *MacKay*, 1946 S.C. 78.
[89] *Cooper* v. *Cooper*, 1987 S.L.T. (Sh.Ct.) 37.
[90] *Sinclair* v. *Sinclair*, 1986 S.L.T. (Sh.Ct.) 54.
[91] s. 8, as read with s. 1(1).
[92] Law Reform (Misc. Provs.) (Scotland) Act 1968, s. 11; Divorce (Scotland) Act 1976, s. 3 and Sched. I, para. 4.

The Divorce (Scotland) Act 1976 provides that decree of divorce may be granted if, but only if, it is established in accordance with the provisions of the Act that the marriage has broken down irretrievably.[93] The seeming concentration on irretrievable breakdown as the sole ground of divorce is, however, misleading. The provisions of the Act on establishing irretrievable breakdown enact that on proof of any one of a series of matters, the marriage is to be taken to have broken down irretrievably with the result that irretrievable breakdown as such does not require to be proved. Each of these matters is, therefore, in effect, a distinct ground of divorce. The grounds so considered are:

   (1)   the adultery of the defender,
   (2)   behaviour of the defender of such a kind that the pursuer cannot reasonably be expected to cohabit with him,
   (3)   desertion of the pursuer by the defender for a period of two years,
   (4)   non-cohabitation for a period of two years combined with the defender's consent to divorce, and
   (5)   non-cohabitation for a period of five years.[94]

If, at any time before granting decree in an action of divorce, it appears to the court that there is a reasonable prospect of reconciliation it must continue the action to enable reconciliation to be attempted. Cohabitation during such a continuation is not to be taken into account for the purposes of the action and does not therefore, whatever its length, constitute condonation of adultery nor bar divorce for desertion.[95] Any ground of divorce, including adultery, may now be established by proof on a balance of probabilities.[96] An action for divorce may still be dismissed if the averments are irrelevant.[96a]

48.22 Divorce for Adultery.—Carnal connection is necessary to constitute adultery. Artificial insemination by a donor is not adultery.[97] The court will not order a wife or child to submit to blood tests for the purpose of obtaining evidence relevant to allegations of adultery.[98] It is no defence to an action of divorce for adultery that there has been adultery on the part of the pursuer: cross actions of divorce are competent.[99] Condonation or forgiveness of the offence by the aggrieved spouse is, however, a good defence.[1] In order that there may be condonation there must have been genuine belief that the adultery alleged to have

[93] s. 1(1).
[94] s. 1(2).
[95] s. 2(1).
[96] s. 1(6).
[96a] *Smith* v. *Smith*, 1994 S.C.L.R. 244.
[97] *Maclennan* v. *Maclennan*, 1958 S.C. 105.
[98] *Whitehall* v. *Whitehall*, 1958 S.C. 252.
[99] See, for example, *Connell* v. *Connell*, 1950 S.C. 505.
[1] s. 1(3). As to onus of proof, see *Andrews* v. *Andrews*, 1961 S.L.T. (Notes) 48; also *Mitchell* v. *Mitchell*, 1947 S.L.T. (Notes) 8.

been condoned has been committed.[2] Mere suspicion of infidelity will not found the plea.[3] Condonation will not be inferred from anything less than cohabitation, by which is meant living together as man and wife.[4] Verbal forgiveness or even sexual intercourse will not alone suffice. It is not essential to the plea of condonation that the spouses should have shared the same bed.[5] Provided the cohabitation is confined to a period of three months from the date of continuation or resumption, continuation or resumption of cohabitation after knowledge of adultery does not amount to condonation.[6] A condition attached to condonation is inept. If the offence is condoned, it can never thereafter be founded on as a ground of divorce but, if there is alleged to have been subsequent adultery, it may be used in evidence as throwing light on suspicious conduct with the same, or even a different, paramour.[7]

Another plea in defence to an action of divorce for adultery is *lenocinium* or connivance.[8] If a husband gives facilities, and creates opportunities, for adultery by his wife, he cannot obtain divorce for the offence at which he has thus connived. But this plea will not be applicable if the husband has done no more than refrain from dissuading his wife: there must be active facilitation of, or encouragement to, commission of the offence.[9] Delay, however long, to take proceedings will not, without other circumstances pointing to acquiescence or condonation, operate as a bar to an action for divorce on the grounds either of adultery[10] or desertion.[11]

48.23 **Divorce for Behaviour Justifying Non-Cohabitation.**—It is a ground of divorce that, since the date of the marriage, the defender has at any time behaved (whether or not as a result of mental abnormality and whether such behaviour has been active or passive) in such a way that the pursuer cannot reasonably be expected to cohabit with the defender.[12] This ground comprehends cruelty, including statutory habitual drunkenness, and also sodomy and bestiality under the previous

---

[2] *Paterson* v. *Paterson*, 1938 S.C. 251; as to knowledge of the extent of the adultery, see *Ralston* v. *Ralston* (1881) 8 R. 371, and *Steven* v. *Steven*, 1919 2 S.L.T. 239.

[3] *Collins* v. *Collins* (1882) 10 R. 250, and (1884) 11 R. (H.L.) 19.

[4] 1976 Act, ss. 1(3) and 13(2).

[5] *Edgar* v. *Edgar* (1902) 4 F. 632, *per* Lord McLaren at p. 635.

[6] Divorce (Scotland) Act 1976, s. 2(2).

[7] *Collins* v. *Collins*, *supra*; *Robertson* v. *Robertson* (1888) 15 R. 1001; also *Nicol* v. *Nicol*, 1938 S.L.T. 98.

[8] 1976 Act, s. 1(3).

[9] *Thomson* v. *Thomson*, 1908 S.C. 179; *Wemyss* v. *Wemyss* (1866) 4 M. 660. See also *Gallacher* v. *Gallacher*, 1928 S.C. 586; 1934 S.C. 339; *Hannah* v. *Hannah*, 1931 S.C. 275. Lenocinium, most inappropriate if the term is used precisely, has been regarded as attributable to a wife: *Riddell* v. *Riddell*, 1952 S.C. 475.

[10] *Johnstone* v. *Johnstone*, 1931 S.C. 60; *Macfarlane* v. *Macfarlane*, 1956 S.C. 472, at p. 476. As to delay in bringing nullity proceedings, see *Allardyce* v. *Allardyce*, 1954 S.L.T. 334.

[11] *Monahan* v. *Monahan*, 1930 S.C. 221.

[12] 1976 Act, s. 1(2)(*b*).

law, but it is broader than these grounds and is not to be equiparated with them. An association by a spouse with another member of the opposite sex, without evidence of adultery can amount to unreasonable behaviour.[13] Unfounded allegations of infidelity and incest, even if unlikely to be repeated, may be sufficient.[14] While it is competent to found on behaviour at any time since the date of the marriage, that behaviour must be such that the pursuer cannot, at the date of the proof, reasonably be expected to cohabit with the defender. Accordingly, behaviour in the remote past, especially if followed by continued cohabitation, will normally be relevant only in so far as it is part of, or throws light on, more recent conduct. In assessing whether it is reasonable to expect the pursuer to cohabit with the defender, however, the court may take into account events occurring since the separation of parties, such as a new association formed by the pursuer with a third party, provided such events can be seen as causally connected with the defender's behaviour.[15] There is no requirement that the behaviour should be extensive in time, and a single serious incident may suffice.[16] Although the behaviour need not have been aimed at the pursuer, the defender's intention is not irrelevant because it may affect the reasonableness of expecting continued cohabitation. Behaviour suggests something more than a state of affairs or a mental or physical condition[17] but, as the behaviour may be passive, it may consist in neglect or inactivity. It is immaterial that the defender's conduct is conditioned by insanity or mental deficiency, but a purely automatic reaction or an action or state of inactivity which is determined by unavoidable physical constraint is probably not behaviour for the purposes of the Act. There will normally be a close relation between the reasonableness of the defender's conduct and the reasonableness of expecting the pursuer to cohabit with him, but if in any case that relation should be lacking it is only the latter which requires to be considered.

48.24   **Divorce for Desertion.**[18]—The Divorce (Scotland) Act 1938, by section 7, repealed the Act 1573, c. 55, which was the foundation of divorce for desertion, and section 11 of the Conjugal Rights (Scotland) Amendment Act 1861, which amended it. The 1938 Act has in turn been repealed by the Divorce (Scotland) Act 1976 which provides for divorce where the defender has wilfully and without reasonable cause deserted the pursuer

---

[13] *Stewart* v. *Stewart*, 1987 S.L.T. (Sh.Ct.) 48.
[14] *Hastie* v. *Hastie*, 1985 S.L.T. 146.
[15] *Findlay* v. *Findlay*, 1991 S.L.T. 457.
[16] Although see *Gray* v. *Gray*, 1991 G.W.D. 8–477—single incident held, in the circumstances, to be insufficient.
[17] See *Katz* v. *Katz* [1972] 1 W.L.R. 955, *per* Sir George Baker P. at p. 960; *cf. Thurlow* v. *Thurlow* [1975] 2 All E.R. 979; *H.* v. *H.*, 1968 S.L.T. 40; *Grant* v. *Grant*, 1974 S.L.T. (Notes) 54.
[18] See Clive pp. 413–426.

and (1) during a continuous period of two years thereafter the parties have not cohabited and (2) the pursuer has not refused a genuine and reasonable offer by the defender to adhere.[19] Until 1964 the law had required the pursuer to prove not only the initial wilful desertion but also the pursuer's willingness to adhere throughout the period necessary to qualify for a right to divorce.[20] That rule is now abrogated and the pursuer's state of mind after the date of the initial separation is no longer a relevant consideration except only for the purpose of assessing the credibility and reliability of the pursuer with a view to ascertaining, *inter alia*, whether or not the pursuer was truly a consenting party to the initial separation.

'Desertion is a bilateral transaction which involves a spouse who deserts and a spouse who is simultaneously willing to adhere.'[21] The 1976 Act does not alter the meaning of 'desertion' as used in the 1938 Act, which 'connotes a parting from the deserted spouse in breach of matrimonial duty.'[22] Accordingly, the pursuer must still prove that the defender separated from him or her against the pursuer's will and not by agreement. Conversely, the defence of voluntary separation is open to the defender. Refusal of sexual intercourse *per se* is not desertion.[23] There must be something akin to a complete withdrawal from the society of the other spouse; but there may be desertion although the spouses continue to reside under the same roof.[24]

There must be a deliberate intention to desert and the desertion dates from the time when the intention to desert is established, provided that there is at that time *de facto* separation, whether voluntary or compulsory.[25] It is not desertion where the absence arose from some necessary cause or duty, nor where a wife refuses to live with relatives of her husband with whom he does not propose to live.[26] Refusal by the pursuer of a genuine and reasonable offer of adherence by the defender will terminate desertion.[27] Insanity may preclude the formation of the *animus deserendi*.[28]

'Reasonable cause' for non-adherence includes all such grave and weighty conduct of the pursuer as would make it unconscionable to

[19] s. 1(2)(c).
[20] *Macaskill* v. *Macaskill*, 1939 S.C. 187; *Borland* v. *Borland*, 1947 S.C. 432. This rule was modified by the Divorce (Scotland) Act 1964.
[21] *Burrell* v. *Burrell*, 1947 S.C. 569, per Lord President Cooper at p. 578.
[22] *Wilkinson* v. *Wilkinson*, 1942 S.C. 472, per Lord President Normand at pp. 476 *et seq*.
[23] *Lennie* v. *Lennie*, 1950 S.C. (H.L.) 1.
[24] *Ibid.*, per Lord Normand at p. 5, and per Lord Reid at p. 16.
[25] *Trondsen* v. *Trondsen*, 1948 S.L.T. (Notes) 85; see also *Beeken* v. *Beeken* [1948] P. 302 (C.A.); as to the inference to be drawn from the silence of the absent spouse, *cf. Lough* v. *Lough*, 1930 S.C. 1016, with *Lench* v. *Lench*, 1945 S.C. 295.
[26] *Young* v. *Young*, 1947 S.L.T. 5; *cf. Stewart* v. *Stewart*, 1959 S.L.T. (Notes) 70.
[27] 1976 Act, s. 1(2)(c)(ii); as to bona fides, see *Martin* v. *Martin*, 1956 S.L.T. (Notes) 41; as to reasonableness, see *Burnett* v. *Burnett*, 1958 S.C. 1.
[28] *Mudie* v. *Mudie*, 1956 S.C. 318; and see *Crowther* v. *Crowther* [1951] A.C. 723, per Lord Reid at p. 736.

ordain the defender to adhere.[29] It probably extends, exceptionally, to a condition for which the other spouse is not responsible and to behaviour before marriage. The remedy of divorce is not available until the expiry of two years from the date of the initial act of desertion, after which the pursuer acquires a vested right to divorce and any offer of adherence thereafter comes too late.[30] Section 2(4) of the 1976 Act permits spouses to resume cohabitation for a period or periods not exceeding six months in all without interrupting the continuity of the period of non-cohabitation required by the Act, but such periods of cohabitation cannot count towards the required period of non-cohabitation. Cohabitation for any greater length of time will interrupt the statutory period of non-cohabitation and so terminate the emergent right to divorce. Since sexual intercourse *per se* does not amount to cohabitation, an act or, it may be, acts of sexual intercourse without resumption of cohabitation have no effect. After expiry of the qualifying period of non-cohabitation, a resumption of cohabitation will bar divorce unless the cohabitation is confined to the period of three months following the resumption.[31] The adultery of the pursuer before or at the time of separation, if uncondoned, affords reasonable cause for non-adherence by the defender and so bars divorce. Adultery of the pursuer thereafter is irrelevant.

48.25   Divorce of Consent.—There is ground for divorce if there has been no cohabitation between the parties to the marriage at any time during a continuous period of two years after the date of the marriage and immediately preceding the bringing of the action and the defender consents to the granting of decree of divorce.[32] Consent must be indicated in the prescribed manner and may be withdrawn at any time before decree is granted.[33] Failure to defend or even known absence of objection is not enough. There is no provision for dispensation with consent, and so this ground of divorce is not available where the defender lacks capacity. The period of non-cohabitation is calculated and allowance made for intervening periods of cohabitation on the same principle as described in the next paragraph.

[29] *Richardson* v. *Richardson*, 1956 S.C. 394; *McMillan* v. *McMillan*, 1962 S.C. 115, conduct suggestive of adultery; *Hamilton* v. *Hamilton*, 1953 S.C. 383, confession of adultery; *A.B.* v. *C.B.*, 1959 S.C. 27, murder, while insane, of a child of the marriage; *Cameron* v. *Cameron*, 1956 S.L.T. (Sh.Ct.) 21, intolerable conduct held to fall short of legal cruelty; *Hastings* v. *Hastings*, 1941 S.L.T. 323, fraud on defender; *cf. Brown* v. *Brown*, 1955 S.L.T. 48, where Lord Wheatley held embezzlement not to be 'reasonable cause' but suggested that indecent practices might be; see also *White* v. *White*, 1966 S.L.T. 288.

[30] *Bell* v. *Bell*, 1941 S.C. (H.L.) 5; see also *Scott* v. *Scott*, 1908 S.C. 1124, *re* insanity of defender.

[31] 1976 Act, s. 2(3).

[32] 1976 Act, s. 1(2)(*d*). On the meaning of cohabitation and whether or not a mental element is required, see para. 48.26 and n. 39, *infra*.

[33] *Ibid.*, s. 1(4).

48.26 **Divorce for Non-Cohabitation.**—It is a ground for divorce that there has been no cohabitation between the parties at any time during a continuous period of five years after the date of the marriage and immediately preceding the bringing of the action.[34] The right to bring an action emerges on the day after the fifth anniversary of the separation.[35] Periods of cohabitation not exceeding six months in all do not interrupt the continuity of the non-cohabitation but are left out of account in measuring its length.[36] Cohabitation means that the spouses are in fact living together as man and wife.[37] It is undecided whether a mental element is required for non-cohabitation, so as to exclude cases where the separation is involuntary or without intention of breaking the consortium, as in absence because of imprisonment, illness or the exigencies of military, professional or other duties.[38]

The court has a discretion to refuse decree in an action on this ground, if to grant it would result in grave financial hardship to the defender. Hardship for this purpose includes the loss of the chance of acquiring any benefit.[39] There are conflicting decisions on whether or not a defender who fails to oppose the grant of decree can advance at appeal reasons which would have justified refusal of decree by the court.[40]

48.27 **Effect of Divorce on Property.**—Prior to the Succession (Scotland) Act 1964 a decree of divorce granted on any ground other than incurable insanity had the same effect as regards the property of the parties and their rights and interests in any property as if the decree had been granted on the grounds of adultery.[41]

Part IV of the Succession (Scotland) Act 1964[42] introduced new provisions governing the financial rights and obligations of spouses on divorce, except for incurable insanity, and terminated the right of the innocent spouse to claim legal rights in actions commenced on or after September 10, 1964. The provisions of that Act were replaced by section 5 of the Divorce (Scotland) Act 1976 under which the court, on granting decree of divorce might, *inter alia*, order either spouse to pay to the other such periodical allowance as it thought fit, having regard to the means of the parties and to all the circumstances of the case.[43] Section 5

---

[34] *Ibid.*, s. 1(2)(*e*).

[35] *i.e.* by the *civilis computatio; cf. Warr* v. *Warr* [1975] 1 All E.R. 85.

[36] 1976 Act, s. 2(4).

[37] *Ibid.*, s. 13(2).

[38] *Cf. Santos* v. *Santos* [1972] Fam. 247. The 1976 Act is, however, stronger against a mental element in non-cohabitation than was the corresponding wording of the Divorce Reform Act 1969 in England and Wales.

[39] 1976 Act, s. 1(5). *Nolan* v. *Nolan*, 1979 S.L.T. 293.

[40] *Colville* v. *Colville*, 1988 S.L.T. (Sh.Ct.) 23 and *Norris* v. *Norris*, 1992 S.L.T. (Sh.Ct.) 51.

[41] Divorce (Scotland) Act 1938, s. 2(1). As to that effect, see 6th ed. of this book, p. 615, and *Coats' Trs.* v. *Inland Revenue*, 1965 S.L.T. 145.

[42] ss. 24, 33(2) and 38(3).

[43] ss. 5(1)(*a*) and (2).

has now been repealed by the Family Law (Scotland) Act 1985 so far as actions of divorce raised after the commencement of that Act are concerned but remains in operation in relation to earlier actions.[44] The section therefore continues to apply to applications made in connection with such actions for variation or recall of orders for a periodical allowance or for the making of such an order subsequent to divorce. In contrast to the 1985 Act,[45] the 1976 Act does not confer upon the court any power to backdate the variation of an award of periodical allowance; to seek to backdate the variation of an award made under the 1976 Act is therefore incompetent.[46] The 1985 Act does, however, confer upon the court the power to make or to vary an award under the 1976 Act for a definite or indefinite period, or until the happening of a specified event.[47] The power to impose a time limit does not amount to a power to terminate periodical allowance;[48] a time limit may itself be varied or revoked on a subsequent change of circumstances.[49] In varying awards made under the 1976 Act, the court should not have regard to the principles governing the award of financial provision under the 1985 Act.[50] An application for an order for a periodical allowance under the 1976 Act may be made after decree of divorce only if there has been a change in the circumstances of either party.[51] An order already made is subject to variation or recall by the court on a change of cirumstances,[52] may be enforced under the Maintenance Orders Act 1950,[53] and terminates on the remarriage or death of the person in whose favour it was made.[54]

Financial provision on divorce, and also on the granting of declarator of nullity of marriage, is now governed by the Family Law (Scotland) Act 1985.[55] The parties remain free to negotiate their own financial settlement; where they have reached an agreement during the course of the action and a joint minute has been lodged disposing of the financial claims, there is no remaining duty on the court to make financial provision and the parties will be bound by the joint minute,[56] unless they can successfully seek an order under section 16 of the Act[57] setting aside the agreement on the grounds that it was not fair and reasonable when entered into.[58] The 1985 Act provides for the making of (1) an

---

[44] Family Law (Scotland) Act 1985, s. 28(3).
[45] s. 13(4)(b).
[46] *Abrahams* v. *Abrahams*, 1989 S.L.T. (Sh.Ct.) 11; *Wilson* v. *Wilson*, 1992 S.L.T. 664.
[47] s. 28(3).
[48] *Wilson* v. *Wilson*, 1987 S.L.T. 721.
[49] *Macpherson* v. *Macpherson*, 1987 S.L.T. 231.
[50] *Wilson* v. *Wilson*, 1987 S.L.T. 721; *Collins* v. *Collins*, 1989 S.L.T. 194.
[51] 1976 Act, s. 5(3).
[52] s. 5(4).
[53] 1976 Act, Sched. 1, para. 1.
[54] s. 5(5)(b).
[55] ss. 8 to 17.
[56] *Horton* v. *Horton*, 1992 S.L.T. (Sh.Ct.) 37.
[57] Discussed, *infra*.
[58] *Young* v. *Young (No. 2)*, 1991 S.L.T. 869.

order for payment of a capital sum, (2) an order for the transfer of property, (3) an order for a periodical allowance, and (4) certain incidental orders.[59] The court is to make such order under those heads as is reasonable[60] having regard to the resources of the parties and is justified by certain principles, namely (a) that the net value of the matrimonial property should be shared fairly, (b) that fair account should be taken of any economic advantage derived by either party from the contributions of the other and of any economic disadvantage suffered by either in the interests of the other party or of the family, (c) that any economic burden of caring, after divorce, for a child of the marriage under 16 should be shared fairly, (d) that a party who has been dependent to a substantial degree on the financial support of the other party should be awarded such financial provision as is reasonable for adjustment, over a period of not more than three years, to loss of this support, and (e) that a party likely to suffer serious financial hardship as a result of divorce should be awarded such financial provision as is reasonable for relief of that hardship over a reasonable period.[61] The net value of the matrimonial property is ascertained by deducting outstanding debts.[62] The date at which the value of the matrimonial property should be ascertained is termed 'the relevant date' and is defined as whichever is earlier of the date on which the parties ceased to cohabit, and the date of service of the summons for divorce.[63] Thus, any increase or decrease in the value of the matrimonial property between the relevant date and the date of divorce must be left out of account in determining what amounts to fair sharing of the net value of the matrimonial property,[64] although a decrease may be a relevant factor when the resources of a party are considered.[65] Matrimonial property means all the property belonging to the parties or either of them at the relevant date which was acquired (otherwise than by gift[66] or succession from a third party) either (i) before the marriage for use as a family home or as its furniture or plenishings or (ii) during the marriage.[67] A house acquired for use as a family home prior to a previous marriage between the same parties will still be matrimonial property.[67a] It includes the proportion of any rights or interests of either party under a life policy or pension scheme built up during the

---

[59] s. 8(1).

[60] The reasonable course may be to award no financial provision at all—*White* v. *White*, 1992 S.C.L.R. 769.

[61] ss. 8(2) and 9.

[62] s. 10(2). There is a conflict of authority on whether or not a tax liability should be deducted—*Buchan* v. *Buchan*, 1992 S.C.L.R. 766; *cf. McCormick* v. *McCormick*, 1994 S.C.L.R. 958.

[63] ss. 10(2) and (3).

[64] *Wallis* v. *Wallis*, 1993 S.L.T. 1348.

[65] Under s. 8(2)(*b*). *Welsh* v. *Welsh*, 1994 S.L.T. 828.

[66] See *Latter* v. *Latter*, 1990 S.L.T. 805—house excluded where purchase price paid by wife's family; also *Whittome* v. *Whittome (No. 1)*, 1994 S.L.T. 114.

[67] s. 10(4).

[67a] *Mitchell* v. *Mitchell*, 1995 S.L.T. 426.

marriage.[68] It is not clear whether or not this definition covers prospective widows' rights under a pension scheme.[68a] The matrimonial property also includes a claim for damages or other compensation for an accident or injury sustained during the marriage,[69] but not compensation paid after the relevant date for an accident before the marriage.[70] It includes a refund of income tax paid by one party during the marriage, although the refund is paid after the relevant date,[70a] but not a redundancy payment received by a spouse after the relevant date.[71] The net value of the matrimonial property is to be taken to be shared fairly if it is shared equally or in such other proportions as are justified by special circumstances including (a) the terms of any agreement on ownership or sale, (b) the source of funds or assets used to acquire the property if not derived from the income or efforts of the parties during the marriage,[72] (c) any destruction, dissipation or alienation of property[73] by either party, (d) the nature of the property and the use made of it and the extent to which it is reasonable to expect it to be realised or divided or used as security,[74] and (e) actual or prospective liability for expenses of valuation or transfer in connection with the divorce.[75] The increase in value of an asset between the relevant date and the date of divorce is not a special circumstance.[75a] It is not necessary for the court to value each and every asset, and to arrive at a global sum; it may in some circumstances be fair to examine and adjudicate upon individual assets according to their nature.[76] Where only very limited assets can be identified at proof, but the evidence justifies the inference that one party has other undisclosed assets, the identified assets may be awarded solely to the other party.[76a] In applying the principles set out in the Act, the court is not to take into

[68] s. 10(5); see Nichols, paras. 3.29–3.30 and *Bannon* v. *Bannon*, 1993 S.L.T. 999 for discussion of the valuation of such interests.
[68a] *Bannon* v. *Bannon, supra; Welsh* v. *Welsh, supra; cf. Gribb* v. *Gribb*, 1994 S.L.T. (Sh.Ct.) 43.
[69] *Skarpaas* v. *Skarpaas*, 1991 S.L.T. (Sh.Ct.) 15 and 1993 S.L.T. 343.
[70] *Petrie* v. *Petrie*, 1988 S.C.L.R. 390.
[70a] *MacRitchie* v. *MacRitchie*, 1994 S.L.T. (Sh.Ct.) 72.
[71] *Tyrrell* v. *Tyrrell*, 1990 S.L.T. 406.
[72] For example, the sale or conversion of an asset acquired by one spouse before marriage (*Budge* v. *Budge*, 1990 S.L.T. 319; *Latter* v. *Latter, supra; Jesner* v. *Jesner*, 1992 S.L.T. 999) or the provision of funds by the family of one spouse (*White* v. *White, supra*).
[73] Not necessarily matrimonial property, and not necessarily deliberate dissipation (*Geddes* v. *Geddes*, 1991 G.W.D. 16–990—appealed, on another point, 1993 S.L.T. 494), but more than merely failing to pay the mortgage (*Park* v. *Park*, 1988 S.C.L.R. 585).
[74] For example, a pension (*Muir* v. *Muir*, 1989 S.L.T. (Sh.Ct.) 20 and *Carpenter* v. *Carpenter*, 1990 S.L.T. (Sh.Ct.) 68; *cf. Little* v. *Little*, 1990 S.L.T. 785 and *Latter* v. *Latter, supra*); a croft (*Budge* v. *Budge, supra*); an award of solatium (*McGuire* v. *McGuire's C.B.*, 1991 S.L.T. (Sh.Ct.) 76; *Skarpaas* v. *Skarpaas*, 1991 S.C.L.R. 423 appealed on another point *supra*); a family business (*Crockett* v. *Crockett*, 1992 S.C.L.R. 591, upheld June 30 1993, (I.H.), unreported).
[75] ss. 10(1) and (6).
[75a] *Welsh* v. *Welsh*, 1994 S.L.T. 828.
[76] *Little* v. *Little, supra.*
[76a] *Shand* v. *Shand*, 1994 S.L.T. 387.

account the conduct of a party unless it has adversely affected the financial resources or, in relation to periodical allowance awarded on particular grounds, it would be manifestly inequitable to disregard it.[77] The court cannot make an order for financial provision if a party has not included such a claim in his pleadings.[77a]

An order for a capital sum may be made on granting of decree of divorce or within such period as the court may then specify.[78] The court may stipulate that it should come into effect at a specified future date[79] or may order payment of the capital sum by instalments.[80] The specified date or the method of payment of the capital sum may subsequently be varied in the event of a material change of circumstances.[81] An order for a periodical allowance may be made when decree of divorce is granted or within such period thereafter as is specified then, or after decree of divorce if no such order has been made previously and there has been a change of circumstances.[82] An order for a periodical allowance is not, however, to be made unless the court is satisfied that an order for a capital sum is inappropriate or insufficient.[83] It may be for a definite or indefinite period or until the happening of a specified event and on a material change of circumstances may be varied or recalled or converted into an order for payment of a capital sum or for transfer of property.[84] In appropriate circumstances, periodical allowance may still be awarded until the death or remarriage of the pursuer.[85] It ceases to have effect on the remarriage or death of the party receiving payment.[86]

By an incidental order is meant an order for sale or valuation of property, for determining any dispute on property rights, for regulating the occupation of the matrimonial home (including the exclusion of either party) or the use of its furniture or plenishings or the liability as between parties for outgoings connected therewith,[86a] for requiring security for any financial provision,[86b] for requiring payment, or transfer of property, to a *curator bonis* or trustee or like person, and for setting

---

[77] s. 11(7). In *Evans* v. *Evans* [1989] 1 F.L.R. 351, under similar English legislation, it was held manifestly inequitable to leave out of account in reassessing financial provision the fact that a wife had been convicted of soliciting others to murder her husband.

[77a] *Muir* v. *Muir*, 1994 S.C.L.R. 178.

[78] s. 12(1).

[79] s. 12(2). See *Little, supra*, where part of payment superseded to reflect non-realisable nature of some matrimonial property, and *Gulline* v. *Gulline*, 1992 S.L.T. (Sh.Ct.) 71, where payment superseded until date when defender's pension payable.

[80] s. 12(3).

[81] s. 12(4).

[82] s. 13(1).

[83] s. 13(2). *McKenzie* v. *McKenzie*, 1991 S.L.T. 461.

[84] ss. 13(3) and (4).

[85] *Johnstone* v. *Johnstone*, 1990 S.L.T. (Sh.Ct.) 79.

[86] s. 13(7)(*b*).

[86a] Which cannot relate to amounts already paid: *Macdonald* v. *Macdonald*, 1995 S.L.T. 72.

[86b] As in *Macdonald, supra*.

aside or varying any term in an ante-nuptial or post-nuptial marriage settlement, for regulating the date from which interest is to run,[87] and for any ancillary order which is expedient to give effect to the principles of the Act on financial provision.[88] An incidental order may be made on or after, with certain exceptions, granting or refusing of decree of divorce.[89] It may subsequently be varied or recalled on cause shown.[90]

The court is empowered to set aside transactions with the actual or likely effect of defeating a claim for financial provision.[90a] An agreement between the spouses as to financial provision on divorce may be varied or set aside by the court, on granting decree of divorce or within such time thereafter as the court then specifies, if the agreement was not fair and reasonable when entered into.[91] After decree of divorce has been granted the court may set aside or vary a term relating to periodical allowance if the agreement expressly provides that that may be done.[92] The provisions regarding variation may not be available where one party has gifted his share of the matrimonial property to the other.[93] A term relating to periodical allowance may also be varied or set aside in the event of bankruptcy of the person liable for payment.[94] Where parties have been divorced or a marriage has been annulled abroad, power is conferred upon the Scottish courts in certain circumstances by the Matrimonial and Family Proceedings Act 1984 to make orders for financial provision.[95]

48.28   Dissolution of Marriage on Presumed Death of Spouse.—Where a person who is missing is thought to have died or has not been known to be alive for a period of at least seven years, any person having an interest, including a spouse of the missing person, may raise an action of declarator of his death.[96] Decree in such an action will be effective for all purposes including the dissolution of a marriage to which the missing person was a party.[97] The marriage is not revived if the decree is subsequently recalled or varied, or if it appears that the missing person was in fact alive.[98]

---

[87] Suggestions that the court is limited in awarding interest from the date of citation or the date of decree are erroneous: *Geddes* v. *Geddes*, 1993 S.L.T. 494.

[88] s. 14(2).

[89] ss. 14(1) and (3).

[90] s. 14(4).

[90a] s. 18; *Tahir* v. *Tahir* (No. 2), 1995 S.L.T. 451.

[91] ss. 16(1) and (2). See *Gillon* v. *Gillon*, 1994 S.L.T. 978 and 984, 1995 G.W.D. 4–193.

[92] *Ibid.*

[93] *Anderson* v. *Anderson*, 1991 S.L.T. (Sh.Ct.) 11.

[94] s. 16(3).

[95] See *Tahir* v. *Tahir*, 1993 S.L.T. 194.

[96] Presumption of Death (Scotland) Act 1977, s. 1. See para. 43.1, *supra*.

[97] *Ibid.*, s. 3(1).

[98] *Ibid.*, s. 3(4).

Further Reading

Bennett, *Divorce in the Sheriff Court* (4th ed., 1994).
Clive, *Husband and Wife* (3rd ed., 1992).
Nichols and Meston, *The Matrimonial Homes (Family Protection) (Scotland) Act 1981* (2nd ed., 1986).

CHAPTER 49

PARENT AND CHILD: GUARDIANSHIP

I. PARENT AND CHILD

Formerly, the concept of parentage was a straightforward one, with no difficulty in identifying the person in law entitled to be regarded as the mother of a child and certain rules for establishing who was the father. The development of alternative scientific techniques of fertilisation has, however, rendered necessary the enactment of provisions identifying the parents of children born as the result of the use of such techniques.[1] Unless a child is adopted, the mother is the woman who is carrying or has carried a child as a result of the placing in her of an embryo or of sperm and eggs.[2] Where a pregnancy results from the placing in a married woman of an embryo or of sperm and eggs, or from her artificial insemination, but her husband is not the genetic father of the child, he will nevertheless be treated as the father unless it is shown that he did not consent to the procedure.[3] Similar provisions apply where treatment is provided to an unmarried couple together.[4] These statutory rules regarding paternity do not apply, however, where by virtue of another enactment or rule of law the child is to be treated as the child of the parties to a marriage,[5] or where the child is subsequently adopted.[6] Where a child is the genetic child of one or both of the parties to a marriage but was carried by a woman other than the wife, and certain other statutory requirements are fulfilled, a court may make an order declaring that the child is the child of the married couple.[7]

49.1 Legal Equality of Children: Legitimacy and Illegitimacy.—At common law a distinction in status was made between legitimate and illegitimate children. Some of the more far-reaching effects of that distinction were abolished by the Bastards (Scotland) Act 1836 but it remained of fundamental importance in determining the legal incidents of the relationship of parent and child and in questions of succession and of

---

[1] Human Fertilisation and Embryology Act 1990.
[2] *Ibid.*, s. 27.
[3] ss. 28(1) and (2).
[4] s. 28(3).
[5] s. 28(5)(*b*).
[6] s. 28(5)(*c*).
[7] s. 30.

legal rights on a parent's death. Modern statute has, however, shown a progressive trend to modify or eliminate the remaining points of distinction and thus assimilate the legal positions of illegitimate and legitimate children. The Law Reform (Parent and Child) (Scotland) Act 1986 represents the culmination of that trend. Section 1 of the Act lays down that the fact that a person's parents are not or have not been married to one another is to be left out of account in establishing the legal relationship between that person and anyone else; accordingly, any such relationship is to have effect as if the parents were or had been married to one another. In any enactment or deed any reference to a relative, however expressed, is, unless the contrary intention appears, to be construed in accordance with that principle.

The Act, although retaining provision for declarators of legitimacy, illegitimacy and legitimation, in general avoids the terms legitimate and illegitimate in relation to children and that terminology is now largely otiose. The abolition of distinctions on the ground of status is not, however, complete. The legal equality of children does not apply to the construction or effect of (a) any enactment passed before the commencement of the Act unless the enactment has been amended and, as amended, otherwise provides, (b) any deed executed before that date or (c) any reference, however expressed, in any deed executed thereafter, to a legitimate or illegitimate person or relationship.[8] The result of the last provision is that, in the construction of deeds executed after the commencement of the Act, words of relationship are not to be taken as by implication confined to legitimate relationship but grantors remain free to distinguish on the former grounds of status if they expressly so provide. It is doubtful if that result is materially different from that already achieved by the Law Reform (Miscellaneous Provisions) (Scotland) Act 1968 under which, in the construction of deeds executed after the commencement of that Act, words of relationship were to receive effect notwithstanding that the relationship was illegitimate, unless the contrary intention appeared.[9] Nor does the 1986 Act confer on the fathers of illegitimate children the parental rights enjoyed by the fathers of legitimate children.[10] Moreover, the legal equality of children does not affect (a) the rule by which a child born out of wedlock takes the domicile of its mother as its domicile of origin or dependence, (b) the law on adoption of children (with the result, inter alia, that the agreement of the father of an illegitimate child is not, qua parent, required in connection with the child's adoption), (c)

---

[8] s. 1(4). See *Wright's Trustees* v. *Callender*, 1993 S.L.T. 556 where a deed to be construed according to Scots law raised a question of legitimacy to be decided by English law, which had been amended between the death of the testator and the vesting of the fee of his estate.

[9] s. 5, applied in *Russell* v. *Wood's Trs.*, 1987 S.L.T. 503.

[10] s. 2(1)(*b*).

questions of title, coat of arms, honour or dignity transmissible on the death of the holder and (d) rights of legitim and succession relating to estates of persons who died before the commencement of the Act.[11]

Because of the various exceptions to the principle of the legal equality of children, questions of legitimacy and illegitimacy are discussed in the following paragraphs. The expressions 'child born in wedlock' and 'child born out of wedlock' are not strictly equivalent to the categories of legitimacy and illegitimacy but are employed as equivalents unless the context requires otherwise.

49.2 Legitimacy: Presumption of Paternity.—In accordance with the brocard *pater est quem nuptiae demonstrant*, the child born of a married woman during the subsistence of the marriage is presumed to be the child of the woman's husband and so to be legitimate.[12] This presumption holds also in the case of a child born after the dissolution of the marriage if its birth takes place at a date which allows of conception while the marriage subsisted.[13] But at common law the presumption applies only where the child may have been conceived during the marriage,[14] and it is, therefore, inapplicable where the child is born within so short a period after the celebration of the marriage, or at a date so long after its dissolution, as to make it impossible that it was conceived in wedlock.[15] Where the child is born shortly after the celebration of the marriage an inference, although technically not according to common law rules a presumption of law, may however be drawn in the circumstances of the case that the husband is the father.[16] The Law Reform (Parent and Child) (Scotland) Act 1986 now provides that a man is to be presumed to be the father of a child if he was married to the mother at any time beginning with the conception and ending with the birth of the child.[17] At common law there was authority to the effect that the presumption did not hold where the marriage was irregular;[18] and it was not applicable where the question at issue was whether there ever was marriage between the parents of the child.[19] The 1986 Act, however, enacts that the presumption shall apply in the case of a void, voidable or irregular marriage as it applies in the case of a valid and regular marriage.[20] In the case of void marriages the operation of the

---

[11] s. 9.

[12] Stair, III, iii, 42; Erskine, *Inst.*, I, vi, 49; Bell, *Prin.*, § 1626.

[13] Fraser, *Parent and Child*, p. 2. This work is hereafter referred to as Fraser.

[14] See the opinions in *Gardner* v. *Gardner* (1876) 3 R. 695.

[15] Stair, *supra*; *Lepper* v. *Watson* (1802) Hume 488; *Aitken* v. *Mitchell* (1806) Hume 489.

[16] *Gardner* v. *Gardner, supra*; *Imre* v. *Mitchell*, 1958 S.C. 439, *per* Lord President Clyde at p. 464; *Brooke's Exrx.* v. *James*, 1971 S.C. (H.L.) 71.

[17] s. 5(1)(a).

[18] *Swinton* v. *Swinton* (1862) 24 D. 833; *Baptie* v. *Barclay* (1665) M. 8431; but *cf.* Stair, III, iii, 42, and IV, xlv, 20.

[19] *Deans' J.F.* v. *Deans*, 1912 S.C. 441.

[20] s. 5(2).

presumption does not, however, by itself conclude the question of legitimacy.[21] Where there is no presumption arising from marriage, a man is presumed to be the father if both he and the mother have acknowledged his paternity and he has been registered as the father in any register of births kept under statutory authority in any part of the United Kingdom.[22] The presumption of paternity, formerly rebuttable only by proof beyond reasonable doubt, may now, however it arises, be rebutted by proof on a balance of probabilities.[23] Provision is also made for a party to civil proceedings to be requested to provide a sample of blood or other body fluid, or body tissue, for testing; if such a request is refused, the Court has a discretion to draw such inference, if any, as is appropriate.[24] A relative of the alleged father sued in a representative capacity can still be a party to the proceedings and, therefore, requested to provide a sample; in cases of doubt as to the course to be followed, the child's best interests should rule.[25]

Where a child is born before the marriage there is no presumption, arising from the fact of the subsequent marriage, that the husband is the father of the child.[26]

49.3 Children of Putative Marriage: Voidable Marriage.—A putative marriage is one contracted in the bona fide belief on the part of one, or both, of the parties that they are free to marry, whereas there is in fact an impediment to the marriage. In these circumstances, although there is no marriage, yet by reason of the good faith of one or both of the parties, the children procreated before the impediment is discovered are entitled to the status of legitimacy;[27] according to Lord Fraser the marriage must be a regular one and the error must be one of fact and not of law.[28] In *Purves' Trs.* v. *Purves*[29] an averment by the parents of a child, the mother being the niece of the father's deceased wife, that they had married in ignorance that parties so related were forbidden to marry was held irrelevant as an averment of such bona fides as would save the legitimacy of the child. In relation to the enjoyment of parental rights the doctrine of putative marriage is in effect superseded by statutory

---

[21] See para. 49.3, *infra*.

[22] s. 5(1)(*b*).

[23] s. 5(4).

[24] Law Reform (Miscellaneous Provisions) (Scotland) Act 1990, s. 70; *Smith* v. *Greenhill*, 1994 S.L.T. (Sh.Ct.) 22.

[25] *Mackay* v. *Murphy*, 1995 S.L.T. (Sh.Ct.) 30.

[26] *Brooke's Exrx.* v. *James*, 1971 S.C. (H.L.) 71.

[27] Stair, III, iii, 41; Erskine, *Inst.*, I, vi, 51; see *Brymner* v. *Riddell* (1811) Bell's Report of a case of Legitimacy; Fraser, 27; *Smijth* v. *Smijth*, 1918 1 S.L.T. 156; *Petrie* v. *Ross* (1896) 4 S.L.T. 63.

[28] Fraser, 33 and 34, *sed quaere*. See Bankton, I, v, 51, on the significance of regular marriage and *Purves' Trs.* v. *Purves*, *infra*, on *dubium jus* and error in law supported by popular sentiment. In *Philp's Trs.* v. *Beaton*, 1938 S.C. 733, opinions were expressly reserved on the question of *error juris*.

[29] (1896) 22 R. 513.

provisions that for that purpose the father of a child shall be regarded as having been married to the mother at any time when he was party to a purported marriage with her which was (a) voidable or (b) void, but believed by him in good faith at that time to be valid, whether that belief was due to an error of fact or an error of law.[30] A child's mother has those rights whether or not she is married.[31]

By the Law Reform (Miscellaneous Provisions) Act 1949,[32] it is provided that where a voidable marriage is declared null, any child who would have been the legitimate child of the parties had the marriage been dissolved, and not annulled, on the date of the decree is to be deemed to be legitimate notwithstanding the annulment.

49.4 Legitimation *per Subsequens Matrimonium*.—An illegitimate child is legitimated by the subsequent intermarriage of the parents. At common law that is subject to the proviso that they were free to marry at the time when the child was conceived.[33] The grounds on which this rule is based are discussed in *Kerr* v. *Martin*,[34] where the question was whether the marriage of the father of an illegitimate child in the interval between the birth of the child and his marriage to the mother excluded the legitimation of the child. It was held by a narrow majority that it did not, but it was indicated in the opinions of the court that the legitimation of this child could not have the effect of prejudicing the rights of succession of the children of the father's earlier marriage. The offspring of an adulterous or incestuous connection are not legitimated by the marriage of their parents.[35]

The common law rules will continue to apply to cases in which it is necessary to rely on legitimation before June 8, 1968. For all other cases the common law is superseded by the Legitimation (Scotland) Act 1968. Under that Act, legitimation takes place from the date of the marriage, or from June 8, 1968 if the marriage was before then, whether or not the parents were free to marry when the child was conceived.[36] Legitimation may be effected by a putative or voidable marriage as well as by a valid marriage and, if a child has died before the marriage of his parents, the rights and obligations of persons alive at the date of the marriage are to be determined as if the child had been legitimated.[37]

49.5 Pupillarity and Minority.—The age of majority in Scots law is 18.[38] Formerly, a two tier system regulated the status and capacity of those

---

[30] Law Reform (Parent and Child) (Scotland) Act 1986, s. 2(2).
[31] *Ibid.*, s. 2(1)(*a*).
[32] s. 4(1); and see Walton, *Husband and Wife* (4th ed.), p. 235.
[33] Erskine, *Inst.*, I, vi, 52; Bankton, V, 57–8.
[34] (1840) 2 D. 752; see also *McNeill* v. *McGregor* (1901) 4 F. 123.
[35] Erskine and Bankton, *supra*; Bell, *Prin.*, § 1627.
[36] ss. 1, 4.
[37] ss. 8(1) and 3.
[38] Age of Majority (Scotland) Act 1969.

persons under the age of 18. The status of pupillarity applied to girls until they attained the age of 12, when they became minors. In boys, pupillarity lasted until the age of 14. Substantial reform of the law was, however, effected by the Age of Legal Capacity (Scotland) Act 1991.[39] The status of minority has not been abolished; the effect of existing rules of law relating to minors and pupils which are not inconsistent with the provisions of the Act is preserved.[40] The introduction of new rules governing capacity means that the distinction will, however, be of little practical importance.

By section 1(1) of the Act, persons under the age of 16 have no legal capacity to enter into any transaction whereas persons of 16 or over have legal capacity to enter into any transaction. Transaction is defined in section 9 of the Act as any transaction having legal effect, and includes unilateral transactions, the exercise of testamentary capacity or of a power of appointment, the giving of any consent having legal effect and the taking of any step in civil proceedings. Any reference in an existing enactment to pupils or to persons under legal disability by reason of age is to be construed as a reference to a person under 16,[41] and any reference in any rule of law, enactment or document to the tutor or tutory of a pupil child is to be construed as a reference to the guardian or guardianship of a person under 16.[42] The Act does not affect transactions entered into before the commencement of the Act on September 25, 1991,[43] nor the delictual or criminal responsibility of any person.[44] Statutory age limits for particular purposes are unaffected,[45] as is the capacity of persons under 16 to receive or hold any right, title or interest.[46] Existing rules of law or practice permitting the taking of steps in civil proceedings in the name of persons under 16 where necessary, and relating to the appointment of *curators ad litem* and *curators bonis*, are unaffected.[47]

The general rule concerning capacity suffers exceptions which are contained in s. 2 of the Act; transactions by persons under 16 not falling within the exceptions are void.[48] Validity is conferred on a transaction entered into by a person under 16 if it is of a type commonly entered into by a person of his age and circumstances, and the terms are not unreasonable.[49] Persons of 12 or over are to have testamentary

---

[39] See articles at 1991 S.L.T. (News) 395 and 1992 S.L.T. (News) 77 and 91.
[40] As a consequence of s. 1(4).
[41] s. 1(2).
[42] s. 5(1).
[43] s. 1(3)(*a*).
[44] s. 1(3)(*c*).
[45] s. 1(3)(*d*).
[46] s. 1(3)(*e*).
[47] s. 1(3)(*f*); and see paras. 49.17–21, *infra*.
[48] s. 2(5).
[49] s. 2(1).

capacity,[50] and the consent of a person of 12 or over to an adoption order or to an order freeing him for adoption is required.[51] Where he appears to a qualified medical practitioner to have sufficient understanding of what is involved, a person under 16 can consent to medical and similar procedures or treatment.[52]

Some protection against transactions to their detriment is afforded to persons of 16 or 17; until they reach the age of 21 they may apply to court to have a prejudicial transaction set aside.[53] A transaction is prejudicial if an adult exercising reasonable prudence would not have entered into it in the circumstances of the young person at the time, and it has caused or is likely to cause substantial prejudice to the young person.[54] Certain types of transaction are excluded from this provision. Testamentary acts, consent to an adoption order or to medical treatment, steps in civil proceedings, transactions entered into in the course of the young person's trade or business, or induced by his fraudulent misrepresentation as to his age or other material fact, and transactions ratified by the young person or the court cannot be set aside.[55] There are no statutory provisions defining ratification by the young person, but before the right to apply to have the transaction set aside is excluded he must have been aware of his right so to apply.[56] Ratification by the court is available only in respect of proposed transactions by persons of 16 or 17 and will not be granted if it appears that an adult exercising reasonable prudence in the circumstances of the young person would not enter into the transaction.[57] Ratification must be sought in the sheriff court and the sheriff's decision is final.[58]

The Act also introduces a statutory rule for determining age; a person now attains a particular age at the beginning of the relevant anniversary of his birth.[59] In non-leap years, the relevant anniversary for a person born on February 29 is to be March 1.[60]

49.6 Parental Rights and Authority.—At common law the parental authority over a legitimate child belonged exclusively to the father. Such powers as the mother had during the father's lifetime arose by delegation or, in the absence of the father, by principles akin to those on which powers may be vested *in loco parentis*. By the Guardianship Act 1973 it was, however, provided that the rights and authority of a mother and father

---

[50] s. 2(2).
[51] s. 2(3); for adoption, see paras. 49.11–13, *infra*.
[52] s. 2(4).
[53] s. 3(1).
[54] s. 3(2).
[55] s. 3(3).
[56] s. 3(3)(*h*).
[57] ss. 4(1) and (2).
[58] s. 4(3).
[59] s. 6(1).
[60] s. 6(2).

should be equal and exercisable by either without the other.[61] Those provisions have now been replaced by the Law Reform (Parent and Child) (Scotland) Act 1986 which regulates, as the 1973 Act did not, parental rights in relation to children born out of wedlock as well as children born in wedlock. A child's mother has parental rights whether or not she has been married to the child's father.[62] A child's father on the other hand has parental rights only if he is married to the child's mother or was married to her at the time of the child's conception or subsequently[63] or, in the case of certain purported marriages, can be deemed for this purpose to have been so married.[64] Any person claiming an interest, including the father of a child born out of wedlock, may, however apply to the court for an order relating to parental rights.[65] It is now settled that the category of persons who may apply is not restricted to parents or persons claiming to be parents.[66] It does not, however, include the parent of a child in respect of whom an order freeing for adoption or an adoption order has been pronounced.[67] The court can on such an application make such order as it thinks fit but is not to do so unless it is satisfied that that will be in the interests of the child; and in any proceedings relating to parental rights the court is to regard the welfare of the child as the paramount consideration.[68] Thus, where grandparents of a child petitioned for appointment as tutors[69] with full rights but made no averments to support the view that their exercise of full powers of tutory would be in the child's best interests, the petition was dismissed.[70]

Parental rights embrace 'guardianship, custody or access, as the case may require, and any right or authority relating to the welfare or upbringing of a child conferred on a parent by any rule of law.'[71] Where two or more persons have any of those rights, each may exercise that right without the consent of the other (or others) unless any decree or deed conferring the right otherwise provides.[72] Previous references to the *patria potestas* and to the authority of the father must now be read as referring to the authority of each parent or other person holding full parental rights. No specific provision is made for resolving disagreements but an application for an order relating to parental rights appears to be appropriate for this purpose. It is probably not appropriate,

[61] s. 10(1).
[62] s. 2(1)(*a*).
[63] s. 2(1)(*b*).
[64] s. 2(2).
[65] s. 3(1).
[66] *F.* v. *F.*, 1991 S.L.T. 357.
[67] *D* v. *Grampian Regional Council*, 1995 S.L.T. 519.
[68] s. 3(2).
[69] Before the commencement of the Age of Legal Capacity (Scotland) Act 1991, under which the application would be for guardianship—see paras. 49.14–16, *infra*.
[70] *M.* v. *Lothian Regional Council*, 1990 S.L.T. 116.
[71] s. 8.
[72] s. 2(4).

however, for one parent to seek to prevent the other from changing the child's name.[73]

The specific concepts of custody and access, and guardianship, are considered in more detail later. It is, however, the general right of a parent to govern the person of a child and to order its upbringing. In a leading nineteenth century case, parental authority over a pupil child was described as a right of dominion.[74] Parental authority extends to such matters as regulation of the child's place of residence, discipline, schooling and religious upbringing. The parental authority is subject to control in the interests of the child by the court, and terminates, at the latest, when the child reaches majority. It may terminate earlier on the death of the parent or other person in whom it is vested. An order under the 1986 Act vesting parental rights may be varied or recalled.[75] A parent will lose the right of custody if an order is made in favour of the other parent or of a third party. Parental rights may also be assumed by a local authority[76] or limited by compulsory measures of care taken by a local authority.[77]

49.7 Aliment.—A father is under a natural obligation to support his child and at common law his was the primary obligation.[78] The liability of the mother and others on whom the common law imposed an alimentary obligation was postponed to his, except only that in the case of a married daughter the obligation of her husband might take precedence. The whole common law rules on aliment, with the exception of those relating to the transmission of alimentary claims against the estate of a deceased person, were superseded by the Family Law (Scotland) Act 1985. Under that Act an obligation of aliment is owed by, and only by: (a) a husband to his wife, (b) a wife to her husband, (c) a father or mother to his or her child and (d) a person to a child (other than a child boarded-out by a public authority or voluntary organization) who has been accepted by him as a child of his family.[79] Where children are concerned, however, the jurisdiction of the courts has now effectively been superseded, except in limited situations, by the Child Support Act 1991, which provides a new mechanism for the assessment and collection of maintenance from parents. As the operative parts of the Act will only come into force over the period April 5, 1993 to April 6, 1997, and as the courts will retain some limited jurisdiction to deal with the

[73] *F.* v. *F.*, 1995 S.C.L.R. 189.
[74] *Harvey* v. *Harvey* (1860) 22 D. 1198. Dicta in this case should be read with caution, bearing in mind the changes effected by the Age of Legal Capacity (Scotland) Act 1991.
[75] s. 9(2).
[76] Social Work (Scotland) Act 1968, s. 16—see para. 49.15.
[77] 1968 Act, Pt. III.
[78] Stair, I, iii, 3, and I, ix, 1, and Erskine, III, i, 9, speak of this as an 'obediential,' *i.e.* a natural, obligation; *Fairgrieves* v. *Hendersons* (1885) 13 R. 98; *Dickinson* v. *Dickinson*, 1952 S.C. 27. See too National Assistance Act 1948, s. 42.
[79] s. 1(1).

maintenance of children, the remainder of this paragraph deals with the assessment and recovery of maintenance through the courts. The new scheme is considered in the ensuing paragraph.

There is no order of liability where two or more persons owe an obligation of aliment to another, but the court in deciding how much, if any, aliment is to be paid by any obligant is to have regard to the obligation owed by any other person.[80] No distinction is made between children born in wedlock and children born out of wedlock either in respect of the nature and extent of the obligation or in respect of the persons on whom the obligation rests. In a claim based on acceptance of a child into a family, there must have been knowledge of the truth; where a man has treated a child as his own in the belief that he is the father but then discovers that he is not, he will not be held to have accepted the child merely because of his conduct whilst so mistaken.[81] The obligation is to provide such support as is reasonable in the circumstances having regard to the needs, resources and earning capacities of the parties and all the circumstances of the case;[82] the conduct of a party is not to be taken into account unless it would be manifestly inequitable not to do so.[83] The obligation may be owed to a child until he reaches majority or, if he is reasonably and appropriately undergoing instruction at an educational establishment or is training for employment or for a trade, profession or vocation, until he reaches the age of 25.[84] It is, no doubt, still the law that neglect by the mother of contraceptive precautions cannot be assimilated to contributory negligence and is irrelevant.[85]

A claim for aliment may be brought in the Court of Session or the sheriff court and, unless the court considers it inappropriate, may be raised as an ancillary matter in a variety of proceedings.[86] A claim in respect of a child may be brought by the child himself, by his father or mother, by his guardian, by anyone entitled to, seeking or having his custody or care and, if he is incapax, by his *curator bonis*.[87] A woman, whether married or not, may bring an action in respect of her unborn child but no such action can be heard or disposed of until the child is born.[88] An order may be made for the making of alimentary payments of an occasional or special nature, including payments in respect of inlying, funeral or educational expenses.[89] Where the person to be alimented is living in the same house as the defender it is a defence to

---

[80] s. 4(2).
[81] *Watson* v. *Watson*, 1994 S.C.L.R. 1097.
[82] ss. 1(2) and 4.
[83] s. 4(3); see *Walker* v. *Walker*, 1991 S.L.T. 649.
[84] s. 1(5).
[85] *Bell* v. *McCurdie*, 1981 S.C. 64.
[86] ss. 2(1) and (2).
[87] s. 2(4).
[88] s. 2(5).
[89] s. 3(1)(*b*).

the action for aliment that the defender is thereby fulfilling his
alimentary obligation and intends to continue doing so;[90] and it is also a
defence that the defender is making an offer, which it is reasonable to
expect the person concerned to accept, to receive that person into his
household and thereby fulfil his obligation of aliment.[91] That defence is
not, however, open in the case of aliment for a child under 16.[92] The
residence of such a child, if disputed, may be regulated by a custody
order. Awards of aliment and agreements to pay aliment may be varied
or terminated on a material change of circumstances, but a change of
circumstances cannot be constituted merely by demonstrating that the
earlier award was made in reliance on inaccurate or incomplete
information.[93] An award may be backdated, and variation of an award
contained in an interlocutor may also be backdated.[94] Agreements to
exclude future liability for aliment or restrict rights of action in that
respect are of no effect unless in all the circumstances they were fair and
reasonable when entered into.[95]

The statutory formulation of the circumstances in which an obligation
of aliment is owed does not affect the common-law rules 'by which a
person who is owed an obligation of aliment may claim aliment from the
executor of a deceased person or from any person enriched by the
succession to the estate of a deceased person.'[96] Such claims are open
where the deceased person owed an obligation of aliment at common
law or under statutory modifications of the common law prior to the
1985 Act. As the liability is of a representative character it is thought,
however, that it can only arise if the deceased also had an obligation of
aliment under the present law. It is not clear whether the liability of
persons who before the 1985 Act would have had no obligation of
aliment (certain cases of acceptance of a child as a child of the obligant's
family) transmits against the obligant's executors and persons enriched
by succession to his estate. It appears that the provisions of the Act on
determining the amount of aliment and on the absence of any order of
liability where there are two or more obligants apply to representational
as they do to other claims.[97] A parent's obligation will be transmitted
with his estate, and if one child takes the estate he does so with the
corresponding liability to aliment his brothers and sisters out of that
estate. There will be no such liability, however, if in the division of the
estate among the children equality or substantial equality has been
observed.[98] It is also not appropriate to grant aliment where a child's

[90] s. 2(7).
[91] s. 2(8).
[92] *Ibid.*
[93] *Walker* v. *Walker*, 1995 S.L.T. 375.
[94] ss. 3 and 5, see also *Walker* v. *Walker*, 1991 S.L.T. 649.
[95] s. 7.
[96] s. 1(4).
[97] s. 4.
[98] *Mackintosh* v. *Taylor* (1868) 7 M. 67; *Beaton* v. *Beaton's Trs.*, 1935 S.C. 187;
Hutchison v. *Hutchison's Trs.*, 1951 S.C. 108.

claim for legal rights against the estate of the deceased parent is sufficient to satisfy his alimentary needs.[99] The resources of the surviving parent may also be taken into account.[1]

If a child has separate estate and is alimented by a parent, the latter is entitled to be reimbursed out of the income of that estate.[2] And, indeed, in a proper case a parent, although of ample means, may be entitled to be recompensed for the maintenance and education of children out of the capital belonging to those children.[3]

49.8 Child Support Act 1991.—This Act does not alter the substantive law regarding the persons on whom obligations of aliment lie. Rather, it provides a new mechanism for the assessment and enforcement of the contribution of an absent parent or parents towards the maintenance of a child. The scheme will be introduced over a transitional period, which runs from April 5, 1993 to April 6, 1997.[4] Where there is already in force either a maintenance agreement, being an agreement made before April 5, 1993, or a maintenance order, the provisions enabling application for a maintenance assessment to be made by a parent or child will only be available from April 8, 1996, and then only on a gradual basis, depending on the initial letter of the surname of the person with care of the child.[5] During the transitional period, the courts will, therefore, retain jurisdiction to vary maintenance orders or agreements, unless an application for a maintenance assessment has been made in furtherance of a requirement to do so imposed on a person claiming benefit and a maintenance assessment has been made pursuant to that application.[6] A court will also have jurisdiction to make a new maintenance order if, at any time during the transitional period, there is pending before the court an application for a maintenance order or an application for an order varying a written maintenance agreement.[7] Otherwise, orders made under the Family Law (Scotland) Act 1985 cease to have effect, and maintenance agreements become unenforceable, when a maintenance assessment is made under the Act.[8] What follows is a summary of the principal provisions of the Act; for many details of the scheme it is necessary to consult Regulations. The Regulations which have already been made are referred to in outline where relevant.

[99] *Russell* v. *Wood's Trs.*, 1987 S.L.T. 503.
[1] *Ibid.*
[2] *Ker's Trs.* v. *Ker*, 1927 S.C. 52; *Duke of Sutherland, Petr.* (1901) 3 F. 761; *Hutcheson* v. *Hoggan's Trs.* (1904) 6 F. 594.
[3] *Polland* v. *Sturrock's Exrs.*, 1952 S.C. 535.
[4] S.I. 1992 No. 2644 as amended by S.I. 1993 No. 966.
[5] *Ibid.*, Sched. paras. 2–4 as substituted by S.I. 1993 No. 966.
[6] *Ibid.*, para. 5(1) as so substituted.
[7] *Ibid.*, para. 5(2).
[8] ss. 10(1) and (2); S.I. 1992 No. 2645, as amended by S.I.s 1993 No. 913 and 1995 No. 123.

The system will be administered by a Child Support Agency, run by child support officers who are civil servants, based in six regional centres across the United Kingdom. Where the person with care of a child makes a claim for certain social security benefits, that person may be required by the Secretary of State for Social Security to authorise the taking of action in respect of an absent parent,[9] with sanctions for non-compliance with this request in the form of a reduction of benefit.[10] Otherwise, utilisation of the system will be on the application of the parties involved,[11] but where child support officers would have jurisdiction under the Act, the courts can make, vary or revive maintenance orders only in specified limited situations.[12] Child support officers have jurisdiction to make an assessment only if both the person against whom the assessment is made and the child are habitually resident in the United Kingdom.[13] No agreement to oust the jurisdiction of child support officers is valid.[14]

For the purposes of the Act, each parent of a qualifying child is responsible for the maintenance of the child, the responsibility being met by payment of the amounts assessed in terms of the Act.[15] A child is defined as a person under 16, or under 19 and in full-time education,[16] or a person under 18 who fulfils certain criteria.[17] Persons who are or have been married do not fall within the definition.[18] A qualifying child is a child having an absent parent or parents.[19] An absent parent is a parent not living in the same household as the child, where the child is living with a person with care.[20] A person with care is a person with whom the child has his home, who provides day to day care of the child and who does not fall within certain prescribed categories.[21] A person with care does not require to be an individual, thus a parent can be found liable to contribute to the maintenance of a child in the care of a voluntary agency, although no assessment can be levied against an agency.[22] The procedure may be initiated by an application for a maintenance assessment made to the Secretary of State by the person with care, or by the absent parent.[23] In provisions

---

[9] s. 6.

[10] s. 46.

[11] Probably with a charge being made under s. 47 for the service.

[12] s. 8; see *infra.*

[13] s. 44.

[14] s. 9(4).

[15] s. 1.

[16] Not advanced education. Advanced and full-time education are defined in Sched. 1 to S.I. 1992 No. 1813.

[17] s. 55(1). The criteria are set out in Sched. 1 to S.I. 1992 No. 1813.

[18] s. 55(2).

[19] s. 3(1).

[20] s. 3(2).

[21] s. 3(3). The categories are prescribed in S.I. 1992 No. 1813, reg. 51, and cover local authorities and their carers.

[22] s. 44(2).

[23] s. 4(1).

restricted to Scotland, an application may also be made by the child himself if he is over 12.[24]

Applications will be referred by the Secretary of State to the child support officers.[25] The person applying can subsequently request that action cease.[26] Where persons claiming benefit are concerned, the discretion of the Secretary of State to require the parent of a qualifying child to authorise him to proceed is fettered only by a provision that a requirement should not be made if the Secretary of State has reasonable grounds to think that either the requirement or the giving of authorisation would risk the person with care or a child living with her suffering harm or undue distress.[27] There is also a general requirement in the Act that in taking any decision under the Act, the Secretary of State and child support officers are to have regard to the welfare of any child likely to be affected.[28] Once the procedure has been initiated, an interim assessment can be made.[29] There are provisions requiring the disclosure of information needed to trace the absent parent, to assess amounts and to recover maintenance.[30] The formulae by which the assessments will be made are contained in Schedule 1 to the Act and associated regulations.[31] The amount computed will include a basic element and may include an additional element. It will reflect both the amount which the maintenance of the child is deemed to require and the relative wealth of the parents. Provision is made for a protected income level, although this is subject to the power of the Secretary of State to prescribe a minimum amount which is to be paid in respect of a child. In effect, there is also an upper limit, which will operate to restrict the amount which a parent is liable to contribute by way of additional element.[32]

In limited situations the courts will retain jurisdiction to make maintenance orders. These are (1) regarding step children,[33] (2) where payment of an amount additional to the maintenance assessment is justified,[34] (3) to meet the costs of education or training,[35] (4) in respect of disabled children, to meet costs associated with the disability,[36] and

---

[24] s. 7.

[25] s. 11.

[26] ss. 4(5) and 7(6).

[27] s. 6(2).

[28] s. 2. Note that there is no provision requiring that the welfare of the child be seen as paramount.

[29] s. 12.

[30] ss. 4(4), 6(9), 7(5) and 14.

[31] S.I. 1992 No. 1815, as amended by S.I.s 1993 Nos. 913 and 925, 1994 No. 227 and 1995 No. 1045.

[32] Sched. 1, para. 4(3) and S.I. 1992 No. 1815, reg. 6(2)(a).

[33] This follows from the definition of a parent in s. 55 as a person in law the mother or father of the child.

[34] s. 8(6).

[35] s. 8(7).

[36] s. 8(8).

(5) against a person with care.[37] A court may also be permitted by Regulations to make a maintenance order where it reflects the terms of a written agreement.[38]

The Act contains provisions dealing with the termination of maintenance assessments,[39] and with the means of obtaining a review of a maintenance assessment. Assessments will be reviewed periodically,[40] and may also be reviewed on a change of circumstances.[41] There is a general right to apply for a review of a maintenance assessment,[42] of a refusal by a child support officer to make or to review a maintenance assessment,[43] or of a decision to cancel or not to cancel a maintenance assessment.[44] Such a review will take place unless there are no reasonable grounds to suppose that a material fact has been ignored or mistaken or an error of law made,[45] and it will be conducted by a different child support officer.[46] Appeals from the decisions of child support officers will lie to the Child Support Appeal Tribunal,[47] from there, on a point of law and with leave, to a Child Support Commissioner,[48] and from the Commissioner, again on a point of law and with leave, to the court.[49] Remarkably, the appropriate court for Scottish appeals is the English Court of Appeal, unless the Child Support Commissioner directs that in the circumstances of the case the appropriate court is the Court of Session.[50]

Where a dispute arises concerning parentage, no maintenance assessment can be made unless the case falls within one of the six cases set out in section 26. If a child support officer is not satisfied that the dispute falls within one of the six cases, the Secretary of State may bring an action for declarator of parentage,[51] and any action seeking declarator of non-parentage may also be defended.[52]

The Act also confers powers to arrange collection of maintenance.[53] The amounts assessed in terms of the Act may be recovered by

[37] s. 8(10).
[38] s. 8(5).
[39] Sched. 1, Pt. II, para. 16.
[40] s. 16. The period will be 52 weeks—S.I. 1992 No. 1813, reg. 17 although see amendments in S.I. 1993 No. 913.
[41] s. 17; the procedures are set out in S.I. 1992 No. 1813, regs. 19–23 although see amendments in S.I.s 1993 No. 913 and 1994 No. 227.
[42] s. 18(2).
[43] s. 18(1).
[44] ss. 18(3) and (4).
[45] s. 18(6).
[46] s. 18(7). Procedural details for such reviews are set out in S.I. 1992 No. 1813, regs. 24–29 as amended by S.I. 1993 No. 913.
[47] s. 20; except on a question of parentage where appeal is to a court—S.I. 1993 No. 961.
[48] ss. 24(1) and (6).
[49] ss. 25(1) and (2).
[50] s. 25(4).
[51] s. 28(1).
[52] s. 28(2).
[53] s. 29, and S.I. 1992 No. 1989, as amended by S.I.s 1993 No. 913 and 1994 No. 227.

deduction from earnings[54] or from benefit.[55] Alternatively, the Secretary of State can apply to the sheriff for a liability order[56] which enables diligence to be carried out[57] and, ultimately, civil imprisonment sought.[58] When arrears are recovered, they may be retained against benefit paid,[59] and there is also provision for the running of interest.[60]

49.8A   Custody of Children.—Under the common law the father of a legitimate pupil child or, after the father's death, the mother or a custodier appointed by the father, was entitled to its custody. This right was subject to control by the Inner House of the Court of Session in the exercise of the *nobile officium*, but the Court would not interfere with the father's right unless it could be shown that the child's health or morals would be endangered by his remaining in the father's custody.[61] In the case of an illegitimate child it was the mother who was, in general, entitled to custody. The common law has now been replaced by statute. As has been noticed above,[62] custody is among the parental rights which vest in the parents of a child born in wedlock and the mother of a child born out of wedlock and which may, by order of the court, vest in any other person claiming interest.[63] The right to apply for custody is unqualified except that interest must be shown. The parent of a child freed for adoption, or in respect of whom an adoption order has been pronounced, does not have the requisite interest.[64] Notwithstanding that generality, custody of a child is not to be granted to a person other than a parent or guardian unless that person (a) being a relative or step-parent of the child, has the consent of a parent or guardian and has had care and possession of the child for a period of three months preceding the making of the application, or (b) not being a relative or step-parent, has the consent of a parent or guardian and has had care and possession for a period or periods amounting to at least 12 months and including the three months preceding the application, or (c) without the consent of a parent or guardian, has had care and possession for a period or periods amounting to at least three years and including the three months preceding the application, or (d) in any case outwith the previous three categories, can show cause why an order should be made awarding him custody of the child.[65] As the child's welfare is the

[54] ss. 31 and 32, and S.I. 1992 No. 1989, regs. 8–25, as so amended.

[55] s. 43.

[56] s. 33.

[57] s. 38.

[58] s. 40.

[59] s. 41(2).

[60] ss. 41(3) and (4); also Regulations contained in S.I. 1992 No. 1816, as amended by S.I. 1993 No. 913.

[61] *Lang* v. *Lang* (1869) 7 M. 445; *Nicholson* v. *Nicholson* (1869) 7 M. 1118.

[62] Paras. 49.1 and 49.6, *supra.*

[63] Law Reform (Parent and Child) (Scotland) Act 1986, ss. 2 and 3.

[64] *D.* v. *Grampian Regional Council*, 1995 S.L.T. 519.

[65] Children Act 1975, s. 47(2), as amended by 1986 Act, *supra*, Sched. 1 and the Age of Legal Capacity (Scotland) Act 1991.

paramount consideration in any custody proceedings[66] it seems that sufficient cause is shown if an applicant proves that the child's welfare requires an order in his favour.[67] An order may be made giving custody to one party *de jure* on the understanding that *de facto* control is to be exercised by another.[68] It will seldom be appropriate, however, for an award of custody to be made in favour of persons who cannot in practice exercise the right to custody for the time being.[69] The courts are also reluctant to make awards of joint custody.[70]

In 1861 jurisdiction was conferred on the court in actions of divorce or judicial separation to pronounce orders as to the custody, maintenance and education of the pupil children of the marriage;[71] in 1939, the power was extended to children up to the age of 16.[72] The Act of 1861 gave the court in such actions a wide discretion in dealing with these matters.[73] The custody jurisdiction of the Outer House in actions of divorce and separation was extended in 1958 to actions of nullity,[74] and also to cover any child who is the illegitimate child of both parties to the marriage, or is the child of one party (including any illegitimate or adopted child) and has been accepted as one of the family by the other party.[75] The Law Reform (Parent and Child) (Scotland) Act 1986[76] substituted a new section 9 in the 1861 Act. The court in any action for divorce, judicial separation or declarator of nullity of marriage may make in relation to any child of the marriage such order as it thinks fit relating to parental rights. The jurisdiction of the court in such actions does not, however, cover a child who, while accepted as one of the family, is not the child of either party.[77] Where the action is dismissed or decree of absolvitor is granted, the court may nevertheless make provision for the children of the marriage as if the action were still before the court.[78] Furthermore, in actions for divorce, nullity or separation the court may not, under the Matrimonial Proceedings (Children) Act 1958, grant decree unless and until it is satisfied either that arrangements have been made for the care and upbringing of every

---

[66] 1986 Act, *supra*, s. 3(2).

[67] See dicta of Lord President Hope in *F.* v. *F.*, 1991 S.L.T. 357, at p. 362.

[68] *Robertson* v. *Robertson*, 1981 S.L.T. (Notes) 7.

[69] *F.* v. *F.*, *supra*, at p. 363.

[70] See *McKechnie* v. *McKechnie*, 1990 S.L.T. (Sh.Ct.) 75; *cf. Mackenzie* v. *Hendry*, 1984 S.L.T. 322.

[71] Conjugal Rights (Scotland) Amendment Act 1861, s. 9; pupil children then being boys under 14 and girls under 12.

[72] Custody of Children (Scotland) Act 1939. See *Wilson* v. *Wilson*, 1954 S.L.T. (Sh.Ct.) 68.

[73] *Symington* v. *Symington* (1875) 2 R. (H.L.) 41. See discussion of the history of custody jurisdiction in *Hogg* v. *Dick*, 1987 S.L.T. 717.

[74] Matrimonial Proceedings (Children) Act 1958, s. 14.

[75] 1958 Act, s. 7.

[76] Sched. 1, para. 2; in turn repealed and re-enacted as s. 20 of the Court of Session Act 1988.

[77] *Bradley* v. *Bradley*, 1989 S.C.L.R. 62.

[78] 1958 Act, s. 9.

child for whose custody, maintenance and education it has jurisdiction, and that those arrangements are satisfactory or are the best which can be devised in the circumstances, or that it is impracticable for the party or parties appearing before the court to make any such arrangements.[79] Where in an action of divorce, nullity or separation the court considers that there are exceptional circumstances making it impracticable or undesirable for the child to be entrusted to either of the parties to the marriage, it may, if it thinks fit, make an order committing the care of the child to any other individual, e.g. a grandparent, or to the local authority.[80] Alternatively it may, where it considers this desirable, make an order placing the child under the supervision of the local authority.[81]

Similar powers to involve a local authority are also conferred on a court dealing with the question of custody other than in an action of divorce, separation or nullity.[82] The existence of such an order does not, however, entitle the local authority subsequently to become a party to the proceedings.[83] If necessary during a custody dispute, the court can make an order prohibiting the identification of the child in any report of the proceedings.[84]

In any proceedings relating to parental rights, and thus in any proceedings in which custody is claimed, the court is to regard the welfare of the child as the paramount consideration and is not to make an order relating thereto unless satisfied that to do so will be in the interests of the child.[85] The court should also take into account any other orders which have been made by competent courts or authorities,[86] including foreign courts.[87] Factors which may influence the court in deciding to whom the custody of a child should be awarded include the maintenance of the status quo for the child,[88] the desirability of rearing all the children of a marriage together,[89] the views of the child himself,[90] and recognition by the applicant for custody of the need to allow access by a non-custodial parent.[91] There are no presumptions to the effect that a child should be raised by the parent of the same sex,

---

[79] 1958 Act, s. 8(1).
[80] 1958 Act, s. 10, as amended; and see *Smith* v. *Smith*, 1964 S.C. 218 as to third party claim by way of minute.
[81] 1958 Act, s. 12, as amended.
[82] Guardianship Act 1973, ss. 11 and 12.
[83] *Black* v. *Black*, 1988 S.L.T. (Sh.Ct.) 24.
[84] *C.* v. *S.*, 1989 S.L.T. 168.
[85] Law Reform (Parent and Child) (Scotland) Act 1986, s. 3(2).
[86] *F.* v. *F.*, 1991 S.L.T. 357.
[87] *Sinclair* v. *Sinclair*, 1988 S.L.T. 87; note, however, in relation to this case that Germany is now a signatory to the Conventions embodied in the Child Abduction and Custody Act 1985.
[88] See *Whitecross* v. *Whitecross*, 1977 S.L.T. 225; *Breingan* v. *Jamieson*, 1993 S.L.T. 186; *Brixey* v. *Lynas*, 1994 S.L.T. 847.
[89] *e.g. Early* v. *Early*, 1989 S.L.T. 114; 1990 S.L.T. 221.
[90] *e.g. MacQueen* v. *MacQueen*, 1992 G.W.D. 28–1653.
[91] *e.g. Brixey, supra.*

or that very young children should be with their mother.[92] In practice, however, an important factor to be fully taken into account is that during infancy, a child's need for its mother is stronger than the need for a father.[93] It was formerly regarded as very important that the child in its formative years be given the opportunity of a religious upbringing.[94] Now, however, the question of religious upbringing is more likely to be regarded, if at all, as simply one aspect of the welfare of the child. To deny custody to a parent because of his or her religious affiliation is a breach of the European Convention on Human Rights.[95]

ACCESS.—The court has power to make provision for access by a parent to children whose custody is awarded to someone else, and may do so in actions of divorce, nullity or separation whether or not provision is made for the legal custody of the children.[96] As a rule some measure of access is allowed, but the matter is to be decided on the same principles as is custody.[97] Access may be refused if the circumstances, character or conduct of the parent render it undesirable and, in any event, cannot be allowed unless it is in the child's interests to do so.[98] A separate action for access may be raised by one parent against the other.[99] Further, access is one of the parental rights for which application may be made under the 1986 Act, whether or not the applicant is a parent or relative of the child.[1] Where an access order has been made the custodier has a duty to persuade and encourage the child to see the person entitled to access but no duty to apply physical compulsion.[2] The Scottish courts have jurisdiction where divorce is granted in Scotland but the child of the marriage is resident in England.[3] Orders for custody and access, as aspects of parental rights regulated by the Law Reform (Parent and Child) (Scotland) Act 1986, terminate when the child reaches the age of 16.[4]

49.10 Delivery of Children.—Where a child is withheld from the person having right to his custody, that person may obtain from the court an order for the delivery to him of the child.[5] The test to be applied in

---

[92] *Hannah* v. *Hannah*, 1971 S.L.T. (Notes) 42; *Whitecross, supra.*
[93] *Brixey* v. *Lynas*, 1994 S.L.T. 847.
[94] *Mackay* v. *Mackay*, 1957 S.L.T. (Notes) 17; *McClements* v. *McClements*, 1958 S.C. 286.
[95] *Hoffmann* v. *Austria*, [1993] T.L.R. 425.
[96] 1958 Act, s.14(2); *Huddart* v. *Huddart*, 1960 S.C. 300.
[97] 1986 Act, *supra*, ss. 3(2) and 8.
[98] See, *e.g. McCahery* v. *McCahery*, 1991 G.W.D. 31–1828.
[99] *McCann* v. *McCann*, 1987 S.C.L.R. 742.
[1] See para. 49.6.
[2] *Brannigan* v. *Brannigan*, 1979 S.L.T. (Notes) 73; *cf. Cosh* v. *Cosh*, 1979 S.L.T. (Notes) 72.
[3] *Hamilton* v. *Hamilton*, 1954 S.L.T. 16.
[4] *Ibid.*, s. 8.
[5] *Leys* v. *Leys* (1886) 13 R. 1223; *Campbell* v. *Campbell*, 1920 S.C. 31; *Begbie* v. *Nichol*, 1949 S.C. 158 (order made).

such an application is what is in the best interests of the child in the whole circumstances having regard to the parent's prior right to custody.[6] There are also statutory provisions empowering a court to order the delivery of a child. By section 17 of the Family Law Act 1986, one parent may seek an order for delivery of a child from the other parent, even though the order for delivery is not sought to implement a custody order. By sections 51 and 52 of the Children Act 1975, where an application for custody is pending and the applicant has had the care and possession of the child for at least three years, it is an offence to remove the child from his custody and the court may order the return of the child.

The extent to which custody rights can be defeated by removing the child to another jurisdiction has been limited by international conventions on the abduction of children and on recognition of foreign custody orders. The conventions concerned are the Hague Convention on the Civil Aspects of International Child Abduction, and the European Convention on Recognition and Enforcement of Decisions concerning, and the Restoration of, Custody of Children. They are introduced into the law of the United Kingdom by the Child Abduction and Custody Act 1985, in the schedules to which they are set out. They apply to children under the age of 16, and relate to both custody and access.

Under both Conventions, responsibilities are imposed in relation to co-operation and assistance on the central authorities of states and, in relation to enforcement, on the courts. The appropriate authority in Scotland is the Secretary of State,[7] and the appropriate court is the Court of Session.[8] Under the Hague Convention, removal or retention[9] of a child in breach of rights of custody existing and exercised[10] under the law of the state in which the child was habitually resident is wrongful.[11] Return of a child so removed is, in general, mandatory.[12] There are limited exceptions, relating to the passage of time since the removal or retention and the associated settling of the child,[13] to previous non-exercise of the custody rights or to consent to or acquiescence in the removal or retention, to the existence of grave risk

---

[6] *Macallister* v. *Macallister*, 1962 S.L.T. 385.

[7] ss. 3 and 14(2).

[8] ss. 4 and 27(2).

[9] See *Kilgour* v. *Kilgour*, 1987 S.L.T. 568, approved by the House of Lords in *Re H.* [1991] 2 A.C. 476, regarding the concept of 'retention'.

[10] For consideration of whether a party could be described as exercising custody rights see *Bordera* v. *Bordera*, 1994 G.W.D. 32–1891, *Seroka* v. *Bellah*, 1995 S.L.T. 204 and *McKiver* v. *McKiver*, 1995 G.W.D. 8–407.

[11] Sched. 1, Art. 3.

[12] Sched. 1, Art. 12.

[13] *Ibid.* A child has to be so settled in his new environment as to override the otherwise clear duty of the court to order his return: *Soucie* v. *Soucie*, 1995 S.L.T. 414. Such settlement may be difficult to demonstrate where the child is very young: *Perrin* v. *Perrin*, 1995 S.L.T. 81.

to the child should he be returned, and to objection by the child himself to his return.[14]

Under the European Convention, application may be made to have a custody order recognised or enforced in another Contracting State.[15] Duties to take positive steps are imposed upon the central authority in the state to which application is made.[16] Recognition and enforcement are, in general, mandatory.[17] There are limited exceptions, relating to certain orders made in the absence of the defendant,[18] to incompatibility of the order with another order enforceable in the state addressed[19] or with fundamental principles of family law there,[20] to changes of circumstances,[21] and to orders made in proceedings begun when the child had a stronger connection with the state addressed.[22] In the United Kingdom, application may be made to an appropriate court for registration of the foreign order.[23] Registration may be refused if one of the exceptions set out in the Convention is satisfied, if the order is unenforceable in the state in which it originated, or if there is overlap with proceedings under the Hague Convention.[24] Once an order has been registered by a court in the United Kingdom, that court has the same powers of enforcement as if it had made the order.[25]

Chapter V of Part 1 of the Family Law Act 1986 makes provision for cross-border recognition of custody orders within the United Kingdom. The appropriate court for Scotland is the Court of Session.[26] An order is to be recognised in another part of the United Kingdom as if it had been made by the appropriate court in that part.[27] Enforcement proceedings can only be taken if the order is registered[28] but, once registered, the order can be enforced by the registering court as if it had made the order itself.[29] The registering court is not, however, required to enforce the order automatically, and a parent who has removed a child should be afforded the opportunity to be heard.[30]

---

[14] *Ibid.*, Art. 13. See *Zenel* v. *Haddow*, 1993 S.L.T. 975 and *Findlay* v. *Findlay*, 1994 G.W.D. 7–372 (consent); *Soucie, supra* (acquiescence); *Macmillan* v. *Macmillan*, 1989 S.L.T. 350 and *C.* v. *C.* [1989] 2 All E.R. 465 (grave risk); and *Urness* v. *Minto*, 1994 S.L.T. 988 (objection by child).
[15] Sched. 2, Art. 4.
[16] Sched. 2, Art. 5.
[17] Art. 7.
[18] Arts. 9(1)(*a*) and (*b*).
[19] Arts. 9(1)(*c*) and 10(1)(*d*); see also *Campins-Coll, Petr.*, 1989 S.L.T. 33, although the interpretation of Art. 10(1)(*d*) in this case is difficult to square with Art. 9(1)(*c*).
[20] Art. 10(1)(*a*).
[21] Art. 10(1)(*b*), subject to Art. 15. *Campins-Coll, Petr., supra.*
[22] Art. 10(1)(*c*).
[23] s. 16.
[24] s. 16(4).
[25] s. 18.
[26] s. 32.
[27] s. 25(1).
[28] s. 25(3). Registration must proceed in accordance with s. 27.
[29] s. 29(1).
[30] *Woodcock* v. *Woodcock*, 1990 S.L.T. 848.

49.11   Adoption of Children.—The contract of adoption is not recognised in Scots law and, however solemn may be the agreement by which a parent hands over his child to another, it is always open to the parent to reclaim the child.[31] Adoption is a purely statutory process, introduced by the Adoption of Children (Scotland) Act 1930 and now governed by the Adoption (Scotland) Act 1978 in which the law is consolidated. Adoption is effected not by contract but by order of the court.[32] Unless the proposed adopter is a relative of the child, no person other than an adoption agency[33] may make arrangements for the adoption of a child.[34] Thus, a children's hearing[35] is not entitled to take decisions with the aim of facilitating the adoption of a child.[36] Provided certain statutory requirements are met an adoption order may be made extinguishing the parental rights and duties of the natural parents and vesting them in the adopters.[37] An adoption order may be made subject to conditions.[38] A condition has been imposed requiring adoptive parents to raise children with an understanding of their own ethnic origins and traditions.[39] Once an adoption order has been made, the child is treated in law as if he had been born as a legitimate child of the adopters.[40] Accordingly he has the same rights of aliment and to sue for damages for the death of an adoptive parent as any child born to the adopters would have, and the adopters have corresponding rights. Adoption, however, affects the prohibited degrees of relationship for the purposes of the crime of incest and the law relating to marriage only in that the adopted child and the adopters are deemed for all time coming to be within the prohibited degrees.[41] Formerly an adoption order did not deprive the child of his legal rights in his parents' estates or of any right under any intestacy or disposition which he would otherwise have taken; nor did it confer on the child any right in property as a child of the adopter. But under the Succession (Scotland) Act 1964[42] an adopted person is now to be treated as the child of the adopter and not of any other person for all purposes relating to the succession to a deceased person and the disposal of property under an *inter vivos* deed. The adopted person loses all rights in the estate of his natural parents,[43] and any reference in a deed to the

---

[31] *Kerrigan* v. *Hall* (1901) 4 F. 10.

[32] *J. & J.* v. *C.'s Tutor*, 1948 S.C. 636.

[33] Adoption agencies include local authorities and approved adoption societies—s. 1(4).

[34] Adoption (Scotland) Act 1978, s. 11(1).

[35] See para. 2.8.

[36] *A.* v. *Children's Hearing for Tayside Region*, 1987 S.L.T. (Sh.Ct.) 126.

[37] s. 12.

[38] s. 12(6).

[39] *A.H. & P.H. Petrs.*, March 30, 1995 (O.H.), unreported.

[40] s. 39. On the death of the adoptive parent the obligation to aliment will now transmit as in the case of any other child.

[41] s. 41 as amended by the Incest and Related Offences (Scotland) Act 1986, Sched. 1.

[42] See paras. 43.2 and 44.20, *supra*.

[43] For certain transitional provisions see Law Reform (Misc. Provs.) (Scotland) Act 1966, s. 5.

child or children of the adopter is construed as including a reference to the adopted person.[44] When an adoption order is made, the child adopted becomes a British citizen if the adopter, or one of the adopters if there are more than one, is a British citizen.[45] In deciding whether or not to make an adoption order, however, the Court should not take into account benefits accruing to a child from acquisition of British citizenship.[46] An adopted children register (with an index) is maintained in which entries, as directed by adoption orders, are to be made, and the word 'adopted' is to be inserted in the register of births.[47]

49.12 Conditions of Adoption.—Any person who has not attained the age of 18 and who is not and has not been married, may be adopted.[48] The adoption order may be made on the application either of a married couple[49] or of one person.[50] In the latter event the applicant must be unmarried or, if married, the court must be satisfied that the applicant's spouse cannot be found, or is separated from the applicant and living apart and likely to remain separated permanently, or is incapable, by reason of physical or mental ill-health, of applying for an adoption order.[51] Adopters must be 21 or over,[52] except that an application by a married couple may proceed where one spouse is a natural parent of the child and is 18 or over, and the other spouse is 21 or over.[53] There are provisions forbidding adoption by the mother or father of the child alone unless the other natural parent is dead or cannot be found or there is some other reason justifying his exclusion.[54] The consent of a child aged 12 or over to his adoption is required.[55] Unless the child is free for adoption by virtue of an order to that effect, the agreement (which must be in writing) of parents or guardians of the child is also required.[56] The father of an illegitimate child is not a parent of the child for this purpose, and his agreement to an adoption of the child is not required.[57] The agreement of a parent or guardian must be unconditional and given freely and with full understanding of what is involved,[58] but it is not necessary for this purpose that the parent or guardian should know the identity of the applicants.[59] The court may dispense

[44] 1964 Act, s. 23(2).
[45] British Nationality Act 1981, s. 1(5).
[46] *Re K* [1995] 1 Fam. 38.
[47] Adoption (Scotland) Act 1978, s. 45.
[48] ss. 65(1) and 12(5).
[49] s. 14.
[50] s. 15.
[51] s. 15(1).
[52] ss. 14(1A) and 15(1).
[53] s. 14(1B).
[54] s. 15(3).
[55] s. 12(8).
[56] s. 16(1). For freeing for adoption, see para. 49.13.
[57] *A.* v. *B.*, 1955 S.C. 378; *A. and B.* v. *C.*, 1987 S.C.L.R. 514.
[58] s. 16(1)(*b*)(i).
[59] See *A., Petr.*, 1936 S.C. 255.

with the agreement of a child aged 12 or over who is to be adopted only if it is satisfied that he is incapable of giving his consent.[60] The court may dispense with the agreement of a parent or guardian if the parent or guardian is incapable of giving consent or cannot be found, or is withholding consent unreasonably; consent may also be dispensed with on grounds relating to the parent or guardian's previous treatment of the child.[61] The Act provides that in reaching any decision relating to the adoption of a child, a court or adoption agency must give first consideration to the need to safeguard and promote the welfare of the child throughout his childhood and must also give due consideration to the child's wishes having regard to his age and understanding.[62] Where a natural parent is opposed to adoption, the court in reaching the decision whether or not to make the order sought must indulge in a balancing exercise in which the welfare of the child is the first consideration, but 'first' is not synonymous with paramount.[63] The decision is a two stage one: has a ground on which the parent's agreement may be dispensed with been made out and, if so, and having regard to the provisions of section 6 of the Act, should the order be made?[64] The Court will put the welfare of the child before a public policy argument stemming from an irregularity or illegality in the placing of the child for adoption.[65] While it is competent for a married couple to adopt the child of one of them by a former relationship, where the consent of the other natural parent is required and is withheld, the alternative of making a custody order may be preferred by the court.[66] In the absence of a serious factor, the court will not normally extinguish the relationship between a non-consenting parent and his child.[67] The Act imposes a probationary period of 13 weeks, during which the child should at all times have had his home with the applicants or one of them.[68] A *curator ad litem* must be appointed to the child, and all proceedings in the petition are heard *in camera* unless the court otherwise orders.

49.13 Freeing for Adoption.—As a preliminary to adoption an application may be made for an order declaring the child free for adoption.[69] The advantages of using this procedure are that a decision on the child's future can be taken at an early stage, the problems associated with

---

[60] s. 12(8).
[61] ss. 16(1)(*b*)(ii) and (2).
[62] s. 6.
[63] *P.* v. *Lothian R.C.*, 1989 S.L.T. 739.
[64] *L.* v. *Central R.C.*, 1990 S.L.T. 818, *Lothian R.C.* v. *A.*, 1992 S.L.T. 858, concerning freeing orders, where the same approach applies as in the making of an adoption order. Note that, strictly, the considerations set out in s. 6 of the Act are directly relevant only at the second stage; *cf. P.* v. *Lothian R.C., supra.*
[65] *D.* v. *F.*, 1994 S.C.L.R. 417.
[66] *A.B. & C.D.* v. *E.F.*, 1991 G.W.D. 25–1420.
[67] *Ibid.*; see also *A.* v. *B.*, 1987 S.L.T. (Sh.Ct.) 121.
[68] s. 13.
[69] s. 18.

parental agreement being given and then withdrawn are avoided and placing for adoption can proceed without the uncertainty attached to possible withdrawal of parental agreement or dispensing with that agreement. An application for a freeing order can be made only by a local authority providing statutory social work services or by an approved adoption society and, unless the child's parent or guardian consents, must include an application for dispensation with parental agreement to adoption.[70] The court must then be satisfied either that the parent or guardian agrees to the making of an adoption order or that agreement can be dispensed with on one of the specified grounds.[71] Before dispensing with agreement the court must also be satisfied that the child is already placed for adoption or is likely to be placed.[72] As with a decision whether or not to make an adoption order, where a parent does not consent to a freeing order, the court must approach the decision in two stages. Firstly, the court must decide whether or not a ground set out in the Act for dispensing with consent has been made out and, if it has, and bearing in mind the principles set out in section 6 of the Act, whether or not the order should be made.[73] An order declaring the child free for adoption may then be made. The result of such an order is that parental rights and duties vest in the adoption agency, parental agreement to adoption is no longer required and an adoption application may proceed accordingly.[74] The risk that the adoption process may be disturbed by an application by the father of a child born out of wedlock for custody or other parental rights is reduced by a requirement that before making a freeing order the court be satisfied either that the putative father has no intention of applying for parental rights or that any application by him would be likely to be refused.[75] As in the case of adoption, a freeing order cannot be made without the consent of a child under 12 unless he is incapable of giving that consent.[76] Each parent or guardian of the child who can be found is entitled to be given the opportunity to make a declaration that he does not wish to be involved in further questions concerning the adoption of the child.[77] If he has not made such a declaration, he is entitled to receive reports on the progress of the adoption and to apply to the court, at any time more than 12 months after the making of the freeing order, for revocation of the order on the ground that he wishes to resume his parental rights and duties.[78] Such an application can, however, be made only if at that time no adoption order has been made

---

[70] ss. 18(1) and (2).
[71] s. 18(1).
[72] s. 18(3).
[73] *Lothian R.C.* v. *A.*, *supra*.
[74] ss. 18(5) and 16(1)(a).
[75] s. 18(7).
[76] s. 18(8).
[77] s. 18(6).
[78] ss. 19 and 20.

and the child does not have its home with a person with whom it has been placed for adoption.[79]

II. GUARDIANSHIP

As has already been noted,[80] the legal position of those under 18 was altered by the Age of Legal Capacity (Scotland) Act 1991. The implications of the Act for the law of guardianship are now considered.

49.14   **Parents as Guardians.**—At common law, the father is the natural guardian of his legitimate child. By the Guardianship Act 1973 the mother of a legitimate child was given the rights and authority of a guardian equally with the father and these were exercisable by either parent without the other.[81] The effect of the Act was to make the mother a guardian as well as the father. The matter is now regulated by the Law Reform (Parent and Child) (Scotland) Act 1986 under which guardianship along with other parental rights vests in the parents of a child born in wedlock, in the mother of a child born out of wedlock and, by order of the court, in any other person claiming interest.[82] Each person having a particular parental right may exercise his rights in that respect without the consent of any other person having the same right unless the decree or deed conferring the right provides otherwise.[83]

As guardians, the parents manage the estate of the child, and are entitled to recover sums due to the child and to grant discharges therefor. A parent's discharge is, as a rule, a sufficient protection to those who make payment of a sum due to the child; but there are circumstances—as, *e.g.* if they are aware that the parent is insolvent—in which it would be their duty to protect the child's interest by taking such steps as requiring the parent to find caution or refusing to make payment except under a decree of the court.[84] Where it is necessary in the interests of the child, the court may supersede a parent in the exercise of his guardianship and appoint a judicial factor.[85] The former power of a court to appoint a factor *loco tutoris* was abolished by the Age of Legal Capacity (Scotland) Act 1991.[86] If a parent is capable of administering the child's estate, however, it is his responsibility to do so; it is not competent for either the court or the parent to delegate to trustees all the powers and duties of the parent to administer the child's estate.[87] The Accountant of Court has a general duty to superintend the

---

[79] s. 20(1).
[80] See para. 49.5, *supra.*
[81] s. 10.
[82] ss. 2, 3 and 8.
[83] s. 2(4).
[84] *Stevenson's Trs.* v. *Dumbreck* (1861) 4 Macq. 86; *Wardrop* v. *Gossling* (1869) 7 M. 532.
[85] See above.
[86] s. 5(4).
[87] *Scott* v. *Occidental Petroleum (Caledonia) Ltd.*, 1990 S.L.T. 882.

conduct of guardians appointed to children under the age of 16.[88] A guardian, including a father or mother acting as guardian of a child under the age of 16, is a trustee within the meaning of the Trusts (Scotland) Acts 1921 and 1961.[89] Guardians appointed to children under 16 are not required to find caution unless the court so directs.[90]

49.15   Nominated Guardians.—Under the Law Reform (Parent and Child) (Scotland) Act 1986,[91] the parent of a child may appoint any person to be guardian of the child after his death, but the appointment is of no effect unless it is made in writing and the parent at the time of his death was the guardian of the child or, in the case of a posthumous child, would have been the guardian. Such nominations, and appointment by the court on an application under section 3 of the Act, are now the only means of being appointed as guardian of a child.[92]

By the Social Work (Scotland) Act 1968[93] where a child has no parent or guardian, or where the parents have abandoned him or are, on grounds specified in the Act, incapable or unfit to have care of him, power is conferred on a local authority to resolve that parental rights and powers with respect to a child in its care[94] or in the care of a voluntary organisation should vest in the authority or organisation as the case may be. The resolution so to proceed may lapse following service of a counter-notice by the parent;[95] otherwise it remains in force until the child attains the age of 18,[96] unless rescinded[97] by the local authority or determined by the sheriff.[98]

49.16   Termination of Office.—The office of guardian terminates on the death of the child or of the guardian or when the child attains the age of 16. Section 31 of the Judicial Factors Act 1849 empowers the court on cause shown to remove or accept the resignation of any guardian, tutor or curator coming under the provisions of the Act, and to appoint in his place a judicial factor or *curator bonis*. This covers any person appointed to be the guardian of a person under 16.[99] The court also has power to vary or recall an order made under section 3 of the Law

---

[88] Judicial Factors Act 1849, s. 10.
[89] 1921 Act, s. 2; 1961 Act, s. 6.
[90] 1849 Act, s. 25(2).
[91] s. 4.
[92] Age of Legal Capacity (Scotland) Act 1991, s. 5(2).
[93] s. 16.
[94] Under either s. 15 or s. 44 of the Act; *Strathclyde Regional Council* v. *M.*, 1993 G.W.D. 25–1570.
[95] s. 16(7).
[96] s. 18(1).
[97] s. 18(2).
[98] ss. 16(8) and 18(3). See *Dumfries and Galloway Regional Council* v. *M.*, 1990 S.L.T. 272 for discussion of the effect of failure by the local authority to serve notice of the resolution 'forthwith' in terms of s. 16(5).
[99] s. 1.

Reform (Parent and Child) (Scotland) Act 1986[1]; section 3 is probably also wide enough to allow for the removal of a guardian appointed by a will to be sought. At the termination of the guardianship, an action is competent to the child for the purpose of calling the guardian to account and to the guardian for recovering what has been profitably expended for the child in the course of the administration.[2] A guardian covered by the 1849 Act can obtain a discharge by a petition to the court.[3]

49.17 **Curator Ad Litem.**—This is a guardian appointed by the court to protect the interests of a party lacking full capacity in a litigation. Where children are concerned, the Age of Legal Capacity (Scotland) Act 1991 provides that the changes it effects do not affect any existing rule of law or practice (1) enabling civil proceedings or any step in such proceedings to be conducted in the name of a person under 16 who has no guardian or whose guardian is unable or unwilling to act; (2) whereby a *curator ad litem* may be appointed to a person under 16 or, in relation to the Trusts (Scotland) Act 1961, a person of 16 or 17; and (3) whereby a *curator bonis* may be appointed.[4] Where a child under 16 has no guardian, or the guardian refuses to concur, or the action is one in which the guardian is the defender or has an adverse interest, the action may be initiated in the name of the child and application made to the court for the appointment of a *curator ad litem*.[5] The defender, for his own security, is entitled to object to the action proceeding until the guardian concurs or a *curator ad litem* is appointed.[6] Where an action involving a claim on behalf of a child under 16 has been raised in the name of a parent, a *curator ad litem* may be appointed if it is apparent that there is a conflict of interest between the parent and child, or if such an appointment is necessary to secure a determination of the matters in issue.[7] If a pupil child is called as defender in an action, a *curator ad litem* to him may be appointed by the court, although appearance has not been entered for him in the action.[8] Curators of this sort have no right to administer the pupil's estate; they are appointed for the special purpose of the action and with the conclusion of the action their office terminates.

Curators ad litem may be appointed to other persons under legal disability, such as insane persons,[9] although the proper course is to apply for the appointment of a *curator bonis*. If the defender is insane and has a *curator bonis*, the action should be brought against the *curator*

---

[1] 1986 Act, s. 9(2).
[2] Ersk., I, vii, 31 and 32.
[3] 1849 Act, s. 34.
[4] s. 1(3)(*f*).
[5] *Ward* v. *Walker*, 1920 S.C. 80.
[6] McLaren, *Court of Session Practice*, p. 172.
[7] *Brianchon* v. *Occidental Petroleum (Caledonia) Ltd.*, 1990 S.L.T. 322.
[8] *Drummond's Trs.* v. *Peel's Trs.*, 1929 S.C. 484.
[9] McLaren, p. 185. See also Divorce (Scotland) Act 1976, s. 11.

bonis; if the defender has no curator, the action may be raised against the defender and then sisted until a curator is appointed. An action raised in the name of a person who lacks sufficient mental capacity is incompetent, and the incompetency cannot be cured by the appointment of a *curator ad litem* during the action.[10]

49.18 **Persons Under Mental Disability.**—Every person above majority and capable of managing his property has a natural right to do so, and before he can be deprived of this right some procedure is necessary for the purpose of establishing that he is not in a condition properly to exercise it. The method in former times was cognition.[11] Under this process a jury was summoned, and if, after inquiry, the person was found to be 'furious or fatuous or labouring under such unsoundness of mind as to render him incapable of managing his affairs,'[12] the nearest agnate was appointed curator, except where the father or husband of the person was alive, in which case they were preferred to the agnate. The Curators Act 1585 remains in force, and in appropriate cases, the nearest male agnate may be appointed tutor-at-law under the 1585 Act to a person whose incapacity is demonstrated by medical certificates.[13] The appointment of such a tutor supersedes the powers of a *curator bonis* already acting.[14] It also remains competent to seek the appointment of a tutor-dative to a person under mental disability.[15] The powers of such a tutor may be restricted to the person of the ward, and a *curator bonis* can therefore also continue to administer the estate of the ward.[16] Because a tutor has power over the person of the ward, if it appears to the court that management of the ward's estate is the desired object the court may refuse to appoint a tutor and prefer the more established course of appointing a *curator bonis*.[17] Statutory provisions are contained in the Mental Health (Scotland) Act 1984[18] for the admission of persons suffering from mental disorders to hospital and for their detention.

49.19 *Curator Bonis.*—The petition for appointment of a *curator bonis* may be at the instance of anyone interested (such as his next-of-kin, or other relative, or his solicitor) or, where it is satisfied that no such arrangements are being made, by the local authority.[19] It must appear

---

[10] *McGaughey* v. *Livingstone*, 1992 S.L.T. 386.
[11] Erskine, *Inst.*, I, vii, 49.
[12] Court of Session (Scotland) Act 1868, s. 101.
[13] *Britton* v. *Britton's C.B.*, 1992 S.C.L.R. 947.
[14] *Ibid.*; *Young* v. *Rose* (1839) 1 D. 1242.
[15] *Dick* v. *Douglas*, 1924 S.C. 787; *Morris, Petr.*, 1987, unreported, but discussed in 1987 S.L.T. (News) 69. See also cases discussed in 1992 S.L.T. (News) 325.
[16] *Dick, supra.*
[17] *Chapman, Petr.* 1993 S.L.T. 955.
[18] Pt. V.
[19] *Ibid.*, s. 91.

that the person is incapable of managing his own affairs, not necessarily from insanity for it may be due to the loss of sight or speech or hearing, to senility,[20] or the after effects of a stroke,[21] and this must be borne out by the certificates of two doctors. The petition must be served on the party unless the court sees fit in the light of medical certificates to dispense with this. When the petition is opposed on the ground that there is no incapacity, the court may determine what inquiry is necessary for further information on this point. The party has no right to insist on a cognition; and the course usually followed is that of a remit to experts.[22]

49.20 **Powers of *Curator Bonis*.**—The appointment of a *curator bonis* does not divest the incapax of his estate, but his management thereof is superseded in favour of the curator.[23] It is the duty of the curator to manage the estate, and he does so as an agent for the incapax rather than as a trustee.[24] He has no power over the person of the incapax,[25] although his position may entitle him to apply to the court where necessary for the protection of the incapax.[26] The powers of a *curator bonis* are those of a judicial factor, and he is subject to the rules laid down in the Judicial Factors Acts and is a trustee under the Trusts Acts.[27] Specific powers regarding the management of the estate may also be issued by the court.[28]

49.21 **Termination of Office.**—The appointment of a *curator bonis* is superseded by the appointment of a tutor-at-law or of a tutor-dative and it may, on a petition to the court, be recalled if the incapax recovers his power of managing his estate.[29] The curator may obtain his discharge by presenting a petition for that purpose or by applying to the Accountant of Court.[30]

Further Reading

Fraser, *Parent and Child* (3rd ed., 1906).
McNeill, *Adoption of Children in Scotland* (2nd ed., 1986).
Thomson, *Family Law in Scotland* (2nd ed., 1991).
Wilkinson and Norrie, *The Law Relating to Parent and Child in Scotland* (1993).

[20] *Kirkpatrick* (1853) 15 D. 734; *Dowie* v. *Hagart* (1894) 21 R. 1052; *Duncan*, 1915 2 S.L.T. 50.
[21] *Fraser* v. *Paterson*, 1987 S.L.T. 562.
[22] *C.B.* v. *A.B.* (1891) 18 R. (H.L.) 40; *Brown*, 1960 S.C. 27.
[23] *Yule* v. *Alexander* (1891) 19 R. 167; *Mitchell & Baxter* v. *Cheyne* (1891) 19 R. 324; *I.R.* v. *Macmillan's C.B.*, 1956 S.C. 142.
[24] *I.R.* v. *Macmillan's C.B.*, *supra*, at p. 147; *Burns' C.B.*, 1961 S.L.T. 166.
[25] *Robertson* v. *Elphinstone*, 28 May 1814, F.C.; *Bryce* v. *Grahame* (1828) 6 S. 425, 3 W. & S. 323.
[26] See *Gardiner* (1869) 7 M. 1130; *Robertson* v. *Elphinstone,, supra, per* Lord Robertson.
[27] See para. 45.11, *supra*.
[28] See *Fraser* v. *Paterson (No. 2)*, 1988 S.L.T. 124—*curator bonis* empowered to retain shares in a family company.
[29] *Forsyth* v. *Forsyth* (1862) 24 D. 1435.
[30] Rules of Court 61.31–33; Judicial Factors Rules (S.I. 1992 No. 272).

CHAPTER 50

PARTNERSHIP

50.1 Statutory Law.—The general law of partnership was codified by the Partnership Act 1890. Except in minor details it made no change in the existing law. It has no provisions with regard to bankruptcy or goodwill.[1] There is a general provision that the rules of common law prevail except so far as they are inconsistent with the express provisions of the Act (section 46). Further legislative provisions on the subject are found in the Limited Partnerships Act 1907 and the Business Names Act 1985.

50.2 Joint Adventure.—It would appear that under the provisions of the Partnership Act there is no general distinction between an ordinary partnership and a partnership for one particular transaction (known as a joint adventure[2]) except that in the latter case the implied authority of each partner is more limited, and further that, in the absence of any provision to the contrary, the partnership is dissolved by the completion of the transaction in question.[3] A joint adventure is simply a species of the genus partnership, differentiated by its limited purpose and duration (which necessarily affect the extent of the rights and liabilities flowing from the relationship), but in all other essential respects indistinguishable from partnership.[4]

50.3 Definition.—Partnership is defined (section 1) as, 'the relation which subsists between persons carrying on a business in common with a view of profit.' 'Business' includes every trade, occupation or profession.[5] The relationship of the members of a company registered under the Companies Acts, or incorporated under a Private Act, Royal Charter or letters patent, is expressly excluded.[6] From the definition it is clear that there must be at least two persons to form a partnership. A business carried on by one person alone, though in a name indicating a firm, is not a partnership,[7] though it is probably included under the term 'firm'

---

[1] See, as to goodwill, para. 38.10, *supra*.

[2] See, as to joint adventure, Bell, *Prin.*, § 392; *Comm.*, ii, 538; and, as distinct from a contract of service, *Parker* v. *Walker*, 1961 S.L.T. 252.

[3] s. 32. See para. 50.27, *infra*.

[4] *Mair* v. *Wood*, 1948 S.C. 83, *per* Lord President Cooper at p. 86.

[5] s. 45.

[6] s. 1(2).

[7] For the use of the term 'sole partner,' see *Allen & Son* v. *Coventry* [1980] I.C.R. 9, at p. 12 *per* Lord McDonald in an English appeal to the E.A.T.

in certain sections of the Act.[8] Associations formed for purposes other than profit (*e.g.* clubs) do not fall within the Act.[9]

50.4   Limitation of Number of Partners.—By section 716 of the Companies Act 1985 no partnership consisting of more than 20 persons, if for the purpose of carrying on any business which has for its object the acquisition of gain, can be formed unless it is registered as a company or incorporated by letters patent or Act of Parliament. This limit does not apply to partnerships of practising solicitors, accountants, and members of a recognised stock exchange.[10] In addition, the Secretary of State now has power by regulation to remove the limit in relation to any other form of partnership specified in the regulations.[11] These, broadly, now include surveyors, auctioneers, valuers, estate agents, land agents, estate managers, actuaries, consulting engineers, architects, town planners, insurance brokers, loss adjusters, lawyers, member firms of the International Stock Exchange, chartered engineers, patent agents and registered trade mark agents.[12] An unincorporated partnership which exceeds these limits is an illegal association. It cannot sue, and each member, as a partner, is responsible for all its debts.[13] A partnership originally within the statutory limits becomes illegal when, by the admission of new partners, they are exceeded.[14]

50.5   Constitution of Partnership.—A partnership may be constituted orally, or in writing, or may be inferred from the relationship of the parties. It is a question of their intention, to be gathered from the whole circumstances of the case.[15] There is no simple or single test which can be applied in every case.[15a] But, in questions of liability for the debts of a business, a man may be held to be a partner, and therefore liable, if he be judged to have intended to assume the position, in relation to that business, from which the law infers partnership, although he may not have regarded himself as a partner, or may have expressly disclaimed that position.[16] So a partnership may be held to have been created when the question is with creditors, although, on the same facts, it would be

---

[8] *e.g.* ss. 14, 17, 18.

[9] As to such associations, see paras. 52.2–52.4, *infra.*

[10] s. 716(2), as amended by the Companies Act 1989, Sched. 19, para. 15(2) and Sched. 24 with the Companies Act 1989 (Eligibility for Appointment as Company Auditor) (Consequential Amendments) Regulations 1991 (S.I. 1991 No. 1997).

[11] s. 716(2)(*d*).

[12] See the Partnerships (Unrestricted Size) No. 1 Regulations 1968, Nos. 2, 3 and 4 Regulations all in 1970, No. 5 in 1982, Nos. 6 and 7 in 1990, No. 8 in 1991 and Nos. 9 and 10 in 1992 (S.I. 1992 No. 1438 amends the No. 4 Regulations of 1970) and No. 11 in 1994 (S.I. No. 644).

[13] *Shaw* v. *Benson* (1883) 11 Q.B.D. 563; *Greenberg* v. *Cooperstein* [1926] 1 Ch. 657.

[14] *Shaw* v. *Simmons* (1883) 12 Q.B.D. 117.

[15] See *Morrison* v. *Service* (1879) 6 R. 1158.

[15a] *Dollar Land (Cumbernauld) Ltd.* v. *C.I.N. Properties*, 1995 G.W.D. 17–968.

[16] *McCosh* v. *Brown's Tr.* (1899) 1 F. (H.L.) 86; *Adam* v. *Newbigging* (1888) 13 App. Cas. 308, *per* Lord Halsbury L.C. at p. 315; *Charlton* v. *Highet*, 1923 S.L.T. 493.

held that there was no partnership in a question between the alleged partners themselves.[17] The question whether the relationship of parties involves partnership, and consequent liability for debts, where there is no express agreement for partnership, has generally arisen in relation to agreements to share profits. The tendency of the earlier authorities to hold, on very inadequate reasoning, that everyone who in any way shared in the profits of a business must be liable for all its debts,[18] was checked by the decision in *Cox* v. *Hickman*,[19] where it was held that a committee of creditors, who had appointed a manager to carry on their debtor's business, with a provision that all profits should go to meet their debts, were not liable as partners in the business. The Partnership Act 1865, commonly known as Bovill's Act, dealing with the inference of partnership to be drawn from certain specified relationships, was repealed by the Partnership Act, but was substantially re-enacted by section 2. The section is printed below.[20] In the last two cases (d and e)

[17] Bell, *Comm.*, ii, 511; *Clippens Co.* v. *Scott* (1876) 3 R. 651; *Walker* v. *Hirsch* (1884) 27 Ch.D. 460.

[18] See Bell, *Comm.*, ii, 511.

[19] (1860) 8 H.L.C. 268.

[20] RULES FOR DETERMINING EXISTENCE OF PARTNERSHIP. In determining whether a partnership does or does not exist, regard shall be had to the following rules:

(1) Joint tenancy, tenancy in common, joint property, common property, or part ownership does not of itself create a partnership as to anything so held or owned, whether the tenants or owners do or do not share any profits made by the use thereof.

(2) The sharing of gross returns does not of itself create a partnership, whether the persons sharing such returns have or have not a joint or common right or interest in any property from which or from the use of which the returns are derived.

(3) The receipt by a person of a share of the profits of a business is prima facie evidence that he is a partner in the business, but the receipt of such a share, or of a payment contingent on or varying with the profits of a business, does not of itself make him a partner in the business; and in particular:

    (a) The receipt by a person of a debt or other liquidated amount by instalments or otherwise out of the accruing profits of a business does not of itself make him a partner in the business or liable as such;

    (b) A contract for the remuneration of a servant or agent of a person engaged in a business by a share of the profits of the business does not of itself make the servant or agent a partner in the business or liable as such;

    (c) A person being the widow or child of a deceased partner, and receiving by way of annuity a portion of the profits made in the business in which the deceased person was a partner, is not by reason only of such receipt a partner in the business or liable as such;

    (d) The advance of money by way of loan to a person engaged or about to engage in any business on a contract with that person that the lender shall receive a rate of interest varying with the profits, or shall receive a share of the profits arising from carrying on the business, does not of itself make the lender a partner with the person or persons carrying on the business or liable as such. Provided that the contract is in writing and signed by or on behalf of all the parties thereto;

    (e) A person receiving by way of annuity or otherwise a portion of the profits of a business in consideration of the sale by him of the goodwill of the business is not by reason only of such receipt a partner in the business or liable as such.

the lender or seller of goodwill is, in the event of bankruptcy, postponed to all other creditors, whether the contract was in writing or not.[21]

The statutory rules, and the decisions,[21a] seem to justify the following statements: (1) An agreement may create a partnership in a question of liability for the debts of a business but not in a question between the parties themselves.[22] (2) An agreement to share both profits and losses necessarily involves partnership.[23] (3) A lender who stipulates for nothing more than a share in the profits is not a partner.[24] (4) A right to a share in profits, and in addition a right, absolute or conditional, to receive or dispose of the partnership assets, involves partnership.[25] (5) Where a right to a share in the profits is coupled with a power to control the method by which the business is carried on, it is a question depending upon the degree of control whether partnership is involved or not.[26] (6) Creditors appointing a manager to carry on their debtor's business, under an arrangement by which the profits are to go to meet their debts, are not partners in the business.[27] (7) Persons registered as owners of shares in a ship,[28] or employed on board and remunerated by a share in the earnings,[29] are not, merely from their ownership or their method of remuneration, to be deemed partners.

It is unlawful for a firm consisting of six or more partners (or six or more persons proposing to form themselves into a partnership) to discriminate against a person on the ground of race, in the arrangements they make for offering a position as a partner, or in the terms on which the position is offered, or by refusing to offer the position; it is unlawful for a firm of any number of partners to discriminate in the same ways on ground of sex.[30]

50.6 Holding Out.—A person who is not a partner may be liable for the debts of a business on the ground that he has, by words or conduct, held himself out as a partner, or knowingly suffered himself to be so held out.[31] A retiring partner does not knowingly suffer himself to be held out merely because the remaining partner uses notepaper belonging

---

[21] s. 3; *Re Fort* [1897] 2 Q.B. 495.

[21a] Reviewed in *Dollar Land (Cumbernauld) Ltd.* v. *C.I.N. Properties Ltd.* 1995 G.W.D. 17–968.

[22] See note 17, *supra*.

[23] Lindley and Banks, *Partnership*, p. 70.

[24] *Laing Bros. Tr.* v. *Low* (1896) 23 R. 1105. This may be doubtful if the agreement was not in writing.

[25] *McCosh* v. *Brown's Tr.* (1899) 1 F. (H.L.) 86; *Charlton* v. *Highet*, 1923 S.L.T. 493.

[26] *Stewart* v. *Buchanan* (1903) 6 F. 15; *Re Young* [1896] 2 Q.B. 484.

[27] *Cox* v. *Hickman* (1860) 8 H.L.C. 268; *Gosling* v. *Gaskell* [1897] A.C. 575; *Stott* v. *Fender* (1878) 5 R. 1104; *Alna Press* v. *Trends of Edinburgh*, 1969 S.L.T. (Notes) 91.

[28] *Sharpe* v. *Carswell*, 1910 S.C. 391.

[29] *Clark* v. *Jamieson*, 1909 S.C. 132; contrast *Scottish Insurance Commissioners* v. *McNaughton*, 1914 S.C. 826.

[30] Race Relations Act 1976, s. 10; Sex Discrimination Act 1975, s. 11, as amended by Sex Discrimination Act 1986, s. 1(3).

[31] s. 14(1).

to the partnership which, contrary to an arrangement between the partners, has not been destroyed upon the dissolution of the partnership.[32] The liability involved in holding out rests on the principle of personal bar, and is not incurred to persons who have notice of the actual facts. So a trustee in the sequestration of a firm has no title to sue a party alleged to have held himself out as a partner, because he represents all the creditors, some of whom may have had notice.[33] A man may incur liability by holding out either when, having been a partner and known as such, he has retired from the firm without giving notice,[34] or by allowing his name to appear in a business of which he is not a partner.[35] A party whose name is so used without his consent has a title to interdict.[36]

50.7 Limited Partnerships Act 1907.—This Act[37] makes provision for a partnership with limited liability. A limited partnership requires the existence of one or more partners, called general partners, responsible for all debts, and one or more limited partners (who may be corporate bodies), who are liable only to the extent of the amount they have contributed to the firm.[38] To secure this limitation of liability registration with the Registrar of Companies is essential.[39] An application for registration must state the firm name, the general nature and principal place of business, the full name of each partner, the terms, if any, of the partnership, and the date of commencement, a statement that the partnership is limited, and which are the limited partners, and the sum contributed by each limited partner and how it was contributed.[40] Any change in these particulars must, under penalties exigible from the general partners, also be registered.[41] As with ordinary partnerships the number of partners is usually limited to 20, but relaxation has been permitted in certain cases.[42]

A limited partner has no right to withdraw any portion of the capital he has contributed, and if he does so remains liable for the full amount

---

[32] *Tower Cabinet Co.* v. *Ingram* [1949] 2 K.B. 397.

[33] *Mann* v. *Sinclair* (1879) 6 R. 1078.

[34] Para. 50.15, *infra*.

[35] See *Brember* v. *Rutherford* (1901) 4 F. 62.

[36] *Walter* v. *Ashton* [1902] 2 Ch. 282.

[37] See, as to the nature of a limited partnership, *Re Barnard* [1932] 1 Ch. 269. See also, generally, Miller, *Partnership* (2nd ed.), Chap. XIV and Lindley and Banks, *Partnership*, Pt. 6.

[38] s. 4(2), as amended by the Banking Act 1979, s. 51(2) and Sched. 7.

[39] s. 5. The Registrar must keep an index of the names of limited partnerships: Companies Act 1985, s. 714(*d*).

[40] s. 8.

[41] s. 9.

[42] s. 4(2) and Companies Act 1985, s. 717, as amended by the Companies Act 1989, Sched. 19, para. 16(2) and Sched. 24 with the Companies Act 1989 (Eligibility for Appointment as Company Auditor) (Consequential Amendments) Regulations 1991 (S.I. 1991 No. 1997); Limited Partnerships (Unrestricted Size) No. 1 Regulations 1971, No. 2 in 1990 (insurance brokers) and No. 3 in 1992 (member firms of the International Stock Exchange).

of the original sum. He may inspect the books but cannot bind the firm, and is not entitled to take part in the management of the business. Should he do so he incurs liability for all debts incurred during the period while he intervened.[43]

The main distinctions between a limited and an ordinary partnership are as follows: the death or bankruptcy of a limited partner does not dissolve the firm; his insanity is not a ground for an application to the court for dissolution; only the general partner can wind up the affairs of the firm on its dissolution, unless the court orders otherwise.[44] But there may be circumstances in which a limited partner will have to apply to the court to wind up the affairs of the firm, as for instance where the only general partner in the firm dies.[45] In the absence of any agreement to the contrary, the death or bankruptcy of a general partner will dissolve the partnership as to all the partners.[46] Applications for winding up should be made either by means of sequestration under the Bankruptcy (Scotland) Act 1985[47] or by the appointment of a judicial factor.[48]

The relationship between general and limited partners may be settled by their contract, express or implied. In the absence of any such contract the general partners may decide all ordinary matters of business, and may introduce a new partner without the limited partner's consent. A limited partner is not entitled to dissolve the firm by notice.[49]

A limited partner may, with the consent of the general partners, assign his share, when the assignee becomes a limited partner with all the rights of the assigner. Notice of the assignation must be made in the *Gazette*.[50]

50.8 **Business Names Act 1985.**—This Act is designed to prevent possible abuses in connection with the names of businesses, including partnerships. It applies only to certain partnerships. If a firm has a name comprising just the surnames of all the partners, *e.g.* Smith Jones & Brown or the corporate names of all the bodies corporate who are partners, the Act does not apply.[51] Nor does it apply (1) if just the forenames or initials of the forenames of the individual partners are added, *e.g.* Alan Smith, B. Jones & C. Brown, or (2) if, when two or

---

[43] s. 6(1).
[44] ss. 6(2) and (3).
[45] See Lindley and Banks, *Partnership*, pp. 767-768.
[46] Miller, *Partnership* (2nd ed.), p. 623.
[47] ss. 6(1) and (7); *cf. Royal Bank of Scotland* v. *J. & J. Messenger*, 1991 S.L.T. 492. The procedure for winding up under the Companies Acts was abolished by the Bankruptcy (Scotland) Act 1985, s. 75(2) and Sched. 8, repealing in part the Companies Act 1985, s. 665.
[48] *Cf. Muirhead* v. *Borland*, 1925 S.C. 474.
[49] s. 6(5)(*e*).
[50] ss. 6(5)(*b*) and 10.
[51] Business Names Act 1985, s. 1(1)(*a*).

more partners have the same surname, just the letter 's' is added, *e.g.* Smith & Browns,[52] or (3) if there is merely an indication added that the business is carried on in succession to a former owner.[53] But if its name does not conform to these criteria, then the Act applies to the firm.

A firm to which the Act applies cannot, without the Secretary of State's approval, use any name which is likely to give the impression that the business is connected with Her Majesty's Government or local government, or which includes a word or expression proscribed by statutory instrument.[54] Where the Act applies, except for some firms with more than 20 partners,[55] the firm must state certain details on all business letters, written orders for goods or services, invoices, receipts and written demands for payment of debts. The details are the name of each partner and an address for service on him of any document relating to the business.[56] In its business premises, where customers or suppliers have access, the firm must display a notice with the names and addresses.[57] A person doing or discussing business with the firm must be given written notice of the names and addresses on request.[58]

Failure without reasonable excuse to comply with these obligations constitutes a criminal offence,[59] but a breach may also affect the firm's right to take legal proceedings.[60] If, when it enters a contract, the firm is in breach of its obligations under the Act, then any action to enforce a right arising out of the contract will be dismissed if the defender can show either that he has a claim against the firm which he has been unable to pursue because of the firm's breach of those obligations or that he has suffered some financial loss in connection with the contract by reason of that breach, unless the court is satisfied that it is just and equitable to permit the proceedings to continue.[61] Failure to comply with the relevant obligations does not affect the firm where it is the defender in an action and apparently would not prevent the firm from counter-claiming in an action brought against it.[62]

50.9 Firm: Firm Name.—Section 4 of the 1890 Act provides: 'Persons who have entered into partnership with one another are for the purposes of

---

[52] s. 1(2)(*a*).

[53] s. 1(2)(*c*).

[54] ss. 2(1), 3 and 6; Companies and Business Names Regulations 1981 (S.I. 1981 No. 1685), Companies and Business Names (Amendment) Regulations 1982 and 1992 (S.I.s 1982 No. 1653, 1992 No. 1196). Certain firms in business before February 26, 1982 are not covered by s. 2(1) of the Business Names Act: s. 2(3).

[55] s. 4(3). A right of inspection, backed by a criminal sanction, is given by s. 4(4) and (7).

[56] s. 4(1)(*a*).

[57] s. 4(1)(*b*).

[58] s. 4(2).

[59] s. 4(6). See also s. 7.

[60] The wording of the section shows that it does not apply to arbitrations or tribunals, but only to proceedings in court.

[61] s. 5(1).

[62] s. 5(2).

this Act called collectively a firm, and the name under which their business is carried on is called the firm name.' The section expressly preserves the rule of Scots law, but not of English law,[63] that a firm is a legal personality distinct from the persons who compose it.[64] The recognition of the firm as a separate legal personality, important in many questions, bulks most largely in the rules as to actions and diligence; as to prescription[65]; as to ranking in bankruptcy;[66] and in questions of compensation between debts of the firm and debts of partners.[67]

50.10   Actions by Firm.—As the firm is a separate legal personality an individual partner has no title to sue for the enforcement of firm obligations. An action by all the partners is good, provided that there is an indication that they are suing for a firm debt.[68] A firm cannot sue for loss of profit arising out of personal injury to a partner caused by the negligence of an outsider,[69] but the injured partner can sue for his loss of profit.[70] If the firm name be descriptive, *e.g.* the Antermony Coal Co., it is not a sufficient instance without the addition of the names of three partners, or of all the partners, if less than three.[71] If the firm name consists of the names of individuals, action in the firm name alone is competent, although the names may not be those of the existing partners.[72]

The same rules hold with regard to the method by which a firm may be sued; it is not competent to sue an individual partner, even though the firm be dissolved.[73]

50.11   Diligence.—When decree has been obtained against a firm, diligence may proceed against any individual partner, without any further judicial procedure, whether he is named in the decree or not.[74] A party who is charged for payment, and is prepared to maintain that he is not a partner, has his remedy by suspension, and may claim damages. A charge against a party who is not a partner is not justified by proof that he is liable for the firm's debts on the ground that he has held himself

---

[63] Lindley and Banks, *Partnership*, pp. 33–35.

[64] *Jardine-Paterson* v. *Fraser*, 1974 S.L.T. 93.

[65] *Highland Engineering Ltd.* v. *Anderson*, 1979 S.L.T. 122.

[66] Para. 50.19, *infra*.

[67] See para. 14.14, *supra*.

[68] *Plotzker* v. *Lucas*, 1907 S.C. 315.

[69] *Gibson* v. *Glasgow Corporation*, 1963 S.L.T. (Notes) 16.

[70] *Vaughan* v. *Glasgow P.T.E.*, 1984 S.C. 32.

[71] *Antermony Coal Co.* v. *Wingate* (1866) 4 M. 1017; *Hutcheon & Partners* v. *Hutcheon*, 1979 S.L.T. (Sh.Ct.) 61. By r.57 in Sched. 1 to the Sheriff Courts (Scotland) Act 1907, as substituted by Act of Sederunt (Sheriff Court Ordinary Cause Rules) 1993, a firm may sue and be sued in the sheriff court by its trading or descriptive name alone.

[72] *Forsyth* v. *Hare* (1834) 13 S. 42; *Brims & Mackay* v. *Patullo*, 1907 S.C. 1106.

[73] *McNaught* v. *Milligan* (1885) 13 R. 366.

[74] s. 4(2); *Ewing* v. *McClelland* (1860) 22 D. 1347.

out as a partner.[75] A protested bill, signed by all the partners, and followed by a charge against each of them, is a warrant for poinding the assets of the firm.[76]

50.12 Authority of Partners.—In matters of contract the authority of any partner to bind the firm may, in a question between the partners themselves, be regulated by the partnership deed. In questions with third parties every partner is an agent of the firm and of the other partners, and his acts in carrying on in the usual way[77] the business of the partnership,[78] and his signature in the firm name to obligatory documents, bind the firm, unless he had in fact no authority and the person with whom he deals knows this or does not know or believe that he is a partner.[79] A partner's admission is evidence against the firm,[80] and notice on matters connected with the firm's affairs to any partner who habitually acts in those affairs is notice to the firm, except in the case of a fraud on the firm committed by or with the consent of that partner.[81] The extent of the implied authority of a partner as an agent for the firm depends upon the nature of the business.[82] The firm is not bound by an undertaking in the firm name which is known to be granted in the private interests of the partner. Thus, while an obligation to clear the record of burdens on a subject disponed in security is within the implied authority of a partner in a firm of law agents, the firm was not bound by such an obligation when granted by a partner in connection with a loan to himself.[83] And where there are exceptional terms the other party should inquire whether the partner has in fact authority, as where a partner in a firm of builders signed the firm name to a promissory note in terms involving interest at 40 per cent.[84] An obligation in the firm name which is beyond the real or ostensible authority of a partner, and is therefore not binding on the firm, is binding on the partner as an individual.[85]

---

[75] *Brember* v. *Rutherford* (1901) 4 F. 62.

[76] *Rosslund Cycle Co.* v. *McCreadie*, 1907 S.C. 1208.

[77] In *United Bank of Kuwait* v. *Hammoud* [1988] 1 W.L.R. 1051, at p. 1063 Staughton L.J. stressed the need to determine current practice.

[78] *Mann* v. *D'Arcy* [1968] 1 W.L.R. 893; *Mercantile Credit Co.* v. *Garrod* [1962] 3 All E.R. 1103 (sale of car by partner of firm mainly concerned with lock-up garages and repairs held valid, although excluded by term of partnership).

[79] ss. 5, 6; *United Bank of Kuwait, supra.* For the signing of partnership documents see the Requirements of Writing (Scotland) Act 1995, s. 7(7) and para. 2 of Sched. 2.

[80] s. 15.

[81] s. 16. See Miller, *Partnership* (2nd ed.), p. 219; *Campbell* v. *McCreath*, 1975 S.C. 81. As to notice by one partner, in a case of joint tenancy, see *Graham* v. *Stirling*, 1922 S.C. 90; *Walker* v. *Hendry*, 1925 S.C. 855.

[82] Illustrative cases are *Bryan* v. *Butters* (1892) 19 R. 490; *Mains & McGlashan* v. *Black* (1895) 22 R. 329; *Ciceri* v. *Hunter* (1904) 12 S.L.T. 293; *Cooke's Circus* v. *Welding* (1894) 21 R. 339.

[83] *Walker* v. *Smith* (1906) 8 F. 619.

[84] *Paterson Bros.* v. *Gladstone* (1891) 18 R. 403.

[85] *Fortune* v. *Young*, 1918 S.C. 1.

50.13 Liability of Firm for Wrongs.—The firm is liable for any wrongful act or omission of any partner acting in the ordinary course of its business, or with the authority[86] of his co-partners, to the same extent as the partner himself,[87] except that it is not liable to one partner for an injury negligently done to him by another partner acting on the firm's behalf.[88] The question whether a partner can act as a servant of his firm has been raised but not decided.[89] Each partner is liable jointly and severally.[90] The firm is also liable when one partner, acting within his apparent authority, receives the money or property of a third party and misapplies it, or when a firm, in the course of its business, receives the money or property of a third party, and it is misapplied by a partner.[91] The firm may also be liable on the ground that it has gratuitously profited by the wrongful act of a partner, as when a partner, obtaining money by fraud, applies it in meeting debts due by the firm.[92] Where a partner who is a trustee improperly employs trust property in the business or on the account of the partnership, the other partners are not liable unless they had notice of the breach of trust, but the trust money can be followed and recovered from the firm if still in its possession or control.[93]

50.14 Liability of Partners.—Every partner is liable jointly and severally for all the debts of the firm, and the estate of a deceased partner is also liable,[94] but the debt must be constituted against the firm.[95] As between themselves, a partner who has paid the firm debts is entitled to pro rata relief from the other partners.[96] A partner may in serious cases be liable to the other partners for loss occasioned in the firm business by his lack of care or skill.[97] A partner who has retired does not cease to be liable for all debts or obligations incurred while he was a partner,[98] and no arrangement between him and the other partners is of any avail against creditors. He may avoid liability by an arrangement between himself

---

[86] Meaning 'control, direction or knowing approval of the action or actions in question': *Kirkintilloch Equitable Co-op Society* v. *Livingstone*, 1972 S.C. 111, *per* Lord Cameron at p. 122.

[87] s. 10. To act as the secretary of a company is not part of the ordinary business of a firm of law agents, even although the partnership deed provides that any salary thence derived is part of the firm's assets, and therefore the firm is not liable for the fraudulent act of a partner in his capacity as secretary: *New Mining Syndicate* v. *Chalmers*, 1912 S.C. 126. *Cf. Kirkintilloch Equitable Co-op Society* v. *Livingstone, supra.*

[88] *Mair* v. *Wood*, 1948 S.C. 83.

[89] *Fife County Council* v. *Minister of National Insurance*, 1947 S.C. 629.

[90] s. 12.

[91] s. 11.

[92] *New Mining Syndicate* v. *Chalmers*, 1912 S.C. 126. *cf.* para. 29.7 *supra.*

[93] s. 13.

[94] s. 9.

[95] *Highland Engineering Ltd.* v. *Anderson*, 1979 S.L.T. 122.

[96] s. 4.

[97] *Blackwood* v. *Robertson*, 1984 S.L.T. (Sh.Ct.) 68.

[98] s. 17(2). See *Welsh* v. *Knarston*, 1973 S.L.T. 66.

and the firm as newly constituted, and the creditor.[99] Such an arrangement may be inferred from a course of dealing between the firm as newly constituted and the creditor,[1] but the decisions establish that the inference is not easy, and that acceptance of interest or part-payment from a new firm, or ranking in their bankruptcy, is not sufficient.[2] The acceptance of a bill from the new firm has been held sufficient to discharge a partner who has retired, on the principle that he is a cautioner for the firm, and is discharged by the creditor giving time to the principal debtor.[3]

50.15 Liability of Retired Partner: Notice.—A partner who has retired and has failed to give adequate notice of the fact may be liable on obligations incurred subsequent to his retirement.[4] A partner who has become bankrupt, or the representatives of one who has died, are not in any event liable for obligations subsequently incurred by the firm, and in these cases no notice is required.[5] Similarly, a retired partner who was not known to the person dealing with the firm to be a partner, is not liable for partnership debts contracted after his retirement, and does not have to give notice.[6] This provision includes apparent as well as dormant partners, and operates from the date of the dissolution of the partnership.[7] In other cases the Act provides that a *Gazette* advertisement is notice to all persons who had no prior dealings with the firm.[8] With regard to persons who have had dealings, a mere *Gazette* or newspaper advertisement is not sufficient, unless knowledge of it can be brought home to the particular creditor. Intimation by circular, or by an obvious change in the firm name, is required.[9]

Liability of a partner who has retired, but failed to give notice, for obligations subsequently incurred by the firm as re-constituted after his retirement, rests on the principle of holding out or personal bar.[10] It would appear that in Scotland at least it is a joint and several, not an alternative, liability.[11] This proceeds on the principle that, as the retired partner, by his failure to give notice, has held himself out to be a

---

[99] s. 17(3).

[1] s. 17(3).

[2] *Morton's Trs.* v. *Robertson's J.F.* (1892) 20 R. 72; *Smith* v. *Patrick* (1901) 3 F. (H.L.) 14.

[3] *Goldfarb* v. *Bartlett* [1920] 1 K.B. 639; see also *Rouse* v. *Bradford Banking Co.* [1894] A.C. 586.

[4] s. 36.

[5] s. 36(3).

[6] s. 36(3).

[7] *Tower Cabinet Co.* v. *Ingram* [1942] 2 K.B. 397. See also s. 4, and para. 50.6, *supra*.

[8] s. 36(2).

[9] Bell, *Prin.*, § 384; *Comm.*, ii, 530.

[10] See above.

[11] *Black* v. *Girdwood* (1885) 13 R. 243 (in which *Scarf* v. *Jardine* (1882) 7 App. Cas. 345, to the opposite effect, was discussed and disapproved by a majority of the Second Division: but the question was obiter).

member of the new firm so far as the creditor is concerned, he must be regarded as if he were such a member.[12] But he has a right of relief against the actual members of the new firm.[13]

50.16 Liability of New Partner.—The Act provides (section 17(1)): 'A person who is admitted as a partner into an existing firm does not thereby become liable to the creditors of the firm for anything done before he became a partner.' Where the whole assets of a going concern are handed over to a new partnership and the business is continued on the same footing as before, the presumption is that the liabilities are taken over with the stock but the presumption may be rebutted if the new partner pays in a large sum as capital and the other partners contribute merely their shares of the going business.[14]

50.17 Effect of Change in Firm on Contracts.—The Act does not decide the question whether a change in the personnel of a firm has any effect on continuing contracts which involve the element of *delectus personae*. It is expressly provided that a continuing guarantee or cautionary obligation given either to a firm or to a third person in respect of the transactions of a firm is, in the absence of agreement to the contrary, revoked as to future transactions by any change in the constitution of the firm to which, or of the firm in respect of the transactions of which, the guarantee or obligation was given.[15] Otherwise, the general rule is the same as for the assignability of contracts as a whole.[16] Contracts of service are not dissolved by a mere change in the constitution of the firm of employers,[17] except where by the death of one of the partners the partnership necessarily comes to an end.[18] It has been pointed out that while the conversion of a partnership into a limited company releases all servants from their engagements, the retirement of one of the partners, or the adoption of a new partner, would have no such effect.[19] Where a testator authorised his trustees to invest money in a partnership business, it was held that the authority given did not justify a continuance of the investment after one partner had retired. The decision, however, proceeded on the presumed intention of the testator.[20]

[12] *Black* v. *Girdwood, supra, per* Lord Young at p. 249.
[13] *Mann* v. *Sinclair* (1879) 6 R. 1078; *Black* v. *Girdwood, supra, per* Lord Young at p. 249.
[14] *Thomson & Balfour* v. *Boag & Son,* 1936 S.C. 2; *Miller* v. *MacLeod,* 1973 S.C. 172.
[15] s. 18, re-enacting s. 7 of the Mercantile Law Amendment Act, Scotland, 1856.
[16] Bell, *Comm.,* ii, 525–526; *Alexander* v. *Lowson's Trs.* (1890) 17 R. 571, *per* Lord Kinnear at p. 575.
[17] *Campbell* v. *Baird* (1827) 5 S. 335.
[18] *Hoey* v. *McEwan & Auld* (1867) 5 M. 814.
[19] *Berlitz School* v. *Duchene* (1903) 6 F. 181, *per* Lord McLaren at p. 186. See, however, *Garden, Haig-Scott & Wallace* v. *Prudential Society,* 1927 S.L.T. 393.
[20] *Smith* v. *Patrick* (1901) 3 F. (H.L.) 14.

50.18 Partnership Property.—Money or property originally brought into the partnership stock or acquired on account of the firm, or for the purposes and in the course of the partnership business, becomes partnership property, and must be held exclusively for the purposes of the partnership and in accordance with the partnership agreement.[21] Unless the contrary intention appears, property bought with money belonging to the firm is deemed to have been bought on account of the firm.[22] The interest of each partner is a right to a *pro indiviso* share of the firm's assets, with the results: (1) that his interest is moveable in his succession, though the property actually held may be heritable,[23] (2) that the proper diligence to attach a partner's interest is arrestment in the hands of the firm, and not adjudication or poinding of the particular assets.[24] The mere contract under which a partner agrees to contribute property to the firm does not complete the firm's title, or remove the property, as a separate asset, from the diligence of the partner's creditors; a conveyance, in the manner appropriate to the particular property in question, is required.[25] Partnership property, with the exception of land held by feudal tenure,[26] may be held in the name of the firm, or in the name of a partner. In the latter case the former rule[27] limiting proof that the property was really held for the firm to the writ or oath of the partner no longer applies.[28]

50.19 Ranking in Bankruptcy.—In bankruptcy the creditors of the firm rank on the firm's estate to the exclusion of the creditors of an individual partner.[29] Where a creditor ranks on the firm's estate for payment of a firm debt, he does not require to deduct the estimated value of any claim against the estates of the individual partners,[30] since the liability of the firm is the primary liability. Conversely, when a creditor claims for a firm debt against the estate of one of the partners, he must make a deduction in respect of the liability of the firm. Where the estate of the firm has not been sequestrated, the creditor must estimate and deduct the value of the debt due to him from the firm's estate. Where the estate of the firm has been sequestrated, he must estimate and deduct the value of his claim in the firm's sequestration.[31] If the permanent

[21] s. 20.
[22] s. 21.
[23] s. 22; Bell, *Comm.*, ii, 501; *Minto* v. *Kirkpatrick* (1833) 11 S. 632 (legitim).
[24] Erskine, III, iii, 24; *Parnell* v. *Walter* (1889) 16 R. 917.
[25] Bell, *Comm.*, ii, 501.
[26] Bell, *Prin.*, § 357 (in which case it should be taken in the name of the partners as trustees for the firm).
[27] Act 1696, c. 25.
[28] Requirements of Writing (Scotland) Act 1995, s. 1 and s. 14(4).
[29] Goudy, *Bankruptcy* (4th ed.), pp. 578–579.
[30] Bell, *Comm.*, ii, 550.
[31] Sched. 1, para. 6 of the Bankruptcy (Scotland) Act 1985 applied to the submission of claims for a dividend by ss. 48(7) and 22(9). *Cf. Clydesdale Bank* v. *Morison's Tr.*, 1982 S.C. 26, decided on s. 62 of the Bankruptcy (Scotland) Act 1913.

trustee does not accept the creditor's valuation, he may reject the claim.[32]

50.20 **Fiduciary Element in Partnership.**[33]—Partnership is a contract which involves fiduciary duties. A partner must be honest in his accounts with his partners and in his dealings with third persons.[34] He must render to a fellow partner or his legal representatives true accounts and full information on all things affecting the firm.[35] If a partner, without the consent of the others, carries on any business of the same nature as, and competing with, that of the firm he must account for and pay over to the firm all profits made in that business.[36] Each partner must also 'account to the firm for any benefit derived by him without the consent of the other partners from any transaction concerning the partnership, or from any use by him of the partnership property, name, or business connection'.[37] So if a partner supplies goods to the firm without disclosing that they are his he acts as an agent and must account for any profit on the transactions.[38] A partner must account for benefits derived from information obtained in connection with the firm or in the course of its business,[39] but a third party to whom the information has been passed cannot be prevented from using it.[40] This rule applies also, in the case of a firm dissolved by the death of a partner, to any transactions either by the surviving partners, or by the representatives of the deceased partner, before the affairs of the partnership are completely wound up.[41] Though it is not expressly stated in the Act, the rule also applies to the case where a partner, having the right to do so, dissolves the partnership in order to secure for his private advantage some contract which the firm was about to obtain.[42] The phrase, 'transaction concerning the partnership' does not include the purchase, by one of three partners, of the interest of another in the partnership assets, without the knowledge or consent of the third. He is under no obligation to account for his profit to the firm.[43] And where one partner owed a directorship to his connection with the firm, but the business in

[32] s. 49(2).
[33] *Chan* v. *Zacharia* (1984) 154 C.L.R. 178, H.Ct.Aust.; *Roxburgh Dinardo & Partners' J.F.* v. *Dinardo*, 1993 S.L.T. 16.
[34] *Carmichael* v. *Evans* [1904] 1 Ch. 486.
[35] s. 28; *Ferguson* v. *Patrick and James W.S.*, 1184 S.C. 115. In *Sinclair* v. *Sinclair*, O.H., Sept. 24, 1985, unreported (Lord McCluskey) it was held that a partner who was in breach of his own obligations might lose this right.
[36] s. 30; see as illustrations of this section, *Stewart* v. *North* (1893) 20 R. 260; *Pillans Bros.* v. *Pillans* (1908) 16 S.L.T. 611; *Trimble* v. *Goldberg* [1906] A.C. 494.
[37] s. 29(1).
[38] *Kuhlirz* v. *Lambert Bros.* (1913) 18 Com. Cas. 217, at p. 226 *per* Scrutton J.
[39] *Aas* v. *Benham* [1891] 2 Ch. 244; *Phipps* v. *Boardman* [1967] 2 A.C. 46.
[40] *Roxburgh* v. *Seven Seas Engineering*, 1980 S.L.T. (Notes) 49.
[41] s. 29(2).
[42] Erskine, *Inst.*, III, xxv, 4; Bell, *Comm.*, ii, 522; *Featherstonhaugh* v. *Fenwick* (1810) 17 Vesey 298; *McNiven* v. *Peffers* (1868) 7 M. 181—both cases of leases.
[43] *Cassels* v. *Stewart* (1881) 8 R. (H.L.) 1.

which he was a director did not compete with that of the firm, it was held that there were no grounds on which the other could claim a share of the director's fees.[44] The rights of a person who is not a partner, but has lent money on profit-sharing terms, are purely contractual, and no fiduciary duties are owed to him.[45]

50.21 Assignation.—As partnership is a contract involving *delectus personae*, no partner, without the consent of the others, can assign his interest so as to make the assignee a partner in the firm,[46] except under the provisions of the Limited Partnerships Act 1907.[47] The interest of a partner is, however, assignable, absolutely or in security. The assignee has no right to interfere in the administration of the firm, to require any accounts, or to inspect the partnership books. He had, therefore, it was held, no right to object to a resolution by which the partners arranged that they should receive salaries for attending to the partnership business.[48] He is only entitled, while the firm is a going concern, to the share of the profits to which the cedent has right, and must accept the account of profits to which the partners have agreed.[49] An assignee has no power to dissolve the firm, but on its dissolution is entitled to receive the share of the partnership assets to which the cedent is entitled as between himself and the other partners, and, for the purpose of ascertaining that share, to an account as from the date of the dissolution.[50]

50.22 Rights of Partners *Inter Se.*—The interests and rights of partners may be regulated by an agreement, express or implied. The Act provides (section 19): 'The mutual rights and duties of partners, whether ascertained by agreement or defined by this Act, may be varied by the consent of all the partners, and such consent may be either express or inferred from a course of dealing.' But it is conceived that if the partnership agreement were in writing, a merely oral consent to alter its terms would not be binding, unless it had been acted upon.[51] In the absence of any agreement to the contrary, the undernoted rules are provided by section 24 as regulating the relations of partners.[52]

---

[44] *Aas* v. *Benham, supra.*
[45] *Teacher* v. *Calder* (1899) 1 F. (H.L.) 39.
[46] s. 31(1).
[47] Para. 50.7, *supra.*
[48] *Re Garwood's Trusts* [1903] 1 Ch. 236.
[49] s. 31(1).
[50] s. 31(2).
[51] *Barr's Trs.* v. *Barr & Shearer* (1886) 13 R. 1055; *Starrett* v. *Pia*, 1968 S.L.T. (Notes) 28.
[52] (1) All the partners are entitled to share equally in the capital and profits of the business, and must contribute equally towards the losses, whether of capital or otherwise, sustained by the firm (*Garner* v. *Murray* [1904] 1 Ch. 57).
  (2) The firm must indemnify every partner in respect of payments made and personal liabilities incurred by him:
    (a) In the ordinary and proper conduct of the business of the firm; or
    (b) In or about anything necessarily done for the preservation of the business or property of the firm (*Stroyan* v. *Milroy*, 1910 S.C. 174).

50.23 **Expulsion of Partner.**—No majority can expel a partner, unless power to do so is conferred by express agreement.[53] Clauses in a deed of partnership giving power to expel a partner are construed strictly, and the court has power, on English authority, to refuse to give effect to them if satisfied that the expulsion is not in the interests of the firm but for some private reasons.[54] A power of expulsion can continue in a partnership at will.[55] It is unlawful for a firm consisting of six or more persons to discriminate against a person on ground of race by expelling him from the partnership; it is unlawful for a firm of any number of partners to discriminate in the same way on ground of sex.[56]

50.24 **Retirement of Partner.**—Where the partnership is at will, *i.e.* not for any fixed term, any partner may determine the partnership by giving notice to all the other partners of his intention to do so.[57] In the absence of agreement to the contrary the notice may take immediate effect. There is nothing in the Act to preclude a partner from retiring without dissolving the firm, and its competency is recognised at common law, subject to the condition that a provision to that effect has been made in the partnership deed, or that all the partners consent.[58]

50.25 **Tacit Relocation.**—Where a partnership is for a fixed term, which has expired, and the business is carried on without any express agreement by such of the partners as habitually acted in the affairs of the firm, the law will infer continuance of the relationship as a partnership at will.

> (3) A partner making, for the purpose of the partnership, any actual payment or advance beyond the amount of capital which he has agreed to subscribe, is entitled to interest at the rate of five per cent. per annum from the date of the payment or advance.
>
> (4) A partner is not entitled, before the ascertainment of profits, to interest on the capital subscribed by him.
>
> (5) Every partner may take part in the management of the partnership business.
>
> (6) No partner shall be entitled to remuneration for acting in the partnership business (*Pender* v. *Henderson* (1864) 2 M. 1428).
>
> (7) No person may be introduced as a partner without the consent of all existing partners.
>
> (8) Any difference arising as to ordinary matters connected with the partnership business may be decided by a majority of the partners, but no change may be made in the nature of the partnership business without the consent of all existing partners.
>
> (9) The partnership books are to be kept at the place of business of the partnership (or the principal place, if there is more than one), and every partner may, when he thinks fit, have access to and inspect and copy any of them. (As to inspection by accountant or solicitor, see *Cameron* v. *McMurray* (1855) 17 D. 1142; *Bevan* v. *Webb* [1901] 1 Ch. 724.)

[53] s. 25.
[54] *Blisset* v. *Daniel* (1853) 10 Hare 493; *Green* v. *Howell* [1901] 1 Ch. 495; *cf. Re Westbourne Galleries* [1973] A.C. 360, *per* Lord Wilberforce at p. 380.
[55] *Walters* v. *Bingham* [1988] F.T.L.R. 260, at p. 268.
[56] Race Relations Act 1976, s. 10(1)(*d*); Sex Discrimination Act 1975, s. 11(1)(*d*), as amended by Sex Discrimination Act 1986, s. 1(3).
[57] s. 26.
[58] Bell, *Comm.*, ii, 522 and see s. 32.

The terms of the partnership which has expired will prevail, in so far as is consistent with a partnership at will.[59] In order that a partnership may be continued by tacit relocation there must be at least two partners surviving at the expiry of the fixed date. It is not enough that one surviving partner continues the business.[60] From the same case it appears that the business must be carried on for some period long enough to justify the inference that continuance was intended; no inference can be drawn from acts done on a single day. A right of pre-emption conferred on one of the partners and exercisable at the expiry of a fixed period, has been held to survive as a condition of a subsequent partnership by tacit relocation;[61] but a clause under which certain rights depended on notice being given three months before the expiry of the partnership was held inconsistent with a partnership at will, in respect that there was no time from which the three months could be computed.[62]

50.26 Rescission for Fraud: Misrepresentation.—Like other contracts, partnership may be rescinded on the ground that it was induced by fraud or misrepresentation.[63] As it is a contract *uberrimae fidei* (of utmost good faith), proof of the concealment of material facts will justify rescission,[64] and will, where fraud or negligence is proved, found a claim for damages.[65] While no claim of damages can be founded on an innocent and non-negligent misrepresentation, the Act provides (section 41) that the party entitled to rescind shall have the following rights, whether fraud be proved or not: (a) to a lien on, or right of retention of, the surplus of the partnership assets, after satisfying the partnership liabilities, for any sum of money paid for the purchase of a share in the partnership and for any capital contributed; (b) to stand in the place of the creditors of the firm for any payments made by him in respect of the partnership liabilities; (c) to be indemnified by the person guilty of the fraud or making the representation against all the debts and liabilities of the firm.[66]

50.27 Dissolution of Partnership.—The Act provides (section 32): 'Subject to any agreement between the partners[67], a partnership is dissolved—(a) if entered into for a fixed term,[68] by the expiration of that term;[69] (b) if

---

[59] s. 27.
[60] *Wallace* v. *Wallace's Trs.* (1906) 8 F. 558.
[61] *Macgowan* v. *Henderson*, 1914 S.C. 839.
[62] *Neilson* v. *Mossend Iron Co.* (1886) 13 R. (H.L.) 50.
[63] See paras. 9.2–9.12, *supra*.
[64] *Ferguson* v. *Wilson* (1904) 6 F. 779.
[65] Law Reform (Misc. Provs.) (Scotland) Act 1985, s. 10.
[66] The section is mainly founded on *Adam* v. *Newbigging* (1888) 13 App. Cas. 308.
[67] For a case where a contractual right to dissolve could not be exercised by partners in breach of the partnership contract, see *Hunter* v. *Wylie*, 1993 S.L.T. 1091.
[68] *Walters* v. *Bingham* [1988] 1 F.T.L.R. 260, at p. 266.
[69] See, as to continuance by tacit relocation, para. 50.25, *supra*.

entered into for a single adventure or undertaking, by the termination of that adventure or undertaking;[70] (c) if entered into for an undefined time, by any partner giving notice[71] to the other or others of his intention to dissolve the partnership. In the last-mentioned case the partnership is dissolved as from the date mentioned in the notice as the date of dissolution, or, if no date is so mentioned, as from the date of the communication of the notice.' A partnership is also dissolved by agreement, whether express or to be inferred from the partners' actings,[72] in the absence of any agreement to the contrary, by the death or bankruptcy of any partner[73] and, irrespective of agreement, by the happening of any event which makes it unlawful for the business of the firm to be carried on or for the members of the firm to carry it on in partnership.[74] So where, on the declaration of war, one of the partners became an alien enemy, it was held that, as partnership with an alien enemy was illegal, the result was necessarily the instant dissolution of the firm.[75]

50.28 Dissolution by Court.—A partnership may be dissolved by the court,[76] on application by a partner, on the following grounds (section 35): (a) that a partner is of permanently unsound mind; (b) that a partner, other than the partner suing, is permanently incapable of performing his part under the partnership contract; (c) that a partner, other than the partner suing, has been guilty of such conduct as, regard being had to the nature of the business, is calculated prejudicially to affect the carrying on of the business;[77] (d) where a partner, other than the partner suing, wilfully or persistently commits a breach of the partnership agreement, or otherwise so conducts himself in matters relating to the partnership business that it is not reasonably practicable for the other partners to carry on the business in partnership with him; (e) when the business of the partnership can be carried on only at a loss; (f) whenever, in any case, circumstances have arisen which render it just and equitable that the partnership be dissolved.[78]

50.29 Effects of Dissolution.—On dissolution the general authority of each partner to bind the firm is determined. But each partner (unless he is bankrupt) retains authority to bind the firm, in so far as may be

[70] See *Gracie* v. *Prentice* (1904) 42 S.L.R. 9; *Millar* v. *Strathclyde R.C.*, 1988 S.L.T. (Lands Tr.) 9.

[71] For the effect of bad faith see *Walters, supra*, at p. 267.

[72] *Jassal's Exrx.* v. *Jassal's Trs.*, 1988 S.L.T. 757 (not reclaimed).

[73] s. 33; *William S. Gordon & Co.* v. *Mrs. Mary Thomson Partnership*, 1985 S.L.T. 122.

[74] s. 34; *Hudgell Yeates & Co.* v. *Watson* [1978] Q.B. 451. Note also the Iraq and Kuwait (United Nations Sanctions) Order 1990 (S.I. 1990 No. 1651).

[75] *Stevenson* v. *Cartonnagen-Industrie* [1918] A.C. 239.

[76] For the scope of arbitration, see *Roxburgh* v. *Dinardo*, 1981 S.L.T. 291.

[77] *e.g.*, a conviction for dishonesty, though not a matter affecting the firm, *Carmichael* v. *Evans* [1904] 1 Ch. 486.

[78] As to the construction of 'just and equitable,' in company cases, see *Elder* v. *Elder & Watson*, 1952 S.C. 49; *Re Westbourne Galleries* [1973] A.C. 360 and para. 51.47, *infra*.

necessary to wind up the affairs of the partnership, and to complete transactions begun but unfinished at the date of dissolution.[79] So where trust money was lodged with a bank on consignation receipt, payable to a firm of law agents, it was held that the bank was justified in accepting the signature of the firm name by one of the partners, some years after the firm had been dissolved, on the ground that the uplifting of the money was the completion of a transaction left unfinished at the date of the dissolution of the partnership.[80]

On dissolution, the winding up of the partnership affairs is primarily with the surviving partner or partners. Any partner may apply to the court to wind up the business and affairs of the firm,[81] but the court will not readily, or merely on averments that differences have arisen between the partners, accede to the application by one partner for the appointment of a judicial factor.[82]

If a premium has been paid for entering into a partnership for a fixed term, and the partnership has been dissolved before the expiration of that term otherwise than by the death of a partner (e.g. by supervening illegality) the court may order repayment of the whole or part of the premium. This does not apply to the case where the dissolution is due wholly or chiefly to the misconduct of the partner who paid the premium, or where the firm is dissolved by an agreement containing no provision for the return of the premium.[83]

50.30 Carrying on Business after Dissolution.—When any member of a firm has died or ceased to be a partner, and the other partners carry on the business of the firm with its capital or assets without any final settlement of accounts, then, unless there is an agreement to the contrary, or an option to purchase the share of the deceased or outgoing partner has been exercised,[84] he or his estate has the option of claiming such share of the profits made after the dissolution as the court may find to be attributable to the use of his share of the partnership assets, or five per cent. interest on the amount of his share of the partnership assets.[85] So where a partnership was dissolved on the declaration of war on the ground that one partner had become an alien enemy, and the other partners had carried on the business, it was held that a share of the

---

[79] s. 38. See *Welsh* v. *Knarston*, 1973 S.L.T. 66. See also, as to contracts with the 'house,' *Inland Revenue* v. *Graham's Trs.*, 1971 S.C. (H.L.) 1; *Jardine-Paterson* v. *Fraser*, 1974 S.L.T. 93.

[80] *Dickson* v. *National Bank*, 1917 S.C. (H.L.) 50.

[81] See s. 39; but only to the Court of Session, not to the sheriff court: *Pollock* v. *Campbell*, 1962 S.L.T. (Sh.Ct.) 89.

[82] *Schulze* v. *Gow* (1877) 4 R. 928; *Elliot* v. *Cassilis* (1907) 15 S.L.T. 190; *Allan* v. *Gronmayer* (1891) 18 R. 784. A judicial factor was appointed in *Carabine* v. *Carabine*, 1949 S.C. 521, and in *McCulloch* v. *McCulloch*, 1953 S.C. 189, where observations were made on the duties of the factors.

[83] s. 40.

[84] s. 42(2).

[85] s. 42(1). On the definition of assets, see para. 50.31, *infra*.

profits, so far as attributable to the use of the enemy partner's share of the assets, must be set aside for him, and would become payable on the conclusion of peace.[86]

50.31 Settling Accounts.—In the absence of any agreement to the contrary the following rules[87] hold in settling accounts on the dissolution of a partnership:

(a) Losses, including losses and deficiencies of capital, shall be paid first out of profits, next out of capital, and lastly, if necessary, by the partners individually in the proportion in which they were entitled to share profits;

(b) The assets[88] of the firm, including the sums, if any, contributed by the partners to make up losses or deficiencies of capital, shall be applied in the following manner and order:

   1. In paying the debts and liabilities of the firm to persons who are not partners therein;
   2. In paying to each partner rateably what is due from the firm to him for advances as distinguished from capital;
   3. In paying to each partner rateably what is due from the firm to him in respect of capital[89];
   4. The ultimate residue[90] if any, shall be divided among the partners in the proportion in which profits are divisible.

In the absence of agreement to the contrary, where rights in capital fall to be determined by reference to accounts or balance sheets, assets should be entered at their fair market value.[91]

Further Reading

Clark, *A Treatise on the Law of Partnership* (1866).
Gretton, 'Who Owns Partnership Property?', 1987 J.R. 163.
Gretton, 'Problems in Partnership Conveyancing' (1991) 36 J.L.S.S. 232.
Gretton, 'Inhibitions and Partnerships' (1991) 36 J.L.S.S. 471.
Hemphill, 'The Personality of the Partnership in Scotland,' 1984 J.R. 208.
Lindley and Banks, *Partnership* (16th ed., 1990).
Miller, *The Law of Partnership in Scotland* (2nd ed., 1994).
Pollock, *Partnership* (15th ed., 1952).
Underhill, *Partnership* (11th ed., 1981).
Wilson, *The Scottish Law of Debt* (2nd ed., 1991), §§ 30.6–30.14.

[86] *Stevenson* v. *Cartonnagen-Industrie* [1918] A.C. 239.
[87] s. 44. For interest see *Roxburgh Dinardo & Partners' J.F.* v. *Dinardo*, 1993 S.L.T. 16
[88] For the distinction between a firm's assets and its capital, see *Noble* v. *Noble*, 1983 S.L.T. 339 (Appendix), and *Thom's Exrx.* v. *Russel & Aitken*, 1983 S.L.T. 335; Lindley and Banks, *Partnership*, p. 422.
[89] *Garner* v. *Murray* [1904] 1 Ch. 57.
[90] *Rowella Pty. Ltd.* v. *Abfam Nominees Pty. Ltd.* (1989) 168 C.L.R. 301, H.Ct.Aust.
[91] *Noble* v. *Noble, supra; Shaw* v. *Shaw*, 1968 S.L.T. (Notes) 94; *Clark* v. *Watson*, 1982 S.L.T. 450; *Thom's Exrx., supra; Wilson* v. *Dunbar*, 1988 S.L.T. 93. Where, as in calculating remuneration, adjustment to fair market value would cause injustice, the general rule should not be applied: *Lindsay* v. *High*, O.H., May 9, 1984, unreported (decision of Lord Davidson).

CHAPTER 51

COMPANY LAW

51.1 Methods of Incorporation.—Parties who desire to carry on any business or enterprise together, otherwise than as partners, may be incorporated by charter or letters patent from the Crown; by a Private Act of Parliament; or under the provisions of the Companies Acts. A Private Act of Parliament is still necessary in the case of any enterprise where power to take land compulsorily is required. The provisions of such Private Acts, so far as not altered by the particular Act, are set forth by the Companies Clauses Acts, 1845–1889.

The 1985 consolidations of company law, represented by the Companies Act, the Business Names Act, the Company Securities (Insider Dealing) Act, and the Companies Consolidation (Consequential Provisions) Act, have had to be supplemented or replaced by the Insolvency Acts of 1985 and 1986, the Company Directors Disqualification Act 1986, the Financial Services Act 1986 and the Companies Act 1989: this chapter deals only with companies formed by registration under that Act. The Companies Act 1985 remains the principal statute dealing with the establishment, financing, management and general administration of companies. Winding up, receiverships, administration orders and voluntary arrangements are now dealt with in the Insolvency Act 1986.[1] The Financial Services Act 1986 regulates the flotation of companies and the Companies Act 1989, in addition to implementing E.C. Directives on consolidated accounts and audits, amends the Companies Act 1985 and the Financial Services Act 1986 in relation to company investigations, reforms the *ultra vires* doctrine, and will amend the current rules on registration of company charges. Insider dealing is now dealt with in Part V of the Criminal Justice Act 1993. The continuing and ever-increasing role of Community law will ensure further legislation for many years to come. A detailed examination of company law is clearly beyond the scope of this work.

It is not essential to the formation of a company that its objects should be commercial or the making of profit. Any persons associated for any lawful purpose may, by complying with the provisions of the Act as to registration, form an incorporated company, with or without limited liability.[1a] A trade union, however, cannot be registered under the Companies Act.[2]

---

[1] As amended by the Insolvency Act 1994.
[1a] Companies Act 1985, s. 1.
[2] Para. 6.14, *supra*.

51.2 Company Distinct from Members.—A company, once incorporated,[3] is a legal personality distinct from its shareholders.[4] So though all the shareholders may, in the event of war, become alien enemies, the company does not necessarily become so, and may retain its title to sue.[5] And the fact that all the interest in the company's profits is in the hands of one individual does not make him liable for its debts to any extent beyond the amount unpaid on the shares which he has agreed to take. So where the memorandum was signed by A and six members of his family, all the shares except six were held by A, and he held debentures giving him a preferable right to all the company's assets, it was held, in liquidation, that there were no grounds on which he could be rendered personally liable for trade debts.[6] So also the fact that an individual was controlling shareholder and governing director of a company did not preclude the contractual relationship of employer and employee between himself and the company: it was a logical consequence of *Salomon's* case that one person might function in the dual capacities of agent and servant of the company.[7] Similarly, where a firm of solicitors had advised the liquidator of a company, it was the liquidator as agent for the company and not its individual members who had a right to challenge their account for professional fees.[8] And it is probably established that when a wrong such as injury to neighbouring property,[9] or infringement of a patent,[10] is committed in the course of company management, the fact that two persons are the only directors and the only shareholders does not involve them in any personal liability. On the same principle no shareholder has an insurable interest in any asset belonging to the company,[11] and the owner of shop premises which were acquired compulsorily by a local authority and which were occupied not by him but by a company of which he was the principal shareholder was held not to be entitled to compensation for disturbance.[12]

The courts may in certain circumstances be prepared to lift, or pierce, the corporate veil and to look behind the company as a separate legal person to the position of its incorporators.[13] This has been done in cases where the control of the company is in issue, as may arise in connection with the taxation of companies[14] or under the law relating to trading

---

[3] Prior to incorporation a company has no legal existence: see *F.J. Neale (Glasgow)* v. *Vickery*, 1973 S.L.T. (Sh.Ct.) 88.

[4] For discussion of this principle, see Palmer, *Company Law*, paras. 2.1501 *et seq.* A subsequent change of name does not affect this: *Vic Spence Associates* v. *Balchin*, 1990 S.L.T. 10.

[5] *Continental Tyre Co.* v. *Daimler* [1916] 2 A.C. 307.

[6] *Salomon* v. *Salomon & Co.* [1897] A.C. 22.

[7] *Lee* v. *Lee's Air Farming* [1961] A.C. 12.

[8] *Davidson & Syme, W.S.* v. *Kaye*, 1970 S.L.T. (Notes) 65.

[9] *Rainham Chemical Works* v. *Belvedere Co.* [1921] 2 A.C. 465.

[10] *British Thomson Houston Co.* v. *Crowther* [1924] 2 Ch. 33.

[11] *Macaura* v. *Northern Insurance Co.* [1925] A.C. 619.

[12] *Woolfson* v. *Strathclyde R.C.*, 1978 S.C. (H.L.) 90.

[13] For a discussion of this principle, see Gower, Chap. 6.

[14] *S. Berendsen* v. *I.R.C.* [1958] Ch. 1; *Re Nadler Enterprises Ltd.* [1981] 1 W.L.R. 23.

with the enemy,[15] or where the device of incorporation has been used for some illegal or improper purpose.[16] The general rule, however, is that any departure from a strict observance of the principle will be appropriate only where special circumstances exist indicating that the company is a mere façade concealing the true facts.[17]

As a general rule, a company cannot be guilty of an offence which it, unlike its human agents, is incapable of committing as an entity. It cannot, for example, be charged with perjury or an offence for which imprisonment is the only penalty.[18] It has been held competent to charge a company with a common-law offence involving *mens rea*.[19] Corporate criminal liability may be imposed[20] or excluded[21] by statute.

51.3 Kinds of Company.—A company incorporated under the Companies Act may take a variety of forms. The three basic types of company are those with liability limited by shares, those with liability limited by guarantee and those whose liability is unlimited.[22] A company whose liability is limited by shares or by guarantee and having a share capital may be registered either as a private company or as a public company; all other companies registered under the Act are private companies.[23] It is now possible also to incorporate as a single member private company limited either by shares or by guarantee.[24] The Act also provides for the registration of certain companies not formed under the Companies legislation[24a] such as joint stock companies[25] and of companies incorporated elsewhere than in Great Britain which establish a place of

---

[15] *Continental Tyre Co.* v. *Daimler, supra.*

[16] *Merchandise Transport* v. *British Transport Commission* [1962] 2 Q.B. 173.

[17] *Tunstall* v. *Steigmann* [1962] 2 Q.B. 593, *per* Ormerod L.J. at p. 601; *Woolfson* v. *Strathclyde R.C., supra, per* Lord Keith of Kinkel at p. 96. Note also *City of Glasgow D.C.* v. *Hamlet Textiles Ltd.*, 1986 S.L.T. 415; *Adams* v. *Cape Industries plc* [1990] 2 W.L.R. 657; *Multinational Gas and Petrochemical Co.* v. *Multinational Gas and Petrochemical Services Ltd.* [1983] Ch. 258.

[18] *R.* v. *I.C.R. Haulage Ltd.* [1944] K.B. 551; *D.P.P.* v. *Kent and Sussex Contractors Ltd.* [1944] K.B. 146; *Dean* v. *John Menzies (Holdings) Ltd.*, 1981 J.C. 23, *per* Lord Cameron at p. 31. Note also *Richmond-on-Thames B.C.* v. *Pinn & Wheeler Ltd.* [1989] R.T.R. 354.

[19] *Purcell Meats (Scotland) Ltd.* v. *McLeod*, 1987 S.L.T. 528. In *Dean* v. *John Menzies (Holdings) Ltd., supra,* the majority (Lord Cameron dissenting) expressly reserved their opinion on whether a company can be guilty of a common-law offence. In *P. & O. European Ferries (Dover) Ltd.* [1991] 93 Cr. App. Rep. 72, it was held that a company could be guilty of manslaughter. The case arose from the Zeebrugge disaster and the prosecution was, ultimately, unsuccessful.

[20] Insurance Companies Act 1982, s. 92.

[21] Criminal Justice Act 1993 Pt. V, s. 52. Only an 'individual' can be guilty of insider dealing.

[22] s. 1(2); see para. 51.5, *infra.*

[23] s. 1(3); see para. 51.6, *infra.*

[24] The Companies (Single Member Private Limited Companies) Regulations 1992 (S.I. 1992 No. 1699), adding Companies Act 1985, ss. 1(3A), 680(1A). It remains impossible to form a single member limited liability public company.

[24a] *Ibid.*

[25] s. 680; for the definition of joint stock company see s. 683.

business in Great Britain,[26] known as oversea companies.[27] Special provisions apply to oversea companies which are Channel Islands and Isle of Man companies.[28]

51.4 European Economic Interest Grouping.—This new type of business grouping is intended to facilitate collaborative ventures between companies, partnerships and individuals located in the European Community.[29] An E.E.I.G. must be registered with the Registrar of Companies[30] but it is not a company and its members are liable jointly and severally if it cannot meet its debts. An E.E.I.G. cannot be formed for the purpose of making profits but to 'facilitate or develop the economic activities of its members.'[31] The Business Names Act 1985 applies to E.E.I.G.s as do a number of the provisions of the Companies Act 1985 and Part III of the Insolvency Act 1986.

51.5 Limited and Unlimited Liability.—A company which is formed with the liability of its members limited by its memorandum to the amount, if any, unpaid on the shares respectively held by them is known as a company limited by shares.[32] When the liability of the members is limited by the memorandum to such amount as the members may respectively thereby undertake to contribute to its assets in the event of its being wound up, it is known as a company limited by guarantee.[33] A company not having any limit on the liability of its members is known as an unlimited company.[34] A company may also be formed with limited liability as to the shareholders, but unlimited as to the directors,[35] although in practice this is almost never done. A company limited by shares must, by definition, have share capital. A company cannot, with effect from December 22, 1980, be formed as or become a company limited by guarantee with share capital.[36] Unlimited companies may be formed with or without share capital. As a general rule the name of a company limited by shares or by guarantee, not being a public company, must have 'limited' as its last word, and the name of a public company must end with the words 'public limited company' which must not be preceded by the word 'limited.'[37] Abbreviated versions of these words

---

[26] ss. 691–703.

[27] Defined in s. 744.

[28] s. 699.

[29] Council Regulation (E.E.C.) No. 2137/85 implemented by the European Economic Interest Grouping Regulations 1989 (S.I. 1989 No. 638). See Anderson, *European Economic Interest Groupings* (1990); Israel, 'The E.E.I.G.—A Major Step Forward for Community Law' (1989) 9 Co. Law 14.

[30] S.I. 1989 No. 638, regs. 3, 9.

[31] Council Regulation (E.E.C.), art. 3.

[32] s. 1(2)(*a*).

[33] s. 1(2)(*b*).

[34] s. 1(2)(*c*).

[35] s. 306.

[36] s. 1(4).

[37] s. 25. The omission of the word 'limited' in a legal document is not necessarily fatal: see *Whittam* v. *Daniel & Co.* [1962] 1 Q.B. 271; *cf. Wolfe* v. *Robertson* (1906) 8 F. 829.

which may be used are 'ltd' for 'limited' and 'plc' for 'public limited company.'[38] A company which is registered as limited may be re-registered as unlimited, and vice versa.[39]

Certain private companies are exempt from the requirements relating to the use of 'limited' as part of the company name.[40] These are associations for the promotion of commerce, art, science, education, religion, charity or any profession whose memoranda or articles require its profits or other income to be applied in promoting its objects, prohibit the payment of dividends to its members and require its assets on winding up to be transferred either to another body with similar objects or whose objects are the promotion of charity. The company must be registered as a company limited by guarantee.[41] A company which is exempt from the use of the word 'limited' as part of its name is required to state in all business letters and order forms of the company the fact that it is a limited company.[42] In an unlimited company each shareholder is liable for all the debts of the company. In a company limited by guarantee, the liability of each member is limited to the amount he undertakes to contribute in the event of the company being wound up.[43] In a company limited by shares each member is liable only for the amount of the shares which he has agreed to take, the time for payment depending on the regulations of the particular company. If, however, a public company carries on business for more than six months without having at least two members, every person who is a member of the company during the time that it so carries on business after those six months and who knows that it is carrying on business with only one member is liable for all debts contracted by the company during that time.[44] This rule has, however, been abolished in respect of a private limited company.[45]

51.6 Public and Private Companies.—A company having share capital may be registered as a private or as a public company. A public company is a company limited by shares or limited by guarantee and having a share capital the memorandum of which states that it is to be a public company and which has been registered in compliance with the requirements of the Act as to the registration or re-registration of a company as a public company.[45a] These include the requirements that the name under which it is registered must end with the words 'public

---

[38] s. 27.

[39] ss. 49–52.

[40] s. 30; they are exempt also from certain other requirements: see s. 30(7), and are free to adopt a name which does not include the word 'company.'

[41] s. 30(2). Note that this subsection provides that companies limited by shares which were licensed before February 25, 1982 continue to enjoy the exemption.

[42] s. 351(1)(d).

[43] See, as to companies limited by guarantee, Insolvency Act 1986, ss. 74(3), 75; *Robertson* v. *British Linen Co.* (1891) 18 R. 1225.

[44] s. 24.

[45] s. 1(3).

[45a] S.I. 1992 No.1699, reg. 2(1), Sched., para. 2 amending Companies Act 1985, s. 24.

limited company' and that the amount of the share capital stated in the memorandum must not be less than the authorised minimum.[46] A private company is every company that is not a public company. No minimum is prescribed for its share capital if it has any, and its shares need not be paid up. A private company must not issue or cause to be issued in the United Kingdom any advertisement offering securities to be issued by that company.[47]

A company which is registered as a public company may not do business or exercise any borrowing powers unless the Registrar has issued it with a certificate, commonly called a trading certificate, that he is satisfied that the nominal value of the company's allotted share capital is not less than the authorised minimum.[48] The certificate issued by the Registrar is conclusive evidence that the company is entitled to do business and to exercise any borrowing powers. A third party who does business with a public limited company before a trading certificate has been issued to it is protected. The transaction is valid as against the company, and the directors of the company are jointly and severally liable to indemnify the third party for any loss or damage which he has suffered in consequence of the company's failure to comply with its obligations.[49] A private company does not require a trading certificate before it does business or exercises any borrowing powers. A public company must have at least two directors but a private company is required only to have at least one.[50] The minimum number of members needed to carry on business as a public company is two, and one in the case of a private company.[51]

51.7 Registration of Company.—A company, whether public or private, is brought into existence as a corporation by the registration with the Registrar of its memorandum of association and its articles of association if there are to be any. The memorandum must be signed by two or more persons. On the registration of the memorandum the Registrar issues a certificate that the company is incorporated. The certificate of incorporation is conclusive evidence that the requirements of the Act in respect of registration have been complied with and that the company is authorised and has been properly registered.[52] Each signatory to the memorandum must subscribe for at least one share,[53] and his signature must be attested by at least one witness.[54]

---

[46] Defined in s. 118. At present it means £50,000, but this figure may be altered by statutory instrument. A minimum of 25 per cent of the issued share capital must be paid up: s. 101(1).

[47] Financial Services Act 1986, s. 170. For a list of the various advantages which a private company has over a public company, see Palmer, para. 2.111.

[48] s. 117.

[49] s. 117(8).

[50] s. 282. The sole director of a private company cannot also be its secretary.

[51] s. 24.

[52] ss. 10, 12, 13. *Cotman* v. *Brougham* [1918] A.C. 514.

[53] s. 2(5).

[54] s. 2(6), as amended by the Requirements of Writing (Scotland) Act 1995, s. 14(2) and Sched. 5.

51.8 Statutory Requisites of Memorandum.—The memorandum of association must in the case of a company limited by shares or by guarantee state (1) the name of the company; (2) whether the registered office is situated in England and Wales or Wales or Scotland; (3) the objects of the company; (4) that the liability of the members is limited; (5) in the case of a company having a share capital, the amount of share capital with which the company proposes to be registered and the division thereof into shares of a fixed amount; and (6) in the case of a public company, the fact that it is a public company.[55] A statement of the first directors and secretary of the company and of the intended situation of the company's registered office on incorporation requires to be delivered with the memorandum on application for registration of the company.[56]

51.9 Name.—No company may be registered under a name which is the same as a name appearing in the Registrar's index of company names, or the use of which in the opinion of the Secretary of State would constitute a criminal offence or which in his opinion is offensive.[57] A company may change its name by special resolution.[58] It may be required to change its name by the Secretary of State if its name is either the same as one on the index or which ought to have appeared on the index at the time of registration or is, in his opinion, too like such a name.[59] It may also be required to do so if the name by which the company is registered gives so misleading an indication of its activities as to be likely to cause harm to the public or if it is discovered that the company gave misleading information in order to be registered with the name chosen.[60] Where a company changes its name the Registrar is required to enter the new name in the register in place of the former name and to issue an altered certificate of incorporation, and the change of name has effect from the date on which the altered certificate is issued.[61] A change of name by the company does not affect any rights or obligations of the company[62] and does not affect or interrupt its corporate existence.[63] A contract is valid if entered into in the new name even before the altered certificate

---

[55] ss. 2(1), (3), (5) and 1(3)(a). Provision as to the form of the memorandum of association is made by the Companies (Tables A to F) Regulations 1985 (S.I. 1985 No. 805) as amended by the Companies (Tables A to F) (Amendment) Regulations 1985 (S.I. 1985 No. 1052).

[56] s. 10. Notice of any change of the situation of the registered office must also be given to the Registrar of Companies: s. 287; see also *Ross* v. *Invergordon Distillers*, 1961 S.C. 286.

[57] s. 26. As to the requirement to include the words 'limited' or 'public limited company' as the case may be, see para. 51.5, *supra*.

[58] s. 28(1).

[59] s. 28(2).

[60] ss. 32, 28(3). The latter direction cannot be exercised more than five years after the date of registration.

[61] s. 28(6).

[62] s. 28(7).

[63] *Vic Spence Associates* v. *Balchin*, 1990 S.L.T. 10.

of incorporation has been issued.[64] Every company is required,[65] subject to certain penalties,[66] to display its name in legible characters outside every office or place in which its business is carried on, on its seal and on all business letters, official publications, bills of exchange, invoices, etc., of the company. It is also required to mention in legible characters on all business letters and order forms of the company the place of registration and the number with which it is registered, and the address of its registered office.[67] A company may do business under a name other than the one it is registered with.[68] The use of 'business names' is regulated by the Business Names Act 1985. A company trading under a business name must disclose its corporate name in its business letters, invoices, receipts, demands for payment, and also on its premises.[69] It must also state an address at which service of any documents relating to its business will be effective.[70]

51.10   Objects Clause.—The memorandum of association of a company incorporated under the Companies Act 1985 must state what its objects are.[71] As a consequence of the *ultra vires* doctrine, objects clauses became long, detailed, lists[72] of the things which companies had the capacity and the power to do.[73] In addition, it might be stated that each of the acts specified in the objects clause is to be treated as an independent object[74] or it might confer on the directors a discretion to do anything which, in their honest opinion, could be considered as being ancillary to the company's specific objects.[75] It is now competent for the memorandum to specify that the company has the single object of carrying on business as a 'general commercial company.'[76] Such an object clause signifies that the company has power to do anything 'incidental or conducive' to its trade or business.[77] Two observations may be made on this last option: (1) only trade or business companies

[64] *Lin Pac Containers (Scotland)* v. *Kelly*, 1982 S.C. 50.
[65] ss. 348–350.
[66] See *Scottish & Newcastle Breweries* v. *Blair*, 1967 S.L.T. 72; *cf. Durham Fancy Goods* v. *Michael Jackson (Fancy Goods)* [1968] 2 Q.B. 839.
[67] s. 351.
[68] See, *e.g. Maxform SpA* v. *Mariani and Goodville Ltd.* [1981] 2 Lloyd's Rep. 54 where Goodville Ltd. traded under the business name 'Italdesign.'
[69] Business Names Act 1985, s. 4.
[70] *Ibid.*
[71] s. 2(1)(*c*).
[72] The statutory models prescribed in Tables B-F of the Companies (Tables A-F) Regulations 1985, *supra*, are far less detailed.
[73] 'Powers' are distinct from but ancillary to 'objects': *e.g.* powers to borrow, lend, give guarantees and sign cheques. See *Rolled Steel Products (Holdings) Ltd.* v. *British Steel Corporation* [1985] 3 All E.R. 52; *James Finlay Corp. Ltd.* v. *R. & R.S. Mearns*, 1988 S.L.T. 302; *Thompson* v. *J. Barke & Co. (Caterers) Ltd.*, 1975 S.L.T. 67.
[74] *Cotman* v. *Brougham* [1918] A.C. 514; *Re Introductions Ltd.* v. *National Provincial Bank Ltd.* [1970] Ch. 199.
[75] *Bell Houses Ltd.* v. *City Wall Properties Ltd.* [1966] 2 Q.B. 656.
[76] Companies Act 1985, s. 3A: added by Companies Act 1989, s. 110(1).
[77] *Ibid.*

enjoy it, specific objects are still required for non-trading companies;[78] and (2) it is not clear whether a company can add on this general object to a number of independent objects.[79]

As the law once stood, contracts made for any purpose outwith the objects clause were *ultra vires* and void.[80] *Ultra vires* transactions could not be cured by subsequent ratification by the shareholders.[81] Attenuated by statute,[82] the Companies Act 1989 has practically abolished the *ultra vires* doctrine.[83] The current law may be stated in three propositions:

(1) Nothing done by a company, acting beyond the capacity conferred on it by its memorandum, will be void on the ground that it lacked capacity.[84] Neither a third party nor the company itself can plead *ultra vires* and section 35(1) applies to both gratuitous and onerous acts.[85]

(2) Shareholders may apply for an interdict to prevent a company doing some act which goes beyond its stated objects.[86] Interdict cannot, however, be granted after a company has already contracted to do such an act.[86]

(3) Directors are still obliged 'to observe any limitations on their powers' as contained in the memorandum.[87] By special resolution, the members may ratify directors' actions which exceed the company's capacity.[87] But ratification, *per se*, does not relieve the directors of their personal liability for any loss suffered by the company in consequence of their authorisation of acts outwith the company's capacity.[87] To relieve them of such liability, a separate special resolution to that effect must be passed.

Consistent with the abolition of the *ultra vires* doctrine is the complete abolition of the doctrine of constructive notice (whereby anyone dealing

---

[78] Palmer, para. 2.602.

[79] The problem arises because whereas s. 2(1)(c) refers to 'objects,' s. 3A envisages memoranda containing only a single object.

[80] See, *e.g. Ashbury Railway Carriage Co.* v. *Riche* (1875) L.R. 7 H.L. 653; *Re Jon Beauforte (London) Ltd.* [1953] Ch. 131.

[81] *Re Birkbeck Building Society* [1912] 2 Ch. 183.

[82] Companies Act 1985, s. 35(1), re-enacting European Communities Act 1972, s. 9(1).

[83] Companies Act 1989, s. 108, amending by substitution Companies Act 1985, ss. 35–35B. This came into force on February 4, 1991: Companies Act 1989 (Commencement No. 8 and Transitional and Saving Provisions) Order 1990, (S.I. 1990 No. 2569). For transactions made before this date, the law is stated in para. 25.9 of the 9th ed. of this work.

[84] Companies Act 1985, s. 35(1) as amended.

[85] European Communities Act 1972, s. 9(1) and Companies Act 1985, s. 35 (as unamended) both referred to 'dealings' and 'transactions.' There was doubt as to whether a gift was a transaction: *Re Halt Garage (1964) Ltd.* [1982] 3 All E.R. 1016. By referring to an 'act,' the new wording of s. 35(1) resolves the doubt.

[86] s. 35(2).

[87] s. 35(3). On the directors' duty to observe the memorandum, see *Selangor United Rubber Estates Ltd.* v. *Cradock* [1968] 2 All E.R. 1073. The subsection also refers to 'other persons,' this may mean other company officers involved in the directors' actions.

with a company was deemed to know the provisions of public documents such as the memorandum) with regard to both corporate capacity and the board of directors' powers.[87a]

The law is somewhat different for charitable companies. An *ultra vires* act by such a company is unenforceable except in favour of a party who (1) gives full consideration for it, and (2) is either unaware that it is not permitted by the memorandum or that it is beyond the directors' powers or does not appreciate at the time that the company is a charity.[88] The onus of proof rests on the party alleging such knowledge by the third party.[89] This burden may be relatively easy to discharge since if the words 'charity' or 'charitable' are omitted from the company name, its business stationery, invoices and receipts, etc., must state that it is a charity.[90] Where property is sold or transferred *ultra vires* the charitable company, or beyond the directors' powers, a subsequent purchaser's title thereto cannot be disturbed so long as he did not know that the original transaction was *ultra vires*.[91]

A further instance of the survival of the *ultra vires* doctrine concerns transactions between the company and its directors, or the directors of a holding company, or someone connected with a director or company with which he is associated.[92] If such a transaction exceeds the directors' powers as defined, *inter alia*, by the objects clause, it is voidable at the instance of the company.[93] Being voidable, the right to rescind may be lost in the following circumstances:[94] (1) where *restitutio in integrum* cannot be made; (2) where the company has been indemnified in respect of any loss caused by the transaction; (3) where rights have been acquired by a bona fide purchaser who is ignorant of the circumstances rendering the original transaction voidable; and (4) where the transaction has been ratified in the appropriate manner.

51.11   Alteration of Objects.—The objects of a company may be altered, for any purpose, by special resolution.[95] A copy of such a resolution must be delivered to the Registrar within 15 days of its being passed.[96] An alteration may be challenged, within 21 days of the resolution, by the holders of not less than 15 per cent. of the issued share capital (or

---

[87a] s. 35B added by Companies Act 1989, s. 108(1). Note also s. 711A(1) added by s. 142(1) of the 1989 Act: not in force at the time of writing and considered unlikely ever to be brought into force: see Bennett, 1994 *Business Law Bulletin*, No. 12, p. 2.

[88] Companies Act 1989, s. 112(3); Companies Act 1985, s. 35(4) as amended by s. 65(1) of the Charities Act 1993.

[89] s. 112(5).

[90] s. 112(6).

[91] s. 112(4).

[92] s. 322A, added by Companies Act 1989, s. 109(1). 'Connected person' includes spouse and children: 1985 Act, s. 346(2).

[93] ss. 322A(1), (2).

[94] s. 322A(5).

[95] s. 4(1), as substituted by the 1989 Act, s. 110(2). The specific, limited grounds upon which alterations were permitted have been abolished.

[96] s. 380(1), (4).

debentures carrying the right to make such an objection), or, where the company is not limited by shares, by not less than 15 per cent. of the members.[97] The court may confirm or reject an alteration and may order the compulsory purchase of objectors' shares.[98] If there are no objections, a copy of the altered memorandum must be delivered to the Registrar within 15 days after the expiry of the period for objection.[99] The legislation is not restricted to the objects clause of the memorandum but to the company's objects wherever they be stated in that document.[1] A charitable company which alters its objects so as to lose its charitable status does not, thereby, acquire the right to apply property or income donated to it for charitable purposes, before the alteration, to non-charitable aims.[2] A charitable company exempted from the requirement of using the designation 'limited,' and being a company limited by guarantee, is prohibited from altering either its memorandum or its articles of association.[3]

51.12 Provisions as to Shares: Alteration and Reduction of Capital.—The provisions of the memorandum with regard to the share capital of the company may be altered, if power to do so is given in the articles of association,[4] in the following respects: (1) the increase of its share capital by the issue of new shares; (2) consolidation and division of its share capital into shares of larger amount; (3) conversion of shares into stock; (4) subdivision of shares into shares of smaller amount; (5) cancellation of shares which have not been taken with resultant diminution of capital. These powers must be exercised by the company in general meeting[5] and notice of their exercise must be given to the Registrar of Companies.[6] If the capital is divided into different classes of shares and the memorandum or the articles authorise the variation of the rights of any class, and such variation is made, objectors holding a minimum of 15 per cent., in aggregate, of the shares of that class, may apply to the court for its cancellation.[7] The expression 'variation' in relation to the rights of a class includes their abrogation.[8]

---

[97] ss. 5(1), (2), (3). A shareholder who has consented to or voted for an alteration is barred from challenging it.

[98] ss. 5(4), (5).

[99] s. 6(1)(a).

[1] *Incorporated Glasgow Dental Hospital* v. *Lord Advocate*, 1927 S.C. 400; *Scottish Housing Associated Ltd., Petrs.*, 1947 S.C. 17.

[2] Companies Act 1989, s. 112(2).

[3] Companies Act 1985, s. 31.

[4] *Metropolitan Cemetery Co.*, 1934 S.C. 65.

[5] s. 121. Where, however, all the shareholders who have a right to attend and vote at a general meeting assent to a matter which the general meeting could carry into effect, that assent is as binding as assent in general meeting would be (*Re Duomatic* [1969] 2 Ch. 365, *per* Buckley J. at p. 373; *cf. Parker & Cooper* v. *Reading* [1926] Ch. 975).

[6] ss. 122, 123: the latter applies only in the case of an increase of share capital.

[7] s. 127; *Re Sound City Films* [1947] Ch. 169.

[8] s. 127(6); and see also *Frazer Bros., Petrs.*, 1963 S.C. 139. *Cf. House of Fraser plc* v. *A.C.G.E. Investments Ltd.*, 1987 S.L.T. 421.

A company having a share capital may, if so authorised by its articles, reduce its share capital by special resolution, subject to confirmation by the court.[9] The court may order that this company must add to its name the words 'and reduced.'[10] There is no limit to the power of a company to reduce its capital, which it may exercise in any way.[11] But without prejudice to that generality it may extinguish or reduce the liability on any of its shares in respect of capital not paid up, cancel any paid-up share capital which is lost or unrepresented by available assets and pay off any paid-up share capital which is in excess of the company's wants.[12] It may also convert issued shares into redeemable shares with a postponed redemption date.[13] A company which desires to reduce its capital must follow the statutory procedure, and the court must be satisfied that the terms are just and equitable as between the various classes of shareholders,[14] and as respects creditors.[15] In exceptional cases the confirmation of the court to a reduction of capital is not required. A company may exercise the right to forfeit the shares of a shareholder who has failed to pay calls, or may accept a surrender from one who is insolvent.[16] Where a company has issued redeemable shares they may be redeemed if they are fully paid and paid for on redemption, but payment may be made only out of distributable profits of the company or the proceeds of a fresh issue of shares made for the purposes of the redemption.[17] As a general rule, a company limited by shares or by guarantee and having a share capital may not purchase its own shares unless authorised to do so by its articles.[18] The shares must be fully paid up and paid for on purchase, and they must be paid for out of distributable profits or the proceeds of a fresh issue. Shares which are redeemed or purchased by the company are treated as cancelled and the amount of the company's issued share capital is diminished by the nominal value of the shares.[19] A payment out of capital by a private company for the redemption or purchase of its shares must be approved by special resolution and must be accompanied by a declaration of solvency by the directors.[20]

[9] ss. 135–140. *John Avery & Co., Petrs.* (1890) 17 R. 1101.
[10] ss. 137(1), (2)(*a*).
[11] s. 135(1).
[12] s. 135(2).
[13] *Forth Wines Ltd., Petr.*, 1993 S.L.T. 170.
[14] *Balmenach Glenlivet Distillery* v. *Croall* (1906) 8 F. 1135; *Caldwell* v. *Caldwell*, 1916 S.C. (H.L.) 120; *Wilsons and Clyde Coal Co.* v. *Scottish Insurance Corporation*, 1949 S.C. (H.L.) 90.
[15] *Westburn Sugar Refineries*, 1951 S.C. (H.L.) 57; see also *Anderson, Brown & Co.*, 1965 S.C. 81: *Lawrie & Symington*, 1969 S.L.T. 221.
[16] *General Property Investment Co.* v. *Craig* (1891) 18 R. 389, and see Table A, arts. 12–22.
[17] ss. 159–161. See also *Quayle Munro, Petrs.*, 1991 G.W.D. 35–2104, conversion of share premium account into distributable profits.
[18] ss. 143, 162–177. Nor, as a general rule, should a company provide financial assistance to another for the purchase of its own shares: ss. 151–158. See D.P. Sellar, 1993 S.L.T. (News) 357.
[19] ss. 160(4), 162(2).
[20] s. 173.

Except as above indicated, a company has no power to alter its memorandum.[21] This rule applies not only to the particulars required by the Act, but to any provision in fact inserted in the memorandum, unless power to alter it is expressly provided.[22]

51.13 Articles of Association.—Together with the memorandum, articles of association may be registered. This is compulsory in the case of an unlimited company, or a company limited by guarantee, but is optional in the case of a company limited by shares.[23] If no articles are registered, articles in a statutory form, known as Table A, apply to a company limited by shares.[24] If articles are registered, Table A applies so far as not modified or excluded.

The articles regulate the management of the company. When registered, they form a contract between the individual shareholders,[25] and between each shareholder and the company,[26] but not between the company and outsiders. So a solicitor could not enforce a clause in the articles providing that he should be employed.[27] If a provision contained in the articles is contrary to public policy it does not bind the members and will not be enforced by the court.[28]

51.14 Alteration of Articles.—A company has power, by special resolution, but without requiring confirmation by the court, to alter or add to its articles.[29] The power cannot be excluded by any provision in the articles themselves,[30] nor can it be excluded by contract with a third party,[31]

---

[21] s. 2(7).

[22] *Welsbach Incandescent Co.* [1904] 1 Ch. 87.

[23] s. 7.

[24] s. 8(2). Table A is set out in the Companies (Tables A to F) Regulations 1985 (S.I. 1985 No. 805) as amended by the Companies (Tables A to F) (Amendment) Regulations 1985 (S.I. 1985 No. 1052). For model form of articles, in cases where Table A is not adopted, see Palmer, *Company Precedents* (17th ed.), I, 473. The Secretary of State may prescribe by regulations a Table G containing articles which are suited to a partnership company: s. 8A of the 1985 Act as added by the Companies Act 1989, s. 128. No regulations have, as yet, been made. Such a company is defined as 'a company limited by shares whose shares are intended to be held to a substantial extent by or on behalf of its employees: s. 8A.

[25] *Welton* v. *Saffery* [1897] A.C. 299.

[26] s. 14; *Hickman* v. *Kent Sheepbreeders' Association* [1915] 1 Ch. 881; *Alexander Ward & Co.* v. *Samyang Navigation Co.*, 1975 S.C. (H.L.) 26.

[27] *Eley* v. *Positive Life Assurance Co.* (1874) 1 Ex.D. 88; *Alexander Ward & Co.* v. *Samyang Navigation Co., supra*, per Lord Fraser at p. 36.

[28] *St. Johnstone F.C.* v. *Scottish Football Association*, 1965 S.L.T. 171.

[29] s. 9. The courts have no power to alter a company's articles: *Bratton Seymour Service Ltd.* v. *Oxborough* [1992] E.G.C.S. 28. An agreement between all the members of a company acting together and representing their unanimous will has been held to be effective to amend the company's articles even although there was neither a meeting nor a resolution in writing: *Cane* v. *Jones* [1980] 1 W.L.R. 1451; *cf. Scotmotors (Plant Hire)* v. *Dundee Petrosea*, 1982 S.L.T. 445.

[30] *Malleson* v. *National Insurance Corporation* [1894] 1 Ch. 200; *Russell* v. *Northern Bank Development Corporation Ltd.* [1992] 3 All E.R. 161 (H.L.).

[31] *Southern Foundries (1926)* v. *Shirlaw* [1940] A.C. 701. Note also *Russell* v. *Northern Bank Development Corporation Ltd.* [1992] 3 All E.R. 161.

although an action of damages may lie for the breach. There are no statutory limits to the power to alter the articles, but, by the decisions, a resolution to alter is reducible if it is made in the interest of individual shareholders or classes of shareholders and not bona fide for the benefit of the company as a whole.[32] Nor can accrued rights, such as the right to have a transfer registered, be affected.[33] By section 16 no member of a company, unless he agrees in writing, is bound by an alteration of the memorandum or articles made after he became a member, if it in any way increases his liability to subscribe for shares, to contribute to the share capital or to pay money to the company. Where the articles are altered the company is required to send a copy of the articles as altered to the Registrar.[34]

51.15 Company Contracts.—A contract (or any other document) is signed by a company if signed on its behalf by a director, or the company secretary, or by a person authorised to sign on its behalf.[35] Where a contract (or any other document) appears to have been subscribed by a director, or by the company's secretary, or by anyone bearing to have been authorised to subscribe on the company's behalf, and, further, bears to have been signed by a person as witness to such subscription, and there is nothing in the contract (or document) or in any testing clause contained therein to indicate that it was not subscribed or witnessed, then there is a presumption that it was subscribed by the subscriber and by the company.[36] There is no presumption, however, that the person subscribing as a director or secretary was truly such, nor that someone signing as a person authorised to do so, was really so authorised.[37] Similar provisions apply in respect of alterations made to a document after it has been subscribed.[38] Subscription of share certificates in the manner described will be sufficient.[39] All that is required for the valid drawing, acceptance or indorsement of bills of exchange and promissory notes is the signature of someone authorised by the company.[40]

51.16 Resolutions.—Certain acts are required, either by statute or under the articles, to be done not by the directors or others to whom the

[32] *Sidebottom* v. *Kershaw* [1920] 1 Ch. 154; *Greenhalgh* v. *Arderne Cinemas* [1951] 1 Ch. 286, esp. *per* Lord Evershed M.R. at p. 291.
[33] *McArthur* v. *Gulf Line*, 1909 S.C. 732.
[34] ss. 18, 42, 711.
[35] Requirements of Writing (Scotland) Act 1995, Sched. 2, para. 3(1).
[36] 1995 Act, s. 3(1) as substituted by s. 7(7) and Sched. 2, para. 3(5) of the 1995 Act.
[37] 1995 Act, Sched. 2, para. 3(5)(1B).
[38] 1995 Act, s. 5(8), Sched. 1, para. 1(1) as substituted by Sched. 2, para. 3(6).
[39] Reg. 6 of Table A of the Companies (Tables A-F) Regulations 1985 refers to the sealing of share certificates. The procedure for the execution of company documents described in the text are in lieu of sealing. The matter is dealt with in para. 51.23, *infra*.
[40] s. 37; *Brebner* v. *Henderson*, 1925 S.C. 643.

management of the business of the company may have been delegated, but only by the company. The company acts by resolutions of its members passed at a general meeting. Resolutions are of four kinds, namely, ordinary, extraordinary, special, and, but only in the case of private companies, elective. An ordinary resolution is one passed by a majority at a meeting[41] called in accordance with the articles or Table A, if applicable. Certain ordinary resolutions, such as for the removal of an auditor or director, require special notice to have been given to the company.[42] An extraordinary resolution is one passed by a majority of not less than three-fourths of those who being entitled to do so vote at a general meeting of which notice specifying the intention to propose the resolution as an extraordinary resolution has been duly given.[43] A special resolution is one passed by the same majority, and at a general meeting of which not less than 21 days' notice, specifying the intention to propose the resolution as a special resolution, has been duly given.[44] An elective resolution may be passed by a general meeting of a private company for any of the purposes designated by section 379A of the 1985 Act.[45] These include dispensing with the need to present accounts and reports to a general meeting, dispensing with the need to hold an annual general meeting and with the annual appointment of auditors. Unlike the other types of resolution mentioned here, which require only a majority vote to be passed, an elective resolution requires the unanimous assent of all the shareholders entitled to attend and vote at the meeting.[46] By virtue of section 381A of the 1985 Act, a private company may dispense with the need to pass a resolution in general meeting if a written resolution is signed by or on behalf of all the members who are entitled to vote at the meeting. A public company limited by shares may permit the use of written resolutions by its articles.[46a] Otherwise, a resolution can only be passed at a meeting which has been duly convened and is duly constituted. A declaration by the chairman that the resolution has been carried is conclusive evidence of the fact, unless a poll be demanded, when reference must be had to the number of votes to which each shareholder is entitled.[47] Voting by proxy is usually sanctioned by the articles.[48] A printed copy of every special resolution, extraordinary resolution and of certain other resolu-

---

[41] See s. 370 for general provisions as to meetings and votes.

[42] ss. 388(1), (3); 303(2), (4).

[43] s. 378(1).

[44] s. 378(2). As to computation of period of notice and quorum, see *Neil McLeod & Sons*, 1967 S.C. 16. As to procedure at a meeting, see Table A, arts. 40 *et seq.*

[45] Added by Companies Act 1989, s. 116.

[46] 1985 Act, s. 379A(2).

[46a] Companies (Tables A-F) Regulations, *supra*, Table A, reg. 53.

[47] s. 378(4). *Graham's Morocco Co.*, 1932 S.C. 269. Usually the articles provide that on a poll a shareholder shall have one vote for each share. See Table A, art. 54.

[48] Table A, reg. 59. A shareholder who has given a proxy may, though he has not recalled it, attend the meeting and vote: *Cousins* v. *International Brick Co.* [1931] 2 Ch. 90.

tions and agreements must be forwarded to the Registrar of Companies within 15 days and recorded by him.[49]

51.17 **Issue of shares.**—The issue of shares and debentures is now regulated by Parts 4 and 5 of the Financial Services Act 1986.[50] There are three types of issue: (a) shares which are to be admitted to the Official List of the Stock Exchange; (b) offers of securities on the occasion of their admission to dealings on a recognised investment exchange approved by the Secretary of State for Trade and Industry for the purposes of the Act; (c) an offer of securities which is a primary or secondary offer.[51] Shares can be admitted to the Official List of the Stock Exchange only in accordance with listing rules made by the Council of the Stock Exchange.[52] The listing rules may require the submission to and approval by the Council of the Stock Exchange of 'listing particulars' in such form and containing such information as may be specified in the rules.[53] In addition to the information specified by the listing rules, listing particulars must contain all such information as investors and their professional advisers would reasonably require and reasonably expect to find there for the purpose of making an informed assessment of the assets and liabilities, financial position, profits and losses and prospects of the issuer of the securities and the rights attaching to those securities.[54] On or before the date on which listing particulars are published as required by the listing rules a copy of the particulars must be delivered for registration to the Registrar and a statement that the copy has been delivered to him must be included in the particulars.[55] An advertisement cannot be issued in the United Kingdom in connection with an application for the listing of any securities unless the contents of the advertisement have been submitted to the Council of the Stock Exchange and the Council has approved the contents or authorised the issue of the advertisement without such approval.[56] With regard to unlisted securities, no person can issue or cause to be issued in the United Kingdom an advertisement offering any securities on the occasion of the admission to dealings on an approved exchange unless a prospectus containing information about the securities has been submitted to and approved by the exchange and delivered for registration to the Registrar or the advertisement is such that no agreement can be entered into in pursuance of it until such a prospectus has been submitted, approved and delivered.[57] No person can issue an

[49] s. 380.
[50] Not all of the provisions of Pt. 5 are in force: see Palmer, Vol. 1, para. 5.112.
[51] For definitions of these offers see Financial Services Act 1986, ss. 160(2), (3).
[52] *Ibid.*, ss. 142, 143. These rules and the contents of listing particulars are found in the Stock Exchange *Yellow Book.*
[53] *Ibid.*, s. 144(2).
[54] *Ibid.*, s. 146.
[55] *Ibid.*, s. 149.
[56] *Ibid.*, s. 154.
[57] *Ibid.*, s. 159. For exemptions and exceptions, see ss. 160A, 161.

advertisement offering any securities which is a primary or secondary offer unless he has delivered for registration to the Registrar a prospectus relating to the securities and expressed to be in respect of the offer, or the advertisement was such that no agreement can be entered into in pursuance of it until such a prospectus has been delivered by him to the Registrar.[58] A prospectus must contain such information and comply with such other requirements as may be prescribed by rules made by the Secretary of State.[59] In addition to the information required to be included by virtue of the rules a prospectus must contain all such information as investors and their professional advisers can reasonably require and reasonably expect to find there for the making of an informed assessment of the assets and liabilities, financial position, profits and losses and prospects of the issuer of the securities and the rights attaching to those securities.[60]

51.18   Liability for Misleading and Untrue Statements.—Liability for untrue or misleading statements in either listing particulars or prospectuses is covered by the Financial Services Act 1986, the Companies Act 1985, and the common law.[61] The former imposes liability to compensate anyone acquiring[62] securities on the strength of such statements, or the omission of any information required to be included in these documents, on whoever is responsible for the particulars or prospectus. To succeed, the claimant will need to prove that loss was suffered as a result of the misstatement or omission.[63] The persons responsible for listing particulars or the prospectus are—(a) the issuer of the securities to which the particulars or prospectus relate; (b) where the issuer is a body corporate, each person who is a director of that body at the time when the particulars were submitted or the prospectus registered; (c) where the issuer is a body corporate, each person who has authorised himself to be named, and is named, in the particulars or prospectus as a director or as having agreed to become a director of that body either immediately or at a future time; (d) each person who accepts, and is stated in the particulars or prospectus as accepting, responsibility for, or for any part of, the particulars; (e) each person not falling within any of the foregoing paragraphs who has authorised the contents of, or any part of, the particulars.[64]

There are several defences available to those responsible for these documents: (a) that there were reasonable grounds for believing that the statements made therein were true or that the omission was proper;[65]

---

[58] *Ibid.*, s. 160. For exemptions and exceptions, see ss. 160A, 161.
[59] *Ibid.*, s. 162.
[60] *Ibid.*, s. 163.
[61] The Financial Services Act 1986 does not affect 'any liability which any person may incur apart from [this Act].'
[62] Not just 'subscribing.'
[63] Financial Services Act 1986, ss. 150, 166.
[64] 1986 Act, ss. 152(1), 168(1).
[65] ss. 151(1), 167(1).

(b) that the statement purported to be made by or on the authority of an expert and that the responsible parties reasonably believed, and continued to believe until the time when the securities were acquired, that the expert was competent to make or authorise the statement and had consented to its inclusion in the form and context in which it appeared;[66] (c) that a correction, or statement that an expert was either not competent or had not given his consent, was published in a fashion calculated to draw it to the attention of likely acquirers of securities or that the parties responsible took all reasonable steps to publish these and reasonably believed this to have been done before any securities were acquired;[67] (d) that the offending statement was an accurate and fair reproduction of one made by a public official or contained in an official document;[68] (e) that the party who suffered the loss knew that the statement was misleading or untrue or that something had been omitted.[69] Where securities have been acquired because of a misrepresentation in the listing particulars or prospectus, whether fraudulent or not, the misled party may rescind his contract to take them.[70] After the commencement of the winding up of a company, the right to rescind cannot be exercised.[71] It is, however, no longer the law that a shareholder cannot sue the company for damages for fraudulent misrepresentation in a prospectus (or in listing particulars) while still remaining a member of the company.[72] Damages may be claimed for any negligent misrepresentation on the principle laid down in *Hedley Byrne & Co. Ltd.* v. *Heller & Partners Ltd.*[73] It has been held that where a prospectus was issued in connection with a rights issue, for which the plaintiff subscribed, reliance on it several months later for a subsequent purchase of shares on the open market did not justify an action for negligence.[74]

51.19 Shares: Shareholders.—The shares or other interest of any member in a company are moveable property.[75] Unless all the issued shares, or all the issued shares of a particular class, are fully paid and rank *pari passu*, each share must be distinguished by its appropriate number.[76] Shares

---

[66] ss. 151(2), 167(2).
[67] ss. 151(3), 167(3).
[68] ss. 151(4), 167(4).
[69] ss. 151(5), 167(5).
[70] *Mair* v. *Rio Grande Rubber Estates Ltd.*, 1913 S.C. (H.L.) 74; *Liverpool Palace of Varieties Ltd.* v. *Miller* (1896) 4 S.L.T. 153.
[71] *Addie* v. *Western Bank* (1867) 5 M. (H.L.) 80: as to the commencement of winding up, see para. 51.48, *infra*.
[72] Companies Act 1985, s. 111A, abrogating the decision in *Houldsworth* v. *City of Glasgow Bank* (1880) 7 R. (H.L.) 53.
[73] [1964] A.C. 465.
[74] *Al Nakib Investments (Jersey) Ltd.* v. *Langcroft* [1990] 3 All E.R. 321. Note also *Caparo Industries plc* v. *Dickman* [1990] 2 A.C. 605; *Al Saudi Bank* v. *Clarke Pixley* [1990] Ch. 313; *Morgan Crucible Co. plc* v. *Hill Samuel Bank Ltd.* [1991] 1 All E.R. 148.
[75] s. 182(1)(*a*).
[76] s. 182(2).

may be all of the same class, or of different classes, such as founders', employees', ordinary and preference shares—a matter to be regulated by the articles unless this is expressly or impliedly regulated by the memorandum.[77] The creation of preference shares requires a provision in the articles, but such a provision may be added by special resolution.[78] The terms of the articles under which preference shares are issued are exhaustive of the rights of holders of these shares, and, unless otherwise provided, they have no right to any surplus assets which may remain, in liquidation, after all capital has been repaid.[79] In the absence of any provision to the contrary, preference shares are cumulative; if the full dividend has not been paid in any one year the arrears must be paid before any dividend is declared on the ordinary shares.[80]

Each of the subscribers of the memorandum is deemed to have agreed to become a member of the company, and is a shareholder for the number of shares (usually one) which he thereby agrees to take. Other persons are members of the company if they have agreed to be so, and if their names are entered in its register of members.[81] The general rules of contract as to offer and acceptance apply.[82] A statement of willingness to take shares will not readily be construed as an application.[83] In the ordinary case an application for shares, where there is no prior obligation on either party, is merely an offer, which must be accepted by the company, and may be withdrawn by the applicant.[84] But an application is in substance the acceptance of an offer and cannot be withdrawn, if it is made in response to an undertaking by the company to allot a certain number of shares if applied for,[85] or in pursuance of a prior agreement to underwrite the shares.[86] No allotment can be made of any share capital of a public company offered for subscription unless (a) that capital is subscribed for in full, or (b) the offer states that, even if the capital is not subscribed for in full, the amount of that capital subscribed for may be allotted in any event or in the event of the conditions specified in the offer being satisfied and where such conditions are specified, these must be satisfied.[87] Any condition binding an applicant to waive compliance with it is void.[88] An

[77] *Campbell* v. *Rofe* [1933] A.C. 91; *Re Marshall Fleming & Co. Ltd.*, 1938 S.C. 873. Note also reg. 2 of Table A of the Companies (Tables A-F) Regulations 1985, *supra*.

[78] *Andrews* v. *Gas Meter Co.* [1897] 1 Ch. 361.

[79] *Wilson and Clyde Coal Co.* v. *Scottish Insurance Corporation*, 1949 S.C. (H.L.) 90.

[80] *Partick Gas Co.* v. *Taylor* (1888) 15 R. 711; *Ferguson & Forester* v. *Buchanan*, 1920 S.C. 154.

[81] s. 22.

[82] Paras. 4.1 *et seq.*, *supra*.

[83] *Mason, infra; Millen & Sommerville* v. *Millen*, 1910 S.C. 868.

[84] *Mason* v. *Benhar Coal Co.* (1882) 9 R. 883; *Chapman* v. *Sulphite Paper Co.* (1892) 19 R. 837.

[85] *Millen & Sommerville* v. *Millen*, 1910 S.C. 868.

[86] *Premier Briquette Co.* v. *Gray*, 1922 S.C. 329.

[87] s. 84(1). But only in relation to unlisted shares: Financial Services Act 1986, s. 212(3) and Sched. 17. Note also S.I. 1986 No. 2246.

[88] s. 83(6). Note the observations in n. 87 and S.I. 1988 No. 740.

allotment made in contravention is voidable, at the instance of the applicant, within one month of the allotment, and not later, and it is voidable whether or not the company is in liquidation.[89] As a general rule, to which exceptions exist, a company may not give financial assistance to others to help them purchase its shares.[90] Any agreement to this effect is unlawful and unenforceable by the parties to it.[91] If an agreement to provide assistance can be severed from agreement to purchase shares this may be done and the latter will be enforceable.[92]

No one may carry on the business of dealing in securities unless he is an 'authorised person' or an 'exempted person' under the Financial Services Act 1986.[93]

51.20 Liability on Shares.—A shareholder is liable to pay the amount for the time being unpaid on his shares up to the nominal amount of his shares as calls may be made by the company, or ultimately in its liquidation, and the company has a lien over its shares for debts due to it by the holder.[94] Shares may be issued as fully or partly paid up otherwise than in cash in return for goods, services or other consideration, but the company must in that case, within one month, lodge with the Registrar the written contract (if any) under which the shares were allotted, or, if there were no written contract, a note specifying the consideration given for the shares.[95] The rule applies to bonus shares.[96] Failure renders the officers of the company liable to penalties, but does not affect the validity of the allotment, nor, as was the case under an earlier statute, render the allottee liable for the nominal amount of the shares. He may be so liable if the consideration is proved to be non-existent.[97] The issue of shares at a discount is expressly prohibited.[98] This prohibition may cause difficulty in cases where shares are allotted for a consideration other than cash, but a public company which allots shares in this way is required to have the non-cash consideration independently valued before the allotment is made.[99] Subject to power contained in the articles and notice in the prospectus, a commission may be paid by the

---

[89] s. 85. Note the observations in nn. 87 and 88.

[90] ss. 151–58. See Palmer, Vol. 1, paras 6.501–521. Note also *Brady* v. *Brady* [1989] A.C. 755. On the meaning of 'financial assistance,' see s. 152(1) and *Selangor United Rubber Estates Ltd.* v. *Craddock (No. 3)* [1968] 1 W.L.R. 1555. Note also *Wallersteiner* v. *Moir* [1975] 1 W.L.R. 1093.

[91] *Brady* v. *Brady, supra.*

[92] *Neilson* v. *Stewart*, 1991 S.L.T. 523.

[93] s. 3.

[94] *Bell's Tr.* v. *Coatbridge Tinplate Co.* (1886) 14 R. 246. The articles may expressly confer a lien: regs. 8–11 of Table A of the Companies (Tables A-F) Regulations 1985, *supra.*

[95] s. 88.

[96] *Scottish Heritages Co.* (1898) 5 S.L.T. 336.

[97] *Innes & Co.* [1903] 2 Ch. 254.

[98] s. 100. See *Klenck* v. *East India Mining Co.* (1886) 16 R. 271; *Ooregum Gold Mining Co.* v. *Roper* [1892] A.C. 125.

[99] s. 103.

company to any person in consideration of his subscribing or agreeing to subscribe for shares in the company or procuring subscriptions.[1] Unless these conditions are satisfied the company is prohibited from applying any of its shares or capital money in this way.[2] But payment of a brokerage continues to be lawful.[3]

51.21 Register of Shareholders and of Individual Interests.—A company is bound, under penalties, to keep a register of members either at its registered office or, if the work of making it up is done at another office, there, in which the shares held by each shareholder are distinguished by numbers, so long as they have numbers.[4] Where membership of a private company limited by shares or guarantee falls to one this fact must be recorded in the register of members and, should it rise again, the register must be amended accordingly.[5] Any member without, and anyone else on, payment of a fee is entitled to inspect the register.[6] It cannot be subjected to a lien.[7] By section 360 no notice of any trust may appear on the register of a company in England, but this section does not apply to Scotland, where the usual practice is to register trustees as such. A person registered as a holder of shares in trust incurs the same liability as a person holding them for his own behoof.[8] Any person whose name is, without sufficient cause, entered in or omitted from the register may apply to the court for its rectification. The same remedy is open when unnecessary dely occurs in entering on the register the fact that a person has ceased to be a member. The application may be made by the person aggrieved, by any member of the company, or by the company.[9]

Provision is made in Part VI of the Act for the disclosure to and registration by a public company of substantial individual and group interests in shares which carry unrestricted voting rights. A person who to his knowledge acquires any interest in shares in such share capital of a public company or who ceases to be interested in such shares, or becomes aware that he has done so, is under an obligation to notify the company of these interests in certain circumstances.[10] The obligation to notify also arises where he becomes aware of a change of circumstances relevant to the question whether the interest is notifiable.[11] The interest

---

[1] s. 97 as amended prospectively by Financial Services Act 1986 s. 212 and Scheds. 16, 17. See *Australian Investment Trust* v. *Strand Properties* [1932] A.C. 735.
[2] s. 98.
[3] s. 98(3).
[4] ss. 352, 353.
[5] s. 352A, added by the Companies (Single Member Private Limited Companies) Regulations 1992, *supra*, reg. 2.
[6] s. 356.
[7] *Garpel Haematite Co.* v. *Andrew* (1866) 4 M. 617.
[8] *Muir* v. *City of Glasgow Bank* (1879) 6 R. (H.L.) 21.
[9] s. 359; *Re Transatlantic Life Assurance* [1980] 1 W.L.R. 79.
[10] s. 198(1): as amended by the Disclosure of Interests in Shares (Amendment Regulations) 1993, S.I. 1993 No. 1819.
[11] s. 198(3).

is notifiable at any time when the person concerned is materially interested in shares comprised in the relevant share capital of an aggregate nominal value equal to or more than three per cent. of the nominal value of that share capital. A shareholder also has a notifiable interest where, though not a material interest, the aggregate nominal value of the shares in which he has interests is equal to or more than 10 per cent of the nominal value of the share capital.[12] For this purpose an interest in shares includes an interest of any kind whatsoever in the shares, and any restraints or restrictions to which the exercise of any right attached to the interest may be subject are to be disregarded. A material interest in shares is any interest other than one which is exempt.[13] The obligation to notify must be performed within the period of two days next following the day on which the obligation arises, and the notification must be in writing and must specify the relevant particulars.[14] For the purposes of these provisions account must be taken, in determining whether and if so to what extent a person is interested in the shares, of any interest in such shares which belong to his spouse or any of his children (under the age of 18) or to a body corporate over which he himself exercises a substantial measure of control.[15] Elaborate provisions are made for various interests, such as interests under a contract to purchase shares, to be taken into account and for various other interests, such as discretionary interests under a trust, to be disregarded.[16] In certain circumstances the obligation of disclosure may also arise from an agreement between two or more persons (a 'concert party') which includes provision for the acquisition by one or more of them of interests in shares of a particular public company.[16a]

Every public company must keep a register of the information furnished to it under these provisions, which is to be open to inspection by any person without charge.[17] A public company has power to carry out investigations with regard to share acquisitions and disposals, and it may be required to exercise its powers on the requisition of members of the company holding not less than one-tenth of such of its paid-up capital as carries the right of voting at general meetings.[18] On the conclusion of any investigation the information received must be registered and must also be the subject of a report to the members of the company.[19]

[12] s. 199(2)(a), (b) as amended by S.I. 1993 No. 1819, regs. 1, 2, 4(1).
[13] ss. 208(2); 199(2A). The latter details exempt interests.
[14] s. 202, as amended by Companies Act 1989, s. 134, and by S.I. 1993 No. 1819, regs. 1, 2, 6(1).
[15] s. 203.
[16] ss. 208, 209. See Palmer, Vol. I, paras. 7.204–205.
[16a] ss. 204–206.
[17] ss. 211, 219.
[18] ss. 212–214; see *House of Fraser, Petrs.*, 1983 S.L.T. 500; *Re Lonrho plc (No. 2)* (1988) 4 B.C.C. 234; *Malaga Investments Ltd., Petrs.*, 1987 S.L.T. 603.
[19] ss. 213, 215.

51.22 Transfer of Shares.—Shares in a company may be transferred in the manner prescribed in the articles,[20] which may, or may not, provide that the directors shall have a power to decline transfers of which they do not approve,[21] or, as is common in the case of private companies, that the shares shall not be transferred to an outsider before first being offered to the other members.[22] If not, the shareholder has an absolute right to transfer his shares to anyone he pleases, and thereby to escape liability for calls,[23] unless the transfer is presented on the eve of liquidation, when the directors are entitled to refuse registration.[24] The fact that the transferee was induced by fraud to accept the shares cannot be founded on by the company or by its liquidator.[25] If directors have a right to refuse a transfer they must exercise the power for the benefit of the company, and the transferee may insist on registration on proof that they acted arbitrarily or capriciously. The directors are bound to give reasons for refusal.[26] The result of a valid refusal is that the transferor may avoid the contract on repaying the price; if he does not choose to do so he must regard himself as a trustee for the transferee, bound to receive dividends and hand them on.[27]

51.23 Share Certificates.—A company, under the sanction of penalties for the company, its directors and officers, must issue a share certificate within two months after allotment, and within two months of the registration of any transfer, unless the conditions of the issue of shares otherwise provide. Similar rules apply to debentures.[28] By section 186, a certificate under the company's common seal is sufficient evidence, unless the contrary is shown, of a member's title to the shares he holds. If regularly issued it is conclusive against the company, and therefore if a company, deceived by a forged transfer, issues a certificate, it is barred from denying the title of a bona fide transferee, and is liable to him in the value of the shares.[29] A share certificate specifying the shares held by a member and subscribed by the company in the manner prescribed

---

[20] s. 182(1)(*b*). See Table A, regs. 23 *et seq., Lyle & Scott Ltd.* v. *Scott's Trs.*, 1959 S.C. (H.L.) 64.

[21] For the form of transfers, see Stock Transfer Act 1963, as amended by Stock Exchange (Completion of Bargains) Act 1976. Note also *Dempsey* v. *Celtic Football Co. Ltd.*, 1992 G.W.D. 25–1406. For the transfer of certain securities through a computerised system, see Stock Transfer Act 1982, s. 1.

[22] *Borland's Tr.* v. *Steel Bros. & Co.* [1901] 1 Ch. 279; *Rayfield* v. *Hands* [1960] Ch. 1.

[23] *Re Discoverer's Finance Corporation (Lindlar's case)* [1910] 1 Ch. 312; *cf. Re Swaledale Cleaners* [1968] 1 W.L.R. 1710.

[24] *Dodds* v. *Cosmopolitan Insurance Co.*, 1915 S.C. 992; *cf. Lindlar's Case, supra, per* Buckley L.J. at p. 318.

[25] *McLintock* v. *Campbell*, 1916 S.C. 966.

[26] *Bede Shipping Co.* [1917] 1 Ch. 123; *Stewart* v. *Keiller* (1902) 4 F. 657; *Weinburger* v. *Inglis* [1919] A.C. 606, *per* Lord Atkinson at p. 626. But in the case of private companies, the articles may often provide that the directors are not required to state reasons for refusal.

[27] *Stevenson* v. *Wilson*, 1907 S.C. 445.

[28] s. 185.

[29] *Balkis Co.* v. *Tomkinson* [1893] A.C. 396.

by the Requirements of Writing (Scotland) Act 1995 is also sufficient evidence of the member's title to the shares.[29a] And where a company, either owing to a mistake or to fraud on the part of its officials, issues certificates stating, untruly, that the shares are fully paid up, they will be liable to a party who is induced to advance money on the faith of the certificates.[30] But the company is not bound by the issue of share certificates fraudulently issued by the secretary to which the names of directors have been forged.[31] Anyone who sends a transfer for registration impliedly contracts that he will relieve the company of any liability. So where a banker sent for registration a transfer of corporation stock to which the name of A, the holder, had been forged, and the corporation registered the transfer and issued new certificates to transferees, with the result that they were bound to recognise the right both of A and of the transferees, it was held that they had a right of relief from the banker.[32] The stereotyped statement that no transfer will be registered without the production of the share certificate is a mere statement of intention and does not bind the company, nor make them liable to a party who has advanced money on a deposit of share certificates, and whose right is defeated by a registered transfer of the shares.[33]

Where shares are purchased on the general market through the TALISMAN[34] system, they are transferred in the first instance to SEPON Ltd.,[35] a subsidiary Stock Exchange company, which acts as a clearing house for listed and unlisted securities. SEPON Ltd. subsequently transfers these shares to the purchaser. Transfer via the TALISMAN system does not oblige the company, whose shares have been purchased, to provide SEPON Ltd. with a share certificate.[36] It need only issue a certificate to the purchaser from SEPON Ltd. The logical next step, a paperless share trading system which would remove the need for share certificates, was designated TAURUS.[37] Detailed regulations[38] covering the operation of TAURUS came into force in February 1992 but the scheme was abandoned in March 1993.[38a]

51.24   Majority and Minority Rights.—By his contract with the company, each individual member undertakes to accept as binding upon him the decision of the majority of the shareholders, provided that it is arrived

---

[29a] s. 186(2), added by the Requirements of Writing (Scotland) Act 1995, s. 14(1) and Sched. 4, para. 54.

[30] *Clavering* v. *Goodwin, Jardine & Co.* (1891) 18 R. 652; *Penang Co.* v. *Gardiner*, 1913 S.C. 1203.

[31] *Ruben* v. *Great Fingall Consolidated Co.* [1906] A.C. 439.

[32] *Sheffield Corporation* v. *Barclay* [1905] A.C. 392.

[33] *Rainford* v. *Keith* [1905] 2 Ch. 147; *Guy* v. *Waterlow* (1909) 25 T.L.R. 515.

[34] Transfer Accounting Lodgement for Investors and Stock Management.

[35] Stock Exchange Pool Nominees Ltd.

[36] Companies Act 1985, s. 185(4).

[37] Transfer and Automated Registration of Uncertificated Stock.

[38] The Uncertificated Securities Regulations 1992 (S.I. 1992 No. 225).

[38a] A further system, CREST, is under development at the time of writing.

at in accordance with the law and the articles. This principle is often referred to as the rule in *Foss* v. *Harbottle*.[39] In that case, a minority of the shareholders alleged that the company had a claim of damages against certain of its directors, but at a general meeting the majority resolved that no action should be taken against them. An action against the directors by the minority was dismissed, on the ground that the acts of the directors were capable of confirmation by a majority of the members, and that it was not for the court to interfere with their decision as to what was for the benefit of the company. The rule does not, however, apply where the act in question is *ultra vires* of the company, or illegal, or constitutes a fraud on the minority, or one which infringes the personal rights of a particular shareholder, nor will a resolution passed by a simple majority be binding when a qualified majority is required, as in the case of special or extraordinary resolutions.[40] A resolution constitutes a fraud on the minority if its effect is to discriminate against the minority in favour of the majority shareholders and it was not made bona fide for the benefit of the company as a whole.[41] Under English law a derivative action, raised by one shareholder on his own behalf and that of the other shareholders, and alleging some wrong against the company, is competent. Also competent is a representative action in which one shareholder alleges some wrong done to him and the other shareholders. Neither is competent under Scots law and a shareholder with such a grievance must raise an action in his own name.[42]

If the majority of the shareholders acts in oppression of the minority, the minority may apply to the court for the winding up of the company, on the ground that it is just and equitable to do so,[43] or, in exceptional cases, for the appointment of a judicial factor.[44] The court cannot make a winding-up order on the ground that it is just and equitable to do so, if it is of opinion that some other remedy is available to the petitioners, and that the petitioners are acting unreasonably in seeking to have the company wound up instead of pursuing that other remedy.[45]

Any member of a company who complains that the company's affairs are being or have been conducted in a manner which is unfairly prejudicial to the interests of its members generally or of some part of the members including at least himself, or that any actual or proposed

---

[39] (1843) 2 Hare 461; see Palmer, paras. 58–09 *et seq.*

[40] See Palmer, Vol. 2, paras. 8.806 *et seq.* The suggestion that the rule does not apply where this would not be in the interests of justice has been rejected: see *Prudential Assurance Co. Ltd.* v. *Newman Industries (No. 2)* [1982] Ch. 204.

[41] See *Greenhalgh* v. *Arderne Cinemas* [1951] 1 Ch. 286, *per* Lord Evershed M.R. at p. 291.

[42] But *cf.* Companies Act 1985, s. 461(2)(*c*), *infra.*

[43] Insolvency Act 1986, s. 122(1)(*g*), see para 51.47, *infra*; *Lewis* v. *Haas*, 1971 S.L.T. 57; *Teague, Petr.*, 1985 S.L.T. 469; *Jesner* v. *Jarrad Properties*, 1994 S.L.T. 83.

[44] See *Fraser, Petr.*, 1971 S.L.T. 146. Note also *McGuinness* v. *Black (No. 2)*, 1990 S.L.T. 461; *Weir* v. *Rees*, 1991 S.L.T. 345.

[45] Insolvency Act 1986, s. 125(2); *Gammock* v. *Mitchells (Fraserburgh) Ltd.*, 1983 S.C. 39.

act or omission of the company is or would be so prejudicial, may apply to the court for relief.[46] If the court is satisfied that the application is well founded, it may make such order as it thinks fit for giving relief in respect of the matters complained of.[47] The court has unrestricted powers in this regard, but four possible ways[48] in which it may provide relief are to pronounce an order (a) regulating the conduct of the company's affairs in the future, (b) requiring the company to refrain from doing or continuing to do an act complained of or to do an act which the petitioner has complained it has omitted to do,[49] (c) authorising civil proceedings to be brought in the name and on behalf of the company by such person or persons on such terms as the court may direct or[50] (d) providing for the purchase of the shares of any member of the company by other members of the company or by the company itself.[51] Prejudicial conduct is not defined by statute but conduct may clearly be prejudicial without being oppressive. The courts now appear to interpret 'unfairly prejudicial' in a relatively liberal manner. For example, an injunction has been granted prohibiting a pro rata rights issue, which seemed fair since it did not alter the balance of members' voting power, because it was known that the petitioner could not find the money to take up his shares.[52] The 'interests of members' has also received a more liberal interpretation and is not restricted to his rights as a shareholder. Removal from the post of managing director has been held to be unfairly prejudicial on the basis that it deprived the member concerned of a legitimate expectation.[53] Relief is available to a person who is not a member of a company but to whom shares in the company have been transferred or transmitted by operation of law,[54] such as the personal representatives of a deceased shareholder or his trustee in bankruptcy. It is not limited to persons who hold minority interests in the company, and is therefore available to majority shareholders who can claim to have suffered unfair prejudice as a result of the exercise of their rights by a minority.

The remedies referred to in the previous paragraph may be exercised by an individual member of the company. Certain other rights are conferred by the Act on a minority of the members, and may be exercised despite the wishes of the majority. These include the right of the minority of not less than one-tenth of the paid-up capital to

[46] Companies Act 1985, s. 459: as amended by Companies Act 1989, s. 145, Sched. 19, para. 11.
[47] s. 461(1).
[48] See s. 461(2).
[49] e.g. Whyte, Petr., 1984 S.L.T. 330; Re H.R. Harmer [1959] 1 W.L.R. 62.
[50] See n. 42. This is an exception to the position stated in the text.
[51] e.g. Re London School of Electronics [1986] Ch. 211; see also Meyer v. Scottish Co-operative Wholesale Society, 1958 S.C. (H.L.) 40; Ferguson v. MacLennan Salmon Co. Ltd., 1990 S.L.T. 658.
[52] Re A Company [1985] B.C.L.C. 80.
[53] Re A Company [1986] B.C.L.C. 376. Note also Ebrahimi v. Westbourne Galleries Ltd. [1973] A.C. 360; Re Ringtower Holdings plc (1989) 5 B.C.C. 82.
[54] s. 459(2).

requisition the holding of an extraordinary general meeting,[55] of a specified minority to demand a poll,[56] and of 15 per cent. of the holders of special classes of shares to object to a variation of the rights attached to that class.[57]

51.25 Commencing Business: Meetings.—A public company is not entitled to commence business or exercise any borrowing powers until it has obtained a certificate from the Registrar, commonly called a trading certificate, that he is satisfied that the nominal value of the company's allotted share capital is not less than the authorised minimum.[58] There must also have been delivered to him a statutory declaration signed by a director or secretary of the company that the requirements relating to the company's minimum issued and paid up capital have been complied with, and stating the amount of the expenses incurred in the company's formation and any amount or benefit paid or given to any promoter of the company.[59]

A general meeting of every company must be held at least once in every year, and not more than 15 months from the date of the previous meeting.[60] Subject to the articles, two members personally present at a meeting represents a quorum.[61] In the case of a single member private limited company, a meeting is quorate when one member is personally present or represented by a proxy.[62] Failure to hold such a meeting may result in the directors being held to have ceased to hold office.[63] The following must be laid before the meeting: the company's annual accounts, the directors' report and that of the auditors on the annual accounts.[64] It is no defence to a charge of failure to do so, that these documents were not prepared in time.[64] The appointment of an auditor and the election of directors in place of those who retire take place at the annual general meeting.

Every company must deliver an annual return to the Registrar within 28 days after the date to which it is made up.[65] The return must contain the information specified by sections 364 and 364A. Information previously not required includes the principal business activities of the company and the dates of birth of all its directors.

---

[55] s. 368.

[56] s. 373(1)(b).

[57] s. 127.

[58] ss. 117(1), (2); see *supra*, para. 51.6, as to the effect of doing business before a trading certificate is issued.

[59] ss. 117(2), (3).

[60] s. 366. Subject to the right of a private company, by elective resolution, to dispense with annual general meetings: Companies Act 1985, s. 366A, see para. 51.16, *supra*. On the meaning of year, see *Park* v. *Lawton* [1991] 1 K.B. 588.

[61] s. 370(4). Exceptionally, a meeting of a company may be quorate with one member present: ss. 367(2), 371(2).

[62] s. 370A, added by the Companies (Single Member Private Limited Companies) Regulations 1992, *supra*.

[63] *Alexander Ward & Co.* v. *Samyang Navigation Co.*, 1975 S.L.T. 126.

[64] s. 241.

[65] s. 363. Ss. 363–65 are substituted by Companies Act 1989, s. 139(1).

General meetings other than the statutory meetings and annual general meetings are called extraordinary general meetings. The articles usually provide that the directors may call an extraordinary general meeting at any time they think fit. The directors are bound to convene an extraordinary general meeting on the requisition (which must state the object of the meeting) of the holders of not less than one-tenth of the issued share capital. Should the directors fail to do so within 28 days of the receipt of the requisition the requisitionists, or a majority of them in value, may convene the meeting themselves.[66] Meetings of separate classes of shareholders may be required where it is proposed to alter, vary or affect the rights of a particular class.[67]

51.26 **Accounts and Balance Sheet: Directors' Report.**—Every company must keep accounting records sufficient to show and explain its transactions. These require to disclose with reasonable accuracy at any time the financial position of the company at that time, and to enable the directors to ensure that any balance sheet and profit and loss account which are prepared comply with the requirements of the Act.[68] In particular, accounting records must contain daily receipts and expenditure and record the company's assets and liabilities.[69] Directors are responsible for the annual preparation of a balance sheet and profit and loss account. Both must give a true and fair view of the company's state of affairs and profit or loss respectively.[70] Additionally, they must submit a report presenting a fair view of the company's business development during the financial year and its position at its close, stating any proposed dividend and any amount they propose to carry to reserves.[71] This report should also include additional information regarding any changes in asset values, directors' shareholdings, political and charitable gifts, the employment and training of disabled persons, and the health, safety and welfare at work of its employees.[71a] The accounts must also be accompanied by the auditors' report stating if, in their opinion, those accounts give a true and fair view of the company's finances.[72] The accounting records are to be kept at the registered office of the company or such other place as the directors think fit, and are to be at all times open to inspection by the officers of the company.[73] Every officer of the company who is in default as to the keeping of accounting records is guilty of an offence, unless he acted honestly and his default was excusable in the circumstances.[74]

[66] s. 368. See *Ball* v. *Metal Industries*, 1957 S.C. 315.
[67] See s. 125(2).
[68] s. 221(1).
[69] s. 221(2).
[70] ss. 226(1), (2). For group accounts, see s. 227 *et seq.* For small and medium-sized companies and groups, see ss. 246 *et seq.*
[71] s. 234.
[71a] Sched. 7.
[72] s. 235.
[73] s. 222.
[74] s. 222(4).

Having laid the accounts before a general meeting of the company,[75] a copy must be delivered to the Registrar within seven months after the ending of its financial year in the case of a public company, increased to 10 months for private companies.[76] If the requirements for laying and delivering accounts are not complied with within the period allowed, every person who is a director of the company immediately before the end of the period is guilty of an offence, but it is a defence for him to prove that he took all reasonable steps for securing that the requirements would be complied with.[77] Apart from the general requirements that every balance sheet of the company shall give a true and fair view of the state of affairs of the company as at the end of its financial year, and that the profit and loss account shall give a true and fair view of its profit or loss for the financial year, these documents must also comply with the detailed requirements set out in Schedules 4 to 10 to the Act.[78] The accounts must also show separately the aggregate amounts and certain other particulars of the chairman's and directors' emoluments, pensions and compensation for loss of office, as well as loans and other dealings in favour of directors.[79] They must also show any loans and certain other similar transactions or dealings in favour of officers of the company other than its directors.[80] The accounts must also disclose the identities and places of incorporation of (a) the company's subsidiaries and particulars of the company's shareholdings therein, (b) companies, not being its subsidiaries, in which the company holds shares of any class exceeding in nominal value one-tenth of the nominal value of the allotted shares of that class, and (c) the company's ultimate holding company.[81] Special provisions exist for the accounts of banking and insurance companies and groups of these[82] as well as for companies in a group.[83] A copy of the balance sheet, and the documents required by law to be annexed thereto, including the directors' and auditor's reports, must be sent to every member 21 days before the meeting at which they are to be considered.[84]

51.27 Borrowing Powers.—Trading companies have an implied power to borrow and grant securities over any of their assets.[85] Non-trading companies must expressly create such power in the memorandum.

---

[75] *Supra*, para. 25.25.
[76] ss. 242, 244.
[77] s. 242(3).
[78] ss. 226, 227. The schedules are as amended by the Financial Services Act 1986, the Banking Act 1987 and the Companies Act 1989.
[79] s. 232, Sched. 6, Pts. I, II.
[80] s. 232, Sched. 6, Pt. III. The expression 'officer' is defined in s. 744; see also *Re A Company* [1980] Ch. 138.
[81] s. 231; Sched. 5.
[82] ss. 255, 255A, 255B, Sched. 9.
[83] s. 227, Sched. 4A.
[84] s. 238.
[85] *General Auction Co.* v. *Smith* [1891] 3 Ch. 432.

Sections 35 and 35A of the 1985 Act[86] operate in favour of a lender to a company whose objects forbid or limit borrowing or whose directors have exceeded their powers in that respect. The lender is not obliged to inquire as to the company's capacity or the directors' powers. With regard to the latter, the lender is presumed to have acted in good faith unless the contrary is proved.[87] Ratification of an *ultra vires* transaction is possible.[88]

51.28 Floating Charges.—Prior to the Companies (Floating Charges) (Scotland) Act 1961,[88a] a company registered in Scotland not only could not create a floating charge over its assets in Scotland, but could not do so even over its assets in England, nor would a floating charge created by an English company with assets in Scotland receive recognition in Scotland.[88b] To be effective any security given by the company required to be a fixed security by which a real right in the property was constituted in favour of the creditor. Under the 1961 Act, however, it became competent under the law of Scotland for an incorporated company, whether it was an English or a Scottish company, to secure any existing or future debts, including any balance on cash account, by creating in favour of a creditor a floating charge over the whole or any part of the property, heritable and moveable, which might from time to time be comprised in its property and undertaking. That Act was repealed and re-enacted with modifications by the Companies (Floating Charges and Receivers) (Scotland) Act 1972, which also made it competent for the first time for receivers to be appointed in respect of Scottish companies.[88c] The relevant provisions are now to be found in Parts XII (registration of charges) and XVIII (creation and ranking of charges) of the Companies Act 1985[89] and Part III, Chapter II of the Insolvency Act 1986.[90] At the time of writing, Part IV of the Companies Act 1989, dealing with the registration of floating charges and amending the relevant provisions of the 1985 Act is not in force.[90a]

The essence of a floating charge is that it gives the creditor of a company security[91] over the property (excluding, possibly, reserve capital)[92] which is subject to the charge, without the need for delivery,

---

[86] Para. 51.10, *supra*; para. 51.35 *infra*. Note also s. 322A.

[87] s. 35A(2)(c). *Carse* v. *Coppen*, 1951 S.C. 233; see also *Ballachulish Slate Quarries* v. *Menzies* (1908) 45 S.L.R. 667.

[88] s. 35(3): by special resolution.

[88a] 9 & 10 Eliz. II. c. 46.

[88b] *Carse* v. *Coppen*, 1951 S.C. 233; see also *Ballachulish Slate Quarries* v. *Menzies* (1908) 45 S.L.R. 667.

[88c] 1972 Act, Pt. II.

[89] 1985, ss. 410–424; ss. 462–466.

[90] 1986, ss. 50–71; see also Palmer, Vol. I, paras. 13.204–220.

[90a] And may never be brought into force: see p. 947, n.87a.

[91] See para. 20.13, *supra*, for a discussion of the floating charge as a right in security.

[92] At least this has been held to be the case in England: *Re Mayfair Property Co.* [1898] 2 Ch. 28. Property held in trust has been held to be unaffected by the crystallisation of a floating charge on the appointment of a receiver: *Tay Valley Joinery Ltd.* v. *C.F. Financial Services Ltd.*, 1987 S.L.T. 207.

intimation or, in the case of heritage, registration in the Register of Sasines or the Land Register.[93] The charge lies dormant until the company is wound up or a receiver is appointed, leaving the company free in the meantime (subject to any restrictions in the agreement constituting the debt) to dispose of the property over which it extends; if it acquires new property that also may become subject to the charge. On the commencement of the winding up, however, or on the appointment of a receiver, the charge crystallises or attaches to the property then comprised in the company's property and undertaking or such part of it as is subject to the charge.[94] Property which comes into the company's hands after the date of the appointment may also be attached by it if the terms of the charge admit of this interpretation.[95] The charge attaches as if it were a fixed security over the property to which it has attached,[96] but subject to the rights of any person who has effectually executed diligence[97] on the property or any part of it, or who holds a fixed security or another floating charge over the property or any part of it which has priority of ranking.[98] Consignment of funds into court, in order to recall an arrestment and inhibition on the dependence, has the effect of removing them from the company's property to which a floating charge may attach after consignment has taken place.[99] In the case of book debts the attachment has effect as if an assignation of the debt to the holder of the floating charge was duly intimated to the third party on the date of the receiver's appointment, with the result that the debt is no longer capable of arrestment after that date.[1] A debtor will be able to set off debts due to him by the company which were due before the appointment, but not any debts which he may have acquired by assignation after that date.[2] A floating charge is

---

[93] s. 462: this does not define a floating charge.

[94] s. 463(1); Insolvency Act 1986, ss. 53(7), 54(6). When s. 140(1) of the 1989 Act is implemented, the charge will attach if a company passes a resolution for voluntary winding up or a winding-up order is made by the court: this amends s. 463(1) of the 1985 Act and postpones crystallisation until the resolution is passed or the winding-up order is made.

[95] *Ross* v. *Taylor*, 1985 S.L.T. 387; the charge extended to the whole of the property 'which is or may be from time to time' comprised in the property and undertaking of the company. Note also *Scottish & Newcastle plc* v. *Ascot Inns Ltd. (in receivership)*, 1994 S.L.T. 1140.

[96] *National Commercial Bank of Scotland* v. *Liqrs. of Telford Grier Mackay & Co.*, 1969 S.C. 181, *per* Lord President Clyde at p. 194. The appointment of a receiver of an English company has the same effect with regard to its property situated in Scotland: *Gordon Anderson (Plant)* v. *Campsie Construction*, 1977 S.L.T. 7. See 1986 Act, s. 72.

[97] As to the meaning of 'effectually executed diligence,' see *Lord Advocate* v. *Royal Bank of Scotland*, 1977 S.C. 155 (arrestment); *Armour & Mycroft, Petrs.*, 1983 S.L.T. 453 (inhibition); *Taymech Ltd.* v. *Rush & Tompkins Ltd.*, 1990 S.L.T. 681 (inhibition); *Iona Hotels Ltd.* v. *Craig*, 1991 S.L.T. 11; Chap. 48, *supra*.

[98] s. 463(1); Insolvency Act 1986, s. 55(3).

[99] *Hawking* v. *Hafton House Ltd.*, 1990 S.L.T. 496. The case, however, arose from the appointment of a receiver and the effect of the difference in wording between the wording of s. 463(1) of the 1985 Act and ss. 53(7) and 54(6) of the Insolvency Act 1986.

[1] *Forth & Clyde Construction Co.* v. *Trinity Timber & Plywood Co.*, 1984 S.L.T. 94.

[2] *Ibid.*

capable of being assigned.[3] If a company becomes subject to an administration order or goes into liquidation, a floating charge created over its undertaking or property within a certain period of the happening of these events is restricted as to its validity. It is invalid, except to the extent of so much of the consideration for the charge as consists of money, goods or services or of the discharge or reduction of debt given at the same time as, or after, the creation of the charge, together with any interest payable on those amounts.[4] The critical date, referred to as 'the onset of insolvency,' is the date of presentation of the petition for the making of the administration order or the date of the commencement of winding up.[5] The period is two years ending with the onset of insolvency if the charge is in favour of a person connected with the company, and 12 months if the charge is in favour of any other person.[6] However, a charge in favour of a person not connected with the company is not affected unless the company was at the time of the creation of the charge unable to pay its debts or became unable to pay its debts in consequence of the transaction under which the charge was created.[7] A charge which is created at any time between the presentation of a petition for the making of an administration order and the making of the order on that petition is also invalid to the same extent, irrespective of whether or not it is in favour of a person connected with the company.[8]

As regards ranking, a fixed security arising by operation of law, such as a repairer's lien, ranks in priority over a floating charge.[9] Subject to that rule, the instrument creating the floating charge or any instrument of alteration may contain provisions restricting or prohibiting the creation of fixed or floating charges ranking prior to or *pari passu* with the charge, or regulating the order in which the floating charge shall rank with any other subsisting or future fixed and floating charges.[10] If

[3] *Libertas-Kommerz* v. *Johnson*, 1977 S.C. 191. If s. 101 of the 1989 Act is implemented, assignees of a charge will need to be named in the company's register of charges: this would substitute a new s. 411 in the 1985 Act.

[4] 1986 Act, s. 245(2).

[5] s. 245(5).

[6] ss. 245(3)(*a*) and (*b*).

[7] s. 245(4).

[8] s. 245(3)(*c*).

[9] 1985 Act, s. 464(2). Note also *Grampian Regional Council* v. *Drill Stem (Inspection Services) Ltd.*, 1994 S.C.L.R. 36 Sh.Ct. However a 'market charge' which is a floating chargee has priority over an 'unpaid vendor's lien' unless the chargee knows of the lien's existence when the property became subject to the charge: Companies Act 1989, s. 179. 'Market charge' is defined by s. 173(1) of the 1989 Act.

[10] s. 464(1). But only valid charges rank effectively: *Bank of Scotland* v. *T.A. Neilson & Co.*, 1991 S.L.T. 8. Note also *A.I.B. Finance Ltd.* v. *Bank of Scotland*, 1993 S.C.L.R. 851. When s. 140 of the 1989 Act is implemented, ranking agreements adversely affecting existing floating charges or fixed securities will require the consent of their holders: this amends s. 464(1)(*b*) of the 1985 Act. Furthermore, new s. 464(1A) of the 1985 Act (when implemented) makes clear that where a charge contains a restriction or prohibition on the creation of fixed or floating charges ranking prior to or *pari passu* with it, that will confer priority on the said charge over subsequently created fixed and floating charges: 1989 Act, s. 140(4).

no such provisions are contained in the instrument, a fixed security, the right to which has been constituted as a real right before the crystallisation of a floating charge, has priority over the floating charge, while floating charges rank *inter se* according to the time of registration with the Registrar of Companies, charges received by the same postal delivery ranking equally.[11] The holder of a floating charge having a postponed ranking may restrict the preference of a floating charge which has priority of ranking by giving written intimation of the registration of his charge.[12] In the event of a winding up, the provisions of the Act relating to winding up have effect as if the floating charge were a fixed security in respect of the principal of the debt or obligation to which it relates and any interest due or to become due thereon.[13] In the event of a receivership, special provisions apply in order to regulate the distribution of monies received by the receiver.[14] The instrument creating a floating charge or any ancilliary document relating thereto may be altered by the execution of an instrument of alteration by the company, the holder of the charge and by the holder of any other charge which would be adversely affected by the alteration.[15]

51.29   **Registration of Charges.**—The machinery for the registration of charges in Scotland is provided in Part XII of the Companies Act 1985.[16] The leading provision is contained in section 410, which provides that every charge created by a company, being a charge to which the section applies, shall so far as any security on the company's property is conferred thereby be void against the liquidator and any creditor of the company unless the prescribed particulars[17] of the charge together with a copy of the instrument by which it is created are delivered to or received by the Registrar within 21 days after the date of its creation.[18] The section applies to a charge on land, a security over uncalled share capital, a security over certain categories of incorporeal moveable property and a security over a ship as well as to floating charges.[19] The requirement for registration with the Registrar of Companies in Scotland

---

[11] ss. 464(3), (4). When s. 140 of the 1989 Act is implemented, s. 464(3) will emphasise that, save in so far as varied by a ranking clause, the statutory rules of priority apply.

[12] s. 464(5). When s. 140 of the 1989 Act is implemented, a floating charge to secure a contingent liability (but not one arising from future advances) will be restricted to the maximum amount of the contingent liability: 1989 Act, s. 140(6), adding s. 464(5)(e) to the 1985 Act.

[13] s. 463(2); *National Commercial Bank of Scotland* v. *Liqrs. of Telford Grier Mackay & Co., supra; Site Preparations* v. *Buchan Development Co.,* 1983 S.L.T. 317.

[14] Insolvency Act 1986, s. 60(1).

[15] s. 466. For the method of execution of a floating charge by a Scottish company, see s. 462(2), as amended by the Companies Act 1989, ss. 130(7), 212, Scheds. 17, 24.

[16] Pt. XII is substantially amended by the Companies Act 1989, Pt. IV, which is not in force at the time of writing.

[17] For these particulars, see s. 417.

[18] For the meaning of the date of creation of a charge, see s. 410(5). The duty to register is laid on the company creating the charge; but may be effected by others: s. 415.

[19] s. 410(4). A retention of title clause is not a security and cannot be registered as such: *Armour* v. *Thyssen Edelstahlwerke A.G.,* 1990 S.L.T. 891.

applies to charges over heritable property situated in England as well as Scotland, where the company which created the charge is registered in Scotland.[20] The register of charges is kept by the Registrar of Companies, whose certificate of registration is conclusive evidence that the requirements of the Act as to registration have been complied with.[21] Provision is made for the entry on the register of a memorandum of satisfaction where the debt for which the charge was given has been paid or satisfied in whole or part or the property has been released from the charge.[22] If the charge does not fall within the list of charges detailed in the definition, registration with the Registrar of Companies is not required,[23] but every company must keep at its registered office a register of all fixed and floating charges affecting its property, whether registrable under section 410 or not.[24] English companies are no longer required to register in Scotland charges affecting Scottish property,[25] but registration in Scotland is required in the case of charges created by, or on property in Scotland which is acquired by, a company incorporated outside Great Britain which has a place of business in Scotland.[26] The court has power in a suitable case to extend the time for registration or to rectify the register where there has been an omission or misstatement of any particular.[27]

51.30 **Debentures.**—Public companies frequently borrow by the issue of debentures. The term is defined as including debenture stock, bonds and any other securities of a company whether constituting a charge on the assets of the company or not.[28] This definition would seem to include any form of bond or mortgage which imports an obligation to pay.[29] A debenture may be merely a personal obligation of the company, but it is usual for security to be provided in the hands of trustees for the

---

[20] *Amalgamated Securities Ltd., Petrs.*, 1967 S.C. 56.

[21] ss. 417–418. Under the 1989 Act, the certificate of registration would no longer be conclusive evidence of compliance with the requirements for registration. Instead, it would only be conclusive evidence that the particulars of the charge (or other information) were delivered to the Registrar no later than the certificate's date. There would be a rebuttable presumption that these were not delivered before that date: 1985 Act, s. 397(5), added by the 1989 Act, s. 94.

[22] s. 419. Under the replacement section (403) added by the 1989 Act (s. 98), the memorandum of satisfaction would have to be signed by both company and holder of the charge. There is not, however, any requirement that a memorandum of satisfaction be registered: *Scottish & Newcastle plc* v. *Ascot Inns (in receivership)*, *supra*.

[23] *Scottish Homes Investment Co.*, 1968 S.C. 244.

[24] s. 422.

[25] As they were by 1961 Act.

[26] s. 424; for the equivalent provision relating to charges on property in England and Wales, see s. 409. Sched. 15 of the 1989 Act will substitute a new set of provisions in relation to the property of overseas companies: 1989 Act, s. 105.

[27] See s. 420. A court order extending the registration period would no longer be necessary under ss. 399, 400 of the 1985 Act as added by s. 95 of the 1989 Act. Non-timeous registration will result in a charge losing priority in ranking. Defective registration may be cured by court order: s. 402, added by the 1989 Act, s. 97 (not yet in force).

[28] s. 744.

[29] See *Lemon* v. *Austin Friars Co.* [1926] 1 Ch. 1.

debenture holders in the form of a fixed security or a floating charge. They may be irredeemable or redeemable only on the happening of a remote contingency or until expiry of a period however long.[30] Debentures are to be construed according to their terms, so that if the repayment of the capital sum is made optional it cannot be demanded until the company chooses to pay.[31] Provision is made for the reissue of debentures which have been paid off and at common law would be extinguished on the principle of *confusio*.[32] Debentures may be issued payable to bearer, and in that form are negotiable instruments.[33] Debentures payable to bearer and issued in Scotland are valid and binding according to their terms notwithstanding anything contained in the Blank Bonds and Trusts Act 1696 (c. 25).[34]

51.31 Receivers.—The holder of a charge or of a debenture created by a Scottish company has the ordinary remedies available to a creditor. He may raise an action for payment of his debt or petition for the winding up of the company. An additional ground of winding up is available in cases where a floating charge subsists over property comprised in the property and undertaking of a company which the Court of Session has jurisdiction to wind up, namely that the security of the creditor entitled to the benefit of the floating charge is in jeopardy.[35]

The holder of a floating charge, has the power to appoint or to apply to the court for the appointment of a receiver.[36] This remedy is available to the ˊholders of all floating charges including those of subsisting floating charges created under the 1961 Act, and it need not be provided for in the instrument creating the charge. It remains competent for a holder of a floating charge who has secured the appointment of a receiver to apply for an order for a winding up. A receiver may be appointed on the occurrence of any event which is provided for in the instrument creating the charge as entitling the holder to make the appointment; and, in so far as the instrument does not otherwise provide, on the expiry of a period of 21 days after the making of a demand for payment of the whole or any part of the principal sum secured by the charge without payment being made, on the expiry of a period of two months during the whole of which interest due and payable under the charge has been in arrears, on the making of an order or the passing of a resolution for the winding up of the company, or on the appointment of a receiver by virtue of any other floating charge created by the company.[37] The receiver may be appointed either by an

---

[30] s. 193; see also Redemption of Standard Securities (Scotland) Act 1971, s. 2.
[31] *Wylie* v. *Carlyon* [1922] 1 Ch. 51.
[32] s. 194.
[33] *Bechuanaland Exploration Co.* v. *London Trading Bank* [1898] 2 Q.B. 658.
[34] s. 197. As to the 1696 Act, see Gloag, *Contract* (2nd ed.), p. 5.
[35] 1986 Act, s. 122(2); see para. 51.46, *infra*.
[36] Insolvency Act 1986, s. 51(1), (2). See also Insolvency (Scotland) Rules 1986 (S.I. 1986 No. 1915), Pt. 3.
[37] 1986 Act, s. 52.

instrument in writing executed by or on behalf of the holder of the charge,[38] or by the court to whom the holder requires to apply by petition served on the company.[39] The appointment of a receiver requires to be intimated to the Registrar of Companies.[40] On his appointment, the floating charge attaches to the property then subject to the charge as if it were a fixed security,[41] in the same way as on the commencement of a winding up. The receiver is required, within three months after his appointment or such longer time as the court may allow, to send a report to the Registrar and to the holder of the floating charge on matters relating to the receivership. This report is also to be sent to the secured creditors (if their addresses be known) and to their trustees, if any, and also sent or supplied to the unsecured creditors free of charge and laid before a meeting of these creditors unless the court otherwise directs.[42] A committee of creditors may be appointed to exercise the same functions as a committee of creditors in a winding up.[43]

The powers which the receiver is to have in relation to the property attached by the floating charge may be defined in the instrument creating the charge, but he has a wide range of statutory powers for ingathering the property and doing other acts, which may be exercised so far as not inconsistent with any provision contained in that instrument.[44] While a receiver may sue in his own name to ingather the company's property, he may only sue in the name and on behalf of the company in respect of debts owed to it.[45] In the exercise of these powers he is not subject to the control of the directors of the company. The view has been expressed that the appointment of a receiver completely deprives directors of power to deal with company property and affairs.[46] While substantially correct, there may be cases where directors can raise an action on the company's behalf in pursuit of their duty to act in its best interests.[47] His powers are, however, subject to the rights of every person who has effectually executed diligence on all or any part of the property prior to his appointment, and to the rights of the holder of a charge ranking prior to or *pari passu* with the floating

---

[38] 1986 Act, s. 53.

[39] 1986 Act, s. 54; Rules of Court 214–215.

[40] 1986 Act, ss. 53(1), 54(3). The receiver's appointment takes effect from the time he receives the instrument of appointment; and a docquet acknowledging receipt of the instrument, signed by him or on his behalf is conclusive evidence of receipt and also fixes the date of his appointment: *Secretary of State for Trade and Industry* v. *Houston*, 1994 S.L.T. 775; s. 53(6).

[41] 1986 Act, ss. 53(7), 54(6); see *Ross* v. *Taylor*, 1985 S.L.T. 387.

[42] 1986 Act, ss. 67(1), (2).

[43] 1986 Act, s. 68.

[44] 1986 Act, s. 55, Sched. 2.

[45] *Taylor, Petr.*, 1982 S.L.T. 172; *Myles J. Callaghan Ltd.* v. *City of Glasgow D.C.*, 1988 S.L.T. 227.

[46] *Imperial Hotel (Aberdeen)* v. *Vaux Breweries*, 1978 S.C. 86.

[47] *Newhart Developments Ltd.* v. *Co-operative Commercial Bank Ltd.* [1978] Q.B. 814; *Shanks* v. *Central R.C.*, 1987 S.L.T. 410; *Toynar Ltd.* v. *Whitbread & Co. Ltd.*, 1988 S.L.T. 433. *Cf. Tudor Grange Holdings Ltd.* v. *Citibank N.A.* [1992] Ch. 53.

charge by virtue of which he was appointed.[48] In deciding which property of the company to ingather or realise in the interest of the holder of the floating charge he is governed only by the code which the Act provides, which is complete in itself.[49] He is deemed to be the agent of the company in relation to its property and also in relation to contracts of employment adopted by him,[50] but he is personally liable on any contracts entered into by him in the performance of his functions except where the contract states the contrary.[51] With regard to contracts of employment adopted by him, a receiver is not liable for the payment of wages, salaries, or pension contributions prior to adoption.[51a] If the company is not at the time being wound up, he must pay out of any assets in his hands, in priority to the claims of the holder of the floating charge, claims which would have ranked as preferential debts in a winding up, provided they came to his notice by the end of a period of six months after he has advertised for claims.[52] If the company is in the course of being wound up, the receiver is entitled to take control of the property which is subject to the floating charge whether he was appointed before or after the commencement of the liquidation. If he does so he is primarily liable for the payment of the secured and preferential debts of the company.[53] In the distribution of moneys received by him, he is required to give preference to the holders of fixed securities which rank prior to or *pari passu* with the floating charge, persons who have effectually executed diligence over the property, and to creditors in respect of liabilities incurred by him. Thereafter, subject to his own remuneration and expenses, all moneys received by him are to be paid to the holder on account of the debt secured.[54] Any surplus is to be paid in accordance with their respective rights and interests to any other receiver, holder of a fixed security or the company or its liquidator.[55] The Act contains detailed provisions as to the provision of information to the receiver and the provision of information by him to the Registrar of Companies and other interested parties.[56]

51.32   Dividends and Distributions.—A company is prohibited from making any distribution except out of profits available for the purpose.[57]

---

[48] 1986 Act, s. 55(3); see also note 97, *supra* as to the meaning of 'effectually executed diligence.'

[49] *Forth & Clyde Construction Co.* v. *Trinity Timber & Plywood Co.,* 1984 S.L.T. 94, *per* Lord President Emslie at p. 97.

[50] 1986 Act, s. 57(1), (1A), added by the Insolvency Act 1994, s. 3(2). The 1994 Act was passed as a result of the decision of the Court of Appeal in *Paramount Airways* (No. 3) [1994] B.C.C. 172; the presumption is rebuttable: *Inverness District Council* v. *Highland Universal Fabrications,* 1986 S.L.T. 556.

[51] 1986 Act, s. 57(2); as amended by s. 3(3) of the 1994 Act.

[51a] 1986 Act, s. 57(2) and (2A) added by the 1994 Act, s. 3(3), (4).

[52] 1986 Act, s. 59.

[53] *Manley, Petr.,* 1985 S.L.T. 42.

[54] 1986 Act, s. 60(1).

[55] 1986 Act, s. 60(2).

[56] 1986 Act, ss. 65, 66.

[57] Companies Act 1985, s. 263(1).

'Distribution' for this purpose means every description of distribution of a company's assets to its members whether in cash or otherwise, except for the issue of bonus shares, the redemption of redeemable shares or purchase by a company of its own shares, the reduction of share capital and a distribution of assets to members of the company on its winding up.[58] A company's profits available for distribution are defined as being its accumulated, realised profits so far as not previously utilised by distribution or capitalisation, less its accumulated, realised losses, so far as not previously written off in a reduction or re-organisation of capital duly made.[59] No distinction is to be made between capital and revenue profits and losses,[60] and the former common law rules as to what may be treated as profits and what as capital no longer apply.[61] A profit which has not been realised is not available for distribution, nor can it be applied in paying up debentures or any amounts unpaid on the company's issued shares.[62] Provision is made as to how 'realised profits' and 'realised losses' are to be calculated in particular circumstances such as where assets are revalued or distributions in kind are made.[63] Where an unlawful distribution is made to a shareholder who knew or had reasonable grounds for believing that it was unlawful, he is liable to repay it or a sum equal to its value to the company.[64] At common law, directors who were parties to the payment of a dividend which was unlawful were liable jointly and severally to repay the amount,[65] and this rule has been preserved.[66] When the articles provide for payment of dividends in a certain event—provided that event does not amount to a contravention of the rules discussed above—a shareholder, or one class of shareholder may enforce compliance by action.[67]

51.33 Promoters.—The term 'promoter' is no longer defined by statute.[68] It has been judicially referred to as 'a term not of law but of business usefully summing up in a single word a number of business operations familiar to the commercial world by which a company is generally

---

[58] s. 263(2).

[59] s. 263(3). For a completely unhelpful definition of 'realised' profits and losses, see the 1985 Act, s. 262(3): substituted by the 1989 Act, s. 22.

[60] s. 280(3).

[61] See *Dovey* v. *Cory* [1901] A.C. 477; *Ammonium Soda Co.* v. *Chamberlain* [1918] 1 Ch. 266.

[62] s. 263(4); the effect of *Westburn Sugar Refineries* v. *I.R.C.*, 1960 S.L.T. 297, with which the English decision in *Dimbula Valley (Ceylon) Tea Co.* v. *Laurie* [1961] Ch. 353 was in conflict, has been preserved by the statutory rule.

[63] ss. 275–276.

[64] s. 277(1).

[65] *Flitcroft's Case* (1882) 21 Ch.D. 519; *Moxham* v. *Grant* [1900] 1 Q.B. 88; *Liqr. of City of Glasgow Bank* v. *Mackinnon* (1881) 9 R. 535.

[66] s. 277(2).

[67] *City Property Inv. Co.* v. *Thorburn* (1897) 25 R. 361; *Paterson* v. *Paterson*, 1917 S.C. (H.L.) 13.

[68] It was defined by s. 67(3) of the 1985; now repealed by the Financial Services Act 1986.

brought into existence.'[69] The term is probably too vague to admit of an exact definition.[70]

A promoter is neither an agent nor a trustee for the company which he brings into existence.[71] Thus—subject to the necessity of full disclosure of the facts—a sale by a promoter to the company is valid.[72] And where a Private Act gave power to a company to pay the expenses of its formation it was no objection to the charges of the law agent and the engineer that they were promoters of the company.[73] It has been held that a promoter 'must put himself in the position of an agent for the company which he has promoted, and must regulate his relations towards the company according to the duty of an agent.'[74] He stands in a fiduciary position to the company and must disclose all material facts.[75] The principle is not that it is illegal for a promoter to make a profit, but that the nature and source of his profit must be disclosed; and they must be disclosed to the shareholders, not merely to the directors who may be his nominees.[76] So while a man may purchase a property for £10,000 and sell it next day for £20,000, he cannot do so without disclosure of the facts, if he is a promoter and the company the purchaser.[77] The company has in such cases the right, resting on general principles of law and not on any express provision of the Companies Act, either to avoid the contract or to recover from the promoter any benefit he, or a firm of which he is a partner, may have gained.[78] To justify such a claim it is not necessary that the promoter has obtained something from the company, or at its expense. Where what he obtained were debentures, irregularly issued, and really valueless, it was held that the company could recover from him the price at which he had fraudulently sold them to a third party.[79]

51.34   Directors: Appointment.—Every company, other than a private company, registered after November 1, 1929, must have at least two directors; and every company registered before that date and every private company must have at least one director.[80] Every company must

[69] *Whaley Bridge Co.* v. *Green* (1879) 5 Q.B.D. 109, *per* Bowen L.J. at p. 111.
[70] See *Lydney Co.* v. *Bird* (1886) 33 Ch.D. 85; *Jubilee Cotton Mills* v. *Lewis* [1924] A.C. 958.
[71] *Omnium Electric Palaces Ltd.* v. *Baines* [1914] 1 Ch. 332; *Tinnevelly Sugar Refining Co. Ltd.* v. *Mirrlees* (1894) 21 R. 1009.
[72] *Lagunas Nitrate Co.* v. *Lagunas Syndicate* [1889] 2 Ch. 392.
[73] *Edinburgh Northern Tramways Co.* v. *Mann* (1896) 23 R. 1056.
[74] *Per* Lord McLaren, in *Edinburgh Northern Tramways Co.*, *supra*, at p. 1066.
[75] *Erlanger* v. *New Sombrero Phosphate Co.* (1878) 2 App.Cas. 1218.
[76] *Mann* v. *Edinburgh Northern Tramways Co.* (1891) 18 R. 1140; affd. 20 R. (H.L.) 7; *Erlanger* v. *New Sombrero Phosphate Co.*, *supra*; *Re Lady Forrest Mine* [1901] 1 Ch. 582. It may be otherwise if the board of directors is truly independent.
[77] See opinion of Lord Blackburn in *Erlanger*, *supra*.
[78] *Henderson* v. *Huntingdon Copper Co.* (1877) 4 R. 294, affd. 5 R. (H.L.) 1; *Scottish Pacific Coast Mining Co.* v. *Falkner* (1888) 15 R. 290; *Mann* v. *Edinburgh Northern Tramways Co.*, *supra*.
[79] *Jubilee Cotton Mills* v. *Lewis* [1924] A.C. 958.
[80] s. 282.

also have a secretary, and a sole director cannot also be secretary.[81] A register must be kept at the company's registered office of its directors and secretaries, which must contain various particulars with respect to each director and secretary.[82] There is no general rule that a director must be a shareholder in the company. But it is frequently provided in the articles that every director must hold one or more shares, commonly referred to as qualification shares.[83] A director vacates his office if he does not obtain his qualification shares within two months from the date of his appointment, or if after the expiration of that period he ceases at any time to hold his qualification.[84] No person over the age of 70 is capable of being appointed a director of a public company or of a private company which is a subsidiary of a public company unless his appointment has been approved by the company in general meeting and special notice has been given of the resolution,[85] and a person who is subject to this rule is required to give notice of his age to the company.[86] The articles may provide for the disqualification and removal of directors in appropriate circumstances.[87] Under the Company Directors Disqualification Act 1986, the court has power to order that a person shall not be a director of a company, or a liquidator or receiver or manager of a company's property, or be associated in any way with its promotion, formation or management without leave of the court where the person is convicted of an indictable offence, has been persistently in default under the Act, is guilty of an offence under section 458 (fraudulent trading) or of any other fraud or breach of duty in relation to the company while an officer or liquidator of it or receiver or manager of its property.[88] The court must disqualify anyone as being unfit to hold office as a director where (a) he is or has been a director of an insolvent company, and (b) his conduct renders him unfit to be concerned in managing a company.[89] An application for disqualification must, ordinarily, be made within two years of the date on which the company became insolvent.[90] In this particular case, a minimum period of two years disqualification is prescribed.[91] Disqualification may also be imposed after a Department of Trade investigation of a company's affairs.[92] An undischarged bankrupt is disqualified from acting as a

---

[81] s. 283. For the qualifications required by secretaries of public companies, see s. 286.

[82] ss. 288–290.

[83] s. 291. Table A in the 1985 Regulations, however, makes no provision for this.

[84] s. 291(3); see *Holmes* v. *Keyes* [1959] Ch. 199; *Pollock* v. *Garnett*, 1957 S.L.T. (Notes) 8.

[85] s. 293.

[86] s. 294.

[87] See Table A, art. 81.

[88] 1986 Act, ss. 1–5. Where evidence of unfitness is manifest a full hearing may be unnecessary: *Re Carecraft Construction Co. Ltd.* [1993] 4 All E.R. 499.

[89] *Ibid.*, s. 6.

[90] *Ibid.*, s. 7(2): *Secretary of State for Trade and Industry* v. *Josolyne*, 1990 S.L.T. (Sh.Ct.) 48; *Secretary of State for Trade and Industry* v. *Normand*, 1994 S.L.T. 1249.

[91] *Ibid.*, s. 6(4).

[92] *Ibid.*, s. 8.

director or liquidator or being concerned in the formation or management of a company except with the leave of the court by which he was sequestrated, and if he does so without leave he commits a criminal offence.[93] It should be noted, however, that the acts of a director or manager are valid notwithstanding any defect that may afterwards be discovered in his appointment or disqualification.[94]

It is common for the articles to provide for the retiral of all the directors at the first annual general meeting and for one-third to retire at each subsequent annual general meeting and, in both instances, to be reappointed if willing to serve.[95] A separate motion must be made for the appointment of each director.[96] Failure to hold an annual general meeting may result, depending upon the terms of the articles, in the company ceasing to have directors.[97] The members of the company may increase or reduce the number of directors by ordinary resolution, subject to any minimum for the number of directors which may be set by the articles.[98] A director (notwithstanding anything in the articles or in any agreement with the company) may be removed by the company during his term of office.[99] Where a director has been removed from office or has resigned and no official notification of that event has been given, and he continues to act as director, or if he does so within 15 days even if official notification has been given, his acts will bind the company unless the company can prove that the third party knew of the irregularity.[1] Every company must keep and make available for inspection by its members free of charge a record of the terms of the contract of service of each director.[2] The names of all of the directors need no longer be displayed on a company's business letters. However, its correspondence cannot display the names of only some of the directors: either all or none may be displayed.[3] The directors are normally given power to appoint one of their number as managing director, and to fill up casual vacancies on the board.[4]

The remuneration of the directors may be provided for in the articles, or by ordinary resolution of the company,[5] or, in the case of a managing director, by the directors themselves.[6] Although they are the persons by

[93] Ibid., s. 11.
[94] s. 285; Table A, reg. 92; Morris v. Kanssen [1946] A.C. 459; see Freeman & Lockyer v. Buckhurst Park Properties [1964] 2 Q.B. 480. There is also the protection conferred on third parties by Royal British Bank v. Turquand (1856) 6 E. & B. 327.
[95] Table A, regs. 73, 80.
[96] s. 292.
[97] Alexander Ward & Co. v. Samyang Navigation Co., 1973 S.L.T. (Notes) 80.
[98] See Table A, reg. 64.
[99] s. 303. A resolution to remove someone from office as a director, if in fact he turns out to be a director, is invalid: Currie v. Cowdenbeath Football Club Ltd., 1992 S.L.T. 407.
[1] ss. 42, 711.
[2] s. 318.
[3] s. 305, as amended by the 1989 Act, Sched. 19, para. 4.
[4] Table A, arts. 84, 79.
[5] Table A, art. 82.
[6] Table A, art. 84; see also Richmond Gate Property Co. [1965] 1 W.L.R. 335.

whom the company normally acts and by whom its business is carried on as its agents,[7] they are not as such employees of the company.[8] A director may nevertheless be a salaried employee of the company.[9] As a director, though not in all respects a trustee for the company, holds a fiduciary position, he is not entitled to remuneration without contract merely because he has done extra work for the company.[10] And the directors have no power to vote themselves additional remuneration which is not authorised by the articles, *e.g.* travelling expenses to board meetings.[11]

51.35 **Powers of Directors.**—The powers delegated to its directors by a company are set out in its articles. So long as they do not exceed these powers, the directors cannot be prevented by members' resolutions from exercising them.[12] Directors are under a duty to exercise their powers in conformity with any limitations 'flowing from the company's memorandum.'[13] Actions exceeding their powers in the memorandum and articles may be ratified by special resolution.[14] Section 35A protects third parties dealing with companies by deeming the power of the board of directors to bind the company (or to authorise others to bind it) to be free of any limitation in the memorandum or articles.[15] To benefit by this provision, the third party must act in good faith: though good faith is presumed unless the contrary is proved and he is not necessarily in bad faith if he knows of the limitations on the directors' powers.[16] There is no duty to ascertain if a transaction is (a) permitted by the company's memorandum or (b) exceeds the directors' powers.[17] So long as no legal obligation has been incurred, the members may interdict further performance and directors are liable for any loss caused to the company by their conduct.[18] Section 35A does not apply where the third party deals with someone other than the company's directors or authorised agents. Nor does it apply where he acts in bad faith or where limitations on the directors' powers are imposed other than by the memorandum and articles. In such cases, the enforceability or otherwise of the act will depend on the common law of agency. Thus if an agent acts within the scope of his actual, implied, or apparent authority the company is

[7] *Ferguson* v. *Wilson* (1866) L.R. 2 Ch. 77.
[8] *Kerr* v. *Walker*, 1933 S.C. 458.
[9] See *Anderson* v. *James Sutherland (Peterhead)*, 1941 S.C. 203.
[10] If no provision is made for remuneration, this is not available *quantum meruit: Guinness plc* v. *Saunders* [1990] 1 All E.R. 652; *McNaughton* v. *Brunton* (1882) 10 R. 111.
[11] *Marmor* v. *Alexander*, 1908 S.C. 78.
[12] *Quinn & Axtens* v. *Salmon* [1909] A.C. 442; *Alexander Ward & Co.* v. *Samyang Navigation Co.*, 1975 S.C. (H.L.) 26; *Lord Duncan Sandys* v. *House of Fraser*, 1985 S.L.T. 200.
[13] s. 35(3).
[14] *Ibid.*
[15] Added by Companies Act 1989, s. 108.
[16] s. 35A(2).
[17] s. 35B: added by Companies Act 1989, s. 108.
[18] ss. 35A(4), (5).

bound,[19] so long as the third party deals with him in good faith. If the third party is on notice that the agent has no authority to bind the company, then, unless ratified by it, the company is not bound by the transaction.[20] The powers enjoyed by the directors may, however, be restrained in several ways. For example, the members have power to alter the articles[21] or to remove a director at any time,[22] and they may also be entitled to an order under section 459 on the ground of unfair prejudice.[23] Furthermore the directors are required to exercise their powers bona fide for the benefit of the company, and an abuse of their powers may be restrained by the court.[24] The company in general meeting may ratify a voidable transaction made by its directors, unless this amounts to a fraud on the minority.[25]

51.36 **Contracts Between Director and Company.**—At common law a director, or a firm of which he is a partner, cannot enforce any contract made with the company.[26] Such a contract may be ratified by a general meeting,[27] and the objection may be obviated by a provision in the articles.[28] Even with such a provision a contract between a director and the company is one involving *uberrima fides*, and reducible unless all material facts have been disclosed.[29] A director having any interest in a contract or proposed contract is bound, under penalties, to disclose it at a directors' meeting.[30] Disclosure must be to the directors as a whole and not merely to a meeting of a committee of the directors.[31] Material interests in contracts of significance with the company must be disclosed in the directors' report, as must particulars of their emoluments.[32] Loans by a company to any person who is its director or a director of its holding company are prohibited as is a range of analogous transactions.[33] Various other restrictions are imposed on the directors of a

---

[19] *Rolled Steel Products (Holdings) Ltd.* v. *British Steel Corporation* [1986] Ch. 246 (actual and apparent authority); *Paterson's Trs.* v. *Caledonian Heritable Security Co. Ltd.* (1885) 13 R. 369 (implied authority).

[20] *Royal British Bank* v. *Turquand* (1856) 6 E. & B. 327; *A.L. Underwood Ltd.* v. *Bank of Liverpool & Martins* [1924] 1 K.B. 775.

[21] s. 9.

[22] s. 303.

[23] Para. 51.24, *supra*.

[24] *e.g. Hogg* v. *Cramphorn* [1967] Ch. 254; *Pergamon Press* v. *Maxwell* [1970] 1 W.L.R. 1167.

[25] *Bamford* v. *Bamford* [1970] Ch. 212; *Alexander Ward & Co.* v. *Samyang Navigation Co., supra*.

[26] *Aberdeen Railway* v. *Blaikie* (1854) 1 Macq. 461.

[27] *North-Western Transportation Co.* v. *Beatty* (1887) 12 App.Cas. 589.

[28] *Liqr. of West Lothian Oil Co.* v. *Mair* (1892) 20 R. 64. And see Table A, art. 85.

[29] *Imperial Credit Association* v. *Coleman* (1873) L.R. 6 H.L. 189.

[30] s. 317; *Hely-Hutchinson* v. *Brayhead* [1968] 1 Q.B. 549.

[31] *Guinness plc.* v. *Saunders* [1988] 2 All E.R. 940.

[32] ss. 231–232; Sched. 5, Pt. V; Sched. 6, Pt. I.

[33] ss. 330–343; see *Thompson* v. *J. Barke & Co. (Caterers)*, 1975 S.L.T. 67. The prohibition extends to securities for loans made to directors. There are exceptions to this prohibition: *e.g.* small loans of less than £5,000.

company to prevent them from taking financial advantage of their position.[34] For example, it is not lawful for a company to make any payment to a director by way of compensation for loss of office or as consideration for his retirement without particulars of the proposed payment being disclosed to the members and the proposal being approved by the company.[35] This rule does not apply to bona fide payments by way of damages for breach of contract or by way of pension for past services,[36] but an *ex gratia* payment on the eve of liquidation has been held to be unlawful.[37] Transactions between a company and a director, or someone connected with him, in which the board has exceeded any limitation on their powers under the memorandum or articles are voidable at the company's instance.[38] Regardless of whether or not the company avoids the transaction, the director (or the person connected with him) who entered into it and any director who authorised it are bound to account to the company for any gain resulting therefrom and to indemnify it for any loss.[39] A connected person escapes this liability if he can show that he was unaware that the directors were exceeding their powers.[40] Where one of the parties to the transaction is a director and the other is not, the latter does not lose the protection of section 35A. Where this results in the transaction being voidable against the director but valid as regards the other party, the latter, or the company, may apply to the court to determine what will happen. The court may affirm the contract, or set it aside, or sever it on such terms as appear just.[41] Until it is avoided the transaction is valid and the right of reduction is lost where restitution is no longer possible, if the company is indemnified against loss resulting from the transaction, if a third party has acquired rights for value in good faith and these rights would be affected by avoidance, and if the transaction is ratified by the appropriate resolution of the company in general meeting.[42]

Contracts other than ordinary business contracts between a single member company and a director (or shadow director) who is that member should be in writing or its terms should either be recorded in a written memorandum or in the minutes of the first directors' meeting to be held after the contract was made.[43] Failure to disclose the existence of the contract in any of these ways does not invalidate the contract.[44]

[34] ss. 311 *et seq.*
[35] s. 312.
[36] s. 316(3).
[37] *Gibson's Exr.* v. *Gibson,* 1978 S.C. 197.
[38] s. 322A; added by the Companies Act 1989, s. 109(1). 'Connected persons' are defined by s. 346.
[39] s. 322A(3).
[40] s. 322A(6).
[41] s. 322A(7).
[42] s. 322A(5).
[43] s. 322B; added by the Companies (Single Member Private Limited Companies) Regulations 1992, *supra,* reg. 2, Sched., para. 3(1).
[44] s. 322B(6). Default is, however, an offence punishable by a fine: subs. (4).

51.37 **Secret Profits.**—A director is so far in the position of a trustee that he is not entitled to make any undisclosed or secret profit from his position.[45] So a payment by a promoter or vendor to a director may be recovered by the company.[46] When one company takes over the business of another an undisclosed payment to the directors of the latter cannot be justified.[47] As a company is entitled to the unbiased services of its directors any payment by a promoter to a director for acting, or even a guarantee against loss, will entitle the company to recover from the director what he has gained thereby.[48] A director who resigns office in order to take up an opportunity which might otherwise have gone to his former company may be liable to account for any profit he makes. In this context, some of the decisions have rested on misuse of opportunity, others on misuse of information.[49]

51.38 **Share Dealings by Directors.**—A director owes no fiduciary duty to the company with regard to his own shares, qualification or other. He has the same right to transfer them as any other shareholder. In *McLintock* v. *Campbell*,[50] a director, at a time when the board knew the position of the company to be hopeless, transferred his shares, on which there was a large liability, to his housekeeper, using fraudulent devices to induce her to accept them. It was held that there were no grounds on which the liquidator could rectify the register and replace the director's name. Only the party defrauded, not the liquidator, could found on the fraud; apart from fraud the director was within his rights.

A director is required to notify the company of his interests and those of his spouse and children in the shares in or debentures of the company, and of the occurrence of certain events in connection with such interests.[51] The company must keep a register for the recording of that information, and of certain other related particulars.[52] A director and his spouse and children are prohibited from purchasing options to buy or sell shares in or debentures of the company and certain associated companies.[53] A director who is obliged to acquire qualification shares, at a time when he is in possession of non-public, price sensitive information, is not prohibited from acquiring those shares in his company.[54]

---

[45] See *Cook* v. *Deeks* [1916] A.C. 544; *Phipps* v. *Boardman* [1967] 2 A.C. 46; Palmer, Vol. I, paras. 8.536 *et seq.*; *Regal Hastings* v. *Gulliver* [1967] 2 A.C. 134.

[46] *Henderson* v. *Huntingdon Copper Co.* (1877) 5 R. (H.L.) 1.

[47] *Clarkson* v. *Davies* [1923] A.C. 100.

[48] *Archer's Case* [1892] 1 Ch. 322.

[49] *Industrial Development Consultants* v. *Cooley* [1972] 1 W.L.R. 443; *Canadian Aero-Service* v. *O'Malley* [1973] 40 D.L.R. (3d) 371; *Island Expert Finance Ltd.* v. *Umunna* [1986] B.C.L.C. 460.

[50] 1916 S.C. 966. The directors had no discretionary power to refuse a transfer.

[51] ss. 324, 327; Sched. 13.

[52] s. 325.

[53] ss. 323, 327. Note the Secretary of State's power to investigate share dealings under s. 446.

[54] Criminal Justice Act 1993, s. 53(1).

51.39 Liabilities of Directors.—Apart from cases turning on his fiduciary position, a director may incur liability either to third parties or to the company.[55] In entering into contracts on behalf of the company, a director acts as agent for a disclosed principal, the company, and so incurs no personal liability merely because the company may be unable to fulfil the contract.[56] The position where a director exceeds his powers has already been discussed.[57]

51.40 Duties and Liabilities to Company.—A director is required to act honestly in the performance of his duties, and to exercise a reasonable degree of care, diligence and skill.[58] The ordinary common law remedies are available for breaches of these duties and for a breach of the fiduciary duties which a director owes to the company.[59] He is clearly liable for any fraudulent act, and also for his failure to exercise reasonable care in the administration of the company's affairs. The question what amounts to negligence on the part of a director which will render him liable depends so much on the nature of the particular company as to preclude any definite statement.[60] A director is entitled to place reliance on the statement of the manager or of the auditor of the company, if he has no reason to doubt their honesty.[61] Any term of the articles or of a contract made with the company which purports to exempt directors, other officers of the company, and its auditors, from liability for negligence is void.[62] He is liable to the company if he pays dividends out of capital[63] or if he acts beyond his powers and the money of the company is lost.[64] In a winding up, a director who has misapplied, retained, or become accountable for money or company property, or who has been negligent, may be ordered to repay, restore, or account for the money or property or to make compensation by contributing an appropriate sum to the company's assets.[65] There are detailed provisions with respect to the liability of directors and other

[55] As to liability for untruthful statements in listing particulars or the prospectus, see para. 51.18, *supra*.

[56] *Ferguson* v. *Wilson* (1866) L.R. 2 Ch. App. 77, *per* Lord Cairns L.C. at p. 89; *McLean* v. *Stuart*, 1970 S.L.T. (Notes) 77.

[57] Para. 51.35.

[58] See, for a general statement, *Re City Equitable Fire Insurance Co.* [1925] 1 Ch. 407, *per* Romer J. at pp. 426–430; *Dorchester Finance Co Ltd.* v. *Stebbing* [1989] B.C.L.C. 498.

[59] See Palmer, Vol. 1, para. 8.401 *et seq.* Note also, *Bishopgate Investment Management Ltd. (in liquidation)* v. *Maxwell (No. 2)* [1994] 1 All E.R. 261. On the question of whether directors can owe a fiduciary duty to the shareholders, see *Dawson International* v. *Coates Paton plc*, 1988 S.L.T. 854.

[60] *City of Glasgow Bank* v. *Mackinnon* (1882) 9 R. 535; *Caledonian Heritable Securities Co.* v. *Curror's Tr.* (1882) 9 R. 1115; *Re City Equitable Fire Insurance Co., supra.*

[61] *Dovey* v. *Cory* [1901] A.C. 477.

[62] s. 310. An indemnity term is also declared void.

[63] Para. 51.32, *supra*.

[64] *Maxton* v. *Brown* (1839) 1 D. 367. In this case, the director would also be liable under s. 35A(5): see para. 51.35, *supra*.

[65] Insolvency Act 1986, s. 212. See also *Blin* v. *Johnstone*, 1988 S.L.T. 335; *Gray* v. *Davidson*, 1991 S.L.T. (Sh.Ct.) 61.

officers of the company for fraud or deception before and in the course of a winding up and for fraudulent trading.[66] A director who signs a cheque for *ultra vires* expenditure is personally liable, though he may have signed it as a mere matter of form.[67]

51.41   Auditor.—Every company must at each general meeting before which accounts are laid appoint an auditor or auditors to hold office until the next such general meeting,[68] if no appointment is made, the Secretary of State may appoint a person to fill the vacancy.[69] Private companies may, by elective resolution, dispense with annual appointment of auditors.[70] Where no accounting transaction requiring to be shown in the company's books has occurred since the end of its previous financial year, the company is dormant.[71] A dormant company may exempt itself from the provisions of the 1985 Act relating to the audit of accounts[72] and it is consequently exempt from the obligation to appoint auditors. Eligibility for appointment as an auditor depends on membership of a 'recognised supervisory body' and eligibility for appointment under its rules.[73] The following persons are disqualified: (a) an officer[74] or employee of the company; (b) a partner or employee of such a person; (c) a partnership of which an officer or employee of the company is a partner.[75] A company may be appointed as auditor.[76]

The auditor is bound to make a report to the members on the annual accounts to be laid before the company in general meeting.[77] The report must state (1) whether in the auditor's opinion the annual accounts have been properly prepared in accordance with the provisions of the 1985 Act; and (2) whether in his opinion a true and fair view is given, in the case of an individual balance sheet, of the company's affairs at the end of its financial year; in the case of an individual profit and loss account, of the profit or loss for the year; and in the case of group accounts of the state of affairs and profit or loss of the company and its subsidiaries thereby, so far as concerns members of the company. The auditor should consider whether the directors' report is consistent with the

---

[66] Insolvency Act 1986, ss. 212–219; *Rossleigh* v. *Carlaw*, 1986 S.L.T. 204. Note also Company Directors Disqualification Act 1986, which makes further provision with respect to the disqualification of directors; and Insolvent Companies (Reports on Conduct of Directors) (No. 2) (Scotland) Rules 1986 (S.I. 1986 No. 1916).

[67] *Joint Discount Co.* v. *Brown* (1869) L.R. 8 Eq. 381.

[68] ss. 384(1), 385(2). The appointment, rights, and remuneration of auditors, are dealt with by ss. 384–394A of the 1985 Act, as substituted by the Companies Act 1989, ss. 118–124.

[69] s. 387.

[70] s. 386. In this case the auditors at the time of the resolution continue in office until a resolution is passed to terminate their appointment.

[71] s. 250.

[72] s. 388A.

[73] Companies Act 1989, s. 25.

[74] Defined in s. 744 of the 1985 Act.

[75] Companies Act 1989, s. 27.

[76] s. 25(2) states that an 'individual or a firm' may be an auditor and defines firm as 'a body corporate or partnership': see s. 53(1).

[77] s. 235: added by s. 9 of the 1989 Act.

picture revealed by the annual accounts and, if it is not, this should be noted in his report.[78] It is the duty of the auditor in preparing his report to carry out such investigations as will enable him to form an opinion as to whether proper accounting records have been kept by the company and proper returns adequate for their audit have been received from branches not visited by him, and whether the company's balance sheet and profit and loss account are in agreement with the books of account and returns. If the auditor is of the opinion that accounting records have not been kept, or that proper returns have not been received, if the balance sheet and profit and loss account are not in agreement with the accounting records and returns, or if he fails to obtain all the information and explanations which to the best of his knowledge and belief are necessary for the purposes of his audit, he must state that fact in his report.[79] The auditor has a right of access at all times to the company's books, accounts and vouchers and is entitled to require from the officers of the company and from subsidiary companies and their auditors such information and explanations as he thinks necessary.[80] He has the right to attend any general meeting of the company and to be heard on any part of the business of the meeting which concerns him as auditor.[81] As a statement of general principle it can be said that an auditor who is negligent in the preparation of the company's accounts and his report owes a duty of care to the company and may be liable in damages should his negligence result in it suffering loss.[82] It has been held that auditors owe no such duty to individual investors, as distinct from the company (i.e. the shareholders as a whole).[83] If an investor can demonstrate that the auditors know that the accounts and their report will be shown to an investor (or an identifiable class to which an investor belongs), and that such an investor is likely to rely on these in deciding whether or not to invest in the company, then a 'special relationship' exists between auditor and investor and creates a duty of care on the former's part.[84]

51.42 Investigation.—The Secretary of State may on the application of the company or of a proportion of its members, or, if he suspects fraud or the withholding of information from its members, on his own initiative, appoint inspectors to investigate the affairs of a company and report on them in such manner as he may direct.[85] He is bound to do so if the

[78] s. 235, Companies Act 1985.
[79] s. 237. For comment on the general duties of an auditor, see *Re City Equitable Fire Insurance Co.* [1925] 1 Ch. 407, *per* Romer J. at pp. 480–482, 497–499.
[80] ss. 389A(1), (3).
[81] s. 390.
[82] *Re Thomas Gerrard & Son Ltd.* [1968] Ch. 455.
[83] *Caparo Industries plc* v. *Dickman* [1990] 2 A.C. 605. Note also *McNaughton Ltd.* v. *Hicks Anderson & Co.* [1991] 2 Q.B. 113.
[84] *Caparo Industries plc* v. *Dickman, supra, per* Lord Bridge at p. 621. Note also *Morgan Crucible & Co.* v. *Hill Samuel & Co.* [1991] Ch. 295.
[85] ss. 431, 432(2). For powers of inspectors, see ss. 433–436.

court declares that the company's affairs ought to be investigated.[86] He also has power to require a company to produce such documents as he may specify at any time if he thinks there is good reason so to do.[87] Failing production by a company when so required, its premises may be entered and searched, and there are penalties for the destruction, mutilation or falsification of a document affecting or relating to the property or affairs of a company.[88] The Secretary of State has power, in the light of the inspectors' report or of any information obtained by them under these provisions, to bring civil proceedings on behalf of any body corporate.[89]

51.43   Arrangements and Reconstructions.—A compromise or arrangement between a company and its creditors, or any class of them, or between the company and its members,[90] or any class of them, is binding if approved (a) by a majority of three-fourths in value of the creditors or members concerned present and voting either in person or by proxy at a meeting called by order of the court and (b) if it is sanctioned by the court.[91] Before the meeting the creditors or members concerned must be given an explanation of the effect of the compromise or arrangement and of the material interests of the directors and the effect of the scheme on their interests.[92] Where the compromise or arrangement is proposed in connection with the reconstruction of a company or the amalgamation of companies and under the scheme property is to be transferred from one company to another the court may provide for, *inter alia*, the transfer or allotment of shares.[93] The court may provide for those who dissented from the proposed compromise or arrangement and for the acquisition of the shares of the dissenters.[94] But it may refuse to sanction an arrangement or compromise on the application of a dissenting shareholder.[95]

Where a proposed compromise or arrangement has as its purpose (or is connected with) the reconstruction of a company (or companies) or the amalgamation of companies, and would involve the transfer of the undertaking, property and liabilities of one public company to another,

---

[86] s. 432(1).

[87] s. 447.

[88] ss. 448, 450.

[89] s. 438.

[90] See *Singer Manufacturing Co.* v. *Robinow*, 1971 S.C. 11.

[91] s. 425.

[92] s. 426; the requirements of this section as to the giving of information about the scheme, including the notice to be given by advertisement, must be strictly complied with: see *Coltness Iron Co.*, 1951 S.C. 476; *City Property Investment Trust Corporation*, 1951 S.C. 570; *Second Scottish Investment Trust Co., Petrs.*, 1962 S.L.T. 392; *Scottish Eastern Investment Trust, Petrs.*, 1966 S.L.T. 285.

[93] s. 427(3).

[94] s. 427(3)(*e*); *Nidditch* v. *Calico Printers' Association*, 1961 S.L.T. 282; *Standard Property Investment Co.* v. *Dunblane Hydropathic* (1884) 12 R. 328.

[95] *Re Hellenic & General Trust Ltd.* [1975] 3 All E.R. 382.

or to any company formed for the purposes of the scheme, the court cannot sanction it unless: (a) there is a three-quarters majority of each class of shareholder of all the pre-existing companies in favour of the scheme; (b) draft terms of the scheme have been drawn up and adopted by all the directors of the transferor and pre-existing transferee companies involved in the scheme and copies of these sent to the Registrar who must publish a notice of their receipt in the *Edinburgh Gazette*; and (c) detailed reports by the directors of the transferor company and independent experts have been made available for inspection by the shareholders.[96]

51.44   Insolvency.—The law relating to the insolvency of companies has undergone considerable reform and modernisation in recent years, notably as a result of the Insolvency Act 1985, now consolidated by the Insolvency Act 1986. The subject is now very complicated, and a detailed examination of the many statutory provisions and their effect is beyond the scope of this book. What follows is no more than an outline of the more important provisions.

A company could be made notour bankrupt prior to the replacement of this concept by that of apparent insolvency, with the statutory effects on diligence and securities for prior debts,[97] but its property cannot be sequestrated under the Bankruptcy Act as can that of an individual.[98] The statutory procedures which are available to enable a company to meet the demands of its creditors[99] comprise (a) the making of voluntary arrangements for a composition in satisfaction of its debts or a scheme of arrangement of its affairs,[1] (b) the making of an administration order in relation to the company by the court,[2] and (c) the winding up of the company.[3] Provision is made[4] for two forms of winding up, namely (i) by the court, also termed compulsory or judicial, and (ii) voluntary, which may be either a members' or a creditors' winding up. The Court of Session has jurisdiction to wind up any company registered in Scotland, but where the amount of the share capital paid up or credited as paid up does not exceed £120,000 the sheriff court of the sheriffdom where the registered office of the company is situated has concurrent jurisdiction with the Court of Session.[5] The Court of Session may remit any petition, if within this

---

[96] s. 427A, Sched. 15B.

[97] *Clarke* v. *Hinde* (1884) 12 R. 347. As to notour bankruptcy and apparent insolvency, see para. 49.3, *infra*.

[98] *Standard Property Investment Co.* v. *Dunblane Hydropathic* (1884) 12 R. 328.

[99] See also para 51.31, *supra*, for the appointment of a receiver by the holder of a floating charge granted by the company.

[1] Insolvency Act 1986, ss. 1–7; para. 51.45, *infra*.

[2] Insolvency Act 1986, ss. 8–27; para. 51.46, *infra*.

[3] Insolvency Act 1986, ss. 73–251.

[4] Insolvency Act 1986, s. 73.

[5] 1986 Act, s. 120. For a company limited by guarantee and without share capital, see *Pearce*, 1991 S.C.L.R. 861.

limit, to the sheriff court.[6] Winding up subject to the supervision of the court was abolished by the Insolvency Act 1985.[7]

51.45 Voluntary Arrangements.—This procedure is available either in the course of a winding up or while an administration order is in force or at any other time when the directors may think it appropriate. The directors may not, however, propose a voluntary arrangement where the company is already in liquidation or where an administration order is in force.[8] It provides a simple procedure whereby a company may conclude an arrangement with its creditors which will be binding on both the company and those of its creditors who have had notice of it, and may enable a company which is nearly or actually insolvent to rationalise its affairs more speedily and with less formality than if a winding up had to be carried through to its conclusion, which is normally the dissolution of the company. The essential elements are the making of a proposal to the company and its creditors for a composition in satisfaction of its debts or a scheme of arrangement of its affairs, which provides for a nominee, who must be an insolvency practitioner,[9] to act as trustee or otherwise for the purpose of supervising its implementation. The proposal is made by the liquidator, the administrator or the directors of the company as the case may be.[10] The nominee, where he is not the liquidator or administrator, is required to submit a report to the court within 28 days as to whether in his opinion meetings of the company and of its creditors should be summoned to consider the proposal.[11] If he reports favourably on the scheme he is required to summon the meetings for the time, date and place proposed in his report unless the court directs otherwise.[12] The contents of a proposal made by either the liquidator or administrator and proposing either himself or another insolvency practitioner as nominee are the same as where the proposal is made by the directors.[13] In the former case the proposal should also include anything he thinks appropriate to enable members and creditors to reach an informed decision.[14] He may also summon a meeting of these to consider his proposal wherever and whenever he thinks fit.[15] If the composition or scheme is approved by the company and its creditors

---

[6] 1986 Act, s. 120(3). See *Chaney & Bull*, 1930 S.C. 759.

[7] s. 88.

[8] s. 1(1).

[9] Note that it is a criminal offence for a person to act as liquidator or administrator in relation to a company or supervisor of a voluntary agreement when he is not qualified to do so: Insolvency Act 1986, s. 389.

[10] Insolvency Act 1986, s. 1. In the case of the directors, a resolution of the board proposing a voluntary arrangement is probably sufficient: *Re Equiticorp International plc* [1989] 1 W.L.R. 1010.

[11] s. 2.

[12] s. 3(1).

[13] Insolvency (Scotland) Rules 1986 (S.I. 1986 No. 1915), rr. 1.3, 1.10 and 1.12(3).

[14] r. 1.10(*b*).

[15] s. 3(2).

at these meetings, with or without modifications, it takes effect as if
made by the company at the creditors' meeting and binds every person
who had notice of and was entitled to vote at that meeting as if he were
a party to it.[16] Provision is made for the implementation and supervision
of the composition or scheme and for the sisting or other conduct of any
proceedings for the winding up or administration of the company so as
to enable the composition or scheme to be implemented.[17] A
composition or scheme may be challenged on the ground of unfair
prejudice or of some material irregularity at or in relation to either of
the meetings.[18]

51.46 Administration Orders.—This procedure provides another method by
which the affairs of a company which is or is likely to be unable to pay
its debts may be dealt with for the benefit of its creditors. It is available
where the court considers that it would be likely to achieve the survival
of the company as a going concern or a more advantageous realisation
of the company's assets than would be effected in a winding up.[19] It
may also be used in conjunction with an attempt to secure approval of a
composition or scheme of arrangement under the procedure for
voluntary arrangements or the sanction under section 425 of the
Companies Act of a compromise or arrangement between the company
and its creditors.[20] An application to the court for an administration
order may be made by petition at the instance of the company or its
directors or by a creditor or creditors, or by the supervisor acting under
a voluntary arrangement.[21] If an administrative receiver has been
appointed, the court is required to dismiss the petition unless it has the
consent of the person by whom or on whose behalf the receiver was
appointed, except in certain special circumstances.[22] The effect of the
application is that until the order has been made or the petition has
been dismissed no resolution may be passed or order made for the
winding up of the company, and the rights of creditors to enforce any
charge or security over the company's property may only be exercised
with the leave of the court.[23] On the making of an administration order
any petition for the winding up of the company is required to be
dismissed, any administrative receiver of the company must vacate office
and any other receiver must do likewise on being asked to do so by the
administrator. Thereafter, and for so long as the administration order is

[16] s. 5; Rules 1.13–1.17.
[17] ss. 7, 5(3); rr. 1.18–1.24.
[18] s. 6.
[19] Insolvency Act 1986, s. 8. It will not be made where the company is already in liquidation.
[20] ss. 8(3)(b), (c).
[21] ss. 9(1), 7(4)(b). Insolvency (Scotland) Rules 1986 (S.I. 1986 No. 1915), rr. 2.1–2.3; Rules of Court 209, 210.
[22] s. 9(3).
[23] s. 10.

in force, a general moratorium is imposed on all other proceedings whereby creditors may seek to enforce their rights against the company or its assets.[24] The court may grant leave to permit actions which might otherwise be prohibited by this moratorium and the Court of Appeal recently provided a list of guidelines intended to help administrators and others in deciding whether a matter should be made the subject of an application to the court.[25]

An administration order provides for the appointment of an administrator,[26] who has general power to do all such things as may be necessary for the management of the affairs, business and property of the company together with a number of specific powers similar to those given to a receiver or a liquidator.[27] He also has power to remove any director of the company and to appoint any person to be a director, whether to fill a vacancy or otherwise, and to call any meeting of the members or creditors of the company.[28] He is deemed to be an agent of the company in the exercise of the powers which are given to him by these provisions.[29] He is required to take over control of and manage the company's affairs, business and property in accordance with any directions given to him by the court and to carry out an investigation of the company's affairs.[30] His most important function is to prepare proposals for achieving the purpose or purposes specified in the administration order, which he is required to lay before a meeting of the company's creditors.[31] A period of three months is allowed for this purpose, but this is capable of being extended by the court.[32] If the creditors approve his proposals, the administrator is thereafter required to manage the affairs, business and property of the company in accordance with them as revised by him from time to time.[33] If the creditors decline to approve the proposals and no modifications to them can be agreed, the court may discharge the administration order or adjourn the hearing of the application for its discharge or make any interim or other order it thinks fit.[34] A creditor or member of the company may apply to the court for relief on the ground that the company's affairs are being or have been managed by the administrator in a manner which is unfairly prejudicial to his interests.[35] In

---

[24] s. 11.
[25] Re Atlantic Computer Systems plc [1991] B.C.L.C. 606. Note also Scottish Exhibition Centre Ltd. v. Mirestop Ltd., 1993 G.W.D. 9–586.
[26] Note that it is a criminal offence for a person to act as administrator in relation to a company when he is not qualified to do so.
[27] s. 14; Sched. 1.
[28] s. 14(2).
[29] s. 14(5).
[30] ss. 17, 22. Note also Re Charnley Davies Ltd. [1990] B.C.L.C. 729.
[31] s. 23; rr. 2.7 (proposals), 2.9–2.14 (meetings).
[32] s. 23(1).
[33] ss. 24(2), 17(2).
[34] s. 24(5).
[35] s. 27.

exceptional circumstances, the administrator may act to realise assets before the approval of the creditors has been secured.[36]

51.47 **Winding Up by the Court.**[37]—A company registered in Scotland may be wound up by the court by petition presented to the Outer House[38] of the Court of Session, in vacation, to the vacation judge,[39] or, as above stated, to the sheriff.[39a] An unregistered company which is dissolved or has ceased to carry on business may also be wound up by the court in Scotland if there are or may be assets in this country belonging to the company and at least one person in Scotland is interested in the distribution of the assets of the company.[40] The title to petition rests with the company, its directors, any creditor, absolute or contingent, or any contributory who is either an original allottee or has held shares for six out of the preceding 18 months,[41] in certain situations, with the Secretary of State,[42] a receiver,[43] an administrator,[44] or the supervisor of a voluntary arrangement.[45]

A company may be wound up by the court on any one or more of the following grounds:[46] (a) that the company has by special resolution resolved that the company be wound up by the court; (b) that the company, being a public company, has failed to comply with the statutory requirements for minimum capital[47] and more than a year has expired since it was registered; (c) that the company is a company which is an old public company, that is to say a company which existed or had been applied for before December 22, 1980, would not have been a private company within section 28 of the Companies Act 1948 and has not been re-registered as a public company or become a private company;[48] (d) that the company has not commenced business within a year from its incorporation, or has suspended business for a year; (e) that the number of members (except where the company is a private company limited by shares or by guarantee) is reduced below two; (f) that the company is unable to pay its debts; (g) that the court is of opinion that it is just and equitable that the company should be wound up. A company which the Court of Session has jurisdiction to wind up

[36] *Re N.S. Distribution Ltd.* [1990] B.C.L.C. 169; *Re Charnley Davies Ltd.* (1987) 3 B.C.C. 408. *Cf. Re Consumer and Industrial Press Ltd.* (1988) 4 B.C.C. 72.
[37] For detailed discussion of the process of winding up in Scotland, see Palmer Vol. I, paras. 15.601 *et seq.*
[38] Rules of Court 217, 218.
[39] Rule of Court 1.
[39a] See, generally, s. 120.
[40] *Inland Revenue* v. *Highland Engineering*, 1975 S.L.T. 203.
[41] 1986 Act, s. 124.
[42] 1986 Act, s. 124(4).
[43] 1985 Act, ss. 14(1), 42(1), 55(2), Sched. 1, para. 21, Sched. 2, para. 21.
[44] *Ibid.*
[45] s. 7(4)(*b*).
[46] 1986 Act, ss. 122(1)(*a*)–(*g*).
[47] See para. 51.6, *supra.*
[48] See Companies Consolidation (Consequential Provisions) Act 1985, s. 1.

may also be wound up by the court on the ground that the security of the creditor entitled to the benefit of a floating charge over property comprised in the company's property and undertaking is in jeopardy.[49] The construction of the term 'just and equitable' in paragraph (g)[50] has been that it is not confined to cases *ejusdem generis* with the grounds of petition which precede, but covers such cases as the loss of the substantial part of the company's business or abandonment of its objects or impossibility of carrying them out, *i.e.* what is referred to as the disappearance of the 'substratum of the company,'[51] persistent disregard by the directors of the provisions of the Acts or other circumstances sufficient to warrant the inference that there has been an unfair abuse of power and an impairment of confidence in the probity with which the affairs of the company are being conducted;[52] or, in a private company which is in substance a partnership, a division between the directors which brings the affairs of the company to a deadlock[53] or the unjustified exclusion of one of the parties from its affairs.[54] The usual ground for a petition for winding up is, however, that afforded by paragraph (f), namely inability to pay debts. By section 123 of the 1986 Act a company is deemed unable to pay its debts when (1) a creditor, to whom a debt exceeding £750[55] is due, has served on the company a demand to pay, and the company has for three weeks neglected to pay, or to compound or secure the debt on the satisfaction of the creditor; (2) the induciae of a charge for payment on an extract decree, or an extract registered bond, or an extract registered protest, has expired without payment, even although the debt be less than £750;[56] (3) when it is proved to the satisfaction of the court that the company is unable to pay its debts as they fall due.[57] The court will refuse a petition on this ground where the debt is the subject of a genuine dispute with the company.[58]

The court has a discretion to grant or refuse a petition for winding up, but will not readily refuse the application of a creditor,[59] and is directed

---

[49] 1986 Act, s. 122(2); for this purpose the creditor's security is deemed to be in jeopardy if the court is satisfied that events have occurred or are about to occur which render it unreasonable in the creditor's interests that the company should retain the power to dispose of the property which is subject to the floating charge.

[50] See Palmer Vol. 1, paras. 15.619 *et seq. Re Westbourne Galleries* [1973] A.C. 360.

[51] Palmer, *ibid. Galbraith* v. *Merito Shipping Co.,* 1947 S.C. 446; *Levy* v. *Napier,* 1962 S.C. 468.

[52] *Elder* v. *Elder & Watson,* 1952 S.C. 49, *per* Lord President Cooper at p. 55; *Teague, Petr.,* 1985 S.L.T. 469.

[53] *Baird* v. *Lees,* 1924 S.C. 83; *Lewis* v. *Haas,* 1971 S.L.T. 57.

[54] *Re Lundie Bros.* [1965] 1 W.L.R. 1051; *Re Fildes Bros.* [1970] 1 W.L.R. 592.

[55] This amount is subject to alteration by statutory instrument: 1986 Act, s. 123(3).

[56] *Spiers* v. *Central Building Co.,* 1911 S.C. 330.

[57] See *Re Bryant Investment Co.* [1974] 1 W.L.R. 826.

[58] *Cuninghame* v. *Walkinshaw Oil Co. Ltd.* (1886) 14 R. 87; *Re Janeash Ltd.* (1990) B.C.C. 250.

[59] *Gardner* v. *Link* (1894) 21 R. 969; *cf. Foxall* v. *Gyle Nurseries,* 1978 S.L.T. (Notes) 29.

not to refuse it merely on the ground that the company has no assets.[60] Where the application is made by members of the company as contributories[61] on the ground that it is just and equitable that the company should be wound up, the court is not entitled to make a winding up order if it is of the opinion that some other remedy is available to the petitioners and that they are acting unreasonably in seeking to have the company wound up instead of pursuing that other remedy. An alternative remedy to winding up in cases of oppression is provided by section 459 of the 1985 Companies Act.[62]

51.48 Consequences of Winding Up.—If the court grants an order for the winding up of the company, the winding up is deemed to have commenced at the time of the presentation of the petition.[63] Thereafter, no action or proceeding against the company or its property can be commenced or proceeded with without leave of the court,[64] and any disposition of the company's property, or transfer of shares, is void, unless the court otherwise directs.[65] Any person who has at any time mishandled or appropriated property belonging to a company which is being wound up, including a director, manager or liquidator, may be compelled to repay or restore or account for the money or property or to contribute such sum to the company's assets as the court thinks fit.[66] The winding up confers on creditors who are creditors by virtue of a debt incurred on or before its commencement and on the liquidator the same rights as are given in bankruptcy to challenge gratuitous alienations and unfair preferences.[67] It has the same effect as a sequestration with regard to the equalisation of diligences,[68] and it is equivalent to a decree of adjudication of the heritable estates of the company for the payment of its debts.[69] The property of a company in liquidation does not vest in the liquidator. The custody and control of its property are transferred from the company and its directors to the liquidator over whom the company has no control, but the company

---

[60] 1986 Act, s. 125(1); *Spiers* v. *Central Building Co., supra.*

[61] As to the meaning of this expression, see 1986 Act, s. 79.

[62] See para. 51.2, *supra; Gammack, Petr.,* 1983 S.C. 39; *Re A Company* [1983] 1 W.L.R. 927; *Virdi* v. *Abbey Leisure Ltd.* [1990] B.C.L.C. 342; *Hyndman* v. *R.C. Hyndman Ltd.,* 1989 S.C.L.R. 294.

[63] 1986 Act, s. 129. See also *Haig* v. *Lord Advocate,* 1976 S.L.T. (Notes) 16. Where the company has already passed a resolution for voluntary winding up, the date of commencement is the date of the passing of the resolution.

[64] 1986 Act, s. 130(2).

[65] 1986 Act, s. 127; *Site Preparations* v. *Buchan Development Co.,* 1983 S.L.T. 317. See *United Dominions Trust,* 1977 S.L.T. (Notes) 56, where the property was already subject to a standard security and a warrant to sell the subjects had been granted by the sheriff.

[66] 1986 Act, s. 212.

[67] 1986 Act, ss. 242, 243.

[68] 1986 Act, s. 185(1), applying Bankruptcy (Scotland) Act 1985, s. 37(1). A gratuitous alienation by a company may also be challenged at common law: 1986 Act, s. 242(7); see *Johnstone* v. *Peter H. Irvine,* 1984 S.L.T. 209.

[69] 1986 Act, s. 185(1), applying Bankruptcy (Scotland) Act, s. 37(1); *Gibson* v. *Hunter Home Designs,* 1976 S.C. 23.

remains the legal owner of all its assets and interests.[70] A liquidator is merely an administrator, taking the place of the directors, for the special purpose of dividing the company's assets among the creditors and any balance among the contributories.[71] But the court may direct that all or any part of the company's property shall vest in the liquidator.[72] And the compulsory liquidation of a company has been treated, in questions as to the completion of securities, as equivalent to the sequestration of an individual.[73] The court has also power to appoint a provisional liquidator,[74] and, on an application by the liquidator or provisional liquidator, to appoint a special manager of the business or property of the company.[75] Where a liquidator and a receiver have both been appointed to a company the rights of the receiver take precedence over those of the liquidator irrespective of whether he was appointed before or after the commencement of the winding up, and the liquidator is bound to deliver to the receiver the property which is covered by the floating charge.[76] If he does so the receiver is primarily liable for the payment of the secured creditors and those who have preferential claims against the company.[77]

51.49   Liquidators.—When an order for winding up is pronounced an interim liquidator (who must be an insolvency practitioner) is appointed by the court.[78] His function is to summon separate meetings of the company's creditors and contributories for the purpose of choosing a person, who may be the interim liquidator, to be the liquidator of the company in his place.[79] The liquidator is the person nominated by the creditors, or if no person is so nominated, the person, if any, nominated by the contributories.[80] The court may, however, appoint a person as liquidator of a company where he has been acting as administrator under an administration order which has been discharged or as the supervisor of a voluntary arrangement.[81] A person who has been appointed as liquidator is described by the style of 'the liquidator' of the company

---

[70] *Clark* v. *West Calder Oil Co.* (1882) 9 R. 1017, *per* Lord President Inglis at p. 1025, Lord Shand at p. 1030.

[71] *Smith* v. *Lord Advocate*, 1978 S.C. 259, *per* Lord President Emslie at p. 271. For a discussion of the effects of the statutory scheme, see *Ayerst* v. *C. & K. (Construction)* [1976] A.C. 167, *per* Lord Diplock.

[72] 1986 Act, s. 145.

[73] *Clark* v. *West Calder Oil Co.*, *supra*; *Bank of Scotland* v. *Hutchison*, 1914 S.C. (H.L.) 1.

[74] 1986 Act, s. 135; see *Levy* v. *Napier*, 1962 S.C. 468.

[75] 1986 Act, s. 177.

[76] *Manley, Petr.*, 1985 S.L.T. 42; see further as to receivers, para. 51.31, *supra*. Note also *McGuiness* v. *Black*, 1990 S.L.T. 156 regarding the position of a judicial factor and a provisional liquidator.

[77] See para. 51.51, *infra*.

[78] 1986 Act, s. 138(1); Insolvency (Scotland) Rules 1986 (S.I. 1986 No. 1915), r. 4.18(2).

[79] s. 138(3), r. 4.12.

[80] s. 139.

[81] s. 140.

concerned and not by his individual name.[82] A person who acts as the liquidator of a company must be qualified to do so, which means that he must be permitted to act as an insolvency practitioner by or under the rules of a recognised professional body or authorised so to act, that he must have furnished the proper caution for the performance of his functions and not been disqualified from acting on grounds such as that he is an undischarged bankrupt or is mentally incapable of managing his own affairs.[83] A person who is not an individual is not qualified to act as an insolvency practitioner, so it is not competent to appoint a partnership or company to the office of liquidator.[84]

The general function of the liquidator is to secure that the assets of the company are got in, realised and distributed to the company's creditors and, if there is a surplus, to the persons entitled to it.[85] A committee of creditors and contributories may be appointed to act with him by the meetings of creditors and contributories at which he is appointed, or by separate meetings of the creditors and contributories called by the liquidator for the purpose of determining whether such a committee should be established.[86] Its members have no claim to remuneration.[87] The powers of a liquidator in a winding up are set out in Schedule 4 to the 1986 Act. Some of these powers may only be exercised by him with the sanction of the court or of the committee,[88] and he is subject to the control of the court in the exercise of all of them.[89] He may ratify acts or proceedings done or started in the name of the company without proper authority.[90] It is his duty to summon a final meeting of the company's creditors when the winding up is complete, and he vacates office as soon as he has given notice to the court and the Registrar that the final meeting has been held, and of the decisions, if any, which it took.[91] A liquidator may be removed or released from office in various circumstances before the winding up is complete.[92]

51.50 Voluntary Winding Up.—Voluntary liquidation is a step often taken when it is proposed to reconstitute the company with wider powers, when two companies propose to amalgamate, or where for any reason it is desired to bring a company to an end. It is competent in the following

---

[82] s. 163.
[83] 1986 Act, ss. 230, 390.
[84] 1986 Act, s. 390(1).
[85] 1986 Act, s. 143(1).
[86] 1986 Act, s. 142. Note that a committee should consist of more than one individual: *Souter, Petr.*, 1981 S.L.T. (Sh.Ct.) 89. See also Insolvency (Scotland) Rules 1986 (S.I. 1986 No. 1915) Pt. 4, Chap. 7.
[87] *Liquidator of Pattisons* (1902) 4 F. 1010.
[88] 1986 Act, s. 167(1).
[89] s. 167(3).
[90] *Alexander Ward & Co.* v. *Samyang Navigation Co.*, 1975 S.C. (H.L.) 26, *per* Lord Fraser at p. 36.
[91] 1986 Act, s. 172(8); r. 4.31.
[92] ss. 172, 174. See Insolvency (Scotland) Rules 1986, rr. 4.23–4.30.

cases: (1) when the period (if any) fixed for the duration of the company by its articles has expired, or the event (if any) occurs, on the occurrence of which the articles provide that the company is to be dissolved, and the company in general meeting has passed a resolution requiring the company to be wound up voluntarily; (2) if the company resolves by special resolution that it be wound up voluntarily; (3) if the company resolves by extraordinary resolution to the effect that it cannot, by reason of its liabilities, continue its business, and that it is advisable to wind up.[93] A voluntary winding up is deemed to commence at the date of the resolution to wind up.[94] The company is bound to give notice of the resolution by advertisement in the *Edinburgh Gazette*.[95]

When a company is wound up voluntarily it must cease to carry on business from the commencement of the winding up, except in so far as may be required for its beneficial winding up.[96] Any subsequent transfer of shares, without the sanction of the liquidator, is void.[97] The resolution does not bar an action being commenced or proceeded with against the company, but the liquidator may apply to the court to direct that no action or proceeding may be commenced or proceeded with.[98] It is no bar to an application for winding up by the court,[99] but where a majority of the creditors favour a voluntary winding up, the court as a rule has regard to their views.[1]

A voluntary winding up may be either a members' or a creditors' voluntary winding up. It is the former if the directors, at a meeting held before the notices for the meeting at which the resolution to wind up is to be proposed are sent out, make, and deliver to the Registrar of Companies, a declaration, termed a declaration of solvency, to the effect that they have made a full inquiry into the affairs of the company, and that, having so done, they have formed the opinion that the company will be able to pay its debts, with interest, in full within a period, not exceeding 12 months, from the commencement of the winding up.[2] If no such declaration is made and delivered to the Registrar, it is a creditors' voluntary winding up.[3] In a members' winding up the liquidator is appointed by the company in general meeting.[4] Provisions are made for the sale, or transfer to another company, of the company's business,[5] and for its dissolution.[6]

[93] s. 84. As to special and extraordinary resolutions, see para. 51.16, *supra*.
[94] s. 86.
[95] s. 85.
[96] s. 87.
[97] s. 88.
[98] *Sdeuard* v. *Gardner* (1876) 3 R. 577; s. 113.
[99] s. 116.
[1] *Bouboulis* v. *Mann, Macneal & Co.*, 1926 S.C. 637; *Re Home Remedies* [1943] Ch 1.
[2] s. 89.
[3] s. 90; see also s. 95.
[4] s. 91.
[5] s. 110.
[6] s. 201.

In a creditors' voluntary winding up the company must call a meeting of its creditors for a day not later than the fourteenth day after the day on which there is to be held the meeting at which the resolution for voluntary winding up is to be proposed.[7] One of the directors must be appointed to preside at the meeting.[8] The liquidator in a creditors' voluntary winding up is the person nominated by the creditors or, where no person has been nominated by them, the person, if any, nominated by the company.[9] A committee of not more than five persons may be appointed by the creditors to act in the liquidation.[10] The company has the right to appoint no more than five other persons to act as members of that committee.[11] On the appointment of a liquidator, all the powers of the directors cease, except in so far as the committee, or, if none, the creditors, sanction their continuance.[12] A member of a committee is in a position of trust; accordingly, if it is proposed that he should purchase some of the assets of the company, the liquidator ought to have the sanction of the court before the sale is made.[13]

51.51 Ranking of Creditors.—Except in a members' voluntary winding up, a creditor claiming to vote at meetings and to be entitled to payment of a dividend must submit a claim in the prescribed form to the liquidator together with an account or voucher as evidence of his debt.[14] In calculating the amount of his claim he must deduct the value of any security.[15] Priority is given to the payment of preferential debts, which rank equally among themselves and must be paid in full unless the assets are insufficient to meet them in which case they abate in equal proportions.[16] Preferential debts have priority over the holder of a floating charge.[17] Questions as to the liabilities and rights of co-obligants, including cautioners, are dealt with according to the same rules as apply in the sequestration.[18] The funds are distributed by the liquidator in the following order:[19] (a) the expenses of liquidation;[20] (b)

[7] s. 98.
[8] s. 99(1). It has been held in England that the meeting is not invalid because none of the directors are present: *Re Salcombe Hotel Development Co. Ltd.* [1991] B.C.L.C. 44.
[9] s. 100.
[10] s. 101(1); for the proceedings of the committee, see Insolvency (Scotland) Rules 1986 (S.I. 1986 No. 1915), Pt. 4, Chap. 7, as modified by Sched. 1.
[11] s. 101(2).
[12] s. 103
[13] Notwithstanding s. 165(2)(b) and Sched. 4, para. 6; see *Dowling* v. *Lord Advocate*, 1963 S.C. 272.
[14] Insolvency (Scotland) Rules, rr. 4.15, 7.30.
[15] Bankruptcy (Scotland) Act 1985, s. 22(9), Sched. 1, as applied by r. 4.16.
[16] 1986 Act, s. 175; see Sched. 6 for a list of preferential debts; *cf.* Bankruptcy (Scotland) Act 1985, s. 51(1)(e), Sched. 3. See also Insolvency Proceedings (Monetary Limits) Order 1986 (S.I. 1986 No. 1996).
[17] s. 175(2)(b).
[18] Bankruptcy (Scotland) Act 1985, s. 60, as applied by r. 4.16.
[19] r. 4.66.
[20] See r. 4.67.

the expenses of any voluntary arrangement in force at the time when the petition for winding up was first presented;[21] (c) the preferential debts; (d) ordinary debts, *i.e.* debts neither secured nor falling under (a), (b), (c) or (f); (e) interest at 15 per cent. on (i) the preferential debts, (ii) the ordinary debts, between the commencement of the winding up and payment; (f) any postponed debt, *i.e.* a creditor's right to any alienation which has been reduced or restored to the company's assets or to the proceeds of the sale of such alienation.[22] Debts within the same category have the same priority and abate in equal proportions.[23]

51.52 Contributories.—Should the assets of the company in liquidation be insufficient to meet its liabilities, calls may be made on the shareholders as contributories in so far (in a limited company) as the shares are not fully paid up.[24] The primary liability rests on the existing holders of the shares, but should it appear to the court that they are unable to meet their liabilities, calls may be made on those prior shareholders who have held the shares during the 12 months preceding the liquidation. Two lists of contributories may be drawn up, known as the A and the B list, the former containing the names of existing, the latter those of prior, shareholders.[25]

A contributory on the B list is not liable for debts incurred after he has ceased to be a member,[26] and it has been decided that the B list contributories, by paying off the earlier debts, escape liability altogether.[27] When, however, calls are made on the B list the proceeds go to meet the general liabilities of the company, and are not earmarked to meet prior debts.[28] In no case is a B contributory liable for more than the balance unpaid on the particular shares which he formerly held.[29]

51.53 Dissolution of Company.—A company is dissolved automatically on the expiration of three months from the date of registration of a notice by the liquidator that a final general meeting of the company has been held. The procedure is the same in the case of a compulsory winding up[30] as for a voluntary liquidation.[31] The liquidator vacates office as soon as he has given notice to the Registrar, and to the court if it was a compulsory winding up or he was appointed by the court, that the

---

[21] Added by the Insolvency (Scotland) Amendment Rules 1987 (S.I. 1987 No. 1921).
[22] See para. 51.46, *supra.*
[23] r. 4.66(4).
[24] s. 74.
[25] See *Liqr. of Caledonian Heritable Security Co.* (1882) 9 R. 1130; *Re City of London Insurance Co.* [1932] 1 Ch. 226.
[26] s. 74(2)(b).
[27] *Brett's Case* (1871) L.R. 6 Ch. 800; (1873) L.R. 8 Ch. 800.
[28] *Webb* v. *Whiffin* (1872) L.R. 5 H.L. 711.
[29] *Liqr. of Caledonian Heritable Security Co.* (1882) 9 R. 1130.
[30] 1986 Act, s. 205.
[31] 1986 Act, s. 201.

meeting has been held and of the decisions if any at that meeting.[32] A liquidator appointed by the court who finds, after meetings of the creditors and contributories have been held, that the realisable assets of the company are insufficient to cover the expenses of the winding up may apply to the court for an early dissolution of the company.[33] In all these cases the court may, on the application of any person who appears to the court to have an interest, order that the date at which the dissolution of the company is to take effect shall be deferred for such period as it thinks fit.[34] At any time within two years of the dissolution of a company, the court, on the application of the liquidator or of any person interested, may make an order declaring the dissolution to have been void, and thereafter such proceedings may be taken as might have been taken if the company had not been dissolved.[35] If the application is made within two years the actual order may be made after the two years have expired.[36] The court has power, under its *nobile officium*, to declare the dissolution to have been void in a case where the company has failed or omitted to grant a conveyance of property sold,[37] but will not exercise this power if there are other means of completing the title.[38]

While a winding up is the normal process by which a company is dissolved, the Registrar of Companies may take steps which will result in striking a company off the register if he has reasonable cause to believe that it is not carrying on business or in operation. In that case the company may be restored to the register at any time within 20 years if the court is satisfied that the company was carrying on business or that it is just that it should be restored.[39]

When a company is dissolved, and not resuscitated, all property and rights vested in, or held in trust for the company immediately before its dissolution, are deemed to be *bona vacantia*, and belong to the Crown.[40]

Further Reading

Farrar, *Company Law* (3rd ed., 1991).
Gower, *Principles of Modern Company Law* (5th ed., 1992).
Marshall, *Scots Mercantile Law* (2nd ed., 1992), Chap. 3.
Palmer, *Company Law* (25th ed., 1992).
Palmer, *Company Precedents* (17th ed., 1956).

[32] s. 172(8).
[33] s. 204.
[34] ss. 201(3), 204(5), 205(5).
[35] Companies Act 1985, s. 651, as amended by the 1989 Act, s. 141. A company may, for the purpose of raising an action for damages against it, be restored to the register at any time within 20 years of the date of dissolution: s. 141(4).
[36] *Re Scald* [1941] Ch. 386; *Dowling, Petr.*, 1960 S.L.T. (Notes) 76.
[37] *Collins Bros., Petrs.*, 1916 S.C. 620.
[38] *Lord Macdonald's Curator*, 1924 S.C. 163; *Forth Shipbreaking Co.*, 1924 S.C. 489.
[39] s. 653; *Healy, Petr.* (1903) 5 F. 644; *Tyman's Ltd. v. Craven* [1952] 2 Q.B. 100.
[40] s. 654; see *Healy, Petr., supra*.

CHAPTER 52

OTHER PERSONS

52.1 Legal Position.—Unincorporated associations, commonly referred to as voluntary associations, occupy an anomalous position in the eye of the law. Corporate bodies[1] and, in Scotland, partnerships or firms,[2] are recognised as possessing legal personality; but, although the courts may be called on to take cognizance of, and adjudicate on, matters relating to a voluntary association, it is not regarded as having a legal existence distinct from that of its members. Hence, such an association cannot at common law sue or be sued in its collective name alone; the names either of all the members, or of responsible members such as office bearers, must be added.[3] But in the sheriff court an association carrying on business under a trading or descriptive name may sue or be sued in its trading or descriptive name alone, and an extract of a decree pronounced against it under its trading or descriptive name is a valid warrant for diligence against it.[4]

Further, the court will not take any concern with the actions or resolutions of such bodies except in so far as these affect the patrimonial interests or civil rights of its members. Unless such rights are involved, an action for determining questions between a member and the association will not be entertained.[5] 'Agreements to associate for purposes of recreation, or an agreement to associate for scientific or philanthropical or social or religious purposes, are not agreements which courts of law can enforce. They are entirely personal. Therefore, in order to establish a civil wrong from the refusal to carry out such an agreement, if it can be inferred that any such agreement was made, it is

---

[1] See *J.H. Raynen (Mincing Lane) Ltd.* v. *Department of Trade and Industry* [1990] 2 A.C. 418.

[2] Para. 50.9, *supra*; Partnership Act 1890, s. 4(2).

[3] *Renton Football Club* v. *McDowall* (1891) 18 R. 670; *Pagan & Osborne* v. *Haig*, 1910 S.C. 341; *Bridge* v. *South Portland Street Synagogue*, 1907 S.C. 1351. An unincorporated association may nevertheless be liable to assessment to corporation tax in respect of its income or capital gains: see *Worthing Club Trs.* v. *I.R.C.* [1985] 1 W.L.R. 409. *Cf. Conservative and Unionist Central Office* v. *Burrell* [1982] 1 W.L.R. 522.

[4] Sheriff Courts (Scotland) Act 1907, Sched. 1, r. 14, as substituted by S.I. 1983 No. 747.

[5] *Forbes* v. *Eden* (1867) 5 M. (H.L.) 36; *Skerret* v. *Oliver* (1896) 23 R. 468; *Drennan* v. *Associated Ironmoulders of Scotland*, 1921 S.C. 151, *per* Lord Dundas; *Marshall* v. *Cardonald Bowling Club*, 1971 S.L.T. (Sh.Ct.) 56; *Bell* v. *The Trustees*, 1975 S.L.T. (Sh.Ct.) 60; *cf. J.A. & D.S. Rennie* v. *Scottish Milk Records Association*, 1985 S.L.T. 272, where interdict was pronounced against an unincorporated association in relation to its disciplinary proceedings.

necessary to see that the pursuer has suffered some practical injury either in his reputation or in his property.'[6]

52.2 Classes of Associations.—Voluntary associations include bodies of such varied character as social clubs, dissenting churches, and societies formed for charitable or religious or scientific purposes. In practice, trading associations are not found among them, as section 716 of the Companies Act 1985 forbids the formation of unregistered associations of more than 20 persons for the purpose of carrying on business for the acquisition of gain.[7]

As the instances given suggest, there is a broad distinction between two types of association. In the case of the ordinary social club the funds are contributed by the members and are to be applied for their benefit. Any questions which may arise are solved, therefore, by the application of the law of contract and joint property. Another type of association is that which exists for the promotion of some further purpose or object. Here the element of trust is to be discovered, and the general principles of trust law will control the application of the funds contributed or subscribed.

52.3 Clubs.—Most clubs are governed by rules drawn up by the members, and any member who joins is understood to agree to be bound by those rules; they form part of the contract between him and the other members.[8] If the rules contain a provision for their alteration, any alteration made bona fide and in accordance with the rules is binding on all the members unless the alteration is incompatible with the fundamental purpose of the association.[9] An alteration of the rules of a club to allow for its dissolution will not be in conflict with its fundamental objects, since any club can be dissolved by the unanimous will of its members.[10] But where the rules make no provision for their alteration they cannot be altered without the consent of all the members.[11]

The property of the club belongs to all the members, each member having a right with all the other members.[12] 'The right of a member of a

---

[6] *Murdison* v. *Scottish Football Union* (1896) 23 R. 449, *per* Lord Kinnear.

[7] Note the exceptions to this rule in the case of partnerships of solicitors, accountants and members of a recognised stock exchange, and the Secretary of State's power to grant further exceptions by regulation: ss. 716(2), (3). See para. 50.4, *supra*.

[8] *Lyttleton* v. *Blackburne* (1875) L.J.Ch. 219.

[9] *Thellusson* v. *Viscount Valentia* [1907] 2 Ch. 1; *Morgan* v. *Driscoll* (1922) 38 T.L.R. 251.

[10] *Blair* v. *Mackinnon*, 1981 S.L.T. 40. Note, however, that unless there is a provision in the rules to this effect a club cannot be dissolved by a majority of its members against the wishes of a minority: *Gardner* v. *McLintock* (1904) 11 S.L.T. 654.

[11] *Harington* v. *Sendall* [1903] 1 Ch. 921; *Dawkins* v. *Antrobus* (1881) 17 Ch.D. 615, *per* Jessel M.R. But see the observations of Lords Guthrie and Skerrington in *Wilson* v. *Scottish Typographical Association*, 1912 S.C. 534. See also *Martin* v. *Scottish Transport & General Workers Union*, 1952 S.C. (H.L.) 1.

[12] *Graff* v. *Evans* (1881) 8 Q.B.D. 373.

club in the property of the club is of a peculiar description. While the club exists as a going concern he is not entitled to insist on a sale and a division of the price. When he dies his right, such as it is, does not pass to his representatives, and if he retires from the club his whole interest therein ceases. But as long as he remains a member of the club his right is one of common property.'[13] Hence it has been held that, while the wish of the majority of the members will rule in the ordinary administration of the property of the club, it is not competent for the majority gratuitously to alienate club property against the protest of a minority where there is nothing in the constitution of the club giving such a power.[14] If the club comes to an end the property remaining after all the debts and liabilities have been met is distributable among the members at the time.[15]

No member of the club, as such, is liable to pay to it or to anyone else any money beyond his subscription;[16] and if he is to be made liable by a creditor of the club, his liability must be established on the ground that he has undertaken liability or has so acted as to render himself liable under the ordinary rules of the law of agency.[17] He has the unilateral right, not dependent on acceptance by the club, to resign his membership at any time, even though the rules contain no provision as to resignation.[18]

A member who has been expelled from a club may apply to the court to have the resolution of the club set aside; and the court will entertain the action if the club possesses property, for the effect of the expulsion is to deprive the member of his right in that property. The court will not, however, review the merits of the club's decision, and will interfere only if it is not authorised by the rules, or if it is contrary to natural justice (as for example if no opportunity were afforded to the member of defending himself against the charge on which the decision is founded), or if the decision was not arrived at in good faith.[19]

---

[13] *Murray* v. *Johnstone* (1896) 23 R. 981, *per* Lord Moncreiff at p. 990.

[14] *Ibid.*, *Gardner* v. *McLintock, supra. Cf. Hopwood* v. *O'Neill,* 1971 S.L.T. (Notes) 53.

[15] *Baird* v. *Wells* (1890) 44 Ch.D. 661, *per* Stirling J.; *cf. Re Sick and Funeral Society of St. John's Sunday School Golcar* [1973] Ch. 51; *G.K.N. Bolts and Nuts (Automative Division) Birmingham Works Sports and Social Club* [1982] 1 W.L.R. 774. These rules do not, however, apply to a proprietary club, that is, one in which the club premises and what is necessary for the members belong to and are provided by the proprietor, who receives the fees of the members. In this case the members have no right in the property.

[16] *Wise* v. *Perpetual Trustee Co.* [1903] A.C. 139.

[17] *Thomson* v. *Victoria Eighty Club* (1905) 43 S.L.R. 628; *Flemyng* v. *Hector* (1836) 2 M. & W. 172; *Todd* v. *Emly* (1841) 7 M. & W. 427. *Cromarty Leasing Ltd.* v. *Turnbull,* 1988 S.L.T. (Sh.Ct.) 62. A member is not entitled to share in profits arising from the club's activities: *Blackpool Marton Rotary Club* v. *Martin* (1988) T.C. Tax Leaflet No. 3158.

[18] *Finch* v. *Oake* [1896] 1 Ch. 409.

[19] *Anderson* v. *Manson,* 1909 S.C. 838, *per* Lord Dundas; *Dawkins* v. *Antrobus* (1881) 17 Ch.D. 615; *Burn* v. *National Amalgamated Labourers' Union* [1920] 2 Ch. 364; *Young* v. *Ladies Imperial Club* [1920] 2 K.B. 523; *Maclean* v. *The Workers' Union* [1929] 1 Ch. 602; *Bell* v. *The Trustees,* 1975 S.L.T. (Sh.Ct.) 60.

52.4 Religious and other Associations.—Where subscriptions are contributed to an association or society formed for the promotion of a certain object, the sums so contributed are held in trust for that object.[20] Every contribution is an irrevocable appropriation of the donor's money to the purposes of the association, and, so long as these purposes are capable of being effected, the donor is not entitled to repayment of his contribution.[21] Unless it is otherwise provided in the rules of the association or the terms on which subscriptions were invited, the purposes to which the money is to be applied cannot be altered without the consent of all the subscribers.[22]

If it becomes impossible to carry out the purpose for which the subscriptions were given, the disposal of the funds of the association may present great difficulty. Where that purpose is of a public or charitable nature, it would appear from the decision in *Anderson's Trs. v. Scott*[23] that the proper course is that a scheme should be prepared by the court in the exercise of the jurisdiction which it possesses in regard to such trusts. Otherwise the funds would apparently fall, as a rule, to be repaid to the subscribers. 'Where parties join in a subscription to effect a particular object, and place the money subscribed in the hands of certain persons to carry out that object, I think the quasi trust, thereby created, is for the alternative purpose of either carrying out the object of the subscription, or, if that cannot be done, of paying back the money.'[24] There may be great practical difficulties in this course: and if a subscriber could not be traced it is possible that his share would fall to the Crown as *bona vacantia*.[25] The terms on which the funds were contributed may, however, be such as to negative any quasi-trust as, *e.g.* where the contributions are not purely gratuitous but have been finally paid over by the contributors as the consideration for benefits to be received by them, and in that case they would have no claim for the return of their contributions.[26]

In the case of a dissenting church, the funds contributed to it are held in trust, and in case of division among its members any question as to the right to these funds is determined by inquiring which of the parties is adhering to the original principles professed by the church. The

---

[20] *Ewing* v. *McGavin* (1831) 9 S. 622; *Connell* v. *Ferguson* (1857) 19 D. 482, *per* Lord Deas.

[21] *Ewing* v. *McGavin, supra; Peake* v. *Association of English Episcopalians* (1884) 22 S.L.R. 3; 8 S.L.T. 236.

[22] *McCaskill* v. *Cameron* (1840) 2 D. 537; *Steedman* v. *Malcolm* (1842) 4 D. 1441.

[23] 1914 S.C. 942; see also *Gibson* (1900) 2 F. 1195; *Davidson's Trs.* v. *Arnott*, 1951 S.C. 42.

[24] *Per* Lord Deas in *Connell* v. *Ferguson, supra*, and *Mitchell* v. *Burness* (1878) 5 R. 954; *Bain* v. *Black* (1849) 11 D. 1287, *per* Lords Mackenzie and Fullerton, at pp. 1307 and 1310; affd. 6 Bell's App. 317; *Re British Red Cross Balkan Fund* [1914] 2 Ch. 419.

[25] This was the decision of the Lord Ordinary (Cullen) in *Anderson's Trs.* v. *Scott, supra*; see also Lord President Dunedin's opinion in *Incorporated Maltmen of Stirling*, 1912 S.C. 887, and Lord Sands' opinion in *Caledonian Employees' Benevolent Society*, 1928 S.C. 633.

[26] *Smith* v. *Lord Advocate* (1899) 1 F. 741; *Cunnock* v. *Edwards* [1895] 1 Ch. 489.

constitution of the church may provide for the disposal of the property in the event of a schism or may give the church the power of altering its principles; but, in the absence of such provisions, where the property is claimed by different sections of those who formed the church, the property will be held to belong to those who adhere to those principles.[27]

If a clergyman wrongfully expelled from a church or a member from an association applies to the court for redress he must show that he has suffered some patrimonial loss; but under such loss is included the deprivation through the expulsion of some particular status, *i.e.* the capacity to perform certain functions or to hold certain offices.[28] The court will award damages for any wrong done in this way, but will not pronounce decree ordaining the church or association to re-admit the expelled member.[29] The court will not interfere with the judgments of an ecclesiastical tribunal, unless the tribunal has acted clearly beyond its constitution and has affected the civil rights and patrimonial interests of a church member, or its proceedings have been grossly irregular or contrary to natural justice.[30]

52.5 Societies Regulated by Statute.—There are certain associations which hold an intermediate position between corporate and unincorporated bodies. They have no corporate existence, but the legislature has intervened for their regulation and assistance. The most important of these are Trade Unions.[31]

At common law a trade union, if its rules and objects were open to objection as being in restraint of trade, was an illegal association in the sense that it could not sue or enforce contracts,[32] or be sued in respect of an alleged breach of contract with a member.[33] By the Trade Union Act 1871[34] it was enacted that the purposes of any trade union should not be illegal on this ground so as to render any member liable to criminal prosecution, or any agreement or trust void or voidable. This dispensation has been preserved in subsequent legislation,[35] and

---

[27] *Free Church of Scotland* v. *Lord Overtoun* (1904) 7 F. (H.L.) 1.

[28] *Skerret* v. *Oliver* (1896) 23 R. 468, *per* Lord Kincairney; *Bell* v. *The Trustees*, 1975 S.L.T. (Sh.Ct.) 60.

[29] *Ibid.*, *Gall* v. *Loyal Glenbogie Lodge of the Oddfellows' Friendly Society* (1900) 2 F. 1187, *per* Lord Trayner.

[30] *McDonald* v. *Burns*, 1940 S.C. 376; *Brentnall* v. *Free Presbyterian Church of Scotland*, 1986 S.L.T. 471.

[31] Building societies are incorporated under the Building Societies Act 1986. Societies regulated by the Industrial and Provident Societies Act 1965 are incorporated on registration (s. 3).

[32] *Wilkie* v. *King*, 1911 S.C. 1310, *per* Lord Dunedin; *Shanks & McKernan* v. *United Operative Masons Society* (1874) 1 R. 453 and 823. Not all trade unions were illegal—*Russell* v. *Amalgamated Society of Carpenters and Joiners* [1910] 1 K.B. 506.

[33] *Bernard* v. *National Union of Mineworkers*, 1971 S.C. 32.

[34] ss. 2 and 3.

[35] See Industrial Relations Act 1971, s. 135; Trade Union and Labour Relations Act 1974, s. 2(5).

extended so as to cover any rule of a trade union. Any such rule is not to be held to be unlawful or unenforceable by reason only that it is in restraint of trade.[36] A major reform of the law relating to trade unions was attempted by the Industrial Relations Act 1971, which gave preferential treatment to organisations registered under its provisions and accorded to them corporate status.[37] That Act was, however, repealed, following a change of government, by the Trade Union and Labour Relations Act 1974[38] by which the unincorporated status of trade unions was restored. Trade unions and employers' associations within the meaning of that Act[39] have, however, certain attributes and privileges in consequence of which, although unincorporated, they may be said to have a legal entity.[40] For instance they are capable of making contracts and, subject to certain immunities, of suing and being sued in their own name, and any judgment, order or award made against them is enforceable against any property held in trust for them as if they were bodies corporate.[41] Statutory rights[42] not to be excluded or expelled from a trade union by way of arbitrary or unreasonable discrimination have been repealed[43] but in some circumstances protection may be afforded at common law[44] and in the case of any employment in which it is the practice, in accordance with a union membership agreement, for employees to belong to a specified trade union or one of a number of specified trade unions, anyone who is or seeks to be in such employment has a right not to have an application for trade union membership unreasonably refused and not to be unreasonably expelled from membership.[45] A member of a trade union has the right, on giving reasonable notice and complying with any reasonable conditions, to terminate his membership.[46] He also has rights that there will be a ballot before industrial action, that he is not denied access to the courts and that he will not be unjustifiably disciplined.[47]

---

[36] Trade Union and Labour Relations (Consolidation) Act 1992, s. 11; see *Faramus* v. *Film Artistes Association* [1964] A.C. 925; *Edwards* v. *Society of Graphical and Allied Trades* [1971] Ch. 354.

[37] s. 74.

[38] That Act was amended by the Employment Protection (Consolidation) Act 1978 and the Employment Acts of 1980, 1982, 1988, 1989 and 1990. The law has now been consolidated by the Trade Union and Labour Relations (Consolidation) Act 1992. See also Trade Union Act 1913 and Trade Union (Amalgamations etc.) Act 1964 as amended. Certain trade unions which are 'special register bodies' may be incorporated (1992 Act, s. 117).

[39] For definition of these expressions, see 1992 Act, ss. 1, 122.

[40] *Taff Vale Rly. Co.* v. *Amalgamated Society of Railway Servants* [1901] A.C. 426; *Bonsor* v. *Musicians Union* [1956] A.C. 104.

[41] 1992 Act, ss. 10, 12.

[42] 1974 Act, s. 5.

[43] Trade Union and Labour Relations (Amendment) Act 1976, s. 1.

[44] *e.g.* on grounds of natural justice, of *ultra vires* or of a public policy against arbitrary exclusion: *Nagle* v. *Feilden* [1966] 2 Q.B. 633; *McGregor* v. *N.A.L.G.O.*, 1979 S.C. 401.

[45] 1992 Act, ss. 174–177.

[46] 1992 Act, s. 69.

[47] 1992 Act, ss. 62–67.

52.6 Friendly Societies.—Friendly Societies are, broadly speaking, constituted for the maintenance and relief of members and their families in sickness or old age and distress and to a limited extent for certain methods of insurance. The Friendly Societies Act 1974, a consolidation statute, contained provisions whereby societies could register and obtain certain privileges and duties. Under the Friendly Societies Act 1992, societies fulfilling prescribed conditions can be registered and on registration become incorporated.[48] The permissible purposes and powers of incorporated friendly societies are extended and they may form subsidiaries.[49] They are subject to supervision by the Friendly Societies Commission.[50]

52.7 Building Societies.—A building society is not a company but it must have a memorandum and rules and it may raise funds by issuing shares, including deferred shares at a premium, to its members.[51] The principal purpose of a building society is secured lending on land bought for residential use[52] but it can also provide other financial services (*e.g.* banking, estate agency, insurance, and investment) so long as lending is not made conditional on the borrower being restricted to making use only of the financial services offered by the lender.[53] A building society may, subject to satisfying requirements laid down by the 1986 Act,[54] transfer its business to either an existing public company limited by shares or such a company specifically formed for the purpose of taking over and running its existing business.[55] Both borrowing members' and shareholders' special resolutions must be passed approving such a transfer. Where the proposed transfer is to an existing company, there is a requirement that the shareholders' resolution must be passed either by not less than 50 per cent. of those qualified to vote or by those holding a minimum of 90 per cent. of the total value of the shares. Where the proposed transfer is to a company formed in order to take over the society's business, the resolution must be passed on a poll of which not less than 20 per cent. of the members of the society qualified to vote have voted.[56]

---

[48] Friendly Societies Act 1992, ss. 5–6.
[49] 1992 Act, ss. 7–17.
[50] 1992 Act, Pt. V.
[51] Building Societies Act 1986, s. 5, Sched. 2; ss. 7(1), (2A). This last is added by the Deregulation and Contracting Out Act 1994, s. 15.
[52] s. 5(1).
[53] ss. 34, 35, Sched. 8, Pt. I.
[54] ss. 97–102.
[55] s. 97.
[56] s. 97(4), Sched. 2, para. 30.

PART IX—DILIGENCE AND INSOLVENCY

CHAPTER 53

DILIGENCE[1]

53.1 **Meaning and Forms of Diligence.**—Diligence has been defined as 'the legal procedure by which a creditor attaches the property or person of his debtor, with the object of forcing him either (1) to appear in court to answer an action at the creditor's instance, or (2) to find security for implement of the judgment which may be pronounced against him in such an action, or (3) to implement a judgment already pronounced.'[2] Various forms of diligence of creditors[3] are recognised, according to the nature and situation of the property to be attached, or according to the nature of the claim in respect of which diligence is to be used. The following forms require notice: (1) Civil Imprisonment; (2) Arrestment; (3) Diligence against Earnings; (4) Personal Poinding; (5) Adjudication; (6) Inhibition; (7) Poinding of the Ground; (8) Mails and Duties; and (9) Sequestration for Rent.[4]

In granting decree against an individual for payment of certain types of debt, the court may make a 'time to pay direction' to the effect that the sum will be payable by instalments or in a lump sum after a specified interval.[5] After diligence has commenced the court may make a 'time to pay order' to the same effect.[6] While a direction or order is in force it is not competent to serve a charge for payment or to commence or execute an arrestment and furthcoming, a poinding and sale, an earnings arrestment or an adjudication for debt to enforce payment of the debt concerned.[7]

I. CIVIL IMPRISONMENT

53.2 **Imprisonment.**—Imprisonment for debt was recognised in the law of Scotland on the theory that after a charge for payment had been given

---

[1] All diligence is subject to the provisions of the Reserve and Auxiliary Forces (Protection of Civil Interests) Act 1951, ss. 7–9.

[2] Stewart, *Diligence*, p. 1.

[3] Contrast diligence for such matters as citation of witnesses and commission and diligence to examine witnesses and to recover documents: see Maclaren, *Court of Session Practice*, pp. 342, 1029, 1058.

[4] See para. 41.12, *supra*. The diligence known as interdiction was abolished by the Conveyancing (Scotland) Act 1924, s. 44.

[5] Debtors (Scotland) Act 1987 (hereafter referred to as 'the 1987 Act'), ss. 1–4.

[6] *Ibid.*, ss. 5–11.

[7] *Ibid.*, ss. 2(1), 9(1).

in the royal name, and had not been implemented, the defaulter was in rebellion.[8] The power to imprison for debt has, however, been considerably restricted by statute, and is now rarely exercised. By the Debtors (Scotland) Act 1880[9] imprisonment for debt was abolished, except in the case of taxes, fines or penalties due to the Crown, rates and assessments, and sums decerned for aliment. For these debts imprisonment was limited to 12 months. Imprisonment for failure to pay rates or any tax is now abolished.[10] Imprisonment is still competent for failure to pay fines imposed for contempt of court or under section 45 of the Court of Session Act 1988.[11] The Civil Imprisonment (Scotland) Act 1882 abolished the general power to imprison for sums decerned for aliment, but the sheriff is empowered to inflict imprisonment for a period not exceeding six weeks, in the case of wilful failure to pay sums decerned for as aliment (including expenses), or such instalments thereof as the sheriff shall appoint.[12] Failure to pay is deemed to be wilful unless the debtor proves want of means, but a warrant for imprisonment may not be granted where the sheriff is satisfied that the debtor has not possessed or been able to earn the means of paying the sum in question since the commencement of the action in which the decree was pronounced.[13] To render imprisonment competent under this provision there must be a direct claim for aliment; not merely a claim by a local authority for reimbursement of money expended in aliment,[14] or a claim for arrears after the right to aliment has ceased.[15] Imprisonment does not operate as a satisfaction or extinction of the debt or interfere with the creditor's other rights and remedies for its recovery.[16] The abolition of imprisonment for debt leaves untouched the power of the court to imprison for failure to implement a decree *ad factum praestandum*.[17] By the Law Reform (Miscellaneous Provisions) (Scotland) Act 1940,[18] however, no person may be imprisoned on account of his failure to comply with a decree *ad factum praestandum* unless the court is satisfied that he is wilfully refusing to comply with the decree. In the case of wilful refusal the term of imprisonment is limited to six months, but the court is required to order immediate liberation if satisfied that the person undergoing imprisonment has complied or is no

---

[8] See Stair, IV, xlvii.

[9] s. 4.

[10] 1987 Act, s. 74(3).

[11] 1880 Act, s. 4, as amended by 1987 Act, s. 108(1), Sched. 6, para. 8.

[12] 1882 Act, s. 4. The Act does not apply to sums decerned for as a periodical allowance on divorce: *White* v. *White*, 1984 S.L.T. (Sh.Ct.) 30. For the procedure which is followed in an application for imprisonment, see *Hardie* v. *Hardie*, 1984 S.L.T. (Sh.Ct.) 49.

[13] 1882 Act, s. 4(3). As regards means, certain state benefits are not to be taken into account: see Social Security Act 1975, s. 87(3).

[14] *Mackay* v. *P.C. of Resolis* (1899) 1 F. 521.

[15] *Glenday* v. *Johnston* (1905) 8 F. 24; *cf. Tevendale* v. *Duncan* (1882) 10 R. 852.

[16] 1882 Act, s. 4(5).

[17] Debtors (Scotland) Act 1880, s. 4.

[18] s. 1.

longer wilfully refusing to comply with the order.[19] Such imprisonment does not operate to extinguish the obligations imposed by the decree on which the application for imprisonment proceeds.[20]

II. ARRESTMENT

53.3 Nature of Arrestment.[21]—Arrestment is the appropriate diligence for the attachment of a debtor's moveable property which is in the custody of a third party.[22] Formerly, if the creditor was a seller of goods, the property in which had passed to the debtor, he could, by virtue of a special statutory provision, arrest the goods while in his own hands or possession, but the provision has now been repealed.[23] If the property is in the debtor's own custody personal poinding is the appropriate diligence, except in the case of a ship.[24] Arrestment operates not *in rem* but *in personam*, amounting to a prohibition against the arrestee from parting with the property and rendering him liable to a penalty if he does so.[25] In order to transfer the property arrested to the creditor and thus to complete the diligence it is necessary that the arrestment be followed by a process of furthcoming.[26] It is used either in security on the dependence of an action, so that the debtor's property may be secured for the benefit of the creditor before judgment is obtained, or in execution. If the ground of debt is liquid, as in a bond or bill, but the term of payment has not yet come, a warrant for arrestment in security may be obtained by letters of arrestment on averments that the debtor is *vergens ad inopiam* or *in meditatione fugae.*

53.4 Arrestment on the Dependence.—This is the usual form of arrestment in security. To render it competent there must be conclusions for payment of money, other than the conclusion for expenses.[27] It is competent even if the dispute between the parties which forms the subject matter of the action falls to be resolved separately by means of arbitration.[28] Arrestment on the dependence of an action for payment of a future debt, including the payment of a periodical allowance or capital sum on divorce, is also competent, but only in special circumstances such as where there are averments that the defender is *vergens ad inopiam* or *in meditatione fugae.*[29] In an action in the Court

---

[19] 1940 Act, s. 1(1)(ii).
[20] 1940 Act, s. 1(1)(iii).
[21] For arrestment to found jurisdiction, see *supra*, para. 2.19.
[22] Stewart, *Diligence*, p. 105.
[23] Sale of Goods Act 1979, s. 40, repealed by 1987 Act, s. 108(3), Sched. 8.
[24] *Clan Line Steamers* v. *Earl of Douglas S.S. Co.*, 1913 S.C. 967.
[25] Stair, III, i, 25–26.
[26] See *Lord Advocate* v. *Royal Bank of Scotland,* 1977 S.C. 155.
[27] See *Stafford* v. *McLaurin* (1875) 3 R. 148; *Ellison* v. *Ellison* (1901) 4 F. 257; *Fisher* v. *Weir*, 1964 S.L.T. (Notes) 99.
[28] See *Motordrift A/S* v. *Trachem Co. Ltd.*, 1982 S.L.T. 127.
[29] *Gillanders* v. *Gillanders,* 1966 S.C. 54; *Brash* v. *Brash,* 1966 S.C. 56.

of Session application for a warrant for arrestment on the dependence may be inserted in the summons before it is signeted;[30] in the sheriff court it should be craved in the initial writ.[31] The procedure for execution of the arrestment is similar to that for arrestment in execution.[32] A high degree of precision and accuracy is required if the arrestment is to be valid, and if the action is raised in the wrong name the arrestment is liable to be recalled.[33] An arrestment on the dependence used prior to service of an action in the Court of Session or an ordinary action in the sheriff court falls unless the action is served within 20 days of the execution of the arrestment.[34] If arrestments on the dependence are duly laid, and decree in the action is ultimately obtained, the arrester has a preferable right over the subjects arrested, even although the debtor may have been sequestrated before the decree was obtained, provided that the arrestment was used more than 60 days before sequestration[35] and that the action was carried on without undue delay.[36] At common law all personal debts due to the common debtor, *i.e.* the defender in the action for payment, or moveable property belonging to him in the hands of an independent third party may be arrested on the dependence.[37] By statute, however, it is no longer competent to arrest on the dependence of an action any earnings or any pension.[38] For this purpose 'earnings' means any sums payable by way of wages or salary, and 'pension' includes any annuity in respect of past services and any pension or allowance payable in respect of disablement or disability.[39]

53.5 Arrestment in Execution.—Arrestment in execution may proceed (1) on an extract of a decree of any court; (2) on a warrant inserted in an extract from the Books of Council and Session or sheriff court books, in which has been registered either a deed such as a bond, lease or other agreement with pecuniary conclusions containing a clause consenting to registration for execution, or a protest by a notary public of a bill for non-payment;[40] and (3) on a summary warrant for the recovery of rates

[30] Rule of Court 74. A warrant for arrestment on the dependence may also be obtained on a counter claim or a third party notice in the Court of Session: Rules of Court 84(*c*), 85(*b*).
[31] Sheriff Courts (Scotland) Act 1907, Sched. I, rr. 3 and 8.
[32] See para. 53.5, *infra.*
[33] *Richards & Wallington (Earthmoving) Ltd.* v. *Whatlings Ltd.,* 1982 S.L.T. 66.
[34] Debtors (Scotland) Act 1838, s. 17; Sheriff Courts (Scotland) Act 1907, Sched. I, r. 112. For summary causes in the sheriff court the period is 42 days: Summary Cause Rules, r. 47.
[35] Bankruptcy (Scotland) Act 1985, s. 37(4); see Bankruptcy, para. 54.23, *infra.*
[36] *Mitchell* v. *Scott* (1881) 8 R. 875; *Benhar Coal Co.* v. *Turnbull* (1883) 10 R. 558 (liquidation).
[37] See para. 53.8, *infra.*
[38] Law Reform (Misc. Provs.) (Scotland) Act 1966, s. 1.
[39] 1966 Act, s. 1(2).
[40] Writs Execution (Scotland) Act 1877, s. 3; Conveyancing (Scotland) Act 1924, s. 10(5). As to protest of bills, see para. 23.25.

or taxes obtained on application to the sheriff.[41] The former procedures by letters of horning, letters of horning and poinding, letters of poinding and letters of caption have been abolished.[42] A schedule of arrestment is served on the arrestee, who must be subject to the jurisdiction of the court from which the warrant to arrest has been obtained, specifying the debt or other subject arrested and arresting generally all goods, debts, rents, and every other thing in the hands or custody of the arrestee pertaining and belonging to the debtor. A decree from one sheriff court can be enforced in another sheriffdom without a warrant of concurrence.[43] When the arrestee is a body of trustees a schedule should be served on each trustee;[44] in the case of a corporate body, service at its place of business is sufficient.[45] If the arrestee has no liability to account to the common debtor at the date when the arrestment is served on him the arrestment will fall.[46]

Warrants for arrestment emanating from the Court of Session can be executed only by messengers-at-arms,[47] except that in any sheriff court district in which there is no resident messenger-at-arms, or in any of the islands of Scotland, a sheriff officer duly authorised to practise there has all the powers of a messenger-at-arms in regard to the execution of or diligence on any decree, warrant or order.[48] Warrants for arrestment in execution emanating from the sheriff court must be executed by a sheriff officer.[49] The same applies to warrants for arrestment on the dependence granted by a sheriff.[50] It is competent to serve schedules of arrestment proceeding on any warrant or decree of the sheriff in a summary cause by registered post or by recorded delivery.[51] An officer must not act in a case in which he has a personal interest.[52] If the sheriff is satisfied that no messenger-at-arms or sheriff officer is reasonably available to execute an extract decree or warrant, he may grant authority to any person whom he may deem suitable to execute such

[41] 1987 Act, s. 87; Local Government (Scotland) Act 1947, ss. 247(2) and (3); Taxes Management Act 1970, s. 63. Local Government Finance Act 1992, s. 97(5), Sched. 8. Where the warrant is granted under the 1992 Act for payment of council tax the debtor is obliged to give information to the levying authority as to his employer and bank accounts: Council Tax (Administration and Enforcement) (Scotland) Regulations 1992 (S.I. 1992 No. 1332).

[42] 1987 Act, s. 89.

[43] 1987 Act, s. 91.

[44] *Gracie* v. *Gracie*, 1910 S.C. 899. The capacity in which the subject is held by the arrestee need not be specified in the schedule, although it is normal practice to do so: see *Huber* v. *Banks*, 1986 S.L.T. 58.

[45] *Campbell* v. *Watson's Tr.* (1898) 25 R. 690; *Abbey National Building Society* v. *Strang*, 1981 S.L.T. (Sh.Ct.) 4.

[46] See para. 53.9, *infra*.

[47] Rule of Court 67.

[48] Execution of Diligence (Scotland) Act 1926, s. 1.

[49] 1987 Act, ss. 91(1)(*a*), (*b*).

[50] *Ibid.*, s. 91(1)(*d*).

[51] Execution of Diligence (Scotland) Act 1926, s. 2 as amended by Sheriff Courts (Scotland) Act 1971, Sched. 1; Recorded Delivery Service Act 1962, s. 1.

[52] *Dalgleish* v. *Scott* (1822) 1 S. 506; *Lawrence Jack Collections* v. *Hamilton*, 1976 S.L.T. (Sh.Ct.) 18; *British Relay* v. *Keay*, 1976 S.L.T. (Sh.Ct.) 23.

decree or warrant, and the person so authorised shall have all the powers of a messenger-at-arms or sheriff officer as regards any diligence or execution competent on such decree.[53]

53.6 Preference Secured by Arrestment.—Arrestments, whether in security or in execution, are preferred *inter se* according to their date of service,[54] the date of any decree of furthcoming being irrelevant for this purpose. Where two or more arrestments are served on the same date they rank *pari passu*. A Crown arrestment is not now preferred to an ordinary arrestment which has not been followed by a decree of furthcoming by the date when the Crown arrestment is executed.[55] In order to secure a preference to the arresting creditor in competition with a poinding the arrestment must have been followed by a decree of furthcoming prior in date to the completion of the poinding.[56] Arrestments used within 60 days prior to the constitution of the apparent insolvency of the debtor or within four months thereafter are ranked *pari passu* as if they had all been used of the same date.[57] Arrestments executed within 60 days of sequestration or the commencement of a winding up are ineffectual to secure any preference to the arresting creditor in competition with other creditors.[58] Where a receiver is appointed to a company an arrestment which has not been followed by a decree of furthcoming will not be effective so as to exclude the power of the receiver to take possession of the property of the company[59] unless the arrestment was executed prior to the registration of the floating charge.[60] Furthermore the receiver's appointment has effect as if an assignation to the holder of the floating charge of all debts owed to the company which are subject to the charge has been duly intimated to the company's debtors on the date of the appointment, with the result that such debts are no longer capable of arrestment.[61]

The service of a schedule of arrestment confers on the arrester a personal right to the subject arrested preferable, where there is no question of bankruptcy, to an inchoate right granted by the debtor, such as an unintimated assignation[62] or a delivery order for goods in a store not completed by intimation to the storekeeper.[63] The rights of the

---

[53] Execution of Diligence (Scotland) Act 1926, s. 3.

[54] *Hertz* v. *Itzig* (1865) 3 M. 813.

[55] ss. 30 and 42 of the Exchequer Court (Scotland) Act 1856 were repealed by 1987 Act, s. 108(3), Sched. 8.

[56] Stewart, *Diligence*, p. 159.

[57] Bankruptcy (Scotland) Act 1985, Sched. 7, para. 24; see further para. 54.4, *infra*.

[58] Bankruptcy (Scotland) Act 1985, s. 37(4); Insolvency Act 1986, s. 185.

[59] Insolvency Act 1986, s. 55, Sched. 2; *Gordon Anderson (Plant)* v. *Campsie Construction*, 1977 S.L.T. 7; *Lord Advocate* v. *Royal Bank of Scotland*, 1977 S.C. 155.

[60] *Iona Hotels Ltd.*, 1991 S.L.T. 11.

[61] *Forth & Clyde Construction Co. Ltd.* v. *Trinity Timber & Plywood Co. Ltd.*, 1984 S.C. 1.

[62] *Gracie* v. *Gracie*, 1910 S.C. 899.

[63] *Inglis* v. *Robertson & Baxter* (1898) 25 R. (H.L.) 70.

debtor are transferred to the arresting creditor, so that, in the case of the arrestment of an illiquid claim, the arrester may vindicate it by action.[64] An arrestment prescribes in three years from its date, if not pursued or insisted on within that time or, in the case of the arrestment of a future or contingent debt, from the date when the debt became due or the contingency was purified.[65] An arrestment in security prescribes in three years from the date of the decree which constitutes the debt.

53.7 Breach of Arrestment.—Arrestments which have been regularly executed render the subject arrested litigious so far as the arrestee and other parties who have knowledge of the arrestment are concerned.[66] The arrestee is prohibited from parting with the arrested subjects to the prejudice of the arresting creditor, but he is under no duty to invest the arrested funds and is not liable to pay interest to the common debtor in the event of their being released from the arrestment.[67] An arrestee who in the knowledge of an arrestment parts with the funds or subject arrested to the prejudice of the arresting creditor is liable to him for the value of the funds or subject arrested up to the limit of the amount secured by the arrestment, or, if the value of the funds or subject cannot be ascertained, for payment of the amount of the debt owed to the arresting creditor.[68] A party to an action who had received payment of funds from an arrestee in breach of an arrestment on the dependence of the action was ordained to repay the funds to the arrestee, on the ground that it had accepted the funds in the knowledge of the arrestment and to the prejudice of the arresting creditor.[69] An arrestee who acts in breach of an arrestment is also theoretically in contempt of court and liable to a fine or imprisonment.[70]

53.8 Action of Furthcoming.—An arrestment is not a perfected diligence, and does not give the arrester a complete right to the subject arrested unless it is followed by decree in an action of furthcoming. 'An arrestment and furthcoming is an adjudication preceded by an attachment, and the essential part of the diligence is the adjudication.'[71] Where a liquid debt has been arrested an action of furthcoming may proceed as soon as the arrestments are laid; if the debt is future or contingent the furthcoming, if brought, will be sisted until the debt becomes liquid.[72] The purpose of the action is to ascertain precisely the

[64] *Boland* v. *White Cross Insurance Co.*, 1926 S.C. 1066.

[65] 1838 Act, s. 22, as amended by 1987 Act, Sched. 6, para. 3; *Jameson* v. *Sharp* (1887) 14 R. 643.

[66] Stewart, *Diligence*, p. 127; see also *High Flex (Scotland)* v. *Kentallan Mechanical Services Co.*, 1977 S.L.T. (Sh.Ct.) 91.

[67] *Glen Music Co. Ltd.* v. *City of Glasgow D.C.*, 1983 S.L.T. (Sh.Ct.) 26.

[68] Stewart, *Diligence*, p. 222.

[69] *High Flex (Scotland)* v. *Kentallan Mechanical Services Co, supra.*

[70] See *Inglis & Bow* v. *Smith* (1867) 5 M. 320.

[71] *Lucas's Trs.* v. *Campbell* (1894) 21 R. 1096, *per* Lord Kinnear at p. 1103.

[72] *Boland* v. *White Cross Insurance Co., supra.*

nature and extent of the obligation to account which has been arrested and to adjudge to the arrester so much as may be required to make payment to him of the principal debt with interest and expenses.[73] Where the subjects are not a debt but consist of corporeal moveable property or incorporeal moveable property such as rights under an insurance policy or shares, the arresting creditor may conclude for a sale of the property and payment out of the proceeds.[74] If there are competing claims on the same fund an action of multiplepoinding may be necessary.[75] The expenses of arrestment and furthcoming may be recovered out of the subjects arrested.[76] In a question with the arrestee the arrester takes no higher right than the debtor, and any defence available against the debtor may be pleaded against the arrester in an action of furthcoming.[77]

53.9 Subjects Arrestable.—It has been laid down that the subject attachable by arrestment is 'an obligation to account.'[78] It includes debts unless they are heritably secured (when the proper diligence is adjudication); funds held by a bank in name of the debtor;[79] shares in a company;[80] interests in a trust estate;[81] a policy of insurance, although premiums may have to be paid upon it before it becomes due;[82] and corporeal moveable property belonging to the debtor which is in the hands of an independent third party.[83] Assuming an obligation to account, it is no objection that the debt is contingent and that it may turn out that nothing is due by the arrestee to the debtor.[84] It has been held that a claim of damages for wrongful dismissal might be arrested although at the time of the arrestment the debtor had neither raised an action nor asserted a claim.[85] But in principle it would appear that a claim of damages, whether arising from breach of contract or delict, is not arrestable until it has been asserted and thus made the subject of a claim by the injured party.[86] A debt payable in future (*e.g.* instalments of rent or interest not yet due) cannot be arrested, because there is no

---

[73] Bell, *Comm.*, ii, 63.

[74] *Lucas's Trs.* v. *Campbell, supra; cf. Stenhouse London* v. *Allwright,* 1972 S.C. 209.

[75] Stewart, *Diligence*, pp. 140–141.

[76] Summary Cause Rules, r. 64.

[77] *Chambers' Trs.* v. *Smith* (1878) 5 R. (H.L.) 151.

[78] Bell, *Comm.*, ii, 71; *Shankland* v. *McGildowny,* 1912 S.C. 857; *Agnew* v. *Norwest Construction Co.,* 1935 S.C. 771; *McNairn* v. *McNairn,* 1959 S.L.T. (Notes) 35.

[79] Sums in the creditor's deposit account with the National Savings Bank may be arrested: Law Reform (Misc. Provs.) (Scotland) Act 1985, s. 49.

[80] *American Mortgage Co.* v. *Sidway,* 1908 S.C. 500.

[81] *Learmont* v. *Shearer* (1866) 4 M. 540.

[82] *Bankhardt's Trs.* v. *Scottish Amicable* (1871) 9 M. 443.

[83] *Inglis* v. *Robertson & Baxter* (1898) 25 R. (H.L.) 70.

[84] *Boland* v. *White Cross Insurance Co.,* 1926 S.C. 1066; *Park, Dobson & Co.* v. *Taylor,* 1929 S.C. 571.

[85] *Riley* v. *Ellis,* 1910 S.C. 934.

[86] *Caldwell* v. *Hamilton,* 1919 S.C. (H.L.) 100, *per* Lord Dunedin at p. 109; *Shankland* v. *McGildowny, supra, per* Lord Kinnear at p. 867.

present obligation either to pay or to account.[87] Bills of exchange cannot be arrested;[88] any goods or other moveables may be, unless they are in the hands of the debtor himself (or held by somebody, *e.g.* a bank, on his behalf for safekeeping only with no right of lien over them) when poinding is the proper diligence.[89] Private books and papers, of no commercial value, cannot be arrested, either in execution or to found jurisdiction.[90]

Special rules apply where the subject to be arrested is a ship. At common law the right to arrest a ship was available on the principle that any moveable property of an intended defender within the jurisdiction of the Scottish court might be arrested both in order to found jurisdiction and on the dependence of the action. This right has, however, been restricted by section 47 of the Administration of Justice Act 1956,[91] which provides that no warrant for the arrestment of property on the dependence of an action or *in rem* shall have effect as authority for the detention of the ship unless certain particular requirements are satisfied. The right to arrest a ship in order to found jurisdiction is not affected by this provision, but it limits considerably the circumstances in which a ship may be detained while an action is in dependence. This may now only be done where the action is for the enforcement of a claim to which the section applies, which in effect restricts the claim for which the diligence is available to claims of a maritime nature.[92] In addition the ship itself must be the ship with which the action is concerned and all the shares in the ship must be owned by the defender against whom the conclusion in the action is directed. The list of claims for which the diligence is available includes claims arising from any agreement relating to the use or hire of any ship and to the carriage of goods in any ship whether by charterparty or otherwise,[93] but these provisions have been interpreted in a restricted manner and held not to include contracts for the insurance of a vessel and for the insurance of its cargo on the ground that there was not a sufficiently direct connection between the contract and the activities listed in the subsection.[94] It is usual, though probably not necessary, to obtain a special warrant from the court. Should it be apprehended that the captain will sail in disregard of the arrestment, a warrant to dismantle the ship, by removing some necessary part of her equipment, may be obtained.[95] On the other hand, it is not competent for the court

---

[87] *Smith & Kinnear* v. *Burns* (1847) 9 D. 1344; *Kerr* v. *Ferguson,* 1931 S.C. 736.
[88] Bell, *Comm.,* ii, 68.
[89] Stewart, *Diligence,* pp. 107–109. But some goods are exempted: 1987 Act, s. 99(2).
[90] *Trowsdale's Tr.* v. *Forcett Ry.* (1870) 9 M. 88.
[91] 4 & 5 Eliz. 2, c. 46.
[92] See the list of claims set out in s. 47(2).
[93] ss. 47(2)(*d*) and (*e*).
[94] *West of Scotland Ship Owners' Mutual Protection & Indemnity Association (Luxembourg)* v. *Aifanourios Shipping S.A.,* 1981 S.L.T. 233; *Gatoil International Inc.* v. *Arkwright-Boston Manufacturers Mutual Insurance Co.,* 1985 S.C. (H.L.) 1.
[95] *English's etc., Shipping Co.* v. *British Finance Co.* (1886) 14 R. 220; *Borjesson* v. *Carlberg* (1878) 5 R. (H.L.) 215.

to authorise the seizure of a vessel on the open sea in order to bring it into port for the purposes of arrestment, even if it is within the jurisdiction of the Scottish court.[96]

It is a general principle of Scots law that funds held for a debtor are not arrestable to the extent that they are alimentary. A debt may be alimentary either by some rule of law or by express provision. Subject to the conditions that the capital must be vested in trustees,[97] and must be provided by some person other than the liferenter or annuitant himself,[98] a liferent or annuity may be declared to be alimentary. The effect of such a declaration is that the liferent or annuity is protected from the diligence of creditors in so far as it is a reasonable provision in relation to the beneficiary's station in life.[99] But it remains arrestable in virtue of alimentary debts, such as rent, food and clothing suitable to the debtor's condition in life.[1] It is no objection that the debt was incurred before the instalment of the alimentary fund which is arrested became due.[2] Arrears of an alimentary fund are arrestable.[3]

53.10 Recall and Loosing of Arrestments.—In certain cases arrestments may be recalled or loosed by the court. A recall extinguishes the diligence: a loosing entitles the arrestee to pay to the debtor, but in case he does not do so preserves the security obtained by the arrestment.[4] In the case of arrestment in execution recall or loosing requires payment or consignation. In the case of arrestments on the dependence of an action the debtor may have the arrestments recalled or loosed on caution or consignation.[5] He may have them recalled or loosed without caution on the ground that they are nimious or oppressive,[6] or that the subjects are not arrestable,[7] or on the ground of some procedural invalidity such as that the action on the dependence of which the arrestment has been used was raised in the wrong name.[8] A third party, who alleges that the subjects belong to him, has no title to petition for recall.[9] The arrestee cannot obtain the recall of an arrestment where the subject arrested is a debt, even on averment that no debt is due; where it is some corporeal moveable property it is not enough that he alleges that he has claims

[96] *J.W.A. Upham Ltd.* v. *Torode*, 1982 S.L.T. 229; *cf.* Administration of Justice Act 1956, s. 47(6).

[97] *Forbes's Trs.* v. *Tennant*, 1926 S.C. 294.

[98] *Lord Ruthven* v. *Drummond*, 1908 S.C. 1154.

[99] *Cuthbert* v. *Cuthbert's Trs.*, 1908 S.C. 967; see also *Weir* v. *Weir*, 1968 S.C. 241.

[1] *Lord Ruthven* v. *Pulford*, 1909 S.C. 951.

[2] *Ibid.*

[3] *Muirhead* v. *Miller* (1877) 4 R. 1139.

[4] *Graham* v. *Bruce* (1665) Mor. 792.

[5] Stewart, *Diligence*, p. 202; see also Rule of Court 74 (*g*); *Fisher* v. *Weir*, 1964 S.L.T. (Notes) 99.

[6] *Magistrates of Dundee* v. *Taylor* (1863) 1 M. 701; *Radford & Bright* v. *Stevenson* (1904) 6 F. 429; *Levy* v. *Gardiner*, 1964 S.L.T. (Notes) 68; *Svenska Petroleum A.B.* v. *H.O.R. Ltd.*, 1986 S.L.T. 513.

[7] *Lord Ruthven* v. *Drummond*, 1908 S.C. 1154.

[8] *Richards & Wallington (Earthmoving) Ltd.* v. *Whatlings Ltd.*, 1982 S.L.T. 66.

[9] *Brand* v. *Kent* (1892) 20 R. 29.

over it in a question with the debtor, but if he maintains that the property in question is his own he may have the arrestment recalled unless the arrester can show a prima facie case for holding that it really belongs to the debtor.[10]

III. DILIGENCE AGAINST EARNINGS

53.11 **Earnings Arrestments.**—Arrestment and furthcoming cannot be used against the earnings of the debtor in the hands of his employer, the appropriate diligences for this purpose being an 'earnings arrestment,' a 'current maintenance arrestment' or a 'conjoined arrestment order.'[11] 'Earnings' includes salary, wages, fees, bonuses, commission, pension and statutory sick pay but not a disablement pension or a social security or redundancy payment.[12]

An earnings arrestment may proceed on a decree of any court, as summary diligence, or on a summary warrant for recovery of rates or taxes.[13] An earnings arrestment is appropriate to enforce payment of any debt other than current maintenance which is due as at the date of execution of the diligence. It must be preceded by a charge.[14] It is executed by service of an earnings arrestment schedule on the employer, a copy of the schedule being intimated to the debtor if it is reasonably practicable to do so.[15] It requires the employer, while the arrestment is in effect, to deduct a sum from the employee's net earnings on every pay-day, the sum being calculated in accordance with a statutory table.[16] The employer must pay the sum deducted to the creditor as soon as is reasonably practicable and he is entitled to deduct a fee for each payment from the balance of the debtor's earnings.[17] The earnings arrestment remains in effect until the debt is paid or otherwise extinguished, the employment ceases, the arrestment is recalled or abandoned or the debtor is sequestrated.[18] While it is in effect, any other earnings arrestment against the earnings of the debtor payable by the same employer is not competent but one earnings arrestment and one current maintenance arrestment may be in effect simultaneously against the same earnings, the earnings arrestment being given priority.[19] If the employer fails to comply with the earnings arrestment, he is liable to the creditor for the amount he should have deducted and

[10] *Laing* v. *Barclay, Curle & Co.,* 1908 S.C. (H.L.) 1.
[11] 1987 Act, s. 46. Act of Sederunt (Proceedings under the Debtors (Scotland) Act 1987) 1988 (S.I. 1988 No. 2013), Pt. IV.
[12] *Ibid.,* s. 73(2).
[13] 1987 Act, s. 87. Local Government (Scotland) Act 1947, ss. 247(2) and (3); Taxes Management Act 1970, s. 63; Local Government Finance Act 1992, s. 97(5), Sched. 8.
[14] *Ibid.,* s. 90(1).
[15] *Ibid.,* ss. 47(2), 70.
[16] *Ibid.,* ss. 47(1), 49, Sched. 2.
[17] *Ibid.,* s. 71.
[18] *Ibid.,* ss. 47(2), 72.
[19] *Ibid.,* s. 59.

he cannot recover from the debtor the sums paid in contravention of the arrestment. An employer can execute an earnings arrestment in his own hands to recover a debt due to him by the employee.[20]

53.12 Current Maintenance Arrestment.—A current maintenance arrestment is used to enforce payment of aliment or a periodical allowance on divorce.[21] After intimation to the debtor of the court order and the elapse of four weeks, a current maintenance arrestment schedule is served on the employer who must then make deductions from the debtor's net earnings related to the daily rate of maintenance specified in the schedule. Only one current maintenance arrestment can be in effect against the earnings of the debtor from one employer.

53.13 Conjoined Arrestment Order.—A conjoined arrestment order is appropriate where there is more than one creditor entitled to proceed against the earnings of the debtor.[22] The employer must pay the sums deducted to the sheriff clerk who pays to each creditor an amount in proportion to the amount of his debt.

IV. PERSONAL POINDING

53.14 Nature and Warrants for Poinding.—Personal poinding is the diligence by which moveable property in the possession of the debtor or of the creditor is attached and sold for behoof of the creditor, or, if not sold, made over to him to the extent or to account of his debt.[23] Until followed by a sale of the poinded effects poinding, like arrestment, is an inchoate or incomplete diligence. It confers on the creditor no real security in the effects, but prohibits the debtor from parting with them to the prejudice of the creditor. It is competent in execution only; not in security or on the dependence of an action. An extract decree of the Court of Session or sheriff court is itself sufficient warrant to charge and poind,[24] as is an extract from the Books of Council and Session or sheriff court books in which has been registered either a deed containing a clause consenting to registration and execution or a protest by a notary public of a bill for non-payment.[25] A summary warrant for the recovery of rates or taxes by poinding may also be obtained by the authority or the collector of taxes on application to the sheriff.[26]

---

[20] *Scobie* v. *Dumfries & Galloway R.C.*, 1991 S.L.T. (Sh.Ct.) 33; *Slater* v. *Grampian R.C.*, 1991 S.L.T. (Sh.Ct.) 72.

[21] *Ibid.*, ss. 51–56.

[22] *Ibid.*, ss. 60–66, Sched. 3.

[23] Stewart, *Diligence*, p. 274.

[24] 1987 Act, s. 87.

[25] Writs Execution (Scotland) Act 1877, s. 3; Conveyancing (Scotland) Act 1924, s. 10(5).

[26] Local Government (Scotland) Act 1947, s. 247(2); Taxes Management Act 1970, s. 63; both as amended by 1987 Act, s. 74(1), Sched. 4. Local Government Finance Act 1992, s. 97(5), Sched. 8.

53.15 **Charge for Payment.**—A poinding must be preceded by a charge, or formal requisition for payment. The charge, in the prescribed form, is executed by delivery of a schedule of charge by an officer of court.[27] It may be given to the debtor personally, or left at his dwelling-place or place of business if this is in Scotland.[28] If his address is unknown, the sheriff may grant warrant for his citation by publication in a newspaper circulating in the area of his last known address, and if he is resident outwith Scotland it may be served on him either personally or by registered or recorded delivery post at his residence or place of business.[29] After the charge has been given certain days of charge within which payment may be made, known as induciae, must elapse before the poinding is executed. The period for payment specified in any charge in pursuance of a warrant for execution is 14 days if the debtor is within the United Kingdom and 28 days if he is outside the United Kingdom or his whereabouts are unknown.[30] The poinding must be executed within two years after service of the charge.[31] The right to poind can be reconstituted by service of a further charge.[32] A debtor who has already satisfied in full the decree upon which the charge proceeds may obtain suspension of the charge on application to the court.[33]

53.16 **Execution of Poinding.**—On the expiry of the days of charge, if no payment is offered, the poinding may be executed by the officer. The execution must commence between 8 a.m. and 8 p.m. and cannot take place on a Sunday or public holiday.[34] The officer, accompanied by one witness, must first exhibit to any person present the warrant to poind and the certificate of execution of the charge relating thereto; he then demands payment of the sum recoverable from the debtor, if he is present, or from any person appearing to be authorised to act for the debtor, and makes inquiry of any person present as to the ownership of the goods proposed to be poinded.[35] He then poinds articles to the extent necessary to realise the sum recoverable if they are sold at the valuation made by him which is to be according to the price they would be likely to fetch if sold on the open market.[36] The officer then prepares

---

[27] For persons empowered to execute a warrant to charge and poind, see para. 53.5, *supra*; Execution of Diligence (Scotland) Act 1926.

[28] Sheriff Courts (Scotland) Act 1907, Sched. 1, r. 10; Stewart, *Diligence*, p. 290.

[29] *Ibid.*, Sched. 1, rr. 11, 12.

[30] 1987 Act, s. 90(3).

[31] *Ibid.*, s. 90(5).

[32] *Ibid.*, s. 90(6).

[33] Sheriff Courts (Scotland) Act 1907, Sched. 1, r. 108; *Dickson* v. *United Dominions Trust Ltd. (No. 2)*, 1983 S.L.T. 502; the suspension of charges on decrees granted by the Sheriff may be applied for in the sheriff court: 1907 Act, s. 5(5), as amended.

[34] 1987 Act, s. 17; Act of Sederunt (Proceedings in the Sheriff Court under the Debtors (Scotland) Act 1987) 1988 (S.I. 1988 No. 2013), Pt. III. The procedure for poinding on a summary warrant is found in s. 74(2), Sched. 5.

[35] *Ibid.*, ss. 20(2), (3).

[36] *Ibid.*, ss. 19(1), 20(4); *MacIver* v. *Strathclyde R.C.*, 1992 S.L.T. (Sh.Ct.) 7.

a schedule specifying the identity of the debtor and the creditor, the articles poinded and their respective values, the sum recoverable and the place where the poinding was executed.[37] The officer and the witness sign the schedule and deliver it to the debtor. The poinded articles are left at the place where they were poinded. Removal, damage or destruction of the articles by the debtor or anyone who knows they have been poinded is a breach of the poinding and may be dealt with as contempt of court.[38] The debtor may redeem any article at its specified value within 14 days.[39] The officer reports the execution of the poinding to the sheriff. On application by the creditor, the sheriff may grant a warrant of sale providing that the sale shall be by public auction and specifying the location of the sale which shall not be a dwelling-house except with the written consent of the debtor and the occupier;[40] if such consent is not given, articles poinded in a dwelling-house must be sold at an auction room specified in the warrant.[41] Where the aggregate value of the poinded articles exceeds £1,000, the warrant appoints an auctioneer to conduct the sale; in other cases the sale is conducted by the officer.[42] There need not be a reserve price unless the creditor so chooses but, if there is one, it must not exceed the specified value of the article.[43] An article may be purchased by the creditor or by any other creditor or by a person who owns the article in common with the debtor.[44] If the sum recoverable has not been realised by the sale, ownership of unsold articles passes to the creditor if he uplifts them within a specified time; the debtor is credited with the specified value of the article.[45] The officer pays to the creditor the proceeds of sale so far as necessary to meet the sum recoverable and any surplus is paid to the debtor.[46] The officer must make a report of the sale to the sheriff within 14 days.[47] If a third party satisfies the sheriff before the sale that a poinded article belongs to him, an order is made releasing the article from the poinding.[48] An article owned in common by the debtor and a third party may be released from the poinding before the sale if the third party pays the officer a sum equal to the value of the debtor's interest in the article or if the sheriff is satisfied that the continued poinding of the article would be unduly harsh to the third party.[49]

53.17 Preference Secured by Poinding.—As with arrestments, poindings used within 60 days prior to the constitution of the apparent insolvency of the

[37] *Ibid.*, s. 20(5).
[38] *Ibid.*, s. 29.
[39] *Ibid.*, s. 21(4).
[40] *Ibid.*, ss. 30–32. As to intimation and advertisement see s. 34.
[41] *Ibid.*, s. 32(2), but see s. 32(3).
[42] *Ibid.*, s. 31.
[43] *Ibid.*, s. 37(3).
[44] *Ibid.*, s. 37(5).
[45] *Ibid.*, ss. 37(6), (9).
[46] *Ibid.*, s. 38.
[47] *Ibid.*, s. 39.
[48] *Ibid.*, s. 40.
[49] *Ibid.*, s. 41.

debtor and within four months thereafter are ranked *pari passu* as if they had all been used of the same date.[50] Sequestration or the winding up of a company are equivalent to a completed poinding, and poindings executed on or after the sixtieth day prior to the date of the sequestration or winding up are ineffectual to secure any preference to the poinding creditor except for the expenses *bona fide* incurred by him in using the diligence.[51] The preference of poinding in competition with a completed diligence depends upon the date when the poinding has been completed by a sale or the handing over of the goods to the creditor.[52] In competition with other inchoate diligences it is determined by priority in date of execution. A poinding which has not been completed before the appointment of a receiver will not be effective so as to exclude the power of the receiver to take possession of the property of the company[53] unless the poinding was executed prior to the registration of the floating charge.[54] Claims by the Inland Revenue for arrears of any tax, for not more than one year's arrears, are accorded a preference by statute over the goods and effects belonging to the debtor at the time the tax became in arrear or was payable, and are recoverable from the poinding creditor.[55] The similar preference for rates has been abolished.[56]

53.18 Subjects Poindable.—In general, any corporeal moveable property which is of commercial value, and capable of being sold by auction under warrant from the sheriff, may be poinded. Clothing, tools of trade, medical equipment, educational books, toys, and articles required for the care and upbringing of a child are exempt.[57] Also exempt are food and essential furniture such as beds, chairs, tables, curtains, floor coverings and refrigerators if they are at the time of the poinding in a dwelling-house and are reasonably required for the use in the dwelling-house of the person residing there or a member of his household.[58] The list may be added to by regulations.[59] The debtor or any person in possession of a poinded article may within 14 days after the poinding apply to the sheriff for an order releasing the article from the poinding on the ground that it is exempt.[60] Bills of exchange, cheques, certificates and other such documents cannot be attached by private diligence, and the competency of poinding money or notes is doubtful. Growing crops may be poinded.[61]

[50] Bankruptcy (Scotland) Act 1985, Sched. 7, para. 24.
[51] 1985 Act, s. 37(4); Insolvency Act 1986, s. 185.
[52] Stewart, *Diligence*, p. 365; see also para. 53.6, *supra*.
[53] 1986 Act, s. 55(3); *Lord Advocate* v. *Royal Bank of Scotland,* 1977 S.C. 155.
[54] *Iona Hotels Ltd.,* 1991 S.L.T. 11.
[55] Taxes Management Act 1970, s. 64.
[56] 1987 Act, s. 74(4), repealing Local Government (Scotland) Act 1947, s. 248.
[57] *Ibid.,* s. 16(1).
[58] *Ibid.,* s. 16(2).
[59] *Ibid.,* s. 16(3).
[60] *Ibid.,* s. 16(4).
[61] *Elder* v. *Allen* (1833) 11 S. 902.

V. ADJUDICATION

53.19 Nature and Grounds of Adjudication.—Adjudication is the diligence by which heritable property may be attached either in payment or in security of debt. It operates so as to bind the property which is attached by it until the whole debt on which it proceeded has been satisfied. It is based on the Adjudications Act 1672 (c. 19), by which it is substituted for the earlier process of apprising, thereby abolished.[62] In form an action, adjudication in execution may be founded on any decree or liquid document of debt.[63] Adjudication in security may be used where the debt is future or contingent, but it is competent only where the debtor is *vergens ad inopiam* or has had other adjudications led against him.[64] The action must be raised in the Court of Session.[65]

53.20 Subjects Adjudgeable.—Any right to land, whether infeftment has been taken or not, and whether in liferent or fee; leases, where judicial assignees are not excluded; heritable securities, although moveable in succession;[66] the stock of a chartered body where the charter excludes arrestment—not the shares of a company under the Companies Act[67]—are adjudgeable.

53.21 Effect of Adjudication.—The service of a summons of adjudication, if followed by a registration of a notice in a statutory form in the Register of Inhibitions and Adjudications,[68] renders the subject litigious, that is to say, it impliedly prohibits voluntary alienation, and any disponee takes subject to the diligence. Such a notice prescribes, and is of no effect after five years, and litigiosity is not pleadable and cannot be founded on to any effect, after the expiry of six months from and after final decree in the action creating it.[69] Decree in the action is equivalent to a conveyance of the subjects and, when followed by recording of the decree in the appropriate Register of Sasines or by its registration in the Land Register[70] vests them in the creditor, subject to the right of redemption. The adjudger takes the subjects *tantum et tale* as they are vested in the debtor and subject to all the conditions and qualifications which attach to them.[71] In a competition between adjudgers all

---

[62] See *Lord Adv.* v. *Marquess of Zetland,* 1920 S.C. (H.L.) 1.

[63] In the case of a liquid document of debt, the debt must have been constituted by decree, or be a *debitum fundi* or the document must have been registered for execution: 1987 Act, s. 101.

[64] Stewart, *Diligence*, p. 665; Bell, *Comm.*, i, 752.

[65] Bell, *Comm.*, i, 714. The rule is preserved by the Sheriff Courts (Scotland) Act 1907, s. 5(4).

[66] See Titles to Land Consolidation Act 1868, s. 117; *Hare* (1889) 17 R. 105.

[67] *Sinclair* v. *Staples* (1860) 22 D. 600.

[68] Conveyancing (Scotland) Act 1924, s. 44.

[69] *Ibid.*

[70] 1924 Act, s. 44(5); Land Registration (Scotland) Act 1979, s. 29(2).

[71] Stewart, *Diligence*, p. 620.

adjudications prior to that first made effectual, *i.e.* by recording in the General Register of Sasines or the Land Register as the case may be, and all those subsequently led within a year and a day, rank *pari passu*.[72] Those outwith the year and a day rank according to the date of the recording of the decree. Sequestration is equivalent to a decree of adjudication of the debtor's heritable estate which has been duly recorded on the date of sequestration, and any adjudications which have not been made effectual more than a year and a day before that date confer no preference on the adjudger.[73]

53.22 **Right of Redemption.**—A decree of adjudication vests the property adjudged, subject to redemption within a period of 10 years, known as the 'legal.' After that period has expired the creditor may raise an action of declarator of expiry of the legal, decree in which excludes the right of redemption. Should no such proceedings be taken, the subjects remain redeemable although the legal has expired.[74] If, however, the title of the adjudger has been duly recorded in the Register of Sasines or the Land Register and possession has followed theron for 10 years from the date of the expiry of the legal, positive prescription applies, and the debtor's right of redemption is excluded.[75]

VI.   INHIBITION

53.23 **Nature of Inhibition.**—Inhibition has been defined as 'a personal prohibition, prohibiting the party inhibited to contract any debt, or grant any deed by which any part of his lands may be alienated, or carried off, to the prejudice of the creditor inhibiting.'[76] It is competent on any liquid debt, such as a decree, bond or bill, or on the dependence of an action containing conclusions for payment of money alleged to be presently due, other than the conclusion for expenses.[77] If used for a debt payable in future (*e.g.* future instalments of sums decerned for as aliment) an application for inhibition requires averments of special circumstances sufficient to justify it, of which the most commonly recognised are that the debtor is *vergens ad inopiam* or *in meditatione fugae*.[78] The procedure is either by letters of inhibition passing the Signet,[79] or by warrant for inhibition inserted in the summons of an

[72] Diligence Act 1661 (c. 62); Adjudication Act 1672 (c. 45).
[73] Bankruptcy (Scotland) Act 1985, s. 37(1); Insolvency Act 1986, s. 185.
[74] *Govan* v. *Govan* (1759) 2 Paton 27.
[75] *Hinton* v. *Connell's Trs.* (1883) 10 R. 1110; Prescription and Limitation (Scotland) Act 1973; ss. 1(1) and (3).
[76] Erskine, II, xi, 2.
[77] *Burns* v. *Burns* (1879) 7 R. 355.
[78] *Symington* v. *Symington* (1875) 3 R. 205; *Wilson* v. *Wilson*, 1981 S.L.T. 101. In such cases procedure must be by petition, not by warrant inserted in the will of the summons. Inhibition in security is not competent on a summary warrant for recovery of value added tax: *Commissioners of Customs and Excise, Applicants*, 1992 S.L.T. 11.
[79] Titles to Land Consolidation Act 1868, s. 156; for form of letters of inhibition, see Sched. QQ.

action raised in the Court of Session on the dependence of which an inhibition is sought.[80] The letters or summons must be served on the debtor, and a notice of inhibition or the inhibition itself and the execution thereof registered in the Register of Inhibitions and Adjudications. If the inhibition and the execution thereof is registered not later than 21 days from the date of registration of the notice of inhibition the inhibition takes effect from the date of registration of the notice, but otherwise it takes effect only from the date of registration of the inhibition and execution. Without such registration an inhibition has no effect.[81] It prescribes in five years from the date when it takes effect by registration of the notice or of the inhibition and execution as the case may be.[82]

53.24 Effect of Inhibition.—The effect of an inhibition, if duly registered, is to render any voluntary deed affecting the debtor's heritable property, whether he has a completed title to it or not,[83] voidable at the instance of the inhibitor (*ex spreta inhibitione*) in so far as his interests are prejudiced, and no further.[84] Heritable property acquired after the date of the inhibition is not affected, unless it was destined under a prior indefeasible title, as in the case of an entail.[85] The right of a purchaser of heritable property which was still only a right under missives at the date of recording of the inhibition, no disposition of the heritage having yet been delivered to him, is not capable of being affected by the inhibition.[86]

An inhibition strikes at any sale, or heritable security, not at a lease, unless its terms are such as in substance to amount to an alienation.[87] It has no effect on prior debts, and therefore where heritable security had been given for a cash credit bond before the inhibition, advances made after it were not affected.[88] It does not affect rights which are not due to any voluntary act of the debtor, such as the granting of a disposition in implement of the missives completed prior to the inhibition.[89] So also it is no bar to adjudication; and when the debtor in a bond paid the sum due and obtained an assignation to a third party, it was held that as the creditor in a bond is bound to accept payment and grant an assignation the fact that he was subject to a prior inhibition did not invalidate the

---

[80] Rule of Court 74. A warrant for inhibition on the dependence may also be obtained on a counter claim or third party notice in the Court of Session: Rules of Court 84(*c*), 85(*b*).

[81] Titles to Land Consolidation Act 1868, s. 155; Conveyancing (Scotland) Act 1924, s. 44.

[82] 1924 Act, s. 44(3)(*a*).

[83] *Dryburgh* v. *Gordon* (1896) 24 R. 1.

[84] See *Lennox* v. *Robertson* (1790) Hume 243.

[85] Titles to Land Consolidation Act 1868, s. 157.

[86] *Leeds Permanent Building Society* v. *Aitken Malone & Mackay*, 1986 S.L.T. 338.

[87] *Earl of Breadalbane* v. *McLachlan* (1802) Hume 242.

[88] *Campbell's Tr.* v. *De Lisle's Exrs.* (1870) 9 M. 252.

[89] *Livingstone* v. *McFarlane* (1842) 5 D. 1.

transaction.[90] Likewise it is no bar to the exercise of a power of sale conferred on a heritable creditor prior to the inhibition. Such a creditor is entitled to be paid in full from the proceeds of the sale if there are sufficient funds. But an inhibition subsequent in date to the heritable security will secure for the inhibitor a ranking to the free proceeds of sale after the heritable creditor has been paid in full preferential to that of ordinary creditors who have taken no steps to secure their debts and also to that of other creditors who have sought to obtain a preference, *e.g.* by arrestment, but whose preferences postdate that of the inhibitor.[91] Similarly a receiver appointed to a company which has granted a floating charge over its heritable property may take possession of and sell that property even although affected by an inhibition, provided the floating charge was granted prior to the date of registration of the inhibition.[92]

53.25 Inhibition when Debtor Sequestrated.—Inhibition is only a negative or prohibitory diligence; it precludes the party inhibited from contracting any debt, or granting any voluntary deed by which any part of his heritable property may be alienated or otherwise affected to the prejudice of the inhibitor; it has no positive effect in giving the inhibitor any real right in any part of the debtor's estate. Its effect is to preserve the heritable property as part of the debtor's estate, and therefore attachable by the inhibitor by adjudication. If there is no question with other creditors, but only with persons who have acquired rights to the debtor's heritable estate, the inhibitor is entitled to any preference which adjudication would confer without the actual use of that diligence.[93] If the debtor is sequestrated the order of the court awarding sequestration has the effect of an adjudication for the benefit of all creditors, including the inhibitor.[94] The exercise by the permanent trustee of his powers in respect of the heritable estate is not challengeable on the ground of any prior inhibition, but the effect of the inhibition is preserved in the ranking on the estate.[95] The principle of ranking has been decided to be that as a first step all creditors should be ranked *pari passu* on the proceeds of the heritable estate; that the right to participate in that ranking of creditors whose debts were contracted anterior to the inhibition is not affected by inhibition; and that the

[90] *Mackintosh's Trs.* v. *Davidson & Garden* (1898) 25 R. 554.

[91] *Bank of Scotland* v. *Lord Advocate and others,* 1977 S.L.T. 24; *Abbey National Building Society* v. *Shaik Aziz,* 1981 S.L.T. (Sh.Ct.) 29.

[92] Insolvency Act 1986, ss. 55 and 61; *cf. Lord Advocate* v. *Royal Bank of Scotland,* 1977 S.C. 155.

[93] *Lennox* v. *Robertson* (1790) Hume 243.

[94] Bankruptcy (Scotland) Act 1985, s. 37(1); see Insolvency Act 1986, s. 185, as regards the winding up of a company. For the effect of an inhibition in the event of the debtor being adjudged bankrupt in England, see *Morley's Tr.* v. *Aitken,* 1982 S.C. 73.

[95] 1985 Act, s. 31(2). The phrase 'any prior inhibition' in this subsection is thought to refer to any inhibition prior to the date of sequestration, as from which the estate vests in the permanent trustee by virtue of the act and warrant issued to him on confirmation.

inhibitor is entitled, at the expense of the ranking awarded to posterior creditors, to the difference between an equal dividend to all and the dividend which he would have drawn had there been no debts contracted subsequent to the inhibition.[96]

53.26 Recall of Inhibition.—An inhibition duly registered forms an incumbrance to title which a seller of lands under the ordinary obligation of warrandice is bound to remove by procuring a discharge; and, in a question with the purchaser, it is immaterial that the inhibition may be open to objection.[97] When an inhibition is used on the dependence of an action, and the defender is ultimately assoilzied, the court, on motion to that effect, will grant an order on the Keeper of the Register to have the inhibition marked as recalled.[98] When the debt on which the inhibition is used has been paid the creditor is bound, at the debtor's expense, to clear the record by recording a discharge. Should he refuse to do so, the party inhibited may present a petition for recall, and the creditor will be liable for the expenses of the petition and for all expenses necessarily incurred in having the inhibition completely removed.[99] The creditor is not entitled to recover the expense of using the diligence.[1] An inhibition may be recalled, with or without caution, if the court is satisfied that in the circumstances its use is nimious or oppressive.[2] The partial recall of an inhibition is also competent.[3] An inhibition on the dependence of an action will usually be recalled on caution or consignation.[4]

VII. POINDING OF THE GROUND

53.27 Title to Poind the Ground.—Poinding of the ground is a real diligence for attaching moveables. In form it is an action, competent either in the Court of Session or sheriff court.[5] It is open only to a creditor holding a *debitum fundi*, that is one who has his debt secured upon land. Such a creditor is a superior for his feuduty, a heritable creditor unless under an *ex facie* absolute disposition, the creditor in a real burden secured over land[6] or the creditor in a ground annual,[7] but not the creditor

---

[96] Bell, *Comm.*, ii, 408; *Baird & Brown* v. *Stirrat's Tr.* (1872) 10 M. 414; *Scottish Waggon Co.* v. *Hamilton* (1906) 13 S.L.T. 779.

[97] *Dryburgh* v. *Gordon* (1896) 24 R. 1.

[98] *Barbour's Trs.* v. *Davidsons* (1878) 15 S.L.R. 438.

[99] *Robertson* v. *Park, Dobson & Co.* (1896) 24 R. 30; *Milne* v. *Birrell* (1902) 4 F. 879.

[1] *Milne* v. *Birrell, supra.*

[2] *Mackintosh* v. *Miller* (1864) 2 M. 452; *Burns* v. *Burns* (1879) 7 R. 355.

[3] *McInally* v. *Kildonan Homes Ltd.*, 1979 S.L.T. (Notes) 89.

[4] For procedure, see Rules of Court 74 (*g*) and (*h*); *cf. Fisher* v. *Weir*, 1964 S.L.T. (Notes) 99.

[5] Bell, *Prin.*, § 2285. For history of this form of diligence see opinion of Lord Deas, *Royal Bank* v. *Bain* (1877) 4 R. 985.

[6] *Scottish Heritable Security Co.* v. *Allan Campbell & Co.* (1876) 3 R. 333; *Scottish Union & National Insurance Co.* v. *James* (1886) 13 R. 928.

[7] *Bell's Trs.* v. *Copeland* (1896) 23 R. 650.

under an assignation in security of a lease registered under the Registration of Leases Act 1857.[8] No one whose title is that of a proprietor, as in the case of the holder of an *ex facie* absolute disposition qualified by a back bond, can poind his own ground,[9] but a creditor who has obtained a decree of maills and duties, and is therefore to a certain extent in possession, retains the right to poind.[10] The action, which is competent both in the Court of Session and the sheriff court, is for warrant to poind and distrain all moveables belonging to the debtor, or to his tenants or possessors of the lands, which are on the lands over which the *debitum fundi* is constituted. Unlike personal poinding, it does not require a charge for payment before the extract decree is executed.[11] It may be carried into effect by procedure similar to that in personal poinding.[12]

53.28 Subjects Poindable.—The subjects attached by a poinding of the ground are all moveables in fact situated on the ground at the date of service in the action, and belonging to the proprietor of the lands. He need not be the debtor, if he is proprietor of the lands over which the poinder's bond extends.[13] Moveables belonging to tenants may be attached, in so far as their value does not exceed rents due and unpaid.[14] Moveables belonging to a third party cannot be poinded;[15] but where lands belonged to a firm, and the title was in the name of the two partners, it was held that moveables belonging to one of them, as he was in substance a proprietor, might be attached.[16] The right to poind the ground in effect amounts to a floating charge over moveable property, but until it is put in force by action it does not give the creditor a nexus over any particular articles, and consequently it does not give any right over articles which have been removed before the action was raised.[17] If they have been removed unlawfully the creditor may have an action of damages against the party responsible; he cannot maintain that his poinding covers goods not in fact on the ground, or insist on their being restored.[18] Service of the summons or initial writ completes the nexus of the creditor over the moveables on the ground, and he has a preferable right to them, or to their proceeds, if sold in a question with anyone who may have obtained possession of them.[19]

[8] *Luke* v. *Wallace* (1896) 23 R. 634.
[9] *Scottish Heritable Security Co.* v. *Allan Campbell & Co.* (1876) 3 R. 333.
[10] *Henderson* v. *Wallace* (1875) 2 R. 272.
[11] Bell, *Prin.*, § 2285.
[12] Para. 53.16, *supra*.
[13] Erskine, IV, i, 13; *Millar's Trs.* v. *Miller & Son's Tr.* (1886) 13 R. 543.
[14] Diligence Act 1469 (c. 36).
[15] *Thomson* v. *Scoular* (1882) 9 R. 430.
[16] *Kelly's Tr.* v. *Moncreiff's Tr.*, 1920 S.C. 461.
[17] *Traill's Trs.* v. *Free Church*, 1915 S.C. 655.
[18] *Urquhart* v. *Macleod's Tr.* (1883) 10 R. 991.
[19] *Lyons* v. *Anderson* (1880) 8 R. 24.

53.29 **Poinding in Competition with Other Rights.**—Questions as to the preference obtained by a poinding of the ground are to be decided on the principle that the creditor, in poinding, is not acquiring any new right but merely putting in force a right which is immanent in the charge on land which constitutes the *debitum fundi* and in respect of which he poinds. On this principle it is held that the date of the poinding is the date when that charge was completed by infeftment, not the date when the action of poinding of the ground was raised.[20] In a competition between creditors, both using the diligence, a superior poinding for feuduty is preferable to any bondholder, because feuduty is a charge upon land necessarily prior in date to any right granted by the vassal.[21] Between bondholders, the holder of the prior bond is preferred irrespective of the date of their diligence.[22] There is no race of diligence between poinding of the ground and personal poinding; the former dates from the constitution of the real right, the latter from the date of the diligence.[23] The same rule applied at common law to sequestration: if a creditor had a real right completed before the sequestration, his right to poind the ground was not affected by it.[24] But in this particular the law has been altered by legislation. Section 37(6) of the Bankruptcy (Scotland) Act 1985, which restated earlier legislation in a simplified form,[25] provides that no poinding of the ground in respect of the estate of the debtor executed within the period of 60 days before the date of sequestration or on or after that date shall be effectual in a question with the permanent trustee, except for the interest on the debt of a secured creditor, being interest for the current half-yearly term and one year's arrears. The same rule applies in the case of the winding up of a company registered in Scotland.[26]

53.30 **Liability of Poinder for Rates and Taxes.**—As with personal poinding, claims by a rating authority for arrears of rates and by the Inland Revenue for arrears of any tax, in each case for not more than one year's arrears, are accorded a preference by statute over the goods and effects belonging to the debtor at the time the rates or tax became in arrear or were payable, and are recoverable from the poinding creditor.[27] In the case of claims for arrears of rates, the poinding creditor is entitled when accounting to the rating authority to deduct the expenses of and incidental to the taking of the goods and effects and their preservation and sale.[28]

---

[20] *Athole Hydropathic Co.* v. *Scottish Provincial Assurance Co.* (1886) 13 R. 818.
[21] Bankton, II, v, 22; *Royal Bank* v. *Bain* (1877) 4 R. 985, opinion of Lord Deas.
[22] *Bell* v. *Cadell* (1831) 10 S. 100; *Nicol's Tr.* v. *Hill* (1889) 16 R. 416.
[23] *Bell* v. *Cadell, supra.*
[24] *Royal Bank* v. *Bain* (1877) 4 R. 985.
[25] See Bankruptcy (Scotland) Act 1913, s. 114.
[26] Insolvency Act 1986, s. 185.
[27] Local Government (Scotland) Act 1947, s. 248; Taxes Management Act 1970, s. 64.
[28] 1947 Act, s. 248 proviso, added by Valuation and Rating (Scotland) Act 1956, s. 34.

VIII. MAILLS AND DUTIES

53.31 **Maills and Duties: Title.**—An action of maills and duties[29] is the diligence by which the creditor in a heritable security may attach rents due by the tenants of the subjects over which his security extends. The action may be brought by the holder of a real right in lands if he has the right to enter into possession, but not by the creditor in a real burden, who has no such right.[30] The clause of assignation of rents in a bond and disposition in security provides the legal basis for the creditor's right in the event of the debtor's default to enter into possession and uplift the rents.[31] The creditor in a standard security has a statutory right under Standard Condition 10(3) to enter into possession of the security subjects and to recover the rents where the debtor is in default.[32] It is settled that this diligence is not open to a superior,[33] though he may obtain the same result by an action of poinding of the ground followed by an arrangement with the tenants under which they agree to pay their rents to him rather than have their effects sold under the poinding.[34] The creditor in a ground annual may raise an action of maills and duties,[35] but it is not competent for the creditor under an assignation in security of a registered lease to do so since the Registration of Leases (Scotland) Act 1857 provides a special procedure whereby the creditor may enter into possession and uplift the rent.[36] The holder of a disposition *ex facie* absolute qualified by a back bond has a direct right to exact the rents, and an action of maills and duties by him is unnecessary, and probably incompetent.[37]

53.32 **Procedure.**—In its earlier form an action of maills and duties was directed against the tenants, the proprietor being called for his interest. This procedure is still competent, but has been superseded in practice by the forms introduced by the Heritable Securities Act 1894.[38] Under that Act the action is directed against the proprietor of the lands covered by the security, and the tenants need not be called as defenders. Instead, notice of the raising of the action may be given to the tenants by

[29] See, on this subject, Rankine, *Leases* (3rd ed.), p. 360. The expression 'maills and duties' is the old form for 'rents,' 'maills' being the money payment and 'duties' the personal services.
[30] Stair, IV, xxxv, 24.
[31] Titles to Land Consolidation (Scotland) Act 1868, s. 119; Conveyancing (Scotland) Act 1924, s. 25(1)(a); see *McAra* v. *Anderson*, 1913 S.C. 931.
[32] Conveyancing and Feudal Reform (Scotland) Act 1970, ss. 20, 24.
[33] *Prudential Assurance Co.* v. *Cheyne* (1884) 11 R. 871; *Nelson's Trs.* v. *Tod* (1896) 23 R. 1000.
[34] *Aberdeen Corporation* v. *British Linen Bank*, 1911 S.C. 239.
[35] *Somerville* v. *Johnston* (1899) 1 F. 726.
[36] 1857 Act, s. 6; *Dunbar* v. *Gill*, 1908 S.C. 1054.
[37] *Scottish Heritable Securities Co.* v. *Campbell* (1876) 3 R. 333; *Crichton's Trs.* v. *Clarke*, 1909 1 S.L.T. 467.
[38] s. 3.

registered letter in a statutory form (Schedule B), and this has the effect
of interpelling them from making payment of their rents to the
proprietor. When decree is obtained, a similar notice (Schedule C) gives
the creditor the right to the rents. Neither the original nor the statutory
form is available against a proprietor who is in personal occupation of
the subjects,[39] but the Act contains a separate provision under which he
may be ejected if he is in default.[40]

53.33   **Effect of Decree.**—The effect of the decree in an action of maills and
duties is to transform the preference over the rents given to the holder
of the heritable security into an active right to uplift the rents. After
service in such an action, or a notice under the Heritable Securities Act
1894, he, and not the proprietor, is the creditor of the tenant, and the
latter therefore cannot plead compensation on a debt due by the
proprietor, and incurred after the date of the service or notice.[41] He has
the same right of hypothec that the proprietor possessed, and may
sequestrate for rent, whether the tenant be the recipient of the original
notice or an assignee.[42] He is so far in possession of the lands that he
may remove tenants,[43] and grant leases,[44] but he was held not to be a
possessor of the subjects so as to render it incompetent for him to raise
an action of poinding of the ground.[45] If a creditor enters into the actual
possession and management of the subjects he incurs the liabilities of a
proprietor to third parties for injuries resulting from their defective
state, but this would probably not apply if all that he did was to obtain a
decree of maills and duties and to uplift the rent.[46]

53.34   **Effect of Sequestration.**—On the analogy of cases relating to poinding
of the ground, and on the principle that an action of maills and duties
merely puts in force a right already conferred by the heritable security,
the right of the creditor in the security to use this form of diligence is
not affected by the fact that the debtor has been sequestrated.[47]

Further Reading

Graham Stewart, *Diligence* (1898).
Gretton, *The Law of Inhibition and Adjudication.*
Maher and Cusine, *The Law and Practice of Diligence* (1990).

[39] *Smith's Trs.* v. *Chalmers* (1890) 17 R. 1088.
[40] 1894 Act, s. 5.
[41] *Chambers' Factor* v. *Vertue* (1893) 20 R. 257.
[42] *Robertson's Trs.* v. *Gardner* (1889) 16 R. 705.
[43] *Forsyth* v. *Aird* (1853) 16 D. 197.
[44] Heritable Securities Act 1894, ss. 7, 8; see, as regards standard securities,
Conveyancing and Feudal Reform (Scotland) Act 1970, Standard Conditions 10(4) and
(5).
[45] *Henderson* v. *Wallace* (1875) 2 R. 272. See para. 53.27, *supra.*
[46] *Baillie* v. *Shearer's Factor* (1894) 21 R. 498; see opinion of Lord Trayner.
[47] Stewart, *Diligence,* p. 524.

CHAPTER 54

LAW OF BANKRUPTCY

54.1 History of the Law.—In the earlier history of the law of Scotland there was no provision whereby a party who had become insolvent might obtain a discharge from his debts without actual payment, or the favour of his creditors. And, while creditors as a body might be ranked on the heritable estate by the process of ranking and sale, the moveable estate was open to the diligence of the individual. Where a debtor was imprisoned, release was attainable by the process known as *cessio bonorum*, whereby the debtor, on giving up all his property, was released from imprisonment, and could not be afterwards imprisoned in respect of pre-existing debts. He did not, however, obtain a discharge, and any property which he might afterwards acquire could be attached by his creditors by the use of the appropriate diligence. Sequestration, a process under which a bankrupt's estate is transferred to a trustee, was introduced in 1772, by a statute confined to living debtors who were engaged in trade. By subsequent Acts, the most important being the Bankruptcy (Scotland) Acts of 1856 and 1913,[1] the process was extended to all debtors and to the estates of those deceased. The process of *cessio bonorum* was preserved in name until it was abolished by the Act of 1913 and replaced by a process termed summary sequestration.

The law relating to sequestration and personal insolvency was reformed by the Bankruptcy (Scotland) Act 1985,[2] which provides a comprehensive restatement of the law of bankruptcy in Scotland. It repealed the Act of 1913, apart from some parts of it which are preserved by re-enactment.[3] It also repealed two Acts of the Scots Parliament, which had been passed to protect creditors; the Bankruptcy Act 1621, (c. 18) which provided for the reduction of gratuitous alienations in favour of conjunct or confident persons, and the Bankruptcy Act 1696 (c. 5) which provided for the reduction of fraudulent preferences. The common law basis for the challenge of such transactions remains, but new statutory provisions have been introduced.[4] The 1985 Act made a number of important innovations on the

---

[1] 19 & 20 Vict., c. 79; 3 & 4 Geo. 5, c. 20.
[2] As amended by the Bankruptcy (Scotland) Act 1993. See also Bankruptcy (Scotland) Regulations 1985 (S.I. 1985 No. 1925).
[3] See Sched. 7, Pt. II.
[4] ss. 34–36.

existing law. These included the introduction of an interim trustee, who
had to be appointed by the court in every case on sequestration being
awarded or as soon as possible thereafter,[5] the re-designation of the
trustee who is elected by the creditors at the statutory meeting as the
permanent trustee,[6] provision for the automatic discharge of the debtor
without application to the court on the expiry of three years from the
date of sequestration[7] and new provisions with regard to voluntary trust
deeds for creditors including the concept of the protected trust deed.[8]
The Bankruptcy (Scotland) Act 1993 altered the provisions for the
appointment of interim and permanent trustees,[9] introduced a procedure
for the summary administration of the sequestration[10] and altered the
conditions for a sequestration petition by the debtor himself.[11] Where
the debtor has been engaged in transactions in financial markets the
provisions of the 1985 Act are modified and the transactions are taken
out of the general insolvency law.[12] Similar arrangements apply under
drug legislation where a confiscation or restraint order has been made.[13]

The word 'bankruptcy' has no technical meaning. It is not defined in
the Act, which uses the term 'debtor,' not 'bankrupt,' to describe the
person whose estate may be sequestrated.[14] In common usage it may be
employed to describe three different situations, namely insolvency in the
absolute sense, apparent insolvency and sequestration.

54.2   **Insolvency.**—Insolvency may mean that at a particular date the debtor's
assets, if realised, would not meet his liabilities, although he may have
been able to meet all debts which were presented for payment; or it
may mean inability to meet debts of which payment is demanded,
although, when the assets are realised, they may exceed the liabilities.
In questions between creditors as to the validity of deeds granted by a
party alleged to be insolvent, insolvency usually has the first meaning; in
questions between the debtor and his creditors, e.g. as to what was
previously known as 'notour bankruptcy' but is now described in the Act
as 'apparent insolvency,' it always has the second.[15] Insolvency in the
first sense, which is known as absolute insolvency, is proved by a report
as to the debtor's assets and liabilities at the material date; insolvency in
the second sense, which is known as practical insolvency, by his refusal

[5] See para. 54.10, *infra.*
[6] See para. 54.15, *infra.*
[7] ss. 54, 55.
[8] See para. 54.38, *infra.*
[9] ss. 1, 2, 5–9.
[10] s. 6.
[11] ss. 3, 4.
[12] Companies Act 1989, Pt. VII; Financial Markets and Insolvency Regulations 1991
(S.I. 1991 No. 880) as amended by S.I. 1992 No. 716.
[13] Criminal Justice (Scotland) Act 1987, s.45(5)(*b*); Criminal Justice Act 1988, s. 85,
Sched. 15.
[14] s. 73(1).
[15] See Goudy, *Bankruptcy*, p. 17; 1985 Act, s. 7.

or failure to pay a debt admittedly due and presented for payment. As a general rule insolvency does not in either sense affect the capacity or the rights and duties of the debtor or terminate any legal relations which may have arisen from contract with him. In itself it is not a bar to a debtor pursuing or defending an action, although he may in certain cases be required to find caution for expenses. It does not prevent a debtor from entering into contracts or from continuing with his business with the purpose and intention of recovering his commercial position.[16] It may, however, affect the rights and obligations of parties to contracts such as those of sale, partnership and lease which may according to their terms become altered once insolvency has occurred. An unpaid seller may exercise the right of stoppage in transit against a buyer who has become insolvent,[17] and insolvency may give rise to an irritancy under a lease.[18] In addition, insolvency has special effects in relation to gratuitous alienations by the debtor and voluntary transactions between him and his creditors.[19]

54.3 Apparent Insolvency: Notour Bankruptcy.—The phrase 'notour bankruptcy' was originally used to describe the condition of a man who, to avoid imprisonment for debt, had retired to the sanctuary, the Abbey of Holyrood. His insolvency thereby became notorious or notour.[20] Notour bankruptcy had important consequences under the law prior to the 1985 Act. It had a statutory meaning,[21] and was constituted in the case of individuals by sequestration or its equivalents in England and Wales, or by practical insolvency[22] concurring with indications that the debtor was unwilling or unable to pay his debts upon the taking of steps by any of his creditors for recovery of their debts, of which the most important was a charge for payment followed by expiry of the days of charge without payment.[23] In the case of a company, notour bankruptcy could be constituted in any of these ways, or by any of the partners being rendered notour bankrupt for a company debt.[24] A company registered under the Companies Acts could be made notour bankrupt,[25] although such companies could not be wound up except under the special provisions of those Acts. Notour bankruptcy was a pre-requisite to sequestration when applied for by the creditors, although not when applied for by the debtor himself with the concurrence of creditors.[26] It

[16] *Ehrenbacher & Co.* v. *Kennedy* (1874) 1 R. 1131.
[17] Sale of Goods Act 1979, s. 44.
[18] para. 41.25, *supra*.
[19] See paras. 54.18 to 54.21, *infra*.
[20] Bell, *Comm.*, ii, 192.
[21] Bankruptcy Act 1913, s. 5.
[22] Meaning inability to meet current obligations, *Teenan's Tr.* v. *Teenan* (1886) 13 R. 833; or refusal to do so, *Scottish Milk Marketing Board* v. *Wood*, 1936 S.C. 604.
[23] For evidence of execution of charge, see *I.R.* v. *Gibb*, 1963 S.L.T. (Notes) 66.
[24] Bankruptcy Act 1913, ss. 2, 6.
[25] *Clark* v. *Hinde, Milne & Co.* (1884) 12 R. 347.
[26] Bankruptcy (Scotland) Act 1913, s. 11.

had the effect of equalising diligences used within 60 days prior to its constitution or within four months thereafter,[27] and it enabled creditors to reduce preferences struck at by the Bankruptcy Act 1696 (c. 5). It was held to commence from the time when its several requisites concurred, and once constituted it continued in the case of sequestration until the debtor obtained his discharge, and in any other cases until his insolvency had ceased.[28]

The concept of notour bankruptcy was replaced by the 1985 Act with that of apparent insolvency. The importance of this condition lies in the fact that apparent insolvency of the debtor is necessary where a petition for his sequestration is presented by a creditor.[29] And it has the same effect on the equalisation of diligences used within 60 days prior to its constitution or within four months thereafter as notour bankruptcy under the previous law.[30] But, unlike the previous law relating to fraudulent preferences, it does not have any effect on the time limit for the cutting down of unfair preferences under statute, as to which the date of sequestration or the granting of a trust deed which has become protected is now the determining factor.[31] Apparent insolvency is constituted[32] whenever (a) the debtor's estate is sequestrated, or he is adjudged bankrupt in England or Wales or Northern Ireland, or (b) he gives written notice to his creditors that he has ceased to pay his debts in the ordinary course of business, or (c) any of the following circumstances occurs, namely, he grants a trust deed for the benefit of his creditors generally, a charge for payment is served on him followed by the expiry of the days of charge without payment, a poinding or seizure of any of his moveable property occurs for payment of rates or taxes followed by the expiry of 14 days without payment, a decree of adjudication of any part of his heritable estate is granted for payment or in security, his effects are sold under a sequestration for rent due by him or a receiving order is made against him in England or Wales, unless it is shown that at the time when any such circumstance occurred the debtor was able and willing to pay his debts as they became due,[33] or (d) a creditor in respect of a liquid debt of not less than £750 has served on the debtor personally a demand requiring him either to pay the debt or to find security for its payment and within three weeks the debtor has not either complied with the demand or intimated to the creditor by recorded delivery that he denies that there is a debt or that the sum

---

[27] 1913 Act, s. 10.
[28] 1913 Act, s. 7.
[29] Bankruptcy (Scotland) Act 1985, s. 5(2)(*b*).
[30] Sched. 7, para. 24; para. 54.4.
[31] s. 36(1).
[32] See the full definition of 'apparent insolvency' in s. 7.
[33] See *Scottish Milk Marketing Board* v. *Wood*, 1936 S.C. 604. If the debtor does not suspend the charge, he cannot subsequently prevent sequestration by an interdict: *Wilson* v. *Bank of Scotland*, 1987 S.L.T. 117.

claimed is immediately payable. The condition of apparent insolvency continues until, if he has been sequestrated or adjudged bankrupt, he is discharged, and in other cases until he becomes able to pay his debts and pays them as they become due.[34] A partnership and an unincorporated body may be made apparently insolvent,[35] and the condition is also applicable to companies incorporated under the Companies Acts although separate legislation exists for their winding up in the event of their insolvency and for the protection of their creditors.[36]

54.4 Effect of Apparent Insolvency on Diligence.—Apparent insolvency, in addition to providing the basis for a petition for sequestration by a creditor has the effect of equalising diligence. Arrestments and poindings executed within 60 days prior to the constitution of apparent insolvency, and within four months thereafter, rank *pari passu* as if they had all been executed on the same date; and any creditor judicially producing in a process relative to the subject of such arrestment or poinding liquid grounds of debt or decree of payment, is entitled to rank as if he had executed an arrestment or a poinding.[37] Put otherwise, since sequestration is equivalent to an arrestment on behalf of all creditors, if sequestration occurs within four months after apparent insolvency an arrester within the period of 60 days before or four months after apparent insolvency ranks *pari passu* with the other creditors.[38]

54.5 Sequestration and its Administration.—The 1985 Act makes provision for the sequestration of the estates of persons who are subject to the jurisdiction of the Courts of Scotland, and for the administration of bankruptcy generally. The administration of sequestration and personal insolvency is subject to the supervision of the Accountant in Bankruptcy.[39] His duties consist of the supervision of the performance by interim trustees, permanent trustees and commissioners of their functions under the Act and the maintenance and publication of records and statistics relating to insolvencies. Protected trust deeds are sent to him for registration, although trustees acting under such trust deeds are not subject to his supervision. The day to day administration of sequestrations is conducted by officers known as interim trustees and

[34] s. 7(2).
[35] See s. 7(3).
[36] s. 7(4) and Sched. 7, para. 24(5); see, as regards winding up and its effects, paras. 51.44 *et seq., supra.*
[37] Bankruptcy (Scotland) Act 1985, Sched. 7, para. 24; *Clark* v. *Hinde, Milne & Co.* (1884) 12 R. 347. This does not apply to diligence against earnings: Debtors (Scotland) Act 1987, Sched. 6, para. 28(*b*).
[38] *Stewart* v. *Jarvie,* 1938 S.C. 309.
[39] s. 1A (inserted by 1993 Act, s. 1).

permanent trustees, and commissioners may also be appointed. An interim trustee must be appointed by the court in every sequestration.[40] His functions are to safeguard the debtor's estate pending the appointment of a permanent trustee, to ascertain the reasons for the debtor's insolvency and the state of his liabilities and assets and to administer the sequestration process until a permanent trustee has been appointed. He must be resident within the jurisdiction of the Court of Session and qualified to act as an insolvency practitioner. In every sequestration there must be a permanent trustee to be elected by the creditors at the statutory meeting.[41] The functions of the permanent trustee, in whom the whole of the debtor's estate vests as at the date of sequestration,[42] are to recover, manage and realise the debtor's estate and to distribute it among the debtor's creditors according to their entitlements. He must also make his own inquiries as to the reasons for the debtor's insolvency and the state of his liabilities and assets, and is required to have regard to advice offered to him by commissioners, if any, in performing his functions under the Act. The general function of commissioners, if elected, is to supervise the intromissions of the permanent trustee with the sequestrated estate.[43] The creditors may if they wish elect one or more but not more than five commissioners from among the creditors or their mandatories at the statutory meeting or at any subsequent meeting of creditors, but the election of commissioners by them is not compulsory.

54.6 Petitions for Sequestration.—The initial step in the sequestration of the estate of a debtor is the presentation to the court of a petition for sequestration. Both the Court of Session and the sheriff court have jurisdiction in sequestration proceedings.[44] In the case of a living debtor, the petition may be at the instance of the debtor himself with the concurrence of one or more creditors whose debts in all amount to not less than £1,500. If there is no such concurrence, the following conditions must be satisfied—(a) the total amount of his debts (including interest) at the date of the petition is not less than £1,500;[45] (b) an award of sequestration has not been made against the debtor in the preceding five years; (c) the debtor either is apparently insolvent or has granted a trust deed and the trustee has been notified that a majority in number or not less than one-third in value of the creditors object to the

[40] ss. 2 (subst. by 1993 Act, s. 2), 13 (subst. by 1993 Act, Sched. 1, para. 2); see also paras. 54.10 et seq.
[41] ss. 3, 24; see also paras. 54.15 et seq.
[42] s. 31.
[43] ss. 4, 30; see also para. 54.16.
[44] See further para. 54.8.
[45] ss. 5(2)(a), (4) (subst. by 1993 Act, s. 3(2), (2B), (4)). The debts may be liquid or illiquid, provided they are not future or contingent: s. 5(4); *Forbes* v. *Whyte* (1890) 18 R. 182. There must not be a time to pay direction or time to pay order (see para. 53.1, *supra*) in effect in relation to the debt: Debtors (Scotland) Act, 1987, s. 12(1).

trust deed and do not wish to accede to it; for purposes of this condition, neither the granting of a trust deed nor giving of notice to creditors that he has ceased to pay debts constitutes apparent insolvency.[46] The debtor must lodge with the petition a statement of assets and liabilities and send copies of the petition and statement to the Accountant in Bankruptcy.[47] The petition may also be presented by one or more creditors who are qualified as for concurrence, that is to say whose debts in all amount to not less than £1,500, but in this case there is the additional requirement that the debtor must be apparently insolvent.[48] The trustee appointed under a voluntary trust deed granted by or on behalf of the debtor for the benefit of his creditors generally has the right to petition for the debtor's sequestration only if the debtor has failed to comply with his obligations under the trust deed or with the trustee's reasonable instructions or requirements or if the trustee avers that it would be in the best interests of the creditors that an award of sequestration be made.[49] In the case of a deceased debtor those who may petition for the sequestration of his estate are his executor, one or more qualified creditors or the trustee acting under his trust deed.[50] Apparent insolvency is not required in any case where the debtor is deceased, but the existence or absence of apparent insolvency is relevant to the time limits within which a creditor's application may be made.[51] A petition for the sequestration of the estate of a living or deceased debtor may be presented at any time by the debtor himself, if he is alive, by his executor if he is deceased or by the trustee acting under his trust deed.[52] A petition at the instance of creditors may be presented during the debtor's lifetime only if the apparent insolvency founded on in the petition was constituted within four months before the petition is presented.[53] Where the debtor is deceased his creditors may present the petition at any time if the apparent insolvency of the debtor was constituted within four months before his death, but in any other case a petition by them may not be presented earlier than six months after the debtor's death.[54] The presentation of, or the concurring in, a petition for sequestration has the effect of interrupting the prescription of the debt of those creditors who petition or concur.[55] In all cases a petitioning or concurring creditor must produce an oath made by him or on his behalf in the prescribed form and an account or voucher which

---

[46] s. 5(2A), (2B) (inserted by 1993 Act, s. 3).

[47] s. 5(6A) (inserted by 1993 Act, s. 3).

[48] s. 5(2)(b). There cannot be a single petition to sequestrate spouses who are not in partnership: Campbell v. Dunbar, 1989 S.L.T. (Sh.Ct.) 29.

[49] ss. 5(2)(c), (2C) (subst. by 1993 Act, s. 3(2)).

[50] s. 5(3).

[51] s. 8(3).

[52] ss. 8(1)(a), (3)(a).

[53] s. 8(1)(b); see Burgh of Millport, Petrs., 1974 S.L.T. (Notes) 23.

[54] s. 8(3)(b).

[55] s. 8(5); see also Prescription and Limitation (Scotland) Act 1973, s. 9(1)(b).

constitutes prima facie evidence of the debt,[56] and a petitioning creditor must in addition produce such evidence as is available to him to show the apparent insolvency of the debtor.[57]

54.7   Estates Which May be Sequestrated.—In addition to the estates of living or deceased individuals, the estates belonging to or held for or jointly by the members of various other entities may be sequestrated under the 1985 Act. These are a trust in respect of debts incurred by it, a partnership including a dissolved partnership, a body corporate or unincorporated body but not a company incorporated under the Companies Acts, and a limited partnership including a dissolved partnership within the meaning of the Limited Partnerships Act 1907.[58] Prior to the 1985 Act an unincorporated body such as a club could not be sequestrated[59] and there was doubt as to whether the process was available in the case of a body established by Private Act of Parliament.[60] It is not competent, however, to sequestrate an entity in respect of which an enactment provides either expressly or by implication that sequestration is incompetent, for example friendly societies and overseas companies.[61] Apparent insolvency must be constituted in each case if the petition is presented by creditors. A majority of the trustees, the partnership or a person authorised to act on behalf of the body corporate or unincorporated body may petition, with the concurrence of a qualified creditor or creditors.

54.8   Jurisdiction.—The primary rule is that the Court of Session has jurisdiction in respect of the sequestration of the estate of a living debtor or of a deceased debtor if the debtor had an established place of business in Scotland or was habitually resident there at the relevant time.[62] These requirements mean that occasional, temporary or transitory presence of the individual in Scotland will not be sufficient to found jurisdiction, and that something more substantial and permanent is necessary. In the case of other entities, the requirements are that they had an established place of business in Scotland at the relevant time, or that the entity was constituted or formed under Scots law and at any time carried on business in Scotland however temporary or transitory that may have been.[63] The relevant time for these purposes is any time

---

[56] ss. 11(1), (5); *Ballantyne* v. *Barr* (1867) 5 M. 330; *Blair* v. *North British and Mercantile Insurance Co.* (1889) 16 R. 325.

[57] s. 11(5); *Drummond* v. *Clunas Tiles Co.*, 1909 S.C. 1049.

[58] s. 6(1). There cannot be one award of sequestration in respect of the estates of a partnership and the individual partners: *Royal Bank of Scotland plc* v. *J. & J. Messenger*, 1991 S.L.T. 492.

[59] *Pitreavie Golf Club* v. *Penman*, 1934 S.L.T. 247.

[60] *Haldane* v. *Girvan and Portpatrick Rly. Co.* (1881) 8 R. 1003.

[61] s. 6(2).

[62] s. 9(1).

[63] s. 9(2); see the definition of 'business' in s. 73(1).

within the year immediately preceding the date of presentation of the petition or the date of death, as the case may be.[64] The same rules apply in the case of applications to the sheriff, with the substitution of the words 'the Sheriffdom' for 'Scotland,'[65] and the sheriff court and the Court of Session thus have concurrent jurisdiction. For the most part, however, sequestration is a sheriff court process, because although the Court of Session may award sequestration and deal with various applications and appeals, and only the Court of Session may recall a sequestration, confirmation of the election of the permanent trustee is always a matter for the sheriff court. Normally any incidental applications will be dealt with there, because where the Court of Session has awarded sequestration it is required to remit the sequestration to such sheriff as it considers appropriate,[66] and it has power at any time after sequestration has been awarded, on application being made to it, to transfer the sequestration from one sheriffdom to another.[67] Provision is made for the possibility that other proceedings are before a court for sequestration or an analogous remedy affecting the same debtor or his estate. It is the duty of the petitioner, the debtor or any creditor concurring in the petition to bring the existence of such proceedings of which he is aware to the notice of the court,[68] which has power to take appropriate steps to deal with the situation. An order made by a court in any part of the United Kingdom in the exercise of jurisdiction in relation to insolvency law is enforceable in any other part of the United Kingdom as if it were made by a court exercising the corresponding jurisdiction there, and courts having jurisdiction in relation to insolvency law in any part of the United Kingdom are required to assist the courts having jurisdiction in any other part of the United Kingdom, the Channel Islands or the Isle of Man.[69]

54.9 Award of Sequestration.—Where the petition is presented by the debtor the court must award sequestration forthwith if it is satisfied that the petition has been presented in accordance with the provisions of the Act, and that the conditions imposed upon the debtor's right to petition[70] are fulfilled, unless cause is shown why sequestration cannot competently be awarded.[71] Where the petition is by a creditor or by a trustee acting under a trust deed, the first order is an order to cite the debtor to appear before the court to show cause why sequestration

[64] s. 9(5).
[65] s. 9(4).
[66] s. 15(1).
[67] s. 15(2).
[68] s. 10.
[69] Insolvency Act 1986, s. 426.
[70] See para. 54.6, n. 46.
[71] s. 12(1) (subst. by 1993 Act, s. 4(2)). See *Royal Bank of Scotland* v. *Aitken*, 1985 S.L.T. (Sh.Ct.) 13, where a motion for continuation for eight weeks was held to be incompetent.

should not be awarded.[72] The first order should require appearance by the debtor on a specified date not less than six or more than 14 days after the date of citation.[73] On the expiry of the induciae, if the court is satisfied that there has been proper citation of the debtor, that the petition complies with the provisions of the Act, that the requirements as to apparent insolvency are satisfied (or, in the case of a petition by a trustee under a trust deed, that his averments as to the debtor's conduct or the interests of creditors are true) sequestration must be awarded forthwith unless cause is shown why it cannot competently be awarded or the debtor forthwith pays or satisfies,[74] or produces written evidence of payment or satisfaction of, or gives or shows that there is sufficient security for the payment of the debt in respect of which he became apparently insolvent and any other debt due to the petitioner and any concurring creditor.[75] In all cases where the date of sequestration is material, this is to be taken to be the date on which sequestration is awarded, if the petition is presented by the debtor, and the date of the order for warrant to cite the debtor, if the petition is presented by a creditor or a trustee acting under a trust deed, or the date of the first such warrant if there is more than one.[76] Where sequestration has been awarded by the Court of Session it must remit the sequestration to such sheriff as it considers appropriate for further procedure.[77]

54.10   Appointment of Interim Trustee.—An interim trustee may be appointed before sequestration is awarded, where the petition is by a creditor or a trustee acting under a trust deed, if the debtor consents or the trustee or any creditor shows cause for the making of a provisional appointment at this stage; if the petition nominates to be interim trustee an eligible person who has given a written undertaking to act as interim trustee, and, where no permanent trustee is elected, as permanent trustee, the court may appoint that person;[78] otherwise the Accountant in Bankruptcy is apponted.[79] If no such appointment is made, a person nominated in the petition who satisfies the conditions stated above may be appointed interim trustee when sequestration is awarded;[80] if the court does not make such an appointment, the Accountant in

---

[72] s. 12(2).
[73] See *Hill* v. *Hill*, 1984 S.L.T. (Sh.Ct.) 21; *Hodgson* v. *Hodgson's Tr.*, 1984 S.L.T. 97.
[74] s. 12(3) (subst. by 1993 Act, s. 4(4)). See *Royal Bank of Scotland* v. *Forbes, supra.*
[75] s. 12(3A) (inserted by 1993 Act, s. 4(4)). The insertion of the words 'or shows' into the wording of what was s. 12(3)(*b*) of the 1985 Act is to indicate that a pre-existing security suffices—a point on which there were conflicting views—*Royal Bank of Scotland plc* v. *Forbes*, 1988 S.L.T. 73; *National Westminster Bank plc* v. *W.J. Elrick & Co.*, 1991 S.L.T. 709; *cf. Bank of Scotland* v. *Mackay*, 1991 S.L.T. 163; *Dryburgh & Co. Ltd., Petrs.*, 1989 S.C.L.R. 279.
[76] s. 12(4) (subst. by 1993 Act, s. 4(5)).
[77] s. 15(1).
[78] s. 2(5) (s. 2 subst. by 1993 Act, s. 2).
[79] s. 2(6).
[80] s. 2(1).

Bankruptcy is appointed.[81] The interim trustee can resign office if authorised to do so by the court.[82] The court has power on the application of the Accountant in Bankruptcy to remove from office an interim trustee who has failed to perform a duty imposed on him without reasonable excuse,[83] and it may replace an interim trustee by appointing another interim trustee to act in his place in various other circumstances including the inability of the interim trustee to act from any cause whatsoever.[84] The interim trustee is required to notify the debtor as soon as practicable after the date of his appointment.[85]

54.11 Registration of Court Order and its Effect.—The clerk of the court which awards sequestration is required to send forthwith after the date of sequestration[86] a certified copy of the relevant court order to the keeper of the Register of Inhibitions and Adjudications for recording in that register, and also to send a copy of the order to the Accountant in Bankruptcy.[87] The publication of a notice in the *Edinburgh Gazette* stating that sequestration has been awarded is the responsibility of the interim trustee, but this step does not require to be taken until an award of sequestration has actually been granted.[88] The recording of the certified copy of the court order in the register has the effect, as from the date of sequestration,[89] of an inhibition and of a citation in an adjudication of the debtor's heritable estate at the instance of the creditors who subsequently have claims in the sequestration which are accepted by the permanent trustee.[90]

54.12 Recall of Sequestration.—An award of sequestration is not subject to review, but a petition for recall may be presented to the Court of Session by the debtor, any creditor or any other person having an interest nowithstanding that any of these persons was a petitioner or concurred in the petition for sequestration, or by the interim or permanent trustee or the Accountant in Bankruptcy.[91] The court is given a wide discretion as to the grounds upon which an award of sequestration may be recalled and as to what further orders should be made in the circumstances,[92] but three particular grounds which are provided by the Act[93] are (a) that the debtor has paid his debts in full

[81] s. 2(2).
[82] s. 13(3) (s. 13 subst. by 1993 Act, Sched. 1, para. 2).
[83] s. 1A(2).
[84] s. 13(2).
[85] s. 2(7).
[66] For the meaning of this expression, see s. 12(4); para. 54.9, *supra*.
[87] s. 14(1).
[88] s. 15(6) (subst. by 1993 Act, Sched. 1, para. 4).
[89] See note 86, *supra*.
[90] s. 14(2).
[91] s. 16(1).
[92] ss. 17(1), (3).
[93] ss. 17(1)(*a*)-(*c*).

or given sufficient security for their payment,[94] (b) that a majority in value of the creditors reside in a country other than Scotland and that it is more appropriate for the debtor's estate to be administered in that other country, and (c) that one or more other awards of sequestration of the estate or analogous remedies have already been granted. A defect in the procedure leading up to sequestration may also provide a proper basis for recall,[95] but the court has a discretion in the matter and may decline to recall the sequestration especially if the defect is trivial and a recall would prejudice creditors.[96] Time limits are set for the making of an application for recall. The general rule is that the petition must be presented within 10 weeks after the date of the award of sequestration,[97] but it may be presented at any time if it is presented on any of the particular grounds provided by the Act which are mentioned above.[98] Special rules apply where the application is made by the non-entitled spouse who has occupancy of a matrimonial home.[99] Publication of an application for recall must be made by notice in the *Edinburgh Gazette*, and any person having an interest as well as those on whom the petition is served may lodge answers to the petition.[1] The Court of Session also has power to reduce an award of sequestration at common law or to deal with or cure defects in procedure under the *nobile officium*,[2] but these are exceptional remedies which are unlikely to be granted if a petition for recall is still competent.

54.13 Interim Preservation of Estate: Duties of Interim Trustee.—The first duty of the interim trustee, as soon as an award of sequestration has been made, is to publish a notice in the *Edinbugh Gazette* in the prescribed form stating that sequestration has been awarded and inviting the submission of claims to him.[3] He make take steps for the interim preservation of the estate; one of his functions being to safeguard the debtor's estate pending the appointment of a permanent trustee.[4] In this regard he may give general or particular directions to the debtor relating to the management of the estate, and although he is not vested in the

---

[94] The debtor's ability to pay the debts will not be sufficient if he refuses to pay them: *Scottish Milk Marketing Board* v. *Wood*, 1936 S.C. 604.

[95] *Ballantyne* v. *Barr* (1867) 5 M. 330; *Hodgson* v. *Hodgson's Trs.*, 1984 S.L.T. 97.

[96] *Nakeski-Cumming* v. *Gordon*, 1924 S.C. 217.

[97] The amendment of s. 16(4) by the 1993 Act, Sched. 1, para. 5, deals with the situation disclosed in *Wright* v. *Tennent Caledonian Breweries Ltd.*, 1991 S.L.T. 823, so that the 10 weeks runs from the award of sequestration and not the 'date of the sequestration.' A reasonable explanation for failure to lodge a petition for recall of an award must be advanced where the petition is lodged outwith the 10 week period: *Brown* v. *Middlemass of Kelso Ltd.*, 1994 S.L.T. 1352.

[98] s. 16(4); the grounds are those set out in ss. 17(a)-(c).

[99] s. 41(b).

[1] s. 16(3).

[2] e.g. *Central Motor Engineering Co.* v. *Gibbs*, 1917 S.C. 490, 1918 S.C. 755.

[3] s. 15(6) (subst. by 1993 Act, Sched. 1, para. 4).

[4] See s. 2(1)(a); para. 54.5, *supra*.

estate[5] he has power to require the debtor to deliver up to him any money or valuables or documents relating to his business or financial affairs and to place them in safe custody, to require him to deliver up to him any perishable goods and arrange for their sale or disposal, to make up an inventory of any property belonging to the debtor, to require the debtor to implement any transaction entered into by him, to effect insurance policies in respect of the debtor's business or property, to close down the debtor's business and to carry on the debtor's business or borrow money in so far as is necessary to safeguard the estate.[6] Certain additional powers may be given to the interim trustee by the court either on his own application or at the request of the petitioner for sequestration.[7] These include power to enter the debtor's house and business premises and to search for and take possession of any money, valuables, documents and perishable goods which the trustee is entitled to require the debtor to deliver up to him. A debtor who fails without reasonable excuse to comply with the interim trustee's directions or requirements or obstructs the interim trustee in the exercise of a power of search commits an offence.[8]

One of the other functions of the interim trustee is to ascertain the state of the debtor's liabilities and assets.[9] If the debtor is the petitioner for sequestration he must, within seven days of the interim trustee's appointment, send to the trustee the statement of assets and liabilities which was lodged with the petition; in other cases, the debtor must, within seven days of the interim trustee notifying him of his appointment, send to the interim trustee a statement of assets and liabilities containing a list of assets and liabilities, a list of income and expenditure and other prescribed information.[10] In addition, the interim trustee may conduct a private examination by requiring the debtor, or his spouse or any other person whom he believes can give such information, to appear before him and give information relating to the debtor's assets, his dealings with them or his conduct in relation to his business or financial affairs.[11] The interim trustee must prepare a statement of the debtor's affairs so far as within his knowledge and indicate therein whether, in his opinion, the debtor's assets are unlikely to be sufficient to pay any dividend in respect of preferred and ordinary debts.[12] Not later than four days before the date of the statutory meeting, he must send to the Accountant in Bankruptcy the statement

---

[5] Unlike the permanent trustee: see para. 54.17.
[6] s.18(2) (as amended by 1993 Act, Sched. 1, para. 6). Note that he may obtain supplies of gas, electricity and water and telecommunication services on condition that he personally guarantees payment of any charges in respect of the supply; s. 70.
[7] s. 18(3). See as to power to sell heritage, *Scottish & Newcastle plc*, (O.H.) 1992 S.C.L.R. 540.
[8] ss. 18(5), (6).
[9] s. 2(4)(c).
[10] ss. 19, 73 (as amended by 1993 Act, Sched. 1, para. 29(5)).
[11] s. 20(4).
[12] s. 20(3).

of assets and liabilities, a copy of the statement of affairs and his written comments indicating what in his opinion are the causes of the insolvency and to what extent the conduct of the debtor may have contributed to the insolvency.[13] His functions continue until the confirmation in office of the permanent trustee, whereupon he must cease to act in the sequestration unless he himself has become the permanent trustee and must submit an account of his intromissions and a claim for outlays and remuneration to the Accountant in Bankruptcy.[14]

54.14   Statutory Meeting of Creditors.—Where the interim trustee is not the Accountant in Bankruptcy he must call a 'statutory meeting'[15] of creditors to be held within 28 days, or such longer period as the sheriff on cause shown may allow, at such time and place as the interim trustee determines.[16] He acts as chairman of the meeting.[17] He is required to give not less than seven days' notice of the date, time and place of the meeting to every creditor known to him and to the Accountant in Bankruptcy, and to invite the submission of such claims as have not already been submitted to him and inform them of his duties as regards providing them with information as to the debtor's affairs; the creditors have power to continue the statutory meeting to a date not later than seven days after the end of the period within which it requires to be held.[18] For the purposes of voting at the statutory meeting each creditor must submit a claim to the interim trustee either at or before the meeting.[19] This is done by producing to the interim trustee a statement of claim in the prescribed form and an account or voucher, according to the nature of the debt, which constitutes prima facie evidence of it.[20] The interim trustee may allow a creditor who neither resides nor has a place of business in the United Kingdom to submit an informal claim in writing.[21] At the commencement of the meeting the interim trustee is required to accept or reject in whole or part the claim of each creditor in order to determine the creditor's entitlement to vote, and to arrange for a record to be made of the proceedings.[22] He is also required to invite the creditors thereupon to elect one of their number as chairman in his place and to preside over the election, but if a chairman is not elected he must remain the chairman throughout the meeting.[23]

---

[13] s. 20(2).
[14] s. 26; see also s. 27 as regards discharge of the interim trustee.
[15] s. 20A.
[16] ss. 21(1), (1A).
[17] s. 23(1).
[18] ss. 21(2), (3).
[19] s. 22(1).
[20] s. 22(2); he may submit a different statement of claim specifying a different amount from his claim at any time before the statutory meeting: see s. 22(4).
[21] s. 22(3).
[22] ss. 23(1)(a) and (c), (2). For further provisions as to the procedure to be followed at the meeting, see Sched. 6, Pt. II.
[23] s. 23(1)(b).

Thereafter his duties at the meeting are to make the debtor's statement of assets and liabilities and his own statement of the debtor's affairs (which he may revise at, or as soon as possible after, the meeting) available for inspection by the creditors and to answer to the best of his ability any question and consider any representations put to him by them relating to the debtor's assets, business or financial affairs or his conduct in relation thereto and to indicate whether in his opinion the debtor's assets are unlikely to be sufficient to pay any dividend.[24] The meeting then proceeds to the election of the permanent trustee,[25] and it may also elect commissioners.[26] The debtor has no right to attend or address the meeting.

Where the interim trustee is the Accountant in Bankruptcy he must, within 60 days of the date of sequestration, or such longer period as the sheriff may allow, give notice to the creditors of whether he intends to call a statutory meeting; he must call a meeting at the request of not less than one-quarter in value of the creditors.[27]

54.15 Election and Replacement of Permanent Trustee.—The permanent trustee is elected by the creditors at the statutory meeting at the conclusion of the proceedings for the provision of information by the interim trustee.[28] The result of the election is determined by a majority in value of such creditors or their mandatories as vote on the question; creditors who acquired a debt due by the debtor after the date of sequestration other than by succession are not entitled to vote in the election, and no creditor is entitled to vote to the extent that his debt is a postponed debt.[29] A person must be qualified to act as an insolvency practitioner in order to be eligible for election as permanent trustee; the debtor himself is not eligible, nor is a person who holds an interest opposed to the general interests of the creditors or a person who resides outwith the jurisdiction of the Court of Session or a person who has not given an undertaking, in writing, to act as permanent trustee.[30] The election of the permanent trustee by the creditors requires to be confirmed by the sheriff.[31] An opportunity is given to the debtor, the creditors, the interim and permanent trustee and the Accountant in Bankruptcy to object to any matter connected with the election within four days after the statutory meeting and to be heard thereon. If there is no timeous objection the sheriff must forthwith declare the elected

[24] s. 23(3).
[25] s. 24; para. 54.15.
[26] s. 30.
[27] s. 21A.
[28] s. 24(1).
[29] s. 24(3); Sched. 6, paras. 11 and 13.
[30] s. 24(2) (as amended by 1993 Act, Sched. 1, para. 12). It is incompetent to elect two persons jointly: *I.R.C.* v. *MacDonald*, 1988 S.L.T. (Sh.Ct.) 7.
[31] s. 25.

person to be the permanent trustee. If there is a timeous objection which the sheriff sustains, a new meeting for the election of a permanent trustee must be held.[32] The permanent trustee, if he is not the same person as the interim trustee, must publish a notice in the *Edinburgh Gazette* that he has been confirmed in office as the permanent trustee.[33]

If no creditor entitled to vote attends the statutory meeting, or if no permanent trustee is elected, the interim trustee must forthwith notify the Accountant in Bankruptcy and report the proceedings to the sheriff who is required thereupon to appoint the interim trustee as the permanent trustee.[34] The sequestration then continues under the modified procedure set forth in Schedule 2[35] to the Act[36] but the interim trustee when making his report can apply for the summary administration of the sequestration.[37] The application is granted if it appears that the debtor's aggregate liabilities do not exceed £20,000 and his aggregate assets do not exceed £2,000.[38] Where a certificate for summary administration is granted, the permanent trustee's duties are modified in terms of Schedule 2A.[39]

Where the Accountant in Bankruptcy is the interim trustee and does not call a statutory meeting or no creditor entitled to vote attends the meeting or no permanent trustee is elected there is a report to the sheriff,[40] the Accountant in Bankruptcy or his nominee is appointed as permanent trustee, Schedule 2 applies to the sequestration[41] and there may be an application for summary administration.[42]

The confirmation in office of the permanent trustee marks the end of the functions of the interim trustee, who, where he has not himself become the permanent trustee, must hand over to the permanent trustee everything in his possession which relates to the sequestration and cease to act as trustee.[43] Provision is made for the death, resignation and removal from office of the permanent trustee.[44]

54.16 Election and Removal of Commissioners.—The creditors may elect up to a maximum of five commissioners to act in the sequestration; but the election of commissioners is not compulsory.[45] The election may be

[32] s. 25(4).
[33] s. 25(6).
[34] s. 24(4).
[35] As amended by 1993 Act, Sched. 1, para. 30.
[36] s. 24(5).
[37] s. 24(4A).
[38] s. 23A (inserted by 1993 Act, s. 6).
[39] s. 23A(4).
[40] s. 21B (inserted by 1993 Act, s. 5).
[41] s. 25A.
[42] s. 21B(2).
[43] s. 26.
[44] s. 13 (subst. by 1993 Act, Sched. 1, para. 2).
[45] s. 30.

made either at the statutory meeting or at any subsequent meeting of creditors, but creditors who acquired a debt due by the debtor after the date of sequestration other than by succession are not entitled to vote in this matter and no creditor is entitled to vote to the extent that his debt is a postponed debt. The debtor himself is not eligible for election as a commissioner nor is a person who holds an interest opposed to the general interests of the creditors or a person who is an associate of the debtor or the permanent trustee.[46] A commissioner may resign office at any time, and may be removed from office by the creditors at a meeting called for the purpose; if he is a mandatory of a creditor he may be removed from office by the creditor recalling the mandate and intimating its recall to the permanent trustee.[47] The general functions of the commissioners are to supervise the intromissions of the permanent trustee with the sequestrated estate and to advise him.[48]

54.17   Vesting of Estate in Permanent Trustee.—The whole estate of the debtor vests as at the date of sequestration in the permanent trustee for the benefit of the creditors.[49] Property which is exempted from poinding for the purpose of protecting the debtor and his family[50] and property held on trust by the debtor for any person[51] do not vest in the trustee. The deduction to be made from injury compensation awards in respect of social security benefits does not form part of the estate;[52] nor will a statutory criminal injuries compensation award.[53] The interest of the debtor under an assured, protected or secure tenancy does not pass to the trustee until he serves notice on the debtor to that effect.[54] The whole estate of the debtor for this purpose means his whole estate at the date of sequestration, wherever situated,[55] including any income or estate vesting in the debtor on that date and the capacity to exercise all such powers in, over or in respect of any property as might have been exercised by the debtor for his own benefit as at or on the date of sequestration, such as the exercise of a right to vote in respect of shares held by him, the claiming of legal rights or completing title to

[46] s. 30(2).
[47] ss. 30(3), (4).
[48] s. 4.
[49] s. 31(1). For the meaning of the expression 'date of sequestration' see s. 12(4) and para. 54.9, *supra*.
[50] s. 33(1)(*a*). The exclusion extends to wearing apparel, working tools of the trade and certain items of household furniture; see Diligence, para. 53.18, *supra*.
[51] s. 33(1)(*b*). Property held on trust by the debtor was previously excluded from vesting in the trustee by the common law: *Heritable Reversionary Co. Ltd.* v. *Millar* (1892) 19 R. (H.L.) 43; *Bank of Scotland* v. *Liqrs. of Hutchison, Main & Co. Ltd.*, 1914 S.C. H.L.) 1. Funds in a solicitor's client account do not vest in the solicitor's trustee in sequestration: *Council of the Law Society of Scotland* v. *McKinnie*, 1993 S.L.T. 238.
[52] Social Security Administration Act 1992, s. 89(2).
[53] Criminal Justice Act 1988, s. 117.
[54] 1985 Act, ss. 31(9), (10).
[55] See Insolvency Act 1986, s. 426, which provides for co-operation between courts in the United Kingdom in relation to insolvency law.

heritage.[56] The estate vests in the permanent trustee by virtue of the act and warrant issued on confirmation of his appointment. So far as the heritable estate of the debtor is concerned, the act and warrant has the same effect in respect of his heritable estate in Scotland as if a decree of adjudication in implement of sale as well as a decree of adjudication for payment and in security of debt, subject to no legal reversion, had been pronounced in favour of the permanent trustee.[57] The effect of these provisions is to give to the permanent trustee a personal right to the heritage, which he requires to complete by registration in the Register of Sasines or the Land Register for Scotland using the act and warrant as a link in title in order to obtain a real right.[58] The debtor is reduced to the position of a squatter in the property without any title to remain there.[59] The permanent trustee is not affected by any prior inhibition in the exercise of any powers which he is given by the Act in relation to the heritable estate.[60] So far as the debtor's moveable estate is concerned, any such property in respect of which delivery or possession or intimation of its assignation would be required in order to complete title to it vests in the permanent trustee by virtue of the act and warrant as if at the date of sequestration the permanent trustee had taken delivery or possession of the property or had made intimation of its assignation to him, as the case may be.[61] The effect of this provision is to give to the permanent trustee a real right in all such moveable property, although, if some additional formality is required, such as registration as in the case of shares in a company or patents or registered designs to which special rules apply these formalities must be completed in order to obtain the real right.[62] Any non-vested contingent interest which the debtor has vests in the permanent trustee as if an assignation of that interest had been executed by the debtor and intimation thereof had been made at the date of sequestration.[63] Any estate other than income acquired by the debtor after the date of sequestration and before the date of his discharge vests also in the permanent trustee.[64] Any income arising from the estate which is already vested in the permanent trustee vests in him also, but any other income of whatever nature vests in the debtor subject to the right of the permanent trustee to apply to the sheriff for payment to him of the excess over a suitable amount to allow for the aliment of the debtor and for any obligations of aliment or to make payment of a periodical

[56] s. 31(8).
[57] s. 31(1)(b).
[58] See also s. 31(3), by which the permanent trustee is enabled to complete title to any heritable estate in Scotland to which the debtor had an incomplete title.
[59] *White* v. *Stevenson*, 1956 S.C. 84.
[60] s. 31(2).
[61] s. 31(4).
[62] See para. 54.24.
[63] s. 31(5).
[64] s. 32(6).

allowance which may be owed by him.[65] Any order as to what is a suitable amount of income for this purpose may be varied on change of circumstances.[66] If the debtor raises an action to recover solatium in respect of personal injuries, the claim becomes an asset in the sequestrated estate and the trustee can be sisted in place of the debtor.[67] The debtor cannot raise an action to enforce a claim which the trustee has taken up.[68]

Any person claiming a right to any estate claimed by the permanent trustee may apply to the court for the estate to be excluded from vesting under these provisions.[69] As mentioned above, any property held on trust by the debtor for any other person is specifically excluded by the Act from vesting in the permanent trustee.[70] If the debtor has paid money held by him in trust into an account which is not earmarked with the trust, and also keeps money of his own in the same account, the court will, if it can disentangle the account, separate the trust funds from the private moneys and award the former specifically to the beneficiaries.[71] A trust may be held to have been created by the debtor over incorporeal moveables such as debts owed to him in the course of his business, but it is necessary for this purpose that there should have been an unequivocal declaration of trust by the debtor over such assets together with delivery or its equivalent in order to constitute the trust.[72] The common law rule remains that the trustee takes the estate *tantum et tale* as it stood in the debtor,[73] and that he cannot maintain a right to property which is reducible on the ground of the debtor's fraud.[74] In the absence of fraud, however, there is no rule in Scotland that the trustee cannot assert a claim which it would have been dishonourable for the debtor to make.[75]

54.18   Safeguarding of Interests of Creditors.—Although insolvency does not in itself prevent a person from entering into contracts or incurring obligations, it has important effects so far as gratuitous alienations by debtors and voluntary transactions between debtors and their creditors are concerned. These effects are provided for both under the common law and by statute. The general principle of the common law is that

---

[65] ss. 32(1)–(3).

[66] s. 32(4).

[67] *Watson* v. *Thompson*, 1991 S.L.T. 683.

[68] *Dickson* v. *United Dominions Trust*, 1988 S.L.T. 19.

[69] s. 31(6).

[70] s. 33(1)(*b*).

[71] *Macadam* v. *Martin's Tr.* (1872) 11 M. 33; *Smith* v. *Liqr. of James Birrell*, 1968 S.L.T. 174. As to following trust money, see Trusts, para. 46.14, *supra*.

[72] *Allan's Trs.* v. *Lord Advocate*, 1971 S.C. (H.L.) 45; *Tay Valley Joiners Ltd.* v. *C.F. Financial Services Ltd.*, 1987 S.L.T. 207.

[73] *Davidson* v. *Boyd* (1868) 7 M. 77.

[74] *Colquhoun's Tr.* v. *Campbell's Trs.* (1902) 4 F. 739; *Gamage* v. *Charlesworth's Tr.*, 1910 S.C. 257.

[75] *Clyde Marine Insurance Co.* v. *Renwick*, 1924 S.C. 113.

from the moment of insolvency a debtor is bound to act with regard to the interests of his creditors.[76] He ceases to be entitled secretly to set his funds apart for his own use, and is no longer entitled to alienate them voluntarily whether by giving away his assets gratuitously and voluntarily to third parties or by conferring a preference upon a particular creditor which is voluntary.[77] Gratuitous alienations which were made to a conjunct or confident person could also be challenged under the Bankruptcy Act 1621 (c. 18), by which all alienations made by a debtor to a conjunct or confident person without true just and necessary cause and without a just price being paid could be declared null, the debtor's insolvency at the date of making the challenge being presumed.[78] And preferences granted by a debtor on the eve of or during his notour bankruptcy were reducible under the Bankruptcy Act 1696 (c. 5).[79] The Acts of 1621 and 1696 were repealed by the 1985 Act, which contains new provisions for the challenge of gratuitous alienations and unfair preferences by a debtor during his insolvency. But the common law basis for challenging such transactions remains unaffected by these changes in the statutory framework.

54.19 **Gratuitous Alienations.**—As has just been noticed, it is a general principle at common law that from the moment of his insolvency a debtor is bound to administer his estate for behoof of his creditors. While he may continue with his trade with the intention of making gain for his creditors and for himself, his funds are no longer his own to give away as caprice or affection may dictate.[80] Accordingly, every voluntary alienation of property by a debtor, being an alienation for no consideration or for no adequate consideration, while in a state of insolvency to the prejudice of his creditors is fraudulent and may be the subject of challenge at common law. Thus, an alienation of goods or money, if it was in the nature of a gift,[81] or a gratuitous surrender of rights,[82] or a purchase at an exorbitant price[83] is reducible either at the instance of creditors, prior or posterior,[84] or of the permanent trustee in his subsequent sequestration or the trustee acting under a protected trust deed or a judicial factor appointed under section 11A of the Judicial Factors (Scotland) Act 1889 on the estate of a person deceased.[85] The onus of proof that the transaction was in substance

---

[76] Bell, *Comm.*, ii, 170.

[77] *Nordic Travel Ltd.* v. *Scotprint Ltd.*, 1980 S.C. 1, *per* Lord President Emslie at p. 10.

[78] Goudy, pp. 43 *et seq.*

[79] Goudy, pp. 78 *et seq*; as to notour bankruptcy, see para. 54.3, *supra.*

[80] Bell, *Comm.*, ii, 170; Goudy, p. 22. See also *Nordic Travel Ltd.* v. *Scotprint Ltd.*, 1980 S.C. 1, *per* Lord President Emslie at p. 10, Lord Cameron at p. 24.

[81] Bell, *Comm.*, ii, 184; *Wink* v. *Speirs* (1867) 6 M. 77; *Main* v. *Fleming's Trs.* (1881) 8 R. 880; *Boyle's Tr.* v. *Boyle*, 1988 S.L.T. 581.

[82] *Obers* v. *Paton's Trs.* (1897) 24 R. 719; *Thomson* v. *Spence*, 1961 S.L.T. 395.

[83] *Abram S.S. Co.* v. *Abram*, 1925 S.L.T. 243.

[84] *Wink* v. *Speirs, supra, per* Lord Justice-Clerk Patton at p. 80.

[85] Bankruptcy (Scotland) Act 1985, s. 34(8).

gratuitous and that the debtor was insolvent at the date of the alienation rests upon the challenger. It is not, however, necessary to prove that the alienation was made with fraudulent intention. A presumption of fraud, in the sense of breach of trust, is created by proof that the alienation was made without onerous consideration when the debtor was insolvent.[86] The right to challenge a transaction as a gratuitous alienation at common law is not subject to time limits, and remains available until it has been cut off by the negative prescription.

It is a good answer to a reduction at common law that the deed in question was granted for some true, just and necessary cause. The fulfilment of an obligation, undertaken during solvency, is not struck at.[87] Provisions in ante-nuptial marriage contracts made for the purpose of securing the party to be benefited against the financial risks of marriage were regarded as having been made for a true and just cause, but marriage is not now regarded as an onerous consideration.[88] A provision for a wife by a post-nuptial marriage contract may be sustained,[89] though made at a time when the husband was insolvent, provided that it is reasonable in amount and is not to take effect until after the dissolution of the marriage.

Gratuitous alienations are also challengeable, within certain time limits, under the statute.[90] The right of challenge is available only where the debtor's estate has been sequestrated, or he has granted a trust deed which has become a protected trust deed, or he has died and his estate has been sequestrated within 12 months after his death, or he has died and a judicial factor has been appointed under section 11A of the Judicial Factors (Scotland) Act 1889 to administer his estate within 12 months of his death and the estate was absolutely insolvent at the date of death.[91] The title to challenge is given to any creditor who is a creditor by virtue of a debt incurred on or before the date of sequestration[92] or before the granting of the trust deed or the debtor's death as the case may be, to the permanent trustee, the trustee acting under the trust deed or the judicial factor.[93] The alienations which may be challenged are any alienation whereby any of the debtor's property has been transferred or any claim or right of the debtor has been discharged or renounced which became effectual on a day not earlier than two years before the date of sequestration, the granting of the trust deed or the debtor's death as the case may be, except that this time limit is extended to five years if the alienation was to an associate of the

[86] McCowan v. Wright (1852) 14 D. 901.
[87] Pringle's Tr. v. Wright (1903) 5 F. 522.
[88] McLay v. McQueen (1899) 1 F. 804; Gilmour Shaw & Co.'s Tr. v. Learmonth, 1972 S.C. 137; Law Reform (Husband and Wife) (Scotland) Act 1984, s. 5(1)(b).
[89] Robertson's Tr. v. Robertson (1901) 3 F. 359.
[90] 1985 Act, s. 34.
[91] s. 34(2)(b).
[92] For the meaning of this expression, see s. 12(4) and para. 54.9, supra.
[93] s. 34(1).

debtor.[94] An associate of the debtor for this purpose is, if the debtor is an individual, a husband or wife or other close relative. A person is an associate of a person with whom he is in partnership and of an associate of any person with whom he is in partnership, and a firm is an associate of any person who is a member of a firm.[95] A person is also an associate of any person whom he employs or by whom he is employed, any directors or other officers of a company being treated as employed by the company.[96] The onus lies on the person who seeks to uphold the alienation to establish either that immediately or at any other time after the alienation the debtor's assets were greater than his liabilities,[97] or that the alienation was made for adequate consideration[98] or that it was a birthday, Christmas or other conventional gift or a gift made for a charitable purpose to someone who was not an associate which it was reasonable for the debtor to make.[99] The advantage of the statutory challenge over the common law is that these matters are presumed unless the contrary is proved. If any one or more of these matters is not established the remedy to be granted by the court is that of reduction or restoration of property to the debtor's estate or such other redress as may be appropriate, but a third party who acquired any right or interest in good faith and for value from the transferee in the transaction is protected.[1] Reduction so as to restore the property to the debtor's estate is the primary remedy; the court does not have an equitable discretion to grant some other remedy where reduction is available.[2]

54.20 Unfair preferences.—Transactions entered into by a debtor which have the effect of creating a preference in favour of a creditor to the prejudice of the general body of creditors are known as unfair preferences and are challengeable under the statute.[3] The right to challenge such transactions is available where the preference was created not earlier than six months before the date of sequestration[4] of the

---

[94] ss. 34(2)(a), (3).

[95] ss. 74(1)–(4) as amended by Bankruptcy (Scotland) Regulations 1985, reg. 11; see the definition of 'relative' in subs. (4).

[96] s. 74(5).

[97] See *Lombardi's Tr. v. Lombardi*, 1982 S.L.T. 81; *Hunt's Tr. v. Hunt*, 1984 S.L.T. 169.

[98] See Goudy, p. 46 for a discussion of what was regarded as adequate consideration in the context of the 1621 Act. See also *Matheson's Tr. v. Matheson*, 1992 S.L.T. 685. The 1985 Act does not define what constitutes consideration. The term has, however, been judicially defined to mean 'something of material or patrimonial value which could be vindicated in a legal process', whether by being claimed or possibly by being pled in answer to another's claim: *MacFadyen's Tr. v. MacFadyen*, 1994 S.L.T. 1245 *per* Lord McCluskey, at p. 1248, delivering the opinion of the court. There cannot be adequate consideration on facts which show that no consideration was given: *ibid.*

[99] s. 34(4).

[1] s. 34(4).

[2] *Short's Tr. v. Chung*, 1991 S.L.T. 472.

[3] 1985 Act, s. 36.

[4] For the meaning of this expression, see s. 12(4) and para. 54.9, *supra*.

debtor's estate, or the granting by him of a trust deed which has become a protected trust deed[5] or his death where within 12 months after his death his estate has been sequestrated or a judicial factor has been appointed under section 11A of the Judicial Factors (Scotland) Act 1889 to administer his estate and his estate was absolutely insolvent at the time of his death.[6] As in the case of gratuitous alienations, the title to challenge is given to any creditor who is a creditor by virtue of a debt incurred on or before the date of sequestration or before the granting of the protected trust deed or the debtor's death as the case may be, and to the permanent trustee, the trustee acting under the trust deed or the judicial factor.[7] The remedy to be granted by the court, if satisfied that the transaction is one to which the section applies, is that of reduction or restoration of property to the debtor's estate or such other redress as may be appropriate, but this is without prejudice to any right or interest acquired by a third party in good faith and for value from or through the creditor in whose favour the preference was created.[8] The right of creditors to challenge fraudulent preferences at common law is preserved, and this right is extended to the permanent trustee, the trustee appointed under a protected trust deed and a judicial factor appointed under section 11A of the 1889 Act.[9] The advantage of the statutory challenge over that available at common law is that it is necessary for the challenger at common law to prove that the debtor was absolutely insolvent at the time of the transaction or as a consequence of it and was also absolutely insolvent at the time of challenge,[10] whereas under the statute it is necessary only to prove that the day on which the transaction became effectual was not earlier than six months before the events referred to above.[11]

The section does not attempt to define more closely the kinds of transactions which may be challenged under it. In terms of the Bankruptcy Act 1696 (c. 5) the transaction required to have been voluntary in order to be the subject of challenge,[12] but the word 'voluntary' is not used in this context by the 1985 Act. The only requirement is that the transaction should have had the effect of creating a preference in favour of a creditor to the prejudice of the general body of creditors. This description is so broad as to cover every form of alienation by which a right to heritable or moveable property may be transferred from one person to another, whether directly or

---

[5] Note that the trust deed must have become protected, but that the time limit runs from the date of the granting of the trust deed.

[6] s. 36(1).

[7] s. 36(4).

[8] s. 36(5).

[9] s. 36(6).

[10] *McCowan* v. *Wright* (1853) 15 D. 494; Goudy, p. 41.

[11] ss. 36(1), (3).

[12] See *Taylor* v. *Farrie* (1855) 17 D. 639; *Stiven* v. *Scott and Simson* (1871) 9 M. 923; Goudy, p. 82.

indirectly. Such transactions may include, for example, the delivery or disposition of property in security of a prior debt,[13] the indorsation of a bill or cheque for a payment not yet due[14] and an arrangement with a debtor to pay a creditor direct.[15] Any transaction which results in giving a creditor, or it would seem a class of creditors, until then unsecured or imperfectly secured, a security for his or their debt is reducible.[16]

A mere acknowledgement of an existing debt, which enables a creditor to obtain no more than an ordinary ranking and does not confer on him any preference is not struck at by the Act.[17] Nor is the substitution for an existing security of another of equivalent value.[18] It is specifically provided that the right of challenge does not apply to four classes of transactions. These are: (1) a transaction in the ordinary course of trade or business; (2) a payment in cash for a debt which when it was paid had become payable, unless the transaction was collusive[19] with the purpose of prejudicing the general body of creditors; (3) a transaction whereby the parties thereto have undertaken reciprocal obligations, unless the transaction was collusive; and (4) the granting of a mandate by a debtor authorising an arrestee to pay over arrested funds or part thereof to the arrester, provided there has been a decree for payment on a summary warrant for diligence which was preceded by an arrestment on the dependence of the action or followed by an arrestment in execution.[20] The first three of these classes of transaction amount to a restatement of categories already recognised by the existing law as exempt from challenge at common law and under the Bankruptcy Act 1696 (c. 5), the third being described as *nova debita*.[20a] They are dealt with more fully in the following paragraph. The fourth enables the debtor to avoid the expense of a furthcoming in circumstances where the diligence of arrestment has been taken sufficiently far for it not to be unfair to other creditors for a mandate to be granted.

54.21   Fraudulent Preferences at Common Law.—Any transactions by an insolvent debtor which have the effect, whether directly or indirectly, of conferring a benefit on one creditor in preference to others are challengeable as frauds at common law. Although a creditor has a legal claim on the debtor, it is the duty of the debtor once he is insolvent to

[13] *Stiven v. Scott and Simson, supra; T. v. L.*, 1970 S.L.T. 243.
[14] *Blincow's Tr. v. Allan* (1828) 7 S. 124; *Carter v. Johnstone* (1886) 13 R. 698, distinguished in *Whatmough's Tr. v. British Linen Bank*, 1934 S.C. (H.L.) 51. See also *Raymond Harrison & Co.'s Tr. v. North West Securities*, 1989 S.L.T. 718.
[15] *Newton & Sons' Tr. v. Finlayson & Co.*, 1928 S.C. 637.
[16] *McCowan v. Wright, supra; Thomas v. Thomson* (1866) 5 M. 198; *Mackenzie v. Calder* (1868) 6 M. 833.
[17] *Matthew's Tr. v. Matthew* (1867) 5 M. 957.
[18] *Roy's Tr. v. Colville* (1903) 5 F. 769.
[19] As to the meaning of collusion, see *Nordic Travel Ltd. v. Scotprint Ltd.*, 1980 S.C. 1, *per* Lord President Emslie at p. 19.
[20] s. 36(2).
[20a] See *Nicoll v. Steelpress (Supplies) Ltd.*, 1992 S.C.L.R. 332.

abstain from any act which interferes with the preferences or rights of the creditors *inter se*.[21] Such transactions are not *pacta illicita*,[22] but they are reducible at the instance of other creditors and others with a title to do so on behalf of creditors, such as the permanent trustee in the debtor's sequestration and the liquidator or administrator if the debtor is a company. Examples of such transactions are where during his absolute insolvency a debtor gives security for what was formerly an unsecured debt or an obligation to grant a security is undertaken,[23] or where he facilitates a creditor's efforts to exercise diligence or to obtain a decree against him.[24] Once it has been proved that the transaction was entered into voluntarily, during absolute insolvency and while the debtor was conscious of his insolvency, fraud is presumed and it is unnecessary to prove an intention of fraud on his part or any collusion or concert on the part of the favoured creditor.[25] The debtor must also be shown to be absolutely insolvent at the time when the transaction is challenged.[26] Once these requirements are satisfied, all such voluntary transactions are liable to be reduced unless they fall within one or other of the following classes: (1) payments in cash of debts due and payable; (2) transactions in the ordinary course of trade; and (3) *nova debita* or transferences for a consideration given at the time.[27]

A payment in cash includes, besides currency, cheques drawn by the debtor on his banker. The transfer of a cheque received by the debtor from a third party, and indorsed by him, was held, where it was used as a method by which one dealer paid another, not to be protected as a payment in cash.[28] But it has since been explained that the decision proceeded on the ground that such a method of payment was unusual in the trade, and a similar payment, but made to a banker to meet an overdraft, was held good.[29] The transfer of a bill of exchange, in which the primary debtor is a third party as acceptor, and which is not instantly payable, is not a payment in cash, and is not safeguarded as a transaction in the usual course of business, by proof that it was the method of paying his business debts usually adopted by the particular trader.[30] As a general rule payment of a debt before it is due is not protected.[31] Payment in cash of a debt which is due is reducible only if

---

[21] Bell, *Comm.*, ii, 226; *McEwen v. Doig* (1828) 6 S. 889.
[22] *Munro v. Rothfield*, 1920 S.C. (H.L.) 165.
[23] *McCowan v. Wright* (1853) 15 D. 494; *Thomas v. Thomson* (1866) 5 M. 198.
[24] *Lauries' Tr. v. Beveridge* (1867) 6 M. 85.
[25] *McCowan v. Wright, supra per* Lord Justice-Clerk Hope at p. 504; *Whatmough's Tr. v. British Linen Bank*, 1932 S.C. 525, *per* Lord President Clyde at p. 543; see also *McDougall's Tr. v. Ironside*, 1914 S.C. 186; *Nordic Travel Ltd. v. Scotprint Ltd.*, 1980 S.C. 1.
[26] *McCowan v. Wright, supra*; Goudy, p. 41.
[27] Bell, *Comm.*, ii, 201.
[28] *Carter v. Johnstone* (1886) 13 R. 698.
[29] *Whatmough's Tr. v. British Linen Bank*, 1934 S.C. (H.L.) 51.
[30] *Horsburgh v. Ramsay* (1885) 12 R. 1171.
[31] *Blincow's Tr. v. Allan & Co.* (1828) 7 S. 124; *Whatmough's Tr., supra, per* Lord Thankerton at p. 59; Goudy, p. 85.

collusion or consent between the debtor and the favoured creditor (with the object of defrauding the equal rights of the debtor's other creditors) is proved.[32] The fact that both parties were aware of the insolvency or impending bankruptcy does not, by itself, infer collusion;[33] the decisions leave it in doubt what further evidence is necessary.[34]

Transactions in the ordinary course of trade include payments for goods supplied on credit, or delivery of goods already paid for,[35] if, in the latter case, the transfer is in fulfilment of a definite obligation, and does not amount to an attempt to complete a security under which the creditor had no real right.[36] Where goods were sent to be bleached, and thereby subjected, according to the established usage of the trade, to a lien for a balance due on prior transactions of the same kind, a challenge of the lien, as in substance a security for a prior debt, failed.[37] And an auctioneer, conducting a displenishing sale for a farmer, is entitled to retain enough of the money received to satisfy the prior balance due by the farmer, unless some unusual procedure can be founded on to take the transaction out of the ordinary course of trade.[38] In general, direct payments in cash are in the ordinary course of trade or business when they are made by a party who is still in the administration of his estate and in funds, in discharge of debts past due.[39]

Nova debita include transactions where the bankrupt and the party whose right is challenged incurred reciprocal obligations at the same time, or with an interval so short as to admit of the application of the term *unico contextu*.[40] To these, though the party may have been insolvent at their date, the common law does not take any objection. So a party lending money, and taking a security for it in return which is duly completed in the way appropriate to the particular subject, obtains a good security, although he may have known that the borrower was insolvent.[41] Where a bank had, within 60 days of their debtor's

---

[32] *Whatmough's Tr.*, *supra*, *per* Lord President Clyde, 1932 S.C. at p. 543; 1934 S.C. (H.L.) 51.

[33] *Coutts' Tr. & Doe v. Webster* (1886) 13 R. 1112; *Pringle's Tr. v. Wright* (1903) 5 F. 522; *Nordic Travel Ltd. v. Scotprint Ltd.*, *supra*, *per* Lord President Emslie at p. 19, Lord Cameron at p. 27.

[34] See *Jones' Tr. v. Jones* (1888) 15 R. 328; *Craig's Tr. v. Macdonald, Fraser & Co.* (1902) 4 F. 1132; *Newton & Son's Tr. v. Finlayson*, 1928 S.C. 637, where the payment was reduced; *Crockart's Tr. v. Hay*, 1913 S.C. 509; *Angus' Tr. v. Angus* (1901) 4 F. 181; *Whatmough's Tr. v. British Linen Bank*, 1932 S.C. 525; 1934 S.C. (H.L.) 51, where it was sustained.

[35] *Taylor v. Farrie* (1855) 17 D. 639.

[36] *Jones & Co.'s Tr. v. Allan* (1901) 4 F. 374.

[37] *Anderson's Tr. v. Fleming* (1871) 9 M. 718.

[38] *Crockart's Tr. v. Hay*, 1913 S.C. 509, distinguishing *Craig's Tr. v. Macdonald, Fraser & Co.* (1902) 4 F. 1132.

[39] *Nordic Travel Ltd. v. Scotprint Ltd.*, *supra*, *per* Lord President Emslie at p. 20; as to the meaning of 'ordinary course,' see also Lord Cameron at p. 29.

[40] See *Cowdenbeath Coal Co. v. Clydesdale Bank* (1895) 22 R. 682.

[41] *Price & Pierce v. Bank of Scotland*, 1910 S.C. 1095, affd. 1912 S.C. (H.L.) 19; *Thomas Montgomery & Sons v. Gallacher*, 1982 S.L.T. 138.

bankruptcy, taken an assignation in security of the overdraft standing against him, but thereafter that overdraft was paid and it was arranged that a new advance should be covered by the assignation, it was held that as at the date of the ultimate bankruptcy the bank held the assignation for the new advance, a *novum debitum*, it was not open to challenge under the 1696 Act.[42]

54.22 **Capital Sum on Divorce.**—Provision is made by the 1985 Act for the recall of an order by the court for the payment by the debtor of a capital sum on divorce or for the transfer of property by him on divorce.[43] It is a requirement of the right to apply for the recall of such an order that the debtor was absolutely insolvent at the date of the making of the order, or was rendered so by implementation of it.[44] It is also necessary that within five years after the making of the order the debtor's estate should have been sequestrated other than after his death, or that he should have granted a trust deed which has become a protected trust deed, or that he should have died and within 12 months after his death his estate has been sequestrated or a judicial factor has been appointed under section 11A of the Judicial Factors (Scotland) Act 1889 to administer his estate.[45] The only parties who are entitled to apply for a recall of the order are the permanent trustee, the trustee acting under the trust deed or the judicial factor,[46] no right of application being given in this instance to any creditor. The court has a discretion as to whether or not to make an order for recall, having regard to all the circumstances including those of the person against whom the order for recall would be made,[47] who will normally be the debtor's former spouse.

54.23 **Effect of Sequestration on Diligence.**—The order of the court awarding sequestration has the effect, as from the date of sequestration,[48] in relation to diligence done, whether before or after that date, in respect of any part of the debtor's estate of (a) a decree of adjudication of the heritable estate of the debtor for payment of his debts which has been duly recorded in the Register of Inhibitions and Adjudications on that date, and (b) an arrestment in execution and decree of furthcoming, an arrestment in execution and warrant of sale and a completed poinding, in favour of the creditors according to their respective entitlements.[49] As has already been noticed, apparent insolvency has the effect of

---

[42] *Robertson's Tr.* v. *Union Bank*, 1917 S.C. 549.
[43] s. 35.
[44] s. 35(1)(*b*). Note that there is no presumption as to insolvency in this case, so this must be proved by the party who seeks recall.
[45] s. 35(1)(*c*).
[46] s. 35(2).
[47] s. 35(2) proviso.
[48] For the meaning of this expression, see s. 12(4) and para. 54.9.
[49] s. 37(1).

equalising diligence executed within 60 days prior to the date when it occurs or within four months thereafter.[50] The effect of the order awarding sequestration within four months after apparent insolvency is to make the debtor's estate available to all the creditors equally as if they had all arrested and poinded for their respective claims, and to suspend diligence during the sequestration.[51] In addition, no arrestment or poinding of the debtor's estate executed within 60 days before the date of sequestration or on or after that date is effectual to create a preference for the arrester or poinder, and the estate so arrested or poinded, or the proceeds of sale thereof, must be handed over to the permanent trustee, subject to the right of the arrester or poinder who is thus deprived of his diligence to payment of his expenses.[52] The order awarding sequestration also affects inhibitions, it being provided that no inhibition on the estate of the debtor which takes effect within 60 days before the date of sequestration shall be effectual to create a preference for the inhibitor.[53] Any right to challenge a deed voluntarily granted by the debtor which vested in the inhibitor by virtue of the inhibition vests instead in the permanent trustee, as does any right of the inhibitor to receive payment for the discharge of the inhibition.[54] These provisions apply also to the estate of a deceased debtor which has been sequestrated within 12 months after his death or which was absolutely insolvent at the date of death and to which within 12 months a judicial factor has been appointed under section 11A of the Judicial Factors (Scotland) Act 1889.[55] The effects of sequestration on poinding of the ground, maills and duties[56] and the landlord's sequestration for rent[57] have already been noted.

54.24 Effect of Sequestration on Personal Rights.—A party who has an incomplete or personal right to any property falling under the sequestration cannot, as a general rule, complete his right after the date of the order awarding sequestration. The statutory effect of the order, as vesting in the permanent trustee the whole property of the debtor, forms an impediment.[58] Thus, in the case of moveable property the permanent trustee is vested with a right completed by possession or intimation, as the nature of the property may demand.[59] The vesting

---

[50] Sched. 7, para. 24; see para. 54.4, *supra.*

[51] *Stewart* v. *Jarvie*, 1938 S.C. 309.

[52] ss. 37(4), (5). This does not apply to diligence against earnings: Debtors (Scotland) Act 1987, Sched. 6, para. 27. Where an arrestment executed prior to the 60-day period still subsists at the date of sequestration the fund vests in the trustee but he must give effect to the preference: *Berry* v. *Taylor*, (O.H.) 1992 S.C.L.R. 910.

[53] s. 37(2).

[54] ss. 37(2), (3).

[55] s. 37(7).

[56] Diligence, paras. 53.29 and 53.34, *supra.*

[57] Leases, para. 33.14, *supra.*

[58] s. 31.

[59] s. 31(4).

clause in the case of heritable property[60] gives the permanent trustee an immediate and completed right to a lease held by the debtor, preferable to the right of any assignees who have not entered into possession.[61] But there is an exception in the case of property where the title of a transferee or disponee is completed by entry in a register. So it was held that a party who, at the date of the sequestration, held a transfer of shares duly executed by the debtor, might complete his right by sending in the transfer for registration after the sequestration, provided that he did so before the permanent trustee had been registered as the owner of the shares.[62] In the case of heritable property, sequestration is not a bar to the completion of title by recording a disposition in the Register of Sasines. The right of a party so recording, in competition with the permanent trustee depends, not the date of the sequestration, but on priority of registration.[63]

54.25 **Administration by Permanent Trustee.**—The principal functions of the permanent trustee are to recover, manage and realise the debtor's estate so far as vesting in him under the Act, and to distribute it among the debtor's creditors according to their entitlements.[64] He is required to make up and maintain an inventory and valuation of the estate, to maintain a sederunt book for the purpose of keeping an accurate record of the sequestration process and to keep regular accounts of his intromissions with the debtor's estate.[65] He is entitled to have access to all documents relating to the debtor's assets, business or financial affairs which may be sent by or on behalf of the debtor to a third party and to make copies of any such documents.[66] He is also entitled to require delivery to him of any title deed or other document of the debtor notwithstanding that a right of lien is claimed over it, but this is without prejudice to any preference to which the holder of the lien may be entitled.[67] A right of lien is a security within the meaning of the Act and the holder of it is a secured creditor,[68] who is entitled to a preferential ranking on the estate.[69] As soon as possible after his confirmation in office the permanent trustee must consult with the commissioners, or, if there are none, with the Accountant in Bankruptcy, concerning the exercise of his functions with regard to the management and realisation of the estate, and he is required to comply with any general or specific

---

[60] s. 31(1)(b).
[61] *Clark* v. *West Calder Oil Co.* (1882) 9 R. 1017.
[62] *Morrison* v. *Harrison* (1876) 3 R. 406.
[63] *Cormack* v. *Anderson* (1829) 7 S. 868; *Clark* v. *West Calder Oil Co., supra.*
[64] ss. 3(1)(a), (b); see also s. 38.
[65] ss. 3(1)(e), (f) and 38(1); see also s. 62.
[66] s. 38(2).
[67] s. 38(4).
[68] s. 73(1).
[69] *Adam & Winchester* v. *White's Tr.* (1884) 11 R. 863; *Findlay* v. *Waddell*, 1910 S.C. 670.

directions given to him in this regard by the creditors, by the court on the application of the commissioners or by the Accountant in Bankruptcy, except in the case of the sale of perishable goods.[70] Various powers may be exercised by him if he considers that their exercise would be beneficial for the administration of the estate, but consent to their exercise is required if there are commissioners.[71] He may obtain supplies of gas, electricity and water and telecommunication services for the purposes of any business which has been carried on by the debtor or on his behalf, on condition that he personally guarantees payment of any charges in respect of the supply.[72] Special rules apply to the sale by the permanent trustee of any part of the debtor's estate over which a heritable security is held by a creditor or creditors,[73] and where he proposes to sell or dispose of any right or interest in the debtor's family home.[74] He has power to adopt any contract entered into by the debtor before the date of sequestration where he considers that this would be beneficial to the administration of the debtor's estate, unless its adoption is precluded by the express or implied terms of the contract.[75] All money received by him in the exercise of his functions must be deposited by him in the name of the debtor's estate in an appropriate bank or institution.[76] He may also obtain an order from the court with respect to any transaction for, or involving the provision of, credit to the debtor if that transaction is or was extortionate and was not entered into more than three years before the date of sequestration.[77] The order may provide for the setting aside of any obligation created by the transaction in whole or part, for varying the terms of the transaction or the terms on which any security for it is held, for the payment by any party to the transaction to the permanent trustee of any sums paid to that party by the debtor by virtue of the transaction or for the surrender to the permanent trustee of any property held as security for the transaction.[78]

54.26 Examination of the Debtor.—Among the general functions of the permanent trustee are those of ascertaining the reasons for the debtor's insolvency and the circumstances surrounding it, and to ascertain the state of the debtor's liabilities and assets.[79] To enable him to perform these functions he may request the debtor or the debtor's spouse or any

---

[70] ss. 39(1), (6).
[71] s. 39(2).
[72] s. 70.
[73] See s. 39(4).
[74] s. 40; see also para. 54.27.
[75] s. 42; note that any party to a contract by the debtor may require the permanent trustee to take a decision on this matter within 28 days: s. 42(2).
[76] s. 43.
[77] s. 61; note the provisions of s. 61(3) as to the meaning of 'extortionate' in this context. The transaction is presumed to be extortionate unless the contrary is proved.
[78] s. 61(4).
[79] ss. 3(1)(c), (d).

other person who he believes can give such information to appear
before him and give information relating to the debtor's assets, his
dealings with them or his conduct in relation to his business or financial
affairs.[80] If necessary he may apply to the sheriff for an order for a
private examination of these persons to be held before the sheriff,[81] and
he may also, and must if requested to do so by the Accountant in
Bankruptcy, or the commissioners, or one-quarter in value of the
creditors, apply to the sheriff for an order for a public examination.[82]
Unlike a private examination, a public examination is held in open court
and notice of it requires to be published in the *Edinburgh Gazette* and
given to every creditor known to the permanent trustee. Provision is
made for the granting of warrants to require the attendance of the
debtor or other persons for examination before the sheriff and for the
appointment of an examining commissioner if he is for any good reason
unable to attend.[83] The examination before the sheriff or examining
commissioner is taken on oath, and the Act lays down rules as to who
may ask questions at the examination and limits the scope of these
questions to matters relating to the debtor's assets, his dealings with
them and his conduct in relation to his business or financial affairs.[84] No
such rules apply to any attendances by the debtor or other person at the
request of the permanent trustee to give information to him privately.

54.27 **Duties and Position of Debtor and his Spouse and Family.**—The debtor
is under a general duty to take every practicable step, and in particular
to execute any document which may be necessary to enable the
permanent trustee to perform the functions conferred on him by the
Act.[85] If necessary, the permanent trustee may apply to the sheriff for
an order on the debtor to do so, and the sheriff may authorise the
sheriff clerk to execute any documents which the debtor has failed to
execute with the like force and effect in all respects as if the document
had been executed by the debtor himself.[86] The debtor commits an
offence if he makes a false statement in relation to his assets or his
business and financial affairs to any creditor, or any person concerned in
the administration of his estate such as the permanent trustee, after his
sequestration unless he shows that he neither knew nor had reason to
believe that the statement was false, as does the debtor or any other
person acting in his interest whether with or without his authority who
destroys, damages, conceals or removes from Scotland any part of the
debtor's estate or any document relating to his assets or business unless

[80] s. 44(1).
[81] s. 44(2).
[82] s. 45.
[83] s. 46 (as amended by 1993 Act, Sched. 1, para. 20).
[84] s. 47; *cf. Delvoitte & Co.* v. *Baillie's Tr.* (1877) 5 R. 143, *per* Lord President Inglis at
p. 144.
[85] s. 64.
[86] s. 64(2).

he can show that this was not done with intent to prejudice creditors.[87] It should be noted that the period during which these offences may be committed is the period commencing one year immediately before the date of sequestration and ending with the debtor's discharge.[88] And a debtor who is engaged in a trade or business is guilty of an offence if at any time within the period of two years ending with the date of sequestration he fails to keep or preserve such records as are necessary to give a fair view of the state of his assets or his business and financial affairs, unless he can show that this failure was neither reckless nor dishonest.[89] The Act makes provision for various other offences in relation to the failure of a debtor who is absent from Scotland to come to Scotland for any purpose connected with the administration of his estate when required to do so by the court, the falsification of documents by the debtor or any other person acting in his interest and the failure of the debtor to report any falsifications of which he is aware to the permanent trustee, and also the making of transfers for inadequate consideration or the granting of unfair preferences to any creditor by a person who is absolutely insolvent.[90] It is also an offence for a person whose estate has been sequestrated, or has been adjudged bankrupt in England and Wales or Northern Ireland, and who has not been discharged to obtain, either alone or jointly with others, credit to the extent of £250 or more without giving the person from whom he obtains it information about his status as an undischarged bankrupt.[91] The permanent trustee must report any offences of which he is aware to the Accountant in Bankruptcy, who is under a duty to report them to the Lord Advocate with a view to prosecution.[92] A debtor whose estate has been sequestrated is disqualified from sitting or voting in Parliament, from being elected a member of the House of Commons or any local authority and from holding certain specified offices.[93] He commits an offence if, prior to his discharge, he acts as director or liquidator of, or directly or indirectly takes part in or is concerned in the promotion, formation or management of, a company.[94]

So far as the debtor's spouse is concerned, her consent, failing which the authority of the court, is required before the permanent trustee may sell or dispose of any right or interest in the family home, and similar provisions apply when the debtor occupies the family home in which his spouse has no rights so long as he does so with a child of the family.[95]

[87] ss. 67(1), (2).
[88] s. 67(11).
[89] s. 67(8).
[90] See generally s. 67.
[91] ss. 67(9), (10). See Bankruptcy (Scotland) Amendment Regulations 1986 (S.I. 1986 No. 1914), reg. 3.
[92] ss. 3(3), 1(4).
[93] Local Government (Scotland) Act 1973, s. 31. Insolvency Act 1986, s. 427; District Courts (Scotland) Act 1975, s. 13A.
[94] Company Directors Disqualification Act 1986, s. 11.
[95] s. 40. *Salmon's Tr.* v. *Salmon*, 1989 S.L.T. (Sh.Ct.) 49.

A petition for sequestration whose purpose was wholly or mainly to defeat the occupancy rights of a non-entitled spouse within the meaning of the Matrimonial Homes (Family Protection) (Scotland) Act 1981 may be recalled or such other order made by the court as it thinks fit to protect those rights.[96]

54.28   Submission and Adjudication of Claims.—A creditor who wishes to vote at a meeting of creditors other than the statutory meeting or to draw a dividend out of the debtor's estate for any accounting period must first submit a claim to the permanent trustee for adjudication, together with any further evidence which the permanent trustee may require to satisfy himself as to the amount or validity of the claim.[97] It is not competent to refer to the oath of the debtor for this purpose,[98] and a written acknowledgement by him if dated after the date of sequestration is not competent as proof of a loan.[99] The claim must be submitted at or before the meeting in order to entitle the creditor to vote, or not later than eight weeks before the end of the accounting period to entitle him to draw a dividend in respect of it. A claim submitted to and accepted by the interim trustee at or before the statutory meeting or submitted to the permanent trustee and accepted by him for the purpose of voting or drawing a dividend is deemed to have been re-submitted to the permanent trustee for the purpose of any subsequent meeting or accounting period,[1] but the creditor is free at any time to submit a further claim specifying a different amount.[2] The permanent trustee is required to accept or reject the claim of each creditor at the commencement of every meeting for the purposes of the creditor's right to vote at it, and to accept or reject any claim submitted or deemed to have been re-submitted to him not later than four weeks before the end of each accounting period. He is not bound by any decision of the interim trustee or any adjudications which he may have made for the purposes of earlier meetings or accounting periods.[3] Reasons must be given to the creditor by the permanent trustee when he rejects a claim, and the debtor or creditor may appeal to the sheriff against the acceptance or rejection of any claim within certain time limits.[4] In calculating the amount of his claim for the purposes of these rules a secured creditor must deduct the value of any security as estimated by him or the amount, less expenses, which he has received or is entitled to receive on the realisation of his security.[5]

---

[96] s. 41.
[97] ss. 48(1), (5).
[98] *Adam* v. *Maclachlan* (1847) 9 D. 560.
[99] *Carmichael's Tr.* v. *Carmichael*, 1929 S.C. 265.
[1] s. 48(2).
[2] s. 48(4).
[3] ss. 49(1), (2).
[4] ss. 49(4), (6).
[5] Sched. 1, para 5.

54.29   Entitlement to Vote and Draw Dividend.—A creditor who has had his claim acccepted in whole or in part by the permanent trustee, or on appeal to the sheriff, may vote on any matter at the meeting of creditors for the purpose of which the claim is accepted.[6] The acceptance of his claim in whole or in part in respect of an accounting period entitles him to payment out of the debtor's estate of a dividend for that accounting period in so far as the estate has funds available to make the payment, having regard to his position in the order of priority for distribution.[7]

54.30   Distribution of the Debtor's Estate.—The procedure which the permanent trustee must follow in the performance of his function of distributing the estate among the debtor's creditors is set out in the Act by reference to accounting periods. He is required to make up accounts of his intromissions with the debtor's estate in respect of periods of six months, the first period commencing with the date of sequestration,[8] until the funds of the estate are exhausted.[9] He has power with the consent of the commissioners or the Accountant in Bankruptcy to shorten the length of any accounting period other than the first, if he considers that it would be expedient to accelerate payment of any dividend, and he also has power to postpone payment of a dividend to the next accounting period.[10] Within two weeks after the end of an accounting period he must submit to the commissioners, or if there are none to the Accountant in Bankruptcy, his accounts of his intromissions with the debtor's estate for audit, together with a scheme of division of the divisible funds and a claim for his outlays and remuneration.[11] Provision is made for the taxation of accounts for legal expenses, and for the audit and determination of the permanent trustee's outlays and remuneration by the commissioners or the Accountant in Bankruptcy, and also for appeal not later than eight weeks after the end of an accounting period against their determination in fixing these amounts.[12] After these procedures have been completed, the permanent trustee must pay to the creditors their dividends in accordance with the scheme of division.[13] Any dividend which is not cashed or uplifted must be deposited by him in an appropriate bank or institution, and the same procedure is followed if the permanent trustee has decided to exercise his power to set aside an amount for a creditor pending the production of evidence in support of his claim.[14] Certain outlays and expenses may be paid by the permanent trustee at any time, as also may the preferred

---

[6] s. 50(a).
[7] s. 50(b).
[8] For the meaning of this expression, see s. 12(4) and para. 54.9, *supra.*
[9] s. 52 (as amended by 1993 Act, Sched. 1, para. 21).
[10] ss. 52(5), (6).
[11] s. 53(1).
[12] ss. 53(2)–(6) (as amended by 1993 Act, Sched. 1, para. 22).
[13] s. 53(7).
[14] s. 53(8); see also s. 52(8).

debts with the consent of the commissioners or the Accountant in Bankruptcy.[15]

The order of priority in the distribution is as follows:[16] (a) The outlays and remuneration of the interim trustee; (b) the outlays and remuneration of the permanent trustee; (c) where the debtor is a deceased debtor, deathbed and funeral expenses reasonably incurred and expenses reasonably incurred in administering the estate; (d) the expenses reasonably incurred by a creditor who is a petitioner, or concurs in the petition, for sequestration; (e) preferred debts,[17] excluding interest accrued to the date of sequestration; (f) ordinary debts, that is, debts which are neither secured debts nor any of the debts mentioned in any other heading of this sentence; (g) interest on the preferred debts and the ordinary debts between the date of sequestration and the date of payment;[18] and (h) any postponed debt,[19] such as a loan made to the debtor by his spouse or a loan made to the debtor in consideration of a share of the profits in his business, which is postponed by section 3 of the Partnership Act 1890 to the claims of other creditors. Any debt falling within any of the heads (c) to (h) has the same priority as any other debt falling under the same head, and where the funds of the estate are inadequate to enable them to be paid in full they abate in equal proportions.[20] Any surplus, other than an unclaimed dividend, which remains after all these debts have been paid in full falls to be made over to the debtor or to his successors or assignees.[21]

The rights of secured creditors whose rights are preferable to those of the permanent trustee and the preference of the holder of a lien over a title deed or other document required to be delivered to the permanent trustee are not affected by these rules.[22] A secured creditor whose rights are preferable to those of the permanent trustee is in a position at the outset of the sequestration to enforce the security to obtain a payment of his debt, subject to special procedures whereby the permanent trustee may take the initiative and require any part of the debtor's heritable estate which is subject to such a security to be sold.[23] At any time after the expiry of 12 weeks from the date of sequestration the permanent trustee may require a secured creditor to discharge the security at the expense of the debtor's estate irrespective of whether it relates to

---

[15] s. 52(4).
[16] s. 51(1).
[17] For the meaning of preferred debts, see Sched. 3 and para. 54.31.
[18] As to the rate of interest, see s. 51(7). The prescribed rate of interest is 15 per cent. per annum, in terms of reg. 8 of the Bankruptcy (Scotland) Regulations 1985 (S.I. 1985 No. 1925), but the rate applicable to the debt apart from the sequestration prevails if it is higher than the prescribed rate.
[19] For the meaning of postponed debts, see s. 51(3).
[20] s. 51(4).
[21] s. 51(5).
[22] s. 51(6). As to the position of the holder of a lien, see para. 54.25, *supra*.
[23] See s. 39(4).

heritage or moveables or to convey or assign it to the permanent trustee on payment to the creditor of the value specified by the creditor, whereupon the amount in respect of which the creditor is entitled to claim in the sequestration is any balance of his debt remaining after receipt of such payment.[24]

54.31   **Preferred Debts.**—Preferred debts are those listed in Schedule 3 to the Act,[25] all of which rank equally *inter se*.[26] These comprise (a) sums due to the Inland Revenue at the date of sequestration or the date of death of a deceased debtor on account of deductions under the pay-as-you-earn scheme or in respect of deductions from payments to subcontractors in the construction industry during the period of 12 months next before that date;[27] (b) any value added tax referable to the period of six months next before the date of sequestration or death as the case may be, and any car tax, general betting duty or bingo duty due within the previous 12 months;[28] (c) social security contributions due in or in respect of the previous 12 months;[29] (d) contributions to occupational pension schemes and state scheme premiums;[30] (e) amounts owed by the debtor by way of remuneration or accrued holiday remuneration to any person who is or has been his employee in respect of the whole or any part of four months before the date of sequestration or death, not exceeding £800;[31] (f) so much of any sum owed in respect of money advanced for the purpose as has been applied for the payment of a debt which, if it had not been paid, would have been a debt falling within (e) above; (g) sums due in respect of levies on coal and steel production.[32] It should be noted that local rates and assessed taxes, which were included among the list of preferred debts for the purposes of the Bankruptcy (Scotland) Act 1913, are not included in Schedule 3 and are therefore no longer preferential claims in the event of the debtor's sequestration.

54.32   **Co-obligants.**—Special provision is made by the Act with regard to the liabilities and rights of co-obligants of the debtor including his cautioners.[33] First, the co-obligant or cautioner is not freed or discharged from his liability for the debt by reason of the discharge of the debtor or by virtue of the creditor's voting or drawing a dividend or assenting to or not objecting to the discharge of the debtor or any

---

[24] Sched. 1, para. 5(2).
[25] s. 51.
[26] s. 51(4).
[27] Under Income and Corporation Taxes Act 1988, ss. 203, 559.
[28] Betting and Gaming Duties Act 1981, ss. 12 and 14.
[29] Under Social Security Act 1975.
[30] Under Social Security Pensions Act 1975.
[31] Bankruptcy (Scotland) Amendment Regulations 1986 (S.I. 1986 No. 1914), adding reg. 14 to Bankruptcy (Scotland) Regulations 1985 (S.I. 1985 No. 1925).
[32] Insolvency (E.C.S.C. Levy Debts) Regulations 1987 (S.I. 1987 No. 2093).
[33] s. 60.

composition.[34] In these respects, therefore, the creditor's position in a sequestration is protected against any results which might otherwise have flowed from these actings under the common law.[35] Second, where a creditor has had a claim accepted in whole or in part and a co-obligant of the debtor or his cautioner holds a security over any part of the debtor's estate, the co-obligant or cautioner must account to the permanent trustee so as to put the estate in the same position as if he had paid the debt to the creditor and thereafter had his own claim accepted in whole or in part in the sequestration after deduction of the value of his security.[36] This means that the co-obligant or cautioner is not entitled to the benefit of his security unless the creditor claims against him in the first instance and not in the sequestration. Third, the co-obligant or cautioner is entitled to require and obtain at his own expense from the creditor an assignation of the debt on payment of the amount thereof in full, and thereafter to submit a claim, vote and draw a dividend on that debt if otherwise legally entitled to do so.[37]

54.33   Rule Against Double Ranking.—The common-law rule that no debt can be ranked twice on a sequestrated estate is of practical importance in the case where a principal debtor and cautioner are both bankrupt. The creditor may then rank on each estate; but the cautioner's estate has no ranking on the estate of the principal debtor. To allow such a ranking would mean that a higher dividend would be paid on the debt in question than is paid on the other debts. Nor can the cautioner's estate obtain the result of a ranking by deducting the amount paid from separate claims in which the principal debtor was a creditor of the cautioner.[38] The rule rests on the theory that when a debt is ranked in sequestration it is, so far as the sequestrated estate is concerned, to be treated as paid. It does not apply where the principal debtor is not sequestrated but compounds with his creditors.[39]

54.34   Automatic Discharge of the Debtor.—It has been held that a debtor is not discharged automatically on the expiry of three years from the date of sequestration, but that discharge is subject to an application, by the permanent trustee or any creditor, to the sheriff for deferment of the discharge.[40] An application for deferment must be made no later than two years and nine months after the date of sequestration[41] and the sheriff has power to defer the discharge for a maximum of two years.[42]

---

[34] s. 60(1).
[35] See Cautionary Obligations, para. 20.20, *supra*.
[36] s. 60(2).
[37] s. 60(3); *cf.* Cautionary Obligations, para. 20.15, *supra*.
[38] *Anderson* v. *Mackinnon* (1876) 3 R. 608.
[39] *Mackinnon* v. *Monkhouse* (1881) 9 R. 393.
[40] *Clydesdale Bank plc* v. *Davidson*, 1994 S.L.T. 225, considering s. 54(1).
[41] s. 54(3).
[42] ss. 54(4), (6); *Pattison* v. *Halliday*, 1991 S.L.T. 645.

When an application for deferment is made timeously, discharge does not occur until the court pronounces an order under section 54.[43] The permanent trustee or any creditor may apply for further deferments provided the application is made not later than three months before the end of the current period of deferment.[44] A discharged debtor can apply to the Accountant in Bankruptcy for a certificate that he has been discharged, in order to obtain evidence of this fact.[45] A debtor whose discharge has been deferred may petition the sheriff for his discharge at any time thereafter, and the question whether or not he should be granted his discharge will then be considered in the light of the debtor's declarations to the effect that he has made a full and fair surrender and disclosure of his estate, a report by the permanent trustee and any representations by the debtor, the permanent trustee or any creditor.[46] The effect of the discharge is that the debtor is discharged within the United Kingdom of all debts and obligations contracted by him, or for which he was liable, at the date of sequestration.[47] There are some exceptions, however: he is not discharged from any liability to pay a fine or other penalty due to the Crown or to forfeiture of any bail; or any liability incurred by reason of fraud or breach of trust; or any obligation to pay aliment under any enactment or rule of law or periodical allowance on divorce; or his obligation to co-operate with the permanent trustee in the performance of his functions under the Act.[48] The discharge removes the disability of the debtor from holding public or other offices, and he is once more enabled to acquire estate without that estate vesting in the permanent trustee.[49]

54.35 Discharge of the Debtor on Composition.—The debtor may also obtain his discharge at any time after the sheriff clerk has issued the act and warrant to the permanent trustee, by making an offer to the permanent trustee in respect of his debts and specifying the caution or other security to be provided for its implementation.[50] If such an offer is made the permanent trustee must submit the offer along with a report thereon to the commissioners or, if there are none, to the Accountant in Bankruptcy. It is then for the commissioners or the Accountant in Bankruptcy to decide whether the offer should be placed before the

---

[43] *Clydesdale Bank plc* v. *Davidson, supra.*
[44] s. 54(9).
[45] s. 54(2).
[46] s. 54(8).
[47] s. 55(1).
[48] s. 55(2). The discharge does not affect any right of a secured creditor to enforce his security for payment of a debt and any interest due and payable thereon until the debt is paid in full: s. 55(3) (inserted by 1993 Act, Sched. 1, para. 23). He is not discharged from liability in respect of a student loan made after sequestration: Education (Student Loans) Act 1990, Sched. 2, para. 6.
[49] ss. 32(6), (10).
[50] s. 56; the procedure is set out in Sched. 4 (as amended by 1993 Act, Sched. 1, para. 31).

creditors. If they consider that the offer will be timeously implemented and that its implementation would secure payment of a dividend of at least 25p in the £ in respect of the ordinary debts and are satisfied with the caution or other security specified in the offer, they are required to recommend that it should be placed before the creditors, and it is then for the permanent trustee to arrange for this to be done. The permanent trustee must publish a notice in the *Edinburgh Gazette* stating that an offer of composition has been made and where its terms may be inspected and invite every creditor known to him, to whom he must send a report on the matter, to accept or reject the offer. If the permanent trustee decides that a majority in number and not less than two-thirds in value of the creditors known to him have accepted the offer he must submit a statement to the sheriff that he has so determined together with his report. The sheriff must then fix a date and time for a hearing to consider whether or not to approve the offer, notice of which must be given to the creditors by the permanent trustee. If the sheriff is satisfied at the hearing that a majority in number and not less than two-thirds in value of the creditors known to the permanent trustee have accepted the offer and that its terms are reasonable he may approve the offer. His order approving or refusing to approve the offer is subject to appeal. If it is approved, and once steps have been taken for payment of or provision for all necessary charges in connection with the sequestration and for lodging the bond of caution or other security with the sheriff clerk, the sheriff is required to make an order discharging the debtor and the permanent trustee. An order of the sheriff approving the offer of composition and discharging the debtor and permanent trustee may be recalled by the Court of Session if it is satisfied that there has been or is likely to be default in payment of the composition or any instalment thereof, or that for any reason it cannot be proceeded with or cannot be proceeded with without undue delay or injustice to the creditors. The effect of a recall is to revive the sequestration and, if the permanent trustee has been discharged, the Court of Session may appoint a judicial factor to administer the estate. Where an offer of composition is made the sequestration must nevertheless proceed for the time being as if no such offer had been made until the discharge of the debtor becomes effective. A debtor may make two, but not more than two, offers of composition in the course of a sequestration.

54.36 **Discharge of Permanent Trustee.**—After the permanent trustee has made a final division of the debtor's estate and has inserted his final audited accounts in the sederunt book he may take steps to obtain his discharge.[51] He must first deposit any unclaimed dividends and any

---

[51] s. 57. If the permanent trustee is the Accountant in Bankruptcy his discharge is governed by s. 58A (inserted by 1993 Act, Sched. 1, para. 26).

unapplied balances in an appropriate bank or institution. Once this has been done he must send to the Accountant in Bankruptcy the sederunt book, a copy of the audited accounts and a receipt for the deposited moneys, and at the same time apply to him for a certificate of discharge. An opportunity is given to the debtor and to all the creditors known to the permanent trustee to make representations on his application within 14 days to the Accountant in Bankruptcy. On the expiry of that period the Accountant in Bankruptcy must, after examining the documents sent to him and considering any representations duly made to him, grant or refuse to grant the certificate of discharge. There is a right of appeal to the sheriff against his decision. The effect of the grant of a certificate of discharge is to discharge the permanent trustee from all liability, other than liability arising from fraud, to the creditors or to the debtor in respect of any act or omission by him in exercising the functions conferred on him by the Act. The same rights of application for a discharge are given to the executor of a permanent trustee who has died and to a permanent trustee who has resigned office.[52]

54.37 Voluntary Trust Deeds for Creditors.—The estates of a party who is insolvent may be wound up by some private arrangement with his creditors without resorting to sequestration. The methods usually selected are a private trust deed for creditors[53] or a composition contract. The Act makes no provision for the latter of these arrangements, but it contains a number of provisions relating to private trust deeds generally as well as particular provisions whereby a private trust deed may become protected against the possibility of being superseded by a sequestration.[54]

A trust deed for creditors is carried out by a conveyance by the debtor to a trustee, with the accession of some, or all, of the creditors. Under the Act a 'trust deed' means a voluntary trust deed granted by or on behalf of the debtor whereby his estate (other than such of his estate as would not vest in the permanent trustee if his estate were sequestrated)[55] is conveyed to the trustee for the benefit of his creditors generally.[56] Such a trustee has no statutory title, and must complete his right to the various subjects conveyed to him by the appropriate methods. He may register a notice of inhibition in the Register of Inhibitions and Adjudications at any time after the trust deed has been delivered to him, which has the same effect as the recording of letters of inhibition against the debtor.[57] Should the trustee fail to take these

---

[52] s. 57(7).

[53] For a form of trust deed, see Burns, *Conveyancing Practice* (4th ed.), p. 151.

[54] Known as a protected trust deed: see para. 54.38.

[55] See para. 54.17, *supra*.

[56] s. 5(4A) (inserted by 1993 Act, s. 3(4)).

[57] 1985 Act, Sched. 5, para. 2. See Rule of Court 201 A (3), inserted by Act of Sederunt (Rules of Court Amendment No. 1) (Bankruptcy Forms) 1986 (S.I. 1986 No. 514), as regards the form of notice to be recorded in the Register.

steps, the subjects left in the debtor's possession may be attached by diligence at the instance of creditors who have not acceded to the trust deed or of creditors to whom the debtor may have subsequently become indebted.[58] When the trustee has completed his title nothing is left with the debtor which can be attached by diligence. The granting of a trust deed is no bar to sequestration, which may still be applied for at any time by a non-acceding creditor;[59] by the debtor, with concurrence of a non-acceding creditor;[60] or by a creditor who has acceded, in the event of non-acceding creditors taking proceedings which might result in giving them preferential rights.[61] The trustee himself may also present a petition for the debtor's sequestration at any time.[62] The act of granting a trust deed for his creditors renders the debtor apparently insolvent, thus opening the way for a petition for his sequestration by any of his creditors whose debts exceed £750 if they wish to proceed in this way.[63] Where sequestration is awarded, the trust deed falls without any reduction, the estate must be wound up by the permanent trustee in the sequestration, and any rights acquired under the private trust deed must be asserted in the sequestration proceedings.[64] The trustee under the private trust deed has, in the event of sequestration, a lien for any expenses he may have incurred.[65] But, like other liens, this requires possession; where the trustee in a private trust deed granted by a farmer had advanced money for the administration of the farm, but had not obtained a completed assignation of the debtor's lease, it was held that as he had no possession he had no lien, and that there were no grounds on which he could claim any preferential ranking in the ensuing sequestration.[66]

In dividing the estate the trustee in a trust deed for creditors is bound to provide for all claims intimated to him. He was held personally liable when he rejected a claim which the creditor was able to prove to be well founded.[67] Unless the trust deed otherwise provides, the provisions of Schedule 1 to the 1985 Act must be applied for the purposes of determining the amount of each creditor's claim.[68] The submission of a claim by a creditor to the trustee acts as a bar to the effect of any enactment or rule of law relating to limitation of actions in any part of the United Kingdom.[69] Even although a particular creditor may not have acceded to the trust deed, he is entitled to be ranked in the

---

[58] *Gibson* v. *Wilson* (1841) 3 D. 974.
[59] *Kyd* v. *Waterson* (1880) 7 R. 884.
[60] *Macalister* v. *Swinburne* (1874) 1 R. 958; *Salaman* v. *Rosslyn's Trs.* (1900) 3 F. 298.
[61] *Jopp* v. *Hay* (1844) 7 D. 260. See *Munro* v. *Rothfield*, 1920 S.C. (H.L.) 165.
[62] s. 8(1)(*a*).
[63] ss. 5(2)(*b*), 7(1)(*c*)(i).
[64] *Salaman* v. *Rosslyn's Trs., supra.*
[65] *Thomson* v. *Tough's Tr.* (1880) 7 R. 1035.
[66] *Mess* v. *Sime's Tr.* (1898) 1 F. (H.L.) 22.
[67] *Cruickshank* v. *Thomas* (1893) 21 R. 257.
[68] Sched. 5, para. 4.
[69] Sched. 5, para. 3.

distribution of the estate.[70] The trustee under a private trust deed has no title to challenge illegal preferences granted by the debtor, unless a creditor entitled to challenge has acceded to the trust, and has assigned his title to sue to the trustee.[71] The debtor, the trustee or any creditor may at any time before the final distribution of the debtor's estate among the creditors have the trustee's accounts audited by and his remuneration fixed by the Accountant in Bankruptcy.[72] The trustee under a private trust deed has the same power as the permanent trustee in a sequestration to obtain supplies of gas, electricity and water and telecommunication services for the purposes of any business which has been carried on by the debtor or on his behalf, on condition that he personally guarantees payment of any charges in respect of the supply.[73]

54.38 **Protected Trust Deeds.**—A private trust deed may be protected to some extent against the possibility of sequestration by being made a protected trust deed.[74] In order to obtain this benefit it is necessary that the deed should comply with the statutory definition,[75] that the trustee would not be disqualified from acting as permanent trustee if the debtor's estate were being sequestrated, that he should forthwith after the delivery to him of the trust deed have published a notice in the *Edinburgh Gazette* and within one week have sent to every creditor known to him a copy of the trust deed, a copy of the notice and other prescribed information and that within the period of five weeks from the publication of the notice, the trustee has not received notification in writing from a majority in number or not less than one-third in value of the creditors that they object to the trust deed and do not wish to accede to it. If these requirements are satisfied the trustee must immediately send a copy of the trust deed to the Accountant in Bankruptcy for registration together with a certificate that he has not received such notification from the creditors. The trust deed is then protected. Any creditor who has received a copy of the trustee's notice and has not notified the trustee that he objects to it is treated as if he has acceded to the trust deed.[76] A creditor who has not been sent a copy of the trustee's notice or who has notified the trustee of his objection to the deed shall have no higher right to recover his debt than a creditor who has acceded to the deed. The debtor may not petition for sequestration of his estate while the trust deed subsists.[77] A creditor who has not been sent a copy of the trustee's notice or who has notified the trustee of his objection loses the right to petition for sequestration after six weeks have elapsed

---

[70] *Ogilvie* v. *Taylor* (1887) 14 R. 399.
[71] *Fleming's Trs.* v. *McHardy* (1892) 19´R. 542.
[72] Sched. 5, para.1.
[73] s. 70.
[74] Sched. 5, para. 5(1) (as amended by 1993 Act, Sched. 1, para. 32(2)).
[75] See para. 54.37, n. 54, *supra.*
[76] Sched. 5, para. 5(2).
[77] Sched. 5, para. 6 (as amended by 1993 Act, Sched. 1, para. 32(3)).

from the date of publication of the notice inviting accession unless he avers that distribution of the estate is or is likely to be unduly prejudicial to a creditor or class of creditors, and the court may award sequestration in these circumstances only if it is satisfied that the averment is correct.[78] Where the trustee under a protected trust deed obtains a discharge from the creditors who have acceded to the protected trust deed he must give notice of the discharge to every creditor known to him and to the Accountant in Bankruptcy.[79] The sending of such a notice to a non-acceding creditor is effective to make the discharge binding on him, subject, however, to the right to apply to the court within 28 days for an order that the discharge should not be binding on him on the ground that the trustee's intromissions with the estate have been so unduly prejudicial to his claim that he should not be bound by it.[80] In addition to the benefits mentioned above, the fact that a trust deed has become a protected trust deed enables the trustee acting under it to challenge gratuitous alienations and unfair preferences without resorting to sequestration.[81]

54.39 Composition Contracts.—An insolvent estate may, alternatively, be wound up without depriving the debtor of his estates, through the medium of a composition contract. Under its usual form the debtor agrees to pay so much in the pound to each creditor, and grants bills payable in instalments for that amount thereby conferring on each creditor, in the event of failure in payment, a liquid debt on which diligence may at once proceed. In the absence of any provision to the contrary, the full debt revives on failure in payment of any instalment.[82] As the debtor under the process is not deprived of his estate it remains open to the diligence of any creditor who is not barred by his accession to the composition contract. Each creditor who accedes does so on the implied condition that the accession of all is obtained.[83]

Further Reading

Goudy, *Bankruptcy* (4th ed., 1914).
McBryde, *Bankruptcy* (1989).
Stair Memorial Encyclopaedia Vol. 2, Bankruptcy.

[78] Sched. 5, para. 7.
[79] Sched. 5, para. 10.
[80] Sched. 5, paras. 11, 12.
[81] See paras. 54.19 and 54.20.
[82] Bell, *Comm.*, ii, 400.
[83] Bell, *Comm.*, ii, 395, 400.

INDEX